Teacher's Wraparound Edition

Introduction to Business
Our Business and Economic World

Betty J. Brown
Ball State University

John E. Clow
State University of New York
College at Oneonta

GLENCOE
McGraw-Hill

New York, New York
Columbus, Ohio
Woodland Hills, California
Peoria, Illinois

Glencoe/McGraw-Hill

A Division of The **McGraw-Hill** Companies

Introduction to Business:
Our Business and Economic World
Teacher's Wraparound Edition

Send all inquiries to:
Glencoe/McGraw-Hill
936 Eastwind Drive
Westerville, OH 43081

ISBN 0-02-814150-4

Printed in the United States of America.
3 4 5 6 7 8 9 10   027/046   02 01 00 99

Contents

Student Components

Teacher Components

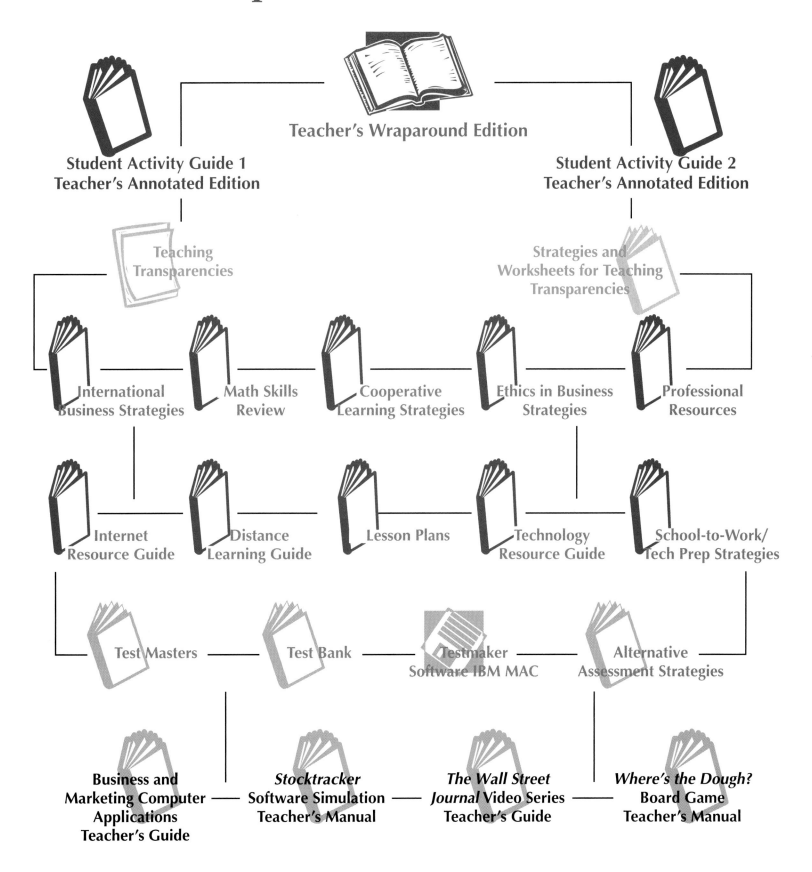

Teacher's Wraparound Edition

Student Activity Guide 1
Teacher's Annotated Edition

Student Activity Guide 2
Teacher's Annotated Edition

Teaching
Transparencies

Strategies and
Worksheets for Teaching
Transparencies

International
Business Strategies

Math Skills
Review

Cooperative
Learning Strategies

Ethics in Business
Strategies

Professional
Resources

Internet
Resource Guide

Distance
Learning Guide

Lesson Plans

Technology
Resource Guide

School-to-Work/
Tech Prep Strategies

Test Masters

Test Bank

Testmaker
Software IBM MAC

Alternative
Assessment Strategies

Business and
Marketing Computer
Applications
Teacher's Guide

Stocktracker
Software Simulation
Teacher's Manual

*The Wall Street
Journal* Video Series
Teacher's Guide

Where's the Dough?
Board Game
Teacher's Manual

Using the Teacher's Wraparound Edition

Introduction

The *Teacher's Wraparound Edition of Introduction to Business: Our Business and Economic World* is a comprehensive resource designed to make the teaching of the course easy and efficient for you, whether you are a novice business teacher or have many years experience. You'll find extensive material "wrapped around" beside and below each student page facsimile. Here are a wealth of ideas, including a variety of strategies helpful in teaching the basic business concepts that are the core of this introductory course. You'll want to tailor your teaching to your own preferences and to your students by choosing among the many activities and strategies offered for each unit and chapter. The *Teacher's Wraparound Edition* also shows you how to integrate the various additional components of the *Introduction to Business: Our Business and Economic World* program into your teaching.

Unit Features

Four pages open each unit in the *Teacher's Wraparound Edition*. The first two offer a chart that organizes the elements of each chapter in the unit and correlates these elements to the National Standards for Business Education. The following two pages offer a brief review of the preceding unit and a preview of the coming one. A unit cooperative learning project is also presented here. Each unit project makes use of blackline masters found in the separate *Cooperative Learning Strategies* booklet. Each unit closes with specific suggestions for extending the Business Issue in the student edition with additional projects.

Chapter Features

The *Teacher's Wraparound Edition* presents a five-step teaching plan for each chapter: **Focus, Teach, Close, Apply,** and **Assess.** Subheadings under these steps are shown in boldface type in the descriptions that follow.

CHAPTER 23

FOCUS

The purpose of this step is, as its title implies, to help students focus their attention on the chapter and help motive their learning.

Follow the suggestions in **Introduce the Chapter** to center students' attention on the chapter. **Major Concepts** lists the main ideas of the chapter. **Introduce the Topic** suggests ways to preview the chapter content. **Use Business Terms** presents methods to introduce the chapter terms. **Use Visuals** contains ways to connect the opening visual to the chapter.

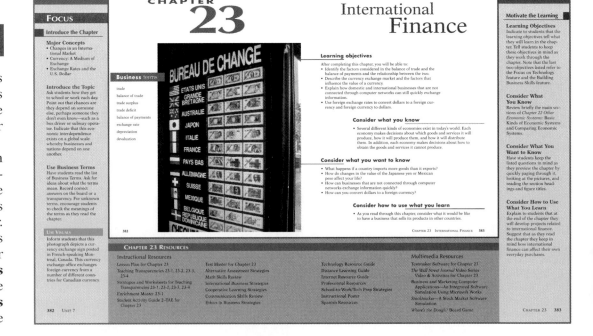

Apply the hints in **Motivate the Learning** to direct students' study of the chapter. **Learning Objectives** helps you remind students what they will learn. **Consider What You Know** lets you activate previous learning. **Consider What You Want to Know** helps you set the purpose for reading the chapter. **Consider How to Use What You Learn** helps you prepare students for the chapter projects.

For your convenience, a list of the **Chapter Resources** is provided below the chapter opener pages. Use this list to preview and choose among the program components to use with the chapter.

TEACH

The **Teach** portion of the teaching plan is the heart of the chapter lesson. It always begins with a **Business Connection.** Use the information in this element to demonstrate to students current facts from the business world that reflect the thesis of the chapter.

For every section of the student edition chapter, the Teacher's Wraparound Edition provides a **Develop Concepts** element. You can use the strategy suggested here to demonstrate the basic concepts in the section. You'll find additional strategies for teaching concepts in the **Learning Activity** and **Teaching Tip** elements interspersed throughout the chapter; use them as additional ideas and strategies to amplify the chapter concepts. **Business Brief** offers additional information from the business world pertinent to the content of the chapter; use it to spark students' interest in ways to connect the textbook to current business.

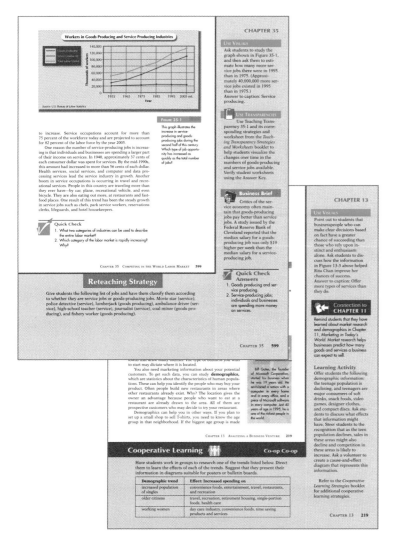

Near each figure or photograph of the student edition, the *Teacher's Wraparound Edition* provides a **Use Visuals** element; use this to present the visual with a reinforcing strategy. Use Visuals also supplies the answer to the question asked in the caption in the student edition. **Use Transparencies** explains at the point of suggested use which *Teaching Transparencies* and activities from the *Strategies and Worksheets for Teaching Transparencies* booklet are appropriate. Occasionally a tie to the concepts in another chapter is worth making to students; use **Connection to Chapter XX** to point these out. Finally, every section of the student edition ends with a **Quick Check;** for your convenience, the Teacher's Wraparound Edition provides the answers to these questions.

More About Teach . . .

Below the student page facsimiles throughout the **Teach** section are additional teaching options. These strategies include **Global Perspective, Reteaching Strategy, Meeting Student Diversity, Curriculum Connection, Making Connections, Enrichment Strategy,** and **Cooperative Learning.** Use these options with students who have particular needs or interests.

With each Focus on Technology, Focus on Entrepreneurs, and Focus on Careers feature, the *Teacher's Wraparound Edition* offers **Discuss** and **Follow Through.** The first helps you get students started with the topic; the second suggests ways to extend it.

For the Building Business Skills features, the *Teacher's Wraparound Edition* **Model** section helps you demonstrate to students how the skill is done. **Practice** suggests ways for you to help students practice the skill. Note that a Skill Reinforcement Activity is offered as part of the Chapter Review to follow up with additional practice of the Business Skill.

CLOSE

You can wrap up the **Main Ideas** of the lesson content with this step of the teaching plan. It includes an answer to the **Case Analysis** and a **Quick Quiz** that you can give to students as a brief diagnostic tool. Students who don't do well with these several questions have missed the major concepts of the lesson; they'll need to re-examine the chapter thoroughly before proceeding to carry out the **Chapter Review** on the following two pages of the student text.

APPLY

The **Apply** step covers the student text **Chapter Review** and provides the answers to the exercises there: **Use the Language of Business, Review What You Learned, Understand Business Concepts, Think Critically,** and **Use What You Learned.** You can use the Chapter Review and these answers in several ways: Have students write all answers as a pre-test of the chapter; provide the answers to students to check their own responses as a comprehensive review; give cooperative learning groups each one of the sections to do and have them share their answers with the whole class as a final learning exercise, and so on. Note that **Use What You Learned** stresses projects that you may choose to have pairs or groups of students carry out together in any case. The Skill Reinforcement Activity here offers additional practice in the business skill taught in the Building Business Skills section of the student book; you may want to assign this to all students or specifically to those who had difficulty with the skill when it was presented earlier in the chapter. For **Independent Practice,** assign students to complete the *Student Activity Guide* activities.

ASSESS

Currently many teachers are expanding their assessment tools by using student portfolios, into which students put evidence of work they've done. **Portfolio Assessment** offers some suggestions for you to correlate the **Use What You Learned** projects with information in the *Alternative Assessment Strategies* booklet to enhance students' portfolios. You can use the rubrics in this booklet to evaluate different kinds of projects. Specific rubrics are suggested in the *Teacher's Wraparound Edition* **Use What You Learned** section.

Teaching Resources

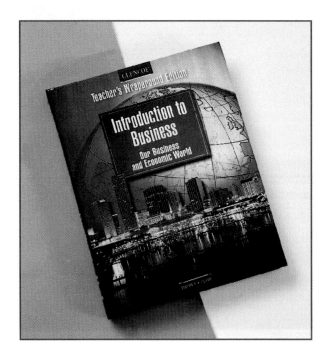

Teacher's Wraparound Edition

The *Teacher's Wraparound Edition* provides a variety of teaching strategies and support alongside facsimiles of the student book pages. You can use the ideas provided to develop and enhance your lesson plans.

Student Activity Guides

The *Student Activity Guides* include consumable worksheets that provide additional practice and application activities for each chapter of the student text. Use these exercises to offer students practice with business vocabulary, reading comprehension, problems, projects, and simulations of business and economic situations. Separate Teacher's Annotated Editions provide answers.

Teaching Transparencies

Use these 100 transparencies to enhance and expand your teaching of each chapter. Each *Teacher's Wraparound Edition* chapter provides a specific strategy that explains how to use each transparency at an appropriate point in the lesson. Eighty of the transparencies are in full color; the remaining 20 are presented as blackline forms for students to use to practice filling in such items as blank checks or sample budgets. You can use these 20 on the overhead projector; you may also make photocopies for distribution to students.

Strategies and Worksheets for Teaching Transparencies

This booklet provides suggested strategies for your presentation of each teaching transparency. Additionally, it includes a blackline master worksheet to accompany each of the 80 color transparencies. The 20 blackline forms are already usable as worksheets.

Cooperative Learning Strategies

This booklet has two parts. The first explains what cooperative learning is and describes several types of classroom management techniques for cooperative learning. The second includes blackline masters students can use as they carry out the unit projects explained in the *Teacher's Wraparound Edition* at the beginning of each unit.

Enrichment Masters

The blackline masters in the *Enrichment Masters* offer extension activities for every chapter in the student text. Photocopy these for students and use them to expand the *Teacher's Wraparound Edition* lessons, where a suggested use is provided for each one.

International Business Strategies

For many reasons, international business has grown in importance in recent years. This booklet offers you some background to enable you to give students the wider perspective they will need as they enter the business world. Sixteen blackline masters give students practice in considering issues important in the global market—and workplace.

Math Skills Review

Use the blackline masters in the *Math Skills Review* to aid students who need to review basic business math concepts or who need reinforcement of those skills.

Communication Skills Review

The *Communication Skills Review* blackline masters can be used to provide students practice in numerous basic business reading, writing, speaking, and listening skills.

Ethics in Business Strategies

Everyone in business must choose the right way to handle thorny business issues. This booklet offers some general background on ethics and provides a decision-making model for ethical dilemmas. Students use the model as they work through blackline masters with several different scenarios.

Internet Resource Guide

Many teachers and students wonder about the Internet and how to use it as a source of information. This booklet provides clear explanations and some ideas that may help you and your students connect yourselves, the Internet, and your business curriculum.

Professional Resources

This annotated bibliography suggests resources pertinent to each chapter of *Introduction to Business: Our Business and Economic World.* Included are books, periodicals, and multi-media resources. Use it to expand your own knowledge of various business topics and/or to share with students.

Distance Learning Guide

What *is* distance learning? This booklet tells you not only what it is, but also how you can involve your class and your school in this innovative use of technology to communicate with other classrooms.

School-to-Work/Tech Prep Strategies

Teachers of business, more than most other curricula, are keenly aware of their students' preparation for the workforce. This booklet describes many programs and strategies regarding preparing students who will either go directly into the workforce or into postsecondary training. Use it as a resource to help those students avail themselves of helpful programs. You may also use the information to set up useful programs within your school and community.

Technology Resource Guide

The array of technological marvels is bewildering and continues to change. This booklet can help you and your students understand some of the basics: what they are and how you might use them in the business classroom and curriculum.

Spanish Resources

Use these for Spanish-speaking students who may benefit from the translation of the Business Terms, Lesson Objectives, and Main Ideas of each chapter.

Instructional Poster

You'll want to display one of the two sides of the poster during study of chapters that are connected to its content. One side focuses on global business, identifying such factors as members of NAFTA. The other side of the poster displays several checklists pertinent to personal finance. Use the poster to motivate students and enhance classroom instruction.

Lesson Plans

The Lesson Plan for each chapter provides a checklist of the components of the program for that chapter. You may want to check off which components of the student edition, the *Teacher's Wraparound Edition* lesson, and other resources you particularly like or want to use as you plan your lessons. Or you may choose to check those that you have done with students.

Multimedia Resources

The Wall Street Journal Video Series

This series of videos is based on *The Wall Street Journal Classroom Edition.* The videos are correlated to the content of the 38 chapters in *Introduction to Business: Our Business and Economic World.* The videos may be used to introduce, reinforce, extend, or close the chapter. A teacher's manual provides strategies, activities, and reproducible blackline masters.

Business and Marketing Computer Applications—An Integrated Software Simulation Using Microsoft Works

This template application software introduces students to the basic functions of Microsoft Works, an integrated software program. The templates are designed for use with Microsoft Works 3.0 for DOS, Microsoft Works 3.0 for Windows, and Microsoft Works 4.0 for Macintosh. In this simulation, students assume the role of a trainee in a media store and perform various job-related activities within the accounting, advertising, human resources, inventory, and sales departments. Included is a series of Quickstart activities for each of the three versions and a teacher's manual with teaching tips, evaluation guidelines, and solutions.

Where's the Dough? Board Game

This board game exposes students to the knowledge needed to prepare a business plan and the process of starting a business. Players use a die and cards to advance through the segments on the board. A profit must be made at the end of the game in order to win. The game may be played in a 5-day format for in-depth learning or in a 1-day format as an overview to starting a business. A teacher's manual contains instructional strategies and orientation and closing activities.

Stocktracker—A Stock Market Software Simulation

This software can simulate several weeks or months of the stock market in a period of a few days. The menu-driven program allows you and your students to control the fluctuations in market prices by choosing news releases that affect the prices of corporate stock. Included with the software is a teacher's manual with reproducible student activities.

Assessment Resources

Test Masters

Use these blackline masters to give students objective tests covering each chapter and unit of *Introduction to Business: Our Business and Economic World.* Also included are Unit Tests and Mid-Term and Final Tests. Answers are provided.

Test Bank

This is a printed version of the database in the *Testmaker* software. It includes every question in the Test Masters—Chapter Tests, Unit Tests, Mid-Term Test, and Final Test—plus 100 additional questions.

Testmaker Software IBM

Testmaker Software MAC

Create your own customized tests by using this software. You can edit or add items or print multiple versions of the same test. Use the printed *Test Bank* described above to preview test items.

Alternative Assessment Strategies

This booklet describes ways to assess students' progress in addition to the traditional objective tests. It includes a variety of rubrics to help you assess such student projects and activities as creating posters, charts and tables, and bulletin boards, as well as writing paragraphs. You will use the rubrics to assess student responses to the Use What You Learned section of the Chapter Reviews.

National Standards for Business Education

A New Era for Business Education as Seen Through the Standards for Business Education

In this era of accountability for education and the interest in upgrading the skills/knowledges of our nation's youth, there has been a groundswell of interest in the development of standards. Due to the request of many of its members, the National Business Education Association updated their standards through a national project involving hundreds of professionals throughout the nation. The National Business Curriculum Model, the format for the standards, procedures for developing the standards, and ways to use the standards will be explained.

National Business Curriculum Model

To gain an overall view of the purposes and scope of the standards for business education, the National Business Curriculum Model (shown in Figure 1) is a good starting point. The outer circle which is continuous is assessment, certainly one of the purposes of developing standards. The next inner circle includes areas which should be pervasive throughout the entire business education curriculum—human relations, communications, technology, quantitative methods, and international business. The third inner circle includes all of the standard areas—twelve in number which include:

1. Accounting
2. Business Law
3. Career Development
4. Communication
5. Computation
6. Economics and Personal Finance
7. Entrepreneurship
8. Information Systems
9. International Business
10. Marketing
11. Management
12. Interrelationship of Business Functions

For purposes of clarification, several of the standards—computation, communication, and international business—are standards areas as well as topical groupings which need to be integrated into the entire business education curriculum. The logic supporting this position is that each of these areas can and should be major units or course of study in the curriculum. Furthermore, in each of the standards areas, there will be some performance expectations focusing on these particular areas.

Most of the nomenclature for the standards are common descriptors for the business education curriculum. An exception is the interrelationships of business function which shows how the various underpinnings of business education relate to one another, i.e. how accounting practices affect marketing and visa versa. These interrelationships are important if students are to gain the breadth of understanding how businesses operate and function. The inclusion of this area is consistent with the current educational reform movement which focuses on showing relationships between different concepts in various disciplines.

FIGURE 1

National Business Curriculum Model

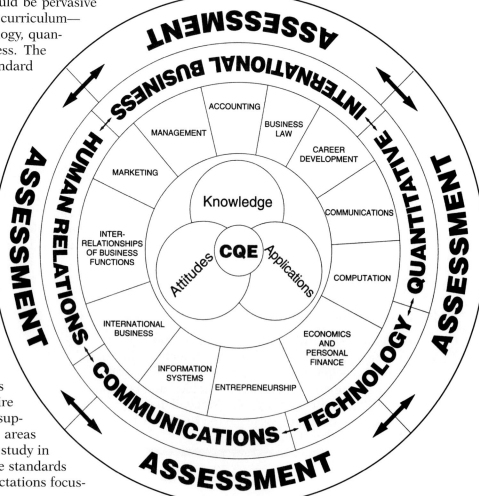

The next inner part of the circle includes the generic goals of business education which are to develop knowledges, application skills and knowledges (such as decision making and problem solving) and the development of attitudes to appreciate and use these knowledges and skills. The CQE in the most inner circle stands for continuous quality education which is the goal of the standards project.

Format of the Standards

For the most part, eleven standards areas follow a consistent format which is demonstrated by the following section taken from the international business standards area. The interrelationships standards area is an exception which will be described later.

Each of the standards areas has achievement standards which are broad standards encompassing a considerable number of performance expectations. For example, there are nine achievement standards for the international business area which are:

1. Explain the role of international business and analyze its impact on careers and doing business at the local, state, national, and international levels.
2. Apply communication strategies necessary and appropriate for effective and profitable international business relations.
3. Describe the social, cultural, political, legal, and economic factors that shape and impact the international business environment.
4. Describe the environmental factors that define what is considered ethical business behavior.
5. Explain the role, importance, and concepts of international finance and risk management.
6. Address special challenges in operations and management of human resources in international business.
7. Apply marketing concepts to international business.
8. Relate balance of trade concepts to the import/ export process.
9. Identify forms of business ownership and entrepreneurial opportunities available in international business.

For each achievement standard, there can be performance expectations for four educational levels. For example, one of the areas under the fifth achievement standard for international business is currency and exchange which have a number of performance expectations that are listed in Figure 2. The designated level numbers correspond to the following grade levels:

Level 1—Elementary (K–6)
Level 2—Middle School/Junior High (6–9)
Level 3—Secondary (9–12)
Level 4—Postsecondary—Community College or Technical School (13–14)

The development approach to learning is exemplified through these performance expectations. As shown in Figure 2, students are expected to know what is a currency and different types of currency at the elementary level. At the middle school level, some general problems/risks of dealing with foreign currencies is developed. At the secondary level, students are expected to explain how different economic situations will affect a currency, such as prevailing economic conditions in a country and balance of payments deficits/surplus of a country. At the two-year college level, students are expected to use effective financial strategies to manage various foreign currencies considering the changes in value caused by economic conditions.

FIGURE 2

Performance Expectation for Currency and Exchange

Level 1—Performance Expectations:

Define basic terms, such as currency and currency exchange.

List the currencies of various countries.

Calculate simple currency exchange.

Level 2—Performance Expectations:

Explain how currency exchange rates affect companies.

Identify potential problems of dealing in foreign currencies.

Level 3—Performance Expectations:

Describe how economic conditions, balance of payment situations, and political issues affect currency values.

Distinguish between currencies (e.g., hard vs. soft, convertible vs. non-convertible).

Level 4—Performance Expectations:

Define interest rate parity and explain how fluctuating interest rates affect international trade.

Compare operations of foreign exchange markets to domestic markets.

Apply international financial strategies to manage foreign exchange risks (e.g., hedging, third-party help, pooling risk, and diversification).

The format for the information processing area is a bit different. The performance expectations are written for more than one educational level because of new technology and the fluidity as to the level where these abilities should be developed. The section on computer architecture appears in Figure 3. Notice that identifying appropriate hardware components for specific tasks is suggested for all levels. Obviously, the complexity of the decision depends on what hardware is available and at what educational level information processing is being taught at a particular time.

The standards are not teaching activities. Rather, they are competencies that experts believed should be developed at a particular grade level. Also, the standards are not overly specific. They are not traditional behavioral objectives. For example, the performance expectation of determining hardware components for specific tasks does not name the hardware components. It is expected that the curriculum developers at a district or state level will add more specifics if they would like to do so.

The interrelationship area is dissimilar from the other eleven standards areas. It includes some activities which can be pursued to show the interrelationships between the vari-

ous areas. These activities focus on analysis, application, and the utilization of those knowledges in a situation which would be commonly used by business (called impact). Figure 4 shows an example which interrelates the economics and marketing areas.

Procedures for Developing the Standards

The development of the standards for business education involved a multistage process gaining input from a considerable number of professionals in both education and in business. An administrative committee was named by the NBEA Executive Board to develop the procedures and oversee the implementation of the various steps of the project. The committee had representation from the secondary, two-year college, four-year college, business teacher education, and supervisors at the district and state department levels.

Two groups—one in Georgia and one in California—developed some initial performance expectations for the various standards areas. A panel of experts representing grade levels K-14 was then called together for a three to four-day meeting to review and revise what was developed. The resulting product was then shared with a panel of business educators and business leaders for review. Revisions were then made. Each draft of standards was then shared with the attendees at the NBEA Conventions; further input was gained. The last group to review the standards was the administrative committee of the project.

Ways to Use the Standards

There are a number of ways in which the standards can be used.

1. Use the standards document to show to your various publics (administrators, guidance counselors, other teachers, parents, business leaders, curriculum developers, etc.) the breadth and depth of business education. The standards publication amply demonstrates that business education is a multifaceted discipline including more than keyboarding, computers, and accounting. The stereotype that business education is only secretarial science is still a prevailing conception among many of our publics.

2. Develop new courses of units of study. If you find that your curriculum is not offering some of the content listed in the standards, develop a unit or course which incorporates the development of the competencies included in the document. International business is a relatively new curriculum area where this could be applicable. The interrelationships section also has some content plus activities where this could be done.

FIGURE 3

Computer Architecture

Achievement Standard: Describe current and emerging computer architecture; configure, install, and upgrade hardware systems; and diagnose and repair hardware problems.

Level 1–4—Performance Expectations:

Identify hardware components appropriate for specific tasks.

Explain the purpose, operation, and care of hardware components.

Identify examples of emerging hardware technology.

Diagnose hardware problems.

Level 2–4—Performance Expectations:

Illustrate various configurations of hardware components.

Describe ergonomic principles in the configuration of computer work stations.

Level 3–4—Performance Expectations:

Remove, upgrade, store, and install computer hardware.

Repair computer hardware problems.

FIGURE 4

Sample Activities Showing Interrelationship Between Economics and Marketing

Economic Trends strongly influence marketing strategies.

Analysis—Explain why the equilibrium price changes for a given product.

Application—Plot the supply and demand curve for a product/service.

Impact—Based on data, develop a marketing strategy to stimulate demand.

3. Evaluate your current courses. Use the performance expectations as criteria to evaluate your curriculum as to breadth and depth of coverage. As an example, if you are teaching about credit in personal finance, you could determine whether your coverage includes all of the performance expectations listed for the credit area and whether you develop the performance expectations suggested for the educational level being taught.
4. Use as a vehicle to develop a coordinated business education curriculum from grades Kindergarten through the second year of college. The developmental approach for the various

discipline areas is given. Work with current teachers or work in developing new courses/units of study at various levels in order to meet the goal of a developmental approach for business education.

To obtain a copy of *National Standards for Business Education,* contact:

National Business Education Association
1914 Association Drive
Reston, VA 22091-1596
Tel. 703-860-8300
Fax 703-620-4483

Business Skills

The importance of basic business skills in the work-place is well known. In fact, lack of such skills in many entry-level employees is well publicized as a current problem for many businesses. It's a problem not only for these businesses, but for the United States as well. The global marketplace makes it more and more imperative that our country's businesses compete successfully—and, ultimately, successful competition is the result of each individual employee's contribution. Specific job training cannot take place if an employee doesn't have basic math and communication skills. Employers also find that too many entry-level employees lack "employability" skills such as making decisions, being on time, being self-directed, and so on. Basic analytical abilities are often needed, too, so that employees can do such things as evaluate information or interpret different points of view.

Introduction to Business: Our Business and Economic World supports development of students' basic business skills through the inclusion of a Building Business Skills feature in each chapter of the student edition. The *Teacher's Wraparound Edition* augments each feature with a **Model** section, which provides suggestions for you to demonstrate the skill, and a **Practice** section, which offers ideas to help students carry out the Practice activity of the feature. Additional practice of the business skill is offered in the **Skill Reinforcement Activity,** part of the **Use What You Learned** section of the **Chapter Review.** Guidelines for evaluating student responses are also provided in the *Teacher's Wraparound Edition.*

The Building Business Skills features emphasize four important categories of basic business skills: employability, analysis, math, and communication. Some topics covered in these features include:

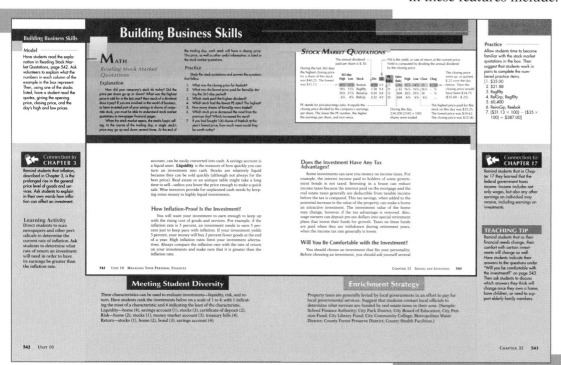

Employability: problem solving, making informed judgments, resolving team conflicts, ethical behavior, dealing with diversity

Analysis: inferring, recognizing cause and effect, interpreting statistics, distinguishing between relevant and irrelevant information

Math: reconciling a checking account, reading stock market quotations, computing finance charges, exchanging foreign currency

Communication: developing listening skills, locating and verifying information, identifying main and subordinate ideas, choosing appropriate forms of business communication.

Cooperative Learning

Studies show that students learn faster and retain more information when they are actively involved in the learning process. In a classroom setting, adolescents often learn more from each other about subject matter than from a traditional teacher-led lecture and discussion. Cooperative learning is one method that gets students actively involved in learning and at the same time allows for peer teaching. The *Cooperative Learning Strategies* booklet can help you find out more about this teaching method. The booklet describes many cooperative learning strategies.

What Cooperative Learning Is

Cooperative learning strategies are team-oriented approaches to learning. They emphasize positive interdependence, heterogeneous groupings, group problem-solving, group evaluation, and individual accountability. The strategies are characterized as follows:

1. Students must perceive that they "sink or swim together" as they work to reach their goals.
2. Students are responsible for ensuring that

everyone in the group, including themselves, learns the assigned material.
3. Students divide tasks and share responsibilities equally among group members.
4. Students are given an evaluation or reward that applies to the entire group.
5. Students share leadership and acquire collaboration skills.
6. Students are held individually accountable for their work.

The Benefits of Cooperative Learning

Cooperative learning is particularly suitable for the business education classroom because it models real-life experiences in the business world. Employees are typically expected to work cooperatively and to use appropriate social skills in a business environment. Teamwork, problem-solving skills, and the ability to adapt to new technologies are essential for success in business.

Research-Supported Benefits of Cooperative Learning for Students

• Increased time on task
• Higher self-esteem
• Improved attitude toward school and attendance
• Lower drop-out rate
• Greater acceptance of individual differences
• Less disruptive behavior
• Reduced interpersonal conflict
• Less apathy
• Deeper comprehension
• Greater motivation
• Higher achievement
• Longer retention of learned material
• Increased kindness, sensitivity, and tolerance

Tips for Getting Started

It is important to remember that while cooperative learning seems to be a simple concept, its implementation can be complex. Most teachers find that the methods evolve over time and become more effective once both the teacher and the students are familiar with them. Each time you use cooperative learning, you are reinforcing the teamwork skills that will make the next cooperative learning session even more successful.

Prepare Your Class Preparation is a crucial step. Discuss with your students the format, the division of tasks, the evaluation procedures, and the goals of cooperative learning strategies. Explain the three basic rules of cooperative learning:

1. Stay with your group.

2. Ask a question of your group first before you ask the teacher.
3. Offer feedback on ideas; avoid criticizing people.

Classroom Arrangement Arrange the furniture in the room so students face each other as they work together.

Group Size Groups work best when they are composed of two to five students.

Group Assignments Each group should be mixed racially, socially, ethnically, and by gender and range of ability.

Rotation of Group Members Change groups periodically. For example, you can change the groups every four to six weeks, every quarter, every semester, or for every new teaching unit.

Student Preparation Prepare students for cooperation. Students need to understand that they are part of a group. Students work with each other to accomplish the same goal, but each student is individually accountable for learning.

Group Roles Explain group roles. Students need to learn the cooperative skills that are fundamental to each role before they begin. Roles should be rotated among group members daily or weekly. Following are suggested roles:

• Recorder or Secretary—Records group answers and serves as spokesperson for the group when appropriate.
• Gatekeeper—Ensures that all members participate and that no one individual dominates.
• Praiser or Cheerleader—Makes sure each group member's contribution is appreciated.
• Taskmaster—Guides the discussion or work to keep the group on target and encourages everyone to participate.

Responsibilities of the Teacher

The success of cooperative learning groups depends on the teacher's ability to coach the groups. The teacher creates the environment and structures the process of learning, then guides the student's learning. Specifically, the teacher:

• Motivates the students to learn.
• States the goals of the instruction.
• Teaches the fundamental concepts.
• Interacts with and guides the work of many groups.
• Acts as a resource as needed.
• Monitors student behavior.
• Evaluates the group process.

Evaluating Cooperative Learning Groups

A fundamental part of cooperative learning is evaluating how well the groups function as a unit. Specific suggestions are provided in the *Cooperative Learning Strategies* booklet.

Alternative Assessment

Evaluation of students' performance is fundamental to the teaching and learning process. Traditional tests are directed at individual students, and they provide a formal assessment of student performance. Such tests, however, do not evaluate students' communication and critical-thinking skills or problem-solving abilities. If classroom instruction is to parallel real-world applications, the evaluation of student performance should also relate to the skills that students will apply in the real world.

Tasks that lend themselves to alternative assessment strategies include the following attributes:

- Reflect the goals, objectives, and content of the curriculum.
- Are realistic, interesting, and thought-provoking.
- Allow students to demonstrate their thinking and understanding of a business problem or situation.
- Are open-ended with more than a single answer.
- Stress depth more than breadth and mastery more than speed.
- Are representative enough to allow generalizations to be made about a student's performance.
- Raise other questions or lead to other problems.

Specific Assessment Strategies

Case Studies

The analysis of case studies, or realistic, extended situations involving problems, has long been used in business education at all levels. Students are required to identify the problem, examine possible solutions and their consequences, and come to a decision about solving the problem. A Case Analysis is presented at the end of each chapter in the student edition.

Cooperative Learning

Cooperative learning activities require students to work together to achieve a common goal. They help students learn effective interpersonal communication skills. Though the assessment of such activities is usually based on the outcome or product of the group effort, each student is individually accountable for his or her work within the group.

Observation and Questioning

Observing and questioning as assessment tools will be encountered by students in the world of work. Observation helps you determine how well an individual understands material to be learned and how he or she goes about solving problems; it enables you to guide group members in reaching their goal.

Asking the right questions can show how well individuals are able to think for themselves and apply their knowledge creatively. Ideas for documenting assessment of these activities can be found in the *Alternative Assessment Strategies* booklet.

Oral Presentations and Discussions

Oral presentations and discussions can be valuable assessment tools because they allow you to hear what and how students think. In addition, they are the primary vehicle for students to share their ideas with classmates. Ample opportunities for oral interaction in class will help students practice and hone important communication skills they will be using in the business environment.

Projects and Investigations

Projects and investigations can be defined as extended activities involving in-depth research as well as problem solving. They may be individual or team efforts. Many ideas for student projects are provided in *Introduction to Business: Our Business and Economic World*. In the student edition, for example, every Chapter Review ends with a set of projects under the title Use What You Learned. In the *Teacher's Wraparound Edition*, every unit opener includes a unit cooperative project.

Portfolios

A portfolio is more than a folder containing a student's work. It is a representative sample of work collected over a period of time. The pieces in it are chosen as illustrations of a student's best work at a particular time and should be carefully dated. The whole portfolio thus can be used to record a student's growth and development as he or she progresses through the business course.

Using Rubrics

A rubric is a set of descriptions of the quality of a product and/or process, covering a continuum of quality from superior to poor. The rubrics presented in the *Alternative Assessment Strategies* booklet can be used to evaluate many demonstrations of student work. The sixteen rubrics are designed for assessing specific kinds of work such as graphs, essays, oral presentations, and models. One is devoted to assessing how well an individual works on cooperative tasks, and another covers portfolio evaluation. Most of the rubrics are geared to the activities and projects described in the **Use What You Learned** section of each student edition **Chapter Review.** The *Teacher's Wraparound Edition* lists possible rubrics to use with each of these activities and projects.

Block Scheduling (90-minute periods for nine weeks, meeting alternate days, or meeting every day for 90 minutes a day for nine weeks)

CHAPTERS	CLASS PERIODS
Unit 1—Introduction to the Global Economy	
Chapter 1—Business in Today's World	2
Chapter 2—Economic Challenges Facing Business	2
Chapter 3—Measuring Economic Performance	2
Unit 2—The Private Enterprise System	
Chapter 4—Motivations of Business	2
Chapter 5—How the Market Works	2
Chapter 6—The Private Enterprise Environment	2
Simulation—Interdependence in the Marketplace (Student Activity Guide 1)	1
Unit 3—Dynamics of Business in a Changing World	
Chapter 7—Building a Business Organization	2
Chapter 8—Managing a Diverse Workforce	2
Chapter 9—Managing Business Finances	3
Chapter 10—Producing Goods and Services Worldwide	2
Chapter 11—Marketing in Today's World	2
Simulation—Providing Services (Student Activity Guide 1)	1
Unit 4—Entrepreneurship and Small Business	
Chapter 12—What Is Entrepreneurship?	2
Chapter 13—Analyzing a Business Venture	2
Chapter 14—Organizing a Business	2
Chapter 15—Financing a Business	2
Simulation—Entrepreneurship (Student Activity Guide 1)	3
Unit 5—Government and Business	
Chapter 16—How Government Affects Business	2
Chapter 17—Taxes and Taxation	2
Chapter 18—Government Spending and the Economy	2
Unit 6—Financial Institutions in the Global Economy	
Chapter 19—Money and Banking	3
Chapter 20—The Federal Reserve System and Monetary Policy	3

END OF NINE WEEKS OR END OF SEMESTER

CHAPTERS	CLASS PERIODS
Unit 7—International Business	
Chapter 21—The Global Market	2
Chapter 22—Other Economic Systems	2
Chapter 23—International Finance	2
Chapter 24—Global Economic Challenges	2
Unit 8—Consumers in the Global Economy	
Chapter 25—Buying Goods and Services	2
Chapter 26—Consumer Rights and Responsibilities	2
Chapter 27—Protecting Consumers	2
Unit 9—Using Credit to Buy Goods and Services	
Chapter 28—Credit: A Promise to Pay	2
Chapter 29—Getting and Keeping Credit	2
Chapter 30—Credit and the Law	2
Simulation—Using Credit as a Consumer (Student Activity Guide 2)	2
Unit 10—Managing Your Personal Finances	
Chapter 31—Planning a Budget	2
Chapter 32—Saving and Investing	2
Chapter 33—Using Banking Services	3
Simulation—Developing Good Banking Habits (Student Activity Guide 2)	1
Chapter 34—Dealing with Risks	2
Unit 11—Working in the Global Economy	
Chapter 35—Competing in the World Labor Market	3
Chapter 36—Job Considerations	2
Unit 12—Planning a Career in Today's World	
Chapter 37—Developing a Career Plan	3
Chapter 38—The World of Work	2

Six-Week Grading Period

GRADING PERIOD	CHAPTERS	CLASS PERIODS
1	**Unit 1—Introduction to the Global Economy** Chapter 1—Business in Today's World Chapter 2—Economic Challenges Facing Business Chapter 3—Measuring Economic Performance **Unit 2—The Private Enterprise System** Chapter 4—Motivations of Business Chapter 5—How the Market Works Chapter 6—The Private Enterprise Environment *Simulation—Interdependence in the Marketplace* (Student Activity Guide 1)	 3 5 5 5 5 5 2
2	**Unit 3—Dynamics of Business in a Changing World** Chapter 7—Building a Business Organization Chapter 8—Managing a Diverse Workforce Chapter 9—Managing Business Finances Chapter 10—Producing Goods and Services Worldwide Chapter 11—Marketing in Today's World *Simulation—Providing Services* (Student Activity Guide 1)	 5 5 6 6 6 2
3	**Unit 4—Entrepreneurship and Small Business** Chapter 12—What Is Entrepreneurship? Chapter 13—Analyzing a Business Venture Chapter 14—Organizing a Business Chapter 15—Financing a Business *Simulation—Entrepreneurship* (Student Activity Guide 1) **Unit 5—Government and Business** Chapter 16—How Government Affects Business Chapter 17—Taxes and Taxation Chapter 18—Government Spending and the Economy	 4 4 4 4 3 4 4 3
4	**Unit 6—Financial Institutions in the Global Economy** Chapter 19—Money and Banking Chapter 20—The Federal Reserve System and Monetary Policy **Unit 7—International Business** Chapter 21—The Global Market Chapter 22—Other Economic Systems Chapter 23—International Finance Chapter 24—Global Economic Challenges	 5 6 5 4 5 5
5	**Unit 8—Consumers in the Global Economy** Chapter 25—Buying Goods and Services Chapter 26—Consumer Rights and Responsibilities Chapter 27—Protecting Consumers **Unit 9—Using Credit to Buy Goods and Services** Chapter 28—Credit: A Promise to Pay Chapter 29—Getting and Keeping Credit Chapter 30—Credit and the Law *Simulation—Using Credit as a Consumer* (Student Activity Guide 2)	 3 4 5 4 5 5 4
6	**Unit 10—Managing Your Personal Finances** Chapter 31—Planning a Budget Chapter 32—Saving and Investing Chapter 33—Using Banking Services *Simulation—Developing Good Banking Habits* (Student Activity Guide 2) Chapter 34—Dealing with Risks **Unit 11—Working in the Global Economy** Chapter 35—Competing in the World Labor Market Chapter 36—Job Considerations **Unit 12—Planning a Career in Today's World** Chapter 37—Developing a Career Plan Chapter 38—The World of Work	 2 3 4 2 4 4 4 3 4

Nine-Week Grading Period

GRADING PERIOD	CHAPTERS	CLASS PERIODS
1	**Unit 1—Introduction to the Global Economy**	
	Chapter 1—Business in Today's World	3
	Chapter 2—Economic Challenges Facing Business	4
	Chapter 3—Measuring Economic Performance	4
	Unit 2—The Private Enterprise System	
	Chapter 4—Motivations of Business	3
	Chapter 5—How the Market Works	4
	Chapter 6—The Private Enterprise Environment	4
	Simulation—Interdependence in the Marketplace (Student Activity Guide 1)	2
	Unit 3—Dynamics of Business in a Changing World	
	Chapter 7—Building a Business Organization	4
	Chapter 8—Managing a Diverse Workforce	4
	Chapter 9—Managing Business Finances	4
	Chapter 10—Producing Goods and Services Worldwide	4
	Chapter 11—Marketing in Today's World	4
	Simulation—Providing Services (Student Activity Guide 1)	1
2	**Unit 4—Entrepreneurship and Small Business**	
	Chapter 12—What Is Entrepreneurship?	4
	Chapter 13—Analyzing a Business Venture	4
	Chapter 14—Organizing a Business	4
	Chapter 15—Financing a Business	4
	Simulation—Entrepreneurship (Student Activity Guide 1)	4
	Unit 5—Government and Business	
	Chapter 16—How Government Affects Business	5
	Chapter 17—Taxes and Taxation	5
	Chapter 18—Government Spending and the Economy	4
	Unit 6—Financial Institutions in the Global Economy	
	Chapter 19—Money and Banking	5
	Chapter 20—The Federal Reserve System and Monetary Policy	6
3	**Unit 7—International Business**	
	Chapter 21—The Global Market	4
	Chapter 22—Other Economic Systems	4
	Chapter 23—International Finance	5
	Chapter 24—Global Economic Challenges	4
	Unit 8—Consumers in the Global Economy	
	Chapter 25—Buying Goods and Services	3
	Chapter 26—Consumer Rights and Responsibilities	4
	Chapter 27—Protecting Consumers	4
	Unit 9—Using Credit to Buy Goods and Services	
	Chapter 28—Credit: A Promise to Pay	4
	Chapter 29—Getting and Keeping Credit	5
	Chapter 30—Credit and the Law	4
	Simulation—Using Credit as a Consumer (Student Activity Guide 2)	4
4	**Unit 10—Managing Your Personal Finances**	
	Chapter 31—Planning a Budget	4
	Chapter 32—Saving and Investing	5
	Chapter 33—Using Banking Services	5
	Simulation—Developing Good Banking Habits (Student Activity Guide 2)	2
	Chapter 34—Dealing with Risks	6
	Unit 11—Working in the Global Economy	
	Chapter 35—Competing in the World Labor Market	6
	Chapter 36—Job Considerations	6
	Unit 12—Planning a Career in Today's World	
	Chapter 37—Developing a Career Plan	6
	Chapter 38—The World of Work	5

One-Semester Course Emphasizing Personal Finance

Unit 1—Introduction to the Global Economy
Chapter 1—Business in Today's World
Chapter 2—Economic Challenges Facing Business
Chapter 3—Measuring Economic Performance
Unit 2—The Private Enterprise System
Chapter 4—Motivations of Business
Chapter 5—How the Market Works
Chapter 6—The Private Enterprise Environment
Simulation—Interdependence in the Marketplace
    (Student Activity Guide 1)

Unit 8—Consumers in the Global Economy
Chapter 25—Buying Goods and Services
Chapter 26—Consumer Rights and Responsibilities
Chapter 27—Protecting Consumers

Unit 9—Using Credit to Buy Goods and Services
Chapter 28—Credit: A Promise to Pay
Chapter 29—Getting and Keeping Credit
Chapter 30—Credit and the Law
Simulation—Using Credit as a Consumer
    (Student Activity Guide 2)

Unit 10—Managing Your Personal Finances
Chapter 31—Planning a Budget
Chapter 32—Saving and Investing
Chapter 33—Using Banking Services
Simulation—Developing Good Banking Habits
    (Student Activity Guide 2)
Chapter 34—Dealing with Risks

Unit 11—Working in the Global Economy
Chapter 35—Competing in the World Labor Market
Chapter 36—Job Considerations

Unit 12—Planning a Career in Today's World
Chapter 37—Developing a Career Plan
Chapter 38—The World of Work

One-Semester Course Emphasizing Entrepreneurship

Unit 1—Introduction to the Global Economy
Chapter 1—Business in Today's World
Chapter 2—Economic Challenges Facing Business
Chapter 3—Measuring Economic Performance
Unit 2—The Private Enterprise System
Chapter 4—Motivations of Business
Chapter 5—How the Market Works
Chapter 6—The Private Enterprise Environment
Simulation—Interdependence in the Marketplace
    (Student Activity Guide 1)

Unit 3—Dynamics of Business in a Changing World
Chapter 7—Building a Business Organization
Chapter 8—Managing a Diverse Workforce
Chapter 9—Managing Business Finances
Chapter 10—Producing Goods and Services Worldwide
Chapter 11—Marketing in Today's World
Simulation—Providing Services (Student Activity Guide 1)

Unit 4—Entrepreneurship and Small Business
Chapter 12—What Is Entrepreneurship?
Chapter 13—Analyzing a Business Venture
Chapter 14—Organizing a Business
Chapter 15—Financing a Business
Simulation—Entrepreneurship (Student Activity Guide 1)

Unit 5—Government and Business
Chapter 16—How Government Affects Business
Chapter 17—Taxes and Taxation
Chapter 18—Government Spending and the Economy

Unit 6—Financial Institutions in the Global Economy
Chapter 19—Money and Banking
Chapter 20—The Federal Reserve System and
    Monetary Policy

One-Semester Course Emphasizing the Economic System

Unit 1—Introduction to the Global Economy
Chapter 1—Business in Today's World
Chapter 2—Economic Challenges Facing Business
Chapter 3—Measuring Economic Performance

Unit 2—The Private Enterprise System
Chapter 4—Motivations of Business
Chapter 5—How the Market Works
Chapter 6—The Private Enterprise Environment
Simulation—Interdependence in the Marketplace
    (Student Activity Guide 1)

Unit 3—Dynamics of Business in a Changing World
Chapter 7—Building a Business Organization
Chapter 8—Managing a Diverse Workforce
Chapter 9—Managing Business Finances
Chapter 10—Producing Goods and Services Worldwide
Chapter 11—Marketing in Today's World
Simulation—Providing Services (Student Activity Guide 1)

Unit 5—Government and Business
Chapter 16—How Government Affects Business
Chapter 17—Taxes and Taxation
Chapter 18—Government Spending and the Economy

Unit 6—Financial Institutions in the Global Economy
Chapter 19—Money and Banking
Chapter 20—The Federal Reserve System and
    Monetary Policy

Unit 7—International Business
Chapter 21—The Global Market
Chapter 22—Other Economic Systems
Chapter 23—International Finance
Chapter 24—Global Economic Challenges

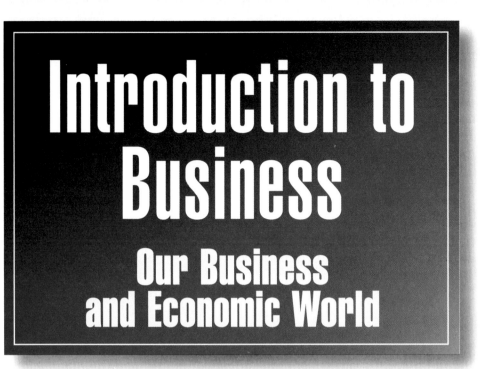

Introduction to Business
Our Business and Economic World

Betty J. Brown
Ball State University

John E. Clow
State University of New York
College at Oneonta

GLENCOE
McGraw-Hill

New York, New York
Columbus, Ohio
Woodland Hills, California
Peoria, Illinois

Authors

Dr. Betty J. Brown is Professor of Business Education and Office Administration at Ball State University, Muncie, Indiana. She was formerly Associate Professor of Technological and Adult Education, Business Education, and Office Systems Management, at the University of Tennessee, Knoxville. In addition to teaching at the secondary and postsecondary levels, Dr. Brown has written numerous articles, delivered speeches, and conducted workshops on the teaching of business.

Dr. John E. Clow is Professor and Director of Business Education at the State University of New York, College at Oneonta. Prior to that, he was President of Berkeley College of Manhattan. He has also served as Director of the Business and Consumer Economics Programs at the National Council on Economic Education. Dr. Clow has taught at both the secondary and postsecondary levels, and has to his credit numerous speeches and publications in the areas of business and economic education.

Introduction to Business:
Our Business and Economic World
Student Edition

Send all inquiries to:
Glencoe/McGraw-Hill
936 Eastwind Drive
Westerville, OH 43081

ISBN 0-02-814149-0

Printed in the United States of America.
5 6 7 8 9 10   027/046   02 01 00 99

Reviewers

Table of Contents

UNIT 3

DYNAMICS OF BUSINESS IN A CHANGING WORLD

UNIT 4

ENTREPRENEURSHIP
AND SMALL
BUSINESS

UNIT 5

GOVERNMENT AND BUSINESS

UNIT 6

FINANCIAL INSTITUTIONS IN THE GLOBAL ECONOMY

UNIT 7

INTERNATIONAL BUSINESS

UNIT 8

CONSUMERS IN THE GLOBAL ECONOMY

18% of nations

25% of world's population

26% of world GDP

ix

UNIT 9

USING CREDIT TO BUY GOODS AND SERVICES

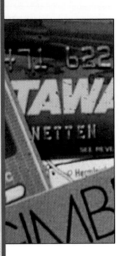

UNIT 10

MANAGING YOUR PERSONAL FINANCES

UNIT 11
WORKING IN THE GLOBAL ECONOMY

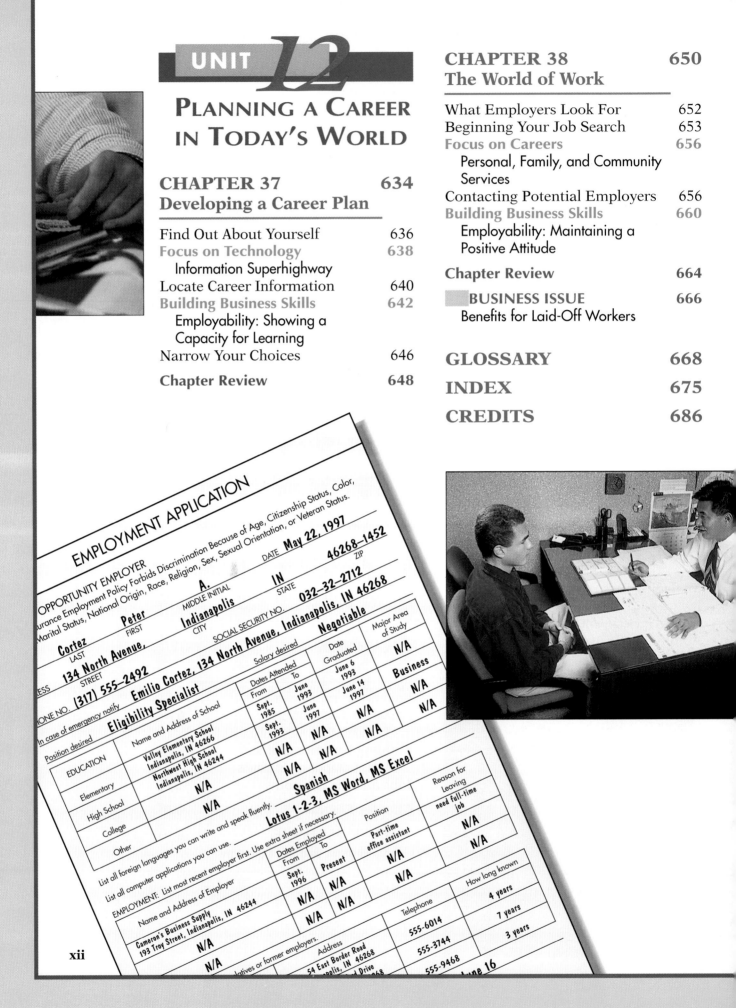

FOCUS ON **Careers**

FOCUS ON **Entrepreneurs**

FOCUS ON **Technology**

Building Business Skills

Inside Your Book

Structure of This Book

Your book contains 12 units. Each unit is divided into chapters; each chapter is divided into sections. There is a total of 38 chapters. This structure, together with numerous special features, helps you learn and apply the business and economic concepts that will enable you to become part of the global economy.

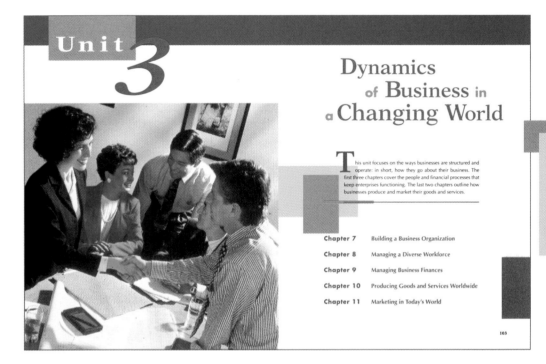

The **Unit Opener** lists the chapters found in that unit. A short introduction and a colorful topic photograph set the stage for what you will learn in the unit.

The **Chapter Opener** helps you organize your study of the chapter concepts. Business terms, learning objectives, and a review of previous learning preview what you will learn in the chapter. Purpose-setting questions guide your study and application of chapter concepts.

Inside Your Book

Channels of Distribution

Manufacturers/ Producers

Wholesalers

Distributors

Consumers

Retailers

FIGURE 11-3

Producers of goods u... eral main channels of ... bution to get their pro... to consumers. Which ... nel do consumers deal directly with?

Each chapter is divided into two to six sections, each ending with a Quick Check. Photographs, graphics, and maps expand and reinforce the business and economic concepts presented in the chapter.

- Distributors are intermediaries who represent a single manufacturer in a specific geographical area. Cosmetics, cars, furniture, and shoes are sold through distributors.
- Wholesalers are another kind of intermediary. They receive large shipments of products from many different producers. They break the shipments into smaller batches for resale. A company that makes canned peas may sell a truckload of its peas to a wholesaler. The wholesaler, in turn, will sell a few cases of peas to each of several local supermarkets.
- Retailers are intermediaries who sell goods directly to the consumer, the final stop in the channel of distribution. When you buy something in a supermarket, drugstore, or department store, you are dealing with a retailer.

GLOBAL VIEW

In labeling and advertis-ing, color... icant. Yet ... different ... ferent cul... ple, in th... often ass... black with... in Brazil ... ered a ... Japan the ... ing is whi... cultures lo... color that

F.Y.I.

Companies try to bridge the gap between con-sumers' rational and emo-tional sides. Lever Brothers is a company that has done so by using an effec-tive product symbol. It cre-ated an advertising cam-paign to promote fabric softener using a teddy bear named "Snuggle." The teddy bear was de-signed to appeal to con-sumers' emotions. It is also a good image for a fabric softener because it is soft and cuddly.

Special Features

Appearing throughout your book are numerous special features that reinforce and enhance your understanding of the business and economic concepts presented. Each feature will help you connect what you are learning to school and to work.

 Quick Check
1. Name the three types of intermediaries that direct products to consumers.
2. What part of the marketing mix does distribution address?
3. What is a channel of distribution?

SPECIAL CONCERNS FOR INTERNATIONAL MARKETERS

Marketers dealing with international markets face special challenges. These include communication difficulties, varying

CHAPTER 11 MARKETING IN TODAY'S WORLD **183**

A **Quick Check** helps you determine how well you understood the concepts presented in the section.

Margin features enhance your learning with interesting tidbits of information.

Building Business Skills

COMMUNICATION
Developing Listening Skills

Explanation

Listening is something you do every day. You prob-ably can't remember a time when you weren't listen-ing—to your mom, your best friend, your coach, your favorite singer, or a TV comic. What more can you pos-sibly learn about listening—something you've done all your life? The answer is "a lot." Most of the listening we do is passive. It just happens. We use our ears but not our minds. However, passive listening is not enough for business or for school.

It takes practice to use your mind to listen actively, but the rewards are great. In business, good communi-cation spells success, and good communication includes listening as well as speaking, reading, and writing. Active listening can help you brainstorm new ideas suc-cessfully, learn new procedures quickly, and understand a customer's complicated request.

Practice

Just how do you turn passive listening into an active skill? Use this checklist to help yourself become an active listener. On a separate sheet of paper, answer each question A (always), F (frequently), S (sometimes), or N (never).

ACTIVE LISTENING CHECKLIST

When you are listening, do you:
1. Determine a purpose for listening? A F S N
2. Avoid doing something else at the same time? A F S N
3. Screen out sights or sounds that could distract you? A F S N
4. Keep your eyes on the speaker? A F S N
5. Concentrate on what the person is saying? A F S N
6. Pick out the important ideas and think about how they are related? A F S N
7. Summarize the ideas in your head? A F S N
8. Take notes to help you focus and remember? A F S N
9. Ask the person to repeat or explain something that isn't clear to you? A F S N
10. Avoid interrupting before the speaker is finished talking? A F S N
11. Avoid thinking of what you will say next? A F S N
12. Pay attention even if you think the person's words don't interest you? A F S N
13. Listen carefully even if it takes time and effort to understand what the person is saying? A F S N

If all your answers are A or F, you have great listening skills! If not, you need practice. Each week choose two questions you answered S or N. Practice these skills in school, at home, and as you watch TV. Keep notes to see how you improve. Now you're on your way to becoming an active listener for school and your business career.

Building Business Skills presents important skills that are necessary for success in school and on the job.

product. A change in consumer demand may affect the price the seller has set.

Price can be used as a competitive strategy. Marketing spe-cialists may try to lure consumers away from their favorite brands by offering nearly identical products at slightly lower prices. Marketing people also use pricing to make products more appealing. They might offer special sale prices on certain products.

FIGURE 11-2

FOCUS ON **Careers**

Manufacturing Technology and Construction

It's almost impossible to imagine a world without tele-vision sets, clothes, cars, buildings, and roads. Yet we tend to take the existence of such material goods and structures for granted. We seldom give a thought to the complex and exacting work that produces them. The people who do this work are employed by manufactur-ing and construction businesses. They work at construc-tion sites as carpenters, plumbers, and operators of cranes and bulldozers. They hold jobs in plants making tiny electronic chips or putting together huge jet engines. They maintain and repair the machines that keep manu-facturing and construction going.

**HELP WANTED
APPRENTICE CARPENTER**
Carson Builders has opening for apprentice carpenter. No experi-ence needed. Earn money as you learn a useful trade by working with experienced carpenter to build house frames and install rafters and joists. Construct stair folds, walkways, and molds for concrete.
High school diploma or GED required. Good math and measur-ing skills, physical strength and flexibility, and excellent hand-eye coordination are musts. You'll need your own hand tools.

Careers in this area are often as high tech as they come. After all, the robots and comput-erized machines that have reduced the drudgery of manu-facturing tasks need skilled workers to operate and maintain them. Though some entry-level positions are open to people with high school diplomas, many require or welcome technical school training. Math, science, computer, machine shop, and mechanical

PRODUCT ASSEMBLER
Are you good at math? Skillful with tools? Mechanically inclined? Do you enjoy a team approach to your work? Then a job assembling electrical equipment at ReliaSoft Electric may be in your future! If hired, you'll have an active role in our team manufacturing process.
Ideal candidate will be a high school graduate with courses to stop, computers, and physics. Good communication skills and basic knowledge of electricity important.

drawing courses are a good starting point for anyone considering a career in manufactur-ing and construction.

Beginners in the building trades often start out as appren-tices working closely with experienced pro-fessionals on the job. Apprentice plumbers and electricians may also attend classes.

Whether the job involves assembling and testing a robot or building and installing fine wood cabinets, a high degree of precision is required. Success calls for mechanical aptitude, manual dexterity, and good eye-hand coordination—not to mention patience, per-

sistence, and self-control. Product assemblers today are often members of teams and need to work cooperatively and communicate well.

Help wanted ads for three entry-level jobs and a job post-ing for a more advanced posi-tion in manufactur-ing technology and construction are presented here.

ROBOTICS TECHNICIAN
ROBO...Robotics... for metal parts to be... a skilled individual to... robotics technician...diploma and technical... Courses on electronics... required. Must have... detailed ability to commu...
Robot...ics engineers to design and build robots...and operating systems, and maintaining...replacing faulty parts and...

CHAPTER 11 MARKETING IN TODAY'S WORLD **181**

**HELP WANTED
DELTA MANUFACTURING
JOB VACANCY POSTING**
Title: **Tool Programmer,
Numerical Control**
Salary Level: 12 E
Key Job Responsibilities:
Individual will analyze blueprint for metal parts to be produced. Will figure size and position of cuts to be made. Will determine order of machine operations, choose cor-rect tools for producing parts, and calculate machine speed. Using correct programming language, will write computer numerical con-trol (CNC) program to direct machine to make parts according to specifications. Will write instruc-tions to aid machine operator and monitor setup and trial run of machine.
Minimum Requirements:
Must have experience as a CNC machine-tool operator running a number of machines that produce metal parts and correcting flaws in programs that control machines. Must have knowledge of metal properties and technical school training in program tool program-ming. For complex projects, must work well with others. Must be will-ing and able to upgrade skills as new machinery is introduced. Must be detail-oriented and able to think logically.
If you feel you meet the mini-mum requirements, apply to the Human Resources Department by April 5.

Focus On features highlight entrepreneurs, careers, and technolo-gies that have had a significant impact on the global economy.

Materials Requirement Planning One technique used to control inventory is called *materials requirement planning* (MRP). This is a method of getting the correct materials where they are needed for production and doing it on time and with-out unnecessary stockpiling. In other words, end products are analyzed to determine the materials needed to produce them. A computer program generally determines when certain mate-rials are needed, when they should be ordered, and when they should be delivered so that they won't cost too much to store.

Manufacturing Resource Planning This inventory control technique is an extension of materials requirement planning. *Manufacturing resource planning* (MRPII) goes beyond MRP to include input from other departments including finance and marketing. Instead of focusing only on material requirements, it focuses on all available resources. A computer program ana-lyzes data from various departments to compare end product requirements to known company resources. This analysis then translates into forecasts of materials requirements and inven-tory needs.

Just-in-Time Planning Another method for managing inven-tory is the *just-in-time* (JIT) system. In this system, materials arrive precisely when they are needed on a production line, and finished goods are delivered "just in time" for usage. In other words, the system is designed to reduce a company's inventory to zero. Just-in-time planning requires that the production sys-tem be simple and well coordinated. It also requires clockwork timing and coordination within the operations system and between the company and its suppliers. For example, at one time, an automaker would order a truckload of parts for delivery within a two- or three-day window of time. Now that the same company will order a one-quarter load for delivery within a two- to three-hour window. Computer-controlled systems alert managers when it is time to order needed materials.

Quick Check
1. What methods do managers use to control production?
2. Give definitions for *production forecasting, inventory,* and *inventory control.*

Reviewing and Applying What You Know

Review and application activities encourage you to apply the business concepts and skills you have learned.

Chapter Summary lists the main ideas of the chapter for quick review and recall.

Case Analysis offers you an opportunity to apply your decision-making skills based on the chapter concepts.

Chapter Review activities and questions help you review important business and economic terms and concepts.

Chapter 11 **Summary**

Main Ideas

1. The marketing mix is made up of product, price, promotion, and place.
2. Market planning involves deciding whether to produce consumer or industrial goods and services and considering the life cycle of the product.
3. Producers of goods and services must understand the physical, social, and psychological needs of consumers and their rational, emotional, and patronage motives for buying goods and services.
4. Market research helps producers determine what people need and want to buy.
5. Products are priced, packaged, and promoted to persuade customers to buy them.
6. People who work in marketing need to be able to communicate well, to get along with people, to have good math skills, to be motivated, and to have creativity and problem-solving skills.
7. Businesses use electronic databases to quickly find specific information to help them make sound business decisions.
8. Active listening is a communication skill that is important in business.

CASE ANALYSIS   Marketing

Assume that you are a market researcher. Choose a product that you know your classmates use, such as clothing, pens, sunglasses, or shampoo. Design a survey to find out why people prefer certain brands. Then ask five classmates to take your survey. Ask them about brands, price, color, style, durability, and other qualities. Also ask them how their own needs and motives as well as advertising affect their buying decisions. After you complete the survey, analyze your results. What did you learn about your classmates' likes and dislikes? Do you think they were honest in answering your questions? Could you have designed your survey to obtain more information? If you were a marketer, how would you use the information you gathered?

Chapter 11 **Review**

...age of Business

...market goods and services ...ng terms. See how well you ...tch each term to its defini-

demographics
logo
marketing mix
market research

...bol,
...oduct, price, promotion,
and place.

3. Group of intermediaries who direct products to consumers.
4. Study of population.
5. Paid promotion.
6. Study showing what types of products and services people like to buy.
7. Point at which money from sales equals the costs of making and distributing a product.
8. Items that are sold to individuals and families.

Review What You Learned

1. Name the four elements of the marketing mix.
2. Name the four phases of a product's life cycle.
3. What information do product labels provide?
4. List three types of intermediaries between a producer and a final user.

5. List three concerns of international marketers.
6. List the five traits that marketing employees need to have.
7. Define the terms *data, database, record,* and *field.*
8. Explain the difference between active and passive listening.

Understand Business Concepts

1. How does placement affect the sales of a product?
2. Which of the four marketing elements do you think is the most important? Why?
3. How are convenience goods and shopping goods different? Give examples.
4. List a product that you think might have a short life cycle and one that might have a long life cycle. Explain your choices.
5. Give examples of products or services that people buy to satisfy physical, social, and psychological needs. Use examples that are not in the text.

6. How might products and services for people's physical, social, and psychological needs vary between countries? Give some examples if you can.
7. What could market researchers learn about a group of people by studying the foods they bought in the last year?
8. Why do you think companies try to design easily recognizable logos?
9. What do you think are some ways businesses could make use of databases?
10. What advantages do you think an active listener has in business?

Think Critically

1. **Analyze.** Choose a ...uct you bought recently. How did price, packaging, advertising, and placement affect your decision to buy the product?
2. **Classify.** Locate several magazine advertisements. What type of advertisements appeal to consumer motivations

in the three basic categories: rational, emotional, and patronage?
3. **Recommend.** Some companies plan special events to draw publicity for a new product. What kind of event could a shoe company hold to attract publicity for a new line of athletic shoes?

Use What You Learned

1. **Group Project.** Work in teams to conduct a survey of other students, teachers, family members, and people in the community to find out what factors are most important in their buying decisions. Find out:
   - Which stores they shop in most frequently.
   - What types of advertising they pay most attention to.
   - What factors are most important to them when making decisions about convenience goods and services, shopping goods and services, and specialty goods and services.

   Keep a copy of your survey and the results. Summarize the results in a chart to display in your classroom.
2. Find out more about current market research techniques, including database marketing. Use articles from newspapers and business magazines. Write a one-paragraph summary and share it with the class.

3. Write a job description for an entry-level position with a top advertising agency. Include a description of the job duties required as well as a description of the ideal applicant.
4. **Computer Application.** Using on-line research, access government/priv... databases to obtain the ...the top ten companies a... processing software to p... in table format. Then wr... tively format a one-paragraph a... of the kinds of companies that fa... within the top categories. Print o... table and your analysis.
5. **Skill Reinforcement.** Review you... answers to the Active Listening Ch... list on page 181, especially those th... indicated you needed to practice ... listening skills. Then write a short p... graph describing those situations in ... which you can best practice those skills and explain why.

Chapter Review activities and questions encourage you to apply the concepts and skills you learned in the chapter.

Save your work in ...

Business Issue

DOWNSIZING

When a company drops employees from its payrolls to cut costs, it is called *downsizing.* Should American companies use downsizing to help them become more cost-efficient and increase their competitive edge in the global marketplace?

Pro

Companies that are carrying too much debt, have increased their use of technology, or eliminated product lines often must reduce staff in order to remain efficient. Because employees' wages, salaries, and benefits account for a major portion of a company's budget, management can achieve savings by eliminating jobs. If the company's competitors in the United States and abroad are able to produce a product or service for less money, a company unable to match that lower price may not survive.

Although no one relishes taking away people's jobs, corporations need to show a profit in order to stay in business. Stiffer competition from the global market in the 1990s made profits harder to come by and demanded extreme measures. If a loss of profits forces enough American companies out of business, the whole United States economy will suffer. This means that many more people than those who lose their jobs through downsizing will find themselves without work.

Reductions in staff can actually improve the quality and delivery of products and services to customers. One hotel chain, for example, employed 40 managers and 200 other employees for a 300-room hotel. A careful examination of operations showed that those operations could be streamlined considerably. The chain trimmed the staff to 14 managers and 140 employees. As a result of the downsizing, both customer and staff satisfaction increased.

In addition, people who lose their jobs because of downsizing can be retrained or hired in other jobs that use their skills to better advantage. Downsizing can also lead to an increase in entrepreneurship. Some workers have turned their job losses into personal opportunities by starting their own business ventures. An increase in new businesses creates new jobs.

Downsizing is a positive practice that results in long-term benefits for everyone by allowing the United States to remain a competitor in the global market.

Con

According to one statistic, since downsizing began in the early 1990s about 75 percent of the companies that reduced their workforces did not improve productivity or profitability. Several theories help explain this.

When a company's managers find that they must cut costs, they often panic and let 20 to 25 percent of their workforce go without examining the best ways to economize. Nor do they find out exactly how employees contribute to the overall operations of the company. As a result, they sometimes cut necessary employees.

After downsizing, the tasks of the dismissed staff must be performed by the remaining employees. These workers are often not able to do these tasks, let alone add them to their own workloads. As a consequence, they do not work as effectively as they did before. Instead of seeing gains in productivity and efficiency, companies become less productive and may even lose business as a result of downsizing.

Even if a company can show that downsizing has cut costs, the strategy may have a negative effect on the remaining employees' morale and confidence in the company. Since they suspect that their jobs will be eliminated, workers may doubt the worth of their efforts. They may work less hard and be less productive.

Low morale can also lead the employees who remain to take their talents elsewhere. Often, these are the very people expected to lead the downsized company to greater productivity and efficiency. Companies then find themselves without some of their best employees. In some cases, downsizing has led to the departure of a company's top people.

Mass layoffs are not a long-term answer to increased profitability. Companies that value the importance of their human resources have found alternatives to downsizing, such as retraining and moving employees to other divisions. Instead of eliminating jobs, some companies have replaced part of their employees' salaries with shares of stock. This strategy gives workers part ownership and a real stake in their company's success.

Downsizing is a negative practice that hurts employees as well as the productivity and profitability of the companies that downsize.

A **Business Issue** concludes each unit. Each focuses on the pros and cons of a timely economic issue that businesses face.

Unit 1 Introduction to the Global Economy

Chapter	Learning Objectives
1 **Business in Today's World** pp. 2–19	• Explain the differences between wants and needs. • Discuss what businesses do to provide goods and services. • Describe some steps in planning for a career. • Identify some jobs and skills in business and financial operations. • Explain the steps in the decision-making process.
2 **Economic Challenges Facing Business** pp. 20–35	• Identify the four factors of production • Explain why the scarcity of economic resources is a problem for every country. • List the three basic questions regarding the production and distribution of goods and services. • Explain the circular flow of economic activity. • Identify the basic components of a computer. • Describe how to evaluate information.
3 **Measuring Economic Performance** pp. 36–51	• Describe the four phases of the business cycle. • Explain how economic activity is measured. • Explain how the federal government tries to maintain stability in our economy. • Describe how one inventor became an entrepreneur. • Explain what inflation is and how it affects the economy.

Business Issue: Full Employment, pp. 52–53

National Standards for Business Education*	Focus on Features	Building Business Skills	Visual Learning	Case Analysis
CD: I A, II A, III A, IV A, VI B; *EPF:* II, V, XIII A; *MGMT:* I A	Careers: Business and Financial Operations Support, p. 6	Employability: Making Decisions, p. 10	Career Clusters, p. 16	School-to-Work Goals, p. 17
COMM: I D; *EE:* I A, III; *EPF:* I, IV, V, VIII, X C; *IS;* I	Technology: Basic Computer Components, p. 24	Analysis: Evaluating Information, p. 28	Factors of Production, p. 23 Population of World Regions, p. 27 Circular Flow Model, p. 32	Factors of Production, p. 33
EE: I A, III; *EPF:* III, IV, XI, XII; *IBF:* EPF, EE	Entrepreneurs: Dean Kamen— DEKA Research & Development Corporation, p. 40	Math: Understanding Inflation, p. 44	Business Cycle Model, p. 39 U.S. Gross Domestic Product, p. 43 Rate of Inflation in the United States, p. 46	The Business Cycle, p. 49

* Level 3 Performance Expectations: Career Development (CD), Communications (COMM), Economics and Personal Finance (EPF), Entrepreneurship Education (EE), Information Systems (IS), Management (MGMT). See page T14 for all 12 content areas.

Unit 1

Look Back

Point out to students that whenever they buy goods such as blue jeans, or services such as tickets to movies, they are participating in our economic system as a consumer. Point out to students that millions of dollars are spent each year in an attempt to influence teenage consumers to buy various goods and services such as clothing, cosmetics, and soft drinks.

UNIT 1 COOPERATIVE LEARNING PROJECT

Categorizing Activity

Preparation: Photocopy and distribute to each student a copy of BLM 1 from the *Cooperative Learning Strategies* booklet. Photocopy and distribute one copy of BLM 2 to each group. Provide students with colored pencils or markers. This project will take approximately one class period.

Guidelines: Have students begin the project at home by using BLM 1 to make a list of common household products for which they can determine the country of origin. Then have students get together with their groups to combine their lists

Introduction to the Global Economy

Look Ahead
Explain to students that many of the goods we buy to satisfy our wants and needs come from other countries. Our country also sells many of our products to other countries. The goods and services a country is able to provide depend on that country's factors of production—the natural, human, capital, and entrepreneurial resources that a country can use to produce goods and services.

T his unit introduces the role and function of business in today's international economy. The first chapter introduces basic business concepts and the relationship between businesses and consumers. The last two chapters explain the components of the business process and economic cycles that affect it.

TEACHING TIP
Use the videos and activities from *The Wall Street Journal* Video Series to introduce, reinforce, extend, or close the chapters in each unit. This series of videos is based on *The Wall Street Journal Classroom Edition.* The videos are correlated to the content of the 38 chapters in *Introduction to Business: Our Business and Economic World.*

1

and categorize the items according to function—clothing, furniture, electronics, and so on. Ask groups to come up with a symbol for each category. Then have group members use the colored pencils and markers to add the symbols to the world map shown on BLM 2. Students should use the symbols to try to identify patterns of world trade. Do some nations or regions seem to specialize in a particular kind of product? Have groups compare information with other groups and continue to look for patterns.

FOCUS

Introduce the Chapter

Major Concepts
• Wants and Needs
• Making Choices
• What Is Business?
• You and the Business World
• From School to Work

Introduce the Topic
Write the following statements on the board and have students complete them.
Things I need in order to survive include _____ .
Things I want to have include _____ .
Ask volunteers to read their statements. Discuss with students how they distinguished between those items they want and those that they need.

Use Business Terms
Have students look at the Business Terms and note any that are familiar to them. Ask them to define these terms or try to recall the context in which they were used. For those terms that are unfamiliar, have students venture a meaning. Reinforce correct definitions. For terms that they cannot define, advise students to note the definitions in the chapter.

USE VISUALS

Have students study the photo for a few moments and then ask them how business affects the lives of ordinary people like those in the photo? What effect do these people have on businesses?
(Answers will vary.)

Business terms

wants

needs

goods

services

resource

opportunity cost

business

ability

aptitude

career clusters

2

CHAPTER 1 RESOURCES

Instructional Resources

Lesson Plan for Chapter 1

Teaching Transparency 1-1

Strategies and Worksheets for Teaching Transparency 1-1

Enrichment Master 1-1

Student Activity Guide 1–TAE for Chapter 1

Test Master for Chapter 1

Alternative Assessment Strategies

Math Skills Review

International Business Strategies

Cooperative Learning Strategies

Communication Skills Review

Ethics in Business Strategies

Business in Today's World

Learning objectives

After completing this chapter, you will be able to:
- Explain the differences between wants and needs.
- Discuss what businesses do to provide goods and services.
- Describe some steps in planning for a career.
- Identify some jobs and skills in business and financial operations.
- Explain the steps in the decision-making process.

Consider what you know

- You and your family buy things like clothes, groceries, and gas for a car. You pay other people to do things such as cut your hair or give you a bus ride. In these and other ways, you are participating in businesses as a consumer.

Consider what you want to know

- What are wants and needs?
- How do people decide which goods and services to purchase?
- What is involved in providing goods and services for a worldwide market?
- How can you participate in the business world by building career skills while you are still in school?
- What skills and abilities are needed for different careers in the business and financial operations support field?
- What are the five steps in the decision-making process?

Consider how to use what you learn

- As you read this chapter, think about how you make decisions and choices. What motivates you to shop at a particular store?

Multimedia Resources

Technology Resource Guide

Distance Learning Guide

Internet Resource Guide

Professional Resources

School-to-Work/Tech Prep Strategies

Instructional Poster

Spanish Resources

Testmaker Software for Chapter 1

The Wall Street Journal Video Series
Video & Activities for Chapter 1

Business and Marketing Computer Applications—An Integrated Software Simulation Using Microsoft Works

Stocktracker—A Stock Market Software Simulation

Where's the Dough? Board Game

Motivate the Learning

Learning Objectives
Point out to students that the learning objectives show what they will learn in the chapter. Tell students to keep these objectives in mind as they work through the chapter. Note that the last two objectives listed refer to the Focus on Careers feature and the Building Business Skills feature.

Consider What You Know
Ask students what they think of when they think of business. Have they ever thought about their role in business? Point out to students that they are making a business transaction whenever they buy a good or a service. Students who have jobs already have business responsibilities.

Consider What You Want to Know
Ask students to read the questions, then page quickly through the chapter to get an idea of how the chapter will help them discover answers.

Consider How to Use What You Learn
Explain to students that at the end of the chapter they will develop some projects related to how they interact with the business world. Suggest that as they read the chapter they think about how their values and goals motivate the decisions they make.

Business Connection

The marketing strategy of the Home Depot chain of home center stores consists of offering prices 20 to 30 percent lower than the competition and a huge variety of products displayed in no-frills warehouse-sized stores. Low prices often go with minimal levels of customer service, but at Home Depot, employees are trained in home-repair techniques, and stores offer free clinics for customers on topics from plumbing to decorative tiling. Employees are encouraged to spend as much time as it takes to educate customers. Workers get stock shares in the company, so they have a personal interest in seeing the company do well.

Develop Concepts

Wants and Needs

Ask students to list ten things they do not have now that they would like to have. Ask them to classify each item as to whether it is a want of an individual or of an entire society. Then ask them to classify each item as absolutely necessary or not.

Help students distinguish between needs and wants in specific categories. For example, a person may *need* a warm winter coat, but may *want* a certain brand or style. Have students think of other examples.

How often do you play a part in the world of business? Whether you know it or not, you, your friends, and your family interact with the business world every day. You even interact with businesses on the other side of the world. As consumers, you are important participants in a global market that includes goods and services from all over the world. Look at the tag on your shirt or the label on your backpack. You make choices about the clothes you buy and the music you play. When you travel to visit a friend, you choose one mode of transportation over another.

You, along with your friends and family, interact with the business world every time you make choices about goods and services. Businesses, too, make decisions every day that affect you. New products, higher prices, and the supply of products affect you, your family, and friends. In this chapter you will explore your roles and choices in today's business world.

WANTS AND NEEDS

Suppose you have $5 to spend. You could use it to buy lunch or a magazine. You could rent a movie. What is the difference between what you want and what you need? How can you satisfy wants and needs with the money you have available?

An Abundance of Wants

Wants are the things we wish we could have. Every individual person has wants. However, some wants are shared by people in families, businesses, or groups. A family might want a new car, a company might want a more advanced computer system, or an athletic club might want a swimming pool. Although these wants are shared, they are still considered private wants of the family, business, or group.

On the other hand, some wants are shared so widely by so many people that they are really no longer private. They become public wants. Highways, drinking water, and education are examples of public wants. For the most part, public wants are satisfied by local, state, and federal governments.

Wants can also be classified as necessary or optional. Necessary wants are **needs,** or things we must have to survive. Food, shelter, and clothing are the most basic of these needs. Optional wants are things that are not necessary for our survival. Many

Global Perspective

Someone living in a rain forest does not have the same needs as does someone in Northern Canada. Discuss how needs vary depending on environment. Have groups of students choose a country or a region of the world and speculate about the climate and economic conditions of that area. Have them develop a list of needs for survival in that climate based on what they have discussed.

Refer to the *International Business Strategies* booklet for additional strategies and activities.

of the items that are important to our daily lives are actually optional wants.

Satisfying Wants: Goods and Services

Most of our wants—whether private or public, necessary or optional—can be satisfied by some type of good or service. **Goods** can be physically weighed or measured. We may buy goods or someone else may buy them for us. Bicycles and skates are goods—so are groceries and telephones. Goods satisfy some of our wants and needs for material things—things we can see or touch.

We also want people to do certain things for us for a fee: cut our hair or teach us how to play a guitar. These are wants for **services,** which are tasks that people or machines perform. Services satisfy some of our wants for nonmaterial things—that is, things we cannot see or touch.

The activities of business do not satisfy every kind of desire. Think about your own wants. Could each of them be satisfied by a good or a service? Although many could be, some could not. All of us want things that cannot be valued in terms of money. For example, we all want to be loved, respected, and have our achievements recognized. When we talk about wants in this book, we are not talking about these intangible kinds of desires. We are talking about those wants that goods and services can satisfy.

Unlimited Wants, Limited Resources

Everyone wants goods and services. Few people, however, have enough resources to satisfy all of their wants. A **resource** is anything that people can use to make or obtain what they need or want. The problem of unlimited wants and limited ways to satisfy those wants affects everyone, from individuals to companies to nations.

The number of wants we can satisfy is limited by our resources. For example, you may want some new clothes and a new camera, but you may have only enough money to buy one of these things. You may also want to earn a lot of money, but have only so much time to work after school and on Saturdays. Businesses and government agencies are affected by the same problem. They lack the resources to do all the things that they want to do.

Quick Check

1. Define *wants, needs, goods, services,* and *resource.*
2. What is the difference between private and public wants?

Some sociologists classify consumer needs as lower-order and higher-order needs. Lower-order needs are food, shelter, and the need to feel safe and protected from danger. Higher-order needs are generally more psychological, for example, the desire for self-fulfillment, success, and respect. In countries like the United States, Canada, England, and Japan, the majority of consumers have satisfied their lower-order needs, so marketers promote goods and services that will appeal to higher-order needs.

TEACHING TIP
Reinforce students' understanding by having them classify the following businesses according to whether they provide goods or services:
- automatic car wash (service)
- health club (service)
- hot dog stand (goods)
- movie theater (service)
- supermarket (goods)
- pet shop (goods)

Learning Activity
Have the class brainstorm a list of classroom resources. (The list might include audiovisual equipment, computers, books, desks, tables, board, and so forth.) Have students describe how each of the resources helps satisfy the need of getting an education.

 Quick Check Answers
1. The desire for things people wish they could have; things people must have to survive, such as food, clothing, and shelter; items that can be weighed or measured; tasks done by people or machines; anything that people can use to make or obtain what they want or need.
2. Private wants are the wants of an individual or people in a group, such as a family or business. Public wants are shared by many people, for example, the desire for public highways or schools.

Making Connections ➤ Community Issues

Have students brainstorm some wants of their community that are not universally agreed upon. For example, some people may think the community needs another elementary school; others may think it isn't necessary. Have students choose a community issue and discuss why community members take different sides on the issue and what resources are involved. How much of the disagreement is about the use of the community's resources?

FOCUS ON **Careers**

Discuss

Discuss with students the kinds of skills people in the business and financial operations support field use. Ask students what courses in school could help them prepare for entry-level business and financial operations support jobs. How do people advance in such careers?

Develop Concepts

Making Choices

Most choices businesses and governments make affect many people. Trying to make a decision that will please everyone is sometimes extremely difficult. Ask students to describe some of the strategies they have used in their own lives to reach compromises in group decisions. Divide the class into groups of five, and have them suppose that their group has been awarded $25 for the best float in the school's homecoming parade. Have the group decide how they should spend their award money. Remind groups that every member has an equal voice in the decision. Allow groups 10 minutes to decide what they will do with the money. Then have a volunteer from each group explain how the group plans to spend the money and how students arrived at their decision.

Business and Financial Operations Support

Banks, insurance companies, law firms—and just about any other enterprise you could name—depend on support personnel to keep them in business. Without processing clerks, administrative assistants, bank tellers, and others, much of the world's work would simply not get done. People who hold support positions help their companies by monitoring goods and payments sent out and received, keeping careful track of information and money, and acting as channels to connect outsiders with business.

Once, business and financial operations support was carried out largely "by hand." Today, as processes become computerized, training in keyboarding and experience with a variety of software is a necessity. Basic skills, such as reading, writing, and math are also essential. The ability of employees to read and record words and numbers quickly and accurately keeps business transactions flowing smoothly.

Many business and financial support workers spend their hours behind the scenes processing

HELP WANTED

LEGAL SECRETARY

Earn high pay, high respect. Doe, Roe, and Poe, Attorneys at Law, are seeking outstanding individual with general secretarial experience to be a legal secretary. Excellent keyboarding skills and knowledge of most popular word processing and spreadsheet software a necessity. Good English language skills required. Technical school course in legal terminology/procedures a plus.

Ideal candidate will be well-organized, independent, able to work under stress, willing to work long hours when needed.

MAKING CHOICES

Having limited resources means that we must make choices. We have to decide which wants are most important to us and which wants we will choose to satisfy and why. We can then choose the goods or services that will best meet those wants. Making decisions is an important part of life.

Decision making is the process of determining which wants and needs to meet at a particular time. Wise decision makers want to gain as much satisfaction as possible from their limited resources. To do so, they must set priorities—that is, determine the order of importance of doing things at a particular time. How do you determine your priorities?

The Cost of Choosing

What makes one choice more desirable than another? Which will give you the most satisfaction? Suppose that a new CD costs $15. That is also the cost of getting the film from last week's game developed. You want both, but you have only $15 to spend. You decide to buy the CD and get the film developed later.

6 UNIT 1 INTRODUCTION TO THE GLOBAL ECONOMY

Reteaching Strategy

Have students write about a recent situation in which they had to make one choice over another. What criteria did they use to make the choice? What did they give up? If the situation arose again, would they make the same choice? Why or why not?

checks, recording deposits, inputting data, and preparing letters and forms. Others need well-developed interpersonal skills as they greet their business's visitors, solve customer problems, and communicate with clients on the telephone. It almost goes without saying that all these jobs require organizational skills.

nesses. These positions may offer a variety of career paths and often give employees an unparalleled view of the "inner workings" of a particular business.

Help wanted ads showing four entry-level jobs in business and financial operations support are presented here.

Trustworthiness, ethical behavior, and reliability are vital for people in support positions, particularly those in financial operations. The rewards for doing these jobs well include pride in your contribution, as well as higher pay and advancement. Entry-level support jobs requiring a high school diploma are available in most busi-

There is another cost besides the $15 involved in your decision. In buying the CD, you gave up the opportunity to get the film developed, at least for the moment. What you give up when you make one choice instead of another is called the **opportunity cost.**

Sometimes the opportunity cost is not money or another item. For example, you may decide to go to the library to study for a math test instead of inviting some of your friends over. The opportunity cost of passing the test is having friends over. Choosing between alternatives involves more than just knowing what you give up. It also involves knowing what you gain.

Values and Goals

You may value a classmate as a friend because that person has a refreshing sense of humor. Perhaps you admire a particular teacher because of her ability to keep cool when the class gets out of hand. Hiking in the woods is your favorite sport because you love being outdoors and away from crowds and traffic. For you, a sense of humor, an even temper, and being out in the woods are all values, things you prize and think are important.

Some of our values come from the people around us and other outside influences. Others are the result of our personal

Curriculum Connection   Economics

The so-called "guns or butter" dilemma is often used to illustrate the economic opportunity costs governments face when deciding how to spend federal money. High levels of military spending (guns) come at the cost of civilian uses and social programs, such as health care or economic development (butter). Do countries need to spend so much on military costs during peacetime, or should the governments use tax money to pay for social and economic programs? Have groups of students take a position on the guns or butter issue. Groups should gather evidence and examples to support their position and develop and present their argument to the class. As a class, evaluate the evidence presented on both sides of the issue.

People's values and goals can affect the kinds of jobs they want to do. What are some of the values this young woman probably has?

Business & HISTORY

Through the ages, people have made decisions in many different ways. Some people let others make decisions and choices for them. For example, in ancient times, people consulted the Oracle at Delphi in Greece. The oracle was a woman trained from a young age to answer people's questions and to help them make difficult decisions. Her answers were often given in the form of a riddle. People who consulted the oracle had to interpret the riddle. Naturally, their own values entered into their interpretation of the riddle. As a result, they often ended up making their own decisions without realizing it.

interests and abilities. No two people have exactly the same set of values. Your own values help guide you in making decisions. When you choose between two alternatives, you place one of your values ahead of another.

Your goals, or aims or objectives, also play a role when you make decisions. Your goals may include passing an English test, getting a good job, or owning your own car. Some goals, such as getting a good job, are long-term goals. Others, such as doing well on a test, are short-term goals.

The goals you set for yourself can tell you something about your values. For example, if one of your goals is to continue your education after high school, you obviously value learning new skills. Sometimes you have goals that conflict with each other. Suppose you want to continue your education after high school, but you also want the income you could earn if you worked full time. You cannot manage both goals at once, no matter how much you want them. You must deal with conflicts concerning resources. When conflicts occur, you must make choices.

Meeting Student Diversity

Having values and goals is not enough. You have to recognize what they are, and you need to know which ones are most important to you. If you do not know what your values and goals are, it is difficult to set priorities or to determine the opportunity costs of your choices. You really need to know yourself before you can make wise decisions.

Quick Check

1. Give definitions for *decision making, priorities, values,* and *goals.*
2. What costs do you encounter when you give up one choice in favor of another?

WHAT IS BUSINESS?

Business is all of the activities of an individual or group of individuals involved in producing and distributing goods and services to customers. Businesses profit from the goods and services they provide. In order to have a profitable business, whether it is a florist's shop or a software manufacturer, the business must figure out what people want to buy. You participate in deciding what a business will produce every time you buy something. When people do not buy a good or service at a price at which a profit can be made, it indicates that the good or service is not wanted. Usually businesses stop producing it.

Businesses are interested in your values and goals because they contribute to the decisions you make to buy certain things. When a business decides to produce a new good or service, the people who run the business want to be sure that there are people who will buy the product. If you are a runner, a business that manufactures running shoes is interested in your values and goals and will try to produce a shoe that will appeal to you. Marketing research is one of the tools businesses use to identify potential buyers. Businesses must also consider the resources they will use to produce goods and services. They must make decisions about how to use the resources most effectively.

Some form of business activity occurs in every country on earth. In fact, today more business activity occurs among different countries than ever before. Many goods and services are a combination of business activities involving many different countries. If you regularly read a major newspaper, you have some experience with global business activity. The newspaper company in a large U.S. city may print the newspapers on materials produced by a Canadian company. A special feature in the paper might be written by a journalist in Europe. You

Curriculum Connection   History

Have students work in teams to research how people from various parts of the world conducted business during different times of history. Assign each team one of the following topics: Egypt from about 2600 to 2500 B.C., the Roman Empire from about 300 to 100 B.C., Northern Europe during the 1500s, England from about 1750 to 1850, and the United States from about 1850 to 1920. Suggest that teams include in their reports such information as what kind of work people did, how business activities were organized, the tools people used, the goods or services that were produced, and how the goods and services were distributed.

Quick Check Answers

1. The process of determining which wants and needs will be met at a particular time; the order of importance of doing things; things a person prizes and thinks are important; a person's aims or objectives.
2. Opportunity costs.

Develop Concepts

What Is Business?

Have students think about products and services they see advertised in magazines or on television. Ask students what methods marketers and advertisers use to appeal to teenage consumers. Ask students if, in their opinion, such marketing strategies work.

Business Brief

Good customer service is more important in the 1990s because increased competition is stimulating companies to work harder in order not to lose customers to the competition. BancOne has been recognized in its industry for its exceptional customer service. BancOne surveys 35,000 of its customers four times a year to find out what the customers want. For example, customers requested more convenient hours. As a result, about 60 percent of BancOne's branches are open on Saturday, and 20 percent are even open on Sunday.

Building Business Skills

Model

Tell students to suppose that in order to prepare for a career, they want to take an accounting class offered in the evenings at a junior college. However, they would have to give up a part-time job in order to take the class. Guide the class through the steps of the Decision-Making Process, helping volunteers provide responses for each of the steps in the situation.

EMPLOYABILITY

Making Decisions

Explanation

You've been making decisions all your life. As you grow older, the decisions you make will be more and more important. When you make important decisions, such as choosing a career or a place to live, you will want to make them carefully.

Effective decision-makers in business, government, and daily life follow a simple step-by-step procedure. The procedure can help you identify available alternatives and analyze the effect of each. It will also enable you to identify the opportunity cost, or what you give up when you eliminate a choice. Here are the steps.

1. Identify the problem.
2. List the alternatives.
3. Determine the pros and cons.
4. Make the best decision.
5. Evaluate your decision.

Practice

Apply the steps of the decision-making process to this situation. You must decide between an after-school job that pays very well and one that pays less but will help prepare you for a career you are interested in.

Business Brief

The temporary help/staffing services industry is rapidly expanding, and the number of jobs in the temporary staffing industry is expected to grow throughout the 1990s. Companies are using temporary staffing services because such services are less costly than full-time employees. Temporary services can provide businesses with highly skilled personnel on an as-needed basis, giving businesses greater flexibility for responding to the constantly changing needs of their operations.

read the paper and then put it in a recycling bin. The newspaper is collected, sold, and shipped to an Asian country where it is recycled into new paper. This is one of many examples of goods and services that combine the business activities of different people and countries.

Providing Goods and Services

Businesses provide goods and services based upon what people need and want. Today, the number of goods and services provided by business is huge. Different people have different needs and wants. Their needs and wants change as time passes. Businesses are aware of people's changing wants and needs. New businesses often come into being because of these changing wants and needs.

The development of information technology—computers, software, and telecommunications—has created rapid production of a variety of goods and services. You might depend on a specific software program to complete schoolwork. People working in homes, libraries, or other workplaces use on-line information services that use a computer, telephone lines, and software. Banks rely on computers and software to update

Reteaching Strategy

Have students use the Decision-Making Process to identify and make a decision about the following problem. Customers at Yuri's Yogurt Shoppe frequently tell him he should serve soup and sandwiches. A new sandwich shop recently opened across the street, and Yuri is afraid he will lose some of his business. Expanding the menu will mean hiring workers and remodeling the shop, which would strain Yuri's budget at this time.

Decision-Making Process

Step 1. Identify the problem. Whether the decision-making problem is one that occurs daily or comes up only a few times in a lifetime, this is the first step. It is often the easiest.

Step 2. List the alternatives. Take time to think the problem through, so you come up with a good range of alternatives. Try to include all the important ones.

Step 3. Determine the pros and cons. Write down and weigh the advantages and disadvantages of each alternative. Your values and goals now become part of the decision-making process.

Step 4. Make the best decision. Determining the best alternative is the key step in the process. Rank the alternatives according to their pros and cons. After you pick a winner, ask yourself what you'll lose if you give up your second choice. Do you really want to give up that alternative?

Step 5. Evaluate your decision. After you've put your decision into effect, ask yourself whether you achieved the results you expected. Would you make the same choice again?

Write a response to each step of the process to make your decision. As you use the process, you'll realize that the steps aren't new to you. You probably use a version of them almost every time you make a decision.

Practice

Have students review the steps in the Decision-Making Process and then use the process to describe how they would arrive at a decision.
(1. Which part-time job would be best for me now?
2. I can take a job that pays well, or I can take a job that pays less but will help me train for a future career.
3. Students' answers will vary.
4. Students' answers will vary.
5. Students' answers will vary.)

financial information for customers. Companies in every industry use information technology to be more competitive in their businesses. The number of service businesses providing information services is growing so rapidly that some business leaders refer to our era as the "information age."

What Business Does

How do you learn about new products or services? Why are some goods not available when you visit a store? You might be surprised to learn about all that happens before a product makes it to a store near you.

When a product such as a soft drink is available to buy, many business activities have taken place so that you could buy it. A company *organized* the people and machinery to provide the product. Within that company, businesspeople *managed* the company's human, financial, and production resources and *produced* the drink. Then the company *marketed* the drink by advertising it and selling it to stores where it is available for you to buy. Every business uses this combination of organizing, managing, producing, and marketing its goods and services to consumers.

CHAPTER 1   BUSINESS IN TODAY'S WORLD   **11**

Enrichment Strategy

Have interested students interview a small business owner about how he or she uses information technology in his or her business. Business owners who have been in business for ten years or more can explain how technology has changed the way they do business. Students should share the information they obtained with the rest of the class.

Business Brief

By 1995 America Online (AOL) managed to increase its subscriber list fourfold since its launch in 1992. However, competition among on-line services was stiffening considerably. Microsoft Network and new on-line services offered by telecommunications companies that allow users to directly access the Internet have more appeal for business and academic customers than AOL, which is geared primarily toward the consumer market.

Use Transparencies

Use Teaching Transparency 1-1 and its corresponding strategies and worksheet from the *Teaching Transparency Strategies and Worksheets* booklet to help students better understand how businesses coordinate resources and activities. Verify student worksheets using the Answer Key.

F.Y.I.

Two people who successfully responded to people's wants and needs were Levi Strauss and Jacob Davis. Strauss and Davis became partners in 1873 and soon began selling work pants to miners, surveyors, cowboys, and other hard-working westerners. Early buyers called the denim pants "Levi's," and the name stuck. Levi Strauss & Company remains one of the world's largest manufacturers of jeans.

Resources Businesses Use

No business can produce goods and services without resources. The salesperson at your favorite store is a resource—so is the building that houses that store and the factories around the world that produce the goods sold there. The energy it takes to produce an aluminum can is a resource too. The bauxite mined from the earth to make aluminum and even the earth itself are resources. People who come up with new ideas for goods or services or think of ways to improve business provide a less obvious, but extremely valuable, resource. Without innovation, or new ideas, we would not have many of the goods and services that we take for granted today. Balancing the use of resources to make a product can be a challenge. Businesses make choices about how to use resources every day; they decide whether it costs too much to use one resource over another.

Quick Check
1. Explain the term *business*.
2. What activities must all businesses engage in when providing goods or services to consumers?

YOU AND THE BUSINESS WORLD

Business affects you and you affect business. Your decisions now and in the future affect business. Business decisions, in turn, will affect you in the present and in the future. It is important to see these interrelationships to understand the importance of various decisions that you and business make, both now and in the future.

Even though you might not have thought about it much before, you have already made countless business decisions. As a consumer, you evaluate the cost and value of products and buy some, but not all that are available. Your family makes decisions about where to live and when and how to purchase food and clothing. Your friends make consumer decisions to buy the goods necessary to enjoy a hobby or play a sport.

Your Role As a Consumer

You have a certain power as a consumer. Every time you buy a good or service, you are supporting the company that produces it. When you buy a soft drink, you are sending a message to the company that you like its product. And if enough people support the product, the company will continue to produce it. You and other consumers are responsible for the company's success or failure.

On the other hand, suppose that few consumers purchase the item that you like. Eventually, the business will discontinue making the item because of little or no profitability. The business's choice of discontinuing the item thus affects your choices. Or if the business finds that its location fails to attract a large volume of customers into the store, the owners may move the store to another location that can attract more potential customers. You may have liked the original location, but the business chose a different location which, in turn, affects you.

Your Role As a Wage Earner

If you have a part-time job or provide baby-sitting or lawn-care services, even if you make and sell a product like pizza, you are already familiar with the world of work and earning a wage. Your work responsibilities will increase as you get older. And so will the challenges. To develop your primary life's work—your career—you will need to consider what you would like to contribute and what you would like to gain. Some people work to gain recognition, respect, or a great deal of money. Other people work to help others and to make a living. The kind of lifestyle you would like to have will also be a factor as you enter the workforce. What you can afford to buy will be tied directly to how much you earn.

To make decisions about your future, you will need to consider at least four factors: your skills, the job market, your personality, and your interests. You could choose to work for a small local business or for a large corporation located in another country. You might even decide to become an entrepreneur and start a business of your own. Throughout this book, you'll read about the special skills and aptitudes of some people who started their own businesses in the Focus on Entrepreneurs features.

Your Role As a Citizen

One of your primary obligations as a citizen is to participate in government. It is your duty to make sure you vote for the candidates you think are most qualified to run the government and make important policy decisions affecting the public. You and all other citizens also share the responsibility of paying the taxes that help the government carry out those policies. The

Many teenagers have part-time jobs. What advantages can such a job offer you besides the money you earn?

Business Brief

Before a company introduces a new product to the general market, it does market research to find out what consumers would be likely to buy. Even so, products frequently fail. Consumers failed to buy NutraSweet's Simple Pleasure ice cream, which was made with a fat substitute. It seemed like a sure bet, given America's obsession with health and diet. But it seems that when it comes to ice cream, most Americans accept no substitutes!

USE VISUALS

Point out to students that being able to follow instructions is an important job skill. Have students suggest other skills and personality traits that are important in the workplace.
Answer to caption: Answers will vary but might include the opportunity to learn skills that will be helpful in future jobs.

TEACHING TIP

Remind students that part of being a consumer involves carefully weighing the opportunity costs of purchasing decisions. Have students suppose that Marcus had decided to spend $10 either for a pair of cycling gloves or to go to a movie with friends. Tell students Marcus decided to go to the movie. Ask: What was the opportunity cost of going to the movie? (Marcus had to give up having a new pair of cycling gloves.)

Reteaching Strategy

Have students think of successful businesses that have been a part of the community for many years. Ask students to brainstorm reasons the businesses have been successful for so long. Why do consumers continue to patronize those businesses? Do people frequent them because of prices, services, or locations?

Quick Check Answers

1. A person's own skills, personality, and interests, as well as the job market.
2. Consumer, wage earner, citizen.

Develop Concepts

From School to Work

Discuss with students how abilities and natural aptitudes often influence people's career choices. For example, a person who enjoyed math in high school might pursue a career as an accountant. Ask students to provide examples of relatives or friends who pursued a career that made use of their abilities and aptitudes.

TEACHING TIP

If your state or district has not yet implemented a school-to-work or tech program, refer to the *Tech Prep/School-to-Work Applications* booklet for suggested strategies to implement such a program.

---

taxes you pay help pay for the costs of government. For example, if you attend a public school, you are receiving a government-funded education.

The people you elect to the government determine the current public wants—the kinds of policies the majority of people want and would benefit from—and work toward establishing those policies. Many of these policies affect business and are affected by business. Stricter environmental laws may increase costs for those businesses whose production processes are affected. Less business profits may mean less tax dollars for state and local governments.

Business plays an important role in your life today and will play an increasingly important role in it in the future. Likewise, you affect what business does now and will do in the future. It's important to know how business ticks and how you can relate to the business world.

Quick Check

1. What are four factors to consider when making decisions about a future career?
2. What three roles will you assume in the business world?

FROM SCHOOL TO WORK

To make a successful transition from school to the world of work requires solid decision-making and planning. A high school business course is one way to learn more about the world of business and how you might fit into it. A business course will also help you build skills for your roles as consumer, wage earner, and citizen.

No matter what you decide to pursue as a career, you will need skills and knowledge. School is the first place that you can gain those skills and knowledge. You will also learn while you are working on the job. In addition, some employers provide training programs and reimbursement for college tuition as benefits for employees.

The job you have will be based, in part, on your ability. **Ability** is any physical or mental activity that an individual performs well. **Aptitude** is a natural talent. When you begin to think about the career you would like to pursue, you should consider your abilities and your aptitudes. You should also think about what interests and personal values you have. Would you like to work helping people in a health-care setting? Do you enjoy working on projects or working with data? If you can

Cooperative Learning Make and Defend

Have teams evaluate and take a pro or con position regarding the following statement. "It is more important to make a lot of money than to find a job that you enjoy." Have a volunteer from each team summarize the reasons for the team's position for the class.

Refer to the *Cooperative Learning Strategies* booklet for additional cooperative learning strategies.

Many young people begin some job training through courses in high school. What courses in your school might be helpful for someone moving into the workforce?

match your abilities, aptitudes, values, goals, and interests to a career, you probably will be happy and successful in your career choice. Some people know early which career they would like to pursue. Other people discover the career they enjoy by trying different courses and investigating different career opportunities in different industries. You should start to develop a career strategy now.

Some states and localities have set up school-to-work programs to help students make the transition from school to high-skill, well-paying careers. These programs can include youth apprenticeships, tech prep education, business-education compacts, career academies, and cooperative education. Planning to participate in any of these programs usually requires making a career cluster choice. A **career cluster** is a group of related occupations in an industry or field that requires similar skills and aptitudes. States and localities all organize their career clusters differently to meet their particular business and employment needs.

Figure 1-1 on page 16 shows one possible organization of career clusters. A nurse's assistant or pharmacy technician is found in the Health and Biomedical Services cluster. Most of the occupations in this cluster require strong aptitude and ability in the sciences. You can match your abilities, aptitudes, interests, goals, and values to the career clusters. It is important to remember that concentration in one skill does not mean you do not need skills from other areas. However, some skills are needed more than others for a particular career.

CHAPTER 1   BUSINESS IN TODAY'S WORLD   **15**

USE VISUALS
Explain to students that job training includes not only learning about equipment, but also involves learning how to get along with others.
Answer to caption: Answers will vary.

Learning Activity
Have a class discussion about the jobs students have or have had previously. Discuss responsibilities of the job, skills needed for the job, and skills developed on the job. Then discuss with students the kinds of jobs they might like to have as a career. Ask students what factors make those careers appealing.

Business Brief
What Color Is Your Parachute? A Practical Manual for Job Hunters & Career-Changers by Richard N. Bolles has been updated and published annually since 1970. It is recognized as one of the most straightforward and practical career guides available. Bolles strongly recommends that people take an inventory of their interests, skills, abilities, and aptitudes when they go about choosing a career.

Enrichment Strategy

Invite a school career counselor to class to speak to students about how they might begin to consider a career cluster. Ask the counselor to discuss aptitude tests students may be able to take. If possible, provide a variety of career information for students.

Suggested materials helpful for you and for students can be found in the *Professional Resources Guide.*

Have students study Figure 1-1 to get an idea of the kinds of jobs found in certain career clusters. Remind students that this chapter's Focus on Careers feature described occupations in the business and financial operations support field. Review some of the skills and abilities used by people in that field. (Computer, communication, organizational, and math skills are necessary. Attention to detail, accuracy, and trustworthiness are also important.)
Answer to caption: Wholesale and Retail Trade.

Learning Activity

Distribute copies of Enrichment Master 1-1, which provides information about which of the jobs in the ten career clusters belong to the goods-producing sector and which are part of the service sector.

TEACHING TIP

The job clusters included in Figure 1-1 were developed in coordination with the U.S. Department of Labor SCANS report, the National Alliance of Business, and the U.S. Employment Service.

Quick Check Answers

1. Any physical or mental activity that a person performs well; a natural talent.
2. Groups of occupations with similar skills and aptitudes arranged by industry or field.

FIGURE 1-1

Each of these ten career clusters includes occupations in the named industry or field. What cluster includes jobs such as customer service representative and merchandise distributor?

	CAREER CLUSTERS
Industry Field	**Examples of Jobs**
Agribusiness, Forestry, Wildlife, and Mining	Agricultural Laboratory Technician Greenhouse Production Assistant Soil Conservation Technician
Business and Financial Operations Support	Account Coordinator Insurance Underwriting Clerk Legal Secretary
Communication, Entertainment, and the Arts	Advertising Creator Apprentice Photographer Theme Park Supervisor
Food and Hospitality	Catering Assistant Food Service Manager Reservations Clerk
Government and Public Administration	Office Clerk of the Court Patrol Officer Recreation Specialist
Health and Biomedical Services	Emergency Medical Technician Pharmacy Technician Production Scientist
Manufacturing Technology and Construction	Apprentice Carpenter Equipment Mechanic Robotics Technician
Personal, Family, and Community Services	Electronics Technician Jeweler Library Assistant
Transportation and Public Utilities	Flight Attendant Surveying Technician Utility Worker
Wholesale and Retail Trade	Customer Service Representative Direct Sales Representative Merchandise Distributor

Source: ENTER HERE™ © ENTER HERE L. L. C.

You will find out more about these clusters in the Focus on Careers features found throughout this book.

Quick Check

1. Define *ability* and *aptitude*.
2. What are *career clusters*?

Curriculum Connection   English and Communications

Have students write a 100-word profile of themselves describing their abilities, aptitudes, values, goals, and interests. Students may also include in the profile any ideas they have about possible career choices.

Chapter 1 **Summary**

Main Ideas

1. Wants are things we wish we could have. Wants may be necessary or optional.
2. People have to make choices about the goods and services they will buy. When making choices, people set priorities and consider their own values, goals, and the opportunity costs involved.
3. Businesses produce the goods and services they think people will buy. Consumers indicate what they want by what they buy. Businesses must adapt the way they produce and market things as the market changes.
4. You can gain valuable career skills by taking classes in school that are related to the career cluster you want to pur-

sue. You can obtain experience by taking a part-time job in the field that interests you.
5. Businesses affect and are affected by consumers, wage earners, and citizens—the common roles we assume.
6. Banks, insurance companies, and law firms are some places that offer entry-level jobs in the field of business and financial operations support.
7. Effective decision-makers follow a simple step-by-step procedure: (1) identify the problem, (2) list the alternatives, (3) determine the pros and cons, (4) make the best decision, and (5) evaluate the decision.

CASE ANALYSIS   School-to-Work Goals

One important decision to make early on is to choose a career cluster that you really like and to develop each day the skills you need to excel in that career cluster. Setting goals helps you know what you have to do to get what you want. There are different levels of goals: Long-term—two to five years; Intermediate—three to four months or one semester or term; Short-term—one week; Immediate—today.

Suppose your goal is to work in manufacturing technology and construction and to eventually own a construction company. Your long-term goal over two to five years could be to get work-related experience and a certificate of mastery in building trades; your intermediate goals could be to take the courses that will lead to a certificate; your short-term goals could be to complete the assignments and projects in your courses; and your immediate goals could be to complete the daily tasks in your classes.

Decide now where you want to be in two to five years, and set your career development goals to get there.

Main Ideas

Main Ideas summarizes the key information in the chapter. It is a useful tool for reinforcement and review.

CASE ANALYSIS

Case Analysis provides a chapter-related case for student analysis and application of decision-making skills.

Answer
Students' answers will vary according to the career cluster they choose.

QUICK QUIZ

1. Differentiate between private wants and public wants. (Private wants are the wants of an individual or group, such as a family or business. Public wants are shared by many people, for example, the desire for public highways or schools.)
2. What is an opportunity cost? (What a person gives up when he or she makes one choice instead of another.)
3. How do consumers' changing wants affect business? (As consumers develop different wants, new businesses start up to meet those wants.)
4. What are two things you can do while still in school to prepare for a particular career field? (Take courses to gain skills needed for the field and get a part-time job related to the field.)

Chapter 1 **Review**

Use the Language of Business

In today's business world, people often use the following terms. See if you can match each term to its definition.

ability   needs
aptitude   opportunity cost
business   resource
career clusters   services
goods   wants

1. Things we must have to survive.
2. Things we wish we could have.
3. Objects you can weigh or measure.
4. Anything that people can use to make or obtain what they want or need.
5. Cost of making one choice over another.
6. Tasks people or machines perform to satisfy wants for nonmaterial things.
7. All the activities of an individual or group involved in producing and distributing goods and services.
8. Physical or mental activity that a person performs well.
9. Natural talent.
10. Groups of occupations arranged by industry or field.

Review What You Learned

1. Explain how a family, a business, or a club could have private wants.
2. What is the difference between wants and needs? Give two examples of each.
3. Explain the major difference between goods and services, and give two examples of each.
4. Why must we choose how to use our resources?
5. Describe the relationship between values and goals.
6. How does the fact that people's wants and needs change affect business?
7. Why is it important to know how businesses interrelate with consumers, wage earners, and citizens?
8. How can investigating different classes at school help you identify a career cluster you would enjoy?
9. List some jobs in the field of business and financial operations support.
10. What are the five steps in the decision-making process?

Understand Business Concepts

1. Explain why opportunity cost is not necessarily expressed in money.
2. Can two people with similar values have different goals?
3. Why will different people with the same alternatives make different choices?
4. How do values and goals affect the way you look at the opportunity cost of a decision?
5. Why do some people say we are living in the information age?

Chapter 1 **Review**

6. How do the purchases you and other consumers make contribute to a company's success or failure?
7. Explain why computer skills are necessary for jobs in the business and financial operations support field.

8. Why is it important to evaluate a decision you have made?

Think Critically

1. **Hypothesize.** List three situations in which goals affect how a person lives.

2. **Apply.** What are some of your aptitudes and abilities? Give examples of jobs in which you could use them.

Use What You Learned

1. **Group Project.** With your group, choose one of the ten career clusters from Figure 1-1 on page 16 to study more thoroughly. Research ways to prepare for jobs in that cluster. Some of these questions may be helpful:

   - What classes can help you develop needed skills?
   - What community resources are available to identify aptitudes and abilities useful for jobs in this cluster?
   - What part-time jobs in the community could provide experience?
   - Can a person do volunteer work in this field in order to gain experience? If so, what kinds of work? Where?

   Using the information your group gathered, develop a career-plan strategy for your career cluster. Compare your group's strategy with other groups'.

2. List five businesses you are familiar with in your community. Identify whether the businesses provide goods

or services. Do any provide both? For example, many hair salons not only provide the service of cutting and styling hair but also sell hair-care products, which are goods. List the kinds of decisions that the five businesses might have made in choosing what to provide for customers. What opportunity costs may have been involved?

3. **Computer Application.** Select from the classified employment section of your local newspaper an industry or field that interests you. Read through the jobs listed and begin to compile an electronic database of jobs that you find appealing.

4. **Skill Reinforcement.** Think of a decision you'll make soon. Copy the five steps in the decision-making process on page 11 onto a separate sheet of paper. Leave room to write after each step. Make your decision, filling in the information at each step.

Save your work in your Business Portfolio.

Use What You Learned
1. Make sure all students participate in the group project. Possible Rubrics: Charts and Tables, Essay, Oral Presentation.
2. Let students choose the method they use to share their results. Possible Rubrics: Booklet, Charts and Tables, Diagram, Essay, Oral Presentation.

3. Students with no access to a computer may manually prepare a jobs chart. Rubric: Charts and Tables.
4. Students' answers will vary, but should include the five steps of the decision-making process. Rubric: Note Taking.

Think Critically
1. Answers will vary depending on goals chosen by students.
2. Answers will vary depending on students' aptitudes and abilities.

Independent Practice

Use the Chapter 1 worksheets in *Student Activity Guide 1* for additional practice and application activities. *Student Activity Guide 1* provides vocabulary exercises, reading comprehension checks, problems, projects, and simulations of business and economic situations. A Teacher's Annotated Edition provides answers.

ASSESS

Portfolio Assessment

The portfolio projects are designed to lead students to develop a collection of their best work to submit to you for assessment. You and your students should decide which projects will be included in their respective Business Portfolios. Refer students to the specific rubric(s) from the *Alternative Assessment Strategies* booklet listed with each of the project notes below. These rubrics will alert students to the criteria you will use to assess their projects.

Chapter Assessment

Use the Chapter 1 Test from the *Test Masters* booklet to evaluate students' understanding of the chapter concepts. An answer key is provided. Or create your own customized test using the *Testmaker* software.

FOCUS

Introduce the Chapter

Major Concepts
- Economic Systems
- Factors of Production
- The Problem of Limited Resources
- Making Decisions About Production
- The Circular Flow of Economic Activity

Introduce the Topic
Hold up five inexpensive items that interest students. Ask students how many would like to have one or more of the items. Indicate that there are not enough items to go around. Ask students for ideas about how the items could be allocated and record the suggestions. Take a vote to decide the most acceptable method. Explain that because economic resources are limited, we have to decide how to allocate resources.

Use Business Terms
Have students read the list of Business Terms. Ask for ideas about what the terms mean. Record answers on the board or a transparency. Advise students to note the meanings of the terms as they read the chapter.

USE VISUALS
Point out to students that forests provide us with very important natural resources. Ask students to explain how forest products are used. Why do businesses that provide wood products replant forests? (Answers will vary.)

CHAPTER 2

Business terms

economic system

economic resources

factors of production

natural resources

nonrenewable resources

renewable resources

human resources

labor

capital resources

entrepreneurship

scarcity

20

CHAPTER 2 RESOURCES

Instructional Resources

Lesson Plan for Chapter 2

Teaching Transparencies 2-1, 2-2, 2-3

Strategies and Worksheets for Teaching Transparencies 2-1, 2-2, 2-3

Enrichment Master 2-1

Student Activity Guide 1–TAE for Chapter 2

Test Master for Chapter 2

Alternative Assessment Strategies

Math Skills Review

International Business Strategies

Cooperative Learning Strategies

Communication Skills Review

Ethics in Business Strategies

Economic Challenges Facing Business

Learning objectives

After completing this chapter, you will be able to:
- Identify the four factors of production.
- Explain why the scarcity of economic resources is a problem for every country.
- List the three basic questions regarding the production and distribution of goods and services.
- Explain the circular flow of economic activity.
- Identify the basic components of a computer.
- Describe how to evaluate information.

Consider what you know

- Consumers make choices to satisfy their wants and needs. Businesses adapt the way they produce and market products in response to consumers' choices and the cost and availability of resources.

Consider what you want to know

- What are the four factors of production?
- How do countries use their economic resources to produce goods and services?
- What kinds of problems do all countries face because of the scarcity of economic resources?
- How do parts of an economic system depend on each other?
- What are the basic parts of a computer?
- How can you evaluate information to determine if it is reliable?

Consider how to use what you learn

- As you read this chapter, consider how the four factors of production are used in your community.

Learning Objectives
Point out to students that the learning objectives show what they will learn in the chapter. Tell students to keep these objectives in mind as they work through the chapter. Note that the last two objectives listed refer to the Focus on Technology feature and the Building Business Skills feature.

Consider What You Know
Review briefly the main sections of *Chapter 1 Business in Today's World:* Wants and Needs; Making Choices; What Is Business?; You and the Business World; From School to Work.

Consider What You Want to Know
Ask students to read the questions, then page quickly through the chapter to get an idea of how the chapter will help them discover answers.

Consider How to Use What You Learn
Inform students that at the end of the chapter they will develop some projects related to business and economics. Suggest to students that as they read the chapter they think about how businesses in their communities use the four factors of production.

Multimedia Resources

Technology Resource Guide

Distance Learning Guide

Internet Resource Guide

Professional Resources

School-to-Work/Tech Prep Strategies

Instructional Poster

Spanish Resources

Testmaker Software for Chapter 2

The Wall Street Journal Video Series Video & Activities for Chapter 2

Business and Marketing Computer Applications—An Integrated Software Simulation Using Microsoft Works

Stocktracker—A Stock Market Software Simulation

Where's the Dough? Board Game

Business Connection

Many people in Madagascar depend on the country's rain forests to make their living. They cut trees for firewood and plant rice and cassava in the clearings. By the 1990s, deforestation was costing the country between $100 million and $300 million a year in decreased crop and forest yields and damage to the country's precious natural resources. With the financial help of several countries and the World Bank, the government of Madagascar began a program designed to protect and improve the environment while working for sustainable economic development.

Develop Concepts

Economic Systems

Introduce the concept of economic systems by asking students the following questions: Do you know what economics is? Could you describe the central problem of economics? Are you familiar with what an economic system is? Do you know what big questions an economic system must find answers to? Advise students that Chapter 2 will provide information to help them answer these questions.

In the preceding chapter, we discussed several basic ideas of economics that you have known about since you were very young. First, there are a lot of things you would like to have. Second, you cannot have everything you want—you have to make choices. If you have $1, you could spend it on a 79-cent ballpoint pen or an 89-cent bottle of apple juice. You cannot buy both. You must make a choice.

This decision assumes that both the pen and the juice are available. In fact, almost all our economic decisions take for granted that we can find the things we want to buy. However, before we can buy goods and services to satisfy our wants, someone must make the goods or offer to provide the services. To do this, they must have access to certain resources.

This chapter focuses on economic systems and the economic resources that can be used in the production of goods and services. We will see that all countries face the same problem as individuals. Because economic resources in our world are limited, every society must make choices about which goods and services it will produce and distribute.

ECONOMIC SYSTEMS

There are more than 180 independent countries in the world. The societies of these countries have developed different types of economic systems. An **economic system** is a set of rules by which a nation decides how to distribute its resources to satisfy its people's wants. Each country, however, faces the same economic question. How can it satisfy the unlimited wants of its citizens with limited productive resources? All countries must make decisions about how the factors of production—natural, human, capital, and entrepreneurial resources—will be used to provide goods and services for their people.

Because each country has a limited amount of resources from which to provide the goods and services to satisfy people's wants, every society must make decisions about the following questions:

- Which goods and services will be produced?
- How will these goods and services be produced?
- How will the goods and services be distributed?

22   UNIT 1   INTRODUCTION TO THE GLOBAL ECONOMY

Cooperative Learning Group Discussion

Have groups discuss how they view the future. Emphasize the idea that decisions made in the present affect the future. Do they think our country's natural resources have been used wisely? What benefits or drawbacks have they experienced from the previous generation's use of the nation's natural resources?

Refer to the *Cooperative Learning Strategies* booklet for additional cooperative learning strategies.

In this chapter, we will discuss the factors involved in answering each of these questions. The answers for a particular country depend on its priorities and the kind of economic system it has. The way countries answer questions about the production and distribution of their resources may be influenced by history, culture, geography, political situation, and a number of other factors. The decisions that a country makes will determine the type of economic system it has as well as how businesses will operate within that system.

Quick Check

1. What is an *economic system*?
2. What three basic questions concerning limited resources do societies need to address?

FACTORS OF PRODUCTION

The goods and services a society can produce depend on its **economic resources.** These are resources that could be used to produce or create goods and services. Economic resources can be used in different ways or not used at all. For example, a tree could be cut into boards or left standing in the forest.

When economic resources are actually used to produce goods or services, they become **factors of production,** or productive resources. Figure 2-1 below depicts the four kinds of economic resources: natural, human, capital, and entrepreneurial. All of these economic resources are considered essential for the production of goods and services. Let's take a closer look at each of them.

FIGURE 2-1

The four factors of production are natural resources, human resources, capital resources, and entrepreneurial resources. What kind of resource is coal? A delivery van?

Factors of Production			
Natural Resources	Human Resources	Capital Resources	Entrepreneurial Resources

Quick Check Answers

1. A set of rules by which a nation decides how to distribute its resources to satisfy its people's wants.
2. Which goods and services will be produced? How will these goods and services be produced? How will the goods and services be distributed?

Develop Concepts

Factors of Production

Have students suppose that Leng tells Andrew she thinks they should set up a lemonade stand near where the track team practices. What four factors of production would be involved? (Natural resources: lemons, water, sugar; human resources: Leng and Andrew; capital resources: table, signs, pitchers, cups; entrepreneurial resources: Leng's idea for the stand.)

USE VISUALS

Challenge students to think of several goods or services and ask them to think how each of the factors of production in Figure 2-1 contributed to making the good or service available.
Answer to caption:
Natural; capital.

USE TRANSPARENCIES

Use Teaching Transparency 2-1 and its corresponding strategies and worksheet from the *Teaching Transparency Strategies and Worksheets* booklet. Verify student worksheets using the Answer Key.

Reteaching Strategy

Have students compile a list of all the resources they come into contact with in one day. Ask them to classify each resource as a natural, human, capital, or entrepreneurial resource. (Some examples might be water, salespeople, cash register in a store, and a new product or service.)

Discuss

Ask volunteers to provide definitions in their own words for *hardware, software, processor, memory, random access memory, computer storage, hard drive, floppy disk drive, input device, keyboard, mouse, output device, monitor,* and *printer*. If you have access to a computer in your classroom, you can use it as a visual aid for those components that are visible, such as input and output devices.

Learning Activity

Have groups of students make posters illustrating and describing several examples each of both non-renewable resources and renewable resources. Display the posters in the classroom and discuss the problems presented by the limited supplies of some of the resources depicted in students' posters.

TEACHING TIP

Discuss with the class the question of whether our society should use scarce resources to produce so many different versions of one product. (An example might be plastic toys for children.) Would our society be "better off" if fewer versions of some products were made, particularly if they use products or resources that are difficult or impossible to recycle or renew?

FOCUS ON **Technology**

Basic Computer Components

Nowadays computers are everywhere and come in many different shapes and sizes. Even so, all computers have four physical components, called *hardware*. Basic hardware includes a processor, memory, storage, and input and output devices.

The fifth basic computer component is *software*. All computers are run by software, or computer programs. Software contains the instructions that tell the computer what to do. Without software the computer is just a collection of parts.

The *processor* is the key to a computer. It interprets and carries out instructions from the software and performs calculations and logical comparisons at extremely high speeds. The processor is the "brain" of the computer.

The computer's *memory* can be thought of as a sort of scratchpad. The computer uses memory to hold all the data and program instructions required during operation. The memory hardware is called *RAM*, which stands for *random access memory*.

There is an important characteristic about RAM: it remembers information only while the computer is on. If you need to turn the computer off, you'll need to save your results or store the data. *Computer storage* devices hold data the computer isn't currently using. Storage is something like a file cabinet. Memory is rather like a scratchpad for calculations.

The most common type of memory is a magnetic disk. The computer keeps or holds that disk in a disk drive. Generally a personal or home computer comes

Natural Resources

Natural resources are things that come from the air, water, or earth. Plants and trees are natural resources, as are the coal and iron ore that we take from the land and the fish we get from the sea. Natural resources are often basic elements that can be combined in various ways to create goods. Even synthetic or artificially produced materials are made by combining or changing natural resources. For example, nylon is a synthetic material derived from coal, water, and air.

It is important to realize that some natural resources can be used only once. The world has a limited supply of coal, oil, and other minerals. Since these resources cannot be replaced or renewed, they are often called **nonrenewable resources.**

Other natural resources renew themselves, or can be renewed through the efforts of people. Water, air, and growing things such as trees, fruits, and vegetables are all examples of **renewable resources.** The supply of a renewable resource may vary. In some areas, for example, water is plentiful during the spring rains, but scarce in the summer or fall.

24   UNIT 1   INTRODUCTION TO THE GLOBAL ECONOMY

Curriculum Connection   Science

Have pairs of students choose one of the United States' natural resources and find out more about it. Topics students could explore include: renewal practices for renewable resources; conservation efforts being made for nonrenewable resources; products made from the resource; environmental or other problems connected with the use or extraction of the resource; and the role of the resource in our economy. Ask pairs to share their findings with the class.

with two kinds of disk drives. A *hard drive* is permanently installed in the machine and can be thought of as a large immovable bank of filing cabinets. The second kind of drive is a *floppy disk drive,* so called because it reads and writes information stored on floppy disks, which are also called diskettes. You might think of the floppy disks as file folders, easily movable from one location to another.

There are many ways a computer user can get information into the computer. Each of them is called an *input device.* The most common input device is the *keyboard.* In addition, many computer users rely on a *mouse* to give the computer commands.

As the computer completes instructions or calculations, it presents the completed information through an *output device.* The most common output devices are the *monitor* and the *printer.* Information displayed on the monitor exists only while the computer is on. To keep the information, the user must save it to a hard disk or floppy disk. If the user needs a hard, or paper, copy of the information, he or she can direct the computer to print the information out on a *printer.*

Output

Disk Storage

Processing

Input

Memory

Follow Through
Divide the class into teams and have each team make a set of flash cards with the terms on the front and definitions on the back. Enrichment Master 2-1 contains additional terms and definitions. Encourage teams to include some of the terms from the Enrichment Master in their sets of cards. Have teams challenge each other to see how well they know the terms. For additional information about current technology, refer to the *Technology Resource Guide.*

The amount of natural resources available to a society has a direct effect on its production of goods and services. Without natural resources, production would not be possible at all.

Human Resources

Most natural resources need to be processed, refined, or somehow changed to make them useful. These processes do not occur automatically. People need to make them happen. The term **human resources** means the people who contribute physical and mental energy to the production process. Human resources are also called **labor.**

Individual workers use their skills to provide services or change natural resources into goods. For example, a number of different workers turn crude oil, a natural resource, into gasoline. Oil field workers drill wells and pump oil from the ground. Other workers refine the oil into gasoline, and still others transport it to service stations or pump it into the tanks of cars.

Human resources include the managers and supervisors who direct production. Changing natural resources into goods

CHAPTER 2   ECONOMIC CHALLENGES FACING BUSINESS   **25**

Business Brief
Alan Thein Durning, executive director of Northwest Environment Watch, has developed a list of "sustainable wonders"—common items taken for granted that can help conserve natural resources. One of the items on his list is the bicycle, which doesn't pollute the air or contribute to global warming and requires only small amounts of resources to produce. Another item on his list is the clothesline. Clotheslines and clothespins are extremely low-tech and have an extremely low impact on the environment. They require few resources to manufacture, last a long time, and require no fuel.

Cooperative Learning Brainstorming

Have groups of students imagine that they have been stranded on an uninhabited tropical island. What kinds of decisions would they have to make for survival? What resources might be available to them? What might be the first thing they would do? What problems and questions would arise? After 15 minutes, bring the class back together and have a volunteer from each group discuss his or her group's results.

Refer to the *Cooperative Learning Strategies* booklet for additional cooperative learning strategies.

Learning Activity

Discuss with students how some goods can be either consumer goods, that is, goods bought by consumers for personal use, or capital goods, that is, goods purchased by businesses for use in that business. For example, the same personal computer used by a small business might also be purchased by a college student for doing schoolwork. Ask students to provide some more examples and describe how they might be used by consumers and how they might be used by a business.

Business Brief

In 1992 students from Los Angeles' Crenshaw High School had an idea for a new product. Straight Out 'the Garden All Natural Creamy Italian bottled salad dressing was the result of the idea. By 1995 the salad dressing was being sold in 2000 grocery stores in California and in some stores in other parts of the country. Profits of $35,000 had been set aside for college scholarships.

Quick Check Answers

1. Natural resources, human resources, capital resources, and entrepreneurial resources.
2. Nonrenewable resources cannot be replaced; renewable resources can be replaced or renewed.
3. Labor.
4. The initiative to combine natural, human, and capital resources to produce goods or services.

and services also requires people who research and develop new methods of production. Capable and skilled people are key to efficient production.

Capital Resources

The third factor of production is **capital resources.** These are all the items other than natural resources that are used to produce goods and services. They include buildings, machines, equipment, and tools. Capital resources, often referred to as capital goods, do not satisfy our wants directly. Instead, they make it possible to produce the desired goods and services. For example, the pineapple peeler, orange juice squeezer, and blender owned by a fruit juice bar are capital resources. They do not directly satisfy your desire for a nutritious beverage. They are, however, useful—even necessary—in producing it.

Some people think of money as a capital resource, but this is not strictly correct because money does not directly *produce* goods and services. Money is, of course, important to production because it is used to *buy* capital resources, as well as labor and natural resources.

Entrepreneurial Resources

The fourth factor is entrepreneurial resources. The initiative to combine natural, human, and capital resources to produce goods or services is called **entrepreneurship.** People who start new businesses; introduce new techniques, products, or services; or improve management strategies provide the entrepreneurial resources that keep an economy healthy.

As you learned in the last chapter, consumers' wants and needs change over time. In addition, consumers in one country have very different wants and needs from those in other countries. Recognizing changes and differences in wants and needs is usually the first step in entrepreneurship. Entrepreneurs are the people who recognize a new want or need and find ways to combine natural, human, and capital resources to fulfill the want or need.

Quick Check

1. Name the four factors of production.
2. What is the difference between *nonrenewable* and *renewable* natural resources?
3. What is another name for *human resources?*
4. What is *entrepreneurship?*

Reteaching Strategy

Organize students into small groups of four or five and have them use a local telephone directory to find listings of local business firms. Ask each group to select one firm and describe a product of that firm. What natural, human, capital, and entrepreneurial resources does the firm use to produce the product? How does the firm produce it? Does it use local natural resources or are some resources brought in from another region or country? Where is the product sold—locally, regionally, nationally, or worldwide? Each group should present their findings to the class in an oral presentation.

THE PROBLEM OF LIMITED RESOURCES

The limited supply of resources is a global problem. Every country in the world has the same problem: the wants of the people are greater than the country's economic resources. This scarcity of resources—natural, human, capital, and entrepreneurial—limits the quantity of goods and services that can be produced. **Scarcity** is the lack of something that can be used to satisfy the wants of a group of people.

Scarcity is not the same as poverty. Poverty is usually thought of as the lack of basic necessities, such as food, shelter, and clothing. These basic needs have always existed and still exist in many parts of the world. However, in many societies like our own, people's wants have expanded well beyond the basic necessities to thousands of items. This is why the problem of having unlimited wants and limited resources is referred to as scarcity.

When you look at the problem of scarcity, it is important to examine population growth in the world. Figure 2-2 below shows the 1995 population figures for various parts of the world and the estimated population figures for those regions in the year 2000. By the year 2000, the population of the world will have increased by about 500 million. Population growth indicates how many more people will be living on earth in the future. This in turn shows how many more needs and wants must be fulfilled by limited resources.

Population growth, however, also gives an idea of the possible growth in the labor supply, which can help produce more of

Desertification—nondesert land becoming desert land as a result of misuse—is depleting a vital resource in parts of Africa. That resource is soil. In the Sudan, desert area is increasing at a rate of two to six miles per year. Practices such as overgrazing and timber and brush cutting have led to erosion. Eroded land becomes desert and no longer supports plant life. Many Sudanese have had to abandon once-fertile farmland and no longer have a livelihood.

POPULATION OF WORLD REGIONS

Geographic Area	1995 Population	2000 Population (Estimated)
Asia	3.3 billion	3.7 billion
Africa	701 million	826 million
Europe	509 million	518 million
Latin America	474 million	519 million
North America	289 million	305 million
Commonwealth of Independent States	287 million	298 million
Oceania	28 million	31 million

Source: U.S. Bureau of the Census

FIGURE 2-2

The scarcity of natural resources could increase as population increases. By how many more people will the population of Africa increase by the year 2000?

Global Perspective

More than 233 million people in 26 countries (mostly in Africa and the Middle East) live in "water-scarce nations" and lack access to clean, drinkable water. As populations increase during the 21st century, water will become more scarce. Have students report on which countries face the most severe water scarcity problems. They should include in their reports potential methods for regulating water consumption, improving water reuse, and eliminating wasteful use of water.

Refer to the *International Business Strategies* booklet for additional strategies and activities.

Develop Concepts

The Problem of Limited Resources

Help students distinguish between shortages and scarcity. Scarcity always exists and, in fact, intensifies as time goes by. For example, the world's supply of petroleum is limited, and its extraction for use as a fuel has caused petroleum to become increasingly scarce. Shortages, on the other hand, are temporary. Shortages of goods and services often occur after natural disasters, like hurricanes and tornadoes, when businesses that provide goods and services have been destroyed. Write the headings "Scarcity" and "Shortages" on the board and have students think of other examples for each category.

USE VISUALS

Have students use Figure 2-2 to compare increases in population around the world. Ask students to calculate the percentage by which North America's population is expected to change between 1995 and 2000. (289 million ÷ 305 million = 1.05 × 100 = 10.5 percent.)
Answer to caption: 125 million.

USE TRANSPARENCIES

Use Teaching Transparency 2-2 and its corresponding strategies and worksheet from the *Teaching Transparency Strategies and Worksheets* booklet to help students compare statistics of population for various parts of the world. Verify student worksheets using the Answer Key.

Building Business Skills

Model

Present the following scenario: Dirk overheard two students talking about a pop quiz in a math class taught by Ms. Lallans, his algebra teacher. Can Dirk expect a pop quiz this afternoon? Work through the questions in the box, asking volunteers to explain why or why not the information is valid. (Dirk's sources aren't reliable. They may be in another kind of math class. His sample isn't large enough.)

ANALYSIS
Evaluating Information

Explanation

On the job you'll often depend on information from other people and sources. You'll need to evaluate it to determine whether it is reliable. This is especially necessary when information is contradictory or it doesn't make sense to you. Asking questions about the information can help you evaluate it.

Practice

Before you accept the validity of a piece of information, evaluate it. Use the questions in the box as you evaluate each of the following items. On a separate sheet of paper, write whether the information is valid or not and explain why.

1. The mayor of Smithson says his city would be an excellent place to open a new business.
2. You're looking for a city to start a branch office. One city you're considering has a major league baseball team.
3. There has been one pizza shop in your town for the last ten years. You're considering opening another one and need information about the town's population. You check the records at the town hall and find out that the population has doubled in the last two years.

Evaluating information before you act on it can save you costly mistakes. Always thoroughly check the information you use to make decisions.

Business Brief

Countries establish priorities for resources according to their needs. In Sweden, where 15 percent of the country lies within the Arctic Circle, energy costs for heating buildings could be astronomical. To conserve energy and keep costs down, most buildings in Sweden have triple-glazed windows and insulated window shades to hold in the heat. Swedish buildings are among the most energy efficient anywhere in the world.

Quick Check Answers

1. The lack of something that can be used to satisfy wants or needs.
2. Make choices about how resources will be used.

the wanted goods and services. A resource such as labor can be used to satisfy many different wants. For example, a carpenter's labor can be used to build a new home. It can also be used to build a store or a school. Iron ore, a natural resource, can be used to make steel for building bridges or constructing skyscrapers.

If the world had an unlimited supply of labor, there would be enough workers to build all the schools, homes, and stores that people wanted. If there was an unlimited supply of iron ore, everyone's demand for skyscrapers, bicycles, and bridges would be satisfied. The fact of the matter is simple. The world has only a limited supply of each of the factors of production. Countries must make choices about how these resources will be used. That means some wants will be satisfied, while others will not.

Quick Check

1. Define *scarcity*.
2. What do countries have to do because their supply of the factors of production is limited?

Reteaching Strategy

Have students determine which information is valid in the following situation: John is looking for an inexpensive restaurant for the evening of the homecoming dance.

- His friend Lisa suggests her favorite restaurant, Andie's. (Invalid. The fact that it is Lisa's favorite restaurant is not relevant.)
- A newspaper ad for Andie's mentions low prices. (Invalid. The ad is biased.)
- John's dad said he ate at Andie's when he and John's mother first got married, and it was pretty cheap. (Invalid. The information is not current.)
- John checks the menu posted outside Andie's Restaurant and finds it suits his budget. (Valid. The source is official.)

How to Test Information

1. *Does the source of the information have real knowledge about the subject?* Carefully consider credentials of your sources. A famous chef might be a good source of information about preparing food that looks and tastes good, but may not necessarily be a nutrition expert.
2. *What are your source's personal biases?* What elements in your source's life and career could influence his or her thinking? A TV network spokesperson and an elementary school teacher might each have strong feelings that would determine the way they present facts about the quality of children's TV programming.
3. *Is the information as current as it needs to be?* If you're researching a historical event, your best source of information might be documents that are hundreds of years old. But if you need to know the population of an area where you plan to open a new branch office, you'll need the most up-to-date population figures.
4. *Is the information based on a large enough sample?* If you're relying on a survey, for example, how many people were interviewed?
5. *Is the information relevant to your problem?* A statement like "Our product is the best in its field" is a generalization that doesn't tell you anything about whether the product will be welcomed by your own customers. You need to know specifics such as features, price, and reliability.

Practice

Instruct students to evaluate and give reasons why the information given in each of the three statements on page 28 is valid or not valid. (1. Not valid. The mayor may be biased. 2. Not valid. The information is irrelevant. 3. Valid. The source is official, and the information is up-to-date.)

MAKING DECISIONS ABOUT PRODUCTION

The problem of scarcity forces societies to answer some basic economic questions. No society has enough productive resources available to produce everything people want. Every society must, therefore, make choices. The choices are determined by its answers to the three basic questions referred to earlier in this chapter.

Which Goods and Services Will Be Produced?

Every country must decide how to use its resources to meet the needs of its people. It has to determine what to produce and how much to produce. The resources used for one purpose cannot also be used for something else. For example, a piece of land could be used to grow wheat or corn. It could also be used as the site of a factory, a housing development, or a park. However, the land can only be used for one of these things at a time. Deciding to use it for one purpose means giving up the

Reteaching Strategy

The imaginary country of Marstinia is ideally suited for growing tomatoes, grapes, plums, apricots, peaches, and oranges. It also has a beautiful seacoast. Based on this information about some of Marstinia's resources, have students think of some possible goods and services that might be produced by the country. (It might produce canned tomato products, canned fruits, jams, and jellies. It might also have a fishing industry and a tourist industry because of the seacoast.)

Develop Concepts

Making Decisions About Production

Explain to students that it is rare for all people involved in a decision about using resources to agree. To show this point, give students the following example. A mining company wants to open a new mine in a rural area. The area is mostly agricultural and has several rivers. A significant number of businesses in the area (hotels, restaurants, crafts shops) depend on visitors to a large state park in the area. Have students brainstorm the possible pros and cons to opening a mine in the area. (Possible answers: Pros: The mine would create jobs and stimulate the local economy. Cons: The mine could cause pollution problems near the rivers, and residents may object to having industry located so near them. The state park might become a less attractive destination once a mine had been established nearby and the businesses that rely on tourists might suffer.)

CHAPTER 2

Business Brief

The research and development (R&D) departments of major corporations are the places where new products are developed. They are also often involved in designing new ways to produce products. Many companies use their R&D teams to create more cost-efficient technology and improve manufacturing processes. Researchers at the pharmaceutical company DuPont Merck use specialized eyeglasses to view and manipulate multi-colored, three-dimensional models of various chemical compounds involved in disease. Such techniques speed up the process of developing new and more potent medicines.

Learning Activity

Japan is a good example of a country that is deficient in one of the factors of production—natural resources. Have students research Japan's economy to find out how it answers the three economic questions, and how it managed to become a major economic power despite the fact that it lacks many natural resources.

Business & SCIENCE

Even though most of the southwestern United States is a desert, the area produces much of the vegetables, fruits, and beef we eat. Agricultural scientists have worked with farmers to design and engineer special irrigation systems that include dams, aqueducts, and reservoirs. These systems divert water from dozens of western rivers, so that the farmers' land can be agriculturally productive.

opportunity to use it for something else. As with all choices, there is an opportunity cost involved.

The same principle is true for the other factors of production. A person can work at building cars, making clothing, or selling vacuum cleaners—but, usually, only one of these at a time. Because natural, human, capital, and entrepreneurial resources are limited, every society must decide which of the many possible goods and services to produce. A country cannot produce everything.

A society must also answer questions about quantity. How much of this good should be produced? How much of that service? The answers to these questions depend on the priorities the society has established.

How Will Goods and Services Be Produced?

When a society decides what to produce, it must address another series of questions: Who will produce these goods and services? What methods will they use? How many people will work on the production? What will be the quality of the items produced?

A society answers these questions according to the economic resources it has at its disposal. Some countries have a large labor force, a generous supply of capital goods, rich natural resources, or a plentiful number of entrepreneurs. A few countries may have an abundance of just one factor of production.

Most goods and services can be produced using more than one mix of resources. In fact, different nations may produce similar goods by using different combinations of resources. Take as an example the way two different countries might produce clothing. One may use hundreds of workers to sew with needles and thread. The other may use fewer workers who operate automatic sewing equipment. Both countries produce the same good using a different mix of resources.

Production methods change as countries discover new ways to combine their economic resources. The development of the computer, for example, has dramatically changed the way goods and services are produced in the world. In the future, new technology will have an even greater influence on how people's wants are satisfied.

How Will Goods and Services Be Distributed?

A country cannot produce everything its residents want. A typical country can produce many goods and services. How

Cooperative Learning   Group Discussion

Tell groups that they each represent a governing body and they need to consider the three economic questions in order to solve the following problem. Some citizens feel that the northern part of the country is being destroyed by sheep grazing and should be preserved by turning it into a national park, which would help the country's tourist economy. Sheep farmers feel they have the right to continue using the land to produce wool, which is part of the country's economy. After 15 minutes, have groups explain how they used the basic economic questions to address this issue.

Refer to the *Cooperative Learning Strategies* booklet for additional cooperative learning strategies.

should these be divided among the residents? Since there are not enough goods and services to satisfy everyone's wants, the society must find a way of determining who gets them and who does not.

Although the first two basic economic decisions are important, choosing how goods and services are distributed probably interests people most. In most societies, people can have as many goods and services as they can afford to buy. Thus the amount of income people receive determines how many goods and services they can have. This solution raises many questions. Should everyone receive the same income so that goods and services can be distributed equally? Should the people who work hardest receive the most income? Who should answer these difficult questions? Should it be the government, businesses, or individuals? You will find in later chapters that countries answer these questions in different ways.

Quick Check

1. When a society chooses to use a resource for one purpose and gives up the opportunity to use it for some other purpose, what cost is involved?
2. What happens to production methods when a country discovers new ways to combine its economic resources?
3. In most countries, what determines how many goods and services a person can buy?

THE CIRCULAR FLOW OF ECONOMIC ACTIVITY

Figure 2-3 on page 32 shows the connection of the different parts of an economic system like ours. Individuals sell the factors of production (natural, human, capital, and entrepreneurial resources) to businesses and, in return, gain income such as wages, rents, and profits. Businesses buy the factors of production and use them to produce goods and services. Businesses sell the finished products to individuals who buy the goods and services with their income. Businesses pay taxes on their income and property to the government which provides public services and payments to individuals. Individuals, in turn, pay taxes to the government and provide it land and labor, thus completing the circle.

As you can see from looking at the chart, there is a large degree of dependence among the different parts of an economic system. Suppose you (an individual) take a job as a salesperson

F.Y.I.

Modern telecommunications systems are vital to most technology today. The People's Republic of China has made updating its telecommunications systems one of its top economic priorities. In 1995, China had only two phone lines for every 100 people. In addition the technology of the phone systems dated back to the 1950s. It has allocated resources to purchase such devices as digital switches and fiber optic cables in order to establish a state-of-the-art telecommunications system.

Quick Check Answers

1. An opportunity cost.
2. Production methods change.
3. Amount of income.

Develop Concepts

The Circular Flow of Economic Activity

To help students understand their own role in the circular flow of economic activity, ask a group of students to dramatize how the Circular Flow Model in Figure 2-3 on page 32 works. Students could carry or wear tags indicating their roles as wage earner (provider of labor), employer, and so on. Students could include a picture of money or a paycheck and show how and where they might spend the money.

Global Perspective

Inform students that economies of the world are also dependent on one another. For example, the United States serves as a buyer when it imports automobiles from Japan. However, the United States serves as the seller when it sells citrus fruit to Japan. Invite interested students to do some research to find other examples of economic interdependence among countries. Have students share their findings with the class.

Refer to the *International Business Strategies* booklet for additional strategies and activities.

CHAPTER 2

Use Figure 2-3 to help students visualize the degree of dependence among the different parts of an economic system. Ask students to identify the arrows that represent the flow of money, and then ask them to identify the arrows that represent the flow of goods and services and the flow of the factors of production. Answer to caption: They provide land, labor, capital, or entrepreneurial skills to businesses and produce their goods and services. They also pay taxes to the government and provide it labor and land, and receive services and payments.

USE TRANSPARENCIES

Use Teaching Transparency 2-3 and its corresponding strategies and worksheet from the *Teaching Transparency Strategies and Worksheets* booklet to help students see the connection between different parts of an economic system. Verify student worksheets using the Answer Key.

Quick Check Answers

1. Economic activity consists of businesses and individuals. They interrelate and are dependent on one another. Their relationship is a continuous relationship.
2. By selling labor (a factor of production) to business.

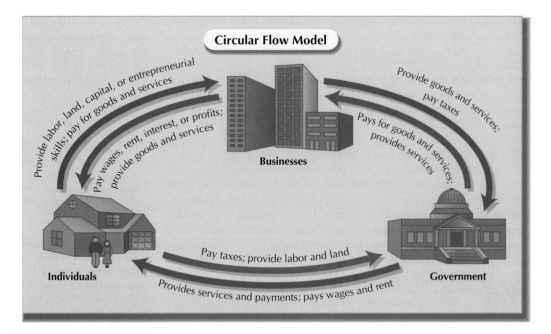

Circular Flow Model

Provide labor, land, capital, or entrepreneurial skills; pay for goods and services

Pay wages, rent, interest, or profits; provide goods and services

Businesses

Provide goods and services; pay taxes

Pays for goods and services; provides services

Individuals

Pay taxes; provide labor and land

Provides services and payments; pays wages and rent

Government

FIGURE 2-3

The circular flow model shows the high degree of dependence among the different parts of an economic system. How do individuals contribute to the flow of economic activity?

at a bookstore. You are a factor of production to the store because you sell your labor to it. You receive paycheck from the store and money flows back to you. Some of your paycheck flows to the government in taxes to provide for public services. With some of your paycheck you buy a tennis racket. Money flows from you to the business selling it. Taxes on the sale and the business's profits flow to the government, completing the circle.

The dependency expressed in the Circular Flow Model helps us to better understand various situations that occur in our economy. Suppose that people begin to worry about the economy. They may decrease their spending, which in turn means fewer goods and services need to be produced, which means fewer resources will be needed, which means less income is earned and distributed. On the other hand, suppose that people have a positive outlook about the economy. They may be apt to increase their spending which could lead to increased total income put into the economy in a reversal of the sequence outlined above.

Quick Check

1. What is meant by the circular flow of economic activity?
2. How does a person taking a job become a factor of production?

Meeting Student Diversity

Students with reading or organizational difficulties may have trouble understanding the interdependence of economic activity. Go over the material, using Figure 2-3 as a visual aid, to show them that the circle on the left represents all businesses and the circle on the right represents all households or individuals. Explain that businesses cannot exist without individuals who provide labor and who buy their goods or services. In turn, individuals cannot buy goods and services unless they gain income from providing labor to businesses.

Chapter 2 **Summary**

Main Ideas

1. To produce goods and services, a society must have access to economic resources.
2. The four main economic resources are natural resources, human resources, capital resources, and entrepreneurial resources, often referred to as factors of production.
3. Every country faces the problem of scarcity, which means it must make decisions about what goods and services to produce, and how to produce and distribute these goods and services.
4. Decisions about using resources are part of the basic economic structure of a society.

5. There is a high degree of dependence among the different parts of an economic system as shown through the circular flow of the economy.
6. Computer hardware consists of memory storage, input devices—keyboard and mouse—and output devices—monitor and printer.
7. When evaluating information you should consider the source of the information and the source's personal bias, the current relevancy of the information, and, in some cases, the size of the sample the information was based on.

CASE ANALYSIS Factors of Production

Phil O'Neil's class voted to take a trip to Washington, D.C., over spring break. The class plans to raise the money by starting a business selling school hats. Phil was put in charge of the project. What part does Phil have in the production process? Where can he get the money to buy the hats? What factor of production are the hats when he buys them? Are there any natural resources involved? What could Phil do if he has trouble getting enough people to work on the project? How will Phil determine the price?

CLOSE

Main Ideas

Main Ideas summarizes the key information in the chapter. It is a useful tool for reinforcement and review.

CASE ANALYSIS

Case Analysis provides a chapter-related case for student analysis and application of decision-making skills.

Answer
Phil has the role of entrepreneur because he must organize the factors of production to set up the business. He could put his own money into the business, borrow it, or ask several people to invest their money. When he buys the hats, they will be a capital resource produced from natural resources. Phil might have to pay people to get them to work or offer them reduced prices on their hats in return for their labor. He will have to charge enough to cover all costs plus enough extra to build up the funds for the class trip.

QUICK QUIZ

1. What three basic questions about limited resources must societies address? (Which goods and services will be produced? How will these goods and services be produced? How will the goods and services be distributed?)
2. What are the four factors of production? (Natural, human, capital, and entrepreneurial resources.)
3. What does scarcity mean? (That there is a lack of something that can be used to satisfy wants and needs.)
4. In most countries, swhat factor determines how many goods or services someone can buy? (Amount of income.)

Chapter 2 **Review**

APPLY

Answers

Use the Language of Business

1. Natural resources, **2.** capital resources, **3.** scarcity, **4.** labor, **5.** economic resources, **6.** nonrenewable resources, **7.** human resources, **8.** factors of production, **9.** renewable resources, **10.** entrepreneurship, **11.** economic system.

Review What You Learned

1. Natural, human, capital, and entrepreneurial resources.

2. A factory or a machine.

3. Natural resources such as coal are nonrenewable—they cannot be replaced; natural resources such as trees are renewable—they can be replaced by replanting.

4. Scarcity of resources.

5. Which goods and services will be produced? How will goods and services be produced? How will goods and services be distributed?

6. All the factors in the circular flow model of economic activity are dependent on one another.

7. Input: keyboard and mouse; output: monitor and printer.

8. Source; possible personal bias; currency; sample size; and relevancy.

Understand Business Concepts

1. A country may be considered poor because it may not have the education or technology to make use of natural resources or because the government limits the resources put into making consumer goods.

2. Possible answer: In some cases, a machine can do the work of many people. In other cases, without the labor force available to do the work, goods and services will be limited.

3. Most people are more concerned about distribution because it affects most people directly.

Use the Language of Business

On a separate sheet of paper, rewrite the sentences below, using the correct term to complete each one.

capital resources
economic resources
economic system
entrepreneurship
factors of production
human resources

labor
natural resources
nonrenewable resources
renewable resources
scarcity

1. _____ come from the air, water, or earth.
2. Machines, buildings, and equipment used to produce goods and services are _____.
3. _____ is the lack of something that will satisfy our wants.
4. The work done by people to produce goods and services is called _____.
5. _____ can be used to produce or create goods and services.
6. _____ cannot be replaced.
7. The people whose efforts go into producing goods and services are _____.
8. The _____ are economic resources used to produce goods and services.
9. Natural resources that can be replaced, either by themselves or through the efforts of people, are _____.
10. The initiative to combine natural, human, and capital resources to produce goods or services is called _____.
11. A[n] _____ is a set of rules by which a nation decides how to distribute its resources to satisfy its people's wants.

Review What You Learned

1. What are the four main economic resources?
2. Give an example of a capital resource.
3. Explain the two types of natural resources and give an example of each.
4. What resource problem is faced by all societies?
5. What are the three economic questions every society must answer?
6. What is the relationship among goods and services, individuals, factors of production, and businesses in the circular flow model of economic activity?
7. Name two computer input devices and two output devices.
8. What five factors should you consider when evaluating information?

Understand Business Concepts

1. Some countries have many natural resources such as oil, timber, and coal. Yet they are described as "poor" countries. Why do you think these countries are described as such?
2. What happens when human resources are scarce?
3. Why are most people more concerned about the distribution than the production of goods and services?
4. Why should a society be careful in using its natural resources?
5. Why is software vital to a computer's ability to function?

4. If a country's natural resources are used without careful planning, the resources may be used up before nature has time to replenish them, or before an alternative resource is found.

5. It contains instructions that tell a computer what to do.

6. That society might not be able to produce what it needs in the future.

7. Economic activity would not take place because all parts are dependent on each other.

8. Your friend is a reliable source because he has the computer you want. However, the price information is out of date. It is also possible that his computer model is no longer available.

Think Critically

1. Answers will vary, but should include the natural, human, capital, and entrepreneurial resources.

2. Answers will vary, but might include the following: airplanes are responsible for goods being distributed to many more areas than in the past; freezers are responsible for the production of processed frozen food; microwave ovens are responsible for food products specifically designed for microwaves.

3. Your wants on the island would be for necessities such as food, clothing, and shelter. You would not be able to purchase goods and services from others. You would have to satisfy your wants and needs in other ways.

6. What might happen if a society conserved economic resources by limiting the number of new factories?
7. What would happen to the flow of economic activity if one part of the circular flow model was removed?

8. Suppose you wanted to buy the same kind of computer your best friend has and you want to know how much it will cost. He tells you what he paid two years ago. Evaluate his information using the checklist on page 29.

Think Critically

1. **Analyze.** Think about one of your favorite foods. What are the specific factors of production necessary to make this product?
2. **Explain.** The development of the computer has had a dramatic effect on the way goods and services are produced and distributed. Name another invention that has caused a dramatic change in the way goods and services are produced or distributed.
3. **Hypothesize.** Suppose you are stranded on a small, uninhabited tropical island. How would satisfying your wants there be different from satisfying them in your own community?

Use What You Learned

1. **Group Project.** With your group, choose a foreign country and research the country's economic resources. Assign research topics to each member, such as:

   • What natural resources are plentiful?
   • What does the country produce with its natural resources?
   • What kind of human resources does the country have?
   • How does the country make up for resources that are in short supply?
   • What impact do entrepreneurial resources have on its economy?

   Display your group's findings, including graphics or photos.
2. All businesses need at least some of the four main economic resources. To see these resources at work, meet with the owner or manager of a local business.

Find out how the business uses economic resources to create a good or provide a service. Write a 200-word report and share it with the class.
3. **Computer Application.** Use charting/graphing software to convert the data in the table in Figure 2-2 on page 27 to a bar graph. Retain the same title and use attractive data formats to distinguish the bars representing the years. Check the graph to assure that your data is correct, and then print out the results.
4. **Skill Reinforcement.** Interview the manager or owner of a local small business. Find out about the sources of information he or she uses in making business decisions. Ask how he or she evaluates the information before acting upon it. Write a 200-word report about the ways that person evaluates information.

Save your work in your Business Portfolio.

Use What You Learned
1. Make sure all students participate in the group project. Possible Rubric(s): Charts and Tables; Photo Essay; Poster.
2. Advise students to draft a list of questions to use during the interview. Rubric: Essay.
3. Students with no access to a computer may make their graphs by hand. Rubric: Graph.
4. Answers will vary, but students should report on certain kinds of information sources the businessperson uses and how that person evaluates the information. Rubric: Essay.

Independent Practice

Use the Chapter 2 worksheets in *Student Activity Guide 1* for additional practice and application activities. *Student Activity Guide 1* provides vocabulary exercises, reading comprehension checks, problems, projects, and simulations of business and economic situations. A Teacher's Annotated Edition provides answers.

ASSESS

Portfolio Assessment

The portfolio projects are designed to lead students to develop a collection of their best work to submit to you for assessment. You and your students should decide which projects will be included in their respective Business Portfolios. Refer students to the specific rubric(s) from the *Alternative Assessment Strategies* booklet listed with each of the project notes below. These rubrics will alert students to the criteria you will use to assess their projects.

Chapter Assessment

Use the Chapter 2 Test from the *Test Masters* booklet to evaluate students' understanding of the chapter concepts. An answer key is provided. Or create your own customized test using the *Testmaker* software.

FOCUS

Introduce the Chapter

Major Concepts
- Economic Activity
- Measuring Economic Activity
- The Federal Government and Economic Stability

Introduce the Topic
Make copies of a current magazine or newspaper article about economic conditions and distribute the article to students. Discuss the article. Ask: How would you describe today's economy? What terms might you use? What factors mentioned in the article seem to be indicators of the state of the economy?

Use Business Terms
Have students look at the Business Terms and brainstorm associations with each term. Ask them where they have heard or seen the term used. Reinforce correct associations. Advise students to note the meanings of the terms as they read the chapter.

USE VISUALS
Explain to students that the manufacturing sector, represented by the aerospace industry depicted in the photograph, as well as the auto industry, has had an important impact on the economy of the United States. Ask students if they can think of reasons why manufacturing is so important to our economy. (Answers will vary.)

CHAPTER
3

Business terms

economic fluctuations

business cycle

expansion

peak

contraction

trough

recession

depression

recovery

economic indicators

gross domestic product

standard of living

inflation

inflation rate

unemployment rate

36

CHAPTER 3 RESOURCES

Instructional Resources
Lesson Plan for Chapter 3

Teaching Transparency 3-1

Strategies and Worksheets for Teaching Transparency 3-1

Enrichment Master 3-1

Student Activity Guide 1–TAE for Chapter 3

Test Master for Chapter 3

Alternative Assessment Strategies

Math Skills Review

International Business Strategies

Cooperative Learning Strategies

Communication Skills Review

Ethics in Business Strategies

Measuring Economic Performance

Learning objectives

After completing this chapter, you will be able to:
- Describe the four phases of the business cycle.
- Explain how economic activity is measured.
- Explain how the federal government tries to maintain stability in our economy.
- Describe how one inventor became an entrepreneur.
- Explain what inflation is and how it affects the economy.

Consider what you know

- A country uses its economic resources to produce goods and services. Societies have to make decisions about which goods and services to produce and how to produce and distribute them.

Consider what you want to know

- What are the phases of the business cycle?
- How do economic systems measure economic activity?
- How does the federal government try to regulate business cycles?
- How did an inventor who also was a physicist build a successful business?
- What effect does inflation have on economic activity?

Consider how to use what you learn

- As you read this chapter, think about the comparisons the media makes between the state of the economy now and in previous years.

Multimedia Resources

Technology Resource Guide

Distance Learning Guide

Internet Resource Guide

Professional Resources

School-to-Work/Tech Prep Strategies

Instructional Poster

Spanish Resources

Testmaker Software for Chapter 3

The Wall Street Journal Video Series
   Video & Activities for Chapter 3

Business and Marketing Computer
   Applications—An Integrated Software
   Simulation Using Microsoft Works

Stocktracker—A Stock Market Software
   Simulation

Where's the Dough? Board Game

Motivate the Learning

Learning Objectives
Point out to students that the learning objectives show what they will learn in the chapter. Tell students to keep these objectives in mind as they work through the chapter. Note that the last two objectives listed refer to the Focus on Entrepreneurs feature and the Building Business Skills feature.

Consider What You Know
Review briefly the main sections of *Chapter 2 Economic Challenges Facing Business:* Economic Systems; Factors of Production; The Problem of Limited Resources; Making Decisions About Production; and The Circular Flow of Economic Activity.

Consider What You Want to Know
Ask students to look through the chapter to get an idea of how the chapter will help them answer the questions.

Consider How to Use What You Learn
Explain to students that at the end of the chapter they will develop some projects related to patterns of economic activity. Suggest that students pay attention to news reports that provide information about the current state of the economy.

TEACH

Business Connection

The U.S. economy experienced steady growth from 1992 to 1995. One hazard that often accompanies economic growth is inflation. In order to engineer a "soft-landing" of the economy—that is, a moderate slowing of the economy without an increase in inflation—the Federal Reserve Board increased interest rates six times in 1994, thereby tightening the supply of credit and reducing the negative effects of continued unharnessed growth.

Develop Concepts

Economic Activity

Ask students to think about their favorite sports team. Does the team always win? Discuss winning and losing streaks and emphasize that, like sports teams, the economy sometimes does well and sometimes does less well. Business cycles are not regular, nor are they all of the same intensity. Ask students what phase they think the economy is in now. What kinds of economic activity do they hear discussed on television or radio news reports?

Business Brief

Fluctuations in the United States economy have occurred almost from the moment our country declared its independence. Severe recessions in the 1820s and in 1873 caused thousands of companies to go into bankruptcy and hundreds of banks to close.

If you were to describe our economic system, you might start with what it produces. You will remember that a major purpose of an economic system is to produce the goods and services wanted by people. You might say that the United States places a priority on consumer satisfaction and that most of our production is privately owned. You might also say that almost anyone can start a business in our economy. Those are some ways of describing it. You can probably think of others.

There are some other features of our economic system that we need to know about as well. How well does the system operate? What are its advantages? Does it have any problems? If so, what are they and how are they resolved? How can we measure the performance of our economic system? In this chapter you will learn what methods can be used to answer some of these questions.

ECONOMIC ACTIVITY

Every day economists and business leaders provide forecasts, reports, and predictions about the state of the economy. These reports appear as often as reports about the weather. Why does the state of the economy require daily attention? What is so important about economic information?

History has taught the world a great deal about the effects of changes in the state of the economy. The Great Depression that began in 1929 is the most striking example of economic decline in the twentieth century. Many people did not have jobs. Many goods and services were hard to find. In the 1970s, people waited in long lines to buy gasoline due to an oil shortage in the United States. These two events represent sizable changes or fluctuations in the state of the economy. Some economic changes affect only one sector or group of people. Other changes can affect many people all over the world. **Economic fluctuations** are the ups and downs in economic activity.

The Business Cycle

If you study the economic changes that have taken place in the past, you will see an irregular pattern of many ups and downs. The repeated rise and fall of economic activity over time is called a **business cycle.**

Global Perspective

Assign groups the task of researching and analyzing the business fluctuations in the economy of another country during the past 10 years and how that fluctuation affected, if at all, the U.S. economy. Ask each group to explain to the class why some of the economic fluctuations occurred and in what way the country responded to these economic fluctuations.

Refer to the *International Business Strategies* booklet for additional strategies and activities.

Figure 3-1 below is a model of a business cycle. The figure charts a common pattern for the ups and downs of a business cycle over a period of time.

- expansion
- peak
- contraction
- trough

A rise in business activity could indicate either a period of **expansion** or of recovery. The rise indicates economic growth. A **peak** is the highest level of economic activity in a cycle. A peak indicates prosperity and means the economy is expanding rapidly. At the peak phase, new businesses open, production of goods and services is high, many jobs are available, and employment is high. A **contraction** is a noticeable drop in the level of business activity, which indicates a slowdown in the growth of the economy. A contraction may mean stable or falling prices for goods and services or it may mean unemployment is increasing. A **trough** is the lowest level of business activity in a particular cycle.

Every phase indicates changes to an economy, to industries, and to working people. Changes in the economy can affect some industries, such as the manufacturing industry or the health-care industry, more than other industries. An economic expansion may affect the auto and steel industries more than the health-care industry. And economic changes can also affect working people. A period of expansion or economic growth affecting the auto industry may mean more job opportunities and higher employment in that industry.

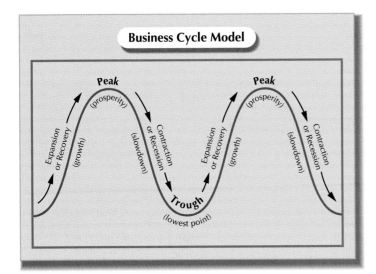

Business Cycle Model

Peak (prosperity)

Peak (prosperity)

Expansion or Recovery (growth)

Contraction or Recession (slowdown)

Expansion or Recovery (growth)

Contraction or Recession (slowdown)

Trough (lowest point)

FIGURE 3-1

The repeated rise and fall of economic activity over time is called a business cycle. A business cycle is made up of four phases: expansion, peak, contraction, and trough. What phase of the business cycle indicates prosperity?

TEACHING TIP

Make sure that students understand that the intensity of each phase of the business cycle can vary. For example, a recession might be very severe or very mild. Ask students what factors might help gauge the severity of a recession. (Possible answers: The number of people who lose their jobs; the number of businesses that close.)

USE VISUALS

Reinforce the concept of the four phases of the business cycle represented in Figure 3-1 by pointing out to students that different terms are sometimes used to mean the same thing. For example, a contraction of the economy can also be called a slowdown or downturn. Ask students what other terms might be used when talking about economic growth. (Expansion or recovery.)
Answer to caption: Peak.

USE TRANSPARENCIES

Use Teaching Transparency 3-1 and its corresponding strategies and worksheet from the *Teaching Transparency Strategies and Worksheets* booklet to help students visualize the four phases of the business cycle. Verify student worksheets using the Answer Key.

Reteaching Strategy

Ask students how the following businesses might fare during a recession: a shop that sells gourmet baked goods and a store that sells discounted clothing. (Possible answer: The baked goods shop might have very poor sales, because consumers have less money to spend and would probably not buy luxury items like gourmet baked goods. The discount clothing store would probably weather the recession better because clothes are a necessity and people would probably try to save money by shopping at a discount store.)

FOCUS ON **Entrepreneurs**

FOCUS ON **Entrepreneurs**

Discuss

Ask students if they would like to visit Dean Kamen's hands-on science museum or one of the U.S. First festivals. What is intriguing about Kamen's uses of science and technology? Ask students to brainstorm a list of businesses that use sophisticated technology in their work.

Dean Kamen—DEKA Research & Development Corporation

"We need to demonstrate to kids that technology is productive and fun." When Dean Kamen isn't working in his home machine shop or firing off suggestions to his 80 employees at DEKA Research and Development, he's putting those words into action.

In 1986 this physicist/inventor/entrepreneur opened a hands-on science museum. Then he set up a nonprofit organization called U.S. First (United States For Inspiration and Recognition of Science and Technology).

The goal of U.S. First is to turn kids on to technology through a yearly festival in which groups of high school students work with engineers "donated" by well-known corporations. Teams design and build robots that compete in remote-controlled ball games, a kind of techno–World Series. Winners have been honored at the White House. "The goal," says Kamen, "is to get [the competition] on TV so that thousands of kids can see it."

People have said that Kamen is a genius, but as a child he sometimes doubted his own intelligence. His mind wandered in school, and his grades were low. School left him with more questions than answers about science and technology. To get those answers he began reading works by scientific "greats" such as Archimedes, Galileo, Newton, and Einstein. They became his heroes.

Kamen turned inventor after high school, when he designed, built, and sold control systems for audiovisual shows. His medical-student brother provided the idea for his next invention: an automated device to give small

Business Brief

From July 1990 to March 1991, the United States economy was in a recession. About 1.5 million workers lost their jobs, which was a lower figure than in past downturns. However, the job losses occurred in a greater number of industries than in past recessions, and more time elapsed before workers were rehired. Workers in the finance, insurance, and real estate industries were especially hard hit during the 1990–91 recession.

Learning Activity

To provide a historical perspective on the economy, have students research times of major economic downturns in the United States (the 1820s, 1870s, 1890s, and 1930s). Ask students to find out what caused each economic decline, how the economy recovered, and how the economy changed afterward. Have students present their findings in an oral or written report.

Business & HISTORY

During the Great Depression, the federal government sponsored many public works projects to relieve unemployment. In 1938, 1000 workers were sent to rural Monmouth County, New Jersey—to build a new town! The workers built 200 homes, a clothing factory, and a community farm. The factory and the farm failed, but the town lived on. In 1945, when President Franklin D. Roosevelt died, the town changed its name to Roosevelt.

The economic ups and downs of one country can affect other countries, too. In a global economy, in which several countries are trading goods and services with one another, one country's economy can affect its other trading partners. If the U.S. economy is in a period of economic expansion, the United States may purchase more goods and services from other countries—promoting expansion in those countries. In today's global economy, most countries are *interdependent;* that is, their economies are linked together.

Pattern of Cycles

Economists study the changes in business cycles very carefully and also discover trends. There is a long history of economic ups and downs in the United States and in many other countries. Economic ups and downs that last for an extended period of time indicate an economic trend. Economists noted long trends of U.S. economic contraction in the 1820s and in 1873. The Great Depression was a prolonged economic trough that spanned the years 1929 to about 1939.

40   UNIT 1   INTRODUCTION TO THE GLOBAL ECONOMY

Cooperative Learning   Make and Defend

Divide the class into groups and have them evaluate the following statement: "Are there any measures you can take to protect yourself from the ups and downs of the business cycle?" Have a spokesperson from each group present and explain his or her group's position.

Refer to the *Cooperative Learning Strategies* booklet for additional cooperative learning strategies.

doses of medicine to patients intravenously. With family and friends as employees, he successfully produced his portable medicine infusion pumps. At age 31, eleven years after he invented that first pump, Kamen was a multimillionaire. He eventually branched out into improving helicopter design and climate-control systems. All told, he holds over 30 patents.

At DEKA, which is his latest venture, Kamen and his engineers have designed a kidney dialysis machine so small that patients can use it outside the hospital. They're also working on a project Kamen won't describe except to say that it involves principles used in an almost forgotten hot-air engine invented in 1816.

Kamen would like to see today's young people inspired as he was by past and present scientific achievements. As he said recently to a group of engineers: "I'm asking all of you to help us make the next hero a scientist or a technologist—*real* heroes."

Follow Through

Have students find articles about recent advances in technology and bring them to class. Discuss with students how the technology will be used and what led to its development. Which of the inventions are designed for consumers and which are designed for businesses? What factors seem to initiate new inventions?

The terms recession and depression are often used to describe long trends of an economic condition. A **recession** is a period of severe economic decline—spending decreases, so fewer goods and services are demanded, and unemployment rises. A **depression** is a very severe recession that lasts for several years. A **recovery** is a period of economic growth or expansion following a recession or depression.

There was a peak of economic prosperity in the summer of 1929. A few months later, on a day that has become known as Black Thursday—October 24, 1929—stock prices collapsed. From this point in 1929 to about 1939, the United States economy was in a depression. Investors lost millions of dollars. Great declines in production and in employment occurred. Factories shut down. Businesses and banks also failed. As businesses failed, more and more people lost their jobs. By 1932, 12 to 15 million people were unemployed, or 25 to 30 percent of the workforce.

During World War II, production increased and more people were employed to support the war effort. The economy experienced small ups and downs throughout the 1940s and

Enrichment Strategy

Encourage students to gain an understanding of the changes that began to occur in the U.S. economy during World War II. Have them research the production increases that occurred between the years 1940–45. Suggest that students address the following questions in a brief written essay. What goods did the United States begin producing because of World War II? Who composed the workforce? What were the major effects of World War II on the American economy?

Business Brief

During World War II, many countries redirected the output of their manufacturing industries. The United States and Great Britain converted some automobile factories into facilities for manufacturing military materials. The British government built "shadow factories" adjacent to their automotive plants. Workers from the nearby automotive plants transferred to the shadow factories and manufactured aircraft and tanks for wartime needs. The automotive industry in the United States retooled plants so they could manufacture tanks, armored cars, machine guns, and even army helmets.

Quick Check Answers

1. Ups and downs in economic activity.
2. Expansion, peak, contraction, and trough.
3. They are interdependent.
4. Period of severe economic decline; very severe decline in economic activity that lasts for several years; period of economic growth or expansion following a recession or depression.

Develop Concepts

Measuring Economic Activity

Be sure that students understand that no one can predict with certainty what the economy will actually do. Economists, businesspeople, and the government are all interested in forecasting economic conditions, so they look for clues to help them make informed predictions. One such clue is unemployment. High unemployment figures usually indicate that the economy is contracting. Invite interested students to look for economic forecasts in news articles and explain to the class which economic indicators were used to make the forecast.

TEACHING TIP

An important thing to know about a country's GDP is that it includes only goods produced in that nation. For example, the GDP of the United States does not include cars and trucks made at a U.S.-owned plant in Canada but does include Hondas made in Ohio using Japanese funds.

1950s. Recessions occurred in the middle and late 1950s. The 1960s were marked by just one trough, or downturn, in February of 1961. There have been several short recessions since the 1960s, which have all been followed by recoveries. The recession of 1990–91 was difficult to define because the peaks and troughs in that period were not very dramatic, so recovery was slow.

Quick Check

1. Describe what is meant by *economic fluctuations*.
2. What are the four phases of a business cycle?
3. What is the economic relationship of countries that trade with each other?
4. Explain the terms *recession, depression,* and *recovery.*

MEASURING ECONOMIC ACTIVITY

You have seen how economists study and define economic activity. But how do economists determine the future state of the economy? Remember that the overall objective of an economy is to produce goods and services that satisfy people's needs and wants. How do economists understand how the economy is doing today? Or how it will do tomorrow? What factors in the economy will affect you?

To determine how well the economy is satisfying people's wants and needs, economists study factors, or indicators, of the economy. **Economic indicators** are important data or statistics that measure economic activity and business cycles. Leading economic indicators are economic factors or conditions that normally change before the rest of the economy does. You may be familiar with some indicators such as stock prices and profits. Each month the Department of Commerce publishes statistics for more than 250 economic indicators. We will discuss three major economic indicators:

- gross domestic product
- inflation
- unemployment

Gross Domestic Product

Goods and services that satisfy our needs and wants are the final output of our economy. They are the result of all the economic activity in the country. One way of telling how well our economy is performing is to determine how many goods and

F.Y.I.

Today, computers in business are taken for granted, but before the 1950s, they were hardly used in businesses at all. The first computers weighed about 30 tons and required 18,000 vacuum tubes to operate! Although they could perform as many calculations in a day as one person could do in 20 years, they were too expensive—and too big—to be of practical use to businesses.

Cooperative Learning 👥   Co-op Co-op

Distribute copies of Enrichment Master 3-1, which lists some of the economic indicators used by economists to forecast economic conditions. Then, explain that economic indicators can be divided into three categories: leading—those that point to what will happen to the economy; coincident—those that indicate activity occurring at the same time as changes in the business cycle; and lagging indicators—those that occur after a change in the business cycle. Have groups research one category of indicators. Suggest they find some current statistics for indicators in their category, explain the meanings of the indicators to the class, and tell how the indicators can be interpreted given current economic conditions.

Refer to the *Cooperative Learning Strategies* booklet for additional cooperative learning strategies.

U.S. GROSS DOMESTIC PRODUCT (IN BILLIONS OF DOLLARS)					
1970	**1980**	**1990**	**1991**	**1992**	**1993**
$1011	$2708	$5546	$5723	$6039	$6378

Source: Statistical Abstract of the United States

FIGURE 3-2

Gross Domestic Product (GDP) is the sum of the dollar value of consumer goods and services, business goods and services, government goods and services, and goods and services sold to other nations. An increase in GDP from one year to the next is an indicator of economic growth. By how much did the GDP increase from 1992 to 1993?

USE VISUALS
Use Figure 3-2 to demonstrate to students the changes in gross domestic product from 1970 to 1993. To help students visualize the changes in gross domestic product, have them use the values given in the figure to make a bar graph. Students may want to use a computer to make their graphs.
Answer to caption: $339 billion.

services it produces during a certain period of time. **Gross domestic product,** or GDP, is the dollar value of all final goods and services produced in the nation in a single year. This measure has replaced the GNP, or gross national product, which was previously used and was similar to the GDP.

To calculate the GDP, economists compute the sum of goods and services. They include four main areas:

- consumer goods and services
- business goods and services
- government goods and services
- goods and services sold to other countries

A dollar value is assigned to the goods and services to find the sum. Figure 3-2 above lists the GDP for several years. The GDP in 1980 was just over $2.7 trillion. In 1993 the GDP was over $6.3 trillion. The change in GDP from one year to the next is one way to determine whether or not there has been economic growth. So, even though the GDP has gone up from one year to the next, the GDP is rising rather slowly. Many economists think that the rate of growth has slowed during the past two decades.

GDP is one way to measure how well people are living in a particular country. The **standard of living** of a particular country is another measure of how well the people in an economic system live. The standard of living depends on the amount and kinds of goods and services the people of a country enjoy. An economic system that can provide for its people's basic needs and can produce the goods and services its people want and can afford probably will have a high standard of living.

Inflation

Business and government leaders also consider the inflation rate to be an important general economic indicator. **Inflation** is a prolonged rise in level of prices for goods and services. A rise in the price of hamburgers or shampoo does not mean

Learning Activity
Suggest that students consult statistical resources such as *The Statistical Abstract of the United States* or *The World Almanac* to verify the categories that comprise the gross domestic product.

Global Perspective

Have students find current articles about the standard of living in other countries. Ask them to find out what factors are evaluated to determine the level of a country's standard of living. Then have students choose a foreign country and study their standard of living. Suggest that they research the factors that determine its standard of living. Have students write a paragraph evaluating the overall standard of living of the country. They should include statistics in their paragraph that support their evaluation.

Refer to the *International Business Strategies* booklet for additional strategies and activities.

Building Business Skills

Have students study the effects of inflation on people and the economy as shown in the box on page 45. Ask students which effects seem unclear to them. Ask volunteers to give a real-life example or provide one yourself for any of the effects students don't understand.

TEACHING TIP

Emphasize that inflation is *not* part of the business cycle, although it is common, at least to some extent, in most economic systems. Point out that inflation can occur during contractions or expansions of the business cycle.

Business Brief

Economists have invented some descriptive terms for the varying degrees of inflation. *Creeping inflation* refers to annual increases in overall prices in the range of 1 to 3 percent. *Galloping inflation* describes severe inflation in the neighborhood of 100 to 300 percent per year. *Hyperinflation* is the most severe form of inflation, with annual rates reaching beyond 500 percent. Hyperinflation occurs during times of extreme economic crisis.

MATH
Understanding Inflation

Explanation

A nickel has always been worth five cents, but the value of five cents has changed over the years. During the Depression in the 1930s, a nickel could buy a loaf of bread. How much does a loaf of bread cost today?

Over the years prices for most products have steadily risen. A general rise in prices is called *inflation*. Inflation reduces the value of money because it means you can buy less than you could earlier for the same amount of money. The price increases during inflation have nothing to do with the goods themselves. If the price of your favorite pizza goes up from $7.50 to $7.75, is the pizza different?

Inflation generally is reported in terms of annual rates of change. *Mild inflation* occurs when prices increase from 2 to 4 percent a year. When the price increases range from 5 to 9 percent, *modest inflation* occurs. If the annual rate is 10 percent or higher, *severe inflation* occurs. This type of inflation is sometimes called *double-digit inflation*.

As long as your wages rise at the same rate as inflation, you'll be able to buy and save as much as you did before. But if you lived on a fixed income—one that didn't change from year to year—you couldn't.

inflation. But if prices rise for most goods and services and they continue to rise for an extended period of time, then the conditions for inflation exist. Inflation reduces the "purchasing power" of money. Your money buys less. Sometimes people describe inflation as a time when "a dollar is not worth a dollar anymore."

Inflation is a problem for most consumers. People who live on a fixed income are hurt the most. Many retired people, for instance, cannot count on an increase in income as prices rise. Retirement income or any fixed income usually does not rise as fast as prices. Many retired people have fewer goods and services to enjoy because of the rising prices.

Even for working people whose incomes are going up, inflation can be a problem. The cost of living goes up, too. People must have even more money to keep up their standard of living. Just buying the things they need costs more. When incomes do not keep pace with rising prices, the standard of living goes down. People may be earning the same amount of money, but they are not living as well because they are not able to buy as many goods and services.

44   Unit 1   Introduction to the Global Economy

Cooperative Learning   Group Discussion

Remind the class that natural, capital, human, and entrepreneurial resources are the four factors of production. Then divide the class into groups, and ask the following question. "What happens to the prices of products as a result of increases in the costs of one or more factors of production?" Have each group answer the question and give reasons for their answers.

Refer to the *Cooperative Learning Strategies* booklet for additional cooperative learning strategies.

EFFECTS OF INFLATION

On People:

- People on fixed incomes are able to buy fewer goods and services.
- Individuals and banks suffer reduction in the purchasing power of their money when they receive payment of a loan.
- People make necessary purchases quickly, then cut back on spending.
- Interest rates rise and discourage people from borrowing and spending.
- People lose their jobs as businesses lay off workers.

On the Economy:

- Workers ask for wage increases to keep up with inflation.
- Business owners raise prices of goods and services to pay for wage increases.
- Increasing inflation reduces consumers' ability to buy goods and services.
- Reduction in quantity of products sold leads to unemployment and a downturn in the economy.
- Interest rates rise discouraging businesses from borrowing and spending to expand.

Practice

Use the information in the box to decide how inflation might affect the following situations.

1. A borrower about to repay a loan.
2. A retired factory worker on a fixed pension.
3. A person who has just withdrawn a large sum of money from a savings account.
4. A person with a three-year contract guaranteeing fixed payment for a job.

Most people have a basic understanding of inflation and how it can affect how much they can buy. But computing and measuring inflation can be difficult. The **inflation rate** is the percentage by which the average level of prices in an economy rises; it is usually expressed as a percentage per year. The inflation rate is the speed at which prices in general are rising. Suppose food is the only good that people buy. And suppose that there was a 10 percent increase in the average level of food prices during the year. This increase means that you would spend $1.10 at the end of the year to buy the same food that $1.00 would have bought at the beginning of the year.

Economists measure inflation by looking at the average prices of one group or type of goods such as the consumer price index or the producer price index. Figure 3-3 on page 46 shows inflation rates in the United States for 1960–1995. An inflation rate of 10 percent or higher is considered severe inflation. During such a period, prices rise much faster than wages, and purchasing power decreases rapidly. The inflation rate rarely has risen above 10 percent a year in the United States. But, in 1980 it did reach 13.5 percent. Some countries have had much

Have students review the effects of inflation listed in the box, and then instruct them to answer the practice questions. (1. Money paid back will have less value than that borrowed. 2. Will have less buying power; may have to make changes in lifestyle. 3. Money will have less buying power than when it was originally saved. 4. Buying power of money paid at the end of the contract will be less than at the beginning.)

Learning Activity

Ask students to choose an item such as a loaf of bread or a pound of sugar and find the current price for it. Then have students use the library to research prices for the item 5, 10, and 25 years ago. Have students display their findings in graphic form and post the graphs in the classroom. Discuss with the class the conclusions that can be drawn about prices from the information displayed in the graphs.

Reteaching Strategy

Have students refer to the Effects of Inflation box above to evaluate how inflation might affect the following situations.

- A couple who wants to get a loan to buy a house. (Interest rates will be high, which will make the cost of buying a house more expensive.)
- A person looking for a job. (Fewer businesses may be hiring, because their current expenses are increasing.)

Use Figure 3-3 to help students see how the inflation rate has fluctuated since 1960. Ask students how they would characterize the trend in the inflation rate from 1990 to 1995.
Answer to caption: 1980.

Connection to
CHAPTER 36

In Chapter 36, students will learn how the government calculates the unemployment rate. Ask students to decide whether they would be more concerned if the unemployment rate increased as the result of people losing their jobs due to automation or if the rate went up during the winter because, traditionally, fewer construction workers, farmers, and service workers are employed during those months.

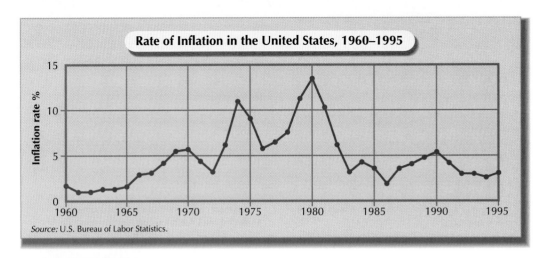

Rate of Inflation in the United States, 1960–1995

Source: U.S. Bureau of Labor Statistics.

FIGURE 3-3

The inflation rate is the percentage by which the average level of prices in an economic system rises. In what year was the inflation rate the highest?

higher rates of inflation. For example, in 1994 Peru had an inflation rate of 20 percent and Poland's inflation rate was nearly 30 percent.

Unemployment

Another important economic indicator is the number of people who are unemployed during a given period of time. The U.S. Bureau of Labor Statistics gathers data related to employment and unemployment in our economy each month. Its findings are then published very early in the next month. When the findings are released, the news media usually report the rate of unemployment. They often compare the rate with the previous month's rate or the previous year's. The **unemployment rate** is the percentage of the unemployed workforce looking for jobs.

In 1994, the unemployment rate in the United States was about 6.1 percent. Previously, in 1982 and 1983, the United States had an unemployment rate near 10 percent, which is considered high.

Business and government leaders are interested in how many new jobs the economy creates during a period of time, because this is one indicator of economic growth. They are also interested in the total number of people employed in various sectors, or areas, of the economy—goods-producing, service, public, and private sectors. Changes in these totals reveal which sectors of the economy are growing and which ones are not.

Value of Economic Indicators

A number of people have been disappointed with some of the economic indicators. The indicators are not overly exact

Curriculum Connection   **History**

Have students find unemployment statistics for the following years: 1933, 1944, 1955, 1966, 1977, 1988, and the most recent year for which statistics are available. Instruct students to present their information in a bar graph. Discuss the reasons for the differences shown in the graph.

because of data which has not been reported or things which have been left out. Yet, they are exact enough to show what is generally happening in a segment of the economy. For example, the unemployment rate in most cases is stated at a lower rate than what it actually is in the nation. The rate shows only those who are without a job but are looking. It does not include those who have given up looking for a job outside the home. Yet, if the rate increases one can conclude that unemployment is rising.

All kinds of people use and study these indicators. Government officials look at them in order to plan governmental policy. If the indicators show that inflation is rising, they will want to implement policies to combat inflation. Such policies are generally not the same policies used to combat increased unemployment. Businesspeople check economic indicators all of the time. If it looks like there will be an economic slowdown, businesses will cut back on their orders because they don't want to have an inventory that may become old and stale. Investors look very carefully at these indicators to determine when to buy or sell stocks. If it looks like a period of prosperity is over the horizon, investors might well want to buy stocks because profitability is probably ahead.

1994 Unemployment Rates Around the World

Japan	2.9%
United States	6.1%
Germany	6.5%
Netherlands	7.7%
Sweden	7.8%
United Kingdom	9.5%
Canada	10.4%
Italy	11.4%
France	12.3%

Quick Check

1. Name three economic indicators.
2. What four factors are used to figure gross domestic product?
3. What does a country's standard of living measure?
4. Define *inflation rate* and *unemployment rate*.

THE FEDERAL GOVERNMENT AND ECONOMIC STABILITY

Changes in our business and economic world are expected—and are normal. However, too many ups and downs are not desirable. Beginning with the Great Depression of the 1930s, the federal government has taken an increasing role in managing the economy. When the economy is in a recession, the government actively tries to prevent a depression and bring about a recovery. In a period of prosperity, the government attempts to maintain it. The government also tries to keep the rate of inflation down.

The federal government uses two main ways to influence the economy: (1) fiscal policy and (2) monetary policy. *Fiscal policy*

Making Connections   Economic Forecasts

Have students find out how well economists were able to predict the recession of 1990–91, which officially began in March 1990, by having them look for economic forecasts for the 12 months preceding the onset of the recession. How accurately were economists able to predict the recession? Did all economists agree on the direction the economy would take? What indicators did economists base their predictions on?

The Federal Reserve System (the Fed) conducts monetary policy, and Congress and the president are responsible for fiscal policy. Monetary and fiscal policy can interfere with one another and often do. For example, during an election year, a president may want to implement policies such as lowering taxes and approving federal spending projects that will stimulate the economy and enhance his chances for re-election. The Fed may see inflation as a problem and decrease the supply of money in order to rein in inflation. The Fed might raise interest rates to tighten the money supply, which would work against the expansion efforts attempted by fiscal policy. Many people believe that fiscal policy should be handled by an independent agency rather than by Congress and the president.

Quick Check Answers

1. Fiscal policy and monetary policy.
2. Fiscal policy.

involves using government spending and taxation to influence the economy. *Monetary policy* involves controlling the supply of money and credit to influence the economy. A number of economists believe that a major reason for business cycles is the changing economic policies of the federal government.

Fiscal Policy

One way the federal government tries to either stimulate or dampen the economy is through how it collects its revenues (taxes) and how it spends its money. For example, cutting taxes is one way to indirectly increase consumer spending. If the government cuts taxes, workers have more take-home pay. Their increased spending for goods and services may help the economy out of a recession. Of course, that plan works only if consumers spend, rather than save, their money.

Sometimes the government acts to slow down the economy. If inflation is a problem, the government may cut its own spending. Since the government is a big consumer of goods and services, less government spending will mean fewer dollars spent in those segments of the economy. The economy thus slows down. The federal government can also increase taxes, which takes money out of the economy. However, if the government wants to curb inflation, it has to use that additional money to balance its budget rather than spend it. You will learn more about government's role in our business and economic world in Unit 5.

Monetary Policy

The second way the federal government tries to stabilize the economy is through controlling the supply of money and the cost of borrowing money—credit—according to the needs of the economy. If the federal government wants to slow down the economy, for instance, it may tighten the supply of money and credit available to businesses and individuals. If, on the other hand, it wishes to stimulate the economy, it may expand the money supply. The federal government does all this through the Federal Reserve System which you will learn more about in Unit 6.

Most Latin American countries relied on government-run industries and high taxes on imported goods. This led to large national debts and extreme inflation rates. It also discouraged trade and investment from abroad. In the mid-1990s, many Latin American countries restructured their economies. Reforms included reducing high import taxes, opening markets to foreign competition and investment, restructuring national debt, and privatizing state-run industries. By 1995 these actions had helped most Latin American countries reduce their inflation rates and increase foreign investment in their economies.

Quick Check

1. What are two ways in which the federal government tries to stabilize the economy?
2. Under which policy would the government cut taxes?

Enrichment Strategy

Voters tend to oppose tax increases. Divide the class into groups and have them survey ten adults about recent local or state tax issues. Have students ask for opinions about whether the taxes were needed, whether taxes are too high, and whether tax dollars are put to good use. Compare the groups' findings in a class discussion.

Chapter 3 **Summary**

Main Ideas

1. The repeated rise and fall of economic activity over time is called a business cycle.
2. During a business cycle there may be a period of expansion in which the economy grows. The peak of the expansion is the highest level of activity in a cycle. A drop in business activity is a contraction. The lowest level of business activity in a business cycle is the trough.
3. The United States economy has experienced many economic fluctuations. In the 1930s the economy was in a very severe decline known as a depression. The economy has also experienced shorter, less severe economic declines called recessions. When economic growth returns following a depression or recession, there is an economic recovery.
4. Economists use economic indicators such as gross domestic product, inflation, and unemployment to measure the performance of the economy.
5. The federal government attempts to stabilize the economy in two main ways: (1) fiscal policy involves using government spending and taxation; (2) monetary policy involves controlling the supply of money and credit.
6. Dean Kamen is a successful entrepreneur, inventor, and physicist who also helps young people become interested in science and technology.
7. Inflation is a lengthy period of rising prices that decreases purchasing power.

CASE ANALYSIS | The Business Cycle

A business cycle has four major stages: expansion, peak, contraction, and trough. Describe what you think will generally happen during each stage to each of these factors:

a. Jobs—increase in number, decrease, or stay the same?
b. Prices for consumer goods—decrease, increase, or stay the same?
c. Consumers' buying habits—buy less, buy more, or no change?
d. Number of business firms in the market—decrease, increase, or stay the same?

QUICK QUIZ

1. What are the four phases of the business cycle? (Expansion, peak, contraction, and trough.)
2. List three economic indicators. (Gross domestic product, inflation, and unemployment.)
3. Explain what standard of living measures. (How well the people in a country live.)
4. What can the federal government do to control inflation? (Cut government spending or raise taxes.)

CLOSE

Main Ideas

Main Ideas summarizes the key information in the chapter. It is a useful tool for reinforcement and review.

CASE ANALYSIS

Case Analysis provides a chapter-related case for student analysis and application of decision-making skills.

Answer:
a. During a *contraction* or when the business cycle is in a *trough,* consumers spend less and production is decreased, so the number of jobs decreases. During an *expansion,* or when the business cycle is at a *peak,* more workers are hired to meet increased demand.
b. During a *contraction* or when the business cycle is in a *trough,* prices tend to decrease. One reason for this decrease is that businesses may have an oversupply of goods because consumers have less money to spend. To get rid of the items, businesses decrease prices. During periods of *expansion* or when the business cycle is at a *peak,* prices stay the same or increase. **c.** During a *contraction* or when the business cycle is in a *trough,* consumers buy less. During *expansion* or when the business cycle is at a *peak,* consumers have more money, so they buy more. **d.** During a *contraction* or when the business cycle is in a *trough,* the number of businesses decreases, whereas in an *expansion* or when the business cycle is at a *peak,* the number of businesses increases.

Chapter 3 **Review**

APPLY

Answers

Use the Language of Business

1. expansion, **2.** trough, **3.** standard of living, **4.** business cycle, **5.** gross domestic product, **6.** peak, **7.** inflation, **8.** contraction, **9.** economic fluctuations, **10.** recession, **11.** economic indicators, **12.** inflation rate, **13.** depression, **14.** unemployment rate, **15.** recovery.

Review What You Learned

1. Expansion, peak, contraction, and trough.
2. It declines.
3. Gross domestic product, inflation, and unemployment.
4. Consumer goods and services; business goods and services; government goods and services; and goods and services sold to other countries.
5. It decreases it.
6. Cut government spending; raise taxes.
7. Control systems for audiovisual shows and a portable medicine infusion pump.
8. A prolonged period of rising prices.

Understand Business Concepts

1. A country whose economy is expanding may buy more goods and services from its trading partners. Because their economies are interdependent, trading partners will benefit from another country's prosperity.
2. A recession or depression.
3. Yes. Exports are part of the gross domestic product.
4. Food and shelter are basic needs. If people can't afford basic needs, the standard of living is not high.
5. No. Inflation is a prolonged rise in price levels of most goods and services. If the other items were the same price, the circumstances would not indicate inflation.

Use the Language of Business

When talking about business cycles and the factors that determine an economic system's health, people use the following terms. See how well you know them by matching each term to its definition.

business cycle	inflation
contraction	inflation rate
depression	peak
economic fluctuation	recession
economic indicators	recovery
expansion	standard of living
gross domestic product	trough
unemployment rate	

1. Rising level of business activity.
2. Lowest level of business activity in a business cycle.
3. Measure of how well the people in an economic system live.
4. Repeated rise and fall of economic activity over time.
5. Monetary value of all final goods and services produced in a country for a stated time period.
6. Highest level of economic activity in a business cycle.
7. Prolonged rise in level of prices for goods and services.
8. Noticeable drop in the level of business activity.
9. Ups and downs in economic activity.
10. Period of severe economic decline.
11. Important data used to measure economic activity and business cycles.
12. Percentage by which the average level of prices in an economy rises.
13. Long period of very severe economic decline.
14. Percentage of the workforce looking for work that does not have jobs.
15. Period of economic growth following a recession or depression.

Review What You Learned

1. What four phases occur in a business cycle?
2. What happens to economic activity during a recession or depression?
3. List three economic indicators.
4. What four parts of the economy do economists look at to calculate gross domestic product?
5. What effect does inflation have on the purchasing power of money?
6. What might the government do if inflation is a problem?
7. What inventions began Dean Kamen's business career?
8. What is inflation?

Understand Business Concepts

1. In our global economy, how are countries affected by the economic prosperity of a trading partner?
2. What event might follow a contraction in the economy?
3. Would the money received for American cars exported to Italy be part of the U.S. gross domestic product? Why or why not?
4. If many people in a country were able to afford only a few food items and

6. Economic growth. During a time of economic growth, consumers want more goods and services. This, in turn, means that people will be working to produce the goods and services, resulting in lower unemployment.
7. To keep inflation down.
8. Possible answer: They invent things or discover ideas that improve the quality of life.
9. Because they are on fixed incomes.

Think Critically

1. Possible answer: Some will believe that it is a good idea since inflation affects almost everyone, and the government should use its power to attack a problem that affects everyone.
2. Possible answer: The country probably has a fairly high standard of living since all residents' basic needs seem well provided for. The fact that few people can afford luxuries does not indicate a low standard of living.

there was a severe housing shortage, would that country have a high or low standard of living? Explain.

5. Suppose you go to a drugstore to buy toothpaste, blank cassettes, and film. You also consider buying a can of soda, but you notice that the price is 20 cents higher than it was last week. The prices of the other items seem the same as always. Is the soda price increase an example of inflation? Why or why not?

6. Would a country with a low unemployment rate most likely be experiencing economic growth or decline? Explain your answer.

7. In what instances might the federal government cut its own spending to enhance the health of the economy?

8. Why does entrepreneur Dean Kamen want to make our next heroes scientists and technologists?

9. Why is inflation often especially difficult for retired people?

Think Critically

1. **Judge.** Do you think it is a good idea for the government to take measures to curb inflation when the inflation rate climbs? Why or why not?

2. **Assess.** How would you rate the standard of living for a country in which all the residents have adequate housing, ample food to eat, and good medical care, but in which few people have expensive cars, boats, or jewelry?

Use What You Learned

1. **Group Project.** Work as a group to find graphs, tables, and charts showing GDP and other economic indicators over the past few years. Use the library and any computer search resources you can. Create a wall display of your findings. Note and discuss the changes that have taken place. What phase of the economic cycle are we in now? What phase were we in five years ago?

2. **Computer Application.** In addition to the Consumer Price Index, the federal government uses many other economic indicators to measure how well the economy is doing. Among these indicators are the following: number of building permits issued; the average workweek for production workers in

manufacturing; plant and equipment contracts and orders; and the change in manufacturers' unfilled orders for durable goods. Do on-line research to retrieve government databases of these indicators from 1980 to the present. Present the data in chart form and analyze in a brief paragraph what the numbers indicate about the economy.

3. **Skill Reinforcement.** Choose five products that you frequently buy. Find out how prices for these products have changed since you were born. Determine if the rise in price is the result of inflation or other factors. Present your data graphically and write a short summary of about 100 words.

Save your work in your Business Portfolio.

Independent Practice

Use the Chapter 3 worksheets in *Student Activity Guide 1* for additional practice and application activities. *Student Activity Guide 1* provides vocabulary exercises, reading comprehension checks, problems, projects, and simulations of business and economic situations. A Teacher's Annotated Edition provides answers.

ASSESS

Portfolio Assessment

The portfolio projects are designed to lead students to develop a collection of their best work to submit to you for assessment. You and your students should decide which projects will be included in their respective Business Portfolios. Refer students to the specific rubric(s) from the *Alternative Assessment Strategies* booklet listed with each of the project notes below. These rubrics will alert students to the criteria you will use to assess their projects.

Chapter Assessment

Use the Chapter 3 Test from the *Test Masters* booklet to evaluate students' understanding of the chapter concepts. An answer key is provided. Or create your own customized test using the *Testmaker* software.

Use What You Learned

1. Make sure all students participate in the group project. Rubrics: Bulletin Board; Charts and Tables.

2. Students with no access to a computer may use periodical and newspaper indexes to retrieve information and make their charts by hand. Rubrics: Charts and Tables; Paragraph.

3. Students' answers will vary. Rubrics: Graph; Essay.

Business Issue

Business Issue

FULL EMPLOYMENT

Highlight the Issue

Before students read pages 52–53, take a poll to discover how many students think the government should provide jobs for people who can't find work in the private sector and how many think full employment is not the government's responsibility. Have students explain their stances and record their reasons on the board. After students finish reading the Business Issue, conduct another poll to find out how many students have changed their opinion regarding full employment.

FULL EMPLOYMENT

When the unemployment rate rises, there are many people willing to work who can't find jobs. Should the government guarantee full employment to all Americans who want to work?

Pro

Government job-creation programs have been successful in the past. During the Great Depression of the 1930s, the federal government sponsored several programs to put the unemployed back to work. The Works Progress Administration (WPA) employed more than eight million Americans in public works projects, building hospitals, schools, roads, bridges, and airports. The Civilian Conservation Corps (CCC) put more than three million unemployed Americans to work planting trees, fighting forest fires, and taking care of public parks. In the 1970s, the Comprehensive Employment and Training Act (CETA), put about 750,000 people on the public payroll. Programs such as these not only employed people in useful work, but also gave them skills they could use when they left their government jobs.

Public works projects don't benefit only the unemployed, however. The CCC built shelters and trails in state and national parks that millions of Americans still enjoy. The WPA constructed hospitals, schools, and airports that are still in use. Workers in a new government jobs program could build affordable housing, restore the environment, teach literacy skills, or tackle any number of projects that would benefit all Americans.

Government jobs programs also strengthen the economy and society as a whole. People who are confident they will have jobs spend more money on goods and services, boosting the economy. Working people also pay taxes, increasing government revenue. Furthermore, when more people are working, fewer people are on welfare or receiving other government aid. People are more hopeful, and social problems lessen.

A federal job-creation program is not only necessary it's also affordable. One economist calculated the cost of a federal jobs program large enough to eliminate unemployment. He found that the bill for full employment was several billion dollars less than the government actually spent on the unemployed!

If the market economy is not creating enough jobs to go around, then it is up to the government to do so.

52   UNIT 1   INTRODUCTION TO THE GLOBAL ECONOMY

Extend the Issue

Have students increase their understanding of the issue of full employment by finding out more about government employment plans of the past. Groups of students who are in favor of full employment may work together to put together a more detailed oral presentation on the benefits of the public works projects of the 1930s and 1970s. Groups not in favor of government-sponsored jobs pro-

Con

Although it's appealing to say the federal government should eliminate unemployment by creating millions of jobs, there is plenty of evidence that such programs don't really work. Federal jobs programs may provide employment, but they do little to stimulate the overall economy. Jobs programs such as the WPA and CCC did not restore prosperity. Many workers who left the WPA to look for jobs in the private sector couldn't find work and had to return to the government payroll. Programs such as the WPA, the CCC, and CETA don't strengthen the economy, they simply create a huge government workforce.

Government jobs are often "make-work" jobs that are low paid and require few skills. They are little more than a handout disguised as a paycheck. Such jobs do little to improve workers' chances of landing a better paid job in the private sector.

In addition, providing full employment for all Americans would cost billions of dollars more than the government collects in taxes. Spending on such a scale would drastically increase the national debt and the portion of the federal budget that goes to pay the interest on that debt—an expense we can ill afford.

Increased government spending on a jobs program would also lead to inflation. When employment is guaranteed, employers must pay more to keep their employees. As wages rise, prices go up and inflation sets in.

Government jobs programs also take work away from the private sector. For example, when the government sponsors a public works project, such as building a new highway, private contractors have no opportunity to do the work.

The guarantee of full employment would also undermine the work ethic and reduce the productivity of American companies. When people know they will always have a job, they may not work as hard or be as productive.

Government jobs programs are not the answer to unemployment. A better solution would be to provide incentives, such as investment tax credits, for businesses to grow and create new jobs. Such measures lead to a stronger economy overall.

Update the Issue

Have students check current news sources for articles about the current rate of unemployment and measures being taken to create jobs. Students should find out what percentage of jobs being created are in the private sector and what percentage are in the public sector. Students may want to explore how the federal government's attempts to balance the budget have affected government jobs programs. Have students summarize their findings in a brief essay.

UNIT 1   INTRODUCTION TO THE GLOBAL ECONOMY   **53**

grams may gather economic evidence from historical sources about the effect of public works projects on the federal budget. Have groups on each side of the issue present their evidence to the class. Discuss the relevance their findings have in today's business and economic climate.

Unit 2 The Private Enterprise System

Chapter	Learning Objectives
4 **Motivations of Business** **pp. 56–69**	• Describe the private enterprise system. • Explain what motivates business. • Describe some benefits businesses provide. • Decide how to organize your work for yourself. • Discuss how entrepreneur Gertrude Boyle used the motivations of business to make Columbia Sportswear a success.
5 **How the Market Works** **pp. 70–85**	• Explain how prices affect consumers and producers. • Discuss how prices are determined. • Identify several circumstances that will cause prices of goods or services to change. • Describe the cause-and-effect relationship of consumers and producers in our market economy. • List the four stages the American economy has gone through. • Name and describe several kinds of electronic transmission media. • Interpret information on a line graph.
6 **The Private Enterprise Environment** **pp. 86–99**	• Describe the rise of business in the United States. • Enumerate the five basic types of businesses. • Explain how consumers benefit from business competition. • Identify skills needed in health and biomedical services. • Explain why observing details and making inferences is an important skill for people in business.

Business Issue: **Family-Friendly Benefits, pp. 100–101**

National Standards for Business Education*	Chapter Highlights			
	Focus on Features	**Building Business Skills**	**Visual Learning**	**Case Analysis**
EE: I A, I C, I D; *EPF:* V, IX, X C, XIII A; *MGMT:* VII D	Entrepreneurs: Gertrude Boyle—Columbia Sportswear, p. 60	Employability: Completing Self-Directed Tasks, p. 64	New Businesses, 1990–1994, p. 62 Businesses and Business Failures, p. 63	Marketing, p. 67
EE: III B, III C, III D; *EPF:* IV, V, VII, VIII, IX; *IS:* V	Technology: Electronic Information Transfer, p. 80	Math: Interpreting Line Graphs, p. 76	Demand, p. 74 Supply, p. 75 Equilibrium Price, p. 78	Marketing, p. 83
CD: II A; *EPF:* III, IX; *MGMT:* I C, IV A	Careers: Health and Biomedical Services, p. 90	Analysis: Observing and Inferring, p. 94	Leading U.S. Businesses, p. 93	Private Enterprise, p. 97

*Level 3 Performance Expectations: Career Development (CD), Entrepreneurship Education (EE), Economics and Personal Finance (EPF), Information Systems (IS), Management (MGMT). See page T14 for all 12 content areas.

Unit 2

Look Back

Ask students to recall that, as consumers, they participate in the global economy. Every country has its own economic system, or set of rules by which the nation decides how to distribute its limited resources to satisfy its people's wants. In the United States, businesses aim to be efficient, provide employment, and grow and expand.

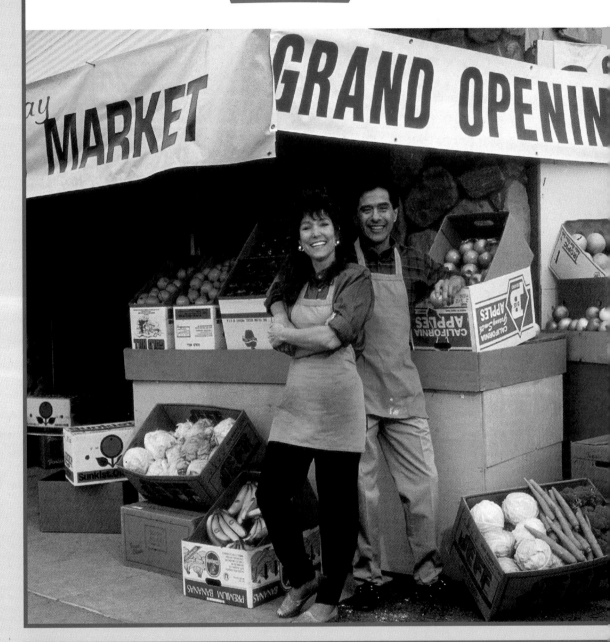

UNIT 2 COOPERATIVE LEARNING PROJECT

Corners/Teammates Consulting Activity

Preparation: Photocopy BLMs 3 and 4 from the *Cooperative Learning Strategies* booklet for each group. Provide each group with a cupful of dry beans to use as currency and one ingredient from the cookie recipe given on BLM 3. Have one group be in charge of "renting" baking supplies—mixing bowls and spoons, measuring cups and spoons, and baking trays. This activity will take approximately two or three class periods.

Guidelines: Each group represents a business that sells a cookie ingredient or rents out baking supplies. For example, one group could sell flour, another could sell eggs, and so on. To make a batch of cookies, each group must use its

The Private Enterprise System

Look Ahead
Explain that businesses in the private enterprise system are motivated by the desire to meet consumer demand for goods and services and the desire for profit. Prices are an important aspect of the private enterprise system. Prices affect consumer demand and how much businesses supply. Businesses in the private enterprise system can be divided into five types: producers, processors, manufacturers, intermediaries, and service businesses.

This unit discusses the private enterprise system. The first chapter covers the role of profits and competition as motivators of businesses. The next chapter describes the laws of supply and demand. The final chapter describes the structure of most businesses and the roles of managers.

55

beans to "purchase" other ingredients and "rent" supplies from other groups. The prices and rental rates (in beans) are listed in the recipe on BLM 3.

Have each group decide how to acquire ingredients, how to sell its "product" to others, and what jobs each member will have. Once each group has its supplies, have students follow the recipe and mix the cookie dough. Make arrangements with the school cafeteria for students to bake the cookies after school. Groups can share their cookies during the next class period while they work together to complete BLM 4.

Alternative: Instead of baking cookies, have groups use a similar process to complete another project, such as an art project.

Introduce the Chapter

Major Concepts
- What Motivates Business?
- Who Benefits from Business?

Introduce the Topic
Ask students if they might someday like to have their own business. What type of business? For what reasons are they interested in running a business? In Chapter 4 students will learn about some of the reasons, or motivations, people have for operating their businesses.

Use Business Terms
Have students look at the Business Terms and brainstorm associations with each term. Ask them where they have heard or seen the terms used. Reinforce correct associations. Advise students to note the meanings of the terms as they read the chapter.

USE VISUALS

Have students examine the photo and then ask: How does this business compete with other sporting goods stores that sell the same items? (By offering some items at lower prices.)

CHAPTER 4

Business terms

private enterprise system

motivation

competition

profit

social responsibility

green products

56

CHAPTER 4 RESOURCES

Instructional Resources

Lesson Plan for Chapter 4

Teaching Transparency 4-1

Strategies and Worksheets for Teaching Transparency 4-1

Enrichment Master 4-1

Student Activity Guide 1–TAE for Chapter 4

Test Master for Chapter 4

Alternative Assessment Strategies

Math Skills Review

International Business Strategies

Cooperative Learning Strategies

Communication Skills Review

Ethics in Business Strategies

Motivations of Business

Learning objectives

After completing this chapter, you will be able to:
- Describe the private enterprise system.
- Explain what motivates business.
- Describe some benefits businesses provide.
- Decide how to organize your work for yourself.
- Discuss how entrepreneur Gertrude Boyle used the motivations of business to make Columbia Sportswear a success.

Consider what you know

- The major purpose of business is to produce the goods and services people need. In the United States, the businesses that produce goods and services aim to be efficient, provide security and employment, and grow and expand.

Consider what you want to know

- What is the private enterprise system?
- How do consumers motivate business?
- What part does profit play in motivating business?
- What are ways businesses benefit society in general?
- How can a business act in a socially responsible manner?
- How can a plan help a person complete a task or an assignment?
- What makes a person a successful business owner?

Consider how to use what you learn

- As you read through this chapter, think about what might motivate you to start your own business. Then decide how many of your reasons match the motivations of business given in this chapter.

CHAPTER 4 MOTIVATIONS OF BUSINESS **57**

Multimedia Resources

Technology Resource Guide

Distance Learning Guide

Internet Resource Guide

Professional Resources

School-to-Work/Tech Prep Strategies

Instructional Poster

Spanish Resources

Testmaker Software for Chapter 4

The Wall Street Journal Video Series
 Video & Activities for Chapter 4

Business and Marketing Computer
 Applications—An Integrated Software
 Simulation Using Microsoft Works

Stocktracker—A Stock Market Software
 Simulation

Where's the Dough? Board Game

Motivate the Learning

Learning Objectives
Remind students that the learning objectives highlight what they will study in the chapter. Ask students to bear these objectives in mind as they read the chapter. Note that the last two objectives listed refer to the Focus on Entrepreneurs feature and the Building Business Skills feature.

Consider What You Know
Review briefly the main sections of *Chapter 3 Measuring Economic Performance:* Economic Activity; Measuring Economic Activity; and The Federal Government and Economic Stability.

Consider What You Want to Know
Have students keep the listed questions in mind as they preview the chapter by quickly paging through it, looking at the pictures, and reading the section headings and figure titles.

Consider How to Use What You Learn
Explain to students that at the end of the chapter they will develop some projects for which they will need to think about the *motivations* and reasons they might have for starting a business. Suggest that as they read the chapter they consider what kinds of businesses already exist in their community. Ask also to think about the location and the length of time some of those businesses have been operating.

TEACH

Develop Concepts

What Motivates Business?

Write the following headings on the board: Wants and Needs, Competition, and Profit. Have the class name three local businesses. Ask students to think of the ways each business satisfies people's wants and needs, how it competes with similar businesses, and how the business makes a profit. Discuss with the class why each of these motives is related to a business's success.

What makes business owners want to start businesses and keep them going? In this chapter you will find out what keeps businesses going and what makes people strike out on their own to provide new products and services. You will also look at the many ways business benefits society. First, we will take a look at how our economy encourages business efforts.

WHAT MOTIVATES BUSINESS?

Our economic system is often called a **private enterprise system.** What does that mean? First, our economy is primarily private rather than public. Most economic resources and businesses are owned by individuals and groups rather than by government. Second, private individuals and groups, not the government, make decisions about what they buy, where they work, and what enterprises, or businesses, they are involved in. Because people are free to make their own economic decisions, the private enterprise system is also known as the free enterprise system.

The private enterprise system has features that distinguish it from other types of systems. Some of the most important are the freedom to buy, the freedom to produce and sell goods, and the freedom to choose a job.

- *Freedom to buy.* In our system, you may buy whatever you want as long as you have the money to pay for it, it is legal, and it is available. If you want to use your money to buy food or clothing, you can. If you want to go to a concert and you have the money, you can do that, too.
- *Freedom to produce and sell.* In our economic system, if you have a business, you are free to produce any goods and offer any services that are legal. You can charge whatever you want for your goods or services. However, you are limited by what people are willing to pay.
- *Freedom to choose a job.* In our system, you may choose the type of work you want to do. If you want to do yard work and you can find someone to hire you, you are free to do it. You could, however, also start a baby-sitting service. You are free to be a truck driver, a ballet dancer, or an accountant. You are not guaranteed a job, of course, but you have the freedom to choose.

Understanding these freedoms helps you to understand the **motivations,** or forces, that cause businesses to act. Because

Reteaching Strategy

List on the board or on an overhead transparency the three freedoms of the private enterprise system discussed on page 58. Ask students how these freedoms have affected their families, friends, and themselves during the past year. Have volunteers suggest activities that might have been impossible without these freedoms.

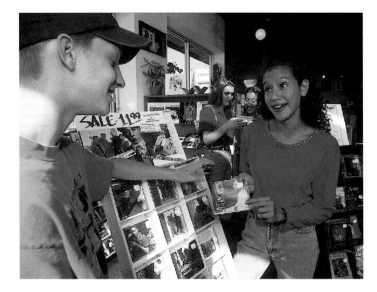

Businesses are motivated by the wants and needs of buyers. Why is variety important in businesses such as music stores?

USE VISUALS
Have students look at the photograph and describe what features or characteristics of a music store attract the most customers. Answer to caption: To appeal to the largest number of consumers.

Learning Activity
Explain that our economy has public and private sectors. Federal, state, and local governments make up the public sector. Governments are consumers because they buy goods and services from private individuals and businesses—the private sector. Have students brainstorm some goods and services your community's government might buy from private businesses. (Possible answers: building materials, trees and bushes for a public park, street lamps, signs, trucks, automobiles, and computers.)

people have the freedom to buy, businesses are motivated by the needs and wants of consumers. The freedom to produce and sell products creates a climate that is favorable to the creation of businesses. In fact, businesses are encouraged in our economic system. Because individuals are free to choose their own careers, businesses generally have a more motivated workforce since individuals act to choose the jobs that they wish to pursue.

Satisfying Wants and Needs

One factor that motivates businesses is the wants and needs of buyers. Buyers include consumers, other businesses, and different levels of government. The largest and most important of these groups is consumers. The goods and services that people are willing to buy are the ones that most businesses produce.

Consumers' wants and needs are very important to business. If consumers do not buy an item at a price that provides a sufficient profit level, businesses will no longer produce it. If enough consumers want a product, however, some company is likely to find a way to produce and sell it.

When the wants and needs of consumers change, businesses are motivated to change along with them. For example, many people today are concerned with health and fitness. This has prompted the establishment of health food stores and many supermarkets now offer whole-grain snacks and low-fat baked

Business & HISTORY

Successful businesspeople are often shrewd enough marketers to develop a need or want that consumers didn't know they had. For example, several years ago an enterprising company used advertising and clever packaging to persuade people to buy a "pet rock."

Global Perspective

China has one of the fastest growing economies in the world, which makes it an attractive market for foreign investors. Because China does not operate under the private enterprise system, American companies must adapt their business practices. Many find it helpful to develop a relationship with a particular government ministry or bureau. These agencies are known as "mothers-in-law" and serve as cultural and political liaisons for helping smooth the path for new joint ventures. Have students check current publications to find out more about how American companies have dealt with the challenges of doing business in China, and have them present their findings to the class.

Refer to the *International Business Strategies* booklet for additional strategies and activities.

FOCUS ON **Entrepreneurs**

Discuss

Ask students what consumer wants and needs Gert Boyle's company fulfills. How are Columbia's products different from those of the competition? (One difference is they cost less.) How has the company's humorous ad campaign helped it sell its products?

TEACHING TIP

Ask students to identify stores, restaurants, or other businesses in your area that compete with each other. Discuss how prices of similar goods have been affected by this competition. What can happen when there are two gas stations across the street from one another? (One gas station might lower its prices to draw customers away from the other station.)

Learning Activity

Divide the class into teams to brainstorm ideas for a new business in your community. Encourage them to think about the amount of competition already in existence. What kinds of consumers are they trying to reach? Where would be a good location for their business? Have a volunteer from each group summarize their group's ideas for a new local business.

Gertrude Boyle— Columbia Sportswear

L ong before she starred in her own company's commercials as "Mother Gert," Gertrude Boyle was a strong businessperson as well as a mother. Now a grandmother, Gert owns Columbia Sportswear, a Portland, Oregon, company that makes moderately priced parkas, raincoats, and other outerwear. In 1994, the firm's revenues topped $250 million.

Gert took over as CEO of her family's hat company in 1970. The first year wasn't easy. "In those days," she says, "they thought women didn't know anything about running a business." She proved that "they" were wrong. She renamed the company Columbia Sportswear and got started.

Columbia really began to take off in the early 1980s when Gert and the company developed a real winner: the Bugaboo, a parka with a zip-out lining that doubled as a separate jacket. Buyers loved the Bugaboo for its warmth—and because it cost half as much as competitors' jackets. As if producing quality products at affordable prices weren't enough, Columbia also started a winning advertising campaign.

In 1983, Gert Boyle and her son Tim, now Columbia's president, began to appear in a series of funny commercials. In one TV spot, Tim demonstrates the waterproofing of a jacket by walking through a car wash—at Mother Gert's insistence. A print ad for a line of sports shorts begins with Tim's words, "One day Mother made us change our shorts three times."

goods. Gyms and fitness centers have also been started to satisfy individuals' desire for fitness.

The Role of Competition

Competition is the contest between businesses to win customers. If you go into a store for a loaf of bread and there is only one kind, that is the only kind you will be able to buy. If there is more than one kind of bread to choose from, however, you can buy the cheapest one, or the one that is the right size for your family, or the one that is made from the grain you prefer, or the one that is the best quality. Businesses compete in many different ways. Their competition is a direct response to the needs and wants consumers possess.

If competition is a contest, the real winner is the consumer. Competition encourages businesses to be efficient and to produce the highest quality product at a given price. Companies find ways to differentiate their products from the others in such areas as price, quality, or extra features. Only then can they compete successfully with other companies that are producing the same product.

60 UNIT 2 THE PRIVATE ENTERPRISE SYSTEM

Global Perspective

To make American-made products more competitive in the global market, the federal government has announced that most goods it buys must now use the metric system of measurement—the system used by most of the rest of the world. The U.S. government is one of the biggest consumers of American goods, so this is a strong motivation for businesses to "go metric." Have students interview contractors or government employees about how a change to the metric system would affect them. Students should report their findings in class.

Refer to the *International Business Strategies* booklet for additional strategies and activities.

The buying public worldwide loved this ad campaign. At first, some at Columbia were afraid that other countries might not warm to the Mother Gert commercials. But they turned out to be wrong. The ads and the company's products have become very popular in Japan, France, and elsewhere. In fact, overseas sales tripled to $30 million in just two years.

Columbia's success goes well beyond advertising, however. Its rugged clothing designs appeal to a wide range of buyers, from suburbanites to city dwellers, all around the globe. Moreover, Columbia has kept prices low by catering to the realistic needs of average customers. In other words, its gear will see you through a Chicago or Tokyo winter, but it's not made for Mt. Everest. As Mother Gert cheerfully puts it, "If you went to the North Pole, you wouldn't take my stuff. Don't! Because you'll die."

Follow Through
Ask students if they think Gert Boyle's decision to not sell outdoor wear suited for extreme conditions was a good decision. Have the class give possible reasons for her decision. (Possible answer: Fewer people would buy her sportswear because most people do not need specialized clothing for extreme weather conditions.)

Profit As a Motivation

Why would a person or a business be willing to supply goods and services that you want to buy? The main reason is to earn money. If you work for someone, you expect to be paid for your work through the wages you earn. If a business produces goods and services, it expects to be paid for them. **Profit** is the amount of money left over after a business has paid for the cost of producing its goods or services. Profit is the motivation for taking the risk of starting a business. It is the reward for taking that risk. It is also the reward for satisfying the needs and wants of consumers. Look at Figure 4-1 on page 62 to see how many new businesses have been started in recent years.

Some people feel that businesses take advantage of consumers and earn huge profits. A few believe that a business charges whatever it wants for its goods and services. Actually, most businesses do not earn huge profits over a long period of time. When businesses do earn large profits, others notice and enter the field. This competition tends to lower profits.

Even though a person may like having a business, there are risks. The chief risk is failure. If customers do not buy the

Learning Activity
Provide students with the following problem: Yeong and Christopher need to raise $100 for their cross-country ski club's next outing. They plan to make and sell giant chocolate-chip cookies in their school cafeteria. They spend $22 on ingredients and price the cookies at 75 cents apiece. How many cookies do they need to sell to make a $100 profit? ($122 ÷ 0.75 = 163 cookies [rounded up])
For students who need to sharpen their math skills, choose among the worksheets in the *Math Skills Review* booklet.

Cooperative Learning Group Discussion

The profit motivation has sometimes been characterized as leading to greed and selfishness. Divide the class into groups and have them discuss the validity of this characterization. Encourage students to back up their opinions with examples. Have a member of each group write a summary of the group's discussion.

Refer to the *Cooperative Learning Strategies* booklet for additional cooperative learning strategies.

As students look at Figure 4-1, ask them to think of some businesses that started up within the past year in your community. Ask: What wants and needs do these businesses fulfill? Answer to caption: Consumer wants and needs, competition, and profit.

USE TRANSPARENCIES

Use Teaching Transparency 4-1 and its corresponding strategies and worksheet from the *Teaching Transparency Strategies and Worksheets* booklet to help illustrate the quantity of new business startups each year. Verify student worksheets using the Answer Key.

Quick Check Answers

1. Free enterprise system.
2. Freedom to buy; freedom to produce and sell; freedom to choose a job.
3. Satisfying wants and needs, competition, profit.
4. Force that causes businesses to act; contest between businesses to win customers; amount of money left over after paying cost of producing goods or services.

FIGURE 4-1

Hundreds of thousands of new businesses start up each year. What motivates people to start these businesses?

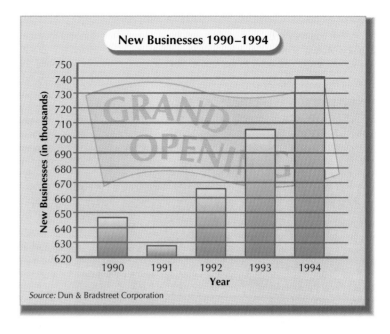

New Businesses 1990–1994

Source: Dun & Bradstreet Corporation

GLOBAL VIEW

What children wanted and demanded last year, this year sits gathering dust on the shelf. One toy, however, has managed to beat the odds and remain a favorite through 30 years—the Barbie doll. In order to keep Barbie a profitable product, Mattel has responded to the desires of American consumers for Hispanic, African-American, and Asian Barbies. In addition, Barbie is now meeting the wants of children in Europe, Eastern Europe, and the Far East.

product, the business may fail. Customers may turn away if prices are too high. The profit motive, however, is often enough to get people to take risks. As you can see in Figure 4-2 on page 63, the percentage of business failures varies from year to year.

Profits are good for our economy in many ways. As you have seen, the concept of profit is an energizing force. It encourages people to develop new products and services in the hope of making a profit. Without profit, few new products would be introduced.

Profits remain high when sales are high, and costs are kept low. This encourages companies to work in an efficient way that helps to conserve precious natural resources. Profits provide money for a company to keep its facilities and machinery up to date. Then the business can produce goods more efficiently. Profits also become income to the owners of a business. Some successful business owners live entirely off the profit from their businesses.

Quick Check

1. What is another name for our economic system?
2. What three features distinguish our economic system?
3. What three factors motivate businesses?
4. Define *motivation, competition, profit.*

Enrichment Strategy

Discuss with students some of the small businesses they consider most successful in your community. Invite an owner of one of these businesses to discuss with the class what motivated him or her to start a business. Allow time before the speaker arrives for students to prepare a list of questions.

BUSINESSES AND BUSINESS FAILURES			
Year	Total Number of Businesses	Number of Failures	Failures as a Percentage of Total Businesses
1989	7,748,000	50,361	0.65
1990	8,209,000	60,747	0.74
1991	8,237,000	88,140	1.07
1992	8,824,000	97,069	1.10
1993	7,902,000	86,133	1.09

Source: Dun & Bradstreet Corporation

FIGURE 4-2

Nearly 100,000 businesses are likely to fail in the next year. What kinds of circumstances can contribute to a business's failure?

USE VISUALS

As students look at Figure 4-2, ask them to think of some local businesses that have closed down or failed. Have students consider how consumer wants and needs, profit, and competition may have contributed to these businesses' failure.
Answer to caption: Product may not sell; price may be too high; management may be poor.

WHO BENEFITS FROM BUSINESS?

As previously indicated, businesses are motivated by consumers' wants and needs. They produce the goods and services that consumers want. Because they are constantly trying to find out what new products consumers want, businesses are innovative forces in the economy. As a result of competition, businesses efficiently produce the goods and services at various quality levels that consumers want. In addition to these benefits that businesses are motivated to provide, there are other benefits that businesses provide.

Business Owners

Business owners gain a lot from business. Besides income and the chance to grow, owners gain a sense of satisfaction from "running their own show." Research has proved that the chance to be your own boss is the most commonly given reason for starting one's own business. Business owners also benefit from knowing they are providing a needed product or service.

Employees

People need money to pay for housing and to buy food, clothing, and other items. People earn money by working at their jobs. Businesses provide workers with the money to purchase the things they need and want. Because of their jobs, workers are able to make choices about where they want to live and the things they want to have.

Develop Concepts

Who Benefits from Business?

Point out to students that aside from the obvious benefit of profit, business activity also benefits communities and society in general. Ask students if they have ever attended an event in which food or funding was donated by a business. Have them think of other benefits businesses provide and list the results on the board.

CHAPTER 4   MOTIVATIONS OF BUSINESS   **63**

Making Connections ➤ Diversity in the Workforce

Levi Strauss was one of the first American companies to take on social responsibilities. In the 1920s, this company offered English and citizenship classes to its immigrant factory workers. During the 1940s and 1950s, it was among the first companies to integrate workers in its factories in the South. Levi Strauss carries on that tradition today with its policy of "responsible commercial success." It instituted a Diversity Council, which represents African American, Asian, Latino, gay, and female employees' interests and sees that they have a voice in management decisions. Have students speculate on the kinds of benefits Levi Strauss receives from encouraging diversity and empowerment of its workforce.

Building Business Skills

Model

Choose a classroom task such as planning a lesson or a field trip. Describe how you would follow the steps listed in the Plan of Action on page 65 to complete the project. Ask volunteers how they would use the steps to help them organize their next big homework assignment.

Connection to CHAPTER 36

Wages and salaries, on average, account for only about 70 percent of an employer's payroll costs. Providing benefits costs employers the substantial additional amount of money. In Chapter 36, students will learn in detail about some of the common benefits offered to employees, including insurance, paid leave, pension plans, tuition reimbursement plans, child-care provisions, and wellness programs.

EMPLOYABILITY
Completing Self-Directed Tasks

Explanation

In school, you have two kinds of tasks—things you do in class, following your teacher's instructions, and homework assignments you do on your own. The work that is not directly supervised by your teacher is a *self-directed task*. You have a specific job, but it's up to you to decide how and when you will get the project done.

Whether you're a business owner or an employee, you'll find that many of your tasks in the workplace are self-directed. You may have to rearrange merchandise, make a certain number of phone calls, or write a report. You will determine for yourself what process you will follow and how you will fit the task into your schedule.

Completing self-directed tasks starts with planning. You'll have to decide up front "what to do when" in order to finish on time. You may often find yourself working on several tasks at once. Put your priorities in order by making schedules showing when you'll work on various assignments. You can keep things straight by preparing detailed "to do" lists for each day's work.

Making the most of the time you have for each task is a necessity. After planning and gathering materials, plunge right into the task at hand. Follow this Plan of Action for your next big homework assignment. Find out how it helps you get better at completing self-directed

Many businesses also provide training to their employees. This training may allow the employees to progress in the company or to find jobs with other firms. In addition, the possibility of learning new skills and knowledge and having the opportunity to use them provide growth or advancement opportunity for the worker, which cuts down on tedium and encourages feelings of personal worth.

Most businesses also provide benefits such as sick days and vacation time. Many offer a health insurance program and retirement plan. A few firms allow their employees to share in the company's profits through a profit-sharing plan.

Government

Businesses also pay taxes—all kinds of them including sales, property, and income taxes at all levels of government. These taxes are used to maintain community facilities and services, such as schools, roads, and police protection. The facilities and services are not just beneficial to the general public. They help business as well. The schools train new workers. Good roads

64 UNIT 2 THE PRIVATE ENTERPRISE SYSTEM

Curriculum Connection   Math

Tell students to suppose that a company called Meinhard Technologies sets aside 15 percent of its annual profits for its profit-sharing program. Last year the company's total profits were $169,340. Each of the 40 employees receives an equal share of the amount set aside for the profit-sharing program. How much money went into Meinhard's profit-sharing program? How much money did each employee receive? ($169,340 × 0.15 = $25,401; $25,401 ÷ 40 = $635)

For students who need to sharpen their math skills, choose among the worksheets in the *Math Skills Review* booklet.

tasks. You'll please not only your teachers and future employers, but yourself!

Practice

Making a plan of action is the starting point for organizing self-directed tasks on your own. Consider the questions in the plan presented here. Number a separate sheet of paper from 1 to 7. Answer the checklist questions to tell how you would put together an oral presentation for your firm's managers about the results of marketing research for a proposed new product. You'll make your presentation in three weeks.

make doing business easier. Police protect business owners as well as the general citizen.

If businesses did not pay these taxes, individuals would have to pay more taxes to maintain a given level of government services. As an example, taxes for schools are generally higher for the individual property owners in an area without major industry when compared to individuals in an area with a considerable amount of industry. Why? In an area with a lot of industry, part of the total tax payments are coming in from businesses.

General Society

At the turn of the twentieth century, most businesses believed that their responsibility to the society was primarily to provide jobs for individuals, produce goods and services wanted by consumers, and pay taxes. Around the middle of the century, governmental legislation and new management attitudes prompted a broader perspective on the role of business in the society. Business was prompted to be more active and involved in a responsible and fair way in the lives of individual

CHAPTER 4   MOTIVATIONS OF BUSINESS   **65**

Making Connections ▪▷◀ Social Responsibility

Nike's Reuse-A-Shoe program began when Nike discovered that used and defective athletic shoes placed in landfills would probably stick around for about 100 years before breaking down. Discarded athletic shoes of any brand are accepted for the program. They, along with waste materials generated from making Nikes, undergo a meltdown procedure and are processed into a resurfacing substance for, appropriately enough, basketball courts. Nike resurfaced about a dozen courts in inner cities and plans to install courts in Moscow and St. Petersburg in Russia, Prague in the Czech Republic, and Paris, France. Ask students how they think this program reflects on Nike's image. What concerns may have motivated Nike to start such a program?

With the help of sophisticated computer databases, marketing researchers have determined a "typical" profile for consumers of green products. Such people are usually single urban dwellers who listen to jazz and modern rock. They also enjoy tennis, racquetball, and aerobics.

Learning Activity

Take a class survey about green products. Find out how many students have bought green products. How many would pay a little extra to buy a product that was easier on the environment? How many would buy green products only if they cost the same or less than competing products? Tally the results on the board and discuss them with the class.

Quick Check Answers

1. Business owners, employees, government, society in general.
2. Idea that businesses act in a responsible and fair way toward their employees and society as a whole; items produced with less negative impact on the environment.

F.Y.I.

Ben & Jerry's ice cream company included social responsibility in its mission statement. The company gives 7.5 percent of its pre-tax profits back to the community. The company uses profits from specific product outlets to fund ventures that fit its social mission. Profits from the scoop shop in Harlem provide training and employment for homeless men in Harlem. At one plant, a greenhouse has been designed to treat waste water.

---

employees and the communities in which they are involved. The idea that businesses act in a responsible and fair way toward their employees and society as a whole is known as **social responsibility.**

Several types of activities were prompted with this broader definition of the social responsibility of business. In the area of employee relations, businesses are acting more responsibly when hiring, promoting, or dismissing employees. Sometimes, for example, companies find that they need to lay off good employees because of financial reasons. In order to act ethically, businesses provide considerable help in securing another position.

Businesses are increasingly becoming more involved in local issues and programs. Large businesses may sponsor a free outdoor concert or may set up job training programs for lower-income citizens. Small businesses, such as restaurants, may donate food or money to fundraising events whose proceeds benefit local organizations. Businesses find that community involvement can lead to increased profits. Their actions put the business in a positive light in the community, making people in the community more likely to purchase the business's goods or services.

Although there are governmental regulations about the environment that businesses must follow, the public also expects business to voluntarily and actively work to eliminate or reduce practices that are detrimental to the environment. Many companies have cut the amount of packaging for products, started recycling their own waste materials, and reduced emissions of pollutants into the air and water.

A number of businesses have begun producing green products. **Green products** are items produced with less negative impact on the environment than competing products. Examples of green products include nontoxic and nonpolluting cleaning products and recycled paper items. Consumers in the United States, Japan, and Europe have shown their support of protective environmental practices by purchasing green products.

Quick Check

1. Who benefits from the actions of businesses?
2. What is meant by *social responsibility, green products?*

Curriculum Connection   Art and Design

Explain to students that the color green is usually associated with the environmental movement. Hence the name *green products.* When marketing green products, the color green is often prominent in the packaging. Ask students to name some other ways marketing and advertising signal that a product is "green." (Some examples include the three-arrow recycling logo and unbleached natural brown paper packaging.) Have students work in groups to select a green product and design an environmentally friendly label or logo that will draw consumers' attention to the product. Display the designs in the classroom.

Chapter 4 **Summary**

Main Ideas

1. The United States has a private enterprise system.
2. In a private enterprise system, people are free to make choices about buying, selling, starting businesses, and choosing where to work.
3. Businesses are motivated to satisfy the wants and needs of consumers.
4. Competition motivates businesses to respond to consumers' wants and needs to win customers.
5. Profit motivates businesses to keep developing new products and services.
6. Businesses provide benefits to business owners, to employees, to governments, and to society.
7. Businesses today are expected to be socially responsible.
8. A worker needs to organize work that is not directly supervised.
9. Many factors helped entrepreneur Gertrude Boyle make her business a success.

CASE ANALYSIS Marketing

Muriel Reyes has recently taken a job in the marketing department of a large film-processing company. Her supervisor has finished teaching Muriel the basic responsibilities of the job, and he is beginning to give Muriel more long-term projects to handle on her own. Right now, in addition to her routine duties, Muriel has a mailing to get out by the end of the day, a report to write by tomorrow afternoon, a telephone survey to complete by the end of the week, and a marketing plan to write by the end of next week. As the number of assignments increases, Muriel finds herself confused about what to do first, and how to get everything done on time. What should Muriel do first to begin organizing her work?

CLOSE

Main Ideas

Main Ideas summarizes the key information in the chapter. It is a useful tool for reinforcement and review.

CASE ANALYSIS

Case Analysis provides a chapter-related case for student analysis and application of decision-making skills.

Answer
Muriel should begin by making a list of the tasks she is working on, along with the deadline for each, starting with the closest deadlines at the top. Then she should list the approximate number of hours (days) each one is going to take. With this information, she can create a work plan that will help ensure that she will complete each project on time.

QUICK QUIZ

1. Name the three motivations of business. (Satisfying wants and needs, competition, profit.)
2. What is *competition?* (Contest between businesses to win customers.)
3. Name four groups that benefit from business activity. (Business owners, employees, government, society in general.)
4. How does a socially responsible business behave? (It is responsible and fair to its employees and to society as a whole.)

Chapter 4 **Review**

CHAPTER 4 REVIEW

APPLY

Answers

Use the Language of Business
1. private enterprise system, 2. competition, 3. profit, 4. motivation, 5. social responsibility, 6. green products.

Review What You Learned
1. Economic resources and businesses are owned by individuals and groups rather than government.
2. Freedom to buy; freedom to produce and sell; freedom to choose a job.
3. Many people are concerned with health and fitness, so stores sell health foods.
4. The business may fail.
5. Consumer wants and needs; desire to make a profit; competition.
6. Employees earn money, get training to help progress in the company, and may receive benefits.
7. Businesses pay taxes, which help fund government services.
8. They provide goods and services; they may also fund community projects and work to eliminate products that are detrimental to the environment.
9. It can help decide how and when to get the project done.
10. She produced affordable sportswear that consumers liked, beat the competition, and made a profit that allowed her company to grow.

Understand Business Concepts
1. We are free to buy whatever we want as long as we have the money to pay for it, it is legal, and it is available. We are free to sell only legal goods and services.
2. Businesses need consumers to buy the goods and services they offer. If consumers do not buy an item, it will no longer be produced.
3. Consumers choose what to buy. When consumers want to buy pizza, for instance, they may choose the pizza place that delivers or the least expensive place. The pizza places must compete to win customers.

Use the Language of Business

Understanding these business terms will help you communicate more easily with others. Rewrite the paragraph. Fill each blank with the term that best completes the sentence.

competition   private enterprise system
green products   profit
motivation   social responsibility

Under the _____, individuals, rather than the government, choose what to buy and sell, and where to work. Under this system, there is _____ between businesses to get customers to buy their products or use their services. The desire to make a(n) _____ is a(n) _____ for many businesses. Some businesses have found that they can fulfill their _____ and make a profit by producing _____, which have less negative impact on the environment than competing products.

Review What You Learned

1. Why is our economic system called a private enterprise system?
2. List three freedoms that distinguish our private enterprise system.
3. Give an example of how businesses respond to consumer wants.
4. What is the chief risk involved in owning your own business?
5. What are the main factors that motivate businesses to supply goods and services?
6. In what ways do businesses benefit employees?
7. How do governments benefit from business?
8. What benefits do businesses provide to society?
9. How can a plan of action help you with a self-directed task?
10. How did Gertrude Boyle use the motivations of business to make Columbia Sportswear a successful company?

Understand Business Concepts

1. What are some limits to the freedoms we enjoy under our economic system?
2. Explain why consumers' wants and needs are very important to business.
3. Explain the role of competition in a free enterprise system.
4. Explain why the consumer is the real winner in the free enterprise system.
5. What is the profit motive? Why are profits good for our economy?
6. Why are businesses usually unable to earn huge profits over a long period of time?
7. Explain why it is to a business's benefit to treat its employees well.
8. Name three ways in which a business can exhibit social responsibility and give an example of each.
9. What is one strategy for planning very large projects?
10. How has Columbia Sportswear kept its prices low and its sales high?

4. They have the freedom to choose, and businesses aim to satisfy consumer wants and needs. In addition, competition among companies helps keep prices low and quality high.
5. Having money left after paying the costs of making and selling a product. Profits encourage businesses to develop new products and work efficiently to continue earning profits.
6. When businesses do earn profits, others notice and enter the field. This competition tends to lower profits.

7. When employees are treated well, they're more likely to do their best. When they do their best, a business thrives.
8. Ethical conduct—being honest and fair about the reasons for a layoff; community involvement—donating goods, services, or money to local fundraising events; environmental protection—reducing the amount of pollution produced.
9. Break a project into small steps and plan each step.
10. By catering to the realistic needs of the average customer.

Think Critically

1. **Apply.** If you were to become a business owner, what type of business would you choose? Why?
2. **Analyze.** A large factory in a community closes, putting 600 people out of work. What are some effects the plant closing will have on the community?
3. **Evaluate.** In some economic systems, individuals do not have as many freedoms as we do in the private enterprise system. In some ways, however, they face fewer risks. For example, in some economic systems, everyone is guaranteed a job. What are the advantages and disadvantages of such a guarantee?

Use What You Learned

1. **Group Project.** Work together to determine what kind of goods or services you would like to offer in a "classroom shopping mall." Make an outline of the kinds of items your store would sell and how much you will spend for stock, rent, and salaries. Determine what you think your profits will be.
2. Survey your classmates to find out what was "hot" two years ago and what's "hot" now. Find out if any items available now were not widely available two years ago. Identify items that were very popular two years ago that are no longer as popular. Use the results of your survey to prepare a three-minute business news report about changing consumer needs and wants.
3. Business owners often make more money than people who work for someone else, but they also have a greater chance of losing their money if their business does not succeed. Would you rather work for a company or be a business owner? Explain your answer in a 100-word paragraph.

4. **Computer Application.** Using E-mail, contact a local business owner and arrange an interview, either in person or through E-mail. Find out the following information:

   - Why did the owner choose to run a business?
   - What are his or her responsibilities?
   - What are some benefits/problems?
   - What recommendations would he or she make to a would-be owner?

   Use word processing software to write and print a report summarizing the interview.
5. **Skill Reinforcement.** Use the Plan of Action on page 65 to carry out one of the projects listed above. Then write a self-evaluation of how well you completed it and whether you met your deadline. Tell how you can improve your planning for your next self-directed task.

Save your work in your Business Portfolio.

1. Answers will vary.
2. Possible answer: Local businesses will lose money. Customers will not have money to spend on things they used to buy. The loss of taxes paid by the factory will decrease the money available to publicly funded services.
3. Possible answer: Advantages: People don't have to worry about losing their jobs. They probably don't have to work as many hours because there would be less competition for jobs. Disadvantages: If people don't fear being out of work, their motivation to do their best may decrease. Job satisfaction is probably low.

Independent Practice

Use the Chapter 4 worksheets in *Student Activity Guide 1* for additional practice and application activities. A Teacher's Annotated Edition provides answers.

ASSESS

Portfolio Assessment

The portfolio projects are designed to lead students to develop a collection of their best work to submit to you for assessment. Refer students to the specific rubric(s) from the *Alternative Assessment Strategies* booklet listed with each of the project notes below. These rubrics will alert students to the criteria you will use to assess their projects.

Chapter Assessment

Use the Chapter 4 Test from the *Test Masters* booklet to evaluate students' understanding of the chapter concepts. An answer key is provided. Or create your own customized test using the *Testmaker* software.

Use What You Learned
1. See that all students participate in the group project. Rubrics: Charts and Tables.
2. Students may want to survey adults or younger siblings as well. Rubric: Survey.
3. Students may want to make a list of pros and cons to help organize their thoughts before writing. Rubric: Paragraph.
4. Students who do not have access to a computer may write to a business owner to set up an interview and may type or write their report. Rubric: Essay.
5. Students' answers will vary, but should include a rating of their completed project, a description of the elements from the Plan of Action they followed, and ideas for planning and improving their efficiency during their next project.

FOCUS

Major Concepts
- Our Market Economy
- How Is Price Determined?
- What Causes Prices to Change?
- The Ever-Changing Market

Introduce the Topic
Have students offer possible explanations for differing prices on similar or identical products. Ask students how they think producers choose a price for goods or services. Record their responses on a transparency or chart. Then ask students how consumers can determine the price of goods and services. Again, record the responses. Students can refine the lists as they work through Chapter 5.

Use Business Terms
Ask students to write a sentence with each of the Business Terms, replacing the term with a nonsense word. Invite volunteers to read aloud their sentences for others in the class to insert the correct term. Advise students to check the meanings of the terms as they read the chapter.

Direct students' attention to the photograph. Ask students to speculate on how consumers can affect the market economy. (Answers will vary, but students should recognize that businesses stop producing goods or services that consumers do not purchase.)

CHAPTER 5

Business terms

market economy

price

market

demand

law of demand

supply

law of supply

surplus

equilibrium price

shortage

70

CHAPTER 5 RESOURCES

Instructional Resources

Lesson Plan for Chapter 5

Teaching Transparency 5-1

Strategies and Worksheets for Teaching Transparency 5-1

Enrichment Master 5-1

Student Activity Guide 1–TAE for Chapter 5

Test Master for Chapter 5

Alternative Assessment Strategies

Math Skills Review

International Business Strategies

Cooperative Learning Strategies

Communication Skills Review

Ethics in Business Strategies

How the Market Works

Learning objectives

After completing this chapter, you will be able to:
- Explain how prices affect consumers and producers.
- Discuss how prices are determined.
- Identify several circumstances that will cause prices of goods or services to change.
- Describe the cause-and-effect relationship of consumers and producers in our market economy.
- List the four stages the American economy has gone through.
- Name and describe several kinds of electronic transmission media.
- Interpret information on a line graph.

Consider what you know

- Businesses in a private enterprise system are motivated by consumers' wants and needs and the desire for profit, which prompts them to produce goods and services.

Consider what you want to know

- How are prices determined? How do prices affect producers and consumers?
- What causes the prices of goods and services to change?
- What kinds of information does a line graph provide?
- What does "electronic information transfer" mean?

Consider how to use what you learn

- As you read this chapter, consider how changes in the market affect you. Also think about ways changes in supply and demand affect consumers and businesses in local and world markets.

CHAPTER 5   HOW THE MARKET WORKS   **71**

Multimedia Resources

Technology Resource Guide

Distance Learning Guide

Internet Resource Guide

Professional Resources

School-to-Work/Tech Prep Strategies

Instructional Poster

Spanish Resources

Testmaker Software for Chapter 5

The Wall Street Journal Video Series
Video & Activities for Chapter 5

Business and Marketing Computer
Applications—An Integrated Software
Simulation Using Microsoft Works

Stocktracker—A Stock Market Software
Simulation

Where's the Dough? Board Game

CHAPTER 5

TEACH

Business Connection

For the first few years of their existence, McDonald's restaurants had little competition from other fast-food restaurants. One reason for this stemmed from their low prices. However, McDonald's prices gradually increased over the years, eventually reaching a level at which competitors could make a profit. Once this occurred, other fast-food restaurants, such as Wendy's and Arby's, entered the market.

Develop Concepts

Our Market Economy

Ask students to report the prices of goods they commonly buy, such as school supplies, blue jeans, cassettes, and CDs. List the various prices on the board or on a transparency. Ask students to indicate whether they feel the prices for these products are low or high. Encourage them to discuss which prices they will not pay because they are too high. Ask if there are any prices which they feel may be too low. Have them explain their choices.

Have you ever wondered why the price of a certain product goes up or down? You may have noticed, for example, that the price of CD players dropped after they had been on the market for a few years. You may have heard about the price of oranges rising sharply after a hard frost in Florida killed part of the crop. Prices constantly change in our economic system.

As you know, the basic economic questions are answered by an economic system. In this chapter, we will look more closely at how our economic system works.

OUR MARKET ECONOMY

You already know that an economic system is a set of rules that answers the three basic economic questions:

Which goods and services will be produced?
How will goods and services be produced?
How will goods and services be distributed?

In the United States, these basic economic questions are answered primarily through a market economy. In a **market economy** the basic economic decisions are based on the actions of buyers and sellers in the market.

What goods and services does a market economy produce? It produces the goods and services that people are willing to buy and that will bring a profit to the sellers or producers. In our market economy, price plays an important role. **Price** is the amount of money given or asked for when goods or services are bought or sold. If producers think the price consumers will pay for a good or service is too low and does not earn them a profit, they will produce little or none of the product. If they think the price is high enough to earn a profit, they will produce the good or service.

In our market system, the consumer is all important. Every time a consumer buys a product, he or she is telling the market to supply more of that product. The same holds true for services. If consumers refuse to buy a product or a service, the market receives the message to supply less of it or to stop producing it.

The Market and Prices

A **market** is any place where individuals buy and sell goods and services. For example, goods and services can be bought at

Cooperative Learning   Pairs Check

Students with language problems often have difficulty seeing differences among similar words. For example, *identify, discuss,* and *explain* are terms that can cause confusion. Provide students with the following guidelines. *Identify* generally means to label or to classify by category. *Discuss* requires a listing of the pros and cons of a situation and/or interacting with the ideas of others. *Explain* requires that the response include reasons or explanations in a complete form. Suggest that students write three questions—one using *identify,* one *discuss,* and one *explain*—for each section in this chapter. Direct students to trade questions with a partner and answer each other's questions.

Refer to the *Cooperative Learning Strategies* booklet for additional cooperative learning strategies.

home, in a store, by telephone, by mail, or even by personal computer through an on-line service. A market may be as small and as close to home as the corner grocery store or as far away as a ranch in Australia. The market is made up of all the different places where buyers and sellers exchange money and goods or services.

There are all kinds of markets in our economic world. There are markets for guitars, television sets, oranges, and cleaning services. All markets, though, have some common economic principles.

Earlier you learned that a basic problem all economies face is scarcity. We cannot have everything we want because there are not enough resources to go around. Price is one indication of the scarcity of an item. If something is in short supply relative to demand, the price will be higher.

Price can be looked at as an unfortunate thing, especially if you do not have enough money to buy something you want. Price can be a discouragement. Sometimes price is *meant* to be a discouragement. However, there are other times when it is meant to be an encouragement. Take a look at how price can be both a discouragement and an encouragement to buyers (consumers) and sellers (producers) in the market.

Prices Affect the Consumer

Consumers are the ones who provide the demand for an item. **Demand** is the amount or quantity of goods and services that consumers are willing and able to buy at various prices. The following examples will show how price affects consumer demand.

Suppose you walked into a store with $15 to buy a CD. You find that the store is having a "two for the price of one" sale, and that you can get two CDs for $15. The chances are pretty good that you would buy two. Many other consumers would do the same thing. The result would be an increase in the number of CDs sold. In this case, the price encourages consumers to buy more CDs.

Here is another example. You have saved $70 to buy a pair of running shoes that you have admired for some time. Suppose that when you get around to buying the shoes, the price has increased to $90. What will you do? Do you want the shoes badly enough? Equally important, do you have the extra $20? You decide to wait and perhaps look for a less expensive brand. You may not buy running shoes at this time. Other consumers are making the same decision. To them, the shoes are too expensive. In this case, price discourages you from buying.

Business & HISTORY

In ancient Greek cities, a bustling marketplace, called the *agora*, was the center of activity. In the agora, merchants sold their wares, citizens debated issues, and friends exchanged news and gossip. Greek civilization developed chiefly in small city-states which consisted of a city or town and the surrounding villages and farmland. The civilization reached its height between 500 and 400 B.C.

Learning Activity
Ask students to generate a list of reasons why large mega-malls and discount shopping malls are popular with consumers. Then have them generate a list of reasons for the increasing popularity of mail order catalogs, television home shopping programs, and computer shopping networks. Have them discuss what part convenience, along with price, plays in the consumer's decision about where and how to make purchases.

TEACHING TIP
Some businesses choose prices for their products using as a guide the phrase, "Whatever the market will bear." Ask students to explain how this phrase reflects the consumer's role in pricing goods and services.

Learning Activity
Use Enrichment Master 5-1, "Shopping for a Good Price," as the basis for a discussion about how students, as consumers, can affect the price of an item. Invite students to offer specific examples for each of the steps listed.

CHAPTER 5   HOW THE MARKET WORKS   **73**

Curriculum Connection   History

Indicate to students that items which were once indispensable to the economy, such as steam locomotives, are no longer manufactured. Ask students to prepare a bulletin board showing pictures of items that are no longer produced. (Examples: carousel horses, phonograph records, horseshoes.) Ask students to discuss why the items are no longer produced.

CHAPTER 5

USE VISUALS

The demand curve in Figure 5-1 illustrates the relationship between demand and price. Consumers are interested in paying the lowest possible price for a good quality product. As the price of Ed's picnic tables rises, consumer demand for the tables falls.

Ask students how many soft drinks they would buy at the following single-can prices: 25¢, 50¢, $1, $1.50, $2.00, and $2.50. Make a chart that records the quantities of soft drinks students would purchase at each price. Ask a volunteer to use the information in the chart to make a graph. Compare the graph to the graph in Figure 5-1. Have another volunteer write a generalization about the relationship between price and demand.

Answer to caption: $100

TEACHING TIP

Indicate to students that there are exceptions to the law of demand. Pose the following question. If doctor's fees dropped suddenly, would there be a corresponding change in the quantity of services demanded? Have a volunteer explain his or her answer. Ask students to name other exceptions to the law of demand.

Your decision and that of other consumers points out an important principle of our market economy: *Generally, the higher the price, the less consumers will buy of an item.* The opposite of this principle also applies: *The lower the price, the more consumers will buy.* At the higher price some consumers will decide not to buy. Others will buy less of the item. Still others may try substitutes. Instead of running shoes, they will buy less expensive sneakers.

The **law of demand** states that consumers will generally buy less of an item at a higher price than at a lower price. It is possible to show how many products could be sold at various prices. Suppose your neighbor Ed makes picnic tables on the weekends. Figure 5-1 below shows how many of Ed's picnic tables can be sold at various prices. Note that people would buy more of Ed's tables at a lower price than at a higher price. This demonstrates the law of demand.

Prices Affect the Producer

Producers are influenced to supply goods or services by the prices in the market. The **supply** is the amount of goods and services that producers will provide at various prices. Producers want to receive a price for their goods and services that will cover their costs and provide a profit. They look at price as a barometer that tells them how much to produce.

FIGURE 5-1

According to the law of demand, consumers will buy less of an item at a higher price than at a lower price. At what price will consumers buy the least number of Ed's picnic tables?

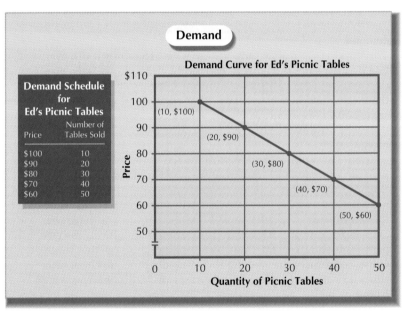

Demand Schedule for Ed's Picnic Tables	
Price	Number of Tables Sold
$100	10
$90	20
$80	30
$70	40
$60	50

Meeting Student Diversity

Less proficient readers may miss the significance of cause-and-effect relationships. Point out to students that a *cause* is any condition, person, or event that makes something happen. What happens as a result of the cause is called an *effect.* The connection between what happens and what makes it happen is known as a *cause-and-effect relationship.* Remind students that clue words—*because, so, led to, produced, brought about, created,* and *therefore*—often signal cause and effect. Suggest that students scan the contents of this chapter looking for words that may signal cause and effect, listing any clue words they find. Point out to students that scanning for cause-and-effect clue words can help them read more efficiently.

Suppose that the price of eggs rises to $4 a dozen. What do you think will happen to the number of eggs produced at that price? The amount will probably increase because egg-producing businesses will see more profits to be made at that price. At that price, producers are encouraged to produce more eggs. Other people who have money to invest may start new egg-producing businesses.

If the price of eggs drops to 50 cents a dozen, what would happen to the amount of eggs supplied to the market? At that price, many producers would not make a profit. Some would sell their chickens, putting their proceeds into another venture. Others would reduce their production of eggs. Therefore, the amount of eggs supplied would decrease.

This example demonstrates another principle of our market economy. *Producers will generally produce less of an item at a lower price than they will at a higher price.* The **law of supply** states that the higher the price, the more producers will supply; the lower the price, the less they will supply. Figure 5-2 below shows how the law of supply works. Ed builds picnic tables on his weekends. If he builds more tables, he has to give up more of his free time. To do this he feels he should be rewarded with higher prices. This demonstrates the law of supply.

Quick Check

1. Define *price, demand,* and *supply.*
2. What are the two principles of our market economy?

FIGURE 5-2

According to the law of supply, producers will supply more of an item at a higher price than at a lower price. At what price will Ed produce the most picnic tables?

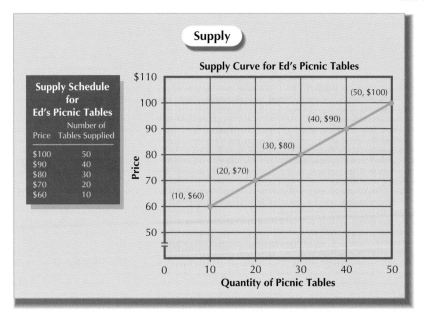

Supply

Supply Curve for Ed's Picnic Tables

Supply Schedule for Ed's Picnic Tables	
Price	Number of Tables Supplied
$100	50
$90	40
$80	30
$70	20
$60	10

(50, $100)
(40, $90)
(30, $80)
(20, $70)
(10, $60)

USE VISUALS

Figure 5-2 shows the supply curve for Ed's picnic tables. In an effort to get the most profit, Ed would prefer to increase the supply of tables when the price is high. Further illustrate the concept of *supply* using a two-column chart on the board or a transparency. Head the columns *Pay per Hour* and *Number of Students Willing to Work.* In the "Pay per Hour" column, list amounts such as $1, $2, $3, and so on to $10. Survey students to find out how many would be willing to work at each wage and record the number in the second column. Ask a volunteer to use the information on the chart to make a graph. Compare the graph to the graph in Figure 5-2. Have another volunteer state a generalization based on the information and the graphs.
Answer to caption: $100

Quick Check Answers

1. Amount of money given or asked for when goods or services are bought or sold; amount of goods or services consumers are willing and able to buy at various prices; amount of goods and services that producers will provide at various prices.
2. Law of demand and law of supply.

Reteaching Strategy

Review the laws of supply and demand by having students discuss how they as consumers can affect the price of an item. Remind students to consider utilities such as gas, electricity, and telephone service as well as retail consumer goods. Have students list the actions consumers can take to lower the price of an item.

Building Business Skills

Model

Once you are confident that students can identify the horizontal and vertical axes of a graph, model each of the interpretation steps. Indicate to students that the title of the graph is generally very important and gives the reader a clue about the data contained in the graph. As you work through each of the bulleted interpretation steps in the explanation, be sure to note both the numerical value and units represented on each axis.

MATH
Interpreting Line Graphs

Explanation

Graphs aren't just for math class. Magazines, business reports, even cereal boxes contain graphs that communicate important information. The line graph is a common kind of graph used to show change over a period of time or direction of change.

The left side of the graph is called the *vertical axis,* and the bottom is called the *horizontal axis.* Both the vertical axis and the horizontal axis have numbers and a label telling what the numbers represent. Dots are frequently used to show numerical information on the graph, and they are connected with a line.

Here's how to interpret a line graph.

- Read the title of the graph.
- Familiarize yourself with the information on the horizontal axis and on the vertical axis.
- Examine where the dots are placed on the graph.
- Determine what the line(s) or curve(s) symbolizes.
- Compare the line(s) in the graph to both axes to determine the point being made.

Practice

Examine the line graph presented here. The number of computers demanded at each price is indicated by

Develop Concepts

How Is Price Determined?

Point out to students that price is determined by producers who wish to sell at the highest possible price and consumers who wish to buy at the lowest possible price. Lead a discussion in which students indicate that there may be a price both consumers and producers are willing to accept, even if the price does not meet their wishes.

Business Brief

Some stores use items called *loss leaders* to lure customers into a store. The loss leaders, products priced noticeably lower than usual, are often popular products such as soda, soap, or soup. Businesses choose to sell these products at a *loss* in order to *lead* customers into the store. The theory is that once inside the store, customers are likely to purchase several items in addition to the items on sale.

HOW IS PRICE DETERMINED?

In the marketplace, both consumers and producers follow their own interests. Consumers want to get as much as possible at the lowest possible price. Producers want to make as much profit as possible. In the marketplace, the prices for all goods and services sold are determined through the actions of buyers and sellers. Take a look at an example.

The Fair Price Supermarket has a supply of 500 roasting chickens that are priced to sell at $1.89 a pound. By the end of the week, only 100 chickens have been sold. Five hundred more are coming in from the producer. There is a **surplus,** or oversupply, of 400 chickens. Evidently the consumer demand is less than the amount supplied at $1.89 a pound.

The Fair Price Supermarket lowers the price to 99 cents a pound. Remember, according to the law of demand, the lower the price, the greater the amount demanded. At 99 cents a pound, all 400 roasting chickens are sold. Let's suppose that everyone who wanted chicken at that price was able to buy

76   UNIT 2   THE PRIVATE ENTERPRISE SYSTEM

Curriculum Connection   Language Arts

Suggest that students survey the non-cable television listings for 14 consecutive days. Have students classify programs into broad categories such as News, Children's Programming, Family Entertainment, Continuing Stories, and Action/Adventure. Direct students to determine the times these categories of programming are most likely to occur. Have students use their findings as the basis of a 200-word summary telling how TV programming is a result of supply and demand.

LINE GRAPH

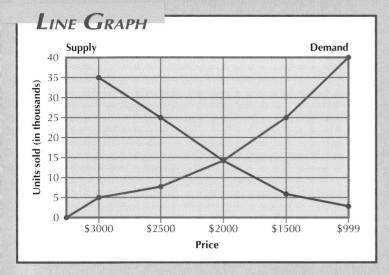

the line labeled *Demand;* the line labeled *Supply* indicates the amount that would be supplied at the various prices. To figure out how many computers are demanded at $3000, find $3000 on the horizontal axis, follow the grid line up to the point on the *Demand* line and then follow the grid line from the point to the vertical axis. How many computers could be sold at $3000? Do the same for the *Supply* line. How many computers would be supplied at a price of $2500?

Practice

Remind students to use each of the interpretation steps to "read" this graph. (Number of computers demanded at $3000: 5000; number of computers supplied at $2500: 25,000) Use the following questions to offer additional practice.

1. How many computers could be produced at $3000? (35,000)
2. What if the price of all computers in the market was $3000? (There would be a surplus.)
3. What is the equilibrium price for the computers? ($2000)

some. The price—at a point where the amount supplied equals the amount demanded—is called the **equilibrium price.** Equilibrium, then, is the price at which the amount supplied and the amount demanded meet, or come together. In a free market, the price of an item moves toward the equilibrium price.

Take a look at another example. In this case, the Fair Price Supermarket started out charging 79 cents a pound for the roasting chickens. In one day the 500 chickens for the whole week were sold. Many shoppers who came later in the week were disappointed. They were looking for roasting chickens at 79 cents a pound. There was, in fact, a real **shortage,** or undersupply, at that price. The seller can see that even more chickens can be sold. What will happen to the price as a result? It will increase to the point where the amount supplied equals the amount demanded, or the equilibrium price.

Naturally the price established at any one store does not go into effect for the entire market. However, if similar surpluses or shortages occurred in many places, the overall price would be affected.

Reteaching Strategy

To increase students' understanding of the effects of a change in supply in a market economy, present the following scenario: A summer of cold and rainy weather prevents much of the South American coffee crop from maturing. How will this affect the price of South American coffee? The demand for substitute products such as Arabian or African coffee? Suggest that students present their responses in the form of a three-minute consumers news brief for the evening TV news. Remind students that graphs and diagrams can help tell a story.

USE VISUALS

The equilibrium price for Ed's picnic tables, shown in Figure 5-3, occurs at the intersection of the supply and demand curves. Remind students that the demand and supply curves in Figure 5-3 are shown in Figures 5-1 and 5-2. Answer to caption: $80

USE TRANSPARENCIES

Use Teaching Transparency 5-1 and its corresponding strategies and worksheet from the *Teaching Transparency Strategies and Worksheets* booklet to increase students' understanding of how equilibrium price is determined. Verify student worksheets using the Answer Key.

Quick Check Answers

1. Buyers and sellers.
2. Quantity of an item that is greater than the consumer demand for the item at a certain price; price at which the amount supplied and the amount demanded meet.

Develop Concepts

What Causes Prices to Change?

Ask students to think of examples of how price is influenced by changes in demand and supply. Offer this example to prime students' thinking: When a new Super Nintendo game is introduced, demand is sometimes so high that stores cannot keep the games in stock. Eventually supply catches up with demand. Later, as interest in a particular game decreases, the price drops.

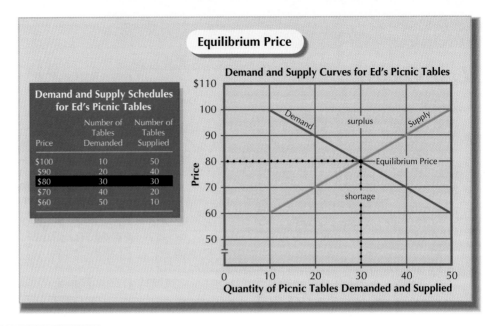

Equilibrium Price

Demand and Supply Schedules for Ed's Picnic Tables

Price	Number of Tables Demanded	Number of Tables Supplied
$100	10	50
$90	20	40
$80	30	30
$70	40	20
$60	50	10

Demand and Supply Curves for Ed's Picnic Tables

FIGURE 5-3

The equilibrium price is the price at which supply and demand meet. What is the equilibrium price for Ed's picnic tables?

To get a better idea of how the equilibrium price is determined, take a look at Figure 5-3 above. It shows the combined demand and supply schedule for Ed's picnic tables. Those are the same demand and supply schedules you saw in Figures 5-1 and 5-2. By drawing demand and supply curves on the same graph, you can determine the equilibrium price.

Quick Check

1. Whose actions determine prices?
2. Define *surplus* and *equilibrium price*.

WHAT CAUSES PRICES TO CHANGE?

You have seen how surpluses and shortages affect price changes. Changes in consumer demand or in amounts produced may also cause prices to change.

Changes in Demand

Fruit-of-the-Sun is a fruit drink sold by Fair Price Supermarket. It is a combination of three natural fruit juices. It sells for $3 a quart. "Independent" laboratory testing recently has

Cooperative Learning   Co-op Co-op

Suggest that students work in teams of four. Have each team research consumer demand for a high-tech product over a recent five-year period. Items may include laptop computers, camcorders, cordless telephones, fax machines, exercise equipment, or some other product of their own choosing. Ask teams to prepare a graph showing annual sales volume and average price and provide a caption explaining the reason for the price/volume relationship illustrated by the graph. Ask volunteer teams to present their findings to the class.

Refer to the *Cooperative Learning Strategies* booklet for additional cooperative learning strategies.

shown that these three juices together are rich in all vitamins required by the average adult. Suddenly consumers develop a taste or preference for Fruit-of-the-Sun over all other competing brands. A shortage of the fruit punch develops at the $3 price, and the price goes up.

Consumer taste or preference can change in the other direction, again affecting prices. Suppose another business produces a new fruit drink to compete with Fruit-of-the-Sun. Consumers prefer this new fruit drink and buy it instead of Fruit-of-the-Sun. Then there would be a surplus of Fruit-of-the-Sun at the $3 price.

Changes in consumer taste and preference that affect prices occur often. This change in preference explains why fad items, such as designer jeans or workout clothes, increase in price when they are popular and decrease in price when they are out of style.

Income can also affect prices. Suppose that the average take-home pay of consumers in your area increases by 6 percent. You now have more money to spend. Would you want to buy more of your favorite foods at the current market price? Most people in your area would. If you all liked the same foods, the food stores might have a shortage in supply. Then prices would increase. On the other hand, if everybody got a cut in pay, the price for food in your area might decrease.

Substitutes also play a role in affecting demand and, therefore, prices. If the price of beef is high relative to that of chicken, consumers might decide to substitute chicken for beef in their diet. Demand for beef at the current prices would decrease. A surplus would result, causing prices to drop. The increased demand for chicken would create a shortage and lead to higher prices for chickens. In our competitive market economy, substitutes exist for most goods.

Changes in Supply

There are some obvious circumstances that cause a change in supply, particularly with food products. For instance, droughts, floods, and even cold weather can affect crops. A heavy frost in Florida can have a severe impact on the citrus crop. Fewer oranges, grapefruit, and lemons are available and the price increases so that a shortage does not occur. Good growing and harvesting weather can have the opposite effect. With a plentiful supply of grains in the market, prices for meat and other food products go down so that a surplus does not occur.

When the costs of producing a product or service change, both supply and price are affected. Suppose that eggs are selling for $2 a dozen. Egg producers have found that their costs

Mattel's Barbie doll has been a best seller in the United States for more than 30 years. The emergence of market economies in Eastern Europe and the former Soviet Union provided new markets for Barbie. In Russia in the early 1990s Barbie dolls were selling for the equivalent of $10. However, an enterprising producer soon placed a "Barbie substitute" on the market. The substitute, Veronika, cost only $1.60. Demand for Veronika increased while demand for Barbie decreased.

TEACHING TIP

Help students understand price changes by discussing seasonal changes in supply and demand for such items as swim wear, convertibles, heating oil, and skis. Note that these changes in demand lead to changes in supply as well.

Learning Activity

Have students name a product they recently purchased because it was on sale. Ask them to identify at least two substitutes for the product. Then ask them to identify instances in which they purchased the substitute product rather than the original item. Ask what motivated them to purchase the substitute product.

Learning Activity

Hold up several examples of a product, such as a candy bar, teen magazine, or video-tape. Ask students to bid on the product by telling you what they would be willing to pay for the product. "Sell" the examples of the product one item at a time. When there is only one item remaining, ask students if they would be willing to pay more than the market price. Help students recognize this as an example of how supply can influence price.

Making Connections ⟡➤ Everyday Living

Supply and demand also influence real estate prices. Direct students to imagine they all work for the same carmaker. The carmaker has built new headquarters in a small town hundreds of miles away. Workers willing to relocate will move to the new location within the next 18 months. Have students describe what they think will happen to the price of homes, the number of new houses being built, and so on at the new location. Then ask students to describe what will happen to real estate prices if the company and its workers relocate a second time. Interested students can check the class predictions about real estate prices by investigating what happened to actual real estate prices in Spring Hill, Tennessee, home of the Saturn car company.

FOCUS ON **Technology**

Discuss

Open a discussion with students by asking them which of the following terms they can define: *data communications, communications channel, twisted-pair wire, coaxial cable, fiber-optic cable, microwaves,* and *communications satellites.* Have students record their ideas on the board or on a transparency.

Business Brief

The principle of interchangeable parts significantly cut suppliers' production costs. First applied to weapons manufacture, the principle was later used in automobile manufacturing and other industries. Today, to strengthen their position in the European market, U.S. manufacturers are producing parts that can be used in European-made machines.

Electronic Information Transfer

These simple words—"Mr. Watson, come here. I want you"—were the first information transmitted by telephone. Alexander Graham Bell's voice was transmitted by wire from one room to the next.

Today, nearly 125 years later, business relies on quick and accurate access to many kinds of information. The national sales manager of a publishing company may use electronic mail to transmit quarterly sales figures to all regional managers. The vice president for development of a computer company might fax an important report to the company's overseas offices. A bank officer in New York City may authorize electronic transfer of funds to the bank's branch in London. All of these business professionals are taking advantage of technology to electronically transmit information from one location to another.

Data communication is the transmission of data over a communications channel between one computer and another. A *communications channel* is the path along which data moves from the sending to the receiving computer. The communications channel may be a simple wire. Or it may be made of one or more transmission media such as twisted-pair wire, coaxial cable, fiber optics, microwaves, or communication satellites.

- *Twisted-pair wire* is made of copper wires twisted and often covered by colorful plastic. It is commonly used in telephone lines. Twisted wire is useful for voice communication but data sent along twisted wire can become garbled.

have risen 10 percent over the last year. To keep their profit at the same level, they will have to increase their price to $2.20 a dozen. However, if the market price stays at $2, some producers will have to decide if it is worthwhile to stay in business for less profit. If many producers leave, the supply will decrease, which will cause a shortage of eggs at the $2 price level, encouraging the price to rise.

In some instances, producers find more efficient ways to produce goods and services so that their costs decrease. A good example has been the rapid developments in the computer industry. Some of the first computers were nearly 60 feet long and weighed over 30 tons. Their energy source was vacuum tubes, and only the government or large companies could afford such computers. Then came the development of the transistor, a complete electrical circuit on a piece of silicon. In a matter of a few years, a microchip of silicon the size of a small postage stamp was designed. Despite its size, it could do more work than 18,000 vacuum tubes. The computer shrank, and so did the price!

Such changes resulted in a greater supply of computers at the prices that were current at the time. As more producers

80   UNIT 2   THE PRIVATE ENTERPRISE SYSTEM

Global Perspective

Across the United States, consumers are able to telephone for take-out or delivery from Chinese restaurants. Recent changes in the economy of China have allowed some Chinese to do the same. However, production costs severely limit what producers are willing to supply. Therefore, service is provided only at lunch and for special occasions such as birthdays or wedding banquets. In addition, only one or two dishes are offered, there must be multiple orders for those dishes, and usually the orders must be received a day in advance. Ask students to discuss what they think will happen to the current take-out industry in China as consumer demand increases and more producers enter the market.

Refer to the *International Business Strategies* booklet for additional strategies and activities.

- *Coaxial cable* consists of a single wire surrounded by insulation and a shield. Coaxial cable is widely used for cable TV, communication lines in offices, and telephone lines under the ocean. Coaxial cable can carry data with little distortion for a distance of about ten miles.
- In a *fiber-optic cable* hair-thin strands of glass conduct light, rather than electric current. A single fiber-optic strand can carry more than 8000 telephone conversations at one time. Fiber optics cable can carry several hundred thousand voice communications at the same time without distortion.
- *Microwaves* are a type of radio wave that does not need wires; voice and data are transmitted the same way radio stations transmit their programs.
- *Communications satellites* are another way to transmit information without wires. Their orbits allow them to rotate with the earth. Dish antenna on earth send and receive radio signals to and from the satellites.

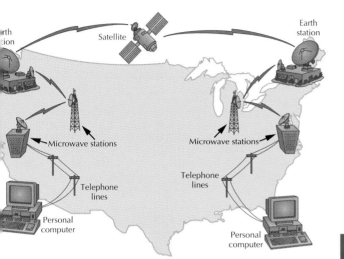

Follow Through

Allow students to review the definitions they presented before reading the technology feature. Ask if there are any definitions they would like to revise or alter. Then ask students to draw a diagram showing how each of these items can be a part of a single electronic information transfer. For additional information about current technology, refer to the *Technology Resources Guide.*

entered the field, a surplus occurred. Prices dropped. The result was that the consumer benefited from lower prices.

Change by Force Controlling Market

For price movements for an item to occur somewhat freely, the market for a good or service must have a lot of buyers and sellers. A number of markets today do not have an abundance of buyers and sellers, especially of sellers. In those cases, prices do not fluctuate as freely as indicated by the theory of supply and demand. For example, there are instances where one or a few firms control the price of an item, resulting in little or no competition. In those situations, the supplier can control the price through controlling the amount of items put on the market.

In some instances, the consumer in our economy wants the government to set the price. Rates for utilities such as water and electricity are generally set by governmental bodies. Rent control laws for apartments in some large cities are another example. In such a case, government is the controlling factor for prices.

CHAPTER 5   HOW THE MARKET WORKS   **81**

Learning Activity
Point out to students that the laws of supply and demand illustrate a cause-and-effect relationship between price and demand. Occasionally a force acts to control the market and interrupt the course of the cause-and-effect relationship. Suggest that students draw a cartoon illustrating how supply and demand are related. Then suggest they revise their cartoon to illustrate how forces might control the market.

Curriculum Connection   Social Studies

Demand for most farm products is relatively constant. Record harvests, therefore, can cause prices of farm products to decline. To ensure that farm revenues remain relatively stable, the United States Agricultural Stabilization and Conservation Service (ASCS) sometimes encourages farmers to limit production through a quota system based on the number of acres the farmer devotes to a single crop. The ASCS also grants loans to farmers and buys excess crops to support the prices farmers receive. Suggest that students find out more about the ASCS and how its programs affect the market for farm products. Have students present and discuss their findings in class.

CHAPTER 5

Quick Check Answers

1. Changes in the supply, changes in the demand, and changes caused by forces which control the market.
2. The price gets lower.

Develop Concepts

The Ever-Changing Market

Emphasize that markets are constantly adjusting many factors to find the equilibrium price. There are changes in producers' supply of a product or service and changes in consumer demand for the product or service. Remind students that as these forces change, the changes will cause the equilibrium price to change as well.

Learning Activity

Have a volunteer begin a supply and demand word web on the board or on a transparency. Ask volunteers, in turn, to complete the diagram so that it shows the relationships of supply, demand, and price. Once the class is satisfied with the diagram, suggest they modify it so that it shows what factors can affect a change in price.

Quick Check Answers

1. Cause-and-effect relationship.
2. Increased competition, increased supply, lower demand.

Quick Check

1. Name three factors that can cause prices to change.
2. What happens to the price of an item if the quantity of an item increases?

THE EVER-CHANGING MARKET

An important point to remember about the market is that prices may change for more than one reason. A situation may occur in which an increase in consumer income increases demand. At the same time, producers may be faced with rising costs for producing goods. In such a case, the change in the equilibrium price can be traced to more than one reason.

As you can see, the market has a lot of cause-and-effect features to it. There generally is no governing board that determines the price of an item, the amount to be produced, or the amount that will be demanded by consumers. Rather, the price goes up or down because of the activities of many consumers and producers. It is a two-way street: Not only do consumers' and producers' activities *affect* price, but those activities are also affected by price.

Take one more look at some of these cause-and-effect relationships in the market. A certain type of fruit drink had an equilibrium price of $3, meaning that the amount supplied equaled the amount demanded at that price. When consumers discovered that the drink had high nutritional value, demand increased. At the available supply, there was a shortage, thus boosting the price. What signal does this development give to producers? At the higher price, more profit can be made. Those already producing the fruit drink will produce even more. Other firms will get into the business. The supply will eventually increase. There will come a time when the available supply is too much for the demand at the market price. The price will eventually decrease, causing some of the inefficient producers to get out of the business.

The market usually determines whether consumers and producers will be satisfied. When Coca-Cola brought out its new formula Coke in 1985, consumers revolted. People began buying and hoarding the old Coke. Many wrote angry letters or called to complain. In less than three months the company brought back the old formula, repackaged as Coke Classic. Both the consumers and the producer won: Coca-Cola's stock price soared to its highest level in 12 years.

Quick Check

1. How would you describe the relationship between producers and consumers in our economy?
2. Suppose the price of an item goes extremely high. What might cause it later to come down?

82   UNIT 2   THE PRIVATE ENTERPRISE SYSTEM

Enrichment Strategy

Ask students to explore the supply and demand relationship in recycling. They may want to explore (1) changing consumer attitudes about products manufactured with recycled materials, (2) the change in producers' demand for raw materials, or (3) the change in production costs of using recycled, rather than raw, materials. Have them concentrate on recyclable products of major raw materials such as crude oil, metals (aluminum, scrap steel), and wood pulp (newspapers, office paper). Suggest they present their data in charts and graphs to be used as a basis for classroom discussion.

Chapter 5 **Summary**

Main Ideas

1. The United States has a market economy in which basic economic decisions are made by the actions of buyers and sellers in the market.
2. Prices affect consumer demand for items, and prices affect how much producers supply.
3. When there is a surplus of goods or services, prices usually come down. A shortage causes prices to rise.
4. Changes in demand that affect prices are caused by consumer preferences, income, and substitutes. Changes in supply that affect prices are caused by weather, the costs of production, and increased efficiency in production.

5. Some prices are not set by the free interaction of supply and demand. They are set by government or by one or a few companies that temporarily control the market for an item.
6. The market constantly changes. It responds to producers and consumers following their own self-interests.
7. A line graph compares two sets of numbers and can be used to show change over time.
8. Electronic information transfer technology allows businesses to use computers to communicate information through several kinds of channels.

CASE ANALYSIS Marketing

Madison's, an upscale women's apparel store, receives a half-dozen tweed jackets with $400 price tags. The store manager prominently displays them at the front of the store where everyone can see them. The first week many people notice them, and several try them on. Two of the jackets sell. In a month or so, the four unsold jackets are moved farther back in the store where they are not so readily seen. Not as many people try them on here. A diligent customer finds them and buys one of the popular sizes. Two months go by and the three remaining jackets are still on the rack. The manager gives a 20 percent markdown and makes the price $320. Two more of the jackets sell. A month later, the last jacket is still in the back of the store. The manager finally marks the price down to $199, about half the original price, and puts it out for a special storewide sale day. The jacket sells. What did the store manager achieve by the markdowns?

CLOSE

Main Ideas

Main Ideas summarizes the key information in the chapter. It is a useful tool for reinforcement and review.

CASE ANALYSIS

Case Analysis provides a chapter-related case for student analysis and application of decision-making skills.

Answer
The jackets had been in the store for a while, and consumers had seen them. The markdown was used as an incentive to consumers to purchase the jackets.

QUICK QUIZ

1. Give two statements that define the market economy. (If a price is high, consumers buy fewer of an item. If the price is low, producers make fewer of an item.)
2. What is the equilibrium price of an item? (The price at which the amount supplied equals the amount demanded.)
3. How can a change in supply increase a price? A change in demand? (A decrease in supply or an increase in demand will increase a price.)
4. Whose actions cause the market to change? (Consumers' and producers'.)

Chapter 5 **Review**

CHAPTER 5 REVIEW

APPLY

Answers

Use the Language of Business
1. demand, 2. law of demand, 3. market, 4. supply, 5. law of supply, 6. market economy, 7. surplus, 8. price, 9. equilibrium price, 10. shortage

Review What You Learned

1. It is based on the actions of buyers and sellers in the market.

2. If the price drops drastically, producers will reduce or eliminate production of the item. This illustrates the law of supply—the lower the price, the less producers will supply of an item.

3. Consumers want to get as much as possible at the lowest possible price; producers try to sell things at the highest price possible to maximize profits.

4. As the item becomes more popular, its price probably will increase.

5. Changes in supply and demand are the major cause, but government intervention and temporary control of the market by one or more firms can also affect price.

6. It is the use of computers to transfer data. Examples could include twisted-pair wire, coaxial cable, fiber-optic cable, microwaves, and communications satellites.

7. The x axis.

Understand Business Concepts

1. By their purchases, consumers indicate what should be produced.

2. They are determined by the actions of buyers and sellers in the market.

3. Children's toys and games are examples of such products.

4. It usually rises in response to strong demand for the product.

5. Children's toys and games are examples of such products.

6. Prices may be set by the government, as in the case of rates charged by public utilities. Rent controls are a way local governments set the price of housing in some areas.

Use the Language of Business

When talking about how the market works, people use the following terms. Match each term to its definition.

demand   market economy
equilibrium price   price
law of demand   shortage
law of supply   supply
market   surplus

1. Amount or quantity of goods and services that consumers are willing and able to buy at various prices.
2. Principle that consumers will generally buy less of an item at a higher price.
3. Any place where individuals buy and sell goods and services.
4. Amount of goods and services that producers will provide at various prices.
5. Principle that producers will generally supply more of an item at a higher price.
6. Economic system in which economic decisions are based on the actions of buyers and sellers.
7. Condition when the supply of an item is greater than the market demand at a particular price.
8. Amount of money given or asked for when goods or services are bought or sold.
9. Price at which the amount of an item supplied is equal to the amount demanded.
10. Undersupply of an item at a particular price.

Review What You Learned

1. Why is the economic system of the United States generally called a market economy?
2. If the price of an item drops drastically, what actions will be taken by many of the producers of that item? What economic law is at work in this example?
3. How do the self-interests of consumers and producers differ?
4. Consumers can get excited about a new fad. What probably will happen to the price of a new item that becomes a fad?
5. What causes prices to change?
6. Tell what electronic information transfer is and name one of the kinds of transmission media.
7. What is the bottom edge of a line graph called?

Understand Business Concepts

1. Why is the consumer all-important in the U.S. market economy?
2. Explain how the prices of items are determined.
3. Clearance sales show the law of demand at work. Explain.
4. Over a long period of time, what happens to the price of an item that is popular and sells quickly?
5. Give an example in which changes in consumer tastes have caused changes in the market for a product or service.

7. As people earn more, they want to buy more of their favorite items. As demand for those items increases, the price increases.

8. It shows change over time or the direction of change.

9. It is the path along which data moves from the sending to the receiving computer.

Think Critically

1. Such price increases are allowed in our market system—especially for nonessential products like toys. In our system, if someone is willing to produce an item, then supply and demand will operate to set the price. What generally happens is that over time more suppliers make this same type of toy, which means increased supply. Assuming that demand does not increase, this increased supply eventually creates a surplus of that toy at the original higher price, so the price comes down.

2. A lower price causes the quantity demanded to increase. As price falls, the quantity supplied falls.

6. Not all prices are set by supply and demand. Give an example in which price is set by other means.
7. How does income cause changes in demand?

8. How does a line graph show the relationship between sets of numbers?
9. Explain what is meant by a communications channel in electronic data transmission?

Think Critically

1. **Evaluate.** Suppose a company produces a new toy that is liked by both adults and children. There is a great demand for it. The supplier raises the price because no other firm produces the toy. In spite of the price increases, the supplier cannot keep up with demand. Some people believe the supplier is taking advantage of the public by increasing its price. Are such price increases allowed in a market system? Should the government control the price? What are other toy producers likely to do?

2. **Compare and Contrast.** How may a lower price affect the quantity of a product demanded? How might it affect the quantity supplied?

Use What You Learned

1. **Group Project.** Supply and demand influence real estate prices. Imagine your team works for a company that has built new headquarters in a small town. You are all going to move to be as close to work as possible. The town does not have enough homes to accommodate so many newcomers. Brainstorm what will happen. Then imagine what might happen if the company decides to relocate again, and all of you want to move along with it. What will be the impact on the prices of homes of so many people trying to move at once? Prepare a brief report explaining what will happen to housing in both cases.

2. **Computer Application.** List five things you buy often. Then list all the places you can buy those items locally. Record the price that each store charges for each item. Do some places charge more than others? What are some reasons that prices differ for identical products? Use word processing software to format your data in a table. Write a 100-word paragraph summarizing your findings. Print out your table and summary.

3. **Skill Reinforcement.** Along with other computer companies, XYZ Computer Company realizes that by cutting prices, it has cut profits drastically. Demand is high, so it raises profits. Soon all computer companies have raised their prices. Copy the graph on page 77 and extend it to show how you predict the laws of supply and demand will affect sales now.

Save your work in your Business Portfolio.

Use What You Learned

1. Be sure students share equally in the group project. Rubrics: Paragraph, Illustration.

2. Students who do not have access to computers can complete the assignment using hand-drawn data tables. Rubrics: Charts and Tables, Diagrams, Paragraph

3. Students' answers will vary, but all graphs should show a drop in sales as the price increases cause a decrease in demand. Rubrics: Graphs

Use the Chapter 9 worksheets in *Student Activity Guide 1* for additional practice and application activities. *Student Activity Guide 1* provides vocabulary exercises, reading comprehension checks, problems, projects, and simulations of business and economic situations. A Teacher's Annotated Edition provides answers.

ASSESS

Portfolio Assessment

The portfolio projects are designed to lead students to develop a collection of their best work to submit to you for assessment. You and your students should decide which projects will be included in their respective Business Portfolios. Refer students to the specific rubric(s) from the *Alternative Assessment Strategies* booklet listed with each of the project notes below. These rubrics will alert students to the criteria you will use to assess their projects.

Chapter Assessment

Use the Chapter 5 Test from the *Test Masters* booklet to evaluate students' understanding of the chapter concepts. An answer key is provided. Or create your own customized test using the *Testmaker* software.

Introduce the Chapter

Major Concepts
• The Rise of Industry
• Types of Businesses
• How Businesses Operate

Introduce the Topic
Ask volunteers to describe occasions when they have developed a better method for accomplishing a certain task. Have them explain what made them look for a better way of doing the task, how they developed the new method, and why the new method was superior to the old method. Tell students that in Chapter 6 they will learn about how innovative techniques helped our country advance through different economic stages.

Use Business Terms
Have students look at the Business Terms and brainstorm associations with each term. Ask them where they have heard or seen the term used. Reinforce correct associations. Advise students to note the meanings of the terms as they read the chapter.

USE VISUALS
The assembly line was one of the techniques that made mass production possible. Although much of manufacturing today is accomplished with machines, people are still key to the manufacturing process. Ask: What can people do that machines cannot do? (Think.)

CHAPTER 6

Business terms

producers

raw goods

processors

processed goods

manufacturers

finished goods

intermediary

wholesaler

retailer

service business

nonprice competition

monopoly

86

CHAPTER 6 RESOURCES

Instructional Resources

Lesson Plan for Chapter 6

Teaching Transparency 6-1

Strategies and Worksheets for Teaching Transparency 6-1

Enrichment Master 6-1

Student Activity Guide 1–TAE for Chapter 6

Test Master for Chapter 6

Alternative Assessment Strategies

Math Skills Review

International Business Strategies

Cooperative Learning Strategies

Communication Skills Review

Ethics in Business Strategies

The Private Enterprise Environment

Learning objectives

After completing this chapter, you will be able to:
• Describe the rise of business in the United States.
• Enumerate the five basic types of businesses.
• Explain how consumers benefit from business competition.
• Identify skills needed in health and biomedical services.
• Explain why observing details and making inferences is an important skill for people in business.

Consider What You Know
Review briefly the main sections of *Chapter 5 How the Market Works:* Our Market Economy; How Is Price Determined?; What Causes Prices to Change?; and The Ever-Changing Market.

Consider what you know

• The market in a private enterprise system changes constantly. Prices affect consumer demand for items, and the prices of items in the market affect how much producers supply.

Consider what you want to know

• What factors have contributed to the growth of industry in the United States?
• What are the five kinds of businesses?
• How do consumers benefit from competition among businesses?
• What jobs are available in health and biomedical services?
• How can the ability to make inferences based on observations help people in business?

Consider What You Want to Know
Ask students to look through the chapter to get an idea of how the chapter will help them answer the questions.

Consider how to use what you learn

• As you read this chapter, think of the products and services you use. What types of businesses produced them?

Consider How to Use What You Learn
Explain to students that at the end of the chapter they will develop projects that will help them better understand how the private enterprise system works. Suggest that as they read the chapter, students think about whether businesses they know of are producers, processors, manufacturers, intermediaries, or service businesses.

Technology Resource Guide

Distance Learning Guide

Internet Resource Guide

Professional Resources

School-to-Work/Tech Prep Strategies

Instructional Poster

Spanish Resources

Multimedia Resources

Testmaker Software for Chapter 6

The Wall Street Journal Video Series
   Video & Activities for Chapter 6

Business and Marketing Computer
   Applications—An Integrated Software
   Simulation Using Microsoft Works

Stocktracker—A Stock Market Software
   Simulation

Where's the Dough? Board Game

TEACH

Business Connection

Small business owners are finding that computerizing their businesses helps level the playing field when competing with larger businesses. Business-accounting software packages designed for personal computers are relatively inexpensive and have proved to be very popular with small business owners. Computerization also allows small businesses to automate the administration of health benefits and inventory control and to maintain customer databases. As recently as the late 1980s, these kinds of money- and time-saving advantages were available only to very large businesses.

Develop Concepts

The Rise of Industry

Explain to students that methods of production have been undergoing change ever since the beginning of the Industrial Revolution. The assembly line, automation, and the use of robots are some examples of innovations that have resulted in increased efficiency. Have students draw a time line from the 1700s to the present year. After they have read the first section of the chapter, have them mark stages of the economy and approximate times when new technology was introduced. Encourage students to add to their time lines throughout their study of the chapter.

In our economic system, businesses are responsible for producing goods and services. If we had no businesses, each individual would have to provide whatever was necessary to satisfy his or her wants and needs. There would be no interdependence, and no relying on someone else to supply a particular item or service. In this chapter, we will take a close look at the five basic types of businesses. We will also examine how businesses operate and how they become successful.

THE RISE OF INDUSTRY

During the early years of the United States, most people made their living from farming. The people who settled the English colonies of North America lived mostly in rural areas where they farmed small plots of land. Some worked as blacksmiths, carpenters, or stonecutters. Some lived in a few urban areas along the Atlantic coast, where they worked in shops, on ships, or in small workshops. By 1700, the colonies had about 250,000 people; by 1775, the population of the colonies was about 2.5 million.

As the number of people in the colonies grew, more and more settlers moved west into the lands on the outer limits of the colonies. Life on the frontier was hard and rugged. Families had to rely on themselves for their needs. They cleared their own land and built their own homes. They made their furniture, raised their food, and made most of their clothes. By 1840, with nearly 70 percent of the U.S. population working on farms, the U.S. economy was clearly an *agricultural economy*.

In the years after the American Revolution, the United States had purchased most of its manufactured goods from other countries. During these years, some manufacturing was done in homes and in workshops. Manufacturing became more important to the economy with the coming of the Industrial Revolution. This was a series of great changes that took place in industry starting in the 1700s with the development of new technology. The changes began in Great Britain with new power-driven machines and later spread to other countries around the world. In the United States, this shift to manufacturing began in the early 1800s. By the time the Civil War began in 1861, our country was on its way to an industrial stage in the economy.

This move to power-driven machines to produce goods brought about many changes in the American economy. Instead

Business & HISTORY

England tried to protect its industrial inventions, but it was inevitable that such innovation would reach other countries. In 1789, a textile worker named Samuel Slater memorized the details of the machinery in an English textile factory. He fled to the United States in disguise, since England did not allow textile workers, plans, or machinery to leave the country. From memory, Slater built the first American cotton textile factory in 1793.

Curriculum Connection   History

Contrast life in past centuries with today to illustrate the rise in business. Have students find out what kinds of stores were common in the United States 200 years ago and 100 years ago. What are some goods and services commonly purchased now that were produced in the home in the past? (Baked goods, clothes, and so on.) What changes have resulted from the growing number of women working outside the home? What differences were there between the goods and services purchased by city and town folk and those bought by rural farmers?

of goods such as cloth being made in homes, they were produced in factories where people came to work. Many people moved off farms and went to work in factories in the cities where they could make more money. The new technology and new work procedures meant that more goods could be produced at lower prices, which meant that more people could afford them. This, in turn, meant that more goods were demanded. In this *industrial economy*, most people worked in manufacturing.

As people bought new manufactured products, their demand for servicing of those products increased. The demand was one factor that contributed to a gradual increase in service industries. In the 1950s, other factors such as an increase in people's leisure time and money brought about the shift to a service stage in the economy. In that *service economy*, more and more people earned a living by producing and selling services.

The demand for services continued to grow into the 1990s. However, another demand became important—the demand for accurate information that was readily available. This caused another shift to our current information stage in the economy. Although the service industry is still growing, today the way most people earn a living depends on the buying and selling of accurate, up-to-date information. That is why we often refer to our economy as an *information economy*.

The changes in the stages of the economy and the new technology and work procedures had a strong impact on farming. Increased use of machinery, fertilizers, and irrigation systems enabled farmers to grow more crops per acre of land. It also enabled any one farmer to farm more acreage. These changes in farming, along with the other changes in the economy, led to a decline in farming as a source of employment. Today less than 2 percent of the labor force work on farms, while almost 70 percent work in service industries. The majority of workers are employed by our nation's several million nonfarm businesses.

Although advances in technology contributed to the growth of industry in the United States, certain other factors also helped make this growth possible. The U.S. economy has developed in a climate that encourages private enterprise. The characteristics of this private enterprise system include the following:

- The right to own property
- The freedom to start new businesses
- The freedom to make agreements
- The right to enter into agreements for producing goods or services
- The right to enter into agreements to provide labor
- The freedom to compete with others in an open market

F.Y.I.

Almost everyone has heard of the Model T, manufactured early in this century by the Ford Motor Company. Ford sold over 15 million of the popular, low-priced cars. Before coming up with the Model T in 1908, Ford had manufactured Models A through S. When the Model T was discontinued in 1927, Ford brought out a revamped Model A. Sales of the Model A were good until the Great Depression hit in 1929.

Learning Activity
Divide the class into five groups and assign each group one of the following inventions to research: walking plow, printing press, spinning jenny, transistor, and fiber-optic cable. Ask groups to present the following information to the class in an oral report: the year of invention and how the invention affected the economy at the time. Ask groups also to tell whether the invention led to other innovations and whether the invention continues to have an impact today.

Business Brief
The common law of England formed the foundation of American private property rights. After the American Revolution, the states carried out land reforms. In the early 1800s, private property rights reinforced the goals of American public policy—economic growth, an expanding population, and a strong middle class.

Learning Activity
Have students brainstorm a list of specific services or products that might have gained popularity as a result of an increase in leisure time and money. (Possible answers: Services—travel agencies, movie theaters, restaurants. Goods—televisions, cars, boats.)

Global Perspective

Organize the class into at least five groups and assign each group a part of the world, such as Northern Africa, Central Africa, Southeast Asia, Central America, and Western Europe. Have each group determine the proportion of countries in the region that have agricultural, industrial, service, or information economies and whether those economies are in the process of change. Have each group present to the class a brief "snapshot" presentation of their region.

Refer to the *International Business Strategies* booklet for additional strategies and activities.

FOCUS ON **Careers**

Discuss

Discuss with students the kinds of skills people in the health and biomedical industries use. Ask students what courses in school could help them prepare for entry-level jobs in health and biomedical services. How do people advance in the field?

Quick Check Answers

1. Agricultural, industrial, service, information.
2. Advances in technology.

Develop Concepts

Types of Businesses

Hand out copies of Enrichment Master 6-1, which lists examples of the five types of businesses and their products. Have students think of other examples of businesses and list their ideas on the board or a transparency. Then help students categorize the businesses according to type. Students may add to and correct, if necessary, the list as they study the section.

Health and Biomedical Services

Health and biomedical services are a major contributor to the growing service business sector of our economy. Many people work in the health and biomedical services, where careers provide a special satisfaction. Whether administering emergency medical treatment, caring for home-bound invalids, dispensing medications from a pharmacy, or drawing blood for transfusions, workers in these fields make a direct contribution to the lives and physical well-being of us all.

Though some health and biomedical personnel spend their working days in laboratories with little patient contact, many more are actively engaged with people, as they test their hearts with EKG machines, X-ray their teeth, or examine their eyes.

Jobs in this area may call for a combination of many different skills and abilities. Workers must be genuinely caring, patient, and able to put others' needs ahead of their own. At the same time, they need an aptitude for science and the ability to make careful, detailed observations of patient symptoms and vital signs. Communication skills are also essential, because health ser-

HELP WANTED

HOME HEALTH AIDE

If you've had some health care training courses and are a compassionate, friendly person with good judgment and physical strength, consider a job with East Branch Home Health Care Services.

The person we hire will: Carry out doctors' and nurses' instructions in patients' homes. Give injections, draw blood samples, take vital signs, help with exercise programs. Report on patient condition and symptoms. Assist patients with baths and meal preparation. Provide caring emotional support.

Quick Check

1. As industry has developed in the United States, through what four stages has the economy moved?
2. What was a major factor in the change from our agricultural economy to our current information economy?

TYPES OF BUSINESSES

There are many different types of businesses in our country and different ways to classify them. One way is to group them by the kind of products they provide.

- producing raw goods
- processing raw goods
- manufacturing goods from raw or processed goods
- distributing goods
- providing services

90   UNIT 2   THE PRIVATE ENTERPRISE SYSTEM

Meeting Student Diversity

Students with reading comprehension problems often don't practice good self-appraisal and self-management skills while reading. Point out to students that they need to be aware of the processes they use to help them understand reading material. Explain that rereading can be very important for understanding. Encourage students to share other techniques they have used.

vice workers are often charged with recording what they observe and passing accurate information on to their colleagues. Physical strength is important for moving ill and injured people. Manual dexterity is necessary in jobs that require activities such as preparing laboratory samples, giving injections, or administering CPR.

With today's team approach to health care, workers are expected to work closely and cooperatively with others. Trustworthiness, punctuality, and a high sense of responsibility are further keys to success in health and biomedical services.

Beginning jobs all require a high school education and, typically, additional training courses or study in technical schools. To advance from these positions, health care workers need continuing education and sometimes certification.

Examples of four entry-level jobs in health and biomedical services are presented in the want ads shown here.

Producers

A farmer in Kansas grows wheat. A petroleum worker in California drills for oil. A miner in Minnesota digs for iron ore. All of these individuals are **producers** because they create or gather products and services for distribution. They are involved in activities related to producing **raw goods**—materials gathered in their original state from natural resources such as land and water. Business firms that perform activities of this sort are producers of raw goods. Agricultural, mining, fishing, and forestry businesses fall into this category.

Processors

Most of the time, we do not use raw goods in the same form that we find them in nature. For example, we usually change wheat into flour. We turn oil into gasoline or some other petroleum product, and we make iron ore into steel. Businesses that change these natural materials from their original forms into more finished forms are **processors.** They are involved in the processing of raw goods. Paper mills, oil refineries, and steel

Follow Through

Explain that health and biomedical services are highly dependent on technology. Invite groups to find out how magnetic resonance imaging (MRI), ultrasound, electrocardiographs, gene mapping, computed tomography (CT), or another technology works. What information do these technologies provide to health-care workers? Have groups present their findings to the class in an oral report.

Business Brief

More and more U.S. manufacturing plants are adopting a method called cell manufacturing, in which small teams of workers produce entire products. Unlike traditional assembly-line techniques, cell manufacturing accommodates product changes and introduces variety for workers without compelling manufacturers to make major changes in work arrangements.

TEACHING TIP

Remind students that we generally don't use raw goods in the same form in which they are found in nature. Have students use encyclopedias to find out how common items such as milk, sugar, and gasoline are processed.

Enrichment Strategy

If possible, arrange for a field trip to a manufacturing facility or a processing facility. Make sure students take notes about the various production operations that take place. Have students choose an aspect of the trip that interested them and write a 100-word report describing the activities and technologies involved in processing the raw goods or manufacturing the finished goods.

TEACHING TIP

Help students distinguish processors from manufacturers by emphasizing that processors of raw goods do not manufacture finished products. They simply make the raw goods into usable resources, which are distributed to manufacturing concerns that will make finished products.

Business Brief

Most people know that paper is made from wood, but processing paper requires an extraordinary amount of other resources. To make a ton of paper a processor typically needs two cords of wood (a cord is a stack of wood 4 ft × 4 ft × 8 ft), 55,000 gallons of water, 102 pounds of sulfur, 350 pounds of lime (a calcium compound), 289 pounds of clay, 1.2 tons of coal, 112 kilowatt hours of power, 20 pounds of pigment, and 108 pounds of starch.

Learning Activity

Have students brainstorm a list of goods or services they could manufacture using only the students in the classroom and the materials available in the classroom. Tell students that they must be able to produce at least 50 units of any good they choose and that any ideas for services must be sustainable.

---

mills are among the businesses that process raw goods. They produce processed goods. **Processed goods** are goods made from raw goods that may require further processing.

Manufacturers

Manufacturers turn raw or processed goods into finished goods. Those goods that require no further processing and are ready for the market are called **finished goods.** Manufacturers are businesses set up to carry out the activities involved in making finished goods out of processed goods. The bakery that makes bread out of flour and other raw or processed goods is a manufacturer. The automobile factory that makes cars out of processed goods such as steel, aluminum, glass, and plastic is also a manufacturer. Many of the leading businesses listed in Figure 6-1 on page 93 are manufacturers.

Intermediaries

An **intermediary** is a business that moves goods from one business to another. It buys goods, stores them, and then resells them. Such a business may also be referred to as a middleman. A **wholesaler** is one type of business that distributes goods. Because they distribute goods, wholesalers are also called distributors. Wholesalers buy goods from manufacturers in huge quantities and resell them in smaller quantities. A clothing wholesaler may, for instance, buy thousands of jackets from several manufacturers. A fruit and vegetable wholesaler may buy oranges and lettuce by the truckload. Wholesalers then divide these large quantities into smaller quantities and resell them to retailers. A **retailer** is a business that purchases goods from a wholesaler and resells them directly to the consumer, the final buyer of the goods. As such, it is another type of business that moves goods. Examples of retailers include gas stations, department stores, and car dealers.

Service Businesses

A fifth type of business, one that is increasing in number very rapidly, is the service business. By the mid-1990s, 75 percent of the workforce was employed by service businesses. A **service business** provides services instead of goods to consumers. Movie theaters, car washes, airlines, lawn-care specialists, mechanics, and doctors all operate service businesses. Service businesses provide for people's wants and needs, but what they sell is intangible, that is, you cannot touch or hold the things they sell.

Making Connections ⇨   Assembly Lines

Explain to students that assembly-line production was introduced in factories in the early part of the 20th century and increased efficiency tremendously. Allow groups to experiment with assembly-line techniques using a simple product and process such as assembling sandwiches. Have groups decide what tasks need to be performed and how they will divide the labor. Ask one group to act as a control group by *not* using assembly-line methods. Give students 15 minutes to assemble as many sandwiches as possible. At the end of the experiment, have groups compare the efficiency of their methods. How do the assembly-line groups' rates compare with the control group's rate? How might students change things to improve efficiency next time?

LEADING U.S. BUSINESSES, 1993

Industry	Business Name	Sales (in millions of dollars)
Aerospace	Boeing	$25,285
Apparel	Levi Strauss	$5,892
Beverages	PepsiCo	$25,021
Chemicals	E. I. du Pont de Nemours	$32,621
Computers, Office Equipment	IBM	$62,716
Electronics, Electrical Equipment	General Electric	$60,823
Food	Philip Morris	$50,521
Forest and Paper Products	International Paper	$13,685
Motor Vehicles and Parts	General Motors	$133,622
Petroleum Refining	Exxon	$97,825
Pharmaceuticals	Johnson & Johnson	$14,138
Rubber and Plastic Products	Goodyear Tire	$11,643
Scientific, Photographic, and Control Equipment	Eastman Kodak	$20,059
Soaps, Cosmetics	Procter & Gamble	$30,433

Source: World Almanac

FIGURE 6-1

Many of the leading businesses in the U.S. are manufacturers; others are producers and processors. Name two processed goods General Motors would use to manufacture cars.

Some service businesses operate to fulfill people's needs for information. Newspapers and television stations fall into this category of service businesses. On-line services, such as America Online, Prodigy, and CompuServe, allow computer users to access all kinds of information from a huge variety of sources and communicate with others by E-mail. In addition to offering photocopying services, copy shops also allow their customers to transmit information by offering faxing services.

Quick Check

1. What type of business produces each of the following: raw goods, processed goods, and finished goods?
2. Name two kinds of intermediaries.
3. Give three examples of service businesses.

Reteaching Strategy

Draw a map of a four-block section of a local shopping district on a transparency. Ask the class to help fill in the types of business firms (by name, if possible) in that area. Have students identify the businesses as producers, processors, manufacturers, intermediaries, or service businesses. (Most will probably be intermediaries or service businesses.) Ask students what other types of businesses they think could succeed in the area. Have students suggest specific locations for the businesses.

USE VISUALS

Have students use the sales figures given in Figure 6-1 to create a bar graph. Have students arrange the graph from highest sales to lowest sales.

USE TRANSPARENCIES

Use Teaching Transparency 6-1 and its corresponding strategies and worksheet from the *Teaching Transparency Strategies and Worksheets* booklet to help students compare sales figures among leading U.S. businesses. Verify student worksheets using the Answer Key.

Learning Activity

Have students consider the business activities that occur prior to the purchasing of ingredients necessary for baking a birthday cake. (Agricultural producers would produce the wheat, eggs, dairy products, sugar, and so forth; wheat, dairy products, and sugar would all need to be processed; manufacturers would package the goods; and a wholesaler or other intermediary would distribute the goods to a retail store where students could purchase the necessary ingredients.)

Quick Check Answers

1. Producers; processors; manufacturers.
2. Wholesalers and retailers.
3. Possibilities: movie theaters, car washes, airlines.

Model

Make sure students understand the relationship between the processes of observing and inferring by providing them with the following example. Cindy sees her mail carrier at the house across the street. She knows from prior experience that that house comes after her house on the carrier's route. Tell students the most likely inference to be made from the observation would be that Cindy's mail has already been delivered.

Develop Concepts

How Businesses Operate

Emphasize to students that competition is one of the major characteristics of a private enterprise system. Point out that competition is beneficial to consumers because it tends to lower prices. Have students suppose that there was only one store that sold CDs. It could charge as much as people were willing to pay since people who really wanted CDs would have no other alternative. If a second store started selling CDs and sold them at a lower price, most people would buy from the second seller. Ask students what the first store would have to do in order to stay in business. (At the least, it would have to match the second company's price.)

ANALYSIS
Observing and Inferring

Explanation

You observe and make inferences every day. Yet these skills, like others, can be improved by practice. People in business need to observe and make inferences to help them analyze graphs or arrays of statistics, find the reason for defects in manufactured goods, and help employees work more productively.

Observing means gathering information from the direct experience of your own senses. Looking at workers assembling cars in a plant is observing. Reading or listening to a description of the same process is not. Observing is more than simply seeing, hearing, and smelling. It is an active skill that involves patience, paying attention, and noting details. Making skilled observations may also mean putting aside prejudices and trusting the evidence of your senses.

Inferring can be thought of as filling in missing information. It is drawing conclusions based on your observations. For example, if you observe workers standing around talking, you might infer that the assembly process at this factory is inefficiently organized. You can use these steps to help you make inferences.

1. Review what you've observed.
2. Use logic or prior knowledge to think of some

HOW BUSINESSES OPERATE

Although large business firms are important in our economic system, the majority of businesses are small. As you will recall from Chapter 2, entrepreneurial resources are one of the factors of production. Individuals who recognize new or changed wants and needs may decide to start a new business to fulfill that want or need. Usually the businesses they start are small. Our private enterprise system encourages entrepreneurship. Small businesses can compete in the market just as large firms do. In fact, some products and services are more suited to production by a small firm. Some people have skills for making products by hand. You might pay more for the handcrafted product than a machine-made product because you might consider its quality and uniqueness worth the added cost.

Both small and large business firms compete for consumers' dollars. If firms are not able to meet the wants of consumers, they go out of business. If they compete successfully, they stay in business and may grow larger. Competition is a way of assuring consumers of the best product or service at the best price.

Cooperative Learning Group Discussion

Have students form groups and ask the groups to assume that they have been asked to select a product or service for a new business firm to sell to the local community. Remind students to consider competition from other businesses when making their decisions. Have groups describe the product or service to the class and explain how and why they made the choice they did.

Refer to the *Cooperative Learning Strategies* booklet for additional cooperative learning strategies.

MAKING INFERENCES FROM OBSERVATIONS

1. **Observation:** You observe that your assistant works hard from 9 to 12. From 12 until she leaves for lunch at 1 P.M., she seems drowsy or inefficient.
   Possible Inferences:
   a. She may suffer from low blood sugar and should eat lunch earlier.
   b. She is lazy and doesn't like to work.
2. **Observation:** Market research indicates homeowners will be eager to buy a new, easy-to-handle garden hose. It reaches stores in the Midwest the third week

in August. You observe that sales figures are low there over the next three months, although sales are good in New England.
   Possible Inferences:
   a. The timing was probably too late in the Midwest, because by August most homeowners have been working in their gardens and lawns for months: They buy hoses earlier.
   b. The market research wasn't accurate for the Midwest, though it was for the New England area.

conclusions it might be possible to draw from your observations.
3. Decide which of your inferences fits best with your observations.
4. If necessary, make further observations.

Practice

Imagine that you observe the cases in the box. Choose which inference you might make accurately about each one. Identify any additional information you think you would need to get a clearer picture.

Businesses usually have several choices when competing on the basis of price. They can:

- Make the same product at a lower price.
- Make a better product at the same price.
- Make a better product at a lower price.

Any business that produces goods or services and wants to remain competitive has to make one of those three choices.

A good example of how competition works comes from the personal computer industry. In the mid-1980s, an IBM personal computer with a single-color monitor cost about $2100. However, IBM-compatible computers, that is, computers made by different companies that use the same operating system and run the same software, sold for about a third less money. The IBM-compatible computers competed with IBMs by making the same product and selling it for less money.

By the mid-1990s, competition was even more intense in the personal computer business. Both IBM and IBM-compatible manufacturers were able to make a better product and sell it at a lower price. Innovations in technology and competition

For years, European airlines operated under a system of controlled competition and charged high fares; however, these controls will end by 1997. By the early 1990s, several new lower-fare airlines had already emerged. EuroBelgian Airlines Express first offered no-frills flights within Europe at prices that were about one-sixth of those of other European airlines. Such low fares caused several major European airlines to start up low-cost services of their own in order to meet the competition.

Practice

Have students use the four steps listed to select the most likely inference for each observation. (1. The (a) inference may be accurate, but more information is needed about her work performance. Since she works well in the morning, there's no real evidence that (b) is likely. 2. Both inferences may be accurate; more information would be needed about the scope of the market research.)

Learning Activity

Provide students with the following scenario: HoHo's Pizza sells a large pepperoni and mushroom pizza for $10.99. Pier-Luigi Pizzeria sells a large pepperoni and mushroom pizza for $9.99. Rocco's Pizza and Pasta sells an extra large pepperoni, mushroom, and green pepper pizza for $9.69. Ask students how Pier-Luigi Pizzeria competes with HoHo's. (It sells the same product at a lower price.) How does Rocco's compete with HoHo's and Pier-Luigi's? (It sells a better product at a lower price.) Ask students which pizza place is the most competitive. (Rocco's.) Which is the least competitive? (HoHo's.)

Reteaching Strategy

Give students the following scenario and have them make inferences based on the observations. Observation: Homer noticed that a new shop called Bart's Bagels opened up two months ago. The shop is a block away from Homer's donut shop. Ever since Bart's opened, fewer customers have been coming into Homer's shop. (Possible inference: Some of Homer's health-conscious customers may have been going to Bart's; however, students should mention that more information is needed.)

CHAPTER 6

USE VISUALS

Ask students what they look for when they buy clothing. Do they make buying decisions based solely on price or do they consider other factors? Have students analyze the influence nonprice competition plays in their own clothes-buying decisions. Answer to caption: By offering features such as pictures of cartoon characters or an attached hood.

Business Brief

Independently owned toy stores find it difficult to compete on a price basis with mass merchandisers. Instead, independent toy stores, which make up between 5 and 10 percent of the market share, use nonprice competition to stay in business. They promote their stores as alternatives to impersonal mass merchandisers and sell educational products, unusual toys produced by small manufacturers or craftspeople, and high-quality toys.

Quick Check Answers

1. Make the same product at a lower price; make a better product at the same price; make a better product at a lower price.
2. Competition based on a product's special features rather than its price.
3. A firm that sells all, or nearly all, of a product has little or no competition and is termed a monopoly.

How does nonprice competition vary the price of children's jackets, for example?

brought the price down. In 1995, it was possible to get an IBM-compatible computer that was much faster and had far more memory and data storage capacity than its predecessors of a few years before. Such a computer also came with features such as a CD-ROM drive, a fax/modem, and free multimedia software. Such a computer sold for well under $1500.

If so many companies had not been making personal computers, the price probably would have stayed high. Technology may not have advanced as quickly, either. As more and more firms entered the market, however, competition forced them to make their products more attractive to the consumer.

If a business sells a product that is exactly like all the others, it must price the product no higher than the going rate. On the other hand, if the business can add a new feature or quality that sets the product apart from its competitors' products, it is now different. Competition based on a product's features rather than its price is **nonprice competition.** The firm charges a higher price because its product offers features competitors' products do not have, and customers may be willing to pay more for the product because of those features.

Businesses can gain some control over their prices simply by becoming larger. When they have a larger share of the market, they can buy supplies for less because they buy in large amounts. They can advertise more. They take the lead in setting prices, and smaller firms have to follow. A smaller firm usually cannot afford a "price war."

In some cases, our economy has so few firms selling one kind of product that they have little or no competition. If one firm sells all or practically all of a product, that firm has a **monopoly.** Because the company has little or no competition, it can determine the price. Since a monopoly usually means higher prices for the consumer, the government may step in. In most cases, it is not legal to control the market through a monopoly. You will learn more about the measures the government takes to ensure fair competition in Unit 5. Although a business's growing larger is not harmful to the economy, controlling prices is. Our private enterprise system favors competition and risk-taking by businesses.

Quick Check

1. What are three choices a business can make when competing on the basis of price?
2. What is nonprice competition?
3. Describe what it means to have a monopoly.

Global Perspective

Competitiveness among nations can be defined by how efficiently a country uses its natural resources, how it develops and uses technology and capital, and how well it uses the skills of its workforce. Have groups of students choose a country and evaluate in what industries it competes, how successfully it competes, and which countries provide competition. Have groups present their findings to the class in an oral report.

Refer to the *International Business Strategies* booklet for additional strategies and activities.

Chapter 6 **Summary**

Main Ideas

1. The U.S. economy has passed through four stages—agricultural, industrial, service, and information.
2. Advances in technology, especially the development of power-driven machinery and new production techniques, were a major factor in the rise of industry in the United States.
3. Certain rights and freedoms that characterize our private enterprise economy provided the environment in which business and industry could develop.
4. The five basic types of businesses are producers, processors, manufacturers, intermediaries, and service businesses.

5. As more and more businesses enter a market, competition increases. Consumers benefit from such competition because businesses may lower prices, increase quality, or add additional features to their products to encourage consumers to buy their products.
6. People who work in the health and biomedical services fields need good communication, science, and observational skills.
7. Because businesspeople do not always have all the information they need, they make reasonable inferences based on observations and prior knowledge.

CASE ANALYSIS Private Enterprise

Jason Simons has just won $100,000 in the state lottery. He is currently working for a retail business as the general manager of one of its stores. He has worked hard and has received promotions as well as increases in salary. Jason knows the retail business very well. The company he works for is growing, and the president has promised Jason that, if the company succeeds in expanding into the other markets, Jason will grow with it. With his newly acquired resources, Jason could go into business for himself. He has sometimes thought about owning his own business. What advice would you give Jason?

CLOSE

Main Ideas

Main Ideas summarizes the key information in the chapter. It is a useful tool for reinforcement and review.

CASE ANALYSIS

Case Analysis provides a chapter-related case for student analysis and application of decision-making skills.

Answer
Students' answers will vary but could include some reference to the characteristics of the private enterprise system that encourage people to go into business.

QUICK QUIZ

1. What four economic stages has the U.S. economy experienced? (Agricultural, industrial, service, information.)
2. Name five types of businesses. (Producers, processors, manufacturers, intermediaries, and service businesses.)
3. What kind of businesses are on-line services? (Service businesses.)
4. What is a monopoly? (One firm that sells all or nearly all of a product.)

Chapter 6 **Review**

CHAPTER 6 REVIEW

APPLY

Answers

Use the Language of Business
1. wholesaler, **2.** retailer, **3.** monopoly, **4.** raw goods, **5.** processed goods, **6.** producers, **7.** service business, **8.** manufacturers, **9.** processors, **10.** intermediary, **11.** finished goods, **12.** nonprice competition.

Review What You Learned
1. Advances in technology.
2. Examples: *producers:* farmers; *processors:* steel mills; *manufacturers:* most factories; *intermediaries:* wholesalers; *service firms:* car washes.
3. A producer grows or gathers goods in their original state; a processor changes these goods into a more finished form.
4. A wholesaler buys goods from manufacturers in huge quantities and resells them in smaller quantities to other businesses.
5. Companies compete by lowering the price of a product, by making a better product at the same price, or by making a better product at a lower price. In all three cases, consumers benefit.
6. Communication skills, observational skills, and the ability to work well with others are important skills.
7. Draws a conclusion based on observations. Prior knowledge also often plays a part.

Understand Business Concepts
1. They hope to attract customers and make a profit.
2. As a result of the shift from an agricultural to a service economy, many more people now work in service industries than in agriculture.
3. *Raw goods:* petroleum, iron ore, wheat; *processed goods:* gasoline, steel, flour.

Use the Language of Business

On a separate sheet of paper, rewrite the sentences below, filling in each blank with the term that best completes the sentence.

finished goods	processors
intermediary	producers
manufacturers	raw goods
monopoly	retailer
nonprice competition	service business
processed goods	wholesaler

1. A(n) _____ sells products to other businesses.
2. A(n) _____ sells goods directly to the consumer, the final buyer of the goods.
3. A firm that is the only seller of a particular product has a(n) _____ .
4. _____ are gathered in their original state from natural resources.
5. _____ are goods made from raw goods that may require further processing.
6. _____ are businesses that create or gather products for distribution.
7. A(n) _____ provides services instead of goods to consumers.
8. _____ turn raw or processed goods into finished goods.
9. _____ turn natural materials into more finished forms.
10. A(n) _____ is a business that moves goods from one business to another.
11. _____ require no further processing and are ready for the market.
12. _____ is based on a product's features rather than its price.

Review What You Learned

1. What was a major factor in the shift in our economy from an agricultural economy to an industrial economy?
2. Give an example of a business in each of the five types of business categories.
3. What is the difference between a producer of raw goods and a processor of raw goods?
4. What does a wholesaler do?
5. How do consumers benefit from price competition among business firms?
6. Name three skills that workers in the health and biomedical fields use.
7. What does a person do when making an inference?

Understand Business Concepts

1. Why do people try new ways of producing goods and services?
2. How did our economy change as a result of the shift from an agricultural orientation to a service one?
3. Give three examples each of raw goods and processed goods.
4. Our business system has millions of businesses. Why are businesses so important to our system?
5. What skills and characteristics are important for health and biomedical service workers who care for homebound elderly patients?
6. What could you do if several inferences are suggested by your observations and you aren't sure which is most likely?

4. They are responsible for furnishing most of the goods and services used by consumers.
5. Workers need to be caring, compassionate, and friendly. They need to be strong enough to move patients.
6. You could make additional observations or obtain more information.

Think Critically
1. Whether there is a demand for the product, whether it can stand up to the competition in the marketplace, and whether the product can be priced so it will be profitable.
2. Some people look at the prices of raw materials and judge profits by the differences between those prices and the prices consumers pay for finished goods. They don't consider the costs involved in producing and distributing the goods.

Think Critically

1. **Evaluate.** What factors should a person choosing a product for a new business consider?

2. **Apply.** Why do many people believe that profits on sales of finished goods are much higher than they actually are?

Use What You Learned

1. **Group Project.** With your group, find out more about how wholesalers or distributors operate. Choose a product such as clothing, food, or equipment. Locate a wholesaler of that product and interview someone there. First, draft some questions about how the company distributes its product to retailers. Start with questions like these:

   - Where does the wholesaler distribute the product?
   - Who sells it to the wholesaler?
   - What is the size of a typical order? Is there a minimum or maximum size for orders?
   - What modes of transportation does the wholesaler use for distribution?

   Work together to write a 400-word report and discuss and compare your report with those of other groups.

2. Prepare a bulletin board or a large chart tracing the route of an item from raw material to consumer product.

3. **Computer Application.** Compile a database of local businesses in which you include fields for the name, the address, the telephone number, and the type of business according to the five categories listed on page 90. Use your local Yellow Pages to locate the information; then identify the category into which each business fits. Try to find at least one business in each category and include a minimum of 10 businesses. Print out your database. If you could not find a local business in one of the categories, explain why you think this may be so.

4. **Skill Reinforcement.** Imagine that you observe what is described in the following case study.

   Your job is to inspect golf carts as they come off the assembly line. You notice an increase in defects in the motors. You know the company has contracted with some new parts suppliers. You also observe a new face among the workers assembling the motors.

   What inferences could you make? What, if any, further observations or information do you think you would need to make better inferences? Write your inferences on a separate sheet of paper.

Save your work in your Business Portfolio

Use What You Learned

1. Make sure all students participate in the group project. Rubric: Essay.

2. Students may want to use a computer to assist them in making their charts. Possible Rubric(s): Bulletin Board; Charts and Tables.

3. Students with no access to a computer may compile their information in a hand-drawn chart or table. Rubric: Charts and Tables.

4. Students might infer that the parts from the new suppliers are the cause of the problem or that the new member of the assembly team is making errors. Students should note that they need more information to decide which of these inferences is correct. Rubric: Paragraph.

Independent Practice

Use the Chapter 6 worksheets in *Student Activity Guide 1* for additional practice and application activities. *Student Activity Guide 1* provides vocabulary exercises, reading comprehension checks, problems, projects, and simulations of business and economic situations. A Teacher's Annotated Edition provides answers.

ASSESS

Portfolio Assessment

The portfolio projects are designed to lead students to develop a collection of their best work to submit to you for assessment. You and your students should decide which projects will be included in their respective Business Portfolios. Refer students to the specific rubric(s) from the *Alternative Assessment Strategies* booklet listed with each of the project notes below. These rubrics will alert students to the criteria you will use to assess their projects.

Chapter Assessment

Use the Chapter 6 Test from the *Test Masters* booklet to evaluate students' understanding of the chapter concepts. An answer key is provided. Or create your own customized test using the *Testmaker* software.

Business Issue

Business Issue

FAMILY-FRIENDLY BENEFITS

Highlight the Issue

Before asking students to read pages 100–101, discuss what they know about the benefits employers offer to their employees. Ask: Should benefits such as child care and parental leave be an essential part of an employee's benefits package? Why or why not? After students have read the pages, ask the question again, and discuss students' responses.

Business Issue

FAMILY-FRIENDLY BENEFITS

More and more children are growing up in households in which the sole parent or both parents work outside the home. These mothers and fathers have to juggle the demands of work and family. To make life easier for working parents, should employers offer parental-leave and child-care benefits?

Pro

According to one study, U.S. businesses lose nearly $3 billion each year because of employees' child-care problems. Concerns about child care can distract workers from their jobs and lower their productivity. Breakdowns in child-care arrangements may even mean workers have to take time off to take care of their children.

By offering employees benefits such as parental leave and child care, companies can reduce the amount of work time lost. Studies show that such family-friendly benefits not only lead to improved worker productivity, but also reduce absenteeism, lower rates of turnover, and increase worker loyalty—all of which contribute to a company's success.

Generous family benefits can also help companies attract and keep skilled workers. A 1993 survey of workers at one company found that 71 percent of workers who used family benefits said the benefits were an important reason for staying with the company. As U.S. firms face increased global competition, their need to keep skilled workers will continue to grow.

Some employers say they can't afford family benefits such as company-sponsored day-care centers or paid parental leave. But there are many less costly alternatives, such as offering employees information about community child-care resources. Another type of low-cost benefit is a reimbursement account, which is an account that employers set up so that employees can pay for child care out of pre-tax income. Flexible hours, job sharing, or work-at-home options also help working parents.

A recent study conducted by a Boston research firm found that family benefits can actually save companies money. For every dollar a company spends on family benefits, it saves $2 to $6 through reduced absenteeism and greater worker loyalty.

Family-friendly benefits not only make good business sense they are also an important investment in the next generation of Americans.

Extend the Issue

Have students work in groups to conduct their own surveys about the pros and cons of offering family benefits. Encourage groups to survey a diverse group of employers and employees. Students may want to contact the human resources departments of some large corporations to find out their policies on child care and family benefits. Have groups compile a report on the results of

Con

Family benefits are nice, but they're too expensive for most businesses to afford. At a time when companies must cut costs to remain competitive, such benefits are a luxury. One survey found that child care costs companies an average of $160 per month per child. If a company employs 2000 workers and those workers have 300 children who need child care, that adds up to $48,000 per month. Such a bill would put many companies out of business and their employees out of work.

Furthermore, if U.S. workers demand such costly benefits, U.S. companies could find that it's too expensive to do business in the United States and decide to move their factories to places where labor costs are lower. The loss of these businesses would put more people out of work.

Parental-leave policies are also bad for business. When its workforce is constantly changing, a business has difficulty running efficiently. The Family and Medical Leave Act, which went into effect in 1993, guarantees some U.S. workers the right to time off without pay for family and medical reasons. The U.S. Chamber of Commerce estimates that this act will cost $16.2 billion a year in lost productivity. Reduced productivity and inefficiency will make it even more difficult for U.S. companies to compete in the world market.

Not only are child-care and parental-leave programs costly to businesses, they are unfair to workers because they don't benefit all workers equally. Only employees who are parents can take advantage of family benefits. Thus workers who don't have children, in effect, receive fewer benefits.

Employers should not bear the responsibility for taking care of their employees' children. Workers don't expect their companies to provide clothing or food for their children. Why should they expect them to pick up the tab for child care? It's up to parents, not businesses, to raise children.

their surveys. Have a volunteer from each group explain his or her group's findings to the class. As a class, discuss the results of the surveys. Discuss the opinions that seemed most common and those that were least common. Encourage students to supply possible reasons for certain people's opinions.

Unit 3   Dynamics of Business in a Changing World

Chapter	Learning Objectives
7 **Building a Business Organization** **pp. 104–117**	• Explain the ways in which businesses organize for management. • Describe the three levels of management. • Identify and give examples of the four functions of management. • List qualities that are essential for all managers. • Describe the advantages and disadvantages of being a manager. • Relate how Urban Miyares built his business organization. • List several functions of leadership in business.
8 **Managing a Diverse Workforce** **pp. 118–135**	• Describe the steps in the employment process. • List the leadership traits of effective human resources managers. • Compare the advantages of using different types of communication in managing a workforce. • Describe virtual reality and explain how it can be used to train certain types of workers.
9 **Managing Business Finances** **pp. 136–151**	• Explain the accounting equation. • Name two kinds of financial statements and describe the information each provides. • Describe the role of the financial manager within a business. • Discuss three main responsibilities of financial management. • Describe the traits of accounting and finance employees. • Explain how to use percents. • Describe electronic spreadsheets and how businesses use them for financial analysis.
10 **Producing Goods and Services Worldwide** **pp. 152–169**	• Identify the three elements of an operations system. • Explain how quality control, maintenance, and cost control contribute to the efficient production of goods and services. • Describe how goods are distributed. • List the special skills that operations and production workers need to have. • Name four problem-solving strategies. • Describe several careers in manufacturing technology and construction.
11 **Marketing in Today's World** **pp. 170–189**	• Identify the four elements that make up the marketing mix. • Define the life cycle of a product. • Discuss the needs and motivations of consumers. • Describe the role of pricing, packaging, and promotion in marketing goods and services. • List the traits that marketing employees need to have. • Describe what an active listener does. • Explain how electronic databases are used for target marketing.

Business Issue: **Downsizing, pp. 190–191**

National Standards for Business Education*	Chapter Highlights			
	Focus on Features	Building Business Skills	Visual Learning	Case Analysis
CD: I A, II A, IV A; *COMM:* II A, V C; *EE:* I A, VI A, VI C; *IBF:* COMM, MGMT; *MGMT:* I A, I B, I C, I D, VI A, VI C	Entrepreneurs: Urban Miyares— Disabled Businesspersons Association, p. 108	Employability: Exercising Leadership, p. 112	Centralized Organization, p. 106 Departmentalized Organization, p. 107 Management Functions, p. 110	Management, p. 115
CD: I A, II A, III C; *COMM:* I C, I D; *EE:* VI C; *IB:* II A, III A; *IS:* VII; *IBF:* CD, COMM, MGMT; *MGMT:* II, V A, V B, V C, V E, V F	Technology: Virtual Training, p. 122	Communication: Choosing Appropriate Forms of Business Communication, p. 126	Sample Job Description, p. 121 A Changing Workforce, p. 125 Maslow's Levels of Needs, p. 132	Management, p. 133
ACCT: I, IV D; *CD:* I A, II A; *COMM:* I B, I C, V D; *COMP:* II, VI E; *EE:* IV B, IV C, V D; *IS:* VIII; *IBF:* ACCT, CD, IS, MGMT; *MGMT:* I A, I B, III A, III B, III D	Technology: Electronic Spreadsheets, p. 140	Math: Learning About Percents, p. 146	Accounting Equation, p. 139 Income Statement, p. 142 Balance Sheet, p. 142 Common Sources and Uses of Funds in a Typical Business, p. 145	Financial Management, p. 149
CD: I A, II A, IV A; *COMM:* I A, II A; *EE:* I D, VII A, VII C; *IB:* VI B, VII G; *IBF:* CD, IB, MGMT, PROD; *MGMT:* II, XI A, XI B, XI C, XI D	Careers: Manufacturing Technology and Construction, p. 160	Employability: Demonstrating Problem-Solving, p. 156	Elements of an Operations System, p. 154 Problem-Solving Flow Chart, p. 157 Modes of Transporting Goods, p. 164	Production, p. 167
CD: I A, II A, IV A; *COMM:* I D; *EE:* II C, V C, VII A, VII C; *IB:* III A, VI A, VII A, VII C, VII F; *IBF:* CD, IB, MGMT, MKTG; *IS:* VII; *MKTG:* I A, III C, III D, IV A, IV B, IV C, IV D, V A, V B, VI, VII A, IX B	Technology: Electronic Databases, p. 176	Communication: Developing Listening Skills, p. 180	Product Life Cycle, p. 175 Break-Even Point, p. 180 Channels of Distribution, p. 183	Marketing, p. 187

* Level 3 Performance Expectations: Accounting (ACCT), Career Development (CD), Communications (COMM), Computation (COMP), Entrepreneurship Education (EE), International Business (IB), Information Systems (IS), Interrelationships of Business Functions (IBF), Management (MGMT), Marketing (MKTG). See page T14 for all 12 content areas.

Unit 3

Look Back

Remind students that in a free enterprise system, businesses have the freedom to choose what they will produce, compete for customers, and make a profit. Although the almost 20 million businesses in the United States vary in size and in what they produce, they all try to satisfy consumer demands, they all take risks, and they all are motivated by profit.

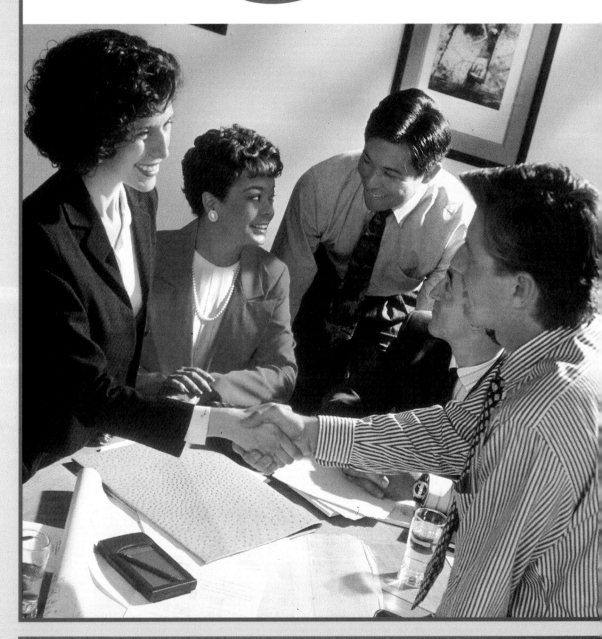

UNIT 3 COOPERATIVE LEARNING PROJECT

Co-op Co-op Activity

Preparation: Photocopy BLMs 5 and 6 from the *Cooperative Learning Strategies* booklet and provide copies of a newspaper job section for each team. This project will take approximately two class periods.

Guidelines: Divide students into five teams, one for each chapter in the unit. Have each team concentrate on the section of its chapter that discusses working in that area of the business world, such as "Is Being a Manager for You?" in Chapter 7. Students should collect samples of want ads that describe jobs like

Dynamics of Business in a Changing World

Look Ahead
Point out to students that *dynamics* are the forces and actions that characterize a system. The dynamics of business are complex. They encompass systems for financing, managing, producing, and marketing goods and services. Business dynamics also include those human resources who weave together the various business systems.

This unit focuses on the ways businesses are structured and operate: in short, how they go about their business. The first three chapters cover the people and financial processes that keep enterprises functioning. The last two chapters outline how businesses produce and market their goods and services.

103

TEACHING TIP

Use the *Business and Marketing Computer Applications* to reinforce and extend the functions of business introduced in Unit 3. This template application software introduces students to the basic functions of Microsoft Works, an integrated software program. In this simulation, students assume the role of a trainee in a media store and perform various job-related activities within the accounting, advertising, human resources, inventory, and sales departments.

those in their team's chapter. Students can analyze the ads as suggested on BLM 5. Have members of each team discuss the ads they found in light of the chapter and BLM 5. Then have teams follow the directions on BLM 6 to draft several want ads of their own for people to work in the kinds of jobs described in their team's chapter. The ads must clearly state the duties and responsibilities of the jobs. All five teams can work together to make a unit bulletin board display of the want ads they found and wrote. As they proceed through the unit, students can add other related want ads they find to the display.

FOCUS

Introduce the Chapter

Major Concepts
- Organizing for Management
- Levels of Management
- Management Functions
- Is Being a Manager for You?

Introduce the Topic
Ask students what they think would be the major responsibilities of a manager of a business firm such as a department store, a fast-food restaurant, or another type of business with which they are familiar. List their responses on the board or a transparency. Ask students to keep those ideas in mind as they read the chapter.

Use Business Terms
Ask students to write a sentence with each of the Business Terms, replacing the term with a nonsense word. Invite volunteers to read aloud their sentences for others in the class to insert the correct term. Advise students to check the meanings of the terms as they read the chapter.

USE VISUALS

Ask students to make some inferences about the organization of the office shown in the photo. Ask students to identify the employee or employees that might have managerial responsibilities. (Possible answer: The people in the office are probably managers; the people at the work stations are probably lower-level employees.)

CHAPTER
7

Business terms

centralization

decentralization

departmentalization

management

top-level manager

middle-level manager

first-line manager

104

CHAPTER 7 RESOURCES

Instructional Resources

Lesson Plan for Chapter 7

Teaching Transparencies 7-1, 7-2

Strategies and Worksheets for Teaching Transparencies 7-1, 7-2

Enrichment Masters 7-1, 7-2

Student Activity Guide 1–TAE for Chapter 7

Test Master for Chapter 7

Alternative Assessment Strategies

Math Skills Review

International Business Strategies

Cooperative Learning Strategies

Communication Skills Review

Ethics in Business Strategies

Building a Business Organization

Learning objectives

After completing this chapter, you will be able to:
• Explain the ways in which businesses organize for management.
• Describe the three levels of management.
• Identify and give examples of the four functions of management.
• List qualities that are essential for all managers.
• Describe the advantages and disadvantages of being a manager.
• Relate how Urban Miyares built his business organization.
• List several functions of leadership in business.

Consider what you know

• In each of the many goods- and service-producing businesses, there are both large and small companies. Consumers benefit from the competition provided by a variety of businesses.

Consider what you want to know

• How are businesses organized?
• What role do managers play in different business organizations?
• What are the four functions of management?
• How did Urban Miyares overcome disabilities to become an entrepreneur?
• How can you exercise leadership when working with others?

Consider how to use what you learn

• As you read this chapter, think about what managers do in businesses or companies you are familiar with. What skills do successful managers have?

Multimedia Resources

Technology Resource Guide

Distance Learning Guide

Internet Resource Guide

Professional Resources

School-to-Work/Tech Prep Strategies

Instructional Poster

Spanish Resources

Testmaker Software for Chapter 7

The Wall Street Journal Video Series
   Video & Activities for Chapter 7

Business and Marketing Computer
   Applications—An Integrated Software
   Simulation Using Microsoft Works

Stocktracker—A Stock Market Software
   Simulation

Where's the Dough? Board Game

TEACH

Business Connection

At one time, top-level management at United Parcel Service (UPS) believed that on-time delivery should always be their first concern. The company clocked the time it took for elevators to open, sawed off the corners of their drivers' van seats so that drivers could hit the pavement faster, and worked out how long it took people to answer their doorbells. These factors all went into a schedule equation designed solely to expedite deliveries and make quotas. Surveys, however, showed that customers often had questions for drivers and felt frustrated by UPS's rigid schedule. UPS now allows drivers 30 minutes of discretionary time for answering customer questions, giving advice, and even bringing in new customers.

Develop Concepts

Organizing for Management

Have students explain in their own terms what *management* means. Build on students' definitions by explaining that *decentralization* of a business organization means that lower-level management has a greater degree of authority. In a highly centralized organization, almost all of the decisions are made by top management. In reality, no business organization is completely centralized or completely decentralized.

A successful business knows what it wants to accomplish and has a plan for meeting its goals. Such a business has some form of organization that identifies who is responsible for which tasks. Usually, a manager or managers direct and coordinate the activities of the workers and deal with any problems that arise. In this chapter, you will look at the ways businesses organize to manage for success.

ORGANIZING FOR MANAGEMENT

Any business that employs more than one person needs some type of organization that lets employees know what their jobs are and how they fit in with company goals. Businesses usually have an organization that establishes which person or group has authority over other persons or groups. These businesses often show the structure on an organizational chart. Figure 7-1 below illustrates how one company is organized.

The type of authority shown here is called line authority because the authority can be traced in a line from the top of the organization to the bottom. The organization shown on this chart is centralized. **Centralization** focuses authority in one place. In this company, that place is the president. The president has authority over the national sales manager. From there, authority fans out to the other parts of the organization. **Decentralization** is a way of organizing a business that gives authority to a number of managers. Businesses with a nation-

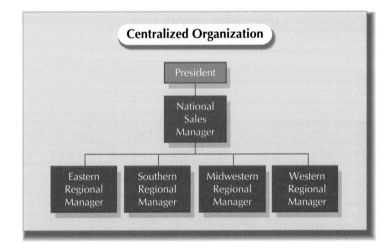

FIGURE 7-1

In a centralized organization, authority can be traced from the top of the organization to the bottom. Who oversees the regional managers in this organization?

Reteaching Strategy

After discussing the differences between centralized and decentralized management, ask students the following questions and have them give reasons for their answers: What kind of management would a car manufacturer with operations in six different countries probably have? (Decentralized. Operations managers located in different countries would have a better idea of market conditions.) What kind of management would a small town newspaper publisher probably have? (Centralized. The organization is small enough for one person to be the major decision maker.)

wide or worldwide market often prefer decentralized organization, because regional managers are more in touch with their region's market conditions. They make major decisions based on what is happening in their market.

Formal Structure

Formal organizations are usually departmentalized. **Departmentalization** is a way of organizing a company that involves subdividing resources and responsibilities to a specific unit, or department, in an organization. The manager has the responsibility for coordinating the department's assigned resources. Figure 7-2 below shows how one computer manufacturer is organized. Notice the three ways (function, product, geographic location) in which the departments are organized.

Informal Structure

Smaller businesses may be organized in a less formal way. Companies that are organized informally usually have a flexible structure. People in this kind of business do not always do the same kind of work.

For example, three partners own a company. They make training videotapes for other businesses. Sometimes one partner works on a project alone. At other times that partner may work as a cameraperson or a writer for one of the other partner's projects. On large projects, the three partners may divide up the work and hire outside people to help. In each case, all

FIGURE 7-2

Departmentalization is a method of organizing a business in which resources and responsibilities are subdivided into specific units, or departments. What four departments make up this computer manufacturer?

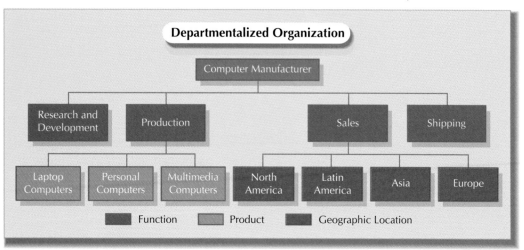

Departmentalized Organization

Computer Manufacturer

Research and Development — Production — Sales — Shipping

Laptop Computers — Personal Computers — Multimedia Computers — North America — Latin America — Asia — Europe

■ Function   ■ Product   ■ Geographic Location

CHAPTER 7

USE VISUALS
Have students compare Figures 7-1 and 7-2. Have them describe the differences between the two ways of organizing. Emphasize that in a departmentalized organization, resources and responsibilities are assigned to specific units, or departments. For example, departments in a hospital could include radiology, critical care, food service, billing, and housekeeping.
Answer to caption for Figure 7-1: National sales manager.
Answer to caption for Figure 7-2: Research and Development, Production, Sales, Shipping.

USE TRANSPARENCIES
Use Teaching Transparency 7-1 and its corresponding strategies and worksheet from the *Teaching Transparency Strategies and Worksheets* booklet to illustrate the structure of a departmentalized organization. Verify student worksheets using the Answer Key.

Cooperative Learning   Co-op Co-op

Tell groups of six to suppose that they are a small company that produces humorous greeting cards. Have them decide what functions their company will perform, perhaps taking into account the talents and interests of individual team members. Encourage them to decide whether their company will be structured formally or informally. Have each team make a chart showing how they organized their company. Teams can present their results to each other.

Refer to the *Cooperative Learning Strategies* booklet for additional cooperative learning strategies.

Discuss

Ask students to describe Urban Miyares' motivations for starting the Disabled Businesspersons Association. What kind of help does his organization provide for businesspeople with disabilities? Discuss with students the ways in which Urban Miyares demonstrates leadership and managerial skills.

Urban Miyares—Disabled Businesspersons Association

With the words "The only one who'll hire me is me" Urban Miyares decided to start his own business. He had recently returned from the Vietnam War and found himself limited to such jobs as loading eggs on trucks. The problem was that Miyares was disabled. He had developed diabetes in Vietnam, and it had left him with kidney disease, deteriorating vision, and loss of feeling in his legs. Nobody would give him a job in which he could use his talents and make a living.

In 1971, Miyares began his entrepreneurial career by starting a small construction company. He enjoyed that business so much that he started others: a hardware company, a real estate business, a public relations firm, and a restaurant.

Then in 1984, Miyares suffered a setback that almost destroyed his spirit. He became totally blind. Over the next six months, he hardly ever left his house. Admission to a rehabilitation center coaxed him back to productive life. There he learned daily living skills to cope with his blindness. He even mastered downhill skiing, eventually becoming the world's best blind skier.

With his confidence restored, Miyares was eager to get back to business. But "the more I searched for resources and assistance to benefit a blind businessperson, the more I couldn't find any," says Miyares. "What

three partners meet weekly to make plans for current and future projects.

Regardless of the structure, however, all forms of business organization depend on good managers within the business.

Quick Check

1. Name three ways to formally structure a business.
2. How does *centralization* differ from *decentralization?*
3. What is *departmentalization?*

Quick Check Answers

1. By function, product, or location.
2. Centralization focuses authority in one place; decentralization gives authority to a number of managers.
3. Subdividing resources and responsibilities to specific departments.

LEVELS OF MANAGEMENT

Management is using human and material resources to accomplish a business's goals. Most businesses have three basic levels of managers:

- Top-level managers
- Middle-level managers
- First-line managers

Develop Concepts

Levels of Management

Point out to students that, for the most part, a company's first-line managers are not primarily concerned with long-term goals. Emphasize that, as a result of the specialization of planning tasks within management, other higher-level managers deal with developing and planning a company's long-term goals.

Reteaching Strategy

To help students differentiate between the kinds of goals levels of managers make, give them the following example. Top management of BossMan Pet Supplies has a goal of making a 5 percent net profit this year. The manager of the pet food division (a middle manager) may set a goal of increasing sales of BossCat cat food by 15 percent and lowering the personnel costs of the division.

Have students discuss what the first-line managers might have to do to carry out these decisions.

I got a lot of was 'sorry' and 'blind people can't do that.'" However, in the midst of his frustration, a former colleague asked Miyares to join him in founding

Nuvenco Group, Inc., a firm that manages new products in the marketplace and does consulting. The enterprise flourished. Miyares was an entrepreneur again, using optical scanners and talking computers to help him "read" materials for his work.

Miyares never forgot the trouble he had trying to return to a business career after he became blind. After giving other disabled veterans free business advice for a number of years, he founded the Disabled Businesspersons Association (DBA). This nonprofit charity helps all "disabled entrepreneurs and professionals maximize their potential in the business world." DBA helped start about 500 businesses by providing members with free expert advice. In return, DBA asks members to become mentors for others, following Miyares's example. As an entrepreneur who guides other entrepreneurs, he proves that disabilities are no barrier to the enterprising spirit.

Follow Through

One of the most important aspects of Urban Miyares' Disabled Businesspersons Association is his mentoring program in which members act as mentors and give advice and encouragement to others who have disabilities. Ask students what kind of problems disabled people might encounter when trying to start up a business. How might a mentoring program help them?

The men and women with the greatest responsibility for planning, organizing, directing, controlling, and evaluating a company's resources are the **top-level managers.** Titles in this group include president, vice president, and chief executive officer (CEO). They think far into the company's future and set the goals and objectives of the company. Top-level managers make up a relatively small group of managers.

Those who carry out the decisions of top-level management are known as **middle-level managers.** Middle management job titles include plant manager, operations manager, and department head. If you took a job in middle management, you would serve as the link with first-line managers. That is, you would take the long-range goals of top-level managers and turn them into short-range goals first-line managers could achieve.

Those who directly assign work duties and oversee workers on the job are **first-line managers.** Some common job titles include supervisor, foreman, and office manager. Your first job in management will probably be as a supervisor. You may have to train a new employee to take on your previous job responsibilities. You may have to oversee a small group of workers who do not have as much experience as you have.

GLOBAL VIEW

Top-level managers at Motorola have adopted a new motivational technique for their workers in Penang, Malaysia. Employees participate in the "I Recommend" program. They receive bonuses and other rewards for their cost-saving ideas. Motorola has found that the program increases employees' sense of importance to the company. The success of the program in Malaysia prompted Motorola to begin a similar program in the United States.

Learning Activity

Have students discuss the following questions: Is a baseball team an informal or a formal structure? (Possible answer: Formal—players usually play the same position in each game.) A fund-raising committee? (Possible answer: Informal—committee members' roles can change, and members will probably take part in different aspects of the fund-raising.) A symphony orchestra? (Extremely formal—musicians always play the same instrument; the orchestra is arranged by section [function]).

CHAPTER 7 BUILDING A BUSINESS ORGANIZATION **109**

Enrichment Strategy

The Americans with Disabilities Act (ADA) of 1990 requires employers to provide accommodations for present and future employees with physical or other disabilities. In addition to installing braille keyboards for the visually impaired, telephones with visual readouts for the hearing impaired, and ramps for wheelchair users, management consultants stress the importance of training all managers to be sensitive and receptive to the needs of employees with disabilities. Encourage interested students to research the impact the ADA has had on businesses and on the employment rate of disabled Americans. Have them share their findings with the class.

Quick Check Answers

1. The process of reaching goals through the use of human and material resources.
2. Top-level, middle-level, and first-line.
3. First-line managers.

Develop Concepts

Management Functions

Focus students' attention on the varied duties of managerial staff by making a chart on the board with the four headings: Planning, Organizing, Leading, and Controlling. Ask students to fill in the chart with examples of each function as they work through the chapter.

USE VISUALS

Have students use Figure 7-3 to describe how the four management functions are interrelated.
Answer to caption: Organizing.

USE TRANSPARENCIES

Use Teaching Transparency 7-2 and its corresponding strategies and worksheet from the *Teaching Transparency Strategies and Worksheets* booklet to reinforce the concept of the four management functions. Verify student worksheets using the Answer Key.

Quick Check

1. Define *management*.
2. What are three levels of management?
3. Which managers work most closely with other workers?

MANAGEMENT FUNCTIONS

How do good managers help a company achieve its goals? Managers at all three levels carry out four types of functions.

- Planning
- Organizing
- Leading
- Controlling

Look at Figure 7-3 below, which shows how these four management functions are related. All these management functions involve making decisions—some fairly routine, some difficult and risky.

FIGURE 7-3

Managers carry out four different functions. Which function involves coordinating resources?

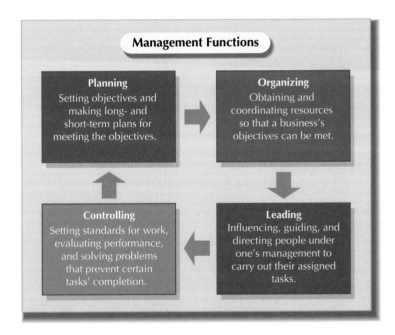

Making Connections — Time Management

Michiko Owada, a manager at Rossville Telecommunications, arrives on a Wednesday morning at 8:00 and writes up the following "to do" list.
- Get figures and statistics from Accounting so budget can be finished. Due Friday!
- Start planning script for presentation in two weeks.
- Job interview at 11:00—review candidate's qualifications beforehand.
- Check 45 pieces of E-mail; answer most pressing ones.
- Sift through 60 resumes and set up two interviews for next week.

Give students Michiko's list and have them rank the tasks according to priority. They should explain why they set the priorities as they did.

Planning

A business must set objectives and make plans for meeting them. Good planning involves setting a realistic goal, which should be written down. The plan for meeting that goal spells out the basic steps to be followed. At the same time, the plan is flexible and allows for change. The plan indicates long-term and short-term strategies for using company resources to meet the goal.

Suppose a company that produces accessories has decided that it should expand. As a long-term goal, the firm decides to produce clothing as well. Many short-term goals will have to be accomplished to successfully reach the long-term goal. The firm will need to study the market to discover the current trends in clothing. If it plans to sell clothing to a worldwide market, it will need to evaluate circumstances in various countries' markets. Then the company will have to develop a marketing strategy to introduce the new line of clothing to the people who already buy the company's products. The firm's management will determine what resources are needed to accomplish these goals.

Organizing

Organizing involves coordinating activities and obtaining and coordinating resources so that a business's objectives can be met. To do this, the manager breaks down the organization's plans into tasks to be performed. Then the manager decides what resources are needed to perform these tasks.

If the resources are available in the company, then the manager makes sure they are applied to the task when they are needed. If the resources are not available, the manager finds out where the resources can be obtained.

Leading

Leading involves influencing, teaching, guiding, and directing people to carry out their assigned tasks to meet the goals that have been set. When most people think of managing, they think of directing employees. Managing, however, is more than directing. Good managers understand and like people. In today's work world, managers need to deal creatively with a diverse workforce. Often managers communicate with employees in several countries. Good managers do not view workers just in terms of what they can produce or what problems they might cause. They recognize each person's potential within the organization and act accordingly.

The increased use of computers and robots in automobile manufacturing plants has required some new management techniques. Those techniques focus more on the needs of the individual worker. For example, at General Motors' Saturn facility in Tennessee, work is done in small teams with a variety of work assignments for everyone.

Business Brief

When planning, managers need to try to project who their future customers and clients will be. Avon Products once relied heavily on door-to-door sales of cosmetics. However, management failed to anticipate the impact of the increased number of women working outside of the home. Door-to-door sales declined, and Avon management had to come up with a new plan for selling their cosmetics. Avon representatives now sell products in the workplace, which accounts for about 25 percent of the company's revenues.

Learning Activity

Have students practice the function of organizing— coordinating activities and resources—by giving them the following objective: You are in charge of demonstrating your company's new telephone system to small groups of employees. Break down the task into steps and indicate what resources you will need to get the job done. (Possible answer: Reserve a time and a meeting room for the demonstration; enlist an assistant to help; notify group members of the time, place, and nature of the demonstration; prepare and make copies of an instruction sheet to hand out.)

Curriculum Connection   Math

A budget is one of the plans a manager makes. A manager at a custom bicycle manufacturer needs to hire new employees because of an increase in orders. The budget for employees' wages each week will be $4000. Currently, four employees work 40 hours/week and earn $18/hour. New employees will be hired at $13/hour. How many employees can be hired without going over budget? ($18 × 40 = $720 × 4 = $2880 for current wages. $4000 − $2880 = $1120 for wages of new employees. $13 × 40 = $520 × 2 = $1040. Two new employees can be hired.)

For students who need to sharpen their math skills, choose among the worksheets in the *Math Skills Review* booklet.

Building Business Skills

Building Business Skills

Model

Have students think about how a football coach might use the leadership checklist to plan a winning strategy or how a drama coach might use the list to rehearse a play. For each question ask students to provide ideas of how a football or drama coach might respond. Ask: In what other situations could people benefit from using the Leadership Checklist?

TEACHING TIP

Point out to students that teaching involves all the functions of management. To illustrate the concept of classroom management, you can give students some examples of how you plan, organize, lead, and control classroom activities and assignments.

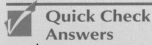

Quick Check Answers

1. Planning, organizing, leading, and controlling.
2. Leading and controlling.

EMPLOYABILITY
Exercising Leadership

Explanation

Being a manager of a business, a department, or a project team requires that you exercise leadership. That's one of the four functions of management. What exactly does it mean?

Deciding what tasks need to be accomplished in what order and by whom are all decisions that go with leadership. "People" skills are a vital part of the picture. To lead effectively, a manager must focus on people. He or she must treat each person as a valued individual, understanding the unique skills, motivations, work habits, and personalities of each. The effective manager uses this understanding to assign and direct tasks in a way that helps each employee contribute most effectively to the job.

Communication forms the link between the leader and the individuals he or she must guide. Exercising leadership means constantly communicating: informing workers of goals and assignments; explaining new procedures and policies; guiding people as they work; evaluating performance clearly and fairly; and encouraging employees to do their best. Leadership communication also involves inviting and actively listening to the ideas, suggestions, and even complaints of other members.

Controlling

Managers assign job responsibilities as part of their organizing function, based on an idea of what they can accomplish with their resources. Controlling involves setting standards for work and solving problems that prevent the completion of required tasks according to these standards. Standards could include sales quotas or project goals. Controlling also involves evaluating or monitoring the activities and procedures employees use in reaching these goals. Managers are expected to review the way workers do their jobs. When they review employees, managers may offer suggestions for improvement or may work with employees to set new goals. Often salary increases are based on such reviews.

Quick Check

1. What are the four functions of management?
2. Which two management functions are most directly involved with other workers in a business?

112   UNIT 3   DYNAMICS OF BUSINESS IN A CHANGING WORLD

Making Connections ➡ Women in Management

"The glass ceiling" is a phrase coined to describe the fact that women are seldom allowed to climb to the top of the corporate ladder. While women do hold a respectable number of lower- and middle-management positions, top management is overwhelmingly dominated by men. In the mid-1990s, only 8.7 percent of executive vice presidents were women. A *Business Week* survey of the country's 1000 largest companies found that only three companies had women chief executive officers. The usual reasons given for the existence of the glass ceiling are preconceptions and stereotypes about women's abilities. Encourage students to find articles about women managers and executives who defied the glass ceiling. Have students present their findings to the class.

LEADERSHIP CHECKLIST

1. I define the job that needs to be done.	Yes	No	5. I maintain constructive relationships with others.	Yes	No
2. I see the relationship between a project and its individual tasks.	Yes	No	6. I motivate others by example.	Yes	No
3. I account for individual differences in assigning tasks.	Yes	No	7. I focus on the situation, not the person, to resolve a conflict.	Yes	No
4. I gear my communication style to my audience.	Yes	No	8. I acknowledge the contributions of others.	Yes	No

Practice

A Leadership Checklist can help you be sure you're exercising leadership effectively. Use the checklist shown here to consider what you would need to do to demonstrate leadership skills. On a separate sheet of paper, respond to each statement as though you were leading one of your school's teams or a class group project.

Use the Leadership Checklist whenever you lead a group project in school or elsewhere. Work to make sure you can answer Yes to all the questions!

Practice

Photocopy Enrichment Master 7-1 and distribute it. Then have students think of a group activity either at school or work that they might lead. Have students respond to each statement in the Leadership Checklist. Instruct students to write a 100-word evaluation of how well they think they can exercise the skills outlined on the checklist. Have them include in the evaluation some ideas for how they might improve their leadership skills.

IS BEING A MANAGER FOR YOU?

Most managers begin their careers as company employees who are promoted after they have gained experience and have shown certain qualities.

- *Ability to perform varied activities.* Managers usually have many tasks to perform at one time. Managers have to plan their time and decide which tasks are the most important at any one time.
- *Ability to work under pressure.* A manager often has to solve many small problems in a fairly short time. For example, a supervisor may have to organize next week's work schedule, solve a production problem, and train two new employees—all in the same workday. Also included might be attending one meeting, writing seven letters, and skimming four industry publications.
- *Effective communication.* Every manager has to communicate well. Communicating might be done on the telephone, by fax or E-mail, in individual or group meetings, or in a written report or a letter. Listening is also an

Develop Concepts

Is Being a Manager for You?

Review with students each of the four management functions: planning, organizing, leading, and controlling. After the discussion, have students work in groups to draw up a plan for a fund-raising car wash for the school's future business leaders club. Groups should include specific steps to be taken for each management function. As a class discuss the feasibility of each group's plan. What improvements might the plans need?

CHAPTER 7   BUILDING A BUSINESS ORGANIZATION   **113**

Curriculum Connection   History

American industrial engineer Frederick W. Taylor developed "scientific management," in which he applied principles of motion and measurement to the functions of planning and organizing. Tasks were broken down into separate motions and timed to determine if they were essential and efficient. Taylor's "time-and-motion" studies did, in some cases, result in better efficiency, and he recommended rewarding efficient workers with higher pay. Some managers, however, applied his principles in order to set high production rates while keeping wages low. Have students research scientific management experiments of the early part of the century and report on methods used, their effect on workers, and the success of the experiments.

CHAPTER 7

Business Brief

PeopleSoft, Inc., a software company, has developed an efficient management system for its foreign operations. When the company opens a new foreign unit, it hires a local manager who is a citizen of that country. The local manager works with others to develop a business plan for the operation. Each operation has its own development, marketing, sales, accounting, training, and support functions. This kind of autonomy allows for more customized service and a quicker response to local market conditions.

Learning Activity

Have individuals or groups of students interview a friend or relative who is a manager about the advantages and disadvantages of being a manager. Students should compile the results of their interviews into a class chart showing the pros and cons of being in management positions.

Quick Check Answers

1. Ability to perform varied activities; ability to work under pressure; ability to communicate effectively; good interpersonal skills; ability to gather and use information.

2. Higher pay, respect, and prestige are some of the advantages. Disadvantages include being a target for criticism and being under more pressure than employees in nonmanagement positions.

Business & COMMUNICATION

In the past, a manager's correspondence may have been handled by an administrative assistant. Today many managers find the quickest and most efficient way of communicating with their employees and business contacts is by E-mail. With E-mail a manager's own communication and writing skills are on display. Managers need to take the time to double-check their spelling and grammar before pushing the "send" button. A piece of E-mail with misspellings will give a poor impression of that manager's abilities.

important part of communication. Most of a manager's day is spent interacting with other people.

- *Interpersonal skills.* Managers work with people and need human relations skills, or skills in dealing with people. For example, a manager may be asked to resolve conflicts among employees.
- *Ability to gather and use information.* Managers must be aware of the events and forces in the global market that affect their business. For example, some managers read local and national newspapers daily. They may also use online services to access international news relating to their company's various markets or products.

If you were offered a job with management responsibilities, would you take it? To help you decide, consider some of the advantages and disadvantages.

Advantages

Managers usually earn more money than employees in nonmanagement jobs. People become managers because they are leaders, and good leaders are respected. So, being a manager has prestige. Because managers are leaders, they have more influence than other employees on how the company is run. That is, managers have more authority than other employees do in planning, organizing, directing, controlling, and evaluating company resources. Managers have varied duties and make decisions about many kinds of things. Managers also have greater control over their time and how they will spend it.

Disadvantages

Managers get the blame when things go wrong, even if another employee caused the problem. Managers are also often targets for criticism. When managers do make mistakes, they can be more costly than other employees' mistakes because their decisions affect many workers. Managers get a lot of pressure to do things right the first time. Finally, some managers feel their relationship with lower-level employees is different from their relationship with fellow managers. Employees are often careful of what they say or do when their manager is around for fear of jeopardizing their jobs.

Quick Check

1. What are five qualities or skills a manager should have?
2. What are the advantages/disadvantages of being a manager?

114 UNIT 3 DYNAMICS OF BUSINESS IN A CHANGING WORLD

Global Perspective

Since World War II, Japanese managers have focused on improving the quality of products by identifying and solving problems in each phase of production. One tool Japanese managers have developed is a cause-and-effect diagram, in which they identify a problem and list all of the probable causes of that problem. Invite students to create their own cause-and-effect diagrams. Have them identify a problem, for example, failure to complete an assignment on time. They should list all possible causes and think of one or more ways to eliminate each cause of the problem. Have them identify possible solutions, select the best solution, and evaluate the solution.

Refer to the *International Business Strategies* booklet for additional strategies and activities.

Chapter 7 **Summary**

Main Ideas

1. Businesses may be organized by function, by product, or by geographic location.
2. The three levels of management are top-level managers, middle-level managers, and first-line managers.
3. The four functions of management are planning, organizing, leading, and controlling.
4. Successful managers are able to perform varied tasks, perform under pressure, communicate effectively, relate to people, and grasp and use information.
5. Managers have prestige, influence, and power; however, they usually have a lot of pressure, too.
6. Successful managers need to exercise leadership skills.
7. Despite his disability, Urban Miyares achieved success as an entrepreneur and helped other disabled entrepreneurs maximize their potential in the business world.

CASE ANALYSIS Management

Today is Betty Barnett's first day as Plant Manager at Logan Plastics. She is the company's first plant manager. The owner, Jake Logan, decided that the company had gotten too big for him to manage by himself. "I want everyone here at 8:00 A.M. sharp," Ed said when he told Betty about her promotion. "Those machines should be up and humming by 8:05. I'd also like you to watch the breaks and lunch hours. We have a big year ahead of us, and the plant has to run at top efficiency. I'm counting on you to whip the company back into shape." Betty will be in charge of five employees. Two of them were just hired, and the other three have been there almost as long as Betty. If you were Betty, how would you let the five employees you have to manage know what is required of them now that you are the new plant manager?

QUICK QUIZ

1. What are three ways in which departments of a formal business might be structured? (By product, by function, or by location.)
2. Name three levels of management. (Top level, middle level, and first line.)
3. What four functions do managers perform? (Planning, organizing, leading, and controlling.)
4. What management function involves coordinating resources so that a business can meet its objectives? (Organizing.)

Chapter 7 **Review**

CHAPTER 7 REVIEW

APPLY

Answers

Use the Language of Business
1. centralized, 2. decentralized, 3. departmentalized, 4. management, 5. Top-level managers, 6. Middle-level managers, 7. First-line managers.

Review What You Learned
1. It can be traced in a line from the top of an organization to the bottom.
2. Lower-level managers.
3. By function, by product, or by geographic location.
4. It involves influencing, teaching, guiding, and directing employees to fulfill company goals.
5. They need to know about the events and forces that affect their businesses.
6. Higher pay, respect, prestige, and power.
7. They set the goals and objectives for the company; plan, organize, direct, control, and evaluate a company's resources; and guide lower-level managers.
8. Getting blamed when things go wrong, being criticized, working under pressure, and having to establish different relationships with different levels of employees.
9. People.
10. To give free expert advice to disabled persons wishing to become entrepreneurs and self-employed professionals.

Understand Business Concepts
1. In a formal organization, it's very clear how each part of the business should function. In an informal organization, the structure is flexible; people don't always do the same work.
2. Good management involves deciding how to reach short-term and long-term goals and how to work with the people and other resources they have.
3. Because they interact with people all day.

Use the Language of Business

When discussing management and how businesses are organized, it is helpful to know the following terms. Copy the paragraphs below on a separate sheet of paper and fill in each blank with the term that best completes the sentence.

centralized	middle-level managers
decentralized	first-line managers
departmentalized	top-level managers
management	

Many formal organizations are _____ so that the authority is focused in one place. In _____ organizations, authority is given to a number of managers. Formal organizations are also usually _____, or organized so that resources are subdivided to a specific department. Some businesses are organized less formally; their authority and organization are usually more flexible.

Both types of business organizations use _____ to reach their goals. There are three basic levels of managers in all organizations. _____ set the goals and objectives of the company. _____ carry out the decisions of top managers. _____ assign work duties and oversee workers.

Review What You Learned

1. What is line authority and how does it look on an organizational chart?
2. Who has the decision-making authority in a decentralized organization?
3. Describe the three different ways in which departments are organized.
4. Describe the function of leading and how it affects a manager's job.
5. Describe the type of information managers need to know.
6. List the advantages of having a job as a manager.
7. What are the primary responsibilities of top-level managers?
8. List the disadvantages of having a job as a manager.
9. What must a business leader focus on to lead effectively?
10. Why did Urban Miyares found the Disabled Businesspersons Association?

Understand Business Concepts

1. What are some of the differences between a business that has a formal organization and one that is informally organized?
2. Explain the importance of good management to a business.
3. Why do managers need to communicate well?
4. Describe the management function of organizing.
5. How do the responsibilities of middle-level managers differ from those of first-line managers?
6. Why do managers have to be able to perform a variety of tasks?
7. Why do business leaders need to have good "people" skills?
8. Which management function do you think Urban Miyares used most often?

4. Organizing involves obtaining and coordinating resources so that a business can meet its objectives. The manager breaks down the organization's plans into tasks that are to be performed.
5. Middle-level managers link levels of management and take long-range goals and turn them into programs. First-line managers directly oversee employees and make sure they carry out middle-level management programs.
6. They usually have many tasks to complete at once and must decide how to complete them.
7. Because interacting with people is basic to helping employees contribute effectively.
8. Answers may vary. Like managers, entrepreneurs such as Urban Miyares must set goals, work with people, and make plans that work toward achieving goals.

Chapter 7 **Review**

Think Critically

1. **Explain.** In which type of business structure would you be more likely to gain a variety of work experiences?

2. **Analyze.** Would you choose to work in a formally or informally organized business? Why?

Use What You Learned

1. **Group Project.** Work with a partner and imagine that one of you is a manager and the other an employee. Choose two business situations that a manager must be able to deal with. Each of you should take the role of manager in one of the situations you chose. After you have acted out the situations, discuss the skills you used. Draw up a list of the management responsibilities and skills that you and your partner think are important for handling the situations you examined.

2. Draw an organizational chart of the administration of your school. Explain what type of organization it has.

3. Top-level managers make major decisions and establish company objectives. For example, top-level managers at Coca-Cola decided to introduce a "new Coke" with a slightly different recipe. It was a disaster. Consumers did not like it. So top management made another decision and brought back the original, calling it "Coca-Cola Classic." Find and bring to class newspaper or magazine articles concerning other similar top-management decisions. In a short paragraph, summarize the management decision and its effect(s) on the company.

4. **Skill Reinforcement.** Interview a manager from a local business to find out how he or she uses leadership skills to manage people and resources on the job. Use the Leadership Checklist on page 113 as a guide. Also ask the manager to determine what percentage of his or her time is spent on each of the four functions of management. Then, using the information you have obtained, write a 250-word report.

5. **Computer Application.** Use the information you obtained from the Skill Reinforcement project to create a pie graph demonstrating the percentage breakdown of the four management functions for the manager you interviewed. Title the graph and include the company name, product, and manager's title. Also, carefully label the sections of the graph. Write a short caption for the graph explaining the percentage breakdown. Print out the finished product.

Save your work in your Business Portfolio.

Think Critically

1. Answers will vary, but students should explain that informal structures usually give workers the opportunity to perform a greater variety of tasks.
2. Answers will vary depending on students' analysis of formal and informal structures.

Independent Practice

Use the Chapter 7 worksheets in *Student Activity Guide 1* for additional practice and application activities. A Teacher's Annotated Edition provides answers.

ASSESS

Portfolio Assessment

The portfolio projects are designed to lead students to develop a collection of their best work to submit to you for assessment. Refer students to the specific rubric(s) from the *Alternative Assessment Strategies* booklet listed with each of the project notes below. These rubrics will alert students to the criteria you will use to assess their projects.

Chapter Assessment

Use the Chapter 7 Test from the *Test Masters* booklet to evaluate students' understanding of the chapter concepts. An answer key is provided. Or create your own customized test using the *Testmaker* software.

Use What You Learned

1. Make sure both partners get a chance to play each role. Rubric: Note Taking.
2. If your school is very large, make a school handbook or directory available to students. Rubric: Charts and Tables.
3. Remind students that both small and large companies have top-level management. They may bring in articles about decisions made by the management of smaller local businesses. Rubric(s): Bulletin Board; Oral Presentation.

4. Students' answers will vary, but should reflect that they have a specific group project in mind. The comment on the first statement, for example, should be the definition of the job to be done. Rubric: Essay.
5. Students may want to use markers or crayons to color code the sections of their graphs. Rubric: Graph.

FOCUS

Introduce the Chapter

Major Concepts
- The Employment Process
- Training and Developing Employees
- Human Resources Managers

Introduce the Topic
Point out that in Chapter 8 students will learn about the aspects of employment from the human resource manager's point of view, learning what factors are important in managing a diverse workforce.

Use Business Terms
Have students look at the Business Terms and note which are familiar to them. Ask them to define these terms or try to recall the contexts in which they were used. For those terms that are totally unfamiliar, have students venture a meaning. Reinforce correct definitions. For terms that they cannot define, advise students to note the definitions in the chapter.

USE VISUALS

Ask how this photograph might represent the chapter. (Managers need to hire individuals with the education, skills, and aptitude to perform the tasks required.) Indicate to students that human resource managers must be sensitive to the feelings and needs of others. Ask: How do you think this characteristic can benefit a business? (Answers will vary.)

CHAPTER 8

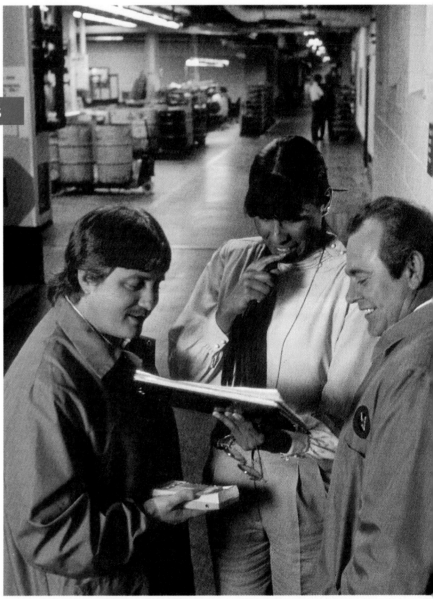

Business terms

job description
hiring from within
application
resume
orientation
on-the-job training
job rotation
performance appraisal
promotion
transfer
layoff
termination

118

CHAPTER 8 RESOURCES

Instructional Resources

Lesson Plan for Chapter 8
Teaching Transparency 8-1
Strategies and Worksheets for Teaching Transparency 8-1
Enrichment Master 8-1
Student Activity Guide 1–TAE for Chapter 8

Test Master for Chapter 8
Alternative Assessment Strategies
Math Skills Review
International Business Strategies
Cooperative Learning Strategies
Communication Skills Review
Ethics in Business Strategies

Managing a Diverse Workforce

Learning objectives

After completing this chapter, you will be able to:
- Describe the steps in the employment process.
- List the leadership traits of effective human resources managers.
- Compare the advantages of using different types of communication in managing a workforce.
- Describe virtual reality and explain how it can be used to train certain types of workers.

Consider what you know

- Managers at all levels have four basic functions: planning, organizing, leading, and controlling. Their skills include the ability to communicate effectively and relate to people.

Consider what you want to know

- What are a manager's responsibilities after hiring a new employee?
- How does a manager build good working relationships with employees?
- How can you choose the appropriate form of communication in business?
- In what ways can virtual training help educate employees?

Consider how to use what you learn

- As you read this chapter, think what it would be like to manage a diverse group of employees. One of the most important resources of any business is the people who work there. The way that these human resources are managed affects many different aspects of a business.

CHAPTER 8 MANAGING A DIVERSE WORKFORCE **119**

TEACH

Business Connection

Computers, specifically data banks, have emerged as a useful hiring tool for companies too small to maintain a personnel or human resources department. Resumes, read by optical scanners, are stored in a data bank. Software retrieves appropriate resumes according to job description. Prospective employers can then review the complete resume of the most promising candidates.

Develop Concepts

The Employment Process

Indicate to students that managers must do some groundwork before they hang out the "Help Wanted" sign. Point out that effective human resource managers

- assess the job requirements,
- budget labor costs,
- recruit employees,
- select employees, and
- orient employees.

Ask students to indicate which of these steps they feel is most important. Have them give reasons for their choice.

In this chapter, you will learn about the employment process—how companies find and hire new employees. You will also examine how companies train and motivate employees, as well as how they evaluate employees. Finally, you will discover the main characteristics of successful human resource managers.

THE EMPLOYMENT PROCESS

At one time, factories in the United States recruited employees by putting up a sign outside the gates and choosing among the potential workers who appeared at the gate. Company managers often enforced work standards in a harsh way. Workers who questioned procedures were usually considered uncooperative and were fired.

Businesses recognize how important human resources management is. They know that the best way to improve operations is to take special care when hiring and training workers. In addition, businesses know that a business's success is often determined by its employees. Employees who are well trained, motivated, and satisfied will help their company succeed.

Two other things have changed today's workplace and made the job of managers even more challenging. Today's workforce is much more diverse than ever. Women and minority groups now play a far greater role in business than in years past. And also, many of today's businesses are global, with offices all over the world. Managers who are sent overseas to work in offices and industries in another country must be well qualified to meet this challenge.

Assessing Job Requirements

Human resource managers need to analyze the jobs in a company before they can choose the right people to do these jobs. This analysis includes all the pertinent information about each job. After analyzing what a job involves, a manager writes a **job description.** A job description lists the duties and responsibilities of a job. A job description may also include the education, skills, and characteristics a person needs to do the job. When managers have a job description to look at, they know what to look for in potential employees. Figure 8-1 on page 121 shows a typical job description.

Cooperative Learning Numbered Heads Together

Organize the class into small groups and ask each group to imagine that it plans to start a business. Have the groups identify the kind of business and list the number of employees they think the business might need, the number of hours each employee would have to work, and what education and skills each employee would need to have.

Refer to the *Cooperative Learning Strategies* booklet for additional cooperative learning strategies.

SAMPLE JOB DESCRIPTION

Position: Shipping Clerk
Department: Shipping and Receiving
Location: "C" Building Warehouse

Job Summary
Under general supervision of warehouse manager, processes shipments to customers in accordance with shipment authorization forms forwarded by the sales department. Together with other clerks and packers, removes goods from shelves by hand or by powered equipment and packs them in containers for shipment by truck, rail, air, or parcel post. Prepares and processes appropriate paperwork and maintains related files.

Education
High school graduate.

Experience
None required.

Duties Performed
1. The following represent 70 percent of working time:
   a. Removing stock from shelves and racks and packing into proper shipping containers.
   b. Weighing and labeling cartons for shipment by carrier designated on the shipping order.
   c. Assisting in loading carriers.
2. The following represent 15 percent of working time:
   a. Preparing and/or processing authorization forms including packing lists, shipping orders, and bills of lading.
   b. Maintaining shipment records by tally sheets or data entry.
   c. Doing miscellaneous typing of forms and labels.
   d. Maintaining appropriate files.
3. The following represent the balance of working time:
   a. Driving company truck to post office or for an occasional local delivery.
   b. Assisting in taking inventory.
   c. Acting as checker for other shipping or receiving clerks.
   d. Keeping workplace clean and orderly.

Supervision Received
Except for general instructions and special problems, works mostly on his or her own.

Relationships
Works in close contact with packers, materials handlers, and other clerks. Has contact with truck drivers when loading. Has occasional contact with order department personnel.

Equipment
Operates mechanized stockpicker, powered conveyor belts, carton sealing machinery, and data entry computer.

Working Conditions
Clean, well-lit, and heated. Requires normal standing, walking, climbing, and lifting. Subject to drafts when shipping doors are open.

FIGURE 8-1

When employers want to hire new employees, the first step is to prepare a job description. What task will take most of this employee's time?

USE VISUALS

Direct students' attention to the Sample Job Description given in Figure 8-1. Ask students how they might use this job description to determine whether they would be well suited for the position of shipping clerk. Answer to caption: 70 percent will be packing stock in shipping containers, weighing and labeling containers, and loading carriers.

Learning Activity

Have students match the items mentioned in the section on Assessing Job Requirements (page 120) with the information provided in the sample job description. Ask students to point to items listed on the description that were not mentioned in the text. (Title, Summary, Working Conditions.) Have students speculate on why these categories were included in the job description.

TEACHING TIP

Ask students to discuss why managers consider the cost of items such as health insurance, life insurance, and child care when they budget labor costs. What effect do these items have on the cost of labor? (They increase its cost.)

Budgeting Labor Costs

Once a manager knows the skills that the job requires, the next step is to calculate the labor costs of the new employee. Wages are only one consideration. The prospective wage is based on many things, including the wage range that is usually offered for this particular position. Other costs also need to be considered. In addition to the wage, company-paid benefits for the employee may include such things as health insurance, life insurance, and child care. In addition, the manager must

Curriculum Connection   Communication

Have students work in groups of four to develop a job description for the position of Business Student. Suggest they follow the sample Job Description shown in Figure 8-1 above. Have teams share their descriptions with another team, asking for comments and suggestions on improving the description. Allow teams to revise and change their initial job description as they wish.

For those students who need to sharpen their written communication skills, choose among the worksheets in the *Communication Skills Review* booklet.

Discuss

Have students write a question that requires one of the following terms—*virtual reality, head-mounted display,* or *data glove*—as an answer. Ask volunteers to share their questions with the class, calling on other volunteers to supply the answers.

Learning Activity

Explain that recruiting employees for jobs is so important that many human resources departments have an employee whose job title is "recruiter." Ask students to bring in examples of job advertisements for recruiters, executive recruiters, or recruitment officers. Have students discuss what each ad tells about a recruiter's job.

Business Brief

Surveys of recruiters from more than 50 companies indicated that the most important skills for management personnel were interpersonal and communication skills.

TEACHING TIP

Ask students to list the advantages associated with hiring a current employee for a vacant position. (Individual knows the company, the company knows the individual's habits and abilities.)

Virtual Training

What do airline pilots, high-school chemistry students, and surgeons have in common? Each can take advantage of the computer's ability to provide an environment for training and practice.

One of the earliest kinds of virtual training was the computer-run flight simulator. The flight simulators allowed pilots the opportunity to learn how to fly aircraft without using the actual aircraft. These devices include a room containing the airplane's cockpit controls as well as a video screen that shows pilots the results of their actions. What's more, the entire room is movable, its motion controlled by a computer so that the pilot can feel the results of pulling out of a spin or rolling to the left.

Schools use computer-based science labs to train and educate students. For example, students can conduct science experiments, complete with mistakes, from the safety of a computer keyboard. A menu selection process allows students to choose which chemicals to combine, in what amounts. No danger of explosion or breaking glass here!

However, it's virtual reality that has captured everyone's attention. *Virtual reality* relies on the computer's ability to recreate physical places and phenomena that seem real to people. A computer, along with specially designed hardware and software, creates the feeling of being inside a computer-generated space or place. This illusionary world uses the body's senses of sight, sound, motion, and touch to simulate real objects or places.

Rather than watching events on a screen, the user views them from inside a head-mounted display, usually

consider the costs of training the new employee to do the job and the money and time lost until the new employee is operating at a productive level.

Recruiting Employees

When there are job openings in a company, the human resources personnel recruit candidates to fill the jobs. Suppose a manager is looking for someone to fill a job opening in the company's accounting department. The manager might begin the search by looking at the individuals who already work for the company and are qualified for the position. This is called **hiring from within.** There are advantages to hiring a current employee. That person is familiar with company operations, and the manager knows the person's work habits and abilities.

It is not always possible to find the right person within the company. In such an instance, the human resources manager might go to other sources:

- Vocational-technical schools, colleges, universities
- Advertisements in newspapers or in trade and professional publications

Meeting Student Diversity

Restating may be difficult for students with language problems. They often have trouble finding synonyms for words in the text and respond with a rearrangement of the words that are given in the text. Explain that the point of restating the text is to use similar language rather than having the restatement sound just like the textbook. Emphasize to students that the directive "Describe *in your own words*" requires the reader to state the idea in his or her own words.

encased in a helmet. Inside the helmet, two miniature television screens show slightly different images to each eye. This arrangement mimics human sight and allows the viewer to see in three dimensions. A *data glove*

replaces the keyboard as an input device. The data glove records the movements of the user's hand and relays them to the computer. The information is processed and relayed to the headset. As a result, the user can "reach into" the three-dimensional scene.

Like the flight simulator before it, virtual reality can assist in pilot training, allowing individuals to learn how to maneuver costly military aircraft without risking lives or equipment. Advancements in the sensitivity of the data glove allow medical schools to train surgeons to practice delicate medical operations without real patients. Business management, particularly human resources and employee development, is exploring the use of virtual reality as a workforce training tool ensuring that in the future more virtual training applications will be developed.

Follow Through

Ask a volunteer to write a single term or concept relating to virtual training on the board. Ask another volunteer to add a term or concept to form the beginning of a word web or diagram that represents the components or uses of virtual training. Continue calling on volunteers until the class is satisfied with the diagram. Suggest that students may want to copy the diagram to use as a study aid.

For additional information about current technology, refer to the *Technology Resources Guide*.

- Former employees or part-time employees
- Drop-in applicants
- Private or state employment agencies
- Labor or professional organizations

Human resources managers explore many sources for prospective employees. After they decide which sources may yield a potential candidate for the job, they must then decide how to select the best candidates. As they select their candidates, they must keep federal and state requirements in mind. Equal opportunity laws state that it is against the law to discriminate against possible candidates because of their sex, age, race, or ethnic background.

Selecting Employees

Selection involves choosing the person for the job who is the best qualified and the most likely to succeed. Certain population trends are changing the characteristics of the pool of applicants. For instance, the workforce is getting older. Because of lower birth rates in the country, fewer young people will be joining the workforce. Employers may be forced to hire older

Business & HISTORY

In the past most employees worked at only one or two different companies during their lifetimes. People just didn't switch jobs very often. As a result, employees felt secure and were loyal to their companies. Today the average employee changes jobs every three to seven years. As a result, managers have to work hard to gain employee loyalty.

Learning Activity

Ask students to speculate on what disadvantages might accompany hiring from within. (Workers may not accept a former coworker as manager, new methods and procedures may be more difficult to implement.) Suggest that students discuss ways managers might avoid each of the disadvantages listed.

Global Perspective

Cross-cultural training is becoming increasingly important to today's managers. When doing business with individuals from other countries, managers must respect cultural differences and be careful not to offend clients or employees, which could jeopardize business activities. Have students research some specifics about cross-cultural training, using business periodicals from the library. Suggest that they present their findings as part of a cross-cultural bulletin board.

Refer to the *International Business Strategies* booklet for additional strategies and activities.

CHAPTER 8

workers and may have to adjust company procedures and policies accordingly. For example, older workers may require flexible work schedules, more say in company management, and adequate retirement plans. Figure 8-2 on page 125 shows how much change in the age of the workforce may occur.

In the past, more men than women were in the workplace, but that has changed, too. Figure 8-3 on page 125 shows that, in the future, more women will be entering the workforce than men. This increase will affect how companies do business. It may become more difficult to transfer a worker to another part of the country or another part of the world. Workers may be unwilling to sacrifice family needs to work overtime. Child care also will become a critical issue.

As Figure 8-4 on page 125 shows, a growing percentage of the U.S. workforce is composed of members from diverse cultural and ethnic backgrounds. Such workers bring with them a wide range of skills, varying attitudes toward the workplace, and a variety of customs and traditions that can affect their work behavior. Managers will have to find ways to effectively communicate with this diverse workforce as well as facilitate cooperation and harmony among all employees.

Because the pool of prospective workers is so diverse, human resources managers want to obtain as much information as possible about a person's skills, knowledge, and attitudes. Hiring someone who is overqualified for a job is usually as unwise as hiring someone who is underqualified. In most companies, the selection process involves a number of activities which may include taking an application, reviewing a resume, conducting an interview, and testing skills and aptitudes.

Application An **application** for employment is a form that all people who are interested in working for a company must complete. Most applications ask for information about three basic areas:

- Personal information: the applicant's name, address, and telephone number.
- Education, training, and work history.
- References: the names of individuals who can give information about the applicant's qualities and abilities.

All this information helps the human resources manager compare the job applicant with other applicants. It also helps the manager see how the applicant organizes and presents the information. Finally the manager often uses the application as a reference during an interview with the applicant.

Resume A **resume** is a detailed summary of the education, work experience, and personal information that highlights an

Cooperative Learning Teammates Consulting

Have students work in groups to collect applications from local businesses. Suggest they try to gather applications from large fast-food corporations, local banks, and nationwide retail stores as well as local "mom and pop" businesses. Each group should gather at least six applications. Suggest that students take note of the kinds of information requested on all applications. Using the sample applications as a base, have students develop an application for a position at school such as band leader, football coach, or school receptionist.

Refer to the *Cooperative Learning Strategies* booklet for additional cooperative learning strategies.

A Changing Workforce

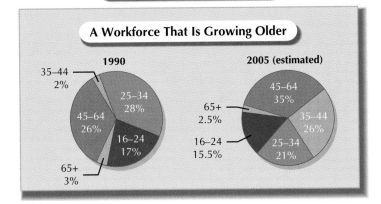

A Workforce That Is Growing Older

1990
- 35–44 2%
- 25–34 28%
- 45–64 26%
- 16–24 17%
- 65+ 3%

2005 (estimated)
- 45–64 35%
- 65+ 2.5%
- 35–44 26%
- 16–24 15.5%
- 25–34 21%

FIGURE 8-2

If you compare the workforce in 1990 and 2005, you can see that there will be more older people as time passes. What age group will grow the most?

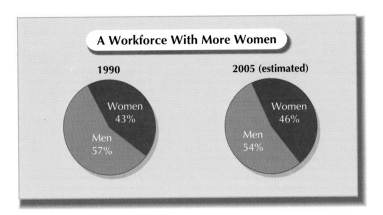

A Workforce With More Women

1990
- Women 43%
- Men 57%

2005 (estimated)
- Women 46%
- Men 54%

FIGURE 8-3

This graph shows that by 2005 there will be a higher percentage of women in the workforce than in 1990. What's the difference between the percentages for men and women in 1990? In 2005?

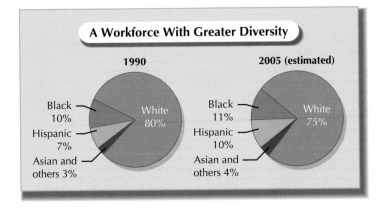

A Workforce With Greater Diversity

1990
- Black 10%
- Hispanic 7%
- Asian and others 3%
- White 80%

2005 (estimated)
- Black 11%
- Hispanic 10%
- Asian and others 4%
- White 75%

FIGURE 8-4

Between 1990 and 2005 the U.S. workforce will become more diverse. Which group will grow the fastest?

CHAPTER 8   MANAGING A DIVERSE WORKFORCE   **125**

Figure 8-2.
Remind students that the title of the figure, "A Workforce That Is Growing Older," gives them a clue to the information in the graphs. Indicate that they can use the title to predict how the graph for 2005 will be different from the graph for 1990.
Answer to caption: 45–64.

Figure 8-3.
Ask students what the title "A Workforce With More Women" tells them about the graphs in the figure. (The second graph will show that there are more women in the workforce.)
Answer to caption: 14 in 1990; 8 in 2005.

Figure 8-4.
Point out to students that this pair of graphs, like the graphs in Figure 8-2 and Figure 8-3, represents the distribution in the workforce. Ask students to indicate which individuals are represented in these graphs. (Individuals with jobs.) Then ask students to identify groups of individuals that are not represented in these graphs. (Nonworking individuals, such as retired people and children.)
Answer to caption: Hispanic.

Curriculum Connection   Mathematics

Have students compare the 1990 and 2005 data shown in Figures 8-2 and 8-4 above in bar graph form. Suggest that they create a bar graph for each pair of circle graphs. Possible graphs are shown here.

For students who need to sharpen their math skills, choose among the worksheets in the *Math Skills Review* booklet.

Growing Older

■ 1990
■ 2005

Greater Diversity

Building Business Skills

Communication

Choosing Appropriate Forms of Business Communication

Explanation

One of the key elements of effective business communication is choosing a form appropriate to each situation. In some cases, the best form of communication will be spoken. In other situations, only a written form will do the job. Sometimes more than one form is needed.

Face-to-face meetings allow you to interact with people, not only noting and responding to words, but also nonverbal cues. In matters related to individual performance, face-to-face communication is effective and shows concern.

A telephone call is ideal for simple one-on-one communications and making initial contacts. Because details of a telephone call can be easily forgotten, however, a written follow-up such as a letter or a memo is often required. The telephone generally wouldn't be appropriate for conducting an interview with a job applicant or firing an employee.

Detailed descriptions, explanations, requests, and instructions should be communicated in writing to avoid error and provide a lasting record. The most common forms are letters to people outside the company, and applicant's qualifications for the job. Like an application, a resume includes personal information, such as name, address, and telephone number. But the resume also provides detailed information about work history, personal traits, and skills that does not appear on an application. For instance, on an application you may list the name of a place where you worked, but on a resume you would detail your job responsibilities there. The main purpose of a resume is to highlight a person's qualifications. The resume is a very personal document and is designed to showcase a person's skills. A resume helps the human resources manager get a better idea of the applicant's skills and work experience and, like the application, can be useful in the interview. Submitting a resume may also make a favorable impression upon a prospective employer, because the applicant has gone a step beyond filling out an application.

Interview An *interview* is a face-to-face meeting between a job applicant and someone from the company. During the interview, the manager can learn much about a person's attitudes, experience, interests, and desire to succeed. The manager tries to put the applicant at ease so that the applicant feels free to ask and answer questions of concern. If the interview is favorable,

Making Connections   Technology in Business

Technology is offering businesses new ways to take applications and process resumes. Telephone application systems allow potential applicants to respond to initial screening questions using a touchtone phone. In another interactive system, job seekers register their resumes in a *New York Times* data base. When they find a help-wanted ad they wish to answer, they contact the *Times* and authorize their resume to be sent to the prospective employer. Have students research other technology-based ways in which businesses can receive and process applications and resumes.

For additional information about current technology, refer to the *Technology Resource Guide.*

FORMS OF COMMUNICATION

- Use **face-to-face** communication for:
  1. Planning projects with your department.
  2. Explaining new policies.*
  3. Individual performance evaluations.*
- Use **telephone calls** for:
  1. Placing an order for supplies.*
  2. Clarifying details in a letter you received.
  3. Asking a coworker for information.

- Use **memos** for:
  1. Telling your department of a meeting.
  2. Describing project schedule changes.
  3. Outlining a new company policy.
- Use **letters** for:
  1. Explaining goods or services to customers.
  2. Informing a job applicant of a hiring decision.
  3. Requesting information from a possible supplier.

*Written follow-up suggested or required.

memos or notices to company employees. Other forms of written communication include job descriptions and notices, outlines of company benefits, instructions for operating machines, and emergency procedures, to name a very small sample.

Practice

For each form of communication, choose one of the listed examples and explain why you think the form is appropriate for it.

the manager may then check the applicant's references before making a final decision.

Testing   Some companies also use *tests* as part of their selection process. The most common type of testing is a job-skills test. This test may measure such things as mechanical aptitude or computer skills. Some companies also require psychological testing and drug testing. Managers use the results of these tests, along with all the other information they have gathered about potential employees, to make their selections.

Orienting Employees

Once new employees are selected and hired, they need to know many things about the company and the job. **Orientation** is the process of helping new employees learn about and adjust to their new company. For instance, new employees need an explanation of what they are to do; an introduction to the employees they will work with; and a review of the conditions of employment, method of pay, deductions, and work, lunch, and break schedules.

Making Connections ▸▷◂   Business Ethics

The federal government has banned the use of lie detector tests as a screening device for most employment situations. As a substitute for these tests, many businesses employ psychological exams. These tests attempt to predict an individual's tendency to steal by matching their test results with those of known thieves. Questions may be obvious—"How often do you tell the truth?" or obscure—"How often do you make your bed?" Ask students to discuss whether they feel this type of testing is appropriate in a business environment.

Refer to the *Ethics in Business Strategies* booklet for additional strategies.

Apply

Remind students that businesses have far more situations that call for communication than those listed here. Invite them to suggest other situations that require clear communication and determine what form of communication—face to face, telephone call, memo, or letter—is most appropriate. Answers will vary but should reflect both the explanation and students' common sense. Students who need additional practice will benefit from the listening activities in the *Communication Skills Review* booklet.

Business Brief

The Americans with Disabilities Act (ADA) prohibits pre-job-offer medical testing or questions about medical conditions. Employers may ask only if the applicant can perform the functions of the job. In addition, the ADA prohibits employers from checking whether the applicant has previously received workers' compensation.

USE VISUALS

Distribute copies of Enrichment Master 8-1, Job Skills Testing. Ask students what kinds of job skills are represented by the sample questions. Have students suggest jobs in which these skills would be required.

Quick Check Answers

1. A full listing of the duties and responsibilities of a job.
2. Personal, education, training, and work history.
3. Details that highlight the applicant's job qualifications.
4. It helps new employees learn about and adjust to their new job.

Develop Concepts

Training and Developing Employees

Point out to students that once an applicant is hired, he or she will likely need some time to learn about the position and its responsibilities. It is in the employer's best interest to make certain that this time is as short as possible. For this reason, many employers offer their employees on-the-job-training. In addition, employers evaluate an individual's performance in order to ensure that the employee is fully productive in the new position.

Business Brief

Motorola Corporation, a manufacturer of cellular phones, computer chips, and other electronic items, has built one of the country's most ambitious job-training programs. The company spends about 4 percent of its payroll for training, well above the industry average of 1 percent. In 1995, the company will deliver a minimum of 40 hours of training to each of its 132,000 employees.

Some companies leave orientation up to the employee's supervisor. Other companies have orientation sessions that are supplemented with written materials, such as an employee manual or handbook.

Quick Check

1. What is a *job description*?
2. What information is included in an *application*?
3. What information is included in a *resume* that is not included in an application?
4. What is the purpose of *orientation*?

TRAINING AND DEVELOPING EMPLOYEES

Whether or not new employees have had prior work experience, they generally receive some type of training. This training may be designed to improve job performance, develop employees for new responsibilities, reduce accidents and inefficient procedures, or teach employees to use new equipment. Also, during orientation managers must remember that the cultural backgrounds of new workers may be different from theirs. For instance, perhaps the new employees use English only as a second language. Managers then have to be sure that the new workers understand information correctly and can effectively communicate with other workers.

If an American company has an office or a division in a foreign country, managers must be sensitive to that country's culture if training is to succeed. In Peru, for example, the culture stresses obedience to authority. In one instance, when a U.S. manager asked workers for their opinions and input about how things were going, the workers quit. They thought the manager didn't know what he was doing! It was his job to tell them, not their job to tell him.

Women make up a significant percentage of the workforce in countries around the world. Here are some examples:

Japan	40%
South Africa	40%
Germany	42%
China	44%
Russia	49%
Mexico	64%

Training

Training employees while they work is known as **on-the-job training.** This method is the most often used and most practical training technique in business. A manager or designated employee explains the steps and demonstrates the job. Then trainees perform the job. They get feedback from the supervisor on their performance and make adjustments as necessary.

Curriculum Connection   Communication

Have students work in groups of four to plan, write, and illustrate a student handbook for first-year students at their school. Suggest that groups decide what information a new student would need about the physical layout of the school (bathrooms, drinking fountains, stairways); behavior expectations (dress code, class attendance); and other useful information (sports teams, extracurricular activities). Allow groups to post their completed handbooks on the bulletin board.

In some businesses, particularly in small businesses, employees must know how to do several jobs. Then, if one employee is absent, another can fill in. To make sure that employees have this flexibility, managers use **job rotation.** Employees move from job to job—or rotate—for several hours, days, or weeks at a time until they learn the various tasks. Job rotation also helps prevent boredom and boosts morale because an employee has a variety of work experiences. Job rotation also helps managers make more effective use of the company's human resources.

Instead of training employees on an individual basis, some managers set up group training sessions. One advantage of this technique is that employees can express their ideas and share their experiences while listening and learning from others. For example, a manager may hold a group training session in order to discuss new products, a special sale, or a change in company policies.

Evaluating Performance

Even after employees are trained and working productively, the manager's job continues. An important responsibility of all managers is to monitor and evaluate employees' performance on a regular basis. Managers do this through evaluation procedures known as **performance appraisals.** Managers gather information about how employees are doing their jobs and then communicate this information to them. During performance appraisals, employees also evaluate their own progress and set

Business Brief

Rohm & Haas, the developer of Plexiglas, practices job rotation at a plant in Connecticut. Workers are cross-trained and work as self-managers. Machinists work on loading docks when needed, and line personnel inspect finished products during peak periods.

Learning Activity
Have students compare their performance appraisals, grades, and parent-teacher conferences with job performance appraisals. Ask students to explain how their grades are similar to a performance appraisal and how the two kinds of evaluation are different.

USE VISUALS

Emphasize to students that during a performance appraisal, supervisors use criteria such as how well employees follow directions and how well they follow tasks through to completion.
Answer to caption: Managers make decisions regarding changes in an employee's assignment. For example, a favorable evaluation often is followed by a raise in salary or wages.

One aspect of a performance appraisal involves the manager evaluating how well employees follow directions and carry through assigned tasks. How does this information directly affect the employee being evaluated?

Global Perspective

Nearly half the computer industry's revenue is generated from markets outside the United States. As a result, individuals who can compete in the international market are in demand. To meet this demand, many hardware and software companies have appointed managers and executives born or trained outside the United States. Ask students to discuss what advantages the companies gain by appointing such individuals to positions in the international market.

Refer to the *International Business Strategies* booklet for additional strategies and activities.

CHAPTER 8

TEACHING TIP

Ask students to draw or illustrate the relationship that exists between the education, training, and experience that might be needed for promotion to a higher-paying job. Then have them indicate how authority and responsibility are related to promotions.

Learning Activity

Have students browse through the business section of local newspapers looking for reports of layoffs and downsizing. Have students record their findings, listing the company, whether it is service- or goods-producing, and the reason given for the layoffs. Invite students to pool their findings. Have them decide what, if any, trends they can find in the reports.

Quick Check Answers

1. Training people while they work; employees move from job to job to learn various tasks.
2. The manager discusses how an employee is doing his or her job; the employee evaluates his or her own progress and discusses long-term goals.
3. Transfer.
4. Workers are asked to leave their jobs temporarily.

goals. Managers use performance appraisals to make decisions on assignment changes such as transfers, wage increases, promotions, layoffs, and terminations.

Sometimes evaluating performance isn't as easy as it sounds, especially in international companies, where culture can affect work behavior. For example, managers usually require that except for specific breaks, workers spend their time on the job working. One American manager in Pakistan had to learn that several times a day all workers would stop work to pray. This was a basic part of their Muslim culture. The manager had to allow for this cultural difference when evaluating each worker's performance.

Promotions   An employee who receives a **promotion** moves to a new job that usually involves more responsibility, higher pay, and more authority. Promotions may be awarded as part of the performance appraisal system in a company. Promoting employees tells them that good work is noticed and rewarded.

Transfers   A **transfer** moves an employee from one job to another within a company. Or a transferred employee may move to a new location. When employees are transferred, they usually work at the same level, for the same salary, and have the same amount of responsibility. Transfers often occur because the company's needs change.

Separations   When a company asks a worker to leave temporarily, the employee has gone through a **layoff.** Such temporary separations result from business slowdowns due to reduced sales, plant conversions, or factory relocations. When conditions improve, workers who have been laid off may be asked to come back to their former jobs. If conditions fail to improve, the layoff may become permanent.

A permanent separation from a company is called a **termination.** A worker may be fired because of excessive lateness or absence, dishonesty, repeated violations of work rules, or poor work performance. Occasionally employees are terminated because of staff reductions or mergers among companies. Some workers voluntarily leave an organization. They may have a job offer at an increased salary; they may want to live in another part of the country; or they may want more challenging work.

Quick Check
1. What is *on-the-job training? Job rotation?*
2. In a *performance appraisal,* what do the manager and the employee do?

130   Unit 3   Dynamics of Business in a Changing World

Cooperative Learning Send-a-Question

Encourage students to work in teams of four. Have each team generate five questions about *job rotation, performance appraisals, promotion, transfer, layoff, termination.* Once the questions are complete, have each team send their questions to another team. Direct the second team to answer each of the questions they receive. Finally, have teams pass the questions, along with their answers, to a third team to evaluate the questions and answers, choosing the best three. Suggest the class pool the best questions to use as study aids.

Refer to the *Cooperative Learning Strategies* booklet for additional cooperative learning strategies.

3. If an employee's job changes but there is no change in the responsibilities, authority, or salary, has the employee had a *transfer* or a *promotion*?
4. What is a *layoff*?

HUMAN RESOURCES MANAGERS

We can look at managing human resources in two ways. In a narrow sense, such management refers to a single department in a company. In a broader sense, human resources management involves the entire company. Even though a human resources department exists in many companies, all managers are involved in the process of selecting, training, and developing workers, evaluating their performance, and motivating them to work as efficiently as possible. When dealing with people, managers need special characteristics to perform their functions as human resources managers. Read through the following list of traits and see if you have any of the characteristics managers need to have.

- *Adaptability.* A manager has to deal with many types of people in many situations. Successful managers are able to adapt their approach as the situation requires.
- *Human relations skills.* Managers who are skilled in human relations are sensitive to the needs and feelings of other people. These managers will respect those needs and feelings and respond to them.
- *Emotional and social maturity.* Good managers can accept their own feelings and control their own behavior. They are able to work with many types of people, some of whom they may not like.
- *Insight.* A good manager should be able to analyze a complicated situation and see relationships, causes, effects, and solutions.
- *Self-motivation.* Good managers do not depend on someone else to motivate them. They have a great determination to work hard and succeed in what they are doing.

Did you find any traits that apply to you? If so, you might be interested in a job in human resources. Of course, you would be unable to step right into the job of human resources manager. But, with good office skills and some experience, you could be part of the human resources team of a company. Many human resources managers began their careers as office support staff or administrative assistants, moved on to become interviewers or office managers, and finally moved into the top spot as

Develop Concepts

Human Resources Managers

Emphasize that at one time or another the actions of the human resources manager affect all other employees in a company. Point out that there are particular skills and character traits that can help an individual be a successful human resources manager.

Learning Activity
Suggest that students scan the Help Wanted section of the local newspapers, paying particular attention to the listings under Human Resources Management. Have students summarize the job titles, descriptions, and qualifications for the jobs listed.

TEACHING TIP

Ask students to generate a list of the qualities that would make an individual a good manager of people. Have a volunteer record the list on the board. Ask students to identify ways in which they could acquire the qualities and skills on the list.

Curriculum Connection   Communication

Have students select one of the characteristics or attributes of human resource managers. Then have them write a newspaper story with headlines and illustrations describing the characteristic and noting its significance for success as a human resources manager.

USE TRANSPARENCIES

Use Teaching Transparency 8-1 and its corresponding strategies and worksheet from the *Teaching Transparency Strategies and Worksheets* booklet to show students the five basic needs that motivate people, as determined by psychologist Abraham Maslow. Verify student worksheets using the Answer Key.

Learning Activity

Ask students to describe the best leader they ever worked with, such as a teacher, coach, or boss. Have them list the traits or personality characteristics of the individual. Then have students discuss how the list of managers' traits applies to this individual.

Quick Check Answers

1. The ability to deal with many types of people.
2. Human relations skills, emotional and social maturity, insight, and self-motivation.

FIGURE 8-5

Maslow believed that five basic needs motivated people and could be arranged in stairstep fashion from lower needs. What needs would have to be fulfilled before self-actualization could begin?

SELF-ACTUALIZATION:
The need to fully realize one's potential, to be the best person one is capable of being, and to do work that is really suited to one's skills and interests.

ESTEEM:
The need for self-respect and for the esteem and respect of others and the desire for recognition as a skilled and useful human being.

BELONGING AND LOVE:
The need to be truly accepted by one's peers, the desire to be liked and loved, and the desire to give love and affection to others.

SAFETY:
The need to be safe from physical danger and to be assured of emotional security.

BASIC NEEDS:
The need for satisfying bodily functions, such as needs for food and drink, shelter, warmth, and rest.

manager or director of the entire department. Some of these jobs do require additional education and training.

• Employees are encouraged to contribute ideas. All employees should have the opportunity to discuss their ideas and bring up problems.

Part of a manager's job is to motivate workers, getting them to do their jobs to the best of their abilities. To motivate people, you must know their needs. Psychologist Abraham Maslow discovered that people have five different levels of needs. These needs are shown in Figure 8-5 above. Maslow believed that lower-level needs had to be satisfied before upper-level needs could be addressed. Understanding Maslow's theories can help managers motivate their employees, because having a job can be the basis of meeting all five levels of need.

Quick Check

1. What is meant by adaptability?
2. Besides adaptability, name four other characteristics a good manager needs.

Reteaching Strategy

Have students write a one-page summary of what they have learned in the chapter that will be helpful to a person thinking about working in the area of human resources management. As guidance, write the following issues on the board and ask students to focus their summaries on any three. Call on volunteers to present and discuss their summaries.

• assessing job requirements
• budgeting labor costs
• recruiting employees
• reviewing applications and resumes

• selecting employees
• designing on-the-job training
• conducting performance reviews

Chapter 8 **Summary**

Main Ideas

1. The steps in the employment process include assessment of job requirements, selection of employees, and orientation.
2. Employment policies must follow federal and state laws regarding equal employment opportunities.
3. Managers train new employees through such techniques as on-the-job training, job rotation, or group training sessions.
4. Managers check and evaluate employees' performance through performance appraisals.
5. Effective managers have leadership traits such as adaptability, human relations skills, emotional and social maturity, insight, and self-motivation.
6. Virtual reality uses computers to simulate the way things look, sound, and feel. It can be used to train people in certain kinds of skills.
7. Choosing the appropriate form of oral or written communication is very important for human resources managers.

CASE ANALYSIS — Management

Paige Engle heads the human resources department at Goldman Enterprises. She has to give Tom Schumann his performance appraisal. Paige has been very pleased with Tom's work. However, because of the financial situation of the company, she can afford to give Tom only a small raise. Paige wants to praise Tom and keep him highly motivated despite the small raise she is able to give him. How can Paige handle this situation?

CLOSE

Main Ideas

Main Ideas summarizes the key information in the chapter. It is a useful tool for reinforcement and review.

CASE ANALYSIS

Case Analysis provides a chapter-related case for student analysis and application of decision-making skills.

Answer
Possible answers: Paige can emphasize the quality of Tom's work and tell him that it is appreciated. She can also emphasize that the small raise is a reflection of the current business situation, not Tom's work. She might also consider promoting Tom to a more prestigious (but not higher-paying) position or recommending him for additional training programs to increase his job skills.

QUICK QUIZ

1. How can managers encourage communication? (By letting employees know what is expected of them, telling employees how they are doing, encouraging employees to contribute ideas, and sponsoring cross-cultural training sessions.)
2. How can managers foster cooperation in a diverse workforce? (By understanding how people react to and influence other people.)
3. When might a layoff occur? (When demand for a company's products or services goes down and the company has to reduce production.)
4. What did Abraham Maslow discover about people and their motivations? (People have five different levels of needs. Lower-level needs must be satisfied before upper-level needs can be fulfilled.)

Chapter 8 **Review**

CHAPTER 8 REVIEW

APPLY

Answers

Use the Language of Business

1. job description; **2.** orientation; **3.** termination; **4.** performance appraisal; **5.** hiring from within; **6.** application; **7.** promotion; **8.** on-the-job training; **9.** layoff; **10.** transfer; **11.** resume; **12.** job rotation

Review What You Learned

1. Recruiting and selecting potential employees, orienting and training workers, and providing leadership in hiring practices.
2. Adaptability, human relations skills, emotional and social maturity, insight, and self-motivation.
3. It prevents boredom, boosts morale, and gives employees more skills.
4. Assessing job requirements, budgeting labor costs, recruiting and selecting employees, and orienting employees.
5. Excessive tardiness or absence, poor work performance, repeated failure to follow work rules, and dishonesty.
6. They need to learn about and adjust to the company.
7. The amount of detail and protection from errors.
8. A computer-driven re-creation of physical places and phenomena that people think are real.

Understand Business Concepts

1. Possible choices: within the company, schools, colleges, and universities; advertisements; former or part-time employees; drop-in applicants; employment agencies; labor or professional organizations.
2. To motivate employees.

Use the Language of Business

Understanding these business terms will help you communicate more easily with others. On a separate sheet of paper, rewrite the following sentences. Fill in each blank with the term that best completes the sentence.

application	orientation
hiring from within	performance appraisal
job description	promotion
job rotation	resume
layoff	termination
on-the-job training	transfer

1. A(n) _____ lists the duties and responsibilities of a job.
2. _____ is the process of helping new employees learn about and adjust to the company.
3. When a person is fired or leaves a company voluntarily, it is called a(n) _____ .
4. A(n) _____ is a manager's evaluation of an employee's performance.
5. _____ takes place when a manager hires someone who is already working for the company.
6. People who are interested in working for a company usually must fill out a(n) _____ .
7. Employees who receive a(n) _____ are given a new position with added responsibilities.
8. _____ occurs when employees are trained at work.
9. During a(n) _____ , workers are asked to leave a company temporarily.
10. An employee who receives a(n) _____ is moved from one job to another within the company, sometimes at a different location.
11. Employers may request a copy of your _____ , a document that provides a summary of your work history and skills.
12. With _____ , employees move from job to job to learn several different jobs.

Review What You Learned

1. What are the responsibilities of a human resources manager?
2. List five leadership traits that human resources managers should have.
3. How can job rotation help employees?
4. What are the steps in the employment process?
5. For what reasons may an employee be terminated?
6. Why is orientation important for new employees?
7. What are two advantages of using written communication instead of telephone communication?
8. What is *virtual reality?*

Understand Business Concepts

1. List four places a human resources manager could go to find potential job applicants.
2. Why do effective managers need to have human relations skills?

3. A current employee is familiar with company operations, and the manager already knows about the person's work habits and abilities.
4. Take an application; review a resume; interview the applicant; test the applicant.
5. So that they can deal successfully with many different types of people in many situations.
6. In person, because then the manager can observe facial expressions and other nonverbal communication.
7. Flying airplanes, constructing or designing buildings, and so on.

Think Critically

1. Answers will vary. Possible responses: They might get recommendations from those employees or invite a part-time employee to fill a full-time job vacancy.
2. Answers will vary. Students may say some needs are simpler than others and must be satisfied before the more complex ones can be fulfilled. Others may feel that the lack of basic needs is a powerful incentive to fulfill higher needs. For instance, the need for basic security can make someone strive to do the best possible work on the job, which will then satisfy esteem needs.

3. What are two advantages of hiring from within?
4. List the four steps generally involved in hiring an employee.
5. Why should managers be adaptable?

6. Would it be better for a manager to interview a job applicant by phone or in person? Why?
7. What are some ways in which virtual reality can be used for training a workforce?

Think Critically

1. **Analyze.** How might human resources managers use former employees and part-time employees to find qualified job applicants?

2. **Enumerate.** List two questions to be asked if you were applying for a job in a fast-food restaurant.

Use What You Learned

1. **Group Project.** Today human resource managers are struggling with issues such as drug use on the job, theft in the workplace, and sexual harassment. Work in teams to choose one such topic. Research the topic in the library and, if possible, interview local business managers about the ways they deal with the issue. Choose sides on the issues and present a classroom debate.
2. **Computer Application.** Select a job, research its requirements, and write a job description of it. Then write a want ad for the job for the newspaper. Use word processing software to attractively format both items and print out the results.
3. **Skill Reinforcement.** In each situation below, decide if the person used an appropriate form of communication. If the person did not, write a paragraph explaining what the person should have done differently and why. Then select

one of the situations and provide an example of appropriate communication for it. If you choose a spoken form, present your example as a written dialogue or script.

(a) *John telephones a clothing store owner describing his company's new line of leather belts. The store owner seems very interested, and John thinks he will call with an order. John never hears from him again.*

(b) *When Joan started working in the company inputting data, she worked faster and more accurately than average. Over the last month, she's frequently been late to work, and her work is not as good as it was. Her supervisor sends her a memo pointing out these problems and threatening to fire her if she doesn't improve.*

Save your work in your Business Portfolio.

Use the Chapter 8 worksheets in *Student Activity Guide 1* for additional practice and application activities. *Student Activity Guide 1* provides vocabulary exercises, reading comprehension checks, problems, projects, and simulations of business and economic situations. A Teacher's Annotated Edition provides answers.

ASSESS

Portfolio Assessment

The portfolio projects are designed to lead students to develop a collection of their best work to submit to you for assessment. You and your students should decide which projects will be included in their respective Business Portfolios. Refer students to the specific rubric(s) from the *Alternative Assessment Strategies* booklet listed with each of the project notes below. These rubrics will alert students to the criteria you will use to assess their projects.

Chapter Assessment

Use the Chapter 8 Test from the *Test Masters* booklet to evaluate students' understanding of the chapter concepts. An answer key is provided. Or create your own customized test using the *Testmaker* software.

Use What You Learned

1. Remind students that current business periodicals may provide the best research sources. Rubrics: Note Taking, Oral Presentation.
2. Students with no access to a computer may complete the project manually on a typewriter or in handwritten form.

3. Possible answers:
(a) After the phone call John should have written a follow-up letter with details about belts, prices, and ordering to the store owner. Students' letters will vary.
(b) The supervisor should have discussed Joan's work problems face-to-face to try to help her improve. Students' dialogs will vary.

FOCUS

Introduce the Chapter

Major Concepts
- Accounting in Business
- Financial Statements
- The Role of the Financial Manager
- Who Works in Accounting and Finance?

Introduce the Topic
Ask students what kinds of items they think might be needed to manage business finances. Allow them to list their ideas. Indicate to students that as they read Chapter 9, they will learn what part accounting plays in business finances.

Use Business Terms
Have students briefly study the list of Business Terms and conjure up mental images of what the terms represent. Invite volunteers to describe one or more of the images they have created. Ask members of the class to match the terms with the descriptions. Advise students to note the meanings of the terms as they read the chapter.

USE VISUALS

Have students look at the photograph and identify any tools they think are important to individuals who manage business finances. Ask what kinds of tools the individuals might be using. What kinds of information might they need? (Answers will vary.)

CHAPTER 9

Business terms

accounting

transaction

asset

liability

owner's equity

fiscal year

net income

net loss

risk

return

forecast

136

CHAPTER 9 RESOURCES

Instructional Resources

Lesson Plan for Chapter 9

Teaching Transparencies 9-1, 9-2, 9-3, 9-4, 9-5

Strategies and Worksheets for Teaching Transparencies 9-1, 9-2, 9-3, 9-4, 9-5

Enrichment Master 9-1

Student Activity Guide 1–TAE for Chapter 9

Test Master for Chapter 9

Alternative Assessment Strategies

Math Skills Review

International Business Strategies

Cooperative Learning Strategies

Communication Skills Review

Ethics in Business Strategies

Managing Business Finances

Learning objectives

After completing this chapter, you will be able to:
- Explain the accounting equation.
- Name two kinds of financial statements and describe the information each provides.
- Describe the role of the financial manager within a business.
- Discuss three main responsibilities of financial management.
- Describe the traits of accounting and finance employees.
- Explain how to use percents.
- Describe electronic spreadsheets and how businesses use them for financial analysis.

Consider what you know

- Businesses need to balance the employment needs of the company, the needs and wants of their workforce, and the costs of meeting those needs and wants as they build the business's workforce.

Consider what you want to know

- How does a businessperson keep track of a business's finances?
- How can you tell if a business is in good financial health?
- How can using percents help in your daily life?
- What are electronic spreadsheets and how do they help managers make business decisions?

Consider how to use what you learn

- As you read this chapter, think about the income opportunities and expenses involved in a business. What do businesspeople do to manage a business's finances?

CHAPTER 9 MANAGING BUSINESS FINANCES **137**

Motivate the Learning

Learning Objectives
Point out to students that the learning objectives show what they will learn in the chapter. Tell students to keep these objectives in mind as they work through the chapter. Note that the last two objectives listed refer to the Focus on Technology feature and the Building Business Skills feature.

Consider What You Know
Review briefly the main sections of *Chapter 8 Managing a Diverse Workforce:* The Employment Process; Training and Developing Employees; Human Resources Managers.

Consider What You Want to Know
Ask students to look through the chapter to get an idea of how the chapter will help them answer the questions.

Consider How To Use What You Learn
Tell students that at the end of the chapter they will develop some projects that will help them explore and apply the principles of business finance. Point out that as they read the chapter they may want to take note of how business finances can affect their lives.

Multimedia Resources

Technology Resource Guide

Distance Learning Guide

Internet Resource Guide

Professional Resources

School-to-Work/Tech Prep Strategies

Instructional Poster

Spanish Resources

Testmaker Software for Chapter 9

The Wall Street Journal Video Series Video & Activities for Chapter 9

Business and Marketing Computer Applications—An Integrated Software Simulation Using Microsoft Works

Stocktracker—A Stock Market Software Simulation

Where's the Dough? Board Game

TEACH

Develop Concepts

Accounting in Business

Emphasize the meanings of *assets*, *liability*, *capital*, and *owner's equity* by starting a chart on the board or on a transparency. Use each term as a column heading. Invite volunteers to fill in the chart with examples. Encourage students to form definitions for the terms in their own words. Visually oriented students can supply drawings or schematics that show money entering and leaving a business, using the terms to label appropriate parts of the drawing.

Strong financial management requires accurate, up-to-date information about a business's financial situation. Company managers use this information to evaluate a company's current financial health and to plan for the company's financial future. When a business needs additional money to grow or expand, financial managers need to supply accurate information to people outside the company. Lenders and investors use the detailed financial records of a company to find out whether it is on sound financial footing and is worth the risk.

In this chapter, you will examine how financial managers analyze and interpret information about their businesses. You will also find out about the decisions financial managers make concerning raising and spending a company's money.

ACCOUNTING IN BUSINESS

Even though the world's six largest accounting firms have their home offices in the United States, they employ more than 72,000 people around the world. The firms provide accounting and consulting services to United States companies engaged in joint ventures and to foreign companies wishing to sell to United States markets.

Keeping track of how a business uses its money is an important part of managing a business. Financial managers need to know how much money the business takes in every week or month and how much the business spends during the same time. Managers use this information to plan a company's future so that the company will always have enough money to meet its obligations and objectives.

Accounting provides a way of keeping tabs on the flow of money in and out of a business. **Accounting** is a system used to record, classify, summarize, and interpret the financial data of a business. These financial data are made up of the transactions that occur in the daily operation of the business. A **transaction** is any activity that has an effect on the financial situation of the business. Each sale, debt payment, or purchase the business makes is a transaction. Businesses record each of these transactions in different accounts. They use the different accounts to track what the business owns, how much money the business takes in, and how much money the business owes.

In accounting, property or any item of value owned by a business is considered an **asset.** Cash, products to sell, equipment, buildings, and land are all assets. Any amount a business owes is a **liability.** If a business buys office equipment on credit, the amount owed the equipment supplier is considered a liability. In other words, the equipment supplier has a claim against the company's assets. There is another claim against the company's assets. The company's owners have invested money and other

Global Perspective

U.S. businesses entering joint ventures with businesses in the former Soviet Union have had to deal with vast differences between U.S. and Soviet accounting standards. As the global market grows, the need for international accounting standards will increase. The International Accounting Standards Committee has been charged with the task of developing accounting standards that can be used by businesses having operations in several countries and in various types of economies. Ask students to speculate on why international accounting standards are necessary.

Refer to the *International Business Strategies* booklet for additional strategies and activities.

resources in the business. Thus, the owners have a claim against the company's assets. This claim, called **owner's equity,** is equal to the total assets of the business less the liabilities.

The relationship between a company's assets and the claims against those assets is expressed by an equation:

ASSETS	=	LIABILITIES	+	OWNER'S EQUITY

Assets always appear on the left side of the equation. Liabilities and owner's equity always appear on the right side of the equation. The two sides of the accounting equation must always balance. This is only logical since the value of the assets must equal the claims (of owners and others) against those assets. Every business transaction that takes place in the company affects this basic accounting equation.

Suppose that a company called Central Cycle Repair is starting up. Out of $12,000 of available cash, the owner spends $3,000 for tools and $4,000 for equipment. Here is how the accounting equation looks:

ASSETS		=	LIABILITIES	+	OWNER'S EQUITY	
Cash in bank	$ 5,000				Owner's claim	
Tools	3,000					
Equipment	4,000					
Total	$12,000				$ 12,000	

Suppose that the owner of Central Cycle then buys $4,000 worth of equipment from Bailey Equipment, paying $3,000 in cash and promising to pay $1,000 to Bailey in the future. Bailey Equipment now has a claim against Central Cycle's assets for $1,000. Remember, Central Cycle's owner also has a claim on the assets. After the purchase of the equipment, the accounting equation for Central Cycle looks like this:

ASSETS		=	LIABILITIES	+	OWNER'S EQUITY	
Cash in bank	$ 2,000		Bailey's claim		Owner's claim	
Tools	3,000					
Equipment	8,000					
Total	$13,000		$ 1,000		$ 12,000	

Quick Check

1. Define *accounting* and *transaction*.
2. What is the relationship between *assets* and *liabilities*?
3. What is meant by *owner's equity*?

Curriculum Connection

Math

Write each of the following math sentences on the board or on a transparency. Ask students to find the missing amount in each equation.

	Assets	=	Liabilities	+	Owner's Equity
1.	$1,000		$150		$(850)
2.	$1,143		$567		$(576)
3.	$800		$(400)		$400
4.	$(900)		$230		$670

For students who need to sharpen their math skills, choose among the worksheets in the *Math Skills Review* booklet.

Learning Activity

Reinforce the *basic accounting equation* by writing the equation ASSETS = LIABILITIES + OWNER'S EQUITY on the board or a transparency. Ask a student volunteer to rewrite the equation, substituting definitions for each of the terms in the equation. Be sure to emphasize that a creditor's claims to the business assets are called *liabilities* and that the owner's claims to those same assets are called *owner's equity.*

TEACHING TIP

Although computers handle most of today's accounting computations, accounting remains based in mathematics. The accounting equation ASSETS = LIABILITIES + OWNER'S EQUITY like any other equation, shows a balanced relationship. Ask students how the basic accounting equation is similar to other equations they have used in algebra or other math classes.

Quick Check Answers

1. System used to record, classify, summarize, and interpret financial data of a business; any activity that has an effect on the financial situation of a business.
2. Assets are property or any item of value owned by a business; liabilities are any amount a business owes.
3. Money and other resources an owner invests in a business.

FOCUS ON **Technology**

FOCUS ON **Technology**

Discuss

Point out to students that a spreadsheet is an effective method of organizing information. Remind them that class schedules and calendars are similar methods of organizing information. Encourage students to describe the terms *spreadsheets, cells,* and *what-if analysis* in their own words.

Develop Concepts

Financial Statements

Direct students' attention to Figures 9-1 and 9-2 on page 142. Explain that these are two of the financial statements, or periodic reports of a firm's financial position, on which financial managers rely.

Business Brief

For financial information to have common meaning from one corporation to another, accounting rules must be standardized and followed by all companies. Accounting organizations, such as the American Institute of Certified Public Accountants and the Financial Accounting Standards Board, contribute to the development of financial accounting standards.

Electronic Spreadsheets

Suppose you are offered two summer jobs. One job, at the corner store, pays $5.60 an hour. The second job, at the mall, pays $6.10 an hour. If you want to earn as much money as you can this summer, which job will you take?

Your choice may seem clear, but you may want to consider some of the other information about each job. What if you can walk to the corner store, and they want you to work 33 hours a week? What if you will need to drive to the mall, pay for your own gas and parking, and they want you to work no more than 30 hours a week? How will you figure out which job to take?

Businesses face questions similar to these every day. They need to quickly calculate their revenue, expenses, and net income and compare alternatives. Accountants often use electronic spreadsheets to help make these calculations. A *spreadsheet* is a computerized version of an accountant's ledger. Spreadsheet software makes the accountant's work easier by providing a visual framework in which to work and the tools to make calculating a breeze.

The spreadsheet is organized into rows and columns. Each row has a number, and each column has a letter. The intersection of a row and a column is called a *cell*. A cell's address is indicated by the column letter and row number. For example, cell B4 is in column B, row 4.

One of four types of information can go into a spreadsheet cell: labels, numbers, dates (or times), and formulas. The spreadsheet can include formulas and functions that automatically make complex calculations for the spreadsheet user. If one or more numbers on the

FINANCIAL STATEMENTS

F.Y.I.

The word *fiscal* refers to financial matters—whether those of a business or of a government. The word comes from the Latin word *fiscus,* which originally meant "basket" and later came to mean "treasury." Apparently tax collectors used a woven basket called a fiscus to hold the tax money they had collected.

A company's owners, investors, and creditors need to know whether the business is making or losing money. They want to know how the transactions made during a time period have affected the company's assets, liabilities, and owner's equity. At the end of an accounting period, a business uses its accounting records to determine its financial condition. The accounting period may be one month, 3 months, or 12 months. A 12-month accounting period is called a **fiscal year.** The federal government begins its fiscal year on October 1. Businesses may begin their fiscal year on a date other than January 1. Many begin their year on July 1.

At the close of a fiscal year, the financial staff puts together all the transactions. The staff then presents financial statements that summarize the year's financial information. There are two main kinds of financial statements: the income statement and the balance sheet.

Reteaching Strategy

Distribute Enrichment Master 9-1, Common Accounting Terms, for students to use as a tool to keep track of the accounting terms introduced in this chapter. Suggest pairs of students take turns rephrasing or explaining the terms to their partner. If students prefer, they can draw an illustration for their terms.

spreadsheet are changed, the program will recalculate all the formulas and totals. Financial managers can use electronic spreadsheets to do *what-if analysis.* By changing one or more variables, they can quickly see the finan-cial effect that results. For example, if sales increase by 10,000 units, what happens to net income?

Another capability available with most spreadsheets is graphics. Spreadsheet graphics present the information contained in the spreadsheet as either a line, bar, or circle graph. This allows managers to graphically present the numbers in the spreadsheet.

Accountants and financial managers aren't the only business professionals who use electronic spreadsheets. The marketing department might use spreadsheets to keep track of sales totals for its sales staff, to calculate commissions to the sales staff, and to forecast materials and product requirements. Marketing managers can create slide shows with graphs of past and future product sales generated by their spreadsheet software. From purchasing to payroll to manufacturing, managers use electronic spreadsheets for easy financial calculation and analysis.

Follow Through

Determine students' understanding of this technology by asking them to supply situations in which they could use a spreadsheet to accomplish a "what-if analysis."

For additional information about current technology, refer to the *Technology Resource Guide* booklet.

Income Statement

The income statement reports net income or net loss over an accounting period. If total revenue is greater than expenses, a business has a **net income.** If expenses are greater than total revenue, the business has a **net loss.** Look at the income statement for Central Cycle Repair in Figure 9-1 on page 142. The statement covers a one-month accounting period. Revenue totals $1,500; expenses total $1,000. Since revenue is greater than expenses, the business has a net income of $500. The income statement provides information concerning a company's revenue. However, it does not give a complete picture of the overall financial health of the company.

Balance Sheet

The balance sheet reports the total in the asset, liability, and owner's equity accounts on a certain date. The balance sheet provides a record of the company's assets and a summary of the claims against those assets. The balance sheet for Central Cycle,

TEACHING TIP

While income statements and balance sheets provide overviews of a business's financial transactions and health, day-to-day transactions may be recorded in a variety of ways. Provide students with an example, using Transparency Master 9-4, Petty Cash Classification. Ask students to discuss why a cashier or accountant might want to use such a form.

Business Brief

A business operating at a loss is characterized as being "in the red." This term is an outgrowth of the accounting tradition of using red ink in ledgers to indicate liabilities.

Meeting Student Diversity

Net income occurs when a business earns more (revenues) than it spends (expenses) during the accounting period. In other words, after all the expenses are paid, there is still some money left. Net income is also called a *profit. Net loss* occurs if a business spends more money than the business earns during an accounting period. Assign two or three of your more proficient students to help students who are having difficulties with these concepts. Allow students to rephrase the accounting equation and the elements in the income statement and balance sheet.

Direct students' attention to the income statement in Figure 9-1. Reinforce the concept of income by reminding students that a service business, such as a bicycle repair service, charges fees. These fees constitute Central Cycle's income.

Answer to caption: Repair fees.

Next, direct students' attention to the balance sheet in Figure 9-2. Remind students that this balance sheet is a representation of the accounting equation Assets = Liabilities + Owner's Equity.

Answer to caption: $13,000; $1000.

Use Teaching Transparencies 9-1 and 9-2 and their corresponding strategies and worksheets from the *Teaching Transparency Strategies and Worksheets* booklet to help students become familiar with income statements and balance sheets. Verify student worksheets using the Answer Key.

Some companies have found that sharing their financial statements with their employees can be a significant tool for motivating employee performance. To help employees who may find the statements difficult to understand, annotations explain the meaning of each line in the statement.

FIGURE 9-1

The income statement for a business reports the revenue and expenses for a specified period of time. What was Central Cycle's source of revenue during the month of June?

INCOME STATEMENT

Central Cycle Repair
Income Statement
For the Month Ended June 30, 19XX

Revenue:		
Repair fees		$1,500.00
Expenses:		
Advertising	$ 25.00	
Gas and oil	100.00	
Rent	800.00	
Utilities	75.00	
Total expenses		1,000.00
Net income		$ 500.00

Figure 9-2 below, shows that Central Cycle's assets total $13,000. The claims against those assets—$1,000 in liabilities and $12,000 in owner's equity—also add up to $13,000. The balance sheet shows that Central Cycle is in good financial condition. The owner has a much larger claim to the assets than the creditors do, and the company can pay its debts.

Business managers use the information in the financial statements to make decisions about the future of the business. These decisions may relate to budgets, ways to cut costs, and tax planning. Managers also give the financial statements to

FIGURE 9-2

A business's balance sheet reports the balances in the company's asset, liability, and owner's equity accounts at a specific time. What is the balance of Central Cycle's asset account? Its liability account?

BALANCE SHEET

Central Cycle Repair
Balance Sheet
June 30, 19XX

Assets			Liabilities		
Cash in Bank	$ 2,000		Accounts payable–Bailey Equipment		$ 1,000
Tools	3,000		Owner's Equity		
Equipment	8,000		Capital invested by owner		12,000
Total assets	$ 13,000		Total liabilities and owner's equity		$ 13,000

Making Connections ⟹   Everyday Life

Use Transparency Master 9-5, Personal Balance Sheet, to model for students how to complete a balance sheet. Have students list their personal assets. Next, have students list any liabilities they might have. Finally, direct students to use the accounting equation to determine their own personal equity. (Students' lists of assets might include clothing, jewelry, sports and audio equipment, and cash in savings accounts. Students' lists of liabilities might include money owed to parents or friends, a layaway, or money owed on an automobile.)

other people and organizations. Stockholders, employees, banks, investment companies, and various government agencies want to know about the financial condition of the business. They can compare the most recent statements with statements from earlier accounting periods. In this way, they can evaluate the progress of the business.

Quick Check

1. On which financial statement is net income or net loss reported?
2. On which financial statement are totals in asset, liability, and owner's equity accounts reported?

THE ROLE OF THE FINANCIAL MANAGER

Whether a business is large or small, one person is normally responsible for financial management of the business. In a small business, the owner may be the financial manager. A small- or medium-sized business may employ a bookkeeper to keep the company's accounting records. Some medium-sized businesses may employ an accountant to act as the financial manager.

In a large corporation, the financial manager may be a vice president of finance who reports directly to the president. The financial manager may have a staff or several assistants including a treasurer and a controller. The treasurer manages the firm's cash and investments. The controller, the company's chief accountant, keeps track of revenue and expenses and is responsible for the company's financial records. In a small business, one person—often the owner—may have all these duties.

Financial management involves three main responsibilities:

- Managing the use of company funds and making sure that the company can meet its financial obligations.
- Obtaining the funds needed to meet the business's financial goals.
- Creating financial plans, setting objectives, and evaluating the progress of the business.

Meeting Financial Obligations

The primary responsibility of a financial manager is to make sure the business can meet its financial obligations and payments.

CHAPTER 9 MANAGING BUSINESS FINANCES 143

Develop Concepts

The Role of the Financial Manager

Reinforce the central role the financial manager plays in both small and large companies. Remind students that businesses are evaluated on their financial growth. To grow, both large and small companies alike need funds. The financial manager is responsible for identifying sources for these funds.

Business Brief

Indicate to students that changes in the standard accounting system occur frequently. One major source of change is in the area of tax law. Whenever the U.S. Congress passes new tax legislation, the Internal Revenue Service makes related changes in the rules affecting accounting practices in an effort to ensure that businesses are adhering to the new tax code.

Curriculum Connection   Social Studies

Have students determine the titles and names of the individuals responsible for managing their home state's or city's finances. State and local governments may have both a treasurer and a controller. Suggest that students determine whether the officials are elected or appointed. Encourage students to contact the offices of these officials and request information concerning the state treasurer's and state controller's duties and responsibilities. Students can present their findings as a bulletin board display or a poster.

Learning Activity

Ask students to name a specific business that interests them. Have volunteers list on the board or a transparency expenses that business would have. For example, a retail sports shoe business might have expenses including stock (shoes, socks, gym bags), shelving, customer chairs, rent, and so on. Help students recognize that although expenses vary from one business to the next, some expenses exist for all businesses.

TEACHING TIP

Help students grasp the idea of exchanging *risk* for *return* by asking them to provide everyday examples. Prime responses by offering the following example: A base runner may risk being thrown out for the return of reaching third base. Ask students to supply other situations in which individuals trade risk for return.

In order to do this, the financial manager determines how money comes to the business and how the business uses that money.

Figure 9-3 on page 145 shows common sources and uses of funds in a typical business. The sources of funds include revenues from the sale of goods and services, profits reinvested in the business, loans and credit received from outside the business, and owner's equity—the money the owner invests in the business. Financial managers must decide the best way to use these combined funds. For example, the business needs money to operate, and a business needs money to grow in order to increase its assets. Where should the money for each of these items come from? How should any surplus funds be used? The financial manager must make these decisions.

Financial managers need funds to pay operating expenses. Operating expenses include wages and salaries of workers, cost of maintaining the machinery and equipment needed to produce goods and services, advertising, rent, electricity, and insurance. Some of these expenses are predictable, but many are not. To pay these expenses, a business needs to have enough cash reserve, or cash that is quickly available.

A business also uses its funds to expand. As you know, the resources a business owns are its assets. To grow, a business must be able to increase its assets. If a business can obtain additional funds, it can purchase additional equipment and machinery and employ additional people to produce more goods and services. In turn, these additional goods and services can generate more income.

At times a business may have excess cash that is not needed to purchase assets or pay expenses. A financial manager will want to use this excess cash to generate additional income. If the company will need the cash in the near future, the manager may temporarily put the funds into a bank account where they earn interest. Here, the funds will be quickly available. If the funds will not be needed in the immediate future, the manager may choose a longer-term, income producing instrument, such as a certificate of deposit.

Investments in stocks and bonds offer another opportunity for increasing a company's excess funds. When financial managers invest company funds, they try to balance risk with expected financial return. **Risk** is the uncertainty of gaining or losing money in an investment. **Return** is the amount of gain or loss an investment yields over a specified period. A desirable investment offers a great return for the risk involved.

Global Perspective

Have students research the future projections of an industry, such as petroleum, and find what the predicted supply/demand balance will be in the years 2000, 2010, and 2020. Have them use the questions below to guide their research and then present their findings as a two-minute Global News Feature for the TV evening news.

- How will supply change?
- Who will the major suppliers be?
- How will new technology affect supply?

- How will demand change?
- How will changes in the global economy affect the price of the product?

Refer to the *International Business Strategies* booklet for additional strategies and activities.

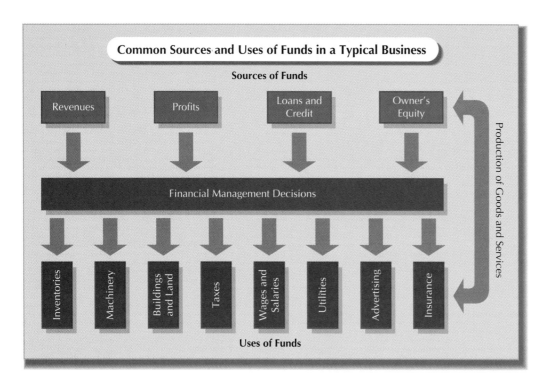

Common Sources and Uses of Funds in a Typical Business

Sources of Funds

Revenues | Profits | Loans and Credit | Owner's Equity

Financial Management Decisions

Inventories | Machinery | Buildings and Land | Taxes | Wages and Salaries | Utilities | Advertising | Insurance

Uses of Funds

Production of Goods and Services

FIGURE 9-3

Financial managers try to balance the flow of funds into and out of a company. What are some of the ways a business might use its funds?

Finding Sources of Funding

To meet all its financial obligations and continue to grow, a business must have an adequate supply of funds. As we have seen, some of these funds come from business revenues—the sale of goods and services. However, a successful company must also have other sources of funds, and the financial manager must find these sources.

Often a company can use its profits—earnings left over after all expenses and taxes have been deducted from the company's revenues—as a source of funds. This kind of financing has a major advantage: The company does not obligate itself to an outside party. Most businesses, however, do not have enough profits to use this method all of the time.

Sometimes a company borrows money to meet its financial needs. The company agrees to repay the borrowed money, plus interest, within a certain time. Financial managers borrow money from many sources, including banks, insurance companies, and investment companies. Each of these businesses makes money by providing funds to businesses that need additional sources of money. The financial manager must

Use Visuals

Direct students' attention to the four sources of funds shown in Figure 9-3. Help students see that revenues and profits are fund sources generated within the business itself, while loans, credit, and owner's equity fuel the business from outside.

Answer to caption: Funds can be used for inventory, machinery, buildings and land, taxes, wages and salaries, utilities, advertising, and insurance.

Use Transparencies

Use Teaching Transparency 9-3 and its corresponding strategies and worksheet from the *Teaching Transparency Strategies and Worksheets* booklet to help solidify student recognition of both sources and uses of funds. Verify student worksheets using the Answer Key.

Business Brief

Using borrowed money to purchase assets that are then used to make more money is called "leverage." A "leveraged buyout" is the use of borrowed money to buy a controlling interest in another firm. However, strict rules and regulations govern the use of borrowed money to purchase stocks in an effort to make money.

Making Connections ➡ Everyday Life

The need and importance of financial management and planning spreads beyond corporations, reaching even to families. Many families prepare and use a financial plan to manage family finances. Although a family's plan may not be quite as formal as a business's plan, the financial principles are the same. The plan includes a budget that identifies short-term funds and expenses. The plan also includes long-term goals, such as owning a home and paying for college education, as well as ways to meet those goals. Individuals and families with financial plans claim that the plan helps them keep their expenses under control and allows them to "plan" for "unplanned" financial emergencies.

Building Business Skills

Model

Each of the numbered Rules for Percents addresses a different type of percent problem. Be sure to model each of the sample problems, making certain students understand each step involved. If any of the problems cause the class difficulty, ask a student volunteer to use his or her own words to model those problems a second time.

TEACHING TIP

Reinforce the responsibilities of a financial manager by asking students: What kinds of information would owners want from the financial manager before contributing more funds to the business? What kinds of information might the government request?

Learning Activity

Encourage students to use a chart or diagram to identify the three ways a financial manager might secure additional funds for the business. Caution students that their chart or diagram should indicate there are three categories of funding as well as include a list of specific methods of funding. Invite volunteers to record their charts or diagrams on the board or a transparency to share with the class.

MATH

Learning About Percents

Explanation

Percents are a useful and efficient way to express the relationship between a part and a whole. They also enable us to compare parts of different whole amounts. They are particularly useful to accountants and other businesspeople. When a business borrows money to buy equipment, it needs to know what interest rate, or percent, the bank will charge.

Percent means the number of parts out of a hundred. If 67 percent of the people in a town own pets, it means that 67 out of every 100 people do. Percents can be expressed as fractions. Seven percent is the same as the fraction 7/100. Percents can also be expressed as decimals. Seven percent is the same as the decimal .07. When figuring percentages, you will usually find it easiest to work with decimals.

Practice

Review the rules and examples for working with percentages. Then try your hand at these problems.

1. Your company borrows $4500 from a bank to help purchase a copier. If the bank charges an annual rate of 9 percent to borrow money, how

be certain that the company, using the borrowed money, will be able to generate enough revenue to repay the loan with the interest.

At other times, the owners of a business may obtain additional funds without borrowing money. Selling stock in the company, looking for new investors, or having the owners contribute more of their money to the business are ways to obtain additional funds. These options allow more owners and investors to share in both the risk and return of the company.

Financial managers must decide which method of financing is best for their businesses and must evaluate their options in light of the business's overall financial plan.

Financial Planning

Financial managers are involved in creating long-range business plans for their firms. A financial plan is a document that specifies what funds are needed by a business and for what period. The plan charts incoming and outgoing funds and outlines the most appropriate uses of these funds. The financial

Curriculum Connection   Communication

Financial professionals are often called upon to state complex financial issues in a simple and straightforward manner. At times they are called to produce a "one-page memo" describing the strategy, financial health, and future outlook of a company. Suggest that pairs of students choose a multi-page business article from a recent periodical. Have the team condense the article into a one-page memo of 250 words or less. Then encourage the team to condense the article further, producing a summary of 100 words or less. Have teams exchange summaries and discuss whether the summary conveys the main idea of the article.

Students who need practice in communication skills will benefit from the activities in the *Communication Skills Review* booklet.

RULES FOR PERCENTS

1. To convert a percent to a decimal, move the decimal point two places to the left:
   25% = .25   8% = .08   175% = 1.75
2. To calculate a percentage of a total, convert the percent to a decimal. Then multiply the total by that decimal: How much is 22 percent of $150?
   a. 22% = .22   b. $150 × .22 = $33
3. To calculate the size of an amount reduced by a percent, calculate the percentage and subtract it from the amount. What is $200 reduced by 25 percent?
   a. $200 × .25 = $50   b. $200 − $50 = $150
4. To determine what percentage of a total a part is, divide the part by the total. Convert that number to a percent. (You may have to add a zero.) What percent of 34 is 17?
   a. Divide the part by the total: 17 ÷ 34 = .5
   b. Convert the decimal to a percent: .5 = 50 percent

much will you owe them at the end of the year over and above the amount you borrowed?
2. The treasurer of World Wide Windows invests $100,000 of the firm's profit in the stock market. One year later, that investment is worth $18,000 more than when it was invested. By what percentage has it increased in value?

Use your skills to figure the cost of the next thing you buy on sale for a certain percentage off.

Practice
Ask students to complete the practice activity in class. Invite them to ask questions if they have any problems understanding the steps involved in solving the sample problems. Have students who are more proficient in working percent problems work as a team with students having difficulty. Suggest each team make up and solve additional percentage problems.
(1. $4500 × .07 = $315
2. 18,000 ÷ 100,000 = .18 = 18%)

plan sets objectives for the business and finds the best ways to accomplish them. Financial managers must also determine whether the objectives are being met.

Financial planning is crucial to a business just getting started. Many businesses fail because they lack financial resources. A detailed business plan allows the owner of a new business to predict how much cash will be needed and to avoid expenses that cannot be met.

To help set objectives, financial managers use a forecast. A **forecast** is an estimate of the future business climate. A useful forecast reflects changes in business conditions in the community, the nation, and the international economy. Such a forecast also evaluates the impact of these changes on the business itself.

Quick Check
1. Define *risk, return,* and *forecast.*
2. What is the primary responsibility of a financial manager?
3. What ways can a business use to obtain additional funds?

Learning Activity
Ask students to compare and contrast weather forecasts with business *forecasts* in terms of information necessary for forecasting, uses of forecasts, and so on. Suggest that they organize their information in table or chart form.

Quick Check Answers
1. Uncertainty of gaining or losing money in an investment; amount of gain or loss an investment yields over a specified period; estimate of the future business climate.
2. To make sure a business can meet its financial obligations.
3. It can use its profits, borrow money, sell stock, look for new investors, or have the owners contribute more money.

Enrichment Strategy

Alert students to the existence of corporations whose charter defines them as a not-for-profit corporation. Often these corporations, such as the United Way or the Red Cross, provide humanitarian services. Assign more proficient students the task of researching four not-for-profit corporations. Have them focus their research on the responsibilities and duties of the financial managers in these corporations and then compare them to their counterparts in for-profit corporations. Allow students time to present their findings in a television news magazine format.

Business Brief

Because of the increasing body of knowledge that Certified Public Accountants (CPAs) must master, approximately half of the 50 states now require that all CPA candidates accumulate 150 hours of advanced education. Typically this means that accounting students will complete an additional year of education beyond the usual four years of undergraduate studies.

✓ Quick Check Answers

1. They must be able to keep errors at a minimum and to correct any errors that do occur. They must work neatly and have a strong sense of order.
2. Ability to analyze.

WHO WORKS IN ACCOUNTING AND FINANCE?

Like workers in other departments of a company, employees in accounting and finance need special characteristics and skills to get the job done. Read through the list below and see if any of these apply to you.

- *Mathematics skills.* Workers in accounting and finance deal with the financial information about a company. They need mathematics skills to process this information. If their company deals with people in other countries, workers may need to understand other currencies and accounting methods.
- *Aptitude for detail.* Accounting and finance employees have to be accurate in recording all the details of a company's financial affairs. These employees must be able to correct any errors and must work neatly and have a strong sense of order.
- *Ability to work with others.* Accounting and finance employees work with people both inside and outside the company. These employees have to be able to deal with many types of people, including those from other cultures.
- *Computer skills.* Most work in accounting and finance departments is done with the aid of computers. Employees in these departments need excellent keyboarding skills. They also need to be familiar with a variety of accounting software.
- *Ability to analyze.* Even though computers can work out the formulas in accounting, accounting and financial workers have to be able to see relationships and draw conclusions. These workers need to understand the numbers and analyze what those numbers mean to the company's financial health.

If you take a job in the accounting or finance department of a company, you might begin as a data entry clerk or an accounting clerk in payroll, inventory, or purchasing. From there you can move to other challenging positions. Accounting and finance departments generally have many kinds of positions available with varying levels of responsibility.

BUSINESS & HISTORY

The accounting system used by most United States corporations has its roots in a system proposed 500 years ago. In 1494, Luca Pacioli, a Franciscan monk working in Venice, published an accounting system designed to measure the flow of money and goods into and out of a corporation—hard assets. Today, some corporations are looking at revising or enhancing this accounting system to include a way to measure "soft assets" such as experience, wisdom, and information in a company's patents, publications, and designs.

Quick Check

1. Why is an aptitude for detail a desirable trait for workers in accounting and finance?
2. Which skill entails being able to see relationships and draw conclusions?

Meeting Student Diversity

Suggest that students interested in accounting, economics, or finance careers actively seek out programs designed to assist students with special needs. Have students find out what kinds of support services local colleges and universities offer to students interested in pursuing a business career. Have them find out who is eligible for these programs and what the programs offer. Students should find out if programs include academics, requisite college course work, or workshops on study skills, time management, and using academic resources. Have students report their findings to the class.

Chapter 9 **Summary**

Main Ideas

1. The accounting equation is: assets = liabilities + owner's equity.
2. An income statement reports a business's net income or net loss over an accounting period.
3. A balance sheet reports the totals in the company's asset, liability, and owner's equity accounts on a certain date.
4. The financial manager must see that funds are obtained and used to fulfill the company's objectives.
5. Financial management involves three main tasks: meeting financial obligations, finding sources of funding, and planning for the future.
6. Accounting and finance employees need to have mathematics skills, an aptitude for detail, the ability to work with others, mechanical coordination, and the ability to analyze.
7. Accountants and financial managers rely on electronic spreadsheets to quickly and accurately forecast the effects and implications of a business transaction.
8. Knowing how to use percents is an important skill for both business and personal situations.

CASE ANALYSIS Financial Management

Amy and Matt Rohr want to go into the restaurant business. They are considering buying Massey's Pizza, a neighborhood restaurant. A little over a year ago, Massey's began offering carry-out service and free delivery within a limited geographic area. Amy and Matt have been given Massey's financial statements for the past 12 months. What should they look for in these statements to help them make a decision about buying the restaurant?

CLOSE

Main Ideas

Main Ideas summarizes the key information in the chapter. It is a useful tool for reinforcement and review.

CASE ANALYSIS

Case Analysis provides a chapter-related case for student analysis and application of decision-making skills.

Answer
Answers will vary but could include these questions. Has income increased, remained the same, or decreased? Have liabilities increased? Has the company earned a net income? How has offering free delivery affected revenue? How has offering carry-out service affected income? Have expenses increased or decreased?

QUICK QUIZ

1. What is the accounting equation? (Assets = liabilities + owner's equity.)
2. What two financial statements give an overview of a company's financial health? (Income statement and balance sheet.)
3. If a business has spent more money than it has earned, has it incurred a net profit or a net loss? (Net loss.)
4. Why are computer skills and the ability to analyze both needed for accounting and financial careers? (Calculations and reports are done by computer and need to be interpreted by an individual.)

Chapter 9 **Review**

CHAPTER 9 REVIEW

APPLY

Answers

Use the Language of Business

1. transaction, **2.** accounting **3.** owner's equity **4.** assets **5.** liabilities **6.** return **7.** net loss **8.** risk **9.** net income **10.** forecast **11.** fiscal year

Review What You Learned

1. Assets, liabilities, and owner's equity.
2. They are created when money is borrowed from an outside source or if items are purchased with credit.
3. To obtain funds and to use them to meet the company's objectives.
4. They balance the sources and uses of a business's funds.
5. It begins on any date decided on by the business.
6. Totals in the asset, liability, and owner's equity accounts on the last day of the accounting period; net income or net loss over an accounting period.
7. Possible answer: use its profits, borrow money, sell stock, look for additional investors, or get more money from the owners.
8. It is a document that specifies what funds are needed by a business and for what period of time.
9. A computerized version of an accountant's ledger; the intersection of a row and a column on a spreadsheet.
10. 17/100; .17.

Understand Business Concepts

1. They use forecasts to help set objectives for the company.
2. Because the assets of a business are equal to the total claims against all those assets.
3. They use it to determine whether the business is making or losing money and to make decisions about the future of the business.
4. They would want to know the financial condition of the company that owes them money.

Use the Language of Business

Rewrite each sentence, filling in each blank with the term that best completes the sentence.

accounting	liabilities	return
assets	net income	risk
fiscal year	net loss	transaction
forecast	owner's equity	

1. An activity that affects the financial condition of a business is a(n) _____.
2. The system used to record, classify, summarize, and interpret the financial data of a business is _____.
3. The money and other resources an owner invests in a business is _____.
4. The _____ of a business are anything of value that a business owns.
5. The _____ of a business are anything a business owes.
6. The gain or loss that results from an investment over a specified period is the _____.
7. A business has a(n) _____ if expenses are greater than total revenue.
8. A business's uncertainty of gaining or losing is its _____.
9. A business has a(n) _____ if total revenue is greater than expenses.
10. A(n) _____, an estimate of the future business climate, reflects changes in business conditions.
11. A 12-month accounting period is a(n) _____.

Review What You Learned

1. What three elements form the accounting equation?
2. How are liabilities created?
3. What is the goal of a company's financial manager?
4. How do financial managers make sure a business is able to meet its financial obligations?
5. How can a company finance its needs?
6. When does a business's fiscal year begin?
7. What information is in a balance sheet? In an income statement?
8. What is a financial plan?
9. Define *spreadsheet* and *cell*.
10. How would you express 17 percent as a fraction? As a decimal?

Understand Business Concepts

1. Why do financial managers use forecasts?
2. Why are the two sides of the accounting equation always equal?
3. How do managers use the information in financial statements?
4. Why would creditors want to have copies of financial statements?
5. What are the main ways a business uses its funds?
6. Why is financial planning crucial to a business that is just getting started?
7. What should a financial manager do with excess cash?
8. What traits do accounting and finance employees need to have?

5. It uses funds to buy the resources it needs to create goods and services and to pay for operating expenses.
6. It can help predict how much cash will be needed and what expenses to avoid.
7. He or she should invest excess cash in a way that balances risk with return.
8. They need math skills, an aptitude for detail, an ability to work with others, computer skills, and the ability to analyze.
9. They make calculations faster and easier and they provide a visual framework in which to work.
10. You earned $2040.

Think Critically

1. Possible answer: No, the owner would have no idea how much money was coming in or going out.
2. Students should suggest that the financial manager's most important task is to make sure the company can meet its financial obligations.
3. Students may mention math or computer skills, analytical abilities, or being detail oriented.

9. Why are electronic spreadsheets so valuable to businesspeople?
10. You earn $200 each week, and during a special sale your boss paid you a two percent commission for selling more than your quota. How much did you earn that week?

Think Critically

1. **Analyze.** Do you think a business could operate without financial management? Why or why not?
2. **Evaluate.** What do you think is the most important task of the financial manager? Give reasons for your answer.
3. **Assess.** What traits do you have that could make you a successful finance or accounting employee?

Use What You Learned

1. **Group Project.** Work in teams to find and review the annual reports of different companies. In each report, find the following information:

   - The value of the corporation's assets.
   - The value of its liabilities.
   - The value of the owner's equity.
   - Add liabilities and owner's equity. Do they equal the assets?

   Evaluate the financial condition of your team's company and tell whether or not you would be willing to invest in the company. Be sure to give reasons for your decision. Write a group report of about 250 words.

2. **Skill Reinforcement.** Accountants often compare two elements from the same year's financial results and state the relationship as a percentage or ratio. One such comparison is the debt-to-total-assets ratio. This ratio is calculated by dividing total liabilities by total assets. Generally the amount of debt should not exceed 50 percent of the total assets. Calculate the debt-to-total-assets ratio on Central Cycle Repair's Balance Sheet on page 142. Show how you calculated the percentage and write your evaluation of the company's debt-to-total-assets ratio.

3. **Computer Application.** Use spreadsheet software to set up a spreadsheet that will calculate the value of Assets in the accounting equation. Title your spreadsheet "The Accounting Equation" and title your three columns "Assets," "Liabilities," and "Owner's Equity." Properly format each column for the values that you will insert. Devise the proper formula to sum each row of values you insert for Liabilities and Owner's Equity; then devise a formula to sum the values of each of the three columns. Format your spreadsheet so that each equation prints with dollar signs and values aligned.

Save your work in your Business Portfolio.

Independent Practice

Use the Chapter 9 worksheets in *Student Activity Guide 1* for additional practice and application activities. *Student Activity Guide 1* provides vocabulary exercises, reading comprehension checks, problems, projects, and simulations of business and economic situations. A Teacher's Annotated Edition provides answers.

ASSESS

Portfolio Assessment

The projects are designed to lead students to develop a collection of their best work to submit to you for assessment. You and your students should decide which projects will be included in their respective Business Portfolios. Refer students to the specific rubric(s) from the *Alternative Assessment Strategies* booklet listed with each of the project notes below. These rubrics will alert students to the criteria you will use to assess their projects.

Chapter Assessment

Use the Chapter 9 test from the *Test Masters* booklet to evaluate students' understanding of the chapter concepts. An answer key is provided. Or create your own customized test using the *Testmaker* software.

Use What You Learned

1. Group students so that all teams have a similar writing skill level. Rubrics: Survey, Essay.
2. Remind students that a ratio is a fraction and implies division. Answer: 7% ($1000 ÷ $13,000); for every dollar of assets, the company is only 7 cents in debt, which is very good. Rubrics: Paragraph, Diagram
3. Students without access to computers may still be able to present spreadsheets with formulas prepared manually. Rubrics: Charts and Tables.

CHAPTER
10

FOCUS

Introduce the Chapter

Major Concepts
- Production and Operations
- Controlling Production
- Making Production Efficient
- Working in Operations and Production

Introduce the Topic
Ask students if they have ever toured a manufacturing plant or factory. Ask them to share their impressions of the production process. How did the plant differ from what they had imagined? What surprised them the most?

Use Business Terms
Ask students to write a sentence with each of the Business Terms, replacing the term with a nonsense word. Invite volunteers to read aloud their sentences for others in the class to insert the correct term. Advise students to check the meanings of the terms as they read the chapter.

USE VISUALS

Have students look at the photo for a few moments and then ask: How does the layout of this production facility help workers do their jobs efficiently? (Students' answers will vary.)

Business terms

operations system

production forecasting

inventory

inventory control

quality control

quality circle

maintenance

variable costs

fixed costs

152

CHAPTER 10 RESOURCES

Instructional Resources

Lesson Plan for Chapter 10

Teaching Transparencies 10-1, 10-2

Strategies and Worksheets for Teaching Transparencies 10-1, 10-2

Enrichment Master 10-1

Student Activity Guide 1–TAE for Chapter 10

Test Master for Chapter 10

Alternative Assessment Strategies

Math Skills Review

International Business Strategies

Cooperative Learning Strategies

Communication Skills Review

Ethics in Business Strategies

Producing Goods and Services Worldwide

Learning objectives

After completing this chapter, you will be able to:
- Identify the three elements of an operations system.
- Explain how quality control, maintenance, and cost control contribute to the efficient production of goods and services.
- Describe how goods are distributed.
- List the special skills that operations and production workers need to have.
- Name four problem-solving strategies.
- Describe several careers in manufacturing technology and construction.

Consider what you know

- In order to produce goods and services, financial managers must understand their business's financial obligations, sources of funding, and plans for future production.

Consider what you want to know

- What are the elements of an operations system?
- How do managers control operations and keep track of what they are producing?
- What are some useful problem-solving strategies?
- What kinds of careers are available in manufacturing and construction?

Consider how to use what you learn

- When reading this chapter, consider the many steps that occur before a product or service is ready for purchase.

Learning Objectives
Point out to students that the learning objectives show what they will learn in the chapter. Tell students to keep these objectives in mind as they work through the chapter. Note that the last two objectives listed refer to the Focus on Careers feature and the Building Business Skills feature.

Consider What You Know
Review briefly the main sections of *Chapter 9 Managing Business Finances:* Accounting in Business; Financial Statements; The Role of the Financial Manager; and Who Works in Accounting and Finance?

Consider What You Want to Know
Have students keep the listed questions in mind as they preview the chapter by quickly paging through it, looking at the photographs, and reading the section headings and figure titles.

Consider How to Use What You Learn
Remind students that they will develop some projects when they finish the chapter. For these projects, they will need to consider the many processes that occur before a product or service is ready for the consumer. Recommend that they pay particular attention to the different ways goods and services are produced.

Multimedia Resources

Technology Resource Guide

Distance Learning Guide

Internet Resource Guide

Professional Resources

School-to-Work/Tech Prep Strategies

Instructional Poster

Spanish Resources

Testmaker Software for Chapter 10

The Wall Street Journal Video Series Video & Activities for Chapter 10

Business and Marketing Computer Applications—An Integrated Software Simulation Using Microsoft Works

Stocktracker—A Stock Market Software Simulation

Where's the Dough? Board Game

TEACH

Develop Concepts

Production and Operations

Discuss with students some simple operations systems, such as that of a potter who makes and sells pottery. Have students think of other simple operations systems and give examples of the facilities, processing, and people elements.

USE VISUALS

Explain that Figure 10-1 shows the three elements of an operations system. Have volunteers explain how the elements of the operations system work together to produce a good or service. Answer to caption: They plan and operate the system.

USE TRANSPARENCIES

Use Teaching Transparency 10-1 and its corresponding strategies and worksheet from the *Teaching Transparency Strategies and Worksheets* booklet to help students understand the elements of an operations system. Verify student worksheets using the Answer Key.

Thousands of factories throughout the world produce the goods you use every day—from the orange juice you drink at breakfast to the mattress you sleep on at night. Businesses also provide the services that you use—from haircuts to bus rides. This chapter will examine how the goods and services you use each day are produced and delivered to consumers.

PRODUCTION AND OPERATIONS

Your local supermarket may stock as many as 30,000 different products. Each one was manufactured or processed in a factory somewhere. In order for a can of peas to appear on your supermarket shelf, a number of steps had to take place. The peas had to be picked, taken to a processing plant, shelled, cooked, and placed in a can. Then the can had to be labeled. All of these steps are elements in the production process.

The production of goods and services has to be planned. People have to make decisions at every step in the process. The planning that goes into producing a can of peas or running a dental office is called an **operations system.** An operations system includes the facilities, the processing, and the people needed to produce goods or services. Figure 10-1 below shows the elements of an operations system. Managers design an operations system so that all of the three elements work together to produce the good or service.

FIGURE 10-1

An operations system includes the facilities needed to produce a product, the processes that are necessary to manufacture the product, and the people needed to make the product. Why are people an important part of an operations system?

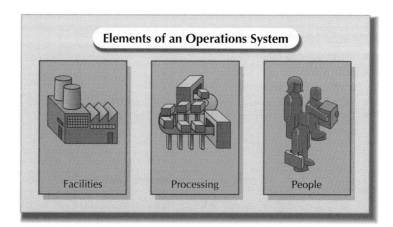

Elements of an Operations System

Facilities · Processing · People

Reteaching Strategy

Distribute Enrichment Master 10-1, which lists a variety of businesses and some of the elements of their operations systems. After students have studied the master for a few moments, ask them to think of a small business with which they are familiar. Have them make a chart similar to Figure 10-1 above showing the specific elements of that business's operations system.

Facilities

Facilities are the physical elements needed to produce a product or provide a service. Some companies have facilities located all over the world. Facilities include factory buildings, warehouses, land, offices, machinery, equipment, and trucks. When managers plan the facilities for a product or service, they must consider the location of the facilities. If you were making computers, you would want to be close to the sources of your computer components. You would also want to be close to major interstate highways and airports so you could ship your products easily. If you were a real estate agent, on the other hand, you would probably want an office near an urban area. You also would want your facility to include parking for your customers so that it would be convenient for them to come to your office.

Once a location has been selected, managers then plan the layout of the facilities. How will the product move through the plant as it goes through the production process? Where will raw materials be stored? How will trucks pick up the finished product? Where will the business offices be located? Some companies have corporate headquarters that are separate from their manufacturing plants. Others house the plant and business offices in the same building.

Layout will differ depending on what production process the company uses and what it is producing. A plant with an assembly line that puts together a product will have a different layout from a plant where each worker assembles a product at a separate workstation. A service layout is usually very different from a production layout. A cement-producing factory needs large open areas, conveyor belts, and loading platforms. A hair salon requires workstations equipped with chairs, mirrors, and electrical outlets.

Processing

The processing part of the operations system is made up of all the activities involved in changing or combining resources to produce a good or service. Processing involves transforming raw materials into finished products so that value is added. Steel, glass, plastic, and fabric become a recreational vehicle. Styling tools, hair products, and the skills of a barber can create a new hairstyle. In each case, the finished product has more value than the sum of the value of its raw materials.

Managers decide what kind of processing is required to produce a good or service. If a factory makes electric guitars, managers must decide how to assemble them, finish them, and ship

Learning Activity
Have students think of some possible situations that might signal that a manufacturing plant needs to redesign its layout. (Possible answers: Increase or decrease in number of employees; new equipment; a decrease in the plant's productivity.)

Business Brief
The cost of land and labor is a major concern when choosing a facility's location. Taxes are also a major consideration. Not all states have the same taxes. South Dakota and Nevada are attractive to some manufacturers because these states do not assess a corporate or personal income tax. They also do not charge taxes on a business's inventory. Such tax advantages are often an incentive for businesses scouting plant locations.

Learning Activity
Have students suggest ways to improve some "facilities" within your school, such as the computer lab, library, or cafeteria. Encourage students to draw floor plans illustrating their ideas for greater efficiency and ease of use. Have them display their plans and describe important features to the class.

Cooperative Learning Debate (Pro/Con)

Group students in pairs and have each pair take a pro or con position on the following statement: "Should manufacturers relocate their facilities to states or other countries with cheaper labor costs?" Have pairs gather evidence and examples to support their position. After students present their arguments, have them evaluate the issues and decide the outcome of the debate.

Refer to the *Cooperative Learning Strategies* booklet for additional cooperative learning strategies.

Building Business Skills

Building Business Skills

Model

Have students brainstorm various problems that they routinely encounter at home, school, or work. Write several examples on the board. Choose two suitable problems—one that students would be able to solve themselves and one that would require outside help. Guide students through the steps listed in the Problem-Solving Flowchart for each of the problems. Be sure students understand how the chart leads them from one step to another.

Business Brief

There are many ways to process raw goods into finished products. Manufacturers may physically or chemically change materials; for example, sugarcane is processed into granulated or powdered sugar. Manufacturers may also combine several raw materials to make a finished product; for example, peanuts, vegetable oil, and salt are combined to make peanut butter. Some manufacturers also use a combination of raw materials and finished goods to make a product. Fruit juice is processed from fruit and then placed in a glass bottle that was produced as a finished good elsewhere.

EMPLOYABILITY

Demonstrating Problem Solving

Explanation

Life is full of little—and big—problems. You solve problems every day, sometimes without even thinking about it. As you look back at problems you've solved, you can probably think of many times when you've found good solutions. You have probably also come up with solutions that turned out not to be such good ideas—and learned what not to do next time.

On the job, employers value employees who demonstrate that they can solve problems. An employee who solves small problems and knows when to ask for help with larger problems is a valuable asset.

Practice

How can you prepare for problems? Often you can't. You can have a strategy for solving problems, though. Study the steps in the Problem-Solving Flowchart. On a separate sheet of paper, use the steps in the chart to solve a problem you currently have.

them. They must also decide how best to use their facilities in the manufacturing process. This may require building a new plant or an addition to an existing plant, retooling the plant's machinery, or reassigning workers to different tasks.

If a company makes products such as automobiles for customers in different parts of the world, managers may decide to standardize designs and parts. By standardizing, or making designs and parts the same, companies can save money. For example, if an auto manufacturer produces a standard kind of windshield for a standard car design, it can use that windshield in cars sold in Europe, Asia, or the United States. It is less expensive to produce a large quantity of one kind of product than to produce smaller quantities of an item that can be sold only in certain markets.

However, businesses producing goods or services for other countries must consider the laws there. For example, other countries may have restrictions on such things as the use of pesticides, additives in foods, and auto emissions. Much United States beef cannot be sold in Europe because of the antibiotics we routinely feed our cattle. Patents and copyrights, too, need to be considered. At one point, Coca-Cola stopped its opera-

Curriculum Connection   Science

Food processors must be particularly aware of the chemical and physical changes that occur as they produce a product. For example, the fat, water, ice, and air ingredients as well as the temperature of ice cream must be carefully balanced during processing. If air bubbles are not incorporated into ice cream, the finished product will be dense and rock hard. Have students select a processed food and research the kinds of scientific operations that make possible the production of the product. Students should write a 250-word report emphasizing the role of science in food processing.

PROBLEM-SOLVING FLOWCHART

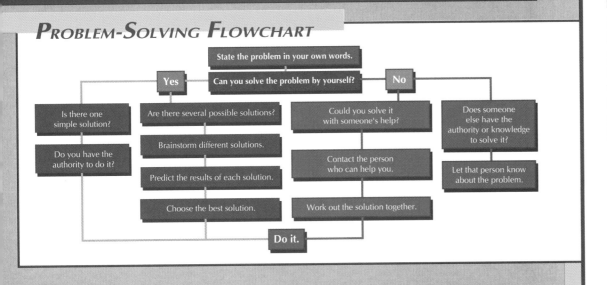

State the problem in your own words.

Yes — Can you solve the problem by yourself? — No

- Is there one simple solution?
- Are there several possible solutions?
- Could you solve it with someone's help?
- Does someone else have the authority or knowledge to solve it?

- Do you have the authority to do it?
- Brainstorm different solutions.
- Contact the person who can help you.
- Let that person know about the problem.

- Predict the results of each solution.

- Choose the best solution.
- Work out the solution together.

Do it.

Practice

Have students use the Problem-Solving Flowchart to solve a problem they have at school or at home. (Students' answers will vary but should show that they have followed one of the problem-solving paths given in the flowchart.)

tions in India when the government there demanded Coke's secret, patented formula.

People

People—human resources—are the most important part of the operations system. Even in factories where machines do much of the work, people are still needed to plan and supervise the processing operation. No matter how automated a factory becomes, people must still program the computers, repair malfunctioning machines, and watch over the processing operations.

Because people are the most important ingredient in the operations system, managers try to plan the content and methods of work in a job. In some factories, the managers focus on the task. They determine how a job can be done most efficiently. Then they train workers to perform the job in just that way. In other plants, the managers focus on the workers. They try to motivate their workers to do the best job they can. They listen to their employees' ideas and may change their assignments frequently. In still other facilities, managers use a combination

Business Brief

The amount of technology and automation used in manufacturing today has changed the people requirements for manufacturers. Many machines can do the work that unskilled workers once did. Businesses that want to keep valued employees sometimes spend money to retrain employees for more challenging work. For example, Boeing paid college fees for its electronics technicians so they could continue to work at Boeing doing more high-skilled work.

Global Perspective

Developing countries such as South Korea, Taiwan, Hungary, India, and Poland have a significant number of well educated and skilled workers. However, many of these workers do not have jobs that let them use their skills to their full potential. U.S. and European businesses have targeted these countries for new joint ventures in order to take advantage of the highly skilled labor force that already exists. Ask students to find out what companies have established joint ventures in some of the countries mentioned above and have them write a 200-word summary of their findings.

Refer to the *International Business Strategies* booklet for additional strategies and activities.

CHAPTER 10

☑ Quick Check Answers

1. Facilities, processing, and people.
2. People.

Develop Concepts

Controlling Production

To help students understand how managers control production, give students the following scenario: Janet is the manager of the concession stand that operates during football games. What factors might she consider when deciding how many hot dogs, bags of pretzels, and cups of hot chocolate she will sell? (How many people have bought tickets for the game; how many people bought food from the concession at previous games; possibly the weather forecast since fewer people will probably attend if the weather is bad.)

Learning Activity

Surveys are one forecasting technique that can be very effective. Have groups of students choose a product that other students would buy, such as the school yearbook or a school T-shirt. Have the groups draft some survey questions for forecasting how many students would probably buy the item. Remind students that they will likely get more reliable results if they survey a large and diverse group of students. Have groups discuss the results of their surveys and their impressions of the survey's effectiveness as a forecasting tool.

158 UNIT 3

F.Y.I.

Loyalty is a two-way street. A survey of employees found that workers who believed their employers were committed to their well-being and job advancement were less likely to use drugs at work, leave early without permission, or call in sick. The findings indicate "an organization's culture can greatly impact employee behavior," according to the survey director.

of these two techniques. In any case, the manager's goal is the same—to produce the most goods or services at the lowest costs.

Some American companies with global operations have found it helpful to diversify management, which means that the company employs managers who are citizens of the country in which they have operations. For example, an American company with manufacturing facilities in China would employ Chinese managers. Companies who have such diversified management allow their local managers to operate with a significant degree of independence. Because locally hired managers better understand their country's cultural concerns, consumer habits, and government regulations, companies have found that the strategy results in greater productivity.

☑ Quick Check

1. What three elements does an operations system include?
2. What part of an operations system is the most important?

CONTROLLING PRODUCTION

How do managers know whether they are producing the right amount of goods at the right rate of speed? Managers use several methods to keep track of the production process and to adjust it to fit their needs.

Production Forecasting

The first thing an operations manager needs to know is just how much of a product to provide. Ideally, a company should produce about the same number of goods or services as consumers want to buy. Managers use forecasting to determine how many units of a product to manufacture. **Production forecasting** is estimating how much of a company's goods or services must be produced to meet future demand. Often the forecasters base their predictions on past demand. If 500,000 consumers bought microwave ovens last year, a similar number may buy microwaves this year. Forecasters also take into account other factors. Do consumers have more money or less money to spend on goods this year than last? Is the economy growing, or is it in a slump? Are interest rates rising or falling? If a forecaster determines that consumer income is falling, the forecaster may recommend that the company make fewer microwave ovens than it made last year.

Cooperative Learning Co-op Co-op

Have students research some of the employee issues facing manufacturers today. Divide the class into teams, and have each team choose one of the following topics: minorities in the manufacturing sector; laws and regulations affecting hiring and safety in factories; women in the manufacturing sector; or upgrading employee skills. Each team should present a four-minute oral presentation explaining their issue and providing examples of how specific manufacturers have addressed the issue.

Refer to the *Cooperative Learning Strategies* booklet for additional cooperative learning strategies.

Scheduling

Once the manager decides how many goods or services to produce, he or she sets up a schedule. The schedule identifies how many goods will be made over a given period of time. It also shows how many of each model, color, and size will be made. Scheduling helps managers decide what facilities, raw materials, and human resources will be needed and when they will be needed. A factory that makes computer games may schedule higher production in the summer and fall to meet holiday shopping demands. The factory may have to hire temporary employees to work during those months. It will also probably have to order more raw materials during that period. Businesses that provide services also have to establish schedules to meet the demands of their customers. For example, the U.S. Postal Service has to hire thousands of temporary workers before the holidays to help deliver greeting cards and packages.

Inventory Management

A factory's **inventory** is the amount of goods—raw materials, supplies, partially completed goods, and finished products—the factory has on hand at any given time. To keep costs down, managers use inventory control. **Inventory control** means balancing the costs of holding raw materials, partially completed goods, and finished goods with the costs of ordering them. For instance, managers must decide which raw materials and supplies to order, how much to order and when to order them, and how to store them. If a bicycle factory does not have enough tires on hand, the workers must wait until the manager obtains more tires before the bicycles can be completed. The delay costs the company money, since the company cannot ship and sell the unfinished bicycles. Some factories keep large quantities of raw materials and partially finished goods on hand to make sure the workers never run out. However, keeping too many raw materials on hand can also cost the factory money. The materials must be bought, then stored until they are used.

Finished goods need to be managed carefully as well. If a factory makes more bicycles than it can sell, it will have to pay to store the extra goods until they can be sold. If the factory makes too few bicycles and there is a demand for them, it will lose the income it would have received from selling more bicycles. Managers hope to avoid having a finished goods inventory that is either too large or too small. In either case, the company loses money.

Ford Motor Company merged its American and European auto operations with the goal of producing global vehicles or "world cars." Designing and producing different car models for each part of its global market is very expensive. The company decided to save production costs by making fewer models and using fewer suppliers for their raw materials. Ford's first world car, the Mondeo, was introduced in 1993 in Europe. In 1994 Ford introduced the Contour in the United States. The two vehicles were virtually identical—except for the name.

Reteaching Strategy

Present students with the following problem, and have them use the Problem-Solving Flowchart on page 157 to solve it. Naomi won't be able to study on Sunday and needs to find two or three hours on Saturday to study for a major math test on Monday. She has to take her dog to the vet at 10:00 Saturday morning and is not sure how long the appointment will take. She is scheduled to work Saturday afternoon from 1:00 to 5:00. Saturday night she has to help at her father's birthday party. Remind students that there may be more than one way to solve the problem. Have volunteers give their solutions and explain how they used the flowchart to find a solution.

FOCUS ON **Careers**

Discuss

Discuss with students the kinds of skills people in the manufacturing technology and construction industries use. Ask students what courses in school could help them prepare for entry-level jobs in manufacturing technology and construction. How do people advance in the field?

Manufacturing Technology and Construction

I t's almost impossible to imagine a world without television sets, clothes, cars, buildings, and roads. Yet we tend to take the existence of such material goods and structures for granted. We seldom give a thought to the complex and exacting work that produces them. The people who do this work are employed by manufacturing and construction businesses. They work at construction sites as carpenters, plumbers, and operators of cranes and bulldozers. They hold jobs in plants making tiny electronic chips or putting together huge jet engines. They maintain and repair the machines that keep manufacturing and construction going.

Careers in this area are often as high tech as they come. After all, the robots and computerized machines that have reduced the drudgery of manufacturing tasks need skilled workers to operate and maintain them. Though some entry-level positions are open to people with high school diplomas, many require or welcome technical school training. Math, science, computer, machine shop, and mechanical

HELP WANTED

APPRENTICE CARPENTER

Conco Builders has opening for apprentice carpenter. No experience needed. Earn money as you learn a useful trade by working with experienced carpenter to build house frames and install rafters and joists. Construct scaffolds, walkways, and molds for concrete.

High school diploma or GED required. Good math and measuring skills, physical strength and flexibility, and excellent hand-eye coordination are musts. You'll need your own hand tools.

TEACHING TIP

Ask students what raw materials might be part of the inventory of a furniture manufacturer. (Possible answers: wood, leather, textiles, plastic, steel, glass.) What would make up the manufacturer's finished goods inventory? (Possible answers: chairs, tables, cabinets, sofas.)

Materials Requirement Planning One technique used to control inventory is called *materials requirement planning* (MRP). This is a method of getting the correct materials where they are needed for production and doing it on time and without unnecessary stockpiling. In other words, end products are analyzed to determine the materials needed to produce them. A computer program generally determines when certain materials are needed, when they should be ordered, and when they should be delivered so that they won't cost too much to store.

Manufacturing Resource Planning This inventory control technique is an extension of materials requirement planning. *Manufacturing resource planning* (MRPII) goes beyond MRP to include input from other departments including finance and marketing. Instead of focusing only on material requirements, it focuses on all available resources. A computer program analyzes data from various departments to compare end product requirements to known company resources. This analysis then translates into forecasts of materials requirements and inventory needs.

Global Perspective

Just-in-time (JIT) inventory control was first developed by an employee at Toyota Motor Company in Japan. When vehicle parts were needed at a plant, they were delivered from other Toyota plants or outside suppliers. JIT is successful because it cuts down on administrative costs and the amount of space needed to store raw materials and finished goods. Because there is very little excess inventory to fall back on, a supply truck stuck in a traffic jam could spell disaster for a plant that uses JIT. Have students hypothesize some other potential problems with using JIT.

Refer to the *International Business Strategies* booklet for additional strategies and activities.

drawing courses are a good starting point for anyone considering a career in manufacturing and construction.

Beginners in the building trades often start out as apprentices working closely with experienced professionals on the job. Apprentice plumbers and electricians may also attend classes.

Whether the job involves assembling and testing a robot or building and installing fine wood cabinets, a high degree of precision is required. Success calls for mechanical aptitude, manual dexterity, and good eye-hand coordination—not to mention patience, persistence, and self-control. Product assemblers today are often members of teams and need to work cooperatively and communicate well.

Help wanted ads for three entry-level jobs and a job posting for a more advanced position in manufacturing technology and construction are presented here.

Just-in-Time Planning Another method for managing inventory is the *just-in-time* (JIT) system. In this system, materials arrive precisely when they are needed on a production line, and finished goods are delivered "just in time" for usage. In other words, the system is designed to reduce a company's inventory to zero. Just-in-time planning requires that the production system be simple and well coordinated. It also requires clockwork timing and coordination within the operations system and between the company and its suppliers. For example, at one time, an automaker would order a truckload of parts for delivery within a two- or three-day window of time. Now that the same company will order a one-quarter load for delivery within a two- to three-hour window. Computer-controlled systems alert managers when it is time to order needed materials.

Quick Check

1. What methods do managers use to control production?
2. Give definitions for *production forecasting, inventory,* and *inventory control.*

Curriculum Connection   Math

Cromwell Bakery bakes 14 dozen loaves of bread a day. Each loaf costs 70¢ to produce. An average of nine loaves are imperfect and have to be discarded. The bakery charges $2.50 per loaf and usually has a dozen loaves left unsold each day. Charlie Stuart's Bakery bakes 13 dozen loaves a day. Usually, all 13 dozen sell. It costs Stuart's 60¢ to produce a loaf, which is priced at $2.25. Which bakery is able to sell the most loaves at the least cost? Remind students that bakeries have to account for the costs of loaves that can't be sold. (Cromwell: 168 × .70 = $117.60. Only 147 loaves can be sold. Stuart's: 156 × .60 = $93.60. All 156 loaves can be sold.)

For students who need to sharpen their math skills, choose among the worksheets in the *Math Skills Review* booklet.

Follow Through

Teamwork is one of the most important skills someone who wants to work in manufacturing technology and construction can develop. Have teams think of something they can "manufacture" together. For example, students could design and produce a newsletter or brochure. Teams might also do something as simple as assembling a fruit salad. Display the teams' projects and discuss the benefits of teamwork.

Business Brief

A survey of 250 American manufacturing firms found that more than 50 percent used just-in-time (JIT) inventory methods, and nearly 35 percent used manufacturing resource planning (MRPII). In addition, about 40 percent also used computers directly in the manufacturing process.

Quick Check Answers

1. Forecasting, scheduling, and inventory management.
2. Estimating how much of a company's goods and services must be produced to meet future demand; the amount of goods a factory has on hand at any given time; balancing the costs of holding raw materials, partially completed goods, and finished goods with the costs of ordering them.

Develop Concepts

Making Production Efficient

Experts define efficient and quality-minded manufacturers as those who

- use up-to-date processing and inventory control systems;
- determine what customers want;
- focus on improving customer satisfaction;
- test, monitor, and evaluate new products; and
- improve programs and procedures continually.

Ask students why it is important for manufacturers to find out what customers want.
(Because if they aren't making a product that satisfies their customers, they will lose business.)

MAKING PRODUCTION EFFICIENT

The most efficient operation is one that can produce the most goods or services at the lowest cost. Managers want to run as efficient a business as possible. They are also concerned with producing high-quality goods and services. Managers focus their attention on the operations activities to attain these goals. Quality control, maintenance, and cost control are their three main areas of concern.

Quality Control

Companies that produce goods and services must assure that their products meet quality standards to remain competitive. The process of **quality control** involves measuring goods and services against established standards. Automakers, for example, set standards for such things as safety, dependability, durability, and comfort. An individual carmaker then might test one out of every 100 cars that roll off the assembly line against these standards.

Quality Assurance   Many companies are setting up a companywide system of practices and procedures to assure that their products meet customers' quality standards. Rather than a random sampling of the tenth or hundredth item, these companies focus on doing the job right the first time and every time thereafter. Redesigning tools and machinery, demanding quality parts from suppliers, and retraining workers encourages such quality production.

Why do you think a group of employees from the same area, a quality circle, would be effective in increasing the standards of quality?

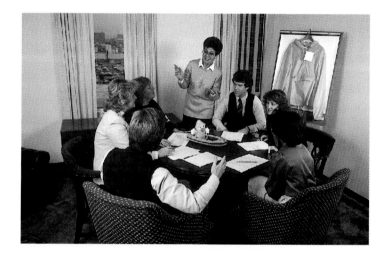

Meeting Student Diversity

Many students who are not good readers can still locate information in the text when their attention is directed to it. Without direction, however, they often cannot make distinctions between important facts and elaboration. The notes they take may contain irrelevant information. Have students read the "Quality Control" subsection and find one sentence in each paragraph that best states the main idea. Have them explain their choices.

To increase employee motivation to meet quality standards, managers use several techniques. One such technique is the **quality circle,** a group of employees from the same work area. Groups of seven to ten people volunteer to meet regularly to define, analyze, and solve quality problems in their area. With one of the members serving as team leader, the circle tackles problems such as reducing defects, boosting morale, streamlining hiring practices, and improving training. Quality circles work closely with their supervisors and inform them of their progress.

ISO 9000 Standards   To compete globally, U.S. companies have to meet certain quality standards. A standard of quality management, known as ISO 9000, is very popular in Europe and is taking hold in the United States and around the world. A committee of examiners studies the operation of a factory, laboratory, or office to determine if it meets quality management requirements set up by the International Organization for Standardization. If the facility passes the examination, it receives a certificate. The certificate lets the company's customers and suppliers know that it meets ISO 9000 standards for testing products, training employees, keeping records, and fixing defects.

Maintenance

In order to be efficient, a plant must be kept running smoothly. **Maintenance** is any kind of activity that keeps a production facility in working condition or puts it back in working condition if it breaks down. Preventive maintenance involves doing things to prevent machinery from breaking down. Breakdown maintenance involves repairing broken machines as quickly as possible.

Preventive maintenance is more efficient and cost effective than breakdown maintenance. Stopping production while a machine is being fixed can cost a factory a lot of money. It has to continue to pay its workers and meet its daily expenses even though no goods are being produced.

Cost Control

When a company makes a product, it must spend money to purchase the raw materials, pay workers, operate the facilities, and transport finished goods. To survive, the company must charge a price that will cover the costs of producing and selling the product. By analyzing costs, managers establish the minimum acceptable price for the product.

Business & Science

Some foods such as seafood, vegetables, and fruits are very perishable and will not stay fresh for very long. Producers who need to store or transport perishable items can control such factors as air pressure and quality, temperature, and humidity to prolong the item's freshness. Iceberg lettuce, for example, will keep fresh six times longer than it would under normal refrigeration in an atmosphere containing specifically controlled amounts of carbon dioxide, oxygen, and nitrogen.

TEACHING TIP

Have students identify and explain the difference between preventive and breakdown maintenance by asking them the following questions. What kind of maintenance is being performed on a car when the owner changes the oil every 3000 miles? (Preventive.) What kind of maintenance is being performed when a cyclist repairs a flat tire? (Breakdown.)

Business Brief

In everyday usage, the terms *price* and *cost* are often used interchangeably. For example, when Uncle Bill says, "The cost of living is going up," he means the prices of goods and services are higher than they were at an earlier time. However, when accountants talk about cost, they mean all the expenses directly related to doing business. Business managers define cost as anything that reduces profits.

Global Perspective

The ISO 9000 standards provide guidelines to manufacturers for how to train employees, test products, fix defects, and keep records. The standards are valuable for establishing universal procedures for goods manufactured around the world. Have a class discussion about the advantages of setting worldwide standards for quality. What could be some disadvantages?

Refer to the *International Business Strategies* booklet for additional strategies and activities.

Connection to CHAPTER 16

Fixed costs also take into account *depreciation*—the gradual wear and tear on the building, office furniture, and equipment that results in those goods losing value. A photocopying machine, for example, will not last forever; eventually it will have to be replaced. A photocopying machine that is six years old is worth much less than a new one because it will need to be replaced sooner. Have students identify some items that are subject to depreciation. (Cars, computers, delivery vans, televisions.)

USE VISUALS

Have students look closely at the advantages and disadvantages listed in Figure 10-2 for the different modes of transporting goods. Explain that most services do not require extensive transportation networks because in most cases consumers go to the service.
Answer to caption: Cost.

USE TRANSPARENCIES

Use Teaching Transparency 18-2 and its corresponding strategies and worksheet from the *Teaching Transparency Strategies and Worksheets* booklet to illustrate the advantages and disadvantages of different modes of transportation. Verify student worksheets using the Answer Key.

Managers must be concerned with two types of costs in producing a product. **Variable costs** are the costs of material, labor, and raw materials that increase or decrease with the number of goods produced. **Fixed costs,** which include the costs of buildings, equipment, rent, insurance, and utilities, must be paid no matter how much is produced. If a plant's sales decrease, it must still pay for telephone service and rent.

Managers in the production department arrange for raw materials and parts to be delivered when needed to produce a product. They also arrange for delivery of the final manufactured products to the customer. They are responsible for selecting the best mode of transportation so that their products reach customers in good condition and at minimum cost. Managers can choose from the four main modes of transportation shown in Figure 10-2 below. Transportation decisions are an important aspect of cost control.

FIGURE 10-2

Each mode of transportation has its advantages and disadvantages. What is the most important consideration for each mode?

Modes of Transporting Goods				
Mode of Transportation	Cost	Advantages	Disadvantages	Types of Goods
Railroad	Low	Shipment of heavy goods over long distances Reliable schedules Little damage to goods	Access to terminals sometimes difficult No service in many small towns Less suitable for small shipments and short distances	Coal Chemicals Iron, steel Automobiles Lumber
Trucking	Moderate	Door-to-door delivery Shipment to and from nearly any point Frequent service Little damage to goods	Less suitable for shipping very bulky or large goods More affected by weather than railroads	Food Large equipment Livestock Paper goods Computers Clothing
Waterways	Low	Can handle very large quantities	Slow speed Infrequent service Not available in many places Damaged goods more likely	Coal Grain Iron ore Petroleum Chemicals
Airline	High	High speed Frequent service Little damage to goods	Access to terminals sometimes difficult Unavailable in many small towns Schedules affected by weather	Perishable foods Flowers Instruments Emergency parts Overnight mail

Making Connections ➡️ Everyday Living

Review with students the difference between fixed and variable costs. Then invite the principal to discuss the kinds of costs of running the school. After the principal's talk, ask volunteers to make a class chart with the headings "Fixed Costs" and "Variable Costs." Have students place each of the costs described by the principal in the proper category. Put the chart on display.

Quick Check

1. What three operations activities contribute to a business's efficiency?
2. How do *quality control, quality circle, maintenance, variable costs,* and *fixed costs* relate to producing a good or service?
3. Name four modes of transporting goods.

WORKING IN OPERATIONS AND PRODUCTION

Like employees in other departments of a company, workers in operations and production need special skills to ensure the quality of their products and services. Some of these skills are mechanical aptitude, problem solving, math and science, communication, and accuracy and attention to detail. Read the following descriptions to learn more about the skills required for jobs in operations and production.

- *Mechanical aptitude.* Workers in operations and production use tools and machines and work with their hands and eyes. They have to be able to work quickly as well as to understand how pieces fit together to form a whole.
- *Problem solving.* People who work in operations and management have to be able to use information to solve a problem. This could include figuring out how to fix a machine that is down or soothe a dissatisfied customer. It may include some knowledge of the requirements and customs of other countries for companies that deal with international markets.
- *Math/science.* Workers in operations and production weigh, measure, sort, cut, and assemble various kinds of materials according to patterns or models. Their math and science skills help ensure a high-quality product or service.
- *Communication.* To improve their products and work environment, employees in operations and production have to have good language skills. These skills include listening, reading, writing, and speaking—sometimes in a language other than English.
- *Accuracy/attention to detail.* Whether the products are large or small, putting them together accurately ensures a high-quality product as well as an efficient operation. People who work in operations or production have to be able to

1. Quality control, maintenance, and cost control.
2. Measuring goods and services against established standards; a group of employees from the same work area who meet to solve quality problems in their area; any activity that keeps a production facility in operating condition or restores it to working condition; the costs of material, labor, and raw materials required to produce a product; the costs of the building, equipment, rent, insurance, and utilities.
3. Railroad, trucking, waterways, and airlines.

Develop Concepts

Working in Operations and Production

Today, people who work in operations and production must be thoroughly familiar with computers and technology. Computer-aided design (CAD) technology aids in the designing and production of goods, and computer-aided manufacturing (CAM) uses computer systems to operate much of the machinery in today's factories. With CAD and CAM, all manufacturing tasks are computer linked. Ask students to list some advantages and disadvantages of these developments.

Enrichment Strategy

Interested students or groups of students can do research to find out about jobs that use computer-aided design (CAD) and computer-aided manufacturing (CAM). What kind of education and training is necessary for employees who work with CAD or CAM? Have students write reports about their research and share their findings with the class.

Higher education skills will help you get a job working in operations and productions, but there are other skills that are required also. Some of these skills are acquired from good school habits. What are some of these skills?

work fast while paying close attention to details. They also must be careful not to make mistakes.

If you decide to pursue a career in operations or production, you may begin work as a materials handler, packager, or delivery truck driver. You could advance to a position as assistant materials clerk, line supervisor, or dispatcher. With more experience and well-developed skills, you could eventually get a job as a warehouse manager, as a production supervisor, or as a distribution manager.

 ### Quick Check

1. What are some skills necessary for workers in operations and production?
2. What specific mechanical skills do workers in operations and production need?

Curriculum Connection   English and Communications

Today's jobs in operations and productions emphasize teamwork. The ability to communicate with team members is crucial. Suggestions for improvement should always be welcome. Tell students to imagine that they have developed a way for improving a procedure. Have students draft a memo in which they tell their supervisor about the idea and set up a time to discuss the idea. Remind students to keep their memo professional, courteous, and brief, and to check their memos for grammar and spelling.

For those students who need to sharpen their written communication skills, choose among the worksheets in the *Communication Skills Review* booklet.

Chapter 10 **Summary**

Main Ideas

1. An operations system is made up of facilities, processing, and people.
2. Businesses use production forecasting, scheduling, inventory management, and planning to determine what goods to produce, how much to produce, and when to produce them.
3. Operations managers can use three methods to manage inventory: materials requirement planning, manufacturing resource planning, and just-in-time planning.
4. Companies employ quality control, maintenance, and cost control techniques to operate their businesses as efficiently as possible and to produce high-quality goods.
5. Many U.S. companies are adopting the ISO 9000 international quality management standards.
6. Producers move goods by railroads, trucks, ships, and airlines.
7. Operations and production workers need to have mechanical aptitude, problem-solving skills, math and science skills, and communication skills. They must also work quickly and accurately while paying attention to detail.
8. Learning how to solve problems is an important business skill.
9. Many careers are available in manufacturing technology and construction that require good skills, a high school education, and on-the-job training.

CASE ANALYSIS Production

Nathan Chu is quality control manager at Grandview Foods. Grandview's products include Krema Peanut Butter, an all-natural product with no additives. Today is Friday, the last day of this week's production, and the schedule calls for overtime to fill a large order for Heartland Health Food Stores. Nathan has performed the usual quality control tests on the peanut butter, and everything seems ready to go. Suddenly, Cathy Bernich, the production manager, rushes in. "Nathan, we've got a problem. Look at the labels on these jars!" Nathan reads one of the labels. Right in the middle, where the words "ALL NATURAL" are printed, there is a mistake. The label says "ALL NATRUAL" instead. "Have you checked our entire stock of empty jars?" asks Nathan. "Yes," says Cathy, "the word is spelled wrong on all of them. I called the supplier right away, but we can't get corrected labels until Monday morning." If you were Nathan Chu and Cathy Bernich, what would you do?

Main Ideas

Main Ideas summarizes the key information in the chapter. It is a useful tool for reinforcement and review.

CASE ANALYSIS

Case Analysis provides a chapter-related case for student analysis and application of decision-making skills.

Answer
Answers may vary. Some students may decide to ship the order with the misspelled labels to avoid possibly losing a valued customer. Others may decide to ship the order late because they are more concerned with the bad image the misspelled label will create.

QUICK QUIZ

1. What are the three elements that make up an operations system? (Facilities, processing, and people.)
2. What are three methods for managing inventory? (Materials requirement planning, manufacturing resource planning, and just-in-time planning.)
3. What are four modes of transporting goods? (Railroads, trucks, ships, airlines.)
4. List the skills and characteristics workers in operations and production need to have. (Mechanical aptitude, problem-solving skills, math and science skills, communication skills, and the ability to work accurately.)

Chapter 10 Review

APPLY

Answers

Use the Language of Business
1. quality control, 2. maintenance, 3. operations system, 4. quality circle, 5. production forecasting, 6. inventory control, 7. fixed costs, 8. inventory, 9. variable costs.

Review What You Learned
1. Facilities, processing, and people.
2. Production forecasting, scheduling, and inventory management.
3. On past demand and on present and future economic factors.
4. Materials requirement planning; manufacturing resource planning; and just-in-time planning.
5. It produces the most goods or services at the lowest cost.
6. ISO 9000 standards.
7. They need to have mechanical aptitude, problem-solving skills, math and science skills, communication skills, and the ability to work accurately.
8. Railroads, trucking, waterways, and airlines.
9. Find one simple solution; find several possible solutions; decide if you can solve the problem with someone else's help; discover if someone else has authority or knowledge to solve the problem.
10. Carpenters, product assemblers, robotics technicians, and tool programmers.

Understand Business Concepts
1. Layout depends on the kinds of production processes a plant uses.
2. They can save money in making them and can use them in more than one application.
3. Forecasting predicts consumer demand for a product. The manager can then make as many goods as consumers are likely to want to buy.
4. Yes. The more goods a company produces, the lower the cost per product unit tends to be because it is spread out over more units.

Use the Language of Business

People who work in production and operations use the following terms. Use each one to best complete one of the sentences that follow.

fixed costs
production forecasting
inventory
inventory control
maintenance

operations system
quality circle
quality control
variable costs

1. _____ is a system for making sure that each product meets the same performance standards.
2. To keep a factory running smoothly, it must have periodic preventive _____ .
3. A(n) _____ identifies the facilities, processes, and people needed to produce goods or services.
4. A group of employees from the same work area form a(n) _____ to solve quality problems.
5. _____ means predicting how many products consumers will want in the future.
6. When managers make sure inventory sizes correspond to production needs and sales needs, they are practicing _____ .
7. The money that is budgeted for buildings, equipment, rent, insurance, and utilities is a company's _____ .
8. The amount of goods a factory has on hand at any given time is its _____ .
9. _____ are the costs of material, labor, and raw materials needed to produce a product.

Review What You Learned

1. Name the three elements of an operations system.
2. What are the methods managers use to control production?
3. On what do production managers base their estimates?
4. What are three methods that operations managers use to manage inventory?
5. Describe some aspects of an efficient production operation.
6. What is the name of the international quality management standards?
7. What skills do operations and production workers need to have?
8. What are the main modes of transporting goods?
9. List four problem-solving strategies.
10. Give several examples of careers in manufacturing technology and construction.

Understand Business Concepts

1. On what factors does the layout of a production facility depend?
2. Why is it a good idea for production managers to standardize designs and parts?
3. How does production forecasting help managers decide how many goods to produce?
4. Is it true that costs decrease as the number of goods produced increases?

5. Preventive maintenance keeps machines operating and producing. With breakdown maintenance, production stops while equipment is being repaired.
6. Fixed costs rise when rent increases.
7. With too little inventory a company loses sales; with too much there are storage costs; a lot of money is tied up in the inventory that can't be used elsewhere.
8. Learning to solve problems makes people valuable to business.
9. Mechanical aptitude, manual dexterity, good eye-hand coordination, patience, persistence, and self-control.

Think Critically
1. Possible answer: It would not be advantageous if prices of supplies rose over a short period. Companies would have no supplies on hand so they would have to purchase supplies at a higher price.
2. Possible answer: Peanuts are shelled, crushed, mixed with other ingredients, and packaged.
3. Answers will vary, but students should say that the defective product would cost the producer money if it is replaced or the money refunded.

Chapter 10 **Review**

5. Why is preventive maintenance more efficient than breakdown maintenance?
6. If a company's building rent goes up, which of the two kinds of costs has risen?
7. Why is it important not to have too much or too little inventory on hand at any one time?
8. Why is it important to learn how to solve problems?
9. What kinds of talents and skills are people in manufacturing technology and construction likely to have?

Think Critically

1. **Judge.** When do you think the just-in-time planning system would not be advantageous?
2. **Analyze.** Describe the steps involved in processing a jar of peanut butter.
3. **Assess.** Have you ever purchased a defective product? Did you exchange or return the product? Do you think the defective product cost the producer money? Why or why not?

Use What You Learned

1. **Group Project.** Work in teams to brainstorm ideas for a product your team could mass-produce and sell to raise funds for an extracurricular activity. Work together to make decisions about the following: quantity to produce, scheduling, and raw materials and supplies.
   Also consider how you will control costs and distribute your product. Draw up a plan and schedule showing how you would produce and distribute your product.
2. Imagine the following businesses were planning to locate in your community: a computer manufacturer, a supermarket, a video store, and a health-food restaurant. Make a list of the pros and cons of various locations for each business. Using your list, make a map of your
   community showing the locations you think would be best for each business.
3. **Computer Application.** Use on-line research to find an article in *The Wall Street Journal* that describes a production problem or innovation. With word processing software, write a 250-word report about the article. List the causes of the problem or the reasons for the innovation and describe how the problem or innovation will affect the company.
4. **Skill Reinforcement.** Interview a production or operations manager to find out the process he or she uses to solve problems. Make a flowchart of the process similar to the flowchart on page 157. Compare the two and describe which one you would prefer to follow. Explain why in a brief paragraph.

Save your work in your Business Portfolio.

Use What You Learned
1. Make sure all students participate in the group project. Possible Rubrics: Charts and Tables; Diagram.
2. Have a map of your community on display for students to refer to as they work on their projects. Rubrics: Note Taking; Map; Paragraph.
3. Students who don't have access to a computer may use a newspaper index to find articles and may write their reports by hand. Rubric: Essay.
4. Students' answers will vary but should include constructive suggestions for solving problems in a workplace. Rubrics: Diagram; Paragraph.

Independent Practice

Use the Chapter 10 worksheets in *Student Activity Guide 1* for additional practice and application activities. *Student Activity Guide 1* provides vocabulary exercises, reading comprehension checks, problems, projects, and simulations of business and economic situations. A Teacher's Annotated Edition provides answers.

ASSESS

Portfolio Assessment

The portfolio projects are designed to lead students to develop a collection of their best work to submit to you for assessment. You and your students should decide which projects will be included in their respective Business Portfolios. Refer students to the specific rubric(s) from the *Alternative Assessment Strategies* booklet listed with each of the project notes below. These rubrics will alert students to the criteria you will use to assess their projects.

Chapter Assessment

Use the Chapter 10 Test from the *Test Masters* booklet to evaluate students' understanding of the chapter concepts. An answer key is provided. Or create your own customized test using the *Testmaker* software.

FOCUS

Introduce the Chapter

Major Concepts
- Elements of Marketing
- Product Planning
- Pricing, Packaging, and Promotion
- Distributing Goods and Services
- Special Concerns for International Marketers
- Working in Marketing

Introduce the Topic
Ask students to describe the best salesperson they have encountered over the past few weeks. What did the person do especially well that impressed them? Point out that in Chapter 11 students will learn about all the aspects of marketing goods and services, including the role of salespeople.

Use Business Terms
Have students look at the business terms and note any that are familiar to them. Ask them to define these terms or try to recall the contexts in which they were used. For those terms that are totally unfamiliar, have students venture a meaning. For terms that they cannot define, advise students to note the definitions in the chapter.

USE VISUALS
Have students look at the photograph and describe what aspect of marketing it conveys. Ask what kinds of products these people are buying. What might have motivated them to shop in this store? (Answers will vary.)

170 UNIT 3

Business terms

marketing mix

consumer goods

market research

demographics

break-even point

logo

advertising

channel of distribution

170

CHAPTER 11 RESOURCES

Instructional Resources

Lesson Plan for Chapter 11

Teaching Transparency 11-1

Strategies and Worksheets for Teaching Transparency 11-1

Enrichment Master 11-1

Student Activity Guide 1–TAE for Chapter 11

Test Master for Chapter 11

Alternative Assessment Strategies

Math Skills Review

International Business Strategies

Cooperative Learning Strategies

Communication Skills Review

Ethics in Business Strategies

Marketing in Today's World

Learning objectives

After completing this chapter, you will be able to:
- Identify the four elements that make up the marketing mix.
- Define the life cycle of a product.
- Discuss the needs and motivations of consumers.
- Describe the role of pricing, packaging, and promotion in marketing goods and services.
- List the traits that marketing employees need to have.
- Describe what an active listener does.
- Explain how electronic databases are used for target marketing.

Consider what you know

- Businesses use forecasting, scheduling, inventory management, and coordinated planning to decide what goods or services to provide, how much of the goods and services is needed, and when to produce them.

Consider what you want to know

- What part does marketing play in delivering goods and services to consumers?
- What four elements do marketers consider when selling to consumers? How do consumers make buying decisions?
- How can you learn to be a good listener in business?
- How do businesses use electronic databases?

Consider how to use what you learn

- As you read this chapter, think about ways marketing affects you and people you know. How are the products and services you and your family use marketed to you?

Multimedia Resources

Technology Resource Guide
Distance Learning Guide
Internet Resource Guide
Professional Resources
School-to-Work/Tech Prep Strategies
Instructional Poster
Spanish Resources

Testmaker Software for Chapter 11
The Wall Street Journal Video Series Video & Activities for Chapter 11
Business and Marketing Computer Applications—An Integrated Software Simulation Using Microsoft Works
Stocktracker—A Stock Market Software Simulation
Where's the Dough? Board Game

Motivate the Learning

Learning Objectives
Point out that the learning objectives show what students will learn in the chapter. Tell students to keep these objectives in mind as they work through the chapter. Note that the last two objectives listed refer to the Focus on Technology feature and the Building Business Skills feature.

Consider What You Know
Review briefly the main sections of *Chapter 10 Producing Goods and Services Worldwide:* Production and Operations; Controlling Production; Making Production Efficient; and Working in Operations and Production.

Consider What You Want to Know
Have students keep the listed questions in mind as they preview the chapter by quickly paging through it, looking at the photographs, and reading the section headings and figure titles.

Consider How to Use What You Learn
Explain to students that at the end of the chapter they will develop projects related to marketing. Suggest that as they read the chapter they keep in mind how marketing of goods and services in today's world affects them.

TEACH

Business Connection

General Motors will end production of the Cadillac Fleetwood, Buick Roadmaster, and Chevrolet Caprice and Impala SS Models after the 1996 model year. Elimination of these big cars was driven by the market, which no longer supported these particular models. At its Arlington, Texas, plant GM will begin manufacturing trucks instead.

Develop Concepts

Elements of Marketing

Emphasize the four elements (product, price, promotion, place) of the *marketing mix* by drawing a chart on the board or a transparency. Have volunteers fill in the chart with definitions and examples. Remind students that the marketing mix is the combination of activities that encourages consumers to buy specific products or services.

Learning Activity

Ask students if they agree or disagree with the following observation: "People used to need products to survive. Now products need people to survive." As students give their reactions, tally the results on the board. Then ask them to explain the relationship between their answers and the marketing of goods and services.

You are standing in a supermarket checkout line. While you wait, you look around and see a display rack holding several different magazines. As an afterthought, you add a magazine to your order of groceries. The placement of that magazine is a marketing device. Merchants deliberately place magazines, batteries, razor blades, and other inexpensive items next to checkout counters. They know that many shoppers, waiting their turn in line, will be tempted to buy one or more of the items even though they had not intended to make that purchase before they got into the line. Placement is just one of many techniques that merchants and manufacturers use to try to persuade consumers in many countries to buy their products. Together, these techniques are known as marketing. In this chapter you will learn how marketing affects your own buying decisions as well as the decisions of other consumers, both in the United States and in other countries.

ELEMENTS OF MARKETING

Just as the production of goods and services requires planning and decision making, so does the marketing of those goods and services. Marketing specialists must ask and answer many questions about the product. Will it appeal to buyers? How much should it cost? How can the seller tell consumers about the product? Where should the product be sold? How can it appeal to consumers in other countries? These factors—product, price, promotion, and place—all make up the **marketing mix,** the activities that go into the selling of a product to consumers.

Product

Marketing specialists do studies and take surveys to find out what goods and services people need or want to buy. Then goods and services are produced to meet those needs and desires. Products are designed to include qualities—such as colors, models, styles, and features—that the business expects will appeal to consumers.

Price

Manufacturers and sellers must determine a price for their products or services. The price must be set at a level to attract buyers. It also must be high enough to generate a profit and cover the costs and expenses that the business has in

Meeting Student Diversity

For some students, taking notes while listening for information can be challenging. Here are some hints to share with students to make note taking easier:
Have pen and paper handy at the beginning of every class. Make up your own "shorthand" using symbols and abbreviations. Write faster, but keep your writing legible. Use an outline format, and use phrases, not complete sentences.

producing, distributing, and selling the product. Price can be set high or low, depending on the customers the business wants to attract and the pricing practices of competitors.

Promotion

Promotion includes all of those activities that go into telling consumers about the product or service and trying to persuade them to buy it. Promotion includes advertising, public relations, in-store displays, sales, coupons, and games. It also includes various kinds of personal selling. When salesclerks in a store help you select an item, they are promoting the product. Promotion includes offering products through catalogs and other direct mailings, on television, or over the telephone.

Place

Place refers to where the product or service is sold. Marketers want to place goods where buyers will find them most conveniently. Fast-food stands and auto dealerships often are located on major highways. Shoe stores, dress shops, and department stores may be located in malls or downtown shopping areas.

Place also means the placement or location of goods within a store. Items in supermarkets and drugstores are often carefully situated to maximize sales. Toys and games, for example, are usually located at the eye level of children because marketers know that they are the ones who are most likely to want those products. Groups of products, such as different brands of shampoos or different brands of T-shirts, are nearly always displayed in the same area. This way shoppers can locate the brands they want and compare prices of different brands.

Quick Check

1. What do marketers mean by the marketing mix?
2. What are the four factors that make up the marketing mix?

PRODUCT PLANNING

Many different elements go into the process of planning products, whether those products are goods or services. Marketing specialists have to consider the type of product they are producing, its life cycle, and the needs and motivations of consumers. Often marketing specialists must consider how the product might suit the needs of the foreign market, too. Study

Hyatt Hotels Corporation has a new way to appeal to traveling families—sell to teens. The Rock Hyatt program, which began at the chain's resort hotels in the early 1990s, is the first in the lodging industry to target teens. Rock Hyatt features excursions, sports clinics, tours, and social events. Parents also benefit. They get a discount on the price of their first room when they book a second hotel room. Hyatt Hotels Corporation hopes the program will create teen loyalty today and adult patronage in the future.

Sometimes the customer and the consumer are separate people. Adults buy most breakfast cereals, but they buy what their children will consume. In businesses, purchasing managers buy products that company employees use. Marketers must be aware of this separation and plan how to focus their product's appeal.

Learning Activity
Ask students: In what ways is placement of a product in a store similar to production layout in a factory? What problems does it cause consumers when a grocery store rearranges items in its aisles?

Quick Check Answers

1. The activities that go into the selling of a product or service to consumers.
2. Product, price, promotion, and place.

Develop Concepts

Product Planning

Point out that finding the right product to meet consumers' needs is a challenge because consumers' needs constantly change. Emphasize that the first decision involves the type of product to be produced. Have students look in their texts for definitions of the three kinds of consumer goods and examples of them. List these on the board or a transparency and encourage students to offer other examples.

Curriculum Connection   Math

Present the following problems to students:
1. A local candy company spent $45,000 on advertising last quarter. Seven percent of this was spent on radio ads. How much money did it spend on radio ads? ($45,000 \times .07 = \$3,150$)
2. If a product sells for $3.10, how much can be attributed to marketing costs if marketing costs are 48 percent of the selling price? ($3.10 \times .48 = 1.488 = \$1.49$)
3. If a shoe manufacturer has a 26 percent market share of the $5.5 billion athletic shoe industry, what is its share in dollars? ($5.5 \times .26 = \$1.43$ billion)

For students who need to sharpen their math skills, choose among the worksheets in the *Math Skills Review* booklet.

of the market helps business produce goods and services that will appeal to consumers.

Types of Products

All goods and services are sold to consumers, to the makers of other goods and services, or to governments. Goods sold to individuals and families are called **consumer goods.** Consumer goods can be divided into the following three categories.

- *Convenience goods and services.* Convenience goods and services are products that consumers use regularly without spending much effort. Convenience products include items such as milk and bread or services such as automatic postage machines. These products are not expensive and are available in many different places. Consumers will usually accept one of several brands.
- *Shopping goods and services.* Shopping products or services are those that consumers purchase after spending some time looking around and comparing similar products. They are usually expensive goods or services, such as vehicles, higher-priced items of clothing, or a disc jockey for a party.
- *Specialty goods and services.* Specialty products are those that consumers often select by brand or by company. They usually require a special sales effort. Specialty goods include cameras, sports and stereo equipment, perfume and fine watches. Specialty services include bicycle repairs or car detailing.

Goods that are sold to the makers of other goods and services are called industrial products. They include supplies, raw materials, and component parts. Supplies are paper, computer disks, order forms, and other products that a company uses to conduct its business. Raw materials are unprocessed natural resources such as oil, wood, iron ore, and wheat, which are processed into a finished product. Component parts are made from raw materials and are used to produce other products. Amplifiers, car seats, and computer keyboards are all component parts. Governments at local, state, and federal levels are also consumers. They need such products as computers, automobiles, and office supplies to carry out their services to the public.

Life Cycle of a Product

When analyzing products, people speak of a product's life cycle. Products come into existence, are popular or fashionable for a while, then fade away. The life cycle of a product goes through the four phases shown in Figure 11-1 on page 175.

Global Perspective

The United States is increasingly part of a global marketplace. A walk down the aisles of any supermarket will likely reveal ethnic foods such as burritos, sushi, and couscous. Ask students how as customers they might influence a supermarket's decision to market such foods. (If such products are popular, owners will continue to stock them and may even expand selections; if not, owners will discontinue them.)

Refer to the *International Business Strategies* booklet for additional strategies and activities.

FIGURE 11-1

The life cycle of a product has four phases. What happens during the growth phase of the life cycle of a product?

Product Life Cycle

Introduction Phase	Growth Phase	Mature Phase	Declining Phase
Product is placed on the market.	Sales and profits increase and competition appears.	Sales level off and profits begin to fall.	Product is no longer profitable and producer stops making it.

Dollars

Time

Product Sales

Product Profits

0

USE VISUALS

Reinforce the concept of the life cycle of a product depicted in Figure 11-1 by pointing out that fad items, such as yo-yos, usually have a short life cycle. Other products, such as cornflakes, have an extended life cycle.
Answer to caption: Sales and profits increase, and competitors appear.

USE TRANSPARENCIES

Use Teaching Transparency 11-1 and its corresponding strategies and worksheet from the *Teaching Transparency Strategies and Worksheets* booklet to reinforce the four phases of the life cycle of a product. Verify student worksheets using the Answer Key.

Learning Activity

Discuss with students that sometimes the products on the market reflect certain social and psychological needs that change. People students' age often want to buy things that "everyone else has," for example, whether those things are items of clothing, certain types of athletic shoes, or even certain types of notebooks or carrying cases. What changes have students observed in items they and their peers want and buy? Have the group list items popular to them as consumers for the last two years.

- *Introduction phase.* The product is placed on the market for the first time. The producer often loses money on the product at this stage because of little revenue compared to costs of development.
- *Growth phase.* If the product becomes popular, it will experience a growth phase. Sales and profits will increase sharply. Other producers will begin to make similar products to compete with it.
- *Mature phase.* Sales level off, and profits begin to fall in a product's mature phase because there are more producers and a steady demand.
- *Declining phase.* Decline is the last stage in the life cycle of the product. It is no longer profitable, so the producer stops making it. The producer may introduce a better-quality or more attractive version of the product to replace it.

Clothing and automobile manufacturers, for example, introduce new products and retire older ones each year because their products go through their life cycles so rapidly. Other products may take several years to go through the life cycle.

Meeting Consumer Needs

To sell products successfully, marketing experts must understand the needs of consumers. As a consumer, you spend your

Reteaching Strategy

Have students draw a comic strip or a series of illustrations or create a collage, based on Figure 11-1 on page 175, portraying the life cycle of one product. Encourage students to show how attitudes change over time. Students may wish to work in groups to divide up the research and illustration tasks. Display completed projects to emphasize the variety of products that have come and gone.

FOCUS ON **Technology**

Discuss

Ask students for other examples of target marketing they have experienced. Have students define the terms *data, database, records,* and *fields* as they pertain to electronic databases. (*Data:* information composed of numbers and letters; *database:* collection of related records; *records:* related data items; *fields:* information in each record.)

Learning Activity

Have students bring in examples of advertising for different products from various sources. Suggest that they prepare a bulletin board display in which they classify the ads into whichever of the three basic needs each ad seems to appeal to the most: physical needs, social needs, or psychological needs. Let students add to the display as they continue to work through this chapter.

Electronic Databases

The mail has just arrived, bringing you a sample of the new concert video featuring your favorite group, Makin' the Grade. As you open the package, you begin to wonder, "Who sent this? How did they know I'd want this concert video? Where did they find my address?"

Congratulations! You've been target marketed. The marketers know not everyone will want "Makin' the Grade—In Concert." Rather than send samples to everyone, the marketer limits the scope of the sampling, targeting people most likely to want that video.

Target marketing depends on the ability of computers to sort through large amounts of data to find bits or pieces of information that match given criteria. *Data* consists of information composed of numbers and letters. For example, your name, your address, and your date of birth are data.

A *database* is a collection of related records. The *records* contain related data items. For instance, records consisting of the names, addresses, and birth dates of your classmates can be collected to form a database. The information in each record is organized in separate *fields*. A student's record in a school's student database might contain seven fields—first name, last name, street address, city, state, zip code, and year of birth.

Information about a person may appear in several databases. For instance, the store where you rent videos keeps your name, address, and a record of what you rent in its customer database. Each time someone uses a credit card to buy a CD, the credit company makes a record of the sale. This record, including the name and

money to meet three basic kinds of needs: physical needs, social needs, and psychological needs. Physical needs include the necessities of life such as food, clothing, housing, and transportation. Physical needs also include the need for health, safety, and security. When you go to the doctor, purchase a life insurance policy, or put deadbolt locks on your doors, you are meeting physical needs.

Social needs are the need to be loved and accepted by others. Out of these needs grow the desire to be attractive, especially to the opposite sex. Marketing specialists appeal to our social needs when they sell such items as cologne, skin care products, and deodorant.

Psychological needs involve the need for approval and prestige. To meet psychological needs, people buy things that show they have accomplished something. One person might buy very expensive shoes. Another might go to a fashionable restaurant.

What "basic needs" are is a debatable issue. Some would say "basic needs" are equally represented in the physical, social, and psychological needs categories. But most experts would say that "basic needs" fall primarily in the physical needs category. These needs must be met before other needs are met.

176 UNIT 3 DYNAMICS OF BUSINESS IN A CHANGING WORLD

Making Connections ⇨ Social Awareness

Direct students to choose a product that is potentially harmful, such as cigarettes or alcoholic beverages, and research the issues involved in marketing the product. Remind students that they must show an awareness of the harm from using the product and then must discuss why they think restrictions on marketing the product are or are not necessary. Have students share their findings in an oral presentation to the class. Encourage members of the class to react to the presentations.

address of the buyer and the name of the CD and the artist, becomes part of their database. When you enter a contest to win tickets to a Makin' the Grade concert, the concert promoter adds your name, address, and age to its database.

Marketing companies buy databases generated by video stores, credit companies, and ticket sellers. Using special software, marketers search the databases looking for matches to their pre-selected criteria. With such software, a high-speed personal computer can check hundreds of thousands of records.

The usefulness of electronic databases reaches far beyond target marketing. Businesses rely on electronic databases for a variety of applications including employee payroll records, merchandise and parts inventories, and company sales records. What's more, businesses are constantly finding new ways to use electronic databases. The ability to search large volumes of data at great speed to find specific information is becoming an important part of making sound business decisions.

Follow Through

Have students speculate about the impact of electronic databases on the way businesses perform routine tasks. How have databases made some tasks easier? (They have made it possible to process large amounts of information in a short time.) Ask students to describe any use of electronic databases with which they are familiar.

For additional information about current technology, refer to the *Technology Resources Guide* booklet.

Learning Activity

Ask students: Do you think it is easier for advertising to appeal to a consumer's physical, social, or psychological needs? Have students explain their answers. Then have students provide examples of current advertising on television, radio, or in print that appeals to physical, social, and psychological needs to illustrate their points.

Since people buy items to meet their needs, a distinction is made between nondiscretionary and discretionary income. *Nondiscretionary income* is used to buy items to meet basic needs. *Discretionary income* is the income left over after the basic needs are met. Knowing this distinction enables the marketer to determine the marketing plan to use. For example, advertising appealing to the emotions is more frequently used for marketing items purchased with discretionary income, rather than nondiscretionary income.

Understanding Consumer Motivations

No two people buy exactly the same goods and services to satisfy their needs. You buy one brand of toothpaste, and your best friend buys another. Both brands, however, meet the same need. Each of us has different motives for buying the products that we do. There are three types of motives:

- *Rational motives.* Consumers are motivated to think logically about a purchase. When you compare the prices and quality of similar products, you are being rational.

Enrichment Strategy

Invite a marketing specialist from a local company to speak to students about the company's market, marketing department, and marketing strategy. Also ask the speaker to emphasize the personal and career qualifications necessary for a marketing specialist. Prior to the visit, ask students to find out as much as they can about the company and have them submit questions that you forward to the speaker.

Quick Check Answers

1. Goods sold to individuals and families; the gathering of information that businesses use to determine what kind of goods or services to produce; the study of population.
2. The type of product they are producing, its life cycle, and the needs and motivations of consumers.

- *Emotional motives.* Feelings or attitudes cause you to buy on impulse or to buy a product when logic tells you that you really cannot afford it. They also influence you to select a particular model, color, or style of a product.
- *Patronage motives.* You may always go to the same hair stylist or drink the same brand of orange juice. Patronage motivation also causes you to be loyal to certain shops and companies. You may like to shop at one clothing store, even though it is farther away than another. Companies spend a great deal of money each year trying to win the loyalty of consumers to their products and services.

Using Market Research

Have you ever been approached by a marketing researcher while you were shopping at a mall? Market researchers commonly ask shoppers to take a few minutes to answer questions, taste a new food, or watch a new commercial.

Market research is the gathering of information that businesses can use to determine what kind of goods or services to produce. Market researchers study people to find out what they want to buy and what they are buying. By using market research, forecasters predict how many goods or services a business can expect to sell.

Market researchers also gather information from a wider group of people. To do this they use **demographics,** the study of population. Where people live, how much income they have to spend, and what newspapers they like to read are just a few examples of information that market researchers collect. Researchers gather such information from maps, census reports, local businesses and chambers of commerce, utility companies, and bus and rail lines.

Some market research studies are elaborate and expensive. Others can be quite simple. For example, in some supermarkets computer-linked cash registers automatically subtract products from the store's inventory. When the results are tallied, managers can see which products (at which prices) are moving the fastest. Then they can make decisions about pricing products and relocating them.

Quick Check

1. Define *consumer goods, market research,* and *demographics.*
2. What elements do marketing specialists consider in planning products and services?

Cooperative Learning   Group Discussion

Divide the class into small groups of three or four students. Assign each group this topic: "Should advertising directed at children be regulated by the government? If regulations are recommended, what specific advertising techniques should not be allowed in advertising directed at children?" Assign a time limit for the group discussions, and when the time limit has expired, ask a representative of each group to share a summary of its discussion.

Refer to the *Cooperative Learning Strategies* booklet for additional cooperative learning strategies.

PRICING, PACKAGING, AND PROMOTION

A producer has decided what type of good or service to produce and found out what the life cycle of the product will be. The marketing specialist has planned the product or service to satisfy consumer needs and appeal to consumer motivations. Market research has confirmed that this product or service has a strong market and should sell well.

What is the next step for marketing specialists? They must make decisions about pricing the goods or services, packaging them, and promoting them so consumers will buy them.

Pricing

Would you pay $15 for a box of popcorn? No, but you might pay $75 for a good pair of shoes. Price is the value that producers and sellers place on goods or services. The pricing of a product or service involves many factors. The price must cover the total costs of producing, shipping, and promoting the product, plus a profit.

Just what exactly goes into figuring the total cost of a product? Of course oil, popping corn, boxes, and salaries of the workers are costs of producing boxed popcorn, but what are some others? Some costs remain the same regardless of how much popcorn is produced. These are called fixed costs. Fixed costs may include rent for work space, cooking equipment, and executive salaries. Variable costs change depending upon how much product is produced. Again, if the product is popcorn, the costs of oil, popping corn, boxes, and salaries for people who are making and boxing the popcorn are included in the product's total costs. The point at which the total cost is equal to the total money the product earns is the **break-even point,** as you can see in Figure 11-2 on page 180.

The way a product is priced delivers certain messages to consumers. If two similar products range widely in price, the consumer may think that the higher-priced product is of better quality. A very high price suggests exclusiveness. A very low price may suggest low quality, even though many low-priced products offer very good value for the money. Businesses must remember that their pricing strategy conveys an image of their product in the marketplace.

Who sets the price on goods and services? In many cases, sellers set the price recommended by the manufacturer. Some sellers base their price on market research that has determined how much consumers are willing to pay for a particular

F.Y.I.

Companies try to bridge the gap between consumers' rational and emotional sides. Lever Brothers is a company that has done so by using an effective product symbol. It created an advertising campaign to promote fabric softener using a teddy bear named "Snuggle." The teddy bear was designed to appeal to consumers' emotions. It is also a good image for a fabric softener because it is soft and cuddly.

Develop Concepts

Pricing, Packaging, and Promotion

Remind students that they have considered how to plan a new product; now they will consider how to price, package, and promote it. Introduce the concept by pointing out that fragrance manufacturers often appeal to customers through packaging. Ask students to think of other examples. List on the board aspects of packaging that students find appealing.

Learning Activity

Ask students to think of products that cost $5, $50, or $500. Have students volunteer products that are "reasonable" at each price, emphasizing that the price of a product should cover the costs of producing, shipping, promoting, and distributing it. List student responses under the three price columns. Then ask students how they think a company determines what the price of a product will be. Use this discussion to lead into the concept of the *break-even point,* the point when the total cost of making a product equals the total money the product earns.

Reteaching Strategy

Tell students that they are a group of market researchers who are brainstorming a survey to help them develop a new breakfast cereal. Tell them that they may suggest anything that they think could help develop and then sell the product, including offering special promotions on the package or special prizes inside. Accept all suggestions and write them on the board or a transparency. When all suggestions have been recorded, have the class decide by a show of hands which suggestions should remain and which should be discarded. Ask a volunteer to prepare a final version of the survey that can be photocopied and distributed by the students.

Building Business Skills

Model

Distribute Enrichment Master 11-1, Active Listening Checklist, to students. Have them complete the list. Then ask them which of the 13 skills listed they identified as S or N. Determine which skills students are deficient in and work through those with the class. Ask students how they could practice the checklist skills in a work situation.

Use Visuals

To reinforce the concept of the break-even point illustrated in Figure 11-2, point out that in order to increase profits, a business must sell more of its products and/or lower its total costs. Answer to caption: You would need to sell 2000 boxes of popcorn to earn $3000. Any boxes more than 2000 would be profit.

Learning Activity

Present this problem to students: A clothing manufacturer plans to produce 25,000 sweatshirts. The sweatshirts will be sold to stores for $16 each. The cost of manufacturing and marketing each sweatshirt is $10. How many sweatshirts must be sold at $16 to reach the break-even point? (25,000 × 10 = 250,000; 250,000 ÷ 16 = 15,625) Refer to the *Math Skills Review* booklet for additional strategies and activities.

COMMUNICATION
Developing Listening Skills

Explanation

Listening is something you do every day. You probably can't remember a time when you weren't listening—to your mom, your best friend, your coach, your favorite singer, or a TV comic. What more can you possibly learn about listening—something you've done all your life? The answer is "a lot." Most of the listening we do is passive. It just happens. We use our ears but not our minds. However, passive listening is not enough for business or for school.

It takes practice to use your mind to listen actively, but the rewards are great. In business, good communication spells success, and good communication includes listening as well as speaking, reading, and writing. Active listening can help you brainstorm new ideas successfully, learn new procedures quickly, and understand a customer's complicated request.

Practice

Just how do you turn passive listening into an active skill? Use this checklist to help yourself become an active listener. On a separate sheet of paper, answer each question **A** (always), **F** (frequently), **S** (sometimes), or **N** (never).

product. A change in consumer demand may affect the price the seller has set.

Price can be used as a competitive strategy. Marketing specialists may try to lure consumers away from their favorite

FIGURE 11-2

The break-even point is reached when the money from product sales equals the costs of making and distributing the product. After that point is reached, businesses begin to make a profit on the product. If the break-even point is $3000, how many boxes of popcorn would you need to sell at $1.50 per box before you make a profit?

Cooperative Learning   Brainstorming

Assign students to teams and ask each team to design an advertising campaign for a product they might produce. Set a time limit, and, when the time limit has expired, ask each team to share its advertising campaign with the class. Vote as a class to find the most effective advertising campaign. If possible, have the entire class implement the winning advertising campaign.

Refer to the *Cooperative Learning Strategies* booklet for additional cooperative learning strategies.

ACTIVE LISTENING CHECKLIST

When you are listening, do you:

1. Determine a purpose for listening?　A F S N
2. Avoid doing something else at the same time?　A F S N
3. Screen out sights or sounds that could distract you?　A F S N
4. Keep your eyes on the speaker?　A F S N
5. Concentrate on what the person is saying?　A F S N
6. Pick out the important ideas and think about how they are related?　A F S N
7. Summarize the ideas in your head?　A F S N

8. Take notes to help you focus and remember?　A F S N
9. Ask the person to repeat or explain something that isn't clear to you?　A F S N
10. Avoid interrupting before the speaker is finished talking?　A F S N
11. Avoid thinking of what you will say next?　A F S N
12. Pay attention even if you think the person's words don't interest you?　A F S N
13. Listen carefully even if it takes time and effort to understand what the person is saying?　A F S N

If all your answers are **A** or **F**, you have great listening skills! If not, you need practice. Each week choose two questions you answered **S** or **N**. Practice these skills in school, at home, and as you watch TV. Keep notes to see how you improve. Now you're on your way to becoming an active listener for school and your business career.

Practice
Have students review their individual answers to the Active Listening Checklist questions, especially those that indicated that they needed to practice their listening skills. Then direct students to write a short paragraph describing those situations in which they could best practice these skills and explain why.

Students who need additional practice will benefit from the listening activities in the *Communication Skills Review*.

brands by offering nearly identical products at slightly lower prices. Marketing people also use pricing to make products more appealing. They might offer special sale prices on certain products.

Packaging

Consumers are strongly influenced by the way products are packaged. A lot of thought goes into the packaging. Packaging must be attractive. If the product is a good, the package must explain clearly how to use it. It must prevent tampering and protect the contents from breaking or spilling. Some goods such as medications are packaged with special tops so that small children cannot open them.

The labels on packages are advertisements for the product. Labels include the **logo,** which is the symbol of the manufacturer, and the brand name of the product. The label also may give directions for using the product and list the ingredients. Many food labels provide nutritional information as well.

CHAPTER 11　MARKETING IN TODAY'S WORLD　**181**

Curriculum Connection　History

Have students choose a product and research advertising for that product from recent sources and from sources 20 or 30 years ago. Students should compare and contrast the techniques and the sources in a presentation to the class. Encourage students to reproduce examples of the advertising to use as part of their presentations.

Learning Activity
Ask students to think about the ways various products they buy are packaged. Have students list on the board different purposes packaging serves. What are some "pet peeves" students have about certain packaging? Why do they think the producers of those goods package them that way? Ask volunteers for examples of changes in packaging that companies have made in response to consumer concerns. (One example is the childproof caps on over-the-counter medicines, and the addition of caps that are not childproof for adults-only households.)

Learning Activity
Have students research the kinds of information on food packages. Ask them to find out about the requirement for the nutritional information on food packages, including the format. Why is it necessary to have foods labeled in a standard fashion? Ask students to bring in several examples of food packages and compare the information on them.

Point out to students that political advertising also sells a product—a political candidate. Such advertising is sometimes controversial. Ask students whether they think advertising is the best way for people to get information about candidates. What other ways can citizens use to get information about candidates in order to cast a well-reasoned vote?

Quick Check Answers

1. The point at which the total cost is equal to the total money the product earns; the symbol of the manufacturer; paid promotion.
2. Pricing, packaging, and promotion.

Develop Concepts

Distributing Goods and Services

Ask students to define the word *distribution*. Guide them to its meaning as the act of supplying products and services to people who want to buy them. Encourage students to supply the names of local companies that are distributors. Have students determine the types of products the companies supply.

Promotion

Promotion includes all of the activities involved in selling a product. Promotion means telling consumers about a product and creating a demand for it. **Advertising** is paid promotion. Businesses and organizations use advertising not only to promote products and services but also to generate ideas and educate the public. For example, soft drink companies spend a lot of money to promote the image of their products.

The people who purchase advertisements are called sponsors. Sponsors advertise in many different ways. They use television commercials, catalogs, magazine and newspaper ads, billboards, direct mail, and even the products themselves. The makers of designer jeans and T-shirts display their logos and brand names in a prominent place on their products. Consumers advertise the product whenever they wear it.

Advertising firms are service businesses that design and produce advertisements. Advertising is a highly competitive business. Some advertisements, particularly television commercials, are very costly to make. A television commercial may cost $1 million to produce. It may cost another $500,000 to purchase air time on television for the commercial. Although television commercials cost a lot to make, they usually generate many millions of dollars in product sales.

Quick Check

1. Define *break-even point, logo,* and *advertising.*
2. What three factors must marketers decide about a product?

DISTRIBUTING GOODS AND SERVICES

Marketers have to decide how and where consumers will buy their goods and services. This is the place decision of the marketing mix. To make this decision, marketers must decide on their channel of distribution. The **channel of distribution** includes all of the people who direct products to consumers. Figure 11-3 on page 183 depicts the channels of distribution that producers use to move goods to consumers. Because these people work at getting the product from the producer to the final user, they are called intermediaries or go-betweens. These intermediaries can include the following:

Curriculum Connection   English and Communication

Ask students to interview owners of local businesses. Have students devise a set of interview questions that will help them establish the channel of distribution that the business employs to obtain its products. Students must submit written answers to their questionnaires as well as write a 100-word report summarizing their findings.

For students who need to sharpen their writing skills, choose among the worksheets in the *Communication Skills Review* booklet.

FIGURE 11-3

Producers of goods use several main channels of distribution to get their products to consumers. Which channel do consumers deal directly with?

- Distributors are intermediaries who represent a single manufacturer in a specific geographical area. Cosmetics, cars, furniture, and shoes are sold through distributors.
- Wholesalers are another kind of intermediary. They receive large shipments of products from many different producers. They break the shipments into smaller batches for resale. A company that makes canned peas may sell a truckload of its peas to a wholesaler. The wholesaler, in turn, will sell a few cases of peas to each of several local supermarkets.
- Retailers are intermediaries who sell goods directly to the consumer, the final stop in the channel of distribution. When you buy something in a supermarket, drugstore, or department store, you are dealing with a retailer.

Quick Check

1. Name the three types of intermediaries that direct products to consumers.
2. What part of the marketing mix does distribution address?
3. What is a *channel of distribution?*

SPECIAL CONCERNS FOR INTERNATIONAL MARKETERS

Marketers dealing with international markets face special challenges. These include communication difficulties, varying

Help students understand the difference among the three kinds of intermediaries (distributors, wholesalers, retailers) shown in Figure 11-3 by having them look through the local yellow pages for names of companies that fall into the three categories. Answer to caption: Consumers deal directly with retailers.

Quick Check Answers

1. Distributors, wholesalers, and retailers.
2. Place.
3. All the people who direct products to consumers.

Develop Concepts

Special Concerns for International Marketers

Reinforce some of the special concerns international marketers face by asking volunteers to provide examples with which they are familiar. Invite students with ties to other countries to contribute to the examples. Students who speak a language other than English also may be able to offer examples of language misunderstandings.

Curriculum Connection   Science

To store goods for a long period, many warehouses must be strictly temperature controlled. Have students select several different products and then research how those products would have to be stored to maintain their product quality. Ask students to present their research in a 250-word report and include diagrams if possible.

CHAPTER 11

Point out to students that an important part of communication with anyone is to consider their point of view and how it might be different from your own. In business communication, especially with people from other countries and cultures, it is important to be prepared. This may mean doing some research in advance when possible.

Business Brief

The competitive environment in other countries is often different from what is common in the United States. In some areas, including Europe and the Middle East, cartels are a standard feature. A cartel is a group of firms (or sometimes even countries) that agree to limit participation in a market. Cartels are illegal in this country in light of antitrust laws. However, U.S. firms often must deal with cartels in overseas markets.

---

traditions and customs, and differences in people's buying habits.

Communication

Certainly understanding the language used by the people you are dealing with is important. Even in the United States, knowing a language other than English can be helpful. For example, knowing Spanish can help any marketer in southern Florida, parts of Chicago and New York City, or the Southwest. United States businesses involved with international trade have learned some difficult communication lessons. Chevrolet tried to market its Nova model in South America, but sales were very slow. Finally, the company realized that the phrase *no va* in Spanish means "does not go."

Traditions and Customs

The culture of a people includes their customs and traditions as well as their language. Often it is cultural differences that are the most troublesome for international marketers. Businesspeople in the United States tend to organize their work by deadlines. Yet those who work in Arabia have learned that Arabians do not like deadlines and may even feel threatened by having to meet specific scheduled dates. In the United States, some businesses consider the giving and receiving of gifts between company and client to hint at bribery. However, in some other countries, such as several in the Middle East, gifts are expected and are exchanged publicly.

Differences in Buying Habits

Part of market research for those businesses offering their products abroad is a careful study of the potential market. Questions like these must be answered by research:

- Is there a need for our product?
- Who are its potential customers?
- What is their level of earnings?
- What are their buying habits?
- What are their motives for buying?

Every country is different. Market research done for one does not provide answers suitable for another. People choose to buy things based on their system of values, and every culture has a different value system. General Foods of the United States tried to market its cakes and cookies in England. The company

Global Perspective

Brand names that are successful in one country may not be so when translated into another language. Here are some examples. The Japanese once tried to sell a baby soap called Skinababe and a hair product called Blow Up in the United States. In Spanish-speaking countries, Ford's Fiera meant "ugly old woman" and General Motors' Nova meant "it doesn't go," if pronounced *no va*. Ask students if they have encountered any other such failure of brand names to translate into another culture.

Refer to the *International Business Strategies* booklet for additional strategies and activities.

When a businessperson is in another country, he or she must know enough about the customs to participate politely and effectively. What are some cultural differences you observe in this photograph of two businessmen in Japan?

discovered too late that English shoppers look for gelatin as an ingredient in those foods, and it was not an ingredient in their offerings.

Quick Check

1. What are the three types of challenges that international marketers face?
2. What kind of differences are the most troublesome for international marketers?

WORKING IN MARKETING

People who like to meet the needs of others often pick a job in marketing. In almost every marketing job, workers come into contact with people every day. In today's business environment, a person who works in marketing needs to enjoy working with people from around the world. Marketing employees have other important traits as well. See if any of them apply to you.

- *Communication.* People who work in marketing spend a lot of time talking to people and writing messages to them. They also spend a lot of time listening to others and reading what others write. Marketers who work with people from other countries need to be especially careful with communication. Often a second language is helpful.

Business & HISTORY

Earl S. Tupper, the plastics engineer who invented Tupperware, also popularized a marketing strategy. He began producing his first polyethylene bowls with sealable lids in 1945. Instead of selling his products to stores or through mail order, he sold his food containers at "Tupperware parties" in people's homes. The parties proved to be a very effective way of distributing and selling his products. Tupperware continues today to be sold at parties.

Ask students what they think businesspeople must do before they travel abroad on business.
Answer to caption: Differences include the surroundings, such as the screen, the floor mat, and the low table; the custom of sitting cross-legged on the mat instead of in chairs.

Quick Check Answers
1. Communication difficulties, varying traditions and customs, and differences in people's buying habits.
2. Cultural differences are the most troublesome.

Develop Concepts

Working in Marketing
Ask students if they have participated in any market research activities (telephone solicitation or samples distributed at the supermarket). Encourage them to describe the process and to analyze their reactions to the marketing activity. Record their responses. Ask students to try to match the activity to one of the traits listed on pages 185–186. Conclude by asking students if they would like to work in marketing.

Making Connections ⇨ Business Ethics

Provide students with the following scenario: You are a marketing specialist with Becker Products. One of your coworkers, Kim Stanley, a part-time data entry clerk, confides that she is also working part-time for Martin-Ames, one of Becker's competitors. Do you see any problems with Kim's working for two companies that are in the same business? (Answer: There may be a conflict of interest. Kim has access to marketing information for both companies. It would be unethical for her to share one company's information with the other, even unwittingly.)

Refer to the *Ethics in Business Strategies* booklet for additional strategies and activities.

Learning Activity

Encourage interested students to find out more about marketing as a career. Point out that one way to start is by working in retail, as a salesclerk or sales associate. Tell students that a valuable sales associate knows the merchandise being sold. Students can develop their interest in a product, such as women's clothing or computers, into specialized knowledge that can help them get and keep a job in that field. Students might also gather job applications from several retail stores and compare the requirements.

Quick Check Answers

1. Because they come into contact with people every day.
2. Communication, human relations, math skills, motivation, and creativity/problem solving.

- *Human relations.* Liking people is not enough to work in marketing. Marketing workers also have to get along well with all of their co-workers. They also have to understand why people do and say certain things. A knowledge of the customs of people in other countries is essential for people working in international marketing.
- *Math skills.* Basic math skills are important in any job, but they are especially important in marketing. Careless mistakes can result in lost sales, overlooked payments, and customer complaints. Anyone who works in international marketing must also understand foreign currencies and exchange rates, too.
- *Motivation.* Marketing workers are very goal-oriented and have a lot of enthusiasm. They want to accomplish something worthwhile by providing goods and services to customers. Those who work in international marketing often have an intense curiosity about the world.
- *Creativity/problem solving.* People who work in marketing use their imaginations to make products attractive to customers. They also answer questions and solve problems for customers. Of course, those who work in international marketing need to be sensitive to other cultures. They can better solve marketing problems if they understand the diversity of their customers.

If you decide to take a marketing job, you have many choices. A look at the yellow pages of the telephone book will give you an idea of the many businesses that provide goods and services and that need workers with marketing skills. You could begin a career in marketing as a salesperson, stock clerk, or display arranger. You might then advance to assistant buyer, aisle manager, or advertising assistant. Finally, with experience and well-developed skills, you could step up to buyer, sales manager, or account executive.

Quick Check

1. Why do people who work in marketing need to enjoy working with people?
2. What are some other important traits of marketing employees?

Curriculum Connection   Geography

Direct students to select an area in your local business district such as a block, a small shopping center, or part of a large regional mall. Instruct students to draw a map of that area and label each business. On the map ask students to identify what each business does. Does it provide goods or services? Does it market to customers or to other businesses? How does its location affect the business?

Chapter 11 **Summary**

Main Ideas

1. The marketing mix is made up of product, price, promotion, and place.
2. Market planning involves deciding whether to produce consumer or industrial goods and services and considering the life cycle of the product.
3. Producers of goods and services must understand the physical, social, and psychological needs of consumers and their rational, emotional, and patronage motives for buying goods and services.
4. Market research helps producers determine what people need and want to buy.
5. Products are priced, packaged, and promoted to persuade customers to buy them.
6. People who work in marketing need to be able to communicate well, to get along with people, to have good math skills, to be motivated, and to have creativity and problem-solving skills.
7. Businesses use electronic databases to quickly find specific information to help them make sound business decisions.
8. Active listening is a communication skill that is important in business.

CLOSE

Main Ideas

Main Ideas summarizes the key information in the chapter. It is a useful tool for reinforcement and review.

CASE ANALYSIS

Case Analysis provides a chapter-related case for student analysis and application of decision-making skills.

Answer
Answers will vary depending on the product chosen and students surveyed. Survey questions might include: What product do you use? What other products have you tried? Why do you prefer one product over the others? What features do you like/dislike? Do you remember any advertisements for this item? After students have conducted the survey, they should analyze the results and suggest how they might have altered their survey to gain more information.

CASE ANALYSIS   Marketing

Assume that you are a market researcher. Choose a product that you know your classmates use, such as clothing, pens, sunglasses, or shampoo. Design a survey to find out why people prefer certain brands. Then ask five classmates to take your survey. Ask them about brands, price, color, style, durability, and other qualities. Also ask them how their own needs and motives as well as advertising affect their buying decisions. After you complete the survey, analyze your results. What did you learn about your classmates' likes and dislikes? Do you think they were honest in answering your questions? Could you have designed your survey to obtain more information? If you were a marketer, how would you use the information you gathered?

QUICK QUIZ

1. Name the four elements of the marketing mix. (Product, price, promotion, place.)
2. List the four phases of a product's life cycle. (Introduction, growth, mature, declining.)
3. What three decisions must a marketer make after the product has been planned? (Pricing, packaging, and promotion.)
4. What is a channel of distribution? (The people who direct products to consumers.)
5. Why is communication especially important for international marketers? (Knowledge of the language of the consumers can help prevent obvious mistakes.)

Chapter 11 **Review**

APPLY

Answers

Use the Language of Business

1. logo, **2.** marketing mix, **3.** channel of distribution, **4.** demographics, **5.** advertising, **6.** market research, **7.** break-even point, **8.** consumer goods

Review What You Learned

1. Product, price, promotion, and place.

2. Introduction, growth, maturity, and decline.

3. They may show a logo, directions for use, safety information, and ingredients.

4. Distributors, wholesalers, and retailers.

5. Communication difficulties, varying traditions and customs, and differences in people's buying habits.

6. They need to be able to communicate well, get along with people, have good math skills, be motivated, and have good problem-solving skills and creativity.

7. Information composed of numbers and letters; collection of related records; related data items; information in each record.

8. Passive listening just happens when we don't use our minds. Active listening requires careful thinking.

Understand Business Concepts

1. It allows consumers to find the product or service conveniently and may even prompt a consumer to buy.

2. Many students will probably feel that the product is most important. They will feel that if a product or service is poor, no other element will cause consumers to continue buying the product.

3. Convenience goods are products consumers use regularly, such as items generally found in the supermarket. Shopping goods are more specific and usually more expensive items that require some looking around to find.

Use the Language of Business

People who market goods and services use the following terms. See how well you know them. Match each term to its definition.

advertising
break-even point
channel of distribution
consumer goods
demographics
logo
marketing mix
market research

1. Company's symbol.
2. Elements of product, price, promotion, and place.
3. Group of intermediaries who direct products to consumers.
4. Study of population.
5. Paid promotion.
6. Study showing what types of products and services people like to buy.
7. Point at which money from sales equals the costs of making and distributing a product.
8. Items that are sold to individuals and families.

Review What You Learned

1. Name the four elements of the marketing mix.
2. Name the four phases of a product's life cycle.
3. What information do product labels provide?
4. List three types of intermediaries between a producer and a final user.
5. List three concerns of international marketers.
6. List the five traits that marketing employees need to have.
7. Define the terms *data, database, record,* and *field*.
8. Explain the difference between active and passive listening.

Understand Business Concepts

1. How does placement affect the sales of a product?
2. Which of the four marketing elements do you think is the most important? Why?
3. How are convenience goods and shopping goods different? Give examples.
4. List a product that you think might have a short life cycle and one that might have a long life cycle. Explain your choices.
5. Give examples of products or services that people buy to satisfy physical, social, and psychological needs. Use examples that are not in the text.
6. How might products and services for people's physical, social, and psychological needs vary between countries? Give some examples if you can.
7. What could market researchers learn about a group of people by studying the foods they bought in the last year?
8. Why do you think companies try to design easily recognizable logos?
9. What do you think are some ways businesses could make use of databases?
10. What advantages do you think an active listener has in business?

4. Students might suggest that a new kind of computer game might have a short life cycle but a large household item, such as a refrigerator, would have a long life cycle.

5. Possible answers: physical—house, dentistry; social—clothing accessories, hairstyling; psychological—fur coat, limousine service.

6. Possible answers: physical—types and preparation of foods; social—clothing styles; psychological—types of jewelry and facial makeup.

7. How much money was spent on food per year; what foods were bought at which times of the year; what sizes or brands were most popular.

8. They want their logos to allow their brands to be picked out from a crowd of other products.

9. Students might suggest that databases could be used to keep track of inventory and sales.

10. Active listeners will understand what is presented to them, enabling them to perform better as employees.

Chapter 11 **Review**

Think Critically

1. **Analyze.** Choose a product you bought recently. How did price, packaging, advertising, and placement affect your decision to buy the product?
2. **Classify.** Locate several magazine advertisements. What type of advertisements appeal to consumer motivations in the three basic categories: rational, emotional, and patronage?
3. **Recommend.** Some companies plan special events to draw publicity for a new product. What kind of event could a shoe company hold to attract publicity for a new line of athletic shoes?

1. Answers will vary.
2. Answers will vary.
3. Answers might include: sponsor a basketball game, have a marathon, or hold a contest.

Use What You Learned

1. **Group Project.** Work in teams to conduct a survey of other students, teachers, family members, and people in the community to find out what factors are most important in their buying decisions. Find out:

   - Which stores they shop in most frequently.
   - What types of advertising they pay most attention to.
   - What factors are most important to them when making decisions about convenience goods and services, shopping goods and services, and specialty goods and services.

   Keep a copy of your survey and the results. Summarize the results in a chart to display in your classroom.

2. Find out more about current market research techniques, including database marketing. Use articles from newspapers and business magazines. Write a one-paragraph summary and share it with the class.

3. Write a job description for an entry-level position with a top advertising agency. Include a description of the job duties required as well as a description of the ideal applicant.

4. **Computer Application.** Using on-line research, access government/private databases to obtain the most recent data on leading U.S. advertisers. Select the top ten companies, and use word processing software to present the data in table format. Then write and attractively format a one-paragraph analysis of the kinds of companies that fall within the top categories. Print out the table and your analysis.

5. **Skill Reinforcement.** Review your answers to the Active Listening Checklist on page 181, especially those that indicated you needed to practice your listening skills. Then write a short paragraph describing those situations in which you can best practice those skills and explain why.

Independent Practice

Use the Chapter 11 worksheets in *Student Activity Guide 1* for additional practice and application activities. A Teacher's Annotated Edition provides answers.

ASSESS

Portfolio Assessment

These portfolio projects are designed to lead students to develop a collection of their best work to submit to you for assessment. Refer students to the specific rubric(s) from the *Alternative Assessment Strategies* booklet listed with each of the project notes below. These rubrics will alert students to the criteria you will use to assess their projects.

Chapter Assessment

Use the Chapter 11 Test from the *Test Masters* booklet to evaluate students' understanding of the chapter concepts. An answer key is provided. Or create your own customized test using the *Testmaker* software.

Save your work in your Business Portfolio

Use What You Learned
1. Make sure all students participate in the group project. Rubrics: Survey, Charts and Tables.
2. Let students choose the method they use to share their results. Possible Rubrics: Bulletin Board, Graph, Charts and Tables, Oral Presentation.
3. Remind students that an entry-level position generally requires no previous experience and only basic formal education. Rubric: Paragraph.

4. Students with no access to a computer may carry out this project with research at the library and prepare the table and paragraph manually. Rubrics: Charts and Tables, Paragraph.
5. Students' answers will vary, but should include an analysis of the importance of listening skills for a job in marketing.

Business Issue

DOWNSIZING

Highlight the Issue

Before students read pages 190–191, ask them what they think the term *downsizing* means. Have them make a chart on the board with the headings *Pro* and *Con*. Hold a brief discussion to elicit ideas students have about the pros and cons of downsizing. Fill in the chart appropriately. After students read the pages, have them add to the chart.

Business Issue

DOWNSIZING

When a company drops employees from its payrolls to cut costs, it is called *downsizing*. Should American companies use downsizing to help them become more cost-efficient and increase their competitive edge in the global marketplace?

Pro

Companies that are carrying too much debt, have increased their use of technology, or eliminated product lines often must reduce staff in order to remain efficient. Because employees' wages, salaries, and benefits account for a major portion of a company's budget, management can achieve savings by eliminating jobs. If the company's competitors in the United States and abroad are able to produce a product or service for less money, a company unable to match that lower price may not survive.

Although no one relishes taking away people's jobs, corporations need to show a profit in order to stay in business. Stiffer competition from the global market in the 1990s made profits harder to come by and demanded extreme measures. If a loss of profits forces enough American companies out of business, the whole United States economy will suffer. This means that many more people than those who lose their jobs through downsizing will find themselves without work.

Reductions in staff can actually improve the quality and delivery of products and services to customers. One hotel chain, for example, employed 40 managers and 200 other employees for a 300-room hotel. A careful examination of operations showed that those operations could be streamlined considerably. The chain trimmed the staff to 14 managers and 140 employees. As a result of the downsizing, both customer and staff satisfaction increased.

In addition, people who lose their jobs because of downsizing can be retrained or hired in other jobs that use their skills to better advantage. Downsizing can also lead to an increase in entrepreneurship. Some workers have turned their job losses into personal opportunities by starting their own business ventures. An increase in new businesses creates new jobs.

Downsizing is a positive practice that results in long-term benefits for everyone by allowing the United States to remain a competitor in the global market.

190 UNIT 3 DYNAMICS OF BUSINESS IN A CHANGING WORLD

Extend the Issue

Ask students to extend the pro and con arguments about the issue of downsizing presented in the text. Students can inverview members of the business community, do research in business periodicals, or find other sources of fact and opinion about the issue. Have students hold a panel discussion to present what they found. Ask students to tally how many people they interviewed and sources they found are *pro* and how many are *con*. Make sure students count themselves on one side or the other.

Con

According to one statistic, since downsizing began in the early 1990s about 75 percent of the companies that reduced their workforces did not improve productivity or profitability. Several theories help explain this.

When a company's managers find that they must cut costs, they often panic and let 20 to 25 percent of their workforce go without examining the best ways to economize. Nor do they find out exactly how employees contribute to the overall operations of the company. As a result, they sometimes cut necessary employees.

After downsizing, the tasks of the dismissed staff must be performed by the remaining employees. These workers are often not able to do these tasks, let alone add them to their own workloads. As a consequence, they do not work as effectively as they did before. Instead of seeing gains in productivity and efficiency, companies become less productive and may even lose business as a result of downsizing.

Even if a company can show that downsizing has cut costs, the strategy may have a negative effect on the remaining employees' morale and confidence in the company. Since they suspect that their jobs will be eliminated, workers may doubt the worth of their efforts. They may work less hard and be less productive.

Low morale can also lead the employees who remain to take their talents elsewhere. Often, these are the very people expected to lead the downsized company to greater productivity and efficiency. Companies then find themselves without some of their best employees. In some cases, downsizing has led to the departure of a company's top people.

Mass layoffs are not a long-term answer to increased profitability. Companies that value the importance of their human resources have found alternatives to downsizing, such as re-training and moving employees to other divisions. Instead of eliminating jobs, some companies have replaced part of their employees' salaries with shares of stock. This strategy gives workers part ownership and a real stake in their company's success.

Downsizing is a negative practice that hurts employees as well as the productivity and profitability of the companies that downsize.

Update the Issue

Have students check current newspapers, news magazines, and other media sources for current news about downsizing. Point out to them that other terms may be used instead of *downsizing*. Some examples are *right-sizing, reductions in force (RIF)*, and *restructuring*. Students will probably discover others. Ask a small group of volunteers to make a presentation about current downsizing issues to the class. They may choose to make an oral report, a poster, or a bulletin-board display.

Independent Practice

As a follow-up activity to Unit 3, have students complete the simulation "Providing Services" found in *Student Activity Guide 1*. The Teacher's Annotated Edition provides answers.

Unit 4 — Entrepreneurship and Small Business

National Standards for Business Education*	Chapter Highlights			
	Focus on Features	Building Business Skills	Visual Learning	Case Analysis
EE: I A, I B, VI A, VI A; *IBF:* CD, EE; *IS:* I; *MGMT:* VII D	Technology: Printers, p. 200	Employability: Making Informed Judgments, p. 202	Calculating Risks, p. 198 Some Inventions of American Entrepreneurial Firms, p. 204 Changes in Employment Between December 1992 and December 1993, p. 204	Entrepreneurship, p. 205
EE: I A, IC, II A, II B, II C, VI A, IX; *IBF:* EPF, MGMT, MKTG; *IS:* II; *MGMT:* I A, I B, VII D; *MKTG:* X	Technology: Computer-Aided Design, p. 212	Analysis: Recognizing Cause and Effect, p. 216	Checklist for Entrepreneurs, p. 210 Overview of a Business Plan, p. 215 Product Description: Comparison to Competitors, p. 219 Population Age Groups of Three Neighborhoods, p. 220	Marketing, p. 221
BL: IV A, IV B; *EE:* I A, I B, VI A, VI B, VIII A, VIII B, IX; *IBF:* MGMT, EE, PROD; *MGMT:* V C, XI	Entrepreneurs: Lisa Hill—Adcor Products, p. 228	Employability: Providing Constructive Feedback, p. 232	Comparing Corporations, Partnerships, and Proprietorships, p. 227 Professional Services, p. 234	Organizing a Business, p. 235
ACCT: III; *EE:* I A, I C, IV A, IV B, IV C, VI A, VIII B, IX; *IBF;* CD, EE, EPF, MGMT; *MGMT:* III A, III B, III C	Entrepreneurs: Don H. Barden—Barden Companies, Inc. (BCI), p. 242	Analysis: Predicting Consequences, p. 246	Sources of Funding for New Businesses, p. 244 Announcement of Stock Offering, p. 249	Financial Management, p. 251

* Level 3 Performance Expectations: Accounting (ACCT), Business Law (BL), Entrepreneurship Education (EE), Interrelationships of Business Functions (IBF), IS (Information Systems), Management (MGMT), Marketing (MKTG). See page T14 for all 12 content areas.

Unit 4

Look Back

Ask students to remember that every business in today's world needs to balance the needs of the business, the needs and wants of its workforce, and the costs of meeting those needs and wants. Running a business requires sound planning from management. Managers must be able to guide workers and must also understand the business's financial obligations. To operate profitably and competitively, a business must accurately estimate the demand for the goods or services it provides and decide how to persuade people to buy its goods or services.

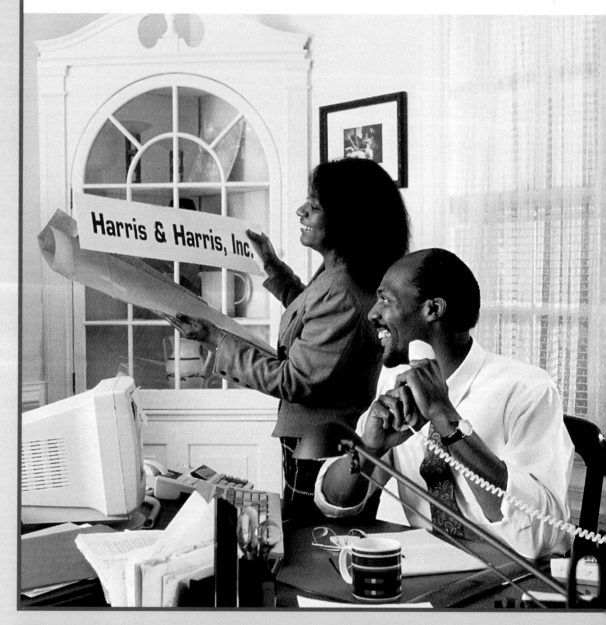

UNIT 4 COOPERATIVE LEARNING PROJECT

Co-op Co-op Activity

Preparation: For each group, photocopy and distribute one copy each of BLMs 7, 8, 9, and 10 from the *Cooperative Learning Strategies* booklet. Refer students to the "Overview of a Business Plan" section in Chapter 13 of their textbooks. For BLM 8, provide phone books for student groups to research local business competition.

Entrepreneurship and Small Business

This unit discusses setting up a new business. The first chapter explains the qualities and habits of successful entrepreneurs. The next chapter introduces the form and purposes of a business plan. The final chapters explain basic types of businesses and the financial considerations facing any new business.

193

Look Ahead

Point out to students that many small businesses are started by entrepreneurs—people who recognize a business opportunity and organize, manage, and assume the risks of a business enterprise. Before starting a business, an entrepreneur must analyze the project very carefully. A business plan is an essential planning tool for establishing a new business. It includes a company description, a product plan, a management plan, an operating plan, a financial plan, and a marketing plan.

TEACHING TIP

Use the board game *Where's the Dough?* to introduce, reinforce, or extend the concept of a business plan presented in Unit 4. This board game exposes students to the knowledge needed to prepare a business plan and the process of starting a business. The game may be played in a 5-day format for in-depth learning or in a 1-day format as an overview to starting a business.

Guidelines: Using BLMs 7 and 8, have students work in groups to think of an idea for a small business and analyze potential competition. Have groups do some research to gather information about their type of business, the competition, and the market interest. Ask groups to use their findings to make decisions for their business plan. Have groups follow the format in BLMs 9 and 10 for developing a business plan.

FOCUS

Introduce the Chapter

Major Concepts
- Entrepreneurship and Small Business
- Characteristics of an Entrepreneur
- Advantages of Entrepreneurship
- Disadvantages of Entrepreneurship
- Entrepreneurship in the United States

Introduce the Topic
Write the following statement on the board for students to complete: "I think that having my own business would be _____ ." Call on volunteers to explain why they completed the statement as they did.

Use Business Terms
Have students look at the Business Terms and note any that are familiar to them. Ask them to define these terms or to try to recall the contexts in which they were used. For those terms that are totally unfamiliar, have students venture a meaning. Reinforce correct definitions. For terms that they cannot define, advise students to note the definitions in the chapter.

USE VISUALS
Point out that entrepreneurs take pride in their work as evidenced by the attitude of this flower shop owner. Ask students to name some other characteristics of entrepreneurs. (Answers will vary.)

CHAPTER 12

Business terms

entrepreneur

small business

self-motivation

self-discipline

calculated risks

194

CHAPTER 12 RESOURCES

Instructional Resources

Lesson Plan for Chapter 12

Teaching Transparency 12-1

Strategies and Worksheets for Teaching Transparency 12-1

Enrichment Master 12-1

Student Activity Guide 1–TAE for Chapter 12

Test Master for Chapter 12

Alternative Assessment Strategies

Math Skills Review

International Business Strategies

Cooperative Learning Strategies

Communication Skills Review

Ethics in Business Strategies

What Is Entrepreneurship?

Motivate the Learning

Learning Objectives
Remind students that the learning objectives listed in the beginning of the chapter tell what they will learn in the chapter. Tell students to keep these objectives in mind as they work through the chapter. Note that the last two objectives listed refer to the Focus on Technology feature and the Building Business Skills feature.

Learning objectives

After completing this chapter, you will be able to:
- Explain what being an entrepreneur means.
- Describe the characteristics of a small business.
- List advantages and disadvantages to a business.
- Explain how entrepreneurial firms influence the U.S. economy.
- List several types of printers and explain how they work.
- Describe the process of making informed judgments.

Consider what you know

- In a private enterprise system, businesses produce the goods and services consumers want. Businesses have the freedom to compete to make a profit and to choose which products to produce.

Consider what you want to know

- Why does an entrepreneur need independence and self-discipline?
- What advantages and disadvantages are there to starting a business?
- How do new small businesses help the U.S. economy?
- What are the different types of computer printers?
- Why is making informed judgments important?

Consider how to use what you learn

- As you read this chapter, think about what it takes to be an entrepreneur. Could you be a successful entrepreneur?

Technology Resource Guide

Distance Learning Guide

Internet Resource Guide

Professional Resources

School-to-Work/Tech Prep Strategies

Instructional Poster

Spanish Resources

Multimedia Resources

Testmaker Software for Chapter 12

The Wall Street Journal Video Series
   Video & Activities for Chapter 12

Business and Marketing Computer
   Applications—An Integrated Software
   Simulation Using Microsoft Works

Stocktracker—A Stock Market Software
   Simulation

Where's the Dough? Board Game

CHAPTER 12

TEACH

Business Connection

Entrepreneurs of the next century are likely to have an MBA degree and to have amassed management and communication skills while working as an employee. As a result, it is likely that entrepreneurs will be older when they strike out on their own, and they will be more likely to rely on deliberation, judgment, planning, experience, control, and organization and less likely to leap spontaneously into the fray. Even so, the new entrepreneurs will need the same enthusiasm, drive, and leadership ability that more traditional entrepreneurs have needed.

Develop Concepts

Entrepreneurship and Small Business

Ask students to develop a list of the businesses in their neighborhood that they frequent and record the names on the board. Have students indicate those businesses for which they know the owner or owners. Point out that these owners do more than accept cash or checks in exchange for merchandise or services. These small business owners organize and manage all aspects of the business. More importantly, these entrepreneurs have decided to assume the financial risk that accompanies owning a small business.

Do you want to see an entrepreneur? Look for the organizer of a school car wash or someone selling customized T-shirts outside a ball game or a concert. In every case some enterprising person decided that there was a need for a certain product and acted to fill that need. These entrepreneurs also hoped that they would make enough money to cover the costs of, for instance, the T-shirts and the screen-printing materials, with some money left over—a *profit*. Every entrepreneur who starts a business does the same thing: identifies an opportunity based on a need, takes the risk of producing a product or a service to meet that need, and hopes for a profit.

ENTREPRENEURSHIP AND SMALL BUSINESS

An **entrepreneur** is a person who recognizes a business opportunity and who organizes, manages, and assumes the risks of a business enterprise focusing on that business opportunity. Every year thousands of entrepreneurs start small businesses. Many of these small businesses won't last more than three years. In 1994, almost 25 percent of businesses failed three years or less after they had begun. If those businesses do succeed, their owners often hope that someday their companies will become industry giants like Microsoft, Kodak, or McDonald's. All of those were started by single entrepreneurs and became more successful than anyone ever imagined. However, there are many entrepreneurs who do not dream of great fame or riches. They simply are people who want to be their own bosses and make their own business decisions.

We usually think of local businesses such as service stations, print shops, appliance stores, restaurants, and video stores as small businesses. These types of businesses follow a common business pattern. A **small business** is an independently owned and managed business that serves a limited geographic area and is not dominant in its industry. Though these businesses are small, they are started and maintained by people with an entrepreneurial spirit.

Small businesses have a tremendous impact on the U.S. economy. Here are some facts about small businesses that show how important they are to our economy.

- Two-thirds of new jobs are created by businesses that employ fewer than 500 people and are less than five years old.

F.Y.I.

Entrepreneurs succeed when they meet the needs of consumers. In 1984, two Israeli immigrants, Avi Ruimi and Avi Fattal, noticed that Los Angeles drivers had hot car seats and steering wheels in the summer. They invented a fanfold auto window shade with a pair of giant sunglasses printed on it. Within two years, they were selling 12 million shades a year. The demand for their product continues today.

196   UNIT 4   ENTREPRENEURSHIP AND SMALL BUSINESS

Enrichment Strategy

Remind students that in Chapter 6 they learned that the free enterprise system has several characteristics. Suggest that volunteers create on the board a concept web or diagram including each of the terms below. Students should place the term *entrepreneurship* in a central circle. Terms related to entrepreneurship can be placed around the central term. Then call on volunteers to explain the relationship of each to the central idea of entrepreneurship.

- Private property
- The right to enter into agreements for providing goods, services, or labor (voluntary exchange)
- Freedom to start new business (economic freedom)
- Freedom to make a profit (profit motive)

196   UNIT 4

- Small businesses employ about 60 percent of the workforce.
- Small businesses contribute about 40 percent of all sales.
- Most young people learn their basic job skills working for small businesses.

There are small businesses in all industries, however the service and retail industries dominate the small business area. More than half of small businesses are found in these two areas. As you may recall, service industries are the fastest growing part of the U.S. economy. It is likely that the number of small businesses in the service industry will increase.

Quick Check

1. What is an *entrepreneur*?
2. Explain the common business pattern of *small businesses*.

CHARACTERISTICS OF AN ENTREPRENEUR

Not everyone is suited to be an entrepreneur—which may be a good thing. After all, if everyone started their own business, there wouldn't be anyone left to work at those businesses! Entrepreneurs are take-charge people who want to work for themselves. Even though they know that many small businesses fail, they are willing to take the risk and face the uncertainty.

Desire for Independence

Of all the characteristics of entrepreneurs, the most consistent one is this: They are very independent. Entrepreneurs simply would rather work for themselves than for someone else. They want to make their own decisions. In fact, some say that people who have been fired are good candidates to become entrepreneurs because they may have proven that they're independent enough to run their own businesses.

Self-Confidence

Entrepreneurs have confidence in their ability to meet the challenges of running a business. They have a great deal of **self-motivation,** that is, they set their own goals rather than having them set by a manager or boss. They work hard to reach their goals, which shows they have **self-discipline.** They

F.Y.I.

One entrepreneur looked at changes in our society to get her idea for a new product. Over the years both parents in more and more households have taken full-time jobs. That has meant many schoolchildren come home after school to an empty house. So Mary Anne Jackson founded a company called My Own Meals, which produced quick, nutritious meals that children could fix themselves.

Learning Activity
Ask students to discuss their agreement or disagreement with the following statement: "Private property gives people the incentive to work, save, and invest." Have students discuss whether or not the right to own property is important to entrepreneurship.

Quick Check Answers

1. A person who organizes, manages, and assumes the risks of a business enterprise.
2. An independently owned and managed business that serves a limited geographic area and is not dominant in its industry.

Develop Concepts

Characteristics of an Entrepreneur

Indicate to students that individuals who become successful entrepreneurs seem to share several personality characteristics. Create for the students a concept web or diagram on the board of the following phrases: desire for independence, self-confidence, self-motivation, self-discipline, and calculated risks. Ask students to supply examples of behavior that exemplify each of the characteristics. Have a volunteer record the examples on the board or on a transparency labeled "Possible Entrepreneur Characteristics." Accept any counter examples students offer. Ask a volunteer to record these characteristics under the heading "Unlikely Entrepreneur Characteristics."

Meeting Student Diversity

Students with problems reading or organizing material can benefit from recognizing the kinds of organization used in their textbooks. Have students rewrite the main headings in the chapter as questions. Then have students list the subheads for each section beneath their questions. Direct students to read the paragraphs to find the answers to their questions, using the subheads as a guide. Ask students to explain how the subheads helped them find the answers to their questions.

USE VISUALS

Direct students' attention to Figure 12-1, Calculating Risks. The figure presents a list of questions potential entrepreneurs can use to calculate the risk involved in the business venture they are considering. Indicate to students that anyone considering going into business for themselves needs to give long, careful, and honest thought to each of the answers.
Answer to caption: To try to ensure the probability of success.

Quick Check Answers

1. Desire for independence, self-confidence, willingness to take risks, and ability to recognize opportunity.
2. Setting one's own goals; working without prompting from someone else; risk that is carefully planned to figure out if the probability of success is high.

FIGURE 12-1

These are some of the questions an entrepreneur must ask when calculating risks. Why is such analysis necessary?

CALCULATING RISKS

1. Is the goal worth the risk?
2. How can I minimize the risk?
3. What information do I need before I take the risk?
4. Why is this risk important?
5. Am I willing to try my best to achieve the goal?
6. What preparation do I need to make before I take the risk?
7. What are the biggest obstacles to achieving my goal?

correct errors and improve their own performance without any prompting from someone else. These are confident people who believe in what they are doing and believe that the job is worth doing.

Willingness to Take Risks

Another characteristic of entrepreneurs is their willingness to take risks. Most successful entrepreneurs say that they don't take risks, they take **calculated risks.** That means that they have thought about their project carefully and tried to figure out in advance that the probability of success is high. Either formally or informally, entrepreneurs conduct market research to be sure that there is a need for their product. Figure 12-1 on the left shows some questions that entrepreneurs can ask themselves when they are calculating risks. That preliminary work can lead them to the conclusion that their businesses have a good chance to succeed.

Even though entrepreneurs work very hard to succeed, they also are willing to fail. They would rather take the risk and learn from their failures than never take the risk at all. And very often, if they fail, they turn around and try again. Many entrepreneurs fail four or five times before they finally become successful.

Ability to Recognize Opportunity

Entrepreneurs are individuals who recognize opportunities on which to build a business. In many instances, they are opportunities that are bypassed by others. These opportunities may include meeting a demand that is not currently being met, putting out a product that is much better than what is currently on the market, or solving a problem or annoyance that consumers have. An entrepreneur not only has the ability to recognize the opportunity, but also has the ability to develop a business that provides goods or services consistent with the opportunity.

Quick Check

1. What are four important characteristics of entrepreneurs?
2. Define *self-motivation, self-discipline,* and *calculated risk.*

Reteaching Strategy

Have students work in groups to identify a potential small business venture such as a grocery store, music store, or math tutoring service. Ask students to compose a want ad seeking a person to start the kind of business they have chosen. Tell students that the ad should name personality characteristics as well as skills they think would be necessary for such an entrepreneur.

ADVANTAGES OF ENTREPRENEURSHIP

Entrepreneurs aren't necessarily people who go into business because they like danger. There are many advantages to having their own business. For instance, many people who have discovered that they don't have enough opportunities in their professions solve the problem by starting businesses of their own. This is especially true for women and members of minority groups. In the 1980s, there was a dramatic increase in the number of women-owned firms, and that trend has continued. The National Foundation for Women Business Owners reported that in 1994 women owned at least 7.7 million businesses and provided employment for 15.5 million people. There are clear benefits to starting a small business.

Satisfaction

Many people start a business when they discover a service or product that can fill a need or want in society. That is true whether the business is a catering service for parties and weddings, a refuge for injured wild animals and birds, or a computer software company. Transforming an idea into a successful business is very rewarding. Owners often think that the reward is well worth the time and effort they devote to their businesses. They like the feeling that they alone have built a business and made it successful.

Full Use of Skills

Many entrepreneurs work for other businesses before they go off on their own. They accumulate experience in their specialty, and they often also gain skills in management, planning, and finances. At some point in their careers, they decide that they want to use those skills in businesses of their own. A hairdresser opens his own shop. A chef opens her own restaurant. A financial manager opens an accounting business.

For similar reasons artistic people also may open their own businesses. They know that they may never make a great deal of money from their paintings, sculptures, jewelry, or music. Nonetheless they have decided that they prefer to use their talents as a business.

Profit

If you work for someone else, you have the security of a regular paycheck. But the profit from the product you produce,

GLOBAL VIEW

Companies start new businesses all over the world. For example, in just a year and a half, 79 Korean businesses set up new factories in Central America. The Korean companies invested $82 million in new facilities in Honduras, Guatemala, Costa Rica, and Panama.

Cooperative Learning   Numbered Heads Together

Ask students to work in pairs to analyze the kinds of rewards entrepreneurs might get from running a business. Suggest that as they form their answers they think about some of the small business owners in their own community. Call on one member of each team to list the rewards on the board. (Sample answers: profits, providing services to others, personal satisfaction, independence.)

Refer to the *Cooperative Learning Strategies* booklet for additional cooperative learning strategies.

Develop Concepts

Advantages of Entrepreneurship

Help students recognize that in addition to satisfaction, use of skills, and profit, there may be many more advantages to entrepreneurship. Ask students to supply examples of specific advantages they would seek if they had their own business. Have a volunteer record the examples in the appropriate column of a chart headed "Satisfaction, Use of Skills, Profit," and "Other." Discuss examples as they are suggested.

TEACHING TIP

Help students recognize that the entrepreneur, seeking profits, is the driving force of the economy. Remind students of the role the consumer plays in deciding what is produced. Ask students to identify what they feel is the government's role in entrepreneurship. (Protector of both business and consumers, regulator of producers, producer, consumer, as well as promoter of national goals.)

Business Brief

There are many entrepreneurs who choose to start a business whose primary purpose is to provide educational, social, religious, or other services. One example is Newman's Own, started in 1982 with actor Paul Newman's salad dressing recipe. All profits go to charity. The company now sells 90 items and by January 1995 had given $62 million to charity.

FOCUS ON **Technology**

Discuss

Ask students to describe how dot matrix and laser printers work and classify each as either an impact or nonimpact printer. If possible, have examples of printout from each type of printer available for student inspection. Ask students to discuss what they see as the advantages and disadvantages of each type of printer.

Quick Check Answers

1. Satisfaction, full use of skills, and profit.
2. Answers will vary.

Develop Concepts

Disadvantages of Entrepreneurship

Discuss with students some of the disadvantages of entrepreneurship: chance of failure, long hours, inadequate financing, poor management, government regulation, too much responsibility. Ask students to speculate on how much profit and satisfaction they would require to balance or outweigh the disadvantages of entrepreneurship.

Printers

Early advocates of the computerized office predicted that computers would lead the way to the "paperless office." Information could be stored on floppy disks, hard drives, and networks. Then anyone in the office could retrieve the information on his or her own computer. There would be no need for filing cabinets full of documents. These advocates believed that mountains of paper would shrink to a molehill. They were wrong.

Instead, computers were accompanied by printers, and the two together have produced a proliferation of printed paper documents. Printers can accomplish their tasks in a variety of speeds. Some low-speed printers print about 300 characters per second. Medium-speed printers produce 300 lines per minute. Very high-speed printers can print more than 3000 lines per minute.

Printers vary in price, quality, and characteristics. However, all can be grouped in two categories: impact and nonimpact printers. An *impact printer* operates like a typewriter—the image of a character is transferred onto paper using a mechanism that strikes paper, ribbon, and character together. *Nonimpact* printers transfer the character image without striking the paper.

An example of an impact printer is a *dot matrix printer*. It uses a print head with 9 to 24 pins. In low-speed printers, the head moves back and forth, printing one character at a time. High-speed dot matrix printers have a print head at each print position, allowing them to print an entire line at once.

With both low- and high-speed dot matrix printers, pins "pop out" from the print head, strike an inked rib-

Business & ECOLOGY

One of the largest solid waste disposal companies in the world was started by an accountant. How did he learn about garbage? He drove a garbage truck in Houston, Texas, for several years before he started his business. He combined his experience and his training to build Browning-Ferris Industries into an international company.

whether it is a new hairdo or an automobile, goes to the company. Your salary is paid out of the money the company makes. Many entrepreneurs decide that they no longer want to work to make a profit for someone else. Even though they are fully responsible for the finances and bills of their own business, many business owners decide they want the full benefits of their own labors.

Quick Check

1. What are three advantages of entrepreneurship?
2. Which advantage is most attractive to you?

DISADVANTAGES OF ENTREPRENEURSHIP

Being successful isn't easy. You don't just start a business and watch the profits roll in. Consider large businesses. There are officers—each has a president, vice presidents, managers.

Making Connections ➪ Business Ethics

Indicate to students that there are at least two ways to view business's responsibility and obligation to society. Some individuals hold that each business has an obligation to be socially responsible—an obligation not to pollute the environment, not to produce harmful or dangerous products, and to continue to produce, even at reduced profits, products and services vital to human life. Other individuals maintain that business, by its very nature, helps society enough by being profitable and hiring workers. Ask students to discuss each of these points of view and determine which is more like their own view of business's responsibility.

Refer to the *Ethics in Business Strategies* booklet for additional business ethics strategies.

bon, and leave a mark on the paper. Dot matrix printers tend to be noisy, and the quality of the printing is relatively low. However, they tend to be inexpensive, and are ideal for businesses that rely on multiple copies—shipping forms, packing lists, invoices, and so on.

Laser printers are examples of nonimpact printers. A laser printer is made up of a small computer, a laser, a heating element, a drum, and a form of dry ink called *toner*. The user's computer sends data to the printer's computer. The printer's computer interprets the data and controls the laser. The laser is pointed at a series of precise locations on the drum. This contact creates a tiny electrical charge on the drum. The toner sticks to the drum at those charged locations, and the image of the characters to be printed appears on the drum. Pressure and heat then transfer the toner image from the drum to paper. Laser printers generally offer high print quality, low noise, and high speed—but all for a higher price.

A second kind of nonimpact printer is the *ink jet* or *bubble jet printer*. These printers create the character image directly on paper, spraying ink through as many as 64 tiny nozzles in the print head. For most characteristics, the ink jet offers a middle ground between dot matrix and laser printers. Also, the ink jet is the primary technology used to produce color documents from a personal computer.

Follow Through

Ask students to speculate why, if so many documents can be read electronically, the consumption of paper has increased. Estimates of annual paper consumption by the world's computers is at 230 million reams or 115 billion sheets. U.S. companies alone use 2 million tons of copier paper a year. (Computers have increased the ease of making documents and encouraged the generation of more drafts and copies.)

There are departments that are responsible for everything from ordering supplies to setting the work schedule for employees. The person who cleans the floor doesn't usually have the responsibility of boxing up the product and shipping it to customers. If you begin your own business, however, those descriptions do not apply.

Total Responsibility

An entrepreneur just starting out is in charge of *everything*. That means that the company's success or failure depends on just one person—the owner. The owner must manage workers, manufacturing, and shipping. He or she has to find customers, sell the product, and be certain that orders are met. The owner of a restaurant must acquire the licenses and permits from the city, handle advertising, order supplies, make sure the food is of high quality, schedule the wait staff, and so on. No matter what size the business is, the owner still has all of the responsibility. If the business grows, the owner may hire people to carry out some of these duties. Even then, the owner is the one who is ultimately responsible.

CHAPTER 12   WHAT IS ENTREPRENEURSHIP?   **201**

Business Brief

The rise of entrepreneurship in the United States has also given rise to a number of periodicals such as *Inc., Entrepreneur, Black Enterprise, Success,* and *The Nation's Business,* which are especially geared toward small businesses. In addition, *Business Week* and *Fortune* often address the challenges and concerns of entrepreneurs.

TEACHING TIP

Write the following statement on the board: "Owning a business means freedom and profits." Have students write a paragraph explaining why the statement is only partially true.

Curriculum Connection   Language Arts

Have students work in small groups to develop print advertising or radio or television spots designed to persuade people to become entrepreneurs. Remind students that while they may want to emphasize the advantages of being an entrepreneur, they will need to be truthful about the disadvantages. Encourage students to display or broadcast their advertisements

Building Business Skills

Model

Photocopy and distribute Enrichment Master 12-1, Checklist for Making Informed Judgments. Have students complete the checklist. Then ask which of the questions they had the most difficulty in answering. Work through these questions with the class, modeling each one in a classroom situation. Then ask students how they might practice the checklist skills in an entrepreneurship situation.

TEACHING TIP

Alert students that under the free enterprise system, individuals are free to risk their savings or any part of their wealth on a business venture. Ask students what incentives exist for entrepreneurs to be willing to take the calculated financial risks. (Possible answers: Opportunity, profit, independence, and challenge).

Learning Activity

Ask students to discuss whether or not the government should offer investment tax credits that give significant tax breaks to businesses that make investments that create jobs. Have them support their opinions with examples.

EMPLOYABILITY
Making Informed Judgments

Explanation

"Use good judgment!" How often have you heard those words? Everybody wants to use good judgment, but how do we do it? Good judgments are *informed judgments,* that is, evaluations based on reliable information and reason. Informed judgments are more likely to be sound because they are made with care and objectivity. The ability to make informed judgments is essential to businesspeople in general and entrepreneurs in particular.

Experience and prior knowledge are the starting point for making informed judgments, but people who possess this skill don't stop there. They recognize where their own knowledge ends and when they must seek further information. Whether they use books, magazines, surveys, or interviews, their sources must be reliable—unbiased and knowledgeable. And the information must be relevant.

Gathering reliable information in surveys and interviews means asking the right questions of the right people. An entrepreneur trying to make a judgment about what shoe care products consumers will buy should probably do some large-scale marketing research rather than rely on opinions and stories of family and friends.

The entrepreneur might also want to get expert information from retailers who sell shoe care products to

Long, Irregular Hours

Being your own boss is a lot of work. Studies show that people who start their own businesses work more hours than those who work for someone else. It isn't unusual for their schedules to extend to more than 60 hours a week. Weekends are often time for work, just as weekdays are. This shouldn't be surprising. If you are responsible for everything, your work is going to take a great deal of time.

Financial Risks

The most serious disadvantage of a small business is the need for money. Chapter 15 will discuss the financing of a small business in more detail. It takes money to get a business going. The owner has to obtain space for the business; furnish it with such things as desks, filing cabinets, and computers; and employ workers. While the business is struggling to get established, the owner has to pay bills and wages.

202 UNIT 4 ENTREPRENEURSHIP AND SMALL BUSINESS

Global Perspective

Governments wishing to promote economic growth recognize that entrepreneurship is key to that growth. After the breakup of the Soviet Union, approximately 516,000 new companies began in Poland; 300,000 sprang up in Czechoslovakia; and 250,000 began in Hungary. Have students use business periodicals and other reference sources to determine the number of new businesses started in the United States as well as in countries such as China, Taiwan, and South Korea since 1990. Have students use graphs to present their information to the class.

Refer to the *International Business Strategies* booklet for additional international business strategies.

CHECKLIST FOR MAKING INFORMED JUDGMENTS

1. I can make an informed judgment based on my own knowledge and experience. Yes No
2. My sources of information are bias-free and knowledgeable. Yes No
3. I know what questions to ask to gather the best information. Yes No
4. I have put my own prejudices aside in making the judgment. Yes No
5. I have applied reason rather than emotion to the process. Yes No

determine what consumers are interested in and how products can best be packaged and displayed.

Obtaining reliable information also helps keep emotions from clouding our reason and helps eliminate prejudice—passing judgment before we have the facts. This is particularly important in working with other people. Our judgments must be based on facts about people's performance, not on our emotional response to their personalities or backgrounds.

Practice

The checklist in the box can help you make informed judgments. Suppose another manager asks your opinion about whether to promote Gary or Meg to the position as assistant manager in his department. You like Meg. Gary rubs you the wrong way. On a separate sheet of paper, work through the checklist to help make an informed judgment. For each statement that you check *No*, explain what you need to do to make it *Yes*.

The owner may try to borrow money from a bank, but banks are often unwilling to lend to a new business because the risks are high. What's more, if the business fails, the owner may have to pay the company's debts out of his or her own pocket.

Quick Check

1. What are three disadvantages of entrepreneurship?
2. Which disadvantage is the greatest?

ENTREPRENEURSHIP IN THE UNITED STATES

As you see, being an entrepreneur is not easy, but it is important. Much of a nation's economic growth reflects the small businesses begun by entrepreneurs. Economic growth helps a nation's standard of living rise. It also makes it more competitive in the global marketplace.

Tom Monaghan started his first pizza parlor in a college town. He took the calculated risk that college students would think *any* food was better than the usual cafeteria food served in dormitories. He was right. Today his company is known as Domino's Pizza and is worth millions of dollars!

Quick Check Answers

1. Total responsibility; long, irregular hours; and financial risks.
2. Answers will vary.

Develop Concepts

Entrepreneurship in the United States

Remind students that there are about 6 million small businesses in the United States. Ask students to list the businesses within a three-block radius of their school or home. Then have them classify those businesses as small or large. Ask students to use their listings to discuss whether the economy in their community revolves around entrepreneurship or large corporations.

Making Connections Technology in Business

The Department of Energy and NASA (National Aeronautics and Space Administration) are interested in meeting with small businesses. The object of these meetings is to introduce some of the technology developed by NASA and contractors working with the Department of Energy. The goal is to find commercial applications for technology originally designed for scientific uses. Information on these technologies is available directly from NASA and other governmental agencies on the Internet. Suggest that students do library research to find examples of technology transfer. They can present their findings as part of a technology fair. (Examples include heart-assist pumps, microwave cardiac catheters, augmented virtual vision.)

CHAPTER 12

USE VISUALS

Figure 12-2
Direct students' attention to the inventions associated with some U.S. entrepreneurs. Have students speculate on how their own lives would be different without these items.
Answer to caption: Answers will vary.

Figure 12-3
Ask students what the information in this figure might mean for their own career choices and opportunities. (They are more likely to find jobs in small businesses.) Answer to caption: Small businesses; large businesses.

USE TRANSPARENCIES

Use Teaching Transparency 12-1 and its corresponding strategies and worksheet from the *Teaching Transparency Strategies and Worksheets* booklet. Verify student worksheets using the Answer Key.

Quick Check Answers

1. They have been a source of many innovations and inventions used around the world.
2. It has been increasing.

FIGURE 12-2

America's smaller entrepreneurial firms have been the source of innovations and inventions used around the world. Which invention do you think has had the biggest impact on the business world?

SOME INVENTIONS OF AMERICAN ENTREPRENEURIAL FIRMS

Air conditioning
Airplane
Automatic transmission
Ballpoint pen
FM radio
Helicopter
Heart pacemaker
Instant camera
Insulin
Jet engine
Penicillin
Personal computer
Xerography (copy machines)
Zipper

FIGURE 12-3

This table shows changes in the number of jobs during one year. In which type of business is employment increasing? In which is it decreasing?

One of the strengths of the U.S. economy has been the way its entrepreneurs create small companies that become industry leaders. The list of successes is impressive. There's Microsoft Corporation, which began in a garage and is now worth billions of dollars. Du Pont Chemical Corporation was started in 1802 with an investment of $3600 from 18 investors. Today it is one of the largest chemical companies in the world. In 1886, David McConnell borrowed $500 from a friend to start Avon Cosmetics. Henry Ford started his motor company with $28,000 invested by Ford and 11 others. Figure 12-2 on the left lists some of the thousands of inventions and innovations that began in America's small entrepreneurial firms.

Entrepreneurs also help the economy in other ways. There are about 20 million small businesses in the United States, and they provide millions of jobs for American workers. In fact, as Figure 12-3 below shows, in 1993 employment in small businesses grew by 1,058,300, while employment in large businesses fell. Small businesses in the United States employ more people than large businesses do.

In the next three chapters, you'll learn specific steps people should take as they start a business. The first step is the research and planning that can reduce an entrepreneur's risk and give a new business a good chance for success.

Quick Check

1. How have American entrepreneurs influenced global business?
2. What has happened to employment in small businesses?

CHANGES IN EMPLOYMENT BETWEEN DECEMBER 1992 AND DECEMBER 1993			
Type of Industry	Total Employment*	Employment Change	Percent Change
Primarily small businesses	38,800,000	+1,058,300	+2.8
Primarily large businesses	28,700,000	−217,200	−0.76

*Total employment: 90.3 million.
Source: The State of Small Business. A Report of the President, 1994. (Washington, DC: GPO, 1995)

204 UNIT 4 ENTREPRENEURSHIP AND SMALL BUSINESS

Curriculum Connection   Social Studies

In an effort to fill a niche, an entrepreneur may invent a machine or device that improves or enhances an existing process. Suggest that students use library reference sources to find out the background of the inventors of the following items. Suggest that students present their findings as a poster or bulletin board. (All are African American.)

- Automatic traffic light (Garrett A. Morgan)
- Portable refrigeration units (Frederick McKinley Jones)
- Electric light bulb (Lewis H. Lattimer)
- Gas mask (Garrett A. Morgan)
- Automatic shoe lasting machine (Jan Matzeliger)
- Process for making refined, white, granulated sugar (Norbert Rellieux)

Chapter 12 **Summary**

Main Ideas

1. An entrepreneur is a person who recognizes an opportunity and organizes, manages, and assumes the risk of a business enterprise focused on that opportunity.
2. Entrepreneurs are independent, self-confident, self-motivated, and self-disciplined people who take calculated risks to open a new business.
3. A small business is an independently owned and managed business that serves a limited geographical area and is not dominant in its industry.
4. The advantages of starting a business are the satisfaction of filling a need, the full use of the person's skills, and the profits secured from the enterprise.

5. The disadvantages of starting a business are that the owner has all the responsibility, must work long hours, and may have difficulties finding the money to get started.
6. Entrepreneurs start businesses that may become very successful companies. They also provide more employment than large businesses.
7. Making informed judgments based on reliable information and reason is especially important for entrepreneurs.
8. Printers are important components of computerized business systems.

CASE ANALYSIS Entrepreneurship

A good friend of yours has an idea to start a small video rental business. She is very excited about this new venture. However, you have heard that small video stores are being replaced by superstores with 10,000 or more tapes in stock. You also have heard that the cost of opening such a store has risen from $50,000 to between $150,000 and $200,000. What would you advise your friend to do before she goes into this kind of business?

CLOSE

Main Ideas

Main Ideas summarizes the key information in the chapter. It is a useful tool for reinforcement and review.

CASE ANALYSIS

Case Analysis provides a chapter-related case for student analysis and application of decision-making skills.

Answer
Answers will vary.

QUICK QUIZ

1. What impact do small firms have on U.S. employment? (They employ nearly 60 percent of the workforce.)
2. What characteristics might an individual need to succeed as an entrepreneur? (Desire for independence, self-confidence, and willingness to take risks.)
3. What incentive often encourages entrepreneurs to take the calculated risks associated with starting a business? (Profit.)

Chapter 12 **Review**

APPLY

Answers

Use the Language of Business
1. entrepreneur, 2. self-motivation, 3. self-discipline, 4. calculated risks, 5. small business.

Review What You Learned
1. Organizes, manages, and assumes the risks of a business enterprise.
2. A person who can set his or her own schedule and who works well without supervision.
3. They wish to be in charge, make their own decisions, and set their own goals and objectives. They are self-motivated, self-disciplined, and confident.
4. One that is taken after research and careful thought.
5. Satisfaction from the work, full use of skills, and profit.
6. Complete responsibility, hard work, and money.
7. They sometimes become very large successful businesses; they also provide more employment than large companies.
8. It is less expensive and is good for businesses that need to make multiple copies, such as labels.
9. It is an evaluation based on reliable information and reason.

Understand Business Concepts
1. Because he or she has to make all decisions and do everything that needs to be done without someone else giving directions.
2. Risks are as likely to fail as succeed—there's no planning involved; a calculated risk is taken only after research and careful thought.
3. You can take advantage of all of your own skills and be proud of successfully reaching your own goals.
4. The owner must take care of all business responsibilities, so he or she must complete all the work.

Use the Language of Business

Use these business terms correctly in the following sentences.

calculated risks	self-discipline
entrepreneur	self-motivation
small business	

1. A(n) _____ is a person who recognizes an opportunity and who organizes, manages, and assumes the risks of a business enterprise focusing on that opportunity.
2. Someone with _____ can work without supervision or schedules set by someone else.
3. People with _____ can correct their own errors and improve their own performance without outside comments or suggestions.
4. Entrepreneurs take _____ to give their business a better chance of succeeding.
5. A(n) _____ is an independently owned and operated business in a limited geographic area.

Review What You Learned

1. What does an entrepreneur do?
2. What is a self-disciplined person like?
3. What are some characteristics of independent people?
4. What is a calculated risk?
5. What advantages are there to being an entrepreneur?
6. What disadvantages are there to being an entrepreneur?
7. How do small businesses help the U.S. economy?
8. What is the advantage of a dot matrix printer over a laser printer for businesses that need multiple copies of forms?
9. Describe an informed judgment.

Understand Business Concepts

1. Why is it important that an entrepreneur be independent and self-motivated?
2. What's the difference between a risk and a calculated risk?
3. Why might it be more satisfying to run your own company than work for someone else?
4. Why does the owner of a business put in more hours at work than an employee?
5. Why can money be such a serious problem for a small business?
6. If you were preparing a very important document, what kind of printer would you use? Why?
7. Why does making informed judgments require using outside sources of information?

5. A great deal is needed to start up a company and keep it going until it makes money.
6. A laser printer, because it produces a very clear, high quality document.
7. Because your own experience and prior knowledge are not usually enough.

Think Critically

1. Self-disciplined means that a person controls his or her own actions without outside direction; self-motivated means that a person does not need the orders of someone else to work on a task.
2. Answers will vary.

Think Critically

1. **Distinguish.** Explain the difference between being self-disciplined and self-motivated.

2. **Analyze.** What skills and attributes do you think a successful entrepreneur needs? Why?

Use What You Learned

1. **Group Project.** In your group, choose an entrepreneur that all of you admire. He or she may be a well-known historical or current figure, or someone in your community. Write a 200-word biography of the person and examine the characteristics that made him or her successful. Include graphics in the biography if possible. Create a bulletin board display with the results.

2. Do some research to find out what kinds of products and services are usually produced by new businesses. Identify two or three types that you think high school students could produce. Give a three-minute presentation to your class explaining these two or three options.

3. Would you be a good entrepreneur? Identify your hobbies and interests. Then list as many business ideas related to your hobbies and interests as you can.

4. Entrepreneurs often look into the future to see where new market needs will be. Describe in writing the kinds of businesses that you think will boom in the next 25 years. Explain why you think they will do so, then develop a plan describing how you would go about getting the knowledge or training to enter one of them.

5. **Computer Application.** Use word processing software to create an attractive letter inviting a local small business owner who started his or her own company to speak to your class. Send the invitation by E-mail.

6. **Skill Reinforcement.** Interview a businessperson about the knowledge and experience he or she uses to make informed judgments. Use the checklist on page 203 as the basis of the interview. Ask the interviewee what he or she might add to the checklist. Rewrite the checklist to include the new information and share it with the class.

Save your work in your Business Portfolio.

Independent Practice

Use the Chapter 12 worksheets in *Student Activity Guide 1* for additional practice and application activities. *Student Activity Guide 1* provides vocabulary exercises, reading comprehension checks, problems, projects, and simulations of business and economic situations. A Teacher's Annotated Edition provides answers.

ASSESS

Portfolio Assessment

The portfolio projects are designed to lead students to develop a collection of their best work to submit to you for assessment. You and your students should decide which projects will be included in their respective Business Portfolios. Refer students to the specific rubric(s) from the *Alternative Assessment Strategies* booklet listed with each of the project notes below. These rubrics will alert students to the criteria you will use to assess their projects.

Chapter Assessment

Use the Chapter 12 Test from the *Test Masters* booklet to evaluate students' understanding of the chapter concepts. An answer key is provided. Or create your own customized test using the *Testmaker* software.

Use What You Learned

1. Be certain each student participates in the groups project. Possible Rubrics: Essay, Bulletin Board.

2. Students will find the greatest amount of information about new businesses and their products and services in one of the periodicals specializing in small business information. Rubrics: Oral Presentation, Note Taking.

3. Encourage students not to edit their thoughts or responses, but to record all the ideas that occur to them. Rubric: Diagram.

4. Remind students that periodicals that cater to entrepreneurs often report trends in business. Rubric: Essay.

5. Students without access to word processing or to E-mail can complete the project manually. Rubric: Paragraph.

6. Answers will vary. Rubrics: Note Taking, Paragraph.

CHAPTER
13

Introduce the Chapter

Major Concepts
- Preparing for Entrepreneurship
- Why Write a Business Plan?
- Parts of a Business Plan

Introduce the Topic
Have students imagine that the class will start a new business. Ask students to name some things they think should be among the first things they need to do. Indicate to them that Chapter 13 will describe the very first thing they need to do: prepare a business plan. The chapter will also describe some of the information in parts of the plan.

Use Business Terms
Have students read the list of Business Terms. Ask for ideas about what the terms mean. Record correct answers on the board or a transparency. For unknown terms, advise students to check the meanings as they read the chapter.

USE VISUALS

Ask students to give their opinions on whether Jay and his family have successfully analyzed their business ventures. (Answers will vary, but students should recognize that the business most likely started as a smaller family business that has managed to prosper through successful management and planning.)

Business terms

franchise

business plan

financing

demographics

208

CHAPTER 13 RESOURCES

Instructional Resources

Lesson Plan for Chapter 13

Teaching Transparencies 13-1, 13-2, 13-3, 13-4

Strategies and Worksheets for Teaching Transparencies 13-1, 13-2, 13-3, 13-4

Enrichment Master 13-1

Student Activity Guide 1–TAE for Chapter 13

Test Master for Chapter 13

Alternative Assessment Strategies

Math Skills Review

International Business Strategies

Cooperative Learning Strategies

Communication Skills Review

Ethics in Business Strategies

Analyzing a Business Venture

Learning objectives

After completing this chapter, you will be able to:
- List four ways to enter into business.
- Describe the purpose of a business plan.
- List the elements of a business plan.
- Describe how computer-aided design can assist in the production of a business's product.
- Explain how recognizing cause and effect can help when making a business plan.

Consider what you know

- Entrepreneurs are people who start their own businesses to provide goods or services. They accept both the risks and the rewards of running their own business.

Consider what you want to know

- Where can you get information about starting a business?
- What should you do before you begin writing a business plan?
- What should be included in a business plan?
- What is computer-aided design and how can it aid in analyzing a design for a product?
- How can your understanding of cause and effect help you analyze a business venture?

Consider how to use what you learn

- As you read this chapter, think how you might begin to prepare a business plan for your own business venture.

Multimedia Resources

Technology Resource Guide

Distance Learning Guide

Internet Resource Guide

Professional Resources

School-to-Work/Tech Prep Strategies

Instructional Poster

Spanish Resources

Testmaker Software for Chapter 13

The Wall Street Journal Video Series
  Video & Activities for Chapter 13

Business and Marketing Computer
  Applications—An Integrated Software
  Simulation Using Microsoft Works

Stocktracker—A Stock Market Software
  Simulation

Where's the Dough? Board Game

Business Connection

Retail franchises, growing in number in the past several years, are poised for even more growth. One reason for franchise popularity with entrepreneurs—franchises have a the lower failure rate than other businesses. Another reason for franchise success is the expanding global opportunities. Elimination of trade barriers and increased access to Eastern European markets have made overseas franchises less difficult to establish. What's more, U.S. entrepreneurial experience is welcome in regions where free market experience is limited.

Develop Concepts

Preparing for Entrepreneurship

Ask students what concerns the owner of a small business in their community might have. Ask a volunteer to list the class responses on the board or on a transparency. Discuss with students the amount and variety of the responsibilities associated with owning a business. Compare students' responses with Figure 13-1, Checklist for Entrepreneurs.

USE TRANSPARENCIES

Use Teaching Transparency 13-1 and its corresponding strategies and worksheet from the *Teaching Transparency Strategies and Worksheets* booklet. Verify student worksheets using the Answer Key.

Most people would like to become wealthy by starting a business that proves to be successful. It's one thing to dream. It's another thing to make that dream become reality. Although it sounds strange, banks report that some people try to start businesses without any specific idea of what that business will do! Such people usually don't succeed.

Once you have decided that you want to start a business, the next step is to analyze what you want to do and find a way to do it. When you begin to plan, you start turning your daydreams into reality.

PREPARING FOR ENTREPRENEURSHIP

Careful planning from the beginning is one way to ensure the success of your business. Figure 13-1 below shows a checklist that you might use to direct your thinking as you get organized. Some of the questions are easy to answer, but others require careful research. One place to start is the local library. Many books have been written about starting a business, with helpful hints and information to assist new business owners.

FIGURE 13-1

A checklist is a good way to organize your thinking when you begin planning your own business. What other questions might help you in your preparations?

CHECKLIST FOR ENTREPRENEURS

What will I produce?

Who are my main competitors?

Why is my product needed?

How much will my product cost to produce?

How many people will I need to run the business?

    Full-time employees:

    Part-time employees:

    Special services:

What physical facilities will I need?

What licenses, permits, or other legal documents do I need?

How much money will I need to get started?

How much profit do I expect to make?

Curriculum Connection   Library Research

Direct students to work in pairs to visit a local library to compile a list of five books about starting a business. For each book, students should read the table of contents and scan the book itself. Then, on an index card or in a computer file, students can identify the book's title, author(s), and library call numbers. Have students write a brief that tells what kind of information the book contains and what special features it has. Keep the book information on file for all students to use and review.

Set up a filing system so that you can organize information about keeping accounts, business taxes, employment guidelines, competing companies, and so on.

There are other sources of assistance. Talk to the owners of other small businesses. Find out how they began. Ask about their successes and failures. Government at all levels also provides help for small businesses. State governments often have their own departments for small businesses. The federal government offers help in the form of loans, management advice, and free information.

Be sure to write down what you learn. Otherwise you may forget something you'll need later. As you gather information, your ideas about your product may change. Your understanding of competing products will become clearer. And you will become very aware that starting up a business requires effort, energy, and discipline.

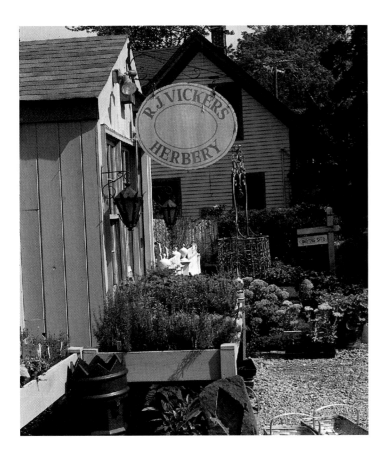

Entrepreneurs often turn a hobby into a money-making enterprise. Do you have a hobby that you could turn into a business?

Learning Activity

Sketch the following chart on the board, pointing out to students that new businesses, like new products, can be classified as one of these types.

Type	Example
new-to-the-world	the first video game
new-to-the-market	Kentucky Fried Chicken in Hong Kong
new and improved	Ultra Super Deluxe Car Wash and Video Arcade
me too	Ajax Bottled Water

Ask students to give additional examples of each kind of business. Then have them tell what they think might be the greatest advantage and disadvantage of each type of business.

USE VISUALS

Ask students to generate a list of their hobbies and outside interests such as gardening, model-making, painting, and drawing. Have them use the items on the list to discuss what new businesses they might form from their hobbies.
Answer to caption: Answers will vary.

Global Perspective

Many individuals in foreign countries get their start as business owners through the assistance of private investment companies in the United States and Europe. Individuals in these investment companies work directly with individuals in towns, villages, and urban neighborhoods in Latin America, Asia, and Africa. Businesses established through this type of cooperative effort include anything from craft shops to small power companies. Ask students to discuss the benefits these new small businesses offer the individuals and their communities. (Individuals get pride of ownership; communities get goods, services, and improved local economies.)

Refer to the *International Business Strategies* booklet for additional strategies and activities.

FOCUS ON **Technology**

FOCUS ON **Technology**

Discuss

Encourage students to use analogies or operational definitions to describe *computer-aided design, computer-assisted engineering, light pen,* and *graphics tablet.* Suggest that students construct a concept or word web on the board or a transparency to show how the devices relate to one another. Then have students use the concept or word web as a basis for an illustration showing how the devices work together.

Learning Activity

Ask students to name some familiar franchises such as Blockbuster Video or Wendy's Restaurants. Ask students to list some characteristics of these businesses and then ask them to use the characteristics to make an operational definition of *franchise.* Have them compare their operational definition with the definition given in the text—grant or right to sell a parent company's product or service within a given area or territory.

Computer-Aided Design

The Wright Brothers built, tested, and analyzed 200 model glider wings before they succeeded in building a glider with the lifting power they desired. The testing took nearly two years to complete. The brothers even built a wind tunnel so they could test the wings' shapes. All this analysis led to a design which flew—even if only for 12 seconds. Such testing and analysis would take far less time today with the help of computers.

In the early stages of manufacturing a product, today's designers use *computer-aided design,* or CAD, to accomplish in seconds what took Orville and Wilbur Wright hours or even days to complete. CAD uses special software that allows a user, typically an engineer, designer, or architect, to create a drawing. From the drawing, the computer generates a three-dimensional model of the object. The user can turn and rotate the model so that it can be viewed from a variety of different perspectives. If the user changes any element in any view, the CAD software responds by making the change in the model. All of this takes place in seconds, saving the time and frustration of producing a different drawing for each view, and, in the case of modifying the design, redrawing every view.

Once the computer model has been completed, *computer assisted engineering,* or CAE, can subject the design to a variety of environments. For example, a design for a military aircraft can be subjected to the electronic equivalent of a wind tunnel, reproducing the effects of wind, temperature, weight, and stress on the design.

In addition to specialized software, CAD users often rely on specialized hardware as well. A *digitizer* works very much like a mouse. In a digitizer, sensors determine

Start a New Business

Thousands of new businesses are started each year. Many of them are new, without any previous business on which to build. If you have ever wished that you were the boss, or had a great idea for a product or service, or like to make your own decisions, you might be one of those people who will start a business from scratch. As you know, everyone in the United States is free to start, own, and operate a business. If you have ever provided babysitting services, mowed someone's lawn, or painted someone's house for pay, you have already been an entrepreneur. Besides starting up a business on your own, there are three other ways to enter business.

Buy a Franchise

If you sometimes eat lunch at a fast-food restaurant, then you are already familiar with one of the most popular franchise businesses. A **franchise** is a grant or right to sell a parent company's product or service within a given area or territory.

GLOBAL VIEW

For the past decade, South Korea has been encouraging its people to start their own businesses. The encouragement has worked—80 percent of money brought into this nation's economy has resulted from those new businesses, small and large!

Cooperative Learning Co-op Co-op

Have the class form small groups to conduct an in-depth interview of a franchise owner in their community. Remind groups to prepare their questions in advance and to make an appointment for the interview. Encourage students to ask the owners what advantages and disadvantages they face owning their franchises. Students can tape their interviews, if possible, for replay in class, or take notes and prepare a written report.

Refer to the *Cooperative Learning Strategies* booklet for additional cooperative learning strategies.

the distance and direction(s) the digitizer has moved. The stopping point is recorded as a pair of coordinates, and a line is drawn between the starting and ending coordinates of each movement. As the user moves the digitizer

from one location to the next, outlining the shape of a box, house, or airplane, the computer responds by connecting the "dots" or coordinates from one location to the next and generating a three-dimensional model of the box, house, or airplane.

A *light pen* touched to the screen allows a user to create or modify drawings and graphics. The pen tip is sensitive; when the activated tip is placed against the screen, the location of its light is transmitted to the computer.

A *graphics tablet* looks a bit like a magnetic sketch pad. Used with a *stylus,* which is an instrument much like a pen, the tablet can create an electronic model of an object drawn on it.

For the Wright brothers, the 12-second flight was the climax of two years of work. For today's designers, 12 seconds of computer-aided design can easily save two years of work.

Follow Through

Engage students in a discussion about the advantages of computer-aided design. Have them speculate about how they might use computer-aided design to design and build a new toy, home, or automobile. Encourage them to discuss what advantages computer-aided design would offer over traditional design methods. For additional information about current technology, refer to the *Technology Resource Guide.*

The *franchisee* (person purchasing the franchise) buys a system of operation that has proven successful over the years. All business planning—called *prepackaging*—is done by the *franchisor*, the owner of the existing business. Prepackaging generally includes management training and assistance with advertising, selling, and day-to-day operations. In return the franchisee agrees to run the business in a certain way. That's why every Wendy's restaurant is almost identical to every other Wendy's.

The biggest advantage of a franchise is that the parent company helps owners start their business. By sharing its experience and proven techniques, the parent company cuts down the risk of failure. In addition, because the name of the parent company is well known, drawing customers is easier.

There are several disadvantages to owning a franchise. The first is the large amount of money needed to purchase most franchises. The second is the share of sales or predetermined yearly fee that franchise owners must pay to the parent company. Also, the franchisor may limit the franchisee's choices as to how the company is run.

TEACHING TIP

Point out to students that some people characterize franchise opportunities as "a way to get maximum market impact for a minimum investment." Ask students to use their knowledge of franchises to explain the statement. Have students make a list of franchises in the community. Direct them to group their list into franchises that offer goods and those that offer services. Then ask students to identify the franchises in which they would be most willing to invest. Have students explain their choices.

Enrichment Strategy

Indicate to students that the startup costs for franchises may range as low as $500 for a Jazzercise franchise to $620,000 for a McDonald's franchise. In addition, the individual purchasing the franchise usually agrees to share the profit or turn over a percent of the sales. Suggest that students prepare a list of questions they might ask about a franchise. Have students trade questions with one another and develop a class list of the ten most important questions. Have students use the questions as a guide to investigate two or three franchises. Students can present their findings as a two-minute "Business Today" segment for the evening news.

Quick Check Answers

1. Start your own business, buy a franchise, buy an existing non-franchise business; take over family business.
2. Grant or right to sell a parent company's product or service within a given area or territory; owner of parent company that sells the franchise; person purchasing the franchise.

Franchisors often advertise prospective franchisees. What is a franchise agreement?

Buy an Existing Non-Franchise Business

You may decide to purchase a non-franchise business from its current owner or owners. When you buy such a business, you must carefully investigate why the business is being sold. You must carefully examine the business records and the condition of the property, equipment, and inventory as well as evaluate the experience and skills of current employees. You must also determine the reputation of the business in the community. A good reputation will work to your advantage; a bad reputation may mean that you will have to work hard to restore customer good will. You usually get little or no help from the previous owner in taking over the business.

Take Over the Family Business

Finally, you might decide to take over your family's business. The same considerations that apply to buying an existing business apply for a family business. You must review business records and the overall condition of the property and equipment. As for any other existing business, you must determine the reputation of the business in the community. In addition, you need to explore possible concerns and conflicts with other family members.

Quick Check

1. Name four ways in which you could enter business.
2. Define *franchise, franchisor, franchisee.*

Meeting Student Diversity

Introduce a focused reading exercise to assist students experiencing comprehension problems. Direct students to read the paragraph "Buy an Existing Non-Franchise Business." Have them write in their notebooks what they remember of the subsection. Suggest that they read their notes to find answers to the following questions: What items should you examine before you purchase the business? How can the business's reputation affect your work? Discuss why any missing information may have been left out of their notebooks.

WHY WRITE A BUSINESS PLAN?

Whether you are starting up a business on your own, purchasing an existing business, or taking over the family business, it is a good idea to develop a business plan. Any prospective entrepreneur needs a guide to follow. A **business plan** is a written description of a new business venture that describes all aspects of the business. It helps you focus on exactly what you want to do, how you will do it, and what you expect to accomplish. The business plan is essential for the potential investors and financing agencies you will go to for start-up funds. Although there is no one standard format, there are many similarities among the general frameworks of most business plans. Figure 13-2 below presents an overview of one such plan. Remember that the business plan for each business venture is unique. Remember, also, that writing a business plan helps you analyze the business venture you want to build.

OVERVIEW OF A BUSINESS PLAN

Summary: A one- to three-page overview of the total business plan. Written after the other sections are completed, it highlights the main points and, ideally, creates enough interest for the reader to continue reading.

Company Description: Explains the type of company and gives its history if it already exists. Tells whether it is a manufacturing, retail, service, or other type of business.

Products and Services Plan: Describes the product and/or service; points out any unique features. Explains why people will buy the product or service.

Marketing Plan: Shows who the potential customers are and what kind of competition the business will face. Outlines the marketing strategy and specifies what makes the company unique.

Legal Plan: Shows the proposed type of legal organization the ownership will take. Points out any special legal concerns.

Management Plan: Identifies the key people who will direct and manage the company. Cites their experience and special skills.

Operating Plan: Explains the type of manufacturing or operating system the business will use. Describes the facilities, personnel, materials, and processing requirements.

Financial Plan: Specifies the financial needs and proposed sources of financing. Presents projections of revenues, costs, and profits.

FIGURE 13-2

A business plan is a proposal that explains every aspect of a new venture to potential investors and guides the opening of the business. What other purpose might the business plan serve?

Curriculum Connection   English and Communication

Have students imagine that they are starting a new manufacturing business called Woofy Widgets that manufactures dog toys. Suggest students work in pairs to answer each of the questions on Teaching Transparency 13-3. Then have students work together to write a descriptive paragraph to satisfy the overview of the company description part of the Woofy Widgets business plan. Direct pairs to exchange completed descriptions with other student pairs for peer review. Suggest that teams use the peer review as a guide for revising or changing the overview of their company description.

For those students who need to sharpen their written communication skills, choose among the worksheets in the *Communication Skills Review* booklet.

Develop Concepts

Why Write a Business Plan?

Ask students to name a single business the class might like to start. Allow students to discuss the business and its characteristics for a few minutes. Following the discussion, project Teaching Transparency 13-2 on the overhead. Ask whether students have considered any of the items listed on the transparency. Exploit any differences of opinion offered by the students to fuel a discussion of the need for a complete and detailed business plan.

USE VISUALS

Ask students how the summary in Figure 13-2 relates to the rest of the business plan. (It contains the highlights of the information listed in detail in the plan, including the business's major goals and objectives.) Answer to caption: It also can be used to manage the business after it is established.

USE TRANSPARENCIES

Use Teaching Transparencies 13-2 and 13-4 and their corresponding strategies and worksheets from the *Teaching Transparency Strategies and Worksheets* booklet to more fully acquaint students with the information contained in a business plan. Verify student worksheets using the Answer Key.

Building Business Skills

Building Business Skills

Model

Each of the numbered items in the list, Things to Remember About Cause and Effect on the opposite page, addresses a different aspect of cause and effect. Be sure to discuss each of the numbered items. If students seem unsure about any of the items, draw a cause and effect diagram or word web on the board to illustrate the relationship discussed in the item.

ANALYSIS

Recognizing Cause and Effect

Explanation

To analyze possibilities and make intelligent decisions, you have to be able to recognize causes and their effects. A *cause* is a condition or action that makes something happen. The thing that happens is the *effect*. An effect can, in turn, become the cause of another effect.

In business, one of the classic cause-and-effect relationships is between price and demand. The lower the price, the greater the demand. If manufacturers can cut the price of their mountain bikes (cause), consumers will purchase more of them (effect).

Cause-and-effect relationships are often more complicated than this. It may take investigation and careful reasoning to recognize the true causes of events and conditions.

Learning to recognize cause-and-effect relationships can contribute directly to business success, especially when you are analyzing a business venture.

Practice

Read the question in the box and answer the questions that follow.

1. You are planning to buy a variety store that sells everything from snacks to film. Here are three things the previous owner noticed about her sales:

- Potato chips sell better when the moon is full.

Learning Activity

Stress to students that simply making the very best product may not be enough for a business to succeed. Offer the following example: John Henry makes the best horseshoes in the country. However, he does not have enough business to make a profit because the horseshoe industry is small and dwindling. Ask students to discuss other instances in which they feel it would be important to consider the state of the industry as well as the state of the individual business.

F.Y.I.

A Boston, Massachusetts, company called Aegis Partners has one primary objective—to help small businesses get started by loaning them money. Over several months, Aegis received 1200 proposals—about 70 a week. The partners read 600 and selected 45 that looked promising. They funded only four! Why did they read only 600? The proposals were written so poorly that Aegis refused to read them all the way through.

A business plan is not a document that you fill with daydreams about instant success. It is a business document—realistic, honest, detailed, and clear-eyed about your plans. This document will help you set your goals and objectives. But the business plan is more than a tool for the owner. It is something that banks and other financial and investment organizations use when they consider giving you **financing,** the money you need to get your business going. These groups need to be assured that they are investing in a business that has a good chance to succeed. Only a clear and logical business plan can persuade them of that.

Quick Check

1. What is a *business plan?*
2. What part does a business plan play in financing the business?

Quick Check Answers

1. A document that focuses on exactly what you want to do, how you will do it, and what you expect to accomplish.
2. Financial organizations base their decision about awarding financing on a person's business plan.

Making Connections Everyday Living

Have students think about and list several inconveniences they experience over the course of a single school day. Have a volunteer collect the lists and record on the board a sample of the inconveniences most commonly listed. Then ask students to invent goods or services to help eliminate or lessen the inconvenience. Have students write the product and services section of a business plan for their product. Remind students that the product and services portion of their plan should include the following:

- Description of similar products on the market.
- Examples of possible uses for the product.
- Prototype of the item to be produced.

THINGS TO REMEMBER ABOUT CAUSE AND EFFECT

1. When obvious cause-and-effect relationships don't seem to work, look for other causes that may be influencing the result. If the price of bikes goes down and demand doesn't rise, perhaps people have less income to spend on leisure equipment.

2. Sometimes effects have more than one cause. An icy road could be the direct cause of a car accident. But indirect causes, such as poor visibility, might also contribute.

3. A cause may have both immediate and long-term effects. If there is a general rise in prices, an immedi-

ate effect might be that businesses take in more money; a long-term effect might be that businesses fail because consumers can't afford to buy.

4. Even when two events occur together, one is not necessarily the cause of the other. The "effect" may be a result of chance or coincidence. Other logical evidence is necessary to connect two events in a cause-and-effect relationship. You may perceive that stock in a corporation seems to go up every time there's a thunderstorm. Since there's no logical way to connect these events, the relationship is a coincidence.

- More people buy film in June and at Christmas.
- Candy sales fell when she raised the price.

What can you infer about cause-and-effect relationships in each observation? Which are true and which are coincidences?

2. Annette learns that there is a new, much cheaper technique for making computer chips. She decides to start a business selling personal computers and software. What reasoning about causes and effects led to her decision?

A business plan must be well-organized, be easy to read, and follow a logical format. Look again at Figure 13-2 on page 215.

PARTS OF A BUSINESS PLAN

A business plan must be well-organized, be easy to read, and follow a logical format. Look again at Figure 13-2 on page 215. This sample format for a business plan has seven parts—Company Description, Products and Services Plan, Marketing Plan, Legal Plan, Management Plan, Operating Plan, and Financial Plan.

In this chapter, we will examine the first three of these parts of a business plan: the company description, the products and services plan, and the marketing plan. In Chapter 14, we will consider the legal plan, the management plan, and the operating plan. Chapter 15 concentrates on the financial plan.

Describing Your Business Venture

As part of your business plan, you first need to give a clear description of your new business. Is this business a start-up, a buyout of an existing business, or an expansion? Has the business started operation, and, if it has, when and where was the business started? What is the basic nature and activity of the

Cooperative Learning   Co-op Co-op

Ask students to work together in teams to generate ideas for an after-school delivery service. Suggest they outline the area they would serve and the extent of services offered. Recommend that they prepare a list of every competitive advantage they think their service can offer to prospective clients. Distribute Enrichment Master 13-1, a Checklist for Entrepreneurs, and direct students to compare the checklist with their own outlines and lists. Encourage them to address each item on the checklist. Then, have students use the information to write a descriptive paragraph for the product and services plan of a business plan.

Practice

Ask students to complete the practice activity in class. Have students more proficient in cause and effect work as a team with students having difficulty. Suggest that each team generate additional examples of cause and effect based on their personal experience. (1. Students should recognize that there is no evidence to show cause and effect in the first observation; it is almost certainly a coincidence. The second observation probably reflects cause and effect: more people buy film because of vacations, graduations, and weddings in June and family gatherings at the Christmas holidays. In the last case, higher prices caused customers to go elsewhere or stop buying candy.
2. The cheaper technology will probably cause computer prices to go down. This, in turn, may mean that more consumers will buy computers—and the software and accessories to go with them.)

Develop Concepts

Parts of a Business Plan?

Indicate to students that for any kind of business, the parts of a business plan generally are the same. Stress that the information in each part of the plan may change but that the overall structure of the plan remains the same.

Business Brief

Not all successful entrepreneurs started their business with a new product or a new service. In some cases the product was well established. The entrepreneur simply thought of another way to distribute the product—Ray Kroc tried delivering the familiar hamburger in a new and innovative fashion. The result was McDonald's.

Learning Activity

Have students explore the concept of a specialized product or a unique service. Ask them to choose a type of business well represented in the yellow pages, such as plumbing contractors or insurance sales. Suggest they list the specialties offered by the companies listed—residential or commercial plumbing, or emergency repair; home and automobile insurance, or life and major medical insurance. Have students organize the information they find in a chart. Use the charts as a basis for discussion concerning the need for the product and services section of a business plan to be detailed and exact.

F.Y.I.

The Center for Entrepreneurial Management in New York reports that most business plans take more than five months to prepare. But most readers, such as bank officers, take less than five minutes to decide whether to read the entire document!

business, and what is its primary product or service? What customers does it serve? What is the company's state of development—beginning, full product line, or what? Readers will come to know whether the business is engaged in retailing, manufacturing, construction, agriculture, or finance. Readers also will know whether it is serving a national or international market.

Other information included in the general company description portion of the business plan applies to an established company. What is its prior history? What achievements has it made to date? What changes have been made in ownership or structure? What is the company's particular competence? Besides giving the history of the company, the general company description should also describe the current state of the industry in which the company is involved.

Products and Services Plan

The next section of your business plan should describe your product, such as a widget for storing loose nails and bolts in a home workshop or a visiting day-care service for people who are recovering from surgery in their homes. A product can be goods—something you make—or a service that you provide. If it is a unique physical product, you need to describe it fully. If necessary, include technical drawings or photographs that will explain and describe the product. Investors will be especially interested in products that have been developed, tested, and found to be totally functional. You should explain any innovative features and identify any trademarks, copyrights, or patents that apply.

Suppose that you want to start a plant nursery, for instance. What will you sell in this business? Some nurseries sell flowering plants, others sell small shrubs, and still others sell small trees for homes. Are you going to specialize? Or are you going to include all kinds of plants?

As you describe your project, you will learn much about what you will need to conduct your business. How many buildings will your nursery require? There will be a shop where customers can buy your plants, of course, but will you need greenhouses? How many? Will you need extra land for shrubs and trees? How many employees will you need? No matter what your project, you need to ask questions like these to make your plans and your needs very clear.

If your product is a service, describe it fully. You may want to include charts that compare your company's services with those of competitors, such as in Figure 13-3 on page 219. Describe what makes your service superior. What gives you the advantage over your competitors?

Curriculum Connection   English and Communication

Present students with the following scenario: A high school class plans to start a car washing business. Ask student pairs to work together to develop the overview statement of the products and services plan for the business. Direct students to write their products and services plan overview on the bulletin board. Have students compare the descriptions. Have them use any differences they identify as a basis for discussion of the importance of a full and complete business description in a business plan.

PRODUCT DESCRIPTION: COMPARISON TO COMPETITORS

	Registered Nurses	Practical Nurses	Physical Therapists	Meal Preparation	Massage Therapy
Home Companion Services	Yes	Yes	Yes	Yes	Yes
Louis Clinic Home Services	No	Yes	No	Yes	No
Practical After-Care Services	No	Yes	Yes	No	No

FIGURE 13-3

Rita Chan used this chart to compare the services that her company—Home Companion Services—provides compared to those of her competitors. How does Rita plan to beat her competitors?

When you describe your product, make clear how it is different from others on the market. This information will help you be sure that your project is as unique as you think it is. And the reader of your business plan will know that you have analyzed your competitors and that you know your product or service well.

Marketing Plan

As you devise your business plan, you need information that will show that a market exists and that customers will buy your product or service. Where is the best location for your business? A plant nursery needs space. A manufacturing company needs to be near good transportation in order to get raw materials in and finished products out. Artisans who make handmade products—weavers, blacksmiths, and quilters, for instance—may need to set up their businesses in places where people purchase these kinds of products, such as historical towns that draw many tourists. The type of business you wish to start may dictate where it is located.

You also need marketing information about your potential customers. To get such data, you can study **demographics,** which are statistics about the characteristics of human populations. These can help you identify the people who may buy your product. Often people build new restaurants in areas where other restaurants already exist. Why? The location gives the owner an advantage because people who want to eat at a restaurant are already drawn to the area. All of them are prospective customers who may decide to try your restaurant.

Demographics can help you in other ways. If you plan to set up a small shop to sell T-shirts, you need to know the age group in that neighborhood. If the biggest age group is made

Business & TECHNOLOGY

Bill Gates, the founder of Microsoft Corporation, started his business when he was 19 years old. He envisioned a nation with a computer in every home and in every office, and a piece of Microsoft software in every computer. Just 40 years of age in 1995, he is one of the richest people in the world.

Point out to students that businesspeople who can make clear decisions based on fact have a greater chance of succeeding than those who rely upon instinct and enthusiasm alone. Ask students to discuss how the information in Figure 13-3 above helped Rita Chan improve her chances of success. Answer to caption: Offer more types of services than they do.

Connection to CHAPTER 11

Remind students that they have learned about market research and demographics in Chapter 11, *Marketing in Today's World*. Market research helps businesses predict how many goods and services a business can expect to sell.

Learning Activity

Offer students the following demographic information: the teenage population is declining, and teenagers are major consumers of soft drinks, snack foods, video games, designer clothes, and compact discs. Ask students to discuss what effects that information might have. Steer students to the recognition that as the teen population declines, sales in these areas might also decline and competition in these areas is likely to increase. Ask a volunteer to create a cause-and-effect diagram that represents this information.

Refer to the *Cooperative Learning Strategies* booklet for additional cooperative learning strategies.

Cooperative Learning Co-op Co-op

Have students work in groups to research one of the trends listed below. Direct them to learn the effects of each of the trends. Suggest that they present their information in diagrams suitable for posters or bulletin boards.

Demographic trend	Effect: Increased spending on
increased population of singles	convenience foods, entertainment, travel, restaurants, and recreation
older citizens	travel, recreation, retirement housing, single-portion foods, health care
working women	day care industry, convenience foods, time saving products and services

CHAPTER 13

USE VISUALS

After students have a chance to study the Population Age Groups shown in Figure 13-4, ask several questions to ensure that they understand the graphs. Which neighborhood has the highest percentage of people under 18 years of age? (A) Which has the lowest percentage of people over 68? (B)
Answer to caption: Possible answers: a children's clothing store; a video or record store; a medium-priced restaurant. Answers should reflect each neighborhood's description.

Business Brief

Point out to students that having extensive business experience and a complete business plan does not guarantee success. Even big business has produced some singularly unsuccessful new products. Among the flops are Ford Motor Company's Edsel and Coca-Cola's reformulated, sweeter Coke.

Quick Check Answers

1. Company description, products/services plan, marketing plan, legal plan, operating plan, management plan, and financial plan.
2. Answers will vary.

Population Age Groups of Three Neighborhoods

FIGURE 13-4

Demographic studies can tell much about neighborhoods. In addition to the age group percentages shown here, a demographic study may provide information about types of buildings. Neighborhood A has a large number of apartments for young families. Neighborhood B includes a technical school and a college. And Neighborhood C has older homes and senior citizens' apartment complexes. What businesses might do well in Neighborhood A? In Neighborhood B? In Neighborhood C?

up of senior citizens, there may not be much interest in your product. An area with a younger group of people may be a better place to set up your shop. You can see this type of information in Figure 13-4 above.

Even national demographics can help you with your planning. If your product is aimed at a certain population group, is that group growing or shrinking? Suppose your product is designed for infants or children. Statistics can tell you that the U.S. birth rate is falling. That means you will be facing strong competition for a shrinking market. That doesn't mean you should give up your project. But it is better to understand what you're up against before you begin. If nothing else, you will need an aggressive marketing and sales plan.

Economic trends are also important. Is the economy growing? If so, then you have a better chance of success. If not, then it will be harder to succeed. Banks will be less willing to loan money to a new business, and your prospective customers will be less ready to buy your product.

Quick Check

1. Name the basic parts of a business plan.
2. Which part of the business plan do you think is most important?

220   UNIT 4 ENTREPRENEURSHIP AND SMALL BUSINESS

Reteaching Strategy

In an effort to distinguish their products from others in the market, sellers often tailor their marketing and advertising to individual markets. Have students choose a common product such as household cleanser or breakfast cereal. Direct students to work in groups to develop a plan to market the same product in each of the three neighborhoods. As part of the plan, have students produce an ad suitable for newspapers or magazines. Post ads on a bulletin board and ask other teams to identify which neighborhood in Figure 13-4 above the ads target.

220   UNIT 4

Chapter 13 **Summary**

Main Ideas

1. Before starting a new business, entrepreneurs should carefully analyze their proposed ventures.
2. Business plans help potential business owners focus on what they want to do, how they will do it, and what they expect to accomplish.
3. A business plan generally includes a company description, a products and services plan, a marketing plan, a legal plan, an operating plan, a management plan, and a financial plan.
4. The company description portion of a business plan explains the type of company and gives its history if it already exists.
5. The products and services portion of a business plan discusses the products/services to be offered, points out their unique features, and tells why people will buy them.
6. The marketing portion of a business plan shows who the potential customers are and what competition the business will face.
7. Computer-aided design (CAD) generates three-dimensional drawings of a product and provides views from several perspectives.
8. A cause is what makes something happen; an effect is the result of the cause. Understanding cause and effect is an important skill in business, especially when planning a business venture.

Main Ideas

Main Ideas summarizes the key information in the chapter. It is a useful tool for reinforcement and review.

CASE ANALYSIS

Case Analysis provides a chapter-related case for student analysis and application of decision-making skills.

Answer
Answers will vary, but students should advise Glenn to narrow his focus, identify a specific market, and then use all his resources to gain a significant portion of it. For example, he should appeal to a single category such as teenagers or senior citizens. Otherwise he may become weak in several areas rather than strong in one.

CASE ANALYSIS Marketing

Glenn McKee is writing the marketing portion of his business plan. He wants to make the business appeal to everyone. Glenn believes that appealing to the widest possible range of consumers is a sure-fire prescription for success. He has demographics for all population groups from teenagers to senior citizens, and he is working on a broad-based advertising campaign that he will use to launch his new business venture. If you were to advise Glenn about his marketing plan, what advice would you give him?

QUICK QUIZ

1. In addition to starting a business, what other ways can you become an entrepreneur? (Buy an existing business, buy a franchise, join the family business.)
2. What part of the business plan contains the description of what you will sell and why people will buy it? (Product and services plan.)
3. What part of a business plan describes how your company, product, or service will be unique? (Marketing plan.)
4. How can you use demographics in a business plan? (Sample: To describe your potential customers.)

APPLY

Answers

Use the Language of Business
1. business plan, 2. franchise plan, 3. demographics, 4. financing.

Review What You Learned
1. Books, owners of small businesses, government agencies and publications.
2. Start a business, buy a franchise, buy a non-franchise business, take over the family business.
3. They can help you predict whether banks will be willing to loan money and customers to buy.
4. A written description of a new business venture that describes all aspects of the business.
5. Company description, products/services plan, marketing plan, management plan, legal plan, operating plan, and financial plan.
6. Drawings, photographs, or charts.
7. In the marketing plan.
8. Light pen, graphics tablet, and digitizer.
9. What makes something happen; the result of the cause.

Understand Business Concepts
1. Possible answers: to learn about the business world, the product and its competitors, and strategies that have succeeded and failed for other business owners.
2. Buy a franchise, buy a non-franchise business, take over the family business.
3. All business planning is done by the parent company, which also assists with training, advertising, selling, and management; initial investment is often high, franchisees have to pay fees or shares of sales to the parent company, and the parent company limits what franchisees can do.
4. To focus your own thinking about your business and to present your plans to organizations that may finance it.
5. Because the people who read it want to know that your ideas are worth their time and money.

Use the Language of Business

It is important for you to know the following terms as they are used in business planning. Complete each sentence with the correct term.

franchise financing
business plan demographics

1. Every business needs to start with a(n) _____, a written description that describes all aspects of the business.
2. A(n) _____ is a grant or right to sell a parent company's product or service.
3. Statistics about the characteristics of human populations are known as _____.
4. _____ is the money to start a business.

Review What You Learned

1. What are some sources of information that help you prepare to become an entrepreneur?
2. Name four ways of getting into business.
3. How can knowing economic trends be helpful in planning a business?
4. What is a business plan?
5. What parts does a business plan generally contain?
6. What materials might you include in the products and services portion of a business plan?
7. In which portion of a business plan would a new owner use demographic information?
8. What are some input devices associated with CAD?
9. Define *cause* and *effect*.

Understand Business Concepts

1. Why is it a good thing to do research before you start a new business?
2. In addition to starting a new business, what are some other ways of getting into business?
3. What are some advantages of a franchise? Some disadvantages?
4. What are two purposes of a business plan?
5. Why is it important that a business plan be detailed and carefully prepared?
6. What kind of information would you find in the marketing portion of a business plan?
7. Why does a business plan need a products and services plan?
8. In addition to making a model of a drawing, how can a computer assist in analyzing a design?
9. How might your understanding of cause and effect help you to analyze your business venture as you develop a business plan?

6. Who a business's customers will be, the marketing strategy, what type of competition there will be, and how the business will best the competition.
7. To explain why people will buy the product or service and to point out any unique features.
8. It can show responses of the model to processes or changes in its environment.

9. Answers will vary; students may mention understanding what affects certain causes, such as how the age of people in a neighborhood might affect the popularity of a product.

Think Critically
1. Answers will vary.
2. Answers will vary.

Chapter 13 Review

Think Critically

1. **Hypothesize.** What kind of business might you like to start? List some specific topics you would need to consider for your business plan.

2. **Assess.** Would you be willing to invest in a new business that has no business plan? Why or why not?

Use What You Learned

1. **Group Project.** Choose a franchise and investigate the franchisor's claims and requirements. Prepare a written report of your findings. Include information on the franchisor, investment requirements, marketability, and territorial protection. Share your report with other groups and compare the similarities and differences among the franchises.

2. Select a product that you use regularly. Suppose you are the owner of the business that produces this product and you want to expand your business. Write a possible Product Plan that explains how you will improve the product to encourage more people to buy it.

3. The U.S. Census Report provides demographic information about the whole United States. Look through this report in your local library. List three or more types of information in it that would be useful if you were planning to open a fast-food restaurant in your town.

4. Assume that you are a prospective entrepreneur who is seeking help in starting a small business. Research the sources of business development information and assistance available in your community. Compile the information you obtain and share it with the class.

5. **Computer Application.** Identify all the competitors in a given geographical area for one type of business. Then use charting software to create a graphic to present the data and write a caption that summarizes the data. Print out the graphic and caption.

6. **Skill Reinforcement.** For each statement, write a sentence that is either a cause or effect of the action or event in the statement.

   a. Cause: The price of rock concert tickets goes up.
   Effect:

   b. Cause:
   Effect: An unusually high number of customers shopped at Keep Cool Appliances today.

   c. Cause: The football star you pay to endorse your fruit drinks demands more money after he is elected to the Pro Bowl.
   Effect:

Save your work in your Business Portfolio

Independent Practice

Use the Chapter 13 worksheets in *Student Activity Guide 1* for additional practice and application activities. *Student Activity Guide 1* provides vocabulary exercises, reading comprehension checks, problems, projects, and simulations of business and economic situations. A Teacher's Annotated Edition provides answers.

ASSESS

Portfolio Assessment

The portfolio projects are designed to lead students to develop a collection of their best work to submit to you for assessment. You and your students should decide which projects will be included in their respective Business Portfolios. Refer students to the specific rubric(s) from the *Alternative Assessment Strategies* booklet listed with each of the project notes below. These rubrics will alert students to the criteria you will use to assess their projects.

Chapter Assessment

Use the Chapter 13 Test from the *Test Masters* booklet to evaluate students' understanding of the chapter concepts. An answer key is provided. Or create your own customized test using the *Testmaker* software.

Use What You Learned

1. Group students having similar language proficiency. Possible rubrics: Note Taking, Essay.

2. Remind students that the business owner is likely to both produce and market the product. Possible rubrics: Essay, Paragraph, Charts and Tables.

3. Suggest that students schedule time among themselves and with the library to ensure that each student has access to the reports. Rubric: Note Taking.

4. Be certain the students understand that business development includes financing for businesses. Possible rubric: Poster, Survey.

5. Students without access to computers can complete the project by making charts or graphs by hand and providing written captions. Rubric: Charts and Tables.

6. a. Answers may vary. Possible response: Fewer people buy the concert tickets.

b. Answers may vary. Possible responses: Local weather forecasters predict a heat wave. Or managers reduce all fans and air conditioners by 30 percent.

c. Answers may vary. Possible response: You decide you can't afford to have the star endorse your fruit drink anymore. This causes sales to decline.

FOCUS

Introduce the Chapter

Major Concepts
- Organizing for Ownership
- Organizing for Management
- Organizing for Operation

Introduce the Topic
Have students complete this sentence: In my opinion, the _____ is probably the best type of business organization. Indicate to them that Chapter 14 will describe the different kinds of organization that new businesses can use.

Use Business Terms
Have students look at the Business Terms and brainstorm associations with each term. Ask them where they have heard or seen the terms used. Reinforce correct associations. Advise students to note the meanings of the terms as they read the chapter.

USE VISUALS

Ask students: If you needed to recruit a partner to start a new business venture, how would you go about looking for that partner? (Answers will vary. For example, some students might only want to recruit friends or relatives. Others may plan to recruit partners from the business field.)

CHAPTER 14

Business terms

sole proprietorship

license

unlimited liability

partnership

corporation

stock

stockholders

corporate charter

board of directors

limited liability

224

CHAPTER 14 RESOURCES

Instructional Resources

Lesson Plan for Chapter 14

Teaching Transparencies 14-1, 14-2

Strategies and Worksheets for Teaching Transparencies 14-1, 14-2

Enrichment Master 14-1

Student Activity Guide 1–TAE for Chapter 14

Test Master for Chapter 14

Alternative Assessment Strategies

Math Skills Review

International Business Strategies

Cooperative Learning Strategies

Communication Skills Review

Ethics in Business Strategies

Organizing a Business

Learning objectives

After completing this chapter, you will be able to:
- List three types of business ownership and explain the advantages and disadvantages of each one.
- Describe how a management plan identifies the key people in a business.
- Tell how an operating plan describes the production requirements of a business.
- Describe how Lisa Hill became an entrepreneur.
- Provide constructive feedback.

Consider what you know

- When starting up a business, you have to analyze the project very carefully by describing the product, evaluating your own abilities, and studying statistics that will influence the business.

Consider what you want to know

- What should you consider when you choose what type of business ownership you will use?
- What are the advantages and disadvantages of the three types of business ownership?
- What is a management plan? An operating plan?
- How did Lisa Hill organize her business around a simple idea?
- How can business owners and managers encourage growth and improvement of company workers through positive feedback?

Consider how to use what you learn

- As you read through this chapter, think how you might choose to organize your business if you decide to become an entrepreneur.

Multimedia Resources

Technology Resource Guide

Distance Learning Guide

Internet Resource Guide

Professional Resources

School-to-Work/Tech Prep Strategies

Instructional Poster

Spanish Resources

Testmaker Software for Chapter 14

The Wall Street Journal Video Series
Video & Activities for Chapter 14

Business and Marketing Computer Applications—An Integrated Software Simulation Using Microsoft Works

Stocktracker—A Stock Market Software Simulation

Where's the Dough? Board Game

Starting your own business is a real challenge. However, it is possible to lower the risk. As you've already learned, careful planning and analysis can help you begin your business right. This includes considering your own abilities and the potential market for your product or service. Another major choice is to determine which type of business ownership best suits your situation. Describing your choice and the reasons for it is an important part of your business plan.

ORGANIZING FOR OWNERSHIP

Just as you can choose which good or service to provide, you also can choose which type of ownership is best suited to your business. The legal form of business organization you choose may make the difference between success or failure. There are three types of business ownership: sole proprietorships, partnerships, and corporations. If you are going to have an auto repair shop, it is more likely that you will be the sole owner. If you plan to have a manufacturing facility, you will probably have partners or form a corporation. You need to assess all the forms of business ownership to decide which is the best for you. Remember that you can change your initial decision about your form of business organization. As your business grows, changing conditions may require you to change your form of ownership.

The Sole Proprietorship

Almost three-fourths of businesses in America are sole proprietorships. A **sole proprietorship** is a business or firm owned by one person. Sole proprietorships are often small service businesses such as travel agencies, florists, and television repair shops. Many farms and home-based businesses are sole proprietorships. Sole proprietorships are especially suited to areas that require personalized service. That's because they are usually small businesses and are flexible enough to meet the specific needs of individual customers. Figure 14–1 on page 227 shows how sole proprietorships compare with other forms of business ownership.

Sole proprietorships have several advantages. First, they are simple to start. Depending on local laws, the only requirement may be a **license,** which is a legal permit for doing business. Second, the owners can manage their businesses as they please.

Curriculum Connection   History

Point out to students that two of the original thirteen colonies established in colonial America were proprietorships. Have students research the Pennsylvania colony or the Maryland colony to find out why these two states were originally established as proprietorships, who granted the proprietorships, and who was the primary beneficiary of the arrangements.

Comparing Corporations, Partnerships, and Proprietorships

Proportion of Businesses

Corporations 18.6%

Partnerships 7.1%

Proprietorships 74.3%

Proportion of Total Business Revenue

Partnerships 4.6%

Proprietorships 5.6%

Corporations 89.8%

Source: Internal Revenue Service Statistics of Income Bulletin. Summer 1995.

FIGURE 14-1

Sole proprietorships are the most common form of business ownership in the United States; however, corporations generate the most revenue. What percentage of total business revenue do proprietorships earn? Corporations?

They can choose their own products, set their own hours, and make all their own business decisions. Another advantage is that the owners receive all of the profits from the business. Finally, sole proprietors pay taxes only once on the income from the company.

Sole proprietorships also have some disadvantages. First, there is the problem of getting started. Where do you get startup capital to buy supplies and materials, rent the space you need, pay for advertising and marketing, and so on? You may have to dip into your personal savings or borrow money from a bank. A shortage of money is a common problem for sole proprietorships because they depend on only one person's resources and abilities.

In some cases, an owner may be good in the "product" of the business—repairing televisions, for instance. But he or she may not have business skills in other areas, such as public relations or tax preparation. Owners may have to seek outside help to keep the business going.

There is another serious financial disadvantage. If your business does not make a profit, you are responsible for *all* of the losses. If the business's debts are greater than the assets the business owns, the owner is responsible for the difference. This responsibility for debts beyond the business's assets is called **unlimited liability.** The owner may lose his or her personal savings or property if the business goes into debt that it cannot repay.

A final disadvantage of a sole proprietorship is its limited life. The business legally ends when the owner leaves or dies.

Reteaching Strategy

Have students imagine that they have decided to start a music store or sporting goods store organized as a sole proprietorship. Suggest that they compose a letter to a bank explaining why they decided to start the business and chose that type of organization for it. Call on volunteers to read their letters to the class and discuss their reasons for starting a sole proprietorship.

Discuss

Discuss with students the chain of events that led Lisa Hill to start her own business. Ask a volunteer to create a flowchart on the board or on a transparency that shows at least four steps in the formation of Adcor Products. (Possible answer: Broken heel tip, expensive repair bill, do-it-yourself idea, market research.)

Lisa Hill—Adcor Products

There they stood in Lisa Hill's closet, ten pairs of high-heeled shoes, with the heel tips worn down. She had been too busy to have them fixed, but she couldn't ignore them any longer. Gathering them up, Hill dropped them off at the shoe repair shop—where she paid a total of $70 for new heel tips!

Hill's reaction to that experience is one that has launched many entrepreneurs: "I thought there had to be a better way," she recalls. She began to work out that better way by doing some research. First, she observed a shoe repair shop replacing heel tips. She was surprised at how easy it was. Her wish for "a better way" grew into a specific idea: "Why doesn't someone make tips so women can repair their own heels?" Shoe repair people advised her that there were too many different heel sizes for her idea to work. That response didn't stop Hill. She did more research and found that 90 percent of the heels on women's shoes come in just four sizes. She learned other things too: Heel tips tend to wear out in four months because an average-sized woman puts 2000 pounds of pressure on them in that time!

Hill didn't ignore market research: She surveyed women at shopping malls to see if they would buy "do-it-yourself" heel tips. The responses she got were so positive that in 1992 she invested $25,000 to produce a batch of "Heel-Tipz." In the first three months, her sales totaled ten times that amount. By the middle of 1995 her company, Adcor Products, had sold 8 million tips.

The success of Lisa Hill's venture began with a great product idea, but it didn't stop there. She developed other good ideas for marketing Heel-Tipz. First, she

Learning Activity

Have students generate possibilities for joint business ventures they might wish to enter. Suggest that they write two profiles of expectations for participation, one for themselves and the other for the business's partners. Ask volunteers to read their lists to the class. Encourage the class to evaluate the profiles for reasonableness, fairness, and workability.

TEACHING TIP

Remind students that most sole proprietorships are small businesses with fewer than 20 employees. Ask students to generate a list of reasons why it might be necessary for more than one person to own and operate a business with more employees. Use the items listed by students to build a discussion about the advantages of partnerships.

Business & TECHNOLOGY

Corey Sandler and Tom Badgett are partners in a company called Word Association. Their business is unusual because Corey lives in Massachusetts and Tom lives in Tennessee! How do they do it? Every day they communicate through computers, modems, and fax machines. They can get in touch with each other as quickly as possible, they live where they please, and they don't have to commute to the office to get things done.

Someone may buy the business from the owner, but the business's success may depend on the owner's special skills.

The Partnership

If starting a sole proprietorship sounds too risky for you, you may decide to share the responsibility and benefit from someone else's skills. Have a partner join you. A **partnership** is a business organization with two or more owners who share the responsibilities and the rewards. Look back at Figure 14-1 on page 227 to see how partnerships compare with proprietorships and corporations.

There are several advantages to a partnership. Starting one has few requirements. Depending on the nature of the business, a partnership, like a sole proprietorship, may need a license. The partners should draw up a partnership agreement, a kind of contract in which they declare certain understandings between themselves. For instance, they might put into writing how they will share the work and profits, and how they will end the partnership. Having this type of written agreement from the start may prevent problems later on.

228 UNIT 4 ENTREPRENEURSHIP AND SMALL BUSINESS

Global Perspective

The number of joint ventures between U.S. and foreign business interests has exceeded the number of mergers and acquisitions. For example, British Telecommunications and MCI Communications Corporation have formed a partnership. Their combined goal is to win the global telecommunications race. Suggest that students scan business periodicals for news of similar joint ventures or partnerships. Remind students that some of these partnerships may be arranged by governments. Students can display their findings on a world map bulletin board.

Refer to the *International Business Strategies* booklet for additional strategies and activities.

priced the tips so reasonably that people could afford to give them a try. Then there was packaging with pizzazz: a lavender card with an aqua image of high heels and detailed instructions attracted buyers. Finally, Hill developed a space-saving display strip to hold the cards, which made Heel-Tipz easy for retail stores to stock.

Success encouraged Hill to continue her entrepreneurial ways and come up with other products that women need for their high-heeled shoes. She's expanded her product line with a cushion to keep feet from slipping forward inside shoes and a transparent heel protector, among other items. And to think that it all began with a little tip!

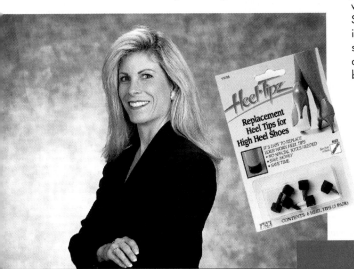

Follow Through
Suggest that students create a diagram that shows how Lisa Hill built Adcor products. (Diagrams should include idea/better way, research, do-it-yourself market, market research, inventive packaging, creative display technique.)

At least two people are needed to form a partnership. Firms may also have dozens of partners. One advantage of a partnership is that each partner can bring special skills to the business. Another advantage is that, unlike sole proprietorships, partnerships can acquire money more easily because there are more owners who can contribute to the business. All partners who share in the business have good reasons to work hard for its success. Each shares in the profits according to the partnership agreement. Like the income of the sole proprietorship, the income of the partnership is taxed only once.

The partnership form of organization has some disadvantages. Like sole proprietors, partners have unlimited liability for debts. Bad decisions may result in the business losing money. Any partner can act for the partnership. That means that if one partner makes decisions that are costly, the other partners are bound by that person's decisions. All partners take responsibility for each others' decisions. For that reason alone, making a partnership agreement is wise. It spells out the duties of each partner so that each person knows exactly what responsibilities are his or hers.

TEACHING TIP
Point out that responsibilities within a partnership are not always divided equally. Ask students to give examples of how business responsibilities in a partnership might be divided or shared.

Learning Activity
Invite students to find out what kinds of companies are generally partnerships. Suggest that they contact a representative of one of these companies to find out what requirements must be met to become a partner. (Accounting firms, management consulting firms, and many law firms often are partnerships.)

Cooperative Learning Numbered Heads Together

Organize the class into groups of four. Direct each group to imagine it is going to form a partnership. Members of each group should determine what goods or services their partnership will provide. Then have each group draw up an agreement between the partners. Remind students that the agreement should address several issues: the role of each partner in providing capital and work; how each partner will share in the profits and benefits; and what will happen to the organization as well as to the assets if one partner leaves the organization. Call on volunteers to read their group's partnership agreement to the class.

Refer to the *Cooperative Learning Strategies* booklet for additional cooperative learning strategies.

Business Brief
Many joint ventures, amounting to billions of dollars, were established between Mexican and foreign companies between 1991 and 1993. The estimated investment in these projects amounted to about $5.6 billion.

Point out that businesses can be reorganized, often growing from sole proprietorships to corporations. Ask students to describe a scenario in which a sole proprietor of a video game software company decides to reorganize to become a corporation. Ask students to generate a list of reasons why the owner might want to change the business organization to that of a corporation, and a list of ways in which the reorganization might benefit the business. Encourage them also to generate a list of ways in which the owner's involvement, responsibility, and liability will change.

Business Brief

The first recorded use of the word *corporation* appeared in the works of Tertullian in 190 A.D. Tertullian employed the term, which he derived from the Latin word *corporare*, "to make into a body," in his writings on church law. The word first appeared in English in the fifteenth century and referred to the trade guilds or merchants. By the seventeenth century, the word had begun to be used in its modern-day sense.

TEACHING TIP

Write the word *corporation* on the board. Ask students to describe what images and phrases come to mind and why. Have students identify the words and images that they feel are positive, and those which might be considered negative. Encourage students to discuss how they formed their opinions.

Even with a partnership agreement, partners may disagree. Those disagreements may become such a problem that the partners can no longer work together. The partnership agreement should provide for adding new partners and for ending the partnership. Partnerships are legally ended if one partner decides to leave the partnership or dies. The remaining partners may reorganize the business, but they really are starting a new business. Many partnership agreements provide a way for the remaining partner or partners to buy the share of ownership of a partner who leaves the business or dies. When an agreement allows the partner to do this, they can keep the business and continue it as a new one.

The Corporation

Suppose that your business has grown and you would like to expand—buy more equipment, add a new location, capture a larger share of the market. What you need, though, is money. You don't want to take on any more partners. You would have to consult with them about every aspect of the business, as you do with your current partners. What you want is for someone to let you use their money, while you run the business. What you are moving toward is a corporation.

A **corporation** is an organization owned by many people, but treated by the law as though it were a person. It can own property, pay taxes, make contracts, and so on. If you want to form a corporation, you issue **stock,** or shares in the ownership of your corporation. The new owners, called **stockholders,** pay a set price for their shares. Each stockholder has one vote in the management of the corporation for each share of the stock he or she owns. Some large corporations have over a million stockholders.

In addition to selling stock in the corporation, its founders have to do two more things—register their company with the state in which they will be headquartered and elect a board of directors. Most state laws governing the formation of corporations are similar. If you and your partners want to incorporate, you will have to file an articles of incorporation application. If the articles are in agreement with state law, the state will grant you a **corporate charter,** a license to operate from that state.

The stockholders of a corporation elect a **board of directors,** a group of individuals chosen to make the major decisions for the company. The board of directors then appoints officers to make the day-to-day decisions for the

The Hudson's Bay Company is a Canadian corporation that is among the oldest commercial enterprises still operating today. Founded in 1670 by a group of merchants and noblemen helped by two French fur traders, the company actually helped settle Canada as it moved farther westward to find more sources of furs. Today, the company is one of Canada's largest corporations. Though its main business now is retail trade, it still ranks as the world's largest fur-trading firm.

Making Connections Business Ethics

Point out that some individuals own a large portion of a single corporation because they own a great deal of stock in the corporation. Ask students to discuss what responsibilities the largest shareholders have towards the corporation and towards society. Ask students to discuss ways in which a large shareholder can influence the actions of a corporation. (By voting for a board of directors who share the stockholder's view.)

company. The officers, such as the president, vice presidents, treasurer, and so on, make most of the day-to-day decisions for the corporation.

There are several advantages to this form of business ownership. It is easy to raise capital, or money, for expansion by issuing stocks. In fact, the corporate form of ownership is often used when large amounts of money are needed to start or expand a business. Each stockholder has **limited liability.** That is, the stockholder is responsible for the losses of the corporation only to the extent of his or her involvement. Because it is a legal entity apart from the owners, the corporation does not end if owners sell shares. Ownership can be transferred to new stockholders, and the corporation goes on.

One major disadvantage of a corporation is that it is subject to special taxes. Owners are taxed on their income from the corporation. Then the corporation itself also is taxed, since it is considered a legal entity, just like a person. In a sense, this is double taxation. A corporation is more difficult to start than a sole proprietorship or partnership. Corporations are more closely regulated by government than other business organizations. And, finally, accounting and recordkeeping are much more complex for a corporation than for the other two forms of business organization.

Although only about 19 percent of all businesses are corporations, they earn about 90 percent of the business income in the United States. Corporations can be very large or very small. If they have offices and plants in more than one country, they are called *multinational corporations.* A few American corporations are so large that their annual sales are larger than the budgets of some small countries! Look again at Figure 14-1 on page 227 to see how corporations compare with proprietorships and partnerships.

Flexibility is important in choosing the legal form of ownership when setting up a new business. Often, a business starts out as a sole proprietorship, grows into a partnership, and ultimately ends up as a corporation. That's what happened to Ray Kroc with his first McDonald's restaurant.

Stockholders elect a board of directors to make major decisions for the company. What is the first action of the new board?

Quick Check

1. Name the three types of business ownership.
2. What is the difference between *limited* and *unlimited* liability for owners of a business?
3. Define *license, stock, stockholder, board of directors,* and *corporate charter.*

Reteaching Strategy

Photocopy and distribute Enrichment Master 14-1, which lists the advantages and disadvantages of different types of business organizations. Then ask students to imagine they wish to start a business that will produce music videos and CDs. Suggest that students use the list as a basis for deciding which type of business organization they would choose for their business. Have them explain the organization and the reason for their choice in the business organization section of the new company's business plan.

USE VISUALS

Direct students' attention to the stockholders' meeting shown in the photograph. Ask students to explain why stockholders might be interested in who runs a company. (Because they are part owners.)
Answer to caption: To elect the board officers.

Learning Activity

Call on volunteers to debate the following: Buying stock in a corporation is a good way to invest money and to promote the entrepreneurial spirit. (Students taking the pro position might indicate that purchasing stock is a good way to help new businesses grow and to make money for oneself. Students taking the con position might indicate that purchasing stocks is risky and that corporations ultimately become too powerful compared to small businesses.)

 Quick Check Answers

1. Sole proprietorship, partnership, and corporation.
2. With limited liability, owners are responsible for debts only up to the amount invested; with unlimited liability, owners are responsible for all business debts.
3. Legal permit for doing business; share of ownership; someone who owns stock; elected group of people that makes major decisions for a company; legal form that gives a corporation permission to operate.

Building Business Skills

Building Business Skills

Model

Have students read the Tips for Providing Constructive Feedback on page 233. Then work through each of the tips, demonstrating how to use each one in a classroom situation. Ask pairs of students to demonstrate or explain the possible use of the tips in a business situation.

Develop Concepts

Organizing for Management

Point out to students that businesses often depend on a number of people to accomplish the daily tasks associated with keeping the business growing. One of the factors for a business owner to consider is that each person in a business may have special skills and knowledge important to the business. The most important factor in managing a business is making sure that business responsibilities and employees' skills are well matched. Clarify this concept by having students compare and contrast the traits necessary for being a good partner with those necessary for being a successful sole proprietor.

EMPLOYABILITY

Providing Constructive Feedback

Explanation

Whenever you communicate your reaction to another person's ideas, actions, or behavior, you are providing *feedback*. Feedback tells people about your reactions and opinions. If you are a business owner or if you are involved in the business world in any way, you'll often find yourself in formal and informal situations that require you to give feedback. A coworker may ask your opinion on his or her way of doing a task. In a meeting, you may be called on to comment on a process or product idea. You may participate in a brainstorming session for new slogan suggestions. Or, if you own your business, you'll need to help workers do the best job they can.

If you become a supervisor, it will be a vital part of your job to give the employees you supervise feedback about job performance. Lack of feedback may make workers feel unsure of themselves. They need to know when they have made a mistake or where there is room for improvement in the way they do things. It's just as important for them to know when they're doing a good job. Positive feedback improves employee confidence and morale, and these in turn can lead to greater productivity.

Practice

How can you give feedback in ways that will help you and your coworkers work together most effectively?

ORGANIZING FOR MANAGEMENT

F. Y. I.

The best leaders of today are those in the business world, according to 1000 Americans surveyed in 1995. About 42 percent rated business leaders as the best, 35 percent chose those in government, and 13 percent preferred sports figures as leaders. Eleven percent identified entertainers as the best leaders!

If you want people to invest in your company, you have to show them that their investment will be well managed. You may have a great idea for a business venture, but that is no guarantee of your ability to manage the business that will produce the good or service you are proposing. Whether you organize as a proprietorship, a partnership, or a corporation, your business plan has to detail the organizational arrangement and the backgrounds of the people who will fill key positions in your company.

Human Resource Planning

In a proprietorship or a very small business, the founder may initially do all or most of the work associated with the business. The owner may not have all the necessary skills to manage the business, however. He or she may be skilled in producing the product the business offers, but may not be able to deal well with the public. Similarly, a person who works well with the public may lack the attention to detail necessary to

232 UNIT 4 ENTREPRENEURSHIP AND SMALL BUSINESS

Global Perspective

McDonald's, one of the world's largest multinational companies, chooses from several structuring options for its overseas operations. In Europe, the company enters a foreign market with a wholly-owned subsidiary, a company owned by McDonald's but with its own management and board of directors. In Asia, the burger giant prefers partnerships. In some Middle-Eastern markets, the company uses no equity capital but licenses its name with strict restrictions. Ask students to discuss what advantages the different management options might offer to McDonald's.

Refer to the *International Business Strategies* booklet for additional strategies and activities.

1. Be honest. People have to know how they're doing in order to do their best work.
2. Remember to give positive as well as negative feedback.
3. Be courteous. Rudeness is counterproductive. Consider the other person's feelings as you choose your words.
4. Frame criticism in a positive manner. Instead of saying "That idea won't work unless you . . .," you might say something like "I think that would work if. . . ."

5. If you are giving negative feedback about an idea or job performance, explain your reasons. Focus your criticism on the idea or performance rather than attacking the person.
6. Provide alternative ideas or specific suggestions for improvement whenever you can.
7. Give feedback in day-to-day work situations as well as formal settings so employees have an ongoing idea of how they're doing. When you think a colleague or coworker has done a good job, let him or her know, even if you're not a supervisor.

Read the Tips for Providing Constructive Feedback. Then number a separate sheet of paper from 1 to 7 and write an example of a situation or comment to illustrate each tip.

Your feedback may not always be what the other person hoped you would say, but if you provide constructive feedback in a positive manner, it will help the other person and the business.

Practice
Ask students which of the tips for providing positive feedback they think might be the most difficult to employ. Discuss these tips with the class, asking students to role-play various situations in which they employ these tips. (Students' answers will vary, but should demonstrate an understanding of each tip and a courteous, caring approach to giving constructive feedback. Students who need additional practice will benefit from the listening activities in the *Communication Skills Review booklet*.)

handle taxes and other recordkeeping tasks. In this case, the proprietor may need to seek outside help.

Many times, people enter into business partnerships to share special skills. Suppose you and a partner open a restaurant. Your special skills include keeping business and financial records. Your partner is a trained chef and likes to work with people in the day-to-day operation of the restaurant. If you had opened a restaurant as a sole proprietor, you would have found that the cooking and operation of the business were your weakest areas. Your partner's special skills, coupled with your expertise, gives the two of you a better chance of making the business a success.

In your business, if you plan to divide responsibility for management among several people, you will have to identify how everyone will fit into the organizational structure. You will have to prepare job descriptions for your partners, employees, and for yourself. After the job descriptions have been prepared, you are ready to develop an organizational chart for your business. If yours is a corporation, your business plan will have to detail the background and special expertise of your company's directors and officers.

CHAPTER 14   ORGANIZING A BUSINESS   **233**

TEACHING TIP
To help students better understand the difference among the types of ownership, lead students in a discussion about how the personality characteristics needed to work for a large corporation might differ from those needed to work for a sole proprietorship. Ask students which type of organization they think they are better suited to work for.

Curriculum Connection   English and Communication

Suggest that students look through recent issues of *Inc., Venture Entrepreneur, Black Enterprise, Success, Business Week, The Nation's Business,* or the business sections of various periodicals. Direct students to review their periodicals to locate articles about sole proprietorships, partnerships, or corporations, making notes on the various items they find. Ask students to write a few paragraphs describing their findings, using business terms such as *sole proprietorship, license, partnership, limited liability, stock, stockholder,* and *corporate charter.*

For those students who need to sharpen their written communication skills, choose among the worksheets in the *Communication Skills Review* booklet.

Quick Check Answers

1. People who invest in a business want to be sure it will be well managed.
2. Accountant, attorney, banker, insurance agent.

Quick Check Answers

1. Location, facilities, equipment, layout, inventory procedures.
2. Service.

FIGURE 14-2

Businesses that are starting up are likely to need a number of professional services. Which of these professionals would you call to help you set up a partnership agreement?

PROFESSIONAL SERVICES	
Professional	**Services Provided**
Accountant	Record-keeping, taxes, cash flow
Attorney	Legal form of organization, contracts, regulations
Banker	Loans, billing services, credit and collection
Insurance Agent	Needs evaluation, insurance, risk management

Outside Professional Resources

There are many professional services that new business owners are likely to need. These must be identified and their responsibilities outlined in your business plan. Some core professionals that assist entrepreneurs are listed in Figure 14-2.

Business owners may also need outside assistance to identify employment practices in their locality or state. For example, new business owners need to be familiar with laws pertaining to minimum wages, occupational health and safety, unemployment compensation, and workers' disability insurance. State and federal government agencies publish free or inexpensive publications to help new entrepreneurs.

Quick Check

1. Why is human resource planning important?
2. What professional services might a new business need?

ORGANIZING FOR OPERATION

Once you have selected your type of business organization, you can then address the operating plan. This section of the business plan explains how you are going to run the day-by-day operations of your business. The operating plan explains the type of manufacturing or operating system you will use. It also describes the facilities, labor needs, raw materials, and process requirements of your business.

Suppose you plan to manufacture a new product. Your operating plan would describe the physical facilities and the location of your factory. Entrepreneurs have to avoid committing to a building space that is too small or too large for efficient operation. Any equipment will have to be planned for and described. For example, general purpose equipment, such as lathes and drill presses may be easier to obtain than special purpose equipment, such as bottling equipment. Layout of the equipment must facilitate production operations and efficient flow of materials.

When planning a service business, describe how, when, and who will provide the services. Compare your services to those of your competitors to show how you will price your service.

Quick Check

1. What kinds of things does the operating plan address?
2. Is customer accessibility more important to a manufacturing or a service business?

Cooperative Learning Co-op Co-op

Group students into teams of four. Direct each team to design an item to be mass produced using only the students and the materials in the classroom. Tell students they should plan to produce 100 units of their items. Encourage the team to describe the item, the materials used, and the assembly process. Then direct teams to produce an operating plan for their product suitable to include in a new business plan.

Refer to the *Cooperative Learning Strategies* booklet for additional cooperative learning strategies.

Chapter 14 **Summary**

Main Ideas

1. Businesses may legally be set up as sole proprietorships, partnerships, or corporations.
2. A sole proprietorship is easy to start. The owner makes all the decisions and earns all the profits. However, it may be hard to raise capital, and the owner has unlimited liability for the business's debts.
3. A partnership is fairly easy to set up and operate. Partners share the risks and the profits. However, partners have unlimited liability for the business debts and may disagree on issues.
4. A corporation has a separate legal existence. Financing is easy to obtain, and investors have limited liability for the company's debts. However, a corporation is taxed at a higher rate and start-up is complex and expensive.
5. A management plan identifies the key people in a business organization and cites their skills and expertise.
6. An operating plan explains the type of manufacturing or operating system a business will use.
7. Resourceful entrepreneurs like Lisa Hill can identify a product need and fill it to begin a business.
8. Business owners and managers need to provide constructive feedback to employees.

CASE ANALYSIS Organizing a Business

Cindy has formed a partnership with her friends Juan and Lisa. They will make and sell works of art. Cindy is a sculptor, Juan is a potter, and Lisa is a painter. Each artist contributed money to the business. The business has been in operation for three months, but the friends are having some difficulties that are threatening their friendship as well as their business.

- Recordkeeping for the business is haphazard. It is irritating to try to figure out the company's taxes and profits.
- Each partner is receiving an equal share of the income. Cindy thinks this is unfair, since she invested the most money.
- Lisa spends very little time at the business and has contributed only three paintings, while Cindy and Juan have stocked the business with their goods.
- Juan decided he wanted a new potter's wheel and a new kiln, so he went out and bought them. Cindy, not realizing that Juan had made these purchases, invested in display counters and carpet for the showroom.

Can the partners save the business? What do you suggest they do in order to save the business? Be specific in your recommendations.

CHAPTER 14   ORGANIZING A BUSINESS   **235**

CLOSE

Main Ideas

Main Ideas summarizes the key information in the chapter. It is a useful tool for reinforcement and review.

CASE ANALYSIS

Case Analysis provides a chapter-related case for student analysis and application of decision-making skills.

Answer
Yes, the business can be saved. The partners should draw up a partnership agreement outlining the responsibilities of each partner. The agreement should specify who will keep records, who will choose and order equipment and materials, and how much time each will spend with the business. This agreement should also specify how much artwork each must contribute, how the partners will share the income, and what will happen if one partner leaves the business.

QUICK QUIZ

1. Which type of business ownership presents the most financial liability to a business owner? (Sole proprietorship.)
2. Who owns a corporation? (Stockholders.)
3. What professional services might a recording company need? (Accountant, attorney, banker, insurance agent.)
4. What kinds of things are important to a business's operation? (Goods producer: Manufacturing facilities, labor, and raw materials; Service provider: accessibility, location, pricing.)

Chapter 14 **Review**

CHAPTER 14 REVIEW

APPLY

Answers

Use the Language of Business

1. partnership; **2.** stockholders; **3.** charter; **4.** unlimited liability; **5.** corporation; **6.** stocks; **7.** limited liability; **8.** sole proprietorship; **9.** board of directors; **10.** license.

Review What You Learned

1. It's simple to start; the owner can make all decisions; profits aren't divided; the owner pays taxes only once on the profits.
2. At least two; no.
3. If the business's debts are greater than its assets, the owners are responsible for the difference.
4. Partnership is legally ended. Remaining partners may reorganize. If not, the business ends.
5. A corporation needs permission to operate, must pay fees before being chartered, and is highly regulated. A partnership may need a license to operate; a partnership agreement is not required, but is an advantageous document to have.
6. The human resources, including owners, directors, managers, and their expertise in running the company.
7. Information about location, facilities, equipment, layout, and inventory management.
8. Heel tips for women's shoes.
9. It encourages improvement.

Understand Business Concepts

1. Advantages: separate legal existence; limited liability; unlimited life; easy to get capital and financing. Disadvantages: taxed at a higher rate; complex and expensive procedures for setting up, operating, and dissolving the business; highly regulated.
2. Possible answer: Many businesses are run more efficiently by one person, and many people prefer to be their own bosses.
3. Risks and rewards are shared; each brings different strengths to benefit the business.

Use the Language of Business

When dealing with organizing a business, it is important to know the following terms. See how well you know them. Complete each sentence with the correct term.

board of directors	partnership
corporate charter	sole proprietorship
corporation	stock
license	stockholder
limited liability	unlimited liability

1. A _____ is a business organization with two or more owners who share responsibility.
2. A person who owns shares in a corporation is a _____ .
3. _____ is the responsibility for debts, even if they are more than the assets of the business firm.
4. A legal form giving a corporation permission to operate is a _____ .
5. A business that is legally regarded as a separate entity is called a _____ .
6. A(n) _____ is a share of ownership in a corporation.
7. _____ means that an owner's responsibility for the debts of a business only extend to the amount of money that the owner has invested.
8. A business owned by one person is called a _____ .
9. A group of individuals called a _____ is elected by the stockholders of a corporation to make major decisions for the company.
10. Any new business may need a _____ , which is a legal permit to operate.

Review What You Learned

1. List four advantages of a business organized as a sole proprietorship.
2. How many people must be involved in a partnership? Is there a limit on the number of partners a firm may have?
3. Sole proprietorships and partnerships both have unlimited liability for the business debts. What does that mean to the owners?
4. What happens when a partner dies or leaves the firm?
5. How is starting a corporation different from forming a partnership?
6. What is included in a business management plan?
7. What should be included in the operating plan?
8. What small item got Lisa Hill's business under way?
9. Why is providing constructive feedback important, especially in business situations?

Understand Business Concepts

1. List the major advantages and disadvantages of a corporation.
2. What do you consider to be the biggest disadvantage of a sole proprietorship?
3. Why would two or more people decide to form a partnership instead of forming a sole proprietorship with one of them as owner?

4. Possible answers include difficulty in raising money; limited life; hard to get discounts; unlimited liability.
5. It is a legal entity—creditors cannot reach beyond the firm's assets to collect corporate debts.
6. They organize important aspects of setting up a new business.
7. To find out if women would buy her product.
8. People are less likely to express their best ideas or do their best work if they feel they might be attacked or ridiculed.

Think Critically

1. Corporations, because they can sell stock to individuals who have limited liability in the firm and do not actively work in the firm.
2. Their skills and abilities contribute to the success of the company and its products.

4. There are more sole proprietorships than partnerships and corporations combined in the United States. Why do you think so many businesses are organized this way?
5. What is the major way in which a corporation is different from a sole proprietorship and a partnership?

6. Why are the legal, management, and operating plans of a business important to its overall business plan?
7. Why did Lisa Hill do market research?
8. Why is constructive feedback more effective than negative comments?

Think Critically

1. **Analyze.** Which of the types of businesses in this chapter would have the easiest time obtaining the money needed to expand a business? Why?

2. **Explain.** The word *resources* makes us think of such things as water or oil. Why are people considered resources in business?

Use What You Learned

1. **Group Project.** Work in three groups to develop a bulletin board display showing the advantages and disadvantages of the three forms of business ownership discussed in this chapter.
2. Interview a local sole proprietor about what he or she enjoys and finds difficult in owning and running his or her own business. Discuss the advantages/disadvantages. Then write a profile of the business owner.
3. **Computer Application.** Suppose that you have $1000 to invest. Check the stock listings in your newspaper and choose one or more corporations in which to invest your money. Follow the

daily progress of your own stock in the financial section of the newspaper for one week. Then use charting/graphing software to create a graph to show whether your stock went up or down in value. Compare your stock selection with others in your class.
4. **Skill Reinforcement.** Work with a partner. Choose one of the examples you used to illustrate the Tips for Providing Constructive Feedback on page 233. Write and present a skit based on that sample situation in which you model how to give constructive feedback.

Save your work in your Business Portfolio.

Use What You Learned
1. Group together students of similar verbal proficiency. Rubric: Bulletin Board.
2. Remind students to prepare questions in advance and to be prompt for their interview appointment. Possible Rubric: Paragraph, Note Taking.

3. Students without access to computers can complete the project by listing the daily quotations of their stocks and making a line graph reflecting the changes in value. Rubric: Charts and Tables.
4. Students' skits will vary. Rubric: Presentation.

Independent Practice
Use the Chapter 14 worksheets in *Student Activity Guide 1* for additional practice and application activities. *Student Activity Guide 1* provides vocabulary exercises, reading comprehension checks, problems, projects, and simulations of business and economic situations. A Teacher's Annotated Edition provides answers.

ASSESS

Portfolio Assessment
The portfolio projects are designed to lead students to develop a collection of their best work to submit to you for assessment. You and your students should decide which projects will be included in their respective Business Portfolios. Refer students to the specific rubric(s) from the *Alternative Assessment Strategies* booklet listed with each of the project notes below. These rubrics will alert students to the criteria you will use to assess their projects.

Chapter Assessment
Use the Chapter 14 Test from the *Test Masters* booklet to evaluate students' understanding of the chapter concepts. An answer key is provided. Or create your own customized test using the *Testmaker* software.

CHAPTER
15

FOCUS

Introduce the Chapter

Major Concepts
- Projecting Expenses and Income
- Sources for Seeking Capital
- Completing the Financial Plan

Introduce the Topic

Ask students to recall a time when they participated in raising money for a school event or other activity or for a personal project. Discuss their responses by posing the following questions: Were the fundraising efforts successful? What did investors gain? (Possible answers: Chance at a raffle prize, cookies, car wash.)

Use Business Terms

Ask students to study the list of Business Terms. Then have each student write a question that requires one of the new terms as an answer. Ask volunteers to read aloud their questions for members of the class to respond. Advise students to check the meanings of the Business Terms as they read the chapter.

USE VISUALS

Entrepreneurs must present a realistic financial plan to those who could provide financial assistance. What do you think is meant by a realistic financial plan? (A realistic financial plan provides an estimate that includes all of the costs for starting a business.)

Business terms
start-up costs
cost of goods sold
operating expenses
cash flow projection
equity capital
debt capital
securities
corporate bond
statement of net worth
net worth

238

CHAPTER 15 RESOURCES

Instructional Resources

Lesson Plan for Chapter 15

Teaching Transparencies 15-1, 15-2

Strategies and Worksheets for Teaching Transparencies 15-1, 15-2

Enrichment Master 15-1

Student Activity Guide 1–TAE for Chapter 15

Test Master for Chapter 15

Alternative Assessment Strategies

Math Skills Review

International Business Strategies

Cooperative Learning Strategies

Communication Skills Review

Ethics in Business Strategies

Financing a Business

Learning objectives

After completing this chapter, you will be able to:
- Describe the content of the financial plan portion of a business plan.
- Identify sources for obtaining capital to start or expand a business.
- Describe several ways in which entrepreneur Don Barden financed his businesses.
- Explain why predicting consequences is important for business-people, especially when financing their businesses.

Consider what you know

- The business plan is a planning tool for establishing a new business. It includes a company description, a product plan, a management plan, an operating plan, and a marketing plan.

Consider what you want to know

- How can you project income and expenses for a new business?
- Where can people get capital to start new small businesses?
- How can an established business obtain money for expansion and growth?
- How did entrepreneur Don Barden finance his first business?
- Why is it important for businesspeople to predict consequences, especially in financing their businesses?

Consider how to use what you learn

- As you read this chapter, think how you might prepare the financial portion of a business plan.

Multimedia Resources

Technology Resource Guide
Distance Learning Guide
Internet Resource Guide
Professional Resources
School-to-Work/Tech Prep Strategies
Instructional Poster
Spanish Resources

Testmaker Software for Chapter 15
The Wall Street Journal Video Series
   Video & Activities for Chapter 15
Business and Marketing Computer
   Applications—An Integrated Software
   Simulation Using Microsoft Works
Stocktracker—A Stock Market Software
   Simulation
Where's the Dough? Board Game

Motivate the Learning

Learning Objectives
Indicate to students that the learning objectives for this chapter are listed at the beginning of the chapter. Encourage students to read and discuss the objectives as a way to tell what they will learn in the chapter. Note that the last two objectives listed refer to the Focus on Entrepreneurs feature and the Building Business Skills feature.

Consider What You Know
Review briefly with students the main sections of *Chapter 14: Organizing a Business:* Organizing for Ownership; Organizing for Management; Organizing for Operation.

Consider What You Want to Know
Have students keep the listed questions in mind as they preview the chapter by quickly paging through it, looking at the graphics, and reading the section headings and figure titles.

Consider How to Use What You Learn
Indicate to students that at the close of this chapter they will develop some projects that will help them investigate different kinds of business funding. Suggest that as they read the chapter they note some of the characteristics of different kinds of funding and the advantages and disadvantages of each.

TEACH

Business Connection

Leslie Johnson received a loan from the Woman's Economic Development Corporation (Wedco) in St. Paul, Minnesota, to purchase roses to sell on Valentine's Day. The $500 Wedco loan had to be repaid within 5 days. Johnson made $2500 selling the roses and paid off the loan. Johnson used a series of such loans to earn and save enough money to start her own floral business. Johnson now has three locations and her business grosses $740,000 a year.

Develop Concepts

Projecting Expenses and Income

Impress upon students that even the smallest businesses, those requiring few supplies or equipment, still have start-up costs, business expenses, and personal expenses. All of these must be covered by the business's income.

Learning Activity

Ask students to keep a record of their personal expenses for two weeks. Invite a volunteer to list on the board some of the categories most students included in their lists. (Lunches, clothes, entertainment, and so on.) Use students' lists as a basis for a discussion on the amount of money a business owner might need to live on while the business is in the start-up phase.

As you've learned in this unit, financing is a key issue for an entrepreneur starting a business. Adequate financing is a key element in a successful company. There are a number of sources of financing, and it's important to consider them when you begin working on the last part of your business plan: the financial plan. The financial plan specifies the financial needs and anticipated sources of income. It presents projections of revenues, costs, and profits.

PROJECTING EXPENSES AND INCOME

Perhaps the hardest part of a business plan is the financial plan. In this document, the prospective owner specifies how much money, or capital, will be required to get the business going and keep it going until it is solidly established.

A well-developed product description, operating plan, management plan, and marketing plan provide much of the background information an entrepreneur can use to write a financial plan. As in all parts of the business plan, the key is to be realistic. Many of the people who read the plan are individuals who hopefully will help finance the company. They expect realism and careful planning.

Start-Up Costs

New small business owners expend money in establishing a business venture. These **start-up costs** must be reflected in the business's financial plan. Some of these costs are one-time only, such as licenses and permits and deposits for telephone service. Others are costs that will continue, such as rent, maintenance, and insurance. If you are starting a new business, you have to estimate your start-up costs and project how much money you will need for your first year of operation. You can get information about start-up costs from people who are already in a similar business, trade associations, or state and local government agencies.

Personal Needs

To produce a sound financial plan for your business venture, you should project your living expenses and household needs for at least your first year of business. You should plan to have enough cash on hand to pay your personal expenses for more

GLOBAL VIEW

The GetAhead Foundation in Soweto, South Africa, gathers funds from all over the world to fund entrepreneurs in South Africa. Many feel that it is entrepreneurs starting small businesses that will bring prosperity to those who suffered most from that country's now discarded policy of apartheid, or separation of races.

Making Connections ⇨   Everyday Living

Have students work in groups of four to develop a realistic and accurate plan for a student's expenses for the school year. Suggest they use as a basis a list of expenses they incur within a two-week period. Remind students they may want to consult the school calendar to consider the costs of scheduled special events they might want to attend. Have groups share their plans with the class. Discuss with students any categories they may wish to add to their original plans.

than your first month of operation. Some experts even suggest that you have enough for the first three months of operation. You might have to lower your current living standards to do this. Setting aside this money in a savings account and not using it for any other purpose will help the new owner get through the start-up period. Many small businesses fail because they do not initially make enough profit to pay their owners' living expenses.

Business Income

In addition to projecting how much money your business will need, you also need to project how much money your business will earn. A major factor affecting the income of your business is the volume of sales. Thus, you need to project the sales volume for your business. You do this by determining what you will charge for the item or service you will sell. You must estimate the number you will sell. This estimate can be gained from trade publications, owners of similar businesses, or industry consultants. To derive your total expected business income, you multiply the price you will charge for items times the number of items you estimate will be sold. This will give you the total yearly sales your business must bring in.

Business Expenses

For any product that a business sells, it must pay certain costs. For instance, a manufacturer must take into account the

Entrepreneurs need a constant source of funds to help their businesses grow. Where would you look first to find investment capital for your new business?

Enrichment Strategy

Discuss

Open a discussion on Don Barden's accomplishments using his quote "Every position is a springboard for the next." Ask students to describe how each of Barden's jobs, positions, or ventures led to another. Encourage students to identify any common thread between successive business ventures or positions.

Don H. Barden—Barden Companies, Inc. (BCI)

As a child growing up in a rural area outside of Detroit, Don H. Barden watched his father work hard at more than one job at a time. The elder Barden worked at an automobile plant, did car repairs, grew crops, and built houses. Don Barden, the ninth of 13 children, has been following his father's example for most of his working life. Today, he is Chairman of The Barden Companies, Inc., with operations in real estate, broadcasting, and entertainment.

In the words of *Black Enterprise* magazine, for Barden "every position is a springboard for the next." After dropping out of college for lack of money, Barden worked at a variety of jobs. At age 21, with $500 in savings, he opened a record store in Lorain, Ohio. "I wanted to control my own destiny," says the entrepreneur. "I said to myself 'I am going to take risks.'" The record store was a springboard to promoting bands and concerts, and then to his next venture, a public relations office.

When he heard that the military recruiting facility across from his office was looking for new space to rent, Barden found a building, secured a $25,000 loan to buy it, and rented it to the U.S. military. Two years later, he sold the building for $50,000 and bought another. He started a county newspaper and served as the first black city councilman elected in Lorain. Meanwhile, he also anchored the local TV news and hosted a talk show in Cleveland. As if this weren't enough, Barden continued to develop real estate.

TEACHING TIP

To help students understand the difference among various kinds of expenses, ask students to imagine they will be opening a music store or a clothing store. Have them diagram the inside of the store, showing how merchandise will be displayed, aisles, counters, checkout cashier's location, and so on. Have them indicate on their drawing which items are likely to be listed as *start-up expenses,* which items contribute to the *cost of goods sold,* and which items are part of the *operating expenses* of a business. (Sample answer: Start-up expenses: goods rack, display cases; cost of goods sold: CDs, jeans; operating expenses: lights, cleaning, security, price tags.)

expenses of producing its goods. A retailer must allow for the expenses of buying merchandise. Any new business owner must predict the **cost of goods sold** that will generate sales volume. That is, he or she must predict the cost of producing or acquiring a company's products for sale during a given period. In addition to the costs directly associated with producing their goods or services, would-be entrepreneurs must account for **operating expenses.** These are all the costs of operation that are not included under cost of goods sold. Operating expenses can include wages and salaries, advertising, insurance, professional services, and supplies.

An important part of any financial plan is the **cash flow projection.** This is a forecast of the funds a business believes it will be receiving and the amount of cash it will be paying out. Generally the cash flow projection is done for each month of one year and for each quarter of a three-to-five year period. Officers of lending institutions and investors in a business are very interested in looking at a business's cash flow estimates.

Curriculum Connection   Social Studies

Ask students to work in groups to contact their local, village, city, or county government or their state government to find out how agencies in these various levels of government establish their cash flow projections. Have students prepare a list of questions before they contact a representative of the controller's or treasurer's office. Students may either interview the representative or submit a list of written questions. Have students prepare a three-minute news brief "Your Government's Cash Flow" for the evening television news.

For students who need to sharpen their writing skills, choose among the worksheets in the *Communication Skills Review* booklet.

Because of his work in broadcasting, Barden came to recognize cable television's business potential and decided to get involved in 1980. By the time he sold his interest in Barden Cablevision in 1994, this multitalented

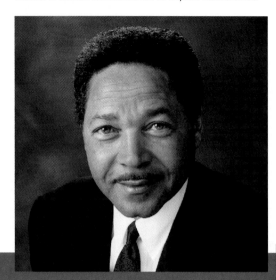

entrepreneur had set up and managed cable systems in several Michigan communities, including Detroit, where he now lives. In eleven years, his companies' revenues increased from $600,000 to more than $90 million.

Success has led to national recognition. Barden has been honored as an entrepreneur by the NAACP, *Black Enterprise* magazine, *The Detroit News*, and *The Wall Street Journal*. With the acquisition of radio stations in Illinois and a $116 million entertainment center under development in Gary, Indiana, Barden Companies, Inc., is thriving, and Don Barden continues to prove that it is possible to do many things at once—and do them all well.

Quick Check

1. Define *start-up costs, cost of goods sold, operating expenses, cash flow projection.*
2. List four items that must be predicted for a financial plan.

SOURCES FOR SEEKING CAPITAL

After you have carefully analyzed your projected income and expenses, you are ready to shop for sources of capital. The most common sources of funds for new businesses fall into two categories: equity capital and debt capital. **Equity capital** is money raised from within the firm or through the sale of ownership (equity) in the firm. **Debt capital** involves funds raised through various forms of borrowing that must be repaid. Most businesses are financed with a mix of equity capital and debt capital. Once the business is launched, it will have a continuing

F.Y.I.

Some banks in Chicago have streamlined the small business loan process. When DeWayne Adamson decided to open a motorcycle customizing shop in 1995, he needed $200,000 to get started. He took his business plan to a local bank. "I . . . walked my banker through the material. After 15 minutes, he . . . told me I had the loan." The competitive banking market has led to better terms for small businesses.

CHAPTER 15   FINANCING A BUSINESS   **243**

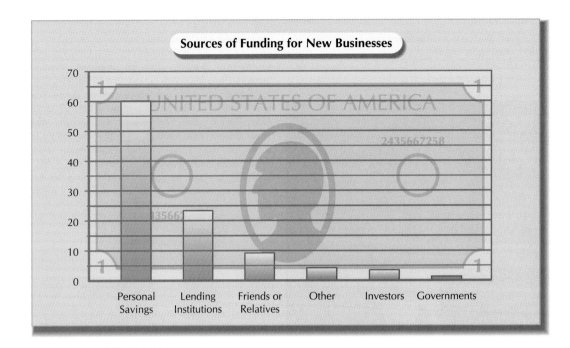

Sources of Funding for New Businesses

FIGURE 15-1

Most businesses are started with relatively little money, and founders generally use their own savings to start their businesses. Which source provides the least amount of funding for new businesses?

need for money. Although some businesses grow through funds created within the company, most need repeated transfusions from outside lenders or investors.

Personal Savings

A financial plan that includes the entrepreneur's personal funds helps build confidence among potential investors. Your prospective investors and creditors expect you to share in the risk. Therefore, as you can see in Figure 15-1 above, about 60 percent of the people who start up new businesses reach into their own pockets.

Lending Institutions

The second most frequently pursued source of loans is lending institutions. Both commercial banks and smaller community banks make small business loans, but entrepreneurs may have greater success with smaller local or community banks because they have a vested interest in the commercial activities of the community. Such banks are often better equipped to make small business loans. In 1994 more than half of the loans made to small businesses came from community banks.

Meeting Student Diversity

Students with limited English proficiency may have difficulty in understanding how a free market economy affects the availability of money for loans. Tell students to imagine they have $10,000 to invest and that five people have each asked for the money they need to expand their businesses. Ask students how they would decide which of the five people would receive their money.

For students who need to sharpen their math skills, choose among the worksheets in the *Math Skills Review* booklet.

It is a good idea to approach several banks when looking for a loan. Rates and terms can vary from bank to bank. Most banks typically charge small businesses relatively high interest to borrow money. Often entrepreneurs report being turned down five or six times before they find a bank that is willing to give them a loan, so it pays to be persistent and not become discouraged. Most banks expect entrepreneurs to put up 25 to 50 percent of the money themselves, and they demand both pledges of assets and personal guarantors to back the loan.

Relatives or Friends

Many people begin their businesses with the help of funds borrowed from relatives and friends. Using such sources of capital can be tricky. Friends or relatives who provide funds may sometimes feel that they have the right to participate in managing the business. Also, hard business times can strain relationships, especially if the business fails, and the loan can't be repaid. The financial plan should provide for repayment of such loans as soon as possible.

Individual Investors

Individuals outside the entrepreneur's circle of friends or relatives are potential sources of funding. These may be local investors such as area physicians or attorneys who invest anywhere from $10,000 to $100,000 in a business venture. The term *angels* is sometimes applied to these private investors. They generally learn about the investment opportunities from

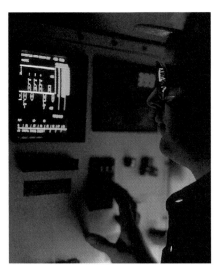

Some entrepreneurs must support their new business ventures with expensive high-tech equipment. Do you think these entrepreneurs have a more difficult time raising money than those who need less to get started?

Curriculum Connection   Theater and the Arts

Investors in commercial theatrical productions are sometimes called *angels.* Ask students to research the cost of financing a Broadway theater production from 1974 to 1994. Suggest that they report their findings in separate graphs for musical and nonmusical productions. Have students include captions detailing the financial return to angels on their investments. Encourage students to share interesting facts about angels that they may learn in their research.

TEACHING TIP

Entrepreneurs often consider four factors when considering a loan: interest costs, market climate, control of the company, and financial condition of the company. Ask students to imagine they are entrepreneurs who are considering applying for a loan. Have them discuss each of the factors, explaining how the factor might influence their decision. (Sample: High interest costs might influence them to look elsewhere for financing.)

Learning Activity

Point out to students that in their lifetimes they will make a large number of financing decisions to purchase things that will last such as major appliances, cars, and houses. Have them imagine that they are business owners who must make decisions about financing. Have students generate a list of the kind of business expansions that might require financing. For each type of business expansion listed, have students suggest what might be the appropriate type of business financing.

USE VISUALS

Remind students that entrepreneurs who purchase the latest technology for their businesses might also need to learn how to use the technology effectively. Ask students how entrepreneurs might fund this learning. (As part of the business's start-up costs.)
Answer to caption: The amount of money that needs to be raised is only one consideration for those who would finance an entrepreneurial venture.

Building Business Skills

Model

Have students read the Steps for Predicting Consequences. Work through each of the tips, modeling each one in a classroom situation. For example, ask pairs of students to propose a business situation and describe how to use the steps in that situation.

ANALYSIS
Predicting Consequences

Explanation

Taking action and making decisions can be risky business. You don't always know what the logical results, or consequences, will be. It *is* possible, however, to improve your skill at identifying the logical consequences of your decisions and actions.

Sometimes it's simple: You attend a rock concert. As a result, you enjoy yourself but have less money to spend next week. You could easily predict these consequences. However, often unforeseen events occur that

don't follow logically or you wouldn't consider likely. For example, at that rock concert someone might tromp on your foot and break it!

People in business find that their success often depends on their ability to predict the probable consequences of business actions and decisions. Making the right predictions is so important that businesspeople need to follow a logical process to predict consequences.

Learning as much as possible about the decision or action is crucial to begin. For example, if you're considering cutting workers to reduce costs and increase productivity, you'll want to look at the experience of other companies. Reading articles analyzing such actions and talking to people from other firms could help.

Armed with your prior knowledge and the information you've gathered, you try to identify what might follow from personnel cuts. The possible consequences

Connection to CHAPTER 9

Review with students the terms *capital* and *owner's equity* from Chapter 9. (Capital is money invested by the company's owners, owner's equity is the owner's claim against the business.) Ask students to supply the equation that shows the relationship between a company's assets and owner's equity. (ASSETS = LIABILITIES + OWNER'S EQUITY)

TEACHING TIP

Invite students with access to the Internet to conduct a 5-minute search for venture capitalists and venture capital companies. Have students take notes on the kinds of funding offered by the individuals and companies, and the kinds of businesses these sources of funding prefer. Suggest that students present the information they find as part of a Venture Capital bulletin board in the classroom.

their business associates. Recently, national networks seeking to match potential investors and entrepreneurs have sprung up.

Venture Capitalists

In addition to seeking funds from individual investors, entrepreneurs may try to attract the interest of venture capitalists. These are individuals or organizations who raise pools of money to fund ventures they think are likely to succeed. Venture capitalists, or VCs as they are sometimes called, become partial owners of the business and have claims on the company's profits. Venture capitalists usually also have a hand in running the business. This might be mutually beneficial, depending on circumstances. As with any other lending source, it is wise to shop around before making a commitment to a venture capitalist. People interested in seeking investors may contact a number of organizations devoted to bringing together prospective business owners and venture capitalists. Some chambers of commerce, universities, and state agencies hold "venture fairs" in which venture capitalists and people planning to start a business can meet and perhaps work out a partnership.

246 UNIT 4 ENTREPRENEURSHIP AND SMALL BUSINESS

Global Perspective

Twenty-five years ago U.S. venture capitalists funded businesses almost exclusively in the United States. In 1990, however, more than half the $80 billion venture capital from venture funds went to businesses outside the United States. Governments have moved to provide entry incentives, lowering costs of initial investments and lowering the risks. Ask students to discuss how this spread of venture capital is helpful to the world's economy.

Refer to the *International Business Strategies* booklet for additional strategies and activities.

STEPS FOR PREDICTING CONSEQUENCES

1. Gather information about the decision or action.
2. Identify as many consequences as possible.
3. Analyze each consequence by asking how likely it is to occur.
4. Figure out ways to ensure favorable consequences and prevent unfavorable ones.

could be opposites: an increase in profits and productivity with waste reduced and people working more efficiently, or no such increase because workers fear they too may lose their jobs.

Analyzing possible consequences in the light of your information can tell you how likely each is to occur and help ensure the best results. For instance, planning and honest communication might keep worker morale up during personnel cuts.

Practice

Develop your ability to predict consequences by working on this problem. You want to start a business producing all-natural jams. Your savings are small and your start-up costs will be large. You could (1) Ask a local bank for a loan. (2) Accept the offer of money from your Uncle Bob, a newly retired successful businessperson. (3) Talk to a venture capital group in your city.

Using what you've learned about financing a business, follow the four-step process to clarify the possible results of each action. Write an explanation.

Practice

Ask students which of the steps for predicting consequence they think might be the most difficult, and which might be the most important. Discuss these steps with the class, asking students to describe various situations in which they already use these steps.
(1. If your personal savings are small and your start-up costs are high, you run the risk of being turned down for a bank loan. You might want to make sure your business plan is strong, or find ways to reduce start-up costs.
2. Uncle Bob's offer would ensure that you'd have enough money to start the business. However, Uncle Bob might try to help you run it. Or he might keep out of it altogether. You could investigate making an agreement to limit his participation.
3. A venture capital group will either accept or reject your application. Your small savings might make rejection more likely. Acceptance would mean that you'd have the funds to start, but you'd probably have to share profits and give them some say in running the business.)

Governments

If you have applied for loans to several banks and been turned down by all of them, you may be able to get a loan backed by the Small Business Administration (SBA), a federal agency. To get such a loan, you apply to a regular bank which actually provides the money; the SBA guarantees the bank it will repay 85 to 90 percent of the loan if you fail to do so. The average SBA-backed loan is about $100,000. The repayment terms are generally longer than for conventional loans—nine years as opposed to two or three. Unfortunately, the demand for SBA-backed loans vastly outstrips the agency's supply of capital, and getting an SBA loan is difficult.

Recently state and local governments have launched programs to help small businesses. Such programs include small-company financing, venture-capital funds aimed at start-ups, and research and development grants. In addition, many state and local development offices are teaming up with universities to form *incubator* facilities. In a typical incubator, new companies lease space at bargain rates and share staff, telephone equipment, and accounting and marketing advice.

CHAPTER 15   FINANCING A BUSINESS   **247**

Curriculum Connection   Communication

Have students make a Funding Sources library for the classroom. Have them write or telephone banks, government agencies, and venture capital firms and request free materials for use in high schools. After students receive the materials, have groups evaluate them, using criteria such as

- easy to read and understand
- technical terms defined

- useful tables, charts, and diagrams
- helpful index or table of contents

Suppliers

One good way to borrow money for your small business is to get credit from your suppliers. That is, you use *trade credit* to purchase the goods needed to operate your own business. For example, you persuade a potential supplier to provide you your beginning inventory on credit. You agree to pay for the inventory at a specified date. The supplier's risk is minimal; the product can always be taken back if you don't sell it. As you pay off the debt, you improve your credit rating and stretch your available cash.

Securities

After a period of several years in business, a company may use another method to raise capital. Companies often try to raise money for expansion by issuing **securities.** Securities are investments sold by corporations and governments to finance their growth. The two most common types of securities are stocks and bonds: stocks represent equity capital; bonds represent debt capital.

Stocks   A company that decides to sell stocks is, in effect, selling off small pieces, or shares, in the ownership of the company. Figure 15-2 on page 249 shows a public offer to sell shares of stock in a corporation. Stockholders buy shares and, because they are helping to finance the company, they usually have a voice in the operation of the company. Issuing stock provides at least two advantages over loans for a corporation. The corporation does not have to repay money obtained through the sale of stocks because stockholders are owners, not creditors. Second, a corporation is not legally obligated to pay an annual return if the company does not make a profit. Disadvantages include the high cost of offering the stock for sale and the owner's loss of control over his or her own company because of having to share decision making with those individuals who puchased the newly issued stock.

Bonds   When corporations need to borrow a large amount of money for an extended period of time, they often issue **corporate bonds.** These are written promises to repay loans or debt. People who buy bonds serve as creditors of the corporation that issued the bonds. In return for the use of the bondholders' money, the corporation promises to repay the buyers of the bonds on the maturity date, which may be 15 to 40 years after the date of issue. Because the bondholders are acting as creditors, the corporation also promises to pay a

Reteaching Strategy

Have students work in groups of four to plan, secure, and conduct an in-class interview of a small business owner who started her or his business. Encourage students to find out

- How the entrepreneur started the business
- How funding was used to start the business
- What sources of financing were used
- What funding was short-term, what was long-term

Suggest that before the interview students investigate local lending institutions and organizations that help people start small businesses. Remind students to write and refine the interview questions in advance.

This announcement is not an offer to sell nor a solicitation of an offer to buy any of these securities. The offering is made only by the Prospectus.

July 8, 1997

Meridian Petroleum Corporation

4,100,000 Shares of Common Stock

Price $2.00 Per Share

Copies of the Prospectus may be obtained in any State from only such of the undersigned as may legally offer these Securities in compliance with the securities laws of such State.

ROBERTSON SECURITIES, INC.

FIGURE 15-2

When a corporation decides to make its stock available to the general public rather than to selected individuals, it is commonly called "going public." How much money will the sale of this stock potentially provide to the corporation selling it?

certain amount of interest. The interest is often paid in installments.

An advantage of issuing bonds is the owner does not give up ownership in the company since the bondholder is not an owner. Disadvantages of bonds include required repayment of the amount loaned plus interest at preset intervals. If the payments are not made in the agreed-upon time frame and amount, bondholders can begin legal action against the company that could force it to close.

Quick Check

1. Differentiate *equity capital* from *debt capital*.
2. List four sources for financing a business venture.
3. What are two ways in which business can obtain capital to expand?

COMPLETING THE FINANCIAL PLAN

After you have identified your source or sources of capital, you have to develop three important financial statements to submit with your business plan—*statement of net worth, balance sheet*, and *income statement*.

Cooperative Learning   Group Discussion

Have groups of students list the different types of financing available to businesses. Ask each group to answer these questions for each type of financing:

- What advantage does a company gain by using this type of financing?
- What is the risk to the company?

Suggest that students use a chart to organize the information and create a poster to present the information to the class.

Refer to the *Cooperative Learning Strategies* booklet for additional cooperative learning strategies.

USE VISUALS

As students study the stock shown in Figure 15-2, be sure they understand that the individuals and organizations purchasing stock in the company expect the company to grow and the stock to increase in value. Answer to caption: $8,200,000 (4,100,000 × $2.00 = $8,200,000.)

USE TRANSPARENCIES

Use Teaching Transparency 15-2 and its corresponding strategies and worksheet from the *Strategies and Worksheets* booklet. Verify student worksheets using the Answer Key.

Quick Check Answers

1. Money raised from or through the firm or through sale of ownership; money raised through various forms of borrowing that must be repaid.
2. Possible answers include: personal savings, lending institutions, relatives or friends, individual investors, venture capitalists, governments, suppliers.
3. By issuing stocks or by issuing bonds.

Develop Concepts

Completing the Financial Plan

Remind students that when they approach the funding resource—bank, friends, or relatives—they will need to present information that will persuade the source that the business venture is a worthwhile financial risk.

Quick Check Answers

1. Financial statement that summarizes an individual's assets and liabilities and indicates the difference between the two.
2. Statement of net worth, balance sheet, income statement.

Statement of Net Worth

The **statement of net worth** is a summary of an individual's current personal financial condition at a point in time. It tells your friend or relative, the loan officer, or an investor about the money you have in savings and in other investments, such as real estate. It also tells what you owe for such things as rent, credit card payments, and car loans. The last line of this financial statement indicates your **net worth,** that is, your assets minus your liabilities. Your statement of net worth is especially important when you are estimating your personal living expenses.

Balance Sheet

As you may recall from Chapter 9, the balance sheet summarizes a business's assets, liabilities, and owner's equity at a point in time. The balance sheet for a new business should project the value of the company's assets, liabilities, and owner's equity for the first year of operation.

Income Statement

You also are familiar with the income statement. It summarizes a business's income and expenses during a specific period of time, such as a month, a quarter, or a year. The income statement for a new business states the earnings projected for the coming year, often by quarters, or three-month periods.

Quick Check

1. What is a *statement of net worth?*
2. What three financial statements should accompany a business venture's financial plan?

Reteaching Strategy

Have students work in groups of four. Ask them to imagine that they own a company that decorates items of clothing with fabric paints, buttons, beads, decorative pins, and so on. Have students determine which type of financing is best for the company's needs. Students should decide if they should borrow or sell shares in the firm and for what length of time money should be borrowed. Remind students to consider such factors as the inventory the company may need, supplies, labor costs, equipment, and cost of borrowing. Have each group of students write a paragraph explaining their financing decisions.

Chapter 15 **Summary**

Main Ideas

1. A financial plan must include projected expenses such as start-up costs, personal needs, and business expenses, as well as projected income from the business.
2. Most people beginning a business depend on their own personal savings for part of the cost. Other sources of funding include loans from banks or other lending institutions, friends and relatives, and other investors such as individuals, venture capitalists, the government, and suppliers.
3. Established businesses may use other ways to raise capital for expansion such as issuing stocks or bonds. Stocks are equity capital, because stockholders own part of the equity of the company. Bonds are debt capital, because they must be repaid as a debt.
4. Three financial statements must be included with the business plan: a statement of net worth, a balance sheet, and an income statement.
5. Don Barden's first business, a record store, enabled him to finance his next business. He followed this pattern to build other businesses.
6. Gathering information prior to making important business decisions can help businesspeople analyze the likely consequences of their actions.

CASE ANALYSIS
Financial Management

Eric Gaines and Jennifer Bradley are partners in a printing business. Their business has grown steadily for 10 years, and they would like to make a major expansion. They determine that their business is worth $200,000, and that they need $600,000 to expand. They decide to form a corporation. The $200,000 value of the current partnership and the $600,000 they must raise total $800,000, the value of the new corporation. If they issue stock at $10 a share, how many shares of stock will there be in the company?

CLOSE

Main Ideas

Main Ideas summarizes the key information in the chapter. It is a useful tool for reinforcement and review.

CASE ANALYSIS

Case Analysis provides a chapter-related case for student analysis and application of decision-making skills.

Answer
80,000

QUICK QUIZ

1. What information do you need to be able to predict to write a financial plan? (Start up costs, personal needs, business income, and business expenses.)
2. How are debt capital and equity capital alike? How are they different? (Both are common sources of new business funding; equity capital comes from the sale of ownership in the firm, debt capital comes from loans that must be repaid.)
3. Is the sale of stocks a way to raise debt capital or equity capital? The sale of bonds? (Equity, debt.)
4. What information is contained in a statement of net worth? (A summary of what an individual owns and what the individual owes.)

Chapter 15 **Review**

CHAPTER 15 REVIEW

APPLY

Answers

Use the Language of Business

1. start-up costs; 2. cost of goods sold; 3. operating expenses; 4. cash flow projection; 5. equity capital; 6. debt capital; 7. securities; 8. corporate bonds; 9. statement of net worth; 10. net worth.

Review What You Learned

1. Start-up costs, personal needs, and business expenses.
2. Figure the amount of money you want or need to earn and divide it by the percentage of the average annual net profit for the type of business you want to start.
3. Equity capital is furnished by people who in return own part of the business; debt capital is simply a loan that must be repaid without any ownership of the business going to the lender.
4. Lending institutions such as local and community banks.
5. Stocks are equity capital—stockholders own a piece of the company; bonds are debt capital—they are a loan that must be repaid on a certain date.
6. Identification of sources of capital, statement of net worth, balance sheet, and income statement.
7. He took out a loan to buy a building and then rented it.
8. Gather information; identify potential consequences; analyze how likely each consequence is; figure out ways to ensure favorable consequences.

Understand Business Concepts

1. Financial needs; anticipated sources of income; projections of revenues, costs, and profits; statement of net worth; balance sheet; income statement.
2. The readers of the plan are usually potential investors, and they expect and need to see realism and careful planning.
3. Potential investors are more willing to risk funds if the people who are going to run the business are willing to risk their

Use the Language of Business

Complete each sentence with the correct term.

cash flow projection   net worth
corporate bonds   operating expenses
cost of goods sold   securities
debt capital   start-up costs
equity capital   statement of net worth

1. _____ are the money that business owners must spend to establish a new business.
2. The _____ is the expense of producing or acquiring a company's products for sale.
3. In addition to the cost of goods sold, a potential business owner must also figure _____, or the costs of operation such as wages, advertising, and so on.
4. A(n) _____ forecasts the funds a business will receive and the amount of cash it will pay out.
5. Money raised by a business from within or by selling ownership in the company is _____ .
6. Money raised by a business by borrowing is _____ .
7. _____ are investments sold by corporations and governments to finance their growth.
8. A corporation might raise money by issuing _____, which are written promises to repay the debt on a certain date.
9. A statement of your current financial condition is a _____ .
10. You can figure your _____ by subtracting your liabilities from your assets.

Review What You Learned

1. What kinds of expenses must be forecast in a financial plan?
2. How can you estimate the sales volume for your first year of business?
3. Explain the difference between equity capital and debt capital.
4. After personal resources, what is the most frequently used source of start-up funds for a new business?
5. What is the difference between stocks and bonds?
6. What do you need to complete a financial plan to start a business?
7. How did Don Barden finance his real estate development business?
8. What steps can you follow to predict consequences?

Understand Business Concepts

1. What are the main components of a financial plan?
2. Why is it necessary to be realistic and careful when projecting financial needs as well as potential income?
3. Why is it important for entrepreneurs to invest their own savings in their new businesses?
4. Depending on friends and relatives for financial support may seem easy, but

own funds. Also, it would be highly unusual for outside investors to provide all the start-up money required.
4. Such investors may feel more able to interfere with the way the business is run; more problems are likely if the business fails or the investment doesn't seem as successful as projected.
5. Stockholders receive dividends if the company is making a profit; bondholders are repaid the full amount plus interest.
6. Equity capital and debt capital.
7. Possible answers: He might not have been able to repay the loan. The building might not have increased in value.
8. Possible answers: They would want to predict the consequences of the release of a new product or the consequences of updating and changing a recognizable logo.

Think Critically

1. Start-up costs are one-time costs, and operating costs are ongoing expenses.
2. Although the start-up costs are high, the company must have information in its business to justify the costs. If the plan demonstrates that the returns from a successful well would be high enough to offset the costs, the investor or bank might approve financing the venture.
3. Answers may vary, but most students will probably list personal resources, SBA-guaranteed loans and bank loans as the most preferable resources, with finance companies and venture capitalists as less desirable.

can present potential problems. Name several.

5. How do stocks and bonds differ in the kind of return an investor receives?

6. What are the two main categories of funds for new businesses?

7. What risk did Don Barden take when he obtained a loan to buy the building he rented to the military?

8. Describe two situations in which a marketing firm would need to predict the consequences of its actions.

Think Critically

1. **Analyze.** An entrepreneur needs long-term finances for both start-up costs and operating costs. What is the difference between them?

2. **Assess.** An oil company pays over a million dollars to build an oil well where the company may or may not find oil. Why would a banker or investor be willing to finance such a risky venture?

3. **Classify.** Suppose you were looking for financing for a new business. Rank the sources listed in the chapter as most preferable to least preferable. Explain why you ranked them the way you did.

Use What You Learned

1. **Group Project.** In your group, choose a successful small business you would all like to know more about. Draw up a list of questions to ask about the company. Here are some examples.

   - Who started the company?
   - Where did the founder get the money to start the business? How difficult was it to find the funding?
   - How did the owner(s) secure additional capital for any expansion?
   - Is it easier or harder for the company to raise capital now compared to when it first started?

   Divide the questions among team members. After securing the answers, write a group report with a time line of the company's history and other illustrations as appropriate.

2. In 200 words, explain what financial considerations would be different when raising capital for a manufacturing company, a restaurant franchise, or a retail business.

3. **Computer Application.** Research sources of start-up business capital in your local area. Use database software to compile the sources. Sort the data according to the categories presented in the chapter.

4. **Skill Reinforcement.** Your business has been doing so well that you want to expand, but you need capital for your expansion. Using the Steps for Predicting Consequences on page 247, on a separate sheet of paper predict the consequences of seeking capital from two of the possible sources described in the chapter.

Save your work in your Business Portfolio.

Use the Chapter 15 worksheets in *Student Activity Guide 1* for additional practice and application activities. *Student Activity Guide 1* provides vocabulary exercises, reading comprehension checks, problems, projects, and simulations of business and economic situations. A Teacher's Annotated Edition provides answers.

ASSESS

Portfolio Assessment

The portfolio projects are designed to lead students to develop a collection of their best work to submit to you for assessment. You and your students should decide which projects will be included in their respective Business Portfolios. Refer students to the specific rubric(s) from the *Alternative Assessment Strategies* booklet listed with each of the project notes below. These rubrics will alert students to the criteria you will use to assess their projects.

Chapter Assessment

Use the Chapter 15 Test from the *Test Masters* booklet to evaluate students' understanding of the chapter concepts. An answer key is provided. Or create your own customized test using the *Testmaker* software.

Use What You Learned

1. Attempt to group students with limited English proficiency with more proficient students. Rubrics: Diagram, Illustrations.

2. Remind students that "explain" generally requires that the response includes reasons in a complete form. Rubrics: Essay, Paragraph.

3. Students without access to a computer can find the necessary information in the library. They can organize the data in categories manually, presenting the data in chart form. Rubric: Charts and Tables.

4. Answers will vary. Rubric: Model.

Business Issue

MAIN STREET VS. THE MEGASTORE

Highlight the Issue

Before students read pages 254–255, ask how many have shopped at "mega-stores" such as Wal-Mart, Costco, and Target. Have volunteers share their opinions of the prices, service, and selection of products available at such stores. Ask students whether they prefer shopping at such discount stores or if they prefer smaller locally based businesses. Have students explain their answers.

Business Issue

MAIN STREET VS. THE MEGASTORE

An increasing number of giant discount stores are moving into small towns and challenging the local "Main Street" merchants for business. Should communities act to protect local businesses from these megastores?

Pro

Small towns across America are fighting off retail giants like Wal-Mart, Kmart, Costco, Target, and others for good reason. Megastores drive small merchants out of business. These big discounters can afford to price popular items below cost to bring in shoppers. Small independent merchants can't match these rock-bottom prices and lose business as a result. Eventually, many of these "Main Street" businesses go under. But the demise of Main Street and locally owned businesses means the loss of something even more fundamental—small town character.

In a study of 30 Iowa towns, one economist found that the average Wal-Mart took in $17 million in its first year in business. About $10 million of that, however, was money Wal-Mart earned at the expense of local businesses. On average, Main Street businesses lose 12 percent of their retail sales when a megastore moves in. In some cases, it's much worse. In one Iowa town, seven downtown businesses closed in the year following the opening of a new Wal-Mart.

But local retailers aren't the only losers when megastores move in. Since most big stores locate along highways on the outskirts of town, they bring increased traffic, noise, and pollution to rural areas. The giant stores—typically 100,000 square feet or more—also gobble up valuable farmlands.

Megastores hurt communities in other ways as well. The jobs that megastores bring to a community are mostly low-paid or part-time with few benefits. The money spent in megastores does not stay in the community. Instead it is sent off to distant corporate banks. This means there is less money in local banks to be used for loans to community members.

A further danger arises when local merchants have been driven out of business and the community becomes dependent on one giant store. If that store closes or raises its prices, the community has nowhere else to shop.

Communities don't have to put out the welcome mat for megastores. They can use zoning laws and other regulations to control development and keep Main Street alive.

254 UNIT 4 ENTREPRENEURSHIP AND SMALL BUSINESS

Extend the Issue

Tell students that some communities have successfully blocked the establishment of megastores in their community. Ask groups to research two or three such communities and give an oral presentation to the class on the economic and social results of taking community action to bar a megastore. After the presentations, discuss with students whether or not they think banning such large stores preserves local character and helps keep the local economy intact.

Con

Megastores beat out Main Street businesses because they offer people what they want—a wider selection of products at lower prices. That's the reason for their success. For people on tight budgets, paying a quarter less for soap or several dollars less for a pair of jeans means their money goes futher. Shoppers also appreciate the convenience of one-stop shopping and easy parking that megastores offer.

Megastores aren't to blame for the disappearance of Main Street. Simply put, the era of small businesses is over. As Sam Walton, the founder of the Wal-Mart empire, wrote, "The small stores were just destined to disappear. It was as inevitable as the replacement of the buggy by the car."

One of the hallmarks of the free enterprise system is competition among businesses. Businesses that can't compete successfully will fail. Communities should not outlaw the big retailers but let the people themselves decide whether to shop on Main Street or at the megastore.

Megastores often bring economic prosperity to the communities they are near. A typical megastore employs hundreds of people and is an important source of jobs in a small town or rural area. Big discount stores also benefit communities with revenues from sales and property taxes. One study found that Wal-Marts tended to improve the overall economy for the communities in which they were located.

The arrival of a megastore in a small town does not have to spell disaster for Main Street businesses. Smart businesses can prosper by offering products and services the big stores don't. In some places local merchants have even benefitted from the increased number of shoppers due to the pull of the megastore.

Communities should not ban megastores. These new stores can benefit communities by boosting the local economy and offering shoppers products and prices they want.

Update the Issue

Sam Walton, the founder of Wal-Mart, stated that "the small stores were just destined to disappear." Have students find evidence in current publications to support or contradict Walton's prediction. Ask students to write an essay summarizing the evidence they found. Encourage students to use specific examples to support their view.

Independent Practice

As a follow-up activity to Unit 4, have students complete the simulation "Entrepreneurship" found in *Student Activity Guide 1*. The Teacher's Annotated Edition provides answers.

Unit 5 Government and Business

Chapter	Learning Objectives
16 **How Government Affects Business** pp. 258–273	• Name four kinds of laws that affect business. • Discuss how government regulates business. • Describe how government regulates business to protect the public. • Explain how government regulation affects business. • List several actions that can help resolve team conflicts. • Identify characteristics needed by workers in agribusiness, forestry, wildlife, and mining.
17 **Taxes and Taxation** pp. 274–291	• Describe the three major types of tax bases in the United States. • Name the major types of taxes levied by governments. • Distinguish among progressive, proportional, and regressive taxes. • Explain how taxes affect economic activity. • Describe how electronic scanning technology helps business. • Explain how withholding tables work.
18 **Government Spending and the Economy** pp. 292–305	• Discuss the government as a provider of goods and services. • List major ways in which governments spend tax money. • Explain why government spending has increased. • Identify some questions to ask when evaluating how the government spends our money. • Describe some careers in government and public administration and explain qualifications for some of those jobs. • Interpret and use data from the Consumer Price Index.
Business Issue:	**User Fees, pp. 306–307**

National Standards for Business Education*	Focus on Features	Building Business Skills	Visual Learning	Case Analysis
BL: I B, II B; *CD:* II A; *COMM:* II B, V D; *EPF:* III, IV, IX; *EE:* III E, VIII B; *IBF:* EE, EPF; *MGMT:* IV A, IX A; *MKTG:* III A	Careers: Agribusiness, Forestry, Wildlife, and Mining, p. 268	Employability: Resolving Team Conflicts, p. 266	Major Federal Regulators That Promote Competition, p. 263 Major Regulatory Agencies That Protect the Public, p. 264 Money Spent on the Reduction of Pollution, 1980–1992, p. 265	Government Regulation, p. 271
COMP: VI C; *EPF:* III, V, X B, XII; *IS:* VIII	Technology: Electronic Scanners, p. 282	Math: Understanding Withholding, p. 278	Sources of Federal Government Revenues, p. 277 Form W-2 Wage and Tax Statement, p. 280 General Sales Tax by State, p. 281 Progressive, Proportional, and Regressive Taxes, p. 286	Tax Incentives, p. 289
CD: II A; *EPF:* V, XII; *EE:* III E; *MGMT:* IX	Careers: Government and Public Administration, p. 296	Math: Interpret the Consumer Price Index, p. 300	Government Services, p. 298 Social Welfare Expenditures, p. 300 Federal Budget Income and Expenses, p. 302	Government Expenditures, p. 303

* Level 3 Performance Expectations: Business Law (BL), Career Development (CD), Communications (COMM), Computation (COMP), Economics and Personal Finance (EPF), Entrepreneurship Education (EE), Interrelationships of Business Functions (IBF), IS (Information Systems), Management (MGMT), Marketing (MKTG). See page T14 for all 12 content areas.

Unit 5

Look Back

Recall with students that entrepreneurs accept both the risks and the rewards of starting a new business. When starting a business, an entrepreneur needs to analyze the project very carefully, which includes developing a viable business plan. Developing a logical and realistic business plan not only ensures that the entrepreneur has planned his or her business carefully, but also serves to persuade banks and other lending institutions that the entrepreneur is a worthwhile credit risk.

UNIT 5 COOPERATIVE LEARNING PROJECT

Make and Defend Activity

Preparation: Photocopy and distribute to groups one copy each of BLMs 11 and 12 from the *Cooperative Learning Strategies* booklet. Have groups collect current articles about cable TV regulation (or another topic relevant to Unit 5).

Guidelines: Have groups identify cable TV regulation issues. Then direct teams to use BLMs 11 and 12 to research the topic, organize and analyze data, choose a group position, and present their position to the class.

Government and Business

Look Ahead
Tell students that local, state, and federal governments may regulate business and enact laws to protect business. Businesses, as well as individuals, pay taxes that raise revenues for the operation of governments. Governments are major consumers of many of the goods and services provided by private businesses.

This unit concentrates on the relationship between government and business in the U.S. economy. The chapters discuss ways that government regulates and promotes business, taxes paid by individuals and businesses, and ways in which government spending affects the national economy.

257

Alternative: Have students research other topics concerning government regulation and taxation, such as current tax proposals in Congress.

CHAPTER
16

FOCUS

Introduce the Chapter

Major Concepts
- The U.S. Legal System
- Government as Regulator
- Government as Promoter and Partner

Introduce the Topic

Encourage students to volunteer information about regulations government imposes on business. Have students explore possible reasons for these regulations. Indicate to students that Chapter 16 presents information about the government's role in business and how it both promotes and regulates business.

Use Business Terms

Have students briefly study the list of Business Terms and conjure up mental images of what the terms represent. Invite volunteers to describe one or more of the images they have created. Ask members of the class to match the terms with the descriptions. Advise students to note the meanings of the terms as they read the chapter.

USE VISUALS

Direct students' attention to the photograph and ask them to describe what aspects of government's effect on business is pictured. (Posting of sign: "Extinguish all smoking materials . . ." Indication under prices that they "include all taxes." Listing of octane ratings, and so forth.)

258 UNIT 5

Business terms

constitution

statute

Uniform Commercial Code

ordinance

common law

administrative law

interstate commerce

antitrust laws

deregulation

patent

copyright

registered trademark

tax abatement

depreciation

258

CHAPTER 16 RESOURCES

Instructional Resources

Lesson Plan for Chapter 16

Teaching Transparencies 16-1, 16-2, 16-3, 16-4

Strategies and Worksheets for Teaching Transparencies 16-1, 16-2, 16-3, 16-4

Enrichment Masters 16-1, 16-2

Student Activity Guide 1–TAE for Chapter 16

Test Master for Chapter 16

Alternative Assessment Strategies

Math Skills Review

International Business Strategies

Cooperative Learning Strategies

Communication Skills Review

Ethics in Business Strategies

How Government Affects Business

Learning objectives

After completing this chapter, you will be able to:
- Name four kinds of laws that affect business.
- Discuss how government regulates business.
- Describe how government regulates business to protect the public.
- Explain how government regulation affects business.
- List several actions that can help resolve team conflicts.
- Identify characteristics needed by workers in agribusiness, forestry, wildlife, and mining.

Consider what you know

- In our free enterprise economy, businesses are generally free to choose which products to produce, when and how to produce them, how to sell them, and at what price to sell.

Consider what you want to know

- What are the different kinds of laws that affect business?
- How does government regulate business to promote competition and protect the public?
- How does government promote business?
- What effects can government regulation have on business?
- What careers focus on the use and preservation of our natural resources?
- What are some actions you can take to resolve team conflicts?

Consider how to use what you learn

- As you read this chapter, note the many ways in which government influences the actions of business. Then watch for references to these situations in business news reports and in business magazines.

CHAPTER 16   HOW GOVERNMENT AFFECTS BUSINESS   **259**

Multimedia Resources

Technology Resource Guide

Distance Learning Guide

Internet Resource Guide

Professional Resources

School-to-Work/Tech Prep Strategies

Instructional Poster

Spanish Resources

Testmaker Software for Chapter 16

The Wall Street Journal Video Series
   Video & Activities for Chapter 16

Business and Marketing Computer
   Applications—An Integrated Software
   Simulation Using Microsoft Works

Stocktracker—A Stock Market Software
   Simulation

Where's the Dough? Board Game

TEACH

Develop Concepts

The U.S. Legal System

List on the board or a transparency the three freedoms of individuals in our society: freedom to buy, freedom to produce and sell, and freedom to work. Then pose the following question: If we have these freedoms, why are there so many laws governing business? Guide students to understand how the laws might provide advantages to businesses and consumers. Ask students if they have heard or seen any news of recent changes in laws that affect business.

USE TRANSPARENCIES

Use Teaching Transparency 16-4 and its corresponding strategies and worksheet from the *Teaching Transparency Strategies and Worksheets* booklet to introduce students to a standard contract. Verify student worksheets using the Answer Key.

If you are looking for a street address in an unfamiliar city, you might go to a police officer for directions. If you are looking for assurance of safety or quality in a product, you might check for FDA approval on the product's label. When looking for a summer job, you might go to a local or state employment agency for job information. In each case, a government agency has helped make your life a little easier.

One of our government's roles is to foster economic prosperity. The economic health of our nation, as well as that of our state and locality, depends on the success of individual businesses. When businesses are creating jobs and making a profit, citizens benefit. To promote this economic growth, government on local, state, and national levels passes laws to both promote and regulate business. A company's success can hinge on its understanding these laws and managing its relationship with all levels of government.

THE U.S. LEGAL SYSTEM

Laws are rules of conduct enacted by a government to maintain harmony, stability, predictability, and justice within a society. In the United States, the primary sources of law are the federal and state constitutions, federal and state statutes, court decisions, and administrative regulations.

Constitutional Law

A **constitution** is the basic law of an entire nation or a single state. The U.S. Constitution establishes the government of the United States and outlines the rights that are reserved for the people. Articles contained in the Constitution give Congress the power to make laws that regulate business. Interpretation of the Constitution is known as *Constitutional law*. In addition, each state has a constitution that establishes the state's governmental structure.

Statutory Law

A **statute** is a law passed by a legislature. In our federal government, statutes are bills written and proposed by Congress and then signed into law by the president. At the state

Curriculum Connection   Social Studies

Encourage students to obtain several copies of their home state's constitution as well as the federal constitution. Suggest that students work in teams of four. Have them identify the parts of each constitution which directly affect business and competition. Have teams explore how the two constitutions are similar and how they are different. Teams can present their findings as a poster or bulletin board display.

Refer to the *Cooperative Learning Strategies* booklet for additional cooperative learning strategies.

level, statutes are enacted by state legislatures and signed by the governor. Statutes may either prohibit activities—for example, banning the use of DDT—or demand activities—for example, wearing seat belts while a driver or a passenger are in a car.

Each year, hundreds of different statutes are passed by the state legislatures. In some cases, important differences in state statutory law exist, causing problems when people from different states do business with one another. To help make interstate trade easier, all states except Louisiana have adopted the **Uniform Commercial Code** (UCC). (Louisiana has adopted parts of the code.) The UCC is a set of uniform laws used to control and regulate business transactions.

Cities, towns, and villages, too, establish laws that govern citizens within their communities. An **ordinance** is a law passed by a local governmental unit. Ordinances address such things as traffic, fire prevention, streets and utilities, and business regulation. Companies wishing to start, maintain, or conduct business in a locality must work within its ordinances.

Court Decisions

Although Constitutional law and statutes are important sources of law, they are not the only sources. Federal and state courts also make laws by following and interpreting common law. **Common law** refers to the legal decisions made by English courts over hundreds of years, as well as the customs of the people. A significant part of common law centered on the commercial rights of merchants and traders. In today's courts, judges often rely on *precedent*, a previous case that a court can follow when considering a similar case.

Administrative Law

Once laws have been passed by a legislature, an administrative agency or commission may take responsibility for enforcing them. The administrative agency writes more specific regulations related to a statute. The Federal Trade Commission, for example, issues regulations and enforces statutes concerning false advertising. The rules, decrees, and decisions of these administrative agencies are known as **administrative law.**

Quick Check

1. What are the sources of law that affect business?
2. What does UCC stand for?

Business & HISTORY

One of the earliest known systems of laws is the code of Hammurabi. Hammurabi was King of Babylon from 1792 to 1750 B.C. The code was found carved on a column of rock. Hammurabi's code covered such matters as family laws, land and business regulations, wages, trade, loans, and debts. A person was believed innocent until proven guilty. The code is famous for the harshness of certain punishments, especially "an eye for an eye." This meant that a person who injured or killed someone suffered a similar fate.

Making Connections Technology in Business

A statute of the UCC requires a contract signed in writing for the purchase of $500 or more worth of goods. Enrichment Master 16-1 will help students become familiar with the elements of a contract. The UCC defines "writing" as including "printing, typewriting, or any intentional reduction to a tangible form." However, corporations and businesses exchange information and data electronically through computers. The information transferred includes inventory control, accounts receivable, and transportation contracts. Invite students to discuss whether any electronic messages received by both buyers and sellers can meet the requirement of the code and meet the requirements of a contract.

For additional information about current technology, refer to the *Technology Resources* Guide.

GOVERNMENT AS REGULATOR

Remind students that in a
market economy, businesses
and consumers answer the
basic economic questions:
• What will be produced?
• How will goods and ser-
  vices be produced?
• Who shall receive the
  goods and services?

From time to time, however,
there may be disagreements
between producers and consumers, or even between
producers themselves con-
cerning the answers to these
questions. It is these
instances that draw government into the role of regulator. Invite students to
suggest analogies which
offer parallels to the business environment. For
example, an umpire in a
tennis tournament or a ref-
eree in a wrestling match.

TEACHING TIP

Emphasize that along with
every freedom or privilege
there is a corresponding
responsibility. Ask students to
identify some of their own privileges and responsibilities.
Then ask if any students have
had privileges taken away
because they did not meet their
responsibilities. Point out that
laws often are enacted to
ensure that individuals and
businesses meet their responsibilities.

Everyone in our economic system buys goods and services
to satisfy wants and needs. Farms, factories, stores, and offices
in this country produce a gross national product of trillions of
dollars a year. For the most part, transactions between the producers of goods and services and the consumers of those items
go smoothly. Disputes between producers and consumers are
handled by the legal system, by government agencies, and even
by trade associations.

The legal system also helps to prevent disputes and other
problems by setting up guidelines and responsibilities for both
business and consumers. Without uniform laws, our economy
would not run as smoothly. From the street vendor to the giant
international corporation, all businesses are subject to government and regulations.

Regulation That Fosters Competition

Competition is a form of consumer protection. Competition
encourages businesses to try to produce the highest-quality
goods or services at the lowest price. When several companies
produce the same item, they try to outdo each other to attract
customers. Price and quality are two major areas in which businesses compete. In our market system, the government's role is
to establish the rules so that all competitors have an equal
chance of producing a product, getting it into the market, and
making a profit.

The federal government first began to regulate business practices during the period of business growth following the Civil
War. Railroads were expanding, and their owners gave little
thought to what was good for the public and focused instead on
making a profit at any cost. Complaints from the public
prompted the federal government to pass the Interstate Commerce Act in 1887. This act created the Interstate Commerce
Commission (ICC), the first regulatory agency in the United
States. The ICC was to regulate all ground transportation in
interstate commerce, or business activities, across state lines.

Following the passage of the Interstate Commerce Act, the
federal government next targeted the unfair practices of trusts.
These were arrangements in which owners of stock in companies gave control of their stock to trustees. The trustees, in turn,
used this control to buy up or drive out smaller companies. The
large companies that remained could control the market, fix
prices, and use other unfair practices. These monopolies made
huge profits.

GLOBAL VIEW

In the early 1990s, the United States and Canada agreed to reduce the levels of acid rain. Each country recognized that its air quality affected and was affected by its neighbor's air quality. The countries agreed to reduce the emissions of sulfur dioxide, the major cause of acid rain, by 40%. In addition, the countries agreed to reduce the level of nitrogen oxide. In order to accomplish these goals, each govern-ment has issued regula-tions for businesses such as utilities, including emission reduction goals and emis-sion limits.

Making Connections → Communications

Remind students that visuals in a presentation help both the presenter and the
listener organize information. Ask students to prepare a short informal business
presentation in which they explain clearly to a foreign client the differences
between constitutional, statute, common, and administrative laws. Suggest that
students design a chart, diagram, or other visual to support their presentation.

For those students whose written communication skills need sharpening,
choose among the worksheets in *Communication Skills Review*.

MAJOR FEDERAL REGULATORS THAT PROMOTE COMPETITION

Name	Responsibilities
Interstate Commerce Commission (ICC)	Regulates all ground transportation across state lines.
Federal Trade Commission (FTC)	Protects businesses from unfair competition; enforces federal antitrust laws; enforces truth-in-lending and truth-in-labeling laws.
Federal Communications Commission (FCC)	Directs all mass communication activities in nation; establishes guidelines and standards for communication via television, radio, telegraph, and satellite; assigns frequencies and call letters; monitors nation's emergency broadcast system.
Securities and Exchange Commission (SEC)	Regulates stock exchanges; oversees investment companies; monitors brokers, dealers, and bankers who sell securities.
National Labor Relations Board	Prevents unfair labor practices; settles labor-union-management disputes; administers federal labor-management laws.

FIGURE 16-1

Congress has established various agencies to regulate parts of the nation's economy. What role of government do these regulators fulfill?

In 1890, a new law, the Sherman Antitrust Act, declared that such trusts and any of their practices "in restraint of trade or commerce" were illegal. For example, it was now illegal for two competing businesses to engage in price fixing. That is, two or more companies could not agree to sell their products at the same prices or to change their prices to control the market.

The Sherman Antitrust Act was the first of many **antitrust laws.** These are laws to prevent monopolies, or businesses that have no competition. Most of the antitrust laws have been at the federal level. In 1914, the Clayton Antitrust Act clarified the illegal practices banned under the Sherman Antitrust Act. Another law, the Federal Trade Commission Act of 1914, set up the Federal Trade Commission (FTC). The FTC was to look for specific unfair methods of competition.

Since 1914, other laws and commissions have been established to further prohibit unfair business practices and promote competition. The latest was the Antitrust Amendments Act of 1990. It raised the limit on antitrust fines. Figure 16-1 above lists the major federal regulatory agencies that foster competition among businesses. In addition to these federal agencies, state governments have set up their own state regulations to limit business practices.

Making Connections

Business Ethics

Wal-Mart's success relies on the strategy of placing stores in or near small towns. Wal-Mart's size allows it to purchase in large quantities and then sell a variety of well-known brands for as much as 15 percent less than smaller retailers. Typically, the mom-and-pop stores which served the region cannot withstand the competition and close. In some cases, nearly all the small businesses that made up a town's business district close two or three years after a Wal-Mart opens nearby, leaving the area entirely dependent on Wal-Mart for general merchandise. Encourage students to discuss the rights and responsibilities of small towns, smaller retailers, consumers, and Wal-Mart in ensuring that consumers continue to have a choice when purchasing merchandise.

Refer to the *Ethics in Business Strategies* booklet for additional activities.

Laws That Protect the Public

Besides assuring that the market system runs smoothly and that businesses can compete, government also protects the people's interests. To safeguard the public, the government has passed laws that protect the environment, protect the consumer, promote fair labor practices, and promote the general welfare.

Just as public outcry led to laws banning unfair business practices, public concerns led to laws that protect society. Sometimes companies lack the perspective or the incentive to consider the public's welfare. As a result, governments have established regulations that protect society. Figure 16-2 below summarizes the major federal regulators set up to protect the public. In many instances, states have their own version of the federal agency.

How Regulation Influences Business

Government regulation influences businesses in many ways. On the positive side, it promotes the market system, promotes competition, and protects the public. On the negative side, government regulation increases the costs of doing business, creates delays, and produces unexpected burdens on certain groups. For example, some manufacturing plants have had to

FIGURE 16-2

Numerous federal agencies set up by Congress are charged with looking out for the public. With which of these agencies are you most familiar?

MAJOR REGULATORY AGENCIES THAT PROTECT THE PUBLIC

Name	Responsibilities
Equal Employment Opportunity Commission (EEOC)	Enforces laws prohibiting job discrimination on the basis of race, color, sex, religion, national origin, age, or handicap by unions or employers.
Environmental Protection Agency (EPA)	Sets and enforces environmental standards and researches effects of pollution.
Occupational Safety and Health Administration (OSHA)	Promotes safety in the workplace; sets and enforces mandatory standards for workplace safety and health; works to eliminate work-related diseases and injury.
Consumer Product Safety Commission (CPSC)	Establishes and enforces safety standards and conducts safety tests on consumer products; initiates recalls of defective products and prohibits sale of unsafe products.
Nuclear Regulatory Commission (NRC)	Issues licenses for nuclear power plants; regulates companies that use, process, and own nuclear materials; investigates nuclear accidents.

264 UNIT 5 GOVERNMENT AND BUSINESS

Reteaching Strategy

Discuss with students how government regulation directly affects both competition and consumers. Have students page through a newspaper and identify two specific businesses regulated by each of the agencies listed in Figure 16-1 on page 263. Then have students scan articles and advertisements for two examples of agencies listed in Figure 16-2 above. Ask students to write newspaper editorials in which they explain why they believe that government regulation either helps or hinders economic activity and the public welfare. Encourage students to support their editorials by citing appropriate examples.

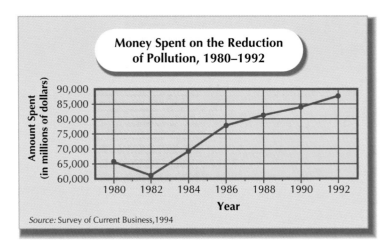

FIGURE 16-3

Each year businesses spend money to clean up the environment and reduce the amount of pollution that manufacturing produces. Which is the only year in which spending decreased?

USE VISUALS

Direct students' attention to the line graph in Figure 16-3. Remind students that a line graph can present a picture of changes over time. Be sure students understand the meaning of the horizontal and vertical axes.
Answer to caption: 1991. For students who need to sharpen their math skills, choose among the worksheets in the *Math Skills Review* booklet.

Quick Check Answers
1. It regulates business activities that might destroy competition or harm the public.
2. Business activities that cross state lines; laws to prevent monopolies; removal or relaxation of rules and regulations affecting business.

spend thousands or even millions of dollars for pollution control devices. As you can see from Figure 16-3 above, millions of dollars have been spent each year to reduce pollution. Environmental protection laws affect business decisions because the managers of a business must decide whether to stop making products whose manufacture causes pollution or to spend the money to install pollution control equipment. The extra costs to business are passed along to the consumer in the form of higher prices.

A move toward **deregulation,** the removal or relaxation of rules and regulations affecting business, began slowly in the 1960s. It gained momentum in the 1970s and 1980s. Those who favored deregulation argued that government regulations were excessive, that they created tangled webs of laws that stifled progress. Opponents of deregulation argued that it dismantled the protection of the health and safety of society, giving business more opportunities for profit.

Regardless of its effect, businesses must adapt to regulation to succeed. On the whole, laws work to promote a positive environment for businesses. Those firms that operate efficiently and make good decisions about how to produce and sell goods and services can compete and earn a profit.

Quick Check
1. Name two general areas in which government regulates business.
2. What do we mean by *interstate commerce? Antitrust laws? Deregulation?*

Cooperative Learning Co-op Co-op

Have student groups work together to decide what kind of small business they wish to operate, for example, auto repair shop, hair salon, or recording studio. Suggest that they research what kinds of government regulations they will encounter as they open and maintain the business: license or permit, zoning permit or other requirement, labor or environmental restrictions. Have students prepare a four-page illustrated booklet indicating what regulations are associated with the business they chose.

Refer to the *Cooperative Learning Strategies* booklet for additional cooperative learning strategies.

Building Business Skills

Building Business Skills

Model

Find out from students who have jobs what kinds of on-the-job disagreements they have experienced in the past few days. Ask volunteers to describe how they resolved those conflicts. Discuss the Key Actions to Resolve Conflict with the class. Then have the class describe how these actions are similar to or different from the methods used by students to resolve conflicts.

Develop Concepts

Government as Promoter and Partner

Engage students in a discussion about the kinds of goods and services provided by governments. Focus the discussion on goods and services that help businesses. Ask students who provides the roads, bridges, and airports businesses use.

USE VISUALS

Direct students' attention to the road reconstruction project shown in the photograph. Ask students what governments are involved in funding the project. (City and county.)
Answer to caption: Better roads promote business by providing easier access to various businesses. The increased revenue brings in more money for the government through taxes.

EMPLOYABILITY
Resolving Team Conflicts

Explanation

One of the things many people enjoy most about their job is working with others. It feels good to be part of a team. Sometimes, though, conflicts arise that cause bad feelings and that affect the performance of the entire team.

When you and another person or a team member have a conflict, it is important to work out the conflict before serious damage is done. You may have noticed that work is not being done correctly, and productivity is slipping. One person may be avoiding you or other members of the team or withholding resources or information. One person may seem unwilling to work with other team members and this creates tension in the team. Even when you feel the conflict is not your fault, you need to take action to resolve the conflict, especially if it causes disruption to others on the team and to the organization as a whole.

Practice

What can you do when you find yourself involved in a team conflict? There are key actions that you can follow to resolve the conflict. If you are the team leader, you can initiate these actions yourself. If you are a mem-

GOVERNMENT AS PROMOTER AND PARTNER

In our private enterprise system, government is expected to provide the kind of environment or circumstances in which businesses can succeed. As you will learn in Chapter 20, the federal government tries to keep the economy growing at a steady

In what way does road reconstruction fulfill government's role as promoter and partner?

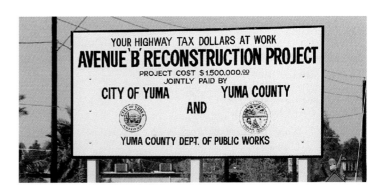

YOUR HIGHWAY TAX DOLLARS AT WORK
AVENUE 'B' RECONSTRUCTION PROJECT
PROJECT COST $1,500,000.00
JOINTLY PAID BY
CITY OF YUMA AND **YUMA COUNTY**
YUMA COUNTY DEPT. OF PUBLIC WORKS

266   UNIT 5   GOVERNMENT AND BUSINESS

Curriculum Connection   Social Studies

Indicate to students that while federal, state, and local governments provide many services, these governments also purchase tremendous amounts of goods and services. Suggest that students contact their local or state governments to find out how much money these governments spend yearly on goods and services such as
- school lunches
- office supplies
- office space rental
- new equipment purchases
- street sweeping service
- building construction

Students can present their findings as part of a poster or bulletin board display.

1. Let the people involved know how their conflict is affecting the team's performance.
2. Set up a problem-solving meeting with all parties to the conflict.
3. Ask all parties involved to take turns calmly and objectively describing the problem as they see it. Assure that each party listens without interrupting as the other person speaks.
4. Get agreement from the parties on the problem that needs to be solved.
5. Have each party propose solutions to the problem.
6. Get an agreement and a commitment as to what each person will do to solve the problem.
7. Summarize what each person will do and set a follow-up date to evaluate progress in resolving the conflict.

ber of the team, you can exercise leadership by going to the team leader to request that action be taken to clear up the conflict and build a stronger team relationship. Here are some key actions that a team leader can take to resolve team conflicts.

In more and more workplaces today, workers are being organized into project teams. Each member brings his or her own special talent to the group to help fulfill its particular goals and responsibilities. If you are a member of such a team, you can make your work experience more enjoyable for yourself and others by resolving conflicts quickly and fairly.

Practice
Suggest that students form teams of five and choose a leader for each team. Ask the teams to follow the Key Actions to Resolve Conflict as they role-play the conflicts and disagreements discussed at the beginning of the skills lesson. Have a member of each team report to the class how using the key actions helped resolve the conflict.
Students who need additional practice will benefit from the listening activities in the *Communication Skills Review*.

pace by adjusting monetary policy. By smoothing out the economic cycle, the government creates a climate that is good for business. By building roads, dams, airports, and such, governments indirectly help business by providing the means to distribute products. Governments also own and operate power plants and schools that supply energy and educate workers.

Government at all levels also purchases goods and services from businesses. Total federal, state, and local government purchases of goods and services account for a significant percentage of all the goods and services produced in the United States. The federal government is the biggest customer for some companies. Automobile companies sell thousands of specially built cars and trucks to police and fire departments and other government agencies. Firms make equipment and uniforms for the armed services. Government pays businesses to construct the highways and build the schools. In all these ways, government depends on business for goods and services.

Creative Property Protection

Government also promotes business firms in another way. Businesses often develop special techniques, inventions, and

Business Brief

The foundation for patent, copyright, and trademark protections can be traced to the U.S. Constitution, Article 21, Section 8, Clause 8. "Congress shall have the power to promote the progress of science and useful arts by securing for limited times . . . the exclusive right to . . . writings and discoveries."

TEACHING TIP

Ask students to identify markets or new product areas in which competition is lively. Mention the intense competition among long distance telephone companies, cellular communications companies, and cable services. Ask students to tell what part they think deregulation played in this competition.

Reteaching Strategy

Have students conduct a survey of family members, students, friends, and teachers on government's role in the economy. Suggest that they ask questions such as the following.
• Do you think there is too much, just enough, or too little government regulation?
• Which regulatory agencies, if any, should be abolished?
• Which regulatory agencies, if any, should have their powers expanded?
• Which government activity do you feel plays the most important role in maintaining competition in the marketplace? Why?

Suggest that students pool their data and share their surveys with the class, presenting the information in charts and graphs.

Discuss

Find out from students what information they already know about agribusiness, forestry, wildlife, and mining careers. Allow students to offer opinions and information they perceive as fact. Suggest that a volunteer record some of the class responses on the board or on a transparency.

Agribusiness, Forestry, Wildlife, and Mining

A s the human population grows, so do the demands we make on the earth for food, shelter, and energy. Careers related to the use and preservation of the natural resources that provide these necessities are found in both private business and government. Because private businesses in this area are involved with scarce or fragile resources and products needed for basic survival, they are often regulated by governmental agencies.

Agribusiness, forestry, wildlife, and mining offer a variety of jobs that provide satisfaction because the jobs are so important to the life of the planet. Some involve the growth and care of living things that feed us or give us pleasure. Others are involved with extracting minerals, gas, and oil from the earth itself. Still others use scientific testing to ensure the safety of our food and to help us use our land wisely.

The settings for these jobs vary from sanitized laboratories to the wide open ranges, but the majority of the entry-level positions require hands-on contact with the outdoors, as well as a love of living things.

HELP WANTED

ANIMAL CARETAKER: VET'S ASSISTANT

Join our team of dedicated animal caretakers! Group of five veterinarians seeks animal-loving high school grad to assist with office exams of small animals and visits to horse farms. You'll start by holding/feeding animals and cleaning cages. More advanced tasks come with experience: preparing medications and immunizations, assisting at surgery; taking X rays.

If you're patient, good with your hands, and have math and science skills, call FiVets Animal Hospital to apply.

USE TRANSPARENCIES

Use Teaching Transparency 16-3 and its corresponding strategies and worksheet from the *Teaching Transparency Strategies and Worksheets* booklet to introduce students to a standard application for patents and copyrights. Verify student worksheets using the Answer Key.

Business Brief

The U.S. Patent Office issued its first patent in 1790. The patent was for a new method of making potash, a potassium compound used in agriculture. Just over 200 years later, in 1991, the U.S. Patent Office issued its 5,000,000th patent—for a genetically engineered microbe.

F.Y.I.

The United States Patent and Trademark Office receives over 100,000 patent applications a year. That's one reason why it takes so long to process applications. Another reason is that for each application, the government needs to be sure that there are no previous patents for similar inventions.

innovations that they want to protect. For instance, entrepreneurs may start a business based on a technique they have invented. So they apply to the U.S. Patent Office for a **patent,** a legal "right" that prevents anyone else from making the same thing for 17 years. Sometimes, if the patent is particularly valuable, a business will decide to sell its patent to other businesses. If other businesses need or want to use the patented item or idea, they must pay for the right to it. If they use the idea without obtaining permission, they violate the law. Issuing patents encourages inventors and entrepreneurs.

A copyright is also a kind of protection. A **copyright** provides protection for authors or creators of books, plays, software, movies, and musical compositions, as well as for photographers, painters, and sculptors. This protection extends throughout the lifetime of the person or persons producing the item and for the fifty years following the person's death. Copyright is a kind of right to property and a protection against persons copying what others have already made. Businesses that may be involved with copyrights are publishers, recording studios, and movie studios. Page *ii* of this textbook has an example of a copyright statement.

268 UNIT 5 GOVERNMENT AND BUSINESS

Enrichment Strategy

Indicate to students that some government regulations, such as those governing media ownership, are designed to ensure that the public has access to a variety of opinions and viewpoints. The original regulations address ownership of radio and television stations, as well as newspapers and other general circulation periodicals. A new service, interactive television programming, requires the participation of television companies, cable providers, and local telephone services. However, the existing government regulations exclude a single company from owning this combination of service companies. Encourage interested students to research the legislation and regulation involving cable providers and telecommunications companies and the controversy surrounding interactive television.

Technology is important, too. Even ranch hands use computers these days, and lab technicians would be lost without them. A strong background in science and math is a key to success in agribusiness, forestry, wildlife, or mining. Workers starting out in this career area will certainly need a high school diploma. Technical school courses or even an associate's degree may be prerequisites for those who plan to test soil, water, and food products.

Another requirement shared by jobs in this area is the ability to make and record accurate and detailed observations. In addition, workers may need to make judgments based on their observations. Trustworthiness and an ability to self-direct tasks are important to those who work without close supervision in forests and oil fields.

Here are ads for four entry-level jobs in agribusiness, forestry, wildlife, and mining.

Government further protects business firms by granting them the sole right to use certain identifying marks. **Registered trademarks** are names, brands, or symbols that a business lists with the government. Other businesses may not use these trademarks.

Tax Advantages

Government at all levels can help business through reduced taxes or special tax treatment. For instance, local governments may give special tax advantages to businesses that want to move into the area. Governments may lower taxes for a certain number of years on property that a new business is using so that new businesses will provide new jobs in the community. Additional jobs will make the community more prosperous. The tax advantage not only attracts business but can also help the local government because jobs are created with taxes paid by job holders. Special limited tax breaks for business like this are called **tax abatements.**

Government offers tax advantages to businesses that borrow money, too. Businesses may deduct interest on loans from

Follow Through

Once students have read Focus on Careers, ask them to identify any information about the careers mentioned that was new to them. Ask students to describe ways in which their views of the careers have changed or expanded. Review the information generated at the beginning of the feature. Suggest that a volunteer revise or enhance the class list so that it reflects students' current views.

TEACHING TIP

Ask students to name several well-known trademarks and to identify the generic class of goods to which they belong. (Example: Jell-O brand gelatin dessert, Kleenex facial tissue.) Ask students why they think companies want to register and protect their product's name as a precious asset.

Business Brief

States such as Ohio have been able to attract and keep businesses by offering enterprise zone agreements. These agreements typically call for tax abatements for up to ten years for businesses moving into the zones. For Ohio, ten years of enterprise zone agreements have netted more than 1000 projects with a corresponding investment totaling more than $15 billion.

Global Perspective

Indicate that most countries have their own versions of copyright and patent laws. In addition, many nations subscribe to international copyright protection laws. Even so, sales of pirated tapes and software for perhaps one-tenth of the normal price cost the industries millions of dollars in lost revenue a year. Concerned nations have indicated that countries that do not enforce protection of creative property may not be welcome in the global marketplace. Suggest students research recording and software industry periodicals to find information concerning the annual cost to U.S. businesses of foreign-made pirated goods. Have them present their findings in a poster or bulletin board display.

Refer to the *International Business Strategies* booklet for additional strategies and activities.

USE VISUALS

Point out to students that, like the business shown in the photo, many businesses need to continually maintain and improve their buildings and grounds. Even with this maintenance, however, buildings and machinery age. Answer to caption: The federal government provides rules for figuring the dollar value of depreciation.

Learning Activity

Emphasize the concept of offering tax advantages to businesses by asking students to suggest strategies that local, state, and federal governments might use to attract corporations. Remind them that they need to consider the overall budget of the government when offering the tax advantage. Have them list ways in which a tax break might ultimately bring revenues to the local, state, or federal government.

Quick Check Answers

1. To provide the kind of environment or circumstances in which business can succeed.
2. a. false; b. true; c. false; d. true.
3. It may lower property taxes for new businesses; it allows businesses to deduct interest or debt from their taxes and allows businesses to deduct the depreciation of their assets from profits to lower their tax bills.

How does a business owner know how much to deduct for depreciation on her or his place of business?

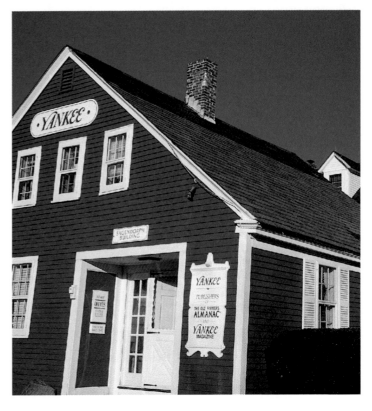

their federal taxes. Tax deductions are also allowed for depreciation of a business's assets. **Depreciation** is the loss of value of an asset. As buildings, machines, computers, and other property grow older, they lose value. This lost value is a cost of doing business. Businesses are allowed to deduct depreciation costs from their profits so the taxes they would have to pay on profits will be lower. From time to time, governments revise the rules for the methods businesses use to figure a dollar value for depreciation.

Quick Check

1. What is expected of government in our private enterprise system?
2. Indicate if the following statements are true or false.
   a. A patent is a symbol used to identify a product.
   b. Depreciation is the loss of value of an asset.
   c. A copyright is a protection for an inventor of a process.
   d. A trademark is the right to protect a written work.
3. What are some tax advantages businesses receive?

Cooperative Learning   Debate (Pro/Con)

In order to meet cleaner environmental standards, many manufacturers have spent millions of dollars to install filters, scrubbers, and other forms of equipment to decrease the amount of air pollution they produce. In some cases, manufacturers need to redesign the entire manufacturing process in order to reduce the amount of solid waste they produce. Have students debate whether or not large manufacturers should get tax breaks for reducing the solid wastes produced during their manufacturing process.

Refer to the *Cooperative Learning Strategies* booklet for additional cooperative learning strategies.

Chapter 16 **Summary**

Main Ideas

1. The primary sources of U.S. law are the federal and state constitutions, federal and state statutes, court decisions based on common law, and administrative regulations.
2. Administrative law is the rules and procedures established by government agencies.
3. Government regulates business to promote competition and to protect the public.
4. Numerous federal agencies regulate business activities.
5. Government regulations influence businesses in both positive and negative ways.
6. There has been a recent move toward deregulation of businesses.
7. Government acts as a promoter and partner to provide an environment in which businesses can succeed.
8. Conflicts that occur in school and in the workplace can be resolved by the people involved in the conflict.
9. Government careers related to the use and preservation of natural resources include agribusiness, forestry, mining, and wildlife.

CASE ANALYSIS — Government Regulation

In recent years, some people have come to believe that governments should apply a cost-benefit analysis to regulation of business activities. Businesses use the principle of cost-benefit analysis to make production, financial, and management decisions. That is, they compare the costs and benefits of a particular action to evaluate the desirability of doing it. For example, before requiring factories to install smokestack scrubbers costing $100 million or more, opponents of tough government regulation say regulators should first measure the installment costs and the costs of people losing their jobs because of loss of company profits against the benefits of cleaner air. Others, on the other hand, say that the benefits of government regulation, such as cleaner air, are intangible and are not easily measured, but are significant. Not all government regulatory agencies are required to perform a cost-benefit analysis of the rules and regulations they write. Do you think regulatory agencies should have to do such an analysis? Why or why not?

CHAPTER 16   HOW GOVERNMENT AFFECTS BUSINESS   **271**

CLOSE

Main Ideas

Main Ideas summarizes the key information in the chapter. It is a useful tool for reinforcement and review.

CASE ANALYSIS

Case Analysis provides a chapter-related case for student analysis and application of decision-making skills.

Answer
Answers will vary.

QUICK QUIZ

1. What kinds of law apply to businesses? (constitutional, statutory, common law, and administrative law.)
2. How does the legal system prevent business and consumer disputes as well as other problems? (It sets up guidelines and responsibilities for both business and consumers.)
3. How do government regulations foster competition? (By ensuring that all competitors have an equal chance of producing a product, entering a market, and making a profit.)
4. Why do government regulations strive to foster competition? (Competition encourages business to work to produce the highest quality goods or services at the lowest price.)

Chapter 16 **Review**

APPLY

Answers

Use the Language of Business
1. interstate commerce, **2.** antitrust laws, **3.** deregulation, **4.** administrative law, **5.** copyright, **6.** tax abatement, **7.** statute, **8.** Uniform Commercial Code, **9.** common law, **10.** constitution, **11.** closed shop, **12.** depreciation, **13.** registered trademark, **14.** ordinance

Review What You Learned
1. The federal and state constitutions, federal and state statutes, court decisions, and administrative regulations.
2. Common law refers to the legal decisions made by English courts over hundreds of years, as well as the customs of the people. A significant part of common law centered on the commercial rights of merchants and traders.
3. Administrative law is the rules, decrees, and decisions; administrative agencies.
4. The Sherman Antitrust Act and the Clayton Antitrust Act.
5. Students may name any two of the agencies in Figure 16-1 on page 263.
6. To protect the public.
7. It provides legal protection including copyrights, patents, and trademarks.
8. Tax abatements and depreciation.
9. Students should list the actions for resolving conflicts on page 267.
10. Each focuses on the use and preservation of our natural resources.

Understand Business Concepts
1. It regulates business to encourage competition and promotes business to keep the economy growing.
2. They could decrease the number of products made, leading to higher prices and fewer products. A consumer has less choice and may be able to afford fewer purchases.
3. Deregulation can help industries by allowing greater freedom. In deregulated industries, competition and supply and demand can encourage efficiency.

Use the Language of Business

Match each term with its definition.

administrative law   interstate commerce
antitrust laws   ordinance
copyright   patent
common law   registered trademark
constitution   statute
depreciation   tax abatement
deregulation   Uniform Commercial Code

1. Business activities that affect people or businesses in two or more states.
2. Federal laws passed to prevent monopolies.
3. Removing of regulations from business activities.
4. Rules and procedures established by regulatory agencies.
5. Protection of creative efforts for the life of the person plus 50 years.
6. Special limited tax break for a business.
7. Law passed by a legislature.
8. Set of laws regulating business activities throughout the country.
9. Source of law based on legal decisions and people's customs.
10. Basic law of an entire nation or single state.
11. Legal right to exclusively use an invention for 17 years.
12. Loss of value of an asset.
13. Name, brand, or symbol used by a business and listed with the government.
14. Law passed by a city or township.

Review What You Learned

1. What are the four sources of law in the United States?
2. Explain common law. Tell how it relates to business.
3. What is administrative law? Who makes administrative laws?
4. Name two federal laws that prevent monopolies and unfair practices.
5. Name two federal regulatory agencies that foster competition in business.
6. Why did the federal government set up agencies such as the Consumer Product Safety Commission?
7. How does government protect the creative property of businesses?
8. Name two tax advantages that government provides to businesses.
9. Describe three possible steps that can lead to the resolution of a conflict.
10. What characterizes agribusiness, forestry, wildlife, and mining careers?

Understand Business Concepts

1. How does government help businesses in our private enterprise economy?
2. How might laws that restrict the products that businesses may make and sell affect the number of different products that you may choose to buy?
3. Deregulation of industries is becoming more common. Why do you think governments are moving in that direction?
4. If the only two businesses that sell television sets in a small town agree to sell their products at the same

4. If the businesses agree on a price, customers have no choice but to pay the price if they want the product. Since they do not compete, the two businesses have a monopoly on television sales in that town.
5. They could offer tax abatements, or reductions in taxes, for a limited period of time.
6. If you have a choice of where to buy and can choose to buy on the basis of price, businesses have incentive to keep their prices as low as possible to attract your business. Competition encourages lower prices, and lower prices promote competition.

7. The consumer—prices are set both to cover the cost of production and to allow a reasonable profit.
8. It consumes many of the goods and services businesses produce and promotes and protects certain business activities.
9. They take attention away from the job at hand and disrupt other workers.
10. Students' answers will vary depending on their self-perception. Answers should indicate such things as a strength in math, a liking for the outdoors, and the ability to make and record accurate and detailed observations.

price, how does that action create a monopoly?

5. Describe how a local government can use special tax treatment to aid new businesses moving into the community.

6. Why does the opportunity for you to compare prices from one business to another promote competition?

7. When a business is required to install pollution control equipment, who

ultimately pays for the cost of that equipment?

8. How does the government act as a partner to business?

9. Why is it important to resolve team conflicts?

10. What characteristics or qualifications do you have that might make you a good candidate for a job in agribusiness, mining, forestry, or wildlife?

Think Critically

1. **Summarize.** Visit two or three local stores and compare their prices on four different products. Be sure to check the same brand and size of product in all the stores. Summarize your findings and compare them with those of your classmates. What reasons can you suggest for any differences you find?

2. **Assess.** Why is it important to government that business prospers?

Use What You Learned

1. **Group Activity.** Within your group, make a list of ways to increase competition among business firms. Make a second list of ways to decrease competition. Compare your lists with those of other groups. Circle the items that are regulated by government. Use your lists as the basis of a class display showing some advantages and disadvantages of government regulation of business.

2. Prepare a five-minute script for an info-mercial on the need to recycle solid waste and the way to best implement such a program.

3. Find out how a law is enacted in your community. Present your findings in a chart.

4. **Computer Application.** Use E-mail to contact and interview a small business

owner in your community. Include questions like these in your interview: What steps did you take before you opened the business? What licenses or permits did you need? What government regulations or inspections apply to your business? Use word processing software to prepare a summary of the interview. Then present an oral report to your class.

5. **Skill Reinforcement.** Role-play a team conflict resolution with two or three classmates and record it on audio- or videotape. Afterward, play the tape and use the Key Actions to Resolve Conflict on page 267 to analyze the role-play. Make notes of how the role-play exhibits the key actions.

Save your work in your Business Portfolio.

Think Critically

1. Prices will depend on the products chosen by students. Reasons for differences in prices may include the type of store and the competition nearby.

2. Possible answer: Because businesses produce the goods and services that governments consume.

Independent Practice

Use the Chapter 16 worksheets in *Student Activity Guide 1* for additional practice and application activities. A Teacher's Annotated Edition provides answers.

ASSESS

Portfolio Assessment

The projects are designed to lead students to develop a collection of their best work to submit to you for assessment. Refer students to the specific rubric(s) from the *Alternative Assessment Strategies* booklet listed with each of the project notes below. These rubrics will alert students to the criteria you will use to assess their projects.

Chapter Assessment

Use the Chapter 16 Test from the *Test Masters* booklet to evaluate students' understanding of the chapter concepts. An answer key is provided. Or create your own customized test using the *Testmaker* software.

Use What You Learned

1. Let students choose the method they use to share their results. Rubrics: Charts and Tables, Diagrams, Oral Presentation.

2. Remind students to indicate which of the three topics they plan to cover in their info-mercial. Rubrics: Script, Video.

3. Indicate to students that a time line is one way in which to chart the progress of proposed law. Rubrics: Charts and Tables, Poster.

4. Students without access to computers can complete this project by submitting a list of written questions to the community business owner. Rubrics: Survey, Script, Paragraph, Oral Presentation.

5. Students' answers will vary, but should expand on the strategies on the conflict resolution checklist or add new strategies. Rubrics: Oral Presentation, Video.

CHAPTER 17

FOCUS

Introduce the Chapter

Major Concepts
- Types of Taxes
- The Basis for Taxation
- Criteria for Taxes
- Effect on Economic Activity

Introduce the Topic
Have students assume that the federal, state, and local governments suddenly stopped collecting taxes. In addition, have students assume all three levels of government also stopped providing services. Direct students to describe what would happen as a result.

Use Business Terms
Ask students to look up the definitions of the Business Terms in a dictionary and jot down all the meanings. Then, as students read the chapter, have them note which dictionary definitions appear in the chapter. Stress that it is important to know which meanings of a word are appropriate to use.

USE VISUALS

While many individuals dread April 15th (the day federal income tax returns are due), the majority of U.S. citizens recognize that paying income tax is the price of receiving services from the government. Ask students to describe the action in the photo. (They are working on their income tax.)

CHAPTER 1

Business terms

tax base

income tax

general sales tax

excise tax

tariff

property tax

benefits-received principle

ability-to-pay principle

direct tax

indirect tax

progressive tax

proportional tax

regressive tax

274

CHAPTER 17 RESOURCES

Instructional Resources

Lesson Plan for Chapter 17

Teaching Transparencies 17-1, 17-2, 17-3, 17-4

Strategies and Worksheets for Teaching Transparencies 17-1, 17-2, 17-3, 17-4

Enrichment Master 17-1

Student Activity Guide 1–TAE for Chapter 17

Test Master for Chapter 17

Alternative Assessment Strategies

Math Skills Review

International Business Strategies

Cooperative Learning Strategies

Communication Skills Review

Ethics in Business Strategies

Taxes and Taxation

Learning objectives

After completing this chapter, you will be able to:
- Describe the three major types of tax bases in the United States.
- Name the major types of taxes levied by governments.
- Distinguish among progressive, proportional, and regressive taxes.
- Explain how taxes affect economic activity.
- Describe how electronic scanning technology helps business input information.
- Explain how withholding tables work.

Consider what you know

- Local, state, and federal levels of government have passed laws to promote business and to assure that competition and business practices are fair. Governments also support business by consuming business products and services.

Consider what you want to know

- What kinds of items or activities are taxed?
- What is the basis for taxing an item or activity?
- How do taxes affect people of different incomes?
- How does electronic scanning work?

Consider how to use what you learn

- As you read this chapter, think about the different kinds of taxes you and your family pay. Keep a record of the money spent on taxes. How does the money your family pays out in taxes affect your family's purchasing power for goods and services in the economy?

Multimedia Resources

Technology Resource Guide

Distance Learning Guide

Internet Resource Guide

Professional Resources

School-to-Work/Tech Prep Strategies

Instructional Poster

Spanish Resources

Testmaker Software for Chapter 17

The Wall Street Journal Video Series
  Video & Activities for Chapter 17

Business and Marketing Computer
  Applications—An Integrated Software
  Simulation Using Microsoft Works

Stocktracker—A Stock Market Software
  Simulation

Where's the Dough? Board Game

TEACH

Some countries use a value-added tax (VAT). In a value-added tax, every business that handles a product from raw materials to finished product pays a tax at each stage of production. For example, in making leather shoes, a VAT would be added after the leather is tanned and again after the shoe is made. The amount of the tax is based on the value a company adds to the product. Each business tries to pass the expense of the tax on to the next buyer.

Develop Concepts

Types of Taxes

Ask students to record the taxes they pay, as well as the taxes they hear mentioned in the news, each day for ten days. Invite a volunteer to create a table on the board or on a transparency. Ask students to organize the information they collected by placing it in the chart. Have students indicate which is the most common type of tax they pay and which is the most common tax in the news. Keep the list handy for reference throughout the chapter.

Learning Activity

Ask students to play a word association game. When you say the word *taxes*, ask students to identify the first word that comes to their minds. List the words. Point out the variety of services provided by the government and comment that these services must be paid for through taxes.

If you go to a private school, you have to pay a yearly fee, or tuition. You do not have to pay tuition if you attend a public school. Does this mean that public education is free? In point of fact, public and private schools have similar costs. In both types of schools, teachers have to be paid, buildings must be cleaned and heated, and supplies need to be purchased. Student tuition helps cover the costs of private school. The government uses tax money it collects to pay the costs of public schools. Everyone, including people who send their children to private school, pays taxes to support public schools. Services such as education are not free. This chapter will examine how you pay for them through taxes and other fees the government collects.

TYPES OF TAXES

The money, or revenue, that the government collects is used to provide all kinds of goods and services. The two major types of revenue are nontax and tax. Nontax revenue includes parking meter fees, postage, fees for various licenses (such as a driver's license), and tuition paid to a state university. Nontax revenues are generally paid by the user or the person who receives the good or service.

Taxes are the major source of revenue for government at all levels. Taxes are payments made to governments that are not necessarily based on how much an individual or business uses the goods and services governments provide. Figure 17-1 on page 277 shows the sources of federal government revenue. In general, taxes have some common characteristics. Each tax is applied to a **tax base,** which is the item or activity that is the source of the tax. Income, purchases of goods and services, and property are the three major types of tax bases. To find the amount of tax to be paid, a tax rate is applied to the base. Suppose, for example, that your state has a tax of 6 percent on purchases of goods and services. If you purchase a $100 portable CD player, you would pay a total of $106. The tax base would be the $100 purchase, and the tax rate would be 6 percent. Six percent of $100 is $6.

Taxes on Income

An **income tax** is a government charge on earnings or other sources of income. The income tax is the primary tool used by the federal government to raise revenue. Both individu-

Reteaching Strategy

Alert students that this chapter presents several ways of looking at taxes. Suggest students use the main headings of this chapter to prepare a diagram or chart as a tool to organize the information they will encounter in the chapter. Write the headings on the board or on a transparency. Work with a volunteer to place the kinds of taxes presented in the first section in the chart. Discuss with students the possibility that they will find several ways to think about each of the types of taxes introduced in the first section.

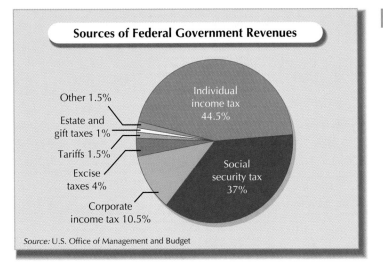

Sources of Federal Government Revenues

Other 1.5%
Estate and gift taxes 1%
Tariffs 1.5%
Excise taxes 4%
Corporate income tax 10.5%
Individual income tax 44.5%
Social security tax 37%

Source: U.S. Office of Management and Budget

FIGURE 17-1

Individual income tax and social security tax are the two largest sources of federal government revenue. What percent of the federal government's revenue comes from these two taxes?

als and corporations pay federal income tax on their incomes. About 55 percent of the federal government's revenue comes from income tax. The majority of states and many large cities also have an income tax.

Federal Individual Income Tax Individuals pay federal income tax on wages and salaries. People may also pay taxes on income from savings accounts, stocks, bonds, and the rent from apartments or houses. Any profits, or capital gains, people make when they sell real estate or other assets are taxed as well.

Federal income taxes are generally paid on a pay-as-you-go basis. When you work for an employer, a certain amount of your pay is withheld each pay period and is forwarded to the federal government. The pay-as-you-go procedure is used for a number of reasons. In the first place, most people do not like to wait until the end of the year to pay all their income tax. They might not have enough money set aside. The pay-as-you-go procedure also provides a steady flow of revenue to the government, which helps the government to operate more smoothly.

State Individual Income Tax State individual income taxes do not differ a great deal from federal income taxes. In fact, the states that tax earnings from work use a pay-as-you-go basis, just like the federal tax. Although some states tax earnings, others tax only the income from savings accounts, dividends on stocks and bonds, and the selling of property or stocks.

Business & HISTORY

The first income tax in the United States was imposed during the Civil War in 1864. In 1872, however, the tax was discontinued. The Sixteenth Amendment to the Constitution, adopted in 1913, allowed the federal government to again collect taxes on income.

CHAPTER 17 TAXES AND TAXATION **277**

Global Perspective

The following list includes some of the top tax rates of industrialized nations.

United States	40%	Sweden	42%	Japan	50%
Germany	53%	France	57%	The Netherlands	70%

Suggest that students survey their friends and relatives asking questions such as those listed below. Encourage students to prepare a three-minute news report, including charts and graphs, describing the results of their survey.
- Do you think your taxes are too high?
- Do you think individuals in most industrialized countries pay more or less taxes than U.S. citizens?
- Would you be surprised to learn that individuals in most industrialized countries pay more in taxes than do individuals in the United States?

CHAPTER 17

USE VISUALS

Direct students' attention to the graph showing sources of federal government revenue in Figure 17-1. Help students recognize that the graph shows two kinds of income tax: individual income tax (44%) and corporate income tax (11%). Ask: What provides the other 45 percent? (Social Security tax, excise tax, tariffs, estate and gift taxes, and other.)
Answer to caption: 81.5%

USE TRANSPARENCIES

Use Teaching Transparency 17-1 and its corresponding strategies and worksheet from the *Teaching Transparency Strategies and Worksheets* booklet to help students understand the sources of revenue for the federal government. Verify student worksheets using the Answer Key.

Business Brief

Taxpayers send their income tax returns to one of the IRS's ten tax processing centers. These centers receive and process some 200 million returns and other related documents each year. Using computers, IRS staff members quickly check each return.

TEACHING TIP

Remind students that income generally refers to any salary, wages, interest, and dividends that an individual earns. For a corporation, income refers to the profits a corporation earns.

CHAPTER 17 **277**

Building Business Skills

Building Business Skills

Model

Direct students' attention to the headings listed in the tables. Ask students to identify any headings they do not understand. Point out to students that the first two columns of numbers give a range of wages for which there is a single withholding amount. Encourage students who have part-time or summer jobs to find their wages, withholding allowances, and withholding amounts in the appropriate table.

Business Brief

Popular belief holds that most U.S. businesses have an after-tax profit of more than 30 percent of sales. In reality, the after-tax profits for U.S. domestic corporations average between 4 and 5 percent.

TEACHING TIP

Point out to students that while Social Security contributions represent about 37 percent of the federal government's revenue, the payments associated with Social Security and Medicare represent about 38 percent of the federal government's expenditures. Use this opportunity to stress to students that without taxes, the government could not provide many of the services that improve the public welfare.

MATH

Understanding Withholding

Explanation

It's exciting to get a new job, and it's especially exciting to find out how much money you will earn. For some people, their first paycheck comes as a shock.

Workers must pay taxes on the money they earn. Employers help the government collect taxes by withholding from employees' earnings their estimated tax payments and sending them directly to the government.

For federal income taxes, the amount of tax to be withheld depends on the amount of earnings, the length of the pay period, the number of withholding allowances, and the employee's marital status. Most employers compute employees' withholding amounts by using tables provided by the federal government.

Practice

To determine the withholding, follow these steps:

1. Choose the proper table based on the pay period and the employee's marital status.
2. Find the line that covers the wages earned. Follow across to the number of allowances claimed. The amount at this point is the tax to be withheld.

Use the tables to answer the following questions.

1. How much federal tax is withheld for a single employee who earns $555 per week and claims one withholding allowance?

Income tax collected by the United States government accounts for 55% of the federal budget. Compare that figure with the figures below.

France	22.2%
Sweden	22.3%
Japan	36.6%
Italy	36.1%
China	89.5%
Egypt	72.3%
Israel	22.9%

City Individual Income Tax Approximately 2000 cities in the United States collect a city income tax. These taxes are based on a variety of income, including salaries, wages, commissions, and money earned by savings and investments. Most of these cities use a pay-as-you-go method to collect the tax.

Corporate Income Tax Corporations must pay a tax on their profits each year. Corporate income tax provides more than 10 percent of total federal revenue. States also tax corporate earnings, but in general, the state rate of taxation is much lower. Corporate income taxes are almost nonexistent at the local level.

Social Security and Medicare Taxes Two other taxes on income handled on a pay-as-you-go basis are the social security tax and Medicare tax. Social security tax is paid into the Federal Insurance Contributions Act (FICA). Money raised through this tax is used to pay retirement benefits. Also, when the primary wage earner in a family covered by social security becomes disabled or dies, the family receives social security benefits.

Medicare tax is money paid to the United States government health insurance program for hospital insurance. This insurance helps pay the cost of hospital care. Nearly all people age

278 UNIT 5 GOVERNMENT AND BUSINESS

Curriculum Connection   Math

Corporations, taxed on yearly income, pay 15 percent tax on income under $50,000; 23 percent on income from $50,000 to $75,000; 34 percent on income between $75,000 and $10 million; and 35 percent on income over $10 million. Have students look at the annual reports of several corporations to determine how much each corporation paid in taxes. Using the figures in the annual report, have students determine the corporation's income, and the approximate tax on that income. (Income × tax rate = tax due.) Have students compare the two figures and offer an explanation for any differences they find.

For students who need to sharpen their math skills, choose among the worksheets in the *Math Skills Review* booklet.

SINGLE Persons—WEEKLY Payroll Period

And wages are–		And the number of withholding allowances claimed is–										
At least	But less than	0	1	2	3	4	5	6	7	8	9	10
		The amount of income tax to be withheld shall be–										
$ 540	$ 550	89	76	64	55	48	42	35	28	22	15	8
550	560	91	79	67	56	50	43	36	30	23	16	10
560	570	94	82	69	58	51	45	38	31	25	18	11
570	580	97	85	72	60	53	46	39	33	26	19	13
580	590	100	87	75	63	54	48	41	34	28	21	14

MARRIED Persons—WEEKLY Payroll Period

And wages are–		And the number of withholding allowances claimed is–										
At least	But less than	0	1	2	3	4	5	6	7	8	9	10
		The amount of income tax to be withheld shall be–										
$ 580	$ 590	70	64	57	51	44	37	31	24	17	11	4
590	600	72	65	59	52	45	39	32	26	19	12	6
600	610	73	67	60	54	47	40	34	27	20	14	7
610	620	75	68	62	55	48	42	35	29	22	15	9
620	630	76	70	63	57	50	43	37	30	23	17	10

2. What is the difference in the withholding amounts for a single and a married employee who each earn $585 a week and claim two withholding allowances?

65 or older are eligible for Medicare. In addition, disabled people who receive social security benefits may be eligible for Medicare benefits.

Many people do not consider social security or Medicare true taxes—these taxes are actually insurance programs run by the federal government. However, these programs are a form of tax because almost everyone who is employed must pay for them. About nine out of ten workers in the United States pay social security taxes. Employers must also pay social security and Medicare taxes equal to the amount the employees pay. Self-employed people pay both of these taxes, but at a higher rate than the individual rate.

Withholding Required by Law Three principal deductions from employees' gross earnings are required by federal law: social security tax (FICA), Medicare tax, and federal income tax withholding. In addition, some states and cities require that state and local income tax be withheld from earnings of employees. After the end of each calendar year, employers must give each employee a Wage and Tax Statement, Form W-2. This is often referred to as a withholding statement and contains

Global Perspective

Have groups of students undertake research on the basic kinds of public and general welfare services provided by the United States federal government as well as the governments of nations such as Sweden, England, Canada, Germany, France, or Japan. Topics they might cover include the history of the social welfare program, original purpose, and variety of benefits received. Suggest that students present their findings in a bulletin board display.

FORM W-2 WAGE AND TAX STATEMENT

1 Control number	22222	For Official Use Only ▶ OMB No. 1545-0008		

2 Employer's name, address, and ZIP code	6 Statutory employee ☒ Deceased ☐ Pension plan ☐ Legal rep ☐ 942 emp ☐ Subtotal ☐ Deferred compensation ☐ Void ☐

Ajax Mail Order Company
111 Main Street
Krum, TX 76249

7 Allocated tips	8 Advance EIC payment

9 Federal income tax withheld 1,300.00	10 Wages, tips, other compensation 16,640.00

3 Employer's identification number 75-7575757	4 Employer's state I.D. number 12-98765	11 Social security tax withheld 1,081.60	12 Social security wages 16,640.00

5 Employee's social security number 123-45-6789	13 Social security tips	14 Medicare wages and tips 16,640.00

19a Employee's name (first, middle initial, last) Cass C. Collins	15 Medicare tax withheld 249.60	16 Nonqualified plans

24 East Oak St.
Krum, TX 76249

17 See Instrs. for Form W-2	18 Other

19b Employee's address and ZIP code		

20	21	22 Dependent care benefits	23 Benefits included in Box 10

24 State income tax 321.00	25 State wages, tips, etc. 16,640.00	26 Name of state TX	27 Local income tax 166.40	28 Local wages, tips, etc. 16,640.00	29 Name of locality Krum

Copy C For Employee
Form W-2 Wage and Tax Statement 19XX
Department of the Treasury—Internal Revenue Service

FIGURE 17-2

Employers use a Form W-2 to report annual wage and tax information to federal, state, and local tax agencies. What percentage of this employee's earnings did the employer withhold for taxes?

information about the employee's earnings and tax withholdings for the year. A Form W-2 is shown in Figure 17-2 above.

Taxes on Goods and Services

Still another tax base includes goods and services that are used. These taxes are a major source of revenue for most state governments. Approximately one quarter of all state revenue comes from the tax on goods and services. The three major types of taxes are general sales tax, excise taxes, and tariffs.

General Sales Tax A **general sales tax** is a tax added to the price of goods and services at the time of purchase. Most states currently have a general sales tax. In some states, local governments receive a share of the revenue collected in their areas. Other local governments collect their own sales tax in addition to the state sales tax.

Sales tax procedures vary from state to state. In most states the purchases of goods, but not of services, are taxed. In some states, food, clothing, and medicine, which are often considered basic necessities, are not taxed. The sales tax rates, which also vary from state to state, are illustrated in Figure 17-3 on page 281.

Cooperative Learning   Co-op Co-op

Work with students to generate a list of the items in your city or town that are subject to a tax levied by the state or the local government. Exclude items that are subject to sales tax only. Be sure students check taxes on items such as tobacco products, gasoline, liquor, electricity, gas, local and long distance telephone service, hotel rooms and service, concerts, sporting events, and soft drinks. Suggest students find out the percent of the tax, or the amount of tax for a single item. Have students display their findings in a poster or on a bulletin board.

General sales tax is collected at the time of purchase. If your purchase of $100 worth of CD equipment is subject to a sales tax of 6 percent, you must pay $106 to the store. The store, in turn, must forward the $6 collected for sales tax to the state government. In this way, the business acts as a tax collector for the government.

Excise Tax An **excise tax** is a tax collected on the sale of particular goods and services. The tax rate is usually a certain percentage of the price, or so much for each item. Alcoholic beverages, tobacco, petroleum products, automobile tires, firearms, and air travel all have a federal excise tax. State governments often tax alcoholic beverages, tobacco, gasoline, and utility services. Many local governments have utility, amusement, and hotel and motel room taxes. In some geographic areas, an item may have an excise tax from all three levels of government—federal, state, and local.

Unlike general sales taxes, excise taxes are automatically included in the price. For instance, the cost of a gallon of

FIGURE 17-3

Many states collect a sales tax of about 5 percent. Which states do not have a sales tax?

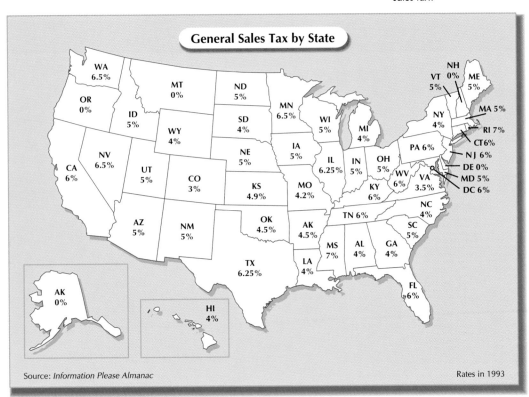

General Sales Tax by State

Source: *Information Please Almanac*

Rates in 1993

Making Connections — Everyday Living

Suggest students find out the local city or town tax rate as well as the rate for neighboring cities, counties, or states. Have students use the tax rates to compute the tax on purchases of $50, $100, $200, $250, and $500. Suggest that they arrange the information in a chart. Have students use the chart to tell when they would consider making purchases outside of their locality. Encourage them to balance the potential tax savings with the time and money needed to travel to the neighboring locality. Have students write a brief paragraph describing the conditions that would lead them to shop in the neighboring locality.

For students who need to sharpen their math skills, choose among the worksheets in the *Math Skills Review* booklet.

Some taxes have been levied as an attempt to change individual behavior. For example, the so-called *sin tax* is a relatively high tax designed to raise revenue as well as reduce the consumption of socially undesirable products such as liquor or tobacco. When Canada quadrupled its tobacco tax, the country raised considerable revenue and reduced per capita cigarette consumption by one-third.

USE VISUALS

Figure 17-3 shows the amount of sales tax varies from state to state. Ask students to identify the amount of sales tax in their home state as well as the amount of tax levied in nearby states. Ask: How might states without a state sales tax, such as Delaware and New Hampshire, obtain the revenues they need to provide governmental services? (Income tax, other fees and taxes.)
Answer to caption: Alaska, Delaware, Montana, New Hampshire, Oregon.

USE TRANSPARENCIES

Use Teaching Transparency 17-2 and its corresponding strategies and worksheet from the *Teaching Transparency Strategies and Worksheets* booklet to help students learn which states have a state sales tax. Verify student worksheets using the Answer Key.

FOCUS ON **Technology**

Discuss

Invite students to supply examples of electronic scanning from their own experiences. Did they feel the scanning accelerated the process? Were they aware the scanning was part of a larger computer-aided transaction? Have students draw diagrams to indicate how bar-code readers, optical character recognition, and imaging technology work.

Connection to CHAPTER 21

Although the United States still collects tariffs on imported goods, the purpose is not to raise revenue. It is to protect certain domestic industries from foreign competition. Tariffs are discussed in more detail in Chapter 21 and Chapter 23.

TEACHING TIP

Present students with the following statement. "Ownership of property is not a true measure of a person's ability to pay taxes." Ask students to discuss what they think the statement means. Then have students indicate whether they think the statement is fact or opinion.

Provide students with the data in the table at right concerning the revenue sources of governments. Ask them to make graphs comparing the data.

Electronic Scanners

They're everywhere! At the grocery store they read the thick and thin black lines on all your cans, bottles, and boxes. Then the computer figures your total bill, including tax. While you wait at the crossing, they read the bars and lines on boxcars zipping by at 60 mph. Even your utility company uses them to record your payments to your account. What are we talking about? Electronic scanners—a technology that shines light onto an image and converts it into an electronic format that can be stored in a computer's memory.

The electronic scanner that you are probably most familiar with is the *bar-code reader* found in supermarkets and department stores. Sometimes the scanner is a flatbed device; sometimes it is a wand. The device converts printed bars on products into a number and feeds that number to the computer, just as though the number had been typed on a keyboard. In fact, after the keyboard and mouse, the bar-code reader is the most widely used input device for data. Besides supermarkets and department stores, other businesses and organizations, including libraries and hospitals, use bar-code readers to assure accurate data entry.

Another type of electronic scanning is *optical character recognition* or OCR for short. Instead of reading only patterns of lines, these devices can "read" printed or typewritten text and convert it into code that you can use on a word processor or that can be stored in a computer file. Some OCR devices are really fast and can scan well-prepared documents at a rate of 500 words a minute! Businesses and other organizations use OCR to

gasoline already includes the excise tax. Any additional general sales tax on the gasoline is added separately.

Tariff Many foreign businesses pay a tax, called a **tariff,** on the goods they want to sell in this country. Tariffs are collected only by the federal government. A tariff may increase the price of the foreign goods sold in our market because the seller may pass the cost of the tariff on to the consumer. Early in our history, tariffs accounted for a major share of federal revenue. That is no longer true. Today tariffs are used as a matter of economic policy to protect United States businesses rather than to collect revenue.

Taxes on Property

Property, all the goods and money owned by an individual, is another source of tax revenue. There are a number of taxes on property, all intended to get revenue from people or organizations that own things.

A **property tax** taxes items owned by a person or business. Local governments—including counties, cities, towns, town-

Curriculum Connection   Math

	Federal	State	Local
FICA	38%		
Corporate Income Tax	9%	3%	
Individual Income Tax	44%	15%	2%
Excise Tax	4%		
Sales Tax		23%	5%
Intergovernmental Revenue		22%	33%

	Federal	State	Local
Retirement Funds		11%	3%
Utilities and Liquor Store Income			9%
Property Taxes			16%
Interest Earnings		4%	5%
Education Charges		4%	
Other	14%	18%	27%

quickly input existing documents without having to have someone sit down and key them in all over again. Credit card companies and insurance companies use OCR to read the payment stubs you send along with your payments and automatically credit your account.

For artists, architects, and engineers, *imaging technology* is an important tool. As a scanner moves over an image, image-processing software converts the image into a digitized format which can then be displayed on a computer screen. Users can manipulate the image in any way they wish.

From bar codes to computerized images, it's clear that businesses will continue to use electronic scanner technology for quick, automatic entry of important data and images of all types.

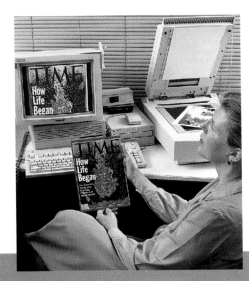

Follow Through
Ask students to speculate on future uses of electronic imaging. What other applications do they think can benefit from electronic or digital imaging? For additional information about current technology, refer to the *Technology Resources Guide.*

ships, and school districts—get a major share of their revenue from property taxes. State and federal governments receive almost no revenue from this tax.

A *real estate property tax* taxes the value of land and anything on the land, such as houses, barns, garages, or other buildings. A *personal property tax* may be levied on machinery used by businesses, as well as on automobiles, furniture, and other personal property of value. Because of the ease with which personal property can be hidden, the personal property tax is used less and less. Therefore, real estate has become the most important property tax base and source of revenue for local communities.

Estate and Inheritance Taxes Estate and inheritance taxes are paid on the value of real estate and personal property left at the time of death. The federal government collects an estate tax on the value of the property left by an individual. Some states also collect an estate tax. Most states collect an inheritance tax, which is paid by the heir or heirs of an estate. An heir is a person who receives part of or all of the estate of another. No tax is collected on estates that are valued below a certain amount.

TEACHING TIP
Have students generate a list of the items they might find in a local restaurant or other small business. Ask a volunteer to classify the property for tax purposes, telling whether the property is *real property* or *personal property.*

Learning Activity
Estate and gift taxes currently provide about 1 percent of the federal revenue. Have students indicate whether or not they think an inheritance or gift tax is fair. Then have them speculate on what other sources of revenue the government could turn to if inheritance and gift taxes were no longer levied.

Reteaching Strategy

Have teams of four students work together to create a crossword puzzle to use as a study aid for this section of the chapter. Have students select the words to be included, including the new tax terms and terms describing the different types of taxes. Then have students fit the terms together in crossword style. Each team must then generate clear definitions. Have teams exchange puzzles with one another. Ask teams to determine whether the directions and definitions of the puzzle they received are clear. Distribute copies of the finished puzzles for students to keep as a study aid.

Quick Check Answers

1. Item or activity that is the source of the tax; government charge on earnings or other source of income; tax added to the price of goods and services at the time of purchase; taxes on items owned by a person or business.
2. Nontax (parking meter fees, postage, fees for various licenses) and tax (income tax, property tax, tax on goods and services).
3. Most of the states' revenues come from taxes on goods and services; local governments tend to rely on property taxes.
4. Salary; wages; income from savings accounts, stocks, bonds, rents on properties, and profits (capital gains) can be taxed as income.

Develop Concepts

The Basis for Taxation

Point out to students that the decision concerning "who pays what" taxes can be traced to two principles that have evolved over the years. Taxes are classified according to how they spread the tax burden among taxpayers. One principle—the benefits-received principle—suggests that those people who receive the benefits of the tax should pay the tax. The second principle—the ability-to-pay principle—suggests that people should be taxed according to their ability to pay.

Gift Tax The gift tax was created because some people tried to give away their property before death, so their heirs could avoid paying estate taxes. Gift taxes are collected by the federal government and some state governments. Only gifts above a certain value are taxed.

Quick Check

1. Define *tax base, income tax, general sales tax,* and *property tax.*
2. What are the two major types of revenue for government? Give three examples of each.
3. What types of taxes do most state and local governments use?
4. What kinds of income are subject to federal income tax?

THE BASIS FOR TAXATION

If you can identify most of the taxes you pay, you can better evaluate them and the effects they have on your personal economic situation. We can make changes in how our government raises revenue through our elected representatives. To make informed decisions, though, all citizens should know some basic principles of taxation.

One principle of taxation is based on the market concept that if you enjoy or use something, you should pay for it. This is called the **benefits-received principle.** People who get benefits from a public service should pay a charge or tax for it. The gasoline tax is an example of revenue obtained according to the benefits-received principle. Money from gasoline taxes is used to build and maintain highways. Therefore, those who pay for fuel contribute directly to good highways.

However, there is a problem with the benefits-received principle of taxation. Sometimes it is hard to know exactly how much benefit has been received and, therefore, how much tax should be collected from an individual. For instance, how would you measure the benefits people receive from public education or parks?

Most of our taxes are based on the **ability-to-pay principle,** which means that those who can afford to pay more taxes should do so. Those with more taxable income, purchases, and property are required to pay more taxes than those with less.

Enrichment Strategy

Excise or so-called "sin" taxes can be said to be based on the benefits-received principle. Long-term cigarette use and alcohol consumption cause a number of illnesses and place extra burdens on the health-care system. Governments sometimes use revenue raised from taxes on cigarettes and liquor to fund health-care programs. Ask students to use newspapers and periodicals to research the health-care costs of treating lung cancer, liver diseases due to alcohol consumption, and injuries from drunk-driving crashes. Suggest they try to determine how much of the burden of health-care costs for these conditions is paid by the federal government. Allow students to produce posters or a bulletin board to share their findings with the class.

Direct and Indirect Taxes

Some taxes are described according to their method of collection. A tax that is charged to the person or persons who pay it is called a **direct tax.** A direct tax cannot be shifted to another party, and it is clear who is paying them. Estate taxes, some property taxes, and the individual income tax are direct.

An **indirect tax,** however, is paid by one party but passed on to another. Sometimes indirect taxes are called hidden taxes. Some examples are excise taxes, customs duties or tariffs, and the property taxes that businesses pay. These taxes are a cost of doing business and are usually passed on to the consumers of goods and services.

Categories of Tax Structure

Some taxes are described by how they are structured to affect people of different incomes. A **progressive tax** is one that imposes a higher percentage rate of taxation on persons with high incomes than on those with low incomes. The federal income tax is an example of a progressive tax. People with very low incomes pay little or no tax. As income increases, so does the tax rate, and of course, the amount of tax collected. For instance, someone who makes $18,000 may pay 15 percent, or $2700 in income tax, and someone who makes $40,000 may pay 28 percent, or $11,200. Some state income taxes are also progressive.

Other states impose the same percentage rate of taxation on everyone, regardless of income. Such a tax is a **proportional tax.** For example, an income of $18,000 and an income of $40,000 would both be taxed at 4 percent. The person making $18,000 would pay a tax of $720; the person earning $40,000 would pay a tax of $1600.

A **regressive tax** is one that imposes a higher percentage rate of taxation on low incomes than on high incomes. A sales tax is an example of a regressive tax. Regressive refers to the effect of the tax, which is harder on those with lower incomes. For example, people with higher incomes generally do not spend as great a percentage of their incomes on necessities as do those with lower incomes. To ease the burden on lower-income families, many states do not tax necessities such as food, medicine, and clothing. The chart in Figure 17-4 on page 285 compares progressive, proportional, and regressive taxes.

F.Y.I.

Inheritance taxes are usually considered to be progressive. That is, the rate of the tax increases as the amount to be taxed increases. An inheritance tax is imposed on a portion of a deceased person's estate that an individual receives. An inheritance tax differs from an estate tax. An estate tax is imposed on the whole estate before it is portioned out to different individuals. Almost all states impose either an estate tax or an inheritance tax—some impose both.

TEACHING TIP

Help students distinguish between the two methods of tax collection. *Direct* taxes are based directly on a person's income or net worth. *Indirect* taxes are taxes on goods and services that are passed along to the consumer. Ask students to name taxes that are direct (income tax, estate tax). Then ask them to name taxes that are indirect (excise taxes, tariffs).

Learning Activity

Although sales tax is both *indirect* and *regressive,* many citizens do not object to paying this tax. Ask students to explain why the sales tax is indirect. (Government collects sales tax from retailers based on their sales volume; retailers collect the tax from the consumers who purchase their goods. In this way, consumers are paying the tax indirectly.) Next, have students explain why sales tax is a *regressive* tax. (Individuals earning $5000 a year pay the same tax on a tube of toothpaste as do individuals earning $50,000 a year.) Then have students generate a list of reasons why many people seem to be willing to pay sales taxes.

Reteaching Strategy

Use Enrichment Master 17-1 to help students recognize that categories such as *direct, indirect, regressive, proportional,* and *progressive* are ways to classify and group taxes, not names of actual taxes. Ask students to identify the taxes as either Direct or Indirect. Have a volunteer label each tax listed on the chart with an *I* or *D* according to the class decision. Then ask students to identify which taxes represent the benefits-received principle *(BRP)* and the ability-to-pay principle *(APP).* Suggest students use the information as a study aid for the classification of taxes.

CHAPTER 17

USE VISUALS

Direct students' attention to Figure 17-4. Make certain students can associate the effects listed at the right of the table with the corresponding term *progressive, proportional,* or *regressive.* Point out to students that all the taxes they have studied can be placed in one of these categories.
Answer to caption: $10,000.

Quick Check Answers

1. People who get benefits from public goods and services pay for those goods and services; people who can afford to pay more taxes should.
2. *Direct tax* is charged to the person or persons who pay the tax; an *indirect tax* is paid by one party but passed on to another.
3. Both the rate and the amount of tax increase as income increases; the amount of tax increases but the rate remains the same; the amount of tax increases as income increases, but the proportion of income paid in tax decreases.

Develop Concepts

Criteria for Taxes

Evaluating taxes requires criteria for fairness, efficiency, and acceptability. Ask students what criteria they think a fair tax might have. Then ask students to name characteristics they think would describe efficient or acceptable taxes.

PROGRESSIVE, PROPORTIONAL, AND REGRESSIVE TAXES			
Tax Structure	$10,000 Income	$100,000 Income	Effect
Progressive Tax Example: Federal Income Tax	$1000 paid in taxes or 10% of total income	$25,000 paid in taxes or 25% of total income	As income goes up, the percent of income paid in taxes goes up.
Proportional Tax Example: City Income Tax of 0.7%	$70.00 paid in taxes or 0.7% of income	$700.00 paid in taxes or 0.7% of income	As income goes up, the percent of income paid in taxes stays the same.
Regressive Tax Example: State Sales Tax of 4%	$5000 spent on food and clothing $200 paid in taxes or 2% of income	$20,000 spent on food and clothing $800 paid in taxes or 0.8% of income	As income goes up, the percent of income paid in taxes goes down.

FIGURE 17-4

All taxes fall into one of three categories of tax structure. Which income, $10,000 or $100,000, pays a higher percentage of its income to a regressive tax?

Quick Check

1. What is the benefits-received principle? What is the ability-to-pay principle?
2. What is the difference between *direct* and *indirect taxes*?
3. Explain how *progressive, proportional,* and *regressive taxes* change as income increases.

CRITERIA FOR TAXES

There are a number of ways of determining how well a tax does the job. No tax is perfect, but some do a better job than others.

Fairness

Fairness relates to whether a tax is just and even-handed in its treatment of all people in our society. As a nation, we have adopted the ability-to-pay rather than the benefits-received principle as a yardstick for most of our taxes. The ability-to-pay principle favors the progressive over the regressive tax. Thus people with higher incomes pay more tax and a greater percentage of their incomes. That is why a progressive income tax is considered fairer than a regressive sales tax.

286 UNIT 5 GOVERNMENT AND BUSINESS

Curriculum Connection   Communication

By now students should recognize that there are several ways to classify taxes: federal, state, and local; regressive, progressive, and proportional; indirect, direct, and so on. Suggest that students review the list of taxes they generated at the beginning of the chapter. Have them choose three taxes from the list. Then have them write an explanatory paragraph evaluating the taxes according to the three criteria of taxation: fairness, efficiency, and acceptability.

For those students who need to improve their written communication skills, choose among the worksheets in *Communication Skills Review.*

286 UNIT 5

Income is generally considered a fairer base to tax than are goods and services purchased or property. The ability to pay is better indicated by income. For example, two families with different incomes may buy the same amount of clothing and pay the same amount of sales tax, but the family with the lower income will have less money left over.

Direct taxes are considered fairer than indirect. People have a better idea of what they are paying to government with a direct tax than with an indirect tax. For this reason excise taxes are often considered unfair.

Efficiency

Another mark of an effective tax is its efficiency—is the tax easy and cost efficient to collect? Government has to rely on somebody else to collect most of its taxes. This is true for such taxes as income, sales, social security, and excise. Sales and excise taxes are paid to the store or manufacturer, who forwards them to the government. Most social security and income taxes are deducted from the employee's wages by the employer and sent to the government.

Property tax is a tax that is not easy to collect. Government must value the property, send out the bills, and then collect the taxes from a variety of individuals and groups. Property taxes are usually more expensive and more difficult for the government to collect than other major taxes. This is especially true of the personal property tax, because establishing the real worth of property is often difficult.

Acceptability

Taxes are generally not very popular, but most people recognize the need to pay them. By and large, the federal income tax, sales tax, and property tax are accepted. Of the three, property taxes are probably the most objectionable. In fact, personal property taxes have become so unacceptable that many local communities have dropped them. At the state level, income and sales taxes are probably the most accepted.

Indirect taxes are generally more acceptable to the public than direct ones. With indirect taxes, the people who pay the taxes to the government know they will be passed along to others in the form of higher prices. However, the people who pay the final price often are not aware that they are paying the tax. Indirect taxes do not provide citizens with a clear idea of how much money they are paying in taxes.

Business Brief

In 1776, Adam Smith, a Scottish economist, published *The Wealth of Nations*. In this book Smith set up a model for evaluating taxes that is still used today.

TEACHING TIP

Remind students how federal and state governments collect individual income taxes. Discuss how requiring employers to withhold federal income tax from a worker's wages satisfies *efficiency*. Ask if this method might also satisfy *acceptability*. Have students speculate why yearly collection might be more difficult.

Reteaching Strategy

Help students understand that fairness does not consider merely the amount of taxes paid, but what percent of an individual's or family's entire income goes to pay taxes. Have students construct a diagram comparing 20 percent of $10,000 and 20 percent of $100,000. Then have students construct a diagram comparing $2000 to $10,000 and to $100,000. Ask students to indicate which diagram represents a relatively fair tax.

Quick Check Answers

1. Fairness: is the tax just and even-handed?; efficiency: is collection of the tax relatively efficient and cost-effective?; acceptability: will people accept the tax as needed and fair?

2. The ability to pay a tax is better indicated by income than by the purchase of goods and services. People of differing incomes may buy the same amount of necessary items and pay the same tax. However, the lower-income people spend more of their income on the tax.

Develop Concepts

Effect on Economic Activity

Point out to students that although taxes and other revenue-raising measures are necessary to support the operations of government, they reduce the income of individuals and businesses. Lower income affects the allocation of productive resources, consumer buying and saving habits, and ultimately the productivity and growth of the economy. Have students discuss how their spending patterns might change if their state levied a 20 percent sales tax.

Quick Check Answers

1. During inflation there is too much money in the economy—if taxes are increased, less money is available.

2. To increase more efficiency by governments and to have more money for people to spend.

Quick Check

1. What three criteria can be used for evaluating taxes? Explain each.
2. Why is a tax on income considered a fairer tax than a tax on goods and services?

EFFECT ON ECONOMIC ACTIVITY

All taxes affect economic activity and thus can be used to try to make changes in the economy. For example, during periods of inflation, there may be too much money in the economy, so taxes may need to be increased. However, during periods of recession, too little money is in the economy, so taxes may need to be decreased.

In recent years, there has been a sustained interest among taxpayers in the United States in cutting taxes or decreasing the amount of tax increase with each tax year. This is evidenced through the tax policies of the representatives American voters have sent to federal, state, and local levels of government in recent elections. Some citizens believe that the only way to encourage governments to be more efficient is to cut back on the money resources (revenue from taxes) that they have to spend.

Determining the amount of the tax burden on the American people is a delicate balancing act. As taxes increase, the economic power of governments increases, and they can buy more resources to provide goods and services to the public. If taxes decrease, individuals and businesses increase their economic power in the marketplace because they have more money to spend. Tax policy, at any one time, depends on the philosophy of the country's citizens in regard to their perceived needs of society in general.

Quick Check

1. How can taxes move the economy away from inflation?
2. What are two reasons some people want taxes to decrease?

Enrichment Strategy

Have students prepare handouts with brief explanations of the three criteria for effective taxes (fairness, efficiency, and acceptability) and the three types of taxes (regressive, progressive, and proportional). Have students distribute the handouts to family members, neighbors, and so on, asking them which type of tax would be best in terms of the criteria. Have students pool their findings and determine which type of tax is most favored.

Chapter 17 **Summary**

Main Ideas

1. The three major types of tax bases in the United States are income, goods and services, and property.
2. The benefits-received principle of taxation is based on the idea that those who get benefits from a public service should pay for them. The ability-to-pay principle means that those who can afford to pay more taxes should do so.
3. With a progressive tax, the rate of taxation increases as income increases. With a proportional tax, the amount of tax increases with income, but the rate stays the same. With a regressive tax, the proportion of income spent on the tax decreases as income increases.
4. Criteria for evaluating taxes are fairness, efficiency, and acceptability.
5. Taxes affect economic activity because they determine how much money is spent by individuals, businesses, and the government.
6. Electronic scanning helps businesses quickly input data and images.
7. Employers withhold required estimated taxes from employees' paychecks to assure government revenues throughout the year.

CASE ANALYSIS   Tax Incentives

State and local governments work hard to attract new industries or to encourage established ones to stay. One technique governments use is to offer companies some form of tax incentives. The incentives can include reducing the company's initial tax rate for a period of years or exempting the company from certain taxes for a specific time period. Governments hope to offset the loss of corporate tax revenue by gaining revenue from taxing the earnings and property of the company's employees and the money employees will spend for goods and services in the local economy. Rival governments sometimes bid against one another in "tax-incentive wars" to attract corporations to their area. For example, in the late 1980s, Chicago offered Sears, Roebuck & Company a tax-incentive package worth $164 million to keep it from leaving the city. However, Hoffman Estates, a Chicago suburb, "won" the bidding war by offering Sears a package of incentives worth about $240 million. Do you think it is a good idea for state and local governments to offer tax incentives to attract or retain businesses? Explain.

CHAPTER 17   TAXES AND TAXATION   **289**

CLOSE

Main Ideas

Main Ideas summarizes the key information in the chapter. It is a useful tool for reinforcement and review.

CASE ANALYSIS

Case Analysis provides a chapter-related case for student analysis and application of decision-making skills.

Answer
Students' responses will vary.

QUICK QUIZ

1. What is a tax base? Give three examples of a tax base. (It is the item or activity that is taxed. Income, purchases, real estate.)
2. Explain how the benefits-received principle differs from the ability-to-pay principle. (Benefits-received; payees receive benefits; ability-to-pay: payees can afford to pay.)
3. Which kind of tax has a tax rate that increases as income increases? Which stays the same as income increases? (Proportional, regressive.)
4. What characteristics can be used to evaluate how well a tax performs? (Fairness, efficiency, and acceptability.)
5. If taxes increase, what will happen to the economic power of the government? (It will increase.)

Chapter 17 **Review**

CHAPTER 17 REVIEW

APPLY

Answers

Use the Language of Business

1. tax base, **2.** indirect tax, **3.** ability-to-pay principle, **4.** regressive tax, **5.** general sales tax, **6.** progressive tax, **7.** direct tax, **8.** proportional tax, **9.** property tax, **10.** excise tax, **11.** benefits-received principle, **12.** income tax, **13.** tariff

Review What You Learned

1. Income: based on the money that an individual or corporation earns; goods and services: based on the value of what is purchased; property: based on items owned.

2. Income tax is the primary means; others include Social Security taxes, tariffs, excise and gift taxes.

3. They pay benefits for retirement, disability, and premature death of primary wage earner in a family. Medicare taxes are used to help pay for hospital costs for senior citizens and people with disabilities.

4. Property is all goods and money owned by an individual. Property taxes include: real estate tax, personal property tax, estate and inheritance taxes, gift tax.

5. Benefits-received principle means that the taxes you pay vary according to the benefits you receive; gasoline tax. The ability-to-pay principle means that you pay taxes according to your income or wealth, regardless of the benefits you receive; progressive income tax .

6. A direct tax is charged to the individuals who pay it; estate taxes, income taxes, and tax on personal property. An indirect tax is paid by one person but its cost is passed on to another party; custom duties, property taxes on apartment buildings, and excise taxes.

7. Fairness, efficiency, and acceptability.

8. Taxes determine the purchasing power of individuals, businesses, and governments in the marketplace.

9. It is money an employer deducts from employees' paychecks; it goes to pay required taxes to governments.

10. It allows businesses to quickly and accurately input large amounts of images and data.

Use the Language of Business

Number your paper 1 through 13. Then write the term that best matches each numbered phrase.

ability-to-pay principle	progressive tax
benefits-received principle	property tax
direct tax	proportional tax
excise tax	regressive tax
general sales tax	tariff
income tax	tax base
indirect tax	

1. Item that is the source of a tax.
2. Tax paid by one party but passed on to another.
3. Those who can afford to pay more taxes should do so.
4. Tax rate decreases as income increases.
5. Tax that is added to the price of goods and services at the time of purchase.
6. The amount of tax paid as well as the tax rate increase as income increases.
7. Tax that is charged to the person or persons who eventually pay it.
8. The amount of tax increases with income, but the rate stays the same.
9. Tax on items owned.
10. Tax included in the price of certain goods and services.
11. Those who use goods and services should pay for them.
12. Government's tax on income.
13. Tax on foreign goods sold in this country.

Review What You Learned

1. What are the three types of tax bases used in this country? Explain each.
2. List four sources used by the federal government to raise revenue.
3. What are the purposes of the social security and Medicare taxes?
4. Define property, and list three kinds of taxes on property.
5. What is the difference between the benefits-received principle and the ability-to-pay principle? Give an example of a tax based on each principle.
6. Explain the difference between indirect and direct taxes. Give examples.
7. List three ways of determining how well a tax does the job.
8. How can taxes affect economic activity?
9. What is withholding and why is it used?
10. Identify a benefit of electronic scanning.

Understand Business Concepts

1. Explain why the pay-as-you-go basis is used for federal income tax collection.
2. Explain how general sales taxes, excise taxes, and income taxes are influenced by the business cycle.
3. Why is the personal property tax not considered a very fair tax?
4. How might varying sales tax rates affect where businesses and individuals locate, what benefits they receive, and their operating expenses or cost of living?
5. Give one advantage and one disadvantage of an indirect tax.

Understand Business Concepts

1. The pay-as-you-go basis makes taxes easier to pay and provides a steady flow of income to the government.

2. In prosperous times, more people have jobs and money to spend. The government receives more taxes on income and goods purchased. The opposite is true in a recession.

3. Estimating the value of some personal property is difficult. In addition, hiding personal property is easy; some individuals may not pay as much tax as they should.

4. States with lower taxes attract businesses and workers. Lower taxes leave businesses and individuals more money to spend. Businesses in these states might be more competitive because they can set lower prices. However, lower taxes can mean fewer or poorer public services. For example, if a state does not spend much on public education, the education of workers may be inferior. Businesses might have to create training programs. This added cost might equal or surpass the higher taxes.

5. An advantage is that it is widely accepted. A disadvantage is that people do not always realize that they are paying the tax.

6. It can be difficult to value property accurately and to enforce collection of the tax.

7. Sales tax is regressive; it takes a greater percentage of income from lower-income taxpayers.

8. Incomes, the price of goods and services, and property values increase during inflation so that even at the same tax levels, tax revenues increase because the tax base increases.

6. Explain why it is difficult for the government to collect the property tax.
7. Explain why many people consider the sales tax unfair.
8. Under our tax system, the amount of taxes collected automatically goes up when we have inflation. Why?
9. Why do governments have employers withhold taxes from workers' paychecks?
10. List some advantages of electronic scanner technology.

Think Critically

1. **Assess.** Compile a list of several goods that have an excise tax included in their prices in your state. Why do you think these goods were selected for taxation?

2. **Judge.** Do you believe more of our taxes should be based on the benefits-received principle rather than the ability-to-pay principle? Explain.

Use What You Learned

1. **Group Project.** With your team, identify three tax bases other than income, goods and services, and property to which governments could levy taxes. For example, people might be taxed according to age, younger people paying a lower tax than older people. Prepare a point-of-view presentation of about 250 words for your classmates. Identify advantages and disadvantages for each tax base you propose.

2. **Computer Application.** Employers compute Social Security and Medicare taxes by multiplying the taxable wages by the tax rate and rounding to the nearest cent. For example, if an employee has taxable wages of $322 and the social security tax rate is 6.5%, the employer multiplies $322 by .065 to get $20.93. Set up a simple spreadsheet program to compute the Social Security and Medicare taxes for the four employees in the chart below. Use Social Security and Medicare tax rates of 6.5% and 1.5% respectively and maintain the same column titles.

3. **Skill Reinforcement.** Use the withholding tables on page 279 to compute the income tax for each of the four employees in the chart below.

Employee	Earnings	Marital Status	Withholding Allowances	Income Tax	Soc. Sec. Tax	Medicare Tax
Earl Echols	$597	Married, wife works	1	$_____	$_____	$_____
Carol Johanson	$576	Single, with children	3	$_____	$_____	$_____
Thach Nguyen	$583	Single	1	$_____	$_____	$_____
Rita Sanchez	$627	Married	2	$_____	$_____	$_____

Save your work in your Business Portfolio

Use What You Learned

1. Make sure all students participate in the group project. Rubrics: Presentation, Illustration, Charts and Graphs.

2. Students with no access to a computer may complete this project using a calculator. Encourage them to place their results in a table. Rubrics: Charts and Tables, Paragraph.

Employee	Earnings	Social Security Tax	Medicare Tax
Earl Echols	$597	$ 38.81	$ 8.96
Carol Johanson	$576	$ 37.44	$ 8.64
Thach Nguyen	$583	$ 37.90	$ 8.75
Rita Sanchez	$627	$ 40.76	$ 9.41

3. Remind students they will need to use all the information provided about each employee. Echols $65; Johanson $60; Nguyen $87; Sanchez $63. Rubric: Charts and Tables.

9. Employers withhold taxes so governments get revenue regularly and to assure payment.
10. It provides a quick and accurate way to input data and images, which can then be manipulated.

Think Critically

1. Frequently taxed items include alcohol, gasoline, tobacco, firearms, and air travel. Students might suggest that goods chosen for excise taxes are nonessential items.
2. Answers should include an understanding of the effects of the two principles.

Independent Practice

Use the Chapter 17 worksheets in *Student Activity Guide 1* for additional practice and application activities. A Teacher's Annotated Edition provides answers.

ASSESS

Portfolio Assessment

These projects are designed to lead students to develop a collection of their best work to submit to you for assessment. Refer students to the specific rubric(s) from the *Alternative Assessment Strategies* booklet listed with each of the project notes below. These rubrics will alert students to the criteria you will use to assess their projects.

Chapter Assessment

Use the Chapter 17 Test from the *Test Masters* booklet to evaluate students' understanding of the chapter concepts. An answer key is provided. Or create your own customized test using the *Testmaker* software.

FOCUS

Introduce the Topic

Major Concepts
- Government as a Provider
- Spending at Different Levels of Government

Introduce the Topic
List the following words on the board or a transparency: *local parks, fire department, public health services, mail service, libraries, schools.* Ask students if they think these services are furnished by government or private business. Tell students that in this chapter they will learn about government services and how they are financed.

Use Business Terms
Have students look at the Business Terms and brainstorm associations with each term. Ask them where they have heard or seen the term used. Reinforce correct associations. Advise students to note the meanings of the terms as they read the chapter.

USE VISUALS
Explain to students that Hoover Dam, located about 25 miles southeast of Las Vegas, Nevada, was a federal project designed to provide water and hydroelectric power to areas in the West. Ask students why large projects such as Hoover Dam are funded by the federal government. (Government provides certain services that are deemed necessary for the well-being of a large number of people.)

292   UNIT 5

CHAPTER
18

Business terms

public welfare

transfer payment

national debt

deficit spending

balanced budget

292

CHAPTER 18 RESOURCES

Instructional Resources

Lesson Plan for Chapter 18

Teaching Transparencies 18-1, 18-2

Strategies and Worksheets for Teaching Transparencies 18-1, 18-2

Enrichment Masters 18-1, 18-2

Student Activity Guide 1–TAE for Chapter 18

Test Master for Chapter 18

Alternative Assessment Strategies

Math Skills Review

International Business Strategies

Cooperative Learning Strategies

Communication Skills Review

Ethics in Business Strategies

Government Spending and the Economy

Learning objectives

After completing this chapter, you will be able to:
- Discuss the government as a provider of goods and services.
- List major ways in which governments spend tax money.
- Explain why government spending has increased.
- Identify some questions to ask when evaluating how the government spends our money.
- Describe some careers in government and public administration and explain the qualifications for some of those jobs.
- Interpret and use data from the Consumer Price Index.

Consider what you know

- The major purpose of taxes is to raise money for local, state, and federal governments. The major taxes that affect business include those assessed to provide revenue for the operations of government and those assessed to regulate business activities.

Consider what you want to know

- How does the government decide which projects will receive our tax money?
- What goods and services do you use daily that are provided by the government?
- What kinds of careers are available in government?
- How can the Consumer Price Index help businesses determine economic trends?

Consider how to use what you learn

- As you read this chapter, think about how government spending affects you and your family. What goods or services do you and your family use that are provided by local, state, or federal governments?

Multimedia Resources

Technology Resource Guide
Distance Learning Guide
Internet Resource Guide
Professional Resources
School-to-Work/Tech Prep Strategies
Instructional Poster
Spanish Resources

Testmaker Software for Chapter 18
The Wall Street Journal Video Series
  Video & Activities for Chapter 18
Business and Marketing Computer
  Applications—An Integrated Software
  Simulation Using Microsoft Works
Stocktracker—A Stock Market Software
  Simulation
Where's the Dough? Board Game

Motivate the Learning

Learning Objectives
Point out to students that the learning objectives show what they will learn in the chapter. Tell students to keep these objectives in mind as they work through the chapter. Note that the last two objectives listed refer to the Focus on Careers feature and the Building Business Skills feature.

Consider What You Know
Review briefly the main sections of *Chapter 17 Taxes and Taxation:* Types of Taxes; The Basis for Taxation; Criteria for Taxes; and Effect on Economic Activity.

Consider What You Want to Know
Direct students to get an idea of what the chapter is about by reading the questions and looking through the chapter to see how it might help them find the answers.

Consider How to Use What You Learn
Explain to students that they will develop some projects when they finish this chapter. Suggest that as they read the chapter, they think about what goods and services they use that are provided either by the local, state, or federal government.

TEACH

Develop Concepts

Government as a Provider

People pay taxes for services provided by the police and fire departments. Ask students why people are willing to pay taxes for government services that they may never need to use. Discuss the nonmaterial benefits of safety and security that some government services provide. Have students think of other examples.

In many cases, when you want something, you can save your money and then buy it. However, you cannot buy some things. For example, you cannot buy highways, bridges, or water treatment plants. The government provides these, along with a large number of other goods and services. Who decides what goods and services the government should provide? Where does the money to pay for them come from? Who decides how much the government should spend?

In a democratic system, people make their collective wants known through their elected officials. These officials try to satisfy as many of the people's wants as possible. However, officials must also consider the **public welfare,** or the well-being of the whole society. Satisfying the wants of many different groups of people as well as providing for the public welfare can be difficult, because the government's funds are limited.

Most government funds come from taxes that people and businesses pay. Government officials, including those you elect to office, determine how tax money will be spent. In this chapter, you will learn about how tax money is spent.

GOVERNMENT AS A PROVIDER

People pay for government-provided goods and services through taxes. You probably pay sales tax when you buy a book, video game, or CD. For some goods, such as gasoline, taxes are included in the purchase price. If you have a job, taxes are deducted from your wages.

The idea behind taxes is to pay for public goods and services and to share the cost among many people. Some people may not receive direct benefits from their tax money. For instance, some people may never need to call on the fire department, but the fire department has value for everyone in the community. Families without children do not directly use the community's schools, but the entire community benefits from having better-educated children and adults.

People who use public goods and services generally do not directly pay the full cost. For example, those who use city parks and libraries usually pay little or no entrance or membership fee. The admission charge for a public museum rarely is enough to cover the museum's costs. The charges people pay for public health services generally are far below the costs. Govern-

Meeting Student Diversity

It is common practice to grade students on their oral participation in class. Students with oral expression difficulties find this hard to do. They need encouragement and, perhaps, special circumstances to contribute to class discussions. It may be helpful to ask factual questions such as "What are three reasons the government provides certain goods and services?" or "What is public welfare?" Allow students time to find the answers in the chapter.

ment uses the taxes it collects from all the people to make up the difference between the actual costs of such goods and services and what the users of those goods and services pay.

Government provides goods and services for a number of different reasons.

- Some services are a necessary part of the function of governing. For example, making and enforcing laws, operating courts, and providing for the security of our nation are part of governing. These services would be impossible for business to provide.
- Certain services are not profitable for business to undertake. For instance, the government has taken over passenger railroad service in many parts of the country. Railroad companies could not operate some of their passenger lines at a profit. Government believed the service should be continued for the well-being of the nation. Government also provides health care for lower-income citizens, people with disabilities, and many senior citizens. A business furnishing the same health care might not be able to recover its costs because the people receiving the care often cannot afford to pay the fees. Government, supported by taxes that many people pay, provides these necessary services.
- People want government to provide certain goods and services so they will remain convenient and available to all citizens. Imagine if all our streets and highways were owned by businesses. We would have to pay tolls or user fees every time we went shopping or ran an errand. People would not be able to come and go as they pleased, and some could not afford to use the streets frequently.

Quick Check

1. Give three reasons why the government provides certain goods and services.
2. Define *public welfare*.

SPENDING AT DIFFERENT LEVELS OF GOVERNMENT

Public goods and services are provided by local, state, and federal governments. Sometimes these goods and services are easy to see and understand. At other times, you may not realize that government is providing particular goods or services.

Certain items are provided only at a particular level of government. For instance, local government provides garbage

F.Y.I.

The Pennsylvania Turnpike, America's first superhighway, stands as a model of real cooperation between state and local government. In one effort to relieve the economic hardship of the Great Depression, the federal government established the Works Projects Administration, or the WPA. The states requested money from the WPA to fund public projects. Pennsylvania requested enough money for a highway through/across the northern part of the state. The opening celebration on October 1, 1940, included postcards showing a moonlit view of the Midway Service Area, located near the midpoint of the highway.

Learning Activity
Have students bring to class current articles relating to different views on how to spend the federal government's tax-generated funds. Point out reasons for differing views. Ask if students believe such differences in views are relatively recent or if they have always been public concerns.

Quick Check Answers
1. Some services are a necessary part of the function of governing; certain services are not profitable for business to undertake; people want government to provide certain goods and services so they will remain convenient and available.
2. The well-being of the whole society.

Develop Concepts

Spending at Different Levels of Government

Total state and city government revenues are substantial. It is often more efficient for a smaller governmental unit such as a state or a city to furnish certain services. Present students with the following examples and ask them which level of government they think would be best equipped for providing the services.
- Sending emergency food supplies to a foreign nation. (Federal)
- Keeping public water supplies pure. (Local)
- Maintaining state parks. (State)

Global Perspective

Some national governments provide more extensive social services to their citizens than the United States does. For example, Great Britain and some other European countries have national health care plans. Have students choose a country and research its government-provided services. Have them write a 250-word report describing some of the country's programs. Ask them also to find out how the government pays for such programs. Do citizens pay higher or lower taxes than in the United States? Is the government currently trying to change its social programs?

Refer to the *International Business Strategies* booklet for additional strategies and activities.

FOCUS ON **Careers**

Discuss

Discuss with students the kinds of skills people in government and public administration need. Ask students what courses in school could help them prepare for entry-level jobs in government and public administration. How do people advance in the field?

Government and Public Administration

I n this land of private enterprise, you might be surprised to learn how many people have careers in state, local, and federal government. Between 18 and 19 million of us pick up our paychecks from the government; that's one out of every seven workers. If this number seems surprisingly large, think of all those teachers and other public school employees. Don't forget collectors and recyclers in city waste management departments and recreation specialists at parks. Or the police officers, court reporters, and clerks who keep the justice system running. The list goes on and on.

People with careers in government and public administration do a variety of work using a vast array of skills. But they share a common goal in their work: to serve us all, either as citizens of the nation or members of smaller communities. Many government jobs add a second aim: to protect the public.

From calming dazed and frightened fire victims to explaining a homeowner's tax bill or teaching young students how to add fractions, successful public servants need well-honed communication skills. In addition to

HELP WANTED

FIREFIGHTER

Are you interested in helping people? Are you physically fit, agile, and strong? Are you a team player with strong communication skills? If so, firefighting may be the career for you! Need high school diploma or GED. Training on the job and special classes provided. Responsibilities include putting out fires using the latest techniques; using high-tech equipment; handling dangerous chemicals; giving emergency medical aid; teaching fire prevention; and conducting safety inspections.

Business Brief

The goods and services provided by the three levels of government can create confusing overlaps. A roadway might have a local name, a statewide route number, and a national highway number. For example, in Raleigh, North Carolina, the Thomas Bradshaw Freeway is also state route 50 and Interstate 40.

collection, and the federal government provides national defense. Sometimes all three levels of government provide similar services, as is the case with roads, court systems, and parks. Highways and streets built and maintained by the local government are used primarily by the people within the local community. State highways link various parts of the state, allowing people living within the state to travel easily from place to place by car or bus. The federal government is concerned primarily with interstate highways. The federal highway system links all the states to make transportation throughout the nation easier.

Sometimes more than one level of government shares financial support for a particular service. This is true for education, aid for lower-income citizens, and assistance for people with disabilities. Every level of government provides some services, and almost every part of society benefits from these services.

The Local Level

You probably notice more of the goods and services being provided at the local level of government than at other levels. A

Global Perspective

Invite students who have lived in other countries to describe the kinds of goods and services provided by the country in which they lived; how efficiently those goods and services were provided; and whether government spending on public goods and services met the needs of the citizens there. Discuss with the class similarities and differences between the countries described and the United States.

Refer to the *International Business Strategies* booklet for additional strategies and activities.

speaking and listening, reading and writing play a large role in jobs that involve laws, regulations, and the maintenance of written records.

Though the majority of beginning positions require only a high school education, applicants may have to pass a civil service examination. Once hired, employees may receive extensive on-the-job training and encouragement to advance by continuing studies outside of work.

As far as personal qualities are concerned, government workers must be especially careful to maintain punctuality and demonstrate trustworthiness. We expect

ethical behavior in our public servants because much of their work relates to institutions and laws that govern us all.

Four entry-level positions in public service are shown here.

variety of local government units, including cities, towns, townships, counties, and school districts, furnish these goods and services. You are probably involved with one or more of these levels of local government more frequently than with the state and federal governments.

The highest percentage of total spending at the local level is for public education—primarily elementary and secondary schools. Support may also go to vocational schools, colleges, and special types of schools. Local governments also fund court systems, libraries, police and fire protection, and the maintenance and building of streets and highways in the community. Water and sewage treatment are other services provided at the local level. Special services for lower-income families and dependent children are usually provided by local government as well. Figure 18-1 on page 298 lists the services provided at the local, state, and federal levels of government.

Local governments vary in the amount, quality, and kinds of benefits provided for their citizens. Some communities have a greater number of modern schools and parks than others. In larger cities, the local government may spend money on

Making Connections ⇨   Government

Establishing community laws and regulations is another responsibility of local government. Local governments establish building codes, waste disposal and recycling regulations, and parking laws. Have students brainstorm a list of other laws or regulations established and enforced by your local government. Discuss why such laws were formulated. How do laws reflect the values or preferences of a community?

USE VISUALS

Explain to students that Figure 18-1 shows how the services of government are distributed among the three basic levels of government. Ask students which level of government is responsible for science and technology programs. (Federal) Answer to caption: Yes, for example, local, state, and federal governments all provide education services.

USE TRANSPARENCIES

Use Teaching Transparency 18-1 and its corresponding strategies and worksheet from the *Teaching Transparency Strategies and Worksheets* booklet to help students identify which levels of government provide which services. Verify student worksheets using the Answer Key.

Learning Activity

Distribute copies of Enrichment Masters 18-1 and 18-2 to provide students with a more detailed picture of the kinds of expenditures states make on services and the sources of state revenue. Have students identify the services on which states spend the most money. Then ask students to calculate what percentage of states' revenues come from various forms of taxes.

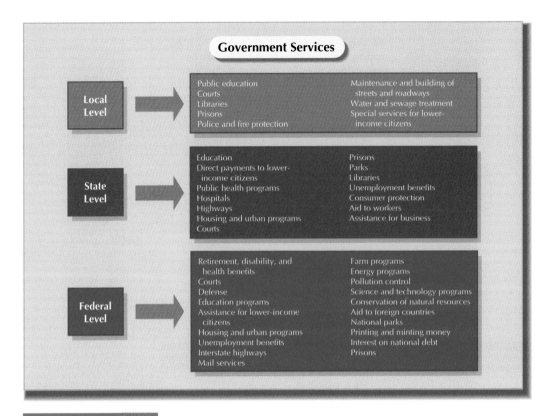

Government Services

Local Level	
Public education	Maintenance and building of
Courts	streets and roadways
Libraries	Water and sewage treatment
Prisons	Special services for lower-
Police and fire protection	income citizens

State Level	
Education	Prisons
Direct payments to lower-	Parks
income citizens	Libraries
Public health programs	Unemployment benefits
Hospitals	Consumer protection
Highways	Aid to workers
Housing and urban programs	Assistance for business
Courts	

Federal Level	
Retirement, disability, and	Farm programs
health benefits	Energy programs
Courts	Pollution control
Defense	Science and technology programs
Education programs	Conservation of natural resources
Assistance for lower-income	Aid to foreign countries
citizens	National parks
Housing and urban programs	Printing and minting money
Unemployment benefits	Interest on national debt
Interstate highways	Prisons
Mail services	

FIGURE 18-1

Local, state, and federal levels provide a variety of goods and services. Do governments at different levels provide some of the same kinds of services?

museums and cultural activities. How a local government spends money depends largely on two things:

- What goods and services the people in the community want.
- How much people are willing to pay for those goods and services.

The State Level

In most states, the greatest chunk of money for services goes for education. This money is used primarily to support state-operated colleges and universities or to provide financial assistance to local school districts. The next largest spending category in most states is direct payments to lower-income citizens and those with disabilities. Figure 18-1 shows some of the other goods and services provided at the state level.

Cooperative Learning   Debate (Pro/Con)

Many states operate lotteries as a means of supplementing tax receipts. The profits from such operations are often spent on education. However, some people object to lotteries as a means of revenue because people who play the lottery are often those who really cannot afford to. Others object on the basis of governmental dependence on gambling. Divide groups of four into pairs and have one pair take the pro position and the other pair the con in regard to state lotteries. Have pairs gather evidence, develop arguments, present arguments, and evaluate the final results.

Refer to the *Cooperative Learning Strategies* booklet for additional cooperative learning strategies.

State governments spend money differently from state to state. The needs of various states and the wishes of their citizens are different. State services are also influenced by the kind of business that generates revenue for the state. In states where the tourist business is important, state government spends much on recreational areas. In states where farming is important, considerable amounts of money may be spent on agricultural services. States, like local communities, provide what the people want most.

The Federal Level

The federal government spends about 48 percent of its budget on transfer payments. A **transfer payment** is money received by people who are not currently producing goods or services to earn it. Transfer payments are made for retirement, disability, health and hospital expenses for senior citizens, unemployment benefits, and assistance to families after the primary wage-earner has died.

The second largest category of government spending is national defense. Currently about 21 percent of the money spent by the federal government goes to some kind of military use. The greatest portion of defense spending goes to operations and maintenance—building ships, airplanes, and tanks, maintaining military bases, and purchasing supplies and equipment. A large share of this money pays the wages of members of the armed services. The remaining money goes to building weapons and conducting research into various new and updated types of systems for our national defense.

The federal government also shares with state and local governments the financing of such services as education, assistance for lower-income citizens, renewal of our cities, and special programs for the unemployed. Much of the money federal, state, and local governments spend goes for social welfare. Figure 18-2 on page 300 compares the expenditures of these levels of government for education, public aid, and other such social welfare areas.

Another large part of the federal budget goes to pay the interest on the national, or public, debt. The **national debt** is the total of all loans made to the federal government by individuals, groups of individuals, businesses, or foreign governments. For instance, if you buy a treasury note or a bond, you are lending money to the federal government. If the government spends less than it brings in, it creates a surplus. However, in recent years the federal government has spent more than it took in.

Business & SOCIAL STUDIES

Recently the United States Park Service embarked on a program to make national parks more accessible to people with disabilities. Each of the more than 360 parks will evaluate how best they can make their facilities accessible to the disabled. Parks such as Shenandoah National Park have been able to add reserve parking for people in wheelchairs. The park has braille booklets and audiocassettes for the self-guided nature trail for the blind. The parks will accomplish these improvements without receiving any specially appropriated government funds.

Learning Activity
Invite students to research how prominent state industries affect state expenditures. For example, in Florida, tourism is important, so the state spends money promoting the tourist industry. Have students describe prominent industries in their home state that affect state expenditures.

TEACHING TIP
To help students consider the cost and efficiency of government services, write the following statement on the board: "Some people say that one problem with government providing goods and services is that there is little or no competition." Have students discuss the statement, considering different government-provided goods and services. Which goods and services could be provided by a private company? Which goods and services probably could not be? Why?

Curriculum Connection   History

In the 1950s, business and industry joined forces in demanding a national highway system. Work on the interstate highway system began in 1956. The 44,000-mile system was 90 percent funded by the federal government and 10 percent funded by state governments. Interstates make it possible for trucks to deliver goods quickly and efficiently; they are also safer than other roads. Opponents of interstates say that such roads have increased air, water, and noise pollution, made the country overly dependent on auto and truck travel, and have scarred the landscape. Discuss these issues with the class.

Building Business Skills

Model

Model how to use the CPI by using it to find the inflation rate for medical care from 1989 to 1990. First, ask students to find on the chart the CPI figure for 1990 (162.8). Then subtract 1989's figure (149.3) from it (162.8 − 149.3 = 13.5). 13.5 is the percentage by which the CPI for medical care increased. To find the *inflation rate* for medical care, divide the CPI increase (13.5) by the previous year's index figure (149.3) and multiply by 100 (13.5 ÷ 149.3 = .09 × 100 = 9%).

USE VISUALS

Explain to students that Figure 18-2 shows how government funds are spent on social welfare. Ask: Which level of government, federal or state and local, spends a larger proportion on health and medical programs? (State and local governments)
Answer to caption: Social insurance; education.

USE TRANSPARENCIES

Use Teaching Transparency 18-2 and its corresponding strategies and worksheet from the *Teaching Transparency Strategies and Worksheets* booklet to illustrate how the federal and state and local governments spend funds. Verify student worksheets using the Answer Key.

MATH

Interpret the Consumer Price Index

Explanation

During inflation, prices for goods and services rise, and dollars buy less than they did before. The government keeps track of inflation by using price indexes to show changes in the costs of goods and services. The most widely known index is the Consumer Price Index (CPI), which shows changes in prices of a "market basket" of 364 consumer goods and services.

Every month, the Bureau of Labor Statistics totals the prices for all the items in the market basket and compares the total to the total for a selected, or base, year, currently 1982. The price total for the base year is given an index value of 100. To compute the CPI for a given period, statisticians divide the price total for the period by the 1982 total and multiply by 100. If the total market basket cost was $1792.00 in 1982 and $2610.94 in October of 1993, the Consumer Price Index for that month was 145.7:

$$\$2610.94 \div \$1792.00 \times 100 = 145.7$$

This means the same goods and sevices cost 45.7% more in October, 1993, than in 1982.

A summary of the monthly CPIs is determined for each year. The complete index is also divided into separate CPIs for different groups of expenditures. The chart shows the CPI for three of these groups for 1984 through 1993.

The inflation rate is the percent change in prices from one year to the next. You can figure out the inflation rate for a group on the chart by dividing its CPI

FIGURE 18-2

Social welfare spending provides financial support for many areas of society. What is the largest social welfare expenditure of the federal government? State and local governments?

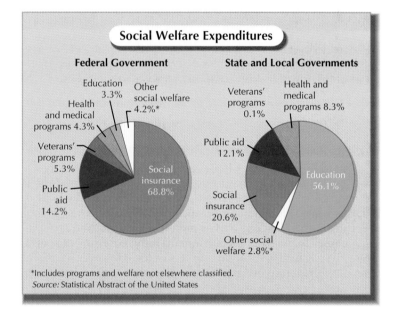

Social Welfare Expenditures

Federal Government
- Education 3.3%
- Health and medical programs 4.3%
- Other social welfare 4.2%*
- Veterans' programs 5.3%
- Public aid 14.2%
- Social insurance 68.8%

State and Local Governments
- Veterans' programs 0.1%
- Health and medical programs 8.3%
- Public aid 12.1%
- Education 56.1%
- Social insurance 20.6%
- Other social welfare 2.8%*

*Includes programs and welfare not elsewhere classified.
Source: Statistical Abstract of the United States

Reteaching Strategy

Ask students to define in their own words the following terms: *country, nation, federal, state, county, city, town, township, village,* and *school district.* Ask students to relate these terms to the three levels of government.

CONSUMER PRICE INDEX

Year	Food	Clothing	Medical Care
1984	103.2	102.1	106.8
1985	105.6	105.0	113.5
1986	109.0	105.9	122.0
1987	113.5	110.6	130.1
1988	118.2	115.4	138.6
1989	125.1	118.6	149.3
1990	132.4	124.1	162.8
1991	136.3	128.7	177.0
1992	137.9	131.9	190.1
1993	140.9	133.7	201.4

increase by the previous price and multiplying by 100. The chart shows that the CPI for food increased 6.9 from 1988 to 1989: 125.1 − 118.2 = 6.9. This means that the inflation rate for food was 5.8%: 6.9 ÷ 118.2 = .058 × 100 = 5.8%.

Practice

Use the explanation of the skill and CPI figures given in the chart to find answers to the following problems.

1. What was the inflation rate for clothing from 1990 to 1991?
2. For which of the three groups did the Consumer Price Index increase the least between 1986 and 1987?
3. For which group has the CPI increased the most over the period from 1984 through 1993? Between what years did it increase the most and what was the rate of inflation?

Learning to use and interpret data from the Consumer Price Index can help people in business determine price trends and understand the economic climate in which they must operate.

Practice

Instruct students to use the chart on page 301 to calculate the answers to the problems.
[1. (128.7 − 124.1) ÷ 124.1 × 100 = 3.7%
2. Food (4.5).
3. Medical care. It increased most between 1990 and 1991 (14.2). The rate of inflation was (177.0 − 162.8) ÷ 162.8 × 100 = 8.7%.)]
For students who need to sharpen their math skills, choose among worksheets in the *Math Skills Review* booklet.

This kind of spending is called **deficit spending.** Figure 18-3 on page 302 shows how the gap between government income and expenses has grown in recent years. Many people are concerned about the debt and want to have a balanced budget. In a **balanced budget,** income and expenses are nearly equal. Since 1985, our presidents and congressional legislators have wrestled with ways to achieve a balanced budget. Nearly all legislators agree that a balanced budget is desirable. However, legislators have not been able to agree on how to achieve that balance—deciding which programs to cut and which expenditures to limit.

Inflation affects government spending. Inflation is a general rise in prices. This means that it costs more now to buy the same goods and services than in the past. The government's cost of providing goods and services is influenced by inflation. As workers' wages and the costs of equipment and supplies increase, the government must pay more to provide the same amount of goods and services.

Learning Activity

In November and December of 1995, the federal government was forced to "shut down" for several weeks because the President and Congress could not agree on what measures should be taken to balance the federal budget. Have students research other previous "shutdowns" and compare those issues with the issues in 1995.

Cooperative Learning   Trade-a-Problem

Ask teams to use the chart above to create an inflation rate problem and a solution. Have each team trade its problem with that of another team. Have teams compare solutions. If solutions agree, teams should exchange problems with another team.

Refer to the *Cooperative Learning Strategies* booklet for additional cooperative learning strategies.

Explain to students that Figure 18-3 shows the gap between the federal government's income and expenses. Ask: What is the term used when the government spends more than it takes in? (Deficit spending.) Answer to caption: 1989: approximately 150 billion; 1993: approximately 250 billion.

Quick Check Answers

1. Money received by people who are not currently producing goods or services; total of all loans made to the federal government by individuals, groups of individuals, businesses, or foreign governments; situation that results when a government spends more than it takes in; situation in which income and expenses of a government are nearly equal.
2. Local, state, and federal governments.
3. Public education.

FIGURE 18-3

The federal government has increased its income in the past 20 years. However, the federal government's expenses have increased faster than its income, leading to deficit spending. How great was the difference between income and expenses in 1989? In 1993?

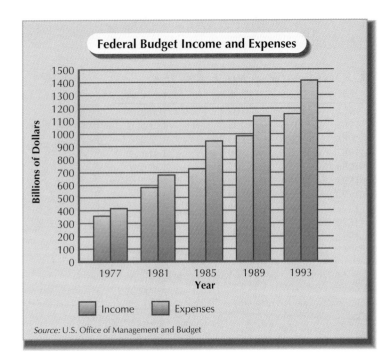

Federal Budget Income and Expenses

Source: U.S. Office of Management and Budget

GLOBAL VIEW

The United States is not the only country to struggle with inflation and enormous federal debt. In the late 1980s, Brazil found itself overwhelmed with debt. Interest payments on Brazil's loans had rocketed $800 million a month and inflation soared to 545%. In order to help Brazil regain economic standing, the international community and Brazil's creditors agreed to forgive much of the debt and restructure the remaining debt. In exchange, Brazil agreed to institute major economic reforms. The debt restructuring was completed in 1994.

Quick Check

1. Define *transfer payment, national debt, deficit spending, balanced budget.*
2. Who provides public goods and services?
3. What does the local level of government spend the highest percentage of its money on?

Cooperative Learning Think-Pair-Share

Ask students why they think mail service is under federal control rather than under the control of individual states. Allow students three minutes to devise an answer. Have each student share his or her answer with another classmate and then have volunteers explain their answers to the class. (Mail must travel between states and all over the country, so central control is more efficient.)

Refer to the *Cooperative Learning Strategies* booklet for additional cooperative learning strategies.

Chapter 18 **Summary**

Main Ideas

1. Most people in a society contribute to paying the cost of public goods and services through taxes.
2. Government provides goods and services that are part of the governing process, that would be unprofitable for business to provide, and that can be provided more conveniently by government than by business.
3. Local governments spend most of their tax money on public education, court systems, libraries, police and fire protection, and streets and highways.
4. State governments spend the largest amount of tax money on education and direct payments to lower-income citizens and those with disabilities.
5. The federal government's largest areas of government spending are for transfer payments and defense.
6. Many people work for governments in a wide variety of jobs.
7. The Consumer Price Index can help businesspeople determine trends and interpret the economic climate.

CASE ANALYSIS — Government Expenditures

Did you buy your lunch in the cafeteria today? Does a grandparent receive benefits from Social Security or Medicare? Have you recently visited a national park or historical monument? These programs and facilities are all examples of government expenditures. What if you wanted to be able to influence how government spends the tax money it collects? What would you do? Here's a list of things you could do to make a difference. Choose the ones that you think are most effective in controlling government spending.

Volunteer in your community.
Organize a neighborhood watch program.
Contribute to charities.
Start a neighborhood garden.
Become an informed voter.
Attend a city council meeting.
Write a letter to the editor.

Write a letter to an elected official.
Work on a political campaign.
Run for local office.
Serve on a school board.
Petition to put an issue on the ballot.

QUICK QUIZ

1. How does the government pay for the goods and services it provides? (By collecting taxes.)
2. What level of government funds elementary and high schools, traffic courts, and fire departments? (Local.)
3. How are governments' costs of providing goods and services influenced by inflation? (Government workers' wages increase and the cost of equipment and supplies increases, which increases the government's cost of providing goods and services.)
4. What is the relationship between income and expenses when a government has a balanced budget? (They are nearly equal.)

Chapter 18 **Review**

CHAPTER 18 REVIEW

APPLY

Answers

Use the Language of Business
1. balanced budget, 2. national debt,
3. deficit spending, 4. public welfare,
5. transfer payments.

Review What You Learned
1. People make their wants known through their elected officials.
2. Individuals and groups pay for all public goods and services through taxes.
3. Government provides certain services that are deemed necessary for the well-being of the nation.
4. Education, aid for lower-income citizens, highways, aid to unemployed people.
5. Public education.
6. Retirement, disability, health and hospital expenses for senior citizens, unemployment benefits, assistance to families after the primary wage-earner has died.
7. Some possibilities: teachers, recreation specialists, police officers, firefighters, court reporters, dispatchers, water plant operators, youth division aides.
8. By subtracting the previous year's CPI from the current year's, dividing the difference by the previous year's CPI, and multiplying by 100.

Understand Business Concepts
1. Private goods and services are paid for by the user. The cost of public goods and services is shared by many, even though those who pay for them do not make equal use of the services.
2. During inflation, prices and wages increase. Since the base for taxation increases, the amount of money collected also increases.
3. Public schools are a public service supported by taxes imposed by government.
4. The cost of providing the services is borne by the tax-paying public.

Use the Language of Business

Understanding these business terms will help you communicate more easily. Fill each blank in the following sentences with the term that best completes the sentence.

balanced budget   public welfare
deficit spending   transfer payments
national debt

1. With a[n] _____, the amount of tax money coming in equals the amount of money going out in spending.
2. The _____ is the total of all loans made to the federal government by individuals or groups of individuals.
3. _____ exists when the government spends more money than it collects in taxes from citizens.
4. The _____ is the well-being of society.
5. _____ are income that people receive from the government without currently producing goods or services to earn it.

Review What You Learned

1. How do people in a democracy make known their social wants so that government can help satisfy them?
2. Why are public goods and services not really free—or even inexpensive?
3. Why does government—not business—provide certain services?
4. Give two examples of public services for which financial support is shared by two or three levels of government.
5. For what purpose does local government spend the most money?
6. A lot of federal money goes for transfer payments. What is included in that category?
7. Give several examples of careers in government.
8. How can you find the inflation rate by using the CPI?

Understand Business Concepts

1. How is paying for private goods and services different from paying for public goods and services?
2. Explain how inflation raises taxes without a change in the tax rate.
3. Why are most elementary and secondary schools referred to as "public schools"?
4. Some people say that public libraries are actually not free to people within a community even though the libraries do not charge fees for each borrowed book. How can this be true?
5. Local, state, and federal governments play an important role in providing public education in this country. Education *could* be provided entirely by business instead. Why do you believe that the people of the United States want government to have this responsibility?
6. A person might say some of the goods and services provided by the government are paid for through loans to the government, not through taxes. What do you think that statement means?
7. What do you think might be some advantages and disadvantages of working in a government job?
8. How do businesses use the data in the Consumer Price Index?

5. Government assumes this responsibility so that education, paid for through taxes, is accessible to all people. Most people believe that no one should be prevented from getting an education because of lack of money.
6. The public debt is actually loans of money to the government. This debt goes toward paying for various goods and services provided by the government.
7. Students' responses will vary but should reflect thoughtful assessment of jobs they know something about.
8. The CPI can help businesses determine price trends.

Think Critically
1. Answers will vary but might include people without children who do not directly use schools. Not everyone uses the services of the fire and police department, and not everyone uses the parks that they help support.
2. Answers will vary depending on students' opinions about the government's production of goods and services. However, students should support their opinions.

Chapter 18 **Review**

Think Critically

1. **Assess.** Think about the people in your community. Make a list of those you know who help to pay the cost of public goods and services but do not directly use them.

2. **Evaluate.** Do you feel that any of the goods and services produced by the government could be produced more efficiently by businesses? Explain your answer.

Use What You Learned

1. **Group Project.** Work in four teams, with each team researching one of the following transfer payment programs: Social Security, Medicare and Medicaid, unemployment compensation, and Aid to Families with Dependent Children. Work together to find the answers to questions such as:

   • Who is eligible for the program? How do benefits reach eligible individuals?
   • How is the program funded? What cost, if any, is there to the individual?
   • What is the annual cost of the program? What concerns, if any, are there about the program and its ability to pay benefits?

   Each team should present a three-minute news report to the class.

2. List at least five services in your community that are provided by both government and business—for example, public and private schools or summer recreation programs. For each service, identify the advantages and disadvantages associated with the government-provided service and with the business-provided service. Do you think the competition between government and business is good? Why or why not? Present

your information in a chart and your analysis in a paragraph of 100 words.

3. Suppose as you look for a summer activity you find the following tennis programs. Lessons at the city's courts cost $50, lessons at the local YMCA are $60, and lessons at Valley Hill, a private club, are $150. Each program has the same number of lessons and the same court times. Tell why the programs differ in price, which programs are likely to be available to more people, and which programs might have more individualized instruction. Write your report as if you were going to present it as part of an evening TV news report on consumerism.

4. **Computer Application.** Use charting software to convert the data in the bar graph in Figure 18-3 on page 302 to a line graph. Use the same title and labels. Print out your completed graph.

5. **Skill Reinforcement.** For 1984 the Consumer Price Index for fuel oil was 98.5; for 1993 it was 87.2. What can you conclude happened to oil prices over this period? How do the price trends reflected by the CPIs of the three groups shown on page 301 differ from that of fuel oil? Does the change in the CPI for fuel oil reflect inflation? Explain your answer.

Save your work in your Business Portfolio.

Use What You Learned
1. Make sure all students participate in the group project. Rubric: Oral Presentation.
2. Provide a local telephone directory to help students identify government and private services. Rubrics: Charts and Tables; Paragraph.
3. Point out that different people have distinct concerns when looking for a place to take tennis lessons and that this should be reflected in students' reports. Rubric: Script.
4. Students who do not have access to a computer may make their line graphs by hand. Rubric: Graph.
5. Oil prices dropped between 1984 and 1993. Food, clothing, and medical care rose in price while oil declined. The oil CPI's do not reflect inflation, because inflation is a *rise* in prices for a period, not a decline. Possible Rubric: Paragraph.

Independent Practice
Use the Chapter 18 worksheets in *Student Activity Guide 1* for additional practice and application activities. *Student Activity Guide 1* provides vocabulary exercises, reading comprehension checks, problems, projects, and simulations of business and economic situations. A Teacher's Annotated Edition provides answers.

ASSESS

Portfolio Assessment
The portfolio projects are designed to lead students to develop a collection of their best work to submit to you for assessment. You and your students should decide which projects will be included in their respective Business Portfolios. Refer students to the specific rubric(s) from the *Alternative Assessment Strategies* booklet listed with each of the project notes below. These rubrics will alert students to the criteria you will use to assess their projects.

Chapter Assessment
Use the Chapter 18 Test from the *Test Masters* booklet to evaluate students' understanding of the chapter concepts. An answer key is provided. Or create your own customized test using the *Testmaker* software.

Business Issue

Business Issue

USER FEES

Highlight the Issue

Before students start reading pages 306–307, ask: What do you think would be the effect of charging a user fee for access to a local beach? For videos from a public library? For checking out books from a public library? After students have read the pages, ask if there are some categories of services that students would be more willing to pay a fee for than others. Have students explain their answers.

USER FEES

More and more public institutions, such as parks and libraries, are asking people to pay for some of the facilities and services they use, such as hiking trails or videotape rentals. Should people have to pay user fees at publicly-funded parks and libraries?

Pro

In many cases, federal, state, and local funding for parks and libraries has been cut. At the same time, costs to run parks and libraries have gone up. In order to continue to remain open and offer people the services they want, these financially strapped institutions have to look elsewhere for money. Why *not* ask people who use parks and libraries to pay for them?

In general, parks and libraries only charge for the use of special facilities or services, such as hiking trails or video rentals. Such fees do not limit basic access. Libraries and parks serve a variety of users, and some users want extra services that they are willing to pay for. For example, although most libraries don't charge patrons for basic services such as borrowing books, many libraries now offer video rentals as a special service for which they charge a fee.

User fees can generate needed revenue to keep libraries and parks open. A Baltimore library began charging for video rentals and was able to pay for all new video purchases and even chip in $350,000 annually to the library's overall budget. In Texas, people who want to enjoy wilderness areas must now purchase a "Passport to Wildlife" to do so. In 1993, the program raised $2.5 million for conservation.

In addition, user fees can help conserve resources by limiting demand for them. By charging for computer printouts, libraries reduce paper waste. By charging for trail access, parks help protect the environment from overuse.

Pay for use is also a fairer way of funding public agencies. Only those who use certain services have to pay for them. People who don't use those services don't pay. In fact, if libraries and parks charged enough in fees, they could pay for themselves, and taxes could be cut—putting more money back into citizens' pockets.

Extend the Issue

Have groups of students investigate user fees in your own community and state. Suggest that groups focus on public libraries, public pools, and city or state recreational areas and parks. Have groups find out if user fees are applied to all services, if they are applied on an annual or per-use basis, and whether the user fees are intended to cover basic operating costs or whether they are meant to provide funds for additional purchases or services. Have each group evaluate the information and present it to the class along with analysis of whether the user fees are fair.

Con

It's unfair and undemocratic for libraries and parks to charge people for services. Charging fees for services discriminates against people who can't afford to pay them. Such discrimination runs counter to the mission of publicly supported institutions: free service to the public. In fact, the Connecticut state attorney general ruled that it was illegal for a library to charge people to reserve books because such fees unfairly limited access to the library's resources.

Furthermore, who will decide which services are basic and which services are special? For instance, if a library decides that access to computer-based information is a special service for which people must pay, then it is limiting access to an important source of information that many people would consider "basic." If libraries can charge for certain services, one day they may charge admission.

Libraries and parks are publicly funded, paid for by our taxes. When users are charged fees, they are essentially paying twice. In 1993, Los Angeles County began charging hikers, bikers, and horse riders a $23 annual fee for the use of public trails and bicycle paths. A family of four would have to pay $92 a year, even if they only used the trails once. Many families could not afford this fee and would be unable to use the public parks that their taxes had already helped pay for.

Finally, who will decide which public services charge user fees and which don't? Like libraries and parks, police and fire departments are public services. If the government expects parks and libraries to charge fees to cover operating costs, perhaps police officers and fire fighters will soon have to bill the people they help for their services!

User fees are not the answer to underfunded public services. If a park or library has a budget shortfall, its leaders need to use our democratic system and convince voters and legislators to provide more funding.

Update the Issue

Have students find out the impact local, state, and federal funding for public services has had on user fees. Some questions students could consider include: Have budget cuts resulted in an increase in user fees? Are user fees limited to "special" services or are they being charged for basic services as well? How have user fees affected the use parks, trails, and libraries get? Have students present a summary of their findings to the class.

Unit 6   Financial Institutions and the Global Economy

Chapter	Learning Objectives
19 **Money and Banking** pp. 310–329	• Describe the functions and characteristics of money. • Explain the three main functions of banks. • Name three types of banks. • Identify at least one way in which the government regulates the banking industry. • Explain how banks use computer networks. • Compute simple interest.
20 **The Federal Reserve System and Monetary Policy** pp. 330–343	• Describe the responsibilities of the Federal Reserve System. • Explain how banks use magnetic ink character recognition and electronic funds transfers. • Identify three kinds of discounts used by manufacturers and wholesalers.

Business Issue: Redlining, pp. 344–345

National Standards for Business Education*	Chapter Highlights			
	Focus on Features	Building Business Skills	Visual Learning	Case Analysis
COMP: IV F; EPF: VI, X; IS: V	Technology: Computer Networks, p. 314	Math: Understanding Interest, p. 318	How Banks Do Business, p. 317 How Banks Create Money, p. 321 Commercial Bank Loans, p. 322	Economics, p. 327
EPF: IV, V, VI, XII; EE: III E; IS: VII, VIII; MGMT: IX A	Technology: Magnetic Ink Character Recognition, p. 334	Math: Understanding Discounts, p. 338	Balancing Monetary Policies, p. 333 The Federal Reserve System, p. 334 Open Market Operations, p. 337	Power of the Fed, p. 341

* Level 3 Performance Expectations: Computation (COMP), Economics and Personal Finance (EPF); Entrepreneurship Education (EE), IS (Information Systems), Management (MGMT). See page T14 for all 12 content areas.

Unit 6

Look Back
Remind students that our government has established laws so that business activities can proceed with harmony, stability, predictability, and fairness. Corporations pay taxes on their profits. State governments may also levy taxes on the goods and services businesses sell. The major purpose of taxes is to pay for government services. All levels of government use revenue from taxes to buy goods and services from private businesses.

UNIT 6 COOPERATIVE LEARNING PROJECT

Planning a Lesson Activity
Preparation: Provide art supplies (poster board, markers, colored pencils) and photocopies of BLMs 13 and 14 from the *Cooperative Learning Strategies* booklet for each group. Schedule a time for students to teach their lessons to a 6th- or 7th-grade class. This project will take approximately three to four class periods.
Guidelines: Assign each group a topic from Unit 6 to teach to a 6th- or 7th-grade class. For instance, one group may focus on the functions of money,

Financial Institutions in the Global Economy

T his unit discusses the role of money, banking, and the Federal Reserve System in the economy. The first chapter describes the services that banks provide and the concept of money. The second chapter discusses ways that the Federal Reserve controls the money supply and the Fed's other tasks, such as regulating banks.

Look Ahead

Explain that money and banking are vital parts of our economy. Banks accept money in the form of deposits and then create money by extending loans to individuals and businesses. The Federal Reserve System (the Fed) is a central system of banks that provides services to other banks. The Fed's responsibilities include controlling the supply of money that circulates in our economy and regulating banks and other financial institutions.

309

another on the organization of the Fed. Groups can use material from the text-book as well as information they find through research. Suggest to groups that they use BLMs 13 and 14 to help them organize their information and structure their lessons.

Alternative: Assign groups topics from Unit 6 and have them make their presentations to other classmates instead of a younger group.

FOCUS

Introduce the Chapter

Major Concepts
- Money
- Banks
- Banking Functions
- Types of Banks
- Regulating the Banking Industry

Introduce the Topic
Students are likely to take for granted the concept of money, the foundations of paper money in the United States, and the amount of money in circulation. Point out to students that money and the banking industry play a central role in the growth of the United States and the U.S. economy. Tell students that Chapter 19 describes the functions and characteristics of money and modern banking services.

Use Business Terms
Ask students to write a sentence with each of the Business Terms. Have students exchange papers with a partner. Call for agreement/disagreement as to use of the terms and an explanation of that position. Advise students to note the meanings of the terms as they read the chapter.

USE VISUALS
Use the chapter-opening photograph to begin a discussion of why people use banking services.

CHAPTER 19

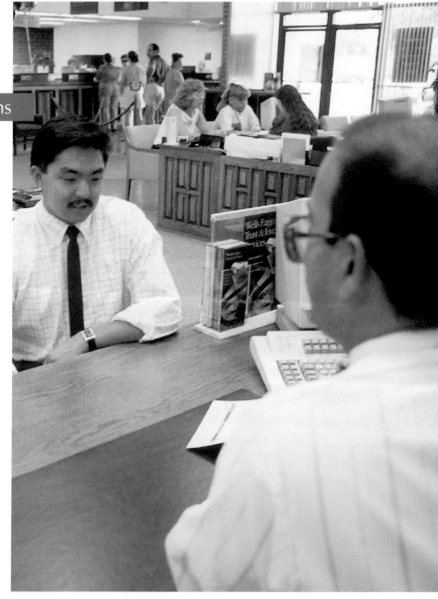

Business terms

money

barter

currency

checkbook dollars

deposit

demand deposit

time deposit

withdrawal

interest

mortgage

line of credit

310

CHAPTER 19 RESOURCES

Instructional Resources

Lesson Plan for Chapter 19

Teaching Transparencies 19-1, 19-2, 19-3

Strategies and Worksheets for Teaching Transparencies 19-1, 19-2, 19-3

Enrichment Master 19-1

Student Activity Guide 1–TAE for Chapter 19

Test Master for Chapter 19

Alternative Assessment Strategies

Math Skills Review

International Business Strategies

Cooperative Learning Strategies

Communication Skills Review

Ethics in Business Strategies

Money and Banking

Learning objectives

After completing this chapter, you will be able to:
- Describe the functions and characteristics of money.
- Explain the three main functions of banks.
- Name three types of banks.
- Identify at least one way in which the government regulates the banking industry.
- Explain how banks use computer networks.
- Compute simple interest.

Consider what you know

- Our government has established laws that affect business so that business can proceed with harmony, stability, predictability, and fairness. In our free enterprise society, government may regulate business or use laws to protect business. Overall, our laws work to promote a positive environment for businesses.

Consider what you want to know

- What is money and what part does it play in our economy?
- What functions do banks fulfill in our economy?
- How is a national bank different from a savings and loan?
- What is the FDIC and how does it affect consumers?
- How are computer networks useful to banks?
- How is simple interest different from compound interest?

Consider how to use what you learn

- As you read this chapter, think about what banking institutions do that affects the everyday life of people.

Multimedia Resources

Technology Resource Guide

Distance Learning Guide

Internet Resource Guide

Professional Resources

School-to-Work/Tech Prep Strategies

Instructional Poster

Spanish Resources

Testmaker Software for Chapter 19

The Wall Street Journal Video Series
   Video & Activities for Chapter 19

Business and Marketing Computer
   Applications—An Integrated Software
   Simulation Using Microsoft Works

Stocktracker—A Stock Market Software
   Simulation

Where's the Dough? Board Game

Motivate the Learning

Learning Objectives
Point out to students that the learning objectives show what they will learn in the chapter. Tell students to keep these objectives in mind as they work through the chapter. Note that the last two objectives listed refer to the Focus on Technology feature and the Building Business Skills feature.

Consider What You Know
Review briefly the main sections of *Chapter 18 Government Spending and the Economy:* Government As a Provider, and Spending at Different Levels of Government.

Consider What You Want to Know
Have students keep the listed questions in mind as they preview the chapter by quickly paging through it, looking at the pictures and reading the section headings and figure titles.

Consider How to Use What You Learn
Explain to students that at the end of the chapter they will be developing some projects concerning the roles both money and banking play in the economy. Suggest that as students read this chapter they take note of the far-reaching influences money and banking exert on business.

TEACH

Develop Concepts

Money

Write the word *money* on the board or a transparency. Ask students to list various definitions of the word. Have students compare their definitions of money with the definition in the text (medium of exchange, standard of value, and store of value). Help them grasp the concept that money is central to an economic system.

Learning Activity

Barter, the exchange of goods and services for other goods and services, exists even in societies where money is used. More than 300 barter exchanges operate worldwide. These exchanges consist of people who barter services or goods that they believe others may want. Members of the exchanges receive trade credits for the value of the items or services they offer. Have students discuss what kinds of things they might include if they were to set up a barter exchange in the classroom.

Although there are places in the world where money and banks play only a small role in the local economy, it is hard for us to imagine life without them. Money enables people and businesses to buy and sell goods and services around the world with easy efficiency. Banks and the banking system play an extremely important role in managing money and controlling and stimulating the economy. In this chapter, we will examine money—its functions and characteristics—and the banking system that helps us manage it.

MONEY

As you already know, money is a convenient item to have. Money can be used as a means of payment for the goods and services people want to buy and sell. To modern Americans, money means paper bills, metal coins, and checks. In other times and places, people have used shells, cows, corn, red parrot feathers, and even gopher tails for money.

Functions of Money

In order for something to be considered money, it must fulfill three functions. **Money** must serve as a medium of exchange, act as a standard of value, and be a store of value. As money performs these functions, it helps today's global economies work smoothly.

Medium of Exchange People use money as a *medium of exchange*, which means that buyers and sellers use money as a means of payment for goods and services. Whether we buy a cola or sell a corporation, money changes hands. Money is the medium, or go-between, that facilitates each exchange. Without money, people would be forced to **barter**—trade goods or services directly for other goods or services. Barter is a clumsy method of exchange. Suppose you've grown an extra bushel of tomatoes. You'd like to use the tomatoes to get new CDs. In a barter economy, you would have to find someone willing to accept your tomatoes for the CDs. If you have particular CDs in mind, you might have to make several trades to acquire something the CD owner would accept. You could spend a lot of time bartering for things you need. With money, however, the exchange becomes easy—you sell your extra tomatoes for money. You then exchange that money for the CDs you want. In

Business & SOCIAL STUDIES

Early peoples in the Americas used a variety of items as money before the Europeans arrived. In much of Central America, cocoa beans served as money. Along the Atlantic and Pacific coasts, beads made from shells were the medium of exchange. *Wampum,* which was strings of tube-shaped shells, was used along the Northeast and Middle Atlantic coasts of North America.

Cooperative Learning Numbered Heads Together

Remind students of the characteristics of a market economy (free to produce any goods or services, free to sell those goods and services at a profit, and free to leave or enter the market as desired). Have students form small discussion groups. Ask them to discuss how the use of money fits into these characteristics. Then ask what characteristics of a market economy would be difficult to achieve in a barter situation (freedom to produce goods and services, freedom to enter or leave the market). Have a representative from each team report his or her team's responses to the class.

a system that uses money, both buyers and sellers agree on exchanging money.

Standard of Value Money also serves as a vehicle for placing value on goods and services. Money thus functions as a *standard of value*. It helps us compare the value of different goods and services. In this country, we measure economic value in terms of our basic unit of money, the dollar. We can quickly figure the relative values of two items by comparing the dollar value of each. We can easily see that $100 worth of CDs costs twice as much as a $50 jacket. Imagine trying to compare CDs worth a bushel of tomatoes with a jacket selling for one tire! People need one standard by which to value goods and services to make exchanges. Money provides that function. Recording and calculating expenses, debts, profits, and losses is simplified when we use standard units of money. Other countries have different basic units of money, of course, but each item used as money still serves as a standard for valuing goods and services in that country.

Store of Value Money has the ability, called *store of value*, to hold its value over time—it doesn't spoil, rot, or disintegrate. If you don't spend all your pay or allowance this month, you can save it to use later. That saved money will have value six months or a year from now. Then you can spend it on those CDs you want. Try that with your extra bushel of tomatoes!

How does money function as a standard of value when purchasing goods and services?

Business Brief

In early Egypt barley was an important source of food. Barley had value and was accepted as payment in exchange for goods and services. By 700 B.C. the Egyptians abandoned barley and adopted gold as their primary instrument of exchange.

Learning Activity
Have students identify a number of items they have recently traded or bartered for other goods or services. Prime their responses by asking if any have traded shirts, hats, CDs, or tapes. List their responses on the board or a transparency. Ask volunteers to detail how each of the items listed does or does not fulfill the three functions of money.

USE VISUALS
Encourage students to describe how the transaction depicted in the photograph would be different if money did not function as a medium of exchange. (The customer would be unsure what to offer in exchange for the merchandise; the clerk would have to decide what to accept in exchange for the merchandise.) Answer to caption: It is used to compare the value of the various goods in the store.

Curriculum Connection   Geography

The triangular trade routes between Africa, the West Indies, and the North American colonies were traveled by ships carrying molasses, enslaved Africans, rum, and Spanish *pesos*. Pesos were often called *dollars* (Spanish *dolár*) by the colonists because they resembled the Austrian *taler*. Eventually the *dollar* became the name of the monetary unit of the United States. Display a world map and ask students to indicate the route of the triangular trade.

FOCUS ON **Technology**

FOCUS ON **Technology**

Discuss

Have students scan the feature and then write a question that requires one of the following terms as an answer—*computer network, file server, nodes, network protocol, local area network,* and *wide area network.* Ask volunteers to share their questions with the class, calling on other volunteers to supply the answers. Ask students familiar with one or more of these terms to describe the situations in which the terms apply.

Computer Networks

The cashier from Uncle Dan's Surplus deposits the morning's cash receipts at the drive-up teller of Allied Bank. At about the same time, Uncle Dan himself is across the street at the walk-up bank—withdrawing funds to make a down payment on a new truck. Within seconds each transaction is recorded in the main bank's computer. How did the information about each transaction travel between the computers at the different locations?

Chances are the bank is using a computer network. A *computer network* is a collection of terminals, computers, printers, and other equipment that uses electronic communications channels to communicate and to share programs, data, and peripheral equipment.

A network allows valuable programs to reside in a shared storage device while allowing several computers and terminals to have access to the same program at the same time. Data can also be accessed and updated from several locations. The shared disk storage device in a network is often called a *file server.* Often, this unit is dedicated to handling the communications needs of the other devices in the network. A centralized location ensures that each device in the network has access to the same current information.

Individual devices—for example, computers, terminals, or printers—on the network are often called *nodes.* Each node in the network needs hardware to transmit and receive data. Each node also needs software capable of translating that data. The network software and the hardware installed in each node follow some standard for communications, called *network protocol.* For

Business Brief

The first coins were minted nearly 2600 years ago when King Croessus of Lydia (now western Turkey) gained control of Asia's richest gold mines. The coins carried the image of a lion and a bull. Coins soon surpassed raw gold in popularity because coins were of a standard value and weight. By the 1500s, commerce expanded and people found that transporting coins over great distances was difficult and dangerous. People deposited their gold at a local goldsmith who issued a receipt in return. Eventually the receipts began to circulate as money because they could be redeemed for the gold itself.

Characteristics of Money

In practically all of the world today, paper money and coins are common forms of money. For money to carry out its functions, it must have several characteristics. No matter what form it takes, all money shares these characteristics.

Money must be *stable in value.* To be used as money, an item must be *scarce.* If the supply of an item is overly plentiful, it loses its value and cannot very well serve as money or a store of value since it would have little worth. People would lose faith in its value as a medium of exchange. Dollars are accepted as money in our society because they are scarce, and they have value.

In addition to being stable in value, money must also be *accepted.* People have to be willing to take it in exchange for goods and services. Before accepting it, they must have faith that the item used as money has value and will continue to hold its value. If they don't have faith in the value of their money, they may try something else like gold or diamonds. To be valuable, money has to be accepted.

314 UNIT 6 FINANCIAL INSTITUTIONS IN THE GLOBAL ECONOMY

TEACHING TIP

Ask students to make up a mnemonic device to help themselves remember the five characteristics of money.

Curriculum Connection   History

Encourage students to study the history of money in the United States during various stages of the country's growth. Organize students into groups and have each group choose a period of U.S. history: the country under the Articles of Confederation, the post-Civil War period, the 1970s, and so on. Groups can assemble pictures or create drawings to illustrate important stages in the development of the monetary standard during their assigned time period. Have groups display their work in chronological order around the classroom.

devices in the network to communicate, they have to follow the same rules or protocol.

Networks are classified as local or wide area. In a *local area network* (LAN) the devices are often physically connected to one another by wire, fiber optic cable, perhaps leased telephone wire, and occasionally microwaves. LANs are generally privately owned and function within a limited geographic area.

A *wide area network* (WAN) covers a wide geographic area and is likely to include communication channels such as phone lines, microwaves, satellites, or a combination of channels.

In the example, Allied Bank probably has a LAN. The drive-up and walk-up facilities include terminals and computers which share printers for issuing receipts for deposits and withdrawals. The network file server is located at the main bank and contains all the bank's customer account information.

Shared printer

Shared printer

Shared file server

Workstation

ared le ver

Workstation

Linear Network

Hub or Star Network

Money should be *divisible* into parts. Suppose you have $20.00 but spend only $4.50. Because money is divisible you can collect $15.50 in return. A money system using coins and bills of different values makes this possible.

Finally, money has to be *portable* and *durable*. A bushel of tomatoes does not make good money because it is not very portable; nor is it durable. An iron bar is pretty durable, but it is certainly not very portable. Coins and paper money serve well enough. They are portable and long-lasting or can be easily replaced.

Kinds of Money

Throughout history, precious metals like gold and silver have been used as money because they have the characteristics money must have. Only recently has paper money replaced gold and silver. Gold and silver, as well as pigs, tomatoes, and diamonds, are considered commodity money. Commodity money has value in itself apart from its use as money. Diamonds, gold, and silver can be made into beautiful jewelry; pigs and tomatoes are used as nourishing food.

Ask a volunteer to write a single term or concept relating to computer networks on the board or on a transparency. Ask another volunteer to add a term or concept to form the beginning of a word web or diagram that represents a computer network. Continue calling on volunteers until the class is satisfied with the diagram. Suggest that students may want to copy the diagram to use as a study aid.

For additional information about current technology, refer to the *Technology Resources Guide.*

Learning Activity
Call on students to name objects that might be used as money today if there were no dollar bills or coins. List 10 responses on the board or on a transparency. Ask the class to select the object that would best serve as money based on their analysis of how well the characteristics of money apply to the object.

Business Brief
The silver mined in South America in the 1500s and 1600s led to massive inflation in Spain after the silver was shipped there. The oversupply of money caused prices to go up and the value of money to fall.

Global Perspective

Nations often use images on their money that reflect their cultural or political interests. For example, money from Islamic countries is not likely to contain images of people because Islam forbids the use of human figures in art or in decoration. With the disintegration of the Soviet Union, churches, saints, poets, and scholars replaced the face of Lenin on the money of the newly formed republics. Refer students to the opening photo for Chapter 23 on page 382 for examples of international currencies. Students can use Enrichment Master 19-1 to become familiar with the names of several kinds of foreign currency.

Business Brief

Metallic content of U.S. coins.

penny	97.5% zinc 2.5% nickel
nickel	75% copper 25% nickel
dime	91.7% copper 8.3% nickel
quarter	91.7% copper 8.3% nickel

Quick Check Answers

1. Serve as a medium of exchange, act as a standard measure of value, and be a store of value over time.
2. Stable in value, a medium of exchange, portable, and divisible into parts.
3. Anything that serves as a medium of exchange, acts as a standard of value, and is a store of value; to trade goods or services directly for other goods or services; the paper money and coins provided by a government.
4. Checkbook dollars.

Develop Concepts

Banks

Point out to students that banks are businesses that provide a safe place for people to deposit their money and lend funds to individuals and businesses temporarily in need of cash. In effect, the banking business brings savers and borrowers together. Banks' profits come from investing depositors' funds, collecting interest on loans and credit cards, and collecting fees for services.

Earlier in our history, the metal content of coins was worth the monetary denomination stamped on it. For example, a nickel contained five cents worth of precious metal. Later on, the United States government and private banks issued paper certificates as money. These certificates were backed by gold or silver on demand. This means that people could exchange their $10 certificate for $10 worth of gold or silver.

Currency is the paper money and coins provided by a government. Most of the currency in circulation throughout the world today does not have the backing of precious metals or other commodities. The money has very little worth in itself. The government has legally ordered that the coins and paper bills that it issues must be accepted as payment of debt. Citizens accept that ruling if they have faith in the government and the economy of the country.

The most common form of money is checkbook dollars. Currency makes up only about 20 to 25 percent of the total money supply in the United States. The remaining 75 to 80 percent is made up of **checkbook dollars** which is the money that people have in their checking accounts. So checking accounts are a major source of money, with bills and coins playing a lesser part. Individuals, families, businesses, and even governmental departments and agencies use checks to pay most of their larger bills. In practice, they do not draw out cash to pay bills. Rather, they write checks for the particular amount of the bill.

The U.S. mint regularly issues new currency and collects and destroys old and worn currency. Even so, there is an estimated $260 trillion worth of currency in circulation. That's over $1000 for each American. However, the government can only account for about $260 per person. Officials believe that the remaining $196 billion dollars is held by people in other countries.

Quick Check

1. What are the three functions of money?
2. Name at least four characteristics of money.
3. Define *money, barter,* and *currency.*
4. What is the most common form of money in the United States?

BANKS

Banks are businesses that sell a variety of services, all of which involve managing money and stimulating the economy. Figure 19-1 on page 317 illustrates some of their primary services—accepting deposits and loaning out part of them to individuals and businesses. Today, most financial transactions—individual and business, national and global—are carried out through the services of banks. As a nation, we rely on the services of banks for millions of business transactions every day. Without

Curriculum Connection   Math

Have students assume that they live in a country where paper money and all forms of checks or other written receipts for money are forbidden. Have them compute the total weight of the silver dollars they would have to carry to purchase the following: television set, round trip plane ticket to Tokyo, new sports car. (The weight of one silver dollar is 0.94 ounces.)

For students who need to sharpen their math skills, choose among the worksheets in the *Math Skills Review* booklet.

How Banks Do Business

Deposits → Bank → Required reserves

Loans

Income → Interest and withdrawals → Profit

Income → Salaries, equipment, other costs

FIGURE 19-1

Banks are businesses that provide financial services to make a profit. What would happen to a bank's profits if deposits suddenly decreased?

banks, buying and selling goods and services within our own economy as well as in the rest of the world would be very difficult.

Bank managers must consider the needs and wants of four different groups of people as they weigh any management decisions affecting their business.

- Banks are businesses. Like other businesses, they try to make a profit on their activities. A bank manager must work to satisfy the bank owners or shareholders.
- Bank depositors want to earn as high an interest return as possible on their deposits.
- Borrowers want banks to provide reliable loans at as low an interest rate as possible.
- Citizens want the local community to grow. Banks help businesses grow and prosper by helping business finance production of goods and services.

The challenge for bank managers is that the needs of these groups can be in conflict. For example, in order to offer shareholders a greater profit, a bank may need to charge borrowers a higher interest rate or pay depositors a lower rate. If the rate of interest is too high, businesses will be reluctant to obtain loans, which could limit their growth. Successful bank managers must find the best middle ground for their decisions.

Quick Check

1. How is a bank like any other business?
2. What four interests must a bank manager satisfy?

CHAPTER 19   MONEY AND BANKING   **317**

USE VISUALS

Ask a volunteer to explain in his or her own words what the diagram in Figure 19-1 depicts. Impress upon students that banks, like other businesses, must make a profit to continue to exist. Answer to caption: Profits would decrease.

USE TRANSPARENCIES

Use Teaching Transparency 19-1 and its corresponding strategies and worksheet from the *Teaching Transparency Strategies and Worksheets* booklet. Verify student worksheets using the Answer Key.

Quick Check Answers

1. It tries to make a profit on its activities.
2. Bank owners or shareholders; depositors; borrowers; citizens in a community.

Building Business Skills

Model

Remind students that to compute interest, they need to change the percent to a decimal. Be sure students correctly convert percents such as 3.5 percent (0.035) and 4¼ percent (0.0425) to decimals. Point out that the method to compute simple and compound interest is essentially the same: Interest = principal × rate × time. In simple interest, the principal stays the same. In compound interest, the principal is increased by the amount of interest due at the end of a specified time period.

Develop Concepts

Banking Functions

List the following chart headings on the board or on a transparency: "Accept Money," "Transfer Money," and "Create Money." Have students generate a list of services they know banks offer. A selection of bank advertisements will help prime student responses. Ask students to classify each of the services they name by writing it in the appropriate section of the chart. Keep the chart accessible as students work through this section of the chapter, allowing them to enhance or revise the chart as needed.

MATH
Understanding Interest

Explanation

If you borrow money, the lender charges a fee. If you deposit money in a bank or other institution, you give someone else the privilege of using your money. Often, the institution pays a fee for the use of your money. In each case, the fee is called *interest*. The rate of interest is expressed as a percent.

There are two types of interest—simple and compound. Simple interest, computed annually, is a percentage of the amount borrowed. The rate of simple interest is sometimes called the Annual Percentage Rate or APR. Compound interest may be computed yearly, monthly—or even daily. The amount of interest due each year, month, or day is computed by using the principal plus interest of the previous time period.

Practice

Read the directions for figuring simple and compound interest. Then answer the following questions on a separate sheet of paper.

1. When you borrow money, would you prefer simple or compound interest?
2. When you lend money, would you prefer simple or compound interest?
3. Find the simple interest on a $2000 loan at 12% interest for 5 years.

BANKING FUNCTIONS

Today's banks are very competitive and offer a range of products and services. However, all banks perform three basic functions. They accept money, transfer money, and create money.

Accept Money

One of the primary functions banks perform is accepting money in the form of **deposits,** or sums of money placed in accounts. The bank holds this money until the depositor needs it. Customers can make two types of deposits. A deposit into a checking account is called a **demand deposit,** because depositors can take the money out of the account any time they wish, on demand. Money in a checking account is like cash. As explained previously, checkbook dollars are the most common form of money in our country. Instead of paying for supplies, salaries, or rent in cash, businesses write a check. When the supplier, employee, or landlord cashes the check, the bank pays

318 UNIT 6 FINANCIAL INSTITUTIONS IN THE GLOBAL ECONOMY

Meeting Student Diversity

Help students understand that diagrams can almost always assist in clarifying information presented in a text. Ask several volunteers to draw on the board or on a transparency a diagram, such as a word web, that indicates the relationship between deposits, demand deposits, checking accounts, time deposits, certificates of deposit, and savings accounts. Then have students discuss the diagrams, indicating ways in which the diagram might be revised to be more helpful. Once students are satisfied with the diagrams, suggest they copy the one that seems most useful to them and use it as a study aid.

HOW TO COMPUTE INTEREST

Simple Interest

Suppose you borrow $1000 for 3 years at a rate of 10% per year. You can find out how much interest you'll pay by multiplying the principal—the amount you borrowed—by the interest rate by the time—length of time it's borrowed. You will need to convert the percent to its decimal equivalent. Use this formula:

Interest = principal × interest rate × time

Principal	x	Decimal Interest Rate	x	Time	=	Interest
$1000	x	0.10	x	3	=	$300

In this example, the simple interest for three years is $300. At the end of three years the cost of the loan would be $300 and you would have paid the lender $1300.

Compound Interest

Suppose you borrow $1000 for 3 years from a lender who charges 10% per year, compounded annually. You already know how to find the amount of interest due the first year: Interest = principal × interest rate × time

	Total Used for Computing Interest	x	Decimal Interest Rate	x	Time	=	Interest	Interest + Principal
1st year	$1000	x	0.10	x	1	=	$100	$1000+$100=$1100
2nd year	$1100	x	0.10	x	2	=	$110	$1100+$110=$1210
3rd year	$1210	x	0.10	x	3	=	$121	$1210+$121=$1331

In this example, the total compounded interest for three years is $331. At the end of three years the cost of the loan would be $331 and you would have paid the lender $1331.

Practice
Have students exchange their responses to the questions in Building Business Skills, allowing them to check one another's arithmetic. Poll the class to find out which of the questions students found most difficult to answer. Then ask a series of volunteers to tell in their own words how they found the answer to the question.
(1. simple
2. compound
3. $1200)

out cash and subtracts the money from the business's checking account. The bank usually charges a fee for servicing the account and may charge a fee for processing each of the business's checks.

The second type of deposit is called a time deposit. **Time deposits** are typically left in the bank for months or years. Money placed in a savings account is a time deposit. Taking money out of a savings account is called a **withdrawal.** In order to make a profit, banks have placed some limits on savings accounts. For instance, some banks require minimum opening balances, restrict the number of withdrawals, and charge penalties for exceeding the number of withdrawals. Some banks no longer offer personal savings account services because the costs of maintaining such accounts are so high that a profit cannot be made from the deposited money.

The advantage of a time deposit is that the money can earn interest. **Interest** is money banks pay to depositors for using their funds. In effect, a savings account depositor is lending money to the bank. The bank, in turn, uses this money to lend to others. In the past, only savings accounts and other time deposits earned interest—checking accounts did not. However,

CHAPTER 19   MONEY AND BANKING   **319**

Curriculum Connection   **Math**

Passbook Savings Account for 5 years ($1175)	3 1/2%, simple interest	($1000 × .035 = $35; $35 × 5 = $175; $1000 + 175 = $1175)
CD on deposit for 12 months ($1071.86)	7%, compounded quarterly	1st quarter ($1017.50), 2nd quarter ($1035.31), 3rd quarter ($1053.43), 4th quarter ($1071.86)
CD on deposit for 12 months ($1100.57)	3 1/2%, compounded monthly	interest at the end of months 2–12: $1008.75, $1017.58, $1026.48, $1035.46, $1044.52, $1053.66, $1062.88, $1072.18, $1081.56, $1091.02, $1100.57

TEACHING TIP
Impress upon students that while both time deposits and demand deposits require the depositor to place money in a bank for safekeeping, the deposits have different characteristics.

Learning Activity
Lead students in a discussion of why banks have imposed some restrictions on savings accounts. Have students generate a list of restrictions—for example, minimum opening balance, or maximum number of withdrawals a quarter. Ask students to speculate on the reason for each restriction. Encourage them to link their speculations to the bank's need to make a profit as a business.

Ask students to use the data in the table at left to compute the total savings on a $1000 deposit at the end of the time periods shown.

CHAPTER 19

TEACHING TIP

Ask the class to describe how a bank, in offering services such as accepting money, transferring money, and creating money, is like other businesses. How is it different? (Like other businesses, its aim is to make a profit. However, the bank makes much of its profit by using other people's money.)

Learning Activity

Stress to students that a bank's function of creating money has nothing to do with printing currency or minting coins. Instead, the function of creating money relies entirely upon the bank's ability to make loans and accept deposits. Point out to students that when a bank customer deposits $1000 in an account, the bank uses most of that money to fund the loans it makes. While it pays the customer for using his or her money, it also charges the loan customer for borrowing the money. Ask students to describe the relationship between the bank's reserves and a customer's wish to withdraw her or his savings. (The bank draws upon its reserves to meet the customer's request).

motivated by the wants of consumers and less restrictive government regulations, some banks have begun to offer interest on certain kinds of checking accounts.

Transfer Money

Another function banks perform is the transfer of money from one person or business to another. Suppose you have a paycheck for $85 from the store where you work. You can take it to your bank, which will accept the check and give you $85 in cash. In this case, the funds will be transferred from the store's payroll account to the bank's cash account, and currency will be paid out to you.

However, most transfers of funds do not involve check cashing. Rather, the transfer involves changes in two separate accounts, usually checking accounts. Suppose you deposited your $85 paycheck in your checking account. The bank increases the balance in your checking account by $85. After the check makes its way through the banking system, the store's payroll account balance will be decreased by $85.

Create Money

A third major function of banks is to create money by making loans. Loans are a bank's primary source of income. Borrowers who receive the loans must pay an interest charge, which is like a rental fee, for the money. The interest earned on a bank's loans is used to pay the interest the bank owes to depositors and to pay bank expenses. Any interest collected in excess of the bank's expenses is the bank's profit. To make a profit, bankers charge borrowers more interest on their loans than the interest they pay savers.

Banks use money deposited by customers to make loans. The government requires the bank to keep a certain percentage of a deposit on hand. This is to ensure that the bank will have enough cash reserves to satisfy depositors who want to make withdrawals. The regulatory agency set up by the government can control the amount of money in the economy by changing the percentage of a deposit banks must keep on hand. The agency can also pump new money into or take money out of the economy.

Figure 19-2 on page 321 shows how banks expand the money supply. Suppose George Smith deposits $10,000 from the sale of some government securities in his checking account at the bank. Suppose also that the bank is required to keep at least $1000 cash reserve on hand. It could then loan out as much as $9000. Assume that Smith's bank decides to lend the

Curriculum Connection   Communication

Have students research the history of a particular bank in the community. Suggest that students use the local library, historical society, or the bank's archives as sources of information. Encourage students to organize their report in three sections that explain how the bank accepted money, transferred money, and created money when it was established and how those functions are accomplished today. Allow students to present their findings as a three-minute news feature complete with a time line.

For those students who need to develop their written communication skills, choose among the worksheets in *Communication Skills Review*.

FIGURE 19-2

How Banks Create Money

New Deposit By	Amount of Deposit	Cash Reserve (10%)	Cash Available for Loans (90%)	New Loan To
George Smith (Bank A)	$10,000	$1000	$9000	Carter Co.
Carter Co. (Bank B)	$9000	$900	$8100	Maria Martini
Maria Martini (Bank C)	$8100	$810	$7290	EFEX,Inc.
EFEX, Inc. (Bank D)	$7290	$729	$6561	Dee Dee Fashions
Possible Totals	$34,390	$3439	$30,951	

Banks accept deposits, and, for each deposit made, banks must keep a cash reserve on hand. The bank is free to loan the remainder of the deposit. If the percentage of money required for reserves is raised, will banks have more or less money to lend? Explain.

USE VISUALS

Have a volunteer explain the parts of Figure 19-2 in his or her own words. Then ask students to write three questions that can be answered using the figure. Have students exchange questions with a partner. Ask the partners to write their answers to the questions and then return the questions to the writer for evaluation.
Answer to caption: Less. The bank will have to keep more on hand, therefore it will have less to loan.

USE TRANSPARENCIES

Use Teaching Transparency 19-2 and its corresponding strategies and worksheet from the *Teaching Transparency Strategies and Worksheets* booklet to help students grasp the concept that banks use loans to create money. Verify student worksheets using the Answer Key.

Connection to CHAPTER 20

Point out to students that the amount of cash reserves a bank must keep on hand is determined by the Federal Reserve Bank. Indicate to students that they will learn more about this and other responsibilities of "the Fed" in Chapter 20.

entire $9000 to the Carter Company. Carter Company then deposits the entire $9000 in its company checking account. Carter Company's bank places $900 in its cash reserves and makes $8100 available for loans. There is now $19,000 circulating in the economic system even though only $10,000 was deposited in cash. The bank has effectively "created" money without printing a single dollar bill.

The money you deposit in a bank helps other people obtain loans. There are four main types of loans, and they vary in purpose and in time allowed for repayment. Figure 19-3 on page 322 shows how the mix of business, real estate, and individual loans has changed in the recent past.

Mortgage Loans   Homes, office buildings, manufacturing facilities, and other properties cost more money to buy than most people or businesses have available. Therefore, they borrow the money from a bank by signing a note and giving a **mortgage** on the property. A mortgage is a pledge of property as a guarantee that the loaned money plus interest will be repaid. The

Making Connections ⬦➤   Everyday Living

Have students form teams of eight, with four students in each group taking the roles of banks and the others the roles of customers. Provide $10,000 in game money for each team or have students make their game money. Have students use the information in Figure 19-2 above to create money within their own teams. Have students accept and lend money in amounts of their own choosing but keep reserves at 10 percent. Encourage them to complete at least four transactions, keeping a record of their transactions. After all transactions are completed, have each team explain how its bank was able to create money.

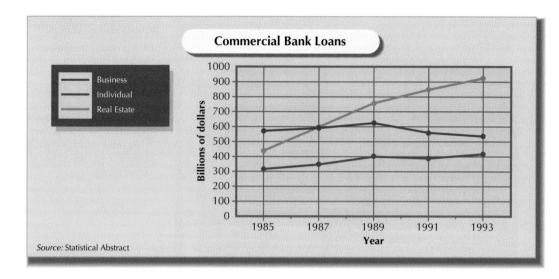

Commercial Bank Loans

Business
Individual
Real Estate

Billions of dollars

1000
900
800
700
600
500
400
300
200
100
0

1985   1987   1989   1991   1993
Year

Source: Statistical Abstract

USE VISUALS

Remind students that line graphs such as the one in Figure 19-3 are useful ways to show how a variable changes over time. Ask students to describe how loans to business changed from 1985 to 1993 and how they know. (They decreased; the graph slopes downward.) Answer to caption: Real estate.

USE TRANSPARENCIES

Use Teaching Transparency 19-3 and its corresponding strategies and worksheet from the *Teaching Transparency Strategies and Worksheets* booklet to help students determine which loans are most common among commercial banks. Verify student worksheets using the Answer Key.

Connection to CHAPTER 6

Remind students that the U.S. private enterprise system includes the following rights:
- the right to own property
- the freedom to start new businesses
- the freedom to make agreements
- the right to enter into agreements for producing goods or services.

Have students discuss how these rights play a central role in the banking industry's ability to create money. Suggest they describe what might happen to the banking industry if any of these rights were revoked by the government.

FIGURE 19-3

Loans to businesses once accounted for the largest share of commercial bank loans. However, in recent years the amounts loaned for real estate—both commercial and residential— and to individuals have increased. What kinds of loans now account for the largest share of commercial bank loans?

mortgage gives the bank the right to take the property if the borrower does not pay as agreed. Because of the large sums of money involved, the time for repaying mortgages may extend for 15 to 30 years.

Business Loans Business loans include loans made to a store to buy goods for its inventory or to an airline to buy new airplanes. The loans for machinery and equipment are often made for long periods. Some businesses, such as farms or resorts, receive a large portion of their income at one time of the year. However, they usually have expenses all year long. A short-term loan from a bank can help them meet their financial obligations between times when they receive income.

Individual Loans An individual loan is made to an individual person to buy a car, pay bills, pay for a vacation, or make major home repairs. The repayment period for an individual loan can range from a few months to several years.

Line of Credit A bank can arrange for its preferred customers to have access to a preset amount of loan money. This loan money is available on demand and is called a **line of credit.** Suppose a bank issues a customer a $15,000 line of credit. The customer can borrow all or part of that money any time the money is needed, and for any purpose. The advantage of a line of credit is that customers avoid the process of applying for a new loan each time they need to borrow some money. Establishing a

Meeting Student Diversity

Use Figure 19-3 above to help students who may have difficulty understanding line graphs by asking general questions about the graph.
- What does the green line on the graph show? (The dollar amount commercial banks loaned for real estate in the years 1985, 1987, 1989, 1991, and 1993.)
- Why are the three lines placed on a single graph? (To compare data.)
- What does the number 500 along the graph's vertical axis represent? ($500 billion).

Ask teams of students to write three questions that can be answered using Figure 19-3. Have teams pass their questions to a second team, which answers the questions and returns them for evaluation.

line of credit requires certain qualifiers such as income, good credit history, and property as security. Of course, the bank charges interest on any amount the customer borrows.

Quick Check
1. Name the three basic functions of a bank.
2. Define *deposit, demand deposit, time deposit, withdrawal, interest, mortgage,* and *line of credit.*

TYPES OF BANKS

Money management is central to our economy, and a variety of financial institutions offer money management services. There are several types of banking institutions, each set up in a different way, and each providing different services.

Commercial Banks

Most of the banks in the United States are commercial banks. They are usually large businesses that provide a wide range of services, many of which have already been discussed. Like many other businesses, banks need charters, or licenses, to conduct business. Commercial banks receive their charters to accept and transfer money and to make loans from either the federal government or a state government. A bank chartered by the federal government is called a national bank and the word *national* must appear in its name. A bank chartered by a state government is called a state bank. A state bank is not required to have the word *state* in its name, but many of them do include it in their titles.

Savings and Loan Associations

Like commercial banks, savings and loan associations accept deposits and transfer and lend money. Traditionally, most of the deposits in these institutions came from individuals and families rather than from businesses and institutions. Individuals and families are still the most common customers of savings and loans. Savings and loan associations make single-family and multi-family mortgage loans. They also finance commercial mortgages and auto loans. These institutions started when members of an association would pool their

Enrichment Strategy

Have students research the trend in the number and kinds of banking services offered through computers. If possible, have them arrange to visit a bank in their community that offers computer banking. Ask students to gather information on costs, ease of access, possibility of outside tampering, special regulations, confidentiality, and the number of customer sign-ups over the past year. Have students plan a brief news report describing how computer banking might become commonplace in the future.

Learning Activity

List the following bank names on the board or on a transparency:

- First National Bank
- First Federal Commercial Bank
- First Security Trust and Savings Bank
- First State Bank
- First Commercial Bank
- First American National Bank & Trust

Ask students to determine which banks have federal charters, which have state charters, and which are not chartered. (Federal: First American National Bank & Trust and First National Bank; State: all others. All banks must have either a state or federal charter to operate.)

Quick Check Answers

1. Commercial banks accept savings and checking deposits, make loans and other investments, and offer services that help people and businesses transfer funds.

2. A thrift institution is a kind of bank that emphasizes savings. Savings and loans and savings banks are two kinds of thrift institutions.

---

money over a period of time. Then members would borrow money, in turn, so that each member could build a home. The interest rates for a loan from a savings and loan association may be slightly less than loans from a commercial bank. Because savings and loans emphasize savings, they are often called "thrifts," or "thrift institutions." Sometimes thrifts pay a higher interest on deposits than commercial banks do.

Savings Banks

Another thrift institution is the savings bank. Like savings and loans, most of the business for savings banks comes from savings accounts and home loans. Savings banks were originally set up to service the smaller-savings customers the commercial banks ignored. Most of a savings bank's loans are for home mortgages, although some do make personal and auto loans. The interest rates for a loan from a savings bank may be slightly less than loans from a commercial bank. In addition, they sometimes pay a higher interest on deposits than do commercial banks.

Other Financial Institutions

A third kind of thrift institution is a credit union. Credit unions are institutions made up of individuals who work for the same company or community organization. In the past, credit unions could only offer savings accounts and make personal loans to members of the credit union. Now credit unions can offer mortgage loans to those members as well. Some credit unions even offer credit cards to their members.

Because of the variety of financial products available for purchase, many other financial institutions specialize in a particular kind of product. Unlike a bank, these institutions do not accept deposits or transfer money; nor do they, in the strictest sense, offer loans. However, institutions such as life insurance companies, investment banks, mortgage companies, and trust companies offer individuals and businesses a variety of options and a range of risks for managing money.

Quick Check

1. What kinds of services do commercial banks provide?
2. What are thrift institutions? Give two examples.

Reteaching Strategy

Emphasize the link between the money deposited by savings and loan customers and the money lent by the institutions by asking students to review Figure 19-2 on page 321. Ask a volunteer to explain what will happen at Bank C if EFEX, Inc. is unable to repay its loan and Maria Martinelli wishes to withdraw the full amount of her deposit. Help students create a diagram to show that many individuals depositing between $1000 and $5000 might be affected if a single $250,000 loan was not repaid.

REGULATING THE BANKING INDUSTRY

During the Great Depression that began in 1929, difficult economic conditions caused many banks to fail. Much of the money that people and businesses had put into these banks was lost. In response to this economic disaster, the federal government set up the Federal Deposit Insurance Corporation, or FDIC, to protect people who use our nation's banks. The FDIC insures each account in a federally chartered bank up to $100,000 per account.

Only two decades ago, government regulation of banks limited the kinds of services and even the interest rates banks could provide customers. As government deregulated the banking industry, savings banks and savings and loan associations began to offer many of the services that commercial banks provided. Competition among banks and other financial institutions increased. As a result, profits decreased. In order to increase their profits, bank managers began to take greater risks both in the loans they approved and the investments they made.

Many savings and loans invested in or made loans to ventures that were quite risky. Also, they continued to put money into mortgage loans. Then the economic downturn of the late 1980s occurred. When borrowers failed to make payments on loans, or business investments failed, the savings and loans had

F.Y.I.

Although the FDIC and SAIF insurance limits a customer's losses to $100,000 per account, customers with more than that to deposit may wish to establish accounts in several institutions. That way the risk is spread out and each account is covered.

What guarantees does the Federal Deposit Insurance Corporation offer people who deposit money in federally chartered banks?

Develop Concepts

Regulating the Banking Industry

Introduce the concepts of regulation and deregulation using examples from students' lives. Ask questions similar to the following: Has the school ever relaxed the dress code for a day? Do some students take advantage of the deregulation or relaxation of the rules to wear something inappropriate? Point out to students that the government relaxed the rules governing the savings and loan industry in the 1980s. The officers of some of those institutions took advantage of the deregulation and acted inappropriately.

USE VISUALS

Ask a volunteer to remind the class why the Federal Deposit Insurance Corporation (FDIC) was established. Ask: What might have happened to the banking industry if the government had not established the FDIC? (Possible answer: People might have been afraid to use banks for fear that their money would be lost. The banking industry could have been permanently damaged.)
Answer to caption: All federally chartered banks are insured for up to $100,000 per account.

Global Perspective

In 1995, Barings, PLC, a British bank that had survived 200 years of revolutions, world wars, and economic depression, went bankrupt. A single bank employee, trading with bank funds, managed to lose more than $1.4 billion through risky trading decisions. The Bank of England, the British government's bank, indicated the problem was due to poor managerial control and lack of regulation. Have students research the collapse of Barings and speculate about what kinds of safeguards might have protected the bank from the bad decisions its employee, Nicholas Leeson, made with bank funds.

Business Brief

In addition to the kinds of services a bank can offer, the federal government demands that certain business practices be enforced. For example, the Bank Secrecy Act requires banks to keep a record of customers' deposits and withdrawals. Banks must keep these records for five years and make them available to federal agencies such as the Internal Revenue Service.

Quick Check Answers

1. During the Depression, many banks failed and individuals and businesses lost money. The federal government set up the Federal Deposit Insurance Corporation, or FDIC, to protect people who use our nation's banks.

2. Their ability to make commercial loans and to fund commercial real estate development are now restricted.

---

no way to get their money back. These institutions could not meet the needs of depositors who wanted to take money out of their accounts. Many savings and loans collapsed, and the government had to step in.

Deposits in these savings and loans had been insured by the Federal Savings and Loan Insurance Corporation (FSLIC). However, so many savings and loans failed that the FSLIC could not cover all the withdrawals requested by customers. The federal government agreed to underwrite the losses by using money from its general revenues. It is estimated that the savings and loan crisis will eventually cost U.S. taxpayers more than $200 billion.

The FSLIC was disbanded by Congress in 1989 and replaced with the Savings Association Insurance Fund (SAIF), which is administered by the FDIC. Like the FDIC, the SAIF insures deposits to a maximum of $100,000. Both the FDIC and the SAIF receive money to operate from insurance premiums paid by member institutions. All federally charted banks must participate in the FDIC program; banks that are not federally charted may choose to enroll. Only financial institutions enrolled in the program are allowed to display the letters FDIC or SAIF on their materials.

Quick Check

1. Why did the government form the FDIC?
2. What kinds of savings and loans activities are now restricted by the government?

Making Connections   Business Ethics

At the heart of the savings and loan collapse was the risky behavior of the management of certain savings and loans. Savings and loan officers approved large loans to businesses that had little chance of succeeding. Often the bankers knew the business's top executives, and loans were made as if between friends. Have students discuss the ethics of these banking practices in light of the fact that the loans were actually funded by the savings and loans' customers' money—not the banks' own money. Have students suggest ways in which the federal government might guard against these kinds of actions in the future.

Refer to the *Ethics in Business Strategies* booklet for additional strategies and activities.

Chapter 19 **Summary**

Main Ideas

1. Money functions as a medium of exchange, standard of value, and a store of value. The characteristics of money include acceptability, divisibility, portability, stability, durability, and scarcity.
2. All banks accept money in the form of deposits to accounts, transfer money between accounts, and create money by extending loans to individuals and businesses.
3. There are three types of banking institutions: commercial, savings and loans, and savings banks.
4. In response to bank failures of the 1930s, the federal government set up the Federal Deposit Insurance Corporation, or FDIC; in response to the failure of savings and loans in the 1980s, the Savings Association Insurance Fund (SAIF) was established.
5. Networks of computer equipment make it possible for businesses such as banks to share information.
6. Simple interest can be computed using the formula: Interest = principal $\times$ rate $\times$ time.

CASE ANALYSIS Economics

Greg Malouf recently received a $10,000 cash gift from his Uncle Alex to use for the education of his children, Zachary and Adam. Uncle Alex had kept the cash in a safe at his home. Like other savers, Uncle Alex did not need to use the $10,000 cash and had set it aside. In this chapter you learned that banks accept cash from savers who do not need to use their cash, reserve a portion of the cash deposited, and loan out the remainder as they see fit. For the privilege of using savers' money, banks pay them interest. Banks then charge borrowers interest for the privilege of having money to put to immediate use. Thus, banks and other financial institutions are financial go-betweens between savers and investors. They gather loanable funds from savers and make them available to investors to use as capital, a factor of production. From an economist's point of view, was Uncle Alex's idea of keeping the $10,000 cash in a safe good for the economy?

CHAPTER 19   MONEY AND BANKING   **327**

CLOSE

Main Ideas

Main Ideas summarizes the key information in the chapter. It is a useful tool for reinforcement and review.

CASE ANALYSIS

Case Analysis provides a chapter-related case for student analysis and application of decision-making skills.

Answer
No. Uncle Alex's money was not being used to help build a stronger and more productive economy. By remaining idle in a safe, it was not available to a borrower, such as a builder constructing new houses. Nor was it a good idea for Uncle Alex. He could have increased his holdings by depositing the money in a financial institution to earn interest.

QUICK QUIZ

1. Name three functions and four characteristics of money. (Medium of exchange, store of value, standard of value; accepted, divisible, stable, portable, and durable.)
2. Why are bank owners and shareholders in the banking business? (To make a profit.)
3. Why are loans important to the banking business? (Loans help banks create money.)
4. Name three kinds of banks. (Commercial banks, savings and loans associations, savings banks.)
5. Who regulates the banking industry? (The federal government.)

Chapter 19 **Review**

APPLY

Answers

Use the Language of Business

1. currency, **2.** line of credit, **3.** mortgage, **4.** withdrawal, **5.** interest, **6.** demand deposit, **7.** barter, **8.** time deposit, **9.** money, **10.** checkbook dollars, **11.** deposit

Review What You Learned

1. Standard of value: money helps us compare the value of different items; store of value: money holds its value over time; medium of exchange: buyers and sellers use money to exchange for goods and services.

2. Currency is paper money issued by a government and has little value in itself; commodity money has value in and of itself, such as gold or silver coins; checkbook money is checks written on balances in a checking account.

3. A depositor wants the highest interest possible; a borrower wants the lowest interest possible.

4. Banks lend money to businesses for supplies and equipment, allowing these businesses to produce more goods and services to be sold.

5. It might cash a paycheck for a factory employee; the bank gives cash to the employee and deducts the amount from the factory's account.

6. Demand deposits can be withdrawn at any time; time deposits must be left in the bank for specified months or years or a penalty will be charged for early withdrawal.

7. A collection of terminals, computers, printers, and other equipment that use communications channels to share data; shared disk storage device in a network; individual devices in a network; standard for communications that acts like a language for communicating data.

8. Interest = Principal × Rate × Time.

Understand Business Concepts

1. A buyer may want to spend only part of the money on hand, for example, a buyer

Use the Language of Business

Understanding these business terms will help you communicate more easily with others. Match each term to its definition.

barter
checkbook dollars
currency
demand deposit
deposit
interest

line of credit
money
mortgage
time deposit
withdrawal

1. Paper money and coins issued by a government.
2. A preset amount of loan money available on demand.
3. A pledge of property or real estate that a loan will be repaid.
4. The process of removing money from a bank account.
5. The money paid to you by the bank for the use of your money.
6. Depositing money into a checking account.
7. Trading goods or services directly for other goods or services.
8. Depositing money in a savings account.
9. Serves as a medium of exchange, acts as a measure of value, and retains its value over time.
10. The form of money used when writing a check.
11. Putting money into a bank account.

Review What You Learned

1. How does money function as a standard of value? A store of value? A medium of exchange?
2. What is currency and how is it different from checkbook money?
3. How might people's needs and wants for banking services conflict?
4. How do banks help increase production of goods and services in the United States economy?
5. Give an example of how a bank might transfer money.
6. What is the difference between a demand deposit and a time deposit?
7. Define *computer network*, *file server*, *node*, and *network protocol*.
8. Give the formula for computing simple interest.

Understand Business Concepts

1. Why does money need to be divisible? Give an example.
2. Banks pay depositors for leaving their money in savings accounts. Why?
3. What is meant by a "thrift" institution? Give three examples.
4. How is a bank's ability to accept money related to its ability to create money?
5. The Spencers have two accounts at the same national bank. The balance in one account is $55,000 and the balance in the second is $65,000. The bank carries FDIC insurance. If the bank fails, how much money would the Spencers get from the insurance?

might have $10.00 and purchase a cap for $4.99; the buyer needs to exchange the $10.00 for the cap and $5.01.

2. Banks want to encourage individuals to put money into savings so that the banks can loan part of that money to others. By charging more interest for the money they loan, banks make a profit.

3. Thrift institutions are those that encourage savings; examples include savings and loans, savings banks, and credit unions.

4. A bank uses money it accepts to make loans and create money. If a bank could not accept money, it would have no resources with which to make loans.

5. The Spencers would get the full amount of both accounts, as each account is insured by the FDIC up to a maximum of

$100,000 per account.

6. Possible answers include: charge more interest on loans; reduce interest on deposits; charge higher fees on services such as safe deposit rental.

7. The account on which interest is compounded daily because it earns interest daily on an amount which increases daily.

8. Your account balance will be increased by the amount of the check; the same amount will be deducted from the Barnett's account.

9. A LAN is local in nature and the devices are often physically connected by wires, or cables; a WAN covers a large geographic area and it is likely to use several communications channels including wires, microwaves, and satellites.

6. Name three things a bank can do to increase its profit.
7. Which will pay more interest, an account whose interest is compounded daily or one whose interest is compounded monthly? Explain.
8. You receive a check from your employer, Barnett's Food Stores, and you deposit the check in your account at the bank. What will happen to your account and to the Barnett's Food Stores account?
9. What is the difference between a LAN and a WAN?

Think Critically

1. **Analyze.** What do you think would happen if all the depositors of a bank requested their deposits?
2. **Evaluate.** Do you think bank owners should be able to borrow money from the bank? Explain your answer.

Use What You Learned

1. **Group Project.** Team with three classmates to form a bank. Open your bank with a deposit of $20,000 in fake game money. Invite classmates to play the roles of business and individual customers in your bank. Determine what interest you will pay on deposits and what interest you will charge on loans. Decide what you will need to do to place $200,000 into the classroom economy. Remember the following may affect your business decisions:

   • Your bank must keep 10% of each deposit on reserve.
   • You will need to pay salaries, rent, FDIC insurance, and other costs.
   • You will compete for customers with other banks in your classroom.

   Write a 300-word report that explains how your bank works.

2. **Computer Application.** Use spreadsheet software to create a spreadsheet that will compute interest using the formula: Interest = principal × rate × time. Be especially careful when you format the "Time" column. Then alternately compare varying interest rates and time periods for the same principal amount. Print out the results.
3. **Skill Reinforcement.** Call several savings institutions to find out how much interest they pay on a regular savings account and whether they offer simple or compound interest on the account. If interest is compounded, find out how often it is done. Make a table to show the results of your research. Then make a summary statement in which you name the savings institution you would choose for your own savings account and tell why.

Save your work in your Business Portfolio

CHAPTER 19 REVIEW

Think Critically
1. Banks would not have enough currency to cover all the withdrawals.
2. Answers will vary.

Independent Practice

Use the Chapter 19 worksheets in *Student Activity Guide 1* for additional practice and application activities. A Teacher's Annotated Edition provides answers.

ASSESS

Portfolio Assessment

These projects are designed to lead students to develop a collection of their best work to submit to you for assessment. Refer students to the specific rubric(s) from the *Alternative Assessment Strategies* booklet listed with each of the project notes below. These rubrics will alert students to the criteria you will use to assess their projects.

Chapter Assessment

Use the Chapter 19 Test from the *Test Masters* booklet to evaluate students' understanding of the chapter concepts. An answer key is provided. Or create your own customized test using the *Testmaker* software.

Use What You Learned
1. Be certain each team member participates in the banking exercise. Possible Rubric: Paragraph, Essay. Remind students that the library is likely to have the references they need to complete this assignment. Possible Rubrics: Charts and Tables, illustration, bulletin board, poster.
2. Students without access to a computer can complete this exercise using a hand-held calculator and creating a spreadsheet manually.

3. Students' answers will vary, but all should include a table with the names of several local savings institutions, the interest rates for a regular savings account, and information about how the interest is compounded. Students should circle the institution that offers the largest amount of interest.

FOCUS

Introduce the Chapter

Major Concepts
- The Fed and the Money Supply
- Organization of the Fed
- Functions of the Fed

Introduce the Topic
Ask students if they have a Federal Reserve Note in their possession. If students seem unsure about the question, suggest that they examine the money in their wallets. Ask students who respond "yes" to indicate where the words identifying the note appear. (At the top.) Then point out that the Federal Reserve System is the nation's central bank and, as such, has a number of responsibilities. One of these responsibilities is managing the amount of money in circulation.

Use Business Terms
Have students briefly study the list of Business Terms and conjure up mental images of what the terms represent. Invite volunteers to describe one or more of the images they have created. Ask members of the class to match the terms with the descriptions.

USE VISUALS
Point out to students that these workers are inspecting new Federal Reserve Notes coming off the press as part of the Federal Reserve System's responsibility to manage the nation's money supply.

CHAPTER 20

Business terms

the Fed

monetary policy

loose money policy

tight money policy

open market operations

government securities

reserve requirement

discount rate

330

CHAPTER 20 RESOURCES

Instructional Resources

Lesson Plan for Chapter 20

Teaching Transparencies 20-1, 20-2, 20-3, 20-4

Strategies and Worksheets for Teaching Transparencies 20-1, 20-2, 20-3, 20-4

Enrichment Master 20-1

Student Activity Guide 1–TAE for Chapter 20

Test Master for Chapter 20

Alternative Assessment Strategies

Math Skills Review

International Business Strategies

Cooperative Learning Strategies

Communication Skills Review

Ethics in Business Strategies

The Federal Reserve System and Monetary Policy

Learning objectives

After completing this chapter, you will be able to:
- Describe the responsibilities of the Federal Reserve System.
- Explain how banks use magnetic ink character recognition and electronic funds transfers.
- Identify three kinds of discounts used by manufacturers and wholesalers.

Consider what you know

- Banks accept money in the form of deposits and then create money by extending loans to individuals and businesses. This makes money and banking a vital part of our economy.

Consider what you want to know

- What other federal agency regulates money and banking and how does it affect the economy?
- How is the Federal Reserve System organized?
- How does technology help the Fed and other banks complete transactions?
- What kinds of incentives and discounts can manufacturers use to attract business customers?

Consider how to use what you learn

- As you study this chapter, keep tabs on the Fed's movements and decisions. Listen to business reports and read business news columns to find out what the Fed is doing.

Multimedia Resources

Technology Resource Guide

Distance Learning Guide

Internet Resource Guide

Professional Resources

School-to-Work/Tech Prep Strategies

Instructional Poster

Spanish Resources

Testmaker Software for Chapter 20

The Wall Street Journal Video Series
Video & Activities for Chapter 20

Business and Marketing Computer Applications—An Integrated Software Simulation Using Microsoft Works

Stocktracker—A Stock Market Software Simulation

Where's the Dough? Board Game

Motivate the Learning

Learning Objectives
Remind students that the learning objectives are an important study tool. The learning objectives show what they will learn in the chapter. Encourage students to keep these objectives in mind as they work through the chapter. Note that the last two objectives listed refer to the Focus on Technology feature and the Building Business Skills feature.

Consider What You Know
Review briefly the main sections of *Chapter 19, Money and Banking:* Money, Banks, Banking Functions, Types of Banks, Regulating the Banking Industry.

Consider What You Want to Know
Have students preview the chapter in order to see how it will provide answers to the questions. They can read the headings and subheadings, look at the graphics and photographs, and read the captions.

Consider How to Use What You Learn
Indicate to students that at the end of this chapter they will develop some projects incorporating what they know about how the Federal Reserve shapes monetary policy and how that policy affects the economy. Suggest that as they read the chapter they keep in mind how the Fed and its actions affect their lives as well as the economy.

TEACH

Many of today's banks are owned by bank holding companies. A bank holding company is an institution that directly or indirectly owns, controls, or exercises a controlling influence over the management policies of a bank. In addition, bank holding companies may make, acquire, or service loans or other credit extensions. They may also supply electronic banking services. About 6500 holding companies control about 8500 banks. Each of these holding companies is under the supervision of the Fed.

Develop Concepts

The Fed and the Money Supply

Introduce the topic by asking: How is the amount of money available to you regulated by the adults central to your life? Encourage students to support their discussion with illustrations. Connect students' experiences to the way regulations are enforced by the Fed.

TEACHING TIP

Write the following phrases on the board: *loose money policy* → large money supply → low interest rates, and *tight money policy* → small money supply → high interest rates. Ask students to explain why the price of credit falls when the money supply increases. (The price of credit—the interest rate—is like any other price. It decreases when supply increases.)

We've discussed commercial banks, savings and loans, and savings banks. You've looked into the kinds of services each of these provide to individuals and businesses. In this chapter, you will learn about one more type of bank. This bank—actually a system of banks—provides services to banks. It is responsible for determining policies and regulating many of the services of banks and other financial institutions.

THE FED AND THE MONEY SUPPLY

The Federal Reserve System is the central banking organization of the United States. Often called **the Fed,** the Federal Reserve System was created by the government in 1913 in an attempt to end the periodic financial panics that plagued business and the nation in the late nineteenth and early twentieth century. The Fed has three major responsibilities: it regulates the nation's money supply, supervises banks, and clears checks. The customers or clients of the Federal Reserve System are commercial banks and the government.

Other nations have central banks as well. For example, the Bank of Japan, the Bank of England, and the Bank of Canada are central banks for their countries. Many of these banks have functions and responsibilities similar to the Fed.

Congress created the Federal Reserve System to oversee banking in the United States. The system also implements monetary policy in an effort to stabilize economic activity. **Monetary policy** is banking policy that affects the supply of money in circulation, which, in turn, affects the amount of credit in the economy and the amount of business activity in the economy. The Fed must ensure that enough money and credit are available to allow expansion of the economy without allowing rapid inflation.

Figure 20-1 on page 333 shows that the goal of monetary policy is to strike a balance between tight and loose money policies. A **loose money policy** is one where a lot of money is available at relatively low interest rates. A loose money policy results in inexpensive and easily available credit. As a result, the economy expands. A **tight money policy** is the opposite—there is relatively little money to lend at relatively high interest rates. A tight money policy makes credit expensive and in short supply. Tight money helps control inflation.

The control of monetary policies makes the Fed a key factor in whether credit is easy or tight, whether prices go

BUSINESS & HISTORY

The camel caravans that crossed the Negev Desert in Israel 2000 years ago had their own banks run by a group of people called the Nabateans. Caravans were easy prey for robbers. The Nabateans set up cities along the caravan routes. A trader could make a deposit in one fortified city. The same trader could make a withdrawal at another heavily guarded settlement. The caravan traders were willing to pay fees for this important service.

Global Perspective

Encourage students to find information about the central banks of European, Asian, African, and South American nations, with individuals choosing the central bank of one nation to research in depth. Suggest they make a chart comparing and contrasting the foreign bank's organization and responsibilities with that of the Fed. Students may find researching the German central bank after reunification or the Russian central bank after the disintegration of the Soviet Union particularly interesting.

Refer to the *International Business Strategies* booklet for additional strategies and activities.

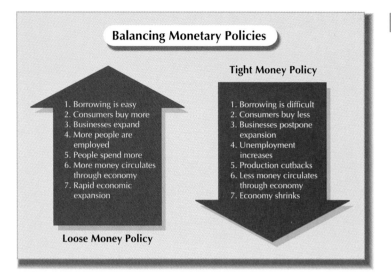

Balancing Monetary Policies

Tight Money Policy
1. Borrowing is difficult
2. Consumers buy less
3. Businesses postpone expansion
4. Unemployment increases
5. Production cutbacks
6. Less money circulates through economy
7. Economy shrinks

Loose Money Policy
1. Borrowing is easy
2. Consumers buy more
3. Businesses expand
4. More people are employed
5. People spend more
6. More money circulates through economy
7. Rapid economic expansion

FIGURE 20-1
Sound monetary policy depends upon the economic condition at any one time. Would you have "tight" or "loose" monetary policies during a time of inflation? Why?

up or down, and essentially whether the economic weather is fair or foul.

Quick Check

1. What is the Federal Reserve System?
2. Define *the Fed, monetary policy, loose money policy,* and *tight money policy.*
3. What are three responsibilities of the Federal Reserve System?

ORGANIZATION OF THE FED

The Federal Reserve System is made up of twelve districts, each with its own Federal Reserve bank, a Board of Governors, and about 5000 member banks. Figure 20-2 on page 334 shows the Federal Reserve districts and their headquarters. The system includes 25 Federal Reserve branch banks. These banks act as branch offices and aid district banks in carrying out their responsibilities.

A Board of Governors directs the operations of the Federal Reserve System. This seven-member board is chosen by the President of the United States and approved by the Congress. The members are appointed for 14-year terms. One member of the board is chosen by the President as the chairperson. The chairperson and board members have one vote each. However,

Making Connections   Communications

Have students make a Federal Reserve and Related Topics library for the classroom. Have them write or phone their district Federal Reserve Bank for a copy of the Public Information Materials, which is a catalog of free materials for use in high school. Because the Federal Reserve Bank of New York has some unique responsibilities concerning the global market, students might also want to request materials from that bank as well. After students receive the materials, have groups evaluate them using criteria such as:

- easy to read and understand
- technical terms defined
- useful tables, charts, and diagrams
- helpful index or table of contents

USE VISUALS

Use Figure 20-1 to help students understand that the choice is not necessarily between loose and tight money policies. Rather, the Fed's monetary policy must strike a balance.
Answer to caption: Tight money policy; to decrease money in the economy.

USE TRANSPARENCIES

Use Teaching Transparency 20-1 and its corresponding strategies and worksheet from the *Teaching Transparency Strategies and Worksheets* booklet. Verify student worksheets using the Answer Key.

Quick Check Answers

1. The central banking organization of the U.S.
2. The Federal Reserve System; banking policy that affects the supply of money, which in turn affects the amount of credit and the amount of business activity; much credit available at low interest rates; very little credit available and at high interest rates.
3. Regulate the nation's money supply, supervise banks, clear checks.

Develop Concepts

Organization of the Fed

Point out to students that the management organization of the Federal Reserve Bank is similar in some ways to the management structure of many corporations. One exception is that the members of the board serve for a specified time— 14 years.

Discuss

Be sure students can identify and describe what the acronyms *ACH*, *MICR*, and *EFT* represent. (Automatic Clearinghouse, magnetic ink character recognition, and Electronic Funds Transfer.) Ask a volunteer to draw a diagram to illustrate each of the terms. Then have a volunteer describe how each of these items might influence his or her individual banking. Have a second volunteer describe how these items can affect a business's banking transactions.

USE VISUALS

Ask students to name the city and state of each of the Federal Reserve Banks represented in Figure 20-2. Then direct students to indicate the approximate location of their community on the map and have them determine which Federal Reserve Bank is most likely to serve their community. Answer to caption: Answers will depend on geographic location.

USE TRANSPARENCIES

Use Teaching Transparency 20-2 and its corresponding strategies and worksheet from the *Teaching Transparency Strategies and Worksheets* booklet to assist students in locating the Federal Reserve Banks. Verify student worksheets using the Answer Key.

Magnetic Ink Character Recognition

Years ago, transactions requiring large amounts of money often required trainloads of money. At $30 an ounce—the price of gold in the 1930s—$1 million weighed more than 2000 pounds. To satisfy debts, tons of gold were physically moved from one location to another. As time passed, the trainloads of gold were replaced with suitcases of currency.

Today, transactions involving large as well as small amounts of money can be accomplished by writing checks drawn on bank accounts. Airplanes carry cargoes of canceled checks from one Federal Reserve Bank to another. In 1993, the Automatic Clearinghouse (ACH) of the Federal Reserve cleared 40 percent of the interbank checks written in the United States; private clearing arrangements processed the remainder. Still, the Federal Reserve cleared 19 billion checks, with a value of over $14 trillion.

As you might imagine, the Federal Reserve and its 46 check processing centers rely on technology to process these hundreds of tons of checks. The key is in the string of characters along the bottom of a check. These characters are printed with magnetic ink. *Magnetic ink character recognition* (MICR) devices interpret the electronic signals generated from the magnetized characters and input the data into a computer. MICR is the banking industry's standard for encoding data on checks.

Characters on the check indicate the bank's identification number, the account number, and the check

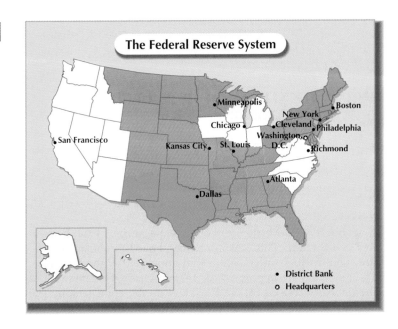

FIGURE 20-2

Many of the twelve Federal Reserve Banks shown here have branch banks that act as branch offices. Which Federal Reserve Bank serves the area where you live?

The Federal Reserve System

- Minneapolis
- New York
- Boston
- Chicago
- Cleveland
- Philadelphia
- San Francisco
- Washington, D.C.
- Kansas City
- St. Louis
- Richmond
- Atlanta
- Dallas

- • District Bank
- ○ Headquarters

334 UNIT 6 FINANCIAL INSTITUTIONS IN THE GLOBAL ECONOMY

Making Connections ➡ Social Responsibility

The Federal Reserve encourages its member banks to work with community organizations to promote local economic development. As part of the bank's annual inspection, the Fed reviews the bank's efforts to serve the credit needs of an entire community, including the extent to which the bank has programs that contribute to the building of affordable housing and to other aspects of community development. Have students contact their Reserve Bank's community affairs officer and ask what community development programs are available in their own community. Suggest that students create posters or bulletin boards to share their findings with the class.

number. When the check is processed, its amount is also added to the string of magnetized characters. MICR readers can process as many as 1200 checks a minute—a speed that allows the Federal Reserve to process and clear checks within two days.

Technology allows the Fed and the banking industry to handle larger numbers of transactions involving increasing numbers of dollars. This speed and accuracy, in turn, allows U.S. businesses to accomplish their banking needs at the touch of a keyboard. Within an instant, banks, their agents, and even consumers transfer millions of dollars around the globe using EFT.

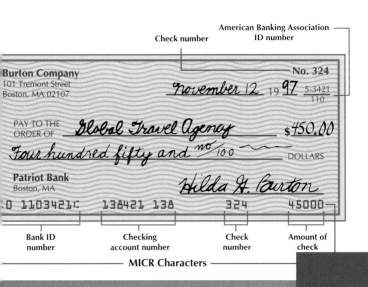

the chairperson is often able to influence decisions made by other board members. For this reason, the Chairperson of the Board of Governors of the Federal Reserve is considered one of the most powerful and important positions in government.

Each Federal Reserve Bank is a corporation owned by its member banks and supervised by its own nine-member Board of Directors. All national banks—banks chartered by the Federal government—are required to become members of the Federal Reserve System by purchasing stock in their district Federal Reserve Bank. Many state banks also belong to their district Federal Reserve Bank. In addition, any institution (member or not) that accepts deposits must deposit its reserves in its district Federal Reserve Bank.

Quick Check

1. How many districts does the Fed have?
2. Who are the members of the Fed?

Encourage students to speculate about the impact of electronic banking on the way businesses conduct their financial transactions. How has electronic banking made some tasks more efficient? (It has made it possible to process large numbers of transactions quickly and accurately.) For additional information about current technology, refer to the *Technology Resources Guide.*

Business Brief

Although foreign banks have been operating in the United States for more than a century, these banks have been subject to regulation only since 1978. The International Banking Act of 1978 requires that foreign banks operating in the United States be subject to the same restrictions and obligations that apply to domestic banking organizations. This act was designed to promote competitive equality between the foreign and domestic banking institutions.

Quick Check Answers

1. Twelve.
2. All national banks are required to be members of the Fed; some state banks choose to belong.

Curriculum Connection   Social Studies

Encourage students to collect a number of articles about the Fed and any recent Fed decisions affecting the economy. Suggest students use both general interest publications and publications specializing in economics. Have students determine the name of the chairperson of the Federal Reserve. Ask them to discuss the implications of the decisions and use the implications to defend or oppose the following statement: The chairperson of the Board of Governors is one of the most powerful positions in the U.S. government.

FUNCTIONS OF THE FED

The federal government collects huge sums of money through taxation. The government deposits some of the collected money in the Fed and distributes the rest among thousands of commercial banks. The Fed keeps track of government deposits and holds a checking account for the United States Treasury. When the government spends money to fund government goods and services, such as social security, tax refunds, and veterans' benefits, the government checks are drawn on this account.

The Federal Reserve also sets standards for consumer legislation dealing with lending and credit. It demands that sellers of goods and services make credit term information—amount of interest, size of monthly payments, number of payments and so on—understandable and available to consumers who buy on credit.

The Fed functions as more than the government's banker and a consumer protector. The Fed must regulate the money supply, supervise banks, clear checks, and supply paper currency.

Regulate the Money Supply

The widespread use of credit cards, debit cards, and electronic funds transfers has changed the way money circulates through the economy. These advances in technology offer new challenges to the Federal Reserve's ability to regulate the supply of money. However, the Fed has several ways in which it can increase or decrease the supply of money in the economy. The Fed can

- buy or sell government securities,
- change the reserve requirement, or
- change the discount rate.

Buy/Sell Government Securities If the Fed buys or sells government securities, the activity is called **open market operations. Government securities,** such as treasury bills, are government security investments the government sells in order to finance growth. In open market operations, the securities are traded in the open market through regular securities dealers; anyone can purchase these government securities. Figure 20-3 on page 337 shows what happens during open market operations. Of the three methods the Fed can use to regulate the economy, buying and selling government securities is the one used most frequently.

In order to decide whether to buy or sell securities, a committee of the Fed looks at what has happened to the money supply in the past, what is happening at the moment, and what is

Making Connections   Technology

Electronic money promises to offer new challenges for the Federal Reserve. Electronic money, also called E-cash, is money that consumers and businesses can send to each other electronically. A credit-card-size piece of plastic can be programmed to be worth $100 or $1000, or even $100,000. (For which the customer pays the face amount in traditional currency.) A business or consumer could then offer that card for payment of goods or services. The purchase amount would be electronically deducted from the card, and electronically added to the merchant's account. The card would be good until all the E-cash was spent. Have students research the current status of E-cash, its availability, its drawbacks, and what the Federal Reserve is doing to ensure that E-cash does not undermine the current monetary system.

Open Market Operations

The Federal Reserve Buys a Security

Federal Reserve — Joe — Joe's Bank

The Federal Reserve buys a government security from Joe. The Fed receives the security and pays Joe.

Joe sells his government security and is paid by the Fed. Joe puts the money in his bank.

With Joe's deposit, the bank now has additional money to make more loans.

The Federal Reserve Sells a Security

Federal Reserve — Frank — Frank's Bank

The Federal Reserve sells a government security to Frank. The Fed receives a check from Frank. The Fed sends the check to Frank's bank for payment.

Frank buys a government security from the Fed. He writes a check for it, so money comes out of his bank and flows to the Fed.

Frank's bank pays the Fed on Frank's check and reduces Frank's account balance. The bank now has less money on deposit, and can make fewer loans.

FIGURE 20-3

Open market operations refers to the sale or purchase of government securities by the Fed. How can buying securities during open market operations put more money into circulation?

likely to happen if the Fed does not act. The committee also considers data such as unemployment level, amount of retail sales, and gross domestic product figures.

If the economy is growing too fast and inflation threatens, the Fed sells securities from its own portfolio holdings. Buyers pay for the securities with checks drawn on their banks. When the Fed presents these checks for payment, the banks draw the money from their reserves. The payment reduces the banks' reserves. However, banks are required to keep reserves at a specified percent of their liabilities. In order to match liabilities to the new, lower reserves, the banks must lower or decrease the amount of loans they make. Fewer loans means less money circulating through the economy, so the economy slows.

If the economy is in a slump, the Fed may decide to buy back government securities. When the Fed pays for these

Reteaching Strategy

Suggest students work in teams to develop a cause-and-effect diagram based on the open market operations depicted in Figure 20-3 above. Have teams choose whether their illustration will show how the Fed uses securities to slow the economy or how the Fed uses securities to move the economy out of a slump. Remind students to include the following in their diagrams: what the Fed does, how the Fed's actions affect the bank's reserves, and how the amount of money in the bank's reserves affects the amount of money available for loans.

USE VISUALS

Remind students of the definition of securities (paper certificates indicating debt or ownership). Provide game money, imitation certificates, and name tags to volunteers. Use Teaching Transparency 20-4 to show students what a buy/sell order for government securities looks like. Have them take the roles of the Fed, and banks and securities buyers and sellers. Suggest they pantomime the information given in Figure 20-3. As the pantomime takes place, have the class identify which part of the figure is being represented. Answer to caption: When the Fed buys securities, its payment increases the amount of money in a bank's reserves. This allows the bank to make more loans.

USE TRANSPARENCIES

Use Teaching Transparency 20-3 and its corresponding strategies and worksheet from the *Teaching Transparency Strategies and Worksheets* booklet. Verify student worksheets using the Answer Key.

Learning Activity

Present the following events to students and have them place them in the correct chronological order.

- Bank reserves are decreased.(4)
- Banks draw money from their reserves.(3)
- Fed presents buyers check for payment.(2)
- Banks have less money available for loans.(5)
- Fed sells securities.(1)

Model

Direct students to read Types of Discounts on page 339. Stress to students that percent off and discount situations usually require two steps: First use the original price and the percent of the discount to determine the dollar amount of the discount. In order to determine the final cost, the dollar amount of the discount must be subtracted from the original price.

Building Business Skills

M ATH
Understanding Discounts

Explanation

Retail businesses often give discounts to attract customers. The discount is usually expressed as a percent off the retail price. Manufacturers also give discounts to the companies they sell to. They give discounts to persuade their customers to do certain things.

Practice

Read about the discounts you may encounter in business. Then answer the following questions on another sheet of paper.

1. A computer manufacturer gives a trade discount of 40 percent on each computer. The list price of a computer is $2000. What is the dollar amount of the retailer's discount?

Jacobs Supply Company			INVOICE NO.	
673 Lynn Lane, Chicago, IL 60620			3027	

SOLD TO: Kelly Cosmetic Company
7609 Wellington
Chicago, IL 60633

INVOICE DATE 8/13/XX
ORDER NUMBER 8119
TERMS 2/10, n/30

QUANTITY	STOCK NO.	DESCRIPTION	UNIT PRICE	AMOUNT
6 Cases	H32	Conditioning formula	190.00	1,140.00
9 Gal	T48	Shampoo concentrate	19.00	171.00
			TOTAL	1,311.00

Connection to CHAPTER 19

Have students make a chart demonstrating how the money supply would increase if the required reserves were 5 percent. Suggest that students use Figure 19-2, How Banks Create Money, as a reference and demonstrate the expansion of money through six loans. For students who need to sharpen their math skills, choose among the worksheets in the *Math Skills Review* booklet.

securities, it places money in the banks' reserves. The increased reserves allow banks to make additional loans, thereby adding money to the economy.

Change Reserve Requirement   The Fed establishes rules for all its member banks. Among these rules is the **reserve requirement.** The reserve requirement specifies the percent of total deposits that must be held either in cash in a bank's own vault or as a deposit in the bank's district Federal Reserve Bank. If the Fed raises the reserve requirement, a larger fraction of each deposit must be placed into the reserve accounts. This leaves less money available for loans.

Controlling the supply of money by changing the reserve requirement is clumsy, and the economy seems to respond slowly. The reserve requirement has remained at 10 percent for several years.

Change Discount Rate   The Fed can act as a "lender of last resort." If a member bank finds its reserves need to be increased, it can borrow money from the Fed. Member banks may also borrow from the Fed if they need funds to satisfy their customers' withdrawals. By making last-resort loans to banks,

Global Perspective

The discount rate at any particular time may vary from one nation to another. At a time in recent years when the U.S. Federal Reserve set the discount rate at 3.0 percent, Canada's discount rate was 4.99 percent, and Germany's was 6.75 percent. Switzerland, the United Kingdom, and Canada have eliminated reserve requirements. Have students list the possible advantages and disadvantages of eliminating the reserve requirements. Encourage them to address how the reserve protects consumers, how it protects the individual banks, and how it protects a nation's economy.

Refer to the *International Business Strategies* booklet for additional strategies and activities.

Types of Discounts

Trade Discount Manufacturers usually set a suggested retail price, called a list price, for their products. To make a profit, the retailer must buy the goods at a cost below the list price. So the manufacturer sells to the retailer at a discount. The discount is a percent off the list price.

Quantity Discount The more merchandise a manufacturer sells to one customer at one time, the better it is for the manufacturer. Less warehouse space is needed, shipping costs are less, and less paperwork is needed for one large order than for several smaller orders. So manufacturers give discounts based on the number of items per order. A shoe manufacturer might give a discount of 5 percent on orders of ten pairs of shoes. An order of fifty pairs might receive a 10 percent discount.

Cash Discount Manufacturers want their money quickly. Customers prefer to keep their money as long as possible. To encourage customers to pay more quickly, manufacturers may allow a customer who pays within 10 days to take a 2 percent discount off the net price—the price after other discounts are taken. If a customer takes the full thirty days to pay, the whole net price is due. This kind of discount may be written as 2/10, n/30.

2. A manufacturer sells T-shirts for $8.00 each. Orders of 10 shirts get a 5 percent discount. How much does a retailer who orders 10 shirts pay for each one?

3. The net price of a grocery store's order for bread is $500. If the manufacturer offers terms of 2/10, n/30, how much can the grocer save by paying the bill within 10 days?

Practice
Use the practice problems to help students understand that often they must determine both the dollar amount of the discount as well as the amount the buyer paid.

1. $0.40 \times \$2000 = \$800$; $\$2000 - \$800 = \$1200$
2. $10 \times \$8.00 = \$80.00$; $\$80 \times 0.05 = \$4.00$; $\$80 - \$4 = \$76$; $\$76 \div 10 = \$7.60$
3. Discount at 10 days $= 0.02 \times \$500 = \$10.00$

the Fed may stop a bank panic or bank run. When the Fed steps in to help a bank meet its obligations, fears are dispelled and depositors are less likely to rush to withdraw their deposits.

Like any other bank, the Fed charges interest. The **discount rate** is the rate of interest the Fed charges its member banks. Lower rates encourage borrowing, and higher rates discourage borrowing. By discouraging borrowing, high discount rates keep the growth of the money supply in check.

Supervise Member Banks

The Fed, along with the FDIC, supervises and regulates member commercial banks. The Fed sets limits for loans and investments by member banks, approves bank mergers, and examines the financial records of member banks. Nonmember commercial banks, savings banks, and even savings and loans and credit unions are regulated by other agencies.

Clear Checks

The Federal Reserve System acts as a central location for clearing checks throughout the nation's banking system.

F.Y.I.

Each of the twelve Federal Reserve banks issues paper money that is identified by a letter of the alphabet. To the left of the portrait on each bill is a circle with a letter in it. Which one did the bills in your wallet come from?

Boston (A), New York (B), Philadelphia (C), Cleveland (D), Richmond (E), Atlanta (F), Chicago (G), St. Louis (H), Minneapolis (I), Kansas City (J), Dallas (K), San Francisco (L)

Learning Activity
Write the following Federal Reserve actions on the board or on a transparency, omitting the words in parentheses:
- The Fed lowers the discount rate (increase).
- The Fed raises the reserve requirement (decrease).
- The Fed sells Treasury bills (decrease).
- The Fed buys Treasury bills (increase).

Call on volunteers to write next to each action whether the effect will likely be an increase or decrease in the money supply.

Cooperative Learning Debate (Pro/Con)

Remind students that in a free market economy the government exercises little control over the economy. Suggest that students list the ways in which the Fed exerts control over the economy and the regulations the Fed imposes on banks. Then ask pairs of students to debate the statement: The role of the Fed in regulating the nation's money supply is in opposition to the principles of a pure market economy. Allow students to evaluate classmates' debate presentations on the following criterion: Do the examples given support the viewpoint expressed?

CHAPTER 20

Business Brief

Value of coins and currency in circulation in selected years (millions of dollars).

	1955	1975	1993
Currency	29,242	68,059	344,465
Coins	1,916	8,285	20,804
Total	$31,158	$76,344	$365,269

✓ Quick Check Answers

1. Act as government's banker, act as consumer protector, regulate the money supply, supervise banks, clear checks, and supply paper currency.
2. Buy or sell government securities, change the reserve requirement, or change the discount rate.
3. Government sale or purchase of government securities; investments the government sells in order to finance growth; the percent of total deposits that must be held either in cash or as a deposit in a Federal Reserve Bank; rate of interest the Fed charges its member banks.

Clearing a check through the Federal Reserve System is a way to insure payment from the financial institutions on which the checks are drawn. This check clearing system maintains the reliability of banks, ensuring that the funds are available for withdrawal. When the system was established, it provided rapid and economical transfer of funds through the economy. Today a check can take only three to five working days to clear.

The Fed also maintains an Automated Clearing House (ACH) to process electronic funds transfers and payment-related information. The government uses Electronic Funds Transfer (EFT) for many large-scale, regular payments such as Social Security and pension payments. Rather than issuing checks, which would be mailed to recipients and then brought to financial institutions for deposit, the ACH allows funds to be deposited directly into the recipients' bank accounts. Many corporations use EFT for payroll, invoices, corporate taxes, and royalty payments. Consumers can use EFT for recurring bills such as insurance, installment loans, and utility payments.

Supply Paper Currency

Each of the twelve Federal Reserve banks in the system issues currency and is responsible for the distribution of that currency. All currency, or dollar bills of all amounts, are Federal Reserve notes. Each Federal Reserve note has a code on it indicating which of the 12 banks issued it. All currency is printed at the Bureau of Printing and Engraving in Washington, D.C. Once the currency is printed, it is shipped from the Bureau to the banks for distribution.

Much of the newly printed currency merely replaces old, torn, or defaced currency. However, each Federal Reserve Bank must have enough paper currency on hand to meet high demands during different times of the year. For example, during winter holidays and vacation time, customers withdraw large amounts of cash from their accounts in commercial banks. The banks borrow from the Fed to help them meet this demand. After the holidays and vacation period, customers deposit money, which allows banks to return to their Federal Reserve Bank the amount borrowed.

GLOBAL VIEW

For most of its existence, the Fed paid little attention to interest rates in other countries. In the 1980s, however, other countries started buying large numbers of U.S. government securities. This made the United States a debtor nation to foreign interests. To encourage foreign interests to borrow money in U.S. money markets, the Fed has to try to assure that interest rates in the United States remain competitive with those in foreign countries.

✓ Quick Check

1. Name six functions of the Fed.
2. What can the Fed do to regulate the money supply?
3. Define *open market operations, government securities, reserve requirement,* and *discount rate.*

Enrichment Strategy

The first U.S. paper money under the Constitution was issued in 1861. All currency ever issued by the U.S. government since then remains valid! Currency in circulation other than Federal Reserve notes includes silver certificates (which have a blue Department of the Treasury seal), United States notes (red seal), and national bank notes (brown seal). Federal Reserve notes, first issued in 1914, have a green seal. In an effort to reduce counterfeiting, the U.S. Treasury began printing newly designed $10, $20, $50, and $100 bills in 1992. Have students research the changes made to the bills' design, including the security strip printed with USA in an alternating up and down pattern. Suggest that students find examples of these new notes and compare them to others, preparing a display showing the differences.

Chapter 20 **Summary**

Main Ideas

1. The Federal Reserve System, the nation's central banking organization, sets monetary policy, supervises banks, and clears checks.
2. The Federal Reserve System is made up of twelve district Federal Reserve banks, a Board of Governors, and about 5000 member banks.
3. The Fed can regulate the money supply by buying or selling securities, changing the reserve requirement, or changing the discount rate.
4. The Fed regulates activities of its member banks, including setting limits for loans and investments, approving bank mergers, and examining financial records.
5. Magnetic ink character recognition allows the Federal Reserve to safely and securely handle billions of transactions a year.
6. Trade discount, quantity discount, and cash discount are three kinds of incentives used by manufacturers and wholesalers to attract business customers.

CASE ANALYSIS Power of the Fed

Although our political system has checks and balances on the powers of the President and Congress, there are few checks on the powers of the Board of Governors of the Federal Reserve System. Under current law, the Board of Governors is free to act within broad limits established by Congress and the President. Actions the Fed takes are important to the success of the government's economic policy, but there is no guarantee that members of the Board of Governors or the Chair will cooperate with Congress and the President in implementing economic policies. Some political leaders think the powers of the Fed's Board of Governors should be limited or that the members should be made responsible to the President. Others are against this because they think it would allow the Fed to be used for political reasons, not the good of our economic system. What would be good or bad about this idea? How would putting the Fed under the control of the President affect you, your friends, or family?

CHAPTER 20   THE FEDERAL RESERVE SYSTEM AND MONETARY POLICY   **341**

Main Ideas

Main Ideas summarizes the key information in the chapter. It is a useful tool for reinforcement and review.

CASE ANALYSIS

Case Analysis provides a chapter-related case for student analysis and application of decision-making skills.

Answer
Students' answers will vary.

QUICK QUIZ

1. What two elements must be balanced in monetary policy? (Sufficient money and credit must be available for economic growth without causing inflation.)
2. How many districts are in the Federal Reserve System? (12)
3. What are the three main responsibilities of the Fed? (Regulate the money supply; supervise member banks, clear checks.)
4. Name three things the Fed can do to control the amount of money in the economy. (Change the reserve requirement, change the discount rate, buy or sell government securities.)

Chapter 20 Review

APPLY

Answers

Use the Language of Business

1. monetary policy, **2.** reserve requirement, **3.** open market operations, **4.** tight money policy, **5.** loose money policy, **6.** discount rate, **7.** the Fed, **8.** government securities

Review What You Learned

1. The Federal Reserve System, which is the central banking organization of the United States.
2. A banking policy that affects the supply of money in circulation, which in turn affects the amount of credit in the economy and the amount of business activity in the economy.
3. Regulating the money supply, supervising banks, clearing checks, and supplying paper currency.
4. Limits loans and investments by member banks, approves bank mergers, and examines the financial records of member banks.
5. Commercial banks and the government.
6. Sell securities from its own portfolio holdings, raise the reserve requirement, and raise the discount rates.
7. Magnetic ink character recognition, used by banks to identify checks as they are processed.
8. Trade, quantity or volume, and cash.

Understand Business Concepts

1. To end financial panics by regulating the nation's money supply, supervising banks, and clearing checks.
2. By purchasing stock in their district Federal Reserve bank.
3. High rates discourage borrowing and thereby limit the growth of the economy.
4. By buying back government securities, thereby pumping money into the economy that is used to create money through the banking system.
5. Buy securities, lower the reserve requirement, or lower the discount rate.

Use the Language of Business

Choose the term that best matches each numbered definition.

discount rate
the Fed
government securities
loose money policy

monetary policy
open market operations
reserve requirement
tight money policy

1. Buying and selling government securities by the Fed.
2. Percentage of a bank's total deposits that must be held in reserve.
3. Policy that affects the money supply and thus credit and business activity in the economy.
4. Policy that discourages lending.
5. Policy that promotes lending.
6. Rate of interest the Fed charges its member banks.
7. Organization that regulates banking and implements monetary policy.
8. Investments sold by the government to finance growth.

Review What You Learned

1. What is meant by *the Fed?*
2. What is monetary policy?
3. What are the major functions of the Fed?
4. What are some of the regulations the Fed can impose on commercial banks?
5. Who banks at Federal Reserve Banks?
6. Name three ways in which the Fed can slow the growth of the economy.
7. What is MICR? How is it used by banks?
8. Name three kinds of discounts manufacturers offer to retailers.

Understand Business Concepts

1. Why was the Federal Reserve System established?
2. How does a national bank become a member of the Fed?
3. How will an increase in the discount rate affect the economy?
4. How does the Fed use open market operations to move the economy out of a slump?
5. What three things can the Fed do to make money more available to consumers and businesses in the country's economy?
6. What is the goal of monetary policy?
7. What is MICR? What advantage does it have for the banks?
8. How might a manufacturer encourage a retailer to pay for materials with cash within 10 days of purchase?

Think Critically

1. **Judge.** Why is the chair of the Federal Reserve System such an important position?
2. **Explain.** How can the Fed use the reserve requirement to slow the economy's growth?

---

6. To ensure that enough money and credit are available to allow expansion of the economy without allowing rapid inflation, monetary policy must balance tight and loose money policies.
7. Magnetic ink character recognition, electronic funds transfer; they enable the Fed to process huge numbers of transactions quickly and accurately.
8. Offer to deduct a specified percent from the cost of the materials if payment is made within 10 days.

Think Critically

1. Answers will vary, but students should mention that as the chair of the Fed a person has an enormous amount of influence over how much money circulates in the economy, and this affects every facet of business.
2. By increasing the reserve requirement. An increased requirement leaves less money for banks to loan and so less money circulates in the economy.

Chapter 20 **Review**

Use What You Learned

1. **Group Project.** Form a four-member team. Plan and organize a model of the Fed. Use your model to show how the Fed can influence the amount of money in the economy. Remember you will need to

   - issue paper money,
   - establish a reserve requirement for banks,
   - determine a discount rate for banks,
   - create some securities that you will either buy or sell.

   Prepare a pamphlet or small booklet for display, explaining how the Fed's monetary policy influences the economy. Include a description of the four activities listed above.

2. Find out the name of the current Chair of the Federal Reserve. Collect several newspaper or magazine articles about recent Fed actions. Determine which articles are critical of the chair's decisions and which support the decisions. List the reasons in each case. Then write a 250-word essay telling whether you agree or disagree with the chair's decision. Give reasons for your opinion.

3. The Bank of England was used as the model for forming and organizing our Federal Reserve System. Choose the central banks of three foreign nations to research. Identify their main functions and responsibilities and compare them to those of the Fed. Prepare a three-minute Global Banking Television News Report for your class.

4. **Skill Reinforcement.** A toy store buys fifty bicycles with a list price of $100 each. If the store gets a 30 percent trade discount and a 10 percent quantity discount, and pays its bill, which is marked 2/10, n/30, within ten days, what is the total cost of the order? Write an explanation of how you arrived at the total.

5. **Computer Application.** Use E-mail to contact the nearest Federal Reserve System branch bank. Request general information about the Federal Reserve System and particular information about that Federal Reserve System branch. Share the information you receive with classmates.

Save your work in your Business Portfolio.

Use What You Learned
1. Be sure that each student takes part in the group project. Possible rubrics: Booklet, Brochure, Model.
2. Remind students that they may find information about the Fed in business and economics sections of newspapers and magazines. Rubrics: Note Taking, Essay.
3. Remind students to keep their final objective in mind as they research the central banks. Possible rubrics: Oral Presentation, Script, Video.
4. Fifty bicycles with a list price of $100 cost a total of $5000. The 30 percent trade discount is $1500. The 10 percent quantity discount is $500. To find the net cost, subtract both discounts from the list price: $5000 − $2000 = $3000. The net price is $3000. Because the retailer pays within ten days, the cash discount is $60, so the total order costs the retailer $2940. Rubric: Paragraph.
5. Students without access to E-mail can complete this project by preparing and mailing a written request to their Federal Reserve branch bank. Rubric: Essay.

Use the Chapter 20 worksheets in *Student Activity Guide* 1 for additional practice and application activities. *Student Activity Guide 1* provides vocabulary exercises, reading comprehension checks, problems, projects, and simulations of business and economic situations. A Teacher's Annotated Edition provides answers.

ASSESS

Portfolio Assessment
These projects are designed to lead students to develop a collection of their best work to submit to you for assessment. You and your students should decide which projects will be included in their respective Business Portfolios. Refer students to the specific rubric(s) from the *Alternative Assessment Strategies* booklet listed with each of the project notes below. These rubrics will alert students to the criteria you will use to assess their projects.

Chapter Assessment
Use the Chapter 20 Test from the *Test Masters* booklet to evaluate students' understanding of the chapter concepts. An answer key is provided. Or create your own customized test using the *Testmaker* software.

Business Issue

Business Issue

REDLINING

Highlight the Issue

Before students read pages 344–355, ask them to discuss the consequences for a person who wants to start a business but cannot obtain a loan to start that business. Discuss also the consequences for a bank that extends credit to someone who later defaults on his or her loan.

REDLINING

When banks systematically refuse to provide credit to low-income or minority neighborhoods, it is called redlining. Should the federal government regulate the lending process to ensure against practices such as redlining?

Pro

Discrimination in lending is a serious problem. At banks across the United States, blacks are turned down for mortgages an average of 2.4 times more often than whites—no matter what their income levels. As one advocate for fair lending said, "It's a simple story: If you're a minority, our nation's banks want only your deposits, not your loan application." Whether banks are discriminating against minorities deliberately or simply as a result of unfair lending requirements, this is a widespread problem that needs to be solved.

The 1977 Community Reinvestment Act (CRA) prohibits redlining and calls on banks to help economically disadvantaged neighborhoods by providing credit. Under this law, banks have a responsibility to make sure they treat all Americans fairly. Since banks have not upheld their end of this bargain, the government must step in to make sure banks offer all Americans an equal opportunity to get a loan.

The CRA sets up reasonable standards, not quotas, for minority loans. Federal bank examiners check to see that banks are indeed making an effort to grant loans to minority applicants. They also evaluate the banks' credit standards to make sure they don't automatically screen out minorities.

Redlining of poor and minority neighborhoods makes problems that those communities already face—run-down buildings, irresponsible landlords, lack of services and employment opportunities—even worse. Home ownership, on the other hand, contributes to neighborhood stability—a goal that benefits all members of society.

Minorities need to be assured of getting fair treatment when they apply for a loan. Since banks have not done this on their own, the federal government should regulate the lending process to ensure against unfair practices.

344 UNIT 6 FINANCIAL INSTITUTIONS IN THE GLOBAL ECONOMY

Extend the Issue

Have a group of students find out the purpose of the Equal Credit Opportunity Act of 1974. Ask them to make a poster that lists and explains the provisions of the act. Discuss with students whether the act is sufficient to protect against discrimination or whether they think certain provisions might be difficult to enforce.

Con

Unfair lending may have been a problem in the past, but it is no longer. A 1994 study of 220,000 Federal Housing Administration mortgage loans found no evidence of discrimination against minorities.

Government claims of discrimination are based on unfair evaluations of bank records. Federal investigators have only looked at income levels when evaluating bank loan applications from whites, blacks, and other minorities. Banks have to consider financial factors other than income in deciding when to grant loans. So while a minority family and a white family may have the same incomes, the white family might qualify for a loan and the minority family might be rejected if the white family has more savings or less debt than the minority family.

Banks are businesses, and they have an obligation to their investors to show a profit and not to make bad loans. Banks need credit standards to determine which loan applicants are most likely to repay their loans. Some loan applicants may have credit problems because of low-paying jobs or limited savings, but these are economic problems banks can't solve.

Federal regulation of the lending process will lead to a system of racial quotas. There already are cases in which banks have been forced into distributing credit by race. The federal government has also misused the Community Reinvestment Act to force banks to open branches in minority neighborhoods and to make loans at rates beneath prevailing interest rates in order to qualify people who wouldn't otherwise meet loan requirements. Credit should be granted based on financial stability, not on race.

It's not fair to expect banks to solve society's civil rights problems. The federal government should leave banks alone to do what they do best—grant loans to creditworthy applicants.

Update the Issue

Have students look for current articles about discrimination in lending to minorities. What new measures, if any, have been taken to ensure fair credit opportunities? Has additional legislation been passed? Have banks become more self-regulating? Have a class discussion about students' findings to decide whether the evidence they found indicates that discrimination in lending practices continues to be a significant problem.

Unit 7 International Business

Chapter	Learning Objectives
21 **The Global Market** pp. 348–365	• Discuss why nations depend on one another for goods. • Compare and contrast free trade and protectionist policies. • Describe how governments can influence the global market. • Describe how a wife-husband entrepreneurial team met the needs of companies doing business internationally. • Identify what type of data is best displayed in a bar, line, or circle graph.
22 **Other Economic Systems** pp. 366–381	• Describe three basic types of economic systems. • Compare and contrast traditional, command, and market economies. • Identify ways to compare economic systems. • Describe the main computer processing components. • Explain how you could use a Venn diagram to compare and contrast systems.
23 **International Finance** pp. 382–397	• Identify the factors considered in the balance of trade and balance of payments and the relationship between the two. • Describe the currency exchange market and the factors that influence the value of a currency. • Explain how domestic and international businesses that are not connected through computer networks can still quickly exchange information. • Use foreign exchange rates to convert dollars to a foreign currency and foreign currency to dollars.
24 **Global Economic Challenges** pp. 398–415	• Identify benefits and challenges to competition in the international marketplace. • Describe the process of economic development and identify characteristics of developing nations. • Identify food and hospitality jobs within the service industry of developed economies. • Discuss how points of view can affect international trade.

Business Issue: Trade Policy, pp. 416–417

National Standards for Business Education*	Chapter Highlights			
	Focus on Features	**Building Business Skills**	**Visual Learning**	**Case Analysis**
EE: I A, II C, VII B, VII C; *EPF:* III, IV, XIV; *IB:* I A, II B, III B, III D, VIII A, VIII B; *MGMT:* IX A	Entrepreneurs: Hughes and Liebling—TLI International Corporation, p. 354	Math: Building Graphs, p. 356	Leading U.S. Trading Partners, p. 351 United States Exports and Imports, p. 353 Tariff Rates in the United States, p. 358 Members of the European Union, p. 359	Global Trade, p. 363
EPF: IV, V, XI; *IB:* III B, III D; *IS:* I	Technology: Computer Processing Components p. 372	Analysis: Comparing and Contrasting Information, p. 374	Basic Economic Systems, p. 369 Total and Per Capita GNP for Selected Nations With Different Economic Systems, p. 377 Change in Per Capita GNP, p. 378	Economic Systems, p. 379
COMP: IV; *EPF:* III, XIV; *IB:* I A, III A, V A, V D, VIII A, VIII C; *IS:* I	Technology: Modems, p. 388	Math: Exchanging Foreign Currency, p. 390	Comparing U.S. Exports/Imports, p. 385 U.S. Balance of Trade, p. 386 Effects of Depreciation of Currency, p. 392 Effects of Devaluation of Currency, p. 393	Marketing, p. 395
CD: II A; *COMM:* I A, II B, I D; *EPF:* V; *IB:* III A, III D, XV; *MKTG:* III D	Careers: Food and Hospitality, p. 404	Analysis: Interpreting Points of View, p. 408	Developed and Developing Countries, p. 403 Per Capita GDP Around the World, p. 406 World Birthrates, p. 411	Marketing, p. 413

* Level 3 Performance Expectations: Computation (COMP), Economics and Personal Finance (EPF); Entrepreneurship Education (EE), IS (Information Systems), Management (MGMT). See page T14 for all 12 content areas.

Unit 7

Look Back

Ask students to recall that money functions as a medium of exchange, a standard of value, and a store of value. Banks sell a variety of services, all of which involve managing money and stimulating the economy. Most financial transactions—both global and national—are carried out by banks. In the United States, the Federal Reserve System has the primary responsibility of controlling the nation's money supply.

UNIT 7 COOPERATIVE LEARNING PROJECT

Trade-a-Problem Activity

Preparation: For each group, make a photocopy of BLM 15 from the *Cooperative Learning Strategies* booklet.

Guidelines: Have students work in groups to create a problem or question related to the topics explored in Unit 7. One example might be: "How do nations benefit from competing in the global market?" Instruct each group to write the problem or question on BLM 15 and pass it to the next group, who will discuss

International Business

This unit examines the global marketplace. The first chapter discusses the purposes of international trade. The next chapter discusses the ways countries can organize their economies to meet their people's needs. The final chapters discuss the balance of trade and challenges facing developing economies.

Look Ahead
Mention to students that all nations face the same economic challenge—they have to satisfy the unlimited wants of their citizens with limited resources. Countries trade goods they can produce efficiently for those they can't produce efficiently. This process is known as world trade. Nations with different economic systems participate in world trade and the international economy to differing extents.

347

the problem and write a response on the BLM. After a group has written a response, it should pass the problem along to another group. Have groups continue exchanging problems until all groups have had the opportunity to discuss and respond to each other group's problem. Monitor groups' problems or questions to ensure that they are realistic and that they address topics discussed in Unit 7.

FOCUS

Introduce the Chapter

Major Concepts
- Global Producers and Consumers
- Free Trade and Protectionism
- Government Influence on the Global Market
- Benefits of Trading in the Global Market

Introduce the Topic
Write the following statement for the students to complete: "Made in America means. . . ." Call on volunteers to read their statements and tell how they would identify an item made in the United States. Then ask them how they would identify an item made in a foreign country. Indicate that Chapter 21 presents information about producers and consumers around the world.

Use Business Terms
Have students read the list of Business Terms. Ask for ideas about what the terms mean. Record correct answers on the board or a transparency. Advise students to check the meanings of the terms as they read the chapter.

USE VISUALS
Ask students to speculate how the photograph might be related to the content of the chapter they are about to study. (Transportation of imported and exported goods.)

CHAPTER
21

Business terms

export

import

trading partner

specialization

comparative advantage

multinational company

free trade

protectionists

quota

tariff

embargo

348

CHAPTER 21 RESOURCES

Instructional Resources

Lesson Plan for Chapter 21

Teaching Transparencies 21-1, 21-2, 21-3, 21-4

Strategies and Worksheets for Teaching Transparencies 21-1, 21-2, 21-3, 21-4

Enrichment Masters 21-1, 21-2

Student Activity Guide 2–TAE for Chapter 21

Test Master for Chapter 21

Alternative Assessment Strategies

Math Skills Review

International Business Strategies

Cooperative Learning Strategies

Communication Skills Review

Ethics in Business Strategies

The Global Market

Learning objectives

After completing this chapter, you will be able to:
- Discuss why nations depend on one another for goods.
- Compare and contrast free trade and protectionist policies.
- Describe how governments can influence the global market.
- Describe how a wife-husband entrepreneurial team met the needs of companies doing business internationally.
- Identify what type of data is best displayed in a bar, line, or circle graph.

Consider what you know

- Everyone in the United States consumes goods and services. The goods and services we decide to produce depend on what must be sacrificed to produce them. Those things we have to give up to get more of what we want are the opportunity costs of our decisions to produce goods and services.

Consider what you want to know

- Why does the United States import and export some goods and services?
- Which policy is best? Free trade? Protectionism?
- How do governments influence the global market?
- How can we benefit from trading goods and services globally?
- How does TLI International Corporation help its clients do business around the world?
- What are the best uses of a bar graph to display information? Line graph? Circle graph?

Consider how to use what you learn

- As you read through this chapter, keep a list of the manufactured products you use each day and the country of their origin.

Multimedia Resources

Technology Resource Guide

Distance Learning Guide

Internet Resource Guide

Professional Resources

School-to-Work/Tech Prep Strategies

Instructional Poster

Spanish Resources

Testmaker Software for Chapter 21

The Wall Street Journal Video Series
   Video & Activities for Chapter 21

Business and Marketing Computer
   Applications—An Integrated Software
   Simulation Using Microsoft Works

Stocktracker—A Stock Market Software
   Simulation

Where's the Dough? Board Game

Motivate the Learning

Learning Objectives
Indicate to students that the learning objectives show what they will learn in the chapter. Tell students to refer frequently to these objectives and to use them to help focus their reading and study of the chapter. Note that the last two objectives listed refer to the Focus on Entrepreneurs feature and the Building Business Skills feature.

Consider What You Know
Review briefly the main sections of *Chapter 20 The Federal Reserve System and Monetary Policy:* The Fed and the Money Supply; Organization of the Fed; and Functions of the Fed.

Consider What You Want to Know
Have students preview the chapter in order to see how it will provide answers to the questions. They can read the headings and subheadings, look at the figures and photographs, and read the captions.

Consider How to Use What You Learn
Remind students that at the end of the chapter they will develop some projects related to the global market and foreign trade. Suggest that as students read the chapter they keep in mind the variety of producers and consumers who trade in the global market.

CHAPTER 21

TEACH

Business Connection

From 1986 to 1994, United States exports more than doubled. This boom was fueled by exports described as "knowledge-intensive" manufactured goods. The value of these goods is derived from the skills that went into making them rather than the cost of the components. Knowledge-intensive products are likely to become a major force in the global market.

Develop Concepts

Global Producers and Consumers

International trade makes up for less than 10 percent of the U.S. economy, yet it affects everyone. Offer examples of products students would not be able to purchase without international trade. Examples may include chocolate (countries along the west coast of Africa and Brazil), and coffee (countries such as Colombia, Brazil, and Nigeria). Note that businesses would be without the magnesium used in batteries and the bauxite ore (Australia, Guinea, and Jamaica) from which aluminum is extracted.

Learning Activity

Ask a volunteer to explain how a product can be both an import and an export. (Sample: the United States may export transportation equipment to Japan. In Japan, that same transportation equipment is an import.) Help students recognize that whether a product is an import or an export depends on the person's—or country's—point of view.

350   UNIT 7

Most countries do not produce everything their citizens want. A country may not have the necessary resources, it may not have the technology, or it may not be interested in making a product. However, most countries can satisfy many of their wants and needs for goods and services by buying them in the global market. The market potential is amazing. The U.S. market includes about 250 million people. The global market, at 5 billion people, has 20 times as many potential customers.

The United States, for example, buys minerals and other natural resources from other countries—tin from China, manganese from South Africa, and bauxite from Australia. We also buy manufactured goods from other countries—jewelry from Mexico, handbags from South Korea, and paper from Canada. In return, we sell items such as wheat, soybeans, corn, cotton, computers, and technology abroad. Countries depend on one another for goods and services. They sometimes compete for markets in which to sell goods and services. Companies in different countries are producing the same type of product or service. With the increased trade and competition, business leaders must have a worldwide perspective.

GLOBAL PRODUCERS AND CONSUMERS

Goods produced in one country and sold in another are **exports** of that country. Foreign-made goods or materials brought into a country are **imports.** Today our country depends on imports as a major source of machinery, metals, other industrial materials, and food products. We use some of these imports in their original forms; others are processed into other goods. For example, bauxite is processed into aluminum and then fabricated into aluminum products such as soft drink cans. In turn, many countries depend on our exports to meet their needs. Some of our major exports include food products, grains, chemicals, airplanes, and computers.

We trade with almost every other country in the world. The countries that are our main producers and consumers are our **trading partners.** Figure 21-1 on page 351 shows the top six U.S. import and export trading partners.

Curriculum Connection   Geography

Have students work in groups of four to generate a list of the ten most common items they purchase in a week. Have them investigate where the items were manufactured and research the origin of raw materials needed to manufacture items made in the United States. (For example, raw materials to make aluminum cans come from Australia, Guinea, and Jamaica.) Suggest that they place a red flag on a world map to indicate the location of each manufacturing nation and use a yellow flag to indicate the location of a nation that supplies raw materials used in manufacturing.

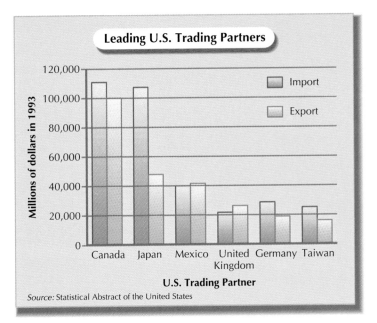

Leading U.S. Trading Partners

Millions of dollars in 1993

- Import
- Export

U.S. Trading Partner: Canada, Japan, Mexico, United Kingdom, Germany, Taiwan

Source: Statistical Abstract of the United States

FIGURE 21-1

The United States trades with a variety of foreign nations. According to this graph, which is greater— the value of the U.S. imports from these countries or the value of the U.S. exports to these countries?

Our economic system is built on **specialization.** Few people produce all of the goods and services that they need. Instead, individuals concentrate their activities in a particular area or field, such as being a carpenter, a doctor, or a secretary. The money that each worker earns is then used to buy goods and services that others have specialized in producing. With specialization, we are all dependent on one another for goods and services.

Countries specialize, too, and trade some of the items that they produce in order to gain the goods and services that the other countries produce. For example, the United States, Japan, and Germany are the world's top automobile producers. They have the resources—materials, technology, factories, and labor force—needed to produce a large volume of cars. Actually, these countries have a **comparative advantage** in producing cars—meaning that this is the one area of production which is a real strength compared to other ways in which they could use their resources. Other countries could produce autos. But many of them have decided that they have a comparative advantage in producing something else, leaving auto production to such countries as the United States, Japan, and Germany.

CHAPTER 21   THE GLOBAL MARKET   **351**

Making Connections ➪ Everyday Living

Point out to students that immigrant communities throughout the United States often have unique imports for sale. Organize students into groups to research and develop lists of the interesting and/or unusual specialty items in their area imported by more recent immigrant groups such as Chinese, Middle Easterners, Southeast Asians, Indians, Pakistanis, Puerto Ricans, Haitians, and others. Students might include natural and prepared foods and various manufactured items such as saris and chadors. Have students stage an "international bazaar" in which a member of each group tells about the items discovered.

USE VISUALS

Determine if students are reading Figure 21-1 accurately by calling on volunteers to use the graph to answer questions such as "What is the value of goods that the United States imports from Canada? (About $110 billion: 110,000 × $1 million.) The value of the goods the United States exports to Canada? (About $100 billion.)

Answer to caption: The value of U.S. imports from these countries is greater than the value of U.S. exports to them.

USE TRANSPARENCIES

Use Teaching Transparency 21-1 and its corresponding strategies and worksheet from the *Teaching Transparency Strategies and Worksheets* booklet to help students become familiar with the trading partners of the United States. Verify student worksheets using the Answer Key.

Learning Activity

Indicate to students that they may already be familiar with the concept of *specialization.* For example, a baseball team has players that specialize in playing a specific position such as first base, pitcher, or catcher. Few players are equally effective at all these positions. Photocopy and distribute Enrichment Master 21-1 which lists additional examples of specialization. Have students use the information to create an operational definition of the economic concept of *specialization.*

The kinds of resources available to a country often influence what it specializes in producing. For example, a major industry for Colombia is the production of coffee. The climate, soil, and environmental conditions are right for them to produce coffee. Few nations in the world have a climate suitable for raising large amounts of coffee. We certainly could raise coffee here in the United States, but it would probably have to be done in a greenhouse, which would make coffee very costly to produce. We don't have the climate, soil, and environment to efficiently produce coffee. Obviously, Colombia has a comparative advantage in producing coffee; the United States does not have that comparative advantage.

As another example, a country that lacks capital and advanced technology but has a large population may specialize in assembling items that require a great deal of manual labor. Because of the abundance of labor, the wages would probably be low. Thus, the cost of the manual labor would be low, contributing to reasonable prices for the item being produced. In South Korea and Taiwan, where there are large numbers of workers, one of their specializations is the assembling of color televisions, videocassette recorders, and computer components sold around the world.

Such specialization could not occur unless we had a lot of trade among nations. Without trade, each nation would try to produce the items that it needs and wants, some of which would not be very natural or efficient for them to produce. Similarly, we as individuals could not specialize in doing one type of job, such as teaching, fixing cars, and building houses, unless we had the opportunity to get other things that we need and want from others.

F.Y.I.

A product shipped from the United States to Japan is considered a U.S. export and a Japanese import. These classifications apply even if the factory in the U.S. is foreign-owned and the purchaser in Japan is a U.S. company.

Products made in the United States are sold to almost every other country in the world. Foreign firms sell to the United States, too. Consumers here are familiar with Colombian coffee, French perfumes, Japanese cameras, and Swiss watches. The graphs in Figure 21-2 on page 353 show what products and services are among our major exports and imports.

Many U.S. companies have established and maintained plants in foreign countries. If resources to make the product exist in the foreign country, a U.S. business may find it more economical to manufacture the product on foreign soil. Most of our large corporations, such as Ford, General Motors, and IBM, have manufacturing and other fabrication plants in foreign countries. In much the same way, foreign companies such as Toyota and Volkswagen maintain plants in the United States. A company that does business in many countries and has plants and offices in many countries around the world is sometimes called a **multinational company.**

United States Exports and Imports

Exports

Chemicals 10%
Electrical machinery 8%
Agricultural products 10%
Machinery 20%
Mineral fuels 2%
Other manufactured goods 50%

Imports

Agricultural products 4%
Machinery 16%
Chemicals 5%
Electrical machinery 8%
Mineral fuels 10%
Other manufactured goods 57%

Source: Statistical Abstract of the United States

Percentage Amounts for 1993

FIGURE 21-2

The United States imports and exports a variety of goods. Which categories of goods does the United States import more than it exports?

Quick Check

1. Define *imports, exports, trading partners,* and *multinational company.*
2. What is meant by *specialization? Comparative advantage?*

FREE TRADE AND PROTECTIONISM

Trade with other countries has often been controlled as a matter of economic or foreign policy. The emerging global market has rekindled a continuing controversy about what kind of foreign trade policy should be in place. Some people favor **free trade,** a policy encouraging few limitations and little government involvement in the trading system. Proponents of free trade cite several advantages:

- Free trade encourages competition among companies producing the same types of goods/services in various nations. When a nation protects a particular industry through governmental policies, it is shielding that industry from competition—thus discouraging efficiency, quality, and lower prices.
- Free trade encourages the most efficient use of limited resources. We do not have enough resources to satisfy all of

CHAPTER 21   THE GLOBAL MARKET   **353**

Curriculum Connection   History

Organize students into several groups, and assign each group a particular period in U.S. history. Have groups research international trade during the assigned historical periods to determine:

- U.S. trading partners of the period
- The revenue that is generated by the trade
- Any trade restrictions or legislation
- The effect of restrictions on U.S. markets.

Groups can report their findings to the rest of the class by presenting a series of news reports called "The United States Trade Story."

FOCUS ON **Entrepreneurs**

FOCUS ON **Entrepreneurs**

Discuss

Ask students to imagine they wish to start an import/export business and identify several tasks for which they might use the services of TLI. Have students discuss how using the services of a company such as TLI can increase the probability of making a profit in a foreign market.

Hughes and Liebling— TLI International Corporation

In 1977, Lyric Hughes and her husband, James Liebling, decided to call their newly formed company Trans-Lingual Communications, Inc. This name proved to be a tongue twister for their Japanese clients, so Hughes and Liebling shortened it to TLI. After all, concern for the problems of people doing business in foreign lands was the reason they got started in the first place.

TLI is still going strong, filling a variety of real needs in today's global economy. It helps its clients understand cultural differences and smooths the path for companies trying to sell their products abroad. To accomplish this,

TLI offers business cards, videos, print material, and consultation, as well as foreign language translation and interpretation services. TLI often works with large firms to train employees who work outside the United States.

Recently TLI has formed a joint venture with China's *People's Daily*, which is the world's largest newspaper with a circulation of five million. The two companies will use the newspaper's resources to help American companies carry out business activities in China.

Going into such a business was a natural for founder Lyric Hughes, who speaks six languages. Because her father worked for the United States foreign service, the family lived outside the United States for some years. She loved foreign travel, and at 16 was an exchange student in Japan.

After she returned to the United States and completed college, Hughes decided she had discovered a

Business Brief

Many countries around the world set aside free trade zones or foreign trade zones to encourage international trade. In these zones goods can be stored, imported, assembled, exhibited or processed without import taxes. Taxes are paid only to the importing country, not to the country where trade is occurring.

Business & FOREIGN LANGUAGES

American companies wishing to sell their products overseas sometimes need to change brand names or slogans when marketing their products in other countries. For example, the phrase "Body by Fisher" became "Corpse by Fisher!" To avoid costly language mistakes, many companies employ translation services to prepare them for entry into a foreign market.

the wants of the people living in the world. Not meeting those needs is compounded when we use resources inefficiently. Free trade encourages people to produce those things they do best and then trade what they produce for the other things that they want. Governmental policies that protect selected industries encourage resources to be used for those areas that might not be the most efficient.

People taking the opposite view are termed **protectionists.** They believe that government should play a major role in regulating trade and subsidizing industry to protect the domestic economy. Protectionists cite several reasons:

- Free trade threatens job security in those industries where there is strong competition from foreign countries. For example, there have been fairly large layoffs in the U.S. textile industry, as the making of cloth and clothing has been more inexpensively completed elsewhere. Those jobs could be saved if the government implemented procedures to protect that industry from the competition. If these jobs are not saved, however, there are more costs to society,

Cooperative Learning Debate (Pro/Con)

Suggest that students, working in groups of four, participate in a debate of the following proposition: "The United States government has a responsibility to offer protection for domestic industries." Students taking the pro position should indicate how the government might fulfill this responsibility. Students taking the con position can suggest ways other than government regulation to protect industries. Have students present their debates for the class and allow the class to judge which side has presented a more persuasive argument.

Refer to the *Cooperative Learning Strategies* booklet for additional cooperative learning strategies.

need. "I thought foreign firms needed help setting up offices and doing business in this country." She attracted her first clients by advertising her consulting services in restaurants visited by Japanese patrons. Next, she offered to soften the culture shock for American firms opening offices abroad. She started by writing letters to companies whose names began with A. She received so many replies that she never moved on to the Bs!

As a lawyer with additional degrees in international relations and international currency, James Liebling, Lyric Hughes' husband, was an ideal business partner. Since the day the husband-and-wife entrepreneurial team opened TLI, Hughes has run the business day to day, and Liebling has traveled extensively to seek out new business opportunities. He also acts as legal counsel. At first, they worked out of their small apartment. Today, TLI has grown. It has a permanent staff of 12 and can call on the services of 2500 freelancers!

As the global marketplace expands, more and more businesses will depend on multicultural understanding for success.

Follow Through
Have students form a concept web that indicates how Lyric Hughes' and James Liebling's experience and education are related to the tasks they perform for clients. Remind students the web should include phrases such as translation services, interpretation services, speaks foreign languages, degree in international relations, and so on.

such as retraining costs, increased social costs, and unemployment costs.

- There are certain industries that should be protected by the government. Some industries, such as steel and defense contractors, are necessary for the protection of the country. These should be protected even though a company in another country may be able to make steel and military arms much better and more cheaply than our own companies. If we need to defend ourselves, for example, we would not want to rely on a company in another country for such items. That country might sympathize with our opponent. Also, new industries have sizable startup costs that may make them fairly uncompetitive at the beginning stages. These fledgling industries need to be protected from foreign competition until they can recover their startup costs and become strong enough to compete effectively in foreign markets.

The pros and cons of world trade will continue to be debated. The debate becomes intensified when new trade agreements are considered or when governments attempt to influence the global market.

CHAPTER 21   THE GLOBAL MARKET   **355**

Global Perspective

Most Japanese firms belong to a *keiretsu* (ky reht soo), a tightly knit group of firms governed by an external board of directors. The keiretsu are often made up of firms that compete with one another. The governing board works to ensure that competition does not force individual firms out of business. In the United States, a similar arrangement among competing firms would be illegal under the antitrust laws. Have students suggest remedies that business and or the U.S. government can take to counter the advantages of the keiretsu.

Refer to the *International Business Strategies* booklet for additional strategies and activities.

Learning Activity
Encourage students to generate a list of ten or more phrases that describe trading, or the effects of trading, in the global market. (Encourages competition, threatens job security, threatens national security, and so on.) Have students categorize their phrases as reasons that support free trade or protectionism.

Business Brief
Protectionism in Japan may help certain segments of the economy, such as the rice farmers or auto workers, but it does not help Japanese consumers. Because foreign competition is limited in Japan, consumer products are generally higher priced. For instance, citrus fruits cost about six times more in Japan than they do in the United States. Even cameras and electronics cost more in Japan than elsewhere.

Model

Stress to students that a useful graph is one in which the data and the graph are each used to their best advantage. For example, a circle graph is best for showing the relationship between the parts and the whole. A bar graph gives a good indication of how one item stacks up against another. A line graph is an excellent choice for showing how a quantity changes as time passes.

Quick Check Answers

1. Few limits and little government involvement in trade; view that governments should regulate trade and subsidize domestic industry.

2. Foreign competition can mean improved products, lower prices for consumers, and more efficient use of limited resources. Free trade threatens the job security of U.S. workers; the economic security of certain industries must be protected; young industries need protection.

Develop Concepts

Government Influence on the Global Market

Stress that governments have a variety of tools at their disposal to influence and regulate foreign trade. In addition to quotas, tariffs, and embargoes that may be placed on goods, governments can enter into trade agreements with foreign nations.

Building Business Skills

MATH
Building Graphs

Explanation

A graph often makes the relationships between numbers much clearer than a string of figures would. Three common types are bar graphs, line graphs, and circle—or pie—graphs.

Practice

Read the information about building graphs. Then choose the appropriate type of graph to present the data in each problem.

Problems

1. Last year MaxiMotors produced a total of 500,000 motor vehicles: 200,000 cars; 50,000 large trucks; 100,000 small trucks; 25,000 buses; and 125,000 vans.

2. Over the last six months, monthly profits for the Pleasing Pets retail stores have been $10,000; $13,000; $11,000; $17,000; $17,000; and $19,000.

3. Your top sellers had the following sales in millions of dollars last year: Brett, $9.5; Pat, 8; Paula, 6.25; Sam, 4.5; Gerry, 3.

Quick Check

1. Define *free trade* and *protectionist*.
2. What reasons do people give to support a free trade policy? A protectionist policy?

GOVERNMENT INFLUENCE ON THE GLOBAL MARKET

Today's world trade involves government regulations and taxes on goods moving from one country to another. An agency of the federal government, the U.S. Customs Office, keeps track of the amount of goods going in and out of our country. Governments can influence the amount of foreign trade by imposing quotas, tariffs, or embargoes to protect domestic businesses. Governments can also influence trade by entering into trade alliances and trade agreements with other nations.

Curriculum Connection   English and Communication

Have students work in pairs to interview three adults about the arguments for and against free trade. Students can create a profile of each of the adults that includes their opinions about free trade issues. Have students make the profiles as complete as possible, including the age, gender, and occupation of the people interviewed. Students can pool their results and present the "typical" profile of a person for or against free trade or present their data in similar graph form.

For students who need to sharpen their written communication skills, choose among the worksheets in the *Communication Skills Review* booklet.

GRAPHS

Bar Graphs
A bar graph compares groups of items in a category. To build a bar graph, draw two perpendicular lines or axes. One represents the number of items in the category (units sold); the other axis is the groups being compared (districts). Using the data given, find the number of items for each group. Draw a bar for each group.

Line Graphs
A line graph shows change over time or direction of change. To make a line graph, draw two axes, one for the numbers of items and one for time periods. For each time period, find the number of items. Make a dot where each number and its period meet. Draw lines connecting the dots. The example shows how the population of a city grew year to year.

Circle Graphs
A circle, or pie, graph shows the parts of a whole. To make a circle graph, change number amounts into fractions or percentages of the total. Divide a circle into pie-shaped sections corresponding to these fractions by drawing lines from the center to the outer edge of the circle. Label the sections. The example shows the part of a company's total budget to be spent on each item.

Laws Restricting Trade

Sometimes a government may place a **quota,** or fixed limit, on the export or import of a product. Countries that export oil, for example, may impose quotas on the amount of oil produced. Remember, if too much is produced, the price of the item declines. So, imposing a quota on oil production can force oil prices to remain high.

A government may put a quota on items imported from a specific country to indicate its disapproval of that country's trade policies. Quotas can be used to protect a country's business firms from too much competition from other countries. In some instances, quotas are used to help protect new industries that have just been established.

Government can also protect domestic businesses by setting a tariff on foreign products. A **tariff** is a special tax on goods made in another country. A tariff effectively increases the price of imported goods because the foreign company paying the tariff generally passes the cost on through higher prices. If increased imports are desired, the government may lower or eliminate the tariff on that product. The item can thus be sold

CHAPTER 21   THE GLOBAL MARKET   **357**

1.

2.

3.

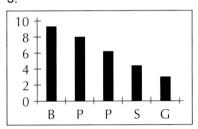

Learning Activity
Ask students to review business periodicals and business and financial sections of newspapers to find evidence of governments' influence on foreign trade. Suggest that they display their findings on the bulletin board.

Cooperative Learning Group Discussion

There are virtually no restrictions on trade within the 50 states. In fact, restrictions are expressly forbidden by the U.S. Constitution. Encourage students to find the section or sections in the Constitution that prohibit at least one restriction on international trade and record their findings. Next have them generate a list of the problems that might arise if the Constitution had been silent on trade among the states, which now number 50.

Refer to the *Cooperative Learning Strategies* booklet for additional cooperative learning strategies.

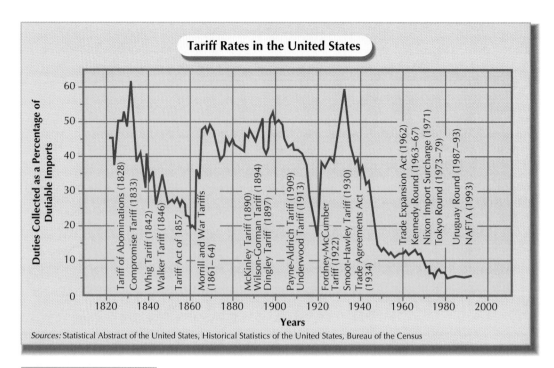

FIGURE 21-3

Tariff rates in the United States have fluctuated greatly over the years. What seems to be the current trend in tariff rates?

at a lower price, making it a more attractive purchase. If reduced imports are desired, a government can increase tariffs, thereby increasing prices on imported items.

Tariff rates can be changed, removed, or added as the government sees a need for increasing or decreasing imports. Today, tariffs account for less than two percent of the federal government's income, but are still used to protect domestic industries. Figure 21-3 above shows how tariff rates have fluctuated in the United States.

If a government wishes to stop the import or export of goods, it places a complete restriction, or an **embargo,** on importing or exporting them. For example, there is an embargo on the exportation of timber cut from federal lands. Oil taken from the North Slope fields in Alaska may not be exported. An embargo may be used to show how a country feels about another's policies. The ban on the sale of Cuban cigars in the United states is an example of an embargo for political reasons. An embargo may be used to prevent foreign firms from competing with a country's own businesses. Occasionally the government considers putting an embargo on some foreign foodstuffs, for example.

Reteaching Strategy

Trade Alliances

Occasionally a group of nations may form an economic community. The goals of the community are to promote the free movement of resources and products among the members of the community and to form common economic policies.

One of the most noteworthy economic communities is the European Union (EU), a trading community of 15 nations of Europe. The EU was formerly known as the European Economic Community, and before that the Common Market. Figure 21-4 below shows which European nations were members of the EU as of January 1, 1995. EU members hope that, by eliminating internal trade barriers and by cooperating among themselves, they can achieve greater efficiency and prosperity. This standardization would eliminate the need to customize products to satisfy regulations and restrictions of each country. What's more, it would eliminate some 60 million custom forms each year!

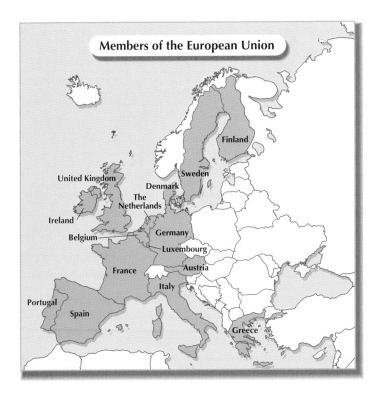

Members of the European Union

FIGURE 21-4

The European Union is the oldest and best known economic community formed to promote free trade among the members of the community and to foster common economic policies. What 15 nations make up the EU?

Enrichment Strategy

The exporting countries with boundaries on the Pacific Ocean are in the process of forming a trade alliance of their own. The Asia-Pacific Economic Cooperation (APEC) is bringing together the emerging nations that border the Pacific. Have students review current periodicals to determine the primary issues facing these nations and the current proposals and guidelines proposed or implemented. (In 1994, APEC nations included Australia, Brunei, Indonesia, Japan, Malaysia, New Zealand, the Philippines, Singapore, Canada, South Korea, Thailand, the United States, China, Hong Kong, Taiwan, Mexico, Papua New Guinea, and Chile.)

Learning Activity

Encourage students to find out the current price of crude oil. Suggest students highlight any references to the trade alliance OPEC. (The 11 members of OPEC are Algeria, Indonesia, Iran, Iraq, Kuwait, Libya, Nigeria, Qatar, Saudi Arabia, the United Arab Emirates, and Venezuela.) Remind students that price is always subject to supply and demand. Then ask students to explain how trade alliances such as OPEC can influence the price of some goods.

Business Brief

As a participant in the European Union, Great Britain has agreed to market food in metric quantities. As of October 1, 1995, soft drinks, ground meat, and snack foods became available in packages measured in liters, kilograms, and grams. Breweries, however, are exempt from the conversion and continue to sell their products in pints and half pints.

Learning Activity

Photocopy and distribute Enrichment Master 21-2, the map of the region covered by the North American Free Trade Agreement. Have students use the map to determine how the market for U.S. goods will change with the agreement.

Some U.S. economists worry that the EU may adopt a protectionist policy—setting high tariffs and imposing harsh trade restrictions on goods from non-EU nations. Such measures would effectively keep non-European goods out of EU member countries.

Concerns also exist about how the EU will deal with countries that are new to democracy and the free market system. East Germany became a member of the EU when it unified with West Germany. Hungary was the first post-communist country to seek membership. Other former Soviet bloc countries seeking membership include Poland, the Czech Republic, and Slovakia. However, the EU's policy on admitting former members of the Soviet bloc is not yet formed.

The world's oil and petroleum producers have come together to protect their common interest: the price of oil. One of the most powerful trade alliances, the Organization of Petroleum Exporting Countries (OPEC), has worked continuously to ensure that its members receive a consistent and adequate price for the oil and petroleum they export.

Trade Agreements

Trade agreements are another way to increase trade among countries. A long-standing trade agreement was formed by the United States and 33 other nations as the General Agreement on Tariffs and Trade (GATT). GATT had set its goal as the reduction or elimination of tariffs and other barriers to world trade. The organization provides a forum for tariff negotiations and a vehicle for settling international trade disputes.

There have been eight "rounds" of negotiations aimed at reducing tariffs. Over the years GATT has reduced the average worldwide tariff on manufactured goods from 45 percent to 5 percent. The most recent round, called the Uruguay round, lasted seven years before its passage in 1994. This round succeeded in lowering trade barriers around the world. Today, 117 nations participate in the World Trade Organization (WTO), the new name for GATT.

While the focus of the WTO is worldwide, the United States has also worked to produce regional trade agreements. Most notable is the U.S. effort to reduce the trade barriers between itself and its nearest neighbors, Canada and Mexico, who are also among its top trading partners. In 1993 these three countries signed the North American Free Trade Agreement (NAFTA). The goal of this agreement is to have free trade among the countries by the year 2009 by eliminating all tariffs on goods produced in and traded between Canada, Mexico, and the United States. In addition, NAFTA is the first trade agree-

Reteaching Strategy

Have students imagine they have an opportunity to increase the sales of a product by exporting it. Suggest that they work in teams to list the laws, customs, consumer preferences, transportation, currency, and political situation they would need to research concerning the country receiving the product. Ask students to report on the difficulties and benefits they experience in their attempts to participate in international trade. Call on volunteers to make suggestions regarding agreements and conventions that might make trading take place more smoothly.

ment in history to take into account specific provisions for protecting the environment.

The first round of tariff reductions on goods traded between the three countries has already been implemented. The outlook for NAFTA is generally hopeful. The United States and Canada agree that both countries have access to petroleum, gas, coal, and electricity produced by either country. Mexico is likely to import more industrial machinery, grain, and even banking services from the United States. At the same time, some industries in the United States may need to adjust to increased competition from imports from Mexico, including footwear, steel, clothes, and citrus fruits.

Quick Check

1. How can governments influence global trade?
2. Define *tariff, quota,* and *embargo.*

BENEFITS OF TRADING IN THE GLOBAL MARKET

World trade can benefit countries in many ways. First of all, it can create jobs in the areas in which the country specializes. As companies sell their products abroad, they may need to expand and hire more workers. For example, aircraft construction is one

A number of U.S. candy products sell well in the global market. Why do you think this is so?

Quick Check Answers

1. Tariffs, quotas, embargoes, alliances, and treaties.
2. A special tax on goods made in another country and sold here; a fixed limit on the export or import of a product; an order to stop the import or export of goods.

Develop Concepts

Benefits of Trading in the Global Market

Indicate to students that the value of U.S. exports in 1994 was $668.6 billion, more than ten percent of the country's total goods and services. What's more, exports supported the equivalent of 10.5 million full-time jobs. Ask students how their life might be different if the money from exports were no longer available.

USE VISUALS

Ask students to describe the kind of trade shown in the photograph. Then have them speculate how this trade benefits the U.S. candy company. (It can sell more candy.)
Answer to caption: Answers will vary. Students may mention most people enjoy candy, and U.S. candy is high in quality, low priced, and comes in a wide assortment.

Global Perspective

Suggest that students choose a region or continent—North America, South America, Europe, Asia, or Africa—to explore in depth. Have them locate and read articles detailing current views on trade in their chosen region. Encourage them to use at least three different newspapers or periodicals. Have them record their findings in a chart indicating how the opinions expressed are alike and how they are different. Then ask them to write a 300-word unbiased news article describing the current free trade views for their region.

Refer to the *International Business Strategies* booklet for additional strategies and activities.

CHAPTER 21

Business Brief

The International Trade Administration (ITA), under the auspices of the Department of Commerce, helps small companies market their products in the global market. The federal assistance takes the form of advice in trade policy development and using export trade intermediaries. As a result, many small U.S. firms are able to use export trade to generate significant profits.

Connection to CHAPTER 24

Ask students to share with the class the brand names of goods they own or admire. Ask students to discuss the reputation of the brand and of the country associated with the brand of each item. Tell students that in Chapter 24 they will explore the impact of international trade upon the quality of life and the economies of the countries producing those exports.

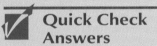

Quick Check Answers

1. Increase in jobs, increase in standard of living, encourage competition, encourage better understanding.
2. Lower prices, greater variety and quality of goods.

Global marketers need to understand the cultural differences that exist within the global marketplace. Cultural variations in body language, greetings, numbers, symbols, and even colors can be important to the acceptance of a product.

area of U.S. specialization. The U.S. market has only so many businesses interested in purchasing aircraft. With worldwide trade, the number of airlines and other businesses interested in new planes expands considerably. In addition, businesses directly related to global trading can prosper. Ports, shipping companies, railroads, and airlines, as well as the banking industry, have an opportunity to expand with global trading.

Another benefit world trade provides is an increased standard of living. Each country specializes in producing items that it can best produce. Then countries trade with one another. This specialization and comparative advantage leads countries to use their resources more efficiently to produce what they do best. Their citizens earn income to buy the goods and services they need, and consumers around the world have more goods and services at lower prices from which to choose.

World trade also encourages competition among similar businesses in different countries. Such competition spurs businesses to operate more efficiently, improve technology, and update production methods. This often means that consumers can find a variety of good products at a lower price.

Finally, world trade helps create better understanding among countries. When we find that other people in the world have the same needs and wants we do, everyone may be brought closer together.

Quick Check

1. How can countries benefit from global trade?
2. What benefit can consumers gain from global trade?

362   UNIT 7   INTERNATIONAL BUSINESS

Enrichment Strategy

The United States government has named 12 countries as emerging markets for U.S. goods: China, Hong Kong, Taiwan, India, Indonesia, South Korea, Argentina, Brazil, Mexico, Poland, Turkey, and South Africa. Suggest that student groups choose one of the nations listed to explore. Have them find out the following:

- What goods the country is most likely to import
- The dollar amount of U.S. goods exported to the country in 1990
- The projected or estimated dollar amount of U.S. goods expected to be exported to the country in 2000 and 2010.

Students can share their findings in the form of a presentation titled "Five Reasons to Develop Trade with [Country]."

Chapter 21 **Summary**

Main Ideas

1. Most countries lack the resources, technology, or comparative advantage necessary to produce all the products their citizens want.
2. The resources available to a country often influence what the country specializes in producing.
3. A free trade policy encourages few limitations and little government involvement in the trading system. A protectionist policy encourages governments to regulate trade and subsidize and protect domestic industries.
4. Governments can influence the global market through trade alliances; trade agreements; and the imposition of quotas, tariffs, or embargoes.
5. World trade encourages specialization of production, competition, higher standard of living, creation of jobs, efficiency of production, and greater understanding among nations.
6. An extensive world marketplace allows all businesses to prosper and grow.
7. TLI is a company that is capitalizing on the increase in international economic interdependence by helping clients understand how to do business in foreign countries.
8. Circle graphs are best for comparing parts to the whole; bar graphs are best for comparing quantities; and line graphs are best for showing changes over time.

CASE ANALYSIS Global Trade

There are advantages to trading in the global market. Some people, however, think there are also disadvantages. Below are two objections they raise. Do you agree or disagree? Explain.

1. Specialization of production among nations encourages interdependency among nations that trade with one another. This interdependency can be good in that it links countries together. However, what happens if the relationship between two trading nations sours? One nation may have to do without certain items if its trading partner decides that it does not want to trade or no longer wishes to produce that particular item. Becoming too dependent on one nation's supply of a product can lead to possible shortages of goods that people want and need.
2. Global trade has increased competition among businesses. Increased competition has resulted in the availability of more goods at lower prices for consumers all over the world. Sometimes, though, the competition has also meant that the more inefficient producer has gone out of business, causing lost jobs, lost profits, and major disruptions to the economies in which the businesses operate.

Main Ideas

Main Ideas summarizes the key information in the chapter. It is a useful tool for reinforcement and review.

CASE ANALYSIS

Case Analysis provides a chapter-related case for student analysis and application of decision-making skills.

Answer
Answers will vary.

QUICK QUIZ

1. What single word can be used to describe goods produced in the United States and shipped for sale in foreign countries? (Exports)
2. Give two examples of comparative advantage. (Sample answer: Colombia, coffee; Taiwan and South Korea, assembling computer components; Switzerland, watches; France, perfume.)
3. Give one protectionist argument and one free trade argument. (Threatens job security; encourages efficient use of natural resources.)
4. What trade alliance determines the price of petroleum? (OPEC)
5. Is an increased standard of living (a) a benefit of the global market, (b) the result of specialization, or (c) an argument for protectionism? (a)

Chapter 21 **Review**

CHAPTER 21 REVIEW

APPLY

Answers

Use the Language of Business

1. export, **2.** embargo, **3.** import, **4.** quota, **5.** tariff, **6.** trading partners, **7.** specialization, **8.** free trade, **9.** protectionists, **10.** comparative advantage, **11.** multinational company.

Review What You Learned

1. Goods produced in one country and sold in another; wheat, soybeans, corn, cotton, computers, and technology; foreign-made goods brought into a country; tin, manganese, and bauxite, jewelry, handbags, and paper.

2. Canada, Japan, Mexico, Germany, the United Kingdom, France, Italy, the Netherlands, Taiwan, South Korea, Singapore, and Mainland China.

3. It allows countries to concentrate on producing the goods and services that they can produce best and for which they have the resources. When countries specialize, they need markets for their goods and want goods that other countries specialize in producing.

4. Policy advocating government regulation of trade to protect the domestic economy; free trade threatens job security, industries vital to the economy should be protected from foreign competition, and new industries should be protected.

5. Free movement of resources and products among the members and formation of common economic policies.

6. To protect prices, to indicate disapproval of another country's policies, or to protect business from foreign competition.

7. Larger markets in which to sell goods and services, larger markets from which to purchase goods and services, increased productivity.

8. Create jobs, raise the standard of living, increased competition, and increased understanding.

9. Foreign language translation, interpretation, print materials.

10. A line graph because it shows best changes over time.

Use the Language of Business

Number your paper 1 through 11. Then write the term that best matches each numbered definition.

comparative advantage
free trade
embargo
exports
imports
multinational company
quota
protectionist
specialization
tariff
trading partners

1. Goods made in one country and sold in another.
2. A government ban that stops the import or export of certain goods or trading with a certain country.
3. Foreign-made goods brought into a country.
4. Fixed limit, set by the government, on the export or import of a product.
5. Special tax on goods made in another country and sold in the United States.
6. Countries that are the United States' main producers and consumers.
7. Concentration of efforts in a particular area or field.
8. Policy encouraging few limitations and little government involvement in trade.
9. View that governments should regulate trade and subsidize industry to protect the domestic economy.
10. Specialization of production by a country in those areas it is best at doing.
11. Firm that does business in other countries and has offices worldwide.

Review What You Learned

1. What are exports? What are imports? Name some of the major imports and exports of the United States.
2. Which countries are the main trading partners of the United States?
3. What is meant by specialization in relation to world trade? Why is trading necessary when countries specialize?
4. What is meant by a protectionist policy? What reasons do free trade opponents give for wanting a protectionist policy?
5. What can countries accomplish by joining a trade alliance?
6. Why might a country impose a quota on certain goods?
7. What benefits can the United States gain from NAFTA?
8. List four benefits of world trade.
9. Give three examples of services offered by TLI International Corporation.
10. What kind of graph would you use to show how U.S. exports have increased over the last 20 years? Explain.

Understand Business Concepts

1. How are we, as consumers and producers, dependent on other countries?
2. What are the advantages of a free trade policy? What are the disadvantages?
3. How might global trading be different if GATT talks had not taken place?
4. Give examples of how the United States has benefited from global trade.
5. What kinds of specialization can occur in a country with limited resources but a large population?

Understand Business Concepts

1. We purchase needed goods from other countries; the sale of our products to other countries helps our economy.

2. Free trade can lead to products improved through competition, lower costs through competition and specialization, and greater efficiency in using scarce resources. Free trade can also lead to business closures, unemployment, a dependence on foreign countries for items needed for national defense, and problems for startup industries.

3. Fewer imports and exports might be exchanged throughout the world because the cost of tariffs might make the purchase price of the goods unacceptable to consumers; trade disputes, which are now settled through GATT, might escalate.

4. Businesses directly related to global trading are expanding, U.S. citizens have an improved standard of living, increased competition allows us to choose from among many good products. We might be able to better understand other people if we understand that they share some of the same needs and wants.

5. Component assembly and other labor-intensive businesses.

6. They feel foreign competition might hurt U.S. businesses and cost jobs.

Chapter 21 Review

6. Why might some raise objections to NAFTA and the foreign competition it might generate?
7. Give arguments for and against having tariffs on imports. Explain.
8. What advantages and disadvantages does the European Union offer the United States?
9. Why are the services offered by TLI International Corporation important in today's global business world?
10. What kind of graph would be best to display the following information? NAFTA created a total market of nearly 374 million people: 27 million live in Canada, 255 million live in the United States, and 92 million live in Mexico.

Think Critically

1. **Analyze.** Should the United States trade with any country that produces the goods and services that we need to import, regardless of that country's political beliefs? Why or why not?
2. **Recommend.** Suppose a country can produce everything its people need at a cost lower than firms in other countries. Should that country trade with other countries? Explain.

Use What You Learned

1. **Group Project.** Use the local telephone directory to locate a business in your community that imports products. Interview the person directly involved with purchasing the products. Prepare your questions in advance, and include questions similar to these:

   - Why did you choose to import the goods?
   - Are goods similar to these made in the United States?
   - What kinds of government licenses and regulations are involved in importing the goods?
   - How did you contact the producer of the goods?
   - What countries produce the goods you import?

   Prepare a chart showing what happens as the business owner places an order for the goods. Share your information with other groups.

2. **Computer Application.** Conduct on-line research to determine how and to what extent your state participates in global trade. Use charting/graphing software to create circle graphs showing (1) the percentage breakdown of the products exported to other countries and (2) the percentage breakdown of export income as a portion of state revenues.

3. **Skill Reinforcement.** Locate a graph in a newspaper or magazine article. Cut it out and attach it to the top of a sheet of paper. Below the graph, write an explanation of the graph. Tell why you think the author of the article chose to use that particular kind of graph.

Save your work in you Business Portfolio.

7. Tariffs protect our businesses and jobs as they help keep prices at desired levels. Tariffs also bring a small revenue to the government. However, doing away with tariffs could increase competition, reduce prices, and improve the quality of goods for sale in our country.
8. The EU offers U.S. businesses the opportunity to trade in a unified market; the EU could pass trade restrictions that could effectively shut the United States out of the EU.
9. Businesses need to be able to compete in foreign markets where language and customs may be different from our own.
10. A circle graph.

Independent Practice

Use the Chapter 21 worksheets in *Student Activity Guide 2* for additional practice and application activities. A Teacher's Annotated Edition provides answers.

ASSESS

Portfolio Assessment

The projects are designed to lead students to develop a collection of their best work to submit to you for assessment. Refer students to the specific rubric(s) from the *Alternative Assessment Strategies* booklet listed with each of the project notes below.

Chapter Assessment

Use the Chapter 21 Test from the *Test Masters* booklet. An answer key is provided. Or create your own test using the *Testmaker* software.

Think Critically

1. Possible answers: Yes, it is to our advantage from an economic standpoint. No, trading would give an implicit approval of the other country's political belief, and withholding trade could give us leverage in trying to change the other country's policies.
2. Possible answer: In economic terms, this is a situation in which the country has an absolute advantage. If it wants to increase its standard of living, its best procedure is to concentrate on the items it produces best and trade them. If it is concerned about depending too much on another country, it should not trade.

Use What You Learned

1. Encourage students to make their list as varied as possible so that it reflects a great number of items and countries. Possible rubrics: Charts and Tables, Paragraph.
2. Students without access to a computer can complete this exercise manually, using the library to collect data and preparing the graphs with compass, rulers, and calculators. Rubric: Charts and Graphs.
3. Students' answers will vary, but all should include a bar, circle or line graph cut from a publication and a paragraph that explains the graph. Both the graph and the paragraph should include the same information. Rubric: Paragraph.

CHAPTER
22

FOCUS

Introduce the Chapter

Major Concepts
• Basic Kinds of Economic Systems
• Comparing Economic Systems

Introduce the Topic
Ask students to think about their shopping experiences: Ask if they have ever been told that the store had no more of the item they wished to purchase. What did they do? Why was the store out of the item? Point out to students that the answers to these questions might be different if they lived in a different kind of economic system.

Use Business Terms
Ask students to write a sentence with each of the Business Terms. Have students exchange papers with a partner. Call for agreement/disagreement as to use of the terms and an explanation of that position. Tell students to note the meanings of the terms as they read the chapter.

USE VISUALS

Inform students that the photograph depicts a neighborhood market in Havana, Cuba. Further inform students that Cuba currently operates under a strong command economic system often referred to as communism. Ask students to compare the market depicted with neighborhood markets with which they are familiar in terms of available items and the general atmosphere.

Business terms

traditional economy

command economy

communism

socialism

capitalism

mixed economy

gross national product

366

CHAPTER 22 RESOURCES

Instructional Resources

Lesson Plan for Chapter 22

Teaching Transparencies 22-1, 22-3, 22-4

Strategies and Worksheets for Teaching Transparencies 22-1, 22-3, 22-4

Enrichment Master 22-1

Student Activity Guide 2–TAE for Chapter 22

Test Master for Chapter 22

Alternative Assessment Strategies

Math Skills Review

International Business Strategies

Cooperative Learning Strategies

Communication Skills Review

Ethics in Business Strategies

Other Economic Systems

Learning objectives

After completing this chapter, you will be able to:
- Describe three basic types of economic systems.
- Compare and contrast traditional, command, and market economies.
- Identify ways to compare economic systems.
- Describe the main computer components.
- Explain how you could use a Venn diagram to compare and contrast systems.

Consider what you know

- An economic system is a set of rules that governs how a country's scarce resources are used to produce goods and services its citizens need and want.

Consider what you want to know

- What kinds of economic systems exist in today's world?
- How are socialism, communism, and capitalism alike? How are they different?
- What characteristics can be used to compare one economic system to another?
- What are the basic components of a computer?
- What organizational tools can you use to compare and contrast information?

Consider how to use what you learn

- As you study this chapter, take time to listen to business news broadcasts or read the business section of the paper. Use what you learn in this chapter to help you identify an example of each of the economic systems described in the chapter.

CHAPTER 22   OTHER ECONOMIC SYSTEMS   **367**

Multimedia Resources

Technology Resource Guide

Distance Learning Guide

Internet Resource Guide

Professional Resources

School-to-Work/Tech Prep Strategies

Instructional Poster

Spanish Resources

Testmaker Software for Chapter 22

The Wall Street Journal Video Series
   Video & Activities for Chapter 22

Business and Marketing Computer
   Applications—An Integrated Software
   Simulation Using Microsoft Works

Stocktracker—A Stock Market Software
   Simulation

Where's the Dough? Board Game

TEACH

Business Connection

On July 1, 1997, after 150 years of British rule, Hong Kong will once again be under the auspices of the central government of China. The Sino-British Joint Declaration allows Hong Kong to keep its capitalist economy within the socialist economy of China for 50 years. The pending reunification prompted thousands of people to leave Hong Kong for Canada, Australia, and the United States. After a time many returned, believing that ultimately, Hong Kong will change China more than China will change Hong Kong.

Develop Concepts

Basic Kinds of Economic Systems

Help students recognize that, like individuals, nations have different wants and needs, and that each nation has a limited amount of resources it can apply to meeting those wants and needs. To make choices among wants, needs, and resources, nations can follow the principles of several different kinds of economic systems.

Learning Activity

Encourage students to provide specific examples for each of the three economic questions. For example, "Shall we make tapes or CDs?" "Shall we use plastic or metal to make car bumpers?" or "Who will receive electricity?"

Today there are more than 180 independent countries in the world. The societies of these nations have developed a variety of economic systems. That is, they have developed a set of rules to allocate scarce resources to produce the goods and services people want and provide the means for people to get them. No matter how much they differ, all nations face the same economic challenge—they have to satisfy the unlimited wants of their citizens with limited productive resources.

In this chapter, we will learn how different countries use their resources to try to satisfy their citizens' wants and needs.

BASIC KINDS OF ECONOMIC SYSTEMS

The wants people have can be unlimited. However, each society has a limited amount of resources from which to provide the goods and services to satisfy these wants. This scarcity of resources forces every society to have a mechanism to help make decisions about the following questions:

- Which goods and services will be produced?

It won't surprise you to know that countries have wants, and like people, different wants. Some countries would like to be very powerful or feel very safe. Such countries might use many of their factors of production to make guns, planes, and ships for defense. Another country might decide to produce mostly basic goods such as food and clothing. Some countries might want both. Still another country might decide to produce the things that people buy to make their lives more pleasant. In whatever way it is done, the question "What goods and services will be produced?" must be answered by any economic system. Since resources are limited, a country must have rules to determine what goods and services will be produced.

- How will these goods and services be produced?

Countries are not equal in the amount or types of resources they have. Some have large numbers of people; some have much technology or capital goods. Others have rich resources of oil, timber, fish, coal, or grain. An economic system provides the means for making decisions about how the factors will be put together to produce goods and services. Some will decide that machinery should do as much of the work as possible. Others with many people may decide to do much of the work by hand.

Curriculum Connection   English and Communication

Encourage students to research current news reports about the economies in several nations. Direct students to classify the information they find, telling which of the three economic questions is asked or answered by the events described in the article. Call on volunteers to justify their classifications in a statement of several sentences.

For those students who need to sharpen their written communication skills, choose among the worksheets in the *Communication Skills Review* booklet.

How the goods and services will be produced is another area in which guidelines must be provided by an economic system.

- How will the goods and services be distributed?

Some people in a society receive many goods and services while others receive only a few. In a country like ours, individuals have a lot of freedom to buy items in the marketplace because much of the income they earn is theirs to spend. In some countries, though, individuals have less income to spend because a greater amount of their income goes to the government. In most societies, people can have as many goods and services as they can afford to buy. The economic system then must have procedures determining how income is to be distributed, since it directly affects who will receive goods and services.

The way a country answers questions about the use and distribution of its resources may be influenced by its history, its culture, its geography, its present political situation, and a number of other factors. The decisions that a country makes determines the type of economic system it has. Figure 22-1 summarizes the major characteristics of the economic systems we will look at.

TEACHING TIP
Help students differentiate between an economic system and a system of government. Remind them *government* refers to the system of political institutions, laws, and customs that a society uses to determine its code of conduct. In contrast, *economic system* describes a way of producing goods and services and providing a means for people to receive those goods and services. Suggest that students make up a mnemonic device to help them remember the difference between *government* and *economic sysem*.

FIGURE 22-1

Each economic system has its particular characteristics. Which system depends most on government planning and guidance?

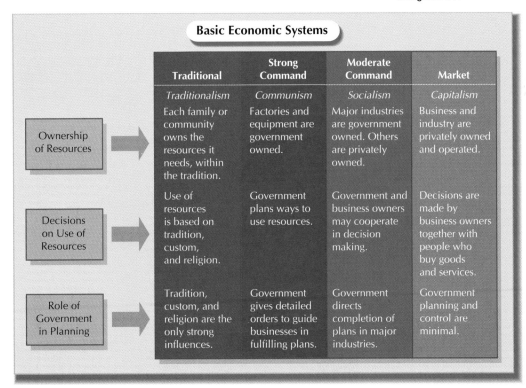

Basic Economic Systems

	Traditional	Strong Command	Moderate Command	Market
	Traditionalism	*Communism*	*Socialism*	*Capitalism*
Ownership of Resources	Each family or community owns the resources it needs, within the tradition.	Factories and equipment are government owned.	Major industries are government owned. Others are privately owned.	Business and industry are privately owned and operated.
Decisions on Use of Resources	Use of resources is based on tradition, custom, and religion.	Government plans ways to use resources.	Government and business owners may cooperate in decision making.	Decisions are made by business owners together with people who buy goods and services.
Role of Government in Planning	Tradition, custom, and religion are the only strong influences.	Government gives detailed orders to guide businesses in fulfilling plans.	Government directs completion of plans in major industries.	Government planning and control are minimal.

USE VISUALS
Direct students' attention to the chart of Basic Economic Systems in Figure 22-1. Indicate to students that this chart provides an overview of the information they will learn in the chapter. Indicate to students that the boxes on the far left of the chart are equivalent to the three economic questions. Ask students to identify which question is associated with each box. Answer to caption: strong command

USE TRANSPARENCIES
Use Teaching Transparency 22-1 and its corresponding strategies and worksheet from the *Teaching Transparency Strategies and Worksheets* booklet to acquaint students with the world's basic economic systems. Verify student worksheets using the Answer Key.

Reteaching Strategy

Review students' understanding of economic decisions by asking why every economic system has to answer the same questions about producing and distributing goods and services. Encourage students to generate a list of reasons. Have a volunteer record the reasons on the board. Lead a discussion in which the students revise or enhance the list until they reach a consensus that all valid reasons are listed and all reasons listed are valid.

Traditional Economy

Suppose you live in a country in which most people do what their parents did before them. If your father is a farmer, you become a farmer. If your mother weaves baskets, you weave baskets. An economy in which people do things the way they have always been done is called a **traditional economy.** People rely on the same tools and methods used by their parents and grandparents. There is little or no change in traditional economies. Most people's methods are based on habit, custom, and religious belief. Individuals are not free to make decisions according to what they want or would like to have. Instead, their roles are narrowly defined. The people know what goods and services they will produce, how to produce them, and how to distribute them.

The main advantage of a traditional economy is that everyone has a role in it. As a result, economic life tends to be stable and community life continuous. The main disadvantage of a traditional economy is that it discourages new ideas and ways of doing things. What would happen in a traditional economy if a new food were discovered? If that food would feed the entire community with half the work and at half the cost, would the traditional economy use it? It probably would not. The community's reasoning might be, "We have never used that food, we have survived without that food, so we do not need that food." Generally, new methods and new products are not accepted in a traditional economy, so the economy does not grow. It falls behind countries with other kinds of economies.

This little girl is learning how to do what her mother does. What is the major advantage of a traditional economy? The major disadvantage?

Tradition is not as influential as it once was. However, it is still a major force in some areas. Some societies living within the rain forests of Latin America, in parts of Africa, and in the Middle East have traditional economies.

Command Economy

Economies influenced by commands, or directives, have been around as long as traditional economies. In a **command economy,** the basic economic questions of what and how to produce and distribute are made by a central authority. The central authority consists of one person or a small group of people who control others in the society. The members of the society in the command economy carry out the commands. Sometimes a command economy is also called a directed or planned economy. Two kinds of command economies exist in the world today.

Strong Command   North Korea and Cuba each have a strong command economy. The economies of these nations call for common ownership of natural and capital resources. The government owns and controls factories, equipment, and land. The leaders of the country answer the three important economic questions: They decide what will be produced, how items will be produced, and who will receive them. An economic and political structure in which the government makes decisions concerning the commonly owned resources is called **communism.**

One advantage of a strong command economy is that, in theory, the economy can make a dramatic change in a short time. Government leaders can decree that factories increase or decrease production. They can even decree production changes—directing, for example, that instead of tractors, resources should now be used for trucks. Another advantage of a strong command system is that the government can provide each person a job with certain medical and social services.

A major disadvantage is that consumer goods and services generally rank low on the list of priorities in most strong command economies. Very few of the citizens' wants are met in a strong command system. A second disadvantage is the lack of incentives to work hard. Workers with differing degrees of responsibility receive the same wages. There is no competition among businesses, and so there is no incentive to improve a product or produce it more efficiently.

Further, the strong command system limits an individual's choice to make his or her own economic decisions. There is little or no room for the entrepreneurial spirit—seeing the need

Business & HISTORY

For most of the twentieth century, people in the former Soviet Union lived with a strong command economy. People were not allowed to own property; there were no enforceable contracts; there was not an independent judicial system; and the currency could not be exchanged for currency of other nations.

Learning Activity
Ask students to suggest words they commonly associate with a strong command economy or a communist political system. Have a volunteer record their suggestions on the board. Point out that in economic terms, communism has become synonymous with lack of incentive, poor quality of products, shortages, and so on. Also remind students of the poorly stocked market in the chapter opening photograph. Ask students to discuss how these characteristics might have contributed to the collapse of communism in many countries.

TEACHING TIP

Point out that the goal of a business in a command economy is to fulfill the government plan and to meet the government quotas. Ask students how this compares to the goals of businesses in the United States. (U.S. businesses have profit as their goal.)

Business Brief

China's leaders have started a slow movement away from a strong command economy. For example, today most Chinese farmers have government contracts to produce a set amount of crops. Any surplus they have after fulfilling their contracts may be sold at "free markets."

Making Connections → ⬨ →   Everyday Living

Pose the following scenario to students: A teacher at school has decided that no matter how clear (or unclear) a report is, how many answers are correct (or incorrect) on a quiz, or how well (or poorly) a student project presents a point of view, the student will receive a grade of "passing." Ask students to describe how this knowledge will affect the effort they put into the report, quiz, or project. Then ask them to discuss how a lack of advancement or increased wage incentive in a strong command economy might similarly affect job performance, productivity, and quality.

FOCUS ON **Technology**

Discuss

Help students understand that without the advances in physics and electronics, technology such as data processing technology would not be possible. Ask students to describe in their own words the terms *transistors, processor, silicon chips, circuit boards, microprocessor, central processing unit,* and *memory.* Have students construct a diagram to show how these terms are related to data processing technology.

Computer Processing Components

L ike televisions, VCRs, and automobiles, computers are made of hundreds of thousands of parts. Some of the most basic processing components of a computer include transistors, silicon chips, processors, and circuit boards. These processing components are common to all computers.

The computer performs all its calculations and operations based on the electrical signals from millions of tiny switches called *transistors*. The signals are called data. The computer translates or processes the data into meaningful information for the computer user.

The *processor,* often referred to as the "brain" of a computer, is the hardware portion of the computer that interprets and carries out instructions from the software and the computer user. The processor contains hundreds of thousands of electrical circuits. Most of these circuits are etched on *silicon chips,* which are slivers of silicon usually smaller than a fingertip. As you might imagine, manufacturing chips is an extremely delicate process, since the components being created are microscopic. A computer chip the size of your fingernail can have more than 1,000,000 transistors etched onto it! The whole manufacturing process takes place in a dust-free, clean room.

Once the chips are manufactured, they are plugged into larger circuits that tie the chips together, linking thousands of circuits to one another. The larger circuits

TEACHING TIP

Point out that moderate command economies can vary widely, from those that allow many private businesses to those in which opportunities for private business are limited. Ask students to speculate on which industries are most likely to be government-owned in a moderate command economy.

Learning Activity

Stress to students that the three economic questions are answered by a central authority in a command economic system. Indicate to students that there are two kinds of command economies: strong and moderate. One way in which strong and moderate command economies differ is in the ownership of natural and capital resources. Ask students to describe how private ownership of natural and capital resources can be used to distinguish strong command and moderate command economies.

F.Y.I.

For Wloclawek, Poland, one benefit of moving toward a market economy comes in the form of hot dogs. American entrepreneur Jacob Sobieraj opened a hot dog factory in Wloclawek. His hot dogs are popular with consumers—they cost less than those made by the government. The hot dogs are popular with farmers—Sobieraj pays more for meat than the government pays. No official word on the government's opinion.

for an item and starting a business to provide it on your own. Yes, the state can do so, but it doesn't move as fast as an individual does when starting a business on his or her own. Also, there are few chances for individual consumers, since consumer goods are not that important in such an economy.

Until recently, the Soviet Union and the countries of eastern Europe operated under strong command economies. However, many of these economies are now being restructured into economies in which individuals make more of the economic decisions.

Moderate Command Sweden and France each have a moderate command economy. The moderate command economy calls for government ownership of major industries including railroads and the steel and iron industries. However, moderate command economies do provide opportunities for private ownership. An economic and political structure in which the government owns major industries but allows for private ownership of other businesses is called **socialism.**

In moderate command economies, government and private businesses work together. Government representatives become

Curriculum Connection   History, Economics

Indicate to students that Karl Marx (1818–1883), a German philosopher and revolutionary, was the chief architect of two powerful movements in history—democratic socialism and revolutionary communism. Suggest that students prepare a three-minute news "flashback" segment on one of the following topics:

- Conditions in czarist Russia at the time of the Social Democratic Party (Bolshevik) Revolution
- Marx's criticisms of the free market economy
- The role production—making the goods necessary to live—plays in society

are usually mapped onto composite cards called *circuit boards,* which themselves contain circuits.

In a personal computer, the processor is usually a single chip and is called a *microprocessor.* In larger computers, the processor may be a collection of several circuit boards and is called a *central processing unit* or CPU.

Two related functions occur inside the CPU. One coordinates the computer's activities—both the instructions for carrying out commands and the directions on how to execute the instructions. Another function in the CPU handles any arithmetic or logic instructions.

Not all the chips on the circuit boards are part of the CPU. While the CPU is working, it needs to be able to access entire programs as well as the data being processed by these programs. Some of the chips on the circuit board provide *memory* for the CPU to use while it is processing data.

While each computer contains these same basic parts, the technology that contributes to computer manufacturing continues to become increasingly complex.

Follow Through

Ask students to speculate on the kinds of advances that might be made in data processing technology in the next few years. Spark the discussion by asking students to describe the changes they have seen in their own lifetime and changes their parents or other family members marvel about.
For additional information about current technology, refer to the *Technology Resource Guide* booklet.

members of the management committees for private business. The committees decide what to produce and how to produce it. However, the government decides who will receive the goods and services that are produced.

Under socialism, workers are taxed at an extremely high rate. The government uses the money it collects from workers to provide medical services, lifelong welfare services, and social security benefits to everyone, workers and nonworkers alike. The government's role in providing for the welfare of all the citizens is an advantage of a moderate command economy. However, the economy does have disadvantages. The high rate of taxation discourages private business and lessens spendable income for individuals. Individuals with less spendable income make fewer choices in the marketplace.

Market Economy

You already know that one way to answer the three basic economic questions is through a market economy. In a market economy, the basic economic decisions are based on the actions of individual people and business firms participating in

During the mid-1900s, socialism started to replace traditional economies in several African nations. However, after the collapse of the former Soviet Union, several African nations seemed to be reevaluating their socialist policies. They appear to be moving toward democracy and free-market economies.

Learning Activity
Present students with a map of the world. As different countries are identified as strong command or moderate command economies, have students locate the countries and place different-colored pins or sticky notes to identify different economies. For example, students might use yellow in locations of strong command economies, blue for moderate command economies, and green for economies in transition. (Countries such as Poland, Czechoslovakia, Ukraine, China, and Singapore.)

Reteaching Strategy

Ask students to list the advantages and disadvantages of strong command and moderate command economies. Remind them to include information on the economy's ability to make changes quickly, job or employment availability, medical and social services, consideration of citizen wants, competition, wages appropriate to work, and individual choice in the marketplace. Suggest that they arrange the information in chart or diagram form.

Business Brief

After World War II, when many of the homes in Europe were destroyed, apartment buildings became more common. In many parts of Europe, the government owns the buildings and leases the apartments inexpensively to citizens of every income level.

Building Business Skills

Model

Draw two completely separate circles on a board. Point out that any information written in one of these circles is distinct from information in the second circle. Then draw two slightly overlapping circles and indicate to students that with this scheme, any information common to both circles can be recorded in the area where the two overlap.

ANALYSIS

Comparing and Contrasting Information

Explanation

Making decisions can be difficult, both on the job and in your daily life. Before you make an important decision, take the time to compare and contrast the alternatives. When you compare, you consider the ways things are alike. When you contrast, you consider the ways things are different.

When you're making a major decision, it helps to organize your thoughts, write down important factors, then consider them carefully. If one factor is more important, give it more weight as you make your decision.

One way to organize your thoughts on paper is to construct a Venn diagram.

Practice

Read the steps for constructing and using a Venn diagram on page 375. Study the sample Venn diagram provided. Then, on a separate sheet of paper, tell which job you would choose and explain your choice.

Learning to compare and contrast can help you make informed decisions in your career as well as in your personal life.

Connection to CHAPTER 6

Remind students that the market economy relies on four factors of production—natural resources, human resources, capital resources, and entrepreneurs. Ask students to compare the roles these four factors play in traditional, strong and moderate command, and market economies.

TEACHING TIP

According to Karl Marx, employers in a market economy take advantage of their employees by paying them less than they are worth in order to make a larger profit. Ask students if they think Marx's opinion is valid in the United States. Encourage them to use examples to support their point of view.

many different markets. A market system may also be referred to as **capitalism.** The United States and Japan are among the countries that have a market economy.

In a market system, the questions "Which goods and services will be produced?" "How they will be produced?" and "How they will be distributed?" are answered by the motivations of businesses interacting with consumers. That is, a market system produces the goods and services that people want or need and that will bring a profit to the sellers.

Businesses figure out how to produce goods and services according to the tastes of consumers, what consumers are willing to pay for a finished good or service, and the cost/profit ratio of producing such items in various ways. Who receives the finished goods and services is also determined by the market. Those who get more income for their input in the market can have more of the resources. For example, the services of certain professionals in the United States are prized more highly than others. These professionals thus receive more income which means that they can secure more of the resources.

As you may recall, price plays an important role in market economies. Producers want the price of a product to be high

Curriculum Connection

Art and Design

Encourage students to work individually or in small groups to review and list the differences between *capitalism, socialism,* and *communism.* Then have them discuss and list what they feel is the most identifiable characteristic of each economy. Ask students if they are familiar with any symbols of the three economic systems. For example, the hammer and sickle is often associated with communism; the dollar sign with capitalism. Suggest that students use the information from their lists to develop logos or symbols for each of the economic systems. Call on volunteers to display and explain their logos or symbols.

VENN DIAGRAM

1. Draw two large overlapping circles, leaving room to write in all three sections.
2. Label one circle with the name of one option. Label the other circle with your other option. Use the overlapping space to write what is true of both choices.
3. Write down all the factors you can think of for each option in the appropriate section. If you have time, work on your chart over a few days.
4. Study the diagram and make notes, marking the options with plus and minus signs. Underline the most important ones. Does one option have more pluses? Does one option outweigh all the others?
5. When you can see your choice clearly, decide.

Job Offers

Wilton, Inc.

Mason Brothers

– some Saturdays and weekends
+ commute 15 min.
+ my own office
+ chance for promotion

+ salary same
+ customer interaction
+ health insurance

+ Mon.–Fri. 9:00–5:00
– commute 1 hour
– share office
+ company car

Practice
Ask a volunteer to explain, in his or her own words, how to complete the diagram. Students' answers will vary, but they should be able to defend their choice of one of the two job offers. Their explanations should refer to the information in the diagram.

enough to make a profit. If producers think the price customers are willing to pay is too low, they will produce little or nothing. If they think the price is high enough, they will produce the good or service. Producers who can make a profit at a price consumers are willing to pay are successful.

Consumers and producers play the two most important roles in a market economy—regulation by government is minimal. If consumers want a certain food, someone will produce it if he or she can make an adequate profit doing so. Every time a consumer buys a product at a certain price, he or she is telling the producers to supply more of that product. The same holds true for services. If consumers refuse to buy a product or a service, the producer receives the message to supply less of it at that price.

A market economy has advantages that traditional and command economies do not. First, a market economy can adjust to change over time as consumer wants and needs change. For example, as automobile production increased, carriage production, buggy whip manufacture, and horseshoe production slowed, then almost ceased. However, the demand for car dealers, gasoline stations, and repair people increased.

CHAPTER 22   OTHER ECONOMIC SYSTEMS   **375**

Learning Activity
Capitalism encourages economic production to profit those who control private ownership. However, to accomplish that production the owners of the production facilities need individuals to work. Ask students to discuss which individuals in a society pure capitalism tends to ignore. (The unproductive or unemployed.)

TEACHING TIP
Encourage discussion by asking students if they agree with the following statement: Consumers have more power than producers in a market economy. Prime the discussion by asking students to think of new products that consumers have encouraged businesses to make.

Global Perspective

Countries such as Russia, Ukraine, Czechoslovakia, and Poland have decided to change their economic systems from command systems to free market systems. As part of this change, many businesses will move from government control to private control. Have students discuss the problems associated with the transition to capitalism. (Privatization, loss of political power, unemployment, social unrest, and learning to accept a new set of economic incentives.) Have student groups use their knowledge of the market economy to generate a list of ways that these problems might be overcome. Direct groups to use their ideas as the foundation of an editorial on how the transition might be made successfully.

Refer to the *International Business Strategies* booklet for additional strategies and activities.

Learning Activity

Ask students to describe aspects of the U.S. economy that are similar to traditional, strong command, or moderate command economies. Then point out to students that pure capitalism does not exist in the world today. Most countries that are essentially capitalist have some government regulation, making them mixed or modified free enterprise economies.

Quick Check Answers

1. Which goods and services will be produced? How will they be produced? How will they be distributed?

2. Traditional, command, and market.

3. Strong command: common ownership of resources and government controls factories, equipment, and land and decides resource allocation; moderate command: government owns major industries, private ownership of other businesses, and government and business decide how to allocate resources; market economy: economic decisions are based on the actions of producers and consumers. Market; strong command, moderate command.

A market economy also offers freedom for everyone involved. Producers may make whatever they think will sell, and they may make it in what they believe is the most efficient way. Likewise, consumers are free to spend their money on whatever goods and services they wish to have. Finally, a market economy is characterized by lack of government control. There is no government unit that dictates what is to be produced, how it is to be produced, and who should receive the output.

A major disadvantage of a market economy is that it rewards only citizens who are productive in the economy. This means that those who do not have factors of production that are wanted, get little income to buy the output of the economy. The wealth of the economy is not evenly distributed throughout the society, and the welfare of some citizens may not be provided for. Just as with command economies, there are different gradations in market economies. For example, Great Britain and Canada have more government controls over resources than the United States and Japan.

Mixed Economy

In reality, no nation has an economy based totally on any one of the approaches just described. Modern economies operate using some elements of traditional, command, and market economies. They are **mixed economies.** However, one of the approaches is dominant. Because of this, economies are described as being traditional, strong command, moderate command, or market to indicate which approach most influences the function of the economy.

Quick Check

1. What three questions must be answered by an economic system?
2. List the basic types of economic systems.
3. What is a strong command economy, a moderate command economy, and a market economy? Which one is associated with capitalism? Communism? Socialism?

COMPARING ECONOMIC SYSTEMS

A society's standard of living is one way to compare economic systems. The standard of living is a measure of how well the people in an economic system live. The standard of living

Cooperative Learning Group Discussion

Suggest that students form groups of four. Ask each group to describe the ways in which people are motivated to produce goods and services in each of the three types of economic systems. Remind students that a chart might help them keep track of the points made during the discussion. Then ask students to create a point/counterpoint segment for a television newsmagazine. The segment should give what each team thinks are the good and bad aspects of each system.

Refer to the *Cooperative Learning Strategies* booklet for additional cooperative learning strategies.

depends on the amount and kinds of goods and services the people of a country enjoy. An economy that can produce the goods and services its people want at a price they can afford probably will have a high standard of living.

Economic systems can also be compared according to their economic efficiency. In a system with high economic efficiency, resources are used to generate the greatest value possible. One indication of economic efficiency is the presence of competition. Healthy competition encourages businesses to produce goods and services efficiently.

Economic equity can also be compared. Economic equity exists when resources are distributed fairly evenly so that all citizens of a society can participate in the benefits of the economy. While equity and efficiency are not necessarily exclusive, an economy that is relatively efficient may not have a high degree of equity. That is, there may be a vast difference between the "haves" and the "have nots."

Finally, economies can be compared by their size and by their economic growth as shown in Figure 22-2 below. The

FIGURE 22-2

When comparing sizes of economies, economists look at the gross national product (GNP). The total GNP can be misleading because of differences in population size. In order to make accurate comparisons, economists calculate a per capita GNP by dividing the total GNP by the nation's population figure. Nigeria's total GNP is slightly larger than Cuba's. Does it have a larger economy? Explain your answer.

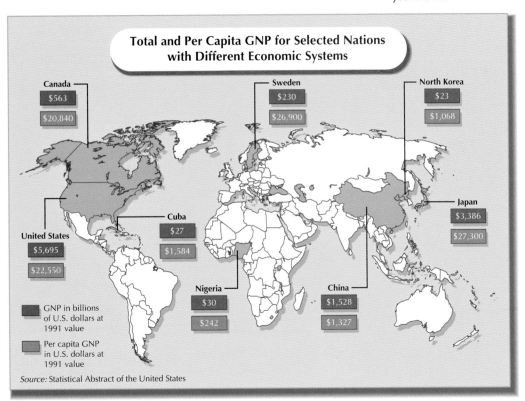

Total and Per Capita GNP for Selected Nations with Different Economic Systems

Canada
$563
$20,840

Sweden
$230
$26,900

North Korea
$23
$1,068

United States
$5,695
$22,550

Cuba
$27
$1,584

Japan
$3,386
$27,300

Nigeria
$30
$242

China
$1,528
$1,327

GNP in billions of U.S. dollars at 1991 value

Per capita GNP in U.S. dollars at 1991 value

Source: Statistical Abstract of the United States

Reteaching Strategy

Organize students into three groups and assign each group one of the three economic systems (traditional, command, mixed). Direct groups to organize a furniture factory appropriate to their assigned system. Have groups consider and then answer the questions below. Have group representatives share their responses with the class.

- How will you get the money to begin production?
- From where will the factors of production come?
- How will workers be paid?

- How much will be produced?
- How will production be organized?
- How will the furniture be distributed?

Develop Concepts

Comparing Economic Systems

Ask students: Which do you think is the best economy? In which economy would you feel most comfortable as a consumer? Have them explain their choices. Then point out that there are several ways to evaluate economies—standard of living, economic efficiency, economic equity, and the economies' size and growth.

USE VISUALS

Direct students to Figure 22-2, which presents information about the total and per capita GNP for selected nations. Remind them that the GNP figure is in billions of dollars while the per capita GNP is in dollars. Answer to caption: No. Nigeria has a much lower per capita GNP.

USE TRANSPARENCIES

Use Teaching Transparency 22-2 and its corresponding strategies and worksheet from the *Teaching Transparency Strategies and Worksheets* booklet to introduce students to the concept of GNP and per capita GNP. Verify student worksheets using the Answer Key.

USE VISUALS

Copy and distribute Enrichment Master 22-1, which compares the economic efficiency and equity of several countries' economies. Use the information presented to help students recognize the difference between economic efficiency and equity. Encourage students to add their own comparisons.

USE VISUALS

Direct students' attention to Figure 22-3. Ask them to describe any similarities in the lines on the graph. Point out that the graphs for Canada, the United States, Germany, the United Kingdom, and Denmark rise at about the same rate and curve at about the same years. Ask students what inferences they can make about economic growth from these graphs. (Economies of different nations are affected in the same way by certain events.)
Answer to caption: Turkey.

USE TRANSPARENCIES

Use Teaching Transparency 22-3 and its corresponding strategies and worksheet from the *Teaching Transparency Strategies and Worksheets* booklet to allow students to become familiar with changes in Gross National Product. Verify student worksheets using the Answer Key.

Quick Check Answers

1. Standard of living, economic efficiency, economic equity, and economic growth.
2. Economic equity exists when resources are distributed fairly and evenly throughout society.

FIGURE 22-3

The growth of an economy can be measured by the change in the GNP of the economy. Which of the nations represented has had the least economic growth in the time shown?

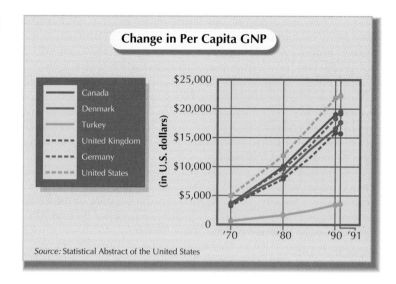

Change in Per Capita GNP

Source: Statistical Abstract of the United States

gross national product (GNP) is one way that has been used to measure the size of an economy. The **gross national product** is the total value of all the final goods and services produced by an economy over a given period of time, usually a year. This figure can be misleading because of differing population sizes. So economists often calculate per capita figures—a nation's total GNP divided by its population. Figure 22-2 shows the total and per capita GNP of the economies of several nations. Figure 22-3 above shows how the GNP for some nations has changed over several years.

In addition to these measures, each type of economy has advantages and disadvantages which have been discussed earlier. What you might think of as advantages or disadvantages in a system depends a great deal on what you consider fair and best for everyone. For example, if you believe that individual freedom to choose is important to have in an economic system, then the market system is one you would prefer. On the other hand, if you believe that resources should be distributed evenly among the citizens of a country, then a command economy would be more to your liking. However, no matter what the advantages or disadvantages, it is best to remember that no economic system is perfect on all accounts.

Quick Check

1. What four characteristics can be used to compare economic systems?
2. What is economic equity?

Global Perspective

Most of the world's economies are converging toward the free market system. One of the most promising of those seems to be China, whose economy is growing at a phenomenal rate. Suggest that students survey recent news periodicals for articles detailing events in China's move toward a market economy. Encourage students to share their findings on a poster or bulletin board exhibit.

Refer to the *International Business Strategies* booklet for additional strategies and activities.

Chapter 22 **Summary**

Main Ideas

1. Countries allocate their resources by making decisions about which goods and services will be produced, how these goods and services will be produced, and how the goods and services will be distributed.
2. The basic types of economic systems are traditional, command, and market.
3. Traditional economies offer everyone a role in the economy but little individual freedom.
4. Command economies range from strong government control to moderate government control of resources.
5. Market economies depend on the interaction of consumers and producers and little interference by government.
6. Economic systems can be compared by the standard of living they offer their citizens as well as by economic efficiency, economic equity, and economic growth.
7. The basic technology of a computer includes components such as transistors, silicon chips, a central processing unit (CPU), and circuit boards.
8. A Venn diagram is a useful tool for comparing alternatives.

CASE ANALYSIS — Economic Systems

Think of your class as a production enterprise. What is the end product? For whom is it produced? How is it distributed? What are the resources it requires? The labor? The capital? The entrepreneurship? After you have answered all these questions, decide into which one of the economic systems described in this chapter your class production enterprise falls.

CHAPTER 22   OTHER ECONOMIC SYSTEMS   **379**

CLOSE

Main Ideas

Main Ideas summarizes the key information in the chapter. It is a useful tool for reinforcement and review.

CASE ANALYSIS

Case Analysis provides a chapter-related case for student analysis and application of decision-making skills.

Answer
Answers will vary.

QUICK QUIZ

1. In what economic system are the resources privately owned? Owned and controlled by the government? (Free market, strong command.)
2. Which economic system is most often associated with communism? Capitalism? Socialism? (Strong command, free market, moderate command.)
3. How can an economic system be efficient but not equitable? (It can make efficient use of resources but not give all members of society access to the goods produced.)

Chapter 22 Review

APPLY

Answers

Use the Language of Business
1. traditional economy; **2.** market economy; **3.** communism; **4.** capitalism; **5.** mixed economy; **6.** socialism; **7.** command economy.

Review What You Learned
1. To satisfy the unlimited wants of citizens with limited productive resources.
2. Possible answer: Advantage—the government, by taxing the population at a very high rate, is able to provide many services and benefits to its citizens. Disadvantage—the high rate of taxation discourages successful private business-people from increasing productivity or personal earnings.
3. It is hard to grow because they see no need for new products or new markets.
4. Consumer goods.
5. The government. In a market economy, consumers and producers decide what will be produced.
6. Major industries, such as railroads.
7. Economic efficiency exists when resources are used to generate the greatest value possible. Economic equity exists when resources are distributed fairly evenly.
8. Most countries have a mixed system, made up of aspects of different systems.
9. Data are electronic signals that the computer processes into meaningful information.
10. A Venn diagram offers a place to record information that is exclusive to each of two alternatives as well as a place to record information common to both alternatives.

Understand Business Concepts
1. It produces the goods and services it has always produced.
2. You probably would not have as large a variety of consumer goods available in the market as you have now. You would have less freedom of choice.

Use the Language of Business

On a separate sheet of paper, rewrite the sentences. Fill in each blank with the term that best completes the sentence.

capitalism
command economy
communism
gross national product
mixed economy
socialism
traditional economy

1. A _____ is an economic system in which people do things the way they have always done them.
2. The _____ is the total value of all the final goods and services produced by an economy over a given period of time.
3. An economic structure in which the government makes decisions concerning the commonly owned resources is called _____ .
4. Another name for a market system is _____ .
5. A _____ is an economic system that combines elements of all the other basic systems.
6. An economic structure in which the government owns major industries but allows for private ownership of other businesses is called _____ .
7. In a _____ , a central authority decides what to produce and how to produce and distribute it.

Review What You Learned

1. What is the major challenge with which all economic systems must deal?
2. What are some advantages/disadvantages of a moderate command system?
3. What problem do most traditional economic systems face?
4. What types of goods may have low priority in a country with a strong command system?
5. What does the government own in a moderate command system?
6. Who decides what will be produced in a strong command system? Who makes the decision in a market system?
7. What are *economic efficiency* and *economic equity?*
8. What type of economic system do most countries have?
9. In a computer, what is the difference between data and information?
10. Explain how a Venn diagram can help compare and contrast information.

Understand Business Concepts

1. How does the traditional system answer the first basic economic question, "Which goods and services will be produced?"
2. How might your life be different if you lived in a country with a strong command economy?
3. Explain how a true market system works.
4. List one problem for a strong command economy and one for a market economy.

3. The key to the operation of a market system is what goes on in the market where buyers and sellers meet. In a market system, goods and services that people are willing to buy and that will bring a profit to sellers are produced. Regulation by government is minimal.
4. Possible answer: In a strong command system, people must follow decisions made by government. This limits individual freedom and can hamper economic growth. In a market system, people are free to make their own decisions. This means they are free to make decisions that may not be good for themselves or those around them.
5. One way in which our market system operates like a command system is in the way government regulates certain industries.
6. No, those who can generate more income can buy more goods and services.
7. It produces the goods and services that consumers are willing to buy and that will bring a profit to the sellers.
8. To coordinate the computer's activities and to handle arithmetic or logic instructions.
9. Draw two circles which overlap slightly. Label one circle "socialism," the other "communism." Record what is common to each in the area that overlaps. Record any other information in the appropriately labeled circle.

Chapter 22 **Review**

5. In what ways do market systems like ours have some strong command characteristics?
6. In a market system, do individuals share equally in the goods produced for that system? Why or why not?
7. Sometimes we describe our economic system as one in which "the consumer rules." How does such a system answer the question, "What will be produced?"
8. What are two functions of the central processing unit of a computer?
9. How would you use a Venn diagram to help you compare socialism and communism?

Think Critically

1. **Observe.** What economic advantages do people have in the United States that people in some other countries do not have?
2. **Synthesize.** What changes would occur if our government began operating our factories, stores, farms, and other kinds of businesses?
3. **Analyze.** How can you evaluate whether an economic system is working well for its people?

Use What You Learned

1. **Group Project.** Work in groups of four. Each group should choose either a traditional, a strong command, or a moderate command economy. Use the game *Monopoly,* which is a model of a market economy, to design a board game to show how the economy your team has chosen works.
2. Choose two countries with different economic systems. Do some research to find out about each of the country's standard of living, economic efficiency, economic equity, and total and per capita GNP. Use your findings to write a 300-word essay comparing and contrasting the countries' economic systems.
3. **Computer Application.** Use word processing software to create a table using the per capita GNP data in Figure 22-2 on page 377. Arrange the data by country in descending order. Be sure that dollar amounts are right-aligned. Attractively format the table and print out the results.
4. **Skill Reinforcement.** Think of a decision you need to make or would like to make, such as choosing a vacation spot or deciding which audio system to buy. On another sheet of paper, construct a Venn diagram to help with your decision. Make your choice and explain it.

Save your work in your Business Portfolio.

Use the Chapter 22 worksheets in *Student Activity Guide 2* for additional practice and application activities. *Student Activity Guide 2* provides vocabulary exercises, reading comprehension checks, problems, projects, and simulations of business and economic situations. A Teacher's Annotated Edition provides answers.

ASSESS

Portfolio Assessment

The portfolio projects are designed to lead students to develop a collection of their best work to submit to you for assessment. You and your students should decide which projects will be included in their respective Business Portfolios. Refer students to the specific rubric(s) from the *Alternative Assessment Strategies* booklet listed with each of the project notes below. These rubrics will alert students to the criteria you will use to assess their projects.

Chapter Assessment

Use the Chapter 22 Test from the *Test Masters* booklet to evaluate students' understanding of the chapter concepts. An answer key is provided. Or create your own customized test using the *Testmaker* software.

Think Critically
1. Possible answer: People in the United States can choose goods and services from a wider variety than in many other countries. People are free to own property and to choose their career. Initiative and creativity can bring recognition and higher earnings in the United States. This is not always possible in other countries.
2. Everyone would work for the government, private ownership of property would decrease, and wages, prices, and production decisions would be determined by the government.
3. Answers may vary, but students may feel one way is by the standard of living and the percentage of people who benefit from and share in the system.

Use What You Learned
1. Circulate to be certain each student participates in the group activity. Possible rubrics: Illustration, Paragraph.
2. Remind students that they are likely to find more current information in periodicals rather than encyclopedias. Rubrics: Note Taking, Booklet.
3. Students without access to computers can create GNP tables by hand. Rubric: Charts and Tables.
4. Students' answers will vary, but they should show a completed Venn diagram with notes in all three sections. Students' explanations should reflect the content of their diagrams. Rubric: Diagrams.

CHAPTER

23

FOCUS

Introduce the Chapter

Major Concepts
- Changes in an International Market
- Currency: A Medium of Exchange
- Exchange Rates and the U.S. Dollar

Introduce the Topic
Ask students how they get to school or work each day. Point out that chances are they depend on someone else, perhaps someone they don't even know—such as a bus driver or subway operator. Indicate that this economic interdependence exists on a global scale whereby businesses and nations depend on one another.

Use Business Terms
Have students read the list of Business Terms. Ask for ideas about what the terms mean. Record correct answers on the board or a transparency. For unknown terms, encourage students to check the meanings of the terms as they read the chapter.

USE VISUALS

Inform students that this photograph depicts a currency exchange sign posted in French-speaking Montreal, Canada. This currency exchange office exchanges foreign currency from a number of different countries for Canadian currency.

Business terms

trade

balance of trade

trade surplus

trade deficit

balance of payments

exchange rate

depreciation

devaluation

382

CHAPTER 23 RESOURCES

Instructional Resources

Lesson Plan for Chapter 23

Teaching Transparencies 23-1, 23-2, 23-3, 23-4

Strategies and Worksheets for Teaching Transparencies 23-1, 23-2, 23-3, 23-4

Enrichment Master 23-1

Student Activity Guide 2–TAE for Chapter 23

Test Master for Chapter 23

Alternative Assessment Strategies

Math Skills Review

International Business Strategies

Cooperative Learning Strategies

Communication Skills Review

Ethics in Business Strategies

International Finance

Learning objectives

After completing this chapter, you will be able to:
- Identify the factors considered in the balance of trade and the balance of payments and the relationship between the two.
- Describe the currency exchange market and the factors that influence the value of a currency.
- Explain how domestic and international businesses that are not connected through computer networks can still quickly exchange information.
- Use foreign exchange rates to convert dollars to a foreign currency and foreign currency to dollars.

Consider what you know

- Several different kinds of economies exist in today's world. Each economy makes decisions about which goods and services it will produce, how it will produce them, and how it will distribute them. In addition, each economy makes decisions about how to obtain the goods and services it cannot produce.

Consider what you want to know

- What happens if a country imports more goods than it exports?
- How do changes in the value of the Japanese yen or Mexican peso affect your life?
- How can businesses that are not connected through computer networks exchange information quickly?
- How can you convert dollars to a foreign currency?

Consider how to use what you learn

- As you read through this chapter, consider what it would be like to have a business that sells its products in other countries.

Multimedia Resources

Technology Resource Guide

Distance Learning Guide

Internet Resource Guide

Professional Resources

School-to-Work/Tech Prep Strategies

Instructional Poster

Spanish Resources

Testmaker Software for Chapter 23

The Wall Street Journal Video Series
Video & Activities for Chapter 23

Business and Marketing Computer Applications—An Integrated Software Simulation Using Microsoft Works

Stocktracker—A Stock Market Software Simulation

Where's the Dough? Board Game

CHAPTER 23

TEACH

Business Connection

The export of services has helped improve the U.S. trade balance. At $56.9 billion in 1993, U.S. exports of business, technical, and professional services led the worldwide market and accounted for nearly one-third of the worldwide service market of $184.9 billion.

Develop Concepts

Changes in an International Market

Indicate to students that the greatest factors or measures of the international market are the balance of trade and the balance of payments. The balance of trade, which is the difference between the value of a nation's exports and the value of its imports, accounts for the exchange of goods between countries. However, countries also exchange services, investments, financial assets, and even tourists. For this reason, the balance of payments presents an expanded view of the trade between nations.

TEACHING TIP

Ask students to classify the following as *trade surplus* or *trade deficit:*

- A nation spends $10 billion on imported goods and gets $12 billion for the exports it sells. (Trade surplus.)
- A nation spends $20 billion on goods made in other countries and sells $15 billion in goods to other countries. (Trade deficit.)

As you have learned, different countries have different resources. Furthermore, because of specialization, some countries can produce goods more economically than others. These factors lead countries to depend on one another to supply goods they cannot produce. World **trade,** foreign trade, and international trade all describe the system by which countries exchange goods and services.

CHANGES IN AN INTERNATIONAL MARKET

As the world's needs for products change, the goods a country can export change as well. Centuries ago, European merchants traveled to foreign ports to obtain salt and spices that they traded for wool and manufactured items.

Today, the basis of trade is still the same; countries trade goods they can produce efficiently for those they cannot produce very efficiently. Most international trade involves the purchase and sale of industrial equipment, consumer goods, oil, and agricultural products. In addition, services such as banking, insurance, telecommunications, engineering, and tourism are part of today's world trade.

Balance of Trade

Goods and services that a country sells to foreign buyers are called *exports;* goods and services that a country purchases from foreign sellers are called *imports.* You probably recall these definitions from Chapter 21. The *merchandise trade balance,* often referred to as the **balance of trade,** is the difference in value between a nation's exports and imports. If a country's exports exceed its imports, a favorable merchandise balance exists. This favorable balance is often called a **trade surplus.** If a country's imports exceed its exports, the balance is considered unfavorable or negative. This condition is called a **trade deficit.**

A country may have a favorable balance of trade with some trading partners and an unfavorable balance with others. For example, Figure 23-1 on page 385 shows the 1993 U.S. trade balance with six of its top trading partners. However, if a country's overall balance of trade is unfavorable—if overall it buys more than it sells—then more of its money leaves the country

Business & GEOGRAPHY

Often the specialization of a country is a result of the country's specific climate, topology, or geologic history. For example, coffee grows best in the mountainous regions near the equator. Amber is found primarily near the Baltic Sea regions of northern Europe. The flat expansive plains in the southwest United States, the Argentine *pampas,* and Australia are ideal for raising cattle.

384   UNIT 7   INTERNATIONAL BUSINESS

Cooperative Learning Debate (Pro/Con)

Ask students to name articles of clothing, watches, shoes, and other items they have with them that are made in other countries. Ask those students who responded why they purchased a foreign-made article rather than one made in the United States. Discuss the reasons with the class. Then conclude by asking students whether they agree or disagree with the statement: Americans depend too much on foreign trade.

Refer to the *Cooperative Learning Strategies* booklet for additional cooperative learning strategies.

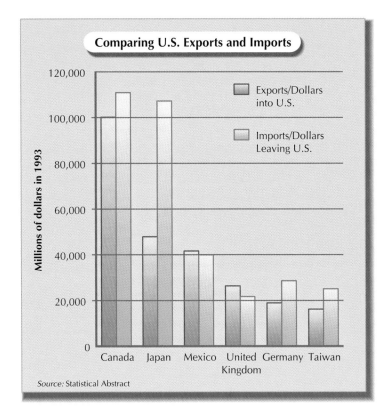

FIGURE 23-1

Comparing U.S. Exports and Imports

Exports/Dollars into U.S.

Imports/Dollars Leaving U.S.

Millions of dollars in 1993

120,000
100,000
80,000
60,000
40,000
20,000
0

Canada   Japan   Mexico   United Kingdom   Germany   Taiwan

Source: Statistical Abstract

The U.S. balance of trade is different with each of the United States' top trading partners. For which partners shown did the United States have a favorable balance of trade in 1993?

than comes into the country. Figure 23-2 on page 386 shows the United States trade balance for the beginning of the 1990s.

There are several factors that have led to the U.S. trade deficit. In some cases, products once produced by the United States are now produced more efficiently by other countries. For example, at one time nearly all the televisions owned by American families were built in the United States. Now, however, foreign countries have the technology and resources needed to manufacture televisions. What's more, those countries can manufacture and sell those televisions at a lower price than U.S. manufacturers can.

Sometimes a country uses certain government actions such as quotas, tariffs, and embargoes to improve its balance of trade. As you recall, a quota is a fixed limit on the import (or export) of a product. A quota on a product can force prices to remain high because outside competition is limited. Tariffs, which are taxes on goods made in other countries, effectively increase the price of imported goods. This tends to lower the

Curriculum Connection   English and Communication

Have students work in pairs within groups of four. Suggest that each pair explore ways in which they think the United States can create a more equal or positive balance of trade. Then have each pair write an essay explaining its suggestions. Partner pairs can exchange completed essays for peer review. Allow time for students to revise or rewrite their essays if they wish.

For those students who need to sharpen their written communication skills, choose among the worksheets in the *Communication Skills Review* booklet.

CHAPTER 23

USE VISUALS

Direct students' attention to Figure 23-2, which shows the U.S. Balance of Trade over a five-year time period. Ask students if they think the trade deficit is increasing or decreasing. (It seems to be increasing slightly.) Answer to caption: 1991

USE TRANSPARENCIES

Use Teaching Transparency 23-2 and its corresponding strategies and worksheet from the *Teaching Transparency Strategies and Worksheets* booklet to acquaint students with the U.S. balance of trade. Verify student worksheets using the Answer Key.

Learning Activity

Emphasize to students that whether an item is an *import* or an *export* depends on a country's point of view. Ask students to name several items they own that were manufactured in other countries. Have them identify the countries and classify the items as imports or exports. (Imports.) Then ask what a student in the country of origin, such as Japan, Taiwan, or Hong Kong, might call them. (Exports.)

FIGURE 23-2

For the five-year period shown here, the U.S. balance of trade has been unfavorable. That is, the United States has imported more goods and services than it has exported. In which year did the value of imports come closest to the value of exports?

Source: Statistical Abstract

F.Y.I.

In the past 25 years, travel to the United States by foreign visitors has grown steadily. Money spent by these foreign tourists for lodging, car rentals, and airline tickets, all helps the balance of payments.

amount of imported goods consumers will purchase and it decreases the dollars a country spends on imported goods. An embargo, which is an order to stop the import of a product, can help control the trade balance by preventing goods from foreign firms from entering the country.

Balance of Payments

Balance of trade does not account for all the exchanges that occur between countries. Countries exchange more than merchandise and services; they exchange investments, financial assets, and tourists. Money also flows from one country to another in the form of military aid, foreign aid, and overseas bank deposits. The difference in the total amount of money flowing in and flowing out is called the **balance of payments.** The balance of payments is the complete summary of all economic transactions.

Balance of payments has two categories.

- The current account records sales of goods, services, and interest payments.
- The capital account includes stocks, bonds, bank accounts, real estate, and factories.

For example, if you purchased a television made in Korea, your purchase would be recorded in the current account. If you purchased the television factory, the purchase would be entered in the capital account. Because both categories make up the

386   UNIT 7   INTERNATIONAL BUSINESS

Cooperative Learning   Teammates Consulting

Remind students they have learned about quotas, tariffs, and embargoes in Chapters 17 and 21. Have students work in groups to discuss how governments use these tools to help improve the balance of trade and what effect these actions might have on consumers. (For example, fixing a quota on imported cars would limit supply so there would be fewer total dollars spent on the cars. Each car might have a higher price because of demand.)

Refer to the *Cooperative Learning Strategies* booklet for additional cooperative learning strategies.

A bottle of Coca-Cola bottled at a bottling plant in Venezuela and purchased in the United States would be recorded in which balance of payments account?

balance of payments, a country can have an unfavorable balance of trade and still have a favorable balance of payments.

Countries try to equalize their balance of payments. One way is to require that any large merchandise trade transaction (current account) include a significant investment transaction (capital account) as well.

For example, Spain agreed to purchase $1.5 billion in jets from a U.S. aerospace manufacturer. To help offset the $1.5 billion going to the United States, Spain required the aerospace manufacturer to help promote U.S. investment in Spain in return. The American aerospace manufacturer complied by helping a U.S. food product company establish a market in Spain. Agreements such as this are called *offset agreements.* They help countries offset the drain of capital to another country in a large purchase transaction.

Just as you cannot continue to spend more money than you earn, a country cannot continue to pay out more than it takes in. If a country has an unfavorable balance of payments over a long period of time, the value of its money in relation to other foreign currencies will probably decrease. When this happens, a country has to look at its trade policies to try to improve the situation.

Quick Check

1. What is the *balance of trade?* How is it related to *trade surplus? Trade deficit?*
2. What is the *balance of payments?* How is it different from the *balance of trade?*

Reteaching Strategy

Direct students to work in pairs within groups of four. Have each pair of partners write a ten-question quiz to cover the terms listed below. Indicate that questions may be true-false or multiple choice. Have partner pairs exchange quizzes, supply answers, and return quizzes to their authors for grading. Suggest that students choose five questions to keep as a study aid.

- Balance of trade
- Trade deficit
- Balance of payments
- Capital account
- Trade surplus
- Negative balance of trade
- Current account

FOCUS ON **Technology**

Discuss

Encourage students to describe in their own words the terms *fax, modem,* and *bit.* Suggest that students illustrate their descriptions.

Modems

Computer networks, like those used by banks, offer a way for several computers at a single location or across a business's many locations to exchange data. Once businesses realized the speed and efficiency of data and document transfer between computers in a network, they began to look for ways in which computers that were not part of the same network could exchange information.

There already existed a potential connection. After all, two individuals at distant locations could communicate over the telephone. The vibrating diaphragm inside a telephone's mouthpiece changes the vibrations in a person's voice into an electric current. At the other end of the call, the receiver changes the current back into the sound vibrations that match the caller's voice.

In fact, technology found a way to send an exact duplicate of a paper document to a remote location over standard telephone lines. During a *facsimile,* or *fax,* transmission, a fax machine translates the image on the paper into electronic signals. The telephone lines carry these electronic signals to the remote location. At the remote location, a second facsimile machine translates the electronic signals back into an image on paper.

Converting information—voice, image, or data—to a signal that can travel a standard phone line is called *modulation.* Converting the signal back—into voice, image, or data—is called *demodulation.*

A *modem* (for *modulator/demodulator*) is the device that converts the digital data a computer uses to a signal that can travel over a phone line. And, at the

Develop Concepts

Currency: A Medium of Exchange

Indicate to students that other nations have their own currencies. These different currencies are often exchanged for one another at a rate called the foreign exchange rate. Like all items, the currency rate is determined by supply and demand. However, a government can take actions to influence the exchange rates for its own currency.

TEACHING TIP

To emphasize the variety of currencies in the world, ask students to name foreign currencies with which they are familiar. Enrichment Master 19-1, from Chapter 19, may provide a useful starting point for discussion.

CURRENCY: A MEDIUM OF EXCHANGE

When buyers and sellers are in different countries, making payments for imported goods and services can be a challenge. Many banks have offices in other countries just to handle foreign payments. These banks are part of a system for changing foreign money into dollars and changing dollars into foreign money. This system is sometimes called international banking. To trade with other countries, a buyer in the United States must pay in the currency, or money, of the other countries.

Types of Currency

Americans buy French cheese and Japanese automobiles. The French and Japanese buy American airplanes and blue jeans. Buyers wishing to purchase goods and services from foreign countries need to pay in the currency of the country. In a similar manner, marketers selling goods and services to these countries will be paid in the currency of the country.

388 UNIT 7 INTERNATIONAL BUSINESS

Global Perspective

Direct students to use business periodicals to find examples of *offset agreements.* Have them note which agreements improve the U.S. balance of payments and which improve a foreign nation's balance of payments. Invite students to post their findings on the class bulletin board. Use the listings to discuss how corporations and governments can work toward a balance of payments.

Refer to the *International Business Strategies* booklet for additional strategies and activities.

other end of the telephone line, a second modem converts the signal into digital data.

Businesses, particularly those working in the global market, need to get information quickly—so one of the most important characteristics of a modem is the speed at which it transmits data. Modem speeds are measured in bits per second or *bps*. A *bit* is an individual piece of data. The higher the bps, the faster the transmission. Because businesses are transmitting increasingly large volumes of data, the generally accepted speed for modems is up to 28,800 bps, sometimes abbreviated 28.8 Kbps.

Armed with a computer, a phone line, and a modem, an individual or business can communicate with any other similarly equipped individual or business. This allows individuals to work at home and literally "phone it in."

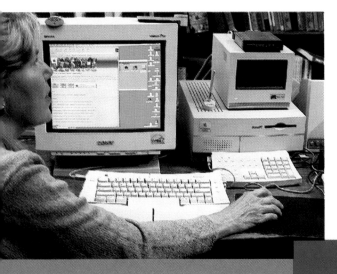

Follow Through

Ask students to speculate on what kinds of improvements or changes in data transmission are likely to occur in the near future. Suggest that they look through computer periodicals or business news sections to locate articles that support their speculations. (Sample answers: Faster transmissions, smaller machines, fiber-optic telephone lines.)

Each country has its own currency that serves as its official medium of exchange. Some foreign currencies and their symbols that you may be familiar with include the Canadian dollar ($), the French franc (F), the Mexican peso ($), the British pound (£), the Japanese yen (¥), and the German deutsche mark (DM).

Foreign Currency Exchange

To buy the currency of a particular country, a business, broker, customer, or central bank turns to the foreign exchange market. This is the place where different currencies are bought and sold. Usually buyers acquire the foreign currency necessary to obtain goods and services from a foreign country. Some participants in the foreign exchange market want foreign currency for other reasons. For example, banks and other financial institutions buy and sell currencies in the market. They hope to earn profits by buying currencies from and selling currencies to customers. Central banks, such as the U.S. Federal Reserve and the Bank of England, also may participate in the foreign exchange market. They buy and sell currencies to influence the exchange rate.

The foreign exchange market is active 24 hours a day. As the market closes in Tokyo and other Pacific Rim locations, London is beginning its market day. When it is 1 P.M. in London, the New York market opens. Later that same business day, as the London markets close, traders in San Francisco begin trading with their Far East counterparts.

Learning Activity

Ask students to find the current exchange rate for several foreign currencies from a newspaper or bank. Have students keep track of the currencies' rates for several days. Have them create a line graph comparing the changes in the rates.

USE TRANSPARENCIES

Ask students to identify articles such as shirts, shoes, watches, and so on that they own and that are foreign-made. Have them enter each item in a chart that indicates its country of origin. Suggest that they group the items into broad categories such as clothing or accessories. Have them locate the country on the world map on Teaching Transparency 23-1 and use a flag to identify the category of the item and the nation's currency. Use Teaching Transparency 23-1 and its corresponding strategies and worksheet from the *Teaching Transparency Strategies and Worksheets* booklet. Verify student worksheets using the Answer Key.

Enrichment Strategy

Photocopy and distribute Enrichment Master 23-1. Indicate to students that they can think of the exchange rates of currencies as "prices" charged for those currencies. Remind students that they learned in Chapter 5 how price changes with supply and demand. If the supply of an item increases, the price decreases; if the demand for an item increases, the price increases. Ask students to use their graphs to identify changes in supply and demand for the currencies listed.

Building Business Skills

Model

Work through the example for students, showing how to determine the number of units of a foreign currency that can be exchanged for a dollar. Then work the problem in reverse, showing how many dollars can be exchanged for a unit of foreign currency. Be certain to remind students that the *unit* is not the name of a currency but a way to indicate the value of one dollar, yen, or peso.

M ATH

Exchanging Foreign Currency

Explanation

Choose a business career today, and chances are that sometime you'll be dealing with people from other nations—most with a currency different from ours. If you travel to another country, you'll have to exchange U.S. dollars for the local money. In conducting business abroad, you'll need to use your ability to "translate" dollars into foreign currency—and vice versa—to carry out transactions and analyze information.

The prices, or exchange rates, may change from day to day. The rates for a variety of foreign currencies are displayed in places where you can exchange money. Foreign exchange rates can be stated in two forms.

1. The number of units of foreign currency that can be exchanged for one U.S. dollar. For example: $1.00 = 6.23 Mexican pesos. Suppose you are in Mexico on the day this rate applies, and you have $100 to exchange for pesos. To find out how many pesos you'll get, multiply the number of dollars times the number of pesos per dollar: $100 × 6.23 pesos per dollar = **623 pesos.**

2. The number of dollars that can be purchased for one unit of foreign currency. For example: 1 Mexican peso = $.1605. If something costs 100 pesos, how much does it cost in dollars? Multiply the price in pesos by the number of dollars per peso: 100 pesos × $.1605 per peso = **$16.05.**

TEACHING TIP

To find out if students grasp the concept of exchange rate, ask: If the exchange rate changed from $1 = 5 clamshells to $1 = 8 clamshells, what would happen to the cost of imports? (Prices would rise.)

Learning Activity

Discuss with students the connection between a lower exchange rate for the dollar and the effect on consumer purchasing imports. (Students should point out that when a currency depreciates, more currency is required to purchase the same amount of imported goods as before.)

Central to international transactions is the **exchange rate,** the price of one currency in terms of another country's currency. Exchange rates for currencies can change from day to day, so there is some risk in dealing with different currencies. A U.S. company selling to a German firm may receive payment in German marks. Those marks must be converted into U.S. dollars. If the value of the mark falls before payment is transferred, the U.S. company will receive fewer dollars for those marks. Companies watch the value of various currencies closely and consider the foreign exchange rate when they trade with other countries. Refer to the Building Business Skills above to learn how to exchange foreign currencies.

Government and Foreign Currency Exchange

Currency exchange rates are affected by a variety of factors: balance of payments, political developments in a country, new tax laws, stock market levels, inflation, and government and central bank policies. However, because currencies are traded in a free market, the most important consideration for the price of currencies is the same as it is for any other good or service.

390 UNIT 7 INTERNATIONAL BUSINESS

Reteaching Strategy

Present students with the following list of events. Have them place the events in chronological order. Caution students that one event does not belong in the list and could lead to a false conclusion. Answers appear in parentheses.

- U.S. company sells $100,000 worth of television parts to Mexico for $623,000 pesos. (1)
- U.S. company receives more than $100,000. (false)
- Pesos are converted to U.S. dollars. (4)
- Peso value decreases before payment is transferred. (3)
- U.S. company receives less than $100,000. (5)
- U.S. company receives $623,000 pesos. (2)

EXCHANGE RATES

National Currencies	[1]Units of Foreign Currency per Dollar	[1]Multiply the rates in this column by the number of U.S. dollars to turn U.S. dollars into foreign currency.
Brazilian real	.9192	
British pound	.6277	
French franc	4.8265	
German mark	1.3803	
Indian rupee	31.385	
Japanese yen	84.88	
Russian ruble	4538.00	
South African rand	3.6317	

National Currencies	[2]Dollars per Unit of Foreign Currency	[2]Multiply the rates in this column by number of foreign currency units to turn units into U.S. dollars.
Brazilian real	$ 1.0879	
British pound	1.5930	
French franc	.2072	
German mark	.7245	
Indian rupee	.0319	
Japanese yen	.011781	
Russian ruble	.000220	
South African rand	.2754	

The box shows exchange rates for the currencies of eight countries on a certain day.

Practice

Use the tables to figure out these problems.
1. Which country gives the most units of currency in exchange for a dollar? Which gives the fewest?
2. The British want 11,200 pounds and the French are asking 88,000 francs for the same machine. Which is offering the best deal? Why?
3. You're selling a Japanese retailer an order of running shoes worth $6597. How much is that in yen?

Ultimately, the exchange rate of foreign currency is determined by supply and demand. If the supply is greater than the demand, prices will fall. If demand is greater than supply, prices will rise.

A government's central bank often buys or sells large amounts of its own currency to influence the supply of the currency available in the exchange market. Remember, if the supply of the currency diminishes, but the demand is constant, the price of the currency will rise. The price of the currency will fall if the supply of that currency increases, and the demand remains the same. The price will also fall if the supply remains the same but the demand decreases.

If the price of a currency falls because of differences in supply and demand, the change is called **depreciation.** For example, if the value of the U.S. dollar depreciates, a single dollar can be exchanged for fewer German marks. Figure 23-3 on page 392 shows how depreciation of the U.S. dollar can make the price of products exported from the United States more attractive to foreign consumers. If more goods are purchased because of the more attractive price, the balance of payments can be favorably affected.

CHAPTER 23   INTERNATIONAL FINANCE   **391**

Global Perspective

Market reforms in the Russian economy caused the value of the Russian currency, the ruble, to tumble. Many Russians avoided using the ruble for transactions. Stores, especially those that sold foreign products, preferred to be paid in dollars, marks, or another stable foreign currency. This drove down the value of the ruble even further. In 1993 alone, the exchange rate for the ruble went from 570 to the dollar to about 1250 to the dollar. To stop the downward spiral, the Russian government ordered stores to accept only rubles or credit cards as payment. Have students discuss what effect the fall of the ruble had on consumers.

Refer to the *International Business Strategies* booklet for additional strategies and activities.

FIGURE 23-3

If the value of the dollar depreciates, the cost of goods imported from the United States decreases. How do overseas consumers benefit from the depreciation of the dollar?

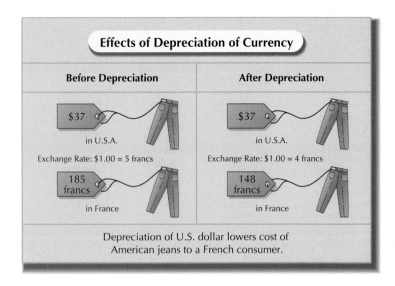

Effects of Depreciation of Currency

Before Depreciation	After Depreciation
$37 in U.S.A.	$37 in U.S.A.
Exchange Rate: $1.00 = 5 francs	Exchange Rate: $1.00 = 4 francs
185 francs in France	148 francs in France

Depreciation of U.S. dollar lowers cost of American jeans to a French consumer.

Keeping Things in Balance

When things in international finance get out of balance, there are automatic mechanisms that "kick in" to bring back the balance. Let's take a look at an example to see how this works.

When a nation has run an unfavorable balance of payments for a number of years, there is an oversupply of their currency in financial institutions throughout the world. The country has had to buy a lot of foreign currencies to purchase goods and services made in other countries and to invest in those countries. Also, the country's currency has not been in demand since their exports to and investments from other countries have been down.

The oversupply of a country's currency causes their currency to lose value in relation to other currencies. That loss of value makes their products lower priced and therefore more attractive to foreign consumers. Also their devalued currency can be more attractive to foreign investors who can get more for their money. These two situations will create more demand for their currency, which over time can bring the country back to more of a balance of payments.

A government can also affect the exchange rate of its currency by issuing an order that changes its currency's exchange rate. If the order lowers the rate, the process is called **devaluation.** For example, if the Japanese yen is devalued, the number of yen that are exchanged for a U.S. dollar is

Reteaching Strategy

Have students describe how a currency is depreciated and list the effects of such a depreciation on import and export prices. Then have students discuss how a currency is devalued and list the effects of such a devaluation on import and export prices. Suggest that students organize their information in a Venn diagram. Finally, have students write a generalization about the effects of devaluation and depreciation on the cost of imported goods.

Effects of Devaluation of Currency

Before Devaluation	After Devaluation
20,000 yen	20,000 yen
in Japan	in Japan
Exchange Rate: 100 yen = $1.00 U.S.	Exchange Rate: 200 yen = $1.00 U.S.
$200	$100
in U.S.A.	in U.S.A.

Devaluation of Japanese yen lowers cost of Japanese VCR to an American consumer.

FIGURE 23-4

The price of a VCR imported from Japan would change if the Japanese government decided to devalue the yen. Why might an American consumer want to buy a VCR after the devaluation took place?

USE VISUALS

Direct students to the diagram in Figure 23-4 that shows what happens to the cost of goods imported to the United States (a Japanese export) when the yen is devalued. Ask students if the value of a yen increases or decreases when it is devalued. (Decreases.) Answer to caption: It would cost less.

USE TRANSPARENCIES

Use Teaching Transparency 23-4 and its corresponding strategies and worksheet from the *Teaching Transparency Strategies and Worksheets* booklet to explore the effects on the U.S. consumer of the devaluation of a foreign currency. Verify student worksheets using the Answer Key.

Quick Check Answers

1. Place where different currencies are bought and sold; the price of one currency in terms of another country's currency.
2. Decrease in a currency's value because of supply and demand; decrease in a currency's value due to government order.

Develop Concepts

Exchange Rates and the U.S. Dollar

Emphasize to students that changes in the exchange rate of currencies, including the dollar, have effects that reach far into the global market. The changes affect consumers who buy foreign-made goods as well as workers who make goods for export.

greater—each yen is worth less. As a result, the cost of goods exported from Japan becomes more attractive, and more exports are likely to be sold. If the cost of imported goods from Japan becomes more attractive to U.S. consumers, purchases of Japanese goods may increase. This increase may have an unfavorable effect on the U.S. balance of payments. Figure 23-4 above depicts an example of such a situation.

Quick Check

1. What is the foreign exchange market? The *exchange rate*?
2. What is *devaluation*? What is *depreciation*?

EXCHANGE RATES AND THE U.S. DOLLAR

Most individuals' learn about exchange rates when they need to exchange money to travel in a foreign country. For example, suppose you decide to travel to Mexico for your vacation. You suspect you will see some handcrafted items you will want to buy. The day before you go shopping you might visit a currency exchange and exchange 50 American dollars for 305 Mexican pesos to pay for goods you wish to buy. Your friend waits until just before leaving for the shopping

Enrichment Strategy

Ask students to imagine that currency is somehow unavailable or that they live in a barter economy. Have them work in groups of four to develop an international rate of exchange involving goods rather than currency. Indicate that the item-based rate of exchange should reflect the values of currency in given countries. Remind students that they will need to find out the relative purchasing power of the currencies of several countries before they can figure out the relative value of items in each country.

Ask students how the activity in the photograph is related to the balance of payments. (Foreign tourists bring money into a country.) Tourism is one way in which international goods and services are purchased. Answer to caption: Because they would be able to get a greater exchange for their currency, therefore, they could buy more goods and services during their trip.

Business Brief

The U.S. dollar reached a post-war low in October of 1994. The large current-account deficit increased from $109 billion in 1993 to $140 billion in 1994. Higher foreign investment and a low savings rate are main causes for the large current-account deficit.

Learning Activity

Ask students to discuss how a high exchange rate for the dollar might affect a foreign visitor's vacation in the United States. (If fewer units of foreign currency are available for each dollar, it would make travel and vacationing more expensive here.)

Quick Check Answers

1. The price of foreign goods and services decreases.
2. Sales may be lower because U.S. goods cost more.

Tourism is one way in which international goods and services are purchased. Why do people who plan to spend money in foreign countries hope their currency is strong in the international marketplace?

Business & HISTORY

In 1295, Europeans were still carrying around heavy gold, silver, and copper coins. During Marco Polo's travels in the Far East, he was startled that the Chinese used paper money in their transactions, which they had done for 600 years. Despite Marco Polo's enthusiastic description of paper money, Europeans were suspicious of it. They didn't begin to use it until some banks in the 1600s issued paper certificates to borrowers and depositors.

expedition. In her case, she exchanges 50 American dollars for 325 Mexican pesos. The exchange rate had changed; the peso had "fallen against the dollar." She could purchase more pesos for each of her dollars.

The example above mirrors what happens in the international marketplace. A stronger dollar—stronger because it can now buy more pesos or more of any other currency—allows U.S. banks and businesses to purchase foreign goods and services more cheaply. This is great news for U.S. businesses that import goods and services and great news for American consumers. However, the balance of trade and the balance of payments may be unfavorably affected. Imports will increase, and American dollars will go abroad.

A stronger dollar also means that consumers and businesses in foreign markets will find U.S. goods and services more expensive. Fewer goods and services may be sold. This may not be good news to businesses that manufacture or sell goods for export. Some consumers who work for those companies may find their jobs in danger. The smaller number of exports sold will also unfavorably affect the balance of trade and the balance of payments.

As you can see, international finance and international trade have a complex and sensitive relationship.

Quick Check

1. How does a strong dollar benefit U.S. consumers?
2. What effect might a strong dollar have on the sales of U.S. exports overseas?

Reteaching Strategy

Discuss with students how the foreign value of a country's currency is related to its domestic economy. Ask students to provide examples of how currency value affects imports, exports, and consumer buying power.

Chapter 23 **Summary**

Main Ideas

1. The balance of trade is the difference in value between a nation's exports and imports. The balance of payments is the complete summary of all economic transactions.
2. Values of foreign currencies, traded in the foreign exchange market, are influenced primarily by supply and demand as well as by the balance of payments, political developments, tax laws, stock market, inflation, and government policies.

3. Changes in the value of a foreign currency can change the prices of goods imported into the United States.
4. Fax technology and modems for computers allow domestic and foreign businesses to use standard telephone lines to exchange information.
5. Exchange rates are stated in terms of the number of American dollars for one unit of foreign currency as well as the number of units of foreign currencies valued at one American dollar.

CASE ANALYSIS Marketing

As a marketer for an international business, you have been asked to develop a promotional campaign for your company's line of cosmetics and fragrances. You know that doing business in another country can be risky, and your company could fail in its marketing attempt if anything is overlooked. What are some of the concerns you should address?

QUICK QUIZ

1. What is the relationship between imports, exports, and the balance of trade? (The balance of trade is the difference between the value of goods exported and the value of goods imported.)
2. How is the balance of payments different from the balance of trade? (It includes investments—stocks, bonds, bank accounts, real estate, factories.)
3. What effects do supply and demand have on a currency's exchange rate? (Supply lowers the rate, demand increases the rate.)
4. What happens to exports when the exporting country's currency is devalued? (Exports cost less and more are sold.)

Chapter 23 **Review**

CHAPTER 23 REVIEW

APPLY

Answers

Use the Language of Business

1. trade; **2.** balance of trade; **3.** trade surplus; **4.** exchange rate; **5.** balance of payments; **6.** trade deficit; **7.** depreciation; **8.** devaluation.

Review What You Learned

1. Tariffs effectively increase the cost of imported goods, which lowers the amount of imported goods purchased and decreases the dollars a country spends on imports. Embargoes prevent foreign-made goods from entering the country. Import quotas can force prices to remain high and help minimize the difference between imports and exports.

2. The balance of payments is the complete summary of all economic transactions. The balance of trade is the summary of imports and exports.

3. Supply and demand.

4. They need to purchase goods from trading partners using these currencies and receive these currencies when they sell products to them.

5. Make purchases overseas; earn profits by buying and selling currencies; influence the value of its own currency.

6. Buy and sell to influence supply and demand; issue an order to change the exchange rate.

7. Each indicates a currency's value has dropped. In depreciation, value drops through supply and demand; in devaluation, value drops by government order.

8. Imports will cost less and may increase.

9. A modem converts the information from a computer into a signal that can be transmitted over standard telephone lines.

10. Find the exchange rates listed in banks or newspapers, multiply the number of yen equal to one dollar times ten.

Understand Business Concepts

1. Payments for services, interest payments, stocks, bonds, bank accounts, real estate, and factories.

Use the Language of Business

Understanding these business terms will help you communicate more easily. Write the term that best matches each numbered definition.

balance of payments	exchange rate
balance of trade	trade
depreciation	trade deficit
devaluation	trade surplus

1. Exchange of goods and services.
2. Difference in value between a nation's exports and imports.
3. Favorable balance of trade, that is, a country's exports exceed its imports.
4. Price or value of one currency in terms of another country's currency.
5. Difference in the total amount of a currency flowing into and flowing out of a country.
6. Excess of a country's imports over exports; also called an unfavorable trade balance.
7. Decrease in the value of a currency caused by changes in supply and demand.
8. Decrease in the value of a currency caused by government order.

Review What You Learned

1. How can tariffs, embargoes, and quotas influence the balance of trade?
2. What is the relationship between the balance of payments and the balance of trade?
3. What is the most important factor in determining the exchange rate or price of a currency?
4. Why are U.S. businesses concerned with the values of foreign currency?
5. Give a reason for a person, a business, and a financial institution to participate in the foreign exchange market.
6. Name two ways in which a government can affect the foreign exchange rate of its own currency.
7. How are devaluation and depreciation alike? How are they different?
8. What effect can a strong dollar have on goods and services imported into the United States?
9. What function does a modem perform in computer communications?
10. How can you find out how many yen you can exchange for $10?

Understand Business Concepts

1. What kinds of things are part of the balance of payments but not part of the trade balance?
2. What is one way in which a company can offset the capital drain of a large international purchase?
3. Who participates in the foreign exchange market?
4. How might the devaluation of a foreign currency affect a U.S. consumer?

2. Require that any large merchandise trade transaction includes a significant investment or capital account transaction as well.

3. Businesses, brokers, customers, and central banks.

4. Imported goods become more affordable.

5. They can buy up a currency, decreasing the supply, thus driving the exchange rate up.

6. The price of the currency will rise.

7. Foreign consumers will be able to purchase U.S. products at lower prices; the balance of payments can be favorably affected.

8. Exported goods become more expensive; imported goods become more affordable.

9. Fax machines and modems allow businesses to use standard telephone lines in place of dedicated network connections.

10. Not necessarily; the exchange rate may have changed.

Think Critically

1. If a currency is weak, the sales of the country's exported goods will increase while the sales of foreign imports will decrease. If the currency is strong, the sales of exports will decrease and the sales of imported goods will increase.

2. Devaluation of a foreign currency may have an adverse or unfavorable effect on the U.S. balance of trade, making goods imported from this foreign country attractively priced.

5. How can governments use supply and demand to influence the foreign exchange rate?
6. What will happen to the price of a currency if the demand for the currency increases and the supply of the currency decreases?
7. How can the depreciation of the U.S. dollar affect foreign consumers? The U.S. balance of payments?
8. How does a strong dollar affect the sale of U.S. goods exported overseas? The

sale of overseas goods imported to the U.S.?
9. How can modems allow businesses to exchange information as if they belonged to the same computer network?
10. On one business day you exchanged $50 for £31. On the next day will you be able to exchange the £31 for $50? Explain why or why not.

Think Critically

1. **Apply.** A few foreign automakers have built automobile manufacturing and assembly plants in the United States. What effect do these plants have on the balance of payments?

2. **Assess.** A foreign government plans to devalue its currency. Why might the U.S. government try to influence the government to reverse its decision?

Use What You Learned

1. **Group Project.** Set up an imaginary business that markets goods to the top U.S. trading partners. Decide the price in dollars of your products; for example, one flamwidget costs $5; one sternbucket costs $10. Find out the current exchange rates in the financial section of the newspaper and use them to compute the amount purchasers in those countries will pay for your product. Then decide how many of each product you will ship to each trading partner. Remember, you will want to sell your product wherever you can make the most profit. Make a chart showing the income your company received from each partner. Compare your chart to the charts of other groups in your class.

2. **Computer Application.** Contact (E-mail, if possible) a local investment expert. Invite him or her to speak to the class about investing in emerging markets in foreign countries. Then prepare a word-processed summary of the presentation.

3. **Skill Reinforcement.** Review the instructions and examples for exchanging foreign currency on pages 390–391. Then suppose that your company is considering opening a plant in Germany. You learn that the average wage for the skilled workers you'll be hiring is 25 marks per hour. How does this compare with the $16.09 per hour that similar workers earn in the United States?

Save your work in your Business Portfolio.

Use What You Learned
1. Each student in the group may be responsible for a different task. Rubrics: Note Taking, Charts and Tables.
2. Students without access to computers can contact their speaker by telephone or in person. The presentation may be prepared manually. Rubric: Presentation.

3. The German workers earn 25 marks × .7245 dollars per mark or $18.11 per hour, $2.02 more than their American counterparts. Rubric: Charts and Tables.

Use the Chapter 23 worksheets in *Student Activity Guide 2* for additional practice and application activities. *Student Activity Guide 2* provides vocabulary exercises, reading comprehension checks, problems, projects, and simulations of business and economic situations. A Teacher's Annotated Edition provides answers.

ASSESS

Portfolio Assessment
The projects are designed to lead students to develop a collection of their best work to submit to you for assessment. You and your students should decide which projects will be included in their respective Business Portfolios. Refer students to the specific rubric(s) from the *Alternative Assessment Strategies* booklet listed with each of the project notes below. These rubrics will alert students to the criteria you will use to assess their projects.

Chapter Assessment
Use the Chapter 23 Test from the *Test Masters* booklet to evaluate students' understanding of the chapter concepts. An answer key is provided. Or create your own customized test using the *Testmaker* software.

Introduce the Chapter

Major Concepts
- Competition in the Global Marketplace
- Developing Nations

Introduce the Topic
Ask students to indicate whether they have heard the term *developing nation*. Point out that in Chapter 24 students will learn about ways in which less developed nations of the world can achieve economic development.

Use Business Terms
Have students look at the Business Terms and brainstorm associations with each term. Ask them where they have heard or seen the terms used. Reinforce correct associations. Advise students to note the meanings of the terms as they read the chapter.

USE VISUALS
Ask students to speculate on how this photograph relates to the chapter title: Global Economic Challenges. Have them discuss whether they think the country pictured is likely to be developed or developing. (Developing.) Remind students that in developing nations, farmers often use little or no mechanical assistance to grow their crops. What type of economy does a developing nation usually have? (Agricultural.)

CHAPTER 24

Business terms

protective tariff

punitive tariff

revenue tariff

developed nation

developing nation

foreign aid

birthrate

398

CHAPTER 24 RESOURCES

Instructional Resources

Lesson Plan for Chapter 24

Teaching Transparencies 24-1, 24-2, 24-3

Strategies and Worksheets for Teaching Transparencies 24-1, 24-2, 24-3

Enrichment Master 24-1

Student Activity Guide 2–TAE for Chapter 24

Test Master for Chapter 24

Alternative Assessment Strategies

Math Skills Review

International Business Strategies

Cooperative Learning Strategies

Communication Skills Review

Ethics in Business Strategies

Global Economic Challenges

Learning objectives

After completing this chapter, you will be able to:
- Identify benefits and challenges to competition in the international marketplace.
- Describe the process of economic development and identify characteristics of developing nations.
- Identify food and hospitality jobs within the service industry of developed economies.
- Discuss how points of view can affect international trade.

Consider what you know

- Imports and exports and the values of foreign currencies can influence a nation's trade balance and its balance of payments. Foreign exchange rates respond to supply and demand as well as to the balance of payments, political developments, tax laws, the stock market, inflation, and government policies.

Consider what you want to know

- How do nations benefit from competing in the global market? What challenges might this competition provide?
- What is a developing country?
- What kinds of jobs are included in the food and hospitality industry?
- How can learning to interpret various points of view help businesspeople as they address global economic challenges?

Consider how to use what you learn

- As you work through this chapter, be aware of news coverage of developing nations and international economic challenges.

Multimedia Resources

Technology Resource Guide

Distance Learning Guide

Internet Resource Guide

Professional Resources

School-to-Work/Tech Prep Strategies

Instructional Poster

Spanish Resources

Testmaker Software for Chapter 24

The Wall Street Journal Video Series
Video & Activities for Chapter 24

Business and Marketing Computer Applications—An Integrated Software Simulation Using Microsoft Works

Stocktracker—A Stock Market Software Simulation

Where's the Dough? Board Game

Motivate the Learning

Learning Objectives
Point out to students that the learning objectives indicate what they will learn as they study Chapter 24. Encourage students to keep the objectives in mind as they work through the chapter. Note that the last two objectives listed refer to the Focus on Careers feature and the Building Business Skills feature.

Consider What You Know
Review briefly the main sections of *Chapter 23 International Finance:* Changes in an International Market; Currency: A Medium of Exchange; and Exchange Rates and the U.S. Dollar.

Consider What You Want to Know
Have students keep the listed questions in mind as they preview the chapter by quickly paging through it, looking at the graphics, and reading the section headings and figure titles.

Consider How to Use What You Learn
Indicate to students that after they have completed this chapter, they will develop projects designed to investigate global economic challenges. Remind them to keep in mind the characteristics of global competition and developing nations as they read the chapter.

Business Connection

Recently Kentucky Fried Chicken's operations in China have faced serious competition from Ronghua Chicken, a Chinese fast-food restaurant that combines Western-style service with Chinese-style food preparation. Ronghua's management has declared that its branches will open everywhere Kentucky Fried Chicken opens.

Develop Concepts

Competition in the Global Marketplace

Indicate to students that, like individuals, nations have needs and wants that they cannot meet themselves. In order to meet those needs and wants, nations participate in a global marketplace. Point out to students that while there are benefits to free trade, there are still many obstacles to free trade as well.

Connection to CHAPTER 6

Remind students that a free market is one in which businesses are free to produce or not to produce a product and are free to enter or leave the market at any time. Ask students to describe how the principles of a free market economy might apply to nations rather than businesses. (Nations acting as consumers can purchase at the best price; nations acting as businesses can sell at the best price.)

As you have learned, *world trade, foreign trade,* and *international trade* all identify the system or process by which nations exchange goods and services. Often this process is described as if it takes place at a specific marketplace, called the global or international market.

As the number of nations participating in the global market increases, we often speak of an "international economy" as if all nations answered questions about production and distribution of goods and services in the same way. They do not. However, nations with traditional, command, free market, and mixed economic systems all do participate in the international economy.

COMPETITION IN THE GLOBAL MARKETPLACE

You have learned that in the free enterprise system, competition is the contest between businesses to win customers. In other words, competition is a direct response to the wants and needs of consumers.

Nations participating in the global market depend on other nations to import foreign goods and services. In one respect, nations that import goods and services can be considered consumers. As nations move to a free enterprise or free market system, they find that the wants and needs of these consumer nations are important to the success of their own economies. Like businesses, nations compete on many different levels. Their competition is a direct response to the needs and wants consumers have expressed.

In the global marketplace, competition is a market system with two main characteristics:

- The market has a large number of buyers and sellers.
- These buyers and sellers may choose to enter or leave the marketplace as they see fit.

When the number of buyers and sellers is large, no single buyer or seller can drastically affect the market price of a particular product or service. This is an important factor in the global market. Remember, nations produce the products that they are best at producing. This is the principle of comparative advantage. In addition, nations import products they need but cannot produce efficiently. A large number of participants in

Enrichment Strategy

A *cartel* is an arrangement among groups of industries or businesses, usually in different countries, to reduce international competition by controlling price, production, and distribution of goods. There are international cartels for resources such as diamonds and petroleum. Direct students to find out more about cartels by investigating the following topics.

- In general, what kinds of products do cartels control?
- What recent production or pricing decisions have cartels made?
- How do cartels use the laws of supply and demand?

the global market helps ensure that one nation cannot bully, intimidate, or threaten other nations by withholding a needed commodity, such as grain or petroleum.

Benefits of Free Trade

As you have already learned, free trade implies that there are few limits and little government involvement in the trading system. Supporters of free trade hold that it can benefit a country in many ways. It can bring improved products at lower costs to consumers. Free trade can help an economy grow by creating jobs. It also can help nations achieve a higher standard of living.

Today, nations around the world are tending toward a free market economy. Many nations are lowering trade restrictions. In one area of the world, for example, three nations—Canada, Mexico, and the United States—have agreed, through the North American Free Trade Agreement (NAFTA), to work toward free trade among themselves. In Europe, members of the European Union have banded together to increase their competitive edge. In addition, around the world, nations who participate in GATT (General Agreement on Tariffs and Trade) are betting that they too will benefit from free trade and increased competition.

Even countries with strong command economic systems are trying out free trade on a kind of trial basis. The countries have established small free trade zones which welcome foreign investment and products. These trade zones offer a way to measure the benefits of free trade.

In all, the global marketplace is moving toward a free market system. The assumption is that, ultimately, free trade will stimulate global economic growth, thus raising living standards for everyone.

Barriers to Free Trade

Some of the barriers to free trade are rooted in outdated habits and practices. For example, a nation's choice of current trading partners is often limited by principles used hundreds of years ago. Most nations have a "home bias" in their trade transactions. They trade most with nations nearest to them in location, culture, and outlook. However, as transportation and telecommunications capabilities expand, nations will need to look farther beyond their neighbors if they wish to fully participate in world trade.

Another stumbling block in global trade has been the lack of knowledge about foreign markets. Businesses wishing to

Japanese officials have proposed a "green code" for Japanese businesses operating overseas. The proposal offers tax breaks to Japanese businesses that adopt environmental protection measures stronger than those required by the host country.

Connection to CHAPTER 21

Review with students the background and members of the North American Free Trade Agreement (NAFTA), pointing out, as shown in Figure 21-1 on page 351, that Canada is the United States' top import-export partner. Ask students to use a globe or world map to find the region covered by the NAFTA agreement. Ask students to write a description of that region without using the names of nations or countries.

TEACHING TIP

Indicate to students that some areas of Western Europe have a high unemployment rate. Ask students to discuss how government policies that restrain free trade can affect unemployment. (Restraints prevent healthy industries from creating jobs to offset losses elsewhere.)

Learning Activity

Suggest that students investigate the primary trading partners of a country in Europe and a country in Asia. Have a world map available for students and ask them to determine whether the principle of "home bias" applies to the trade transactions of the two countries.

Global Perspective

Ask students to use periodicals and other reference materials to investigate the trade barriers to a specific commodity, such as rice. For example, students can research what barriers the Japanese government has set up to prevent U.S. rice from being imported into Japan. Have students find out what impact these barriers have on the Japanese rice consumer and on the United States rice producer. Have them present their findings in a 200-word report that describes both sides of the rice trade situation.

Refer to the *International Business Strategies* booklet for additional strategies and activities.

Business Brief

A joint venture between Israel and Egypt allows the two countries to export more efficiently. It will also open markets for both countries. For example, Israeli exports will now reach countries that are regular destinations of Egypt Air.

CHAPTER 24

Business Brief

In Japan, packaged cake mixes offered as a convenience for homemakers sold poorly. After research, the company discovered that only 3 percent of Japanese homes have ovens suitable for baking the cakes.

Connection to CHAPTER 17

Remind students of the information about tariffs presented in Chapter 17, *Taxes and Taxation*. Remind students that tariffs are one of many ways governments raise revenues. Ask students to use Figure 17-1 on page 277 to find out how much of the federal government's revenue comes from tariffs. (1.5 percent.)

Quick Check Answers

1. Tax on imports designed to protect domestic producers; tax on imports designed to influence the trade-related actions of another country's government; tax on imports designed to raise money.
2. Possible answers: Brings improved products at lower costs to consumers; helps an economy grow by creating jobs; helps nations achieve a higher standard of living.
3. Outdated habits and practices, lack of knowledge about foreign markets, protectionism.

sell to foreign customers need to understand what needs and wants those customers might have. Often those needs may be different from the needs of domestic consumers the business is familiar with. For example, in the Philippines, packages of six sticks of gum from the United States did not sell well. Upon study, the manufacturer learned that the average Philippine consumer interested in purchasing gum had only enough money to purchase a single stick of gum, not a package of six. Businesses entering the global marketplace need information about prospective consumers. Not every domestic product is suitable for export.

Often, the greatest barrier to free trade is protectionism. It generally is implemented by the national government. Even though agreements to foster free trade exist, they are not always popular and have not been easy to carry out. Protectionists hold a view in direct contrast to free trade. They believe that free trade threatens job security and that new domestic industries should be protected from foreign competition. In addition, protectionists believe that any industry vital to the economy should be protected from foreign competition.

The tariffs that governments levy on imports are one form of protectionism. For example, a **protective tariff** is designed to protect domestic producers by raising the cost of imported goods. In addition to protective tariffs, governments occasionally impose a **punitive tariff.** This tariff is designed to influence the trade-related actions of another country's government. For instance, the United States might impose a punitive tariff on goods from a country that duplicates CDs without paying royalties to the U.S. recording artists and companies. The punitive tariff raises the price of imported goods, thus decreasing the amount of those imports sold. Seeing fewer of its goods purchased and its export income decreasing, the foreign country may decide to ban the duplication of those pirated CDs.

Another kind of tariff, the **revenue tariff,** is designed to raise money. A revenue tariff needs to be high enough to generate funds yet low enough to allow continued purchase of the imported goods. Although revenue tariffs are a source of income for some countries, they can prevent a country from fully participating in the global market.

Business & HISTORY

In 1930, the U.S. government levied the Smoot-Hawley Tariff, the second highest tariff in U.S. history. Foreign governments responded to it with retaliatory tariffs of their own. The result was a 60 percent reduction in world trade and a deepening of the Great Depression of the 1930s.

Quick Check
1. Define *protective tariff, punitive tariff,* and *revenue tariff.*
2. Name several benefits of free trade.
3. Describe some barriers to free trade.

Reteaching Strategy

Have students imagine that they live in a country that does not trade with neighboring countries, or even with any distant countries. Direct students to discuss the economic problems the country faces because of the low level of imports and exports. Then have students write a letter to a government official detailing the advantages of foreign trade for the individual and for the country.

DEVELOPING NATIONS

There is an incentive for competition in the global economy and a reason nations seem to be moving to a free market global economy: development. *Development* refers to the economic, social, political, and environmental systems that sustain a high quality of human life. Just as profit works as an incentive for businesses to produce goods and services, economic development offers an incentive for nations to participate in the global marketplace. Nearly all nations now recognize that the process of development is tied to the state of the world's economy.

Characteristics of Developing Nations

Of the almost 180 nations in the world, only about one-fourth of them are considered **developed nations.** These are nations with relatively high standards of living and economies based more on industry than on agriculture. Among these nations are the United States, Canada, most European countries, Japan, and Australia.

The remaining three-fourths of the world's population live in **developing nations.** These are nations with less industrial development and relatively low standards of living. Within this general definition, however, there can be differences. Mexico, while considered a developing nation, is more developed and prosperous than almost all other developing nations. Brazil, Indonesia, China, and India also are considered developing countries. Figure 24-1 below shows the differences.

FIGURE 24-1

As you can see from these graphs, there is a great disparity between developing and developed countries in terms of numbers, population, and gross domestic product. What percent of the world's population is in developed countries? What percent of the world GDP do these countries produce?

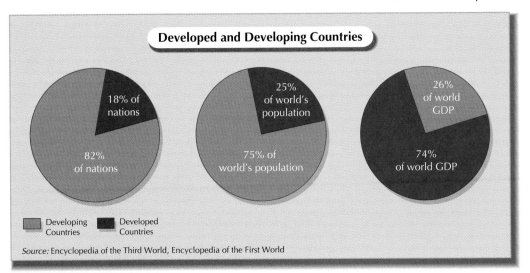

Developed and Developing Countries

18% of nations

82% of nations

25% of world's population

75% of world's population

26% of world GDP

74% of world GDP

■ Developing Countries   ■ Developed Countries

Source: Encyclopedia of the Third World, Encyclopedia of the First World

Curriculum Connection   Mathematics

Suggest students use the information in Figure 24-1 to create bar graph profiles of developed and developing countries. The result should resemble this graph.

Developing Nations

Developed Nations

■ % of World GDP
■ % of Population
■ % of Nations

0 10 20 30 40 50 60 70 80 90

For students who need to sharpen their math skills, choose among the worksheets in the *Math Skills Review* booklet.

Discuss

Ask students to list some of the jobs they are familiar with in the food and hospitality industry. Suggest that for every visible job, one in which the individual works directly with the public, students identify two jobs in which the individuals work behind the scenes.

Food and Hospitality

The food and hospitality industry is labor-intensive. Despite the growing use of computers to control large food-processing machines, keep track of hotel reservations, and monitor inventories, it still takes hardworking humans to keep hungry customers and weary travelers content. "A job well done" means contributing directly to the comfort, pleasure, and even health of others, something workers can take pride in.

When we think of food and hospitality employees, welcoming hotel clerks and knowledgeable, friendly servers spring pleasantly to mind. Many food and hospitality workers, however, hold less visible jobs. Cooks and food preparers make tempting dishes in processing plants as well as in restaurant or supermarket kitchens. Others prepare meals for people in hospitals, nursing homes, and schools. Food service managers and catering personnel orchestrate the complicated teamwork that goes into obtaining, cooking, presenting, and serving food.

There are plenty of beginning jobs in this area, but they can be demanding. Physical stamina and excellent

HELP WANTED

BAKERS

Home and Hearth Bakeries, a commercial maker of whole-grain food products, is looking for three entry-level bakers to do a variety of jobs in our high-tech bakery.

If you are a high school grad with good measurement skills and physical strength, baking might be the profession for you! You'll need to be detail-oriented and handy around machines. If we hire you, we'll train you to prepare ingredients, stir batter, and monitor mixture temperatures. You'll learn how to operate our baking machines.

Business Brief

Many individuals in economically developing countries of Latin America, Africa, and Asia barter to get the bare necessities. Individuals produce barely enough food to meet their own needs, and as a result rarely have any money.

Connection to CHAPTER 23

As students learned in Chapter 23, a traditional economy has a well-defined but limited economic environment. The economy continues to produce the goods it has always produced, does not seek to expand production, and confines its trade to few markets. Ask students to discuss how such a system tends to perpetuate itself. (Sample answers: Lack of communication, lack of entrepreneurs to develop innovations.)

Nations at the beginning stages of development share several characteristics: low gross domestic product, an agricultural economy, poor health conditions, low literacy rate, and rapid population growth. As the development process unfolds, the characteristics of a nation's economy change.

Agricultural Economy   The kinds of jobs present in an economy offer another way to identify a nation's stage of development. As a nation's economy begins development, most of its jobs are in agriculture. As the economy develops, the majority of jobs move to manufacturing. As the economy develops further, the majority of its jobs move to the service sector.

Developing countries are more likely to rely on agricultural goods than on manufactured goods. In addition, they produce their agricultural goods with little or no mechanical or manufactured assistance. Often the level of farming is basic, and the crops yield barely enough to keep the farmer's family from starving. Under these conditions there is little or no possibility of exporting agricultural goods to obtain money needed for more productive farming or for starting up industries.

404   UNIT 7   INTERNATIONAL BUSINESS

Enrichment Strategy

Photocopy and distribute Enrichment Master 24-1 to students to use as they work through this section of the chapter. Ask students to use the information shown in the graphs to compose five questions about developing countries. Have students share their questions with a partner who uses the graphs to answer the questions. Questions should be returned to the writer for evaluation.

health are essential. In fact, passing state or local health certification may be a prerequisite for some food-related jobs. Workers, such as commercial bakers and cheesemakers, need manual and computer skills to work with large food processing machines. Waiters, concessions workers, and desk clerks must have math skills to handle money. In an industry where an unfriendly sneer or rude word to a customer can spell disaster, the ability to communicate and maintain a positive attitude is vital.

Although most food and hospitality workers must start at the bottom, many begin before they graduate from high school, balancing work with school. Advancement definitely depends on hard work and experience. It's not unheard of for someone to advance from waiting tables to owning the restaurant!

Help wanted ads for three starting jobs and a job posting for a more advanced position are shown here.

Poor Health Conditions In general, people in developing countries are likely to experience more health problems and have overall poorer health than their counterparts in developed countries. A number of factors contribute to this characteristic. Many people in these countries tend to be malnourished because they either do not have enough to eat or they do not have a nutritionally balanced array of foods to choose from. These factors weaken individuals and make them more susceptible to illness. Further, because the countries usually lack the revenue and equipment necessary to construct adequate sewage facilities, the people are exposed to a variety of diseases that seldom occur in developed countries. Once people fall ill, it is unlikely they can receive adequate care because physicians, hospitals, and medicines are in short supply in developing countries.

Low GDP Development can be measured by using the nation's gross domestic product (GDP). GDP, you will recall, is the total value of (1) consumer goods and services, (2) business goods and services, (3) government goods and services, and

CHAPTER 24 GLOBAL ECONOMIC CHALLENGES **405**

Making Connections ▪▷ Everyday Living

CHAPTER 24

USE VISUALS

Direct students' attention to the graph in Figure 24-2 that shows the GDPs of several nations. Ask students how the graph can help them distinguish developing nations from developed nations. (Answers will vary, but students should recognize that there is a gap between the GDP of developing and developed nations.)

Answer to caption: Answers will vary but could include poor housing, low income, less food, few consumer goods.

USE TRANSPARENCIES

Use Teaching Transparency 24-2 and its corresponding strategies and worksheet from the *Teaching Transparency Strategies and Worksheets* booklet to assist students in understanding the relationship among the GDPs of several nations. Verify student worksheets using the Answer Key.

TEACHING TIP

To help students understand cause-effect relationships, ask them to create an illustration or drawing that indicates how a low literacy rate can be considered both a cause and an effect of a nation's low GDP. If necessary, review with students clue terms associated with cause and effect, such as *because, so, thus, as a result,* and *as a consequence.*

FIGURE 24-2

This graph shows the marked contrast in per capita GDP between several developed and developing nations. How would economic life differ in developing countries?

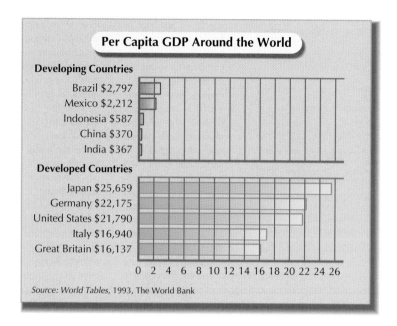

Per Capita GDP Around the World

Developing Countries

Brazil $2,797
Mexico $2,212
Indonesia $587
China $370
India $367

Developed Countries

Japan $25,659
Germany $22,175
United States $21,790
Italy $16,940
Great Britain $16,137

0 2 4 6 8 10 12 14 16 18 20 22 24 26

Source: World Tables, 1993, The World Bank

(4) exports. In a developed nation, GDP ranges from $12,000 per year to around $35,000 per year. (The per capita GDP is the amount of the gross domestic product divided by the number of people in the nation.) The per capita GDP of a developing nation generally is significantly lower—usually less than $3000. A developing country may have many natural or human resources, but may lack the financial and entrepreneurial expertise needed to put those resources to work. This lack of economic output is one of the most significant differences between developed and developing nations. Figure 24-2 above shows the wide range of per capita GDP that separates the people in developed and developing nations.

Low Literacy Rate   In developing nations, governments often have few resources available to build, staff, and maintain schools. Thus, few people have access to schools. In some cases families need their children to work in the fields; families are so poor they would starve if children attended school rather than worked on the farm. As a result, the workforce in a developing country may be relatively unsophisticated and illiterate—unable to read or write. As a consequence, businesses may face difficulty in finding workers they can train for industrial, manufacturing, technical, or engineering jobs.

Rapid Population Growth   Developing countries also tend to have rapid population growth. In some cases the growth is so

Reteaching Strategy

Have students use atlases and encyclopedias to identify three developed and three developing countries. Suggest they use several criteria including GDP, literacy rate, and population growth rate. Call on volunteers to share their findings to explain why particular countries are categorized as either developed or developing, explaining how they used the criteria.

great that the population of a country can double in about 20 years, about the span of a single generation. Even a developed country with medical and industrial facilities in place would have a difficult time supporting a population that is growing this rapidly.

Undertaking Economic Development

The task facing developing nations is deciding how to finance the equipment and training necessary to improve the standard of living of their citizens. The task facing developed nations is deciding how best to assist developing nations in achieving their goal.

Development can be achieved through two possible courses of action: self-sufficiency and international trade. Some nations may choose to develop their resources by focusing on producing goods and services for the domestic market. This economic development path may lead to modest income and economic growth. Also, this choice leads to investment in an array of industries, because nations want a variety of goods and services for domestic consumers.

Other nations may choose to develop their resources by focusing on producing goods and services for international trade. These nations must produce goods or services that are desired by other nations. Once a developing country begins to trade, the income generated by that activity can be used to expand and strengthen its export industries. As the export industries grow, income from exports can be used to make improvements in the country's living conditions. For example, schools, hospitals, roads, and other services can begin to reach larger and larger segments of the population. This is an application of the concept of specialization of production to improve the standard of living. A country specializes in what it does best and buys products and services from other countries.

Development Through Foreign Investment

Developing nations also can move toward development by encouraging foreign investment in their countries. Foreign investment can take the form of aid from developed nations or investment from foreign businesses in developed nations.

Developed nations may offer development help for a variety of reasons. One is humanitarian. Most developed nations feel they have a moral responsibility to help nations with fewer resources. The suffering and starvation of individuals in developing nations often moves individuals and governments of developed nations to offer assistance.

Nine of every 10 children born today are born in developing nations. In the last 20 years of the century, the number of people 20 to 40 years of age will have increased by 630 million in developing nations compared to 20 million in industrialized nations.

TEACHING TIP

To encourage discussion, ask students to explain how foreign trade can help a nation improve its education and health care systems.

Learning Activity

Have students find out the population growth rate of several developing and developed countries. Direct them to present the information in a graph that contrasts the growth rate for developing and developed countries. Suggest they write a generalization for their graph.

Business Brief

In recent years, China's economy has grown at an impressive 10 percent per year. Direct foreign investment is primarily responsible for this growth. In 1994 alone, $33.8 billion poured into the country. Three quarters of foreign investments come from Chinese businesspeople in Asian countries such as Indonesia, the Philippines, Singapore, and Hong Kong.

Business & HISTORY

In 1845, Fredric Bastiat proposed that a law be passed to require people to use shutters on windows and doors so that candlemakers would be protected from the "unfair" competition of the sun. His satire included an argument that this law would be of great benefit to the French candle industry.

Curriculum Connection   Communication

Call on students to identify the priorities for industrialized nations and for developing nations in promoting economic development. Note their responses on the board. Then have students work in small groups to develop a publicity campaign to inform industrialized and developing countries about the steps they could take to encourage development. Have groups present and explain their campaigns.

For those students who need to sharpen their communication skills, choose among the worksheets in the *Communication Skills Review* booklet.

Building Business Skills

Building Business Skills

Model

Ask students to read the explanation of how to interpret points of view. Invite volunteers to share their own experiences with trying to understand different points of view. Then ask volunteers to provide ideas of ways to deal with different points of view in the classroom.

Learning Activity

Have students use current newspapers and periodicals to learn about current foreign investment efforts. Then ask students to classify the articles to provide an example of each of the reasons for such investments—humanitarian, economic, political, or national security. (Sample answers: To assist starving people, to widen a product's market, to gain the friendship of a nation, to decrease civil unrest or turmoil in a region.)

Business Brief

International Development Association, an affiliate of the World Bank, specializes in low cost loans to developing nations. Another affiliate of the bank, International Finance Corporation, stimulates the growth of private capital within developing nations. In the past 20 years these organizations have loaned several billion dollars to member countries.

408 UNIT 7

ANALYSIS
Interpreting Points of View

Explanation

Everybody has his or her own point of view. That's an idea that most of us would agree is true, but we often forget as we go about our daily lives. After all, things would be so much easier if we all shared similar points of view. Work would get done more quickly, and disputes would seldom arise. Unfortunately, this is not the case. If you expect to succeed in business, you'll have to recognize and be sensitive to the points of view of coworkers, suppliers, and customers in order to do your job effectively.

Among coworkers, differences in point of view should be an issue only if they relate to the job. Whether the person at the next desk is liberal or conservative in politics doesn't matter as long as he or she does the job. If, on the other hand, a clerk and store manager have different points of view about how customers should be served, the clerk will have to follow the manager's lead.

In marketing and selling goods and services, you have to be especially alert to different viewpoints. You can't just assume, for example, that because you or your friends respond well to a product or advertisement, everybody will. If a company is active in the global marketplace, it must consider carefully whether its products will appeal to countries with different cultural and social viewpoints. Trying to sell a breakfast cereal in a country where people don't eat breakfast, for example, may be difficult. Sometimes such problems may be solved by

Another reason for offering assistance is economic. Developing nations outnumber developed nations, and their population exceeds that of developed nations by a ratio of nearly 3 to 1. This means that developing nations provide a large market for the goods and services of developed nations.

Politics is a third reason for aid. Many developed nations believe that offering aid to developing nations will influence their political decisions, making them allies. Or developed nations may wish to change certain government policies in developing nations and use development funds as a motivation to change.

Finally, national security also provides a reason for offering aid. The economic difference between developing and developed nations is so great that it can easily be the source of unrest and social turmoil in the developing countries. Developed nations may offer aid in order to avoid that turmoil.

Like individuals and businesses, developing nations can borrow money to meet their development needs. One of the more important international lending agencies is the International Bank for Reconstruction and Development, usually

Cooperative Learning Group Discussion

Direct students to form groups of four. Then ask them to identify which of the four reasons for foreign aid—humanitarian, political, economic, and national security—they think constitutes the most direct path to economic development. Have a volunteer from each group explain the group's choice.

Refer to the *Cooperative Learning Strategies* booklet for additional strategies.

CASE STUDIES

1. 2-B-Me sells blue jeans by suggesting that these well-made, high-fashion jeans will bring teenagers freedom, power, and popularity with their peers. The company hopes to expand its market to several countries that emphasize respect and obedience to elders. Teenagers in these countries spend most of their time outside of school with their families. Teenagers' social lives are carefully chaperoned and monitored.

2. The TV commercials for an American after-shave lotion show a couple watching a football game. The woman expresses her approval of the lotion's fragrance to her male friend. Men in the country to which the manufacturer plans to introduce the product generally don't use after-shave lotion, and women wouldn't comment on the fragrance if they did. Moreover, the country's national sport is soccer.

adapting the product to the market: a cereal could be sold as a snack; a fast-food menu might feature some local items.

In addition, companies must make certain their advertisements and promotions will send the correct message. White flowers, furniture, clothing, and curtains in a TV commercial would convey joy to an American audience; to the people of China they would signify mourning.

Practice

The two case studies relate to marketing products in nations whose cultural or social points of view differ from those in the United States. For each case, tell how you would take the potential customers' point of view into account in marketing the product.

referred to as the World Bank. The World Bank helps developing countries with loans and guarantees of loans from private sources. In the past, many of the loans have been for transportation and energy-related projects such as dams, roads, and factories. Today, the World Bank may offer a loan that can be used for any purpose but that, in addition to repayment, carries with it an obligation to reduce a tariff or work toward establishing financial policies that will reduce inflation.

Foreign aid is the money, goods, and services given by governments and other organizations to help other nations and their citizens. Foreign aid can take a variety of forms.

Economic Assistance The most visible kinds of economic assistance include loans and outright gifts of money or equipment to other nations. The money and equipment generally are applied to the completion of several kinds of projects. Top priority is usually given to transportation and communications systems. As roads, bridges, airports, and telephones begin to link isolated locations, goods and services begin to flow to and from all regions within the nation.

CHAPTER 24 GLOBAL ECONOMIC CHALLENGES **409**

Curriculum Connection   Social Studies

Have students write to their U.S. senator or representative to request copies of recent testimony about some aspect of foreign aid given before a congressional subcommittee. Have students read the materials and share the information with the class. Suggest that students might write a summary, make a poster, or use charts and diagrams in their summary.

Practice
Ask students to present business situations, real or imagined, in which the point of view of the people involved is crucial to the outcome of the transaction. Seed the discussion by asking for points of view on items such as school dress codes, violence on television, or teenage drinking.
(1. Students' answers should suggest that in this market, 2-B-Me might want to emphasize the quality of its jeans rather than the fashion aspects. Advertising should stay away from themes such as social popularity and freedom from family restrictions that might run counter to the values of these countries.
2. Ads for the after-shave should probably show how and why the lotion can be used, emphasizing the way it makes users' skin feel. Women commenting on the fragrance and the American sports background would be meaningless, if not offensive, to potential customers.)

Learning Activity

In recent years, the conditions for development loans for items such as dams, roads, and factories include reassurance about the amount of damage the project will impose on the environment. Today's development loans are often designed to respond to concerns about the environment. Ask students what advantages are associated with evaluating loans and development in light of the development's impact on the environment.

Learning Activity

Suggest students use library resources to find out which of the world's nations have the highest and lowest birthrates. Then have students identify several reasons for the lowest birthrate and the highest birthrate.

Business Brief

In some developed countries officials are concerned about low birthrates. Taiwan and Singapore are among countries whose birthrate is declining. Reasons for the decline include women joining the workforce, becoming more educated, and having children later in life.

TEACHING TIP

To stimulate discussion, present students with the following maxim: Give someone a fish, she'll eat for a day; teach someone to fish, she'll eat for a lifetime. Ask students how this maxim applies to foreign investment and technical assistance for developing countries.

Learning Activity

Have students use newspapers and television news programs to discover which developing nations are currently receiving military assistance from other countries or specifically from the United States. Have students discuss how the military assistance may (or may not) help these nations improve their economies.

Technical Assistance Often professionals, such as engineers, teachers, and medical personnel, work with individuals in developing countries to provide technical assistance. These people teach necessary skills to some of the nation's population and so strengthen the skills and knowledge base of the nation's human resources. Then the people in the developing country are prepared to be effective in a variety of environments for producing goods and services.

Military Assistance Sometimes foreign aid includes military assistance. One goal of this assistance is to foster political stability. If a government is stable, it can create a climate in which an economy can grow and flourish.

Obstacles to Economic Development

In some developing nations, even millions of dollars of foreign investment and aid cannot overcome some obstacles to economic development. Nations wishing to improve the standard of living of their citizens work to overcome a variety of obstacles.

Population Growth The number of people in some developing nations is so great that there is barely enough arable land and other resources available to support them. Residents of these countries often depend on traditional methods of agriculture to supply the food needed to support the population. Families work together to raise food to support the family, viewing each child as another potential farm worker. As a result, many developing nations have a high **birthrate.** The birthrate is the ratio of total live births to total population in a certain country or area over a specified period of time. It is frequently expressed as the number of live births for every 1000 people per year. Figure 24-3 on page 411 compares the birthrates in each of the world's major geographic regions.

F.Y.I.

Several proposals have been made to help developing nations decrease their foreign debt while preserving their natural resources. One plan forgives foreign debt if the nation agrees to set aside, preserve, and maintain its forestland undisturbed.

Limited Resources Limited natural resources pose another obstacle to development. If the land does not have a mineral resource and is unproductive or in a harsh climate as well, the potential for economic growth is limited. If a country is fortunate enough to have a valuable mineral resource, it may be able to finance development. Middle Eastern countries that have a harsh environment and generally little arable land are able to finance development through the sale of their main mineral resource: petroleum. In some cases international efforts assist nations with sparse mineral resources to establish some cash crops not normally found in the region. For example, the World Bank has funded such projects as developing cotton, cashew, and tea crops on opposite sides of the African continent.

Cooperative Learning Numbered Heads Together

Ask students to work in groups of four. Have each team imagine that it is a committee in charge of economic development in a developing country. Ask students to identify the first two obstacles to economic development that the committee would work to overcome. Students should also outline plans for overcoming the obstacles. Call on volunteers to explain their team's choices.

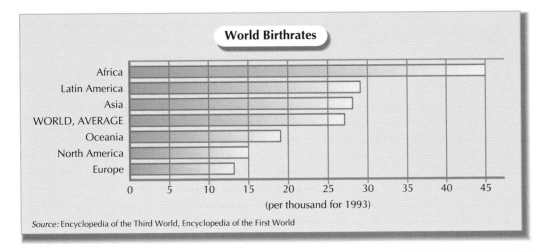

World Birthrates

(per thousand for 1993)

Source: Encyclopedia of the Third World, Encyclopedia of the First World

FIGURE 24-3

This graph shows the birthrates for the world's regions. High birthrate is one of the characteristics of developing countries. Which regions of the world are likely to include developing countries?

Foreign Debt   Foreign debt is a concern for all nations, but it causes particular concern in developing nations. In their rush to development, some countries have relied on massive amounts of money borrowed from foreign investors and foreign banks. Often the amounts are so large that repayment is impossible. For example, Latin American nations accumulated a debt that amounted to 64 percent of the region's income! That is, for every dollar earned in Latin America, 64 cents was owed to someone else.

Loss of Capital   In some developing nations, large numbers of their government officials export the nation's currency. Generally these individuals export the currency for their own benefit, profiting at the expense of their nation. Exporting the currency can lead to a cash/credit shortage within the nation. This, in turn, severely limits the nation's ability to repay its loans.

Lack of Education   Yet another obstacle to progress in developing nations is a lack of education and limited knowledge of technology. An uneducated population hampers a nation's efforts to develop a workforce capable of working in industry. Technical skills are needed to build an industrial society; scientists and engineers are also important in economic development. However, many developing nations do not even have the funds needed to provide a basic education for school-age children. In nations that can provide some schooling, many children do not come to school, but work instead to help provide food for their family.

Direct students' attention to the graph in Figure 24-3. Ask students to use the graph to determine the world's average birthrate. (About 27 per thousand.) Answer to caption: Asia, Latin America, Africa.

USE TRANSPARENCIES
Use Teaching Transparency 24-3 and its corresponding strategies and worksheet from the *Teaching Transparency Strategies and Worksheets* booklet to assist students in comparing the birthrates of various world regions. Verify student worksheets using the Answer Key.

Learning Activity
Point out that investment in people, also known as human capital investment, improves peoples' skills and health. As a result, productivity increases. Ask students to write a paragraph to explain how investment in a school in a developing nation can ultimately improve that nation's economy. Suggest that they diagram a possible sequence of events to illustrate their description.

TEACHING TIP
To help develop students' critical thinking skills, ask students to identify which of the obstacles discussed in the section they think constitutes the greatest barrier to economic development. Have them explain their selection.

Global Perspective

Aware that there is a limited supply of natural resources available, today's developing nations plan to strive for *sustainable development*—economic growth that does not destroy the biological systems on which life depends. Developing nations might emphasize using renewable resources, while developed nations can apply their best efforts to restoring the environment. Ask students to discuss what part they can take in sustainable economic growth.

Refer to the *International Business Strategies* booklet for additional strategies and activities.

USE VISUALS

Ask students to compare the school in the photograph with the school they are attending. Have students describe how both schools can help a country improve its GDP. (A high GDP is associated with a high literacy rate, a low GDP is associated with a low literacy rate.)
Answer to caption: Education will give people in developing countries the resources they need to build an industrial society, thereby improving their economic development.

TEACHING TIP

To help develop students' understanding of foreign economic development, ask them to explain why developed nations have an interest in seeing developing nations repay loans made for economic development. (The developed nations, working through organizations such as the World Bank, lent the money.)

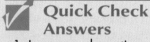

Quick Check Answers

1. Low gross domestic product, agricultural economy, poor health conditions, low literacy rate, and rapid population growth.
2. Through self-sufficiency and through international trade.
3. Resources, goods, or services desired by other nations.
4. Cheap labor, little regulation, raw materials.

In what way can spending money on education help developing countries improve their economic outlook?

Unstable Governments   Another obstacle to development is both domestic and foreign lack of faith in the nation's government. Corrupt or weak governments lack the ability to inspire confidence in economic plans. Foreign investors, financial institutions, and donor nations are unwilling to risk losing their money in a nation whose government may change or fall.

Quick Check

1. List five characteristics of developing nations.
2. How can nations fund their development?
3. What must a country have to fund its development through world trade?
4. What might attract foreign investment to a developing country?

Reteaching Strategy

Have students imagine they are successful entrepreneurs in the United States and they wish to expand and establish a branch of their business in one of the developing countries. Encourage these entrepreneurs to prepare a business plan that discusses the opportunities and obstacles presented by opening a business in that developing nation. Select students to present and explain their plans to the class.

Chapter 24 **Summary**

Main Ideas

1. Benefits of free trade include improved products at lower costs to consumers, economic growth, and personal freedom. Barriers to free trade include "home bias," lack of knowledge about foreign markets, and protectionist attitudes.
2. Developed nations are nations with relatively high standards of living and economies based on industry. They include such countries as the United States, Canada, most European countries, Japan, and Australia.
3. Developing nations are nations with less industrial development and relatively low standards of living. They include such countries as Mexico, Brazil, Indonesia, China, and India.
4. Developing countries are characterized by low GDP, an agricultural economy, poor health conditions, low literacy rate, and rapid population growth.
5. Development refers to the economic, social, political, and environmental systems that sustain a high quality of human life. Developed nations can provide developing nations with economic, technical, and military assistance. Even so, developing nations must offer a safe and stable environment for such foreign investment.
6. Continued global economic development depends on *sustainable development*, which is economic growth without destruction of the environment.
7. Careers in the food and hospitality industry continue to grow, including globally.
8. To be effective in a global or domestic marketplace, businesspeople must be able to understand points of view different from their own.

CASE ANALYSIS Marketing

A customer demands to know where the shirt he wants to buy was made. If it wasn't made in the United States, he will not buy it. You find the label that indicates the cotton shirt was made in a small developing country. What will you say to the customer?

QUICK QUIZ

1. What kind of market has a large number of buyers and sellers who may enter or leave the market at will? (Free enterprise.)
2. How does protectionism influence free trade? (It is a barrier to free trade.)
3. What is a nation's gross domestic product (GDP)? (The total value of consumer, business, and government goods and services and exports.)
4. Name two characteristics of developing countries that are also obstacles to development. (Possible answers can include high population growth rate, lack of education, limited resources, foreign debt, loss of capital, and unstable government.)

Chapter 24 **Review**

APPLY

Answers

Use the Language of Business

1. revenue tariff; **2.** protective tariff; **3.** punitive tariff; **4.** developed nation; **5.** developing nation; **6.** foreign aid; **7.** birthrate.

Review What You Learned

1. The market has a large number of buyers and sellers; buyers and sellers may choose to enter or leave the marketplace as they see fit.
2. Overcoming home bias, learning about foreign markets.
3. Protective, punitive, revenue.
4. 75 percent, 25 percent.
5. Moral responsibility, economics, politics, and national security.
6. Answer should include four of the following: population, limited natural resources, lack of education and technology, immense foreign debt, export of currency, and unstable or corrupt government.
7. Physical stamina, excellent health, manual and computer skills, math skills, and the ability to maintain a positive attitude.
8. It helps you do your job effectively, especially when you need to address clients or consumers from other cultures.

Understand Business Concepts

1. Both respond to the needs and wants of consumers; consumers are nations rather than individuals and businesses.
2. They feel that free trade can threaten job security, that domestic industries as well as any industry vital to the economy should be protected from foreign competition.
3. The tariff raises the price on imported products, making the domestic goods more attractive to consumers.
4. The economic, social, political, and environmental systems that sustain a high quality of human life; it acts as an incentive for nations to participate in the global market.
5. It lowers the risk of losing their investment.

Use the Language of Business

Understanding these business terms will help you communicate more easily with others. Write the term that best matches each numbered definition.

birthrate	protective tariff
developed nation	punitive tariff
developing nation	revenue tariff
foreign aid	

1. Tax on imported goods designed to raise money.
2. Tax on imported goods designed to raise the cost of foreign goods to make the price of similar domestic goods more attractive.
3. Tax on imported goods designed to influence the trade policies of foreign nations.
4. Nation with relatively high standard of living based on industrial development.
5. Nation with relatively low standard of living and less industrial development.
6. Money, goods, and services provided by governments and other organizations to help other nations and their citizens.
7. Ratio of total live births to total population in a certain country or area over a specified period of time.

Review What You Learned

1. What are the two characteristics of competition in the global marketplace?
2. What challenges do businesses in the global market face?
3. Name three different kinds of tariffs.
4. What part of the world's population lives in developing nations? What part of the world's GDP is produced by developing nations?
5. Name four reasons industrialized nations offer assistance for development.
6. Name four obstacles to economic development.
7. What kinds of qualifications and attributes are needed for jobs in the food and hospitality industry?
8. Why is being sensitive to other points of view necessary, especially in the global marketplace?

Understand Business Concepts

1. How is global competition similar to business competition? How is it different?
2. How do protectionists feel about free trade?
3. How can a tariff help protect domestic producers?
4. What is development? What is its place in the global market?
5. Why is a stable environment attractive to foreign investors?
6. How are a punitive and a protective tariff alike? How are they different?

6. Both are taxes on goods and services imported from another country. A protective tariff makes foreign goods more costly, thereby protecting domestic production. A punitive tariff is designed to get a nation to change its trade policies.
7. By making sure the development makes the best use of resources, and uses renewable, rather than non-renewable, resources.
8. It can increase the market for the donor nation's goods.
9. They may have opportunities in other countries as tourism and business travel grows.
10. When the point of view affects how the job is done.

Think Critically

1. Student responses may vary, but they should mention the dangers of accumulating large debts.
2. Student responses will vary. Responses should include recognition that the United States has passed from agricultural through manufacturing to service sector employment.

7. How can a nation develop and still preserve the environment?
8. How can foreign aid help the donor nation as well as the developing one?
9. How might the people in the food and hospitality industry be affected by increased economic activity in developing nations?
10. When should an employee not only understand but also adopt a manager's point of view?

Think Critically

1. **Assess.** A small distant nation has decided to fund all of its development through international loans. Tell whether you think this a wise course of action. Give reasons for your answer.

2. **Apply.** In history class a student suggests that the United States was once a developing country. Decide if you agree or disagree with the statement and give reasons for your opinion.

Use What You Learned

1. **Group Project.** In your group choose a pair of countries to investigate; one should be a developed nation and the other a developing nation. Find out as much as you can about each nation's economic development. Be sure to find at least the following for each country:

   • GDP and annual growth of GDP
   • birthrate and population growth rate
   • literacy rate
   • average annual income
   • major employment area (agriculture, manufacturing, service)

   Compile the information and present it as a TV newsmagazine story. Include maps or other appropriate graphics.

2. As the United States and many nations in Europe developed their economies, they relied heavily on the forests that covered their lands. Countries such as India and Malaysia believe that their development also depends on harvesting their forests. Research the effects of removing large parts of these rain forests. Write a newspaper editorial telling why you think developing countries should or should not cut down their forests as other countries have done.

3. **Computer Application.** Do on-line research to obtain information in magazines about a U.S. company that operates in some developing countries. Prepare a one-page word-processed report of what you learn about that company's global marketing.

4. **Skill Reinforcement.** Imagine you are working for a fast food chain called Toppings to Go. The chain specializes in hamburgers and small pizzas that buyers can customize by adding a wide array of toppings. The company picks you to plan its first franchise abroad. Choose a country in which you think a franchise might work. Write a plan for making Toppings to Go a success in that country.

Save your work in your Business Portfolio.

Independent Practice

Use the Chapter 24 worksheets in *Student Activity Guide 2* for additional practice and application activities. *Student Activity Guide 2* provides vocabulary exercises, reading comprehension checks, problems, projects, and simulations of business and economic situations. A Teacher's Annotated Edition provides answers.

ASSESS

Portfolio Assessment

The portfolio projects are designed to lead students to develop a collection of their best work to submit to you for assessment. You and your students should decide which projects will be included in their respective Business Portfolios. Refer students to the specific rubric(s) from the *Alternative Assessment Strategies* booklet listed with each of the project notes below. These rubrics will alert students to the criteria you will use to assess their projects.

Chapter Assessment

Use the Chapter 24 Test from the *Test Masters* booklet to evaluate students' understanding of the chapter concepts. An answer key is provided. Or create your own customized test using the *Testmaker* software.

Use What You Learned

1. Circulate to ensure that all members of a group participate. Rubrics: Note Taking, Oral Presentation.

2. Point out to students that the factors that affect forests in Malaysia and India may be significantly different from those that affect the forests of Brazil. Rubrics: Essay, Paragraph.

3. Students without access to on-line services can find appropriate research in the library. Students without access to word processing software may prepare their reports on a manual typewriter or in handwritten format. Rubric: Essay.

4. Answers will vary. They should reflect some knowledge and understanding of the particular cultural and social aspects of the country. Rubric: Paragraph.

Business Issue

TRADE POLICY

Highlight the Issue

Before students read about the issue on pages 416–417, poll the class to find out how many think economic sanctions should be used to achieve national political goals. If necessary, explain that sanctions are actions taken by one country to force another to follow certain rules. Ask volunteers to explain their positions. After students have read the pages, poll the class again to find out how many students have changed their views.

TRADE POLICY

In its efforts to influence other nations, the United States has often turned to economic sanctions—using trade policies to pressure other countries to change their ways. Sanctions have been used for many reasons, including to punish nations for invading their neighbors or for repressing their own people. Should the United States use its trade policy as a tool to achieve its foreign policy goals?

Pro

Economic sanctions are useful because they provide a peaceful means of achieving foreign policy goals. As U.S. President Woodrow Wilson said, "Apply this economic, peaceful, silent, deadly remedy and there will be no need for force."

Sanctions also offer policymakers a wide range of responses, from withholding certain types of trade benefits to banning all imports and exports from the offending country. This means governments can choose the most appropriate type of pressure to put on an outlaw nation.

Furthermore, sanctions work. During the 1980s, anti-apartheid activists in the United States urged U.S. companies to stop doing business in South Africa to put pressure on the South African government to end its racist system of apartheid. By the end of the 1980s, 200 U.S. companies had left South Africa, and Congress had imposed a ban on trade and investment in the country. These sanctions helped end apartheid and bring democracy to South Africa. Sanctions have also proven successful in Iraq, where a trade embargo forced the Iraqi government to comply with the terms of the United Nations agreement that ended the Gulf War.

Sanctions can also foster greater international cooperation, because nations must work together to make sanctions effective. In order for the embargo against Iraq to work, the United Nations had to line up support from many nations. Even former enemies, such as the United States and Russia, cooperated to make the sanctions stick.

Trade sanctions may actually help avoid conflicts. When nations know they will be punished for their offenses, they may think twice before acting.

By providing an effective alternative to war, trade policy can be a useful tool for achieving foreign policy goals.

Extend the Issue

Have a group of interested students research more thoroughly one of the sanctions mentioned in the text. Ask the group to provide background information about the sanction, the duration of the sanction, and students' opinion on the political effectiveness of the sanction. Discuss the group's findings and then ask for a show of hands to find out how many students agree and how many disagree with the imposition and the outcome of the sanction.

Con

Sanctions sound like a good idea, but they can end up hurting the people we are trying to help. In general, trade sanctions miss their targets—the people in power—and hurt average citizens instead. When the United States and the United Nations imposed an embargo on Haiti in the early 1990s to protest the military's takeover of that country, it was Haiti's poor who suffered most. The military leaders and their wealthy allies had enough money to buy whatever they needed on the black market or abroad.

Sanctions also hurt U.S. businesses. For example, U.S. sanctions on Vietnam meant that U.S. companies could not compete with companies from other nations that were taking advantage of new economic opportunities in Vietnam. European oil companies, for instance, won the rights to drill for valuable oil and gas deposits, while U.S. companies were shut out of the market by the trade embargo. In one recent year, U.S. companies lost about $7 billion in potential exports, and 175,000 workers lost their jobs because of U.S. sanctions.

Despite the damage they do, sanctions don't work. President Jimmy Carter imposed sanctions (a grain embargo and a U.S. boycott of the 1980 Moscow Olympics) on the Soviet Union after its 1979 invasion of Afghanistan but could not force the Soviets to withdraw their troops. More than 30 years of embargo against Cuba still have not brought about the fall of Fidel Castro. In some cases, sanctions can even strengthen the hand of dictators, who use the economic hardships caused by sanctions to unite their people against a common enemy—often the United States.

U.S. trade policy is not an effective tool for achieving foreign policy goals. In today's global market, the United States is no longer the most important trading partner for many nations. Thus, if the United States alone imposes sanctions, the target country can simply increase its trade with other nations to make up for the economic loss. To be effective, sanctions must have broad support from many nations, a difficult goal when nations have different economic priorities.

Economic sanctions are ineffective and hurt the wrong people. The United States should use diplomacy, not trade policy, to achieve its foreign policy goals.

Update the Issue

Have interested students find out what, if any, trade sanctions or embargoes are now in effect. Students should present their findings in a chart that lists the names of the countries involved, the reason for the sanction, and the hoped-for outcome of the sanction.

UNIT OVERVIEW

Unit 8 — Consumers in the Global Economy

Chapter	Learning Objectives
25 **Buying Goods and Services** pp. 420–435	• Describe choices consumers make when buying goods and services. • Identify types of places in which consumers make purchases. • List some tips on how to be a smart consumer. • Distinguish between what is relevant and irrelevant in the information you hear or read. • Describe how software can control computer viruses.
26 **Consumer Rights and Responsibilities** pp. 436–451	• List your six basic rights as a consumer. • List your six responsibilities as a consumer. • Discuss what consumers can do to conserve natural resources and protect the environment. • Identify main and subordinate ideas in written communications. • Describe the skills necessary for jobs in transportation and public utilities.
27 **Protecting Consumers** pp. 452–465	• Identify various consumer protection sources at the federal, state, and local government levels. • List some of the major private consumer organizations and explain what they do. • Describe actions a consumer might take to handle a problem. • Relate what one entrepreneur did at her company to ensure customer satisfaction. • Identify several sources from which to obtain current business-related information.

Business Issue: **Cost of Environmental Regulations, pp. 466–467**

National Standards for Business Education*	Focus on Features	Building Business Skills	Visual Learning	Case Analysis
COMM: I B, I D; *COMP:* VI G; *EPF:* II, X A (Buying Goods and Services), X C, XIII A, XIII D; *IS:* V	Technology: Antivirus Software, p. 424	Analysis: Distinguishing Between Relevant and Irrelevant Information, p. 426	Checklist for Comparison Shopping, p. 428 Unit Prices, p. 429	Consumer Choices, p. 433
CD: II A; *COMM:* I C; *EPF:* X A (Buying Goods and Services), X C, XIII A, XIII D	Careers: Transportation and Public Utilities, p. 440	Communication: Identifying Main and Subordinate Ideas, p. 442	Consumer Rights and Responsibilities, p. 444 Major Sources of Air Pollution, p. 445	Consumer Issues, p. 449
COMM: I B; *EE:* I B; *EPF:* III A, III B, III C, III D	Entrepreneurs: Kathy Prasnicki— Sun Coast Resources, p. 458	Communication: Locating and Verifying Information, p. 460	Federal Consumer Protection Agencies, p. 455	Consumer Protection, p. 463

* Level 3 Performance Expectations: Career Development (CD), Communications (COMM), Computation (COMP), Economics and Personal Finance (EPF), Entrepreneurship Education (EE), IS (Information Systems). See page T14 for all 12 content areas.

UNIT 8

Look Back

Have students recall that countries may have a variety of economic systems: traditional, strong command, moderate command, and market. The main economic challenge facing all nations is how to produce goods and services with limited resources. Most countries satisfy some of their wants for goods and services by buying them from other countries. Nations that trade with one another are participating in the international economy. One of the greatest global economic challenges is promoting economic development and growth in the developing world. Economic development can be encouraged by foreign investment from developed nations and economic assistance from lending agencies such as the World Bank.

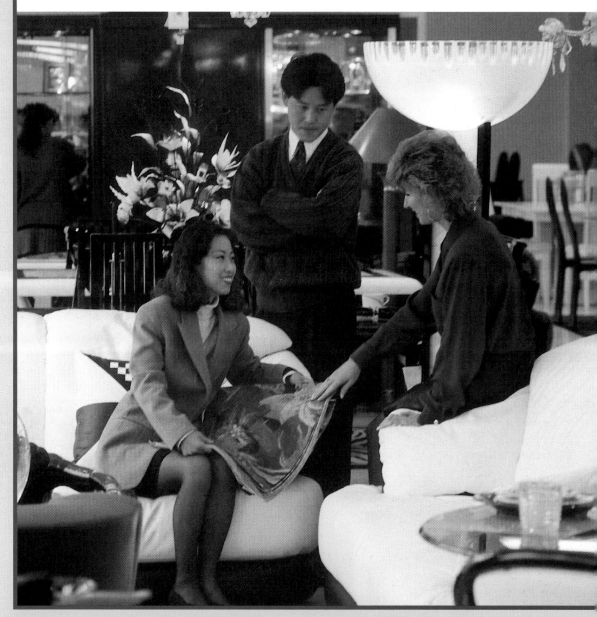

UNIT 8 COOPERATIVE LEARNING PROJECT

Co-op Co-op Activity

Preparation: For each group make one photocopy each of BLMs 16, 17, and 18 from the *Cooperative Learning Strategies* booklet. Provide computer magazines, catalogs, newspapers, and consumer magazines, such as *Consumer Reports,* for research. Assign students to groups of three or four. This activity will take two or three class periods.

Guidelines: Groups will do research to identify the best choice for a classroom computer system and write a proposal describing their recommendation. The

Consumers in the Global Economy

T his unit discusses the global economy and its effect on consumers shopping for goods and services. The first chapter describes store types, advertising, and comparison shopping. The next chapter analyzes wise and responsible consumers and businesses. The final chapter describes federal regulations that protect consumers.

419

Look Ahead
Tell students that smart consumers choose very carefully what they buy and when and how they buy. Consumers have basic rights, including the right to choose, to be heard, to be informed, and to have problems corrected. Along with consumer rights come consumer responsibilities. Consumers are responsible for being informed, choosing and using products safely, and seeking solutions for problems. To ensure that consumers get fair treatment, legislators at all levels of government have passed laws that establish rules and agencies to protect and inform consumers. Many nongovernmental organizations also exist that work on behalf of consumers.

information in BLMs 16, 17, and 18 will guide groups in their research and remind students to consider options such as warranties and service plans. Group members should first determine what kind of equipment would be best for their classroom. Groups eventually will decide which supplier, store, or mail-order catalog offers the best deal on the specific models they recommend. After groups complete their proposals, have them present their recommendations to the class. Suggest that groups compare their research and proposals.

FOCUS

Introduce the Chapter

Major Concepts
- Consumer Choices
- How to Be a Smart Consumer

Introduce the Topic
Ask students to suppose they need to buy some shampoo. Ask them to name all the stores in your area where they could buy shampoo. Record students' ideas on the board. Point out that the list illustrates the wide variety of stores available to shoppers.

Use Business Terms
Ask students to study the list of Business Terms. Then have each student write a question that requires one of the new terms as an answer. Ask volunteers to read aloud their questions for members of the class to respond. Reinforce correct responses. Advise students to check the meanings of the Business Terms as they read the chapter.

USE VISUALS

Direct students' attention to the photograph and ask them what kinds of choices the people in the photo might be making as they shop for shoes. (They might be comparing prices or brands in order to decide which shoes to buy.)

CHAPTER 25

Business terms

consumer

brand name

generic product

comparison shopping

unit pricing

promotional sale

clearance sale

loss leaders

impulse buying

warranty

420

CHAPTER 25 RESOURCES

Instructional Resources

Lesson Plan for Chapter 25

Teaching Transparency 25-1

Strategies and Worksheets for Teaching
   Transparency 25-1

Enrichment Master 25-1

Student Activity Guide 2–TAE for
   Chapter 25

Test Master for Chapter 25

Alternative Assessment Strategies

Math Skills Review

International Business Strategies

Cooperative Learning Strategies

Communication Skills Review

Ethics in Business Strategies

Buying Goods **and** Services

Learning objectives

After completing this chapter, you will be able to:
- Describe choices consumers make when buying goods and services.
- Identify types of places in which consumers make purchases.
- List some tips on how to be a smart consumer.
- Distinguish between what is relevant and irrelevant in the information you hear or read.
- Describe how software can control computer viruses.

Consider what you know

- In the United States, the forces of supply and demand operate in a market economy to provide goods and services. Characteristics of our market economy include private enterprise, freedom of choice, private property, profit incentive, and competition.

Consider what you want to know

- What kinds of choices do consumers make when they buy?
- What are the different places and ways in which a consumer can shop?
- What actions can a smart consumer take when making the decision to buy something?
- How can you separate what is relevant from all the information you receive?
- How can consumers protect their computers from viruses?

Consider how to use what you learn

- As you read this chapter, think about the factors that influence your decisions to buy products. What factors help you decide to buy a certain brand or to shop at a particular store?

Multimedia Resources

Technology Resource Guide

Distance Learning Guide

Internet Resource Guide

Professional Resources

School-to-Work/Tech Prep Strategies

Instructional Poster

Spanish Resources

Testmaker Software for Chapter 25

The Wall Street Journal Video Series
    Video & Activities for Chapter 25

Business and Marketing Computer
    Applications—An Integrated Software
    Simulation Using Microsoft Works

Stocktracker—A Stock Market Software
    Simulation

Where's the Dough? Board Game

Learning Objectives

Point out to students that the learning objectives show what they will learn in the chapter. Tell students to keep these objectives in mind as they work through the chapter. Note that the last two objectives listed refer to the Focus on Technology feature and the Building Business Skills feature.

Consider What You Know

Review briefly the chapters in *Unit 2 The Private Enterprise System:* Motivations of Business, How the Market Works, The Private Enterprise Environment.

Consider What You Want to Know

Have students keep the listed questions in mind as they preview the chapter by quickly paging through it, looking at the photographs, and reading the section headings and figure titles.

Consider How to Use What You Learn

Explain to students that at the end of the chapter they will develop some projects for which they'll need to think about the factors that influence their decisions to buy a certain brand or shop at a particular store.

TEACH

Business Connection

Charles R. Hughes, president of Land Rover North America, defined car buying as "the most horrible retail experience any customer can imagine." Hughes wanted Land Rover customers to feel differently about the experience. By late 1995, about a quarter of U.S. Land Rover dealerships had transformed into "Land Rover Centres"—auto boutiques that showcase both the four-wheel-drive sports utility vehicle and a line of Land Rover brand clothing and accessories. Staff at the centres wear khaki safari outfits and are instructed not to use high-pressure sales tactics.

Develop Concepts

Consumer Choices

Point out to students that we have many choices available to us when making a purchase. Having choices is nice, but sometimes it is difficult to choose wisely. Tell students to imagine they want to buy a new bicycle. On the board write: "What to Buy," "When to Buy," "How to Buy," "Where to Buy," and "What to Pay." Invite students to think of as many considerations as they can for each category and discuss the amount of time it might take to reach a final decision.

When you shop, making choices is not always easy. There are so many different products and services available. Supermarkets, for example, have thousands of different products for sale. Even small neighborhood stores have several hundred different products from which you can choose. In addition, there are many places to look for the best buy.

As a consumer, you also have to face the problem of making your money go as far as possible. If you want to get the most for your money, you have to learn to be a smart consumer.

CONSUMER CHOICES

Being a **consumer**—a person who selects, purchases, uses, and disposes of goods or services—is difficult when you have so many choices. If you had unlimited money, you could buy whatever you wanted, whenever and wherever you wanted. People cannot do that. They have to stretch their income to meet their wants and needs. The first problem of being a consumer is deciding what to buy.

What to Buy

Before you can buy, you have to decide what to buy. This generally means deciding which item has the highest priority as far as you are concerned at any one time. After deciding which goods or services you want, you must then make a selection from various choices. Making choices among brand names can be hard. A **brand name** is a word, picture, or logo on a product that helps consumers distinguish it from similar products. One store may carry eight or ten well-known brands of a product. Which do you choose?

A store also may carry *no-name* products. These items have no brand name, plain labels, and lower prices. They are called **generic products.** For instance, you may be able to buy generic peanut butter, paper towels, canned fruit, and juices. Generic products may differ in size, color, and appearance from brand-name products, but still be of good quality. Sometimes they are exactly the same quality as the brand-name items. However, on average, brand-name products cost about 40 percent more than generic products.

Other decisions you make have to do with price. Should you buy the most expensive product, the least expensive, or one in between? The number of goods available in stores often gives

Making Connections ⇨ Marketing

Note that producers of generic products save money on promotion and package design. Ask students to contrast the marketing process for a brand name bar of soap with that of a generic bar. Ask students if they have ever seen a commercial for a generic product. Why do they think this is so?

you a wide range of prices. Some people think that the most expensive item is always the best quality. That may or may not be true. In fact, the least expensive item or the one in the middle price range may be the best buy. How can you tell? It generally depends on what you plan to do with the product or service you are buying. For example, fresh blueberries are more expensive than frozen blueberries. But frozen blueberries on top of a bowl of cereal would be messy and unattractive. However, if you wanted to make a blueberry pie, the best buy would be frozen blueberries. Fresh blueberries would lose their freshness when you baked the pie, so there would be no need to spend the extra money for fresh berries. Even if you can afford to buy the most expensive item, that does not make the choice easier. The most expensive item may not best fit your wants.

When to Buy

All consumers face problems in deciding how to spend money to get the most from it. For instance, should you buy now or later? Since you usually buy more than one thing at a time, you must decide which goods and services are important to have now, and which can be postponed. Postponing purchases takes will power. Postponing a purchase also involves the risk that the selection may be limited or that the item you want may no longer be available.

How to Buy

Should you pay cash or buy on credit when you make a purchase? Sometimes you do not have a choice. If you do not have enough cash, you may have to use credit. Credit is available at most stores. There is usually a cost for credit, though, and you should consider how that adds to the total cost of the item.

If a product is on sale, should you stock up on it? Special sales may make it possible for you to save money on products you use frequently. However, if you stock up, will you use all of what you buy or will some of it be wasted? If you stock up on one product, will you still have money left over for other things you need?

Where to Buy

You also have to decide where to shop. Do you want to go to a downtown department store, an outlet mall, or a warehouse store, or do you want to stay at home and visit an electronic mall via your computer?

Business & HEALTH

The U.S. Food and Drug Administration (FDA) has issued precise definitions for terminology used on packaged food labels. According to the FDA, a product can only be termed *low fat* if it has less than three grams of fat per serving. A *reduced-fat* product, such as a cookie, must have at least 25 percent less fat than would normally be in the product. A *light* product has half the fat of the regular version of the product.

Global Perspective

FOCUS ON **Technology**

Antivirus Software

You'll see none of the usual symptoms: no fever, no runny nose. It won't act tired or as if it ached all over. So how can you tell if your computer has a virus? What could you do about it? For that matter, what is a computer virus?

Occasionally unscrupulous people want to do malicious or deliberate damage to the data in a computer. One of the most potentially dangerous types of malicious damage is done by a *computer virus,* a computer code that directs the processing system of a computer to change programs or destroy data. Viruses can be programmed to do many things: display false information, destroy existing data files, even erase an entire hard drive.

The damage done by a virus can be extensive because the virus can be designed to copy itself into other software and spread through multiple computer systems. A piece of software that has a virus is called the *host program.* As computer users copy the host program, they unknowingly copy the virus as well. Thus, a computer can "catch" a virus whenever an infected program is copied and shared or downloaded from an electronic bulletin board. The virus can be transmitted by floppy disk or telephone line. There have even been instances of viruses existing in shrink-wrapped disks direct from the factory!

People who copy the host software are often unaware that the virus exists. Executing the legitimate program can activate the virus and damage data. Often damaged data is difficult to detect because data may not be used or reviewed on a regular basis. Frequently, the

Basically, there are three reasons for the different types of places in which to shop: the kinds of goods and services sold, the prices, and the convenience.

- *Department Stores.* Stores that have different departments selling clothing, home furnishings, gifts, jewelry, and services are department stores. They sell moderately priced merchandise but also carry expensive goods such as designer clothing. Department stores generally are service-oriented, with knowledgeable salespeople. Merchandise displays are attractive and creative. Special services, such as delivery, gift wrapping, and wedding gift registry, may be available. Macy's and Marshall Field's are examples of department stores. Because of all the services these stores provide, they generally do not offer the lowest prices.
- *Mass Merchandisers.* Mass merchandise stores sell a wide variety of consumer items at reasonable or low prices. These stores are often nationwide chain stores. The large number of stores makes it possible for these stores to obtain merchandise in large quantities at low prices. Mass merchandisers feature practical rather than elaborate

424   UNIT 8   CONSUMERS IN THE GLOBAL ECONOMY

Cooperative Learning Categorizing

Have groups decide whether a department store or a mass merchandiser would be the better option for purchasing the following items: a gift that needs to be delivered to a person in another state; a pair of athletic socks; a fine watch; a tube of toothpaste. Groups should be able to explain their choices.

Refer to the *Cooperative Learning Strategies* booklet for additional cooperative learning strategies.

virus is designed to hide from computer users for weeks or even months and then attack on a specified date.

Happily, among the goods and services available to computer users is utility software called *antivirus soft-*

ware. The software scans the storage disk and the computer's programs looking for known viruses. The software must be used regularly to afford maximum protection. Once installed, good antivirus software checks for the signs of a virus automatically at every start up, any time a disk is inserted, or any time a modem retrieves a file. The software will alert the user to viruses and remove them.

Regular scanning with antivirus software can offer protection against known viruses. However, new viruses are continually being created. It may be possible for your computer to catch a virus that will not be detected by current antivirus software. There may be no way to protect a computer against a new virus. However, there is a way to protect or limit the damage done by a virus: KEEP ADEQUATE BACK-UP FILES.

If all data is backed up, you have a record that is uncontaminated by viruses introduced later.

Follow Through

Have students name some ways to protect against computer viruses. (Use antivirus software and back up all data.) Ask why antivirus software may not be capable of detecting all viruses. (Antivirus software only protects against *known* viruses; it may not recognize a new virus.)
For additional information about current technology, refer to the *Technology Resource Guide* booklet.

Business Brief

In the mid-1990s, there were approximately 10,000 off-price and outlet stores in the United States, which sold $10 billion of merchandise annually. To keep costs down, many off-price and outlet stores locate in remote shopping areas or outlet malls that charge lower rents.

merchandise displays. Some mass merchandisers are Sears, Target, and Venture.

- *Off-Price and Outlet Stores.* Off-price stores carry well-known brand name and designer goods with prices discounted from 20 to 70 percent. They are able to offer large discounts because they buy merchandise from producers who have surpluses. They also sell merchandise that may be slightly imperfect or is being discontinued by the manufacturer. Examples of off-price stores include T.J. Maxx, Hit or Miss, and Loehmann's. Outlet stores are very similar to off-price stores in that they sell the same types of goods. Outlet stores, however, are operated by the manufacturer so they sell only that manufacturer's goods. Calvin Klein, Jockey, and Nike are just a few examples.
- *Limited-Line Retailers.* Stores that sell only one kind of merchandise are limited line retailers. Clothing and accessory stores, athletic-goods stores, home-appliance stores, and hardware stores are all limited-line retailers. Services and selling methods vary. Pricing policies vary as well. The Limited, Foot Locker, Best Buy, and Ace Hardware are

Reteaching Strategy

Ask students to prepare a list of products that a shopper would tend to buy at the most convenient store. Then have them prepare a list of goods for which a shopper would usually shop around among several stores. Compare and contrast the two types of products.

Model

On the board write the heading "Relevant." Remind students that relevant information is the information they need in order to complete a certain task. Guide students through the first Case Study on page 427, asking students to determine which parts of the conversation are necessary to fill the pizza order. (Relevant: a large pizza, pepperoni, 100 Smith Road.)

Learning Activity

Note that some shoppers feel intimidated by the size of hypermarkets. Ask students what other drawbacks there might be for certain hypermarket shoppers. (Possible answers: People with disabilities may encounter difficulties in such stores; small children could easily become separated from a parent; it could be difficult to locate a salesperson for assistance.)

ANALYSIS

Distinguishing Between Relevant and Irrelevant Information

Explanation

You are constantly being bombarded with information. In most cases you've already learned to automatically distinguish information you need from information you don't need.

On the job, some of the information you'll be confronted with will be relevant, or necessary. Other information will be irrelevant. Irrelevant information may be interesting, but it has no connection to your work. It is important to learn how to disregard irrelevant information.

If you're speaking to someone who is not giving you information you need, ask questions. If you are reading information, write down what you want to know. Then decide which information you need. What defines, explains, illustrates, or gives a cause or effect of the main topic of your question is the relevant information.

Practice

Read each Case Study and decide which information is necessary for the person involved to know. On a separate sheet of paper, write the relevant information from each Case Study.

some examples. Convenience stores are also considered limited-line retailers. Although such stores sell groceries, carry-out food, and nonfood items, the selection is small. People shop at convenience stores like White Hen and 7-Eleven because they are located near residential areas and stay open for long hours. Consumers pay higher prices at such stores because they are paying for convenience.

- *Superstores and Hypermarkets.* Superstores are similar to supermarkets but in addition to groceries they sell mass merchandise items such as clothing, garden products, books, and hardware. Superstores are very large—on average they occupy about 30,000 square feet. Hypermarkets are even larger with stores of 200,000 square feet or more. Hypermarkets carry a larger selection of the items superstores carry and also offer large appliances and furniture to their customers. Kroger and Safeway operate superstores. The appeal of hypermarkets may be limited by the fact that some consumers feel overwhelmed by the size of such stores. Generally speaking, they do not offer a lot of extra services.
- *Warehouse Stores.* For consumers who like shopping in extremely large stores, there are warehouse stores. These

426 UNIT 8 CONSUMERS IN THE GLOBAL ECONOMY

Cooperative Learning Trade-a-Problem

Have teams write a scenario containing relevant and irrelevant information. Teams should trade their scenarios with another team and identify and record the relevant information in each other's scenarios. When teams are finished, have them compare their solutions. Teams can continue trading problems if they need more practice.

Refer to the *Cooperative Learning Strategies* booklet for additional cooperative learning strategies.

1. You are taking orders at the pizza company where you have a summer job. It's dinner time and the busiest part of the evening. You pick up the phone and hear: "Hi! Pizza to Go? My grandkids are in town. They've had a really busy day at the Bell Road pool, and they're starving. They'll need a large pizza. Let's see. I like anchovies myself, but I guess we'll get pepperoni. They'll be at their grandpa's house. That's 100 Smith Road. Boy, it's been a busy day. Can't wait 'til you get here!"

2. You go to an appliance store to buy an inexpensive personal tape player so you can listen to music on the bus. You want to know about a feature mentioned in the ads.

   "I'd like some information about personal tape players," you say to the clerk.

"They're hanging on the wall," replies the clerk.
"First I want to know about a feature," you say.
The clerk interrupts. "We're having a great sale on RealSound brand tape players."
You try again, "What does the antiroll mechanism do?"
"The players on sale don't have that feature, but they're really a good deal," says the clerk.
"I know you're having a sale, but I need to know more: could you tell me what the antiroll mechanism does?"
"Sure. The antiroll mechanism keeps the tape running smoothly when you're, say, running or riding a bike. But these sale players really come in cool colors!"

Practice

Have students separate the relevant from the irrelevant information for the second Case Study on page 427 themselves. (Relevant: The antiroll mechanism keeps the tape running smoothly even when you are moving.)

---

stores are about the size of a football field and carry a huge selection of food and nonfood items at low prices. Food and other merchandise is available in bulk quantities. If you want to buy a case of laundry detergent, a warehouse store is the place to go. Warehouse stores, sometimes called warehouse clubs, require customers to become members of the store by paying a small membership fee. Usually, there are relatively few salespeople to assist customers in these types of stores.

- *Catalogs.* Mail-order houses send out catalogs of limited-line items such as clothing or household items. They may not have a store located anywhere—merchandise is stored in warehouses and sent to customers directly. Some stores, such as Crate and Barrel and Eddie Bauer, also send out catalogs. When ordering from a catalog, a customer can fill out an order form and mail it or fax it. Customers can also call a toll-free number and give the order to an operator. Customers may need to return merchandise, especially clothing, they have ordered from catalogs, because they are unable to examine it in person before delivery.

CHAPTER 25 BUYING GOODS AND SERVICES **427**

Business Brief

Price Co. and Costco Wholesale Corp. were the second and third largest warehouse chains in the country. In 1993, they merged to form Price/Costco, the second-largest warehouse chain, with only Wal-Mart's Sam's Wholesale Clubs having greater revenues.

TEACHING TIP

Tell students that one advantage of shopping by mail is that out-of-state customers do not have to pay a state's sales tax. Have students list other advantages of shopping by mail. What disadvantages are there?

Curriculum Connection   History

The emergence of warehouse stores, superstores, and electronic shopping have all contributed to a shift in the way Americans buy things. Mom-and-Pop corner groceries and five-and-dime variety stores are quickly becoming relics of the past. Have students interview older relatives or acquaintances to find out how consumer buying habits have changed over the years. Some questions they could ask include: How often did people shop? Where did they shop? What kind of variety in goods was available? Have students write a 150-word summary of their interviews.

- *Electronic Shopping.* Personal computer owners can buy items by subscribing to an on-line service. Consumers can choose from a menu of "electronic shops" and order airline tickets, flowers, software, CDs and more. Pictures and product information are displayed on the computer screen. To order, consumers type information into an electronic order form. Because the entire transaction is carried out electronically, consumers cannot use cash. They must make their purchase with a credit or debit card because the card number must be typed into the computer.

What to Pay

Checking the price and quality of a product in more than one store is known as **comparison shopping.** Figure 25-1 below shows factors you should consider when doing comparison shopping. Comparison shopping can really save you money. Comparison shopping is of most value in making a major purchase. Of course, you need to consider the cost of the time and energy you spend in comparison shopping, as well as the money you might save. If you spend $1.25 on transportation to save 50 cents on an item, that is not a bargain.

Products come in many sizes. How do you know which size is the best buy? It can be confusing for a consumer in the supermarket to try to compare a large economy-size package with a smaller regular-size package. If all products of the same kind were priced in terms of ounces, pounds, or liters, consumers

FIGURE 25-1

When comparison shopping, you should check price, features, quality, convenience, and whether the product comes with a warranty. When you are examining the quality of a product, what should you look for?

Checklist for Comparison Shopping	
Price	Keeping within a certain price range is important to most people.
Features	The characteristics of a product or service are important.
Quality	Quality includes how well a product is made, how well it performs its job, and how long it will last.
Convenience	The labor- and time-saving features of a product affect many consumer decisions. A store's location may make a difference.
Warranty	A warranty is a legal document that states the rights and responsibilities agreed to by the consumer and the seller.

Enrichment Strategy

Bring in nutritional labels from two or three boxes of different types of cereal. Pass them around and then discuss how nutritional labels can be helpful in comparison shopping. Ask: Which product would be the best choice for someone on a low-salt (sodium) diet? Which would be best for someone who wants to avoid sugar? Fat?

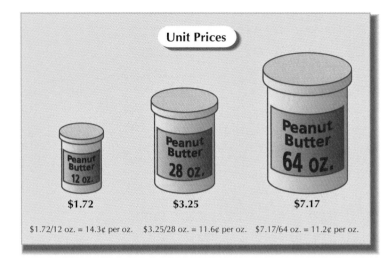

Unit Prices

Peanut Butter 12 oz.
$1.72

Peanut Butter 28 oz.
$3.25

Peanut Butter 64 oz.
$7.17

$1.72/12 oz. = 14.3¢ per oz. $3.25/28 oz. = 11.6¢ per oz. $7.17/64 oz. = 11.2¢ per oz.

FIGURE 25-2

Find the unit price of an item by dividing the price by the weight or volume. The unit price helps you decide which product is the best buy. What size of jar of peanut butter is the best buy?

might have an easier time in comparing sizes and prices. A price expressed in a standard measurement such as per ounce for the same product is called **unit pricing.** Peanut butter, for example, often comes in three or four different-sized containers. Many suppliers offer this range of sizes. If you are comparing one brand of peanut butter with another, it helps to know that Brand A is 14.3 cents per ounce or unit, whereas Brand B is 16.9 cents per ounce or unit.

Generally, the larger the size, the lower the price per unit. This is not always true, though. That is why it is always important to look at the unit price of an item. Some stores provide unit pricing information for various products. If not, you can figure it out yourself by dividing the price of the product by its weight or volume. Figure 25-2 above shows you how to compute the unit price of a product to compare different sizes.

Quick Check

1. Define *consumer, brand name, generic products, comparison shopping,* and *unit pricing.*
2. What are three reasons for different types of places in which consumers may buy products?

HOW TO BE A SMART CONSUMER

As a shopper, you have to decide what a bargain really is for you. To be a good shopper, you cannot buy products that are a waste of your money. If you buy something you cannot use, it is

Curriculum Connection   Math

Give students the following scenario: Shantha needs to buy two pounds of basmati rice. Annapurna Grocery sells basmati rice for $1.39 a pound. Foodstuffs sells 8-ounce packages for 99¢. Grocerola sells a 32-ounce package for $2.89. Have students calculate the unit price in ounces for each choice and find out which store offers the best price. (Annapurna has the best price—$1.39 ÷ 16 = 8.7 cents per ounce; Foodstuffs .99 ÷ 8 = 12.4 cents per ounce; Grocerola $2.89 ÷ 32 = 9 cents per ounce.)

For students who need to sharpen their math skills, choose among the worksheets in the *Math Skills Review* booklet.

Learning Activity

Emotional advertising strategies include the "bandwagon" technique, in which the implication is that everyone is buying the product advertised. Celebrity testimonials are also strategies that are designed to appeal to consumers' emotions. Ask students to think of some current examples of each of these two techniques.

TEACHING TIP

Ask students what other useful material they might find in an ad other than information about price and quality. (Possible answers: Dates that the sale price is offered; coupons; restrictions on the number of items that may be bought.)

Learning Activity

Have students suppose they are in the market for a camera, and they want to have as much information as possible before buying one. What kind of information might be available from advertisements? From salespersons? From consumer publications? From friends and acquaintances? Whose information would be the most trustworthy? Have students explain their answers.

F.Y.I.

A poll of 40,000 consumers in 40 countries identified four major kinds of shoppers. *Deal makers* just like the process of buying things. *Price seekers* feel that price is the most important consideration. *Luxury innovators* want the most up-to-date and prestigious products. *Brand loyalists* insist on buying name brands. Which type are you?

not a bargain at any price. A wise shopper checks that prices really are special and that those special buys are useful.

You can become a smart shopper by planning in advance. You can start by checking to see what the good buys are. Newspapers and magazines include advertising that can help. Big stores often send out their own advertisements.

Study Advertisements

Advertisements are an important source of information for planning your shopping. U.S. companies spend about $150 billion a year on advertising. To be a wise shopper, you should learn how to read advertisements. Here are some hints that will help you analyze and understand advertisements.

Advertisements come in two kinds. Rational advertising attempts to convince you with facts and other information. It tries to persuade you that you should choose a specific product because it is the best one for your purpose. "You can make your decision on the basis of this information," the advertisement implies. On the other hand, emotional advertising appeals to your feelings. It suggests that if you buy something you will be the most popular person in town. "Use this product," the advertisement implies, "and your friends will like you better."

When you look at advertising, decide whether it gives you useful information. An advertisement that simply announces "The best buy in town!" will not necessarily help you become a smarter shopper. Why is it the best buy in town? Is it the cheapest price you can get? Is the quality so good that the item is worth more than you pay for it? On the other hand, an advertisement that says "9 oz. Sparkle-Plenty Toothpaste, $1.99" may be very helpful. If you know that Sparkle-Plenty Toothpaste is good, and that it usually sells for $2.79 for 9 ounces, you know the sale is a good buy.

Also look at the advertisements to determine whether they include any discount coupons. Many businesses use coupons to encourage consumers to buy products, especially when they are new to the market.

Read Consumer Publications

Magazines such as *Consumer Reports* and *Consumers Research Magazine* give detailed information about goods that have been tested and rated by their organizations. When you are considering buying an expensive item, such as a used car, you can find out and compare any car's gas mileage, brake system, body integrity, repair record, comfort, and numerous other facts. The same information is tested and rated for differ-

Making Connections ▪▷◆ Humor in Advertising

Many advertisers use humor as a selling technique. Have students check some newspapers and magazines at home and bring in ads that use humor. As a class, analyze the ads to decide how often the ads give useful information versus how often they appeal strictly to the consumer's sense of humor. Discuss with students the effectiveness of humor in persuading people to buy.

ent brands of products so you can make comparisons easily. Consumer magazines examine and rate everything from bottled iced-tea beverages to expensive products and services like cars and travel agency services. Many specialty magazines, such as those for photographers or hikers, rate equipment such as cameras or hiking boots. Libraries and on-line services are good places to find these sources of consumer information.

Shop at Sales

Some shopping experts say that the average consumer can save up to 15 percent by watching for and taking advantage of sales. Stores may use two different kinds of sales. A **promotional sale** is one that gives you a special buy on a new product or a product that is in season. First check to make sure that the price is lower than usual. In January, for example, many stores have "white" sales. They sell towels, sheets, and other household items at lower prices during the white sale. Promotional sales are usually held at a time when consumer buying is down. After the holidays, a January white sale is intended to bring people into the stores.

A store may also use a **clearance sale** to clear or get rid of goods that are going out of style or that are no longer profitable. Clearance sales may occur at the end of a season or when products have been on the market too long. A clearance sale is a way of moving those products to make room for new merchandise.

During sales, look for products that are advertised as going at a loss or below cost. These advertised specials are called **loss leaders.** Even though a store loses money on these products, the advertised low prices bring customers into the store.

Use Shopping Lists

It is fairly easy to fall into the trap of impulse buying when you do not have a firm idea of what you want before you enter a store. **Impulse buying** is purchasing items on the spur of the moment. Such buying can ruin a budget and encourage purchases you really do not need. To cut down on unplanned buying, wise shoppers prepare shopping lists. A shopping list will help you save time and money. It may keep you from making unnecessary shopping trips because you forgot something you need. A shopping list may help you save money as well, because you have decided ahead of time what items you need to buy.

Resist Pressure and Gimmicks

Some sales representatives use high-pressure tactics to try to insist that you buy what they are selling. These salespeople

GLOBAL VIEW

Consumers are not the same the world over; they have different values and associations. American businesses need to bear this in mind when advertising and marketing products in a variety of countries. When a U.S. business promoted a new perfume in Latin America, sales did not take off as expected. The ad featured pictures of camellia flowers, and the company later discovered that in Latin America camellias are funeral flowers.

CHAPTER 25 BUYING GOODS AND SERVICES **431**

TEACHING TIP

Emphasize to students that taking just 15 minutes to plan a shopping trip can improve their decision making. Have students brainstorm a list of tips to help plan a shopping trip.

Learning Activity

Bonnie has just finished her grocery shopping and is waiting in the checkout line. There is an attractive-looking display of snacks and candy within easy reach. While she is waiting, she adds a king-sized candy bar to her shopping cart—even though it wasn't on her shopping list! Ask: What buying behavior has Bonnie just demonstrated? (Impulse buying.) How did the store contribute to Bonnie's buying behavior? (By purposely placing tempting items in an area where customers have to wait.)

Global Perspective

Promoting American products in Poland's formerly communist economic system has proved difficult. Many Polish consumers distrust advertising and believe that any product that needs advertising must be of poor quality. One advertiser even resorted to beginning an ad with, "This is truth, not advertising." Have students brainstorm ways other than advertising that consumers can obtain information about new products. (By receiving free samples; by reading about them in consumer or other publications; by word of mouth from trusted friends or acquaintances.)

Refer to the *International Business Strategies* booklet for additional strategies and activities.

CHAPTER 25

Business Brief

All products have an implied warranty, or an understanding between the buyer and the seller that the product should perform as expected. Implied warranties are part of state and county civil codes. Products may also come with an express warranty, a written or an oral agreement between a buyer and seller.

Quick Check Answers

1. A sale that gives you a sale price for a new product or a product that is in season; a sale on goods that are going out of style or are no longer profitable; products that are sold below cost in order to bring customers into the store; purchasing items on the spur of the moment; a legal document that states the rights and responsibilities agreed to by the consumer and the store or manufacturer.
2. Rational and emotional.
3. In consumer publications such as *Consumer Reports* and *Consumers Research Magazine.*

Making a list before you go shopping is one way to be a smart consumer. How might this man's list help him in the gocery store?

can be very persuasive. You should always ask yourself if what the salesperson is saying is true, if you need the product or service, and whether you can afford it. If the answer to any of the questions is "no," you should not let the salesperson pressure you into buying what he or she is offering.

Sales gimmicks, such as "free" prizes or prices that are far lower than the going rate, are meant to grab consumers' attention and draw them into making an unwise purchase. You might receive a notice in the mail saying you have won a "free" prize. However, after reading carefully, you realize you will not receive the prize unless you buy what the company is offering. You should always examine closely any deal or bargain that seems too good to be true.

Read Labels and Warranties

Before buying a product, read the label. You may find information on the label that will make you decide not to buy the product. For example, a pair of slacks that needs to be dry-cleaned presents you with the problems of extra expense and inconvenience. You may want to look around for a pair of machine-washable slacks.

Many items such as automobiles, appliances, and electronics come with warranties. A **warranty** is a legal document that states the rights and responsibilities agreed to by the consumer and the store or manufacturer. Full warranties state that the seller will repair a product that does not work—free of charge. It could also offer to replace the product or refund the consumer's money. *Full warranties* are usually in effect for a stated time period, for example, one year. *Limited warranties* cover only certain parts of a product. In addition, the responsibilities of the seller are usually limited, such as replacing a defective part, but requiring the buyer to pay the labor cost for making the repair. Whatever the type of warranty, buyers must register warranted products with the company for the warranty to go into effect.

Quick Check

1. Explain the terms *promotional sale, clearance sale, loss leaders, impulse buying,* and *warranty.*
2. What are the two kinds of advertising?
3. Where can you find information about goods that have been tested and rated?

Chapter 25 **Summary**

Main Ideas

1. When consumers shop, they have choices to make including what to buy, when to buy, how to buy, where to buy, and what to pay.
2. Depending on the type of product, the price, and the convenience, consumers may choose to buy in a number of different types of stores or to order by catalog or from an on-line service.
3. Smart consumers study advertisements, shop at sales, use shopping lists, read consumer publications, resist gimmicks and pressure from salespeople, and read labels and warranties.
4. It is important to develop the ability to distinguish between relevant and irrelevant information.
5. Computers can "catch" viruses whenever programs are shared or downloaded from another source. Wise consumers purchase anti-virus software that checks computers for viruses.

CASE ANALYSIS   Consumer Choices

A factory clothing outlet has just opened on your side of town. Here's the information you've been able to find out about it from some of your friends.

a. It operates from a warehouse.
b. Seconds, not overstocks, are sold.
c. Brand names have been removed from the clothing.
d. All sales are for cash.
e. There are no refunds or returns.
f. Prices offer savings ranging from 30 to 50 percent.

Would you be willing to shop at the outlet to update your wardrobe? Why or why not?

CLOSE

Main Ideas

Main Ideas summarizes the key information in the chapter. It is a useful tool for reinforcement and review.

CASE ANALYSIS

Case Analysis provides a chapter-related case for student analysis and application of decision-making skills.

Answer
Students' answers will vary.

QUICK QUIZ

1. What can you determine by figuring out unit prices for different sized products? (Which product is the best buy.)
2. Name two kinds of advertising. (Rational and emotional.)
3. Where would you look to find information about goods that have been tested and rated? (Consumer publications.)
4. What is a warranty? (Legal document that states the rights and responsibilities agreed to by the consumer and the store or manufacturer.)

Chapter 25 **Review**

APPLY

Answers

Use the Language of Business

1. unit pricing, **2.** clearance sale, **3.** impulse buying, **4.** comparison shopping, **5.** promotional sale, **6.** generic products, **7.** consumer, **8.** brand name, **9.** warranty, **10.** loss leaders.

Review What You Learned

1. They have no brand name, plain labels, and lower prices than brand-name products.

2. It provides a standard measurement for pricing products, allowing shoppers to compare prices and find the best buy.

3. Surplus merchandise, imperfect merchandise, and discontinued merchandise.

4. Rational and emotional.

5. Consumer publications give detailed information about products that have been tested and rated.

6. A promotional sale attracts buyers to merchandise that is in season or that is new in the store. A clearance sale clears out old merchandise to make room for new items.

7. It is information that is not necessary to know in order to complete a task.

8. A computer virus is a computer code that directs the processing system of a computer to change programs or destroy data.

Understand Business Concepts

1. The supermarket may be using the lower price on milk as a loss leader. Management hopes that by advertising a low price on a product such as milk, which is used by most consumers, more customers will come to the store and that while there, they will buy other items.

2. Answers will vary according to students' opinions.

3. By making them so convenient, the store hopes consumers will buy them on impulse.

4. It is wise to buy large quantities of a product at a reduced cost if it is something

Use the Language of Business

Part of being a smart consumer means understanding the terms connected with buying goods and services. See how well you know them. Match each term to its definition.

brand name   impulse buying
clearance sale   loss leaders
comparison shopping   promotional sale
consumer   unit pricing
generic products   warranty

1. Price based on standard measurements of different brands of a product.
2. Sale to clear or get rid of goods.
3. Purchases made on the spur of the moment.
4. Activity in which a consumer checks the price and quality of a product in more than one store.
5. Sale that gives a special buy on a new product or a product that is in season.
6. Products that have no brand name, plain labels, and lower prices.
7. Person who selects, purchases, uses, and disposes of goods and services.
8. Word, picture, or phrase that helps consumers identify a product.
9. Legal document that states the rights and responsibilities of the consumer and the store or manufacturer.
10. Goods that are being sold below cost to bring customers into a store.

Review What You Learned

1. How do generic products differ from brand-name products?
2. Why is unit pricing important in getting the best buy?
3. What three factors make it possible for off-price and outlet stores to offer large discounts?
4. What are two types of advertising?
5. What kinds of information will you find in consumer publications?
6. Compare a promotional sale with a clearance sale.
7. How do you distinguish irrelevant information?
8. What is a computer virus?

Understand Business Concepts

1. At the supermarket, Maria found milk on sale for $1.89 a half-gallon. Other stores were selling milk from $2.09 to $2.39 a half-gallon. Why might the supermarket have a lower price?
2. Of the places where consumers can buy goods and services, which do you think have a bright future? Do you think any will decrease in importance in the next 10 years?
3. In many supermarkets, racks in front of the checkout lanes have a wide range of "convenience" goods on display. Why do you think those products such as candy, magazines, razor blades, and chewing gum are displayed in that way?
4. When does it make sense to buy certain products in large quantities?

you need and will use frequently, if it will store well, and if you will still have money left to buy other items you need.

5. Possible answer: Advantages: You don't have to travel to any stores; items and information about products are clearly displayed on your screen; Disadvantages: You need a computer and an on-line service; you can't inspect items personally; you can't use cash.

6. Lists will vary depending on advertisements students chose.

7. A virus can come from a number of sources; viruses can be inactive until a specified date or time.

Think Critically

1. The 9-ounce package costs the least per ounce, so it is the best buy.

2. Answers will vary. Helpful information may include price, weight, warranty information, ingredients, and nutritional information. Information that is not helpful may include the adjectives companies use to describe their products and puzzles and games on the backs of packages.

5. List some advantages and disadvantages of electronic shopping.
6. Find some advertisements in magazines and make a list showing which information is relevant and which information is irrelevant.

7. Explain why periodic scanning of a computer system with anti-virus software is desirable.

Independent Practice

Use the Chapter 25 worksheets in *Student Activity Guide 2* for additional practice and application activities. *Student Activity Guide 2* provides vocabulary exercises, reading comprehension checks, problems, projects, and simulations of business and economic situations. A Teacher's Annotated Edition provides answers.

Think Critically

1. **Recommend.** Five ounces of toothpaste cost $2.09. Eight ounces cost $2.69, and 9 ounces cost $2.88. Which is the best buy?

2. **Classify.** Bring some labels, tags, seals, or packaging from various products to class. List the information you find on those items. Which types of information are helpful? Which are not?

Use What You Learned

1. **Group Project.** Work with your team to devise a shoppers' survey. Include questions such as these in your list:

   • Do you use a shopping list?
   • Do you compare unit prices?
   • Do you buy large, economy sized products?
   • Do you wait for sales?
   • Do you read consumer publications?

   Each team member can survey shoppers at a different store. Tally your survey results and then write a profile of typical consumer behavior in your community.

2. Visit a grocery store and choose five items that are available as generic products. Record their prices. Find brand-name versions of the same items and record their prices. Calculate the unit prices of the brand-name items and the generic items. Make a chart

showing how much money a person can save by buying generic products.

3. **Computer Application.** Select a big-ticket item that you are interested in purchasing. Use database software to create a database of stores in your area that stock the item you are interested in purchasing. Include names, addresses, telephone numbers, prices and any other information you determine to be relevant to the purchasing decision. Print out the database and use the information to analyze the best place to purchase the item you want.

4. **Skill Reinforcement.** Suppose that yearbook sales in your school have declined this year. As yearbook chairperson, you want to know why. Make a list of relevant information you'll need to find out. Compare your list with others' lists.

Save your work in your Business Portfolio

Use What You Learned
1. Make sure all students participate in drafting survey questions and taking the survey. Rubrics: Survey; Essay.
2. Provide a conversion chart (pounds to ounces, pints to quarts and so forth) for students to use when calculating unit price. Rubric: Charts and Tables.
3. Students who don't have access to a computer may compile

the information in a hand-drawn chart. Rubric: Charts and Tables.
4. Students' answers will vary, but should include information such as how the number of students in previous years compares to this year's population; whether the price has changed; if students find the yearbook easy to order; and how many students are planning to place their orders later. Rubric: Note Taking.

ASSESS

Portfolio Assessment

The portfolio projects are designed to lead students to develop a collection of their best work to submit to you for assessment. You and your students should decide which projects will be included in their respective Business Portfolios. Refer students to the specific rubric(s) from the *Alternative Assessment Strategies* booklet listed with each of the project notes below. These rubrics will alert students to the criteria you will use to assess their projects.

Chapter Assessment

Use the Chapter 25 Test from the *Test Masters* booklet to evaluate students' understanding of the chapter concepts. An answer key is provided. Or create your own customized test using the *Testmaker* software.

FOCUS

Introduce the Chapter

Major Concepts
- Your Rights As a Consumer
- Your Responsibilities As a Consumer

Introduce the Topic

Ask students if they have ever bought items that were faulty or defective. Ask if they think it is their consumer responsibility to return these items. Why or why not? Let students know that in Chapter 26 they will learn about consumers' rights and the responsibilities that go with them.

Use Business Terms

Have students look at the Business Terms and brainstorm associations with each term. Ask them where they have heard or seen the terms used. Reinforce correct associations. Advise students to note the meanings of the terms as they read the chapter.

USE VISUALS

Ask students to describe what is happening in the photo. Ask students how the store may remedy the problem the woman has with the item she is returning. Discuss with students how stores they have visited handle exchanges and returns of merchandise.

Business terms

consumerism

bait and switch

pollution

conservation

recycling

boycott

436

CHAPTER 26 RESOURCES

Instructional Resources

Lesson Plan for Chapter 26

Teaching Transparency 26-1

Strategies and Worksheets for Teaching Transparency 26-1

Enrichment Master 26-1

Student Activity Guide 2–TAE for Chapter 26

Test Master for Chapter 26

Alternative Assessment Strategies

Math Skills Review

International Business Strategies

Cooperative Learning Strategies

Communication Skills Review

Ethics in Business Strategies

Consumer Rights and Responsibilities

Learning objectives

After completing this chapter, you will be able to:
- List your six basic rights as a consumer.
- List your six responsibilities as a consumer.
- Discuss what consumers can do to conserve natural resources and protect the environment.
- Identify main and subordinate ideas in written communications.
- Describe the skills necessary for jobs in transportation and public utilities.

Consider what you know

- Smart consumers choose what they buy, and when and how they buy. They do comparison shopping in order to make smart decisions about purchases.

Consider what you want to know

- What are the six basic rights of consumers?
- What responsibilities do consumers have?
- How can you pinpoint main ideas when reading business communications?
- What kinds of careers are available in transportation and public utilities?

Consider how to use what you learn

- As you read this chapter, think about what happens to products after you use them. How does your community handle waste and environmental problems? Do you consider the impact a product has on the environment before you buy it?

Learning Objectives
Point out to students that the learning objectives show what they will learn in the chapter. Tell students to keep these objectives in mind as they work through the chapter. Note that the last two objectives listed refer to the Focus on Careers feature and the Building Business Skills feature.

Consider What You Know
Review briefly the main sections of *Chapter 25 Buying Goods and Services:* Consumer Choices and How to Be a Smart Consumer.

Consider What You Want to Know
Have students preview the chapter in order to see how it will provide answers to the questions. They can read the headings and subheadings, look at the figures and photographs, and read the captions.

Consider How to Use What You Learn
Inform students that at the end of the chapter they will develop some projects. As they read the chapter, ask them to think about how their roles as consumers affect the environment.

Multimedia Resources

Technology Resource Guide

Distance Learning Guide

Internet Resource Guide

Professional Resources

School-to-Work/Tech Prep Strategies

Instructional Poster

Spanish Resources

Testmaker Software for Chapter 26

The Wall Street Journal Video Series
Video & Activities for Chapter 26

Business and Marketing Computer Applications—An Integrated Software Simulation Using Microsoft Works

Stocktracker—A Stock Market Software Simulation

Where's the Dough? Board Game

TEACH

Develop Concepts

Your Rights As a Consumer

Point out to students that consumer rights issues have had, and continue to have, a major impact on businesses. Consumers have become more aware of unethical sales tactics. Laws are in place that protect consumers' rights and make sure that consumers are able to make informed buying choices. Have students take a look at each of the six rights listed in the section. Invite students to give some examples of what they think each right could refer to.

In 1962, President John F. Kennedy presented a special message to the members of Congress. In his message, President Kennedy outlined what was called the Consumer Bill of Rights. According to the President, every consumer has certain basic rights. These consumer rights have received much attention since the beginning of the consumer movement in the 1960s. Today, there are many consumer-rights groups as well as laws that protect the interests and rights of consumers. **Consumerism** consists of all the activities and measures that protect the rights of consumers.

However, consumer rights are like any other rights. They come with certain responsibilities. In this chapter, we will examine these consumer rights and responsibilities.

YOUR RIGHTS AS A CONSUMER

In addition to your roles as a wage earner and as a citizen, you also have a role as a consumer in our free enterprise economy. As a consumer, you have certain rights that affect how you use goods and services.

The Right to Be Informed

Before deciding which products and services to buy, consumers need information. A wise decision is an informed decision. As a consumer, you have a right to information that is based on facts. For example, you may want to purchase a pure fruit juice, not a fruit drink with ingredients other than fruit juice. You are willing to pay more money for the pure fruit juice than for a fruit drink. A company cannot tell you that its fruit drink is the same as a pure fruit juice, since all of the ingredients in the product must be listed. You have the right to accurate information so you can buy wisely.

The information about products and services should also be clear. It should not be misleading or difficult to understand. In the past, customers were not always told how much interest charges would add to the cost of an item paid for over time. Some businesses hid the interest charges in long, complicated agreements. They may no longer do that because the government passed laws protecting the consumer's right to information presented in a manner that can be clearly understood.

Curriculum Connection   History

The consumer movement began in the 1960s. Most of the rights consumers enjoy today are the results of consumer advocacy during that time. Have students research the history of the consumer movement and prepare an oral report on one of the aspects of the consumer movement. Have students share their reports with the class.

A number of laws protect your right to be informed. Business firms are required to give you certain information about their products. The grocery store or supermarket that sells meat must tell you what grade or quality you are buying. Drug companies must list the minerals and vitamins contained in a vitamin pill. Some laws require clothing manufacturers to specify on labels which natural and synthetic fibers are used in materials. Other laws require the ingredients of packaged foods to be listed on the label in decreasing amounts. For example, a corn-rice cereal might contain the following list of ingredients: corn, rice, brown sugar, salt, malt flavoring, baking soda, turmeric, color.

The Right to Choose

Because the United States has a market economy, you are able to choose from a wide variety of goods and services produced throughout the world. Businesses compete with one another to sell their products to you and other consumers. They try to offer new products, the lowest prices, the highest quality, or the best service. For consumers, competition means choice.

In our system, one business is not allowed to prevent other businesses from competing for customers. If a business tries to reduce competition, we say that it is trying to control the market. If only one company produced television sets, consumers would have to buy the models this company offered and pay the price it was asking. A monopoly arises when one business controls the market. In most cases, the resulting lack of competition hurts the consumer.

As you learned in Chapter 16, the federal government has the power to step in to keep our markets competitive. It can use antitrust laws to break up monopolies into smaller businesses or stop monopolies from forming so that competition in the market is maintained. A competitive market provides lower prices, better services, and a variety of choices for the consumer. In 1994 Microsoft, the world's largest computer software company, attempted to buy Intuit, a software company that produces a top-selling personal finance program. The federal government blocked the merger. The merger would have given Microsoft a virtual monopoly in personal finance software. For consumers, the merger could have resulted in higher software prices and fewer choices.

The Right to Safety

You have the right to buy products that are safe to use. In response to the need for safe products, the government has passed many laws to ensure that clothing, food, drugs, cosmetics,

Anita Roddick works hard to remain conscious of the effect on the global environment of her company, Body Shop International. She cultivates entrepreneurships in developing countries that make products based on environmentally sound practices. For example, one company she helped start in Brazil makes cosmetics from local natural oils. The cosmetics are part of the line of products in the Body Shop stores. Consumer support for these goals is reflected in the company's continuing success.

TEACHING TIP

Make sure students can differentiate between a monopoly and a market leader. Tell students that it is not illegal for a business to be a market leader, only for it to eliminate or disrupt normal competition.

Learning Activity
Emphasize the importance of making realistic buying decisions by contrasting buying a mountain bike and buying a notebook. Have students contrast points such as safety, quality of features, appearance, and how long the purchase must last. Why are some of these considerations more important for some purchases than others?

CHAPTER 26   CONSUMER RIGHTS AND RESPONSIBILITIES   **439**

Cooperative Learning Debate (Pro/Con)

Consumer groups in some states propose that electric utilities monopolies should be opened up to competition from private providers so that consumers can shop around for electricity in the same way they comparison shop for long-distance telephone service. Opponents say that open competition would cause utility stock prices to drop and that cheaper power prices could lead to increased use of electricity, which would add to air pollution. Have groups of students choose a side of the issue to research and debate. After groups have presented arguments, have them decide the outcome of the debate. Take an informal poll to find out whether anyone changed his or her mind as a result of the debate.

Refer to the *Cooperative Learning Strategies* booklet for additional cooperative learning strategies.

Discuss

Discuss with students the kinds of skills people in the transportation and public utilities field use. Ask students what courses in school could help them prepare for entry-level jobs in transportation and public utilities. How do people advance in such careers?

Transportation and Public Utilities

Almost every waking moment of our lives is dependent on some form of transportation or public utility. At home, at school, at work—or on our way—we're all quietly supported by a host of workers in these industries. They keep the energy humming along electrical lines and water flowing through pipes. They help convey us safely, comfortably, and efficiently from coast to coast or just across the city. They distribute raw materials to factories and deliver the finished goods. They also help us find ways to conserve our resources and reduce hazards in the environment. In short, these workers make just about everything in modern life happen.

Although careers in transportation and public utilities range from repairing broken gas mains to assembling airline tickets for travelers, most entry-level positions are open to people with a high school education. Utilities and transportation companies usually train their beginning staff on the job or in more formal classroom settings.

For utility workers, a good background in math and science is often a key to success and advancement.

HELP WANTED

SURVEYING TECHNICIAN
City Engineering Department has opening for surveying technician. High school diploma with strong math background, especially geometry and trig, required. Technical school courses a plus. Applicant should be computer literate, able to visualize/compare shapes and sizes, like working outdoors, be in good physical shape. Long hours sometimes required.

Opportunities to advance to chief of surveying parties or even licensed land surveyor through experience and additional course work.

Learning Activity

The effects of regulations for automobile safety belts, air bags, antilock brakes, food and drug labels, and lead in gasoline are responsible for the prevention of injury and the loss of life. Have students choose one of the above-mentioned topics, or another of their own choosing, and research why regulations were implemented and what effects the regulation has had on consumer safety. Have students present their research in a 200-word report.

toys, and other items will not harm consumers. For example, new drugs must be tested and proved safe before they may be prescribed for the general public. Certain tools and appliances must have safety devices for your protection. Products that could be dangerous if used improperly have instructions that tell consumers how to use the product safely and correctly.

The Right to Be Heard

Consumers who have complaints about products or services have a right to be heard. Suppose that you buy a bike helmet from a store. After wearing the helmet for several weeks, you find that the strap under your chin has become loose at the place where the strap is connected to the helmet. By letting the store know you are unhappy with one of their products, you give them the opportunity to fix the situation. The store manager could offer to order a new helmet or have it fixed for you. Businesses need satisfied customers in order to stay in business. If you are not satisfied, businesses generally want to hear about it and will try to fix the problem so they can keep you as a customer.

Enrichment Strategy

Tell students that manufacturers sometimes recall products that have been discovered to be unsafe. Have students check consumer magazines or a consumer-information site on the Internet for recall notices. Have them describe for the class the product being recalled, the problem with the product, and the procedure for getting the problem resolved.

No matter what the job, computer skills will be useful. The ability to read and observe accurately is necessary in all these jobs, where a mistake could mean snarled travel plans, a broken-down school bus, or a dangerous gas leak. Workers must also be able to communicate clearly and simply with colleagues and the public.

The importance of the services provided by transportation and utilities workers to the entire population can be a great source of job satisfaction. In return, their jobs call for dedication, a sense of responsibility, and trustworthiness. Electrical company employees and the people who keep airports operating must often work long hours in bad or unpleasant weather. Occasionally the work is dangerous. Transportation and utility employees who meet the public face to face must maintain a positive attitude—sometimes under stressful conditions.

For examples of beginning jobs, check the help wanted ads shown here.

Follow Through

Remind students that transportation and public utilities are services that consumers use. Have groups of students gather information for a consumer guide they will design and produce about one of your local utilities. Groups can describe how natural gas, water, or electricity gets to consumers. They may also want to include ideas for saving money and conserving the resources utilities provide.

There are always some businesses that do not operate in the best interests of the consumer. They may place a high price tag on an item and then mark it down to give the impression that the item is "on sale." They may also try a tactic known as **bait and switch,** in which a store advertises a low-priced item in order to lure customers to the store. Once the customers are in the store, the salespeople attempt to get the customers to buy a more expensive item. There are laws to protect consumers from misleading and unfair business practices. You can turn to a number of government or consumer organizations for help. These will be discussed in the next chapter.

The Right to Have Problems Corrected

Sometimes products do not work properly after you buy them. Usually if you take a defective item and your receipt back to the place you purchased it, the business will replace the item or refund your money. Services, too, are not always up to par. For example, say you take a cassette player to a repair shop because tapes keep getting jammed in it. The shop fixes it, you pay the bill, and two days later the problem recurs. You should

Connection to CHAPTER 27

Inform students that in Chapter 27 they will learn about the agencies, organizations, and individuals they can turn to if they have consumer complaints that cannot be remedied through the usual channels. Invite students to name any governmental or nongovernmental organizations with which they are familiar that work on behalf of consumers.

CHAPTER 26 CONSUMER RIGHTS AND RESPONSIBILITIES **441**

Curriculum Connection — Math

Miguel went to Ibex Cycle Shop to buy a pair of Mundane brand bicycle shorts that had been advertised for $19.99. Bart, the salesperson, informed him that they were sold-out of Mundane shorts but that King of the Mountain brand shorts, which were priced at $27.99, were on sale for 30 percent off and that they were really a much better product. Have students calculate the sale price of the King of the Mountain shorts and then ask if Bart was using bait-and-switch tactics on Miguel. (No. On sale, King of the Mountain shorts are actually slightly cheaper than Mundane shorts. $27.99 \times .30 = \$8.40$. $27.99 - \$8.40 = \$19.59$.)

For students who need to sharpen their math skills, choose among the worksheets in the *Math Skills Review* booklet.

Building Business Skills

Model

Have students look at the three sample memos that point out the main ideas. Ask students to focus on the "Policy Statement" memo. Explain that an implied main idea is probably the most difficult to identify. Show students that each of the statements in the memo is about employees' interactions with customers. Ask volunteers if they can deduce the main idea. (In our store, customers must always be treated well.)

Learning Activity

Have students write a sample complaint letter to a manufacturer about a defective CD player. Tell students that discs played on the player are nearly inaudible even when the volume is turned up to the maximum. Students should include the following information in their letters.

- The name of the product, the nature of the problem, and the measures taken so far to correct it.
- The action that should be taken to correct the problem and the time allowed for fixing the problem.
- Copies of receipts and any other documents connected with the problem.

COMMUNICATION

Identifying Main and Subordinate Ideas

The main idea may be directly stated in a sentence, or it may not be stated at all. If it is stated, it can be located anywhere in the communication. Subordinate ideas, or details, can accompany the main idea. They are ideas whose purpose is to tell more about the main idea.

Explanation

You'll communicate with other people constantly during your career. You will receive many written communications such as memos or procedure statements. You'll always need to understand the main idea quickly. You'll need to sort out the main idea and the details that support it.

Practice

Study the sample of business communications in which the main and subordinate ideas have been identified. Then read the memo to all employees about smoking in the workplace. Write its main idea on another sheet of paper. List the subordinate ideas below the main idea.

complain about the repairs performed by the shop. If you have a reasonable complaint, the business will usually try to help you. Many large businesses, especially department stores, have customer service departments to handle complaints and correct problems. If a business refuses to correct a problem, you can write to the manufacturer of the defective product or contact a consumer-interest group (government or private) to find out how to get the problem resolved. Being able to clearly and concisely communicate your problem will speed up having your problem resolved.

The Right to Consumer Education

Consumers have the right to learn how our market system works. Consumers should be able to get the best value and the greatest satisfaction from the goods and services they purchase. When you decide to buy an item, you should know that different stores may charge different prices for the same item. You can comparison shop to find the best deal. Checking the information required by law on labels and fact sheets educates con-

442   UNIT 8   CONSUMERS IN THE GLOBAL ECONOMY

Cooperative Learning Co-op Co-op

Have teams choose a type of product to research. Then have team members visit stores and check catalogs and consumer magazines to collect information about prices and different brands or models of the product. Have team members organize all the information in a chart and agree on which product they would buy and where they would purchase it. Have them explain to the class how they did their research and why they made the decision they did.

Refer to the *Cooperative Learning Strategies* booklet for additional cooperative learning strategies.

BUSINESS COMMUNICATIONS

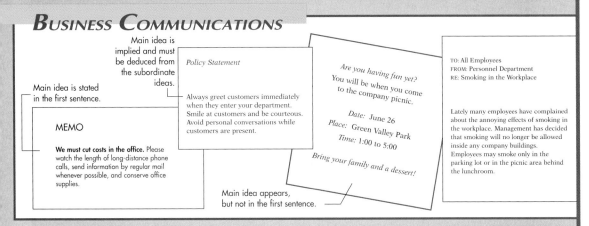

Main idea is stated in the first sentence.

MEMO

We must cut costs in the office. Please watch the length of long-distance phone calls, send information by regular mail whenever possible, and conserve office supplies.

Main idea is implied and must be deduced from the subordinate ideas.

Policy Statement

Always greet customers immediately when they enter your department. Smile at customers and be courteous. Avoid personal conversations while customers are present.

Are you having fun yet? You will be when you come to the company picnic.

Date: June 26
Place: Green Valley Park
Time: 1:00 to 5:00

Bring your family and a dessert!

TO: All Employees
FROM: Personnel Department
RE: Smoking in the Workplace

Lately many employees have complained about the annoying effects of smoking in the workplace. Management has decided that smoking will no longer be allowed inside any company buildings. Employees may smoke only in the parking lot or in the picnic area behind the lunchroom.

Main idea appears, but not in the first sentence.

Understanding what the communication is really about will help you decide what action you need to take and how quickly you need to take it. It will help you file the communication away for future reference—in your file cabinet or in your mind.

sumers about products they are thinking of purchasing. Schools offer consumer education classes. There are also magazines such as *Consumer Reports* and organizations whose goal is to provide consumers with information so they can make educated purchases.

Quick Check

1. What are the six basic consumer rights?
2. Define *consumerism* and *bait and switch*.

YOUR RESPONSIBILITIES AS A CONSUMER

With consumer rights come responsibilities. If information about a product is available, you have the responsibility for reading and using that information. Figure 26-1 on page 444 summarizes major consumer rights and responsibilities.

Reteaching Strategy

Have students practice writing a business memo to employees about upcoming training sessions for the company's new computer system. Students should be sure to include time, place, and topic in their memos. Have students trade memos with a partner. Partners should circle the main idea of the memo or write it at the bottom of the memo if the main idea is implied. Have partners get back together and make any improvements the memos may need.

Practice

Have students read the "Smoking in the Workplace" memo. Then have them write down the main idea and list the subordinate ideas below it. (Main Idea: Smoking is no longer allowed in company buildings. Subordinate Ideas: Employees have complained. People can smoke only in the parking lot or the picnic area.)

Quick Check Answers
1. The right to be informed, to choose, to safety, to be heard, to have problems corrected, to consumer education.
2. All the activities and measures that protect consumers' rights; a tactic in which a store advertises a low-priced item and then attempts to sell customers a higher-priced item.

Develop Concepts

Your Responsibilities As a Consumer

Consumers have rights, but it is the consumer's responsibility to exercise those rights. Ask students to think of times they have exercised their rights. Have students look at Figure 26-1 on page 444. For each right and responsibility, have volunteers give some specific examples illustrating each point.

CHAPTER 26

Use Visuals

Allow time for students to read through the information provided in Figure 26-1. Organize the class into six groups. Assign one of the consumer responsibilities to each group. Have groups work out a role-play in which they demonstrate their assigned consumer responsibility.
Answer to caption: Responsibility to use products safely.

Learning Activity

The Newspaper Association of America reports that advertisers place a high value on newspapers as a way to deliver product information to consumers. Point out that advertisements are only one way of finding out about products. Have students brainstorm other consumer information that could be found in newspapers. (Information about safety or other laws affecting consumers; product recall information; articles about new products and new technology.)

CONSUMER RIGHTS AND RESPONSIBILITIES

Consumer Rights	Consumer Responsibilities
1. *Right to be informed.* Consumers should be provided with the facts needed to make informed choices and be protected against unfair or misleading advertising, labeling, or sales practices.	1. *Responsibility to be informed.* Consumers should compare and evaluate information on different brands and models of products.
2. *Right to choose.* Consumers should have access to a variety of goods and services at competitive prices.	2. *Responsibility to choose carefully.* Consumers should use their buying power to encourage ethical business practices and safe and reliable products.
3. *Right to safety.* Consumers should be protected against goods that are hazardous in any way.	3. *Responsibility to use products safely.* Consumers should use and maintain products as recommended.
4. *Right to be heard.* Consumers should be assured that their interests will be considered in the making of laws.	4. *Responsibility to speak out.* Consumers should keep themselves informed on consumer issues and should report any safety problems with a product to the manufacturer or the proper government agency.
5. *Right to have problems corrected.* Consumers are entitled to quick and fair remedies for consumer problems.	5. *Responsibility to seek remedy.* Consumers should inform businesses when their products and services do not measure up to expectations.
6. *Right to consumer education.* Consumers should be taught how to get the greatest satisfaction and value for each dollar.	6. *Responsibility to learn consumer skills.* Consumers should take advantage of opportunities to develop consumer skills.

FIGURE 26-1

Each consumer right has a corresponding responsibility. What responsibility comes with a consumer's right to safety?

The Responsibility to Be Informed

Responsible consumers know what they are buying. They read the label on every food product to find out what ingredients it contains. They examine nutrition information listing carbohydrate, protein, fat, vitamin, cholesterol, sodium, and sugar content.

Before making a major purchase, responsible consumers check it out. They consult consumer magazines and sources such as the Fact Sheets put out by the government's Consumer Product Safety Commission to find out how the product is rated in terms of safety, performance, and value.

The Responsibility to Choose Carefully

Responsible consumers make comparisons to find the best product or service at the best price. Which stereo company offers the best guarantee? Which cars have the best record for reliability? What computer will best fit your budget and your needs? Taking the time to make comparisons pays off for

444 UNIT 8 CONSUMERS IN THE GLOBAL ECONOMY

Reteaching Strategy

Review students' ability to become informed consumers by asking them how they would find out about each of these purchases: a VCR, a container of yogurt, a computer, and a business suit. Make a chart on the board and have volunteers explain what information they would want to find out and how they would obtain that information.

responsible consumers. They can examine the options and prices and then make an educated choice.

Price and product are not the only thing consumers should be concerned with. Consumers today demand that businesses operate in an ethical and socially responsible way. If a manufacturer adds to the pollution problem by using excess packaging for its products or has a hiring policy that is unfair to women and minorities, the consumer may choose not to buy that manufacturer's products.

One of the most serious concerns facing consumers is the effect that buying patterns have on the environment. Individuals have the right to drink pure water, breathe clean air, and live in a healthful place. However, the environment has been threatened in recent years. The waste from the products that we have made as well as what we have done with those products has caused the **pollution,** or contamination, of our air, water, and land. Most air pollution comes from the exhaust fumes put out by cars and trucks. Figure 26-2 below shows the proportion of air pollution produced by various sources.

At one time, it seemed that the United States had boundless resources. Over the years, however, the population grew and filled up much of the available space. The demands of people also increased. It became clear that we must conserve our natural resources. **Conservation** is the preservation, protection, and planned management of our natural resources. We are faced with a limited supply of many resources and must deal with that issue.

Part of conservation is learning to avoid waste. Consumers can start reducing, reusing, and recycling in their daily pur-

F.Y.I.

In Phoenix, AT&T used its own telecommunications technology to help solve air pollution caused by automobile emissions. It set up a program that enabled 134 state employees to "telecommute." By working at home one day a week, those employees, in six months, drove 100,000 fewer miles—preventing 1.9 million tons of air pollution. They also saved almost 4000 hours of commuting time, thus increasing their job efficiency.

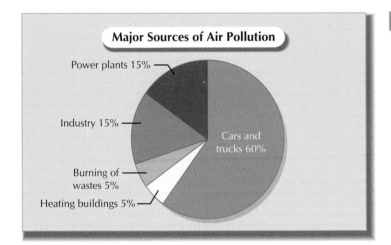

Major Sources of Air Pollution

- Power plants 15%
- Industry 15%
- Cars and trucks 60%
- Burning of wastes 5%
- Heating buildings 5%

FIGURE 26-2

Air pollution caused by cars and trucks, power plants, industry, the burning of waste materials, and the combustion of fuels for heating buildings is a serious threat to our environment. What source produces the most air pollution?

CHAPTER 26   CONSUMER RIGHTS AND RESPONSIBILITIES   **445**

Global Perspective

Citizens of Heilbronn, Germany, agreed to be part of an air-pollution experiment during the summer of 1994. Only cars with special pollution-control devices were allowed to enter the city, and most diesel trucks were banned. After only four days, certain air pollutants decreased by about half. Such experiments may eventually lead to new air pollution regulations in Europe. Have students research some of the other pollution problems facing the European Union. Ask them to write an essay explaining how various governments are attempting to deal with the issues. Topics could include: acid rain, depletion of the ozone layer, climate change, or water pollution.

Refer to the *International Business Strategies* booklet for additional strategies and activities.

CHAPTER 26

USE VISUALS

Have students look at the photo for a few moments. Then ask students to recall that trees are a *renewable resource.* Many resources, however, are nonrenewable. Because nonrenewable resources cannot be replaced once they have been used, conservation methods for nonrenewable resources are crucial. Have students name some ways nonrenewable resources can be conserved.
Answer to caption: Answers will vary.

Business Brief

Today nearly two-thirds of American consumers say that they're willing to pay 10 percent more to buy environmentally friendly products. Areas of the country with the largest concentrations of buyers of environmentally friendly products are: Alaska, California, the Chicago metropolitan area, and New England.

Learning Activity

To comply with consumer safety laws, manufacturers provide purchasers of washing machines with instruction booklets for the safe operation of the units. Tell students that a manufacturer is keeping up its end of the bargain by supplying the booklet. Ask students to identify the consumer's responsibility. (To read and follow the instructions for the safe operation of the machine.)

These young people are planting trees in their local park as one way to conserve natural resources. What are some ways your community conserves resources?

Business & SCIENCE

Most people assume that trash deposited in landfills decomposes into soil. Unfortunately, the trash and the soil covering it combine to keep out moisture and air, which otherwise would allow bacteria to decompose the trash.

chases. **Recycling** involves collecting products for processing so that they can be used again. Many communities have programs to collect newspapers and other paper products, plastic and glass bottles, and aluminum and steel cans.

The Responsibility to Use Products Safely

The government has passed many laws designed to make clothing, food, drugs, cosmetics, toys, and other items conform to certain safety standards. However, consumers must follow the instructions given by the manufacturer for safe use of the products. For example, it is your responsibility to read the label of a cold remedy to find out the recommended dosage. You should also use common sense when handling or storing potentially dangerous chemical cleaning products or electrical devices.

Safety problems can also arise if you buy products from an unreliable source. Some businesses may not be able to provide satisfactory proof that the product you are buying is safe. If you have doubts about the safety of a product a business is selling, do not buy it. In addition, you should contact a consumer protection agency and inform the agency of the situation.

446 UNIT 8 CONSUMERS IN THE GLOBAL ECONOMY

Cooperative Learning 👥 Planning a Lesson

Have teams of students draw up a lesson plan for teaching a group of younger students how to develop good consumer skills. Encourage teams to think of examples and visual aids they could use to help teach some of the concepts.

Refer to the *Cooperative Learning Strategies* booklet for additional cooperative learning strategies.

The Responsibility to Speak Out

As a consumer, you have the responsibility to express your opinion about businesses and their products. Responsible consumers can help improve the policies and products of the businesses they patronize. Consumers can speak out by writing letters to newspapers and magazines, telling others, and, most importantly, letting the company know they do or do not approve of the company's products or policies.

Consumers do have control in the marketplace. Consumers can let a company know that they do not like the way a company does business when they **boycott,** or refuse to buy, its products or services. When a large number of consumers boycott, it can have a very negative effect on a company's business. The company usually responds by changing its policies. In 1994 a consumer-interest group announced that most movie-theater popcorn was popped using large quantities of coconut oil. The group also let consumers know that coconut oil is a saturated fat, which raises cholesterol levels. Consumers immediately began requesting that theaters stop using the unhealthful oil. Theater-chain operators, who earned about $550 million a year from popcorn sales and feared a consumer boycott, quickly switched to canola oil, which is lower in saturated fat.

Business & HISTORY

In the 1800s in Ireland, a landlord named Charles C. Boycott would not lower rents. His tenants refused to have anything to do with him. Activities like theirs bear his name to this day when people *boycott* a product, service, or company they disapprove of.

Until recently, only a small number of food products were low in fat or cholesterol. Today, food companies produce a wide variety of goods that contain low or reduced fat and cholesterol. What do you think caused food companies to change?

Business Brief

Canned tuna producers have been the target of boycotts because tuna fishers used nets that entangled and harmed dolphins. Tuna canning companies responded by changing the way they caught tuna. They made sure consumers knew they had remedied the problem by labeling tuna as "dolphin safe."

Learning Activity

Allow students some library time to research boycotts of the last several years and have them choose one to research more thoroughly. Ask students to find out when the boycott started, how the business being boycotted responded, and whether and how the boycott ended. Have each student give a brief oral report for the class.

USE VISUALS

Have students study the photograph for a few moments. Ask students if they check labels when buying food items. Ask what they look for when they check labels and how the information on the label influences their decision to buy the product.

Answer to caption: Many of today's health-conscious consumers want to limit the amounts of fat and cholesterol in their diets and prefer to buy products that are not high in fat and cholesterol.

Enrichment Strategy

Encourage interested students to collect newspaper and magazine articles from consumer publications that illustrate how consumers influenced businesses to change their policies or improve their products. Have students make a "Consumers Speak Out!" bulletin board to display their articles.

Learning Activity
Ask students to discuss products that broke or malfunctioned shortly after they bought them. Have volunteers describe how they sought to have the problem resolved. Did the store where they made the purchase correct the problem or did students have to seek other help? What was the final solution?

Quick Check Answers

1. To be informed, to choose carefully, to use products safely, to speak out, to seek remedy, to learn consumer skills.
2. Consumers refuse to buy a company's products or services because they oppose something about the way the company does business.
3. Read information on labels and packaging; compare prices and look for sales; consult local media to become aware of illegal practices or scams; acquaint yourself with consumer information and resources; attend consumer issue workshops or classes.
4. The preservation, protection, and planned management of our natural resources; reprocessing used products so they can be used again; the contamination of air, water, and land.

It is also a consumer's responsibility to report unfair and illegal business practices to agencies concerned with protecting consumer rights. Reporting these practices helps protect other consumers from having problems with such businesses.

The Responsibility to Seek Remedy

Because part of being a good consumer is getting the best value for your money, you must be compensated for products that are defective. If you plan to exchange an item or get a refund, it is your responsibility to bring with you the item, the receipt, and any warranties or guarantees that came with the item. You should clearly explain the problem and tell the staff at the store how you expect them to fix the problem. If you follow this procedure, and the store cannot give you a satisfactory remedy, you will need to write to the manufacturer or contact a consumer-interest organization for help.

The Responsibility to Learn Consumer Skills

There is a remarkable amount of information available to consumers. It may be a bit overwhelming to think of trying to research every purchase you make. However, wise consumers follow a few simple tips:

- Read information provided on labels and packaging.
- Compare prices at different stores and look for sales.
- Consult local media to become aware of illegal practices or scams.
- Acquaint yourself with consumer information publications and other consumer resources.
- Attend classes or workshops focusing on consumer issues and problems.

Quick Check

1. List six consumer responsibilities.
2. What is meant by a *boycott*?
3. What are some things a person can do to develop good consumer skills?
4. Define *conservation, recycling,* and *pollution.*

Meeting Student Diversity

Some students are unable to recall words they have heard. To reinforce the chapter terms, create some sentence completion exercises on a tape recorder. Record the definition for each word in a partial sentence. Leave a pause where the student is to complete the sentence. The student can either record the answer on the tape recorder for independent practice, review responses with a partner, or write the answers.

Chapter 26 **Summary**

Main Ideas

1. Consumers' basic rights include the right to choose, the right to be heard, the right to be informed, the right to safety, the right to have problems corrected, and the right to consumer education.
2. Consumers are responsible for being informed, choosing carefully, using products safely, speaking out, seeking remedies for problems, and learning consumer skills.
3. Consumers can conserve resources by conserving energy, avoiding waste, and recycling. They can try to follow the guidelines of consumption: reduce, reuse, and recycle.
4. The main idea of a business communication is supported and explained by the subordinate ideas.
5. People who work in transportation and public utilities jobs need good communication, computer, and observational skills. In addition, math and science skills will help utility workers advance their careers.

CASE ANALYSIS Consumer Issues

The following action could be taken to solve a consumer problem. Choose among the lettered options that illustrate the pro/con viewpoints. Write your answers on a separate sheet of paper.

Action
Initiate pollution standards for the nation that are higher than those required in other nations.

Pro/Con Viewpoints
a. Businesses will become less competitive in the world market.
b. Pollution has caused many problems in society including sickness, premature death, and destruction of property.
c. Production costs for business owners will rise and will be passed on to consumers in the form of higher prices.
d. The United States has always been a world leader in protecting the environment.

CLOSE

Main Ideas
Main Ideas summarizes the key information in the chapter. It is a useful tool for reinforcement and review.

CASE ANALYSIS
Case Analysis provides a chapter-related case for student analysis and application of decision-making skills.

Answer
Pro: b and d; Con: a and c.

QUICK QUIZ

1. Name the six basic consumer rights. (Rights to be informed, to choose, to safety, to be heard, to have problems corrected, to consumer education.)
2. What six responsibilities do consumers have? (Responsibilities to be informed, to choose carefully, to use products safely, to speak out, to seek remedy, to learn consumer skills.)
3. What is a boycott and what can it do? (Consumers refuse to buy a company's products or services because they disagree with the company's policies; it can cause a company to change its policies.)
4. What three things can you do to help conserve resources? (Reduce, reuse, and recycle.)

Chapter 26 **Review**

Answers

Use the Language of Business
1. boycott, 2. bait and switch, 3. pollution, 4. recycling, 5. consumerism, 6. conservation.

Review What You Learned
1. The right to choose, the right to be informed, the right to be heard, the right to be safe, the right to have problems corrected, and the right to consumer education.
2. The first place you should go is to the store where you purchased the item.
3. Reduce, reuse, and recycle.
4. Consumers can organize a boycott.
5. The responsibilities to use information correctly, choose carefully, use products safely, speak out, seek remedies for problems, and learn consumer skills.
6. Subordinate ideas give additional information about the main idea.
7. Math and science skills are helpful for utility workers.

Understand Business Concepts
1. Consumer rights are what people are entitled to; consumer responsibilities are the actions people must take to deserve those rights.
2. Consumers are responsible for following the safety recommendations given by the manufacturer of the products they purchase.
3. Answers will vary depending on the community.
4. Consumers can read labels, consumers' magazines, and information from the government's Consumer Product Safety Commission.

Use the Language of Business

When dealing with consumer rights and responsibilities, it is important to know the following terms. See how well you know them. Complete each sentence with the correct term.

bait and switch consumerism
boycott pollution
conservation recycling

1. The consumer group decided to _____ the food-processing company because of its policy toward workers.
2. When a business advertises a bargain price for an item and then tries to get customers to buy a higher-priced item, it is using the _____ tactic.
3. Auto emissions cause air _____.
4. An important way to conserve resources and reduce the problem of solid-waste disposal is by _____.
5. _____ consists of the activities and measures that protect consumer rights.
6. _____ is the preservation, protection, and planned management of our natural resources.

Review What You Learned

1. What are your basic consumer rights?
2. Where would you go first if you had a problem with an item you purchased?
3. What are some basic consumer guidelines for conserving resources?
4. How can consumers pressure companies to change their policies?
5. What responsibilities do you have as a consumer?
6. What is the purpose of subordinate ideas?
7. What skills are especially helpful for utility workers who want to advance their careers?

Understand Business Concepts

1. What are the differences between consumer rights and consumer responsibilities?
2. Why is safely using products a consumer's responsibility?
3. Describe an environmental problem around your community. List your responsibilities to help solve the problem. What actions could be taken?
4. How can consumers be well informed?
5. How can consumers reduce their use of limited resources?
6. How could you prepare for a career in transportation and public utilities?
7. Why is it important to learn how to identify the main idea of information you hear or read on the job?

5. They can make wise buying decisions and refuse to buy things that are wasteful.
6. By finishing high school, having a good background in math and science, and learning computer skills.
7. Understanding the main idea will help you decide quickly how you need to respond.

Think Critically
1. Answers will vary depending on the area.
2. Answers will vary depending on the labels.
3. Answers will vary depending on the community.

Chapter 26 **Review**

Think Critically

1. **Explain.** Compile a list of sources for consumer information in your city or local area. Then describe how a person would use each of the sources.
2. **Classify.** Bring five labels from various types of appliances to class. What types of information are provided on the labels? What other information is needed or would be helpful?
3. **Recommend.** What measures could your community take to conserve resources?

Use What You Learned

1. **Group Project.** Devise and then conduct a survey with your team members to find out about the environmental awareness of local stores and businesses. Each team member could survey a different business using the team's survey questions. Your survey could include some of the following questions:

   • What methods do you use to conserve resources?
   • Do you recycle? What items?
   • Do you encourage consumers to use reusable bags or offer recycling for plastic or paper bags?
   • Do you use energy-conserving heating and cooling equipment?
   • Did consumers' wishes influence your conservation measures?

   Compile your group's findings in a written report and share it with the class.
2. Go to a supermarket and find a product that you think has too much packaging. Explain how the packaging is wasteful. How would you reduce the packaging on the product so it was not so waste-ful? Sketch the product. Describe the packaging and give your analysis.
3. Investigate the rules your community has established for the responsible disposal of waste. Some examples of things to research include how to handle yard waste; how to sort recyclables; and how to dispose of potentially hazardous substances like motor oil and household chemicals. Make a class poster listing your community's rules.
4. **Computer Application.** Survey five different local stores (department, hardware, computer, clothing, books, shoes, and so forth) regarding their returns policies. Then use word processing software to compile the information in an attractive table format. Print out the results of your survey and share it with the class.
5. **Skill Reinforcement.** Suppose you bought a defective product from a local store and needed to return it. Write a plan of action for getting the problem corrected. Flesh out the main idea of your plan with subordinate ideas that explain the details of the situation.

Save your work in your Business Portfolio.

Use What You Learned

1. Make sure all students participate in the group project. Rubrics: Survey; Essay.
2. Students may choose to compare and contrast the packaging of similar items if they wish. Rubrics: Illustration; Paragraph.
3. Remind students that water and air need to be considered when disposing of waste. Rubrics: Note Taking; Poster.
4. Students who don't have access to a computer may make their tables manually. Rubrics: Survey; Charts and Tables.
5. Plans will vary but should reflect a logical approach. Rubric: Paragraph.

Independent Practice

Use the Chapter 26 worksheets in *Student Activity Guide 2* for additional practice and application activities. *Student Activity Guide 2* provides vocabulary exercises, reading comprehension checks, problems, projects, and simulations of business and economic situations. A Teacher's Annotated Edition provides answers.

ASSESS

Portfolio Assessment

The portfolio projects are designed to lead students to develop a collection of their best work to submit to you for assessment. You and your students should decide which projects will be included in their respective Business Portfolios. Refer students to the specific rubric(s) from the *Alternative Assessment Strategies* booklet listed with each of the project notes below. These rubrics will alert students to the criteria you will use to assess their projects.

Chapter Assessment

Use the Chapter 26 Test from the *Test Masters* booklet to evaluate students' understanding of the chapter concepts. An answer key is provided. Or create your own customized test using the *Testmaker* software.

FOCUS

Introduce the Chapter

Major Concepts
- Federal Consumer Protection Agencies
- State and Local Consumer Protection
- Private Consumer Protection Organizations
- How Consumers Can Handle Problems

Introduce the Topic
Ask students to brainstorm a list of potential consumer problems. Ask what they would do about each problem. Tell students that in Chapter 27 they will learn about the federal, state, local, and private agencies that have been established to protect consumers.

Use Business Terms
Have students look at the Business Terms and brainstorm associations with each term. Ask them where they have heard or seen the terms used. Reinforce correct associations. Advise students to note the meanings of the terms as they read the chapter.

USE VISUALS
Explain to students that government regulations offer consumer protection. Ask: If this new stove doesn't work properly, what can the purchaser do? (Possible answer: Request a replacement; request service to make it operate properly.)

CHAPTER 27

Business terms

consumer advocate

recall

grade label

license

refund

small claims court

452

CHAPTER 27 RESOURCES

Instructional Resources

Lesson Plan for Chapter 27

Teaching Transparency 27-1

Strategies and Worksheets for Teaching Transparency 27-1

Enrichment Master 27-1

Student Activity Guide 2–TAE for Chapter 27

Test Master for Chapter 27

Alternative Assessment Strategies

Math Skills Review

International Business Strategies

Cooperative Learning Strategies

Communication Skills Review

Ethics in Business Strategies

Protecting Consumers

Learning objectives

After completing this chapter, you will be able to:
- Identify various consumer protection sources at the federal, state, and local government levels.
- List some of the major private consumer organizations and explain what they do.
- Describe actions a consumer might take to handle a problem.
- Relate what one entrepreneur did at her company to ensure customer satisfaction.
- Identify several sources from which to obtain current business-related information.

Consider what you know

- Consumers have basic rights including the right to choose, to be heard, to be informed, and to have problems corrected. In addition, consumers are responsible for being informed, choosing and using products safely, and seeking solutions for problems.

Consider what you want to know

- How do government agencies protect consumers' rights?
- What are some non-governmental agencies that help consumers?
- What should consumers do if they have a problem or complaint?
- How can a small business owner keep customers satisfied?
- Where can you find current information about business issues?

Consider how to use what you learn

- As you read this chapter, listen to news broadcasts to learn about pending consumer legislation or consumer issues in your community.

CHAPTER 27   PROTECTING CONSUMERS   **453**

Motivate the Learning

Learning Objectives
Point out to students that the learning objectives show what they will learn in the chapter. Tell students to keep these objectives in mind as they work through the chapter. Note that the last two objectives listed refer to the Focus on Entrepreneurs feature and the Building Business Skills feature.

Consider What You Know
Review briefly the main sections of *Chapter 26 Consumer Rights and Responsibilities:* Your Rights As a Consumer and Your Responsibilities As a Consumer.

Consider What You Want to Know
Ask students to read the questions, then page quickly through the chapter to get an idea of how the chapter will help them discover answers.

Consider How to Use What You Learn
Explain to students that at the end of the chapter they will develop some projects that involve consumer issues in your community. Point out that consumer issues and the organizations that fight for consumer rights are often the subjects of news stories.

Multimedia Resources

Technology Resource Guide

Distance Learning Guide

Internet Resource Guide

Professional Resources

School-to-Work/Tech Prep Strategies

Instructional Poster

Spanish Resources

Testmaker Software for Chapter 27

The Wall Street Journal Video Series
  Video & Activities for Chapter 27

Business and Marketing Computer
  Applications—An Integrated Software
  Simulation Using Microsoft Works

Stocktracker—A Stock Market Software
  Simulation

Where's the Dough? Board Game

TEACH

Develop Concepts

Federal Consumer Protection Agencies

Bring in some grade labels from packages of meat or egg cartons. Pass the labels around the class and then ask students why they think the federal government has established certain standards for food and other products.

What do you do if the inexpensive watch you purchased at a discount store doesn't work? What if the store will not replace the watch?

What do you do if you've paid for a sweatshirt ordered from a TV ad but you never received the sweatshirt? What if the sweatshirt company says the shirt was sent weeks ago? What can you do? Where can you turn?

There are many agencies, organizations, and individuals who work to promote the health, safety, and honest treatment of the public. Legislators at the national, state, and local levels have passed laws that establish rules and regulations to protect and inform consumers. In addition to the government agencies, there are many non-governmental organizations that work on behalf of consumers. Even businesses themselves offer avenues for consumer complaints and concerns.

In this chapter, you will learn about many of the organizations that act as **consumer advocates,** champions on the side of consumers' rights.

FEDERAL CONSUMER PROTECTION AGENCIES

The federal government can take different kinds of action to protect consumers. For example, a number of executive branch cabinet departments oversee agencies that deal with protecting consumers. Alternatively, legislators can pass laws designed to protect consumers and then establish agencies charged with enforcing those laws. Figure 27-1 on page 455 lists some federal consumer protection agencies and tells how they help consumers. Notice that not all of the agencies have the word *consumer* in their names.

The ways in which these agencies enforce consumer protection laws may differ from one agency to the next. Drugs, for example, cannot enter the marketplace without FDA approval. The Consumer Product Safety Commission has the right to remove unsafe products already in the marketplace. The National Highway Traffic Safety Administration may require automobile manufacturers to **recall,** or take back and fix, automobiles with dangerous defects.

Enrichment Strategy

Explain to students that the Food and Drug Administration (FDA) is known for thorough but sometimes slow studies of new drugs and health aids. Sometimes the FDA recalls medications that have been approved or does not approve medications that consumers would like to see approved. Have students do research on a drug or medical device that has been withdrawn from the market or one that is yet to be approved. Students should write up their findings and present the information to the class as a three-minute news report.

FEDERAL CONSUMER PROTECTION AGENCIES

Agency	How It Helps Consumers
U.S. Department of Agriculture (USDA)	Establishes and maintains standards of quality in nation's daily food supply by inspecting and grading meat, fish, dairy products, and produce. Ensures that food production is sanitary.
Food and Drug Administration (FDA) under the direction of the Department of Health and Human Services	Establishes and maintains purity and safety standards for foods, drugs, and cosmetics. Researches and tests new health and drug products. Inspects food and health aid plants. Ensures accurate labeling. Allows safe products on market and removes unsafe ones.
National Highway Traffic Safety Administration under the direction of Department of Transportation	Sets requirements for motor vehicle safety, maintenance, and fuel economy. Tests vehicles and other automobile-related products for compliance. Studies ways to save fuel and increase highway safety. Investigates consumer complaints about vehicle safety.
Consumer Product Safety Commission	Promotes safety in the marketplace by protecting the public from unreasonable risk of injury from products. Sets safety requirements and tests products. Forbids production and sale of unsafe products. Conducts research and education programs.
U.S. Postal Service	Enforces laws against fraud by mail. Acts on complaints from individual consumers. Helps consumers recover money. Provides information on common mail fraud schemes.
Federal Trade Commission	Promotes free and fair competition by enforcing laws and regulations against false or unfair advertising, business practices that cheat and trick consumers, misleading or illegal labeling and packaging. Protects consumers from violations of credit laws.
Consumer Information Center Program	Provides catalog of government publications on topics of interest to consumers.

Some agencies, such as the Federal Trade Commission, are responsible for a wide variety of rules and regulations governing business practices. Other federal organizations may set and maintain standards of quality. The Department of Agriculture, for example, grades foods such as meats and gives them **grade labels,** labels that indicate levels of quality, to help consumers judge the products.

FIGURE 27-1

The federal government has established organizations to protect consumers from unsafe products and dishonest business practices. Which two organizations help keep the food you eat safe?

Quick Check

1. What two federal agencies are concerned with the safety of food?
2. Which federal agency tests products before they go to market?
3. Define *consumer advocate, recall,* and *grade label.*

Reteaching Strategy

Develop Concepts

State and Local Consumer Protection

Since the 1950s, consumer protection has been part of the duties of state governments. States have standards and regulations that apply to any business operating within their borders. Many cities also have enacted legislation that protects consumers—for example, rules regarding the rights of tenants and landlords. Ask students why they think certain consumer protection regulations like these are handled by state or local governments instead of the federal government.

Learning Activity

Public utilities are often in the news. Have students find and bring to class copies of articles about any of your local utilities. Display the articles on a class bulletin board. As a class, identify consumer issues discussed in the articles.

Learning Activity

Continuing education is part of the licensing requirement for many occupations. Ask students why states would require people such as physicians, architects, and building contractors to periodically return to school. (To make sure they learn the newest techniques and to ensure they continue to be qualified to do their jobs.)

STATE AND LOCAL CONSUMER PROTECTION

In Germany, government agencies, various experts, and an independent jury work together to award products a *Blue Angel* mark. The label is awarded to products which, while not necessarily perfectly safe, are less damaging to the environment than other competing products.

There are government-funded consumer affairs or protection offices all over the country at every level of government. Legislators at the state and local levels pass laws or ordinances to protect consumers as well as to help consumers with problems or complaints. In some states, the office of the attorney general handles consumer affairs.

In each state, a public utilities commission regulates the rates of public utilities—companies that provide electricity, gas, and water. In some areas, this includes local telephone service. Utilities are legal monopolies, that is, companies operating without competition. The public utilities commission protects consumers from unfair prices a utility might charge. A utility's request for a rate increase is usually followed by a public meeting. At that meeting, individual consumers and consumer advocate groups have a right to speak out. The commission listens to both sides before making a decision. In a similar way, state insurance commissions control and approve insurance rate increases.

Another protection for consumers comes from a state department sometimes called Weights and Measures or Division of Standards. This agency is responsible for checking scales, packages, gasoline pumps, and labels to insure true weights and measures. A short weight or measure of a product is less than the amount indicated by the scale, package, or gasoline pump. If short weights are being given on products, inspectors from the Department of Weights and Measures have the authority to remove the products from the market.

State governments also work to protect the public from unfair marketplace practices such as false advertising. They may have laws regulating such matters as credit card interest rates and procedures for estimating car repairs. Most states regulate health care businesses. Many protect consumers in areas related to housing such as home rental, repairs, and mortgages.

To guard against unqualified people practicing certain occupations and professions, states issue licenses or permits through their Professional Regulation Department. A **license** gives a person the legal right to conduct a business or practice a profession. State licenses are required for hundreds of professions including those of physicians, architects, teachers, accountants, real estate salespeople, roofing contractors, funeral directors, hair stylists, and even professional wrestlers! Requirements for licensing vary with each occupation or pro-

Making Connections ▸▸   Everyday Living

Provide students with the following situation. Mariel bought three pounds of tomatoes from a local roadside farm stand. When she got home she weighed the tomatoes and found that she had only two pounds of tomatoes. She returned to the farm stand, but the farmer insisted his scales were correct and refused to do anything about the problem. Mariel suspects that the farmer is cheating customers by selling short weights. What should she do? (Possible answer: Because the roadside stand is local, it would not be governed by the FTC. Mariel could file a complaint with her state's department that regulates weights and measures, but it might be more expedient to choose a local consumer protection agency.)

One way government protects consumers is by requiring people practicing certain professions to be licensed. This hairdresser, for example, must have a license that ensures she has had proper training. What other kinds of professions need licenses in your state?

fession. Applicants may need technical training, advanced education, internships, or a passing grade on an exam to qualify.

Quick Check

1. What is short weight? What agencies protect consumers against short weight?
2. What is a professional license? How does it protect consumers?

PRIVATE CONSUMER PROTECTION ORGANIZATIONS

The government is by no means the only source of help for consumers. The telephone directory, under the heading *Consumer*, lists names of many non-government organizations involved with consumer welfare. These private, usually not-for-profit, organizations are dedicated to protecting consumer rights.

The Consumer Federation of America, one of the largest national consumer organizations, has about 50 million members. The Federation consists of national, state, and local non-profit groups that share a common interest in monitoring federal legislation affecting consumers. When Congress considers bills affecting consumers, the federation lets its members know. In addition to keeping members up to date, the federation

Business & SCIENCE

Sometimes government regulation has an economic effect that was unforeseen. In 1978, the Environmental Protection Agency (EPA) banned the use of fluorocarbons in aerosol products such as hairspray. Studies had shown that the fluorocarbons were destroying parts of the earth's protective layer of oxygen. Manufacturers replaced the aerosol spray can with the pump spray bottle. Since the pump bottle costs less to produce than the aerosol can, consumers ended up with a product that worked just as well but that cost less money.

Curriculum Connection   English/Literature

Have students read *The Jungle* by Upton Sinclair, *Unsafe at Any Speed* by Ralph Nader, *Silent Spring* by Rachel Carson, or *The Hidden Persuaders* by Vance Packard and report on the effect these books have had on consumer protection laws.

FOCUS ON **Entrepreneurs**

Discuss

Begin the discussion by having students describe the kind of business Kathy Prasnicki runs. Ask: How did she become an entrepreneur? (She worked as an accounting clerk for an oil company, worked her way up to sales representative, and then decided to start her own distributorship.) How successful is her company? (It is the top-ranking gasoline distributorship in Texas.)

Kathy Prasnicki— Sun Coast Resources

"**I** just take care of my employees," says Kathy Prasnicki, commenting on the success of Sun Coast Resources, the gasoline distributorship she founded and runs. For Prasnicki, taking care of employees means giving her gasoline truck drivers, who serve customers directly, higher wages and better fringe benefits than her competitors. She believes that happy, experienced drivers make for satisfied customers. "I think that's why we provide better service, because people truly like to work here."

Prasnicki also gives her employees every chance to move up to higher paying jobs. Anybody who shows the

potential for it can become a sales rep, where success means more money. When her daughter was born, Prasnicki created a nursery at the firm and opened its doors to all Sun Coast employees' babies.

Hard work is also part of Prasnicki's philosophy. She works 60 to 70 hours a week with few vacations. But she also tries to "work smart." For instance, she has saved a great deal of time by adopting a computerized system to double-check ledgers in the company's accounting department. "Every day I find cracks that have to be fixed, or ways to save time and money."

Prasnicki's approach must be working because her Houston-based enterprise does $200 million a year in business, making it the top-ranking gasoline distributor in the state of Texas. She has made it in a tough business where a woman might not expect to succeed as an entrepreneur. "Sometimes people in the business haven't

TEACHING TIP

Ask: Why do you think businesses are willing to organize and support organizations such as the Better Business Bureau?

Business Brief

There are more than 150 Better Business Bureaus in the United States. In the mid-1990s, they handled about ten million consumer questions a year. The questions were most often about retail businesses, home improvement companies, and service firms.

F.Y.I.

Consumer Reports magazine accepts no advertising and buys all the products it tests. The magazine has no commercial interest in promoting one product over another. Furthermore, it does not allow its ratings or the information from its reports to appear in advertisements. In several cases the magazine has taken legal action against companies that have ignored these rules.

also actively promotes or works against specific legislation. The National Consumers League is another organization that works for or against specific legislation that affects consumers' welfare.

A private, nonprofit organization called Consumers Union publishes the periodical *Consumer Reports.* Subscribers to the magazine are voting members of Consumers Union and can elect the organization's board members. Consumers Union tests and rates products and prints the results in the magazine. Consumers Union also publishes books and pamphlets on subjects of interest to consumers.

Local businesses support another well-known consumer protection agency, the Better Business Bureau (BBB). This nonprofit organization collects information on retail businesses, handles complaints about them, and distributes consumer information. If a consumer has a complaint against a particular business, the Better Business Bureau will try to help the consumer find a satisfactory solution. It will keep the complaint on record. The BBB cannot enforce the law and will not recommend one business over another. However, at the request of a consumer, the BBB will indicate whether it has received prior complaints about a business.

458 UNIT 8 CONSUMERS IN THE GLOBAL ECONOMY

Cooperative Learning Debate (Pro/Con)

Through bioengineering, scientists can manipulate a plant's DNA in order to alter some of the plant's traits and characteristics. Some results of bioengineering include the development of virus- and drought-resistant varieties of plants. The FDA approved selling these bioengineered plants in 1994. However, some ecologists and consumer groups claim that a more thorough examination of the potential risks of the technology should be conducted. Most plant breeders and the FDA maintain that bioengineered plants pose no new risks. Have groups of students choose a side of the issue, gather evidence, present arguments, and evaluate the outcome of the debate.

Refer to the *Cooperative Learning Strategies* booklet for additional cooperative learning strategies.

taken me seriously," she says, "but I'm not sure if it's because I'm a woman or because I'm young."

Kathy Prasnicki was raised in a working-class home in Brookeland, Texas, northeast of Houston. With no thought of becoming an entrepreneur, she earned money in high school by working as an accounting clerk for Jasper Oil Company. She enjoyed the job so much that she stayed on after high school. She worked her way up to sales representative for Jasper, then took the plunge and started her own gasoline distributing business.

For Kathy Prasnicki, success is a matter of taking care of business by taking care of employees. As she says of Sun Coast's nursery, "I think this kind of atmosphere helps us grow."

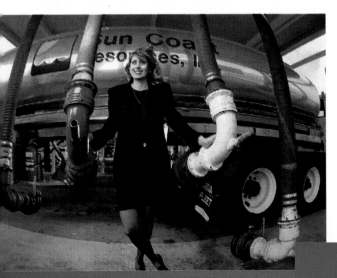

Follow Through
Ask students to describe how Kathy Prasnicki runs her business. What is her philosophy concerning her employees? (She believes in paying higher wages and offering better benefits than her competitors and offering employees the chance to advance within her company.) What is her personal philosophy? (She believes in working hard and "working smart.")

Some industries have consumer assistance panels. One of these is the Major Appliance Consumer Action Program (MACAP). This organization is set up to solve problems involving large appliances such as dishwashers, washing machines, dryers, stoves, refrigerators, and freezers. If the manufacturer is unresponsive to a complaint, MACAP will help.

Local radio and TV stations today often use the power of the press to right consumer wrongs. They may have a consumer advocate or a designated reporter who identifies and reports on consumer problems. The threat of adverse publicity is often enough to persuade companies to settle complaints. Consumer news programs help consumers learn about—and avoid— potential consumer problems.

Numerous large businesses offer consumer assistance. Many packages of consumer products—nearly everything from soup to nuts—list the address or telephone number of the consumer relations representative for that product. These representatives and departments may assist in replacing defective or unsatisfactory products. They also furnish consumer information, including how to get the most for your money with the company's products. Several consumer relations departments

Learning Activity
Provide some time for students to page through issues of *Consumer Reports* or other consumer publications. As a class, discuss how information in the magazines warns consumers against buying products or services that don't perform as advertised, aren't safe, and so on. Have students give specific examples.

Enrichment Strategy

Have students check the labels of shampoo, toothpaste, and packaged food products to find a consumer-relations representative telephone number or address. Have them request consumer information from the manufacturers. Display the information on a bulletin board and have students analyze the usefulness of the information. Decide if it genuinely helps consumers get the most for their money or if it's basically just advertising for the company's products.

Building Business Skills

Model

Arrange to have the class visit the school library. Make sure students know where to find reference sources and how to use them. Ask the librarian to talk to students about other useful references available in your library.

COMMUNICATION

Locating and Verifying Information

Explanation

As you perform your job, you'll rely on your colleagues and others in many ways. One of the most important things you'll depend on others for is to supply information you'll need to complete your own projects.

There are many ways to find or verify information. Some information, like last year's sales figures, will be available from your own company. For other kinds of information, you may rely on many of the same sources you use now for class projects, such as reference books, interviews, and computer services.

Make sure the sources you use are reliable and up to date. Check the copyright date of books or the issue date of periodicals. Verify your information whenever possible by cross-checking in another source.

Practice

How can you be sure you're getting accurate, up-to-date information? The Information Source Guide here suggests some sources of information. Read the guide, then use it to discover how to find the following information:

1. Population of your city.
2. Number of cars your favorite car manufacturer sold last year.

Quick Check Answers

1. Consumer Federation of America monitors consumer legislation; Consumers Union tests and rates consumer products.
2. A nonprofit organization that collects information on retail businesses, handles complaints about them, and distributes consumer information. The Better Business Bureau will try to help the consumer find a satisfactory solution to complaints against a business.

of large businesses provide booklets with consumer hints at little or no cost.

Quick Check

1. What services do the Consumer Federation of America and Consumers Union furnish to consumers?
2. What is the Better Business Bureau? How does it help consumers?

HOW CONSUMERS CAN HANDLE PROBLEMS

Although careful, informed consumers will usually be able to avoid problems, they sometimes do occur. More often than not, such problems are the result of individual error, not defective product lines or substandard business practices. As examples, a faulty product might not be caught by an inspector; a

Develop Concepts

How Consumers Can Handle Problems

Photocopy and distribute Enrichment Master 27-1 and direct students' attention to the section that deals with documentation of a purchase. Point out that when trying to solve a consumer problem, having well-documented facts about the problem is crucial to getting the problem resolved satisfactorily.

Global Perspective

Citizens of former Soviet-bloc countries have been confronted for the first time with the consumer issues associated with a market economy. Consumers in these countries do not have a wide choice of goods and services. Goods are often of poor quality, and counterfeit and unsafe products are often sold. Consumer protection legislation has not yet been established in most of the countries. Have interested students consult some of the sources listed in the Information Resource Guide in Building Business Skills on page 461 to find out about consumer issues faced by former Soviet-bloc countries. Invite students to prepare a report to share with the rest of the class.

Refer to the *International Business Strategies* booklet for additional strategies and activities.

INFORMATION SOURCE GUIDE

Interview. Interview an expert or a person who was directly involved in an event for a first-hand account. Try reaching people who live at a distance by phone or through a computer service.

Newspapers. Recent newspapers contain current information. Many newspapers, including the *New York Times* and *Wall Street Journal,* publish an index that lists articles by subject.

Magazines. Consult the *Reader's Guide to Periodical Literature* for general interest magazines. Search specialized indexes, such as the *Business Periodicals Index,* too.

Directories. Many specialized directories can have exactly the information you need. The Thomas Register of

American Manufacturers, for example, is published annually. You can find companies according to the product they manufacture, by the name of the catalog of their products, or listed alphabetically.

Atlases. Investigate certain kinds of facts and figures in an atlas. Be sure to use the latest edition.

Computer On-line Services. The amount and types of information available through a computer with a modem change daily. Keep up to date by consulting a local expert or reading about available services right on-line.

The United States Government. The Government Printing Office publishes free or inexpensive information about many subjects.

3. Names and addresses of two companies that manufacture a product or provide a service in a career field that interests you.

Practice
Have students find the answers to the three questions on pages 460 and 461, and make sure they note the source of information, page number, and the date of the source or the copyright. (Students' answers will vary, but answers in like categories should be similar.)

salesperson might make false claims about a product; or someone may make a mistake in billing.

If a consumer encounters a problem, he or she has not only the right, but also the responsibility to complain. A well-stated complaint could solve an individual consumer's problem as well as lead a business to correct something that might be a problem for future customers. Often the first and most effective step is to bring the complaint to the business in person along with receipts or other papers involved in the transaction. A valid complaint states the problem—along with a reasonable solution or remedy the business could provide—clearly, firmly, and courteously. For example, a consumer may wish to return a defective product and request a full **refund,** a return of the purchase price (plus sales tax if any) of the product. In most cases, businesses are willing to offer refunds or replacements, make repairs, or take other action in order to satisfy an unhappy consumer.

In some cases, however, a business may not be willing to meet a consumer's expectations. As a final means of securing their rights, consumers can decide to go to court. All states have

Connection to CHAPTER 26

Remind students that "the right to be informed" is a consumer right as they learned in Chapter 26. Ask students how consumer information from local radio and television reports and information available from consumer-relations representatives can protect consumers. Students should provide specific examples from their own experiences, if possible.

CHAPTER 27   PROTECTING CONSUMERS   **461**

Reteaching Strategy

Have students practice finding the following information and noting the source of their information. Have them cross-check the information by finding an additional source.

- Consumer ratings for a used car that is two years older than the current year (Magazines such as *Consumer Reports* or *Car and Driver,* on-line service.)
- The capital of Paraguay (Atlas, encyclopedia.)
- Names and addresses of two consumer organizations in your state (Directories, on-line service.)
- Tomorrow's weather forecast for Denver, Colorado; London, England; and Cairo, Egypt. (Newspapers, on-line service.)

What are some options open to consumers who happen to buy defective merchandise?

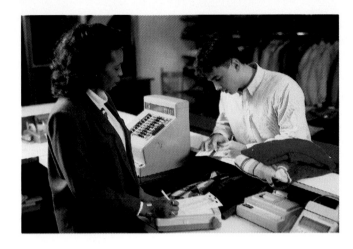

small claims courts that deal with minor legal matters up to a certain amount of money. In most states, a consumer may bring a case to court with little cost and without a lawyer. In fact, some states do not permit lawyers in small claims court. A small claims court can handle consumer problems over money or personal property. The limit of the claims varies from state to state and changes often, but can be as low as $25 and as high as $5,000.

Typical problems include tenant and landlord disagreements and consumers who have trouble with a product or service purchased from a business. Small claims courts also deal with warranties. A warranty is a promise that a product is of a certain quality or will perform in a certain manner. An expressed warranty specifically states in writing what the product is or what it will do. An implied warranty is one that is understood but not necessarily stated in writing. For example, an electrical appliance, even one sold without a written guarantee, should work when it is plugged in and turned on. Both expressed and implied warranties often become a matter of dispute in small claims court when consumers feel they have been cheated.

In some areas, legal aid societies provide legal assistance with consumer problems to people who have little money. People must meet certain requirements before they can use these services.

Quick Check

1. What is a *refund*?
2. Name three typical problems that might be taken to small claims court.

Global Perspective

Although consumer movements gained ground in some African countries in the 1990s, in general African consumers suffer from a lack of money, a lack of goods and services, and an unfamiliarity with consumer rights. In 1994, the International Organization of Consumers Unions opened its first African office in Harare, Zimbabwe. Have students choose a country in Africa and research the state of consumer rights and consumer protection in that country. How could the country benefit from the efforts of a consumers' union that unifies the whole continent? Have students share their findings with the class.

Refer to the *International Business Strategies* booklet for additional strategies and activities.

Chapter 27 **Summary**

Main Ideas

1. Federal consumer protection agencies, such as the Department of Agriculture and the Food and Drug Administration, monitor the quality of food, drugs, cosmetics, and health aids. The National Highway Traffic Safety Administration sets requirements for automobile safety. Other federal agencies promote safety in the marketplace and free and fair competition.
2. At the state and local levels, consumers may get help through consumer protection bureaus, the state attorney general's office, the public utilities commission, the bureau of weights and standards, and consumer affairs offices.

3. Organizations like the Consumer Federation of America monitor legislation concerning consumer protection. The Consumers Union tests and rates products available in the marketplace.
4. Consumers with a complaint about goods or services should first approach the business that provided the goods or services, explain the problem, and tell the solution they expect.
5. Entrepreneur Kathy Prasnicki, owner of Sun Coast Resources, believes that keeping employees happy is one way to ensure satisfied customers.
6. Periodicals, on-line services, and government publications are three sources of current business information.

CASE ANALYSIS — Consumer Protection

Testing by the FDA (Federal Drug Administration) of a new drug can take up to 10 years. First, a drug is used on animals. Then drug companies must pay for three phases of clinical tests on humans. In the first phase, healthy volunteers take increasing doses of the drug to judge its safety. In the second phase, the drug is tested on sick people who take the drug to check its side effects. In the third phase, sick people take the drug for three or four years to judge its long-term effects. Some people think the testing takes too long and argue that lives are lost while extremely ill patients wait for FDA approval. Others think the testing is necessary so that the drug can be safely used as an effective means of treating disease. What do you think?

CLOSE

Main Ideas

Main Ideas summarizes the key information in the chapter. It is a useful tool for reinforcement and review.

CASE ANALYSIS

Case Analysis provides a chapter-related case for student analysis and application of decision-making skills.

Answer
Students' opinions will vary.

QUICK QUIZ

1. What federal agency is responsible for the rules and regulations that govern business practices? (Federal Trade Commission.)
2. What government body regulates public utilities? (State public utilities commissions.)
3. How does Consumers Union provide information to consumers? (By testing and rating products and publishing the results in *Consumer Reports*.)
4. What are three consumer problems that might be resolved in small claims court? (Tenant/landlord disputes, unsatisfactory products purchased from a business, and warranty disputes.)

Chapter 27 **Review**

APPLY

Answers

Use the Language of Business

1. small claims court, **2.** consumer advocate, **3.** grade label, **4.** license, **5.** refund, **6.** recall.

Review What You Learned

1. Some agencies are part of the executive branch cabinets; other agencies are set up to enforce the consumer protection laws Congress passes.
2. The U.S. Postal Service provides information to consumers on common mail fraud schemes.
3. Meat, fish, and dairy. Grade labels help consumers judge the quality of products.
4. Utilities are legal monopolies that could control prices if not closely regulated.
5. Possible answers include: They regulate utility monopolies, license certain professions, and check scales, packages, and gasoline pumps to make sure consumer weights and measures are correct.
6. Possible answers include: Consumers Union, Better Business Bureau, local television and radio shows, and businesses' consumer relations departments.
7. She worked in the accounting department of an oil firm before starting her own business.
8. An index lists articles by their subject.

Understand Business Concepts

1. Consumers base many of their purchases on advertising claims; if these claims are false or misleading, consumers will be purchasing products that may not meet their needs.
2. The manufacturer should not be held responsible for damages caused by the user's carelessness or misuse. The second statement shows the manufacturer's good intentions to stand behind the product, even if the buyer moves away from the vicinity of the seller.

Use the Language of Business

Write the term that best matches each numbered definition.

consumer advocate   recall
grade label   refund
license   small claims court

1. Court that deals with minor legal matters up to a monetary unit.
2. Champion on the side of consumers' rights.
3. Label that indicates the quality level of a food.
4. Permit that gives a person the legal right to conduct a business or practice a profession.
5. Return of the purchase price of a product or service.
6. Manufacturer's action to take back a product for repair or replacement.

Review What You Learned

1. How are federal consumer protection agencies established?
2. How does the U.S. Postal Service protect consumers?
3. What types of products are graded by the U.S. Department of Agriculture? How do its grade labels help consumers choose products?
4. Why are public utilities closely regulated?
5. Give three examples of the ways in which state and local governments protect consumers.
6. Name several additional sources of consumer help besides government agencies.
7. What background did entrepreneur Kathy Prasnicki have when she started her own business?
8. How can an index to a newspaper help you find information?

Understand Business Concepts

1. The Federal Trade Commission monitors advertising claims. How does this help consumers?
2. One warranty states: "This warranty does not cover damage resulting from accident, misuse, or abuse. The warranty covers products purchased and retained within the United States." Why does the manufacturer make these statements?
3. The new CD you purchased skips two of your favorite tracks each time it plays. What should you do?
4. Why do large companies have entire departments devoted to consumer affairs?
5. Why do you think the need for consumer protection has grown over time?
6. Some people say that the government should not be so active in consumer protection. What reasons do you think they might give for their opinions?

3. First go to the store where you purchased the CD and explain the problem. If the store clerk and manager do not help, take your complaint to the district or national sales manager. If that does not help, write to the CD manufacturer explaining the problem.
4. More goods and services are being offered in the marketplace. It would be impossible for individual consumers to know about all areas of product safety and performance.
5. It is a response to consumer demand for information and is good for public relations for getting out information about the quality of the good or service being sold.

6. Some people believe that consumer protection is not an area of government responsibility and that government involvement is expensive and inefficient. Competition is a form of consumer protection in a market where there are a number of suppliers of a product.
7. Employees are encouraged to move to higher-paying jobs. Prasnicki also offers higher wages and better benefits than her competitors.
8. The copyright indicates when the material was published and is an indication of the age of the information contained in the publication.

7. What are some of the ways in which Sun Coast Resources takes care of its employees?

8. What can a copyright date tell you about the information in a book, atlas, or periodical?

Think Critically

1. **Assess.** Some people argue that consumers are intelligent enough to make wise choices in buying goods and services and do not need all of the protection that is provided. Others say that consumer affairs offices and government agencies are needed for consumer protection. With which side do you agree? What points support your side?

2. **Explain.** Some industries feel that government regulations should be abol-ished and that the industries should be self-regulating, establishing their own guidelines, standards, and regulations. How can consumers influence indus-tries to enforce their own guidelines and regulations?

3. **Apply.** Why do you think manufactur-ers of food, drugs, and cosmetics are required to have their products checked by the Food and Drug Administration?

Use What You Learned

1. **Group Project.** Work in teams of four students. Choose a product that a team member or family member has found unsatisfactory. Prepare a short presen-tation showing how to complain about the product or service. Be sure your presentation includes:

   • Description of how to approach the business where the goods or services were purchased;
   • Sample letter describing the problem and a possible solution, and
   • Private, state or local, or federal con-sumer advocate or agency that might handle the complaint.

2. Study an issue of *Consumer Reports* or *Consumers' Research Magazine*. List the types of products that are reported. Write a summary of the kinds of infor-mation provided about each product and indicate how you might find the information.

3. **Computer Application.** Choose from your local newspaper an advertisement for a product or service. Note any spe-cial claims, incentives, or time limits. Contact the seller/supplier/vendor to verify the information in the advertise-ment. Using word-processing software, write and print out a one-paragraph critique of the advertisement from the point of view of a consumer.

4. **Skill Reinforcement.** Find out how to receive a free copy of the brochure *Subject Bibliography Index* from the Government Printing Office and get one. When you receive the brochure, put it in your Business Portfolio to use in future information searches.

Save your work in your Business Portfolio.

Business Issue

Business Issue

COST OF ENVIRONMENTAL REGULATIONS

Highlight the Issue

Before students read pages 466–467, explain that cost-benefit analysis is an evaluation of a plan based on how its costs compare to its benefits. Ask students if they think environmental regulations should be evaluated this way. Why or why not?

COST OF ENVIRONMENTAL REGULATIONS

Over the past 25 years, the federal government has passed many regulations designed to protect the environment. Because so many of these regulations affect business, business leaders, legislators, and others have called for the government to use cost-benefit analysis to assess the value of environmental regulations. Cost-benefit analysis would be used to determine whether the benefits of environmental regulations outweigh the costs to government, businesses, and consumers. Should environmental regulations have to pass the test of cost-benefit analysis?

Pro

Cost-benefit analysis will help weed out excessive regulations that overburden businesses and limit economic development. When regulations cut too deeply into business profits, people lose their jobs and the entire economy suffers. For example, one Pennsylvania steel company had to shut down part of its operations to comply with the Clean Air Act. This put hundreds of employees out of work. According to one congressional leader, regulations cost the private sector about $500 billion each year. Since many business costs are ultimately passed along to consumers, this works out to about $10,000 a year for a family of four.

Costly regulations make it hard for U.S. businesses to stay competitive in the global market. Some businesses may decide regulations are so burdensome that they will take their operations to other countries where there is less regulation. This will mean that even more U.S. workers will lose their jobs.

Many environmental regulations are unreasonable. For instance, the EPA fined one company $5000 just for entering information on the wrong line of a form. Property owners have been arrested for building on wetlands, which according to the government's overly broad definition includes lands that are under water for just 11 days a year.

Other regulations are unnecessary or based on faulty science. Often the risk to the environment is greatly exaggerated, as in the case of acid rain. Such regulations have cost businesses millions of dollars, for questionable benefits.

Cost-benefit analysis will lead to more reasonable environmental regulations and help make government agencies accountable to businesses and consumers.

Extend the Issue

Write on the board the quotation from the text "Protecting the health of the American people cannot be reduced to a game of numbers." Ask students to agree or disagree with this statement. Have students form groups according to their opinions. Instruct groups to gather evidence to develop their argument for or against. Have groups that hold opposing views debate the issue. As a class, discuss and evaluate the outcomes of the debates.

Update the Issue

Suggest that interested students find out how environmental regulations that have been in effect for several years are working. Are the regulations having the desired effect? How costly are the regulations? Have students share their information with the class, and then discuss whether the costs compare favorably with the benefits of the regulations.

Con

Business profits are not the only factor to consider when evaluating environmental regulations. Protection of the environment is also a worthy goal and a popular one. A 1995 Time/CNN poll found that 88 percent of Americans think environmental protection is very important. In response to another question, only 23 percent think that anti-pollution regulations go too far.

If environmental regulations are subject to cost-benefit analysis, many important safeguards will be lost. According to the Environmental Protection Agency (EPA), if cost-benefit rules had been in place years ago, the agency would not have been able to ban lead from gasoline or prohibit the use of dangerous pesticides like DDT.

Without environmental regulations, the environment would be in even greater danger than it is today. It took regulations such as the Clean Water Act to force industry to stop polluting lakes, rivers, and streams. Despite their costs to businesses, such regulations benefit all Americans.

Many environmental problems, such as global warming and pollution, affect the entire world, not just the United States. The U.S. government needs to be able to make and enforce regulations to comply with international agreements in order to address these problems.

Cost-benefit analysis is an unfair test of environmental regulations. How do you weigh the cost of anti-pollution devices against the health of children who will develop asthma unless air pollution is reduced? As one EPA administrator has said, "Protecting the health of the American people cannot be reduced to a game of numbers."

Regulations are not always bad for business, either. New companies, products, and markets can also arise as a result of regulations. For example, because of environmental regulations, a new industry in environmental equipment and services has begun to flourish.

Requiring cost-benefit analysis will simply bog down government agencies in useless paperwork, delaying the passage of important environmental regulations.

Unit 9 Using Credit to Buy Goods and Services

Chapter	Learning Objectives
28 **Credit: A Promise to Pay** **pp. 470–483**	• Describe the nature of credit. • Discuss the advantages and disadvantages of using credit. • Name various sources and types of credit. • Explain how and why businesses and governments use credit. • Describe how using observation to draw conclusions can help you solve problems. • Explain how expert systems help businesses make decisions, including whether to accept your credit cards.
29 **Getting and Keeping Credit** **pp. 484–497**	• Name the three factors creditors examine when determining your credit rating. • Discuss how installment and cash loans work. • Describe what is meant by the cost of credit. • Explain how to manage credit and avoid credit problems. • Calculate finance charges. • Name jobs in wholesale and retail trade and explain how communication skills are used in those jobs.
30 **Credit and the Law** **pp. 498–511**	• Explain why federal and state governments have passed credit legislation. • List federal laws that protect consumers. • Discuss how credit protection laws are enforced. • Identify ways of handling credit problems. • List some tips for ethical business behavior. • Describe several methods a business can use to maintain the electronic security of its computer information system.
Business Issue:	**The Public Debt, pp. 512–513**

National Standards for Business Education*	Chapter Highlights			
	Focus on Features	Building Business Skills	Visual Learning	Case Analysis
COMM: II B; *EPF:* X A (Buying on Credit), XII; *IS:* III	Technology: Expert Systems, p. 474	Analysis: Drawing Conclusions, p. 478	Public Debt of the United States, p. 480	Consumer Credit, p. 481
CD: II A; *COMP:* VI F; *EPF:* X A (Buying on Credit)	Careers: Wholesale and Retail Trade, p. 490	Math: Computing Finance Charges, p. 492	Credit Application, p. 487 Security Agreement, p. 488	Consumer Credit, p. 495
BL: II C, VI D; *COMM:* V E; *EPF:* XIII A, XIII C, XIII D	Technology: Electronic Security, p. 504	Employability: Exhibit Ethical Behavior, p. 506	Maximum Interest Rates Charged for Credit Cards, p. 501 Truth-in-Lending Disclosure, p. 502 Credit Regulators, p. 508	Consumer Credit, p. 509

* Level 3 Performance Expectations: Business Law (BL), Career Development (CD), Communications (COMM), Computation (COMP), Economics and Personal Finance (EPF), IS (Information Systems). See page T14 for all 12 content areas.

Unit 9

Look Back

Remind students that smart consumers use techniques such as comparison shopping to ensure that they get the most for their money. Smart consumers also know their rights and responsibilities as consumers. Many agencies, both governmental and nongovernmental, work to promote the health, safety, and honest treatment of consumers.

UNIT 9 COOPERATIVE LEARNING PROJECT

Make and Defend Activity

Preparation: Before beginning the project, have students collect samples of credit card applications and advertisements from mailings, newspapers, or magazines. Have students place the applications and other materials in a folder to serve as a class resource file. For each group, make photocopies of BLMs 19 and 20 from the *Cooperative Learning Strategies* booklet. This project will take approximately one class period.

Using Credit to Buy Goods and Services

This unit discusses the role of credit. The first chapter describes types of credit. The next chapter discusses the mechanics of applying for a loan, either in the form of money or of goods and services. The final chapter discusses ways to handle credit problems and federal laws regulating credit.

Look Ahead
Explain that people can obtain goods and services on credit by using a credit card or taking out a loan. Using credit allows people to purchase items and use them immediately. However, it is more expensive to buy things on credit, and if credit is not used responsibly, a person's credit rating can be damaged. In our society it is important to establish and maintain a good credit rating.

469

Guidelines: Have students work in groups of three or four. Assign each group one of the consumer credit situations outlined in BLM 19. Have each group use the resource file to research credit options and decide which credit card would be the best choice for its scenario. Groups can use BLM 20 to record and organize their findings. Then have groups defend their choice in a presentation to the class.

CHAPTER 28

FOCUS

Introduce the Chapter

Major Concepts
- The Nature of Credit
- Where to Go for Credit
- Credit and Business
- Governments and Credit

Introduce the Topic

Ask students to list the words they think of when they hear the word *credit*. List their responses on the board or a transparency. Then ask them to compare their list to the Business Terms for Chapter 28. Point out that in this chapter they'll learn how credit fits into our economic system.

Use Business Terms

Ask students to write a sentence with each of the Business Terms. Have students exchange papers with a partner. Call for agreement/disagreement as to use of the terms and an explanation of that position. Tell students to note the meanings of the terms as they read the chapter.

USE VISUALS

Explain that when people use a credit card they are promising to pay later for what they receive now. Ask: Do you think most people buy more with credit than they would otherwise? Why do you think so?

Business terms

credit

creditor

debtor

consumer credit

commercial credit

credit rating

charge account

installment payments

big-ticket items

credit limit

470

CHAPTER 28 RESOURCES

Instructional Resources

Lesson Plan for Chapter 28

Teaching Transparency 28-1

Strategies and Worksheets for Teaching Transparency 28-1

Enrichment Master 28-1

Student Activity Guide 2–TAE for Chapter 28

Test Master for Chapter 28

Alternative Assessment Strategies

Math Skills Review

International Business Strategies

Cooperative Learning Strategies

Communication Skills Review

Ethics in Business Strategies

Credit: A Promise to Pay

Learning objectives

After completing this chapter, you will be able to:

- Describe the nature of credit.
- Discuss the advantages and disadvantages of using credit.
- Name various sources and types of credit.
- Explain how and why businesses and governments use credit.
- Describe how using observation to draw conclusions can help you solve problems.
- Explain how expert systems help businesses make decisions, including whether to accept your credit cards.

Consider what you know

- Federal, state, and local governments have passed laws to protect consumers, whether they are buying goods with cash or credit.

Consider what you want to know

- Who are the two parties in a credit arrangement?
- What are the advantages and disadvantages of using credit?
- What are the different types of credit?
- Why do businesses and governments use credit?
- How can the ability to observe situations and draw conclusions from them help you at school and at work?
- How can computer software help guard against fraud?

Consider how to use what you learn

- As you read this chapter, consider ways in which credit can be useful. When is it a good idea to use credit? When should you avoid using credit? Why?

Multimedia Resources

Technology Resource Guide

Distance Learning Guide

Internet Resource Guide

Professional Resources

School-to-Work/Tech Prep Strategies

Instructional Poster

Spanish Resources

Testmaker Software for Chapter 28

The Wall Street Journal Video Series
Video & Activities for Chapter 28

Business and Marketing Computer Applications—An Integrated Software Simulation Using Microsoft Works

Stocktracker—A Stock Market Software Simulation

Where's the Dough? Board Game

TEACH

Develop Concepts

The Nature of Credit

Ask students whether they have ever bought an item and then found they didn't really want it after all. Discuss how marketing and advertising encourage people to "buy now—and pay later." Have students discuss how easy credit buying might encourage poor consumer habits.

TEACHING TIP

To help students grasp the concept of commercial credit, ask students to think of reasons a small business, such as a restaurant, video store, or doctor's office, might need to obtain credit.

Buying an item now and paying for it later can be an easy and convenient way to make a purchase. Consumers use credit to buy everything from a tank of gasoline to a new car. How does buying on credit work? What are the advantages and disadvantages of using credit?

In this chapter, we will examine different types of credit and discuss their advantages and disadvantages.

THE NATURE OF CREDIT

Credit is the opportunity to obtain money, goods, or services now in exchange for a promise to pay in the future. The one who lends the money or provides the credit is called the **creditor.** The one who borrows the money or uses the credit is called the **debtor.** Because it involves a promise to pay, credit is based on the creditor's confidence that the debtor can and will make the payments. In other words, credit is a matter of trust.

Credit is used by individuals, businesses, and governments. Credit that is used for personal reasons is called **consumer credit.** Credit that is obtained for business purposes is called **commercial credit.** Governments also use credit to provide goods and services for their citizens.

Why Use Credit?

Every year, consumers in the United States purchase goods and services worth more than $750 billion on credit. Why is the use of credit so widespread? Many people like the convenience of buying on credit. They can shop and travel without carrying large amounts of cash. Also, credit can be especially useful in an emergency. Someone may suddenly need to buy a new washing machine or pay to have a car repaired. Buying on credit involves trade-offs. If you buy a new washing machine on credit, you can use the washing machine immediately and can stop going to the laundromat. However, it is more expensive to buy the machine on credit because of the interest charges you must pay.

For very expensive items, such as cars and houses, people frequently need to spread the payments for the item over the lifetime of the item. Suppose a family buys a van that costs $20,000. They expect to keep the van for five years. While they are paying for the van over a period of five years, they are, of

---

Cooperative Learning   Group Discussion

Help students see the positive uses of credit by asking them to imagine our economy without credit. Divide the class into groups and have them think about how people would purchase large appliances, cars, and houses, or pay for a college education if they could not use credit. Have groups come up with several ideas. Bring the class back together and have a member of each group share the group's ideas with the class.

Refer to the *Cooperative Learning Strategies* booklet for additional cooperative learning strategies.

course, using the van. At the end of five years the van will be worth only $8000. Over five years the family will get about $2400 of use out of the van each year. By spreading payments out, each payment is roughly equivalent to the value the family gets by being able to use the van within the time period for which the payment is made.

Advantages of Using Credit

One of the advantages of buying on credit is that you can use the item while you are still paying for it. For example, you can wear your new coat before you have saved up enough money to buy it. A family can live in their new home while they are paying for it. An individual can take advantage of a special promotion on multimedia computer systems without having the money right now.

Another advantage of buying on credit is that you establish a credit rating. A **credit rating** is a measure of a person's ability and willingness to pay. The factors that determine a person's credit rating are income, current debt, information about a person's personal life, and how debts have been repaid in the past. A good credit rating is desirable because it indicates to creditors that you have paid your debts in the past and that you have the ability to pay future debts.

A third advantage is that you don't have to carry around large sums of money to pay for major purchases. For many people this is a great safety and convenience factor in using credit.

Credit also contributes to the growth of our economy. If you can use credit, your ability to buy goods and services increases. Since so many consumers make credit purchases, businesses must hire more workers and produce more goods to keep up with the demand.

Disadvantages of Using Credit

The availability of credit has its disadvantages as well. If a person shops only at stores where he or she has credit accounts, that person will not be able to take advantage of sales or lower prices offered by other stores. Some people cannot resist the temptation to buy things they do not need or cannot afford. As the credit payments pile up, these people may begin to have trouble meeting their obligations. Late or missed payments may lower their credit rating, which will make it difficult for them to obtain credit in the future. If they cannot meet their obligations, the losses to the business are added costs of doing business, which increases prices for other consumers.

Business Brief

Researchers have identified that about 46 percent of American households have a significant amount of outstanding debt on their credit cards. Two groups of people, in particular, maintain high credit card balances: young, single people who live in cities such as Boston, New York City, and Los Angeles, and white-collar suburbanites who dine out often and take expensive vacations.

F.Y.I.

It's estimated that, by the year 2000, there will be 125 million credit card-holders in the United States. These cardholders will spend $1.1 billion using bank, oil company, phone, retail store, and travel and entertainment credit cards.

TEACHING TIP

Note that a credit rating includes records of a person's past loan and credit card payment histories, as well as information about payment of current accounts. For example, several late payments on a car loan two years ago can negatively affect a person's current credit rating.

Reteaching Strategy

Review the advantages of using credit with a comparative chart, listing the pros and cons of using both cash and credit. Add to the chart throughout the discussion of the chapter.

FOCUS ON **Technology**

Discuss

Ask students to explain what an *expert system* is. (Computer software that manipulates and combines the knowledge that a human expert would have in the same subject.) Have students explain why credit card companies use expert systems. (To cut down on fraudulent use of credit cards.) Ask students to name other applications for expert systems. (Physicians and airlines might use expert systems.)

Quick Check Answers

1. The opportunity to obtain money, goods, or services immediately in exchange for a promise to pay in the future; the one who lends money or provides credit; the one who borrows money or uses credit; credit used for personal reasons; credit obtained for business purposes; a measure of a person's ability and willingness to pay.

2. Advantages: a person can use an item while still paying for it; a person can establish a credit rating. Disadvantages: a person may be tempted to buy things on credit that he or she cannot really afford; a person may damage his or her credit rating by missing payments.

Expert Systems

A cashier accepts a customer's credit card, and swipes it through a card reader. A few electronic chirps and beeps later a receipt is printed. The customer signs the receipt and leaves with his or her purchases—usually. This time the cashier hands the nearby phone to the customer. After a short conversation, the receipt appears, and the customer signs. Who was on the phone? What did they talk about?

A credit card, like many other forms of identification cards, carries a small strip of magnetized plastic tape. One side of the tape is coated with a magnetic material, usually iron oxide. The tiny particles of iron oxide are organized in a magnetic pattern. The card reader the cashier uses reads the magnetic pattern embedded in the plastic strip and sends the information to a computer. Software in the computer recognizes that pattern as the account number assigned to a specific customer: name, address, phone number, and so on.

This is just the beginning of the software's role in the purchase. In an effort to eliminate fraud, many credit card companies use an expert system. An *expert system* is computer software that manipulates and combines the knowledge that a human expert would have in the same subject. The software is designed to imitate the decisions that would be made by such an expert.

The expert system used by credit card companies relies on databases as well as some logic operations. Once the customer is identified, the system checks the database to determine that the card and the account's payments are current and that the card is not reported stolen. The system continues checking—reviewing the

Another disadvantage of using credit is that credit costs money. Creditors charge a fee for loaning you the money to make a purchase. The fee is based on the interest rate that the creditor charges and increases the total amount you pay. For example, a television set may cost $350 if you pay cash for it. Purchased on credit at 18 percent interest, with payments spread over two years, the finance charge could increase your total cost to more than $419.

Even though the use of credit has its disadvantages, most consumers feel its benefits outweigh the potential problems. The key, of course, is to use your credit wisely. Understanding how credit works can help you make responsible decisions.

Quick Check

1. Define *credit, creditor, debtor, consumer credit, commercial credit,* and *credit rating*.
2. Name two advantages of using credit and two disadvantages of using it.

Global Perspective

Have students work in groups of four to research the kinds of consumer credit used in various countries in the Eastern Hemisphere (Europe, Asia, Africa, and Australia) and Western Hemisphere (North, Central, and South America). See that each group chooses a different country. Suggest that groups include information about restrictions on the use of personal consumer credit and also the effect of credit use on saving. After each group presents its information, have the class discuss whether Americans could learn some credit lessons from other nations.

Refer to the *International Business Strategies* booklet for additional strategies and activities.

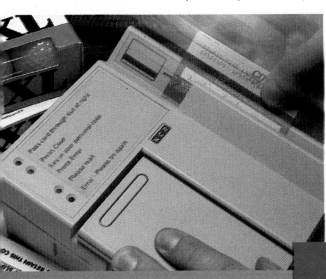

customer's purchase patterns to determine whether the current purchase fits the customer's profile.

For example, if a customer's clothing purchases have been limited to T-shirts and jeans, the system is designed to question a fur coat purchase and alert a service representative. The representative may interrupt the sale and ask to speak to the customer. After a few questions and answers, the service representative may be satisfied that the customer is the authorized card user and approve the sale.

In other businesses, expert systems sift through highly detailed databases to help users narrow the field of possibilities. For example, a medical expert system can compare hundreds of symptoms as well as medical histories to help a physician diagnose an illness. Airlines, too, have developed expert systems to help determine the most cost-efficient use of an airport's terminal gates.

Follow Through

Ask students if they think expert systems could replace human experts. Why or why not? Ask students to name some potential disadvantages to using expert systems in retail stores. (Possible answer: If an expert system detects the possibility of fraud, the checkout process gets slowed down; customers could become angry.)

WHERE TO GO FOR CREDIT

Many kinds of credit are available from a number of different sources. Long-term credit is available from lending institutions, such as banks and credit unions. Long-term loans are used for large purchases, such as houses and businesses, and are paid back over a period of more than five years. Short-term credit is offered by many institutions. Charge accounts and credit cards are examples of short-term credit. Short-term credit is usually repaid in fewer than five years. The risk a creditor takes in lending money or selling on credit is one of the most important factors in determining the cost of credit. Consumers who have a good credit rating will usually pay less than those who have a poor rating. In general, the lower the risk, the lower the cost of obtaining credit.

Lending Institutions

Financial institutions such as commercial banks, savings and loan associations, credit unions, and savings banks offer

Develop Concepts

Where to Go for Credit

Ask students to imagine that they need money quickly and that the only way to get the amount they need is to borrow it. Direct them to name all the places people could go to borrow the money. Record students' ideas on the board and ask them to offer opinions about the various options. Photocopy and distribute Enrichment Master 28-1 and have students compare the information provided by the master with the ideas on the board.

Enrichment Strategy

Have students interview an officer or manager in a credit union or savings and loan about the services offered. Topics they could explore in their interview include the advantages and disadvantages there are to using the services of a credit union or savings and loan compared with using those of a commercial bank. Have students summarize their interviews in a written report.

Business Brief

On-line shopping has increased the use of credit cards to a certain extent, since it is impossible to use cash when ordering something electronically. The Electronic Business Co-op has developed a simplified plan for making transactions over the Internet, and reports that the most popular commodity sold in cyberspace is pizza!

Learning Activity

Have students visit businesses such as clothing stores, department stores, and gas stations to collect charge account applications. Have students make a display of the applications, and allow time for students to study the display. Ask students what they think the creditors are trying to determine by asking for certain kinds of information.

BUSINESS & HISTORY

The Bank of England was chartered in 1694 to make loans to the British government. The bank advanced more than one million pounds to the government. In exchange, it received certain privileges, such as the right to issue money. The Bank of England is sometimes known as The Old Lady of Threadneedle Street. This is because its main office is located on a London street by that name.

long-term credit. They will loan specific amounts of money to people for stated purposes. Many people purchase expensive items by obtaining a loan. The main advantage of a loan is that you can get the loan from a financial institution and buy the item from a different business. That way you can shop around for the loan with the lowest fees. You can also shop around, compare the prices of an item, and find the lowest price. Loans can be used to pay for cars, household improvements, vacations, educational expenses, medical bills, and more.

Consumer Finance Companies

Consumer finance companies specialize in loans to people who cannot get credit elsewhere. Consumers may have trouble borrowing from other sources if they do not have steady jobs or if they have a poor credit rating. The cost of a loan from a consumer finance company is higher than the cost of a loan from other sources, since this loan involves a greater risk. The interest rate a consumer finance company charges varies from state to state and can be more than 20 percent.

Charge Accounts

One of the most common types of short-term credit is the **charge account.** Customers who have charge accounts at a store can use their credit to "buy now and pay later." When the bill for the purchases arrives in the mail, the customer can pay some of or all of the amount owed. Many department stores, large chain stores, and some small stores offer charge accounts. There are three main types of charge accounts—regular, revolving, and installment.

- Regular charge accounts require that people pay for purchases in full within a certain period of time, usually 25 or 30 days. If the bill is paid on time, they do not have to pay interest. If they do not pay the entire bill, interest will be charged on the amount that has not been paid.
- Revolving charge accounts allow people to pay a portion of the amount owed each month. However, interest (usually 1.5 to 2 percent per month) is charged on the unpaid portion.
- Installment charge accounts permit people to pay for costly items with equal **installment payments** spread out over a period of time. Each installment payment includes part of the amount due on the purchase as well as part of the interest. Large home appliances, cars, and furniture are frequently purchased this way and are referred to as **big-ticket items** because of their high prices.

Making Connections ➤ Advertising

Tell students that there is a great deal of competition among credit card issuers and that advertising plays a large role. Some cards use direct mail to offer special introductory rates or credit protection services. Others use glossy ads in magazines intended to promote the prestige of using their card. Over a few weeks have students bring in credit card ads or offers. Have students evaluate the way cards are advertised. Are some of the offers actually good deals? How often do the ads and offers seem less appealing once students read the small print?

Most charge accounts combine both regular and revolving features. You have a choice of paying the entire balance and avoiding paying interest or paying only a portion of the money you owe and paying interest charges on the amount unpaid.

Credit Card Companies

Credit card companies issue cards that can also be used to buy goods and services on credit. These cards work like charge accounts, but some of the cards have annual fees, which may range from $25 to $80. Credit card companies earn money from the interest they charge. In addition, businesses that accept credit cards for purchases pay a certain percentage of the purchase price to the credit card company or bank that issued the card. When issuing credit cards to individuals, credit card companies set a **credit limit,** which is the maximum amount of purchases a person can charge at any given time. A person with a $1000 credit limit would not be able to charge more than that amount. Credit cards can be divided into three types: single-purpose cards, multipurpose or bank credit cards, and travel and entertainment cards.

- Single-purpose credit cards can only be used to buy goods or services at the business or branches of the business that issued the card. Single-purpose cards operate like revolving charge accounts. Each month you receive a statement listing all the purchases you made in the past 30 or so days. You can pay part or all of the total amount you owe. Credit cards issued by oil companies are examples of single-purpose credit cards. There is no annual fee for single-purpose cards.
- Multipurpose cards are also called bank credit cards because they are issued by banks. Multipurpose cards work like a revolving charge account. These cards may be used at many different stores, restaurants, and other businesses all over the world. MasterCard and Visa are examples of multipurpose cards. Customers may pay an annual fee of about $20, but many credit card companies have phased out the fee in order to attract more customers.
- Travel and entertainment cards are offered by companies that specialize in the credit card business. These cards usually operate like regular charge accounts. You must pay the full amount due each month. Cards such as American Express and Diners Club are examples. Typical annual fees for these cards range from $50 to $80. They are accepted worldwide for purchases connected with travel, business, and entertainment such as restaurant and hotel bills, car rentals, and airline tickets. Many people use these cards for more general purchases as well.

F.Y.I.

The first credit cards came into use in the 1920s. They were single-purpose cards issued by businesses, such as hotel chains and oil companies. In 1950 Diners Club introduced the first card that could be used at a variety of businesses. American Express introduced its card in 1958.

Learning Activity
Have groups make a "Consumers' Guide to Credit and Charge Cards" booklet. In the booklet they should explain the differences between regular, revolving, and installment credit. Encourage groups to use real examples and illustrations in their booklet.

Learning Activity
Have students take a survey of friends and relatives to find out what kinds of big-ticket items they have bought using an installment charge account. Record students' results on the board or a transparency and have students conclude which kinds of items are most frequently purchased using an installment charge account.

Business Brief

According to a survey conducted by American Express in late 1994, the percentage of businesses giving employees cash or travelers' checks to pay for their business-travel expenses declined from 30 percent in 1990 to 17 percent in 1994. Instead of giving employees cash, more companies are giving them corporate credit cards to pay for their business expenses.

Global Perspective

Consumer credit card debt in Japan has skyrocketed in recent years. One reason debt has increased is that interest rates charged by credit cards are very high. Have interested students research credit card use in Japan to find out other reasons credit card debt has increased. Have students summarize their findings in an oral report.

Refer to the *International Business Strategies* booklet for additional strategies and activities.

Building Business Skills

Building Business Skills

Model

Emphasize to students that people often are able to draw conclusions by piecing together what they know and analyzing how those pieces of information fit together. For example, if you noticed that your friend Dan was coughing and knew that Dan's sister was absent because she had a cold, you might draw the conclusion that he had caught his sister's cold.

Analysis

Drawing Conclusions

Explanation

Whether you work in the loan department of a bank or the accounts receivable section of a department store, you may find that many parts of your job will not be spelled out for you. It would be almost impossible for another employee to teach you every single thing you need to know. The same thing is true in everyday life. There will be many things you'll just have to figure out for yourself.

Figuring things out for yourself is one way of drawing conclusions. You observe the things around you and put the information together to make an educated, logical guess.

Some of the conclusions you draw will be about people and policies in the office. Sometimes you'll need to draw conclusions as part of your personal life.

Practice

Drawing conclusions is a process of making decisions through an analysis of available information. Read the following observations and then draw a conclusion from the information or clues they contain. Write your conclusions on a separate sheet of paper.

Quick Check Answers

1. A kind of short-term credit offered to store customers; equal payments that include part of the purchase price and part of the interest and are spread out over a period of time; high-priced items frequently purchased by using installment payments; the maximum amount of purchases a person can charge at any given time.
2. Commercial banks, savings and loan associations, credit unions, and savings banks.
3. Regular, revolving, and installment.
4. Single-purpose, multipurpose, and travel and entertainment credit cards.

Quick Check

1. Explain the terms *charge account, installment payments, big-ticket items,* and *credit limit.*
2. What kinds of institutions offer long-term loans?
3. What are the three kinds of charge accounts?
4. Name three types of credit cards.

Credit and Business

Businesses often use credit for the same reasons that individual consumers do. For instance, they may need to buy goods on credit, or they may need short- or long-term loans to pay salaries or to buy property. Manufacturers borrow money to buy raw materials, new machinery, factories, or trucks. When businesses borrow money, however, they can pass along the cost of credit by charging higher prices on their own products.

Businesses also use credit to help sell their products. For instance, stores that accept credit cards or sell on an installment

478 Unit 9 Using Credit to Buy Goods and Services

Reteaching Strategy

Horace Porterfield's charge account bill at Bryson's department store records last month's payment of $8.00 and interest charges of $2.34 on his unpaid balance of $117.00 from last month. The bill requests that he make a minimum payment of $8.00 this month. Have students review the information about drawing conclusions given above and then have them use what they have learned so far in the chapter to draw a conclusion about whether Horace's account is revolving or regular. (The account is a revolving account, because Horace paid only a portion of the bill, has been charged interest on the unpaid balance, and may continue to pay off only a portion of his bill.)

OBSERVATIONS AND CONCLUSIONS

1. *Observations*
   - The used-car salesperson gives you a credit application to finance the car you want to buy through the dealership.
   - The bank where you have your checking and savings accounts advertises short-term loans.
   - You know your credit rating is excellent.

   Which place do you conclude will probably give you the best deal on a car loan?

2. *Observations*
   - There have been several brake problems fixed in your auto repair shop in the last few weeks.
   - Three times in the past week customers have returned, complaining that their brakes squeak, even after your shop has repaired them.
   - All three jobs were done by different mechanics.

   - When you check your orders, you find that the replacement parts for all three brake jobs came from the same manufacturer.

   What do you conclude about the probable source of the problem?

3. *Observations*
   - In your first week on the job, you notice that one employee is consistently five or ten minutes late.
   - After the first few days, the supervisor checks at nine o'clock to see whether the employee is at his desk.
   - You think the supervisor looks angry.

   On the next Monday morning, that employee is gone.

   What's your conclusion about this situation?

basis make it easier for consumers to buy. In addition to increased sales of products, businesses handling their own credit make money from interest. In general, the more credit that businesses sell to consumers, the more they make on interest.

Although there are advantages to businesses in offering credit, there are also disadvantages. Any business that accepts multipurpose or travel and entertainment credit cards must pay a percentage of each credit purchase to the credit card company or bank that issued the card. A business that offers credit on its own to customers can make additional income, but it also has additional costs. Employees must be hired to keep records of payments and to send out bills. The business will also have to take additional risks. When people do not pay their bills, profits are reduced. Businesses that are well run, however, usually make money offering credit.

Quick Check

1. How do businesses use credit?
2. Name two disadvantages for businesses that allow customers to use credit cards.

The World Bank is an international organization that makes loans to countries for stated economic development projects such as building roads or improving agricultural practices. The bank is part of the United Nations, and more than 160 countries are members. The World Bank obtains its funds from member countries and from borrowing in the world market. The bank extends loans to countries not otherwise able to get loans with reasonable interest rates.

Making Connections — Everyday Living

Explain that businesses usually benefit by offering credit. Provide students with the following hypothetical situation. Deb was shopping for a winter coat in Lemmon's department store. Deb saw only one coat she liked, but it cost $20 more than she had. Since she didn't have any credit cards, Deb decided she wouldn't be able to buy the coat and started to leave the store. As she neared the exit, a customer service representative offered her instant credit with a Lemmon's charge card. Deb signed up for the card and charged the coat. Have students analyze the situation and explain how the store benefited from offering credit and whether they think Deb benefited from obtaining credit to buy the coat.

Develop Concepts

Governments and Credit

One way the federal government borrows money is by selling securities such as Treasury bills and savings bonds to individuals and businesses. State and local governments borrow money by selling municipal bonds. Have students choose a government security and investigate how governments pay back their creditors. What incentives do governments offer to encourage people to buy government securities? (Government securities are fairly low-risk investments; they also have tax advantages.)

Quick Check Answers
1. The federal government.
2. Highways, housing, and water systems.

USE VISUALS

To help students visualize the size of the public debt, direct them to the line in Figure 28-1 that represents debt as a percent of federal outlay. Ask: Between which years did the percentage of debt nearly double? (1980–1990.)
Answer to caption: 1980–1990.

USE TRANSPARENCIES

Use Teaching Transparency 28-1 and its corresponding strategies and worksheet from the *Teaching Transparency Strategies and Worksheets* booklet to help students visualize the size of the public debt of the United States. Verify student worksheets using the Answer Key.

During World War II, the federal government used credit to finance military spending, and the national debt increased enormously. Since that time, the public debt, or the amount owed by any level of government, has grown at a rapid rate. By far, the largest share of the public debt is the result of the federal government's spending. Figure 28-1 below shows how the public debt has grown.

The federal government uses credit to pay for many of the services it provides to American citizens, largely because it is unwilling to sufficiently increase its income by raising taxes to pay for those services. State and local governments more often balance their budgets. However, they too may use credit to pay for such things as highways, housing, stadiums, and water systems. Like the federal government, state and local governments collect taxes to help pay for these services. Just as part of the federal budget goes to pay interest on the national debt, state and local governments must also set aside part of their budgets to pay interest on their outstanding debts.

FIGURE 28-1

The public debt of the United States federal government has grown rapidly, both in dollars and in percent of the outlay of dollars of the federal budget. In which decade did the debt first increase more than $2000 billion?

Quick Check
1. Which level of government has the largest share of the public debt?
2. What items might state and local government pay for with credit?

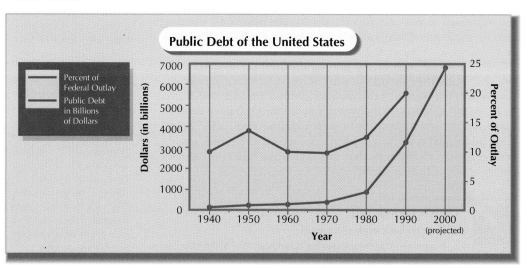

Public Debt of the United States

Global Perspective

The United States isn't the only country that uses credit to pay for many of the services it provides to its citizens. Have students choose another country and find out the amount of public debt for the most recent year available. Students should present their findings in bar graph form showing both the monetary amount of the debt and the debt as a percentage of that government's budget.

Refer to the *International Business Strategies* booklet for additional strategies and activities.

Chapter 28 **Summary**

Main Ideas

1. Credit is the opportunity to obtain money, goods, or services now by promising to pay in the future.
2. Credit allows people to use things while they pay for them and take advantage of sales, but credit can also lead people to buy things they cannot afford.
3. Long-term loans can be obtained from commercial banks, credit unions, savings and loan associations, and savings banks.
4. Charge accounts and credit cards allow you to buy items and pay for them after the bill arrives.
5. Companies may benefit by increased business when they allow customers to buy on credit, but it also increases the cost of doing business.
6. Governments use credit to pay for some of the services they provide.
7. The ability to draw conclusions by observing situations is an important skill.
8. An expert system is computer software designed to imitate the decisions that would be made by a human expert.

CASE ANALYSIS — Consumer Credit

The Martini family's washing machine has broken down. They can get it repaired, but since it is quite old it may not be worth it. A new washing machine will cost $390, but it will take 8 months for them to save the money. In the meantime, the family will have to take their clothes to a laundromat. They can instead buy a new machine on credit now for $498, which includes the finance charges. For each of the three different choices below list the advantages and disadvantages.

    a. Repair old washing machine.
    b. Buy new washing machine on credit.
    c. Save to buy new washing machine for cash.

Which choice do you suggest? Why?

QUICK QUIZ

1. What are four sources of loans? (Commercial banks, credit unions, savings and loan associations, and savings banks.)
2. What are the three types of credit cards? (Single-purpose, multipurpose, and travel and entertainment.)
3. What are two disadvantages businesses might encounter when they allow customers to use credit cards? (They pay a percentage of each card purchase to the issuer. Extra employees need to be hired to keep records of credit payments and bills.)
4. What level of government has the largest portion of the public debt? (The federal government.)

Chapter 28 **Review**

CHAPTER 28 REVIEW

APPLY

Answers

Use the Language of Business

1. creditor, **2.** big-ticket items, **3.** credit, **4.** commercial credit, **5.** credit rating, **6.** installment payments, **7.** consumer credit, **8.** charge account, **9.** debtor, **10.** credit limit.

Review What You Learned

1. For convenience, in emergencies, and for expensive purchases.

2. Advantages: You can use the item while paying for it; you can take advantage of sales; credit generates sales, which encourages the production of more goods and services and creates jobs. Disadvantages: Credit provides a temptation to buy unnecessary or unaffordable things; credit costs money in interest charges.

3. Single-purpose cards are issued by business firms to be used only at that firm. Examples include oil company cards and department store cards. Multipurpose, or bank, cards are accepted by a wide variety of businesses. Examples include Visa and MasterCard. Travel and entertainment cards are accepted worldwide. Examples include Diners Club and American Express.

4. Short-term credit is usually repaid in fewer than five years. Short-term credit purchases are anything that might be charged to a charge account or credit card. Long-term credit requires payment over many years and might be used to purchase a house or a business.

5. Commercial banks, credit unions, savings and loan associations, and savings banks.

6. Firms must pay the cost of offering credit. They take additional risks; when people do not pay their bills, profits are reduced. Workers must be paid to prepare bills and keep credit records.

7. Because consumer finance companies often lend to people who cannot get credit elsewhere. They charge higher interest rates to cover the risk involved in making these loans.

Use the Language of Business

See how well you know these credit terms. Complete the sentences by using the following terms.

big-ticket items	credit limit
charge account	credit rating
commercial credit	creditor
consumer credit	debtor
credit	installment payments

1. A(n) _____ lends money or provides credit.
2. _____ are high-priced items that are often paid for in installments.
3. _____ is the opportunity to obtain money, goods, or services now in exchange for a promise to pay later.
4. _____ is used by businesses.
5. Your _____ is a measure of your willingness and ability to pay.
6. _____ are equal payments you make over a period of time.
7. Credit used for personal reasons is _____ .
8. With a(n) _____, you can purchase up to a certain amount in a specific store.
9. A(n) _____ borrows money or uses credit.
10. The maximum amount of credit you can use in a specified time period is your _____ .

Review What You Learned

1. Why do consumers use credit?
2. What are the advantages and disadvantages of using credit?
3. What are the three types of credit cards? Give an example of each.
4. What is the difference between short-term and long-term credit?
5. What are four sources for loans?
6. In what ways can the use of credit be a disadvantage to business?
7. Why do consumer finance companies have higher finance charges than other places?
8. List two services for which governments use credit.
9. What is a person doing when he or she makes an educated, logical guess based on observations of a situation?
10. How do credit companies use information technology to guard against fraud?

Understand Business Concepts

1. Why is credit important to our country's economy?
2. What is risk? How does risk affect the cost of credit?
3. Convenience is one of the reasons for using credit, but cash is also convenient. Describe two situations in which cash would be more convenient. Next, describe two situations in which credit would be the better choice.
4. Why are credit cards so popular? Who benefits from their increased use?
5. If people use credit, does that mean they have money problems? Explain.
6. What advantages would the ability to draw conclusions from observations have for a new employee at a job?
7. How does an expert system provide information to its users?

8. Highways and housing.

9. The person is drawing conclusions about the situation.

10. To determine if a purchase matches a customer's buying pattern; purchases that do not match the pattern are suspect.

Understand Business Concepts

1. Credit increases the demand for goods and services because people can obtain items before they have enough money to purchase them. This creates jobs producing and selling these goods and services.

2. Risk refers to the probability that a loan will be repaid. The higher the risk, the higher the interest charge.

3. Possible answer: Cash is more convenient when paying cab, bus, or subway fares, tips, and using vending machines. Credit is more convenient when ordering items by phone, when taking advantage of sales, and when making expensive purchases.

4. Credit cards are popular with consumers because they are convenient, and with businesses because they can increase sales and store loyalty. Issuers of credit cards benefit by making a profit.

5. The use of credit does not indicate money problems. Credit is used wisely and efficiently by many people.

6. Being able to draw conclusions from observations would help a new employee adapt to the work environment more quickly.

7. It sifts through a highly detailed data base imitating the thought process of an expert in that field of knowledge.

Chapter 28 **Review**

Think Critically

1. **Evaluate.** Bring in newspaper articles and advertisements that show uses of credit by consumers, businesses, and government. Who benefits the most from these examples of credit?
2. **Judge.** "Everyone would gain if there were no consumer credit. Consumers would benefit because goods and services could be sold at a lower price. The lower price means that businesses would sell more goods and services." Do you agree or disagree? Explain.

Use What You Learned

1. **Group Project.** In your group, discuss whether you agree or disagree with the following statements. Record the reasons for your group's opinions. Share the results with other groups.
   - The use of credit is usually justified for necessities but not for luxuries.
   - The best way to minimize the cost of credit is to borrow at the lowest available interest and repay the loan in the shortest possible time.
   - A good credit rating is a valuable thing to have, so a consumer should protect that rating.
   - It is best to shop for credit just as you shop for any major purchase.
2. Find out the cost of credit from each of the sources listed below. Then rank them in order, from the lowest interest rates to the highest interest rates.
   - Consumer finance company
   - Revolving charge account
   - Travel and entertainment credit card
   - Credit union
   - Commercial bank
3. **Computer Application.** Most installment contracts require a percentage of the total price as a down payment. Use spreadsheet software to set up a spreadsheet that will compute the down payment for each of the items in the chart below.
4. **Skill Reinforcement.** Think of a problem you have to solve or something you would like to understand better. Spend several days making observations about the situation. Record your observations on a sheet of paper in a manner similar to the observations on page 479. Spend some time studying the observations you have made. Then draw a conclusion from them that you can use to solve your problem or increase your understanding.

Item	Price	Required Down Payment	Amount of Down Payment
CD player	$295	10%	$_____
Color TV	298	10%	_____
Electric stove	489	20%	_____
Desk and chair	263	15%	_____
Used car	5495	25%	_____
Sofa	995	17%	_____

Save your work in your Business Portfolio

Think Critically
1. Answers will vary.
2. Possible answers: Disagree: Curtailing credit could cause an increase in prices because demand might fall off. Agree: People would not have to pay interest on their purchases, thus keeping prices lower. Also, they would not have to pay their share of the bad debts.

Independent Practice

Use the Chapter 28 worksheets in *Student Activity Guide 2* for additional practice and application activities. A Teacher's Annotated Edition provides answers.

ASSESS

Portfolio Assessment

The portfolio projects are designed to lead students to develop a collection of their best work to submit to you for assessment. Refer students to the specific rubric(s) from the *Alternative Assessment Strategies* booklet listed with each of the project notes below. These rubrics will alert students to the criteria you will use to assess their projects.

Chapter Assessment

Use the Chapter 28 Test from the *Test Masters* booklet to evaluate students' understanding of the chapter concepts. An answer key is provided. Or create your own customized test using the *Testmaker* software.

Use What You Learned
1. Make sure all students participate in the group project. Rubric: Note Taking.
2. Point out to students that interest rates may vary according to the circumstances of the loan. Rubric: Charts and Tables.
3. Students with no access to a computer may complete the down payments manually or with a calculator. Answers: CD Player: $29.50; color TV: $29.80; electric stove: $97.80; desk and chair: $39.45; used car: $1373.75; sofa: $169.15. Rubric: Charts and Tables.
4. Students' answers will vary. Rubric: Note Taking.

CHAPTER 29

Introduce the Chapter

Major Concepts
- Establishing Credit
- Managing Your Credit

Introduce the Topic
Begin discussion of the chapter by having students review the advantages and disadvantages of using credit, as introduced in Chapter 28.

Use Business Terms
Have students read the list of Business Terms. Ask for ideas about what the terms mean. Record correct answers on the board or a transparency. For unknown terms, advise students to check the meanings of the terms as they read the chapter.

USE VISUALS
Explain to students that if you buy things with a credit card or a charge card, you will receive a monthly statement detailing the purchases and payments that have been posted to your account. Ask students why this woman is checking her monthly statement against her own records. (To make sure no mistakes have been made.)

Business terms

collateral

down payment

principal

interest rate

secured loan

unsecured loan

cosigner

finance charge

annual percentage rate

garnishment

repossess

484

CHAPTER 29 RESOURCES

Instructional Resources

Lesson Plan for Chapter 29

Teaching Transparencies 29-1, 29-2, 29-3, 29-4, 29-5, 29-6, 29-7, 29-8

Strategies and Worksheets for Teaching Transparencies 29-1, 29-2, 29-3, 29-4, 29-5, 29-6, 29-7, 29-8

Enrichment Master 29-1

Student Activity Guide 2–TAE for Chapter 29

Test Master for Chapter 29

Alternative Assessment Strategies

Math Skills Review

International Business Strategies

Cooperative Learning Strategies

Communication Skills Review

Ethics in Business Strategies

Getting *and* Keeping Credit

Learning objectives

After completing this chapter, you will be able to:
- Name the three factors creditors examine when determining your credit rating.
- Discuss how installment and cash loans work.
- Describe what is meant by the cost of credit.
- Explain how to manage credit and avoid credit problems.
- Calculate finance charges.
- Name jobs in wholesale and retail trade and explain how communication skills are used in those jobs.

Consider what you know

- People can obtain goods and services on credit by using charge or credit cards or taking out a loan. Using credit allows people to purchase items and use them immediately. However, it is more expensive to buy things on credit, and if credit is not used responsibly, a person's credit rating can be damaged.

Consider what you want to know

- How can you apply for and establish credit?
- What can you do to make sure you manage credit responsibly?
- How can you calculate how much finance charges will add to the cost of an item you buy on credit?
- What kinds of jobs are available in wholesale and retail trade?

Consider how to use what you learn

- As you read this chapter, think about items you might purchase with credit. What do you need to find out first before using credit?

Motivate the Learning

Learning Objectives
Point out to students that the learning objectives show what they will learn in the chapter. Tell students to keep these objectives in mind as they work through the chapter. Note that the last two objectives listed refer to the Focus on Careers feature and the Building Business Skills feature.

Consider What You Know
Review briefly the main sections of *Chapter 28 Credit: A Promise to Pay:* The Nature of Credit; Where to Go for Credit; Credit and Business; and Governments and Credit.

Consider What You Want to Know
Have students keep the listed questions in mind as they preview the chapter by quickly paging through it, looking at the pictures, and reading the section headings and figure titles.

Consider How to Use What You Learn
Inform students that at the end of the chapter they will complete projects related to establishing and maintaining credit. Suggest that as they read the chapter they keep a running list of tips to remember about using credit.

Multimedia Resources

Technology Resource Guide

Distance Learning Guide

Internet Resource Guide

Professional Resources

School-to-Work/Tech Prep Strategies

Instructional Poster

Spanish Resources

Testmaker Software for Chapter 29

The Wall Street Journal Video Series Video & Activities for Chapter 29

Business and Marketing Computer Applications—An Integrated Software Simulation Using Microsoft Works

Stocktracker—A Stock Market Software Simulation

Where's the Dough? Board Game

TEACH

Business Connection

Some financial advisers suggest that, as young adults, people take out a small loan and pay it off on time in order to establish a good credit rating. People sometimes have trouble obtaining credit simply because they don't have a credit history, and creditors are unable to determine whether they would be a good credit risk.

Develop Concepts

Establishing Credit

Ask students to write responses to the following questions: When someone asks you for a loan, what factors make you decide to say yes or no? How and when would you expect the person to repay the loan? Tell students that lending institutions use similar criteria to determine whether they should give someone a loan. Explain that these criteria and the responsibilities of a borrower will be described in this section of the chapter.

Buying on credit involves a choice. "Should I use my emergency cash reserves to pay for the new refrigerator or use the dealer's installment plan?" "Should I pay for this gasoline with a credit card and save my cash for something else?"

The decision to buy or not to buy on credit can be difficult to make. Paying later may mean paying more. Buying a $195 coat on credit will probably mean an additional interest charge. You must also keep track of how previous credit purchases may affect your ability to pay bills on time. Missed or late payments can harm your credit rating and will affect your ability to use credit in the future.

In this chapter, you will learn how to apply for, establish, and maintain credit, and how to use credit responsibly.

ESTABLISHING CREDIT

To take advantage of the benefits of using credit, you need to know how to apply for credit. When you fill out an application to obtain credit, the bank, store, or credit card company needs to establish if you are a good credit risk. They will use the information you put on your application to find out about your income, any debts you currently have, and how well you have paid previous debts. These factors help you establish credit.

Business & Social Studies

The word *credit* comes from the Latin word *credo*, meaning "I trust." Banks and other lending institutions trust borrowers to pay them back. Merchants give credit to buyers because they trust that they will be paid back.

Applying for Credit

Whether you decide to open a credit or charge account, you will be required to fill out a credit application. Figure 29-1 on page 487 is an example of an application for a charge account. The form requests information about where you live and work and what other credit you have received. You will also be asked to sign the application, which indicates that the information on the form is correct and that you agree to have your credit checked. The creditor also checks with a credit bureau, an agency that collects information about you and other consumers of credit. Creditors then use this information to examine three factors when determining whether or not you are a good credit risk.

- *Capacity to pay.* Your income and the debt you already have will affect your ability to pay additional debts. If you already have a large amount of debt in relation to your income, creditors will be unlikely to extend you more credit.
- *Character.* Creditors want to know what kind of person they will be lending to. They may ask for personal or profes-

Enrichment Strategy

Students can obtain the following materials on responsible credit use: (1) "Credit Cards: What You Don't Know Can Cost You," available for $1 from Bankcard Holders of America, 524 Branch Dr., Salem, VA 24153; "A Student's Plain English Dictionary of Credit Terms," available at no cost from American Express, Office of Public Responsibility, Dept. CT, 200 Vesey St., New York, NY 10285-4850. Have students prepare an oral presentation for the class about the information they receive.

HERE'S HOW TO GET YOUR CARD

1. APPLY FOR INSTANT CREDIT NOW. COMPLETE THIS FORM. GIVE IT TO A SALES PERSON.
2. APPLY BY PHONE TODAY. CALL 1-800-555-4422
3. APPLY BY MAIL. COMPLETE THIS FORM AND MAIL IT.

You must be 18 or older to apply.
You must have at least one of these credit references.
Check all that apply. List one below.

☐ American Express   ☐ JC Penney   ☒ Montgomery Ward
☒ VISA   ☐ Discover   ☐ Major Store Card
☐ Master Card   ☐ Sears

Montgomery Ward
CREDITOR'S NAME

7846 920 847 933   **2-02**
ACCOUNT NUMBER   EXP. DATE

Tell us about yourself
Hood
LAST NAME (As you would like your name to appear on the card)

Anne   **G.**
FIRST NAME   MIDDLE INITIAL

476-03-1102
SOCIAL SECURITY NUMBER

1270 E. Continental #102
ADDRESS (Home/Number & Street/Apt. No.)

Glenfield,   **WA**   **97849-7936**
CITY   STATE   ZIP CODE

(208) 769-6604
TELEPHONE (Home)

NAME PHONE LISTED UNDER (If different from applicant)

(208) 769-2050
TELEPHONE (Business)

Cantwell Insurance Agency
EMPLOYER NAME

50 W. Center St. Suite 400
STREET

Glenfield   **WA**   **97849-1149**
CITY   STATE   ZIP CODE

ISSUE AN ADDITIONAL CARD
IN AUTHORIZED USER'S NAME   ☐ Yes   ☒ No

AUTHORIZED USER'S NAME

RELATIONSHIP   MIDDLE INITIAL

Read the fine print
I am applying to American Family National Bank for a Credit Card for personal, family or household use. The information that I have supplied is true and correct. I agree that a credit report may be used in making the credit granting decision. I agree to be bound by the terms of the Credit Card Agreement. I acknowledge that I will receive a Credit Card Agreement upon arrival.

Sign here
Anne G. Hood   **10-6-97**
APPLICANT'S SIGNATURE   DATE

There are costs associated with the use of this card. You may contact us to receive information about the costs at 1-800-555-3257, or write us at American Family National Bank, PO Box 720711, Fairwood, WA 90879-1200. If you are married you may apply for a separate account. Wisconsin Residents Only: No provision of a marital property agreement (including a Statutory Individual Property Agreement) pursuant to Section 766.587 Wisconsin Statutes) a unilateral statement classifying income from separate property under Section 766.59 or a court decree under Section 766.70 adversely affects the creditor unless the creditor is furnished with a copy of the document prior to the credit transaction or has actual knowledge of its adverse provisions at the time the obligation is incurred. Wisconsin law requires us to inform your spouse that we have opened a credit account for you. If you are married please give us the following:

SPOUSE'S NAME

SPOUSE'S ADDRESS

FOR STORE USE ONLY   ID:

ST.#   EMP.#   MGR.:   ACCT.#

FIGURE 29-1

The information you put on an application for credit gives a creditor details about where you live and work and whether you have other credit or charge accounts. What kind of credit does this applicant already have?

sional references to establish a person's trustworthiness. They may also check to see if a person has a criminal record or a history of problems with the law.

- *Collateral.* Creditors look at what kinds of property or savings you already have. Money you have in the bank or big-ticket items, such as a car, can be offered as **collateral.** Collateral is a form of security to help guarantee that the creditor will be repaid. It indicates that if you lost your source of income, you could repay your loan from your savings or by selling some of your property. If a creditor requires that you put up collateral, they may have the legal right to take it if you do not repay as agreed.

Making Connections ⟳   Everyday Living

Homeowners often borrow money with a home equity loan—such loans allow homeowners to borrow against the value of their home. Home equity loans often have low interest rates, because a home is a very secure form of collateral. Homeowners can estimate how much they could borrow against their home by using the following formula: Calculate 80 percent of the home's value and subtract the current mortgage balance to find the loan amount. Have students use the formula (value of home × .8 − current mortgage balance = loan amount) to find out how much a family with a home valued at $98,000 with a current mortgage balance of $27,800 could borrow with a home equity loan. ($98,000 × .8 = $78,400 − $27,800 = $50,600.)

USE VISUALS
Have students study Figure 29-1 to discover what kind of information is requested on charge and credit card applications. Ask students what pieces of information on the application are related to the applicant's capacity to pay. (The information about the applicant's other credit or charge cards and current job and salary information.)
Answer to caption: She has a Visa credit card and a Montgomery Ward charge card.

USE TRANSPARENCIES
Use Teaching Transparencies 29-1 and 29-2 and their corresponding strategies and worksheets from the *Teaching Transparency Strategies and Worksheets* booklet to show students examples of the kinds of applications they would fill out if applying for a credit card or a loan, respectively. You may want to distribute photocopies so students can practice filling out such forms. Verify student worksheets using the Answer Key.

Learning Activity

Have students evaluate their own creditworthiness by making a chart with the following headings: Credit History; Capacity to Pay; Character; and Collateral. Have them list loans from relatives or friends they repaid and their current pay or allowance. Have them evaluate their determination to repay a loan and whether they have anything that could be offered as collateral. Suggest assigning one point to each item in each category and have students add up their scores. Higher scores indicate a better risk. Ask students for suggestions to improve their creditworthiness.

USE VISUALS

Use Figure 29-2 as an example of the kind of information contained in a security agreement. Have students review the agreement, and then ask a volunteer to explain what is meant by the "grace or free ride" period. (The period of time during which a person can pay in full and not be charged a finance charge.) Answer to caption: A late payment fee of $5 or 5 percent can be applied to payments more than 10 days late in all states where late payment fees are allowed by law.

Business Brief

Countries can be creditors and debtors, too. Part of a proposed $52 billion loan from the United States to Mexico included, among other things, a request that Mexico use one of its natural resources—oil—as collateral to secure the loan.

The information gathered from your application and the credit bureau establishes your credit rating. If you always make your payments on time, you will probably have an excellent credit rating. If not, your credit rating will be poor. Creditors are happy to extend credit to people with a good rating, but usually refuse those with a low rating.

The creditor will also use the information from your credit application and credit history to decide how much you can borrow. As you remember from Chapter 28, the amount of credit a creditor will extend to you at any one time is your credit limit.

When a credit card company or a store's charge account department accepts your application, you will receive a security agreement that explains how interest will be charged on the account. When you signed your name on the application, you agreed to follow the rules described in the agreement. Figure 29-2 below shows a sample security agreement for a charge account.

Buying on Credit

Credit cards and charge accounts are commonly used, convenient ways to make relatively inexpensive purchases. For

FIGURE 29-2

Security agreements explain how interest charges will be figured for a credit or charge account. What is this store's policy regarding late payments?

SECURITY AGREEMENT — Important Charge Credit Terms

Regardless of your state of residence there is
• NO Annual or Membership Fee.
• NO Transaction charges and NO Over Limit Fee.

THERE IS ALWAYS A GRACE OR FREE RIDE PERIOD—If you pay the full account balance within 30 days of the billing date you will not be charged a finance charge.

IF YOU DON'T PAY THE BALANCE WITHIN THE GRACE OR FREE RIDE PERIOD, A FINANCE CHARGE WILL BE ADDED.

FINANCE CHARGE INFORMATION—Finance Charge Rates vary by state. The ANNUAL PERCENTAGE RATE IS 21% unless you reside in a state shown below:

Alabama . . . . .21% to $750, 18% on excess
Alaska . . . . .18% to $1000, variable rate on excess
Arkansas . . . . .Variable rate not to exceed 17%
California 19.2%
Connecticut 15%
Florida, Hawaii, Louisiana, Maine, Mass., Minnesota, No. Carolina, No. Dakota, Penn., Rhode Island, Texas, Wash., W. Virginia,
Wisconsin 18%
Iowa 19.8%
Kansas . . . . .21% to $1000, 14.4% on excess
Michigan 20%
Missouri, Puerto Rico 20.4%
Nebraska . . . . .21% to $500, 18% on excess

A MINIMUM MONTHLY FINANCE CHARGE OF 50¢ applies in all states except Ark., Conn., Hawaii, Maryland, Neb., Nevada, No. Carolina, No. Dakota, Rhode Island, Virginia, District of Columbia, and Puerto Rico. The Finance Charge is applied to the Average Daily Balance including current charges, except in Maine, Mass., Minn., Miss., Montana, New Mexico, No. Dakota, where current charges are excluded.

A LATE PAYMENT FEE OF THE LESSER OF $5 OR 5% MAY BE APPLIED IN ALL STATES WHERE AUTHORIZED BY LAW ON PAYMENTS MORE THAN 10 DAYS LATE.

ILLINOIS RESIDENTS ONLY: Residents of Illinois may contact the Illinois Commissioner of Banks and Trust Companies for comparative information on finance charges, fees and grace periods 1-800-555-1234.

OHIO RESIDENTS ONLY: The Ohio laws against discrimination require that all creditors make credit equally available to all creditworthy customers, and that credit reporting agencies maintain separate credit histories on each individual upon request. The Ohio Civil Rights Commission administers compliance with this law.

WISCONSIN RESIDENTS ONLY: Wisconsin law provides that no agreement, court order or individual statement applying to marital property will affect a creditor's interests unless prior to the time credit is granted the creditor is furnished with a copy of the agreement, court order, or statement, or has actual knowledge of the adverse provision.

NEW YORK RESIDENTS ONLY: A consumer credit report may be ordered in connection with this application, or subsequently in connection with the update, renewal or extension of credit. Upon your request, you will be informed whether or not a consumer credit report was ordered, and if it was, you will be given the name and address of the consumer reporting agency that furnished the report. See chart for other important information.

New York Residents:				
Annual Percentage Rate	Variable Rate	Annualized Membership Fee	Grace Period	Late Fees or Other Charges
21%	None	None	30 Days	None

Curriculum Connection   English and Communication

Have students compile their own glossaries of credit terms. In addition to the chapter's Business Terms, they should include and define other words they encounter when collecting information for projects and learning activities. Students may use a computer and word processing software to format and design their glossaries.

expensive items—such as automobiles, furniture, and large appliances—many consumers spread out the cost over a period of months or even years by taking out a loan.

One kind of loan is an installment loan. When you use an installment loan, you usually make a **down payment** on your purchase. The down payment is a portion of the total cost paid with cash or a check. The balance of the cost, plus the interest, is divided into monthly or weekly installment payments. All the financial details of your purchase and the installment loan are spelled out in an installment contract. It specifies the rate used to calculate the interest, the date your payments are due, the penalty for late payments, and the cost of the credit.

Getting a cash loan is another way to pay for an expensive item. Cash loans can be obtained from banks, credit unions, savings and loan associations, and consumer finance companies. Consumers can also get cash from their bank credit cards. In this case, the payments are billed on the monthly credit card statement. The interest charged for cash loans varies widely. Credit card companies charge a higher interest rate than banks and credit unions.

The amount you borrow, the **principal,** is the amount of money owed as a debt upon which interest is calculated. The principal is one of three factors that determine the cost of buying on credit. The other two factors are the **interest rate,** which is a stated percentage of the principal, and the length of the loan. The cost is calculated using the simple interest method, which multiplies the principal, the interest rate, and the length of the loan.

When you receive a cash loan, you must sign a written agreement to repay the loan within a certain period of time. If the cash loan is backed by collateral, it is called a **secured loan.** If not, it is called an **unsecured loan.** Because of the increased risk to the creditor, the finance charge on an unsecured loan is often higher than on a secured loan. Collateral for cash loans could be cars, stocks and bonds, or property. A loan used to buy a house, office building, manufacturing plant, or other type of property is called a mortgage, which is secured by the property itself.

A creditor can also reduce the risk of a loan by asking you to have a **cosigner** to the loan. The cosigner agrees to make the payments if you cannot make them. A cosigner may be a relative or a close friend who not only knows you, but also knows that you can be relied on to pay your debts. The cosigner is actually lending his or her ability to secure credit to you. Many first-time borrowers obtain their first loans with the help of a cosigner.

F.Y.I.

Some creditors use a "scorecard" system for determining whether to give an individual a loan. The creditor assigns a number, or score, to each of the credit factors analyzed—capacity to pay, character, and collateral. If the sum of the numbers is below a predetermined number, the loan is denied; if it is above the number, it is approved.

Learning Activity

Lyudmila put a $795 down payment on a computer system that cost $2795. Ask: What is the principal of the loan? ($2000.) The interest rate of her loan is 12 percent and the length of the loan is one year. Ask: What will Lyudmila's monthly payments be? ($2000 × .12 = $240 (interest) + $2000 (principal) = $2240 ÷ 12 months = $186.65.)

TEACHING TIP

Tell students to imagine that someone has asked them to cosign a loan. Have them list reasons why they would or would not be willing to cosign. Discuss cosigning from the standpoint of both the borrower and the cosigner.

USE TRANSPARENCIES

Use Teaching Transparency 29-3 and its corresponding strategies and worksheet from the *Teaching Transparency Strategies and Worksheets* booklet to show students the kind of information that is contained on a retail installment contract. Verify student worksheets using the Answer Key.

Global Perspective

The International Monetary Fund (IMF) is an agency of the United Nations that works to help developing countries achieve economic growth, a high level of employment, and an improved standard of living. Have students find articles about recent IMF loans and explain the reason for the loan, the terms of the loan, and what criteria the IMF used in deciding to make the loan. Have students summarize their findings in a paragraph.

Refer to the *International Business Strategies* booklet for additional strategies and activities.

Discuss

Discuss with students the kinds of skills people in the wholesale and retail trade industries use. Ask students what courses in school could help them prepare for entry-level jobs in wholesale and retail trade. How do people advance in the field?

Wholesale and Retail Trade

I n wholesale and retail trade, buying and selling is the name of the game. Whenever we purchase a new pair of running shoes, drop clothes off at the cleaners, rent a movie at the video store, or order a sweatshirt from a catalog by phone, we become customers in retail business transactions.

The sales associates, agents, and telemarketers we interact with play a vital role in making sure we get the goods and services we need promptly and pleasantly. Behind these employees stand many more we may not encounter directly—the people who perform services, distribute merchandise, send out orders, and arrange and stock store shelves. Other workers in this area of business may be engaged in buying merchandise—either for resale in stores or for use in operating organizations.

For people interested in how businesses function, an entry-level job in wholesale and retail trade can be an ideal introduction. Many such jobs are open to students on a part-time

---

HELP WANTED

SALES ASSOCIATE

BWG Cycles, this area's biggest retailer of fine bicycles, is looking for bike enthusiast to work full-time as sales associate for salary plus commission.

We'd like to hire someone with knowledge of all aspects of cycling from serious racing to pleasure riding. Must have superior command of details of imported/domestic bikes/equipment; be willing and able to keep up with new product developments; able to fit customers for bikes. Outgoing, friendly personality and clean, neat appearance also necessary. Hours flexible.

If you think you fit our bill, call for an appointment.

USE TRANSPARENCIES

Use Teaching Transparencies 29-4 and 29-5 and their corresponding strategies and worksheets from the *Teaching Transparency Strategies and Worksheets* booklet to illustrate how an interest rate of 15 percent compares with a rate of 9 percent for the same type of loan. Verify student worksheets using the Answer Key.

USE TRANSPARENCIES

Use Teaching Transparency 29-6 and its corresponding strategies and worksheet from the *Teaching Transparency Strategies and Worksheets* booklet to model how to calculate the cost of credit with varying interest rates. Verify student worksheets using the Answer Key.

The Cost of Credit

The simplest measure of how much you will pay for credit is called the dollar cost of credit. This is the difference between the cost of an item if you pay for it in cash and what it will cost if you buy it on credit. For example, a used car may cost $5000 if you can pay cash for it. However, you might need to buy the car on an installment plan. You could make a down payment of $1000 and then pay $160 a month for 36 months. Your total cost would then be $6760. The difference between $6760 and $5000 is $1760, which is the dollar cost of credit.

When you are given credit, the security agreement explains the interest rate and finance charges. The **finance charge** is the cost of credit stated in a dollar and cents figure. The creditor imposes a finance charge on any unpaid balance. The finance charge is calculated using the **annual percentage rate** (APR), which indicates how much credit costs you on a yearly basis. For example, an APR of 18 percent means you pay $18 per year, or $1.50 per month, on each $100 you owe. Every organization that extends credit of any kind must state the true annual percentage rate it charges its customers. This makes it

Making Connections ▷ Mortgage Loans

Organize the class into three groups and have them investigate three common types of mortgage loans: 30-year fixed-rate, 15-year fixed-rate, and adjustable-rate mortgages. Groups may research the loans by contacting various lending institutions or by using library resources. Have groups explain the loan they researched to the rest of the class, noting the terms and the advantages and disadvantages of the loan.

basis with flexible hours. Many others provide strong opportunities for advancement and require a high school diploma to start.

Although jobs in this area range from selling goods and services directly to customers to managing merchandise in a warehouse, all require communication skills. Forklift operators must read and record data about the shipments they move. Customer service representatives need to listen carefully and speak clearly to customers—and resolve conflicts. For workers engaged in buying and selling, detailed knowledge of the products they handle is often the key to success.

Keeping track of merchandise, money, and credit options is essential to wholesalers and retailers, and today this means using computers. Most employees in wholesale and retail trade will be using some form of computerized equipment daily in their jobs.

Presented here are help wanted ads for three entry-level jobs and a job posting for a more advanced position.

Follow Through

Emphasize the importance of good communication skills by having students discuss some of the ways employees who have the jobs mentioned in the text might communicate with customers and with business associates. Have students work with partners to role-play situations such as calming down an angry customer, helping a customer select merchandise, and giving precise delivery instructions to a business associate.

easy to compare the cost of credit at several businesses or between several different credit cards.

Quick Check

1. What three factors do creditors examine when deciding if a person is a good credit risk?
2. Define the terms *collateral, down payment, principal, interest rate, secured loan, unsecured loan,* and *cosigner.*
3. What is a *finance charge?*
4. What does an *annual percentage rate* indicate?

MANAGING YOUR CREDIT

More than likely, the first type of credit you will use will be short-term credit—the kind of credit available from charge cards and credit cards. If you are going to purchase goods and services with credit, you must also take on the responsibilities that go along with using credit. It is important to pay your bills

Quick Check Answers

1. Capacity to pay, character, and collateral.
2. Property or savings that could be offered to repay a loan; a cash or check payment that is a portion of the total cost; the sum of money owed as a debt upon which interest is figured; a stated percentage; a cash loan backed by collateral; a cash loan that is not backed by collateral; someone who agrees to make payments if a debtor is unable to make them.
3. The cost of credit stated in dollars and cents.
4. How much credit costs on a yearly basis.

USE TRANSPARENCIES

Use Teaching Transparency 29-7 and its corresponding strategies and worksheet from the *Teaching Transparency Strategies and Worksheets* booklet to model how to calculate the cost of credit for loans with varying time periods. Verify student worksheets using the Answer Key.

Curriculum Connection   Math

"Safe debt load"—the debt a person can take on after accounting for all necessary expenses can be calculated the following way.

- Calculate annual income after taxes and estimate annual expenses.
- Subtract total expenses from after-tax income and divide the difference by 3.

Ask students to find Bob Smauwg's safe debt load. His income is $23,980. He pays $4800 for housing, $4900 for food, $950 for clothes, and $1280 for transportation. ($23,980 – $11,930 = $12,050 ÷ 3 = $4016)

For students who need to sharpen their math skills, choose among the worksheets in the *Math Skills Review* booklet.

Building Business Skills

Building Business Skills

Model

Begin by reminding students that when you multiply by a percent you move the decimal point two places to the left: 2% is .02 when multiplying. Have students work out on paper the first two months on the Installment Payments Chart on page 493 by multiplying the unpaid balance of $500 by .02 to get $10. Point out that the finance charge of $10 gets added to Month 2's starting principal and ask students to calculate the finance charge for Month 2.

Develop Concepts

Managing Your Credit

The number of businesses and organizations that exist to help consumers mend their ruined credit ratings reflects the fact that it's easy to get in over your head when using credit. Photocopy and distribute Enrichment Master 29-1 and have students read through the tips for using credit. Record on the board any additional tips or ideas from students.

USE TRANSPARENCIES

Use Teaching Transparency 29-8 and its corresponding strategies and worksheet from the *Teaching Transparency Strategies and Worksheets* booklet to show students how to calculate finance charges using the adjusted daily balance and the average daily balance methods. Verify student worksheets using the Answer Key.

MATH

Computing Finance Charges

Explanation

As soon as you begin working, you may be eligible for credit. Opening charge accounts may seem like a good idea. You can get things you want and use them immediately. There is one drawback, though—the finance charge.

At first glance, finance charges may not seem very high. If you buy a $1000 TV and VCR with your credit card at a finance charge of 1.5 percent per month, you'll pay only $15.00 interest for the first month.

$1000 × 1.5% = $15

But what if you don't pay off that $1000 before next month? Or what if you buy other items and increase your debt? If your credit card charges 1.5 percent a month, you would be paying 18 percent per year in finance charges:

1.5% per month × 12 months = 18%

Keeping an unpaid balance of $1000 on your credit card bill for a year would cost you $180!

18% × $1000 = $180

Many credit cards demand a minimum monthly payment, but they don't require you to pay the balance. This is revolving credit, and with it finance charges can build up if you aren't careful.

promptly and keep records of the purchases you make using credit so you will know when you cannot afford to take on any more debt.

Many American businesspeople use major credit cards to buy goods and services in other parts of the world when they are on business trips. Credit card companies convert their credit transactions made in other countries into U.S. dollars before they send out the customers' monthly statements.

Pay on Time

When you use a charge account or a credit card, you receive a monthly statement that lists the charges and payments for the previous month. Regardless of whether a statement is from a store or a bank, it usually includes the following information:

- Previous balance, or the amount owed at the end of the last billing period.
- New purchases, including each item bought during the past month. Each purchase increases the amount you owe.
- Payments, which are the money paid on the account, and credits, which are goods returned to the store or business for credit. These decrease the amount you owe.
- Finance charges, if any, that were added to the bill. These charges increase the amount you owe.

492 UNIT 9 USING CREDIT TO BUY GOODS AND SERVICES

Meeting Student Diversity

Calculating interest and finance charges can be confusing to students whose math skills are below average. Make sure they know how to use the formulas for determining the cost of credit. Have them go through an exercise in which they make an imaginary credit purchase and must calculate and compare the costs using different interest rates. Explain that knowing how to find the best credit bargain can save them hundreds of dollars.

INSTALLMENT PAYMENTS CHART

	Month 1	Month 2	Month 3
Starting principal	$600.00	$510.00	$418.20
Less your payment	100.00	100.00	100.00
Unpaid balance	500.00	410.00	318.20
2% finance charge	10.00	8.20	6.36

Practice

Suppose that you buy a stereo system that costs $600 including tax. You charge the stereo on your E-Z Pay credit card, since you have a steady job and can afford to pay $100 a month. E-Z Pay will charge you 2 percent each month. Here's how E-Z Pay will figure your finance charge: When you get your first month's bill, you'll owe $600. When you make your $100 payment for that month, E-Z Pay will subtract that amount, leaving an unpaid balance of $500. Then they'll multiply $500 by 2 percent to get a finance charge of $10. They'll add that charge to the $500 unpaid balance. The sum, $510, will become the starting principal for the next month, and so on. Study the chart to follow the process through three months. Copy it and extend it until the debt is paid off. Then answer the questions.

1. How long will it take to pay off the stereo?
2. What is the total finance charge?
3. What is the total cost of the stereo?

Practice

Have students copy the Installment Payments Chart on page 493 and calculate how long it will take to pay off the debt. Then have them answer the questions.

	Month 5	Month 6	Month 7
Starting principal	$229.05	$131.63	$ 32.26
Less your payment	100.00	100.00	32.26
Unpaid balance	129.05	31.63	00
2% finance charge	2.58	.63	—

(1. Seven months.
2. $32.26 (Add the finance charges for each month.)
3. $600 + $32.26 = $632.26)

- Current balance, or the total amount you owe. When you receive your statement, check all the information to make certain it is correct.
- Due date for payments.

Paying on time keeps the costs of offering credit down. Businesses have to spend money to collect outstanding amounts when payments are late. Businesses pass these extra costs on to the consumer. Paying on time also protects your credit rating.

Keep Accurate Records

If you use charge accounts or credit cards, you need to keep records of the charges you make. You should keep all your receipts so you will know how close you are to your credit limit. When you get your monthly statements, you should compare your receipts with the charges listed on your statement. If you think there is a mistake on your statement, you should write the card issuer and find out how to resolve the error.

CHAPTER 29 GETTING AND KEEPING CREDIT **493**

Reteaching Strategy

Give students the following problem to practice computing finance charges.
1. Guillermo's unpaid credit card balance is $387.92, and interest charges each month are 1.75%. Find the finance charge on Guillermo's unpaid balance. ($387.92 × .0175 = $6.78.)
2. Add the finance charge to Guillermo's balance to find his new starting principal. ($387.92 + $6.78 = $394.70.)
3. Guillermo sends in a payment of $200. What is his new balance and what will the finance charge be on it? ($394.70 − $200 = $194.70 [new balance] × .0175 = $3.40 [finance charge].)

TEACHING TIP

According to a survey conducted by Princeton Survey Research Associates, some 40 percent of credit cardholders have no idea how much interest they are paying. To illustrate the danger of such ignorance, have students calculate the finance charges for a year for someone who carried an average balance of $650 with an interest rate of 8 percent. Then have them do the same calculation using an interest rate of 19 percent. ($650 × .08 = $52; $650 × .19 = $123.50.)

Quick Check Answers

1. Previous balance, new purchases, payments, finance charges, current balance, and due date for payments.
2. Report the loss to the credit or charge card issuer immediately.
3. Creditor takes part of the debtor's wages in payment; creditor may take back an item if a debtor fails to pay.

If you discover that your card is missing or has been stolen, it is your responsibility to notify the card issuer immediately. Card issuers have 24-hour phone numbers you can call to report lost or stolen cards. As soon as you notify the company, it will deactivate your card so that no one can make any further charges on your card. You will not have to pay more than $50 of unauthorized charges if you report the loss immediately. It is a good idea to keep a record of these phone numbers in a safe place so you will be able to report losses as soon as they are discovered.

Avoid Credit Problems

Credit cards and charge accounts are useful financial tools, but they can easily be misused. The more credit cards you have, the more you might be tempted to make impulse purchases. To protect your credit rating, you must be careful to buy only the things you can afford.

Taking out a loan can also present problems. It is important to read the fine print on the loan contract carefully before signing it. The contract may say that the lender can ask for full payment of the entire loan amount if one payment is late. Some contracts allow the creditor to take part of your wages if you miss a payment, a practice known as **garnishment** of wages. If you can't live with these clauses in your contract, delete them or don't sign the contract.

When you buy an item with a loan, the item you buy serves as collateral to help guarantee that the creditor will be repaid. Suppose you fail to make the installment payments on a new car. Your installment contract gives the creditor the legal right to **repossess,** or take back, the collateral, which in this case is the car. The business can sell the car to someone else to obtain the money you still owe. Because creditors report missed payments, wage garnishment, and repossessions to credit bureaus, all these problems will cause your credit rating to drop quickly.

Quick Check

1. What six items do most monthly credit statements show?
2. What is the first thing you should do if your credit card is lost or stolen?
3. Explain the terms *garnishment* and *repossess.*

Cooperative Learning Make and Defend

Some banks offer a *secured credit card.* With a secured card, a person sets up a savings account with a bank. The amount deposited in the account serves as collateral for the balance on the card. Secured cards are attractive to people who have been turned down for other credit cards. Secured cards usually charge an annual fee and have a higher APR than other cards; individuals must also keep a substantial amount of money tied up in the savings account to maintain credit. However, keeping the secured account in good standing can help rebuild a damaged credit rating. Have teams evaluate the pros and cons of a secured card and explain whether they would advise someone with a poor credit rating to obtain a secured credit card.

Refer to the *Cooperative Learning Strategies* booklet for additional strategies.

Chapter 29 **Summary**

Main Ideas

1. Capacity to pay, character, and collateral are the three factors creditors look at when determining a person's credit rating.
2. For very expensive items, people often get an installment loan or a cash loan.
3. The difference between the cost of an item in cash and what it costs on credit is known as the cost of credit.
4. Being able to calculate how much finance charges add to the cost of a purchase helps people decide whether or not they should use credit.
5. The principal, the interest rate, and the length of the loan are the three factors that determine the cost of credit.
6. A security agreement explains the terms on which credit is extended and explains how interest charges will be computed. Signing the agreement means you agree to follow the rules described in the document.
7. Responsible consumers use credit wisely by paying on time, keeping accurate records, and avoiding credit problems.
8. For people who have good communications skills and enjoy working with the public, there are many opportunities available in wholesale and retail trade.

CASE ANALYSIS Consumer Credit

Reva Alhusen recently bought some new living room furniture on credit from Belair's Furniture Store. Belair's had a sale and offered special credit terms for qualifying buyers. Reva's total purchase came to $1036.29, and she qualified for the special credit program that offered no finance charges if the entire amount financed was paid within 12 months. Reva made a down payment of $36.29 and agreed to pay $50 twice a month until the $1000 balance due was paid. The security agreement she signed said in part, "No finance fee if amount financed is paid in 12 months." Belair's told Reva that her account would be serviced by Triangle Financial Services, a finance company that handled the store's credit sales. When her payment book arrived from Triangle Financial Services, Reva found 24 monthly payment coupons each in the amount of $49.92. What should Reva do?

QUICK QUIZ

1. What three factors do creditors consider when determining whether to extend credit? (Capacity to pay, character, and collateral.)
2. What is a finance charge? (The cost of credit stated in dollars and cents.)
3. Name two actions a creditor could take if a borrower failed to make payments on a loan. (A creditor could repossess the item purchased on credit or could garnishee the debtor's wages.)
4. What is the maximum amount of charges you will be liable for if you report a lost or stolen credit card immediately? ($50.)

Chapter 29 **Review**

CHAPTER 29 REVIEW

APPLY

Answers

Use the Language of Business

1. collateral, 2. annual percentage rate, 3. unsecured loan, 4. interest rate, 5. down payment, 6. finance charge, 7. repossess, 8. cosigner, 9. secured loan, 10. garnishment, 11. principal.

Review What You Learned

1. Creditors check a person's capacity to pay, character, and collateral.
2. The rate used to calculate interest; the date payments are due; the penalty for late payments; and the cost of the credit.
3. Previous balance, new purchases, payments, finance charges, current balance, and due date for payments.
4. A creditor could repossess the item purchased on credit or could garnishee the debtor's wages.
5. They increase the cost.
6. A customer service representative needs to listen carefully and speak clearly. He or she also needs to communicate effectively when resolving conflicts.

Understand Business Concepts

1. Yes, a person is really borrowing when using credit. The money to buy the goods or services must be repaid.
2. If the bill is paid in full each month, the user pays no finance charge. The user gets to use someone else's money for a period of time, often 30 days, with no additional charge.
3. Employment information and length of time at an address help a creditor determine the debtor's stability. Financial information helps determine the applicant's financial resources.
4. You could ask yourself a series of questions such as: Do I really need this TV right now? Do I have enough saved for a down payment to keep monthly payments at an affordable level? How much more will it cost to buy with credit than with cash?

Use the Language of Business

When establishing and using credit, it is important to know the following terms. Match each term to its definition.

annual percentage rate
collateral
cosigner
down payment
finance charge
garnishment

interest rate
principal
repossess
secured loan
unsecured loan

1. Property or savings that could be offered to repay a loan.
2. Cost of credit on a yearly basis.
3. Cash loan not backed by collateral.
4. Stated percentage of the principal.
5. Cash or check payment that is a portion of the total cost.
6. Cost of credit stated in a dollar and cents amount.
7. Creditors take back items if debtors fail to make payments.
8. Someone who agrees to make payments if a debtor is unable to do so.
9. Cash loan backed by collateral.
10. Creditors take part of a debtor's wages when he or she misses payments.
11. Sum of money owed as a debt upon which interest is computed.

Review What You Learned

1. What three factors do creditors check to determine a person's credit rating?
2. Name four pieces of information concerning the terms of an installment loan that are generally contained in an installment loan contract.
3. What six items are on a statement for a charge or credit card account?
4. List two measures a creditor might take if a debtor did not make payments on a loan.
5. What effect do finance charges have on the cost of an item bought on credit?
6. Describe two situations in which workers in wholesale and retail trade would need good communication skills.

Understand Business Concepts

1. When a person uses credit, is he or she really borrowing? Explain your answer.
2. "The real benefit of credit cards comes when a consumer pays his or her bill in full each month." What does this mean?
3. Why do you think years on the job, years at present address, and owning your home or car help your credit rating? What other factors might affect it?
4. Suppose you want a TV but have saved only part of its cost. How would you decide whether to buy on credit?
5. What is the role of a cosigner of a loan?
6. Should repossession of goods bought on installment be allowed if the buyer cannot make payments? What problems are not solved by repossession?
7. What is the best way for consumers to compare interest rates?
8. How much would you pay in finance charges in 8 months on a balance of $500 for a credit card that charged 1 1/2 percent interest per month?
9. Why would getting a part-time job in wholesale or retail trade be a good way to learn about business?

5. The cosigner is a person who agrees to repay a loan if the borrower cannot. The cosigner lends his or her ability to secure credit to the borrower.
6. Possible answer: Repossession should be allowed so that the creditor can regain some value on a loan that a debtor is unable to pay.
7. Consumers should compare the annual percentage rate of various forms of credit.
8. The finance charges would come to $60.
9. Possible answer: A part-time job allows a person to see the

factors involved in selling goods and services and to decide if he or she would like to pursue such a career.

Think Critically

1. Answers will vary depending on students' values. Generally, however, the most expensive items are most likely to be purchased on credit.
2. Summaries will vary depending on the adults surveyed.

Think Critically

1. **Evaluate.** Many items can be bought with cash, with installment payments, or with a credit card. Decide what you think is the best way to purchase each of the following items: a swimming pool, a bag of groceries, a car, a pair of shoes, a refrigerator, books for school, a sofa and chair, and a CD player. Give reasons for each option that you chose.

2. **Synthesize.** Survey a number of adults on their opinions about buying expensive items. Do they favor using credit for such purchases? For what types of items would they pay only cash? Write a summary of your survey.

Use What You Learned

1. **Group Project.** As a team, choose a high-priced item such as a used car, sound system, or computer system that would probably be purchased with credit. Each team member should investigate the terms of credit from a different credit source, such as commercial banks, credit unions, or savings and loans. Consider these questions:

   - Is credit available from the seller?
   - Is a down payment required? If so, how much is it?
   - What is the annual percentage rate?
   - What would monthly payments be?

   Make a chart of the information you and your team have gathered. Use the chart to decide which source offers the best credit terms. Write a paragraph describing your group's decision.

2. **Computer Application.** Create a spreadsheet to compare varying financing plans offered by local car dealers on new car purchases. If the dealer offers leasing, also include the financing rates for lease plans on new cars. Print out the information in the spreadsheet and use it for classroom display or discussion.

3. **Skill Reinforcement.** Select two different credit card applications in local stores or banks. Check their monthly finance charges and their annual percentage rates. Using the information from the applications, determine for each of the cards how long it would take to pay off a $700 purchase if you made a $75 payment each month. What would you pay in finance charges for each of the cards? Create a table to compare the numbers and write a short paragraph to tell which card you would choose and why.

Save your work in your Business Portfolio.

CHAPTER 29   GETTING AND KEEPING CREDIT   **497**

Independent Practice

Use the Chapter 29 worksheets in *Student Activity Guide 2* for additional practice and application activities. *Student Activity Guide 2* provides vocabulary exercises, reading comprehension checks, problems, projects, and simulations of business and economic situations. A Teacher's Annotated Edition provides answers.

ASSESS

Portfolio Assessment

The portfolio projects are designed to lead students to develop a collection of their best work to submit to you for assessment. You and your students should decide which projects will be included in their respective Business Portfolios. Refer students to the specific rubric(s) from the *Alternative Assessment Strategies* booklet listed with each of the project notes below. These rubrics will alert students to the criteria you will use to assess their projects.

Chapter Assessment

Use the Chapter 29 Test from the *Test Masters* booklet to evaluate students' understanding of the chapter concepts. An answer key is provided. Or create your own customized test using the *Testmaker* software.

Use What You Learned
1. Make sure all students participate in the group project. Rubrics: Charts and Tables; Paragraph.
2. Students with no access to a computer may make their comparison charts by hand. Rubric: Charts and Tables.
3. Students' answers will vary depending on the terms offered, but their calculations should indicate that they can compute finance charges. Rubrics: Charts and Tables; Paragraph.

FOCUS

Major Concepts
• Protecting Your Credit Rights
• Enforcing the Laws
• Handling Your Credit Problems

Introduce the Topic
Ask students to imagine there were no laws regulating lenders and credit card issuers. How could lenders abuse their power? Discuss students' responses. Explain that in Chapter 30 students will learn how state and federal laws protect consumers from unethical lending practices.

Use Business Terms
Have students read the list of Business Terms. Ask for ideas about what the terms mean. Record correct answers on the board or a transparency. For unknown terms, advise students to check the meanings of the terms as they read the chapter.

Explain that the Consumer Credit Protection Act requires that all costs of borrowing be made known to the borrower. These costs must be provided in a *written* truth-in-lending disclosure that shows both the dollar cost of credit and the annual percentage rate. Ask students to recall why it is important to know these costs before using credit. (So you will know exactly how much you will have to pay.)

CHAPTER
30

Business terms

usury law

truth-in-lending disclosure

credit bureau

collection agent

credit counselor

consolidation loan

bankruptcy

498

CHAPTER 30 RESOURCES

Instructional Resources

Lesson Plan for Chapter 30

Teaching Transparency 30-1

Strategies and Worksheets for Teaching Transparency 30-1

Enrichment Master 30-1

Student Activity Guide 2–TAE for Chapter 30

Test Master for Chapter 30

Alternative Assessment Strategies

Math Skills Review

International Business Strategies

Cooperative Learning Strategies

Communication Skills Review

Ethics in Business Strategies

Credit and the Law

Learning objectives

After completing this chapter, you will be able to:
- Explain why federal and state governments have passed credit legislation.
- List federal laws that protect consumers.
- Discuss how credit protection laws are enforced.
- Identify ways of handling credit problems.
- List some tips for ethical business behavior.
- Describe several methods a business can use to maintain the electronic security of its computer information system.

Consider what you know

- In our society it is important to establish and maintain a good credit rating. Part of maintaining a good credit rating is understanding the cost of credit and whether you can afford the extra cost. Wise consumers weigh the costs of using credit carefully before borrowing.

Consider what you want to know

- What credit laws exist to protect consumers?
- What strategies can consumers use to deal with credit problems?
- How can employees make sure they are behaving ethically on the job?
- What security measures have been developed for electronic data?

Consider how to use what you learn

- As you read this chapter, think about how you might advise someone who has problems with credit. Where could they get help and advice?

CHAPTER 30   CREDIT AND THE LAW   **499**

Multimedia Resources

Technology Resource Guide

Distance Learning Guide

Internet Resource Guide

Professional Resources

School-to-Work/Tech Prep Strategies

Instructional Poster

Spanish Resources

Testmaker Software for Chapter 30

The Wall Street Journal Video Series
  Video & Activities for Chapter 30

Business and Marketing Computer Applications—An Integrated Software Simulation Using Microsoft Works

Stocktracker—A Stock Market Software Simulation

Where's the Dough? Board Game

TEACH

In 1994, Congress passed a revision to the Fair Credit Reporting Act of 1971, making it easier for consumers to correct errors in credit reports provided by credit bureaus. The revision was deemed necessary because consumer advocates found that 61 percent of the people denied credit, jobs, or housing were turned down because of errors in the bureaus' reports.

Develop Concepts

Protecting Your Credit Rights

Credit rights are another aspect of consumer rights. In fact, some of the same agencies involved in protecting consumers' rights also oversee lending institutions. Various agencies enforce the laws that have been passed to ensure people are treated fairly when applying for and using credit. Ask students why it is important for people who use credit to know what their rights are. Ask students if they think that laws alone will ensure that a person's credit rights aren't abused. (No. There are many examples of lending institutions and other creditors that do not obey the laws. It is up to consumers to *know* their rights and take the proper action to make sure they are treated fairly.)

Credit is widely used in our economy today. However, the reliance on credit has created certain problems. Billing mistakes, unfair credit charges, misleading claims, hidden costs, and refusal to extend credit are just a few of the problems faced by consumers.

In this chapter, you will learn about the laws that have been passed to protect consumers from credit abuses. You will also find out how those laws are enforced by various levels of government.

PROTECTING YOUR CREDIT RIGHTS

Consumers have specific rights where credit is concerned. To protect consumers, both the federal and state governments control and regulate the credit industry. Most states, for example, have set a maximum on the interest rates charged for certain types of credit. A law restricting the amount of interest that can be charged for credit is called a **usury law.** Figure 30-1 on page 501 shows the maximum rates of interest some states allow for credit cards.

Concern about consumer problems also resulted in the passage of a series of federal laws. Among other things, these laws helped inform consumers about the costs of credit. The laws also established rules and regulations concerning credit application, credit history information, and debt collection. More important, they provided for a smoother running of the nation's economic machinery.

Business & HISTORY

In Europe there were no real laws about charging interest on loans until the 1500s. Up until that time, most people thought that interest should not be charged. In 1545 King Henry VIII of England passed laws that allowed some forms of interest. The laws also set a maximum rate for the amount of interest—the first usury law.

Consumer Credit Protection Act

At one time, consumers who bought credit did not know how much the credit would cost. In one place, credit was available for $10 down and $2 a week. Another advertisement said "12 percent add-on interest." A department store promoted charge accounts ". . . with only 1 1/2 percent per month carrying charge." How could you figure out all of this? To make comparing credit costs easier, Congress passed the Consumer Credit Protection Act, commonly known as the Truth in Lending Law.

The most important part of the Consumer Credit Protection Act is the requirement that *all* costs of borrowing be made known to the consumer. These costs are provided in the

Enrichment Strategy

Usury and indebtedness are frequently found as themes in literature. Invite students to post descriptions on a bulletin board of some examples from readings in their English classes. As students progress in the chapter, have them decide which laws they have studied are designed to prohibit such practices.

MAXIMUM INTEREST RATES CHARGED FOR CREDIT CARDS

State	Maximum Rate	State	Maximum Rate	State	Maximum Rate
Alabama	No limit	Kentucky	21%	Ohio	25%
Alaska	17%	Louisiana	18%	Oklahoma	30%
Arizona	No limit	Maine	No limit	Oregon	No limit
Arkansas	17%	Maryland	24%	Pennsylvania*	12%, 18%
California	No limit	Massachusetts	18%	Rhode Island	18%
Colorado	21%	Michigan	18%	South Carolina	No limit
Connecticut	19.8%	Minnesota	18%	South Dakota	No limit
Delaware	No limit	Mississippi	21%	Tennessee	24%
District of		Missouri	22%	Texas	22%
Columbia	24%	Montana	No limit	Utah	No limit
Florida	No limit	Nebraska	No limit	Vermont	18%
Georgia	No limit	Nevada	No limit	Virginia	No limit
Hawaii	24%	New Hampshire	No limit	Washington**	25%, no limit
Idaho	No limit	New Jersey	30%	West Virginia	18%
Illinois	No limit	New Mexico	No limit	Wisconsin	No limit
Indiana	36%	New York	25%	Wyoming	36%
Iowa	No limit	North Carolina	18%		
Kansas	18%	North Dakota	No limit		

*12% loans, 18% purchases
**25% loans, no limit purchases

FIGURE 30-1

truth-in-lending disclosure that a creditor gives to a borrower. The Truth in Lending Law requires costs to be expressed in two ways. One is the dollar cost of credit, or the total finance charge. The other is the annual percentage rate, or APR, which you learned about in Chapter 29. A truth-in-lending disclosure, such as the one shown in Figure 30-2 on page 502, shows the total finance charge so the borrower can determine whether buying on credit is worth the extra cost. In addition, the disclosure shows the APR so the borrower can compare it with interest rates at various banks, credit unions, and finance companies. The truth-in-lending disclosure also states the credit terms and conditions. For instance, what happens if a payment is late? Is the finance charge reduced if the loan is paid off earlier than agreed? If so, by how much is it reduced? Or is there a penalty for paying off the loan ahead of time?

Many states have laws establishing the maximum interest rates that can be charged for credit cards. What is the maximum rate of interest in your home state?

Curriculum Connection   Math

Have students use Figure 30-1 above to find the maximum annual finance charge that could be charged in Connecticut for someone who maintained a credit card balance of $750 for a year. ($750 × .198 = $148.50.) What would the finance charges be for the same balance in New Jersey? ($750 × .3 = $225.)

For students who need to sharpen their math skills, choose among the worksheets in the *Math Skills Review* booklet.

Business Brief
In 1994, Italy's economy was in the midst of a recession and usury had reached disturbing levels. It was estimated that about 15 percent of small businesses in Rome had fallen prey to "loan sharks" who charged illegal interest rates. The crime was often carried out by organized crime groups.

Use Figure 30-2 as an example of the kinds of information contained in a truth-in-lending disclosure. Have students study the figure and then ask: How would paying off the debt early affect the borrower's contract? (He or she would be entitled to a refund of part of the finance charge.) Answer to caption: $1178.06.

Use Teaching Transparency 30-1 and its corresponding strategies and worksheet from the *Teaching Transparency Strategies and Worksheets* booklet to help students better understand the provisions contained in a truth-in-lending disclosure. Verify student worksheets using the Answer Key.

Learning Activity

Ask students to collect newspaper ads or direct-mail offers that demonstrate compliance with the Truth in Lending Law. Discuss these advertisements with students.

Point out that consumers need to read all advertisements concerning credit terms and interest rates extremely closely. Have the class discuss how information can be concealed. (Fine print and confusing "legalese" are two examples.)

FIGURE 30-2

Truth-in-lending disclosures must be provided to borrowers. They spell out all the costs involved in borrowing money or in purchasing items on credit. What is the dollar amount the borrower will pay in finance charges on this loan?

TRUTH-IN-LENDING DISCLOSURE

ANNUAL PERCENTAGE RATE The cost of your credit as a yearly rate.	FINANCE CHARGE The dollar amount the credit will cost you.	AMOUNT FINANCED The amount of credit provided to you or on your behalf.	TOTAL OF PAYMENTS The amount you will have paid after you have made all payments as scheduled.
13.50%	$1,178.06	$5,314.90	$6,492.96

Your payment schedule will be:

Number of Payments	Amount of Payments	When Payments Are Due
36	$180.36	Commencing monthly 9-16-97

SECURITY: ☒ right of set-off against any moneys, credits, or other property of yours in the possession of Holder, on deposit or otherwise.

LATE CHARGE: If a payment is late, for more than 10 days, you will be charged $5.00 or 5% of the payment, whichever is less.

PREPAYMENT: If you pay off early, you will be entitled to a refund of part of the finance charge. See your contract terms for any additional information about nonpayment; default; any required repayment in full before the scheduled date; and prepayment refunds and penalties.

Another important condition in the Truth in Lending Law involves the advertising of credit. An advertisement must tell the number of payments, the amount, and the period of payments if the amount of the down payment is given. In other words, if an ad states "$10 down and $2 a week," the number of weeks must also be given.

Finally, the Truth in Lending Law protects credit card customers. If your card is lost or stolen and used by someone else, your payment for any unauthorized purchases is limited to $50. Some credit card companies do not make you pay the $50 if you report the loss immediately. Also, credit card companies may not send unrequested cards to consumers.

Equal Credit Opportunity Act

When you apply for a loan or a credit card, you must provide certain information. This information is evaluated to determine whether you are a good credit risk. The Equal Credit Opportunity Act says that the application for credit must be judged only on the basis of financial responsibility. No person may be denied credit or discriminated against on the basis of

Enrichment Strategy

The Truth in Lending Law didn't come into effect until 1968. Invite interested students to search the archives of the local newspaper or historical society or to use microfilm versions of *The New York Times* or other large metropolitan newspapers to find earlier advertisements for credit that would not be allowed today. Suggest that students concentrate their search on the business, automobile, and home sections of the newspapers. Have students take notes and present their findings to the class.

age, sex, marital status, race, religion, or nationality. The Equal Credit Opportunity Act allows only three reasons for denying credit:

- low income
- large current debts
- poor record of payments in the past.

The Equal Credit Opportunity Act also requires that all credit applicants be informed of their acceptance or rejection within 30 days. Any person who is denied credit must be given a written statement listing the reasons for the rejection.

The Equal Credit Opportunity Act pays special attention to the credit rights of women. It says that it is illegal to deny a person credit just because she is a woman. It is also illegal to deny credit to a woman because of marital status. In addition, a married woman can use either her maiden name or her married name when applying for credit.

Fair Credit Reporting Act

When a person applies for and uses credit, the information goes into a file at one or more credit bureaus. A **credit bureau** is an agency or firm that collects and maintains information about the paying habits of consumers. A credit file includes personal, employment, and financial information. In the past there has been a lot of concern about the accuracy of credit file information. Information that was merely hearsay or gossip was often included in the file. For these and other reasons, the Fair Credit Reporting Act was passed.

The Fair Credit Reporting Act gives you the right to know what is in your credit file. If incorrect information is found, it must be removed from your file after an examination of the situation. If there is disagreement between you and the credit bureau as to the correctness of the information, you have the right to have your version of the situation placed in your file. For example, suppose you stopped payments on a stereo system because you believed it was defective. The store you bought that system from made a report on the situation. Both your version and the store's version must be included in your credit file if no agreement is reached.

The Fair Credit Reporting Act also states that you must be notified when an investigation is being conducted on your credit record. If you are denied credit, insurance, or employment because of a credit report, you must be given the name and address of the credit bureau that provided the report.

The privacy of the information in your credit file is important. According to the law, only authorized persons may see a

In some countries in the Middle East, businesses are not allowed to charge interest because the Islamic religion forbids it. To cover their costs for extending credit, businesses frequently charge two different prices for the same item. The lower price is charged when the item is paid for with cash. The higher price is charged when a customer buys with credit.

CHAPTER 30

Learning Activity
Have students describe situations of discrimination and consumer rights' violations that are outlawed by the Equal Credit Opportunity Act. Discuss whether or not the law might be difficult to enforce in certain cases.

Business Brief
One way of uncovering discrimination involves the use of people called "testers." For example, a Latino couple might believe that they have been denied a loan because of their ethnic background. To test for discrimination, a white couple would present credentials to the same lending institution listing the same income, job history, educational background, and credit history as the Latino couple. If a loan was approved for the tester couple, it serves as strong proof that the Latino couple was discriminated against on the basis of race since the two couples' credentials were identical.

CHAPTER 30   CREDIT AND THE LAW   **503**

Curriculum Connection   History

Tell students that the Equal Credit Opportunity Act was passed in 1974. Have students research the origins of the act and find out why such a law became necessary. Have them report their findings to the class.

Discuss

Some students will be familiar with the process of logging on to on-line computer services. Ask a volunteer to describe the procedure to the rest of the class. Have students define the terms *user identification code, log on, password, encryption,* and *software piracy.* (Code needed to gain access to a computer's files; gain access to a computer's files; name or number that identifies the user; process of encoding and decoding data; illegal copying or using of programs.)

Learning Activity

Photocopy and distribute Enrichment Master 30-1 so students can see an example of a credit report. Then have students find out how someone would investigate the contents of his or her credit file. Suggest that they look in the Yellow Pages under Credit Rating or Credit Reporting Agencies to find out where the nearest credit clearinghouse is located. Have them find out what information they would need to provide to obtain the report and whether or not there is a fee.

Electronic Security

Piracy! Theft! Breaking the code! Elements of a new spy thriller? No, unfortunately these activities are everyday occurrences in the world of electronic data and computers. Computer criminals have been known to steal thousands of credit card numbers, resulting in millions of dollars of fraudulent charges. Sensitive programs have been stolen from security experts' computers. Irreplaceable credit records have been erased.

To limit the amount of damage that can be done by computer thieves, companies take steps to secure their computers and the data in them. Among the most basic security steps is the requirement that all users of a computer have a *user identification code.* In order to *log on,* or gain access to the computer's files, a user must supply the appropriate identification code.

In addition to the identification code, most systems require that each user also give a password before gaining access. A *password* may be a name or number that identifies the user. (See computer screen showing user ID and query for password.) Generally a user's password is known only to the user, the data processing manager, and the computer's security system. If the user's identification code or password does not match records within the computer's security software, the user is locked out of the system.

Even if the user identification code and the password are correct, the user may not have access to all the files in a system. For instance, personnel files may not be accessed by people in accounting. Accounting records and reports may be inaccessible to sales and marketing.

Another method used to ensure the security of data is data encryption. *Encryption* is a process of encoding

copy of your credit report. People may legally obtain your credit report when you apply for additional credit, a job, or insurance.

Fair Credit Billing Act

Every month millions of credit card and charge account customers receive their monthly statements. Most of the time these bills are correct, but occasionally a billing error can occur. Errors may be due to a computer problem. They may include the listing of incorrect amounts or charges to your account that are not yours. The Fair Credit Billing Act states the steps to be followed when errors occur. The law also requires that consumers be notified regularly of the steps to take to get an error corrected.

The first step in correcting errors is to notify the creditor in writing. In the letter, you must give your name, account number, an explanation of the error, and the amount of the error. While waiting for a reply, you do not have to pay the part of the bill that you believe to be in error. However, you still have to make any other payments that are due. The creditor must either correct the error or explain in writing why the account is

504   UNIT 9   USING CREDIT TO BUY GOODS AND SERVICES

Curriculum Connection   English and Communication

Give students the following scenario: A few years ago, Ralph Weiss withheld a portion of his rent because his landlord refused to make necessary repairs to his apartment. Last month Ralph was denied a loan; he checked his credit report and found a statement saying he hadn't paid his rent. According to the landlord-tenant laws in Ralph's city, withholding rent was the correct action to take in his situation. Have students draft a letter explaining Ralph's side of the issue. Students may use their imaginations to fill in reasonable details.

For those students who need to sharpen their written communication skills, choose among the worksheets in the *Communication Skills Review* booklet.

and decoding data. It is used most often in systems such as electronic mail. Advanced software for encryption can encode a message in more than 72 quadrillion ways. This means that, even if a computer thief found a file of credit card numbers, the information would need to be decoded before the numbers were usable.

While criminal hackers and their exploits often make headlines, they are not the most pressing security problems for the computer industry. *Software piracy,* the illegal copying or use of programs, is a widespread problem. It is easy to copy a program; it is also illegal. Like books, videotapes, and CDs, software is copyrighted and covered by the Copyright Act of 1976. Software development is a business: software companies invest huge amounts of time and money to develop software in the hopes of making a profit. The laws against software piracy are designed to protect the enormous investment of time and money spent by software developers. Without the protection of the law, software development would not be profitable. Without the profit incentive, software development would cease and the advancement of technology would stop.

Integrated Criminal Justice Information System

CJIS

User ID: Investigator
Password: *******

(Level 3 Encryption Enforced)

Career Criminal
Involved Person
Inquiry

OK

Follow Through

Have students research real-life examples of what has happened when a business's computer data has been destroyed or illegally tampered with. Suggest that students focus on what measures the business took to secure its files from future tampering. Have students share the results of their research with the class.

correct. Your account cannot be closed for refusal to pay the amount in question during that time. If the creditor made the mistake, you will not have to pay any finance charge on the part in error. If there was no error, you may have to pay a finance charge for any late payments.

This law, like the Fair Credit Reporting Act, allows consumers to tell their side of the story. Any information sent to a credit bureau must report that the consumer believes there is an error in the bill.

The Fair Credit Billing Act permits consumers to stop a credit card payment for items that are damaged or defective. Before stopping payment, however, you must attempt to return the item to the place where you bought it.

Fair Debt Collection Practices Act

A **collection agent** is a person who has the job of collecting debts that are overdue. Consumers who get behind in their credit payments may be called on by such an agent. At one time, collection agents could use almost any method they chose to collect overdue bills. They could call late at night, use threats

CHAPTER 30   CREDIT AND THE LAW   **505**

Meeting Student Diversity

Students with limited proficiency in English may have trouble distinguishing among the different federal acts. Have them copy the main points of each act onto different colored paper to "color code" the information. They will then be able to associate the different colors with the information for different acts.

Building Business Skills

Building Business Skills

Model

Have students read the Tips for Ethical Business Behavior listed on page 507. Provide students with some additional examples if necessary. For instance, you might tell them it would be ethical to acknowledge the work of teammates when being praised for a group project. Encourage students to describe other examples of ethical behavior.

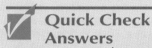

Quick Check Answers

1. Consumer Credit Protection Act, Equal Credit Opportunity Act, the Fair Credit Reporting Act, Fair Credit Billing Act, and Fair Debt Collection Practices Act.

2. Law restricting the amount of interest that can be charged for credit; an agency or firm that collects and maintains information about paying habits of consumers; a person who has the job of collecting debts that are overdue.

3. Annual percentage rate, finance charges, amount financed, and total of payments.

EMPLOYABILITY

Exhibit Ethical Behavior

Explanation

Ethics are values, or moral standards. Behaving ethically is nothing new for you. You have been setting standards and living by your values every day of your life. So why is it necessary to discuss ethics on the job?

Business ethics may include ideas you never thought of before. For example, talking on the phone with a friend seems harmless. You might be shocked to be accused of stealing from your employer—but isn't using company time for personal business the same thing? Your employer pays you to work for a certain period of time every day. Taking long breaks means you are not doing your work. In addition, your company pays the phone bills!

When you accept a job, you become part of the company. Your behavior reflects on your company's reputation as well as your own. Consider how your behavior appears to colleagues, customers, and suppliers.

Practice

How can you avoid ethical pitfalls on the job? Read the Tips for Ethical Business Behavior. Then number a separate sheet of paper from 1 to 4. Read the following case studies and answer the questions.

1. You just had your performance review and found out you're getting a raise. You can't wait to tell someone. What should you do?

of jail or seizing property, and even try to collect more than was owed. The Fair Debt Collection Practices Act made all of these practices illegal.

This act protects consumers from collection agents in several ways. First, collection agents must identify themselves to the people whose bills they seek to collect. They cannot tell others about the debt. This is considered a violation of privacy and is forbidden by the law. They cannot contact people at work, if that is not permitted by the employer. Collection agents are not allowed to make telephone calls without identifying themselves. They cannot keep calling or pretend to be someone else. Finally, they cannot use postcards that mention the amount of the debt owed.

Quick Check

1. Name five federal laws that protect consumers' credit rights.
2. Define *usury law*, *credit bureau*, and *collection agent*.
3. What four amounts appear as part of a truth-in-lending disclosure?

Reteaching Strategy

Have students briefly review the section and then have them imagine the following situations. Ask students what law offers protection in each case.

- A debt collector calls you several times a day at work and at home in the evenings. (Fair Debt Collection Practices Act.)
- You discover a mistake on your credit card bill. (Fair Credit Billing Act.)
- You have been refused a loan but given no reason. (Equal Credit Opportunity Act.)
- You find out the interest on your loan is not what you were told. (Consumer Credit Protection Act, also called Truth in Lending Law.)
- You checked your credit report and found some incorrect information. (Fair Credit Reporting Act.)

2. You know the employee at the next desk is unhappy on the job. Today at lunch you saw him with a business competitor. What should you do?

3. Your friend who moved out of state leaves a voice mail message on your office phone and asks you to call back. The message says it is not urgent. What should you do?

4. You work at a credit bureau that charges a fee to provide individuals with an updated report concerning their own credit rating. Your friend wants to apply for a loan and asks you to show her a copy of her credit report. What should you do?

ENFORCING THE LAWS

As you may recall from Chapter 16, the federal government has established numerous agencies to regulate business activities. One agency already discussed is the Federal Trade Commission (FTC). In addition to its responsibilities to assure competition, it is also responsible for enforcing the laws on credit. The FTC helps consumers with credit problems. It handles complaints about being unfairly turned down for credit, being overcharged on a bill, or being bothered by collection agents. Several other federal government agencies deal with specific credit matters. Figure 30-3 on page 508 lists some credit regulators.

As you can see, the federal government is concerned with consumer credit protection. On the state level, you can contact your state banking department about credit problems. In addition, a consumer protection division of the state attorney general's office deals with complaints that may not be handled by other government agencies. Many cities and other local governments also have consumer credit protection agencies.

F.Y.I.

If you need a credit counselor, you should shop around for one. Keep in mind that counselors should not charge more than 12 percent of your debt as a fee. You might want to consider checking out one of the nonprofit credit counseling agencies in the United States. For a list, write to the National Foundation for Consumer Credit, 8611 2nd Avenue, Silver Springs, MD 20910.

Making Connections ➡️   Classroom Ethics

Bruno is in Mr. Ladislaw's 10:00 algebra class. Bruno's good friend Jim is in Mr. Ladislaw's 2:00 class. Jim has been having trouble with algebra and asks Bruno to slip him some of the answers to the test at lunchtime. Bruno likes Jim and doesn't want to see him fail algebra. Have students evaluate the situation and describe what would be the ethical way of handling the situation. (Possible answer: Bruno should tell Jim that it would not be honest or ethical to give him the answers to the upcoming test. Bruno could, instead, offer to help Jim study for future tests.)

Refer to the *Ethics in Business Strategies* booklet for additional strategies and activities.

Quick Check Answers

1. It enforces the laws concerned with credit.
2. The state banking department and the consumer protection division of the state attorney general's office.

Quick Check Answers

1. Someone who assists people with their credit problems; one loan that brings all a person's debts together.
2. It has a very negative effect on a credit rating and makes it very difficult to reestablish credit.

FIGURE 30-3

The federal government is concerned with consumer credit protection and has established several agencies for enforcing credit laws. Name three situations in which the Federal Trade Commission could step in to help consumers with credit problems.

CREDIT REGULATORS

Federal Agency

Federal Trade Commission

Comptroller of the Currency

Federal Reserve Bank

Federal Deposit Insurance Corporation

Office of Thrift Supervision

Final responsibility for credit protection rests with you. After all, a law can help you only if you know about it in the first place. You have credit rights. Insist on those rights, and the laws will protect you.

Quick Check

1. What credit-related function does the Federal Trade Commission perform?
2. At the state level, what help is available for consumers with credit concerns?

HANDLING YOUR CREDIT PROBLEMS

What can you do when you have a credit problem or when you have gone too far in your use of credit? Of course, it is best to avoid a credit problem in the first place. If you are already in difficulty, however, there are ways to deal with your problem.

If you cannot meet your payments, the first thing you should do is contact the creditor. Talk to the credit manager and try to work out a plan that will make your payments easier. Consumers who cannot work out their own credit problems should talk to a **credit counselor.** This person assists consumers with their credit problems. A credit counselor might help you revise your budget, contact creditors to arrange new payment plans, or help you find additional sources of income.

Another possible solution is to bring your debts together in one loan, called a **consolidation loan.** There are two dangers with a consolidation loan. First, it carries a high interest rate, because the people who get such loans are generally poor credit risks. Second, because there is only one monthly payment, the debtor may feel that the credit problem is under control and make new purchases.

The last resort is to declare **bankruptcy.** This is a legal process in which some or all of the assets of the debtor are distributed among the creditors. Individuals as well as businesses can declare bankruptcy. When bankruptcy is declared, the debtor, the creditor, and a federal court-appointed trustee compose a plan to repay the debt on an installment basis. Bankruptcy should be avoided if possible, because it leaves a permanent record of credit failure in a person's credit history.

Quick Check

1. Explain the terms *credit counselor* and *consolidation loan.*
2. What effect does declaring *bankruptcy* have?

Global Perspective

Many developing nations borrow money for economic development from the World Bank and the International Monetary Fund (IMF). Sometimes, for a variety of reasons (war, economic instability, natural disaster, other debt), a country falls behind in payments or is unable to pay the loan back in time. Have students find out what measures the World Bank and the IMF take when a country has trouble repaying a loan. Suggest that students find specific examples and explain the reason the country had trouble repaying its loan and the action taken by the lending agency.

Refer to the *International Business Strategies* booklet for additional strategies and activities.

Chapter 30 **Summary**

Main Ideas

1. Federal and state governments have passed laws to help consumers with credit problems.
2. Federal laws that protect consumers include the Consumer Credit Protection Act, the Equal Credit Opportunity Act, the Fair Credit Reporting Act, the Fair Credit Billing Act, and the Fair Debt Collection Practices Act.
3. Numerous federal agencies, including the Federal Trade Commission, enforce federal credit laws.
4. If you have a credit problem, the first thing you should do is contact the creditor.
5. Consumers who cannot work out their own credit problems should talk to a credit counselor.
6. Declaring bankruptcy is a last resort for solving credit problems because it has a very negative effect on a person's credit rating.
7. Three tips for ethical business behavior are: be honest, be discreet, and follow company policies.
8. The sophisticated computer technology businesses use to manage information requires equally sophisticated security measures.

CASE ANALYSIS   Consumer Credit

You have applied for a charge account at Stern & Mann's Department Store. You find out that the store has turned down your application for "insufficient credit history." You ask for and get an appointment with the credit department manager. How will you convince the manager that you are a good credit risk? Describe any preparations you will make for the interview. Are there any documents that you might want to bring along?

CHAPTER 30   CREDIT AND THE LAW   **509**

CLOSE

Main Ideas

Main Ideas summarizes the key information in the chapter. It is a useful tool for reinforcement and review.

CASE ANALYSIS

Case Analysis provides a chapter-related case for student analysis and application of decision-making skills.

Answer
Students' answers will vary.

QUICK QUIZ

1. How does a truth-in-lending disclosure allow consumers to compare the cost of credit? (It requires businesses to reveal the total finance charge and annual percentage rate for any loan, so consumers can compare credit costs.)
2. Name six examples of credit discrimination. (Refusal to offer credit on the basis of age, sex, marital status, race, religion, or nationality.)
3. What credit-related function does the Federal Trade Commission perform? (It enforces the laws concerned with credit.)
4. What happens to a person's credit rating if he or she declares bankruptcy? (That person will be rated as a very poor credit risk and will have great difficulty obtaining credit.)

APPLY

Answers

Use the Language of Business

1. collection agent, 2. usury law, 3. truth-in-lending disclosure, 4. credit counselor, 5. consolidation loan, 6. bankruptcy, 7. credit bureau.

Review What You Learned

1. It is designed to curb excessive interest rates.

2. It requires businesses to reveal the total finance charge and annual percentage rate for any loan. Consumers can use these figures to compare credit costs.

3. Refusal to offer credit on the basis of age, sex, marital status, race, nationality, or religion.

4. He or she may revise clients' budgets, contact creditors to arrange new payment plans, and help clients find sources of extra income.

5. Federal Trade Commission, Comptroller of the Currency, Federal Reserve Bank, Federal Deposit Insurance Corporation, Office of Thrift Supervision.

6. It has a very bad effect on a consumer's credit rating. The record of credit failure remains on a credit record, making it difficult or impossible to obtain credit in the future.

7. Being honest and discreet and following company policies.

8. By having user identification codes, passwords, or data encryption.

Understand Business Concepts

1. People in such circumstances have a poor chance of repaying debts. The act protects them from further problems with credit. The law also protects people who might be able to handle credit but who have been discriminated against in the past.

2. Request the written report that gives the reason for denial. If you think a mistake has been made, you may request a copy of your record from the credit bureau and

Use the Language of Business

Match each term to its definition.

bankruptcy
collection agent
consolidation loan
credit bureau

credit counselor
truth-in-lending disclosure
usury law

1. Person who has the job of collecting debts that are overdue.
2. Law designed to limit rates consumers can be charged for credit.
3. Document that lists all costs of borrowing for consumers.
4. Person who helps people with credit problems.
5. Loan that brings together all of a person's debts.
6. Legal procedure that distributes a debtor's property or money among the creditors.
7. Agency that collects information about the paying habits of consumers.

Review What You Learned

1. What is the purpose of a usury law?
2. How does a truth-in-lending disclosure help consumers compare credit costs?
3. Give six examples of credit discrimination.
4. How does a credit counselor help people with their credit problems?
5. What federal government agencies oversee major credit institutions in the United States?
6. Why is bankruptcy a last resort for a consumer with debt problems?
7. What three tips will help you behave ethically on the job?
8. Identify several ways by which companies can secure their data.

Understand Business Concepts

1. A person may be denied credit only if he or she has a low income, owes large sums of money, or has a poor credit record. Why do you think the Equal Credit Opportunity Act allows credit to be denied for these reasons? In what other ways does the act protect consumers?
2. You have applied for credit at a department store. The store has denied you credit because of your credit rating. Since you know that you have always paid your bills on time, what action should you take?
3. For a fee, you can receive a copy of the information in your credit file at the credit bureau. Why would you want to check your credit record?
4. How can consumers become better informed about credit laws?
5. What procedures does the Fair Credit Billing Act provide for?
6. A truth-in-lending disclosure shows consumers the dollar cost of credit and the annual percentage rate. How can this information help protect consumers from credit problems?

have incorrect information removed from your file or have your version of the situation added to your record.

3. To check the information in your file if you believe it is incorrect or to make sure that your version of a disputed payment is registered.

4. By obtaining copies of the laws about credit and reading them. Consumers should also pay attention to media reports about consumer credit laws.

5. It establishes steps to follow when billing errors occur and requires that consumers be notified regularly of the steps to take to correct an error.

6. Knowing the dollar costs of credit and the annual percentage rate helps consumers know how much using credit will cost them. That information can save consumers from having to make higher payments than they may have anticipated or can handle.

7. Kristin behaved ethically by using her own time and money to make the copies.

8. Software development would not be profitable. Without the profit incentive, software development would stop and the advancement of technology would slow.

7. Kristin wanted to make 100 copies of her prize-winning short story to distribute to her friends and relatives. Even though her office has a photocopy machine, she went to a copy shop on her lunch hour to make the copies. Was this ethical behavior? Why or why not?

8. What might happen if the procedure of pirating software were not outlawed?

Think Critically

1. **Analyze.** The Truth in Lending Law requires that consumers be given complete credit cost information in advertisements that mention credit sales. Decide whether each of the following statements gives complete credit information. Explain your answers.

   • "$20 down, $43 a month."
   • "Finance charge is $10 a month, 18.15% APR."

   • "$35 down, $14 a month for 2 years."
   • "Payments for 52 weeks, and only $15 down payment."

2. **Classify.** Consult your local telephone book and compile a list of all the agencies that provide consumer credit protection for people in your community. Organize the list as local, state, or federal agencies.

Use What You Learned

1. **Group Project.** Work with a partner to role play a consumer or credit problem situation. You are a credit counselor, and your partner is seeking advice about a credit problem. After your partner explains the problem, outline several possible strategies for dealing with the problem based on what you learned in the chapter. Then switch roles. Write a one-paragraph evaluation of the advice your partner gave you to solve your credit problem.

2. Contact a consumer credit counseling service in your area. Find out what services it offers and what fees it charges. Ask the service for copies of any educational materials it has available about the wise use of credit. Write a summary of the services available and list some situations in which a consumer could benefit from the counseling service.

3. **Computer Application.** Use E-mail to contact your state consumer protection agency. Retrieve information regarding consumer credit laws in your state. Then use word-processing software to create a chart summarizing the laws and their provisions. Print out the chart for posting in the classroom.

4. **Skill Reinforcement.** Interview several businesspeople whom you know and respect. Ask each one to tell you the most important advice about business ethics he or she would give a new employee. Make a list of the tips you receive.

Save your work in your Business Portfolio.

1. Students' answers should contain the following information for each of the bulleted examples.
• Incomplete information; number of monthly payments is not given.
• Incomplete information; number of monthly payments is not given.
• Complete information; for advertisements, the law does not require that the APR be given.
• Incomplete information; monthly payment is not given.
2. Students' lists will vary.

Independent Practice

Use the Chapter 30 worksheets in *Student Activity Guide 2* for additional practice and application activities. A Teacher's Annotated Edition provides answers.

ASSESS

Portfolio Assessment

The portfolio projects are designed to lead students to develop a collection of their best work to submit to you for assessment. Refer students to the specific rubric(s) from the *Alternative Assessment Strategies* booklet listed with each of the project notes below. These rubrics will alert students to the criteria you will use to assess their projects.

Chapter Assessment

Use the Chapter 30 Test from the *Test Masters* booklet to evaluate students' understanding of the chapter concepts. An answer key is provided. Or create your own customized test using the *Testmaker* software.

Use What You Learned

1. Make sure all students participate in the group project. Rubric: Paragraph.
2. Advise students to seek out a not-for-profit consumer credit service. Rubric: Essay.

3. Students with no access to a computer may write the state consumer protection agency and make their charts by hand. Rubric: Charts and Tables.
4. Students' answers will vary but should include several tips about ethical conduct on the job. Rubric: Note Taking.

Business Issue

Business Issue

THE PUBLIC DEBT

Highlight the Issue

Before assigning the reading on pages 512–513, ask volunteers to explain what they know about the public debt and deficit spending. Record students' ideas on the board. After students have read the pages, ask them to vote on whether they think the budget should be balanced.

THE PUBLIC DEBT

Each year the federal government spends billions of dollars more than it collects in taxes and other revenues. This deficit spending has created a national debt that totalled nearly $4.8 trillion by 1995. Some fear that such a huge debt will eventually undermine the health of the U.S. economy. Should the federal government have to balance its budget—in other words, spend no more each year than it takes in?

Pro

Debt is bad for the economy. Just like a business or household, the government can't keep spending more than it takes in. When a business or household borrows money, it eventually has to pay back the loan or go bankrupt. By racking up a large national debt now, we're burdening future generations with the task of paying it off or heading for bankruptcy. As the experiences of debtor nations like Brazil and Mexico show, huge national debts lead to long-term economic problems.

Each year of deficit spending adds to the national debt because the government must borrow more money to make up the budget shortfall. Like any other borrower, the government must pay interest on these loans. Each year a larger part of the federal budget goes to pay the interest on the debt. In 1995, the government paid $235 billion in interest on its $4.8 trillion debt. If things don't change, the Congressional Budget Office estimates that by 2002 interest payments will reach $334 billion, and eventually the entire budget will be needed just to pay interest on the debt. That's real money that can't be spent in more productive ways—to build new roads, fund education, or provide health care.

When the government is borrowing so much money, interest rates rise, making it harder for businesses to afford loans. If businesses can't borrow money, they can't expand or create more jobs, and the entire economy suffers.

All Americans would benefit from a debt-free America. One economist estimates that a balanced budget would create 2.4 million jobs and increase America's economic output by about 2.5 percent, resulting in an average of an extra $1000 per family annually.

Extend the Issue

Organize students into groups to research issues related to balancing the federal budget. Topics students could choose include: how funding should be allocated between social needs and national defense; whether a balanced budget is desirable or even possible; and ways to control or reduce deficit spending. Have groups present their findings in a class discussion.

Con

Governments aren't exactly like households or businesses, and a balanced budget is not always a wise policy for government finances. If each year's spending is limited only to revenues collected, the government won't be able to respond to changes in the economy. In the past the federal government has been able to prevent serious recessions by increasing spending, thus stimulating the economy.

Government spending provides a safety net in economic hard times. One reason the economy has been relatively stable since the Great Depression is that the government has been able to respond to economic downturns with deficit spending. During a recession, when many people are out of work, the government collects less in taxes, yet it needs more to pay for unemployment benefits, food stamps, and other programs that aid the jobless. Through deficit spending, the government can put money back into the economy where it is needed. Deficit spending during the 1970s and 1980s helped prevent recessions from turning into depressions. If deficit spending is prohibited, the economy will be less stable.

Debt is not all bad. In fact, it's beneficial to go into debt if you're investing in programs that will pay off in the future. Consider a household with a mortgage. Although the household is in debt and paying back the loan, the investment should yield future wealth as the value of the property increases. If the federal budget is cut and tax revenues aren't raised to pay for investments, the United States will be unable to remain competitive in the world economy.

Budget cuts also tend to unfairly affect some Americans. The programs most often cut are those that benefit the poor, such as Medicaid, welfare, and food stamps.

According to some economists, the deficit is not even growing that rapidly. When considered as a percent of the nation's gross domestic product, the deficit has remained relatively steady in recent years, and the U.S. debt is still less than that of most other industrial nations.

A balanced budget is not necessary for a healthy economy. In some cases, it can even lead to economic problems. Thus the federal government should not have to balance its budget each year but be able to use deficit spending wisely.

Update the Issue

Provide students with the amount of the current national debt. Is the amount greater or less than the figure given in the text? Have interested students find articles that explain how the federal government is currently handling deficit spending and the national debt. Have students give a brief oral summarization of the information contained in their articles. Discuss with the class whether the articles support the pro or con position in the text.

Independent Practice

As a follow-up activity to Unit 9, have students complete the simulation "Using Credit as a Consumer" found in *Student Activity Guide 2*. The Teacher's Annotated Edition provides answers.

Unit 10 Managing Your Personal Finances

Chapter	Learning Objectives
31 **Planning a Budget** pp. 516–533	• Explain how a particular lifestyle can affect your budget. • Explain how budgeting can be helpful. • Identify the five steps in planning a budget. • Develop a budget based on goals, income, expenses, and savings. • Compute two kinds of averages—mean and median—that you might use as you plan a budget. • Identify some advantages of portable or notebook computers.
32 **Saving and Investing** pp. 534–553	• Give three reasons why people save. • Describe the differences between saving and investing. • List six guidelines to wise investing. • Identify and describe three common choices for investments. • Describe how technology assists stockbrokers and investors. • Explain the information contained in stock market quotations.
33 **Using Banking Services** pp. 554–573	• List the major services banks and financial institutions provide. • Enumerate the factors consumers should consider when choosing among banking services. • Describe how electronic banking provides customers with quick, timely access to their bank accounts. • Explain how to reconcile a check register with the checking account statement issued by the bank.
34 **Dealing with Risks** pp. 574–591	• Explain how insurance can help people protect themselves against possible financial loss. • Describe the process of purchasing insurance, and identify the more common types of insurance. • Identify the factors that affect the cost of insurance. • Explain important steps to follow to interpret a statistical table.

Business Issue: National Health Care, pp. 592–593

National Standards for Business Education*	Focus on Features	Building Business Skills	Visual Learning	Case Analysis
COMP: VI C, VI D; *EPF:* X B (Spending Plans); *IS:* I	Technology: Electronic Notebooks, p. 520	Math: Determining Averages, p. 526	Lifestyle Costs, p. 519 Check and Pay Statement, p. 523 Percentage of Income for Expenses, p. 525 Budget, p. 528 Statement of Net Worth, p. 530	Budgeting, p. 531
COMP: VI B; *EPF:* X B (Saving and Investing); *IS:* VII	Technology: Electronic Ticker Tape, p. 538	Math: Reading Stock Market Quotations, p. 542	Selected Investments Ranked by Risk and Potential Return, p. 541 Median Home Price in the United States, p. 549	Saving/Investing, p. 551
BL: V B; *EPF:* X B (Using Financial Services); *IS:* VII	Technology: Electronic Banking, p. 558	Math: Reconciling a Checking Account, p. 562	Checking Account Fee Schedules and Information Guide, p. 557 Check, p. 561 Check Register, p. 563 Bank Statement, p. 563 Savings Account Interest Rates, p. 565 Annual Interest Rate, p. 565	Endorsements, p. 571
COMP: V; *EE:* I A; *EPF:* X B (Protecting Against Risks)	Entrepreneurs: Cecil F. Hess— MetroLaser, p. 578	Analysis: Interpreting Statistics, p. 582	Automobile Insurance Coverages, p. 580 Losses Covered by Homeowner's Policy, p. 584	Insurance Coverage, p. 589

* Level 3 Performance Expectations: Business Law (BL), Computation (COMP), Economics and Personal Finance (EPF), Entrepreneurship Education (EE), IS (Information Systems). See page T14 for all 12 content areas.

Unit 10

Look Back

Ask students to recall that using credit allows people to purchase items and use them immediately. Wise consumers understand how to calculate interest rates and know exactly how much extra they pay when they use credit. Using credit is a privilege. Consumers who don't make credit card or loan payments on time will damage their credit rating and may be denied credit in the future.

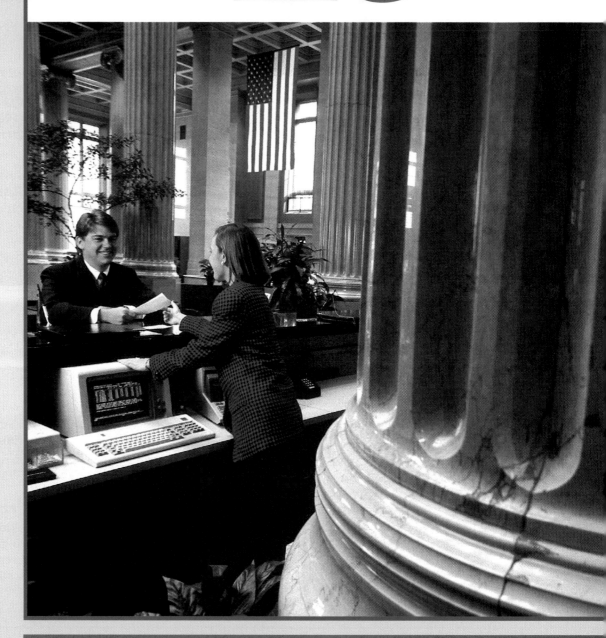

UNIT 10 COOPERATIVE LEARNING PROJECT

Viewpoint Activity

Preparation: Distribute to each student a photocopy of BLM 21 from the *Cooperative Learning Strategies* booklet.

Guidelines: Have students work in groups of four to research different investments. Assign each student in each group one of four investments to research:

Managing Your Personal Finances

This unit concentrates on personal finances. The first chapter discusses analyzing personal lifestyle to prepare a useful budget. The next two chapters describe how to save for the future and manage a checking account. The final chapter discusses how insurance protects life and property.

515

Certificates of Deposit, Real Estate, Bonds, or Stocks. Group members must each be prepared to explain to the rest of their group why their investment is a good choice.

FOCUS

Introduce the Chapter

Major Concepts
- Lifestyle Costs
- The Importance of Budgeting
- Steps in Planning a Budget
- A Sample Budget

Introduce the Topic

Ask students to play a word association game. When you say the word *budget*, ask students to identify the first word that comes to their minds. List the words on the board or on a transparency. Many words supplied by the students may have negative connotations. Point out that the purpose of a budget is to help individuals and families achieve their own financial goals.

Use Business Terms

Have students briefly study the list of Business Terms and conjure up mental images of what the terms represent. Invite volunteers to describe one or more of the images they have created. Ask members of the class to match the terms with the descriptions. Advise students to note the meanings of the terms as they read the chapter.

USE VISUALS

Ask students how the people in this photo might be planning for their financial future. Point out that most people plan a budget to get the most from their money.

516 UNIT 10

Business terms

money management

lifestyle

budget

gross pay

deductions

net pay

516

CHAPTER 31 RESOURCES

Instructional Resources

Lesson Plan for Chapter 31

Teaching Transparencies 31-1, 31-2, 31-3, 31-4, 31-5, 31-6, 31-7

Strategies and Worksheets for Teaching Transparencies 31-1, 31-2, 31-3, 31-4, 31-5, 31-6, 31-7

Enrichment Master 31-1

Student Activity Guide 2–TAE for Chapter 31

Test Master for Chapter 31

Alternative Assessment Strategies

Math Skills Review

International Business Strategies

Cooperative Learning Strategies

Communication Skills Review

Ethics in Business Strategies

Planning a Budget

Learning objectives

After completing this chapter, you will be able to:
- Explain how a particular lifestyle can affect your budget.
- Explain how budgeting can be helpful.
- Identify the five steps in planning a budget.
- Develop a budget based on goals, income, expenses, and savings.
- Compute two kinds of averages—mean and median—that you might use as you plan a budget.
- Identify some advantages of portable or notebook computers.

Consider what you know

- A good credit rating is achieved by paying bills on time. If you can't pay your bills, you will have a bad credit rating.

Consider what you want to know

- How can you analyze your lifestyle so you can set priorities as you manage your money?
- How can you develop a budget?
- What happens if you can't live according to your budget?
- How can you determine how much you are worth?
- What is the difference between a mean and a median?
- What's the smallest computer you might use to plan a budget?

Consider how to use what you learn

- As you read this chapter, think how you can manage the money you have. Do you often wonder where all your money went? Is there a way to stretch your money so that you can buy the goods and services that are most important to you?

Multimedia Resources

Technology Resource Guide

Distance Learning Guide

Internet Resource Guide

Professional Resources

School-to-Work/Tech Prep Strategies

Instructional Poster

Spanish Resources

Testmaker Software for Chapter 31

The Wall Street Journal Video Series
Video & Activities for Chapter 31

Business and Marketing Computer
Applications—An Integrated Software
Simulation Using Microsoft Works

Stocktracker—A Stock Market Software
Simulation

Where's the Dough? Board Game

CHAPTER 31

Motivate the Learning

Learning Objectives
Remind students that, as with previous chapters, the learning objectives indicate what they will learn as they study Chapter 31. Encourage students to keep these objectives in mind as they work through the chapter. Note that the last two objectives listed refer to the Focus on Technology feature and the Building Business Skills feature.

Consider What You Know
Review briefly the main sections of *Chapter 30 Credit and the Law:* Protecting Your Credit Rights; Enforcing the Laws; and Handling Your Credit Problems.

Consider What You Want to Know
Ask students to look through the chapter to get an idea of how the chapter will help them answer the questions.

Consider How to Use What You Learn
Mention to students that at the completion of the chapter they will develop some projects for which they will need to know the steps needed to plan a budget. Suggest that as they read the chapter they keep in mind the information that forms the basis of a reasonable budget.

Business Connection

When you prepare a budget, you are acting as a manager for your own business, which is your lifestyle. A budget is a financial plan that sets forth management's (or personal) expectations for revenues, and allocates use of specific resources. A master budget includes an operating budget (rent, food, clothing), cash budget (miscellaneous), and capital budget (large purchases such as cars, stereo). Just as in business, some elements considered in developing a financial plan or budget for an individual or family include short-term and long-term forecasting.

Develop Concepts

Lifestyle Costs

Ask students to list some of the extracurricular activities they enjoy—watching sports, playing sports, going to concerts, and so on. Have a volunteer record the responses on the board. Point out that the differences among the students' choices reflect the differences in lifestyles among all individuals.

Learning Activity

Marketers often target advertising and products to markets with a specific lifestyle. *DINK* is an advertising acronym for one of those lifestyles: Double Income No Kids. Have students collect advertisements from newspapers and magazines that reflect this lifestyle.

Money is a limited resource. Most people want more goods and services than they can buy with their money. However, with planning, you can figure out how to use the money you have to buy the things you really need or want. Good planning helps.

Money management is the process of planning how to get the most from your money. Good money management can help you keep track of where your money goes so you can make it go further.

LIFESTYLE COSTS

Before you can manage your money, you need to set priorities about your spending. Think seriously about this question: If you could live any way that you want, what would your life be like? Everyone will have different answers. Many people want to have a family. Some people want a loft in a city. Others would rather have a cabin on a cliff by the ocean. Some people want a speedboat, and others want a canoe. Some people want a state-of-the-art computer, and others want a grand piano. Others would prefer buying vacations.

A person's **lifestyle** is his or her way of living that reflects that person's attitudes and values. Most people know how they want to live, but not as many people try to determine how much it will cost. It's important to learn how much your lifestyle will cost. If you do some planning to achieve your desired lifestyle, you will get more out of life. You will spend money on things that are important to you. Begin by considering these questions.

- Where will you live, and will you rent or own? Some people want to rent a house or apartment, but others want to own their own homes. Some want to live alone, and others want to share expenses by living with others.
- What do you prefer in clothing? Do you want to dress in the latest style? Or would you rather wait for sales? Some people even hunt for clothes at resale shops.
- What are your tastes in food? Do you like to eat in restaurants? Perhaps you work long hours and are willing to settle for a quick meal warmed up in the microwave. Or would you rather fix meals "from scratch" at home?
- What transportation will you use? Some people insist that they have to have their own cars, but remember that this choice also involves insurance and maintenance costs. Is public transportation an option for you? How about biking to school and work?

Making Connections ⇨ Everyday Life

Suggest students investigate what costs they would incur if their current lifestyle included a car. Have them choose a late-model used car to "purchase." Then have them find out the average monthly cost of owning the car, not counting the cost of the car itself. Remind students to research items such as those listed below by consulting consumer and automobile periodicals.

- Insurance costs for make and model year of the car, as well as sex and age of driver.
- City sticker, state license.
- Cost of gasoline based on average 12,000 miles a year.
- Regular maintenance costs: oil changes, coolant, etc.

- How will you use your leisure time? Everyone needs time off from work. Do you go to movies? Would you rather stay home with family and friends? Some people belong to health clubs or play a sport. Others like to take long walks or take photographs of wildlife.
- What type of vacations do you prefer? Do you want to travel to another country, or is your favorite vacation time spent at home with your family?
- Will there be other lifestyle costs, such as health care and savings for retirement, major purchases, or emergencies? It is important to be realistic about health care costs and savings, because life isn't predictable. A new set of brakes for a car is an expensive repair, but it also is an expense that can't be put off.

The answers to these questions will tell you a great deal about your lifestyle. And your lifestyle will determine how you will spend your money. Figure 31-1 below is a sample lifestyle analysis done by Shelly Becker. She thought carefully about the kinds of things that she likes to do as she estimated her costs.

TEACHING TIP

In some areas of the country, biking to work has become quite popular. Ask students how they would compute the cost per month of biking to work using the following information: Bicycle cost: $400; tires and repair: $65 per year; bike lock $55; bus fare on rainy or snowy days: $120 a year. (Average the tire, repair, lock, and bus fare costs to find the cost per month; determine how long a bicycle will last to compute the average cost per month.)
For students who need to sharpen their math skills, choose among the worksheets in the *Math Skills Review* booklet.

LIFESTYLE COSTS	
Category	**Lifestyle Costs per Month**
Housing: *I rent a three-bedroom apartment with two roommates.*	$300
Furnishings: *Although the apartment is furnished, I do like to add my own furnishings now and then.*	$60
Clothing: *I don't spend much on clothes for work, but I do like to buy clothes for evenings and weekends.*	$120
Food: *I like to cook, so during the week I fix my own meals. On the weekends, however, I do like to go to a restaurant for dinner.*	$300
Transportation: *Because the bus stop is just down the street, I take the bus to work and to go shopping.*	$100
Health Care and Recreation: *I am lucky because my job provides health insurance. I ride my bike and go to aerobics class for exercise. I go to about two movies a month. And I want to save some money for a short vacation every year.*	$120
Other Costs: *My other costs include household supplies and gifts.*	$100
Total Lifestyle Costs:	$1,100

FIGURE 31-1

Shelly Becker is a 22-year-old single woman who works as a radiology technician. She shares an apartment with two other roommates. When Shelly decided to make up a budget, she thought carefully about her lifestyle. Look carefully at the descriptions she wrote in each category. How would your descriptions be different from hers? How would they be the same?

USE VISUALS

Direct student attention to Figure 31-1, which lists some lifestyle costs for a single person. Help students understand that the dollar amounts listed reflect monthly averages, and in any given month the actual cost might be slightly higher or lower.
Answer to caption: Answers will vary.

USE TRANSPARENCIES

Use Teaching Transparency 31-1 and its corresponding strategies and worksheet from the *Teaching Transparency Strategies and Worksheets* booklet to assist students in recognizing lifestyle costs. Verify student worksheets using the Answer Key.

Reteaching Strategy

Suggest that students make a chart with headings reflecting the seven categories mentioned in Figure 31-1 above: *Housing, Furnishings, Clothing, Food, Transportation, Health Care and Recreation,* and *Other Costs.* Ask students to enter their own lifestyle descriptions for at least three categories. (Students need not include their name on the listing.) Have students post their listings on the bulletin board. Ask volunteers what lifestyle differences they can detect using the posted listings. Have students suggest what an individual's economic goals reveal about a person's values.

Discuss

Ask students to discuss the meanings of the terms *downloading, byte, kilobyte,* and *megabyte (downloading:* transferring data to another computer; *byte:* the equivalent of a single character; *kilobyte:* 1024 bytes of information; and *megabyte:* 1024 kilobytes of information.)

For additional information about current technology, refer to the *Technology Resource Guide* booklet.

FOCUS ON **Technology**

Electronic Notebooks

For a while, business believed that bigger was better. Now opinion seems to be going in the opposite direction. Certainly the move in computers has been toward smaller and smaller equipment. What's more, the equipment is able to do as much as—sometimes even more than—its larger brothers and sisters.

Among the most popular of technology's smaller products is the notebook or laptop computer. *Notebook* computers measure about 8½ × 11 inches—about the size of an average notebook. Meant to be portable, these computers have a lightweight battery pack that allows them to function for a number of hours without recharging.

A notebook computer also has a pop-up display and a built-in keyboard for input. Some models also come with a *trackball,* the notebook equivalent of a mouse. Size notwithstanding, these computers are fully functional and popular with people who need computers wherever they go.

Many businesspeople who rely on their laptops out in the field also have access to larger equipment such as personal computers or networks. Information stored on the laptop can be downloaded and distributed to multiple users. *Downloading* is the process of transferring data from the laptop to another computer, usually a personal computer, with increased storage capabilities. Of course, a notebook, laptop, or powerbook computer can also be plugged into an ordinary power source and used in an office.

Learning Activity

Have students page through a newspaper or magazine and collect pictures and prices of big-ticket items they want to own. For each item have students figure out the equivalent cost in movies (at $7 per movie) or dinners out (at $10 per dinner). For example: if a stereo system costs $350, its cost-equivalent is 50 movies. Then have students determine how long it would take to save enough money to purchase the item. (Twenty-five months of giving up two movies a month.) Ask them to discuss their findings and how they feel about trading movies, sports events, or dinners out for more expensive items.

You will not be able to do everything you want. So you will need to set priorities. You may want a new car and a new computer. Which is more important to you? What will you be willing to give up? If you like to go to movies, perhaps you are willing to give up going out to eat. After all, it costs less to eat at home, and the money you save can be spent at the theater. It is your lifestyle that will help you set up a budget.

Quick Check

1. What is meant by *lifestyle?*
2. What is money management and why is it important?

THE IMPORTANCE OF BUDGETING

A **budget** is a plan for using your money in a way that best meets your wants and needs. It is like a road map or guide that you set up and then try to follow. A budget includes a record of your probable income, your planned expenses, and your planned savings over a certain period of time.

520 UNIT 10 MANAGING YOUR PERSONAL FINANCES

Quick Check Answers

1. Way of living that reflects a person's attitudes and values.
2. Process of planning how to get the most from your money.

Curriculum Connection   Communication

Have students choose an item they wish to own that costs at least $100, such as a leather jacket, boom box, athletic shoes or similar item. Direct them to write a persuasive paragraph either to themselves or to their family telling how the students can finance the item by cutting back on other expenses. Remind students to be specific and indicate how many movies, movie rentals, or football games will they would be willing to give up in order to finance the purchase of the item.

For those students who need to sharpen their written communication skills, choose among the worksheets in the *Communication Skills Review* booklet.

Until now, the primary limitation of the laptop was in storage capability. Most laptops relied on 3½-inch floppy disks for data storage. Typically these disks hold a little over one megabyte of information. A *byte* is the equivalent of a single character. A *kilobyte* (kb) is 1024 bytes of information. A *megabyte* (mb) is 1024 kilobytes or 1,048,576 bytes of information.

The floppy disk may soon be replaced by a memory advancement called *flash memory*. A flash memory card is about the size of a credit card, yet it holds 14 times as much data as the 3½ inch floppy disk. Flash memory can be described as a cross between RAM memory and storage. It can retrieve stored information with the speed associated with RAM chips.

Some business computers are even smaller than notebooks. *Personal data assistants* (PDAs) are about the size of a checkbook. These computers, less powerful than notebooks or laptops, are used for special applications such as small spreadsheets, phone numbers, agendas, and calendars. As with notebooks, many PDAs can exchange data with larger computers.

Budgets can be helpful in a number of ways. Most people do not have enough money to buy all of the goods and services that they want. A good budget makes you set goals and priorities for spending your money. In other words, you plan to spend money only on those things that you want or need and that are most important to you. Because you determine in advance how you will use your money, you avoid wasting money on things that are not very important to you.

A budget also provides a reference that tells you how well you are managing your money. For example, if you decide to spend $25 a month on movies and videocassette tapes and you spend that amount during the first week of the month, the budget acts as a means of control. You then have several options.

- You might decide to increase the amount in your budget for these items and decrease the amount budgeted for something else.
- You might decide to stop spending money on movies and videocassette tapes for the rest of the month because you used all of the $25 during the first week.

F.Y.I.

Businesses, like people, use budgets for financial planning and forecasting. Most of the quantities in business budgets are expressed in money, as are those in personal budgets. However, a labor budget may be presented in hours of work. Other business budgets may use units of production materials, such as pounds or yards.

Ask students to speculate on the kinds of tasks a personal data assistant might accomplish. Encourage students to describe situations in which small hand-held computers can keep track of a series of numbers simultaneously. Spark students' imagination by indicating that these kinds of computers are planned for use on the floor of the stock exchange and are also used by hot dog sellers at athletic stadiums!

Develop Concepts

The Importance of Budgeting

Indicate to students that a budget is a voluntary tool that helps individuals accomplish their financial goals. A budget helps people control their spending and avoid spending money on items that are not among their highest priorities. Stress that budgets are tailored to an individual's or family's lifestyle—they are designed not to deprive but rather to assist in reaching some financial goals.

Connection to CHAPTER 15

Remind students that in Chapter 15, Financing a Business, they learned about projecting income and expenses for a business. Remind them that the financial plan of a business allows management to list its expectations of revenue. Ask students in what ways a personal budget is like the financial plan.

Meeting Student Diversity

Students with weak study skills might benefit from making a time budget for longer assignments. Suggest that students choose an assignment due in two or more weeks. Then suggest that they make a list of the steps—and time—needed to complete the project (time expenses), and the time available to complete the project (time income). Have students make a chart or calendar showing which steps should be completed by which date so that the entire assignment can be completed on time.

Learning Activity

Suggest that students interview the school's budget officer or the sports department's budget officer. Have them find out how this year's budget is different from last year's and from the budget five years earlier. Encourage students to ask how often during the school year the budget is changed or revised to take advantage of new opportunities or to respond to new challenges. Be certain students remember to ask what goals drive the budget.

Quick Check Answers

1. A plan or guide for using your money.
2. It sets goals and priorities, and it is a reference to see how well you are managing your money.
3. It must be able to change as circumstances change.

Develop Concepts

Steps in Planning a Budget

Remind students that business managers control human and financial resources. When students prepare a personal budget, they are acting as a manager for their own business—their life. Stress to students that planning a budget is best accomplished in steps. Most important of these steps is to establish goals. Indicate to students that as time passes their goals and priorities might change and as this happens their budget, too, should change.

- You might decide to figure out a way to increase your income—by working extra hours or doing odd jobs—so that you will have more money to spend on these items in future months.

This example points out an important principle of budgeting—flexibility. You should never consider a budget permanently fixed or unchangeable. As different circumstances arise, budgets can and should be changed. Of course, you should have a good reason for changes, such as changes in income or priorities. Otherwise, you will not be meeting your most important wants and needs.

Keep in mind that budgeting is a way of being good to yourself because it helps you buy or save for the goods and services that are most important to you. The budget that you develop for yourself should reflect your personal goals and priorities. Your budget will probably be different from all of your friends' budgets because each one of you has a different set of goals and priorities.

Quick Check

1. What is a *budget?*
2. List two reasons to use a budget.
3. Why should a budget be flexible?

STEPS IN PLANNING A BUDGET

Planning a budget is easier if you divide the process into several steps. Follow the five steps listed here as you plan your budget:

- Set your goals.
- Estimate your income.
- Estimate your expenses.
- Plan for savings.
- Balance and adjust your budget.

Set Goals

Ask yourself the following questions as you prepare to set your goals.

- What do you want to accomplish in the next month? The next year? The next five years?
- What is important to you?
- Are your goals practical?

Making Connections ▪▷ Everyday Living

Suggest that students interview adult family members, friends, or teachers to find out their attitudes about budgets. Have groups of students compose four or five survey questions about budgets that can be answered "Always," "Sometimes," or "Never." (Samples: Do you use a budget? Do you ever change your budget? Does your budget meet your needs?) Have students pool their findings and prepare a poster, complete with graphs, for display in the classroom.

It is useless to set a goal of buying a computer in one year if your total income for the year is less than the price of the computer. A budget should help tell you which goals you can meet with the amount of money you have.

Estimate Income

Knowing how much money you have available is an important step in the budgeting process. Your income is the actual amount of money you earn or receive during a given time period. If you get a weekly allowance at home, that is income. Wages you earn as a stock clerk at a supermarket are income, as is the interest you earn on a savings account. If you have any investments, any income they earn is also part of your income.

If you have a job, you may remember your surprise when you got your first paycheck. Your **gross pay,** the total amount of money you earned for a specific time, may have seemed like a lot of money. For example, if you worked 20 hours a week at $5.50 an hour, your gross pay would be $110 for the week. However, your gross pay is reduced by various **deductions,** or certain amounts that are subtracted from your pay before you receive your paycheck. As you can see from the sample paycheck in Figure 31-2 below, all deductions are listed with your paycheck. Deductions include such things as taxes, insurance payments, retirement payments, union dues, and others. Your

FIGURE 31-2

Your employee pay statement attached to your check tells you the amount of your gross pay, your deductions, and your net pay. How is net pay determined?

Blue Chip Software, Inc.
Three Beacon Street
Boston, MA 02215

Check no. 1348

Date: January 10, 1997

Pay to the
Order of: James Sikora _____ $ 237.67
** Two hundred thirty-seven and 67/100************************************** Dollars

Second National Bank
Boston, MA 02215

FOR: Period Ending 01/10/97

Samuel Rosen

⑆0193001201⑆ 627 ⑈20527 ⑊1348

Employee Pay Statement
Detach and retain this statement

Check no. 1348
Period Ending: 01/10/97

| EARNINGS | DEDUCTIONS | | | | | | TOTAL | NET PAY |
	SOC SEC	MEDICARE	FIT	SIT	HEALTH	OTHER		
333.52	20.68	4.84	40.65	16.68	13.00	0.00	95.85	237.67

Curriculum Connection   Math

Remind students that often a graph or diagram helps people understand numerical information. Suggest that students use the information at the bottom of the pay stub shown in Figure 31-2 above to make a pie chart. If feasible, suggest that students construct their pie chart using graphing software. Ask students how the diagram can help them better understand the relationship between total pay, deductions, and take home pay.

For students who need to sharpen their math skills, choose among the worksheets in the *Math Skills Review* booklet.

CHAPTER 31

net pay, then, is your gross pay minus deductions. Net pay is sometimes called "take-home" pay.

If your own take-home pay is the only income you have to consider, then it is easy to figure your total income. On the other hand, if you are figuring the budget for a family, and other family members contribute to total income, include their take-home pay when you figure total income. However, when you make a budget, do not count on gifts or unusual income. And if part of your income consists of tips, do not overestimate how much you expect to receive. Use a figure that is lower than what you think you may receive. By making your estimates "honest," your budget will be as accurate as possible.

Estimate Expenses

As with business, every household has two types of expenses. Fixed expenses must be paid regularly. The amount of a fixed expense may change from time to time, but it is usually the same over long periods. For a business, a fixed expense might be yearly license fees. For a household, fixed expenses include such things as rent or mortgage payments, insurance premiums, and car payments. You cannot reduce or avoid such fixed expenses without creating problems. Variable expenses are expenses over which you have more control. As with a business, they include expenses such as food, long-distance telephone charges, entertainment, and gifts. The amount of these expenses usually varies from month to month. One good way to begin estimating your expenses is to look at what you have paid out for similar items in the past. The more expenses you can document, the easier it will be to estimate expenses.

Fixed expenses make up a large share of a typical family's spending. In some cases, families' estimated fixed expenses are almost as great as their incomes. When that happens, they must find ways to increase their incomes, or they will have few choices in how they spend their money. They might have to make some lifestyle changes, such as moving to a less expensive house or apartment if their current mortgage or rent payments are too high. Figure 31-3 on page 525 shows the ways in which an average family spends its income.

If a budget does not include all estimated expenses, a real problem can arise. It is essential to plan for insurance payments, regular visits to the doctor or dentist, or other expenses that occur less often. Take into consideration the increasing costs of some expenses. When expenses increase or are unplanned, they can wreck a budget.

Reteaching Strategy

Present students with the following scenario: Ingrid started as a waitress at a local restaurant just after Thanksgiving. In January she made a budget, projecting her income based on the tips she made in December, as well as the gifts she received from her aunts. Have students discuss what problems this might cause in Ingrid's budget. Then have students suggest ways in which Ingrid can more accurately predict her income.

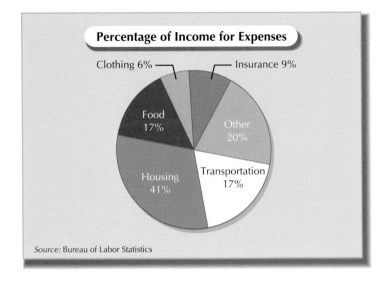

Percentage of Income for Expenses

Clothing 6%
Insurance 9%
Food 17%
Other 20%
Housing 41%
Transportation 17%

Source: Bureau of Labor Statistics

FIGURE 31-3

This graph shows how an average household in the United States spends its money. If you earned about $1200 a month, how much, on the average, would you spend on housing?

Plan for Savings

A budget really is not complete without a regular plan for savings. Not only are savings valuable for future wants, but they also protect you against expenses that you did not budget for and expenses that are higher than you budgeted.

Balance and Adjust the Budget

The most difficult step in the budgeting process is balancing and adjusting the budget. The total estimated income for the budget period—usually a month or a year—should equal the total estimated expenses for that same period, plus the savings. If total estimated expenses and savings are greater than total income, you will have to make some changes in the budget. You must cut some expenses or savings, or you must increase income by either doing extra work or finding a higher-paying job.

For example, suppose you budget $20 each week for transportation expenses. At the end of the month, you find that you have spent more than this amount each week. If you cannot reduce this expenses, you will have to decrease some other item of your budget to make up the difference, or you will have to increase your income.

Quick Check

1. List the five steps of making a budget.
2. Define *gross pay, deductions,* and *net pay.*

The Japanese save more than Americans and Europeans—about 20 percent of their income! There are many reasons. For instance, the Japanese rarely use credit cards. Since they pay for things such as furniture in cash, they have to save for them in advance. Car and home loans in Japan require very large down payments, so the Japanese must save a great deal before they can buy either of these things.

CHAPTER 31 PLANNING A BUDGET **525**

CHAPTER 31

USE VISUALS

Have students determine which combined expenses in Figure 31-3 use more than half a household's income. (Housing, food, and beverage or housing and transportation.) Answer to caption: About $492 a month.

USE TRANSPARENCIES

Use Teaching Transparency 31-3 and its corresponding strategies and worksheet from the *Teaching Transparency Strategies and Worksheets* booklet. Verify student worksheets using the Answer Key.

Connection to CHAPTER 19

Remind students that for investment to take place, someone in the economy must save. If people spend all of their income, a bank may not have any funds to loan. Savings provide the financial resources for borrowing and therefore make investments possible. Have students use Figure 19-2, on page 321 to show how the increased savings allows for increased business expansion.

Quick Check Answers

1. Set goals, estimate income, estimate expenses, plan for savings, balance and adjust the budget.
2. The total amount of money earned for a specific time; certain amounts that are subtracted from your pay before you receive your paycheck; your gross pay minus deductions.

Meeting Student Diversity

Some students have difficulty mastering the skill of differentiation. Present students with the following general reasons for saving: (1) for a purchase; (2) for emergencies; or (3) for financial security. Then provide the list of goals below. Have the students provide the general reason for saving associated with each of the goals.

a. Unexpected medical bills (2)
c. Vacation trip (1)
e. Unplanned repairs of water pipes (2)

b. Retirement home (1 or 3)
d. College education (1)

CHAPTER 31 **525**

Building Business Skills

Model

Have students read the items listed in Working with Averages, page 527. Then work through each of the items, asking students to present a classroom or sports situation in which they would need to know the *mean* and the *median*. Then ask pairs of students to propose a business situation and describe how to find the mean and the median in that situation.

Develop Concepts

A Sample Budget

Point out that not all budgets set aside the same amounts for each category. The Morales family has tailored a budget to meet its needs by setting goals, estimating income, estimating expenses, planning for savings, and periodically checking the budget against actual income and expenses. Ask students to offer suggestions for adapting a budget similar to the Moraleses for seasonal changes in such expenses as gifts, utilities, and vacation.

MATH

Determining Averages

Explanation

An average is a single number that summarizes a group of numbers. Averages are useful in business: A sales manager compares the average monthly sales of an outlet in a suburban mall and one in an urban center. An office worker calculates the average number of pages per week turned out by the firm's copier.

If you've ever figured out your average grade for a series of math tests or your average weekly earnings for a summer job, you're familiar with a kind of average called a *mean*. To calculate a mean, you add up all the items in a series and divide by the number of items.

Another kind of average is called a *median*. The median is used in cases in which the mean may be misleading. This happens when one or two numbers in a series are much larger or smaller than the others. If you worked 45 hours each week for several weeks and 25 to 35 hours a week for the rest of the summer, the median might be a more accurate reflection of your weekly earnings. To find the median, you list your wages for each week in order of amount; the middle item on your list is the median.

Practice

Review the rules and examples for computing means and medians in the box. Then practice by doing the problems.

A SAMPLE BUDGET

Let's follow the steps a young couple, Michael and Anita Morales, used to set up a budget. Michael and Anita decided to set up both an annual and a monthly budget. First, they drew up a list of their short- and long-term goals by deciding which of their wants were most important to them. Setting such goals is the first step in developing a spending plan to use their available money to meet as many financial goals as possible.

Next, they estimated their income for the year to know how much money they would have available during the planning period. Michael, who is a salesperson, earns a gross annual pay of $19,000. Anita is a management trainee and earns $21,500 a year. Michael and Anita include only their take-home pay as income. Although they earn a total of $40,500 a year, their net income is about $31,200. They use that amount in their planning, since it is what they actually have to spend. Look again at Figure 31-2 on page 523 to review how take-home pay is determined.

If the Moraleses had a large, steady income from investments, or if they had income from rents, bonuses, or monetary gifts, they would include this income in their budget. They do

Global Perspective

Americans save about 5 percent of their income. Individuals in many other countries save a larger percentage of their income. As a result, these countries have a larger pool of financial capital that can be used to fuel economic growth. Other countries that have notably higher percentage of savings include Belgium 22 percent; Denmark 16.2 percent, Japan 15.7 percent, and Canada 8 percent. Have students research the average per capita savings in several other nations and display their findings in a bar graph.

Refer to the *International Business Strategies* booklet for additional strategies and activities.

Working with Averages

1. **The *mean* is the average of a series of items.**
   Over the years, Sam has earned the following hourly wages: $4.75, 6.68, 7.36, 9.57, and 10.19. What is Sam's mean hourly wage?
   a. Add up the different wages:
      $4.75 + 6.68 + 7.36 + 9.57 + 10.19 = $38.55
   b. Divide the total by the number of different wages:
      $38.55 ÷ 5 = **$7.71**

2. **The *median* is the midpoint of a series of items arranged in order.**
   Using the previous numbers, find Sam's median hourly wage.
   a. Arrange the different items in order:
      $4.75, 6.68, 7.36, 9.57, 10.19
   b. The middle item is the median: **$7.36**

3. **If the number of items is even, the median is the mean of the two middle items.**
   If Sam is promoted to a job paying $10.90 an hour, what will his median wage be?
   a. Arrange the different items in order:
      $4.75, 6.68, 7.36, 9.57, 10.19, 10.90
   b. Compute the mean of the middle items:
      7.36 + 9.57 = 16.93; 16.93 ÷ 2 = **$8.47**

Problems

1. Six stores charge different prices for jeans: $25.95, $24.50, $27.95, $24.36, $26.00, and $29.95. What is the mean price? The median?

2. Compute the mean and the median. $16,545; $19,227; $14,278; $23,950; $20,772; $14,922; and $14,673.

---

not have a large savings account because they used most of their savings when they recently rented a new apartment and purchased a new car. They do not, therefore, include interest from their savings account in their budget. When they have built up their savings again, they may be able to add interest income to their estimated total income.

Next, the Moraleses estimated their expenses for the planning period. To help them set up their budget, Michael and Anita kept a record of their actual expenses for the past several months. The couple made a list of planned expenses and savings for the year. This list included their fixed expenses, such as rent payments; variable expenses, such as clothing and food; and savings.

When Michael and Anita prepared their budget, they took their goals into consideration. You can see this in their savings budget. For example, they want more new furniture for their apartment. To begin saving for a vacation, they are cutting their entertainment expenses. Michael and Anita know that to save money, they have to have a regular, systematic plan.

In developing their budget, the Moraleses had to make sure that the total income figure was the same as the total for

Making Connections ▶︎ Everyday Living

Photocopy and distribute Enrichment Master 31-1. Have students use it as a guide to planning a cost of living budget for an average month. Point out to students that the most common errors in planning a budget include failure to plan for predictable expenses that occur perhaps quarterly or semi-annually (insurance, property taxes, tuition); failure to be realistic when estimating the amount of expenses; and failure to be specific in setting up budget categories (such as $100 "extras.") Have students discuss how to avoid these errors when planning their budget.

Practice
Suggest that students work in pairs to complete the numbered practice items. Then direct students to make up three problems that require finding the mean and the median. Have them exchange problems with a partner, work their partner's problems, and turn the problems back to their partner for evaluation.
(1. Mean: $26.45; Median $25.98.
2. Mean: $17,767; Median: $16,545.)

Use Transparencies
Use Teaching Transparency 31-4 and its corresponding strategies and worksheet from the *Teaching Transparency Strategies and Worksheets* booklet to help students create a record of their expenses. Verify student worksheets using the Answer Key.

Learning Activity
Ask students to record the amount of money they spend on lunch each day, including weekends, for two weeks. Ask them to use their records to compute the average amount they spend on lunch—the amount they would include in a budget. Ask "On what days did you spend (exactly) what you budgeted for lunch?" Use their answers as a basis for extending the discussion about variable and fixed expenses.

528   UNIT 10

USE VISUALS

Be sure that students understand that the budget in Figure 31-4 contains both monthly and yearly estimates of expenses. Ask students to explain why this is so. (The Moraleses' income is the same month-to-month but some of the expenses, such as insurance, may occur only twice a year.) Point out that the Moraleses have a combined income of over $40,000. Ask students to explain why they have budgeted only $31,200 of their income. ($31,200 is their combined take-home pay.) Answer to caption: $100 monthly or $1200 yearly.

USE TRANSPARENCIES

Use Teaching Transparency 31-5 and its corresponding strategies and worksheet from the *Teaching Transparency Strategies and Worksheets* booklet. Verify student worksheets using the Answer Key.

TEACHING TIP

Ask students to describe how they think the Moraleses' budget would change if the family's goals changed. For instance, suppose the Moraleses decide that they wish to send Michael to tech school and to buy a home computer. Have students decide if these changes affect long-term or short-term goals. (Both.) Then ask students to indicate what items in the budget might change to accommodate these changes in goals. (Sample: More savings, a dedicated education account, less on clothes and travel.)

FIGURE 31-4

A budget should be broken down into annual and monthly amounts for each category. How much money does the Morales family plan to spend on insurance payments?

BUDGET		
	Annual	Monthly
Income (after taxes)	$ 31,200	$ 2,600
Fixed Expenses		
Rent payments	7,800	650
Insurance payments	1,200	100
Loan and credit card payments	2,220	185
Variable Expenses		
Food	4,800	400
Utilities (heat, phone, electricity)	1,920	160
Car repair/transportation	1,860	155
Contributions/Gifts	720	60
Health and personal care	1,140	95
Travel	600	50
Entertainment	900	75
Clothing	2,040	170
Household (furniture, supplies)	3,000	250
Savings	3,000	250
Total Expenses	$ 31,200	$ 2,600

planned expenses and savings. If their planned expenses and savings had been more than their income, they would have had to cut some expenses or find some other source of steady income. The Moraleses' budget is shown in Figure 31-4 above.

Checking Out the Budget

The Moraleses were very careful. After their budget was prepared, they kept records of their actual expenses. They organized their spending records by breaking down their expenses into various categories, including car expenses, rent payments, and so on.

After they had estimated annual expenses and income, the Moraleses developed a monthly budget. They divided the yearly figures by 12 to get an estimate of how they planned to manage their money from one month to the next. At the end of each month, Michael and Anita totaled their actual expenses for each item. They then compared these totals with their budgeted amounts to see whether they were keeping within their budget.

When they compared their monthly budgeted amounts with their actual expenses, the Moraleses found that they spent less than they had budgeted for food, utilities, car repair and transportation, contributions and gifts, entertainment, and travel. On the other hand, they spent more than their budgeted amounts for health and personal items, clothing, and house-

Cooperative Learning   Group Discussion

Organize students into groups to conduct a panel discussion on issues related to the sample budget in Figure 31-4. Topics might include how the Moraleses might change the amounts they budget for food and rent, how to keep the budget balanced even with increasing health care, or how to control deficit spending (depending on loans and credit cards for purchases).

Refer to the *Cooperative Learning Strategies* booklet for additional cooperative learning strategies.

hold expenses. Even with these differences, Michael and Anita had money left at the end of the month. Their total actual expenses were close to their total income for the month. They are living within their budget.

After looking at their actual expenses, the Moraleses decided to make some changes in their budget. They chose to decrease the amount budgeted for food. They decided not to decrease the other budgeted amounts, since their utility bills or car repair expenses may be higher in the future. Using the amount taken out of the food budget, the Moraleses increased the budgeted amounts for clothing and household expenses, the two main areas in which their expenses were higher than the amounts first budgeted.

The Moraleses have adjusted their budget according to their needs. A budget works only if it meets your needs. A budget provides a warning signal for rising costs, and it identifies trouble spots.

How Does It All Add Up?

Many families do not know the actual state of their financial affairs. They need to develop a statement of net worth. You may recall that a statement of net worth summarizes an individual's assets and liabilities and indicates the difference between the two. Providing a statement of net worth is an important part of an entrepreneur's business plan. Such a financial statement is an important part of an individual or family money management plan.

The family's statement of net worth has three kinds of information. First, it contains a list of money and items or property owned. How much cash does the family have on hand? How much savings, clothing, and furniture? These are the family's assets. Next, the statement of net worth lists amounts of money owed. Is there a mortgage, a loan, or a balance owed on a charge account? These are the liabilities. When you subtract liabilities from assets, you learn the third piece of information, the family's net worth.

To balance the statement of net worth, you add total liabilities and net worth. You will see that the bottom line of both columns contains the same dollar amount. Take a look at the statement of net worth for the Morales family in Figure 31-5 on page 530. It contains information that a budget does not have, such as the value of recreational equipment they own and the total amount that they owe on their car. A budget and a statement of net worth together provide a very effective set of tools for managing financial affairs. A family's statement of net worth is also a very important document to

USE TRANSPARENCIES

Use Teaching Transparency 31-6 and its corresponding strategies and worksheet from the *Teaching Transparency Strategies and Worksheets* booklet to help students plan a budget. Verify student worksheets using the Answer Key.

TEACHING TIP

Emphasize the importance of budget review. Simply preparing a budget is not enough—the Moraleses must compare their actual spending against the budget to determine how the budget needs to be adjusted. Ask what the Moraleses should do to ensure that the budget reflects the actual expenses they incur. (Keep records.) If the Moraleses find that they are spending more than the budgeted amount on health care, what steps should they take? (Review the expenditures to see if there were extraordinary or emergency expenditures. If not, the Moraleses should increase the amount they budget for health care and decrease some other amount in their budget.)

Learning Activity

Prepare slips of paper and write on them changes to items in the Moraleses' budget. Have groups select one or more slips and determine how the family's budget will change.

Business & History

The word *budget* meant "leather purse or wallet" in England in the Middle Ages. Later, when the English finance minister—called the chancellor of the exchequer—presented his annual spending plan to Parliament, he was said to be "opening his budget." Now *budget* means a plan for using money.

Enrichment Strategy

Have students work in groups to design a board game called Budget This. Students will need to prepare a selection of lifestyle cards, such as family of four or single working parent with three children, income cards, and cards listing annual expenses. On the board students can include events that impact a family's budget, such as car repairs $600, Aunt Celia's gift $300, new job, pay raise, and so on. As students move around the board they will need to make adjustments in their budgets to accommodate changes. Have groups share completed games with other groups and determine which games are the most exciting to play.

Connection to CHAPTER 9

Remind students of the definitions of *assets* and *liabilities* from Chapter 9: Property or any item of value (cash, products to sell, equipment, buildings, and land) owned by a business is considered an *asset*. Any amount a business owes is a *liability* (equipment purchased on credit).

USE VISUALS

Ask students to indicate what items comprise the Moraleses' assets. (Cash in checking accounts, savings, life insurance, car, household furnishings, recreational equipment, and clothing.)
Answer to caption: By subtracting total liabilities of $6200 from total assets of $15,300.

USE TRANSPARENCIES

Use Teaching Transparency 31-7 and its corresponding strategies and worksheet from the *Teaching Transparency Strategies and Worksheets* booklet to give students more experience with net worth statements. Verify student worksheets using the Answer Key.

Quick Check Answers

1. A document that details your financial state.
2. Subtract liabilities from assets.
3. Provide quick input of expense amount, quick analysis of expenses, and "what if" analysis of possible changes.

FIGURE 31-5

A statement of net worth summarizes assets and liabilities and indicates the difference between the two. How was the Moraleses' net worth determined?

Morales Family
Statement of Net Worth
December 31, 1997

Assets		Liabilities	
Cash in checking account	$ 600	Midtown Savings Bank	
Savings	2,000	automobile loan	$ 4,200
Life insurance (cash value)	3,500	furniture store	2,000
Car	4,200	Total Liabilities	$ 6,200
Household furnishings	3,000		
Recreational equipment	500	Total Assets	$ 15,300
Clothing	1,500	Total Liabilities	$ 6,200
Total Assets	$ 15,300	Net Worth	$ 9,100

provide if, for instance, Michael and Anita go to the bank for a loan.

Using a Computer for Budgeting

Many people have computers in their homes today. Several kinds of software programs are available so that people can set up and maintain a household budget on their computer. With a computerized budgeting program, you can store your budgeted amounts and enter your expenses either as they occur or at the end of the month. The computer can give you a quick analysis of total expenses, including amounts that are over or under the budget.

In addition, the computer can help with "what if" situations. For example, what if Anita Morales's income increased by ten percent? With a computer, the Moraleses could easily find out how much more they could save each month. What if their rent also went up—by $50 each month? What if they also wanted to save for a compact disc player? How much would they have to cut their entertainment and travel expenses in order to buy this item in one year? By using a computer, the Moraleses could quickly see how such changes would affect their budget.

Quick Check

1. What is a statement of net worth?
2. How do you figure net worth?
3. How can a computer help the budgeting process?

Making Connections ⟶ Technology

Point out that computerized budget programs work along the same principles as business accounting programs and spreadsheets. When an entry in one classification is changed, other categories are automatically adjusted. Ask students whether they think they would be more or less likely to stick to a budget developed on the computer. Have them explain their answers.

Chapter 31 **Summary**

Main Ideas

1. Your lifestyle, which is based on your values and attitudes, often determines how you spend your money.
2. Budgeting helps you set priorities for spending and saving your money.
3. Budgeting provides a reference so you can see how well you are managing your money.
4. The five steps in planning a budget are setting goals, estimating income, estimating expenses, planning for savings, and adjusting the budget.
5. You can figure out the state of your financial affairs by comparing your assets and liabilities and computing your net worth.
6. A computer can be helpful in budgeting because it stores information, can give a quick analysis of expenses, and can show you how changes in income and expenses will affect your budget.
7. To find a mean average, add all the items and divide by the number of items; to find a median average, list all the items according to their amount and find the item in the middle.
8. Advances in computer technology allow computers the size of notebooks to be as powerful as full-size units.

CASE ANALYSIS   Budgeting

Listed below are some points of view about budgeting. Give your opinion of each statement. Then defend your position.

1. "I pay all of my bills by check. My checkbook's my record of expenses."
2. "I have a complete record of every penny I've spent for the past 10 years."
3. "I know how much I earn and how much I can spend. Why should I keep a record?"
4. "I keep a record of major expenses only. There's no point in bothering with nickel-and-dime items."
5. "I'm just not good with numbers. I buy what I want and hope I have enough money."

CHAPTER 31   PLANNING A BUDGET   **531**

CLOSE

Main Ideas

Main Ideas summarizes the key information in the chapter. It is a useful tool for reinforcement and review.

CASE ANALYSIS

Case Analysis provides a chapter-related case for student analysis and application of decision-making skills.

Answer
Answers will vary.

QUICK QUIZ

1. What tool can help you use your money to meet your needs and wants? (A budget.)
2. What five steps are part of the budget process? (Set goals, estimate income, estimate expenses, plan savings, balance and adjust budget.)
3. What part does saving play in a budget? (Helps protect against unplanned expenses.)
4. What is a family's statement of net worth likely to include? (Assets—money and property owned, liabilities—money owed, and the dollar difference between the two.)

Chapter 31 **Review**

CHAPTER 31 REVIEW

APPLY

Answers

Use the Language of Business
1. lifestyle; 2. money management; 3. budget; 4. net pay; 5. gross pay; 6. deductions.

Review What You Learned
1. To show where money will be spent and help you plan your spending more carefully.
2. Estimated income, expenses, and savings.
3. It helps you set goals and priorities for spending money; it helps cut down on money wasted on things that are not so important to you; it provides a reference to check on how well you are managing your money.
4. Yes, to reflect new circumstances that arise.
5. Set goals, estimate income, estimate expenses, plan for savings, and balance and adjust the budget.
6. To provide money for long-term goals, for emergencies, and for extras.
7. Either cut expenses or savings, or increase income.
8. All the money, items, and property owned (assets); all the bills or debts owed (liabilities); the difference between assets and liabilities (net worth).
9. 20; 18.
10. Storage space needed for a single character; 1024 bytes; more than a million bytes.

Understand Business Concepts
1. It should allow you to buy or save for things you find most important.
2. The budget is your money management plan. Money management also includes other activities, such as getting the best buy on an item and keeping records of where you spend money.
3. Knowing previous income and expenses gives you some idea of what your budget should be for a future period.

Use the Language of Business

When you are trying to manage your money, it is important to know the following terms. See how well you know them. Complete each sentence with the correct term.

budget	gross pay	money management
deductions	lifestyle	net pay

1. The way of living that reflects a person's attitudes and values is called that person's _____.
2. Planning how to get the most from your money is called _____.
3. An important part of managing money is making a plan, or _____.
4. To estimate your income, you use the figure of your pay after deductions, or your _____.
5. Do not use the figure of your _____ because that is not the amount available to spend.
6. Use the amount your employer subtracts for state and federal taxes, and other _____.

Review What You Learned

1. What is the purpose of a budget?
2. What are three categories of items that should be included in a budget?
3. What are three advantages of using a budget to help you manage your money?
4. Should a budget ever be changed? Why?
5. List the steps that you should always follow in planning a budget.
6. Why is it important to save part of your income on a regular basis?
7. If your personal budget does not balance, what two possibilities for change do you have in order to make it balance?
8. What three kinds of information are contained in the statement of net worth?
9. What is the mean average of 25, 22, 18, 20, and 15? What is the median?
10. Define *byte*, *kilobyte*, and *megabyte*.

Understand Business Concepts

1. How should a budget relate to your values and goals?
2. Why is budgeting your money only a part of money management?
3. Why is it important to look at previous income and expenses in developing a budget?
4. List five examples of fixed expenses.
5. List five examples of variable expenses.
6. When should income from savings and investments be included in a budget? When should such income not be included?
7. Why is follow-up an important step in the budgeting process?
8. If a family has total assets of $33,600 and liabilities of $27,350, what is its net worth?

4. Fixed expenses include such things as rent or mortgage payments, insurance, taxes, loan payments, and car payments.
5. Variable expenses include such items as food, clothing, utilities, entertainment, and recreational activities.
6. Income from savings or investments should be included only if it is substantial and steady.
7. Follow-up is important for determining how well you are following the budget and for deciding whether the budget should be changed.
8. Its net worth is $6250.
9. When the mean is misleading because a few numbers in the series are either much higher or much lower than the rest of the numbers.

10. They can go most anywhere business people want to go and they can exchange data with larger computer systems.

Think Critically
1. Higher-than-expected or unplanned for expenses could wreck a budget if the person has very little income left over after providing for fixed expenses.
2. The budget shows the money the Moraleses expect to earn and spend in the near future. The statement of net worth lists their actual assets and liabilities for the present.
3. By looking at what was spent in the past for similar items.

9. When would it be best to find a *median average* instead of a *mean average?*

10. What are two advantages of notebook computers?

Think Critically

1. **Assess.** In planning a budget, why is it important that the figure for net pay—not the figure for gross pay—be used as income?

2. **Compare and Contrast.** Compare the statement of net worth in this chapter with the budget for the Morales family. How do the two differ?

3. **Analyze.** When setting up a budget, how can an individual or family know how to estimate the expenses that will occur?

Use What You Learned

1. **Group Project.** Each member of your group should keep a list of his or her expenses for one week to find out how much is spent on such things as food, transportation, clothing, and entertainment. At the end of the week, meet to evaluate how each member's spending satisfied lifestyle goals. Summarize your group's lifestyle spending in a paragraph to share with other groups.

2. Write a description of your "dream lifestyle." Include things such as housing, clothing, food, transportation, leisure, vacation, and savings. Check newspapers and magazines to determine the cost of your dream lifestyle. The ads may also give you ideas about other costs. How much income would you need to earn each month to achieve your dream lifestyle?

3. Select a vocational/technical school or college that you would like to attend after high school. Obtain information on tuition and other fees. Add to these amounts the costs of food, shelter, clothing, books and supplies, transportation, and any other items you believe are part of the cost of the education you would like to receive. Estimate the total cost of this education. Then estimate how you will pay for your education. Include income from parents or relatives, loans, scholarships, personal savings, and earnings while attending school. Prepare a budget for the length of time that will be needed to finance and complete your education.

4. **Computer Application.** Prepare a personal budget and present it in a spreadsheet format.

5. **Skill Reinforcement.** Review the difference between the mean and the median on pages 526–527. Though each is relatively easy to determine, what might cause you to make an error in determining either the mean or the median?

Save your work in your Business Portfolio.

Use What You Learned

1. Be certain that each student participates in the group activity. Rubric: Paragraph.

2. Encourage students to find realistic prices, not just sale prices, for items they include in their "dream lifestyle." Rubrics: Note Taking, Essay.

3. Remind students to be specific about all expenditures, replacing gasoline, snack food, and so on for the unspecific "miscellaneous." Rubrics: Note Taking, Charts and Tables.

4. Students without access to computers can create a spreadsheet manually. Rubric: Charts and Tables.

5. Miscounting the number of numbers in the group and thus dividing by the wrong number; making an error in addition.

Use the Chapter 31 worksheets in *Student Activity Guide 2* for additional practice and application activities. *Student Activity Guide 2* provides vocabulary exercises, reading comprehension checks, problems, projects, and simulations of business and economic situations. A Teacher's Annotated Edition provides answers.

ASSESS

Portfolio Assessment

The projects are designed to lead students to develop a collection of their best work to submit to you for assessment. You and your students should decide which projects will be included in their respective Business Portfolios. Refer students to the specific rubric(s) from the *Alternative Assessment Strategies* booklet listed with each of the project notes below. These rubrics will alert students to the criteria you will use to assess their projects.

Chapter Assessment

Use the Chapter 31 Test from the *Test Masters* booklet to evaluate students' understanding of the chapter concepts. An answer key is provided. Or create your own customized test using the *Testmaker* software.

FOCUS

Introduce the Chapter

Major Concepts
- Why Should You Save?
- Starting Your Savings Program
- Guidelines for Investing
- Common Investment Choices

Introduce the Topic

Ask students to describe what they think is the difference between saving and investing. Then ask students to describe some kinds of investments they have heard mentioned in the news.

Use Business Terms

Have students look at the Business Terms and note any of the terms that are familiar to them. Ask them to define these terms or try to recall the contexts in which they were used. For those terms that are totally unfamiliar, have students venture a meaning. Reinforce correct definitions. For terms that they cannot define, advise students to note the definitions in the chapter.

The individual in this photograph is comparing the interest rate on several types of savings accounts. How can people make the money they save "work" for them? (By investing the money so that it earns income.)

Business terms

saving

investing

rate of return

fixed rate

variable rate

liquidity

maturity date

dividend

capital gain

equity

534

CHAPTER 32 RESOURCES

Instructional Resources

Lesson Plan for Chapter 32

Teaching Transparencies 32-1, 32-2

Strategies and Worksheets for Teaching Transparencies 32-1, 32-2

Enrichment Masters 32-1, 32-2

Student Activity Guide 2–TAE for Chapter 32

Test Master for Chapter 32

Alternative Assessment Strategies

Math Skills Review

International Business Strategies

Cooperative Learning Strategies

Communication Skills Review

Ethics in Business Strategies

Saving and Investing

Learning objectives

After completing this chapter, you will be able to:
- Give three reasons why people save.
- Describe the differences between saving and investing.
- List six guidelines to wise investing.
- Identify and describe three common choices for investments.
- Describe how technology assists stockbrokers and investors.
- Explain the information contained in stock market quotations.

Consider what you know

- You have learned that planning a budget is a useful way to make sure that you can meet your expenses. A budget also lets you prepare for future financial needs. However, budgets are not only about spending; they are also about saving.

Consider what you want to know

- Why should you save?
- What's the difference between saving and investing?
- What do you need to know before you invest?
- What kinds of investments do most people make?
- Can a computer help you buy stocks?
- What information is in the daily stock quotations? What do all the symbols and numbers mean?

Consider how to use what you learn

- As you read this chapter, watch for advertisements in your local newspapers and on television. Take special note of the advertisements of banks and investment companies in your area. Try to decide which ones might become part of your saving and investment plans.

CHAPTER 32   SAVING AND INVESTING   **535**

Multimedia Resources

Technology Resource Guide

Distance Learning Guide

Internet Resource Guide

Professional Resources

School-to-Work/Tech Prep Strategies

Instructional Poster

Spanish Resources

Testmaker Software for Chapter 32

The Wall Street Journal Video Series
  Video & Activities for Chapter 32

Business and Marketing Computer
  Applications—An Integrated Software
  Simulation Using Microsoft Works

Stocktracker—A Stock Market Software
  Simulation

Where's the Dough? Board Game

TEACH

Business Connection

McDonald's Corporation offers a direct investment service to nonemployees. Through Mc-Direct, potential investors can purchase up to $250 worth of McDonald's stock per year. The transactions carry a 10¢ per share fee with a maximum fee of $5, well below traditional transaction fees.

Develop Concepts

Why Should You Save?

Ask students to list some of the major purchases they wish to make in the next year or so. Ask how many students already have the money for these purchases and how many will need to save. Use students' responses as a springboard for discussing reasons for savings: major purchases, emergencies, and retirement.

Learning Activity

Have students imagine that they wish to purchase $500 worth of sound equipment 12 months from now. Have them compute how much money per month they would need to save to be able to make the purchase. ($500 ÷ 12 = $41.66, or about the cost of five movies or ten fast-food lunches.) Then have students compute the cost of buying the system on credit and paying it off within a year. Remind students that many credit cards charge an interest fee of 18 percent. ($500 × .18 = $590; $590 ÷ 12 = $49, or about seven movies.)

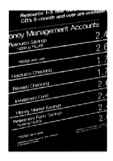

As you learned in Chapter 31, a personal budget is not complete without a plan for regular savings. **Saving** is putting money aside for future use. However, saving is not just a matter of putting money aside. Money should be working by earning income. Then saving becomes **investing.** There are various ways of saving and investing. Some ways may earn more money than others. Some may involve risk.

In this chapter you will discover how money set aside can work and grow until it is needed. You will also learn some general guidelines to help you balance risks against earnings to make the best—and safest—use of your savings and investments.

WHY SHOULD YOU SAVE?

Saving makes sense for everyone. Each of us may need a large amount of money sometime in the future—maybe for education expenses, a vacation, or a car. You may want to plan for the proverbial "rainy day" and save money in case of a financial emergency.

Individuals set up and maintain savings plans for three main reasons: to make purchases, to provide for emergencies, or to have income for retirement. A specific plan will give you the motivation you need to save your money now and in the future.

For Major Purchases

Suppose you would like to have a really nice sound system, a first-class guitar, a car, or a two-year degree from a technical college. You will probably need to save money before you can buy items like these. You may even need to save for an entire year. Even if you want to buy new clothes or holiday gifts, you may need to save. Saving for your education after high school involves putting money aside for several years.

Remember, if you purchase items on credit or borrow money to make purchases, you will have to pay a finance charge. If you use cash for the purchase, you do not have to pay the finance charge. Finance charges may average 17 percent, much higher than the interest on a savings account. So saving money can help you save money! You should save for major purchases, even if you save money for other reasons as well.

Making Connections ➡ Everyday Life

Have students conduct an informal poll among family members, neighbors, and friends to discover how many save and for what reasons. Suggest that students pool their results and present them along with graphs or diagrams as a poster for classroom display.

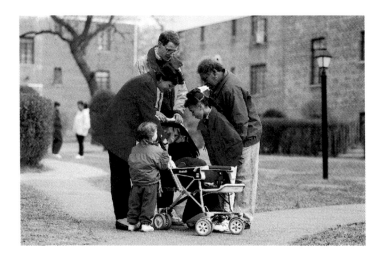

An addition to a family, such as a new baby, can change a family's financial needs. How might a family have prepared for such a change?

For Emergencies

You may face a financial emergency in the future. You may be ill for several weeks and unable to work. Or you may need to make an unexpected trip to visit a friend or relative. Your car may need an expensive repair. Sometimes you need emergency money so quickly that you do not have time to arrange for a loan. It is a good idea to try to have some money set aside as an "emergency fund" to take care of these unexpected needs.

For Retirement

It might seem early to think about saving for retirement, but it's best to begin early. It's possible that when you do retire, some income will be paid to you by the federal Social Security program. You may also be covered by a retirement plan provided by your employer. However, these sources of retirement income may not be adequate. If you haven't worked regularly, or long enough for a single employer, or if your employer didn't have a pension plan, you may have trouble meeting your expenses. Starting a savings plan now will enable you to supplement your income when you retire.

Quick Check

1. Name three major reasons people save money.
2. How can saving for purchases save you money on a purchase?
3. How does *investing* differ from *saving?*

Curriculum Connection   English and Communication

Have students work in groups of four to design, write, and produce a brochure titled "Savings, the Key to Your Future." Suggest that in the brochure students indicate reasons to save and ways to make saving a regular habit. Encourage them to include examples of how saving helps individuals meet their financial goals.

For those students who need to sharpen their written communication skills, choose among the worksheets in the *Communication Skills Review* booklet.

Direct students' attention to the photograph. Ask students to speculate on how this family's financial needs have changed in the past five years and how they will change in the next five years.
Answer to caption: Through savings and investments.

Business Brief

Savings and investment objectives often change as people age. People in their 20s and 30s use their savings to purchase homes, automobiles, and appliances. They also use savings for vacations and visits to relatives. They may also use savings to fund their children's education. As people age, their savings and investment goals include money for retirement.

TEACHING TIP

Ask students for ways, aside from automatic payroll deductions, that they could make savings a habit, setting aside a certain amount on a daily, weekly, or monthly schedule.

Quick Check Answers

1. Purchases, emergencies, retirement.
2. You do not pay for the interest charged for credit purchases, therefore you save that money.
3. Invested money is saved money that earns income.

FOCUS ON **Technology**

Discuss
Ask students to discuss the meanings of the terms *30-day moving average, quote,* and *real-time,* with respect to computer stock information.
For additional information about current technology, refer to the *Technology Resources Guide* booklet.

Electronic Ticker Tape

Stockbrokers have always needed to know the current price of stocks and bonds. Early in this century, stockbrokers hovered around a ticker tape machine as it printed information about stocks on a one-inch ribbon of paper. These machines announced their messages by the ticking sounds they made as they tapped out the stock's symbol, the number of shares traded, and the price per share.

Today, the same stock information is still distributed in ribbons of information. Today's ticker display is a large electronic ribbon. Information moves silently across the ribbon as it hovers above the trading floor at stock exchanges, letting traders at the exchanges know the current price of stocks.

Brokers use computers to access data about the performance of the stock market itself or of an individual stock. The broker can request a graph showing the average price for 30 days. This information is updated daily and is called a 30-day moving average. The broker can call to the screen graphs showing the average price for the last 60 days or 90 days as well. This kind of visual information helps the experienced stockbroker identify *trends,* or the general direction of prices in the stock market or of an individual stock. That information is useful when advising a customer on when to purchase or sell stocks.

In addition to graphs, stockbrokers can access news items related to a specific company such as any new products, marketing campaigns, mergers, and so on. All of this information helps the stockbroker better inform the customer about which stocks to buy or sell.

Develop Concepts

Starting Your Savings Program

Indicate to students that one of the easiest ways to save is to have savings automatically deducted from a paycheck. Some banks will arrange to transfer a predetermined amount from an individual's checking account to his or her savings account. Stress to students that automatic deductions help individuals save regularly.

STARTING YOUR SAVINGS PROGRAM

The amount of money you save depends on how much of your income you are willing *not* to spend. All saving involves some sacrifice. The key to an effective savings plan is to set a goal and keep working toward it. A goal will help motivate you and keep you from forgetting. You may want to choose a dollar goal, one that you could use to buy something expensive like a car. Remember to make saving a habit. Each week or month, set aside a certain percent of your income—before you spend it. For example, you may be able to save 10 percent of your income. If you make $220 a week, you would put $22 into savings. Once you have the savings habit, you will find it easy to save.

A savings plan might start with regular deposits to a savings account at a bank, a savings and loan association, or credit union. These institutions pay you for the use of your money, which they lend out to other customers. The amount of interest earned and the requirement for depositing and withdrawing

Learning Activity
Suggest that students use the text example to make a graph of savings vs. time. Have students use the graph to answer the following: How much savings will they have in six months? ($528) How would the graph change if their savings earned interest? (The line would be steeper.)

Reteaching Strategy

Explain to students that individuals in the United States save about 5 percent of their income. In contrast, individuals in many other countries save a larger percentage of their income. Encourage students to acknowledge that they live in a country where people save very little. Direct students to discuss the economic problems the country faces because of the low level of savings. Then have them write a letter to a friend detailing the advantages of savings for the individual and the country.

The most important information is the *quote,* or price of the stock. It must be current. Prices in stock, bond, currency, and commodity markets change every minute, sometimes every second. Stock exchanges are required, by law, to record transactions within 90 seconds of completion. The exchanges use *real-time* information—that is, the transaction information is transmitted to the ticker display instantaneously.

Brokerage houses spend millions of dollars to make certain they have access to absolutely up-to-the-second information. They use high-speed communication links to gather and transmit information from the exchanges. Old information is useless, even costly. A 2:30 P.M. purchase of stock based on a 2:15 P.M. price can produce disastrous results. For example, if the price of a share increases a quarter point (25¢ a share), and the transaction purchased 100,000 shares, the stockbroker could have to make up a difference of $25,000 to complete the purchase.

Follow Through
Ask students who have witnessed electronic ticker tape displays, either on television or in windows of brokerage houses, to describe the information they observed. Ask students to speculate on what other technological advancements might affect stock purchases in the future.

money vary from one institution to the next. Generally, though, savings accounts are very liquid, meaning a depositor can get cash out of a savings account quickly and easily.

Many banks and investment companies offer money market accounts. These usually pay a higher rate of interest than do savings accounts. However, to get that higher rate of interest, these accounts require a significant minimum balance, for example $2500. You may withdraw the entire balance of a money market account at any time without penalty. However, there may be restrictions on the number of partial withdrawals you may make within a month or a quarter.

Making the decision to save is only the first step. You must also decide what to do with the money you save. You can, of course, simply hide the money somewhere. When you need it, the money will probably be exactly where you left it. However, you will have only as much money as you hid. In fact, economic factors may have reduced the buying power of your money. A better way to save requires investing your money so that it earns extra income.

Connection to
CHAPTER 19

Remind students that Chapter 19 explained how banks rely on savings deposits to fund loans they make to other bank customers. Ask a volunteer to describe for the class how banks create money. Then have students design a symbol or logo that illustrates the relationship between depositors' savings and bank customers' borrowing.

Making Connections ⟡ **Communication**

Suggest that students search local television listings to find what, if any, channels in their area broadcast continuous stock quotations throughout the day. Have students prepare an oral report on what kinds of information are presented, for example New York Stock Exchange (NYSE) quotes, Chicago Board of Trade (CBOT) quotes, and commodity prices. Encourage students to report on what, if any, analysis the programs provide.

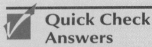

Quick Check
Answers

1. A savings goal can keep you motivated.
2. Interest, minimum deposits, if any, and any other requirements.

Develop Concepts

Guidelines for Investing

Point out to students that there are more considerations to investing than asking "How much will this investment make?" A wise investor considers a number of factors, among them risk, rate of return, availability of money, resistance to inflation, and tax considerations.

TEACHING TIP

Point out to students that different kinds of investments have different levels of risk associated with them. For example, General Motors or IBM may lose rather than earn money on any given day, but the overall risk for investment in such companies is relatively minimal. Ask students to describe financial risk in their own terms.

Connection to
CHAPTER 19

Remind students that many savings account deposits are insured by agencies of the federal government, for example the Federal Savings and Loan Insurance Corporation (FSLIC). Ask students how the protection of these agencies affects the risk associated with savings accounts. (It lowers the risk. Savings up to $100,000 are guaranteed safe.)

Quick Check

1. How can setting a goal help you save money?
2. As you plan your savings program, what kind of information should you get from banks?

GUIDELINES FOR INVESTING

Any potential investor can choose among many investment options. Some are safe: The amount of money you invest is secure, and it might increase at a steady rate of return. Other investments are risky: They offer the potential of sizable gains, but you could lose your original investment. The key to wise investing is knowing what investment options are available to you, what goals you have, and what amount of risk you will accept. Before you make an investment, ask yourself the following questions.

What Is the Risk?

Risk is the possibility that you may lose your investment. Few investments are entirely risk-free. Even established banking institutions and corporations occasionally fail. The economic climate can change suddenly, turning relatively safe investments into risky ones. Some investments, however, always involve less risk than others.

Many investments offer no guarantees. You risk losing some or all of your money. If you have money invested in a business that has a bad year, your investment will probably decrease in value. If the business fails, you may lose your entire investment. Real estate and collectible items such as baseball cards may increase in value, but then again they may not. Before making any investment, evaluate the risk.

What Is the Rate of Return?

The **rate of return,** or yield, on an investment is the amount of money the investment earns. The rate of return is always expressed as a percent of the original investment. The rate of return is figured on an annual basis. For example, suppose $1000 in a savings account earns a $50 interest payment for one year. The rate of return on the investment is 5 percent. A single share of stock whose value increases from $50 to $60 in a year has a 20 percent rate of return.

Enrichment Strategy

Investment periodicals and advisors point out that successful investors seem to follow two common investment rules: (1) invest regularly and (2) invest for the longer-term. Direct students to use several news and investment periodicals to learn some tips or pointers about investing. Have students use their findings to compose a Top Ten list of investment rules.

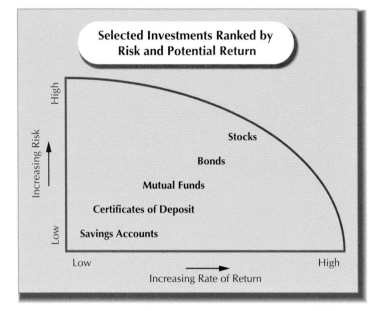

Selected Investments Ranked by Risk and Potential Return

Increasing Risk — Low to High

Stocks

Bonds

Mutual Funds

Certificates of Deposit

Savings Accounts

Low ——— Increasing Rate of Return ——— High

FIGURE 32-1

This chart reflects the general rule that lower-risk investments have lower rates of return. The lowest risk investment is a savings account. Potentially it will yield a relatively small return. What does the chart show about the possible risk and potential return for investing in stocks?

A **fixed-rate** investment is one that yields an unchanging return. You can predict with a high degree of accuracy the rate of return on fixed-rate investments, such as some savings accounts and bonds. With **variable-rate** investments, the rate of return changes depending on the average yield of the investment. You cannot predict, for example, how much stock in a corporation will increase in value, if at all.

In return for a higher rate of return on your investment, you may need to accept greater risk. In general, the greater an investment's risk, the greater the possibility of a higher rate of return. Like all general rules, this one is not always true. Sometimes the yield on a risky investment is lower than the yield on a safe investment. Figure 32-1 above shows the general yield-to-risk relationship of some common types of investments. In this chapter we will look more closely at how these investments work.

How Available Is the Money?

You should design a savings plan that can respond to emergencies. For example, you may need money from your investments to make an unplanned purchase or to deal with a medical emergency. Some investments, such as a savings

Reteaching Strategy

Direct students to work in groups of four to search local newspapers for advertisements for investments such as stocks, bonds, mutual funds, and so on. Have students collect the ads and highlight or circle the terms *rate of return, yield, fixed rate,* and *variable rate.* Have students rewrite the advertising copy, substituting their own words for the highlighted terms. (Students might also find examples giving *return on investment (ROI).* ROI is the same as yield or rate of return).

USE VISUALS

Direct students' attention to Figure 32-1, Selected Investments Ranked by Risk and Potential Return. Have students describe what happens as the rate of return of an investment increases. Then ask them to describe what happens as the risk of an investment increases. Ask volunteers to state the information in Figure 32-1 in a single sentence. (Higher rates of return involve higher risk; lower rates of return involve lower risk.) Answer to caption: Although the risk of investing in stocks is high, the returns also may be high.

USE TRANSPARENCIES

Use Teaching Transparency 32-1 and its corresponding strategies and worksheet from the *Teaching Transparency Strategies and Worksheets* booklet to assist students in understanding the relationship between risk and return. Verify student worksheets using the Answer Key.

Learning Activity

Discuss the concept of *liquidity* with the class. Then ask students to create a drawing or picture that illustrates the meaning of liquidity. Invite volunteers to share their drawings with the class. Post the most descriptive illustrations for the class to use as a study aid.

Building Business Skills

Building Business Skills

Model

Have students read the explanation in Reading Stock Market Quotations, page 542. Ask volunteers to explain what the numbers in each column of the example in the box represent. Then, using one of the stocks listed, have a student read the quotes, giving the opening price, closing price, and the day's high and low prices.

Connection to CHAPTER 3

Remind students that inflation, described in Chapter 3, is the prolonged rise in the general price level of goods and services. Ask students to explain in their own words how inflation can affect an investment.

Learning Activity

Direct students to scan newspapers and other periodicals to determine the current rate of inflation. Ask students to determine what rate of return an investment will need in order to have its earnings be greater than the inflation rate.

Math

Reading Stock Market Quotations

Explanation

How did your company's stock do today? Did the price per share go up or down? What was the highest price it sold for in the last year? How much of a dividend does it pay? If you are involved in the world of business, or have invested part of your savings in shares of corporate stock, you must be able to understand stock market quotations in newspaper financial pages.

When the stock market opens, the stocks begin selling. In the course of the trading day, a single stock's price may go up and down several times. At the end of the trading day, each stock will have a closing price. This price, as well as other useful information, is listed in the stock market quotations.

Practice

Study the stock quotations and answer the questions that follow.

1. What was the closing price for Reebok?
2. What was the lowest price paid for ReinsGp during the 365-day period?
3. Which stock paid the highest dividend?
4. Which stock had the lowest PE ratio? The highest?
5. How many shares of ReinsGp were traded?
6. Which stock price decreased the most from the previous day? Which increased the most?
7. If you had bought 100 shares of Reebok at the year's lowest price, how much more would they be worth today?

account, can be easily converted into cash. A savings account is a liquid asset. **Liquidity** is the measure of how quickly you can turn an investment into cash. Stocks are relatively liquid because they can be sold quickly (although not always for the best price). Real estate or an antique table might take a long time to sell—unless you lower the price enough to make a quick sale. Wise investors provide for unplanned cash needs by keeping some money in highly liquid investments.

How Inflation-Proof Is the Investment?

You will want your investment to earn enough to keep up with the rising cost of goods and services. For example, if the inflation rate is 5 percent, an investment needs to earn 5 percent just to keep pace with inflation. If your investment yields 3 percent, your money will buy 2 percent fewer goods at the end of a year. High inflation rates limit your investment alternatives. Always compare the inflation rate with the rate of return on your investments and make sure that it is greater than the inflation rate.

Meeting Student Diversity

Three characteristics can be used to evaluate investments—liquidity, risk, and return. Have students rank the investments below on a scale of 1 to 4, with 1 indicating the most of a characteristic and 4 indicating the least of the characteristic.
Liquidity—home (4), savings account (1), stocks (3), certificate of deposit (2).
Risk—home (2), stocks (1), money market account (3), treasury bills (4).
Return—stocks (1), home (2), bond (3), savings account (4).

STOCK MARKET QUOTATIONS

The annual dividend paid per share is $.30.

Yld is the yield, or rate of return at the current price. Yield is computed by dividing the annual dividend by the closing price.

During the last 365 days the highest closing price for a share of this stock was $40.25. The lowest was $31.13.

The closing price went up, or gained, $.25 over the day before. Then the closing price would have been $34.75 ($35.00 – $.25).

365-day High	Low	Stock	Div	Yld	PE Ratio	Sales (hds)	High	Low	Close	Chng
40¼	31⅛	Reebok	0.30	0.9	13	2342	35¼	34⅝	35	+ ¼
18¾	15⅛	RegRlty	1.58	9.4	21	63	16⅞	16⅝	16¾	– ⅛
30⅜	21⅞	ReinsGp	0.24	0.8	12	604	30¼	29¾	30	– ¼
6¾	4⅞	RelGrp	0.32	4.9	10	604	6⅝	6⅜	6½	...

PE stands for price/earnings ratio. It equals the closing price divided by the company's earnings per share. The *lower* the PE number, the *higher* the earnings per share, and vice versa.

During the day, 234,200 (2342 × 100) shares were traded.

The highest price paid for this stock on this day was $35.25. The lowest price was $34.63. The closing price was $35.00.

Practice

Allow students time to become familiar with the stock market quotations in the box. Then suggest that students work in pairs to complete the numbered practice items.

[1. $35.00
2. $21.88
3. RegRlty
4. RelGrp; RegRlty
5. 60,400
6. ReinsGp; Reebok
7. ($31.13 × 100) – ($35 × 100) = $387.00]

Does the Investment Have Any Tax Advantages?

Some investments can save you money on income taxes. For example, the interest income paid to holders of some government bonds is not taxed. Investing in a house can reduce income taxes because the interest paid on the mortgage and the real estate taxes generally are deductible from taxable income before the tax is computed. This tax savings, when added to the potential increase in the value of the property, can make a home an attractive investment. The investment value of the home may change, however, if the tax advantage is removed. Also, wage earners can deposit pre-tax dollars into special retirement plans that invest their funds for growth. Taxes on these funds are paid when they are withdrawn during retirement years, when the income tax rate generally is lower.

Will You Be Comfortable with the Investment?

You should choose an investment that fits your personality. Before choosing an investment, you should ask yourself several

CHAPTER 32   SAVING AND INVESTING   **543**

Connection to CHAPTER 17

Remind students that in Chapter 17 they learned that the federal government taxes income. Income includes not only wages, but also any other earnings an individual may receive, including earnings on investments.

TEACHING TIP

Remind students that as their financial needs change, their comfort with certain investments will change as well. Have students indicate their answers to the questions under "Will you be comfortable with the investment?" on page 543. Then ask students to discuss which answers they think will change once they own a home, have children, or need to support elderly family members.

Enrichment Strategy

Property taxes are generally levied by local governments in an effort to pay for local governmental services. Suggest that students contact local officials to determine what services are funded by real estate taxes in their area. (Sample: School Finance Authority; City Park District; City Board of Education; City Pension Fund; City Library Fund; City Community College; Metropolitan Water District; County Forest Preserve District; County Health Facilities.)

CHAPTER 32

Quick Check Answers

1. Its risk, rate of return, liquidity, how its return compares with inflation, its tax advantages, whether you can be comfortable with its level of risk.
2. The income earned by the investment, expressed as a percent of the original investment; the rate may rise as the risk increases.

Develop Concepts

Common Investment Choices

Indicate to students that there are many kinds of investments available today. Among the most common are certificates of deposit; securities, including stocks and bonds; and real estate, including home, income property, and undeveloped property. Stress to students that each of these investment choices is associated with a particular rate of return and risk.

Learning Activity

Photocopy and distribute Enrichment Master 32-1, Different Types of Investments. Suggest to students that as they read this section about Common Investment Choices, they make notes about the type of investment that most closely meets their savings and investment goals. Indicate to students that they may want to rate each of the investments based on their own willingness to take risks with their invested money.

questions. The answers will help you decide what kind of investment to make.

- Am I willing to take a smaller return in exchange for a smaller risk?
- Am I willing to take a greater risk in exchange for a greater return?
- Will I spend time worrying about whether my investment is safe?
- Am I depending on the investment to fund a known future expense?
- Can I afford to lose all the money I'm investing?
- Do I have enough information about the investment to make an informed decision?

Quick Check

1. What do you need to know about an investment before you invest?
2. What is meant by the *rate of return?* As the risk of an investment increases, how might the rate of return change?

COMMON INVESTMENT CHOICES

There are many ways you can invest your money. The type of investment you choose depends on your goals. Do you want a return in the quickest time possible? Or do you want a steady, reasonably predictable flow of cash? We will look at several common ways in which many people invest their money. After you have studied these options, you can tailor an investment program to meet your individual needs.

Certificates of Deposit

If you are willing to sacrifice some liquidity, but earn a higher rate of interest, you may want to buy a *certificate of deposit,* or CD. This is a type of time deposit that requires you to leave your money in the bank for a specified period of time. The end date of this time period is called the **maturity date.** You can cash in the certificate for the full amount of your original savings and the interest earned at the maturity date. Certificates of deposit have higher interest rates than do savings or money market accounts, but your money may be tied up for 18 months to 5 years. There is a significant penalty for withdrawing the money early, which is usually deducted from the amount you deposited, not from the interest you earned.

More than 40 percent of Americans put their savings in certificates of deposit (CDs). There are several reasons for their popularity. First, they usually pay higher interest rates than traditional savings accounts and money market accounts. Second, people who are saving for long-term goals want accounts that have low liquidity. Since the money in a CD is deposited for a specific length of time, people cannot spend it sooner than they intended.

Reteaching Strategy

Suggest that students find out the current rates offered by local banks on certificates of deposit. Remind students that each bank or savings institution may offer a variety of CDs, each with a different *maturity date.* Have students pool their information in a chart or table. Ask volunteers to make a generalization about the relationship between the interest rate and the maturity date. Also ask for a generalization about the interest rate and the current rate of inflation. (Longer-term CDs offer higher interest rates; the interest rate is/is not enough to cover inflation.)

Certificates of deposit are a relatively low-risk way to invest your money. Suppose you want a greater return on each dollar you invest—and you want it faster. If you are willing to take more risk, you may want to invest in securities.

Securities

As you learned in Chapter 15, securities are investments sold by corporations and governments to finance growth. Securities may be purchased either as stocks or as bonds. The money earned by a security generally depends on the degree of risk involved.

Stocks Corporations can sell stocks to raise money to finance their expansions. An investor who buys a corporation's stock becomes a shareholder of the company. Shareholders earn money from the investment in two ways. **Dividends,** distributed to shareholders quarterly, are returns on each share of stock the investor holds. The amount of money paid to a shareholder depends on the size of the dividend as well as the number of shares the investor holds. The size of the dividend depends on how much profit the company has made. If the company has suffered a loss, stockholders may receive no dividend at all. Furthermore, the board of directors of the corporation may decide to reduce the dividend or not pay it at all, choosing instead to put the money into company operations.

Investors can also sell their stock. If they sell the stock at a price higher than the price they paid for the stock, they will make a profit. If an investor pays $25 for a share of stock and sells the stock for $40 a share, the investor has made a profit of $15 per share. This profit is called a **capital gain.** Of course, there is always the possibility that a stock will decrease in value. This makes stocks a relatively risky form of investment. If investors sell a stock for less than they paid for it, they take a *capital loss.* In the jargon of the stock market, people aim to "buy low and sell high."

There are two types of stocks that investors can purchase—common and preferred. *Common stock* is the stock that all corporations must issue and, in fact, many corporations issue only common stock. Common stock entitles shareholders to take part in the selection of the company's board of directors and to speak out on other issues such as mergers, acquisitions, and takeovers. Common shareholders, however, enjoy no special privileges as far as dividends or company assets are concerned.

A company also may issue *preferred stock.* Preferred stock, as its name implies, gives its holders certain privileges that common stockholders do not have. Dividends on preferred

Business & JOURNALISM

As you check the Dow Jones averages, you might wonder who Dow and Jones were. Charles Henry Dow and Edward D. Jones founded Dow Jones & Company, a firm that provided financial news services. Dow Jones & Company delivered bulletins to Wall Street financial firms by messenger. The last delivery of the day consisted of a news sheet that later became *The Wall Street Journal.* Dow was this newspaper's first editor, from 1885 to 1891.

Business Brief

The Dow Jones average can be used as a measure of the stock market's movement. The 30 stocks used in the average are Allied Signal; Alcoa; American Express; AT&T; Bethlehem Steel; Boeing; Caterpillar; Chevron; Coca-Cola; Disney; DuPont; Exxon; Eastman Kodak; General Electric; General Motors; Goodyear; IBM; McDonald's; International Paper; Merck; Minnesota Mining and Manufacturing; J.P. Morgan; Philip Morris; Proctor and Gamble; Sears; Texaco; Union Carbide; United Technologies; Westinghouse; and Woolworth.

Learning Activity

Use Glencoe's *Stocktracker*—A Stock Market Software Simulation to simulate several weeks or months of the stock market in a period of a few days. The menu-driven program allows you and your students to control the fluctuations in market prices by choosing news releases that affect the prices of corporate stock. Included with the software is a Teacher's Guide with reproducible student activities.

Global Perspective

Stock markets have national, regional, and even local bases. However, stock market trading routinely crosses national boundaries. United States stock brokers sometimes buy and sell stock in the middle of the night in order to do business as soon as Japanese markets open each day. Suggest that students consult the business section of the local newspapers to find the Japanese and London equivalents of the Dow Jones Averages. (Nikkei 225; FT-SE 100, often called "Footsy.")

Refer to the *International Business Strategies* booklet for additional strategies and activities.

Ask students what kind of stocks are shown in the photograph. What privileges do the owners of this stock have? (Common; they can select the company's board of directors and vote on mergers, acquisitions, and takeovers.)
Answer to caption: When the stock price is higher than the purchase price.

Learning Activity

Have students choose three stocks in which they are interested. Encourage students to imagine they had purchased 500 shares of each of the stocks one year ago and plan to sell that stock today. Direct students to use stock quotations from the business section of today's newspaper to determine the amount of capital gain (or capital loss) associated with the sale of the stock.

Business Brief

Most stock market investors never actually possess the stock certificates they own. Because stocks are often bought and sold at a moment's notice, the certificates are generally held in the investor's name at the stock or brokerage house that completes the stock transactions. The name assigned to the numbered stock certificate is the name of the brokerage house and is called a "Street Name."

Shareholders have the option of holding their stock for as long as they want. When is the best time to sell stock?

F.Y.I.

One inexpensive and informative way to invest in stocks is to join an investment club. For $25 a month, about a dozen club members research stocks, choose purchases, and pool their money to make purchases. Some investment clubs have done remarkably well.

stocks must be paid before any dividends are paid on common stocks. If a company fails, preferred shareholders have the right to receive their share of whatever assets are left (after the company's debts have been paid) before common shareholders receive anything. However, preferred stockholders receive limited voting privileges and so play a smaller role in the company's affairs. In some companies, preferred shareholders have no voting privileges at all.

Proof of stock ownership is provided through a document called a *stock certificate*. The stock certificate shows the name of the shareholder, the number of shares held, the type of stock, and any other special details. The certificate has no maturity date, that is, no end date on which the stocks have to be cashed in. They can be held as long as the shareholder wants them.

Most individuals who invest in stocks use the services of a stockbroker, a dealer who specializes in stock transactions. Many stockbrokers advise investors on which stocks to buy and when to buy them. Stockbrokers also process the purchase and sale of stocks. Stockbrokers charge a percent of the value of the stock as a fee for this service. If you invest in stock, you have to deduct these fees from any gains you might receive in selling your stock.

Most stocks are bought and sold through a trading market known as a stock exchange. These exchanges provide a central place where the brokers, buyers, and sellers of stock meet to buy and sell stocks. Stock traders use a complicated process somewhat like an auction to determine the prices of stocks

Curriculum Connection   Communication

Ask students to find out what financial information and advice are available to potential investors on the radio, television, in magazines and newspapers, and, if feasible, via computer. Have students write a brief report and critique one example of each kind of resource they discover.

traded on these exchanges. Some of the best-known exchanges are the New York Stock Exchange (NYSE) and the American Stock Exchange (AMEX), both located in New York, the London Stock Exchange, in London, and the Nikkei Exchange in Tokyo.

Stocks not listed on one of the major exchanges can be bought and sold through the over-the-counter (OTC) market. To buy or sell an unlisted stock, a stockbroker checks the latest price. If the price is acceptable to the investor, the broker will complete the transaction. Some stocks are available directly from the corporation involved. For instance, stock in a local bank may be available at the bank itself.

An investor can participate in the stock market without actually buying stocks in one specific corporation by purchasing shares in a stock mutual fund. The mutual fund is a pool of money used by an investment company to purchase the securities of many corporations. Mutual funds are a way to limit risk in the stock market. Because mutual funds buy from many companies at the same time, the investment risk due to a single stock's poor performance is limited.

Bonds If a corporation or government needs to borrow a large amount of money for a long time, it may issue bonds. As you know, bonds are written promises to repay loans. Investors who purchase bonds expect the loan will be repaid in full. Investors also expect to receive a fixed amount of interest, usually paid in installments.

Bonds issued by corporations are called corporate bonds. Various governments and government agencies also issue bonds. Local or state governments and certain government agencies issue municipal bonds. Money from these bonds finances highway construction and other government projects. Municipal bonds have earned a reputation as safe investments. Although these bonds usually offer a rate of return lower than investments such as stocks, the interest earned by a municipal bond is free from federal income taxes.

The federal government issues U.S. Savings Bonds, which can be bought at a bank or through a payroll-deduction plan at work. Investors must pay federal taxes on the interest bonds earn. However, the earnings are exempt from state or local taxes, and there is no fee for buying or selling a U.S. Savings Bond. The U.S. Treasury also issues three kinds of bonds, which are classified according to the amount and the length of the loan: (1) treasury bills (or T bills) are issued for periods of three months to one year; (2) treasury notes are issued for two to ten years; and (3) treasury bonds are issued for ten or more years.

Learning Activity
Direct students to determine which of the following investments will result in the greatest gain: a $10,000 corporate bond offering 7 percent or a $10,000 municipal bond paying 5 percent. The investor pays a tax of 31 percent on her income. (Municipal bond will pay $10,000 × 0.05 = $500 interest; corporate bond will pay $10,000 × .07 = $700 interest; the investor's tax will be .31 × 700 = $217, leaving $483 return.) For students who need to sharpen their math skills, choose among the worksheets in the *Math Skills Review* booklet.

Business Brief
Unlike stocks, bond prices are generally quoted as a percent of face value. A bond quote of 98 indicates that a bond with a value of $1000 is being sold for $980.

Learning Activity
Suggest that students work in pairs to research some of the terms associated with bonds, finding out the definitions of the terms *coupon, maturity,* and *par value.* (*Coupon:* stated interest on the debt; *maturity:* length of time until the debt is repaid; *par value:* the amount that will be repaid to the lender at maturity, often called face value.)

Global Perspective

Mutual funds with largely foreign assets are gaining in popularity among U.S. investors. The assets usually are in emerging areas of the world such as Latin America and Asia. The fast-growing economies of these areas usually mean high returns for investors. Have students discuss how investment in mutual funds helps the economies of developing nations.

Refer to the *International Business Strategies* booklet for additional strategies and activities.

TEACHING TIP
Ask students to explain why treasury bonds, notes, and bills are considered part of the national debt.

Learning Activity

Photocopy and distribute Enrichment Master 32-2, which lists the advantages and disadvantages of home ownership. Have students use the listing as a basis for discussing their own desire to own (or not to own) their own home.

TEACHING TIP

Ask students to list some of the reasons the prices of homes have increased in the past 25 years. (Example: Increased population in urban areas.)

Business Brief

In an effort to assist individuals and families in fulfilling their dreams of owning their own home, many social and governmental agencies have instituted programs to help first-time home owners and others who meet specific financial criteria.

GLOBAL VIEW

Not all cultures of the world have the same concepts about owning land that we do. In Australia, a group of indigenous people believe in owning land in common rather than as individuals. Each group of Aborigines lives within a particular geographic area. The group owns the land in common and cannot sell the land to anyone else. Aborigines believe they hold the land in trust and are responsible for taking care of it.

Real Estate

Real estate is land and all the buildings that are attached to it. The reasons that people invest in real estate vary from person to person. Some people buy real estate because they see it as a safe investment. For others, investing in real estate, especially housing, represents security. Others invest with the hope of making a lot of money.

Some people invest in real estate to build up **equity**—the difference between the value of the property and the amount owed on the mortgage. If the property increases in value while they are repaying the mortgage, this increases their equity. Figure 32-2 on page 549 shows how the median home price has increased since 1970. Other investors like the tax advantages of home ownership. Home owners can generally deduct the interest payments they make on their mortgage loan and their real estate taxes from their taxable income.

Home Ownership Because different people have different needs, a variety of homes are available. There are single- and multiple-family houses, as well as condominiums, cooperatives, and manufactured houses. Condominiums are individually-owned units in a building or group of buildings. Condominium owners pay mortgage and taxes on their units and a share of the upkeep on common areas such as entrances and grounds. Cooperatives are physically similar to condominiums. However, rather than buying their units, investors buy shares in the non-profit organization that owns and maintains the building.

No matter what type of home you buy, it is likely to be the single most expensive purchase of your life. Few buying decisions require as much planning and careful choice. You need to think about many things when you are buying a home. You will need to address two major considerations when purchasing a home:

- How much will it cost you to buy and keep the house?
- How much will you be able to sell the house for?

Once you own the home, you must be prepared to pay certain continuing costs. The largest of these will be the monthly mortgage payments. The size of these payments depends on the cost of the home, the amount of your down payment, the amount of your mortgage loan, and the rate of interest. Payments for home insurance and property taxes are also continuing costs of home ownership.

Furthermore, the cost of maintaining and repairing a home should be considered. Over the years you may need to repaint, put on a new roof, replace windows, or install a new furnace. These expenses will be in addition to the payments for mortgage, insurance, and taxes.

Cooperative Learning Numbered Heads Together

Have students work in teams of four. Allow each team to choose a type of home ownership, such as single family home, multifamily building, condominium, cooperative, and manufactured house or trailer. Encourage students to scan the real estate section of the local newspapers to learn some of the advantages and disadvantages of the type of housing chosen by their team. Have a designated team member present each team's findings to the class.

Median Home Price in the United States

Source: National Association of Realtors

FIGURE 32-2

The steady increase in median home prices over the years suggests that purchasing a home is a good investment. By how much did the median home price rise between 1980 and 1994?

USE VISUALS

Point out to students that Figure 32-2 shows the increase in median home price in the United States. Ask students to describe how the median home price is determined. (The median is the home price in the middle of all the home prices; there are as many homes priced higher than the median price as there are homes priced lower.) Answer to caption: The median home price rose by about $48,000.

USE TRANSPARENCIES

Use Teaching Transparency 32-2 and its corresponding strategies and worksheet from the *Teaching Transparency Strategies and Worksheets* booklet to assist students in recognizing how the cost of homes has increased. Verify student worksheets using the Answer Key.

Learning Activity

Suggest that students research the kinds of home owner assistance available in their area, such as HUD (U.S. Department of Housing and Urban Development) homes, first time mortgage programs, and guaranteed mortgages. Have students present their findings in an oral report to the class.

The home's future selling price also plays a role in your decision. Clearly, the type, size, location, and condition of the house will affect its overall selling price. Timing of the sale will also affect the price. A house may sell for one amount this month and for a very different amount a year from now. Certain locations may become more or less desirable with the passage of time, and this, too, affects the selling price.

Income Property Many people are not content to wait to get a return on their investment by selling their property. These people prefer to invest in *income property,* property on which rent or some other form of payment is earned. Farms, stores, factories, shopping centers, and apartment and office buildings are some types of income properties for investment. Two- or three-family homes are income property as well. You can occupy one floor or unit and rent out the other units. The rental income then can be used to help you pay off the mortgage. You may choose to manage income property yourself or hire a management company.

CHAPTER 32   SAVING AND INVESTING   **549**

Curriculum Connection   English and Communication

Suggest that students interview several home owners to find out how they feel about owning their own home. Students should focus on questions such as: Is owning a home more expensive than you thought it would be? Knowing what you know now, would you buy a home again? What advice would you give to someone thinking about buying a home? Have students pool their findings and present them in a poster or bulletin board display.

USE VISUALS

Direct students' attention to the family in the photograph. Remind students that homes often represent a combination of savings and investment.
Answer to caption: As a safe investment; for security.

Learning Activity

Have students scan newspapers and other periodicals for articles describing land speculation—the purchase of undeveloped property in the hopes of development. Direct students to write a 200-word summary of the articles they find and post the article along with the summary on a bulletin board.

Quick Check Answers

1. Certificates of deposit, securities, and real estate.
2. Stocks and bonds.
3. Bonds are likely to be lower risk than stocks.
4. Home, income property, undeveloped land.

Buying a home is the single most expensive purchase for many people. Why do you think this family chose a home as an investment?

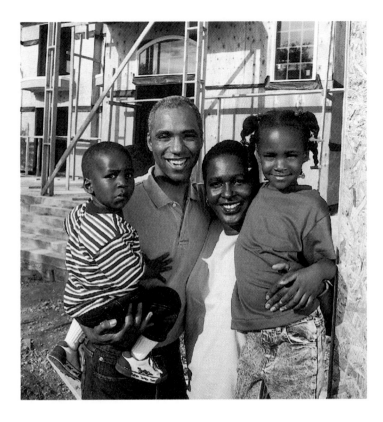

Undeveloped Property   Undeveloped property offers another opportunity for investment. Undeveloped property is land that generally is in its natural state. Usually the land is not cleared, has no access by road, and has no utility services such as water. Often, but not always, such land may be fairly inexpensive.

Investors in undeveloped property generally hope that its value will increase sharply over the years. Sometimes it does. The land may be chosen as the site of a shopping center, housing development, or industrial park. In other cases, however, the land's value may stay the same or even decrease. For example, a planned highway may never be built, leaving the land along its route undeveloped.

Quick Check

1. Name three common types of investments.
2. What are two kinds of securities investors can purchase?
3. Which kinds of securities are lower risk? Higher risk?
4. Name three kinds of real estate investments.

Reteaching Strategy

Have students write a "biography" of an investment such as a bond, stock, or real estate. Suggest that students include in their biography information such as the investment's history, its major characteristics, and the investment's risks and benefits. Call on volunteers to present and discuss their biographies to the class.

Chapter 32 **Summary**

Main Ideas

1. People save money for major purchases, emergencies, and retirement.
2. Investing money is more than just saving money—it's placing money where it can earn income.
3. An informed investor knows the risk, rate of return, availability of the money, and how the rate of return compares to inflation before making an investment. In addition, the investor evaluates his or her own comfort level with the risk potential of the investment.
4. Common investments people choose include certificates of deposit, securities, and real estate.
5. Certificates of deposit are time deposits in a bank that pay the investor a relatively high interest rate for a fixed period of time and restrict withdrawals to a specified time.
6. Investment choices in securities include stocks and bonds.
7. People invest in real estate because they see it as a safe investment, they want security, they want to build up equity, or they hope to make a lot of money.
8. Computers provide instant information about stock prices to stockbrokers.
9. Daily newspapers summarize the day's stock market activity in stock market quotations that are followed by investors.

CASE ANALYSIS   Saving/Investing

Eric and Allison Moser are both 25 years old. They have been married for three years and have one child. Their annual income is $33,000. Two years ago they bought a house. The mortgage will be paid up in 18 years. The Mosers have life insurance of $60,000. They have just made the last payment on their two-year-old car. The Mosers' budget shows that they can now save $100 a month. What kind of savings/investment plan would you recommend that they begin?

QUICK QUIZ

1. How are saving and investing alike? How are they different? (Each is setting aside money for future use; invested money earns income, saved money does not.)
2. What is the rate of return? (The amount of money an investment earns expressed as a percent of the original investment.)
3. How can you become an owner of General Motors? (Purchase stock.)
4. How can you lend money to a city to build a stadium? (Purchase municipal bonds.)

Chapter 32 **Review**

CHAPTER 32 REVIEW

APPLY

Answers

Use the Language of Business

1. saving; **2.** investing; **3.** rate of return; **4.** fixed rate; **5.** variable rate; **6.** liquidity; **7.** maturity date; **8.** dividend; **9.** capital gain; **10.** equity.

Review What You Learned

1. Saving is simply putting money aside; investing earns income.

2. What is the risk? Rate of return? Availability of funds? What are the tax advantages? How does it compare to inflation? Does it fit my personality?

3. The greater the rate of return, the greater the risk involved.

4. Certificates of deposit, securities, and real estate.

5. Current price; 30-day average price; background information such as high, low, change ratio, and dividend.

6. Dividend, Yield or Rate of Return, Price/Earning ratio, Change.

Understand Business Concepts

1. Investors can lose all their money in a high-risk investment.

2. Sometimes people need to have quick or immediate access to cash.

3. Bondholders lend money to corporations and expect the stated interest payment and eventual return of their loan. Shareholders own stock in the corporation and expect dividends and a capital gain when they sell the stock.

4. Pride of ownership, increase in equity, tax deductions, the opportunity for financial gain upon sale, secure shelter.

5. The graph can help the stockbroker identify trends and tell whether the stock price is moving up or down.

Use the Language of Business

On a separate sheet of paper, rewrite these sentences filling in each blank with the term that best completes the sentence.

capital gain	investing	rate of return
dividend	liquidity	saving
equity	maturity date	variable rate
fixed rate		

1. _____ is putting money aside for future use.
2. _____ is using money so that it earns income.
3. An investment that has _____ can be turned into cash quickly.
4. The _____ is the end date of the time period of a time deposit.
5. An investment that yields an unchanging return is a(n) _____ investment.
6. With a(n) _____ investment, the rate of return changes depending on the average yield of the investment.
7. The amount an investment earns, expressed as a percent of the original investment, is called the _____ .
8. The periodic return on a share of stock is a(n) _____ .
9. If an investor sells a stock for more than the original purchase price, the investor has made a(n) _____ .
10. Value of property minus the amount owed on mortgage equals _____ .

Review What You Learned

1. What is the difference between saving and investing?
2. What six questions should you ask about any possible investment?
3. What is the usual relationship between return and risk of an investment?
4. What three common kinds of investments do most people make?
5. What information is available to a stockbroker by computer?
6. What do the symbols *Div, Yld, PE ratio,* and *Chng* mean?

Understand Business Concepts

1. If you have only a small amount of savings, why might you decide to avoid a high-risk investment?
2. Why is liquidity sometimes more important to an investor than the rate of return?
3. What is the difference between being a bondholder and being a shareholder?
4. Instead of rent, a homeowner pays for a mortgage, homeowner's insurance, real estate taxes, maintenance, and repairs. What advantages can owning a home offer to balance these expenses?
5. Why would a stockbroker want to see a graph of the average price of a stock for the last 30 days?
6. When investing in stocks, which of the following numbers would an investor want to be low rather than high: dividend, yield, PE Ratio? Explain.

Think Critically

1. **Evaluate.** What types of investments do you believe are the safest? Why?
2. **Explain.** What risks are involved in investing in undeveloped land?

6. PE ratio because it is the price of the stock divided by the earnings per share; either low price or high earning will make the ratio small.

Think Critically

1. Students' choices will vary.

2. Its value may decrease; planned development may not take place.

Use What You Learned

1. **Group Project.** In your group, select an industry in the business world. Each member of the group should collect current information on the stock and bond prices for one individual company in that industry. Then search issues of newspapers from a year ago and six months ago. Find your company among the listings of stock market quotations. Use the information from the back issues to help you answer these questions.

   • What was the selling price of the stocks six months ago? A year ago?
   • What rate of return or yield do the companies report?
   • What was the amount of the most recent dividend the companies distributed?
   • What were the high and low prices during the year?
   • How did the performance of the companies your group researched compare? Was any one much better than the others? Much worse?

   Use the information you collect about the companies to make an industry profile. Tell whether you think companies in this industry might be a good investment and why.

2. **Computer Application.** Survey banks, savings and loan associations, or credit unions about the interest they pay on their savings accounts, certificates of deposit, and money market accounts. Also compile information on their min-

imum deposits and balances, allowable number of transactions, minimum balances to earn interest, and limits on withdrawals. Set up a spreadsheet with the information you gather that will calculate the return for each of the kinds of saving/investing plans you discover. Input varying amounts of money from small to very large and print out the results. Then determine which institutions are best for growth when smaller amounts are invested; which are best for larger amounts.

3. **Skill Reinforcement.** Study the stock listings below and answer the questions that follow.

365-Day High	Low	Stock	Div	Yld	PE Ratio	Sales (hds)	High	Low	Close	Change
18 ⅝	11 ⅞	K Mart	0.48	3.0	35	16010	16 ¼	15 ⅞	16	− ⅛
28 ⅝	19 ¹⁹/₃₂	Mattel	0.24	0.9	24	4760	28 ¾	27 ¾	27 ⅞	− ¾
39 ½	25 ⁹/₁₆	McDonalds	0.27	0.7	22	11692	39 ⅝	38 ¾	39 ⅛	0
69 ⅝	58 ⅛	Texaco	3.2	4.8	17	4875	66 ¾	65 ¾	66 ¾	+ 1

   A. Which stock traded the most shares on this day? How many?
   B. Which stock lost the most from the day before? How much did it lose?
   C. What was the closing price for Texaco on this day?
   D. What was the lowest price paid for McDonalds' stock during the 365-day period?
   E. Which stock paid the highest dividend? The lowest?
   F. If you had bought 100 shares of K Mart at the year's lowest price, how much more would it be worth at the end of this particular day?

Save your work in your Business Portfolio.

Use What You Learned
1. Make certain that all students in the group participate. Rubric: Essay.
2. Students without access to a computer can complete this assignment using a hand-drawn spreadsheet and a calculator. Rubric: Charts and Tables.

3. A. K Mart; 1,601,000; B. Mattel; $.75; C. $66.75; D. $25.56; E. Texaco, Mattel; F. $412.50. Rubric: Charts and Tables.

Independent Practice

Use the Chapter 32 worksheets in *Student Activity Guide 2* for additional practice and application activities. *Student Activity Guide 2* provides vocabulary exercises, reading comprehension checks, problems, projects, and simulations of business and economic situations. A Teacher's Annotated Edition provides answers.

ASSESS

Portfolio Assessment
The portfolio projects are designed to lead students to develop a collection of their best work to submit to you for assessment. You and your students should decide which projects will be included in their respective Business Portfolios. Refer students to the specific rubric(s) from the *Alternative Assessment Strategies* booklet listed with each of the project notes below. These rubrics will alert students to the criteria you will use to assess their projects.

Chapter Assessment
Use the Chapter 32 Test from the *Test Masters* booklet to evaluate students' understanding of the chapter concepts. An answer key is provided. Or create your own customized test using the *Testmaker* software.

CHAPTER
33

FOCUS

Introduce the Chapter

Major Concepts
• Checking Accounts
• Savings Accounts
• Other Banking Services

Introduce the Topic
Ask students to describe what they know about banks and the kinds of services banks offer. Allow students with savings or other accounts to describe their banking activities. Point out to students that in Chapter 33 they will learn about several different kinds of banking services. They will also learn how to use some of the most common services.

Use Business Terms
Ask students to write a sentence with each of the Business Terms. Have students exchange papers with a partner. Call for agreement/disagreement as to use of the terms and an explanation of that position. Tell students to note the meanings of the terms as they read the chapter.

USE VISUALS

The people in this photo are taking advantage of the bank's many services. Why do you think banks offer their customers a variety of services? (Banks are businesses, and like many other businesses, they offer services to attract the greater number of customers.)

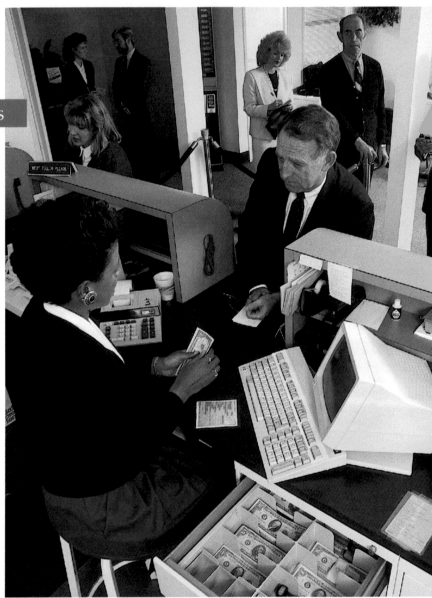

Business terms

overdraft protection

signature card

joint account

deposit ticket

check register

endorsement

bank statement

canceled check

554

CHAPTER 33 RESOURCES

Instructional Resources

Lesson Plan for Chapter 33

Teaching Transparencies 33-1, 33-2, 33-3, 33-4, 33-5

Strategies and Worksheets for Teaching Transparencies 33-1, 33-2, 33-3, 33-4, 33-5

Enrichment Masters 33-1, 33-2

Student Activity Guide 2–TAE for Chapter 33

Test Master for Chapter 33

Alternative Assessment Strategies

Math Skills Review

International Business Strategies

Cooperative Learning Strategies

Communication Skills Review

Ethics in Business Strategies

Using
Banking Services

Learning objectives

After completing this chapter, you will be able to:
- List the major services banks and financial institutions provide.
- Enumerate the factors consumers should consider when choosing among banking services.
- Describe how electronic banking provides customers with quick, timely access to their bank accounts.
- Explain how to reconcile a check register with the checking account statement issued by the bank.

Consider what you know

- There are a variety of saving and investment plans available. Investments are savings that earn income and, in general, the more income an investment earns, the greater the risk involved.

Consider what you want to know

- What factors should you consider when deciding which bank to use?
- How can you make the best use of the many services banks offer?
- How can technology help you bank at any time of the day or night?
- How can you make sure that the bank and you agree about the amount of money in your account?

Consider how to use what you learn

- As you work through this chapter, ask a friend or relative which banking services he or she uses. Ask what made them choose the bank they use.

Multimedia Resources

Technology Resource Guide

Distance Learning Guide

Internet Resource Guide

Professional Resources

School-to-Work/Tech Prep Strategies

Instructional Poster

Spanish Resources

Testmaker Software for Chapter 33

The Wall Street Journal Video Series
Video & Activities for Chapter 33

Business and Marketing Computer Applications—An Integrated Software Simulation Using Microsoft Works

Stocktracker—A Stock Market Software Simulation

Where's the Dough? Board Game

You've learned about money and banking, the Federal Reserve, and monetary policy. This information should help you get the "big picture" of banking and banking services—how banks and monetary policy can influence the economy. You've also learned what part the banking business, a service-producing business, can play in the economy.

You may already know that banks offer savings and checking accounts. However, banks also offer other services such as credit cards, loans, and financial planning services. You may recall that many of these services are regulated by the Federal Reserve System, the central banking authority in the United States. As part of the federal government, "the Fed" oversees and establishes financial policy for banks that serve the public. In this chapter you will learn how you, as a consumer, can participate in the variety of services offered by banks and other financial institutions.

CHECKING ACCOUNTS

F.Y.I.

The word *check* comes from an Arabic word, *shah*, which has several translated meanings, including "king." In the game of chess, *check* means a move that makes an attack on an opponent's king. In banking, it means an order or a demand to pay—something once only kings, perhaps, could do.

One of the most important services banks provide is the convenience of checking accounts. It would be impossible to imagine businesses functioning without the convenience of checks. A customer deposits money in an account and receives a book of checks. Each check the customer writes and signs is an order to the bank to release on demand the specified amount and give it to the *payee*, the person or business indicated on the check. This is why checking accounts are sometimes called *demand deposits*. Checks are the most common medium of exchange. They are more popular than either cash or credit cards. In fact, almost 85 percent of all U.S. households have checking accounts.

Most banks offer several types of checking accounts. Before opening a checking account, a wise consumer investigates what kinds of accounts are available, as well as their advantages and costs. The customer service personnel at financial institutions are available to answer questions about account services, fees, and charges. In addition, you may wish to ask parents and friends about their experiences with different banks and different types of accounts. Shop around and compare financial institutions and what they have to offer.

Curriculum Connection   English and Communication

Point out to students that a *check* is a specialized type of draft ordering one person to pay another. On a check, the writer of the check orders a bank to pay someone on the writer's behalf from the writer's account. Have students work in groups to list the characteristics and uses of a check. Suggest they limit their list to single words or short phrases. Have teams work together to write an *operational definition* of a check. Ask students to explain why a checking account is known as a *demand deposit*. Encourage teams to share their definitions with one another and allow them to revise their definitions.

For those students who need to sharpen their written communication skills, choose among the worksheets in the *Communication Skills Review* booklet.

Types of Accounts

A financial institution may offer an array of checking accounts like those shown in Figure 33-1 below. Each type of account has different advantages and requirements. A basic checking account, like the one described in Figure 33-1, is designed for customers who write few checks each month and do not keep a minimum balance in the account. If a customer can afford to keep a minimum balance—ranging from $50 to $500—other options are available. Withdrawal transactions include checks the customer may have written on the account; any automatic deductions, such as utility, mortgage, or automobile payments; and any ATM (automated teller machine) withdrawals. If the balance falls below the minimum, a service charge is deducted from the account. A service charge is a fee for the paperwork the bank does in record keeping and in maintaining the account. This charge may be a flat fee, such as $5 or $10 per month. In addition, there may be an individual fee for

FIGURE 33-1

This brochure shows the different types of checking accounts available at this bank. Which type of account requires the least amount of money to open?

CHECKING ACCOUNT FEE SCHEDULES AND INFORMATION GUIDE

	Basic Checking	Unlimited Checking	Deluxe Checking
Minimum opening deposit	$50	$250	$500
Requirements for no monthly service fees and no transaction charges	Not available	$750 minimum daily balance–OR–$1,500 monthly average balance	$1,500 minimum daily balance–OR–$3,000 monthly average balance
Monthly Service Fee	None	$6.00	$10.00
Item charges (No charge for deposits)	35¢ each withdrawal transaction–check, automatic payment, or ATM	None	First 50 withdrawal transactions–check, automatic payment, or ATM–free, 25¢ each additional withdrawal transaction
Interest earned	None	2.5% if minimum balance is maintained throughout statement period	2.5% if average minimum balance is maintained throughout statement period
Bank credit card available	Yes, $1.50 monthly fee	Yes, $1.50 monthly fee	Yes, no charge
Debit card available	No	Yes, $50 annual fee	Yes, no annual fee
Overdraft protection available	Yes, $250 maximum; $2.50 monthly fee	Yes, $500 maximum; $2.50 monthly fee	Yes, $1,000 maximum; no monthly fee
Returned and overdraft items	$25 per item/Maximum: three items per quarter	$25 per item/Maximum: three items per quarter	$25 per item
Stop payment charges	$20 per item	$20 per item	$20 per item

Curriculum Connection   Math

Ask students to use the information in Figure 33-1 above to answer the following question: In the unlimited checking account, what minimum balance does a customer need to have in order to earn enough interest to cover the monthly service fee? ($240; $6.00 = .025 × (min. bal.); min. bal. = $6.00 ÷ .025 = $240.)

For students who need to sharpen their math skills, choose among the worksheets in the *Math Skills Review* booklet.

FOCUS ON **Technology**

Electronic Banking

On a warm Sunday afternoon, you wander past a yard sale. Suddenly they catch your eye. Dozens of classic Marvel Comics, some with titles you've wanted for years, and in mint condition! You reach into your pocket for the amount the seller is asking—$30.00. Alas! you have only $10, and the seller wants cash only, no checks. What can you do?

Swipe! Beep. Beep. ATM to the rescue. You go to the nearest automated teller machine (ATM) location and withdraw $20 from your checking account. That very evening you're enjoying your classic comics.

The ATM process relies on a terminal, a connection to a banking network, a mainframe computer, and transaction processing or interactive software. The ATM user needs an approved ATM account, an ATM card, and a personal identification number (PIN).

The terminal is the visible equipment at an ATM location. It is an input/output device that acts as a doorway or window to another computer in a different location. A communications network connects the ATM terminal to a mainframe computer at the network's electronic headquarters. The *mainframe computer* is large, powerful, and able to serve hundreds of users at the same time.

A mainframe that services ATM machines contains a database of customer accounts and identification codes as well as interactive processing software. *Interactive processing* acts immediately upon receiving input. For an ATM transaction, the interactive program retrieves customer records from the bank's database, presents a menu of options suited to the

each check paid from the account. The variety of checking account options makes it worthwhile to compare the features of the checking accounts offered by several banks.

Many banking institutions also offer NOW accounts, in addition to regular checking accounts. A NOW account, or negotiable-order-of-withdrawal account, is an interest bearing checking account. It has a minimum balance requirement, but generally allows unlimited writing of checks.

The advantage of a NOW account is that the balance in the account is always earning interest. The minimum account balance for a NOW account may be much higher than for a regular checking account, ranging from $1000 to $10,000. Most savings banks, savings and loan associations, and commercial banks offer NOW accounts.

Account Features

Banks offer other features and options for checking accounts. Overdrawing your checking account is poor financial management. If an account has insufficient funds when a check is presented for payment, the bank may mark the check NSFC

Discuss

Have students scan the feature and then write a question that requires one of the following terms—*ATM, EFT, PIN, CPU, terminal,* and *mainframe*—as an answer. Ask volunteers to share their questions with the class, calling on other volunteers to supply the answers. Ask students to describe the situations in which the terms apply and what the acronyms represent.

TEACHING TIP

Have students find out at what age an individual may open a checking account. Ask students to find out whether the age varies from one bank to another or if the minimum age is set by a banking regulation.

Business Brief

Federal law once prohibited interest-paying checking accounts. In 1980, Congress lifted the ban on these accounts, authorizing banks to offer *negotiable order of withdrawal* accounts —usually referred to as NOW accounts. Like savings accounts, NOW accounts pay interest. Unlike savings accounts, depositors withdraw funds by writing negotiable orders of withdrawal similar to checks.

Enrichment Strategy

Remind students that they learned in Chapter 19 that money serves three functions (medium of exchange, standard of value, and store of value) and that for money to be effective, it must have several characteristics (stability, acceptability, divisibility, portability, and durability). Ask students to discuss how checkbook dollars, the most common form of money in the United States, perform all the functions and have all the characteristics of money.

customer's accounts, and acts on the customer's menu choices.

You have arranged through your bank to have ATM access to your savings, checking, and money market

accounts. You have an ATM card which has a plastic strip embedded with a magnetic pattern that identifies you. You have been assigned a personal identification number (PIN) that acts as a computer password. You step up to the terminal, press "Transaction start" and swipe your ATM card through the card reader. As the terminal prompts, you follow the steps.

After you choose to withdraw $20 from checking, the software checks the balance in your account. Because the balance is greater than $20, the software deducts the amount from the account, directs the dispensing mechanism at the terminal to dispense $20 in cash, and issues a receipt for the transaction.

At the software's prompting, you close the transaction. The mainframe computer places your records back into the database. You take your $20, your ATM card, and your receipt. You return to the yard sale, able to make the purchase.

Follow Through

Ask a volunteer to write a single term or concept relating to electronic banking on the board. Ask another volunteer to add a term or concept to form the beginning of a word web or diagram that represents the elements needed to accomplish electronic banking. Continue calling on volunteers until the class is satisfied with the diagram. Suggest that students may want to copy the diagram to use as a study aid. For additional information about current technology, refer to the *Technology Resource Guide* booklet.

("not sufficient funds") and return it to the individual or business who tried to cash it. In addition, the bank will charge a returned check fee to the account with insufficient funds. Some banks may charge from $10 to $20 per returned check.

Some institutions offer a service, for a fee, that covers this situation. **Overdraft protection** is a prearranged line of credit for overdrawn checks. If you write a check with insufficient funds in your account, the funds will be drawn from the line of protection. The amount of the line of protection varies from hundreds to thousands of dollars. The line of protection is similar to a loan or credit card limit. You pay a service fee for the overdraft protection and interest on the overdrawn amount until it is repaid.

There may be a time when you will want to stop payment on a check. A stop payment order is a request for an institution not to cash a particular check. For example, you may have misplaced the check, sent a check for an incorrect amount, or sent it to an incorrect address. If you wish to stop the check, contact the bank immediately. If the check has not yet been processed, the bank will issue a stop payment order. Fees for stop-payment orders vary from one institution to the next.

Connection to CHAPTER 20

Ask students whether they have heard people mention that they need to "make sure their check clears." Ask a volunteer to reiterate for the class the check clearing process. Enrichment Master 20-1 from Chapter 20 provides an overview of the process.

Learning Activity

Have students inquire at local banks about the difference between "Not Sufficient Funds" and "Uncollected Funds." Suggest they ask under which of these conditions checks will be returned unpaid and for which the bank will charge an additional fee. (In most cases, checks will be returned and a fee assessed for either reason.)

Cooperative Learning Group Discussion

Collect for students or ask students to obtain information about *overdraft protection* from several banks. Have them use the information to discuss the following questions for each institution. Suggest students arrange their findings in a chart or poster.
- Which institution charges a monthly fee for overdraft protection, even if you have not overdrawn your account?
- What is the annual interest rate on the overdraft balance?
- What would it cost to overdraw your checking account by $100?
- When does the bank begin to charge interest on the overdraft balance?

Refer to the *Cooperative Learning Strategies* booklet for additional cooperative learning strategies.

Other services may come along with checking account privileges. Some banks offer credit cards. Many banks also offer check cards or debit cards. These cards look like credit cards and allow the funds to be withdrawn directly from a checking account and applied to the place of purchase. No check is written and no paper is processed, although the customer does receive a receipt. Then, just as you would record a written check, you write the amount in your checkbook register.

Opening an Account

Once you decide which checking account is best for your banking needs, how do you open an account? The first step in opening an account is to fill out a **signature card.** This is the card that the bank uses to verify your identity. You will be asked to supply basic information—your name, address, and telephone number, and the name and address of your employer—and to sign your name. At that time the bank will assign a checking account number to your account.

Your signature is the most important part of the signature card. You should write your name as it will appear on your checks. The bank may check your signature card when one of your checks is presented for payment. If the signatures match, the check will be cashed. If they do not match, the bank will not make payment on the check. This helps prevent other people from cashing checks against your account.

It is also possible to open a **joint account,** an account shared by two people. In this case both signatures appear on the signature card. Then either person can write checks on the account.

To open, or add to, an account, you must make a deposit by completing a **deposit ticket.** The deposit ticket lists the cash, amount of each check, and the total amount of the deposit. After making the deposit, you record it in your **check register.** This is the section of the checkbook where you keep track of all your transactions. Periodically you will receive bank statements that list all of the activity on your accounts.

Writing a Check

There are several different kinds of checking accounts. However, the information on the front of a check and the steps in writing a check are the same. There are usually three people, or parties, named on a check. The party who gets the money and to whom the check is written is called the *payee*. The party on whose account the check is written and who signs the check

F.Y.I.

Experts suggest that you keep canceled checks that relate to your tax returns for at least three years, in case your tax return is audited. Canceled checks for major improvements to your home should be kept for as long as you own the house, plus three years. It may also be wise to keep canceled checks for major purchases, such as appliances. If you have to file a homeowner's insurance claim because of theft, damage, or fire, a canceled check can be used to verify the purchase price.

Making Connections ➪ Everyday Living

Photocopy and distribute Enrichment Master 33-1, Steps in Writing a Check. Have a volunteer read the steps and demonstrate them on Teaching Transparency 33-1, a blank check. After the demonstration is complete, ask students if they have any questions about how to write a check. Call on volunteers who understand check writing to demonstrate the process while describing it in their own words.

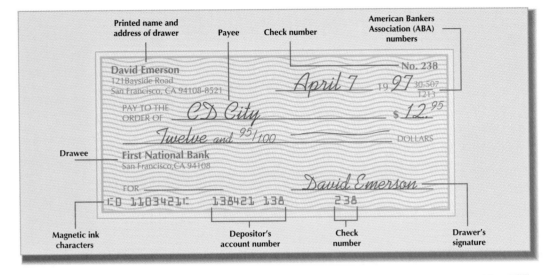

Printed name and address of drawer

Payee

Check number

American Bankers Association (ABA) numbers

David Emerson
121 Bayside Road
San Francisco, CA 94108-8521

No. 238

April 7 19 *97* 30-507 / 1213

PAY TO THE ORDER OF *CD City* $ *12.⁹⁵*

Twelve and ⁹⁵/100 DOLLARS

Drawee

First National Bank
San Francisco, CA 94108

FOR *David Emerson*

⑆ 1103421 ⑆ 138421 138 238

Magnetic ink characters

Depositor's account number

Check number

Drawer's signature

FIGURE 33-2

Most checks have the same kind of preprinted information and are designed so that it appears in about the same location. To be negotiable, that is for the check to be able to be transferred to a person or business, it must contain certain essential elements: drawee, payee, name and signature of drawer, date, and amount. Who is the payee on this check?

is called the *drawer*. The third party is the *drawee*, the financial institution that holds the drawer's account. Figure 33-2 above shows the information commonly appearing on a check as well as the three necessary parties to a check.

Before you write a check, record it in the check register. If you don't register the check immediately, you might find later that you have forgotten some information about the check. The Building Business Skills feature on page 563 shows a sample check register and how to record checks and deposits.

Some checks also have a line in the lower left corner where you can indicate the purpose or reason for the check. This line is also for indicating the account number when making utility, insurance, or loan payments.

Endorsing a Check

When you deposit a check in your account, you need to endorse, or sign, it on the back. The **endorsement** always includes the signature of the payee, the party to whom the check has been written. An endorsement is necessary for cashing a check. Certain rules should be followed in making any kind of endorsement.

- Write the endorsement on the left end of the back of the check, on the lines printed for endorsement. Do not write below the printed lines.
- Use a pen so your signature cannot be erased.

CHAPTER 33 USING BANKING SERVICES **561**

Curriculum Connection English and Communication

Have students interview a bank officer or personal banker to investigate the most common mistakes made when writing a check. Students might also ask what they should do if they make a mistake while writing the check, for example, writing $27.95 for $29.75. Students can compile their information in a booklet titled "The Top Ten Check-Writing Errors."

USE VISUALS

Indicate to students that the parts of a check are illustrated in Figure 33-2. Ask students to speculate why preprinted checks always have preprinted information in the same location. (Ease and accuracy of processing.)
Answer to caption: CD City.

USE TRANSPARENCIES

Use Teaching Transparency 33-2 and its corresponding strategies and worksheet from the *Teaching Transparency Strategies and Worksheets* booklet to assist students in understanding the standard parts of a personal check. Verify student worksheets using the Answer Key.

TEACHING TIP

Ask students to form their own definitions of *drawee, payee,* and *drawer.* Encourage them to illustrate their definitions.

Learning Activity

Point out to students that individuals occasionally write a check to the order of "Cash." Ask students to discuss why this might not be a good idea.

Learning Activity

Some checkbooks are made so that when an individual writes a check, a duplicate slip remains, showing the date, payee, and amount of the check. Ask students to explain why these checks still require the use of a check register. (Deposit and current balance information is kept in the register.)

Building Business Skills

Model

Point out to students that reconciling a checkbook is similar to "balancing the books" in a business. The goal is to add up all the income (interest and deposits), then subtract all the expenses (checks and service fees). The result should be the amount of money available.

Use Teaching Transparency 33-3 and its corresponding strategies and worksheet from the *Teaching Transparency Strategies and Worksheets* booklet to familiarize students with check registers and checking account statements. Verify student worksheets using the Answer Key.

Independent Practice

Have students complete the simulation "Developing Good Banking Habits" found in *Student Activity Guide 2.* Answers are provided in the Teacher's Annotated Edition.

MATH

Reconciling a Checking Account

Explanation

Reconciling a checking account means making certain that the information, including the balance, in the checkbook agrees with the information and balance given on the monthly bank statement.

Every time you write a check, you should record it in the check register. Include the date, to whom it was written, and the amount. Subtract the check amount from the account balance recorded in the register. Record each deposit you make and add it to the balance. Note the example here of a well-maintained check register.

Your bank statement lists the checks and deposits processed that month by number and amount. It subtracts service charges from your account and gives the balance as of the date of the statement. Compare the example of the bank statement to the check register.

How to Reconcile a Checking Account

1. Match the check numbers and amounts in your checkbook with those on the statement. Mark the checks in your checkbook that the bank has processed.
2. Do the same with deposits.
3. Deduct service charges from the balance in your checkbook. Add interest, if applicable.
4. Add to the bank statement balance deposits that the bank has not yet processed.
5. Subtract from the bank statement balance any checks that the bank has not yet processed.

- If you are depositing the check by mail, write "For Deposit Only" above or below your signature.
- Sign your name exactly as it is written on the front of the check. If your name is misspelled on the front, the endorsement should include the incorrect spelling, followed by the correct spelling.

Using Bank Statements

Banks issue statements to customers periodically—usually once a month. The **bank statement** lists all of the activity in the account—each withdrawal, deposit, interest amount, or fee is recorded in the statement.

You should review every statement to make sure that the bank's listing agrees with your records. A bank statement is especially useful for verifying the activity of a checking account. Once the check clears, it is canceled and returned to the drawer, the individual who wrote it. **Canceled checks** indicate that payment was made by the bank and that the amount of each check was deducted from the account balance

Enrichment Strategy

The banking industry loses about $85 million a year through consumer fraud and forgeries. Suggest that students interview local bank officials to find out how often the bank receives notice of forged checks and what procedure it follows when dealing with forgery. Have students work in pairs to present their findings as a two-minute "Crime Stoppers" feature for the evening news.

CHECK REGISTER/ BANK STATEMENT

		CHECK REGISTER			Balance	
Number	Date	Description	Payment/Debit	Deposit/Credit	914	32
116	1/27	George's Foods	37 92		876	40
117	2/1	Rent	525 00		351	40
—	2/2	Paycheck		600 26	951	66
118	2/3	Cash	60 00		891	66
119	2/9	Phone Bill	58 34		833	32
120	2/15	Clothes Horse	42 27		791	05
—	2/18	Mom's Check		25 00	816	05
121	2/20	Bakery Yum	16 95		799	10
122	2/24	CD City	25 32		773	78
123	3/1	Rent	525 00		248	78

FIRST NATIONAL BANK OF CHICAGO

Allison M. Barrett
95 West End Avenue
Chicago, IL 60614

123-456-7 ACCOUNT NUMBER
1 MAR 1999 STATEMENT DATE

SUMMARY OF ACCOUNTS

ACCOUNT NUMBER	PREVIOUS BALANCE	TOTAL CREDITS	TOTAL DEBITS	TOTAL CHARGES	CURRENT BALANCE
123-456-7	914.32			3.00	

PREVIOUS BALANCE	914.32	CURRENT BALANCE	830.00

DEBTS		CREDITS		BALANCE
FEB 1	116	37.92		876.40
			FEB 2	600.26	1476.66
FEB 3	117	525.00		951.66
	118	60.00		891.66
FEB 14	119	58.34		833.32
			FEB 18	25.00	858.32
FEB 27	122	25.32		833.00
	SC	3.00		830.00

When you have completed these steps, your checkbook balance should match the bank statement balance.

Practice

Reconcile the check register balance ($248.78) with the sample bank statement balance ($830.00) using the five steps.

of the drawer. Canceled checks may be used as proof of payment, and should be kept in a safe place.

Most banks send canceled checks along with the bank statement. Although bank statements may vary in the period covered and the type of account described, most statements provide the kinds of information shown in the sample statement above. Some financial institutions do not return canceled checks with the checking account statement. In these cases the statement includes not only the amount of each check but also the name of the party to whom the check was written. Then the statement serves the same purpose as the canceled checks and can be used to prove that money has been paid to the various parties.

Quick Check

1. What is the most common medium of exchange?
2. Who are the three parties to a check?
3. What is required to open a checking account?
4. What checking account characteristics can vary from bank to bank?

Curriculum Connection   English and Communication

Direct students to work in groups of four to plan and design storyboards for a documentary called "A Day in the Life of a Check" that describes a check's life from writing through canceling and return with the bank statement. Students can use Enrichment Master 20-1 from Chapter 20 to review the check-clearing process. If feasible, have students videotape their productions.

Practice

Ask students to suggest reasons why many individuals often find that their checkbooks do not reconcile on the first attempt. (Incorrect arithmetic, incorrect amounts recorded in register, overlooking service fees.)
(Step 1: Checks 120, 121, and 123 have not yet been processed. Step 2: Both deposits are shown on the statement. Step 3: $248.78 − $3.00 = $245.78. Step 4: No unprocessed deposits. Step 5: $42.27 + $16.95 + $525.00 = $584.22; $830.00 − $584.22 = $245.78. Step 3 agrees with Step 5, so the checkbook register agrees with the statement.)

Connection to CHAPTER 20

Processing checks written on an account in one bank but presented for deposit at another bank requires a way to exchange the checks and transfer the funds involved. Ask students to identify the main agency involved with clearing checks. (The Fed.)

Quick Check Answers

1. Checks.
2. Payee (person to whom check is paid); drawer (person who writes the check); drawee (financial institution that holds the account).
3. Deposit with a deposit ticket and a signed signature card.
4. Minimum deposit, service charge, overdraft protection, charges for credit and debit cards.

SAVINGS ACCOUNTS

Remind students that banks and other deposit institutions offer a variety of ways to save and a variety of interest rates. Some of the more common forms of savings accounts include passbook savings, money market accounts, and certificates of deposit.

Connection to CHAPTER 19

Remind students of the different kinds of banking institutions: commercial banks, savings and loan associations, savings banks, and credit unions. Encourage students to list what they, acting as individual depositors, might consider as the advantages and disadvantages of each type of bank. Help students choose a way to organize and present their responses.

TEACHING TIP

Indicate to students that the method to compute simple and compound interest is similar: Interest = principal x rate x time. Ask them to use this equation as the basis of an explanation of how the two kinds of interest are different. (In simple interest, the principal stays the same; in compound interest, the principal on which interest is computed increases after each time period.)

Business & HISTORY

To help pay the costs of the Civil War (1861-1865), the federal government issued about $430 million in notes guaranteed by the U.S. government rather than by deposits in a bank. Because the back of each of these government-issued notes was printed in green, the paper money quickly became known as *greenbacks*. The value of the greenbacks depended on the people's confidence in the government. That confidence rose and fell with the victories and defeats of the Union army.

Banks hold much of the nation's wealth in savings accounts. These are *time deposits* that pay interest and restrict withdrawals to a specific time. Savings accounts are a way to save money and have that money earn income at the same time. Banks use the money you deposit in your savings account. In return, they pay interest on the money you deposit. The amount of interest varies from one account to another and from one financial institution to another.

Financial institutions usually require a minimum opening balance, for example, $250. Other characteristics of savings accounts include a required minimum balance and service fees. A wise saver compares the rates and requirements of several financial institutions before opening a savings account. At one time such accounts were called "passbook accounts" because savers carried a passbook to the bank along with their deposits and had the amount recorded in it. Today, most savings accounts are called statement accounts because the record of deposits appears on a period statement, not in a passbook.

The rate of interest paid should be a major factor in your decision. Keep in mind that as a general rule, larger balances earn higher interest rates. The length of time you intend to leave your savings in an account may also affect the interest rate. If you agree to leave your money on deposit for 3, 6, 12, or 24 months, the interest rate will probably increase as the time period lengthens. This is partly because the bank is assured that it will have your money to use without the record keeping costs of recording money in and out of the account. Savings accounts have had interest rates ranging from low to high to low. Take a look at Figure 33-3 on page 565 to see how interest rates have varied over the years.

The rate of interest is not the only factor to consider when opening a savings account. Two banks may announce the same interest rate, but may use different methods of calculating interest. The interest for some accounts is computed from the date of deposit to the date of withdrawal, the *DD/DW method*. With this method, money earns interest every day it is in the bank. In contrast, some banks credit interest only on certain days, for example the 15th and the 30th of the month. If you make a withdrawal on the 29th, your money will have earned interest only to the 15th of the month.

Withdrawals may also affect the amount of interest paid. Some banks compute the interest earned using the lowest balance occurring in a month or a quarter, even if the average balance is higher. For example, if your account balance dips to

Curriculum Connection   Communication

Direct students to collect information from local banks concerning the method each uses to compute interest. Have students highlight information in banking brochures that tells whether the bank computes interest using the *DD/DW* method or compounds interest only on the 15th and 30th of the month. Have students discuss whether the banks' materials clearly state the method used to compute interest. Allow students to propose revised information for those brochures they feel are unclear.

Savings Account Interest Rates

Year	Rate	Year	Rate
1935	2.5	1984	5.5
1957	3.0	1989	6.10
1963	4.0	1990	5.83
1970	4.5	1991	4.30
1973	5.0	1992	2.88
1980	5.25	1993	2.46

Source: Federal Reserve Board

FIGURE 33-3

Interest rates have varied over the last 60 years. In which year did statement savings accounts have the highest rate of return? What comparison can you make between 1993 and 1935?

$200 during a period, you are paid interest on $200, even if you kept an average of $500 in the account.

Nearly all financial institutions offer *compound interest.* Compound interest is a multi-step process for computing interest. First the interest on a balance is computed. That interest is added to the balance. The next time interest is computed, the new, larger balance is used. These steps may take place every quarter, every month, or even every day.

Competing banks may compound interest at different time periods. The stated rate is an annual rate and is the percentage used to calculate the interest. The rate of return for deposits earning compound interest is actually higher than the stated rate. Information from a bank may read: "Savings accounts earn 5% interest, compounded daily, for an annual yield of 5.13%." Figure 33-4 below compares the annual interest

FIGURE 33-4

Today, most savings accounts earn compound interest, but that interest may be computed at different intervals, changing the amount of interest earned. Which method of compounding, quarterly or daily, earns the most interest?

Annual Interest Rate Compared With Rate of Return for Compound Interest

Stated Annual Interest Rate	Growth of $1000 savings if interest is compounded		Rate of return (yield) if interest is compounded	
	Quarterly	Daily	Quarterly	Daily
4.00%	$1040.60	$1040.80	4.06%	4.08%
4.50%	$1045.80	$1046.00	4.58%	4.60%
5.00%	$1050.90	$1051.30	5.09%	5.13%
5.50%	$1056.10	$1056.50	5.61%	5.65%
6.00%	$1061.40	$1061.80	6.14%	6.18%

Reteaching Strategy

Ask students to explain how each of the following banking advertisement statements can be accurate. "Acme Bank, a leader in your community, offers the highest return possible on savings accounts—6 percent APR and an annual yield of 6.18 percent." "Ace Trust and Savings currently offers a whopping 6 percent annual interest on passbook savings. Start saving now and get an annual yield of 6.14 percent." (The banks compound interest at different intervals.)

Use Visuals

Direct students' attention to Figure 33-3, Savings Account Interest Rates. Ask students in which years individuals were more likely to place money in savings accounts. (Those with higher interest rates, 1989 and 1990.)
Answer to caption: They're nearly the same.

Learning Activity

Ask students to explain why a consumer might be wise to withdraw from his or her savings account on the 1st of April rather than on the 29th of March.

Use Visuals

Direct students' attention to Figure 33-4, which compares simple and compound interest rates. Indicate to students that compounded interest offers a better return than simple or annual interest.
Answer to caption: Daily.

Use Transparencies

Use Teaching Transparencies 33-4 and 33-5 and their corresponding strategies and worksheets from the *Teaching Transparency Strategies and Worksheets* booklet to acquaint students with the fluctuations in interest rates and the difference between simple and compound interest rates. Verify student worksheets using the Answer Key.

rate with the rate of return for compounded interest. The more frequently interest is compounded, the greater the rate of return.

Finally, banks' charges and service fees vary. Savers should ask about these when opening an account. An account that earns a high interest rate compounded daily, but has fees and charges, may not be the wisest choice.

Most savings accounts are insured by the FDIC or SAIF, agencies of the federal government. This means that if the savings institution fails, depositors can recover their account balance up to $100,000. Some banks offer additional insurance to recover amounts in excess of $100,000.

Money Market Accounts

Many financial institutions and investment firms offer savings accounts in the form of money market accounts. A money market account is a kind of time deposit in which the interest rate generally varies from month to month. However, the interest rate is usually higher than for traditional savings accounts. Money market accounts often require a relatively high minimum amount to open and maintain. Withdrawals from a money market account may be accomplished by writing a check against the balance in the account. Most money market accounts limit the number of withdrawals per month. If the number of withdrawals exceeds the limit or if the balance falls below the minimum, the bank or financial institution may request a service charge or check processing fee. The money market accounts of investment firms are not insured by the FDIC.

Certificates of Deposit

Certificates of deposit (CDs) are another type of savings account banks and other financial institutions offer. Like money market accounts, CDs require minimum deposits. Unlike money market accounts, funds in a certificate of deposit must remain in the financial institution for a specified time ranging from several months to several years. During that time money cannot be added to the account nor can it be withdrawn without a penalty for withdrawal. Certificates of deposits are increasing in popularity among depositors who want to earn more interest on their money, but want to do it in a low-risk environment. Rates of interest paid on these savings plans vary according to the amount deposited and the time period for which it is deposited.

Global Perspective

Swiss bank accounts have earned a reputation throughout the world for safety and intrigue. The accounts, coupled with other financial, insurance, and real estate services, comprise 13 percent of Switzerland's gross domestic product (GDP). (The GDP is the total value of consumer goods and services, business goods and services, government goods and services, and services sold to other nations.) Direct students to prepare an oral report on one of the following topics:
• How to open a numbered Swiss bank account.
• What part international politics plays in the Swiss banking system.
• What part banking services play in the Swiss economy.

Refer to the *International Business Strategies* booklet for additional strategies and activities.

Quick Check

1. List three types of savings accounts generally available to savers.
2. Why should savers find out how their bank computes savings account interest?

OTHER BANKING SERVICES

Commercial banks and other financial institutions offer a broad range of opportunities for handling your money. Savings and checking accounts offer "places" to keep your money safe, allow you to earn interest, and provide you with an efficient way to pay bills. Banking technology offers customers quicker and easier methods of completing bank transactions and accessing information. Banks also offer services that allow you to borrow and invest funds.

Electronic Banking

The fastest and most efficient way of transferring money is by electronic funds transfer (EFT), an electronic, computer-based process. There is some flexibility in the way EFT operates. You are already familiar with some of the applications of EFT. Large-scale, regular payments such as Social Security and pension payments, payroll, invoice, and corporate tax payments are some of the applications for which government and businesses use EFT.

However, EFT is also available to individual consumers. You probably have automated teller machines (ATMs) in banks, malls, or grocery stores. These machines allow customers to make deposits or withdrawals 24 hours a day, seven days a week. Customers can also transfer funds from one account to another in the same bank, such as from a savings account to a checking account, and find out the balance in each account. Some banks offer this service without charge. Others charge only if the ATM terminal is not part of the bank's own network. Still other banks charge for each ATM transaction as if it were a check.

Consumers can also use EFT at the point of sale. Suppose you want to buy some clothes at a store that has installed an EFT system. Instead of paying cash for your purchase or writing a check, you could transfer funds electronically from your checking account to the store's bank account. You would just give the salesclerk your debit card, which is a plastic card resembling a credit card. The store issues a receipt showing the

CHAPTER 33   USING BANKING SERVICES   **567**

Reteaching Strategy

CHAPTER 33

Business Brief

The European Savings Bank Group, a consortium of banks in 12 countries, has created an organization to manage ATMs in several countries.

Business Brief

Some banks operating in foreign countries have imposed a higher than average fee ($5) on ATM withdrawals at foreign locations. Banks are noticing that ATM use has reduced revenues previously obtained from teller-assisted currency exchanges.

Learning Activity
Credit cards, such as MasterCard, Discover, or Visa, are actually short term loans. Some larger banks process credit card payments for major credit card issuers such as oil companies and large retail operations. Have students use a Venn diagram (described in Chapter 22) to show how bank credit cards and loans are similar and how they are different.

USE VISUALS

Ask students what kinds of services the bank might have that would probably interest the family in the photo. (Investment, savings.)
Answer to caption: Funds for retirement, for traveling, for an emergency, for the education of the child.

transfer. The transfer appears on your bank statement as a withdrawal.

Some individuals use EFT to do much of their banking from their home computer. Customers reach their banks' computers by telephone and pay bills and transfer money from one account to another. A home computer cannot, however, be used to obtain cash.

Bank Credit Cards

Banks offer credit card services to their customers. These credit cards, like credit cards issued by other institutions, can be used to delay payment for purchases. Some of the credit cards may be used to access emergency cash through ATM machines. The amount of purchases made on a credit card is like a loan, and credit cards charge interest.

Banks require an application for a credit card. They may also require that you maintain a savings account, with a minimum balance equal to your credit limit, at the bank.

Loans

Commercial banks and other financial institutions also provide loan services to individuals and to businesses. The majority of loans issued by banks are mortgages, which are loans for the purpose of buying real estate such as houses. Banks also issue loans for the purchase of automobiles, education

Banks offer investment services to their customers. What future goals might be included in an investment plan for this family?

Reteaching Strategy

Ask students to work in teams of four to develop a quiz for the material on checking accounts, savings accounts, and other services offered by banks. Suggest they include five true or false questions and five multiple choice questions. Have student groups exchange quizzes and determine which ones would make good study aids.

expenses, and home renovation. Banks prefer to make *secured loans,* which are loans backed by something valuable such as property. *Collateral* is the individual's property that is used to secure or help guarantee the repayment of a loan. For example, if you were to apply for a car loan, the car would serve as collateral. If you fail to repay the loan, the bank has the legal right to repossess, or take, the car. A bank may issue an unsecured loan, which is a loan not backed by any collateral.

Each bank offers different interest rates and terms of repayment. A wise consumer compares the rates and terms offered by several banks before taking out a loan.

Financial/Investment Planning

Banks and other financial institutions also offer services to help you plan your investment goals. People decide to invest their money for many reasons—to accumulate money for retirement, for traveling, or for an emergency. To develop an investment plan, you should meet with a financial planner at a bank. Banks can offer a variety of savings and investment plans, which have varying degrees of risk. A financial planner at a bank can offer comprehensive services and design an investment plan that meets your goals.

Special Bank Services

In some situations cash and personal checks will not be accepted as payments. One reason is a concern there may be insufficient funds to cover the check. When that happens people use other forms of payment that are available through banks and other financial institutions. Using these forms of payment has certain advantages: The money is available almost immediately, and these kinds of payment are guaranteed by the financial institution that issued them.

Bank Checks   A *certified check* is a personal check that a bank has stamped with a guarantee indicating that there is enough money in the depositor's account to cover it. A bank deducts the amount of the check from the depositor's account at the time the check is certified. In this way the person or business receiving the check is assured that the money has been set aside. A certified check is often required when a large sum of money is involved.

A *cashier's check* is written on the bank's own accounts. A cashier's check is a request for money drawn from the bank's own funds. A *bank draft* is a request for funds from an account in another commercial bank or the Federal Reserve bank in the

Cooperative Learning   Debate (Pro/Con)

Ask students to work in pairs to prepare for a debate on the following statement: Modern banking services have improved life for consumers. One partner should take the *pro* position, the other the *con* position. Pairs of students should gather evidence and develop arguments supporting their positions. After each partner presents his or her argument, the other evaluates the presentation to determine whether the evidence supports the position.

Refer to the *Cooperative Learning Strategies* booklet for additional cooperative learning strategies.

Quick Check Answers

1. Electronic banking, credit cards, loans, investment planning, and other special services.
2. Certified, cashier's, and bank draft.

GLOBAL VIEW

Before traveler's checks, individuals and businesses relied on *letters of credit* to purchase items in locations far from home. The letter of credit, written from one bank to another, allowed the person named in the letter to withdraw money from the new bank. These letters of credit were phased out soon after 1891, when the first American Express Traveler's Cheque appeared. Now American Express Traveler's Cheques, as well as traveler's checks issued by other concerns, are available throughout the world and can be converted into dollars, drachmas, yen, rupees, and several other currencies.

district. Both the cashier's check and the bank draft are made payable to the party indicated by the purchaser of the check. Both are considered to be safe, since the banks themselves guarantee the funds are available. Either a cashier's check or a bank draft may be used if large sums of money are transferred and a personal check will not be accepted. In some cases the bank charges a service fee.

Traveler's Checks   It is not wise to carry a large amount of cash when traveling because of risk of theft or loss. In addition, personal checks may not be accepted outside one's city or state, or in foreign countries. A traveler's check is a draft for funds issued by a bank or other financial institution in predetermined amounts such as $25, $50, or $100. A traveler purchases these checks and signs them at the time of purchase. The checks are signed again when they are used. Keeping a record of the check numbers separate from the checks themselves is important. In that way, if the checks are lost or stolen, the identification numbers of the missing checks can be reported and the checks will be replaced by the issuing company.

Money Orders   A money order, like a check, is a form of payment that can be purchased for an exact amount at banks and at other locations such as post offices, travel agencies, department and grocery stores. The purchase price of the money order will be the amount of the money order plus a service fee. The organization that issues the money order promises the payment of money from its funds. Generally money orders are used to transfer relatively small amounts of money. Money orders are very safe to use, since they are payable only to the party named on the order. If lost, they can be replaced easily.

Quick Check

1. In addition to checking and savings accounts, what other services do banks provide?
2. Name three kinds of checks issued by banks.

Enrichment Strategy

Have students research the trend in the number and kinds of banking services offered through computers. If possible, have them arrange to visit a bank in their community that offers computer banking. Ask students to gather information on costs, ease of access, possibility of outside tampering, special regulations, confidentiality, and the number of customer sign-ups over the past year. Have students plan a brief news report describing how computer banking might become commonplace in the future.

Main Ideas

1. One important service banks offer is checking accounts. Checking accounts are safe and convenient and are the most common medium of exchange.
2. Some checking accounts may pay interest and may offer a plastic debit card that can be used as a check.
3. Much of the country's wealth is held in time deposits in bank savings accounts that pay interest—a number of which restrict withdrawals.
4. Interest rates on savings and checking accounts vary among financial institutions according to the minimum deposits required, the manner in which the interest is computed, and the length of time the deposit is held.
5. In addition to checking and savings accounts, banks also offer electronic banking, credit cards, loans, investment planning, and other special bank services.
6. Special forms of payment that banks and other financial institutions provide include certified checks, cashier's checks, traveler's checks, and money orders.
7. Matching or reconciling a check register against the bank statement for the same account involves checking that each transaction amount has been processed and that the balances of the register and the statement agree.
8. Electronic banking in the form of ATMs (automated teller machines) allows depositors to access their savings and checking accounts at times that are convenient for them.

CASE ANALYSIS Endorsements

Helen Thomas just received her paycheck. To get cash in the amount of the check, she has to endorse it. By signing only her name, Helen writes a *blank endorsement*. If the check is lost or stolen, it can be cashed by someone else. If she writes her name followed by "For Deposit Only," she has created a *for-deposit-only endorsement*. Helen is ordering the bank to deposit the full amount of the check in her account. If Helen writes "Pay to the Order of Brian Mackin" and signs her name, she writes a *third-party endorsement*. Brian can cash or deposit her check. Decide which form of endorsement is best for each situation that follows:

1. You want to mail a check to the bank for deposit.
2. You want to give a friend a check made out to you so your friend can cash it.
3. You are at the bank and want to cash your check.

CLOSE

Main Ideas

Main Ideas summarizes the key information in the chapter. It is a useful tool for reinforcement and review.

CASE ANALYSIS

Case Analysis provides a chapter-related case for student analysis and application of decision-making skills.

Answer
1. For-deposit-only; 2. third-party; 3. blank.

QUICK QUIZ

1. What banking services do you use? What services do the adults in your family use? (Answers will vary.)
2. Where can consumers find a list of the checks they wrote last month? (Check register.)
3. Where can a consumer find a list of the checks that cleared in the last month? (Checking account statement.)
4. How does a certified check differ from a cashier's check? (A certified check is a personal check guaranteed by the bank; a cashier's check is drawn against the bank's funds.)

Chapter 33 **Review**

APPLY

Answers

Use the Language of Business

signature card, joint account, deposit ticket, endorsement, overdraft protection, check register, bank statement, canceled check.

Review What You Learned

1. Savings and checking accounts, credit cards, loans, financial planning services.
2. They are safe and convenient; checks are the most common medium of monetary exchange.
3. A depositor can withdraw (within limits) from a money market account; money in a certificate of deposit must remain there for a specified time.
4. Certified checks, cashier's checks, traveler's checks, and money orders.
5. There may not be sufficient funds to cover the check.
6. A terminal connected to a banking network, an account approved for ATM use, ATM card, and PIN.
7. Match all deposits and deposit amounts; match all withdrawals and withdrawal amounts; add/subtract uncleared checks, service charges, fees, and interest earned.

Understand Business Concepts

1. Because the features and charges of a certain kind of account at one banking institution may fit your needs best.
2. A little of both. It earns interest like a savings account, but withdrawals can be made by writing checks against the account.
3. To make sure that your records and the bank's match.
4. To keep your record of the activity in your checking account, such as checks you have written and deposits you have made.
5. Interactive software immediately processes input data. It helps call up and verify customer bank records and immediately makes additions/subtractions based on customer choices.
6. When you receive your bank statement.

Use the Language of Business

Understanding these business terms will help you communicate about banking. Write the term that best completes each sentence.

bank statement   endorsement
canceled checks   joint account
check register   overdraft protection
deposit ticket   signature card

The bank uses a(n) _____ to ensure that the signature on a check is the signature of the customer holding the account. Sometimes a checking or savings account is a(n) _____ that is used by more than one person. To open an account, you fill out a(n) _____, a form that lists the cash and checks you wish to deposit to your account. Your signature, or _____, is recorded on the back of a check before you deposit it. You may arrange for _____ in case you write a check with insufficient funds in your account. Each time you write a check, record the pertinent information about the check in your _____. A(n) _____ is a listing from the bank showing all transactions in your bank account including _____, or those checks that have been paid.

Review What You Learned

1. What major services do banks provide?
2. Why do businesses and most people have checking accounts?
3. What is the difference between a money market account and a certificate of deposit?
4. Name four methods of payment that banks can provide in addition to personal checks.
5. Why are personal checks not accepted as payment by some individuals?
6. Name four things needed to complete a transaction at an ATM.
7. Describe three main steps in reconciling a check register to the bank statement for the same account.

Understand Business Concepts

1. Why should you shop around before opening a checking account?
2. Is a money market account a savings account or a checking account? Explain your answer.
3. Why is it important to review your monthly bank statement?
4. What is the purpose of a check register?
5. What is *interactive software?* How does it aid in ATM transactions?
6. When do you record and subtract bank charges and fees associated with your checking account?

Think Critically

1. Possible answers: **a.** The amount will decrease because more payments will be made electronically. **b.** Fewer tellers will be needed because of increased use of ATMs. **c.** More bank employees will need to know about computer operations as the use of EFT increases. **d.** Individuals will visit banks less often as use of EFT increases. Bank lobbies will be smaller because there will be less traffic.
2. The account might have insufficient funds if another check is cashed before the date on which the check is to be paid.

Think Critically

1. **Analyze.** Electronic Funds Transfer (EFT) has had and could have many effects on our society and the banking community. Predict what you think will happen as EFT becomes more popular. Give reasons for your responses.

2. **Assess.** Banks will not accept a check that has been *postdated*, that is, dated for a future date. Why do you think banks have this policy?

Independent Practice

Use the Chapter 33 worksheets in *Student Activity Guide 2 for* additional practice and application activities. *Student Activity Guide 2* provides vocabulary exercises, reading comprehension checks, problems, projects, and simulations of business and economic situations. A Teacher's Annotated Edition provides answers.

Use What You Learned

1. **Group Project.** In your team choose a local bank to research. Each team member should concentrate on a different service offered by the bank. Visit or telephone the bank for information. Create a chart of the bank's services to share with the class.

2. Two factors affecting the rate of interest paid on a savings account are the amount that you deposit and the length of time you are willing to keep that money deposited. In a paragraph or so, explain which of these factors is more significant in influencing the amount of interest earned.

3. Survey local merchants and banks. Make a list of the different kinds of ATM networks available in your area. Indicate which locations are open 24 hours a day, 7 days a week, and which locations accept the most types of ATM cards.

4. **Computer Application.** Some banks do not return canceled checks to their customers. Use online research to collect information about the pros and cons of this practice. Then use word

processing software to write a two-page report about the advantages and disadvantages of this practice for both banks and their customers.

5. **Skill Reinforcement.** Review the check register, bank statement, and steps for reconciling a checking account presented on page 562. Then reconcile the balance on the check register shown below with a bank statement balance of $844.71. The bank has taken out its service fee of $4.00. The statement does not show checks 578 or 581. Also missing is the deposit in the amount of $47.86. Write an explanation of what you did.

Number	Date	Description	Payment/Debit		Deposit/Credit		Balance	
							624	83
575	6/27	Sam's Good Gifts	22	95			601	88
—	7/1	Paycheck			650	77	1252	65
576	7/1	Finer, Fresher Foods	42	13			1210	52
577	7/10	Cash	100	00			1110	52
578	7/15	Rent	435	00			675	52
579	7/21	Phone Bill	34	67			640	85
580	7/25	World Wide Airlines	227	14			413	71
581	7/29	Electric Bill	32	90			380	81
—	7/31	Al's check			47	86	428	67

Save your work in your Business Portfolio.

ASSESS

Portfolio Assessment

The portfolio projects are designed to lead students to develop a collection of their best work to submit to you for assessment. You and your students should decide which projects will be included in their respective Business Portfolios. Refer students to the specific rubric(s) from the *Alternative Assessment Strategies* booklet listed with each of the project notes below. These rubrics will alert students to the criteria you will use to assess their projects.

Chapter Assessment

Use the Chapter 33 Test from the *Test Masters* booklet to evaluate students' understanding of the chapter concepts. An answer key is provided. Or create your own customized test using the *Testmaker* software.

Use What You Learned

1. Suggest that students might want to collaborate so that they get information from several different banks. Rubric: Charts and Tables.

2. Remind students that they may want to use Money Market Accounts and Certificates of Deposits as examples in their paragraph. Rubric: Paragraph.

3. Indicate to students that specific networks include Cash Station, Novus, and so on. Suggest they look for the logos on the ATM machines. Rubrics: Note Taking, Paragraph.

4. Students without access to computers can accomplish this task manually by using library research materials to find data and by writing the report manually. Rubrics: Note Taking, Essay.

5. Steps 1 and 2 are given in the problem. Step 3: Deducting the $4.00 service charge from the checkbook balance leaves $424.67. Step 4: $844.71 + $47.86 = $892.57. Step 5: $435.00 + $32.90 = $467.90; $892.57 − $467.90 = $424.67. The balance in the checkbook (Step 3) agrees with the bank statement balance (Step 5), so the account is reconciled. Rubrics: Charts and Tables, Paragraph.

FOCUS

Introduce the Chapter

Major Concepts
- Managing Risk
- Automobile Insurance
- Real and Personal Property Insurance
- Life, Health, and Income Insurance

Introduce the Topic
Ask students to describe insurance advertisements. Have them tell what kinds of things the ads seem to be selling. Point out that in Chapter 34 students will learn about how insurance helps people manage their financial risks.

Use Business Terms
Have students briefly study the list of Business Terms and conjure up mental images of what the terms represent. Invite volunteers to describe one or more of the images they have created. Ask members of the class to match the terms with the descriptions. Advise students to note the meanings of the terms as they read the chapter.

USE VISUALS

The family in this photograph may face several economic hardships in the coming years—accident, illness, or natural disaster. How can a normally healthy, financially stable family benefit from owning insurance? (Anyone can benefit from insurance because insurance protects against financial losses due to accidents, emergencies, and natural disasters.)

Business terms

insurance

insurable interest

policy

insurer

insured

claims

premium

deductible

proceeds

beneficiary

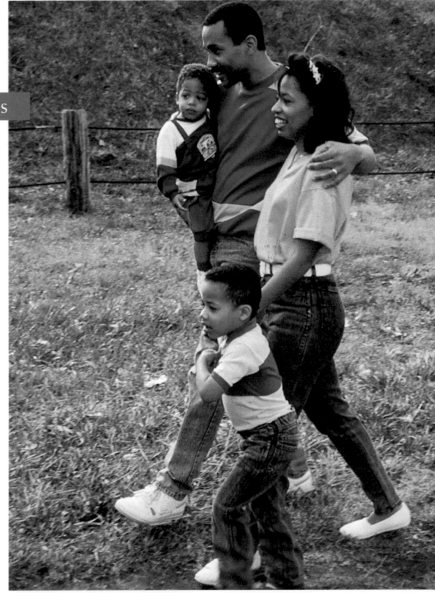

574

CHAPTER 34 RESOURCES

Instructional Resources

Lesson Plan for Chapter 34

Teaching Transparencies 34-1, 34-2

Strategies and Worksheets for Teaching Transparencies 34-1, 34-2

Enrichment Master 34-1

Student Activity Guide 2–TAE for Chapter 34

Test Master for Chapter 34

Alternative Assessment Strategies

Math Skills Review

International Business Strategies

Cooperative Learning Strategies

Communication Skills Review

Ethics in Business Strategies

Dealing *with* Risks

Learning objectives

After completing this chapter, you will be able to:
- Explain how insurance can help people protect themselves against possible financial loss.
- Describe the process of purchasing insurance, and identify the more common types of insurance.
- Identify the factors that affect the cost of insurance.
- Explain important steps to follow to interpret a statistical table.

Consider what you know

- People begin savings and investment plans for many reasons, including purchase of a home, education for their children, emergency expenses, and retirement. To effectively manage their financial affairs, they use the services of banks and other financial institutions.

Consider what you want to know

- What can minimize the risk of financial loss?
- Where can you buy insurance? What are the differences among the many kinds of insurance available?
- What factors affect the cost of insurance?
- How can you interpret a statistical table?

Consider how to use what you learn

- As you work through this chapter, check the newspapers and magazines for insurance advertisements. Clip the ads and see how they match the kinds of insurance mentioned in the chapter.

Multimedia Resources

Technology Resource Guide
Distance Learning Guide
Internet Resource Guide
Professional Resources
School-to-Work/Tech Prep Strategies
Instructional Poster
Spanish Resources

Testmaker Software for Chapter 34
The Wall Street Journal Video Series Video & Activities for Chapter 34
Business and Marketing Computer Applications—An Integrated Software Simulation Using Microsoft Works
Stocktracker—A Stock Market Software Simulation
Where's the Dough? Board Game

Motivate the Learning

Learning Objectives
Point out to students that the learning objectives tell what they will learn in the chapter. Encourage students to keep these objectives in mind as they work through the chapter. Note that the last two objectives listed refer to the Focus on Entrepreneurs feature and the Building Business Skills feature.

Consider What You Know
Review briefly the main sections of *Chapter 33 Using Banking Services:* Checking Accounts, Savings Accounts, and Other Banking Services.

Consider What You Want to Know
Direct students to get an idea of what the chapter is about by reading the questions and looking through the chapter to see how it might help them find the answers.

Consider How to Use What You Learn
Indicate to students that at the end of the chapter they will develop projects related to managing risk. Suggest that as they read the chapter they think about how they might take advantage of products offered to reduce risk.

TEACH

Develop Concepts

Managing Risk

Insurance is a way to reduce an individual's financial risk. The customers who purchase insurance pay money in the hope that if they suffer a loss, the insurance coverage they purchased with their premiums will cover their financial loss.

Learning Activity

Invite a volunteer to draw a diagram or illustration for the "principle of large numbers." Ask another volunteer to describe the principle in his or her own words.

These headlines—"House Burns in Midnight Fire" "Three-Car Pileup Injures Five" "Business District Hit Hard by Tornado"—represent common emergencies and disasters. Individuals and businesses may work hard to protect themselves against disasters or emergencies. They may periodically inspect electrical wiring to see that their home or factory is safe from fire, drive defensively to avoid accidents, and establish businesses where tornadoes are unlikely. Nevertheless, disasters and emergencies can strike even the well-prepared. This chapter examines one way in which individuals and businesses can protect themselves against the financial losses associated with emergencies and disasters. Such protection is important to individuals, families, businesses, and society as a whole.

MANAGING RISK

Financial risks are handled most effectively when large numbers of individuals or businesses participate in sharing the risk. Purchasing insurance is one way to share risk—**insurance** distributes a possible loss among a large number of people.

In the insurance process, each individual pays a fee for protection. The individual fee for this protection is usually much less than the total financial cost of losses from a disaster or emergency would be. However, because large numbers of people pay the fee, there is enough money available to cover the cost of a loss for those few people who actually have a disaster or emergency. This "principle of large numbers" means many individuals share a loss so that any one individual suffers less. It is a basic concept of insurance.

Some people believe that they are not getting their money's worth if they purchase insurance but never file a claim. These people have forgotten that insurance is a way of managing the *risk* of financial loss, a way of managing the financial risk associated with unplanned and unforeseen events. Individuals and businesses purchase insurance because they do not know how great a loss they might suffer, but if they incur a loss, they wish to share that loss with large numbers of people. The financial consequences of experiencing a major loss without the protection of insurance are generally far greater than the amount paid for insurance.

There are some people who feel that because they have insurance, they no longer need to be careful. However,

BUSINESS & HISTORY

Insurance is thousands of years old. The ancient Greeks and Romans had a form of life insurance. People would join burial clubs to which they would contribute money. When a member died, the burial club would pay for funeral expenses. It also would arrange for payments to be made to the member's survivors.

Reteaching Strategy

Ask students to offer a response to the following statement: "I've wasted my money on insurance. I've had a policy for 20 years, paid $50 a month, and never filed a claim. The insurance company is sure making a profit at my expense."

insurance is intended to cover financial losses that occur because of accidents or unexpected events. Carelessness drives up the cost of insurance. When losses increase, costs go up and all insurance customers pay more to cover these costs.

Insurance companies provide a risk management service. For a fee, they offer to reduce the financial risk their customers might face. In order to manage financial risk for their customers, insurance companies estimate the probability rate at which an emergency or disaster will occur. For example, an insurance company might keep track of the number of house fires occurring in a community during the past 20 years. The data might indicate that in a community of 5000 families, fire destroys an average of one family home each year. That data helps the insurance company determine the risk of fire for a single home in that community. Then the company uses the risk of fire for a single home and the estimated value of the home to determine the fee they will charge for insuring a home against the financial risk associated with a fire in that community.

Purchasing Insurance

To buy insurance, an individual or business generally must have an **insurable interest** in the person or item covered by the insurance. In other words, the customer must be able to prove that the loss of the person or item insured would cause a financial loss to the customer. For example, you have an insurable interest in all of your personal property, your clothes, CDs, and so on. If your property were destroyed or stolen, you would suffer a financial loss. However, you do not have an insurable interest in your best friend's property. If that property is lost or stolen, you yourself would not suffer a financial loss. An insurable interest is not necessarily required with life insurance. The reason for this exception is explained later.

Most insurance is purchased through an insurance agent, who is a representative of the insurance company. Agents offer information, help, and guidance to customers to help them plan the best insurance program for their needs. After a plan is complete, the agent prepares an application for the customer. If the application is accepted, the insurance company issues a policy. A **policy** is a formal written agreement between the purchaser and the company.

The policy identifies the insurance company as the **insurer** and the customer or policyholder as the **insured.** The policy states in detail all of the protection, costs, rights, and responsibilities the insured can expect. The policy also lists the conditions under which the insurer will—and will not—honor

One of the most famous insurance organizations in the world is Lloyd's of London. This institution began in Edward Lloyd's Coffee House in about 1688. Lloyd's is not an insurance company, but an association of 26,000 members that buy and sell risks. At one time, Lloyd's was considered the insurer of last resort, covering risks few, if any, other companies would insure. However, after huge recent claims, Lloyd's has refused to insure some risks.

Cooperative Learning   Group Discussion

Point out to students that some insurance companies do not hire outside agents and require their agents to sell only their products. These agents are often called *career agents* or *direct writers.* Ask students how purchasing insurance through one of these agents might affect the price and policies available to them.

Refer to the *Cooperative Learning Strategies* booklet for additional cooperative learning strategies.

Discuss

Point out to students that office and lab space is often a costly start-up item for small businesses. Loans for these kinds of expenses are considered risky and are hard to get. Ask students how Cecil Hess of Metro-Laser reduced his financial risk and found lab and office space. (He worked with universities so that his company could use their labs.)

Cecil F. Hess—MetroLaser

Lasers. The word conjures up images of intense beams of light zapping across merchandise bar codes, burning away damaged tissue, or even cutting holes in diamonds. For entrepreneur Cecil F. Hess, president of MetroLaser, lasers are the precise measuring and diagnostic devices that his successful research and development company specializes in. Its instruments are used in such high-tech areas as combustion research, structural analysis, and measurement of gas particles and temperatures.

Born in the Dominican Republic, Hess earned his Ph.D. at the University of California in mechanical engineering. When he made the decision to become an entrepreneur, he was doing lab work and writing as a senior scientist at a "think tank." (Think tanks are organizations that do research projects using specialists in a variety of fields.) When his firm was acquired by a large aerospace corporation, it lost some of the freedom it had had as a smaller organization. Hess and a fellow scientist began to talk about starting their own company. Within seven months they had taken the plunge.

"We had a business plan and a lot of faith," says Hess, describing MetroLaser's modest beginnings in 1988. They had plenty of ideas, too, but they lacked vital lab space—and paying clients. However, Hess had a winning attitude: MetroLaser "just wasn't going to fail." The company began by working with universities so that it could use their laboratories, and it grew. By 1995, MetroLaser had plenty of labs and more than 30 employees, seven of them Ph.Ds.

Business Brief

Individuals purchasing insurance in Florida pay about 40¢ of every premium dollar to a storm insurance fund. Insurers calculate this amount by looking at 20-year trends and determining the probability of the disaster occurring.

Learning Activity

Ask a volunteer to draw a word or concept web showing what a *premium* is and its uses. (Money charged by insurer; costs of services, claims, disaster reserves, profit.)

claims. **Claims** are requests for payment to cover financial losses. An insurance policy is a legal contract between the insured and the insurer. Anyone purchasing insurance should read his or her policy carefully, asking the agent to explain any unclear items.

Once a policy is signed, the policyholder must pay a fee for the risk management service the insurance company has agreed to provide. The amount of money charged by the insurance company for protection during a certain period of time is called a **premium.** Part of the premium is used to cover the cost of the services the customer receives from the agent and the company. Some of the premium, of course, goes to pay claims. Some may be held in reserve to cover large disasters, such as hurricanes, earthquakes, or floods. The reserves generally are invested to earn income. Part of the premium is profit to the insurance company that writes the policy.

Most insurance policies, with the exception of life insurance, specify a deductible. A **deductible** is the amount the policyholder must pay first, before the insurance company pays anything. If the policy has a $250 deductible, the policyholder

578 UNIT 10 MANAGING YOUR PERSONAL FINANCES

Curriculum Connection   Math

Insurance companies rely on the laws of probability. These laws enable an insurance mathematician, called an *actuary,* to determine the likelihood that an event will actually take place. Ask students to explore probability and to present their findings as a bulletin board or poster display.

Hess and MetroLaser also built a reputation for completing contracts on time and within budget. Among their satisfied clients was the federal government. According to Hess, the government makes a fine client but sets up strict rules for its contractors. MetroLaser has played by these rules so well that in 1995 it was named National Small Business Prime Contractor of the Year. (A prime contractor controls a project and hires other firms as subcontractors to complete different phases.) In that year Hess and MetroLaser's projects included designing instruments for the Air Force's flying optical lab, the KC-135 aircraft.

Though Cecil Hess spends less time in the lab than he'd like to, he likes having his own company. His message to prospective entrepreneurs is strong: "I would encourage anyone to do this."

pays the first $250 of insurance claims. Depending on the type of insurance, the deductible must be paid every calendar or policy year or for every incident. Generally, a policy with a larger deductible has smaller premiums.

Regulating Insurance

States regulate the insurance industry. In order to conduct business, an insurance company must obtain a license from each state in which it operates. The state insurance department reviews insurance companies' operations on a regular basis. Each state has an insurance supervisor, often called a commissioner, who is responsible for applying and enforcing the rules and regulations established by the state.

An important area of regulation is policy premiums. Some states require that premiums be approved by the insurance commissioner. In other states, premiums can be set without approval of a commissioner, but the data used to determine the rates are still subject to review. In any case, the insurance companies are closely supervised by the commissioner.

CHAPTER 34   DEALING WITH RISKS   **579**

Follow Through
Have students prepare a time line showing at least five events that contributed to the beginning and growth of Metro-Laser. (Any five of the following in chronological order: Hess's firm acquired by large corporation, loss of freedom, Hess and partner form company, business plan, working with universities, 30 employees, named National Small Business Prime Contractor of the Year.)

Business Brief
Consumers should evaluate an insurance company as well as the insurance policy. They need to make sure the company is licensed and has adequate financial backing. They should also investigate if the company has a reinsurer and if it has had complaints lodged against it.

Learning Activity
Ask students to identify what role the government plays in regulating the insurance industry. (Issuing licenses, data used to set premiums, and in some cases, premiums.)

Reteaching Strategy

Ask students to imagine that they are responsible for teaching the terms in this section to a group of people for whom English is a second language. Have students work in teams of four to generate definitions, diagrams, or illustrations they could use to present the terms. Display the results and allow the class to choose the best examples to copy and use as study aids.

TEACHING TIP
Help students to understand the cost of insurance by asking them to explain the relationship between premiums and deductibles. (Higher deductibles generally mean lower premiums.)

**Quick Check
Answers**
1. A fee for protection; insurance companies use past figures to predict how many losses might occur in a period of time.
2. Pay business operating costs, pay claims, and invest to earn income.
3. Formal written agreement of insurance between the insurer, or insurance company, and the insured, or customer or policyholder.

Develop Concepts

Automobile Insurance

Students are probably familiar with the concept of automobile insurance. Point out to students that there are several types of auto insurance and that each type has its own costs and deductibles.

USE VISUALS

Direct students' attention to Figure 34-1, which lists a variety of automobile insurance coverages. Ask students to determine what type of coverage they need to minimize their financial risk if their car is stolen. (Comprehensive.)
Answer to caption: Answers will vary.

USE TRANSPARENCIES

Use Teaching Transparency 34-1 and its corresponding strategies and worksheet from the *Teaching Transparency Strategies and Worksheets* booklet to familiarize students with a variety of automobile insurance coverages. Verify student worksheets using the Answer Key.

Quick Check
1. What is a *premium?* How is it determined?
2. What do insurance companies do with premiums?
3. Explain what a *policy* is, and who the *insurer* and *insured* are.

AUTOMOBILE INSURANCE

Automobile accidents can cause damage to property and bodily injury resulting in medical costs and loss of income. Automobile insurance offers protection from these financial risks. In most cases, the driver of an automobile has a legal responsibility, or liability, to pay for any damages that he or she causes in an accident. Most states require proof of the ability to pay for these damages, and an insurance policy is one form of that proof.

FIGURE 34-1

The kinds of automobile insurance coverage listed here are often included in a package policy. Does your state require that motorists carry liability insurance to register a car?

Automobile Insurance Coverages	
Name of Coverage	**Covers Financial Risk Due To**
Bodily Injury	Injury or death to person(s) not in policyholder's car
Property Damage Liability	Damage to another person's property during an accident
Medical Payments	Medical expenses resulting from injury to the driver or others in policyholder's car
Collision	Damage during an accident to the policyholder's car
Comprehensive Damage	Storms, floods, falling objects, fire, vandalism, and theft
Uninsured Motorists	Accidents caused by people who have no liability insurance and no money to pay for the damage they cause

Curriculum Connection   Communication

Have students work in groups of four. Suggest that they call or visit local insurance agents to find out what, if any, special requirements must be met by minors who wish to purchase automobile insurance. Direct them to find out the amounts of premiums at various ages. Suggest that they ask if there are any ways, such as taking a driver education course, to reduce premiums for teenage drivers. Have each group present an oral report.

For students who need to sharpen their communication skills, choose among the worksheets in the *Communication Skills Review* booklet.

Types of Automobile Insurance

Most automobile insurance policies combine coverage for a variety of risks. Figure 34-1 on page 580 shows six basic types of coverage. The owners of motorcycles and motor scooters can purchase policies with similar coverages.

Automobile Insurance Costs

Insurance companies base automobile insurance premiums on the risk of insuring a certain driver in a certain car. As the risk of an accident and the potential cost of the damage increase, so does the premium. Several factors influence the potential cost of the damage, including the cost of the automobile, the number of miles traveled per year, and the driving habits of the policyholder. For example, expensive cars cost more to insure than cars with a low value because replacing or repairing an expensive car usually costs more. Insurance is higher for people who commute by car than for those who use their car only for personal trips. Also, the longer the commute, the higher the cost of insurance.

Some areas of the country record more traffic accidents and higher repair costs than other areas. Insurance in one of these higher-risk, higher-cost areas costs more. Unmarried male drivers under 25 years of age pay high insurance premiums because statistics show that this group has more accidents and causes more damage than any other group of drivers. However, many companies give a discount to young drivers who pass a driver education course or make good grades.

It can take a lot of time and money to decide who is at fault in an accident and, therefore, who should pay for the damage. To avoid this problem, some states have *no-fault* automobile insurance. With no-fault insurance, it does not matter who is legally responsible for the accident. The medical expenses and repair costs of each person are paid by his or her own insurance company.

Quick Check

1. Name the six basic types of automobile insurance coverage.
2. Name three factors that affect auto insurance premiums.

Making Connections ⟶ Everyday Living

Have students find out how many states require that motorists have automobile insurance coverage. Suggest that they also find out how states enforce the law and what penalties are associated with breaking the law.

Learning Activity

Ask students to generate a list of items that can help lower automobile insurance premiums and a list of items that tend to make premiums higher. Suggest that they organize their list in chart form. Then have students indicate which of the items are within their control as consumers.

USE VISUALS

Photocopy and distribute Enrichment Master 34-1, Automobile Insurance Fact sheet. Suggest that students use the fact sheet to generate a multiple-choice quiz to test their understanding of the terms used in automobile insurance. Have students exchange quizzes with a partner and then complete their partner's quiz. Suggest that students exchange completed quizzes with a third partner for grading.

TEACHING TIP

Ask students to use the concepts of *shared risk* and *no-fault insurance* to explain why insurance companies offer special coverage for damage or injury caused by uninsured motorists.

Quick Check Answers

1. Bodily injury liability, property damage liability, medical payments, collision, comprehensive, and uninsured motorist coverage.
2. Possible answers include driving record, type of car, number of miles you drive, where you live, and your age.

Building Business Skills

Building Business Skills

Model

Discuss with students the possible uses for statistics. For example, statistics, along with probability, help insurance companies determine premiums for different kinds of insurance.

Develop Concepts

Real and Personal Property Insurance

Renter's and homeowner's insurance are two of the most common types of real and personal property insurance. As with all other insurance, the costs for these kinds of insurance depend on a variety of factors.

Connection to CHAPTER 17

Suggest that students review the definition of real property as mentioned in Chapter 17. Ask students to explain how real estate property differs from personal property. (*Real estate property* includes land and anything on the land, such as houses, barns, garages, or other buildings.)

Learning Activity

Have students find out what insurance companies in their community offer renter's insurance and what such insurance covers.

ANALYSIS

Interpreting Statistics

Explanation

Statistics are just numbers until you learn how to interpret them. An understanding of statistics can help businesspeople spot trends and patterns of change, understand surveys, and make informed predictions. For example, in the insurance industry statistics about disease and accidents are essential for assessing risks and determining premiums.

Statistics gain meaning when they are compared to each other. You probably couldn't make an intelligent interpretation of a company's sales figures for the past year unless you also knew what sales were in previous years or how this year's sales compare to the competition's. In comparing statistics look at differences over a period of time or for two or more groups.

Sometimes, after you've compared statistics, you'll be able to apply other knowledge to make inferences about them. For example, if prices for a consumer item are declining, you might infer that the item is not selling well. The statistics (falling prices), coupled with your knowledge of the relationship between demand and price, lead you to this inference. Watch out, though. It's possible to make incorrect inferences. If more than one conclusion comes to mind, seek more information.

Practice

Apply the five steps to the life insurance table presented in the box by writing a response to each step as it applies to the table.

REAL AND PERSONAL PROPERTY INSURANCE

Automobiles are not the only possession for which individuals and businesses need protection against loss or damage. Houses, buildings, and other real property, as well as personal property, such as furniture, jewelry, and electronic equipment, also need to be insured.

Renter's Insurance

When people first start out on their own, they usually rent rather than buy a home. The owner or landlord of the building will probably have insurance on the building in which the rental unit is located. However, that insurance will not pay for loss of or damage to personal property of renters. A personal property inventory will help to determine how much coverage is necessary to protect personal possessions such as CD players, televisions, large appliances, or furniture. Renter's insurance

Reteaching Strategy

Suggest that students make an inventory of their personal possessions. Encourage them to include everything they would want to replace if their home were struck by a natural disaster. The inventory should include the name of the item, the approximate cost when new, and the replacement cost. Have students use their lists to discuss whether or not they could benefit from some type of insurance.

STATISTICAL TABLES

Ownership of Life Insurance in the U.S. and Assets of U.S. Life Insurance Companies (millions of dollars)

Year	Purchases of life insurance				Insurance in force					Assests
	Ordinary	Group	Industrial	Total	Ordinary	Group	Industrial	Credit	Total	Assests
1940	6,689	691	3,350	10,730	79,346	14,938	20,866	380	115,530	30,802
1950	17,326	8,068	5,402	28,796	149,116	47,793	33,415	3,844	234,168	64,020
1960	52,883	14,845	6,880	74,408	341,881	175,903	38,563	29,101	586,448	119,578
1970	122,820	63,890*	6,612	193,122*	734,730	551,357	38,644	77,332	1,402,123	207,254
1980	385,575	183,418	3,609	572,602	1,760,474	1,579,355	35,994	165,215	3,541,038	479,210
1990	1,089,660	459,271	220	1,529,151	5,366,982	3,753,508	24,071	248,038	9,392,597	1,408,402
1991	1,041,508	573,953*	198	1,615,659*	5,877,777	4,057,606	22,475	228,478	9,986,338	1,651,201
1992	1,048,135	440,143	222	1,488,500	5,941,810	4,240,919	20,973	202,090	10,405,792	1,664,531
1993	1,101,327	576,823	149	1,678,299	6,428,434	4,458,338	20,451	199,518	11,104,741	1,839,127

*Includes Servicemen's Group Life Insurance $27.8 billion in 1965, $17.1 billion in 1970, $1.7 billion in 1975, and $166.7 billion in 1991.
Source: American Council of Life Insurance

1. What information do the statistics present?
2. Read the headings of the sections, if any, columns (vertical), and rows (horizontal). How is the information being presented? What do the figures at the intersection of each column and row mean?
3. Compare statistics to spot similarities, differences, changes, or trends.
4. Ask yourself the reason for changes and differences.
5. Apply your prior knowledge to make inferences from the statistics.

premiums are based on the amount of coverage, type of building, and location.

Homeowner's Insurance

Many insurance companies offer a combination policy known as a homeowner's policy. This policy protects against most types of losses and liabilities related to home ownership. Among the kinds of protection covered are losses from fire, lightning, windstorm, hail, explosion, riot, aircraft crashes, smoke, motor vehicles, malicious mischief, vandalism, and burglary. Homeowner's policies also cover liability for injuries to other persons while they are on the insured property.

When you buy homeowner's insurance, the number of perils, or risks, covered depends on the form of the policy you choose. There are six standard HO (homeowner) policy options:

HO-1: Basic Form   HO-4: Renters' Form
HO-2: Broad Form   HO-5: Comprehensive Form
HO-3: Special Form   HO-6: Condo Owners' Form

Making Connections ▷▷ Business Ethics

In an effort to control costs, some insurance companies refuse to offer homeowner's or renter's policies in some urban areas. This practice is called *redlining* and is illegal. However, redlining is often difficult to prove because the areas traditionally have a high percentage of crime and many of the individuals in the neighborhood are poor. Have students discuss what effects redlining has on a neighborhood, an insurance company's reputation, and the stockholders of the insurance company. Remind students that they already discussed redlining in reference to bank credit policies in the Business Issue on pages 344–45.

Refer to the *Ethics in Business Strategies* booklet for additional activities.

Practice

(1. Ownership in the U.S. and assets of life insurance companies.
2. Two main columns—*Purchases of life insurance* and *Insurance in force.* Figures are given for certain years from 1940 through 1993. The far right column lists asset totals for U.S. insurance companies. The figures at the intersections of columns and rows show the amount of money in a given year for particular kinds of insurance.
3. Most columns show a steady increase in amounts of money over the years. Exceptions are industrial life insurance in the *Purchases* section where the trend is downwards after 1975, as well as a drop for group insurance purchases in 1992. In the *Insurance in force* section, there is a similar downward trend. This seems to be the case also in the Credit column.
4. Students should consider population growth, inflation, and other indicators.
5. Students may say they think population growth probably accounts for the upward trends, but they need more information about this and the other trends.)

Business Brief

Individuals operating a home-based business should not assume that their homeowner's or apartment dwellers' insurance policy will pay for losses relating to their businesses. The rapid growth of home-based businesses is prompting insurance companies to design and offer policies targeted at home-business owners.

Figure 34-2 lists the perils covered by three different kinds of homeowner's insurance. Ask students which kind of insurance covers most damage from water-related perils. (HO2) Answer to caption: No. Some perils cause such great damage that insurers cannot insure against them at a reasonable cost.

USE TRANSPARENCIES

Use Teaching Transparency 34-2 and its corresponding strategies and worksheet from the *Teaching Transparency Strategies and Worksheets* booklet to familiarize students with the events covered by a variety of homeowner's policies. Verify student worksheets using the Answer Key.

TEACHING TIP

Ask a volunteer to review for the class the terms *premium* and *deductible*.

Learning Activity

Encourage students to discuss why renters or homeowners might want to review their insurance coverage every two years.

Learning Activity

Indicate to students that if a homeowner has a mortgage, the bank or mortgage institution requires that the homeowner carry insurance on the property. Ask students to explain why this is a reasonable demand and an example of insurable interest.

Losses Covered by Homeowner's Policy

Basic (HO-1)	Broad (HO-2)	Comprehensive (HO-5)
1. Fire or lightning 2. Loss of property removed from premises endangered by fire or other perils 3. Windstorm or hail 4. Explosion 5. Riot or civil commotion 6. Aircraft 7. Vehicles 8. Smoke 9. Vandalism and malicious mischief 10. Theft 11. Breakage of glass constituting a part of the building	12. Falling objects 13. Weight of ice, snow, sleet 14. Collapse of building(s) or any part thereof 15. Sudden and accidental tearing asunder, cracking, burning, or bulging of a steam or hot water heating system or of appliances for heating water 16. Accidental discharge, leakage, or overflow of water or steam from within a plumbing, heating or air-conditioning system, or domestic appliance 17. Freezing of plumbing, heating and air-conditioning systems, and domestic appliances 18. Sudden and accidental injury from artificially generated currents to electrical appliances, devices, fixtures, and wiring	All perils EXCEPT: earthquake, landslide, flood, surface water, waves, tidal water or tidal wave, the backing up of sewers, seepage, war, and nuclear radiation

FIGURE 34-2

Categories of insurance policies are determined by the number of perils they insure against. Can homeowner's insurance protect you against all perils?

The key to how these forms differ is in the number of perils the policyholder is insured against. An HO-1 policy is the minimum form, while an HO-5 policy is the broadest. Figure 34-2 above shows the difference in coverage among three of these HO policy options.

Property Insurance Costs

Like automobile insurance, property insurance rates vary. Your costs for different coverages are determined by several factors.

- Payment Terms—Most policies are written for a one-year term; paying semiannually or quarterly increases your costs.
- Construction Materials—Whether your house is built from brick, stucco, wood, or concrete determines what you pay.
- Deductible—Small losses are costly to process. The higher the deductible, the less you pay.

Enrichment Strategy

Indicate to students that financial losses due to flooding are not generally covered by homeowner's policies. Suggest that interested students find out what kinds of government programs and insurance are available to people who live in areas that experience frequent flooding. Suggest that they present their findings in a three-minute "Consumer Watch" segment for the evening news.

- Replacement Value of the Home—The cost of replacing your home with one of similar value at current prices will determine what you pay.
- Preventative Measures—You can get a discount if you install burglar alarms, smoke detectors, fire extinguishers, and deadbolt locks.

It also pays to comparison shop. Insurance rates for the same coverage are not the same for all companies.

Quick Check

1. What two general types of protection does a homeowner's policy include?
2. What are three factors that affect the cost of homeowner's insurance?

LIFE, HEALTH, AND INCOME INSURANCE

Who will pay for an individual's medical expenses if he or she has an accident or becomes ill? What would happen to a family if one or more of the wage earners were to die? What income will a person have if he or she is injured? Life, health, and income insurance can help protect individuals and their families against such risks.

Life Insurance

When a person dies, he or she does not suffer a financial loss. However, family and friends of the deceased may suffer a financial loss if the deceased was their primary means of support. A family thus has an insurable interest in a wage earner's life.

Life insurance is designed to protect the standard of living of the policyholder's survivors. At the policyholder's death, the survivors are paid the face value of the life insurance policy. The money paid to the survivors is called the **proceeds** of the policy. Each person who receives part of the proceeds is called a **beneficiary.** When an individual purchases life insurance, it is best to specify the beneficiaries of the policy. There are several types of life insurance tailored for different situations. Let's look at some of the most common types.

Term Insurance As its name implies, term insurance covers a person for a specific period of time—the term of the policy. If

F.Y.I.

Life insurers predict losses through a table that lists how long people usually live. It is called a mortality table. The earliest known mortality table dates from the year 220. In 1693, 1400 years later, the astronomer Edmund Halley (of Halley's Comet fame) made up a much more useful table. It was based on statistical laws of mortality. In 1756, this table was corrected by Joseph Dodson. Insurance companies continue to update mortality tables as the population changes and lives longer.

Global Perspective

Headquartered in Georgia, AFLAC is the largest supplemental health insurance company in the world. The company receives 79 percent of its revenues from Japan. The company entered the Japanese market offering only cancer insurance policies. Ask students to research how AFLAC approached the Japanese market. Encourage students to discuss the differences between the Japanese and United States insurance markets.

Refer to the *International Business Strategies* booklet for additional strategies and activities.

TEACHING TIP

Ask students to identify what kinds of actions they as renters or homeowners can take to reduce their insurance premiums. (Increase the deductible; install burglar alarms, smoke detectors, fire extinguishers, and so on.)

Quick Check Answers

1. Most types of losses and liabilities relate to home ownership; liability for injuries to other persons while they are on the property.
2. Possible answers include payment terms, construction materials, deductible, replacement value of the home, preventive measures.

Develop Concepts

Life, Health, and Income Insurance

Some of the greatest financial risks to families occur when the income of working family members is no longer available. Insurances available to help reduce the financial risk in the event of loss of a wage earner include life, health, and income insurance.

Business Brief

Term life insurance is generally less expensive than other insurance policies. Some consumers purchase this insurance and invest the difference in premium cost.

CHAPTER 34

the insured does not die before the term expires, the policy has no value. The older the insured, the higher the premium. Many companies provide group term insurance for their employees. These policies guarantee two to three times the insured's annual salary to beneficiaries in case of death.

Whole Life Insurance   This kind of insurance provides death benefits and savings. The policy stays in effect until the insured dies, provided the premiums are paid. In addition to paying death benefits, whole life insurance accumulates value, like a savings account. Whole life insurance is more expensive than term insurance.

Variable Life Insurance   Like whole life insurance, this stays in force and accumulates value until the insured dies. The policyholder, however, decides how to invest the cash value, whether in stocks, bonds, or money market funds. If the insured invests well, the policy's death benefit and cash value will increase; if the investments do poorly, the reverse can occur.

Life Insurance Costs   The amount you pay for insurance depends on many factors. Here are some of them.

- Type of Life Insurance—Whether you buy term, whole life, or variable life insurance will determine the amount of the premiums you pay.
- Age of Insured—Generally, the younger a person is, the less he or she will pay for insurance. As people age, they have a greater chance of dying.
- Insured's Health—If the insured's health is poor, the premium will be higher. If the insured's health is good, the premium will be lower.
- Sex—Women live longer than men. Thus they pay less for life insurance.
- Face Amount of the Policy—The larger the face amount of the policy, the more it will cost.
- Company Selected—Different companies charge different premiums for the same coverage.

Health Insurance

Few people have enough savings to pay the costs of extended medical care. Health insurance provides many types of coverage to protect people against the costs of illness and accident. Most health insurance plans include these five general areas of coverage:

- **Hospitalization insurance** pays the major part of the cost of a hospital stay.

Curriculum Connection   Social Studies

Japan's health care system balances universal coverage at reasonable cost. The government acts as insurer and subsidizes health care spending for the employees of small enterprises and the self-employed. Have students investigate what kinds of health care regulations or assistance the United States government provides to small enterprises, employees of small enterprises, and self-employed individuals.

- **Surgical and medical insurance** pays the costs of surgery and of in-hospital care by physicians.
- **Major-medical insurance** covers all the medical expenses that fall outside the coverage limits of hospitalization insurance and surgical and medical insurance.
- **Dental and vision insurance** cover a fixed percentage of costs for eyeglasses, medically prescribed contact lenses, and various forms of dental work.
- **Mental health insurance** pays for psychological counseling and psychiatric care.

Like other kinds of insurance, most health insurance policies have a deductible that the policyholder must pay first. After the deductible, the insurance company and the policyholder share the remaining costs. This sharing of costs is called *coinsurance*. The insurance company computes the *usual and customary charges* for treatment by finding the average cost of a specific treatment in a specific location or area of the country. Usually the insurer pays 80 percent of the usual and customary charges for any care or treatment. The policyholder pays the remaining 20 percent. This is often written as an 80/20 coinsurance clause. In many policies, the 80/20 clause applies to costs up to a set limit. After the limit is reached, the insurer pays 100 percent of the costs.

Many businesses offer some form of group health plan for their employees. Employers typically pay about 80 percent of the premiums. As costs rise, however, employers are shifting more of the burden to employees by requiring them to pay a larger portion of their premiums. Under some group health

Does health insurance cover only hospital costs?

Reteaching Strategy

Ask students to work in groups of four to develop a ten-question quiz for this section. Direct them to include questions on *proceeds, beneficiary, hospitalization, surgical, major medical, coinsurance,* and *usual and customary.* Have groups exchange quizzes and answer the questions. Suggest that groups pool their efforts and choose the five best questions to keep as a study aid.

Learning Activity
Suggest that students contact local hospitals or hospital associations to find out the cost of a hospital room for one day. Have students use the information as a basis for a discussion about the importance of hospitalization insurance.

TEACHING TIP

Ask students to describe in their own words the difference among *major medical, hospitalization,* and *surgical and medical* insurance.

Learning Activity
Ask a volunteer to create a diagram or illustration for a 75/25 coinsurance policy.

USE VISUALS

Advise students that often medical care requires a team of highly-trained professionals. Ask students how this contributes to the cost of medical care.
Answer to caption: No. Some medical insurance is used to help pay for care administered by a dentist or an eye doctor, also.

Business Brief

Several foreign insurance companies have established operations in Mexico, which is underinsured due to such factors as high inflation. Individuals in Mexico spend an average of $31 a year on insurance in comparison to individual U.S. citizens, who spend $1930 yearly.

CHAPTER 34

Learning Activity
Ask students to discuss why group health insurance policies often offer more benefits for less money than do individual policies.

Business Brief
Deere and Co. created its own health maintenance organization. It is popular with employees and has cut the company's health insurance costs. The HMO serves 300 other companies, but 22 percent of the members are Deere employees.

Quick Check Answers

1. A policyholder does not have an insurable interest in his or her own life. The policy protects family or friends against the economic loss they would suffer from the policyholder's death.

2. By raising the percent of coinsurance the insured must pay and by keeping usual and customary charges low, the benefits paid on a health care claim can be controlled.

3. Disability, worker's compensation, and unemployment.

plans, usually those written by private insurance companies, patients can choose the doctors and hospital they wish to use for their health care. Some companies use health maintenance organizations, or HMOs. An HMO is a prepaid health care plan in which consumers pay a set fee to receive a full range of medical care from a select group of medical practitioners. A patient must go to the HMO's doctors and health centers to receive health care. HMOs tend to be less expensive than traditional group health plans. Some employers opt for preferred provider organizations, or PPOs. These are health care providers who offer reduced-rate contracts to groups that agree to obtain their medical care through those providers.

Income Insurance

Companies that offer health insurance usually also offer disability insurance to provide income for employees who become disabled through injury or a medical condition. Most policies have a waiting period before an individual is eligible for benefits. State governments provide worker's compensation to provide income to workers who are injured on the job. States also provide unemployment insurance, which guarantees workers who are laid off from jobs income for a certain number of weeks. To receive this compensation, workers must be actively looking for another job. In most states, employers make payments to state-run insurance programs or to private companies for both of these programs.

Quick Check

1. How is life insurance an exception to the rule of insurable interest?
2. How can coinsurance and usual and customary charges affect the amount of benefits paid in a health insurance claim?
3. Name three types of income insurance.

Curriculum Connection English and Communication

Have students survey adult family members and friends to determine if they have insurance through their employer and whether it is traditional insurance, an HMO, a PPO, or other. Encourage students to ask respondents if they are satisfied with their coverage. Suggest that students pool their results and make graphs or charts to display their findings.

Chapter 34 **Summary**

Main Ideas

1. Insurance distributes financial risk or a possible loss among a large number of people, reducing the risk to any one individual.
2. Insurance is sold in the form of a policy, generally by an agent, and for a fee called a premium. Common types include automobile, property, life, health, and income insurance.
3. Automobile insurance includes coverage against bodily injury liability, property damage liability, medical payments, collision, comprehensive damage, and uninsured motorists. Its cost is affected by factors such as sex, age, marital status, cost of the automobile, age of the automobile, and number of miles driven.
4. Renter's and homeowner's policies range in coverage from basic to broad to comprehensive. Costs of property insurance are affected by such factors as payment terms, construction materials, replacement value, deductible, and preventative measures.
5. Life insurance protects the standard of living of a policyholder's survivors. Three basic types of life insurance include term, whole life, and variable life.
6. Health insurance protects against the costs of medical care and treatment. Most people are covered through group health plans provided by their employers.
7. Income insurance protects against loss of income due to disability, unemployment, or work-related injury.
8. Entrepreneur Cecil Hess of MetroLaser worked with university laboratories to lower his costs and strictly followed federal government contractor rules to reduce his risk of failure.
9. Interpreting statistics correctly is important to any business, especially one dealing with risks.

CASE ANALYSIS   Insurance Coverage

In 1992, the Kramers bought a house for $100,000 and a homeowner's policy to cover that amount. Suppose that the value of the house went up by 15 percent a year. If the house was totally destroyed eight years later, what amount would the Kramers receive? Would it cover the loss?

CLOSE

Main Ideas

Main Ideas summarizes the key information in the chapter. It is a useful tool for reinforcement and review.

CASE ANALYSIS

Case Analysis provides a chapter-related case for student analysis and application of decision-making skills.

Answer
They would receive $100,000, which would not cover the loss. Since their house was increasing in value, they should have increased the insured amount on their homeowner's policy proportionally.

QUICK QUIZ

1. Define the terms *policy, premium, deductible,* and *claim.* (Formal written agreement between the insured and the insurer; fee or cost of protection paid to the insurer; amount the insured must pay before the insurance pays the claim; request to insurer to cover financial loss.)
2. What kinds of regulations apply to insurance companies? (State-licensing, premium or rate review)
3. Why would an insurance company check how many teenage drivers have car accidents? (To determine teenage insurance premiums.)
4. Name five kinds of health insurance. (Hospitalization, surgical, major medical, dental and vision, and mental health.)

APPLY

Answers

Use the Language of Business

1. premium; 2. insured; 3. policy; 4. insurable interest; 5. insurance; 6. claims; 7. insurer; 8. deductible; 9. proceeds; 10. beneficiary.

Review What You Learned

1. By dividing the cost of a possible loss among a large number of people. Each individual pays a small fee for protection.
2. Automobile, real and personal property, life, health, and income.
3. Bodily injury, property damage liability, medical payments, collision, comprehensive damage, and uninsured motorists.
4. On the number of perils, or risks, covered by your policy.
5. To maintain the standard of living of the surviving dependents; term insurance, whole life insurance, and variable life insurance.
6. Many factors influence the cost of insurance premiums, and costs vary among insurance providers according to these factors.
7. Most people obtain group health insurance through their employers; private insurers, HMOs, and PPOs.
8. Take advantage of disability insurance, worker's compensation, or unemployment insurance funded by their employers.
9. MetroLaser worked with universities and other clients who had lab space available for MetroLaser's use.
10. Statistics only gain meaning when compared so that changes or trends become clear.

Understand Business Concepts

1. One cannot avoid all economic risks. Even with insurance, the risks still exist, and it's impossible to insure against every possible risk.
2. Renter's insurance covers damage to or loss of someone's personal property within a rented unit or injury to someone within the unit. Property insurance covers damage

Use the Language of Business

Match each term to its definition.

beneficiary   insurer
claims   insured
deductible   policy
insurable interest   premium
insurance   proceeds

1. Amount of money charged by an insurance company for protection for a fixed period of time.
2. Policyholder or person who purchases insurance protection.
3. Financial interest in insured property.
4. Formal written agreement between you and the insurance company.
5. Way of sharing economic risks and the resulting losses.
6. Requests to the insurance company for payments because of financial losses.
7. Insurance company that protects against loss.
8. Amount of damage you must pay for first, before the insurance company pays for any part of the claim.
9. Money paid out to the survivors of a life insurance policyholder.
10. Person who receives money from a life insurance policy.

Review What You Learned

1. How does insurance reduce the risk of financial loss?
2. Name five common types of insurance.
3. What are six basic types of coverage that most automobile insurance policies provide?
4. When you buy renter's or homeowner's insurance, what factors affect the type of policy you choose?
5. Why do most people buy life insurance? What are three common kinds of life insurance?
6. Why is it wise to shop around when buying automobile, renter's, and homeowner's insurance, or life insurance?
7. How do most people obtain health insurance? Name some current kinds of health insurance plans.
8. How do some wage earners minimize the risk of lost income when they are disabled from injury or illness or lose their jobs?
9. How did entrepreneur Cecil Hess avoid the financial risk of purchasing laboratory space and equipment?
10. Why is it important to be able to compare statistics?

Understand Business Concepts

1. Do you think it is possible to avoid all economic risks? Why or why not?
2. Explain how renter's insurance is different from homeowner's insurance.
3. Give examples of ways in which you have an insurable interest in someone or some property.

to or loss of the insured's own real and personal property.
3. If you are financially dependent on someone, as a child is on a parent, you have an insurable interest in that person. Anyone who owns property has an insurable interest in it.
4. A new car has a higher cash value than a used car. Most coverages are for reimbursement for losses, thus they are generally greater for new cars than for older cars. Age, sex, marital status of driver; number of miles driven.
5. With a coinsurance clause, the policyholder shares the cost of a loss. The policyholder would pay 20 percent of the remaining $10,000, or $2000.
6. Hire them to complete different phases of his contract work.
7. Because statistics help them assess risks.

Think Critically

1. Answers will vary, but students should point out that fire trucks will arrive at a closer home more quickly. Homes built of brick and stone will not burn as quickly as those built of wood. Many will agree that since these homes are less costly to insurers, they should have lower premiums.
2. Students should indicate that insurance is not merely protection against financial loss, but it is also protection against the possibility of financial loss. They might include analogies such as carrying an umbrella in case of rain.

4. People who buy new cars are often amazed at the increased cost of their automobile insurance. Why is the cost of insurance for a new car higher than for a used car? What other factors affect the cost of car insurance?

5. Explain how the coinsurance clause in a major-medical insurance policy works: Suppose a policyholder's medical bills came to $11,000, and the policyholder paid $1000 deductible. What would the policyholder's share of the remaining $10,000 be if the policy called for 80/20 coinsurance?

6. Now that MetroLaser is a prime contractor, what can Cecil Hess do to help other entrepreneurs?

7. Why do you think the insurance industry depends on statistics?

Think Critically

1. **Assess.** Property insurance rates are sometimes lower for those people who live near fire stations or who have homes built of brick or stone rather than wood or siding. Is this fair? Explain your answer.

2. **Compare/Contrast.** What could you tell a person about the advantages and disadvantages of having insurance? How would you address the complaint "If I never have an accident, I will have wasted my money"?

Use What You Learned

1. **Group Project.** Work in teams of four. Head one sheet of paper "Risks We Face." Head a second sheet of paper "Ways to Avoid or Reduce Each Risk." On the first sheet, list the risks that you might face in a year. Include the time you spend at school, at home, at work, and in sports and fun activities. On the second sheet, list how you might be able to prevent the risks or reduce the seriousness of the risks. Identify each risk for which your team feels insurance might be worthwhile. Compare your lists with the other groups.

2. **Computer Application.** Compile and print out a spreadsheet related to kinds of insurance, coverages, and premiums.

3. **Skill Reinforcement.** The following paragraph contains statistics from the National Safety Council about accidental deaths in the United States. Arrange them in a table with headings and a title. How could you compare the number of deaths in the categories mathematically? Did comparing the statistics lead to any surprises? What were they? Was it easier to deal with the statistics in a table? Why or why not?

The most common types of accidental death in the United States in 1993 were motor vehicle accidents and falls. In that year, about 42,000 people died in motor vehicles, and 13,500 suffered fatal falls. Poison gases accounted for 700 deaths and other poisons for 6500. Forty-eight hundred, 4000, 2900, and 1600 people died from drowning, fires or burns, ingestion of food or other objects, and firearms mishaps, respectively.

Save your work in your Business Portfolio.

Use the Chapter 34 worksheets in *Student Activity Guide 2* for additional practice and application activities. *Student Activity Guide 2* provides vocabulary exercises, reading comprehension checks, problems, projects, and simulations of business and economic situations. A Teacher's Annotated Edition provides answers.

ASSESS

Portfolio Assessment

The portfolio projects are designed to lead students to develop a collection of their best work to submit to you for assessment. You and your students should decide which projects will be included in their respective Business Portfolios. Refer students to the specific rubric(s) from the *Alternative Assessment Strategies* booklet listed with each of the project notes below. These rubrics will alert students to the criteria you will use to assess their projects.

Chapter Assessment

Use the Chapter 34 Test from the *Test Masters* booklet to evaluate students' understanding of the chapter concepts. An answer key is provided. Or create your own customized test using the *Testmaker* software.

Use What You Learned

1. Place students of similar language proficiencies in the same group. Rubric: Note Taking.

2. Students should include data about insurance losses and premium costs to support their opinion. Students without access to a computer can create a spreadsheet manually with pencil and ruler. Rubric: Charts and Tables.

3.

Year	Motor vehicles	Falls	Poisons (solids, liquids)	Drowning	Fires, burns	Food or objects ingested	Firearms	Poison gases
1993	42,000	13,500	6,500	4,800	4,000	2,900	1,600	700

Students should note that more than three times as many people died in motor vehicle accidents as from falls, and more than ten times as many as died from fires or burns. Answers to the question about surprises will vary, but could include the relatively high number of poisonings by solid or liquid substances or the number of accidental deaths from firearms. Answers to the final question may vary, but most students should find it easier to work with the statistics in a table.

Business Issue

Business Issue

NATIONAL HEALTH CARE

Highlight the Issue

Before students read pages 592–593, have a class discussion about what students know about plans for a national health care system. What would be the advantages? What would be the disadvantages? List students' responses on the board. After students have read the pages have them add to the list.

NATIONAL HEALTH CARE

The cost of medical care in the United States continues to rise, and more than 30 million Americans have no health insurance at all. Should the government provide health care for all Americans?

Pro

The current system of health care doesn't work. Although many Americans get health insurance through their employers, more than 30 million Americans have no health insurance at all. A serious illness can wipe out a family's savings.

When health care is tied to employment, a number of problems arise. For example, if you change jobs, your insurance plan will probably also change and you may be denied coverage for a "preexisting condition." If you lose your job, it's even worse. You lose your health care—at a time when you can least afford to pay for your own insurance or medical bills. A national health system would guarantee that all Americans have health care.

A national health care system would also help control costs. The United States already spends more on health care than many countries that offer universal health care. In 1993, health care cost the United States $884.2 billion, or 13.9 percent of the gross domestic product, and still millions of Americans lacked health care. Other industrial nations with national health care plans spend only 6.6 to 10 percent of their GDP on medical care.

Under a national health care system, the government could set limits on what it would pay providers, keeping costs down. Administrative costs would also be reduced, since there would just be one health care system for all Americans. The U.S. General Accounting Office estimates that a national health system could save the U.S. $67 billion each year.

National health care systems have worked well in other countries such as Canada, France, Germany, and Sweden. In these countries, everyone has access to health care, rich or poor. These countries' health care plans offer people their choice of doctors, high quality care, and advanced medical technology.

A national health care system would make sure that all Americans have access to health care. A 1993 New York Times/CBS poll found that 59 percent of Americans want a national health care system like Canada's, which offers equal quality of care for all—not just for those who can pay.

Extend the Issue

Have groups research the national health system of one of the countries mentioned in the text. Suggest that groups consider the cost of the program to taxpayers, the number of people without access to health care, and the quality of care. Have each group present a profile of their country's national health care system to the class. As a class, compare the countries' health care systems with the private health care system of the United States.

Con

America's private, market-based health care system provides Americans with the most advanced health care in the world. Competition among health care providers, drug companies, and insurance companies encourages innovation and high quality care. The government should provide health care for those Americans who are uninsured, but leave the rest of the health care industry alone.

The government has a dismal record as a provider of health services. Two current government medical programs, Medicaid and Medicare, are inefficient and costly. As former Secretary of Health and Human Services Dr. Louis W. Sullivan said, national health insurance would mean "combining the efficiency of the Postal Service with the compassion of the IRS."

Furthermore, our country can't afford a national health system. The government already spends more than it collects in taxes. It would take a huge tax increase to pay for a national health plan and balance the budget. In addition, if health care is included in the federal budget, it will be subject to budget cuts whenever the government tries to reduce spending. These cuts will be reflected in poorer quality health care.

Government-run health care just doesn't work. With national health care, people don't get to choose their doctors, they may not have access to the latest medical treatments, and they may have to wait a long time for care. In Canada, for example, patients can even die before their turn for an operation comes. Countries like Great Britain that had national health care plans are switching back to private health care options.

The costs of the current health care system help make sure that health resources are not overused, but used wisely. If everyone has access to free health care, the system will be overburdened.

The United States currently has an excellent health care system and should not abandon it for a government-run program that would provide poorer quality health care.

Update the Issue

Have interested students search current publications for information about the United States' plans for a national health care system. What seems to be the largest concern about implementing a national health care system? Have students also look for information about related issues such as control of health care costs and other reforms of the health care system. Students may present their findings in a written or oral report.

Unit 11 Working in the Global Economy

Chapter	Learning Objectives
35 **Competing in the World Labor Market** pp. 596–611	• Describe two kinds of job classifications based on end products. • Identify and describe four kinds of occupational groups. • Identify the issues and activities associated with a union contract. • Discuss factors of diversity in the world labor market. • Describe how jobs in the communications, entertainment, and arts industries fit into the world labor market.
36 **Job Considerations** pp. 612–629	• Describe different forms of compensation. • Identify some of the common benefits offered to employees. • Explain why it is important to consider working conditions when choosing a job. • Explain how economic trends affect employment. • Describe CD-ROMs and explain how they work. • Describe how comparing statistics can help you analyze a job offer.

Business Issue: Immigration and the Economy, pp. 630–631

National Standards for Business Education*	Chapter Highlights			
	Focus on Features	Building Business Skills	Visual Learning	Case Analysis
CD: I A; *BL:* III B; *COMM:* I A, II A; *EPF:* XV; *MGMT:* V G, X	Careers: Communications, Entertainment, and the Arts, p. 600	Employability: Recognizing Diversity, p. 604	Workers in Goods Producing and Service Producing Industries, p. 599 Union Membership as a Percent of Total Labor Force, p. 607	Organized Labor, p. 609
COMP: V; *EPF:* XV; *IS:* I; *MGMT:* V E	Technology: CD-ROMs, p. 616	Math: Comparing Statistics, p. 620	The Minimum Wage, p. 615 Average Employer Costs for Employee Compensation, p. 618 Percentage of Full-Time Employees Participating in Selected Benefits, p. 623	Employment Issues, p. 627

* Level 3 Performance Expectations: Computation (COMP), Economics and Personal Finance (EPF); Entrepreneurship Education (EE), IS (Information Systems), Management (MGMT). See page T14 for all 12 content areas.

Unit 11

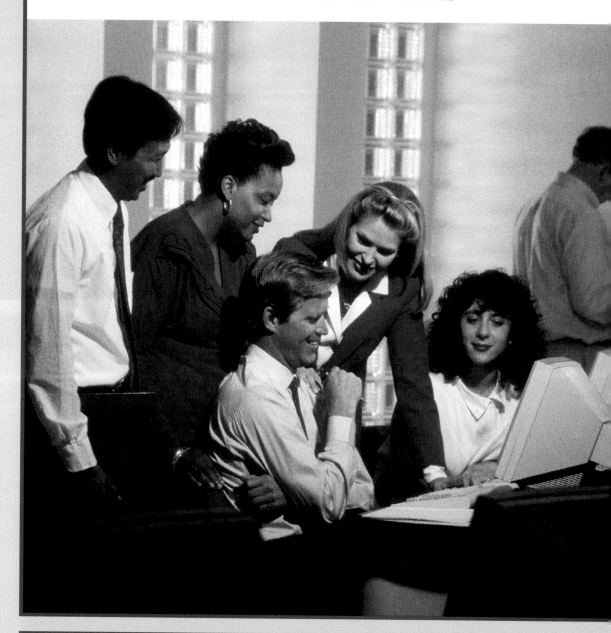

UNIT 11 COOPERATIVE LEARNING PROJECT

Group Discussion Activity

Preparation: Provide career handbooks and related resources for students to use for their research. Pair students who have expressed interest in similar careers. For each pair of students, photocopy and distribute a copy of BLM 22 from the *Cooperative Learning Strategies* booklet. This project will take approximately three class periods.

Working in the Global Economy

This unit discusses the world of work in an international economy. The first chapter discusses the various types and levels of work, from upper-level management to entry-level jobs. The second chapter discusses benefits included in a compensation package, such as pensions, profit-sharing, and insurance.

Look Ahead
Explain to students that the labor market is frequently divided into two sectors: the occupations that produce goods and those that provide services. Occupations can be further classified as white-collar, blue-collar, service, and farm or agricultural occupations. It is important to find a job that fulfills personal needs as well as financial needs. In addition to a salary or wages, jobseekers should consider a company's working conditions and the benefits it offers.

595

Guidelines: Have students work in pairs to research careers that interest them. Direct students to use BLM 22 to organize the information they find. Students can place their completed BLMs in a classroom handbook about different careers.

FOCUS

Introduce the Chapter

Major Concepts
- The Labor Market
- Occupational Profiles
- Organized Labor
- An Overview of the Labor Market

Introduce the Topic
Discuss with students the ways in which the American labor force is changing. What jobs exist now that didn't exist when their grandparents were teenagers? Ask students what kinds of ideas they had about careers when they were in fourth or fifth grade and ask them to discuss how and why those ideas have changed.

Use Business Terms
Have students look at the Business Terms and brainstorm associations with each term. Ask them where they have heard or seen the term used. Reinforce correct associations. Advise students to note the meanings of the terms as they read the chapter.

USE VISUALS

Explain that manufacturing today uses more high-tech methods than were used in the past. Ask: In what way do you think the labor market has been affected by this change? (Possible answer: The level of education or training needed to perform the jobs has increased.)

CHAPTER
35

Business terms

labor market

apprentice

labor union

collective bargaining

strike

arbitration

mediator

turnover

596

CHAPTER 35 RESOURCES

Instructional Resources

Lesson Plan for Chapter 35

Teaching Transparencies 35-1, 35-2

Strategies and Worksheets for Teaching Transparencies 35-1, 35-2

Enrichment Masters 35-1, 35-2

Student Activity Guide 2–TAE for Chapter 35

Test Master for Chapter 35

Alternative Assessment Strategies

Math Skills Review

International Business Strategies

Cooperative Learning Strategies

Communication Skills Review

Ethics in Business Strategies

Competing in the World Labor Market

Learning objectives

After completing this chapter, you will be able to:
- Describe two kinds of job classifications based on end products.
- Identify and describe four kinds of occupational groups.
- Identify the issues and activities associated with a union contract.
- Discuss factors of diversity in the world labor market.
- Describe how jobs in the communications, entertainment, and arts industries fit into the world labor market.

Consider what you know

- The factors of production include natural resources, capital resources, human resources, and entrepreneurial know-how.

Consider what you want to know

- Where do businesses go to find the workers they need?
- What kinds of occupations exist in the labor market?
- What is covered in a union contract?
- Why does the labor market change?
- What kinds of occupations are available in the global communications, entertainment, and arts industries?
- What are some ways to deal with diversity in the workplace?

Consider how to use what you learn

- As you work with this chapter, pay particular attention to the employment and labor reports in the paper and on television news programs. See if you can identify the types of jobs being discussed in the media.

Multimedia Resources

Technology Resource Guide

Distance Learning Guide

Internet Resource Guide

Professional Resources

School-to-Work/Tech Prep Strategies

Instructional Poster

Spanish Resources

Testmaker Software for Chapter 35

The Wall Street Journal Video Series
Video & Activities for Chapter 35

Business and Marketing Computer Applications—An Integrated Software Simulation Using Microsoft Works

Stocktracker—A Stock Market Software Simulation

Where's the Dough? Board Game

Motivate the Learning

Learning Objectives
Point out to students that the learning objectives show what they will learn in the chapter. Tell students to keep these objectives in mind as they work through the chapter. Note that the last two objectives listed refer to the Focus on Careers feature and the Building Business Skills feature.

Consider What You Know
Review briefly the factors of production that societies use to produce goods and services. Emphasize the human resources—labor—factor. Also remind students that the principles of supply/demand also apply to the labor market.

Consider What You Want to Know
Have students keep the listed questions in mind as they preview the chapter by quickly paging through it, looking at the pictures, and reading the section headings and figure titles.

Consider How to Use What You Learn
Explain to students that at the end of the chapter they will develop projects related to various occupational categories. Suggest that as they read the chapter, students try to identify the occupational category for jobs held by people they know.

TEACH

Business Connection

According to projections made by the U.S. Bureau of Labor Statistics, jobs in the health-care industry will increase far faster than jobs in most other fields throughout the 1990s and into the early years of the next century. Demand will be greatest for health-care network managers, nurses, nurse-practitioners, home health aides, and physical therapists. Health-care workers of the twenty-first century must acknowledge the need to control costs and will need to keep up with changing medical technology.

Develop Concepts

The Labor Market

Ask a volunteer to remind the class of the difference between a good and a service. (A good is something tangible; a service is something intangible, like a haircut.) Then have students name jobs held by people they know. Record the jobs on the board or a transparency. Help students classify the jobs according to whether they are goods-producing occupations or service occupations.

TEACHING TIP

Have students brainstorm a list of jobs that have grown as a result of people's increased demands for services. Post the list and encourage students to add to the list as they study the chapter.

Businesses require the assistance of a variety of workers who can bring to their work an array of aptitudes, abilities, skills, education, and training. Careful selection among the available pool of qualified workers will ensure that a company will have the right human resources when it needs them.

THE LABOR MARKET

Business finds the workers it needs in the **labor market,** which includes the number of job seekers and the number of job openings. The labor market changes over time. Population growth, advances in technology, and business trends affect the labor market. Business, government, and citizens all have a responsibility to understand and anticipate the needs of the labor market.

One way to understand the market is to look at the end product produced by various occupations. Some workers are involved in producing goods, and others are involved in providing services. These two broad categories can help organize our view of the labor market.

Goods-Producing Occupations

The workers employed in an automobile plant produce goods. Carpenters, construction workers, steelworkers, and bakers also produce goods. The amount of goods produced in the United States generally increases from year to year. However, because of improvements and automation in manufacturing processes, the total number of jobs in goods-producing occupations has not increased very rapidly in the United States since the 1980s. Also, many goods-producing jobs that were in the United States have been moved to other countries because it is less costly to produce them elsewhere.

Service Occupations

Some workers provide services. The administrative assistant, teacher, lawyer, airline pilot, and police officer all provide services. The automobile mechanic, accountant, nurse, social worker, and dry cleaner also provide services. As you can see in Figure 35-1 on page 599, the number of jobs in the service areas has increased rapidly in the past two decades and will continue

GLOBAL VIEW

After the dissolution of the Soviet Union, skilled workers from Eastern Europe migrated to Germany, France, Italy, and Great Britain. These displaced workers found jobs in the hospitality, machine-building, construction, agriculture, and computer soft- ware industries. These workers contributed to the welfare of their families and gained firsthand knowledge of a market economy.

Cooperative Learning Categorizing

Divide the class into groups and give each group a section of the local help wanted ads. Have each group analyze its section of the ads to determine the proportion of jobs available that are service jobs and the proportion available that are goods-producing jobs. Have each group report its findings to the class. As a class, discuss whether the findings about jobs in your area correspond to the national statistics discussed in the chapter for service and goods-producing occupations.

Refer to the *Cooperative Learning Strategies* booklet for additional cooperative learning strategies.

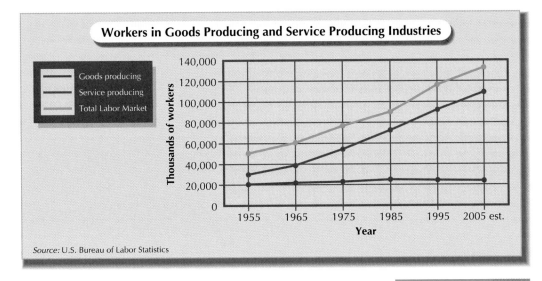

Workers in Goods Producing and Service Producing Industries

Goods producing
Service producing
Total Labor Market

Thousands of workers

140,000
120,000
100,000
80,000
60,000
40,000
20,000
0

1955   1965   1975   1985   1995   2005 est.

Year

Source: U.S. Bureau of Labor Statistics

FIGURE 35-1

This graph illustrates the increase in service-producing and goods-producing jobs during the second half of this century. Which type of job opportunity has increased as quickly as the total number of jobs?

to increase. Service occupations account for more than 75 percent of the workforce today and are projected to account for 82 percent of the labor force by the year 2005.

One reason the number of service-producing jobs is increasing is that individuals and businesses are spending a larger part of their income on services. In 1940, approximately 37 cents of each consumer dollar was spent for services. By the mid-1990s, this amount had increased to more than 56 cents of each dollar. Health services, social services, and computer and data processing services lead the service industry in growth. Another boom in service occupations is occurring in travel and recreational services. People in this country are traveling more than they ever have—by car, plane, recreational vehicle, and even bicycle. They are also eating out more, at restaurants and fast-food places. One result of this trend has been the steady growth in service jobs such as chefs, park service workers, reservations clerks, lifeguards, and hotel housekeepers.

Quick Check

1. What two categories of industries can be used to describe the entire labor market?
2. Which category of the labor market is rapidly increasing? Why?

Reteaching Strategy

Give students the following list of jobs and have them classify them according to whether they are service jobs or goods-producing jobs. Movie star (service), police detective (service), lumberjack (goods producing), ambulance driver (service), high-school teacher (service), journalist (service), coal miner (goods producing), and fishery worker (goods producing).

FOCUS ON **Careers**

Discuss

Discuss with students the kinds of skills people in communications, entertainment, and the arts use. Ask students what courses in school could help them prepare for entry-level jobs in communications, entertainment, and the arts. Which of those mentioned are service jobs? Which are goods-producing jobs? How do people advance in such jobs?

Communications, Entertainment, and the Arts

People who work in communications, entertainment, and the arts have the task of forging links between individuals and the world around them. These workers in the media help bring us information we need to manage our businesses and our lives. Some do this by presenting print and pictures on paper in ways that help us "get the message." Others use the sounds and visual images of radio, television, and film to tell us what we need to know. Communicating information is only part of what these workers do for us: They are also responsible for the entertainment that renews us and the art that gives us a perspective on ourselves, our culture, and our history.

Some workers contribute from behind the scenes in producing and processing videos, live shows, recordings, print materials, and photographs. Others connect with us directly as they perform live on stage or before cameras. Still others interact with us by answering our requests for information in museums or

HELP WANTED

FILM PROCESSING TECHNICIAN

Use your acute vision and color perception to build a career! Chromor Film Labs will train the right high school graduate to be a film processing technician. Learn to run processing machines and maintain chemicals in them. Duties include developing/printing client pictures, making duplicates of photos and slides.

Must have good mechanical, manual skills, be able to follow directions exactly, treat client film as your own.

Develop Concepts

Occupational Profiles

Help students understand that there are different ways of classifying occupations. Point out that many "white-collar jobs" would also be classified as service jobs. Discuss with students the pros and cons of the various ways of classifying jobs. Which method is the most descriptive? How do the different ways of classifying jobs overlap?

OCCUPATIONAL PROFILES

Another way of describing or classifying the labor market involves describing the workers and the work they perform. The types of workers include white-collar workers, who work with other people or the processing of information; blue-collar workers, who work primarily with machinery and equipment; service workers, such as firefighters and hairstylists, who provide personal services; and farm and agriculture workers.

White-Collar Workers

For the most part, white-collar workers are involved in producing services. Opportunities for white-collar workers are likely to grow in the future. White-collar jobs have been increasingly affected by business's use of computers and other types of electronic equipment. Many of these jobs require specialized skills to operate such equipment. For example, many businesses keep all their financial records and product information on computers, so it is especially important for employees

Making Connections ⏩ Performance Appraisals

Explain to students that a performance appraisal is an evaluation of how well an employee performs his or her job. Distribute photocopies of Enrichment Master 35-1 to show students an example of a typical performance appraisal. Discuss some of the jobs described in the Focus on Careers feature above. Then ask students to think of how an employer might evaluate, for example, a film processing technician's work performance. Encourage students to think of other ways they could evaluate aspects of the jobs described in the feature.

shepherding us through theme parks.

Although jobs in this area often have a reputation for glamour, the entry-level positions may require extended hours of hard, unexciting work. Camera operators often start out servicing equipment. Apprentice photographers set up lights. Production assistants in TV do anything that needs doing.

Most beginning jobs in this area are open to people with a high school diploma. Media jobs make use of technical devices, so math and science skills, manual dexterity, and experience with the appropriate

devices—including computers—are necessary. Workers involved in creating photographs, films, and printed pages need an aptitude and training in the visual arts. Aspiring performers, of course, should have experience in their chosen arts. Reliability and the ability to work as a team member are required.

Here are four entry-level jobs.

to know how to use the computer efficiently. There are four basic types of white-collar workers.

Administrative Support Smooth business operation requires a variety of administrative support jobs such as secretary, administrative assistant, bookkeeper, and receptionist. Almost every business, industry, government, medical, and legal concern employs some type of administrative support worker. These workers prepare and maintain records, analyze data, and may indirectly or directly deal with customers. Some administrative support workers operate machines such as word processors, computers, facsimile machines, and copiers. Other workers, such as receptionists, have "people-type" jobs. Most administrative support jobs require a high school diploma, and many require some additional training.

Technical and Professional Lawyers, teachers, computer programmers, engineers, journalists, accountants, actors, and doctors are among the workers included in the technical and professional category. Businesses rely on these workers to express ideas, analyze data, and even create new information. Technical and professional workers often have a lot of contact

Follow Through

Virtually none of the jobs available today in communications, entertainment, and the arts goes unaided by technology. Invite interested students to research a job in communications, entertainment, and the arts that interests them and report on how technology is used in that job. Students may want to compare and contrast the way the job was done prior to the introduction of technological aids.

Business Brief

Rapid technological change is responsible for a 55 percent projected increase in jobs for computer programmers by 2005. Jobs for technicians who come to the rescue when fax machines, computers, and other high-tech equipment temporarily fail are expected to increase by 60 percent by 2005.

Enrichment Strategy

Invite interested students to read an autobiography or biography of a person whose occupation interests them. Ask students to write a 250-word book review. At the end of the review, have students write a summary paragraph explaining whether the book encouraged them to pursue a career in that field or if the book helped them decide that the career might not suit them after all.

Inform students that some people classify jobs according to the level of training or education the job requires. *Unskilled* jobs, for instance, are those that require no specialized training beyond a basic high school education. Examples would include fruit picker or ditch digger. *Semiskilled* jobs are those that require some formal training. Photocopy machine operators and short-order cooks are semiskilled workers. *Skilled* jobs belong to people who have learned a trade or gone to a vocational school, for example, an electrician or a computer technician. *Professional* jobs are those that require at least a college degree and often an advanced degree. Doctors and teachers are professionals.

The nature of blue-collar jobs in manufacturing plants has changed dramatically over the years. Several decades ago, factory workers in an auto plant performed tedious, repetitive tasks and risked injury or death from operating heavy equipment. Today, hydraulic tools lift cars and car parts, while human workers use teamwork and their intellectual powers to solve problems and improve production processes.

F.Y.I.

Years ago people who held certain jobs, particularly in offices, wore white shirts or blouses. The term *white-collar worker* became popular to describe people who worked in offices. The term *blue-collar worker* started in much the same way. Most factory workers, construction workers, and craft workers wore blue shirts, coveralls, or overalls at work.

with other people in the course of their jobs. Jobs in this category cover a wide range of skills and knowledge. An associate degree is required for some, a college degree for many, and graduate study after college for others.

Executive, Administrative, and Managerial Managers, administrators, company executives, school principals, office managers, and small-business owners are among the workers in this category. Analyzing data, coming up with new ideas, making judgments, and dealing with people are important tasks in this occupational group. A college, or even a graduate, degree may be required for high-level managerial jobs.

Clerical and Sales Retail selling and telephone selling are variations of the same occupation. Selling goods and services is the primary responsibility of this white-collar group. Developing new ideas for selling goods and services may be important. In some cases, little formal training is required. However, four years of college can add a great deal to one's selling techniques and provide the background for promotion to management positions.

Blue-Collar Workers

Most goods-producing businesses rely on blue-collar workers to do the physical work needed to produce the goods. Although modern machines and equipment have reduced the amount of physical work required in many cases, working with or operating machinery may still be a large part of a blue-collar worker's job. Approximately 25 to 30 percent of the jobs in the United States are blue-collar jobs, and business's need for these occupations is not increasing as rapidly as the need for service occupations.

Operators, Production and Processing Workers Road building, mining, and construction businesses employ workers to operate cranes, bulldozers, compressors, road pavers, and other similar equipment. People in these jobs are often referred to as heavy-machinery operators or engineers. Manufacturing businesses depend on production and processing workers to use specialized machinery and equipment to produce the desired product. Although applicants may need only a high school education, a fair amount of on-the-job training may be required for some of these jobs. Operators and production workers are considered semiskilled workers. Overall, employment of these workers is decreasing although production output remains nearly steady.

Global Perspective

Asian countries such as Hong Kong, Indonesia, Malaysia, Singapore, South Korea, Taiwan, and Thailand are high-productivity manufacturing countries. Assign groups one of the countries listed, and have them find out how the country develops policies that stimulate industrial productivity. Groups may explore the impact wage rates, technology, education, and population growth have had in shaping the country's workforce and economic success. Ask groups to present their findings to the class.

Refer to the *International Business Strategies* booklet for additional strategies and activities.

Construction, Trades, and Crafts Carpenters, painters, plumbers, bricklayers, electricians, and mechanics are among those included in the crafts and skilled trades category. *Crafts and trades* are old terms used to describe certain kinds of highly skilled or trained workers. For instance, a young person might become an **apprentice,** a person in training for a trade or craft. Years later the apprentice might become a journeyman, or trained worker. The best and most experienced journeymen become master craftsmen.

Nonfarm Laborers Businesses rely on laborers to complete tasks such as loading or unloading trucks, ships, or trains. Some laborers work in stockrooms and warehouses. Very little training, either educational or on-the-job, is usually required. In a matter of hours or days, any skills required can be learned. Many unskilled laborers' jobs have been eliminated due to automation. Need for this type of work is not likely to grow in the future.

Service Workers

This category includes occupations concerned with tasks in and around private households, serving individuals in institutions and commercial establishments, and protecting the public against crime, fire, and accident. For example, gardeners, police, firefighters, pastry chefs, day-care attendants, hairstylists, airline attendants, and food and beverage servers are

Among those employed in various blue-collar occupations, skilled trade workers may experience the least decline in overall employment. Why might this be so?

Learning Activity
Invite a local tradesperson or craftsperson to come in and speak to the class. Ask the person to discuss how he or she learned the skills needed for the job and how long it took to master the skills. Instruct students to prepare some questions for the speaker beforehand.

Business Brief

According to the U.S. Bureau of Labor Statistics, the number of jobs in construction, trades, and crafts is expected to experience moderate growth between 1990 and 2005.

Carpenters	14–24%
Electricians	25–34%
Painters, paperhangers	14–24%
Plumbers, pipefitters	14–24%
Bricklayers, stonemasons	14–24%

USE VISUALS

Ask students to name some of the ways blue-collar workers gain the skills they need to do their jobs. (They might become apprentices or they might get trained on the job.)
Answer to caption: Skilled trade workers are least likely to be replaced by automation.

Reteaching Strategy

Distribute photocopies of Enrichment Master 35-2, which shows some of the jobs available in the four basic occupational profiles discussed in the section, as well as some other jobs and categories. Then have each student write the name of a job that interests him or her on a slip of paper. Collect the slips. Read off the jobs and have the class categorize each one according to occupational profile.

Building Business Skills

Model

Have students think of a situation in which they were working with a group. On a separate piece of paper have them describe how each of the guidelines on page 605 was observed or not observed as the group did the project. Invite volunteers to read their explanations to the class.

TEACHING TIP

Point out to students that although only about 3 percent of the population actually works directly in the agricultural sector, the number of businesses that exist in order to transport, process, distribute, and sell agricultural products is much larger. Other businesses operate in order to supply farms with goods and services, credit, and information. Have students brainstorm a list of businesses indirectly involved in agriculture. (Trucking companies, frozen-food processing plants, grocery stores, banks, farm equipment manufacturers, and so forth.)

Business Brief

Approximately half of the land in the United States is farmland. Despite the fact that only 3 out of 100 workers work on a farm, the United States produces 25 percent of the world's beef and 15 percent of the world's milk, grain, and eggs. The leading agricultural states are California, Texas, Iowa, Nebraska, and Illinois.

EMPLOYABILITY
Recognizing Diversity

Explanation

Diversity is a distinguishing feature of the modern labor force. You're probably well aware by now that no two people are alike. You already have encountered a variety of backgrounds, skills, and viewpoints in your fellow students. When you enter the labor force, you'll find even greater diversity among your coworkers. Your success on the job will depend on how effectively you work with and for people very different from yourself.

Your response to another employee should be based on that individual's words and behavior, not on oversimplified generalizations about his or her ethnic, racial, or gender group. On the other hand, if you find you're having difficulty understanding someone from a different background, take the time to learn where he or she "is coming from." Don't depend on the opinions of others—talk directly to the person about his or her upbringing, education, experiences, and beliefs. Share similar information about yourself. You may find you have more in common than you thought.

Diversity in the workplace also means differences in skills, work habits, and approaches to tasks. Several people with similar assignments may carry them out in members of this occupational group. The amount of general education needed for these occupations varies. However, nearly all of these occupations require some specialized training.

Farm and Agriculture Workers

Farm workers are responsible for tilling the soil and for planting, fertilizing, cultivating, and harvesting crops. They also care for livestock. In addition, farm workers may be involved in planning which crops to plant, managing farm finances, and marketing farm products.

Large farms need many workers to work with tools and equipment. Like big businesses in other areas, big farms need managers and workers who can examine data, plan better methods of producing things, and control operations such as fertilizing and irrigating. These large farms now account for the majority of farm workers in the United States. The industry is now often called "agribusiness."

Better equipment and higher crop yields have combined to decrease the number of farm jobs. In the 1970s, about 4 out of every 100 people in the United States worked in agriculture.

Meeting Student Diversity

Students with difficulty categorizing information will find it helpful to draw a chart comparing the different types of occupations discussed in this section. Suggest that students include three to five examples of specific jobs included in each category.

GUIDELINES FOR RECOGNIZING DIVERSITY

1. Recognize that everyone is different and that people have a right to their differences.
2. Judge people as individuals, not according to stereotypical images of groups they belong to.
3. Communicate with your coworkers to understand your differences and find common ground.
4. Overlook differences that aren't relevant to the job.
5. Adapt your workstyle to your coworkers if it helps get the job done.
6. When assigning tasks, take into account the different skills and talents of others.
7. Let workers work "their own way" as long as they get the right results.

different ways. If you are a supervisor, concentrate on results. There is often more than one way to do a job. Trying to make everyone conform to your methods may hurt efficiency. If a worker's results are unsatisfactory, however, help that person improve. Successful managers make the most of their workers' distinctive skills and aptitudes.

Practice

Listed here are some guidelines to help you recognize diversity in an active and positive way. On a separate sheet of paper, give an example from your own experience in school, your neighborhood, or a job related to each guideline.

Practice

Allow students to work in groups to complete the assignment. Students may share experiences they have encountered and work together to write responses. (Students' descriptions will vary but should reflect the guidelines.)

Now about 3 out of every 100 people work in agriculture—a decrease of 25 percent. Because of increased automation, the percentage of farm workers in the work force is expected to decrease further.

Quick Check

1. Name four basic occupational profiles. In which group would your principal fit?
2. What is an apprentice?
3. Why are nonfarm laborers referred to as unskilled?

ORGANIZED LABOR

Some workers employed in the same types of jobs may be members of a **labor union,** an organization that is formed specifically to represent the workers. A *local* is a small branch union, generally formed by a majority vote of the workers in a company. Most local unions, in turn, are affiliated with a national union.

Business & HISTORY

Craft and merchant guilds were associations formed in western Europe between the eleventh and the seventeenth centuries. Craft guilds were formed to allow workers such as weavers or potters to gain local control over their craft. The guild set standards for the quality and price of the product. The guild also protected the craft from competition.

Global Perspective

Organize students into groups to research organized labor in two countries of their own choice. Have them make a chart comparing the state of organized labor in the two countries. A volunteer from each group should explain the group's chart to the class.

Refer to the *International Business Strategies* booklet for additional strategies and activities.

Quick Check Answers

1. White-collar, blue-collar, service, and farm and agricultural workers. White collar.
2. A person in training for a trade or craft.
3. Their jobs don't require much training.

Develop Concepts

Organized Labor

Provide students with the following historical background to help them better understand why labor unions were organized. Working conditions in factories in the late 1800s were dangerous, pay was low, and job security was nonexistent. Union organizers promoted the idea of workers joining forces to negotiate for better conditions. Factory owners resisted and sometimes violently repressed attempts at organization. It wasn't until the 1930s that legislation guaranteed workers the right to organize and negotiate with employers.

Learning Activity

Have students choose one of the following federal laws that regulate organized labor: the Norris-LaGuardia Act, the Wagner Act, the Taft-Hartley Act, or the Landrum-Griffin Act. Ask students to research and write a brief report that explains the reasons the law was passed, the main points of the law, and the effects the law had on union workers and the economy.

Business Brief

One of the most famous strikes in American history was the Pullman Strike of 1894. The strike started in response to a 25 percent reduction in wages for employees of the Pullman Palace Car Company, a manufacturer and operator of railway cars. The strike was initiated by the American Railway Union (ARU) when the Pullman Company refused arbitration with the union. The strike began in Chicago and soon spread to many areas of the country. Because the strike was disrupting national mail delivery, President Grover Cleveland sent federal troops to Chicago to stop the strike. Violence broke out when the troops arrived; property was destroyed and strikers were arrested. The federal government halted the strike within a week.

Unions may engage in a variety of work-related and social activities. Probably the most important union activity is **collective bargaining.** During collective bargaining, representatives of the union and management come together to negotiate a contract. The contract identifies issues of interest to both the union and management, such as pay, working conditions, and hours of work.

A primary goal of discussions about a contract is to reach agreements that both business management and workers will accept. The average contract length is three years. When a contract nears its end, labor and management begin to talk about extending the contract for another three years. The provisions in the contract are reviewed, some are changed, others are removed, and new ones may be added.

If the contract runs out before a new agreement is reached, unions sometimes call for a work stoppage, or **strike.** Strikes are usually a last resort. They can be effective, but they can also hurt the workers as well as the business. If no products are made because of a strike, then none are sold, and no profit is made. The workers are hurt because they do not receive wages. Workers on strike may, however, receive money from a strike fund set up by the union. The strike fund is financed by the union dues the workers pay. However, the payments to striking workers are usually less than the workers' wages.

When business management and organized labor want a contract but cannot seem to agree on the terms, they may try another procedure. They may try **arbitration,** submitting the disagreement or differences to a third party who acts as a kind of judge. The arbitrator must be approved by both parties. More importantly, both business management and organized labor must agree in advance to accept the provisions decided upon during arbitration.

Another procedure may be used instead of arbitration. It involves bringing in a third party, a **mediator,** who listens to both sides and then suggests what the provisions of the contract should be. Neither side, however, has to accept the mediator's judgment on the contract. Occasionally, federal or state governments are called upon to provide mediation or arbitration services.

Traditionally, most union members held manufacturing jobs and other blue-collar occupations. As the number of such jobs decreases, the number of workers belonging to industrial unions is also decreasing. Figure 35-2 on page 607 shows how the percentage of the labor force made up of union members has decreased since 1930.

Today, the growth area for jobs in the United States is in the service sector. Unions have made some inroads in organizing

Enrichment Strategy

Invite a union organizer to speak to the class about unions. Ask the speaker to describe the history of the organized labor movement, the benefits provided, the membership dues, and the value of negotiating as a group rather than as an individual. Also discuss national affiliations of unions.

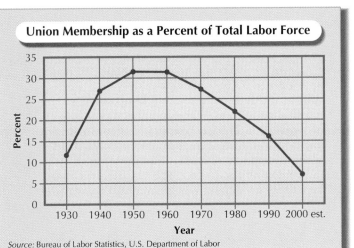

FIGURE 35-2

Union Membership as a Percent of Total Labor Force

Source: Bureau of Labor Statistics, U.S. Department of Labor

The number of people in the workforce has increased since 1930, but union membership has not kept up with this growth. During what 10-year period was union membership at its peak?

USE VISUALS

Use the graph shown in Figure 35-2 to help students visualize the changes that have occurred in union membership over the years. Ask students what union membership is estimated to be for the year 2000. (About 7 percent.)
Answer to caption: 1951–1960.

USE TRANSPARENCIES

Use Teaching Transparency 35-2 and its corresponding strategies and worksheet from the *Teaching Transparency Strategies and Worksheets* booklet to help students evaluate trends in union membership in the United States. Verify student worksheets using the Answer Key.

service workers in government, teaching, food service, and offices. Even so, increases in union membership in service jobs have not kept up with increases in the number of jobs in service areas that have been created.

Quick Check

1. Define each of the following: *labor union, strike, arbitration, mediator.*
2. What are three common issues that might be part of a labor-management contract negotiation?
3. Give three reasons why unions have lost membership in the last few years.

AN OVERVIEW OF THE LABOR MARKET

The outlook for any occupation is affected by a number of factors. Demand, competition, job turnover, and location affect the job market. To be prepared to enter the future labor market, a worker should learn about the kinds of goods and services that will be in demand in the future. Without demand, career opportunities decrease. In the early part of this century, for example, the demand for blacksmiths dropped sharply after the automobile was introduced. At the same time, however, the

Quick Check Answers

1. A union or a number of unions; a work stoppage; submitting a disagreement or difference to a third party who acts as judge; a third party who listens to both sides of a dispute and suggests a solution.
2. Pay, working conditions, or hours of work.
3. The number of manufacturing jobs has decreased; unions have not widely organized service workers; and increases in union membership in service jobs have not kept up with increases in the number of jobs created.

Cooperative Learning   **Debate (Pro/Con)**

Have groups of students debate the following question: "Unions have improved working conditions for employees, but have they outlived their usefulness?" Ask groups to take a position on the topic, gather evidence, develop and support their argument with examples from the past and present, and evaluate the outcome of the debate.

Refer to the *Cooperative Learning Strategies* booklet for additional cooperative learning strategies.

CHAPTER 35

Develop Concepts

An Overview of the Labor Market

Job growth and population growth usually go hand in hand, that is, increases in the number of jobs available in an area usually bring an increase in population. Assign groups a region of the United States. Have teams write to the U.S. Bureau of the Census and the U.S. Bureau of Labor Statistics to request information about trends in population and employment for their assigned region. Have each team display its findings and statistics on a map of the United States.

Business Brief

Twelve out of the twenty metropolitan areas forecast to have the largest gains in employment between 1995 and 2005 are in the South—in Florida, the Carolinas, and Texas. Six are located in the West and Southwest—in Nevada, Arizona, and California.

Quick Check Answers

1. Demand, competition, turnover, and location.
2. The number of people who leave one job for another; advancement, retirement, and dismissal.
3. Increased education can allow a worker to choose from a wider variety of occupations, to advance further in any given occupation, and to increase his or her income.

---

automobile created a demand for mechanics because people needed to have their cars fixed. Today, the demand for instant access to information has created a need for workers who supply, record, process, and distribute information. It has also created a need for workers who can maintain the machines and equipment used in these activities.

Another factor is the amount of competition within a particular field. In some cases, the competition for jobs may come from workers in another country. For example, workers in Pacific Rim countries such as Malaysia, South Korea, and Taiwan now design and manufacture most of the televisions sold in the United States. In fact, the last U.S.-owned business to make televisions, Zenith, was bought by a Korean company in 1995. In some cases, the competition is keen because so many people want to enter a field. That is often true, for example, with writers, artists, and entertainers. For this reason, it may become difficult to obtain steady work in these fields.

A third factor affecting the number of job openings in any one year is the turnover in a field. **Turnover** is the number of people who leave one job for another. People leave jobs for a number of reasons, including advancement, retirement, dismissal, and relocation. There is generally a greater turnover in entry-level positions than in higher-level positions. For example, the turnover rate for bank tellers is likely to be higher than for loan officers.

Location is also a factor. Job opportunities vary from one part of the country to another. In the 1970s and 1980s, many businesses and people moved from the midwestern and northeastern states to southern and southwestern states. As a result, the number of job openings in these areas changed.

An important factor in anyone's job outlook is education. The amount of education a worker has affects both the kinds of occupations open to the worker and the income the worker will receive. Education increases the number of occupations from which a worker can choose. It also often enables a worker to advance to higher positions. Generally speaking, income increases as the amount of education increases.

Quick Check

1. What four factors affect the labor market?
2. What is *turnover?* Give some reasons for turnover.
3. In what ways can education affect a worker's position in the labor market?

608 UNIT 11 WORKING IN THE GLOBAL ECONOMY

Cooperative Learning — Team Word Webbing

Divide the class into teams, and have teams write the main concepts of the chapter and related ideas on a sheet of paper. Team members should work together to make a word web showing connections between concepts and ideas discussed in the chapter.

Refer to the *Cooperative Learning Strategies* booklet for additional cooperative learning strategies.

Chapter 35 **Summary**

Main Ideas

1. Business finds the workers it needs in the labor market, which includes the number of job seekers and the number of job openings.
2. The labor market can be grouped into goods-producing and service-producing occupations.
3. Occupations can be classified as white collar, blue collar, service, or farm.
4. A union contract is the result of negotiations between the union and company management. It usually describes wages, working conditions, and hours of work as well as other items of mutual concern.

5. Demand, competition, turnover, and location are factors that affect the labor market.
6. Recording engineers, electronic production artists, film processing technicians, and theme park supervisors are some occupations in the communications, entertainment, and arts industries.
7. Competing in the world labor market requires workers to recognize and deal with diversity.

CASE ANALYSIS Organized Labor

A union would like to see all workers in a company under its authority. Such a *closed shop*, forcing workers to join the union as a condition of employment, was outlawed by the Taft-Hartley Act. The next best option for organized labor is the *union shop*. This setup allows the employer to hire new workers at will, but after a trial period—usually 30 days—the new workers must join the union. Another option is the *agency shop*, which requires nonunion workers who benefit from union contracts to pay service fees to that union. The least desirable option for organized labor is the *open shop*, in which nonunion workers pay no dues. Twenty-one states have laws that give workers the right to get a job without joining a union. Do you think that workers should have to join a union or pay union fees to get or keep a job? Why or why not?

CLOSE

Main Ideas

Main Ideas summarizes the key information in the chapter. It is a useful tool for reinforcement and review.

CASE ANALYSIS

Case Analysis provides a chapter-related case for student analysis and application of decision-making skills.

Answer
Students' opinions will vary. Some may say that workers should contribute to an organization from which they will benefit. Others may say that workers should not have to join any organization as a condition of employment.

QUICK QUIZ

1. What two classifications of industries can be used to categorize the entire labor market? (Goods-producing and service industries.)
2. What are the four groups of white-collar workers? (Administrative support; technical and professional; executive, administrative, and managerial; and clerical and sales.)
3. What is arbitration? (The submission of disagreements or differences between union and management to a third party. Both sides agree to accept the provisions decided during arbitration.)
4. Name two advantages educated workers have in the job market. (A greater number of jobs are available to educated workers; educated workers usually make more money.)

APPLY

Answers

Use the Language of Business

1. apprentice, 2. turnover, 3. strike, 4. arbitration, 5. labor union, 6. mediator, 7. labor market.

Review What You Learned

1. People have been demanding more services.
2. Develop ideas, analyze data, and create new information or strategies.
3. Blue-collar jobs; manufacturing industries are increasing output without adding additional employees.
4. Reaching an agreement acceptable to both management and workers.
5. Decreasing; the trend to larger, more automated farms is continuing.
6. The number of job openings changes as populations of workers move from one geographic region to another.
7. Possible answer: goods: film processing technician and electronic production artist; services: theme park supervisor and assistant recording engineer.
8. Your job success can depend on it.

Understand Business Concepts

1. By automating many tasks.
2. Prepare and maintain records; analyze data; deal with customers directly or indirectly; operate equipment such as computers, copiers, and fax machines.
3. Some, such as cleaning hotel rooms or serving meals, are not easily automated.
4. A contract identifies how union and management agree to address issues of mutual concern.
5. It makes it more difficult for workers to hold a steady position.
6. It has created a need for workers who supply, record, process, and distribute information, as well as for workers who can maintain the machines and equipment used in these activities.

Use the Language of Business

Understanding these business terms will help you communicate more easily with others. Number your paper 1 through 7. Then write the term that best matches each numbered definition.

apprentice	labor market	labor union
arbitration	mediator	strike
		turnover

1. Person in training for a skilled trade or craft.
2. Number of people who leave one job for another.
3. Work stoppage.
4. Submitting the disagreements or differences to a third party who acts as a judge. The final ruling must be accepted by both.
5. Organization of workers set up to benefit its members.
6. Third party who listens to both sides and then suggests what the provisions of a labor contract should be.
7. The number of job seekers and the number of job openings.

Review What You Learned

1. Why has there been an increase in the number of new job openings in the service occupations?
2. What do workers in the professional and technical category do?
3. Which group of occupations is likely to have about the same number of jobs in the next few years? Why?
4. What is the primary goal of contract negotiation?
5. Is the number of farming jobs in the labor market increasing or decreasing? Explain.
6. How can geography affect the labor market?
7. Name two jobs in communications, entertainment, and the arts that provide goods and two that provide a service.
8. Why is it important to work well with people who are different from you?

Understand Business Concepts

1. How has the United States increased its production without increasing the number of workers?
2. What are some of the responsibilities of administrative support workers?
3. Why have a number of service-producing jobs not become automated?
4. Explain what is meant by a contract between a union and management.
5. How does competition affect the labor market?
6. How has the demand for information affected the labor market?

7. Answers will vary, but students should indicate that geography plays a large role in the labor market for these two industries. Students may indicate that competition for jobs in these parts of the country would probably be much greater than for similar jobs in other locations.
8. Answers will vary, but students may suggest that recognizing that people are different or judging people as individuals is basic to the other guidelines.

Think Critically

1. Opinions will vary. The ability to strike gives those workers more bargaining power. However, those workers' jobs directly affect public welfare because they provide essential services.
2. In addition to the jobs with the new firm, additional new job opportunities would include goods and service occupations to provide food, clothing, recreation, shelter, education, and fire and police protection.

Chapter 35 **Review**

7. Much filmmaking takes place in California, and live theater is concentrated in New York and Chicago. What does this tell you about the labor market for the entertainment industry?

8. Which one of the guidelines for Recognizing Diversity on page 605 do you think is the most important? Why?

Independent Practice

Use the Chapter 35 worksheets in *Student Activity Guide 2* for additional practice and application activities. *Student Activity Guide 2* provides vocabulary exercises, reading comprehension checks, problems, projects, and simulations of business and economic situations. A Teacher's Annotated Edition provides answers.

Think Critically

1. **Evaluate.** Unions are becoming more common among government workers, including those in police and fire departments. Do you think that unionized public employees should be allowed to go on strike? Explain.

2. **Explain.** Suppose a firm requiring 5000 workers moved into your community. How would this move affect the total number of jobs in the community?

Use What You Learned

1. **Group Activity.** Work with three other students. Collect several issues of your local newspaper's help wanted pages. Group the ads into the occupational profile categories used in this chapter. Then review the ads and prepare an occupational profile booklet for your community. Identify the following information in your booklet:

   • Which occupational categories and which jobs have the most openings.
   • Occupations for which the employer will provide training.
   • Occupations that require education beyond high school.
   • Occupations that seem to offer the most advancement.
   • Locations in your community that seem to have a high concentration of job opportunities.

2. **Computer Application.** Find out how many businesses in your community employ union workers. Contact a regional development association, chamber of commerce, or other local business group to obtain the information. Then use charting/graphing software to prepare a graph that shows the percent of union and nonunion workers in your area.

3. **Skill Reinforcement.** Review the Guidelines for Recognizing Diversity on page 605. Write a fictionalized description of a workplace situation in which the characters ignore one or more of the guidelines. Write a second description in which they use the guidelines to help solve the problem. You and some classmates may want to dramatize the situation for the rest of the class.

ASSESS

Portfolio Assessment

The portfolio projects are designed to lead students to develop a collection of their best work to submit to you for assessment. You and your students should decide which projects will be included in their respective Business Portfolios. Refer students to the specific rubric(s) from the *Alternative Assessment Strategies* booklet listed with each of the project notes below. These rubrics will alert students to the criteria you will use to assess their projects.

Save your work in your Business Portfolio.

Use What You Learned
1. Make sure all students participate in the group project. Rubric: Booklet.
2. Students with no access to a computer may make their graphs by hand. Rubric: Graph.

3. Students' descriptions will vary but should reflect the guidelines. Possible Rubrics: Essay; Oral Presentation.

Chapter Assessment

Use the Chapter 35 Test from the *Test Masters* booklet to evaluate students' understanding of the chapter concepts. An answer key is provided. Or create your own customized test using the *Testmaker* software.

FOCUS

Major Concepts
• Looking at the Package
• Jobs and the Economy

Introduce the Topic
Begin discussion of the chapter by asking students to name reasons that people work. As you discuss the reasons with the class, point out that two people might find the same job rewarding for different reasons.

Use Business Terms
Have students look at the Business Terms and brainstorm associations with each term. Ask them where they have heard or seen the term used. Reinforce correct associations. Advise students to note the meanings of the terms as they read the chapter.

USE VISUALS
Explain that the kinds of benefits a company offers is an important consideration when deciding whether to accept a company's job offer. Ask students how much they think a company's benefits package would influence their decision to accept or reject a career position. (Answers will vary.)

CHAPTER
36

Business Terms

compensation

wage

minimum wage

salary

commission

incentive

profit sharing

bonus

benefits

pension plan

612

CHAPTER 36 RESOURCES

Instructional Resources
Lesson Plan for Chapter 36

Teaching Transparencies 36-1, 36-2

Strategies and Worksheets for Teaching Transparencies 36-1, 36-2

Enrichment Masters 36-1, 36-2

Student Activity Guide 2–TAE for Chapter 36

Test Master for Chapter 36

Alternative Assessment Strategies

Math Skills Review

International Business Strategies

Cooperative Learning Strategies

Communication Skills Review

Ethics in Business Strategies

Job Considerations

Learning objectives

After completing this chapter, you will be able to:
- Describe different forms of compensation.
- Identify some of the common benefits offered to employees.
- Explain why it is important to consider working conditions when choosing a job.
- Explain how economic trends affect employment.
- Describe CD-ROMs and explain how they work.
- Describe how comparing statistics can help you analyze a job offer.

Consider what you know

- The labor market can be grouped into goods- and service-producing occupations. Occupations can be further classified as white-collar, blue-collar, service, or farm occupations.

Consider what you want to know

- What are some of the common forms of compensation?
- What are some types of benefits an employee might be offered?
- Why should you consider working conditions when deciding whether a job is for you?
- What are the advantages of using CD-ROMs to store data?
- How can comparing statistics help a person evaluate a job offer?

Consider how to use what you learn

- As you read this chapter, think about your friends and relatives who have jobs. How long have they had their jobs? What do their jobs provide other than a paycheck?

Multimedia Resources

Technology Resource Guide

Distance Learning Guide

Internet Resource Guide

Professional Resources

School-to-Work/Tech Prep Strategies

Instructional Poster

Spanish Resources

Testmaker Software for Chapter 36

The Wall Street Journal Video Series
   Video & Activities for Chapter 36

Business and Marketing Computer
   Applications—An Integrated Software
   Simulation Using Microsoft Works

Stocktracker—A Stock Market Software
   Simulation

Where's the Dough? Board Game

Motivate the Learning

Learning Objectives
Point out to students that the learning objectives show what they will learn in the chapter. Tell students to keep these objectives in mind as they work through the chapter. Note that the last two objectives listed refer to the Focus on Technology feature and the Building Business Skills feature.

Consider What You Know
Review briefly the main sections of *Chapter 35 Competing in the World Labor Market:* The Labor Market; Occupational Profiles; Organized Labor; and An Overview of the Labor Market.

Consider What You Want to Know
Have students preview the chapter in order to see how it will provide answers to the questions. They can read the headings and subheadings, look at the figures and photographs, and read the captions.

Consider How to Use What You Learn
Remind students that at the end of the chapter they will develop projects related to the decisions people make when choosing a job. Suggest that as they read the chapter they consider the criteria they would use in judging whether to take a job.

TEACH

Business Connection

The benefits Chrysler Corporation offers its employees rank among the best of any large corporation in the United States. Chrysler provides medical and dental insurance at no monthly cost to its employees, gives employees up to 16 paid holidays a year including a week between Christmas and New Year's, and makes available education scholarships for employees' children. In addition, employees get discounts on new and used Chrysler vehicles.

Develop Concepts

Looking at the Package

Explain to students that although benefits like health insurance, life insurance, and pension plans may not interest them now, once they enter the workforce such things will become an important consideration. For example, a company that offers a good dental insurance plan can save an employee hundreds of dollars. Have the class brainstorm a list of factors, other than the size of a paycheck, that they feel should be part of a job package.

At this point in your life, you are probably beginning to think about what career path you want to pursue. Choosing a career is a very important and difficult decision—but it is far from the last job-related decision you will make. Your potential workplace, your coworkers, your benefits, and the future outlook of your career are all factors you need to consider right from the beginning of your decision-making process. This chapter will help you begin your job search by outlining these considerations and helping you decide which are most important.

LOOKING AT THE PACKAGE

There are many factors for you to consider in choosing a job. All jobs provide some form of **compensation,** or a combination of payments, benefits, and employee services, for the work performed. The first form of compensation that most people think of is a paycheck. Most companies, however, offer other forms of compensation to their employees—from health insurance to the use of a company car. In addition to compensation, you should also consider your potential working environment, from your surroundings to your coworkers, when choosing a job. There are many different factors that will influence your success and enjoyment at work.

In the same way, employers also consider many different factors when looking for employees. They might be looking for people with a certain amount of experience or a certain type of personality. When choosing a job, you have to consider your potential employer's needs also, making sure that you will be able to fulfill them.

When you take a job, you are taking on more than just a title and the promise of a paycheck. You are taking on a whole package of advantages and responsibilities. You must consider this whole package carefully before you take a job. There are 30,000 possible types of jobs for you to choose from—but probably only a handful of these jobs will really suit you.

Wages and Salaries

Some people think money is the most important consideration in choosing a job. Most people, however, find it more important to have jobs they enjoy rather than jobs that will make them millionaires. Even if your goal is not to become a millionaire, you still need enough money to pay for your basic needs—

Making Connections ⇨ Public Opinion

Ask students to poll at least 10 people of various ages, asking whether they agree with the statement "There should be no minimum wage." Students should encourage respondents to provide one or two reasons to support their opinions. Have students classify the responses and present them to the class. As a class, discuss the responses.

housing, food, and clothing. You need enough money left over for other expenses such as vacations, gifts, hobbies, and entertainment. So, whether or not money is your most important consideration in choosing a job, you should make sure you choose a job that will allow you to satisfy your wants and needs.

Employees receive their payment for work in many different forms. Many workers are paid a **wage,** which is a certain amount of money for each hour the employee has worked or the number of units the employee has produced. For example, if your wage rate is $5 per hour and you work 40 hours in one week, you earn $200. Some companies pay overtime wages to their hourly workers, which is pay at a higher rate for working extra hours. Overtime, most often set at one and one-half times the regular wage, is usually paid for work more than 40 hours a week. So if your wage is $5 an hour and you worked an additional six hours overtime, you would earn—before taxes—an additional $45, for six hours at $7.50 per hour.

In 1938, the federal government passed the Fair Labor Standards Act to protect the nation's workers. One of the things the act called for was a nationwide **minimum wage.** This meant that, by law, employers engaged in interstate commerce had to pay their workers at least the federal minimum wage. Amendments to the law broadened the coverage to many more workers, including certain hospital, retail, hotel, restaurant, and school employees. In 1938, the government set the minimum wage at 25 cents an hour. The government has continued to increase the minimum wage over the years to compensate for inflation. Figure 36-1 below shows the rise in the minimum

Business & Science

At Dow Chemical, salaries and bonuses are linked to how well the company meets its environmental goals. Managers meet with local environmental groups to discuss ways to reduce pollution and waste. With salary increases and bonuses as incentives, workers at a plant in Michigan discovered ways to cut down by 60 percent the amount of waste destined for landfills.

Learning Activity

Tell students that Jim makes $9 an hour. His standard workweek is 40 hours. What does he get paid for a standard workweek? ($9 × 40 = $360.) He gets paid time and a half for each extra hour he works during the week. Suppose he worked 49 hours one week. How much would he get paid that week? ($9 × 1.5 = $13.50 × 9 hours = $121.50 + $360 = $481.50.)

USE VISUALS

Use Figure 36-1 to show students how the minimum wage has increased since 1975. Have students use the numbers in the figure to make a bar graph showing minimum wage increases over time.
Answer to caption: 1981–1990; $3.35.

USE TRANSPARENCIES

Use Teaching Transparency 36-1 and its corresponding strategies and worksheet from the *Teaching Transparency Strategies and Worksheets* booklet to discuss how the minimum wage has increased since 1975. Verify student worksheets using the Answer Key.

THE MINIMUM WAGE

Year	Wage per Hour
1975	$2.10
1976–77	$2.30
1978	$2.65
1979	$2.90
1980	$3.10
1981–1990	$3.35
1990	$3.80
1991–95	$4.25

Source: Congressional Quarterly

FIGURE 36-1

For some low-skill jobs, the minimum wage is an entry-level wage. As workers gain skills, the hourly rate increases. What was the longest time period in which the minimum wage did not increase? What was the minimum wage during that time period?

Cooperative Learning Trade-a-Problem

Have teams devise a math problem and a solution involving how to calculate overtime. Then ask teams to trade their problems with another team. Have teams compare solutions. If solutions agree, have teams continue trading.

Refer to the *Cooperative Learning Strategies* booklet for additional cooperative learning strategies.

FOCUS ON **Technology**

FOCUS ON **Technology**

Discuss

Ask students what "CD-ROM" stands for. (Compact disc-read only memory.) Have students define the term *multimedia* and explain why multimedia applications rely on CD-ROM technology. (Multimedia applications use sound, graphics, and video. CD-ROMs have a large storage capacity and an index that allows users to choose what they want to see, hear, or read.)

CD-ROMs

Now you can hold in one hand not only the complete works of Shakespeare, but also an entire encyclopedia, and all the volumes of case-study law. You can do this even if you're not a weight lifter. All you'll need are a few compact discs.

You're already familiar with compact discs, or CDs, from the music store. The same technology—lasers and optical storage devices—encodes enormous amounts of computer-readable information on thin discs. A single 5 1/2-inch-wide CD-ROM, short for *compact disc-read only memory,* offers 600 megabytes of stored information, or about 400,000 typed pages.

The disc itself consists of a thin layer of aluminum sandwiched between two layers of plastic. To record information on the disc, a laser burns microscopic pits in the surface of the disc. The pits and flat spaces represent data. To retrieve the data from the disc, a lower power laser "reads" the disc by reflecting light from the disc's surface. The pits and flat spaces provide *on* and *off* signals that are connected to standard data bytes that a computer can read.

The data on a CD-ROM is laid out in a spiral that is similar to the spiral on a phonograph record. However, the information on a phonograph record is usually read from beginning to end like the chapters in a novel. The music on a CD may read that way, or may read like a book of short stories, in blocks of information. The blocks may be read out of sequence, but the information in the blocks is read in sequence.

To be useful to a user, the information on a CD-ROM must be able to be read in any order. The user must be able to choose what information he or she wishes to

wage for a recent 20-year period. Currently about 80 percent of the nation's hourly workers are covered by minimum wage laws.

Some factory workers may be paid at a piecework or a per unit rate rather than an hourly wage rate. This means a worker receives a set amount of money for each piece of work completed. Suppose it is someone's job to pack gift boxes of mixed nuts. For each box packed, the worker is paid 10 cents. If the worker packs 70 boxes an hour, he or she would be paid $7.00 an hour. During the next hour, the worker might pack only 62 boxes. For that hour the worker would earn $6.20. Workers who work quickly and accurately can benefit from a piecework rate, because what they earn is linked to the speed with which they perform their jobs.

Some employees earn a **salary.** This means that they earn a certain amount of money each week or month no matter how many hours they work. Salaries are usually figured on an annual basis. The payments are divided evenly and usually paid to the employee every two weeks. For instance, if you earned an annual salary of $16,900, you would receive $650 every two weeks. One disadvantage to working for a salary is that you do

Cooperative Learning Debate (Pro/Con)

Ask volunteers who work at minimum-wage jobs to briefly discuss whether they think the wage they receive is fair. Then select two teams of students to debate the following statement: "It is time for the minimum wage to be increased." Have students not directly involved in the debate act as judges. At the end of the debate, have the judges declare a winner.

Refer to the *Cooperative Learning Strategies* booklet for additional cooperative learning strategies.

access. To accomplish this, CD-ROMs employ a special indexing method.

You may have already guessed that CD-ROM drives are the central component in today's multimedia applications. *Multimedia*—sound, graphics, and video—requires the computer to read and interpret sound and video as well as program data. Video games and multimedia applications, such as virtual reality, rely exclusively on CD-ROMs. These interactive applications store digital audio, full-motion video and graphics, animation, text, and data on a CD that has an index and a program, which allows the user to choose what he or she wishes to see, hear, or read.

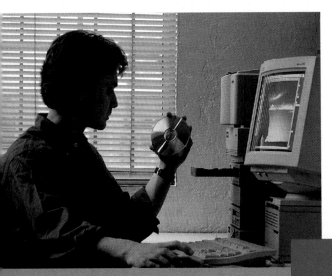

Many businesses have taken advantage of the great storage capacity of CDs to place important reference volumes on CD-ROMs. References, such as encyclopedias and the *Occupational Outlook Handbook*, are now available on CD-ROM. In other businesses, multimedia CDs are turning up as marketing tools. For example, some financial institutions are marketing their services, or even recruiting potential employees, using CD-ROM technology.

Follow Through
Have students brainstorm a list of the advantages of CD-ROM reference sources over traditional print references. Students may also list disadvantages. Encourage students who have used CD-ROM reference sources to share their experiences with the class.

not receive compensation for overtime. But many people like being salaried because of the security of receiving a set amount of pay for each pay period.

Many sales workers earn a **commission,** or a percentage of the value of their sales. Suppose you sell camping equipment at a 10 percent commission. If you sell $200 worth of equipment, you earn $20. Sales workers may also receive a small salary, but usually a substantial part of their pay comes from their commissions. Some people do not like the pressure of working under commission; if sales are slow, a person who relies on commissions will not earn as much. Many people, however, prefer this type of compensation because they receive a concrete payback for extra effort.

Any monetary compensation for extra effort is called an **incentive.** Commission is one type of incentive. When companies make a profit and distribute a specified percentage to their employees at certain intervals, they are offering their employees a type of incentive called **profit sharing.** Profit sharing encourages employees to work harder to increase the company's profits. With profit sharing, employees benefit individually when the company does well.

Learning Activity
Give students the following scenario: Gerri works on commission at a computer equipment retailer. She gets a 6 percent commission on the items she sells. Today, she sold a color monitor costing $997, a scanner costing $629, and a laser printer costing $1299. How much did she make in commissions? ($997 + $629 + $1299 = $2925 × .06 = $175.50.)
For those students who need to sharpen their math skills, choose among the worksheets in the *Math Skills Review* booklet.

CHAPTER 36   JOB CONSIDERATIONS   **617**

Making Connections ➡️ Equal Pay for Equal Work

On average, women make 25 percent less money than men. Have students find out why this is so. Suggest that students address such issues as the connections among gender, occupation, and discrimination. Have students write an essay addressing these issues and proposing solutions for making pay more equitable.

Business Brief

According to a survey conducted in 1994 by *Money* magazine, Proctor & Gamble provides the most lucrative benefits to its employees. Highlights of the benefits package include generous profit-sharing incentives, inexpensive and flexible medical and dental care, and six weeks of vacation time for employees who have worked for the company for 25 years or more.

Use Visuals

Have students study Figure 36-2. Then have students suppose that a company that fit the average profile shown in the figure spent a total of $320,800 for employee compensation. How much would that company pay for retirement and savings? ($320,800 × .03 = $9624.)

Answer to caption: Seven percent.

Use Transparencies

Use Teaching Transparency 36-2 and its corresponding strategies and worksheet from the *Teaching Transparency Strategies and Worksheets* booklet to help students visualize employer cost breakdowns for employee compensation. Verify student worksheets using the Answer Key.

Another type of incentive is a bonus. A **bonus** is similar to profit sharing, because it is extra money earned for helping a company increase its profits. The difference is that the amount of a bonus and the time of payment are not predetermined. A company may give out annual bonuses, or it may distribute bonuses to individual employees who worked hard to complete a particularly successful project.

Benefits

Many companies regularly provide their employees with **benefits,** financial compensation other than wages, salaries, and incentives. Benefits should be carefully considered when you are choosing a job. Although wages and salaries, on average, account for about 70 percent of an employer's payroll costs, providing these benefits, which are sometimes called *fringe benefits,* costs employers a substantial additional amount of money. Often the value of the benefits offered to employees plays a major role in a person's decision to take a job. Figure 36-2 below shows a breakdown of the cost an average employer assumes when employing an average worker.

There are many different types of benefits, and the provisions can vary considerably. Certain companies offer a wide variety of benefits, while others may have a minimal benefits package. Some of the more common benefits are described in detail in this section.

FIGURE 36-2

The average cost of employee benefits and government-required insurance amounts to nearly 30 percent of an average employer's payroll costs. On average, what percentage of compensation goes for paid leave?

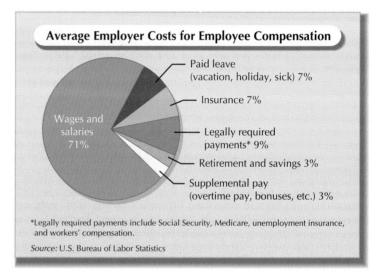

Average Employer Costs for Employee Compensation

Paid leave (vacation, holiday, sick) 7%

Insurance 7%

Legally required payments* 9%

Retirement and savings 3%

Supplemental pay (overtime pay, bonuses, etc.) 3%

Wages and salaries 71%

*Legally required payments include Social Security, Medicare, unemployment insurance, and workers' compensation.

Source: U.S. Bureau of Labor Statistics

Reteaching Strategy

Have a class discussion about the difference between wages and benefits. Ask students to provide examples of how both add to a person's financial stability. After the discussion, have students write a paragraph summarizing the ideas the class discussed.

Insurance Many companies offer their employees health insurance. The types of coverage vary, but it is almost always less costly to enroll in health insurance through an employer than to pay for insurance on your own. Companies may pay a percentage of the monthly health insurance costs, or premiums, while their employees pay the rest. Some companies pay the entire cost of the health insurance premiums. Most companies offer employees a choice of coverages depending on whether they want to be able to choose their own health-care practitioners or whether they are willing to limit themselves to practitioners that belong to an approved network of health-care providers. Some plans also offer dental and eye care, as well as long-term disability. Numerous employers also offer their workers life insurance, which will help support dependents, such as a spouse and children, if the worker dies.

Social Security, Medicare, workers' compensation, and unemployment insurance are financial benefits that employers are required by federal law to provide. Employers pay taxes that fund these programs. Most employees have Social Security and Medicare taxes deducted from their paychecks. However, employers must match the amount of Social Security and Medicare taxes each employee pays.

Employers are also required to pay federal and state taxes that fund unemployment insurance. When workers have been laid off, and in certain other cases, they can collect the equivalent of part of their pay in unemployment insurance. Although workers' compensation and unemployment insurance are part of federal law, the specific terms of these types of insurance vary from state to state. In addition, all 50 states have laws that mandate workers' compensation insurance. These laws require employers to pay for insurance that will repay employees for losses suffered from job-related injuries, sicknesses, or death.

Paid Days Off Almost all companies provide their employees with a certain number of company-wide paid holidays. National holidays, such as Independence Day and Labor Day, are paid vacation days for employees in most companies, and the company is officially closed on those days. Many companies also provide paid time off on religious holidays, such as Christmas. Today, many companies provide "floating" holidays. With floating holidays, workers can choose which days they take as holidays.

Many companies also give their employees a certain number of paid sick/personal business days. Employees can use these days when they are ill or when they have personal business to attend to. Most employers also provide their employees with paid time off for vacations. Generally, you have to work

F.Y.I.

The Families & Work Institute surveyed different categories of employees to find which benefits they would like to have added to their compensation package. Employees with a working spouse and children under age six would like a child-care center at the workplace. Employees with children older than six placed insurance for eye care at the top of their list. Employees with no children would like to work more hours each day in exchange for an additional day off each week.

Business Brief
Less than 25 percent of American households fit the once-prevalent scenario in which a father works outside the home and a mother stays home cooking, cleaning, and taking care of the kids. Today, many employees live with and care for aging relatives or live with a "significant other" of the same or opposite sex. So far, about 150 companies have recognized other definitions of family units by offering employees the option of medical, dental, and life-insurance coverage for their "domestic partners" who are not financially dependent spouses.

Learning Activity
Discuss with students the advantages of floating holidays. Ask: Why do you think employers offer floating holidays? (Possible answers: In recognition of employees' cultural and religious differences. To give employees more flexibility.)

Enrichment Strategy

Invite a human resources representative from a local large business to speak to the class about the benefits offered by his or her company. Ask the representative to cover topics such as how benefits vary according to the length of time an employee has worked and how the company decides on which benefits to offer.

Model

Explain that the more statistics you have from which to make comparisons, the more likely you are to get an accurate assessment. Ask: Is a student who gets a poor grade on an English test a poor student? Point out that academic performance is not based on a single test or a single class. Explain to students other factors (statistics) you would consider in assessing a student's performance.

Business Brief

Many benefits that workers enjoy today are the result of hard-won victories achieved in only the last 65 years or so. These include:

- Workers' compensation
- Equal opportunity hiring practices
- Health benefits
- Five-day workweek and eight-hour workday
- Paid holidays and vacation
- Grievance procedures for filing complaints against employers

Mᴀᴛʜ

Comparing Statistics

Explanation

Where can you get the most for your money when you buy a CD player? What store has the lowest prices on your favorite jeans? Whenever you check the price of an item in different stores to find the best deal, you are comparing statistics. This is a skill you'll use increasingly as you move into the business world.

If you do research into jobs and careers, you'll likely be comparing statistics. You might want to compare growth in various industries to learn which will be offering the most jobs over the next few years. You'll proba-bly also want to find out how wages in a variety of jobs compare. Publications such as the *Statistical Abstract of the United States* and the *Occupational Outlook Handbook* contain such information.

You might want to know how wages compare in different geographic areas. Machine repairers in the Midwest, for example, average around $16.17 per hour, significantly more than they do in the South.

In considering jobs, you'll want to make other statistical comparisons as well. Comparing newspaper, supermarket, and classified ads for different areas can help you compare living costs. If living costs are higher, they may balance out higher earnings. For example, a job that pays $50 a month more won't be an advantage if you have to pay $60 more per month in rent. State and local sales or income taxes also might take more of your wages if you move to another state.

with a company for a certain amount of time before you receive paid vacation time. You may earn a day of vacation time for each month of work time, or you may receive more vacation time after a certain number of years with a company.

Pension Plans Many companies offer their workers a **pension plan** to provide them with income when they retire. In some cases, only the employer contributes to the plan. In other cases, both employers and employees put money into the plan. Usually, a company sets aside a certain amount of money each year for each employee. When the employee retires, that money provides the former worker with a monthly income.

Credit Unions Many large companies also set up credit unions for their employees. As you will recall from Chapter 19, credit unions are cooperatives through which members can save or borrow money at better rates than those of most other financial institutions. The employees pool their money, which is then loaned out to members who need or want loans.

Other Benefits Many companies encourage their employees to further their education by paying all or part of the cost of

Reteaching Strategy

Have students suppose they have two after-school job options: baby-sitting for $4 an hour or walking a neighbor's dog on weekdays for $1 a day. Which offer seems better? (Students should indicate they need more information.) Provide students with additional information: They would have to pay $1.50 bus fare each way to get to the baby-sitting job, which would be for two hours one day a week. Have students compare statistics and decide which offer is better. (When the bus fare is accounted for, both jobs would pay $5 a week. The dog-walking job would be easier and more convenient.)

COMPARING JOB STATISTICS

1. By 2005, there will be 85 percent more jobs available for paralegals, or lawyers' aides, than there were in 1990. There will only be 24 percent more jobs available to retail sales workers. Does this mean there will be more paralegal jobs than retail jobs in 2005? What else, if anything, do you have to know to answer the question?

2. You have been offered two jobs as a machine repairer, one by Southern Industries and one by Midwest Metal. Taking the Midwest job means moving to the Midwest. The statistics are shown in the table. Which job is better financially?

	Southern Job	Midwest Job
Hourly wage per 40-hour week	$14.87	$16.17
Your cost for health insurance	None (Firm pays entire cost)	$10.00 per week
Rent (based on classified ads)	$450 per month	$600 per month
Food (based on food ads)	50 per week	$52 per week
Transportation to job	$2.00 per day (bus fare)	$4.40 per day (car; $.44/mile for 10 miles)

Practice

Work through the problems above that involve making statistical comparisons.

classes taken by their workers. The classes usually must be related to the workers' jobs. For example, an employee who works with computers may take a class to learn a new type of software. A worker who wants to be more efficient may take a class on time management. Both companies and employees benefit from such tuition-reimbursement programs. Employees gain skills and knowledge that help them perform their jobs better. They may also qualify for higher salaries or wages and the opportunity to advance in their careers. Companies gain more competent employees who can do their jobs better.

Another benefit gaining popularity is child care in the workplace. These days, both partners in a marriage are likely to work outside the home. A number of companies are beginning to help these employees by providing care for their children. Sometimes a large company has a day-care center in the building, which its employees can use. Other companies help support their employees' expenses at community day-care centers. In addition, more companies now offer paid leave for new parents.

Also gaining popularity in recent years are employer-sponsored exercise and wellness programs. Many employers have found that helping their workers stay healthy decreases

Meeting Student Diversity

Students with writing difficulties often copy answers directly from the book and have problems when they encounter questions that require some interpretation. Help them practice "reading between the lines" in the text, not only to have students make interpretations but also to help them recognize when information is implied.

Practice

Have students work through the problems to find out how statistics can help them make comparisons.
(1. One would have to know the actual number of jobs for both paralegals and retail sales workers in 1990 to answer the question. 2. The Southern job pays $30,929.60 per year [about $2500 a year less than Midwest at $33,633.60]. Yearly expenses total $8520 for Southern and $11,568 for Midwest. The Southern offer is a bit better.)

Business Brief

Bell Atlantic, headquartered in Philadelphia, is one of a growing number of employers that offers a flexible "menu" of benefits. Bell Atlantic employees may opt for health club discounts, job sharing, stop-smoking programs, or nutrition counseling as part of their benefits package.

Learning Activity

Have several groups of students each contact the human resources department of a large company in the community. Have them ask for a summary of the company's benefits. Ask groups to make a chart of the company's benefits and give a brief presentation to the class. As a class, discuss the benefits offered by each of the companies and take a vote to decide which company offers the "best" benefits package.

CHAPTER 36

Learning Activity

Have students think of some possible answers for the following question: What benefits might employers gain from offering expensive "extras" such as fitness programs, child care, and tuition reimbursement? (Such "extras" will attract more highly qualified job seekers; fitness programs will keep employees in better health and less time will be lost because of illness; tuition reimbursement will encourage employees to become better qualified to do their jobs.)

Employer-sponsored exercise and educational programs are designed to reduce the number of sick days and lower insurance premiums. Can you think of any other possible benefits to having such a program? Can you think of any drawbacks?

the number of sick days and the size of insurance payments. Some large companies have set up fitness centers in their buildings where their employees can use exercise machines and weights. Some companies may not have these facilities but instead sponsor memberships at nearby fitness clubs. Educational programs to control stress, discourage smoking, and encourage healthful diets are also being promoted in an increasing number of companies.

Some companies do not offer all of their benefits immediately. They award them to employees who have been working with them for a certain number of months or years. Some companies even let employees choose which benefits they want. For example, if you are single, you may not want life insurance. Instead of life insurance, your company may allow you to choose a program in which it pays all or part of the tuition for job-related classes you want to take. Figure 36-3 on page 623 shows the percentages of employees nationwide who took advantage of certain kinds of benefits offered by their employers.

Working Conditions

As important as income and benefits are for you to consider in choosing the right job, there are countless other factors you should consider that are not written into a job offer. There may

Curriculum Connection   English and Communication

Have students write a profile of their ideal working conditions. Students may consider such factors as where they would like the job to be located, whether they want to work independently or as part of a team, and whether they would like flexible hours or a predictable 9 to 5 schedule. Ask them what kinds of work responsibilities they would be willing to accept in order to earn such conditions.

For those students who need to sharpen their communication skills, choose among the worksheets in the *Communication Skills Review* booklet.

PERCENTAGE OF FULL-TIME EMPLOYEES PARTICIPATING IN SELECTED BENEFITS

Program	Percentage Participating
Health insurance	92%
Life Insurance	94%
Holidays	97%
Vacation	97%
Sick leave	68%
Pension plans	81%
Tuition reimbursement	69%
Child care	5%
Wellness	23%

Source: U.S. Bureau of Labor Statistics

FIGURE 36-3

Benefits vary from company to company. Certain benefits, such as paid holidays and vacation time, are part of almost every employer's benefits package, and nearly all employees, not surprisingly, take advantage of paid time off. Other programs are not offered or participated in as fully. What percentage of employees took advantage of their companys' wellness programs?

USE VISUALS

Be sure that students understand that the benefits listed in Figure 36-3 are not offered by all employers. Ask students to choose six shown in the table that they personally would consider the most important. Have students rank the benefits and give reasons for their choices.
Answer to caption: Twenty-three percent.

Business Brief

Working outdoors appeals to many people. Outdoor jobs are available in cities, rural areas, remote forests, and even on water! Some outdoor jobs open to people with a high school diploma include mail carrier, oil well driller, commercial fisher, tour guide, and tree surgeon. Jobs such as surveyor, forestry technician, and police officer require additional specialized training. With four or more years of college, a person who enjoys the outdoors could become a conservation scientist, petroleum engineer, or farm manager. (See Focus on Careers—Agribusiness, Forestry, Wildlife, and Mining—Chapter 16.)

be aspects of a job that you like—or dislike—that you might not think to consider beforehand. Do you enjoy the challenge of juggling many tasks at once? Or are you a perfectionist who likes to work on one task until it cannot be improved anymore? You might take on a desk job only to realize later that you would much rather work outdoors. It is not easy to pinpoint the working conditions that are best for you until you have worked for a while, but you should try to assess as many of these factors as possible beforehand by observing your potential workplace carefully when you visit for an interview.

You should also consider carefully not just the indoor, but also the outdoor surroundings at your potential workplace. Is the neighborhood safe, especially if you will have to work late hours? Is it near where you live, or will you have a long—and possibly exhausting—commute in the morning and evening? You may enjoy the convenience of a workplace that is close to a shopping district so you can run errands on your lunch break or after work. Or perhaps you would rather work in a more secluded area with beautiful scenery outside the office windows. Maybe you would rather not work in an office at all. As personal computers and modems, cellular phones, and fax machines are making centrally located offices less necessary, your own home may become your office.

Your coworkers may also have a strong influence on how much you enjoy your day-to-day work. Try to find a workplace

CHAPTER 36   JOB CONSIDERATIONS   **623**

Enrichment Strategy

Distribute photocopies of Enrichment Master 36-1 and ask students to rank the job considerations given on the checklist in order of personal importance. Ask volunteers to explain some of their choices to the rest of the class. Discuss with students the different priorities people have when choosing a job.

CHAPTER 36

Quick Check Answers

1. Combination of payments, benefits, and employer services for work performed.
2. A wage is a certain amount of money paid for each hour of work. A salary is a certain amount of money paid each week or month that does not take into account the number of hours worked.
3. Commission, profit sharing, and bonus.
4. The lowest amount of money per hour certain workers can be paid according to law; special services to employees provided by employers; money contributed to a savings plan that provides an employee with income during retirement.

Develop Concepts

Jobs and the Economy

As students begin to think about entering the labor force, they should be concerned with the future, or outlook, for their career options. Magazines and books are available at libraries and guidance offices that provide people with job outlooks—statistics that forecast employment, salary, and other information for specific jobs. If possible, obtain some job outlook books or magazines for students to examine.

---

that fosters cooperative relationships and teamwork among its employees. You may find that you like working with people who have similar interests, or you may find it stimulating to work with many different types of people you would be less likely to encounter outside of work. If you consider a job in a company that is unionized, remember that strict work rules negotiated as part of the union contract will apply to you. You'll also have mandatory union dues deducted from your paycheck.

Quick Check

1. Define *compensation*.
2. What is the difference between a *wage* and a *salary*?
3. Name three incentives that can motivate employees to work harder.
4. Give the definitions of the terms *minimum wage*, *benefits*, and *pension plan*.

JOBS AND THE ECONOMY

The world of work is constantly changing. Things have been moving especially rapidly in the past few decades, as the United States has entered the global marketplace. As you know, business cycles affect employment. When the economy is experiencing a recession, companies try to save money to survive the economic downturn, which they often do by not hiring any new workers. They might also lay off some of their workers.

There are other economic factors that influence employment. Exceptionally high or low interest rates can also affect the job market. For example, low interest rates may encourage new businesses to start up. Because interest rates are low, businesses can afford to borrow larger amounts of money for expansion. High interest rates can have the opposite effect. Businesses are less likely to borrow money to expand, thereby not increasing the number of available jobs. Although it is difficult to determine exactly how certain economic factors affect employment, evaluating economic conditions and employment trends can help you tailor your job search to fit the times.

Unemployment

The federal government would like to keep every worker in the country employed. This theoretical standard is known as *full employment*. In reality, there will always be some percent-

624 UNIT 11 WORKING IN THE GLOBAL ECONOMY

Curriculum Connection   Economics

Distribute photocopies of Enrichment Master 36-2, which provides definitions of five categories of unemployment: frictional, structural, cyclical, seasonal, and technological. Assign groups one of the categories for more study. Ask groups to find real-life examples of their assigned type of unemployment in newspaper or magazine articles. Groups' examples need not be limited to unemployment in the United States. Have each group give a brief oral summary of their findings to the rest of the class.

age of the population out of work at any given time because there will always be people between jobs and people who do not have the skills and attitudes to hold jobs. Calculating the number of unemployed people in the nation is a difficult task that can never be entirely accurate. But the unemployment rate is the federal government's best estimate of how many people are looking for work and unable to find it.

How does the federal government actually calculate unemployment? It surveys approximately 60,000 households each month. These surveys are used to compile data about people in the labor force and people trying to enter the labor force. People who did any amount of paid work during the survey week are considered employed. Those considered unemployed are those actively looking for work—sending out resumes, making phone calls, or checking in at an unemployment office. Full-time students, people under 16 years old, people hospitalized or in prison, and those not actively seeking work are not considered part of the labor force and are not included in the survey data.

When the U.S. economy is doing well, the unemployment rate is usually low—around 5 percent. This percentage means that 95 percent of the labor force is working, and 5 percent is unable to find work. In times when the U.S. economy was not doing very well, such as in the early 1980s, the unemployment rate has reached over 9.5 percent, meaning that almost one out of every ten people looking for work was unable to find a job.

Employment Trends and the Economy

There have been many different trends and changes in U.S. employment over the years. In the first half of the 1900s, most of the nation's jobs—certainly the higher-paying jobs—were filled by white males. In the 1940s and 1950s, more African-American workers moved from farming jobs into higher-paying manufacturing and office jobs. Before the 1970s, most women in the labor force worked at clerical and service jobs, but were not paid as well as men. Many married women with children did not even work outside the home. During the 1970s, more women and minorities entered the labor force and set out on careers that before had been mostly filled by white men. The 1970s also brought a boom in service industry jobs. The 1980s, however, brought a decline in farming and manufacturing jobs.

Let's look at some employment trends in the 1990s. A continuing increase in demand for services has brought about an increase in service industry jobs. Service workers include accountants, real estate agents, sales associates, and mechanics—to name just a few. Technology is also responsible for some

High unemployment in the mid-1990s caused several European governments to launch programs designed to encourage employment. In 1994, France allowed companies to hire certain workers under the age of 26 at 80 percent of the French national minimum wage. Spain had a similar program that removed restrictions on part-time employment and allowed companies to pay workers between 18 and 25 years old wages that were between 70 and 80 percent of Spain's minimum wage.

Learning Activity
Unemployment can be divided into categories, some of which are more serious than others. Give students the following two situations and have them decide which case is a greater problem. Joe lost his job at Minn's Manufacturers when the company installed machinery that made Joe's job no longer necessary. David's wife, Antoinette, got a job in Chicago, so the couple moved there. David had to quit his job as a computer programmer in Boston and is currently looking for a job in Chicago.

Business Brief
One of the employment trends of the 1990s is *outsourcing*—subcontracting work to outside contractors. Outsourcing saves employers money; since they have fewer full-time employees, employers save on payroll and benefits expenses.

Making Connections 🔁 Job Outlooks

Arrange to have a guidance counselor discuss with students how they can find out about job outlooks. Then have each student select one of the careers they are interested in and prepare a report about the percentage of unemployment in the field, expected growth during the next decade, potential for salary growth, and potential for promotion. Have students write a job outlook report that includes a paragraph explaining whether they are still considering the job after having examined some statistics.

CHAPTER 36

Point out that women sales representatives at car dealerships were at one time very uncommon. Ask students for examples of other occupations in which women are gaining a foothold. (Possible answers: Physicians, real estate agents, firefighters, and police officers.)

Answer to caption: Many more women and minorities have found careers in service industry jobs since the 1970s.

Quick Check Answers

1. Full-time students, people under 16 years old, people hospitalized or in prison, and those not actively seeking work.
2. Generally, it is not considered high.

Many women have taken jobs previously traditionally held by men. What are some examples in addition to this used-car saleswoman?

of the employment trends of the 1990s. Personal computers equipped with modem and fax capabilities have made it possible for more people to work from home.

As the cost of employing full-time workers increases, different workforce management techniques have emerged. Many companies rely on freelancers and part-time workers to give them more flexibility in managing their workforces. When a company has a heavy workload or a peak period, it may employ freelancers or part-time workers to handle the extra work. The company saves money because it generally does not pay benefits for freelancers or part-time workers.

Looking at some of the economic factors that affect the job market will help you determine the kind of economic climate in which you will be conducting your job search. Knowledge of the economy can also provide insight into why some companies are hiring or expanding and others are not. Having some understanding of the economy's workings and how the state of the economy influences the labor market before you start on a job search can help you know what to expect.

Quick Check

1. What groups of people are not counted in the government's calculations of the unemployment rate?
2. Is an unemployment rate of 5 percent considered high?

Global Perspective

One way students can prepare themselves for international careers is through study of foreign languages and travel. Suggest that interested students check issues of the *Occupational Outlook Quarterly* for descriptions of job opportunities abroad and for sources of information about international jobs. Have students work in groups to make posters promoting ways students could prepare themselves for jobs abroad. Posters may include addresses and names of organizations as well as photos and other graphics.

Refer to the *International Business Strategies* booklet for additional strategies and activities.

Chapter 36 **Summary**

Main Ideas

1. Employers compensate employees for their work by paying them and providing them with various benefits.
2. Some employees are paid wages at an hourly rate while others earn a salary, which is figured annually. Workers who do piecework are paid for each piece of work completed. Employees who work on commission earn a percentage of the value of what they sell.
3. Some employee benefits include insurance, paid days off, pension plans, credit unions, tuition-reimbursement programs, child-care facilities, and wellness programs.
4. You should try to assess the working conditions at a potential workplace to determine how they would suit your personality and work habits.

5. The government calculates the unemployment rate by compiling data about people in the workforce and those trying to enter the workforce.
6. Gauging the economic climate by looking at the unemployment rate and other economic factors will help you conduct your job search.
7. CD-ROMs can hold vast amounts of data in the form of text, sound, graphics, and video. They can be useful in job searches in some industries.
8. Comparing statistics about growth, wages, and living costs associated with different industries and geographic locations can help you analyze job offers.

CLOSE

Main Ideas

Main Ideas summarizes the key information in the chapter. It is a useful tool for reinforcement and review.

CASE ANALYSIS

Case Analysis provides a chapter-related case for student analysis and application of decision-making skills.

Answer
Students' opinions will vary.

CASE ANALYSIS Employment Issues

Listed below are a series of questions that relate to issues employers and employees must face. Answer each question, and explain why you answered as you did.

1. Would you be willing to take a cut in pay to save someone else's job? To save your own?
2. Should a company spend time and money training an older worker who will work only a few more years?
3. Does a job that requires simple repetitive tasks and little thought make a good job?
4. Should all workers contribute equally to production and be paid equally?
5. Would you be willing to work at a job that was below your abilities and paid relatively low wages?

QUICK QUIZ

1. What three incentives can motivate employees to do their best? (Commissions, profit sharing, and bonuses.)
2. Name the three types of insurance that employers must provide according to law. (Social Security, workers' compensation, and unemployment insurance.)
3. Name two advantages employers gain from employing freelancers. (Freelancers give employers more flexibility because they can be hired on an as-needed basis. Employers save money because they generally don't provide benefits to freelancers.)
4. What groups of people aren't counted in the government's calculations of the unemployment rate? (Full-time students, people under 16 years old, people hospitalized or in prison, and those not actively seeking work.)

Chapter 36 **Review**

CHAPTER 36 REVIEW

APPLY

Answers

Use the Language of Business

1. bonus, **2.** wage, **3.** minimum wage, **4.** compensation, **5.** pension plan, **6.** salary, **7.** incentive, **8.** benefits, **9.** commission, **10.** profit sharing.

Review What You Learned

1. They pay employees and offer them benefits.

2. A wage is an hourly rate of pay and a salary is figured annually.

3. The minimum wage.

4. They receive a set amount of money for each piece of work completed.

5. Social Security, workers' compensation, and unemployment insurance.

6. A paid day off of an employee's own choosing.

7. In multimedia applications that combine sound, graphics, video, and text.

8. Living costs such as the cost of housing, transportation, and food.

Understand Business Concepts

1. An employee may earn overtime pay for extra hours worked.

2. It encourages employees to work harder at increasing the company's profits, because employees will benefit personally.

3. The company pays all or part of the premiums so the employee benefits financially. Even if employees pay the entire premium, costs are lower for a group policy or an individual policy.

4. Workers' compensation.

5. Employees can gain more skills to perform their jobs better.

Use the Language of Business

Use the following terms to best complete each of the sentences below.

benefits	incentive	profit sharing
bonus	minimum wage	salary
commission	pension plan	wage
compensation		

A company may reward an employee with extra money, or a[n] _____, for helping a company increase its profits. A _____ is a certain amount of money paid for each hour of work. By law, all employers must pay certain classes of workers at least the _____. Jobs provide some form of _____, or payment, for work performed. Many companies offer their workers a[n] _____ to provide them with income when they retire. People who earn a certain amount of money each week or month no matter how many hours they work earn a[n] _____. Some companies provide some type of _____ to encourage employees to work harder. Additional compensation or services companies provide to their employees are called _____. Persons who are paid a percentage of the value of something they sell receive a[n] _____. When a company makes a profit and distributes a percentage of the profit to its employees, it is offering employees an incentive called _____.

Review What You Learned

1. What are two ways employers compensate employees for the work they do?
2. Describe the difference between a wage and a salary.
3. What kind of wage standard was established by the Fair Labor Standards Act?
4. How are workers paid who do piece-work?
5. What three kinds of insurance are employers required by law to provide?
6. What is a floating holiday?
7. For what type of application is a CD-ROM drive a central component?
8. What statistics, other than wages, should you look at when comparing job offers?

Understand Business Concepts

1. What is an advantage of being paid a wage rather than a salary?
2. Why do some companies offer their employees profit sharing?
3. What advantage does an employee usually get from being enrolled in a company-sponsored health insurance plan?
4. What kind of insurance would cover an employee who sprained her wrist when a piece of machinery at her job malfunctioned?
5. Why might a company offer its employees a tuition-reimbursement program?
6. How can a CD-ROM be used as a marketing tool or an employment recruiting tool?
7. Why is it important to find out the cost of living if you are comparing jobs in two different geographic locations?

6. CD-ROMs can act as electronic brochures. People can easily identify what they are interested in and choose those items from the menu.

7. The cost of living could be significantly higher or lower in one of the locations. Lower living costs could compensate for a lower wage or salary.

Think Critically

1. Answers will vary depending on students' preferences.

2. Possible answer: Each worker is different and has different wants and needs. Most potential employees and current employees would see being able to choose which benefits they want as a benefit in itself.

Chapter 36 **Review**

Think Critically

1. **Evaluate.** Would you prefer to get a salary with the possibility of earning an annual bonus or would you prefer to earn an hourly wage with overtime pay for extra hours worked? Explain your answer.

2. **Hypothesize.** Why do you think some employers have begun offering their employees a flexible benefits package in which employees can choose the benefits they want?

Use What You Learned

1. **Group Project.** The labor force has changed radically since the 1940s. With your group, determine the kinds of changes that have taken place. Do some research to find out which population groups made up the labor force in your state for each of the following years: 1950, 1960, 1970, 1980, 1990, and the current year. How culturally diverse was the labor force? How many female workers were in the labor force? Graph your findings and discuss with the class possible reasons for the changes.

2. Interview three people you know who have full-time jobs. Ask them about the benefits they receive. Include questions about health insurance coverage, paid time off, qualification period for benefits, bonuses or profit sharing, and flexible benefits packages.
    Make a chart comparing the benefits statistics of each job.

3. **Computer Application.** Do on-line research to find articles in magazines and newspapers about current trends in employment. Topics you may want to explore include: flexible benefits packages, job enrichment programs, basic skills training, flextime, and job redesign programs. Use word processing software to write a 250-word summary of the information you retrieved.

4. **Skill Reinforcement.** Select two occupations that interest you and research current trends in each occupation. Here are some questions to consider. Will the number of jobs increase by the year 2005? How do the wages or salaries for these jobs compare in different locations? What effect would different living costs in the locations have on the earnings? Make a chart similar to the chart on page 621 comparing the statistics about the two occupations you chose. Then write a paragraph summarizing which job you think is better financially.

Save your work in your Business Portfolio.

Use What You Learned
1. Make sure all students participate in the group project. Rubric: Graph.
2. Students may choose to use a computer to make their charts. Rubric: Charts and Tables.

3. Students with no access to a computer may use periodical indexes to do their research and may write their summaries by hand. Rubric: Essay.
4. Students' answers will vary. Rubrics: Charts and Tables; Paragraph.

Independent Practice

Use the Chapter 36 worksheets in *Student Activity Guide 2* for additional practice and application activities. *Student Activity Guide 2* provides vocabulary exercises, reading comprehension checks, problems, projects, and simulations of business and economic situations. A Teacher's Annotated Edition provides answers.

ASSESS

Portfolio Assessment

The portfolio projects are designed to lead students to develop a collection of their best work to submit to you for assessment. You and your students should decide which projects will be included in their respective Business Portfolios. Refer students to the specific rubric(s) from the *Alternative Assessment Strategies* booklet listed with each of the project notes below. These rubrics will alert students to the criteria you will use to assess their projects.

Chapter Assessment

Use the Chapter 36 Test from the *Test Masters* booklet to evaluate students' understanding of the chapter concepts. An answer key is provided. Or create your own customized test using the *Testmaker* software.

Business Issue

Business Issue

IMMIGRATION AND THE ECONOMY

Highlight the Issue

Before students read pages 630–631, point out that the United States has always been a haven for immigrants. Ask: Is it time for the United States to change its stance toward welcoming immigrants in view of our country's current population and economy? Encourage students to explain their opinions.

IMMIGRATION AND THE ECONOMY

Over the years millions of immigrants from around the world have come to the United States to make new lives. Now some people are concerned that the government is letting in too many immigrants, particularly unskilled immigrants. Should immigration be limited to favor the entry of skilled workers over unskilled workers?

Pro

The U.S. population is growing too rapidly, largely due to immigration. Each year about 880,000 newcomers—legal and illegal—enter the United States. Unfortunately, the U.S. economy can't expand fast enough to provide jobs for all Americans, let alone the new immigrants. Government statistics show that in the next decade the number of new workers will exceed the number of new jobs by more than 1.5 million.

The new immigrants compete with native-born Americans for jobs. Low-skilled American workers are especially likely to be hurt because immigrant workers are often willing to accept very low wages. According to many economists, for every six or seven immigrants, one unskilled American loses a job.

Because they earn low wages, unskilled immigrants are also more likely to use the welfare system. This costs U.S. taxpayers billions of dollars a year. By reforming immigration policies to favor skilled workers, we would get the economic benefits of immigration without the drain on social services.

Immigration policies should also be changed because the needs of the U.S. economy have changed. One hundred years ago, the United States needed laborers to build railroads, mine ore, harvest crops, and work in factories. A lack of skills and education was not such a problem. Today our high-tech industries need skilled workers to help U.S. businesses compete in the global economy.

Skilled immigrants do contribute to the economy, especially in science and engineering. One-third of U.S. engineers and computer-technology designers were born in other countries. This talent helps U.S. industries succeed in world markets.

We must face the fact that the United States can't accept everyone who wants to come here. We need to limit immigration. Favoring those with the skills our society needs makes good economic sense.

Extend the Issue

Have groups of students survey at least 10 people to find out how many favor limiting the number of new immigrants. Be sure that students ask the people they survey to provide reasons for their opinions. Have groups share the results of their surveys with the class. Ask the class to identify commonly held opinions and to evaluate the validity of some of those opinions.

Con

It's just not true that the United States is being overrun by immigrants. From 1980 to 1990, 8.6 million legal immigrants entered the United States, just 3.5 percent of the total U.S. population. The population as a whole is not growing that rapidly either. In the next 60 years, researchers estimate that the U.S. population will grow by about 128 million, roughly the same rate as during the past 60 years.

Immigrants don't take jobs away from Americans. During the 1980s wave of immigration, the 10 states that had the most immigrants also had unemployment rates below average. Each new immigrant is also a new consumer, increasing the demand for goods and services. This increased demand means more jobs for people producing those goods and services. Many immigrants also become entrepreneurs, running their own businesses and creating more jobs.

Immigrants also give more than they take from the economy as a whole. A 1994 study by the Urban Institute found that "immigrants generate significantly more in taxes paid than they cost in services received."

Furthermore, immigration policy should not favor skilled immigrants over unskilled. The United States needs unskilled workers, too. Many industries such as agriculture and garment manufacturing rely on immigrants who are willing to do hard work for low wages—jobs native-born Americans don't want. Employers and consumers benefit from immigrant workers, whose labor keeps costs and prices low for many products.

There's another problem with changing immigration policy to favor skilled immigrants: How do you measure a person's potential for economic success? Many immigrants who came to this country with little formal education or few language skills became very successful. They were hardworking and ambitious even though they didn't have formal resumes.

An important American ideal is summed up in the poem that appears on the Statue of Liberty. It says "Send these, the homeless, tempest-tost to me,/ I lift my lamp beside the golden door." It doesn't say "Send these, the college graduates, computer engineers to me." We should continue to heed the words of Lady Liberty and open the golden door to all immigrants—not just those with diplomas.

Update the Issue

Have students use current publications to find out about the United States' present immigration policies. Suggest that students focus on such issues as whether any quotas have been imposed, what percentage of immigrants use the welfare system, and how many immigrants start new businesses. Have students share the information they find with the class.

Unit 12 Planning a Career in Today's World

Chapter	Learning Objectives
37 **Developing a Career Plan** pp. 634–649	• Explain how taking a self-inventory can help you plan a career. • Identify sources of information that can help you learn about careers and the required education and training. • Describe how computer users can access information from the information superhighway. • Name some strategies that will help you continue to learn and develop skills once you have entered the workforce.
38 **The World of Work** pp. 650–665	• Identify characteristics employers look for in employees. • Describe how to prepare a resume, write a cover letter, and fill out a job application. • List five sources of information about job openings. • Explain how to get ready for an interview.

Business Issue: **Benefits for Laid-Off Workers, pp. 666–667**

National Standards for Business Education*	Chapter Highlights			
	Focus on Features	Building Business Skills	Visual Learning	Case Analysis
CD: I A, II A, IV A, IV B, VI A, VI B; *EPF:* XV; *IS:* VII	Technology: Information Superhighway, p. 638	Employability: Showing a Capacity for Learning, p. 642	Major Types of Abilities, p. 637 Programs That Link School and Work, p. 644	Marketing Careers, p. 647
CD: II A, III A, III B, V B, V C; *EPF:* XV	Careers: Personal, Family, and Community Services, p. 656	Employability: Maintaining a Positive Attitude, p. 660	Resume, p. 654 Cover Letter, p. 658 Employment Application, p. 659	Job Offers, p. 663

* Level 3 Performance Expectations: Career Development (CD), Economics and Personal Finance (EPF), Information Systems (IS). See page T14 for all 12 content areas.

Unit 12

Look Back

Have students remember that most occupations can be classified either as goods-producing or service occupations. In the United States, service jobs account for more than 75 percent of the workforce. All jobs provide some form of compensation. Wages and salaries are compensation, but many companies also provide additional compensation to their employees in the form of benefits such as health insurance and paid leave.

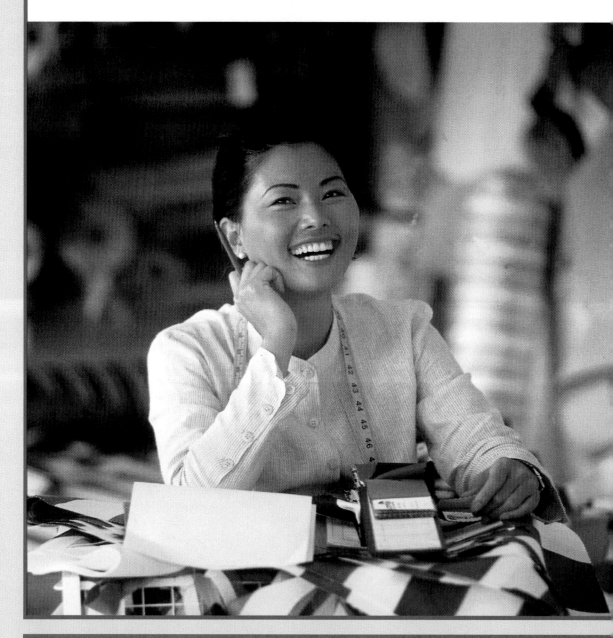

UNIT 12 COOPERATIVE LEARNING PROJECT

Roundrobin Activity

Preparation: Distribute photocopies to each student of BLMs 23 and 24 from the *Cooperative Learning Strategies* booklet.

Guidelines: Have students work in pairs to role play a job interview. One student will be the interviewer and another will portray the interviewee. BLM 23

Planning a Career in Today's World

T his unit discusses strategies for searching for the best job for you. The first chapter describes ways to learn about possible jobs and how to qualify for them. The second chapter discusses mechanisms of a job application, such as interviews, from the perspective of the employer and of the applicant.

Look Ahead
Point out that choosing a career is one of the most important decisions a person will ever make. Anyone planning a career should evaluate his or her interests, abilities, wants and needs, values, and goals. Career planners must also find out the qualifications required for different careers. When looking for a job, many job seekers use a resume, which provides a summary of the potential employee's level of education, skills, work experience, and character.

633

provides a list of questions for the interviewer to ask. Students will take turns playing each role. Students should work individually to do the self-evaluation given on BLM 24.

CHAPTER 37

FOCUS

Introduce the Chapter

Major Concepts
- Find Out About Yourself
- Locate Career Information
- Narrow Your Choices

Introduce the Topic
Give students five minutes to list their favorite activities, both in and out of school. Tell them to keep the list as a reference. Point out that in Chapter 37 they will learn how their interests can be of help in choosing a career.

Use Business Terms
Have students look at the Business Terms and note any of the terms that are familiar to them. Ask them to define these terms or try to recall the context in which they were used. For those terms that are totally unfamiliar, have students venture a meaning. Reinforce correct definitions. For terms that they cannot define, advise students to note the definitions in the chapter.

USE VISUALS

Explain that parents, teachers, and guidance counselors are good sources of career information. Ask: In what places could you find career information? (School guidance office, school library, and public library.)

Business terms

interests

networking

qualifications

entry-level job

career ladder

postsecondary education

associate degree

bachelor's degree

alternative

trade-offs

634

CHAPTER 37 RESOURCES

Instructional Resources

Lesson Plan for Chapter 37

Teaching Transparencies 37-1, 37-2, 37-3, 37-4

Strategies and Worksheets for Teaching Transparencies 37-1, 37-2, 37-3, 37-4

Enrichment Master 37-1

Student Activity Guide 2–TAE for Chapter 37

Test Master for Chapter 37

Alternative Assessment Strategies

Math Skills Review

International Business Strategies

Cooperative Learning Strategies

Communication Skills Review

Ethics in Business Strategies

Developing *a* Career Plan

Learning objectives

After completing this chapter, you will be able to:
- Explain how taking a self-inventory can help you plan a career.
- Identify sources of information that can help you learn about careers and the required education and training.
- Describe how computer users can access information from the information superhighway.
- Name some strategies that will help you continue to learn and develop skills once you have entered the workforce.

Consider what you know

- It is important to find a job that fulfills your personal needs as well as your financial needs. In addition to salary or wages, you should consider a company's working conditions and the benefits it offers to help you determine if you should take the job.

Consider what you want to know

- How can taking a personal inventory help you plan your career?
- What sources of information are available to help you learn about careers and the training and education that they require?
- What resources are available on the information superhighway?
- How can you keep learning new skills once you have started working?

Consider how to use what you learn

- As you read this chapter, think about how the interests, abilities, wants, needs, values, and goals of the people you know are related to the jobs they have or the jobs they would like to have.

Multimedia Resources

Technology Resource Guide

Distance Learning Guide

Internet Resource Guide

Professional Resources

School-to-Work/Tech Prep Strategies

Instructional Poster

Spanish Resources

Testmaker Software for Chapter 37

The Wall Street Journal Video Series
Video & Activities for Chapter 37

Business and Marketing Computer Applications—An Integrated Software Simulation Using Microsoft Works

Stocktracker—A Stock Market Software Simulation

Where's the Dough? Board Game

TEACH

Develop Concepts

Find Out About Yourself

Distribute photocopies of Enrichment Master 37-1 and have students make a personal inventory with the following categories: Interests, Abilities, Wants and Needs, and Values and Goals. Have each student make a personal list for each category. Encourage students to write down as many ideas as possible and to add to the list throughout the study of the chapter. Explain to students that their charts will help them focus on career possibilities.

Choosing a career is a very important decision that each person has to make. The decision will affect the rest of your life. As you learned in Chapter 36, the amount of money you will earn is not the only thing you should consider; you need to think about job satisfaction, working conditions, and the benefits you need.

In this chapter you will begin evaluating and planning what you want from a career. A good career plan has two parts—finding out about yourself and finding out about the work you want to do. The first part requires a clear understanding of your own interests, abilities, wants and needs, values, and goals. The second part involves investigating career resources and requirements and developing a plan that will work for you.

FIND OUT ABOUT YOURSELF

Business & HISTORY

Paul Revere is best known for his midnight ride, but it had little to do with his career, or rather, careers. As a silversmith he crafted some of the finest decorative silver items of his era. He also worked with other metals and made surgical tools, bells, and eyeglasses. When the Revolutionary War began, he became an entrepreneur and set up a gunpowder factory. After the war he discovered a copper-rolling process and built the country's first copper-rolling mill.

Once you know something about the job market, you can take the next step in planning your career. You should start by taking a personal inventory—examining your interests, your abilities, and what you want out of life. To make this inventory count, you have to be as honest with yourself as you can.

Your Interests

What do you enjoy doing? Your answer to this question will tell a lot about your **interests.** Many people's hobbies are their interests. For example, cooking, writing stories, hiking, and playing musical instruments are all hobbies. Each one might suggest a possible occupation.

You should also consider what subjects and activities you enjoy at school. If you like to do science experiments or write articles for the school newspaper, you may find that one of those interests could lead to a career.

In addition, think about any work you have done in your community. This might include volunteering at the local hospital or working part-time at a restaurant. Ask yourself what interests led you to do this work and what you like about it.

Your Abilities

After you have considered what you like to do, ask yourself what you are good at doing. Identifying the things that you do well will help you choose a career. Every person has certain

Cooperative Learning Think-Pair-Share

Have each student get together with another student he or she knows fairly well. Have each partner make up a list of at least five abilities or strengths his or her partner has. After partners have exchanged and discussed their lists, ask students how many were surprised by the information they received from their partners. Have students add the information provided by their partners to their personal inventories.

Refer to the *Cooperative Learning Strategies* booklet for additional cooperative learning strategies.

abilities that are made up of natural aptitudes and learned skills. Aptitudes are very different from skills. In Chapter 1 you learned that aptitudes are talents that come naturally, whereas skills require learning and practice. If you are good at figuring out how to fix things, you probably have mechanical aptitude. You need more than aptitude, however, to repair a sophisticated personal computer. To fix a computer you would need to study electronics.

Abilities may be classified in many ways. Figure 37-1 below provides a classification of five types of abilities and examples of occupations in which each type of ability is very important.

If you are not sure what your strongest aptitudes and skills are, a guidance counselor or teacher can give you information about aptitude and skills tests you can take. If you get top grades in certain subjects, that is an indication that you have aptitudes and skills in those areas. Another way to recognize abilities is to ask yourself what other people have said about your talents and skills. For example, if people often praise your artwork, you probably have creative and artistic abilities. As you examine your abilities, keep in mind that you can develop many skills if you have enough interest. Determination and enjoyment are key factors in the development of skills.

Your Wants and Needs

When you choose an occupation, you should consider whether it can satisfy your own wants and needs. Will you be

FIGURE 37-1

These five major abilities are used to a certain degree in every job, but some abilities are especially important in particular jobs. What ability does a person have who listens well to others and can work well with a variety of people?

Major Types of Abilities

Ability		Explanation	Examples of Occupations
Mechanical		Ability to work well with your hands	Copier Technician Carpenter
Math		Ability to work well with numbers	Retail Sales Associate Insurance Underwriter
Communication		Ability to express yourself in speech and in writing	Writer Customer Service Representative
Human Relations		Ability to understand and get along with people	Supervisor Health-Care Worker
Problem Solving		Ability to apply the reasoning process to problem situations	Manager Systems Analyst

Learning Activity
Have each student gather some background information about a career that he or she finds interesting by interviewing someone who has a job in that field. Suggest that students ask some of the following questions: What tasks do you find most interesting? Least interesting? Which factors helped you choose this career? Is your job related to any of your hobbies? What are the possibilities for advancement?

USE VISUALS
Allow students a minute or so to examine Figure 37-1. Then ask students to think about what ability or abilities might be most important in the following occupations: accountant (math), auto repair technician (mechanical, problem solving), and newspaper reporter (communication). Answer to caption: Human relations ability.

USE TRANSPARENCIES
Use Teaching Transparency 37-1 and its corresponding strategies and worksheet from the *Teaching Transparency Strategies and Worksheets* booklet to help students relate abilities to specific occupations. Verify student worksheets using the Answer Key.

Reteaching Strategy

Have students create a wall chart listing the five types of abilities. Ask students to draw or clip pictures from newspapers and magazines that portray jobs in the skill area and add them to the proper category on the chart.

FOCUS ON **Technology**

Discuss

Ask volunteers who have "surfed the Internet" to describe the features they found most interesting. Have students define the terms *information superhighway* (nationwide computer network that could link all computer users), *information service* (company that provides on-line services for a fee), *Internet* (collection of information available on worldwide interconnected computer networks), and *file transfer protocol* (set of rules that determines the format in which data is sent).

Learning Activity

Have a class discussion about how a job could satisfy nonmaterial needs. Discuss the nonmaterial rewards of occupations such as nurse, newspaper reporter, and musician. Ask volunteers to name some occupations that interest them and to explain what nonmaterial needs could be met by those jobs.

Information Superhighway

What's all this buzz about the "information superhighway"? Where is it? Where does it lead?

The *information superhighway* is a nationwide network that could potentially connect every home, school, business, and organization in the country. The information superhighway has been described as a computerized version of the transcontinental railroad and the interstate highway system because it offers a way for information to travel to millions of locations.

Although the superhighway is still "under construction," much of the initial roadway is in place. For example, many businesses regularly access commercial information services. An *information service* is a company that provides on-line services for a fee. The fee allows a customer access, via telephone lines, to an account that acts as a window to the company's central computers. Businesses reach databases on hundreds of topics, including business news and industry analyses, updates on business law, and newly issued patents.

Another existing element of the superhighway system is the Internet. The *Internet* is a collection of information available on worldwide, interconnected computer networks, with each network having its own rules and policies. The Internet network of resources allows many users to communicate and exchange valuable data among researchers, educators, students, and individuals who are thousands of miles apart. Like commercial information services, access to the Internet is via telephone lines—and computer.

One of the most exciting features of the information superhighway is *file transfer protocol* (FTP). FTP is a set of rules or guidelines that determines the format in

able to earn enough to provide for your basic needs—food, shelter, and clothing—and at least some of your wants? A career can also help you meet your nonmaterial needs:

- Safety—the need to be physically and psychologically safe and secure.
- Belonging—the desire to be accepted, liked, and loved.
- Esteem—the desire to be respected and recognized as a valued human being.
- Self-actualization—the need to achieve your full potential and do work that is suited to your skills and interests.

Everyone has these needs, but different people put them in different orders of importance. You should try to find the career that best matches your individual pattern of needs.

Your Values and Goals

Wants and needs are a result of your values and goals. It is important to make choices that match your values and goals. Different people faced with the same choices will choose differently. When you examine possible careers, you need to ask yourself: "Which one would be best for me?"

638 UNIT 12 PLANNING A CAREER IN TODAY'S WORLD

Enrichment Strategy

Poll the class to see what careers are of most interest. Invite workers in those fields to talk to the class about their work. Topics could include ways to prepare for a career in their field and the projected employment outlook for their field.

which the data will be sent from one computer to another. FTP allows users, no matter what computer or operating systems they use, to download or transfer files from a remote location to their own computer. For exam-

ple, a biomedical drug company can retrieve patent information from the United States Patent Office, a paper on heart-liver transplants from the *Journal of the American Medical Association,* and news articles on the most recent heart-liver transplant.

Newer, more broad-based commercially available information services such as CompuServe, Prodigy, and America Online link the subscriber not only to the service's central computer, but also to every other subscriber to the service. Such services are also a primary way of accessing the Internet.

This electronic information sharing can give businesses, especially those which want to be globally competitive, the edge they need in a worldwide market. All each business needs is a computer, a modem, and access to an on-line service. The wealth of information available from on-line services is also a useful research aid for career planners.

Follow Through

If most students are not familiar with the Internet, arrange for a demonstration on how to use the Internet for research purposes. Ask students what equipment is needed to do this. (Computer, modem, access to an on-line service.) Over a period of a few days, have each student use the Internet to research a career field he or she is interested in. Have a class discussion about the range of sources students found and the variety of materials they were able to access. Refer to the *Internet Resource Guide* booklet for additional information on the Internet.

Now take a different kind of inventory. What is important to you? Do you want to have challenge or adventure in your life? Do good times with family and friends or helping others top your list? Knowing which values and goals are most important to you can help you choose an occupation. For example, being an airline pilot or flight attendant or traveling a lot on business may satisfy your need for adventure. However, if you value spending your evenings at home, such careers probably are not for you.

Some people may place great emphasis on independence and may not want to work for someone else. These people may become entrepreneurs. To them, the risk and hard work involved in owning a business is worthwhile because they are free to make their own decisions. On the other hand, many people prefer working for others because they value the steady income and job benefits.

Quick Check

1. What are a person's interests?
2. Name five major classes of ability.
3. Name four nonmaterial needs.

CHAPTER 37   DEVELOPING A CAREER PLAN   **639**

Business Brief

America Online has a feature geared specifically to career planners. A person can take an on-line aptitude test, complete interest-determining exercises, and even schedule a consultation with an on-screen job counselor.

Quick Check Answers

1. The things he or she enjoys doing.
2. Mechanical, math, communication, human relations, and problem-solving skills.
3. Safety, belonging, esteem, and self-actualization.

Cooperative Learning   Write a Note

Divide the class into teams and have individual members each write a note explaining what they understand about the chapter so far. They should also write a question about a concept that is not clear to them. Team members should trade notes with each other and write answers to other team member's questions.

Refer to the *Cooperative Learning Strategies* booklet for additional cooperative learning strategies.

USE VISUALS

Ask students to study the photo. Ask: How could you begin networking? Point out that many people find out about jobs from friends or acquaintances who tell them about openings at their own workplaces. (Possible answer: Students might say that they would first talk to their friends at school.)
Answer to caption: You might choose to become an entrepreneur.

Develop Concepts

Locate Career Information

Emphasize to students that it is important to be focused when *networking.* Suggest that they develop a list of questions to ask people, for example: Which features of your work are most enjoyable? What are the disadvantages of your job? Their questions could be about the requirements of a specific employer or about the more general requirements of a specific field.

USE TRANSPARENCIES

Use Teaching Transparency 37-2 and its corresponding strategies and worksheet from the *Teaching Transparency Strategies and Worksheets* booklet to show students how they might develop a networking checklist. Verify student worksheets using the Answer Key.

Different people have different sets of values and goals that they use to make career choices. If you value your independence, what career might be good for you?

LOCATE CAREER INFORMATION

Investigating the job market can be overwhelming. After all, there are thousands of different occupations from which to choose. However, career information is plentiful and simple to use if you know how. Here are some sources that can be useful, no matter what career you decide to pursue.

Sources of Career Information

Other people are often your best and most abundant source of career information. Almost all workers are happy to explain what they do. This process of talking to other people about their jobs is called **networking.** The advantage of networking is that your network of contacts is not limited to the people you know personally. Because you have a network of friends, relatives, and acquaintances, you can probably find a person who works at almost any job in which you might be interested. That person can give you an insider's view on the career. In some cases, you may be able to visit the workplace.

Before you talk to people about their jobs, think about the questions you want to ask. Ask about their education and training, both before they were hired and after they started work. Also, try to ask questions that will give you a sense of what the job is like.

Meeting Student Diversity

Presenting information in small units aids students with attention problems. Ask students to read the "Locate Career Information" section and self-monitor their attention to the reading. Ask whether they think it is easier to read through the whole section and then take notes, or if it is better for them to break the section into smaller segments. Emphasize that there is no "correct way." The best approach is the one that works well for them.

Guidance counselors and teachers should be a part of your network as well. The guidance counselors at your school are trained to help you discover and evaluate possible careers. Teachers may be able to suggest careers that would use the abilities and interests you have displayed in class.

Your school guidance office, school library, and public library can be sources of information on careers. Start by looking in the following sources.

The *Occupational Outlook Handbook* (OOH) contains descriptions of more than 400 different occupations in 13 main occupational groups. It lists the fastest-growing job fields and provides addresses of places to write for more information. The OOH is also available on CD-ROM.

The Encyclopedia of Careers and Vocational Guidance is a four-volume encyclopedia that profiles careers in 14 different occupational categories. It contains detailed descriptions of 540 jobs including educational requirements, employment outlook, and opportunities for experience.

The *Vocational Careers Sourcebook* is a valuable career-planning source. For each of the 135 occupations described, the book directs readers to organizations, periodicals, and many other sources where they can obtain additional information about a particular occupation.

While you are in the library, check the catalog for other useful books. Also, ask the librarian about magazines, newspapers, or electronic sources that highlight careers.

For additional free information, you can also attend career days and job fairs that may be held at a local school or community center. At these events many companies display information about the work they do and the kinds of jobs they offer. Some companies hold open houses or give tours of their facilities. Depending on your area of interest, you may be able to volunteer or work part-time in the business that appeals to you.

Job Requirements

As you talk to people, read about jobs, and see workers in action, you will probably be drawn to a particular career field, such as health care or finance. However, hundreds of different jobs are available in each of these fields. To narrow your career choices, you need detailed information about the **qualifications,** or requirements, for specific jobs.

Work Requirements   As you investigate the details of a career that interests you, find out everything you can about the work requirements. Keep the following list of questions in mind when you look at a specific job.

F.Y.I.

It is important to try to determine whether the career you are interested in has a promising future or outlook. Based on factors such as low unemployment, expected employment growth, potential salary growth, and potential for promotion, the ten careers with the best outlooks through the year 2005 are: software engineer, computer systems analyst, psychologist, military officer, computer service technician, patrol officer, attorney, surgeon, podiatrist, and accountant.

Learning Activity

Have students make a list of five people to be part of their career information networks. Emphasize to students that they can list people whose occupations they know and people whose occupations they don't know. Have students write down three questions to ask each person. They may want to vary the questions, depending on how well they know each person. Have students take notes during each interview session. Discuss with students the kind of information they obtained. Ask volunteers to describe the results of some of their interviews.

TEACHING TIP

Obtain a copy of the *Occupational Outlook Handbook, The Encyclopedia of Careers and Vocational Guidance,* the *Vocational Careers Sourcebook,* or another career reference handbook and give a brief demonstration of ways to use the publication to research occupations. Or ask your school's guidance counselor to demonstrate how to use these publications.

Making Connections ▶▷ Technology

If you have the *Occupational Outlook Handbook* available both on CD-ROM and in print, invite students to compare the advantages and disadvantages of print and electronic versions. Which was easier to use? Which was easier to read? Which was faster?

Building Business Skills

Model

Ask students to recall their first days of high school. Then point out that they probably used strategies very similar to the Strategies for Learning shown on page 643 in order to adapt to high school. Ask volunteers to give examples from their own experiences for each of the strategies.

USE TRANSPARENCIES

Use Teaching Transparency 37-3 and its corresponding strategies and worksheet from the *Teaching Transparency Strategies and Worksheets* booklet to show students how they might evaluate the work requirements of a job. Verify student worksheets using the Answer Key.

Learning Activity

Have students interview two relatives or friends who work in different career fields. Students should find out what kind of career ladder there is for each occupation. Ask students to write a 250-word report that highlights the similarities and differences in the career ladders for both jobs.

EMPLOYABILITY

Showing a Capacity for Learning

Explanation

Learning doesn't stop after school. By being alert to what's going on around you and making a conscious effort to understand what you see, you can learn a great deal. By asking questions about what you experience and actively seeking answers, you can develop an inquiring mind and a capacity for learning that will stand you in good stead in your career.

In today's high-tech workplace, no sooner has one technology taken hold than another rises up to replace it. This demands learning and adaptation from workers—so much so that showing a capacity for learning is vital for job success and advancement.

Once you enter the world of work, you'll be taking more responsibility for your own education. Start by learning what's going on around you. Even if you're just beginning in an entry-level position, find out as much as you can about your company. What exactly does it do or make? How is it organized? Who does what?

Be willing to learn on your own. Are there books or videos that can teach you job skills? What periodicals exist for people with your career interests?

To learn about other jobs you might like to have, question people about their work. Think about ways you can get the knowledge to move to different positions.

- What tasks do people in the position typically perform? What are their responsibilities? Do they work with information, people, machines, tools, or a combination of these? Do they perform a variety of tasks, or do they do the same thing many times?
- Which skills do people in the position use? Are these skills learned on the job, or must workers already have these skills to apply for the job?
- What personal and physical characteristics are necessary? What type of personality is best for the position? Do the tasks require problem-solving skills or good manual dexterity?
- Is any previous work experience required or preferred? If so, what kind?

Career Ladders In many occupations, workers who want to move ahead follow a path of advancement. They usually start out in an **entry-level job;** that is, a job at the beginning level. As the workers gain skill and experience and show a capacity to accept responsibility and exercise leadership, they can advance to higher positions within the field. This method of progressing from one level to another is called a **career ladder.**

642 UNIT 12 PLANNING A CAREER IN TODAY'S WORLD

Curriculum Connection　　　English and Communication

Have students suppose that they found out that the amount of competition for jobs in a field they were very interested in was very high. Would they still pursue jobs in that field or would they look for a field with less job competition? Allow students 15 minutes to write a paragraph explaining what they would do and why.

For those students who need to sharpen their written communication skills, choose among the worksheets in the *Communication Skills Review* booklet.

STRATEGIES FOR LEARNING

1. Be alert to what's going on around you.
2. Ask yourself and others questions about what you see and hear—and find the answers.
3. Learn everything you can about the company you work for—its products, structure, personnel, and opportunities.
4. Ask people questions about their jobs to help develop your career plan.
5. Investigate and use educational materials—books, tapes, and periodicals—that can teach you about your career.
6. Take advantage of company training to learn new skills.
7. Take courses outside of work, especially if your firm has a tuition reimbursement policy.
8. Never turn down an opportunity to learn a new skill.

Find out about educational opportunities at your company. Many firms offer in-house training to help employees learn. Don't hesitate to sign up for voluntary training sessions if you think they'll be helpful in any way. In addition, companies often encourage employees to continue their education by reimbursing them for the cost of job-related courses at colleges or technical schools.

Practice

Think about a job you have held or hold now. How could you apply the strategies listed in the box above to this job? How would you prepare yourself to advance to a higher position? Write a short paragraph answering these questions.

Practice
Students who have never held jobs can use a job they would like to have as the basis for writing their paragraphs. (Students' answers will vary but should present specific examples of how they could learn more about a job and other related positions.)

A career ladder describes the typical experience from an entry-level position to the top of the field. It may include many different jobs.

Suppose, for example, that you were interested in working in sales in the computer industry. You might start out working in a store that sells computers. Then, as you gained experience and knowledge of the field through work, training, and further schooling, you might move up the career ladder to become an assistant store manager. Perhaps, after many years, you would end up as the manager of the store or as director of a chain of computer stores or as the sales manager of a company that makes computers.

It is important to study the potential career ladder of the field in which you want to work. You can learn what skills and education you should have if you want to reach the highest levels.

Education and Training Find out the education requirements of the jobs that interest you. If you research a specific occupation using the methods mentioned earlier in the chapter, be sure you take a close look at the information about the level of education and types of high school courses job applicants

TEACHING TIP

Point out to students that advancement on a career ladder is not always within the same company. For example, a person might start out in an entry-level job at one company and a year or two later find a more advanced position with another company. After a few years in that position, the person might once again look for a more advanced position with yet another company.

Reteaching Strategy

Have students investigate the work requirements of a job that interests them. Have them use the bulleted questions given on page 642 as a guide for writing a descriptive 200-word report about the job's work requirements.

Give students some time to read through the information presented in Figure 37-2. Ask students what program or programs would be most suitable for a student who wanted to gain some experience running a business. Have students explain their answers. (Possible answer: School-Based Enterprise gives students a chance to run a business and become familiar with all aspects of the industry.) Answer to caption: Students' answers will vary.

Learning Activity

Students who are considering postsecondary education may want to send for several community college catalogs. Students can use the catalogs to compare programs, costs, financial aid, and other aspects of the different schools. Ask students to share the information with the rest of the class by giving a brief oral report.

should have. Today, virtually all jobs require workers to have at least a high school education.

You may be able to get some work experience while you are still in high school and get education credit for it at the same time. Your school may have a cooperative work or earn-and-learn program already set up. Apprenticeships, private industry programs, and pre-employment training also may be available through businesses in your area. In each of these programs, business and community leaders, teacher coordinators, and the students, themselves, work together to plan the student's work experience and education goals. Figure 37-2 below lists some of the kinds of programs that help students make the transition from school to work.

Many states also have vocational high schools or career centers that specialize in training students for jobs. Still other states have technical high schools. These schools are especially equipped to teach technical subjects such as computer programming or electronics.

Some careers may require **postsecondary education,** or education beyond high school. For some occupations, you may need to take courses at a technical college or community college. Some courses may be short-term, such as six to eight

FIGURE 37-2

There is a wide variation in school-to-work transition programs. Which of these kinds of programs might appeal to you?

PROGRAMS THAT LINK SCHOOL AND WORK

Cooperative Education (Co-op)	Students spend part of their day in high school and the other part at a paid job for which they also earn credit toward high school graduation. Programs normally last one year or less.
Tech Prep	Programs of courses link the last 2 years of high school with community or four-year college programs in specific occupational areas and can lead to an associate degree in a technical field. Work experience is sometimes, but not always, included. Employers participate in developing and designing the programs and may have worked on developing occupational competencies.
Career Academies	Organized as "schools within schools" in comprehensive high schools, each academy has a particular occupational or industrial theme, such as health or computer technology. Local employers serve as advisors to the academy and as mentors to the students and provide jobs and internships for participants. Students may be enrolled in career academies for 2 to 4 years.
Youth Apprenticeship	Employers provide employment and on-the-job training that lead to widely accepted credentials. The goal is to provide youths with opportunities to enter well-paying careers. Employers take part in administering the program. Apprenticeships have generally been offered in building and metal trades and licensed service occupations.
School-Based Enterprise	Students create and operate small businesses such as retail stores and child-care programs. These businesses provide students with an opportunity to learn all aspects of an industry. School-based enterprises contain an academic component as well.

Enrichment Strategy

If your school has a cooperative work program, ask the coordinator of the program to speak to the class about the requirements for the program, the types of experiences offered, and the advantages of the program for career exploration. Allow time for a question-and-answer session.

weeks, and lead to a certificate of completion. Others may be long-term, two-year courses that lead to an **associate degree.** After you work at a career for a time, you may want to learn more to advance to a higher position. This may require a four-year course of study at a college to get a **bachelor's degree.**

For people who do not plan to go to college but are willing to spend some years in training, becoming an apprentice is a good opportunity. An apprentice earns a wage while learning a trade by working with a master worker for a set period. Most opportunities as apprentices are in mechanical and construction occupations. As apprentices' skills increase, so does their pay. In some states workers such as electricians and plumbers must pass a test in order to get a license to work at their trade.

After you find out what additional education or training you will need, figure out how much it will cost. Look at a catalog from a school that you might attend. Keep in mind that public institutions and colleges are usually less costly than private schools. Also, public colleges and institutions usually cost less for residents of the state than for out-of-state students.

As you consider the cost of training and education, remember that people who graduate from a technical school or college usually earn more money than people who do not. Many college and vocational school students receive financial aid such as scholarships, grants, or loans. Your guidance counselor or the financial-aid officer at a local college can explain the options to you. Many libraries and guidance departments have books and other information on how to apply for scholarships and loans.

Quick Check

1. What do you call the process of talking to other people about their jobs?
2. Where does an entry-level job fit on the career ladder?
3. What are *qualifications*?
4. What are two levels of postsecondary degrees?

NARROW YOUR CHOICES

After you have analyzed your interests and abilities, and identified your wants, needs, values, and goals, it is time to start organizing your thoughts. In Chapter 1 you learned about ten career clusters—ten categories or fields of related jobs. These clusters are one way of organizing the many types of jobs in this

As the economy becomes increasingly global, there are more opportunities for careers in which people work outside of the United States. You can gain experience and develop skills for working with people from different cultures by studying foreign languages and enrolling in a study-abroad program. Bookstores, libraries, and guidance offices also have information about international career opportunities.

Business Brief

Apprenticeships date back to about A.D. 1000. A boy would become apprenticed to learn a trade such as metalworking, printing, or weaving when he was a young teen. Usually he went to live with a *master* who would feed, house, and clothe him for the time it took to learn the trade—about seven years. Once the training ended, the apprentice became a *journeyman* and was considered qualified to work at his craft or trade for a wage.

Quick Check Answers
1. Networking.
2. At the beginning level.
3. The requirements for a specific job.
4. Associate and bachelor's degrees.

Develop Concepts

Narrow Your Choices

Ask students why it is important when making decisions to have some alternatives. Point out to students that although they can probably rule out some career choices, it is a good idea to leave their options open. By the time students graduate, they will probably have had some work experience. They will also have gained additional education. These factors and others will influence the kind of career decisions they ultimately make.

Making Connections   ▶ **Postsecondary Education**

Have a representative from a community college or technical institute discuss programs offered, entrance requirements, extracurricular activities, and cost. Have students prepare some questions beforehand for the representative.

Have students work individually to list a few job alternatives that interest them. Collect students' lists and then group together students who have similar career interests. Have groups discuss ways they could work together to gather additional information about the jobs that interest them.

TEACHING TIP

For any careers in which students think they would be interested, ask them to write down some of the values the jobs reflect and some of their goals the jobs would satisfy.

USE TRANSPARENCIES

Use Teaching Transparency 37-4 and its corresponding strategies and worksheet from the *Teaching Transparency Strategies and Worksheets* booklet to show students how they compare different categories of careers. Verify student worksheets using the Answer Key.

Quick Check Answers

1. Another plan a person can put into action if the first plan does not work out.
2. They are making a trade-off.

---

country. One or two of these clusters may appeal to you and give you some ideas to pursue. Through your networking, reading, and researching, you will discover other jobs and careers that interest you. As you will recall, the first step in the decision-making process is identifying the problem. In this case, the problem is fairly obvious—which career field should you choose?

List Alternatives

What do you think are your best alternatives? An **alternative** is another plan you can put into action if your first plan does not work out. When you consider possible career fields or clusters, you should come up with more than one alternative. You do not want to narrow your options too much until you know more about each field. Begin listing alternatives by using interest as the key factor. Ask yourself which career fields really interest you. Then ask yourself which ones would help you satisfy your values, meet your goals, and satisfy your wants and needs. Finally, ask yourself whether you have the aptitude and believe that you have the ability to prepare for the career successfully.

Make Tentative Choices

After you have listed some alternatives, match your own characteristics with career fields to determine which careers seem possible for you. In reaching a decision, look at the advantages and disadvantages of each career from your point of view. Be sure to base your decisions on what matters most to you.

You can start by eliminating the careers that you are only mildly interested in. Then you might want to rule out the careers that would not help you satisfy your wants and needs, and so on. You may not find an occupation that satisfies all your values and goals and also your wants and needs.

Most people have to make **trade-offs** when choosing occupations. You could think of trade-offs as opportunity costs—people have to give up some things they want in a career in order to have other, more important, things. The key is to give up the things that are least important to you.

Quick Check

1. What is an alternative?
2. When people give up one thing they want in a career in order to fulfill another more important requirement, what are they doing?

Cooperative Learning   Group Discussion

Have groups identify the trade-offs in the following situation. Bruce was offered a job that paid $40,000 a year. The job would require that he travel about 40 percent of the time, which would mean he wouldn't be home on some evenings and weekends. He was offered another job that paid $34,000 and wouldn't require any travel. Have groups identify the trade-offs involved in each of the choices. (If Bruce took the first job, he would have to give up some of his leisure time. If he took the second job, instead, he wouldn't sacrifice his leisure time, but he would be making less money.)

Refer to the *Cooperative Learning Strategies* booklet for additional cooperative learning strategies.

Main Ideas

1. Skills generally may be classified as those involving manual dexterity, math, communication, human relations, or problem solving.

2. Other people are one of your best and most abundant sources of career information.

3. The *Occupational Outlook Handbook,* *The Encyclopedia of Careers and Vocational Guidance,* and the *Vocational Careers Sourcebook* are some places to look for information on careers and career planning.

4. A career ladder is a method of progressing from one level to another in a field, with increasing responsibility and increasing pay.

5. You should learn about the education and training required for specific occupations and look into their costs.

6. To help you narrow down your career field choices, you should take into account your interests, abilities, wants and needs, values, and goals.

7. The Internet and commercial information services are part of the information superhighway. Individuals and businesses all over the world exchange and retrieve data using their computers, modems, and telephone lines.

8. You can continue your education once you have started working by reading about your field, learning from more experienced coworkers, and taking advantage of training sessions at work.

CASE ANALYSIS Marketing Careers

Listed below are some sample job titles in several specialty areas of marketing careers. Each has a career ladder with increasing challenges, responsibilities, and salary. In which of these marketing specialty areas do you think you would be interested?

Marketing Research
Market research
    interviewer
Fieldwork director
Research analyst
Associate research director
Director of research

Promotion
Media planner
Assistant account
    executive
Account executive
Art director

Product Management
Marketing analyst
Product manager
Group product manager
General manager (hotel)

Retailing
Department manager
Executive trainee
Assistant buyer
Department store manager
Supermarket store
    manager
Buyer

Sales
Salesperson
Travel agent
Real estate agent
Insurance agent
Sales manager
Broker (stocks and bonds)

Top Management
Public relations director
Senior sales executive
Director of marketing
Vice president of
    marketing

CLOSE

Main Ideas

Main Ideas summarizes the key information in the chapter. It is a useful tool for reinforcement and review.

CASE ANALYSIS

Case Analysis provides a chapter-related case for student analysis and application of decision-making skills.

Answer
Answers will vary.

QUICK QUIZ

1. What are the five major classifications of abilities? (Mechanical, math, communication, human relations, and problem solving.)
2. Explain what networking means. (Talking to other people about their jobs.)
3. What is the first step on the career ladder? (An entry-level job.)
4. What do you call a plan you can put into action if your first plan doesn't work out? (An alternative.)

Chapter 37 **Review**

APPLY

Answers

Use the Language of Business

1. interests, **2.** trade-offs, **3.** alternative, **4.** networking, **5.** associate degree, **6.** entry-level job, **7.** career ladder, **8.** bachelor's degree, **9.** qualifications, **10.** postsecondary education.

Review What You Learned

1. Interests are activities a person enjoys; abilities are things a person is good at.
2. Aptitudes come naturally; skills are learned.
3. The *Occupational Outlook Handbook, The Encyclopedia of Careers and Vocational Guidance,* and the *Vocational Careers Sourcebook.*
4. Work requirements; requirements needed to move up the career ladder; and education and training requirements.
5. How to get started in a career; how to gain skills and experience to advance within the field.
6. Ones that interest you only mildly.
7. They will determine which career fields will satisfy your nonmaterial needs.
8. Collection of information on a global network of computer networks that maintains communications and exchanges data.
9. By reading publications or viewing videos related to your career field.

Understand Business Concepts

1. Interests; abilities; wants and needs; values and goals.
2. It affects income and leisure time.
3. It will help you when you are looking for a job.
4. They are familiar with your aptitudes and abilities as well as a variety of careers. They can help you match your aptitudes and abilities to an occupation.
5. Position at which a person begins a career. A sales representative is usually an entry-level job. Store manager, regional sales manager, and national sales manager could all be steps on that career ladder.

Use the Language of Business

When planning and making decisions about careers, it is important to understand the following terms. Match each term to its definition.

alternative
associate degree
bachelor's degree
career ladder
entry-level job

interests
networking
postsecondary education
qualifications
trade-offs

1. Types of things a person enjoys doing.
2. What a person makes when he or she gives up some things in order to have others.
3. Plan that can be put into action if another plan does not work.
4. Process of talking to other people about their jobs.
5. Result of the successful completion of a two-year postsecondary course of study.
6. Beginning level of the career ladder.
7. Method of progressing from one career level to another.
8. Result of successful completion of four-year course of postsecondary study.
9. Requirements for specific jobs.
10. Education beyond high school.

Review What You Learned

1. Explain the difference between interests and abilities.
2. How are aptitudes different from skills?
3. What are three career publications that you can use as sources of career information?
4. Which specific details concerning job requirements or qualifications should you investigate about the careers you are interested in?
5. What can you learn from studying the career ladder of an occupation?
6. When making tentative choices, which careers should you eliminate first?
7. How will your values affect the career you choose?
8. What is the Internet?
9. How can you learn more about your job on your own?

Understand Business Concepts

1. List the categories that should be included in a self-inventory.
2. How can an occupation affect a person's lifestyle?
3. What is one long-range benefit of developing an extensive network of contacts related to your career interests?
4. Why are guidance counselors and teachers especially helpful in matching your aptitudes to possible careers?
5. What is an entry-level position? Give an example of such a position, and describe what types of jobs it might lead to within the same career field.

6. The education or training will probably allow you to earn more money, which would more than make up for the initial expenses.
7. You also have to look at your interests, abilities, wants, and needs.
8. It acts as an electronic translator so data from different computer systems can be read by any computer user.
9. It will help you be more successful and do your job better. It could also help you advance in your career.

Think Critically

1. Possible answer: Entrepreneurs need to have some of or all of the five skills, but especially problem-solving and human-relations skills. Since entrepreneurs work for themselves, they are responsible for solving problems. They also have to know how to work well with their employees and patrons.
2. Because a person needs to know as many details as possible to make an informed decision.
3. Answers will vary depending on the job chosen.
4. Both require setting goals and devising a plan of action.

6. Why should you evaluate the cost of education or training for a career only after looking at its long-term effects?

7. In reaching a career decision, analyzing your own values and goals and the characteristics of jobs is not enough. Why?

8. Why is file transfer protocol (FTP) a necessary feature of the information superhighway?

9. Why is it worth your time to continue to learn once you have gotten a job?

Think Critically

1. **Evaluate.** What types of skills might entrepreneurs need to have? Why?

2. **Apply.** After making a few tentative career choices, why should a person investigate those careers further?

3. **Assess.** Choose a job you are interested in pursuing. What three qualifications do you think you would need for it?

4. **Explain.** How is a career strategy similar to a strategy for a business?

Use What You Learn

1. **Group Project.** Work in groups of four. Brainstorm a list of ten careers. For each career write the interests, abilities, wants and needs, and values and goals that you think would be relevant. Then divide into pairs. Interview your partner about his or her interests, abilities, wants and needs, and values and goals. Suggest one or two careers from your group's list that you think would be suitable for your partner. Then switch roles. Write a brief essay about the career your partner suggested for you and why you think it might or might not be suitable for you.

2. Use Figure 37-2 on page 644 as a guide in compiling a chart of programs in your state or locality that link school to work. Be sure to include names, addresses, telephone numbers, and other pertinent information.

3. **Computer Application.** Select a career cluster and determine the skills and knowledge necessary for it. Devise your personal plan to achieve competency in that career cluster. Use word processing software to prepare a copy of your plan.

4. **Skill Reinforcement.** Copy the Strategies for Learning on page 643 onto a separate sheet of paper. Use them as a basis for an interview of someone who has worked for several years in a career he or she enjoys. Ask the person to describe how he or she learned what was necessary to hold the job and advance. What suggestions does the person have for developing a capacity for learning? Add these to your existing list of strategies. Then write a short article based on the interview.

Save your work in your Business Portfolio.

Use What You Learned

1. Make sure all students participate in the group project. Rubric: Essay.

2. If students need help getting started, suggest they contact your school guidance office. Rubric: Charts and Tables.

3. Students with no access to a computer may make their plans manually. Rubric: Essay.

4. Students' answers will vary. Rubric: Essay.

FOCUS

Introduce the Chapter

Major Concepts
- What Employers Look For
- Beginning Your Job Search
- Contacting Potential Employers

Introduce the Topic
Ask volunteers to describe the process of applying for and interviewing for a part-time job. What kind of information was requested on the application? What kinds of questions did the interviewer ask? Ask the volunteers what advice they would give to someone applying for a job for the first time.

Use Business Terms
Ask students to look up the definitions of the Business Terms in a dictionary and jot down all the meanings. Then, as students read the chapter, have them note which dictionary definitions appear in the chapter. Stress that it is important to know which meanings of a word are appropriate to use.

USE VISUALS

Direct students' attention to the photo and then ask: What characteristics does this woman possess that might make a good impression on an employer? (Answers may include cleanliness, organization, and ability to work in any environment.)

CHAPTER
38

Business terms

reference

employment agencies

cover letter

650

CHAPTER 38 RESOURCES

Instructional Resources

Lesson Plan for Chapter 38

Teaching Transparencies 38-1, 38-2, 38-3, 38-4

Strategies and Worksheets for Teaching Transparencies 38-1, 38-2, 38-3, 38-4

Enrichment Master 38-1

Student Activity Guide 2–TAE for Chapter 38

Test Master for Chapter 38

Alternative Assessment Strategies

Math Skills Review

International Business Strategies

Cooperative Learning Strategies

Communication Skills Review

Ethics in Business Strategies

The World of Work

CHAPTER 38

Learning objectives

After completing this chapter, you will be able to:
- Identify characteristics employers look for in employees.
- Describe how to prepare a resume, write a cover letter, and fill out a job application.
- List five sources of information about job openings.
- Explain how to get ready for an interview.

Consider what you know

- Other people are one of your best and most abundant sources of career information. When investigating a career, you should consider the education and training required and look at the career ladder to determine how people advance.

Consider what you want to know

- What do employers look for in people they hire?
- What information is included in a resume, a cover letter, and a job application?
- Where can you find out about job openings?
- How should you prepare yourself for an interview?
- What skills are important for jobs in the field of personal, family, and community services?
- What steps can you take to maintain a positive attitude at work?

Consider how to use what you learn

- As you read this chapter, think about what you already know about the job market in your area. How have you or people you know handled job interviews?

Multimedia Resources

Technology Resource Guide
Distance Learning Guide
Internet Resource Guide
Professional Resources
School-to-Work/Tech Prep Strategies
Instructional Poster
Spanish Resources

Testmaker Software for Chapter 38
The Wall Street Journal Video Series
   Video & Activities for Chapter 38
Business and Marketing Computer
   Applications—An Integrated Software
   Simulation Using Microsoft Works
Stocktracker—A Stock Market Software
   Simulation
Where's the Dough? Board Game

Motivate the Learning

Learning Objectives
Point out to students that the learning objectives show what they will learn in the chapter. Tell students to keep these objectives in mind as they work through the chapter. Note that the last two objectives listed refer to the Focus on Careers feature and the Building Business Skills feature.

Consider What You Know
Review briefly the main sections of *Chapter 37 Developing a Career Plan:* Find Out About Yourself; Locate Career Information; and Narrow Your Choices.

Consider What You Want to Know
Have students keep the listed questions in mind as they preview the chapter by quickly paging through it, looking at the pictures, and reading the section headings and figure titles.

Consider How to Use What You Learn
Remind students that at the end of the chapter they will develop projects related to preparing themselves to enter the labor force. Suggest that students think about how they would present themselves to a potential employer at an interview.

TEACH

Develop Concepts

What Employers Look For

Have students imagine that they are a manager of a store that sells athletic goods and clothing. Tell them that they need to hire a floor sales representative who will be responsible for answering customers' questions and working at the cash register. Have students write a profile outlining the kind of education, skills, previous work experience, and personality the ideal candidate would have.

Business & HISTORY

Some people have become successful by recognizing the potential in a seemingly troublesome situation. In 1916 Clarence Birdseye was in Canada studying wildlife. It was so cold that his food supplies froze; however, Birdseye discovered that the food was still good. He worked out a technique for quick-freezing vegetables so they would keep for a long time. He sold the process to General Foods for $1 million. Birdseye's name still appears on a brand of frozen food today.

You learned what to look for in a job and how to plan and choose a career. You will be able to use what you have learned when you go out to look for a job. But how *do* you go about looking for a job? Where do you start?

Fortunately, most employers follow similar procedures when they have job openings to fill. Once you know what those procedures are, you can move through the steps with confidence. This chapter discusses some of the qualities that employers look for in employees and provides some guidelines for starting your job search and succeeding in a job once you have entered the workforce.

WHAT EMPLOYERS LOOK FOR

Different jobs require different qualifications. What is important for one job may be less important for another. There are, however, certain constants. Employers want to know about the applicant's education, skills, work experience, and character. All these factors influence an employer's decision.

Level of Education

For most jobs, employers want applicants who have at least a high school diploma. High school dropouts these days have fewer job opportunities, especially if they have no previous work experience. On the whole, the level of education of workers in our country has risen. Today, nearly 40 percent of the people who work have at least some postsecondary education.

Required Skills

Employers expect workers to have certain basic skills for practically any job. Employees must be able to read at least well enough to function in their jobs. They must be able to communicate with others and do simple mathematical problems. They must be able to follow instructions, and they must be able to get along with others. Employers find these skills essential.

Employers evaluate your skills by looking at the level of your education, your grades in certain subjects, the results of tests you may have taken, and your work experience. Sometimes they check with teachers or former employers.

Curriculum Connection   English and Communication

Ask students to list all the part-time jobs they have held. Students may list jobs they have performed on an informal basis such as babysitting or yard work. Students may find it helpful to break down the jobs according to tasks performed and skills used to perform those tasks. Ask students to analyze the skills they gained and write a brief essay describing how those skills will be of value to them when applying for jobs in the future.

For those students who need to sharpen their communication skills, choose among the worksheets in the *Communications Skills Review* booklet.

Work Experience

Many employers look for people with work experience. Sometimes employers even require that a prospective employee have a certain number of years of experience because an experienced worker brings tested skills, familiarity with work procedures, and knowledge of the field. An experienced worker usually needs less training to take over a new job.

Character and Personality

Though skills are important, employers also look for employees who have certain character traits. Employers value honesty, dependability, and hard work. They also want employees who have a positive attitude toward work, a desire to do the job well, and the ability to get along with other employees.

An employer can learn about these characteristics in several ways. An applicant's behavior during the interview provides some clues. For instance, a person who seems fidgety or bored during the interview will make a poor impression. Employers may check school records for information. If, for example, your grades match what you seem capable of doing, that may show a willingness to apply yourself. Extracurricular activities may indicate both additional enthusiasm and effort as well as possible leadership ability.

Quick Check

1. What characteristics do employers evaluate when considering a job applicant?
2. What is the minimum level of education required for most jobs?

BEGINNING YOUR JOB SEARCH

As you will recall from the previous chapter, before you begin looking for a job, you need to discover which jobs you would like most and would be best able to do. You should, however, avoid limiting yourself to one type of job. Some jobs require little or no experience. Other jobs require work experience. Still others may require certain skills. Do not try to get a job for which you are not qualified. For example, if you try to get an administrative assistant job without keyboarding skills, you would be wasting both your time and the employer's.

GLOBAL VIEW

Many people who want to gain experience working with people of other cultures volunteer for the United States Peace Corps. Peace Corps workers spend two years working in countries in Africa, Asia, and Latin America. Workers and community members work together to improve local agricultural methods, health care, leadership, and education.

TEACHING TIP

Remind students of the employability skills they have learned in the Building Business Skills features: Making Decisions, page 10; Completing Self-Directed Tasks, page 64; Exercising Leadership, page 112; Demonstrating Problem Solving, page 156; Making Informed Judgments, page 202; Providing Constructive Feedback, page 232; Resolving Team Conflicts, page 266; Exhibit Ethical Behavior, page 506; Recognizing Diversity, page 604; Maintaining a Positive Attitude, page 660.

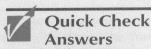

Quick Check Answers

1. Level of education; required skills; work experience; character and personality.
2. High school.

Develop Concepts

Beginning Your Job Search

Remind students that a resume serves as both a summary of a person's qualifications and a potential employer's first impression of a candidate. Obtain a book of sample resumes and copy two or three. Have students critique the resumes for good points and bad points. Point out to students that the resumes of people who have had several years' work experience are somewhat different from those of students who haven't yet acquired much work experience.

Reteaching Strategy

Have students suggest reasons that employers might look for someone with previous work experience for the following jobs: computer programmer, high school teacher, and nurse. Ask: What skills do each of these jobs require and why would previous experience be helpful or required?

After you decide what types of jobs you want to look for, you need to prepare a resume. Then you can begin to look for job openings.

Preparing Your Resume

Your resume highlights your job qualifications. The purpose of a resume is to persuade potential employers to grant you an interview, not to give you a job. When you answer an advertisement, you should enclose your resume with a cover letter. In some cases, prospective employers ask for a copy of your resume during an interview. As you can see in Figure 38-1 below, a resume provides information about your employment objective, education, work experience, skills, other activities,

FIGURE 38-1

A resume tells a prospective employer four things—who you are, what you want to do, what you have done, and what you can do. Why was it a good idea for Peter to list his activities?

PETER A. CORTEZ

134 North Avenue
Indianapolis, IN 46268-1452

Telephone: 317-555-2492
E-mail: pcortez@aol.com

OBJECTIVE To secure an office position with potential for growth.

EDUCATION Northwest High School
Will graduate June 14, 1997

Related Coursework

Accounting	Math With Business
Algebra	Applications
Computer Applications	Microcomputer Keyboarding
Cooperative Office Education	Personal Finance
Introduction to Business	

WORK EXPERIENCE September 1996–present
Part-time Office Assistant
Cameron's Business Supply

Responsibilities

Maintained company files as directed.
Key-entered data for reports, correspondence, and monthly customer billings.

SPECIAL SKILLS Working knowledge of Lotus 1-2-3, MS Word, MS Excel.
Speak and write Spanish fluently.

ACTIVITIES Vice President of local chapter of Business Professionals of America.
Tutored middle school students in math at Hispanic Center.

REFERENCES References will be provided upon request.

Enrichment Strategy

Work with students to create a career information center in the classroom. Encourage students to display anything they think would be helpful to someone looking for work. Students could include addresses and phone numbers for job banks, sample resumes, government publications, and so forth.

and references. A **reference** is a person a potential employer can contact to find out about your work, your skills, and your character. References may be teachers, former employers, or other adults who are qualified to assess your personal and work habits. Before using people as references, be sure to get their permission.

The beginning includes personal information such as your name, address, and telephone number. Some people also include a fax number or an E-mail address. Be sure the resume is neatly formatted and that the information is presented clearly. Also be sure that everything is spelled correctly and that you have made no grammatical errors. It is a good idea to let at least two other people proofread and check your resume.

Looking for Openings

Where can you find out about job openings? The following are good places to start:

Your Network   Talk to your parents, friends, neighbors, and acquaintances. Many times people you know are the best sources of information about job openings.

Your School   Your school may have a work placement office, and someone there can help you look for job leads. Your school may have a cooperative education or work experience program. Besides helping you plan your career, these programs can help you find a job. Also talk with your guidance counselor and teachers about the kind of job you would like to have.

Want Ads   Help-wanted advertisements in newspapers can be useful in several ways. First, you can find out quickly if any jobs are listed in which you might be interested. You can also get a good idea of how much certain jobs pay and what skills or education are required. If you have access to a computer with an on-line service, you can search local and national databases for jobs. The databases are updated very frequently and usually provide detailed descriptions of jobs.

Local Businesses   Some businesses post job notices on supermarket or shopping mall bulletin boards. You can also call a company's personnel or human resources department to see what jobs are open. Some businesses post help-wanted signs in their windows.

Employment Agencies   Organizations set up to help people find jobs are called **employment agencies.** The Federal Job Information Center operates regional agencies that will provide you with information about government job openings. The

F.Y.I.

When a job seems too good to be true, it probably is. A consumer advocate spotted an advertisement offering high-paying jobs around the world. She called the number listed and said she wanted to be a truck driver in Brazil. Even though she had never driven a truck in her life, the "employment agent" assured her that it was not a problem. All she needed to do to get the job was to pay a very large "employment fee."

Learning Activity
Have students prepare a reference list. Students should have a minimum of three references who have given students permission to use them as references. If possible, have students use a computer to make a neatly formatted reference list that includes the names, addresses, and business phone numbers of their references.

Business Brief
Many job seekers have expanded their job prospects by posting their resumes on the Internet. The Internet provides potential employers with the option of viewing part of the job seeker's portfolio. For example, an employer searching for an industrial photographer would want to view some of the photographer's work. The employer would simply click on a "hot link" to have the photos appear on his or her computer screen.

Making Connections   Technology

Many companies now post their help-wanted ads on their World Wide Web "home pages" on the Internet. Suggest that interested students access the following electronic databases to search for specific home pages and employment opportunities:
- Online Career Center at http://www.occ.com
- CareerMosaic at http://www.careermosiac.com
- CareerPath at http://www.careerpath.com

Have students prepare an oral report for the class describing how they found specific job openings and what other useful information they accessed.
Refer students to the *Internet Resource Guide* booklet for more information.

FOCUS ON **Careers**

Discuss

Discuss with students the kinds of skills people in the personal, family, and community services field use. Ask students what courses in school could help them prepare for entry-level jobs in personal, family, and community services. How do people advance in the field?

Personal, Family, and Community Services

Ask an auto mechanic, a real estate agent, a library worker, or an education aide what rewards their jobs bring, and you'll probably hear a variety of answers. One that might be mentioned often is the satisfaction of helping people fulfill their needs.

People engaged in personal, family, and community services do things for us that we might not want or be able to do for ourselves. They keep our automobiles and audio systems functioning. They find us places to live that suit our wants and needs. They help us learn how to exercise our bodies and our minds. Some—jewelers, dog groomers, and electronics technicians, for exam-

ple—may work for private businesses. Others may work in community services helping in classrooms or assisting library patrons find books.

The skills and personal qualities required for entry-level positions in this area are as varied as the jobs themselves. A high school diploma is a prerequisite for almost all of them, and technical or educational jobs may require additional study or certification.

HELP WANTED

LEASING AGENT

If you are an outgoing person with good speaking/selling skills, consider a career in real estate. Culpepper Properties, a real estate and property management firm, now hiring entry-level leasing agents for our large, luxury apartment complex, Lakeside Paradise.

Your duties will include working with prospective tenants, matching their wants and needs to available apartments, checking tenant credit records/reliability, monitoring apartment maintenance.

High school diploma, computer/math skills required. Courses in real estate a plus.

Quick Check Answers

1. Objective; Education; Work Experience; Special Skills; and Activities.
2. Someone who can tell about an applicant's work, skills, and character.
3. Your network of family, friends, and acquaintances; your school; want ads; local businesses; and employment agencies.
4. Organizations set up to help people find jobs.

Develop Concepts

Contacting Potential Employers

Career advisors suggest that job hunters keep a file of job prospects. For each company a person is interested in, he or she should fill out a card stating the name of the business, its address, phone and fax numbers, industry, products, and the names of contacts at the company. Have students establish a job prospect file by asking them to make at least three cards.

agencies do not charge a fee. Private employment agencies, however, usually charge a fee. Often the fee for placing a worker in a job is paid by the employer. At other times, the person looking for the job must pay the fee. If you contact an agency, be sure to find out if they charge you for their services.

Quick Check

1. What five headings might be included on a resume?
2. What is a *reference?*
3. List five sources you could use to find out about jobs.
4. What are *employment agencies?*

CONTACTING POTENTIAL EMPLOYERS

After you have prepared a resume and found several interesting job openings, you need to let potential employers know of your interest. The process of applying for a job includes some or all of the following steps:

656 UNIT 12 PLANNING A CAREER IN TODAY'S WORLD

Making Connections ➤ Equal Employment Opportunity

The Civil Rights Act of 1964 prohibits discrimination in all areas of employment on the basis of sex, race, color, religion, and national origin. The Equal Employment Opportunity Commission (EEOC) is the federal regulatory agency established by the act. Have interested students contact the EEOC and request information about its functions. Have students find out what action a job seeker who suspects discrimination should take. Ask students to present their findings to the class in an oral report.

In many of these careers, mechanical aptitude and manual dexterity are necessary. Math, reading, and computer skills are likely to help applicants land jobs as well as improve chances for advancement.

Most jobs in personal, family, and community services depend on interaction with clients, customers, and students, so listening carefully and speaking clearly are a necessity. The worker who can maintain a friendly, positive attitude while bathing a rambunctious dog, separating squabbling preschoolers, or servicing a demanding customer's car is an asset to an employer. Standards of trustworthiness and ethical behavior for workers in these areas are high, since these jobs often require working in clients' homes and places of business or handling their valuable possessions.

Take a look at the want ads presented here.

- Writing a cover letter
- Filling out a job application
- Taking an employment test
- Going on a job interview

Cover Letter

A **cover letter** is a letter you write to accompany the resume you send to a potential employer. Because it is often your first link with the employer, you want it to make a good impression. When you write a cover letter, be brief but complete. Figure 38-2 on page 658 shows a typical example.

Job Application

Most employers ask job applicants to fill out application forms. Like your resume, this form represents you to a potential employer. For that reason, you should follow the directions carefully, provide the information requested, and write neatly. The process will be easier if you have your resume and your list

FIGURE 38-2

A cover letter introduces you to a prospective employer. It should be tailored to the position you are interested in. What should accompany the cover letter?

PETER A. CORTEZ

134 North Avenue
Indianapolis, IN 46268-1452

Telephone: 317-555-2492
E-mail: pcortez@aol.com

May 12, 1997

Ms. Marcia Chisholm
Director of Human Resources
Oakland Insurance Company
One Acorn Park
Indianapolis, IN 46244–7777

Dear Ms. Chisholm:

When I read the description for the position of eligibility specialist at your company, I just knew that I was the person for the job. I have the technical and computer skills you require as well as the math and written communication experience you desire. As you review my resume, you will see that my education, work experience, and activities have prepared me to be a successful addition to your company.

I will graduate from high school in June. Working as an eligibility specialist at your company will continue to develop the skills I have gained from school and work. I know I am the right person who can do the job for you. I will call you next week to arrange an appointment, or you may reach me at 317-555-2492 after 3:00 p.m.

Sincerely,

Peter A. Cortez

Peter A. Cortez

Enclosure

Besides the knowledge or the skills tested, what do you think an employer looks for on an applicant's completed test?

of references with you so you can refer to them for names, addresses, and dates.

Application forms may look like the one in Figure 38-3 on page 659. Begin by answering each question. If a question does not apply to you, write in N/A (not applicable).

Employment Testing

When you apply for some jobs, you may be asked to take some tests. For example, applicants for desktop publishing or administrative assistant positions may have to take tests designed to determine how well they know various word processing programs. Those looking for jobs involving driving may be asked to take a driving test or obtain a special license.

Meeting Student Diversity

Students who have difficulty paying attention in class can benefit from being given a time limit for a task. Ask students to read the section "Job Interview," which is approximately 500 words. Give students seven minutes to read the section (enough time for average readers). Discuss with students the effect of a time limit on their ability to stay on task.

Job Interview

A job interview is a face-to-face discussion between an employer and a possible employee. It is an exchange of information about the nature of the position and your qualifications for it. Keep in mind a number of things about the interview:

- *Do some homework about the job.* Find out as much as you can about the company or organization. If you have a friend who works for the company, talk with your friend. Visit your library and use their print and electronic indexes to find articles in newspapers and magazines about the

EMPLOYMENT APPLICATION

AN EQUAL OPPORTUNITY EMPLOYER
Oakland Insurance Employment Policy Forbids Discrimination Because of Age, Citizenship Status, Color, Disability, Marital Status, National Origin, Race, Religion, Sex, Sexual Orientation, or Veteran Status.

NAME **Cortez** **Peter** **A.** DATE **May 22, 1997**
      LAST   FIRST   MIDDLE INITIAL

ADDRESS **134 North Avenue,** **Indianapolis** **IN** **46268–1452**
        STREET   CITY   STATE   ZIP

PHONE NO. **(317) 555–2492** SOCIAL SECURITY NO. **032–32–2712**

In case of emergency notify **Emilio Cortez, 134 North Avenue, Indianapolis, IN 46268**

Position desired **Eligibility Specialist** Salary desired **Negotiable**

EDUCATION	Name and Address of School	Dates Attended		Date Graduated	Major Area of Study
		From	To		
Elementary	Valley Elementary School Indianapolis, IN 46266	Sept. 1985	June 1993	June 6 1993	N/A
High School	Northwest High School Indianapolis, IN 46244	Sept. 1993	June 1997	June 14 1997	Business
College	N/A	N/A	N/A	N/A	N/A
Other	N/A	N/A	N/A	N/A	N/A

List all foreign languages you can write and speak fluently. **Spanish**

List all computer applications you can use. **Lotus 1-2-3, MS Word, MS Excel**

EMPLOYMENT: List most recent employer first. Use extra sheet if necessary.

Name and Address of Employer	Dates Employed		Position	Reason for Leaving
	From	To		
Cameron's Business Supply 193 Troy Street, Indianapolis, IN 46244	Sept. 1996	Present	Part-time office assistant	need full-time job
N/A	N/A	N/A	N/A	N/A
N/A	N/A	N/A	N/A	N/A

REFERENCES: Do not list relatives or former employers.

Name	Address	Telephone	How long known
John Durkee	54 East Border Road Indianapolis, IN 46268	555-6014	4 years
Amanda Freymann	1037 Crawford Drive Indianapolis, IN 46268	555-3744	7 years
William Council	468 Center Street Indianapolis, IN 46244	555-9468	3 years

Are you currently employed? **Yes** Date available for work **June 16**

To the best of my knowledge all of the foregoing is true and given voluntarily.
I authorize Oakland Insurance to contact my references, including previous employers, to confirm credentials.

Peter A. Cortez
SIGNATURE

FIGURE 38-3

Most employers ask potential employees to fill out application forms. It is important to read the directions carefully and fill out the form neatly and completely. How many computer applications is Peter able to use?

Global Perspective

Students can get valuable international experience by volunteering for the U.S. Peace Corps. Volunteers accepted into the service live and work in a developing country for two years and receive a $4800 bonus and a college scholarship upon finishing their service. Interested students can obtain more information by contacting the Peace Corps at 1-800-424-8580.

Refer to the *International Business Strategies* booklet for additional strategies and activities.

Model

Give students the following hypothetical situation. Rufus's mom has asked him to stay home and take care of his five-year-old sister next Saturday afternoon. Rufus would prefer not to. Help students apply the hints for maintaining a positive attitude to Rufus's situation.

Learning Activity

Tell students that there has been a recent trend toward more casual dress in corporate offices. Have students suppose they are interviewing at a company where one of their friends has a job. The friend says that employees are allowed to wear jeans to work. Ask students how they would dress for the interview. Should they take their cue from the way employees dress or should they dress more formally? Have students explain their answers.

Employability

Maintaining a Positive Attitude

Explanation

Nobody likes his or her job all the time. In the workplace, as in other areas of life, nothing is perfect. Although these statements may not seem to reflect an upbeat attitude, keeping them in mind can give you a sense of perspective about your work. This perspective can, in turn, help you maintain a positive attitude in your workplace.

Why should you care about maintaining a positive attitude at work? What does attitude matter as long as the work gets done? First, and most obviously, a positive attitude is sure to please your supervisors. In the second place, a positive attitude tends to be contagious. It can produce a pleasant atmosphere in which people can work cooperatively to get the job done. Third, maintaining a positive attitude can help you do better work and enjoy it more.

Practice

Describe a situation in which you might have done better at maintaining a positive attitude. Use the hints in the box to explain what you could have done to improve your attitude.

F.Y.I.

Some large companies electronically scan the thousands of resumes they receive and store them in a database of potential job candidates. The software can be instructed to search the resumes for key words that characterize the applicant's skills and education. For example, a company looking for a sales manager might have the computer scan resumes for key words or phrases such as "exceeded quota," "top sales," and "managed."

company. Lists of the names of officers, department heads, and managers are often available so you can identify to whom you should send your resume.

- *Be on time.* This is the best way to start your interview off right. Not only do employers not appreciate waiting for job applicants, but they will also think you are not careful about being on time for work or meeting deadlines.
- *Wear appropriate clothes.* Dress neatly and in a style appropriate for the job you are seeking. When in doubt, dress on the conservative side.
- *Put your best foot forward.* Remember that one of the most important reasons for the interview is to show that you have the ability to do the job. It is important to be courteous, cooperative, alert, and interested during the interview. Try to leave a good impression by being positive without being boastful.
- *Ask questions about the job.* Show the interviewer that you are interested in the company by discussing some of the information you found when you researched the company.

Reteaching Strategy

Have students evaluate each of the following situations and write a response to each that demonstrates a positive attitude.

- Ralph's supervisor gives him a stack of sales orders to process at 4:00 on Friday afternoon. (Ralph is glad his supervisor trusts him to finish the job on time.)
- Audrey sees that her coworker Bert is having trouble with his computer. (Audrey could offer to help Bert figure out the problem.)
- Molly has been asked to learn a new spreadsheet program. (Molly realizes the program will help her develop her technical skills.)

MAINTAINING A POSITIVE ATTITUDE

1. If your job seems uninteresting, try to imagine what would happen if there were no one to do it. You'll probably conclude that you're doing an important job you can take pride in.
2. Concentrate on the things you like about your job. Although no job is perfect, no job is without its good points. Pluses might be dressing as you please, pleasant surroundings, benefits, flexible hours, friendly coworkers, and so forth.
3. Consider what you're learning on the job. There are few jobs that don't teach us something. Be willing and eager to learn new things.
4. Use your creativity to invent better ways to do your job.
5. Envision your next step. Where can you go from your present job? How will this one prepare you to advance?
6. Try to make someone else's job a little easier. Maybe you can teach a coworker something you've learned about the job that will help that person.
7. Make friends with your coworkers. Good personal relationships at work can improve your outlook. Try to be pleasant and polite—even when you don't feel like it. Other people will probably respond the same way.
8. Avoid complaining about your job to your coworkers. Negative attitudes are contagious, too.
9. When job problems make it difficult to maintain a good attitude, analyze them and try to improve things. If your manager seems difficult to work with, talk to him or her and try to work things out. If your job seems boring, see if there are additional responsibilities you could take on to make it more challenging.

Practice
Allow students a few minutes to review the hints given in the box on page 661 and then have them use the hints to write a 100-word essay describing how they might have reacted more positively in a past situation. (Students' answers will vary, but should present specific examples.)

Ask questions. The interview is a two-way process. Most interviewers appreciate people who ask intelligent questions, since this shows that they have taken time to think about the job.

- *Ask about the pay and benefits.* If the interviewer does not bring up salary or wages, ask about them near the end of the interview. Do not ask about these points too early in the interview.
- *Do not expect a job offer right away.* Most interviewers need some time to think about your qualifications in relation to the job. Interviewers probably have other applicants to consider. Interviewers will often tell you when they expect to make a decision about the job. If they do not bring it up, ask about this at the end of the interview and also ask that you be informed of the decision.
- *Write a thank-you letter.* Write a letter thanking the person or persons you spoke to at the interview. This shows that you are still interested in the job. It also gives you the chance to clarify something you said in the interview or

Learning Activity
Point out that an applicant may have to interview with more than one company representative, for example, a human resources officer and the manager of the department that has the job opening. Ask students how they would prepare for such an interview. Ask any students who have had job interviews to share their experiences with the class.

Curriculum Connection   Career Development

Ask pairs of students to prepare and present a skit portraying a job interview. Tell pairs to include at least one or two lapses or mistakes on the part of the person being interviewed. After each skit have volunteers identify the mistakes and suggest corrections.

USE VISUALS

Have students study the photo for a few seconds. Then ask: What kinds of questions should *you* ask a potential employer? (Possible answer: Questions about information you found when researching the company.)
Answer to caption: Answers will vary.

Learning Activity

Enrichment Master 38-1 lists some frequently asked interview questions. Distribute photocopies to students and explain that they can help prepare themselves for job interviews by reviewing the questions and thinking beforehand about how they would answer the questions.

Quick Check Answers

1. It accompanies a resume and introduces an applicant to a potential employer.
2. You can talk to someone who works for the company. You can use a library or on-line service.
3. Write a thank-you letter to the interviewer.

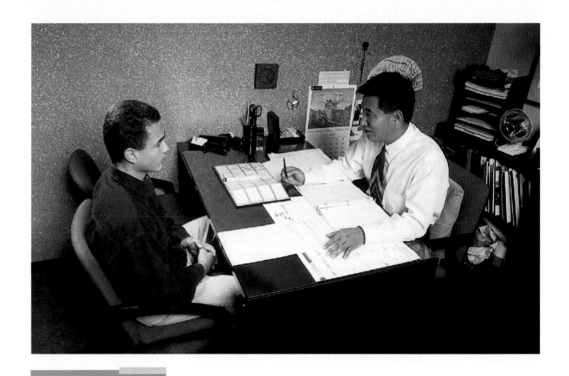

What other helpful hints can you think of that may help in an interview situation?

mention something that may have occurred to you later. Write the letter as soon as possible after the interview. Your letter may be handwritten or typed. Be sure it is neat, clear, and free of grammatical errors.

- *Follow up.* If the interviewer tells you to call back in a few days, wait two or three days to do so. If the interviewer tells you that someone will call you, wait about a week and then call if you have not heard from anyone.

Quick Check

1. What is the purpose of a *cover letter?*
2. Name three sources for researching a company.
3. What should you do as soon as possible after an interview?

Reteaching Strategy

Have groups create a job interview checklist. The list may include hints given in the text as well as insights students have gained from their own experiences. Students may use a computer to format and add graphics to their checklists. Post checklists in the classroom.

Chapter 38 **Summary**

Main Ideas

1. Employers look for certain skills and levels of education; they often require work experience. They also assess an applicant's character and personality.
2. Your resume should present your qualifications clearly and should be neat and free of spelling and grammatical errors. A cover letter should accompany any resume you send out.
3. You can locate job openings in many ways, including talking to family and friends, getting help at school, visiting businesses, checking want ads, and contacting employment agencies.

4. It is important to do some research about a company prior to an interview. You should be able to ask intelligent questions during the interview to show your interest in the job.
5. Skills required for jobs in personal, family, and community services careers include mechanical, math, communications, human-relations, and computer skills.
6. Maintaining a positive attitude pleases managers, makes the workplace more pleasant for others, and can help you do your work better and enjoy it more.

CASE ANALYSIS   Job Offers

Stan Wayne has two job offers. Job A is a sales position that requires travel within a three-state territory. The salary is a commission of 8 percent on sales, which averages about $1700 a month. Job B also is a sales position, but with only local travel and a salary of $1200 per month. Stan supports his family, which includes his wife and eight-month-old son, on his income. Which job do you think he should take and why?

CLOSE

Main Ideas

Main Ideas summarizes the key information in the chapter. It is a useful tool for reinforcement and review.

CASE ANALYSIS

Case Analysis provides a chapter-related case for student analysis and application of decision-making skills.

Answer
Answers will vary. Some students may think Job A is better because it has the potential for more income if Stan can increase the amount of sales. Others may recommend Job B because it has a guaranteed income, and Stan would not have to be away from his family as much.

QUICK QUIZ

1. What is the minimum level of education most employers will accept? (A high school education.)
2. Name two reasons an employer might prefer to hire someone with previous work experience. (They are already familiar with work procedures; they need less training.)
3. What five headings might you include on your resume? (Objective; Education; Work Experience; Special Skills; and Activities.)
4. What is a cover letter? (A letter that accompanies a resume and introduces an applicant to a potential employer.)

Chapter 38 **Review**

CHAPTER 38 REVIEW

APPLY

Answers

Use the Language of Business

1. cover letter, **2.** reference, **3.** employment agencies.

Review What You Learned

1. Want ads in newspapers and on electronic databases are a quick way to check for jobs you are interested in. Want ads give you a good idea of pay, skills, and education requirements for certain jobs.
2. Private employment agencies may charge a fee to help you find a job.
3. Workers should be able to read, to communicate with others, to do simple mathematical problems, to follow instructions, and to get along with others.
4. Honesty, dependability, willingness to work hard, a positive attitude, cooperativeness, and loyalty.
5. Teachers, former employers, or anyone who is qualified to assess your work and personal habits.
6. Leasing agent, aerobics instructor, and security systems installer.
7. It will please your supervisors, prepare you for advancing within the company, and will help you do your job better.

Understand Business Concepts

1. To show that you are still interested in the job and to clarify points made in the interview, if necessary.
2. Your special abilities, experience, and interests.
3. No, because other applicants may be under consideration and most interviewers need time to make the decision.
4. A certain level of education, required skills, work experience, and specific character and personality traits.

Use the Language of Business

Choose the term that best completes each of the following sentences.

cover letter   employment agencies   reference

1. When you send your resume to a prospective employer, you also should send a(n) _____ .

2. You might choose a former employer or a high school teacher to be a(n) _____ .

3. Organizations set up to help people find jobs are called _____ .

Review What You Learned

1. Name two ways in which want ads can help you find a job.
2. What might be a disadvantage of using a private employment agency?
3. What basic skills do employers expect workers to have?
4. What kinds of personality traits do employers look for in an employee?
5. Whom should you use as references?
6. Give three examples of entry-level jobs in the personal, family, and community services field.
7. Name three benefits you and your coworkers receive when you maintain a positive attitude.

Understand Business Concepts

1. Why should you send a thank you letter after an interview?
2. What does the "Activities" section on your resume tell a prospective employer?
3. Should a person expect to be offered a job immediately following an interview? Why or why not?
4. List those things an employer looks for when hiring someone for a job.
5. Why is it difficult for an employer to assess the attitude of a job applicant?
6. Why do workers in personal, family, and community services need to be honest and behave ethically?
7. Name three things you could do to improve your attitude on the job.

Think Critically

1. **Judge.** List five personality characteristics or skills that you think are the most important for an employee to have. Explain your choices.

2. **Synthesize.** Why is it important for you to find out as much as you can about a position before you are offered the job?

5. A person's true attitude generally is shown over an extended period of time. In a job interview, the employer only sees the candidate for a brief amount of time.
6. Many workers are charged with the responsibility of working on or caring for people's valuable possessions, so they must not take advantage of their clients' trust.
7. Possible answers: Concentrate on the things you like about your job; consider what you are learning on the job; and try to make a coworker's job easier by helping him or her.

Think Critically

1. Students may name characteristics such as honesty, cooperativeness, or intelligence, and skills such as communication or math skills. Students should support their choices.
2. Students should point out that they need to find out as best they can whether they will like and be able to do the job before they accept an offer. They might miss an opportunity elsewhere or have a very bad experience if they make a poor choice.

Use What You Learned

1. **Group Project.** Choose a partner to role-play a job interview. Together, choose a position to be filled and the wages or salary that will be offered. The partner who will play the interviewer should prepare a list of questions for the applicant. The applicant should prepare questions and background information. The interviewer should write a 150-word evaluation of the applicant following the interview, and the applicant should draft a thank-you letter to the interviewer. Then switch roles.

2. Study the want ads in your local newspaper for two weeks. What conclusions can you draw about the kinds of jobs in your area; the salary range for various jobs; the benefits available; and the qualifications or work experience required? Write a 250-word summary of local job opportunities for a recent high school graduate.

3. Interview two acquaintances or relatives who are working. Find out what kind of training they had when they began working. Have they received training on the job and what new skills have they developed? How have their job responsibilities and opportunities changed since they first started their jobs? Have they changed jobs? Write a 200-word report explaining the kinds of training the people received and how the training affected their careers.

4. **Computer Application.** Do on-line research to retrieve data on the annual and lifetime earnings for workers with varying levels of education. Create a spreadsheet of the information. Then use charting software to prepare and print out a set of graphs to compare the data.

5. **Skill Reinforcement.** Review the hints for maintaining a positive attitude on page 661. Then read the following paragraph about Pat. Work with a partner to develop a role-play in which a friend helps Pat maintain a positive attitude at work. Feel free to add details about Pat and the work situation. Present your role-play.

> Pat works in a hotel cleaning rooms and making beds daily. The wages for this job are low, but sometimes guests leave tips. The hours of the job are from 8 A.M. until 4 P.M. or until all the rooms are clean. The hotel features scenic views and free lunch for workers. The job takes hard work, cleaning and organization skills, and could lead to a cleaning supervisor's position. Although other workers do the same tasks, they work alone. Pat seldom talks to fellow workers, because everyone is busy. Pat is frequently bored and lonely at work.

Place your work in your Business Portfolio

Independent Practice

Use the Chapter 38 worksheets in *Student Activity Guide 2* for additional practice and application activities. *Student Activity Guide 2* provides vocabulary exercises, reading comprehension checks, problems, projects, and simulations of business and economic situations. A Teacher's Annotated Edition provides answers.

ASSESS

Portfolio Assessment

The portfolio projects are designed to lead students to develop a collection of their best work to submit to you for assessment. You and your students should decide which projects will be included in their respective Business Portfolios. Refer students to the specific rubric(s) from the *Alternative Assessment Strategies* booklet listed with each of the project notes below. These rubrics will alert students to the criteria you will use to assess their projects.

Chapter Assessment

Use the Chapter 38 Test from the *Test Masters* booklet to evaluate students' understanding of the chapter concepts. An answer key is provided. Or create your own customized test using the *Testmaker* software.

Use What You Learned

1. Make sure all students participate in the group project. Rubric: Essay.

2. Students may also want to check the help wanted ads in newspapers that serve surrounding communities. Rubric: Essay.

3. Suggest that students develop a list of questions to ask interviewees. Rubric: Essay.

4. Students with no access to a computer may do conventional library research and may make their spreadsheets and graphs by hand. Rubric: Charts and Tables; Graph.

5. Students' scenarios will vary, but might include Pat and his or her friend listing job pluses; finding new ways to do the job; planning how Pat could advance to a supervisory position; and suggesting to management that cleaners work in pairs. Rubric: Oral Presentation.

Business Issue

Business Issue

BENEFITS FOR LAID-OFF WORKERS

BENEFITS FOR LAID-OFF WORKERS

Each year nearly two million U.S. workers are laid off as companies downsize and make other changes in operations. Should businesses provide retraining and other benefits to help laid-off workers find new jobs?

Highlight the Issue

Before students read pages 666–667, have them speculate on the possible beneficial effects of providing benefits for laid-off workers and the possible negative effects of providing such benefits. Record students' ideas on the board. After students have read the pages, ask students to revise the list.

Pro

An employer has an obligation to help workers who are laid off. In many cases, laid-off workers have given years of service to the company, contributing a great deal to its success. If workers must be laid off, then the least an employer can do is retrain them or help them find new jobs.

Retraining programs don't just benefit laid-off employees, however. Such programs can help a company keep valuable workers by giving them the additional skills they need so they can be transferred to other departments. These experienced employees can help increase a company's competitiveness and save the company the cost of recruiting and training new workers.

Offering benefits to laid-off workers can also improve the morale of the workers who remain with the company. Many of these "survivors" feel guilty and depressed that they still have a job while so many coworkers are out of work. These feelings can lower their productivity. By setting up a program for laid-off workers, a company can keep productivity up.

Helping laid-off workers find new jobs can even save a business money. When one Midwestern hospital laid off 1200 employees, its managers estimated that lay-off costs, including unemployment insurance payments and legal fees for potential lawsuits, would add up to nearly $10 million. In contrast, the cost of a program to help the unemployed workers get back to work was only about $1 million.

Retraining programs can benefit the U.S. economy as a whole by increasing the skills of American workers. This not only improves the nation's productivity and competitiveness in the global marketplace, but also decreases the need for government aid programs such as welfare and unemployment. Furthermore, if companies have to offer such benefits, it may help discourage unnecessary layoffs.

Providing retraining and other benefits to laid-off workers helps workers and businesses. Companies should have to offer such benefits.

Extend the Issue

Ask interested students to find articles about companies that have retraining programs for their workers. Have students prepare a brief oral presentation for the class in which they discuss the cost of such programs, who the programs benefit, and the success of the programs. Discuss with the class whether they think such programs should be implemented in more companies.

Con

Job loss is a fact of life in a free-market system, and a worker must always be prepared to search for his or her next job. Research shows that today's workers will change jobs many times during their careers. Workers need to develop their own skills to weather economic hard times, not rely on their employers to find them new jobs.

Companies don't owe workers more than the wages and benefits they pay them for their work. Companies fulfill their obligation to laid-off workers with severance benefits—often generous packages that include several weeks' salary to help tide workers over until they find new jobs.

A business's primary responsibility is to make profits for its shareholders. Providing retraining programs so laid-off workers can find jobs elsewhere doesn't contribute to a company's profitability. The cost of the retraining programs increases the cost of the goods or services the business produces. This increased cost may make the business less competitive in the global market if other companies can produce the same goods or services for less. Retraining programs and other benefits for laid-off workers may even be so expensive that companies downsizing to stay in business may fail, causing even more workers to lose their jobs.

Gaining new skills and searching for a new job should be the responsibility of the individual worker with the help of the government—not the employer. The government has an obligation to use tax dollars to provide retraining for laid-off workers in order to reduce unemployment and keep the economy healthy.

In any case, retraining and other job-search assistance benefits should not be mandatory. Businesses and their employees should be free to determine their own benefits packages through negotiations.

Update the Issue

Have students find current articles about benefits for laid-off workers and post the articles in the classroom. Discuss with students whether they think there is a trend toward providing benefits for laid-off workers or if such programs are too costly for most businesses to implement. Ask students whether they think employers should be obligated to provide benefits for those employees they lay off. Ask volunteers to explain their positions.

Glossary

A

ability Any physical or mental activity that an individual performs well.

ability-to-pay principle A principle of taxation that says those who can afford to pay more taxes should do so.

accounting A system used to record, classify, summarize, and interpret the financial data of a business.

administrative law A type of law that deals with the regulation of business; it is usually made and enforced by government agencies.

advertising Paid promotion used to promote products and services as well as to generate ideas and educate the public.

alternative A plan you can put into action if your first plan does not work out.

annual percentage rate A charge to the borrower that indicates how much credit costs on a yearly basis.

antitrust laws Laws passed by state and federal governments to prevent monopolies.

application A form that all people who are interested in working for a company must complete; it is a summary of an applicant's personal information, education, training, and work history.

apprentice A person in training for a skilled trade or craft.

aptitude A talent that comes to a person naturally.

arbitration The process of submitting disagreements or differences to a third party who acts as a kind of judge.

asset Anything of value that a business owns, such as cash or equipment.

associate degree A degree a student receives after completing a two-year course of study after high school.

B

bachelor's degree A degree a student receives after completing a four-year course of study at a college.

bait and switch A tactic in which a store advertises a low-priced item and then attempts to sell customers a higher-priced item.

balance of payments The difference in the total amount of money flowing in and out of a country.

balance of trade The difference between the total value of what a country imports and the total value of what it exports.

balanced budget The situation that exists when a government spends the same amount of money it receives.

bankruptcy A legal process in which some or all of the assets of a debtor are distributed among creditors.

bank statement A listing of all the activity in an account issued by the bank every period.

barter Trading goods or services directly for other goods or services.

beneficiary Each person who receives part of the proceeds of a life insurance policy.

benefits Special services provided by a company for their full-time employees.

benefits-received principle A principle of taxation that says those who get benefits from a public service should pay a charge or tax for it.

big-ticket item A costly item, such as a large home appliance or car, that is often bought on credit.

birthrate The number of live births for every 1000 people per year.

board of directors A group of individuals chosen to make major decisions for a company.

bonus An incentive paid to employees for helping increase profits; it may be given out annually or distributed to individual employees who worked on a particular project.

boycott Refusing to buy goods as a way of expressing an opinion about a business or its products.

brand name A word, picture, or logo on a product that helps consumers distinguish it from similar products.

break-even point The point at which money from sales equals the costs and expenses of making and distributing a product.

budget A plan for using your money in a way that best meets your wants and needs.

business All of the activities of an individual or group of individuals involved in producing and distributing goods and services to customers.

business cycle The repeated rise and fall of economic activity over time that includes four phases: expansion, peak, contraction, and trough.

business plan An essential document for a new business that helps focus on exactly what the business wants to do, how it will do it, and what it expects to accomplish.

C

calculated risk Risk that is carefully planned in advance so that the probability of success is high.

canceled check A cleared check that indicates payment was made by the bank and the amount of the check has been deducted from the account balance of the drawer.

capitalism A market economic system in which individuals and companies own and direct most of the resources used to produce goods and services, including land, capital, and labor.

capital gain Profit from the sale of certain investments, such as stocks.

capital resource A resource, such as equipment or a machine, that makes it possible to produce goods and services.

career clusters Groups of related occupations in an industry or field that require similar skills and aptitudes.

career ladder The method of progressing from one level in a field to another.

cash flow projection A forecast of the funds a business believes it will be receiving and the amount of cash it will be paying out.

centralization A way of organizing a company so that authority is focused in one place.

channel of distribution All of the people who direct products to consumers, including distributors, wholesalers, and retailers.

charge account A type of short-term credit that allows a person to make purchases up to a certain amount in a store.

checkbook dollars The form of money used when writing checks.

check register A section of the checkbook where you keep track of all your transactions.

claims Requests for payment to cover financial losses.

clearance sale A sale to clear a store of goods that either are going out of style or are no longer profitable.

collateral A form of security to help guarantee that a creditor will be repaid.

collection agent A person who has the job of collecting debts that are overdue.

collective bargaining The coming together of labor union members and their bosses, or management, to negotiate a contract.

command economy An economic system influenced by the commands, or directives, of a central authority consisting of one person or a small group who controls others in the society.

commercial credit Credit obtained for business purposes.

commission A form of payment in which workers earn a percentage of the value of their sales.

common law The legal decisions made by English courts over hundreds of years, as well as the customs of the people, on which many U.S. laws are based.

communism An economic structure in which the government makes decisions concerning the commonly owned natural and capital resources.

comparative advantage An area of production in which a country excels.

comparison shopping Checking the price and quality of a product in more than one store.

compensation A combination of payments, benefits, and employee services for the work performed.

competition The contest between businesses to win customers.

conservation The preservation, protection, and planned management of our natural resources.

consolidation loan A loan that brings all a person's debts together into one loan.

constitution The basic law of an entire nation or a single state.

consumer A person who selects, purchases, uses, and disposes of goods or services.

consumer advocate A champion of consumers' rights.

consumer credit Credit used for personal reasons.

consumer goods Goods that are sold to individuals and families.

consumerism All the activities and measures that protect the interests and rights of consumers.

contraction A noticeable drop in the level of business activity that indicates a slowdown in the growth of the economy.

copyright A protection for authors or creators of books, plays, software, movies, musical compositions, and art against persons copying what has already been made.

corporate bond A written promise to repay debt on a certain date. Corporations issue bonds to raise money.

corporate charter A legal form or license, granted by a state giving a corporation the permission to operate in that state.

corporation An organization owned by many people, but treated by the law as though it were a person. Such a business is legally regarded as a separate entity—that is, separate from the people who own it.

cosigner A person who agrees to make the payments on a loan if the borrower cannot make them.

cost of goods sold A business owner's prediction of the cost of producing or acquiring a company's products for sale during a given period.

cover letter A letter written to accompany the resume that introduces a prospective employee to an employer.

credit The opportunity to obtain money, goods, or services now in exchange for a promise to pay in the future.

credit bureau An agency or firm that collects and maintains information about the paying habits of consumers.

credit counselor A person who assists consumers with their credit problems.

credit limit The maximum amount of purchases a person can charge at any given time.

creditor One who lends money or provides credit.

credit rating A measure of a person's ability and willingness for making credit payments on time.

currency Government-issued paper money and coins legally ordered to be accepted as payment of debt.

D

debt capital Funds raised though various forms of borrowing that must be repaid.

debtor One who borrows money or uses credit.

decentralization A way of organizing a business that gives authority to a number of managers.

deductible The amount of money the policyholder must pay first before the insurance company will pay anything.

deductions Taxes, insurance payments, union dues, and other amounts subtracted from a person's paycheck.

deficit spending A situation in which the government is spending more than it is collecting.

demand The amount or quantity of goods and services that consumers are willing and able to buy at various prices.

demand deposit A type of bank deposit, such as a checking account deposit, from which account holders can withdraw money at any time they want, on demand.

demographics Statistics about the characteristics of human populations; the study of population.

departmentalization A way of organizing a company that involves subdividing resources and responsibilities to a specific unit, or department, in an organization.

deposit A sum of money placed in a bank account.

deposit ticket An item-by-item record of the amount of money a person is putting in a bank account.

depreciation The loss of value of an asset; when the price of a currency falls because of differences in supply and demand.

depression A very severe recession that lasts for several years—business is bad and unemployment is high.

deregulation The removal of some type of regulation.

devaluation When a government issues an order that lowers its currency's exchange rate.

developed nation A nation with a relatively high standard of living and an economy based more on industry than on agriculture.

developing nation A nation with less industrial development and a relatively low standard of living.

direct tax A tax that is charged to the person or persons who pay it.

discount rate The rate of interest the Fed charges its member banks.

dividend The return on an investment, the size of which depends on how much profit a company has made.

down payment A portion of the total cost of an item that is required at the time of purchase.

E

economic fluctuations The ups and downs in economic activity.

economic indicators Important data or statistics that measure economic activity and business cycles.

economic resource A resource that could be used to produce or create goods and services.

economic system A way of producing goods and services and of providing a means for people to get them.

embargo A method used by a government to stop the import or export of goods.

employment agency An organization set up to help people find jobs.

endorsement The signature of the party to whom a check has been written that is necessary for cashing a check.

entrepreneur A person who recognizes a business opportunity and organizes, manages, and assumes the risks of a business enterprise.

entrepreneurship The initiative to combine natural, human, capital, and entrepreneurial resources to produce goods or services.

entry-level job A job at the beginning level of a field.

equilibrium price The point at which supply and demand meet; the amount of a product supplied equals the amount demanded.

equity The difference between the value of property and the amount owed on the mortgage.

equity capital Money raised from within a firm or through the sale of ownership (equity) in the firm.

exchange rate The price of one currency in terms of another country's currency.

excise tax A tax collected on the sale of specific goods and services, such as tobacco and air travel.

expansion A rise in business activity.

export A good produced in one country and sold in another.

F

factor of production Any of the natural resources, human resources, capital resources, and entrepreneurial resources that are used to produce goods or services.

Fed, the The Federal Reserve System; the central bank of the United States, which regulates the nation's money supply, supervises banks, and clears checks.

finance charge The cost of credit stated in a dollar and cents figure.

financing The money invested by banks and other organizations to help get a new business going.

finished good A good that requires no further processing and is ready for the market.

first-line manager A manager who directly assigns work duties and oversees workers on the job.

fiscal year A 12-month accounting period.

fixed costs An expense, such as rent or insurance premiums, that must be paid regularly.

fixed rate A type of investment that yields an unchanging return.

forecast An estimate of the future business climate.

foreign aid The money, goods, and services given by governments and other organizations to help other nations and their citizens; it can take a variety of forms: economic, technical, and military.

franchise A grant or right to sell a parent company's product or service within a given area or territory.

free trade A policy encouraging few limitations and little government involvement in the trading system.

G

garnishment A practice that allows the creditor to take part of the borrower's wages if a payment is missed.

general sales tax A tax added to the price of goods and services at the time of purchase.

generic products Items that have no brand name, plain labels, and lower prices.

goods Items or products that people may buy.

government securities Security investments, such as treasury bills, that the government sells in order to finance growth.

grade label A label that indicates the quality level of foods such as meat and dairy products.

green products Items produced with less negative impact on the environment than competing products.

gross domestic product The dollar value of all final goods and services produced in the nation in a single year.

gross national product The total value of all the final goods and services produced by an economy over a given period of time, usually a year.

gross pay The total amount of money a person earns for a specific period.

H

hiring from within Filling a job opening with someone already employed by the company.

human resource A person who contributes physical and mental energy to the production process.

I

import A foreign good brought into a country.

impulse buying Purchasing items on the spur of the moment.

incentive Monetary compensation for extra effort on the job, such as commissions, profit sharing plans, and bonuses.

income tax A charge on earnings or other sources of income of individuals and corporations levied by the government and used to raise revenue.

indirect tax A tax that is paid by one party but passed on to another.

inflation A prolonged rise in level of prices for goods and services.

inflation rate The percentage by which the average level of prices in an economy rises; it is usually expressed as a percentage per year.

installment payment A regular payment on a loan or on a large purchase spread out over a period of time.

insurable interest A financial interest in property or another person's life that permits a person to buy insurance to protect against loss.

insurance A protection plan that divides possible losses among large numbers of people.

insured The insurance customer or policyholder.

insurer The insurance company that sells protection, or insurance.

interest Money that banks pay to depositors for the use of their funds.

interest rate A stated percentage of the principal.

interests Any of the things a person enjoys doing.

intermediary A business that moves goods from one business to another.

interstate commerce Business activities that affect people or businesses in two or more states.

inventory The amount of goods a factory has on hand at any given time.

inventory control The act of balancing the costs of holding raw materials, partially completed goods, and finished goods with the costs of ordering them.

investing Using savings so that the savings earn extra income.

J

job description A listing of the duties and responsibilities of a job.

job rotation A process in which employees move from job to job within a company.

joint account A bank account shared by two people.

L

labor Work done by people to produce goods and services.

labor market The number of job seekers and the number of openings in a geographical area; business finds the workers it needs from this pool, which is constantly changing and varies from year to year.

labor union An organization that represents workers who are in the same type of occupation or the same industry.

law of demand A principle stating that consumers will generally buy less of an item at a higher price than at a lower price.

law of supply A principle stating that producers will supply more of an item at a higher price than at a lower price.

layoff The act of asking an employee to leave a company temporarily until business gets better.

liability Anything a business owes.

license A legal permit for doing business; a permit from the state that gives a person the legal right to conduct a business or practice a profession.

lifestyle A person's way of living that reflects his or her attitudes and values.

limited liability The responsibility of the owners of a corporation for the debts of that corporation only to the extent of the amount they have invested.

line of credit An arrangement in which bank customers can borrow a certain amount of money from the bank immediately.

liquidity The measure of how quickly an investment can be turned into cash.

logo A manufacturer's symbol.

loose money policy Monetary policy that allows banks to lend money to all qualified borrowers, usually at relatively low interest rates.

loss leaders Products that are advertised as going at a loss or below cost.

M

maintenance Any activity that keeps a plant in working condition or puts it back in working condition if it breaks down.

management The process of reaching a business's goals through the use of its human and material resources.

manufacturer A business that turns raw or processed goods into finished goods.

market Any place where individuals buy and sell goods and services.

market economy A system in which the basic economic decisions are based on the actions of buyers and sellers; the market produces the goods and services people are willing to buy and that will bring a profit to the sellers and producers.

marketing mix The activities that go into the selling of a product to consumers.

market research The gathering of information that businesses can use to determine what kinds of goods or services to produce.

maturity date The end date of the specified period of time for a certificate of deposit.

mediator A third party who listens to both sides in contract discussions and then suggests what the provisions of the contract should be.

middle-level manager A manager who carries out the decisions of top-level management.

minimum wage The lowest wage an employer in certain industries can pay an employee.

mixed economy An economic system that is made up of parts of several other economic systems.

monetary policy Banking policy set by the Fed that affects the supply of money in circulation, the amount of credit in the economy, and the amount of business activity in the economy.

money Anything accepted as a medium of exchange that acts as a standard of value and a store of value.

money management The process of planning how to get the most from your money.

monopoly A company that sells all or practically all of a product or service and, therefore, has little or no competition.

mortgage A pledge of property as a guarantee that the loaned money plus interest will be repaid; it gives the bank the right to take the property if the borrower does not pay as agreed.

motivation Forces that cause businesses to act, including competition, desire to earn a profit, and the needs and wants of consumers.

multinational company A company that does business in many countries and has facilities in many countries.

N

national debt The total of all loans made to the federal government by individuals, groups of individuals, businesses, or foreign governments.

natural resources A factor of production that comes from the air, water, or earth; something that nature produced.

need A necessary want; something people must have to survive.

net income The difference between total revenue (money coming in) and expenses if revenue is greater.

net loss The difference between expenses and total revenue if expenses are greater.

net pay A person's gross pay minus deductions.

networking The process of talking to other people about their jobs.

net worth The last line in a statement of net worth that shows an individual's assets minus his or her liabilities.

nonprice competition Competition based on a product's features rather than its price.

nonrenewable resource A resource that cannot be replaced or renewed.

O

on-the-job training The training of employees while they work.

open market operations Refers to the sale or purchase of government securities by the Fed.

operating expenses All the costs of operation that are not included under the cost of goods sold.

operations system A system that includes the facilities, processing, and people needed to produce goods or services.

opportunity cost What a person gives up when making one choice instead of another.

ordinance A law or regulation passed by a local governmental unit.

orientation The process of helping new employees learn about and adjust to their new company.

overdraft protection A prearranged line of credit for overdrawn checks.

owner's equity The total assets of a business minus the liabilities.

P

partnership A business organization with two or more owners who share responsibilities and rewards.

patent A legal "right" that prevents anyone except the inventor of a product from making the same product for 17 years.

peak The highest level of economic activity in a cycle indicating prosperity and rapid expansion.

pension plan A plan offered to workers to provide them with income when they retire from work.

performance appraisal A process during which managers evaluate employees' performance.

policy A formal written agreement between the purchaser and the company.

pollution The contamination of air, water, and land.

postsecondary education Education beyond high school.

premium The amount of money an insurance company charges a policyholder for a certain period.

price The amount of money given or asked for when goods and services are bought or sold.

principal The amount of money owed as a debt upon which interest is calculated.

private enterprise system An economic system in which most resources are privately owned and decisions about production are made by individuals and groups rather than by the government.

proceeds The money paid to survivors after a policyholder dies.

processed goods Goods made from raw goods that may require further processing.

processor A business that changes natural materials from their original forms into more finished forms.

producer A business that creates or gathers products and services for distribution.

production forecasting Estimating how much of a company's goods or services must be produced to meet future demand.

profit The amount of money a business has left over after paying the cost of producing its goods and services.

profit sharing A company's distribution of a specified percentage of profits to employees as an incentive.

progressive tax A tax that increases as income increases.

promotion The awarding of a new job, which usually involves more responsibility, higher pay, and more authority, to an employee.

promotional sale A sale that offers people a special buy on a new product or a product that is in season.

property tax A tax on items owned by a person or business.

proportional tax A tax in which the rate of taxation is the same for everyone, regardless of income.

protectionist A person who believes that governments should regulate trade and subsidize industry to protect the domestic economy.

protective tariff A tax designed to protect domestic producers by raising the cost of imported goods.

public welfare The well-being of a whole society.

punitive tariff A tax designed to influence the trade-related actions of another country's government.

Q

qualification A requirement for a specific job.

quality circle A group of employees from the same work area who meet regularly to define, analyze, and solve problems in their area.

quality control The process of measuring goods and services against established standards.

quota A fixed limit on the export or import of a product.

R

rate of return The amount of money, or yield, an investment earns; it is expressed as a percentage of the original investment.

raw goods Materials gathered in their original state from natural resources such as land and water.

recall Take back and fix.

recession A stage in the business cycle in which the economy is in a period of decline—spending falls so fewer goods and services are demanded and unemployment rises.

recovery A period of economic growth or expansion following a recession or depression.

recycling Collecting products for processing so that they can be used again.

reference A person a potential employer can contact to find out about a job applicant's work, skills, and character.

refund A return of the purchase price (plus sales tax if any) of the product.

registered trademarks Names, brands, or symbols that a business lists with the government so they may not be used by other businesses.

regressive tax A tax in which the proportion of income spent on the tax decreases as income increases.

renewable resource A resource that can renew itself or can be renewed through the efforts of people.

repossess Take back collateral if a purchaser fails to pay loan installments.

reserve requirement A rule established by the Fed for all its member banks that specifies the percent of total deposits that must be held either in cash in a bank's own vault or as a deposit in the bank's district Federal Reserve Bank.

resource Anything that can be used to make or obtain a need or want.

resume A detailed summary of facts about a person that highlights the applicant's qualifications; it is used when a person applies for a job.

retailer A business that purchases goods from a wholesaler and resells them directly to the consumer.

return The gain or loss that results from an investment over a specified period.

revenue tariff A tax designed to raise money that needs to be high enough to generate funds yet low enough to allow continued purchase of the imported goods.

risk The uncertainty of gaining or losing money in an investment.

S

salary A form of payment in which employees earn a certain amount of money each week or month no matter how many hours they work; salaries are usually quoted as yearly figures.

saving Putting money aside for future use.

scarcity The lack of something that can be used to satisfy the wants of a group of people.

secured loan A cash loan backed by collateral.

securities Investments sold by corporations and governments to finance their growth.

self-discipline Working without prompting from someone else to achieve one's goals.

self-motivation Setting one's own goals rather than having them set by a manager or boss.

service business A type of business that provides services instead of goods to consumers.

services Tasks that people or machines perform to satisfy wants.

shortage An undersupply of an item at a particular price.

signature card A card a bank uses to verify the identity of a person using an account.

small business An independently owned and managed business that serves a limited geographic area and is not dominant in its industry.

small claims court A court that deals with minor legal matters involving small amounts of money.

socialism An economic and political structure in which the government owns major industries but allows for private ownership of other businesses.

social responsibility The idea that businesses act in a responsible and fair way toward their employees and society as a whole.

sole proprietorship A business or firm owned by one person.

specialization A basic premise of the U.S. economic system that states that individuals concentrate their activities in a particular area or field, and the money that each worker earns is then used to buy goods and services that others have specialized in producing.

standard of living A measure of how well the people in an economic system live.

start-up costs The money new business owners must spend in order to establish their business.

statement of net worth Summary of an individual's current personal financial condition.

statute A law passed by a legislature that either prohibits or demands specific activities.

stock Shares in the ownership of a corporation.

stockholders Those who own shares in a corporation.

strike A work stoppage by members of a labor union.

supply The amount or quantity of goods and services that producers will provide at various prices.

surplus An oversupply of goods or services that occurs when supply is greater than demand.

T

tariff A special tax on goods made in one country and sold in another.

tax abatements Special limited tax breaks used to attract business that also help the local government.

tax base The item or activity that is the source of a tax, such as income.

termination An employee's permanent separation from a company, whether voluntary or involuntary.

tight money policy Monetary policy that allows banks to lend money to only the most trusted borrowers, usually at relatively high interest rates.

time deposit A deposit typically left in the bank for months or years.

top-level manager A manager with the greatest responsibility for planning, organizing, directing, and controlling a company's resources.

trade The system by which countries exchange goods and services.

trade deficit The situation that exists when a country's imports exceed its exports.

trade-off Something a person gives up in order to have something more important.

trade surplus A favorable situation that exists when a country's exports exceed its imports.

trading partner Any of the countries with which the United States exchanges goods.

traditional economy An economic system in which people do things the way they have always been done.

transaction An activity that has an effect on the financial situation of a business.

transfer The moving of an employee from one job to another within a company.

transfer payment Money received by people who are not currently producing goods or services to earn it.

trough The lowest level of business activity in a particular cycle.

truth-in-lending disclosure A document expressing all costs of borrowing that a creditor is required by law to give to the borrower.

turnover The number of people who leave one job for another.

U

unemployment rate The percentage of the workforce without jobs.

Uniform Commercial Code A set of laws that are the same throughout the country and that are used to control and regulate business transactions.

unit pricing Using a standard measurement as a basis for pricing a particular product.

unlimited liability The responsibility of business owners for the debts of their business, even if those debts are greater than the assets of the business.

unsecured loan A cash loan not backed by collateral and that carries an increased risk to the creditor.

usury law A law restricting the amount of interest that can be charged for credit.

V

variable costs The costs of material, labor, and raw materials that increase or decrease with the number of goods produced.

variable rate A type of investment whose rate of return changes depending on the average yield of the investment.

W

wage A form of payment in which employees earn a certain amount of money for each hour they work.

want Anything that people desire or need; things people wish they could have.

warranty A legal document that states the rights and responsibilities agreed to by the consumer and the store or manufacturer.

wholesaler A type of business that distributes goods by buying them from manufacturers in large quantities and reselling them in smaller quantities.

withdrawal The act of taking money out of a bank account.

Index

Disabled Businesspersons Association (DBA), 108-109
discount rates, 338-339
discounts, understanding, 338-339
discretionary income, 177
distribution, 30-31, 182-183
distributors, 92, 183
diversification of employees, 120, 124, 125, 128
diversity, recognition of, 604-605
dividends, 545
Division of Standards, 456
Dow, Charles Henry, 545
Dow Chemical, 615
Dow Jones average, 545
down payment, 489
drawee, check, 561
drawer, check, 560-561

E
E-mail, 114
economic activity, 38-48
  circular flow model of, 31-32
  cycles of, 38-40
  federal government and economic stability, 47-48
  measuring, 42-47
  patterns, 40-42
  taxes, affect on, 288
economic assistance, to developing nations, 409
economic communities, 359-360
economic development in developing nations, 407
economic efficiency, of systems, 377
economic equity, of systems, 377
economic fluctuations, 38
economic indicators, 42-47
  GDP, 42-43
  inflation, 43-46
  unemployment, 46
  value of, 46-47
economic policy, 47-48
economic resources, 22-32
  capital resources, 26
  decision making, 29-31
  entrepreneurial, 26
  factors of production, 23-26
  human resources, 25-26
  limited, problem of, 27-28
  natural resources, 24-25
economic systems, 22-23, 368-376
  command economy, 371-372, 378
  comparing, 376-378
  considerations, 368-369
  defined, 22
  directed or planned, 371-372, 378
  interdependent, 40
  market economy, 373-376
  mixed, 262, 376
  private enterprise systems, 58-62
  traditional, 370-371
economy
  agricultural, 88
  entrepreneurs and, 203-204
  free market, 401

government role in, 267
industrial, 88-89
information, 89
in global marketplace, 400-412
international, 350-362
jobs and, 624-626
service, 89
education
  and job outlook, 608
  as fringe benefit, 621
  consumer, 442-443
  costs of, 645
  in developing nations, 411
  of job applicant, 652
  public, 276, 297
  requirements for job, 643-645
educational programs, employer sponsored, 622
efficiency of taxes, 287
efficiency, production, 162-165
electronic banking, 567-568, 558-559
electronic databases, 176-177
Electronic Funds Transfer (EFT), 340, 567
electronic information transfer, 80-81
electronic notebooks, 520-521
electronic scanners, 282-283
electronic scanning of resume, 660
electronic security, 504-505
electronic shopping, 428
electronic spreadsheets, 140-141
electronic ticker tape, 538-539
embargo, 358, 386
emergencies, saving for, 537
emotional advertising, 430
emotional motives, 178
employees
  benefits for, 618-622
  benefits of business to, 63-64
  diversity of, 120, 124, 125, 128
  in accounting, 148
  in marketing, 185-186
  in operations systems, 157-158
  in production, 165-166
  job considerations, 614-626
  loyalty, 123, 158
  motivation, 132
  recruitment of, 122-123
  relationship with coworkers, 623-624
  selection of, 123-127
  training and developing, 128-130
  training of, 64
employers
  contacting potential, 656-662
  costs, 618-622
  job applicant qualities sought by, 652-653
employment
  economy and, the, 624-626
  encouragement of, 625
  trends and the economy, 625-626
employment agencies, 655-656
employment process, 120-132
  job analysis, 120
  managers, human resources, 131-132
  orientation, 127-128

recruitment, 122-123
selection of employees, 123-127
training and development of employees, 128-130
employment testing, 127, 658
Encyclopedia of Careers and Vocational Guidance, 641
endorsement, 561
entertainment, career in, 600-601
entrepreneurial resources, 26
entrepreneurs, entrepreneurship, 26, 94, 196-220
  advantages of, 199-200
  capital for, 243-249
  characteristics of, 197-198
  defined, 196
  disadvantages of, 200-203
  examples of, 196, 197, 200, 203, 204, 212, 219
  in the U.S., 203-204
  inventions by, 204
  operating expenses of, 242
  personal savings of, 244
  planning for, 210-220
  preparing for, 210-214
  profit, 199-200
  small business and, 196-197
  sources of assistance, 211
  women and, 199
entrepreneurs, focus on, 40-41, 60-61, 108-109, 228-229, 242-243, 354-355, 458-459, 578-579
entry-level job, 642, 643
environment of workplace, 623
Environmental Protection Agency (EPA), 264, 457
environmental protection, 445
  laws, 265
Equal Credit Opportunity Act, 502-503
Equal Employment Opportunity Commission (EEOC), 264
equilibrium price, 77-78, 82
equity, 548
  owner's, 138-139, 142
equity capital, 243
estate tax, 283, 285
esteem needs, 638
estimated income, 241
European Union (EU), 359-360, 401
evaluation, performance, 129-130
exchange, money as medium, 312-313
exchange rate, 390, 393-394
excise tax, 281-282
executives, 602
exercise programs, employer sponsored, 621-622
expansion, 39
expenses
  business, 241-242
  estimate in budget, 524
  fixed and variable, 524
  living, 240-241
  operating, 144, 242
  projecting 240-242
experience, work, 653
expert systems, 474-475

greenbacks, 564
Gross Domestic Product (GDP), 42-43
    in developing nations, 405
Gross National Product (GNP), 43,
    377-378
gross pay, 523
group health plans, 587-588
group training, 129
growth phase in product life cycle, 175
guidance counselors, 641, 645

H

Hammurabi, code of, 261
hard assets, 148
Health and Biomedical Services, career
    in, 90-91
health conditions, in developing nations,
    405-406
health insurance, 586-588
health maintenance organizations
    (HMOs), 588
Hess, Cecil F., 578-579
Hewlett Packard, 124
hierarchy of needs, 132
highway systems, 296
Hill, Lisa, 228-229
hiring from within, 122
holidays, paid, 619
home ownership, 548
homeowner's insurance, 583-584
homes, types of, 548
hospitalization insurance, 586
Hudson's Bay Company, 230
Hughes, Lyric, 354-355
human relations skills, 131, 186
human resources, 25-26, 157-158
    See also employees
human resources management, 120-132
    employment process, 120-128
    managers in, 131-132
    planning, 232-233
    training and development of
        employees, 128-130
Hyatt Hotels Corp., 173
hypermarkets, 426

I

IBM, 95-96
ideas, identifying, 442-443
implied warranty, 462
imports, 350, 351, 384, 385
impulse buying, 431
incentives, 617
income
    ability-to-pay principle, 284, 286, 287
    discretionary, 177
    estimate in budget plan, 523-524
    estimated (for business plan), 241
    fixed, 44
    net, 141
    nondiscretionary, 177
    projection, 240, 241-242
income insurance, 588
income property, 549
income statement, 141, 142, 250
income tax, 276-280
incubator facilities, 247

independence of entrepreneurs, 197
indicators, general economic, 42-47
indirect tax, 285
individual loans, 322
industrial economy, 88-89
industrial products, 174
industry, rise of, 88-89
inflation, 43-46, 542
    government and, 48, 301
    understanding, 44-45
inflation rate, 45-46
information
    analysis of, 426-427
    comparison and contrast of,
        374-375
    consumer's right to, 438-439,
        444-445
    consumer's responsibility to check,
        442-443
    evaluation of, 28-29
    locating and verification of, 460-461
    manager's collection and use of, 114
    sources of career, 640-641
information economy, 89
information superhighway, 638-639
inheritance tax, 283, 285
insight, 131
installment contract, 489
installment payments, 476
insurable interest, 577, 585
insurance, 576-588
    automobile, 580-581
    benefits, 619
    claims, 578
    deductible, 578-579
    defined, 576
    health, 586-588
    homeowner's, 583-584
    in ancient times, 576
    income, 588
    life, 585-586
    premiums, 578, 579, 581, 619
    property, 584-585
    purchasing, 577-579
    regulation of, 579
    renter's, 582-583
insurance agent, 577
insured, 577
insurer, 577, 578
interdependence, 31-32, 40
interest
    charge accounts, 476
    compound, 565
    consumer finance companies, 476
    credit cards, 477
    defined, 319
    on accounts, 319-320
    on bank loans, 320
    paid by government, 480
    understanding, 318-319
interest rates, 332, 339, 340, 489
    bank, 569
    certificates of deposit, 566
    cost of credit and, 490-491
    economy and, 624
    in Europe, 500
    in Middle East, 503

money market, 566
    savings, 564-565
interests, self inventory of, 636
International Bank for Reconstruction
    and Development, 408-409
international banking, 388
international finance, 384-394
international marketing, 183-185
    communication, 184
    difference in buying habits, 184-185
    traditions and customs, 184
International Organization for
    Standardization, 163
international trade, by developing
    countries, 407
interpersonal skills, 114, 148
interstate commerce, 262
Interstate Commerce Commission (ICC),
    262, 263
Interstate Commerce Commission Act,
    262
interstate highways, 296
interview, job, 126-127, 659-662
introduction phase in product life cycle,
    175
inventory, 159
inventory control, 159-161
investing, investments
    availability of money, 541-542
    common choices, 544-550
    defined, 536
    fixed rate and variable rate, 541
    guidelines for, 540-544
    in business venture, 245-246
    individual, 245-246
    inflation and, 542
    real estate, 548
    See also saving(s)
investment clubs, 546
investment planning, 569
ISO 9000, 163

J

job analysis, 120
job application, 124, 657-658
job considerations, 614-626
    benefits, 618-622
    unemployment, 624-625
    unemployment trends and the
        economy, 625-626
    wages and salaries, 614-618
    working conditions, 622-624
job description, 120, 121
job fairs, 641
job interview, 126-127, 659-662
job requirements, 641-645
job rotation, 129
job, applying for a, 652-662
    job qualifications and, 652-653,
        654
    job search, beginning, 653-656
    contacting potential employers,
        656-662
joint account, 560
Jones, Edward D., 545
judgment, skill of informed, 202-203
just-in-time (JIT system), 161

K

Kamen, Dean, 40-41
Kennedy, John F., 438
Korean businesses, 199

L

labels, 181, 432, 455
labor, 25, 28
    costs, 121-122
    organized, 605-607
labor force, 30
labor market, 598-608
labor unions, 605-607
large numbers, principle of, 576
Latin America, reforms in, 48
law(s)
    administrative, 261
    antitrust, 263
    common, 261
    consumers' rights, 439, 441
    credit rights, protection of, 500-506
    protecting public, 264
    small claims court and, 462
    usury, 500
    See also regulation, government
law of demand, 74, 76
law of supply, 75
layoffs, 130
layout of facilities, 155
leadership, skill of, 112-113
leading, 110, 111
learning, strategies for, 642-643
legal aid societies, 462
legal system of U.S., 260-261
lending institutions, 244-245, 475-476, 489
letters of credit, 570
Lever Brothers, 179
Levi Strauss & Co., 12
liabilities, 138, 139, 529, 530
liability
    limited, 231
    unlimited, 227, 229
liability insurance, 580
license, 226, 456-457
Liebling, James, 354-355
life cycle of a product, 174-175
life insurance, 585-586
lifestyle, 518
limited liability, 231
limited resources, 410
limited-line retailers, 425-426
line authority, 106
line graphs, interpretation of, 76-77
line of credit, 322-323
liquidity, 542
listening skills, 113-114, 180-181
literacy rate, in developing nations, 406
living expenses, 240-241
Lloyd's of London, 577
loan(s)
    bank, 568
    bank, example of, 243
    bank, types of, 320-323
    cash, 489
    consolidation, 434-435
    government, 247

mortgage, 321-322, 489
    secured, 489, 569
    small business, 244-245
    unsecured, 489, 569
    See also credit
local consumer protection, 456-457
local government spending, 296-298
locals, 605
location, as factor in labor market, 608
location of facilities, 155
logo, 181
London Stock Exchange, 547
loose money policy, 332
loss leaders, 431
loss, net, 141
loyalty, 158
    of employees, 123

M

magnetic ink character recognition, 334-335
mail order catalogs, 427
maintenance, 163
Major Appliance Consumer Action Program (MACAP), 459
major-medical insurance, 587
management, 106-114
    bank, 317
    financial, 143-147
    functions of, 110-112
    human resources, 120-132
    inventory, 159-161
    levels of, 108-109
    of business finances, 138-148
    organizing, 106-108, 232-234
    See also money management
management plan, 232-234
managers, 602
    advantages vs. disadvantages, 114
    financial, 143-147
    human resources, 120, 131-132
    qualities of, 113-114
manufacturers, 92
manufacturing, 88-89
manufacturing resource planning (MRP II), 160
manufacturing technology and construction, career in, 160-161
market
    defined, 72-73
    ever-changing, 82
    foreign exchange, 389
    global, 350-362
    prices and, 72-75
market economy, 72-82, 373-376
    defined, 72
market research, 178
market system, 262
marketing, 172-186
    distribution, 182-183
    elements of, 172-173
    packaging, 181
    pricing, 172, 179-181
    product planning, 173-178
    promotion, 173, 182

    international, 183-185
    working in, 185-186
marketing mix, 172-173
marketing plan, 219-220
Maslow, Abraham, 132
mass merchandise stores, 424-425
materials, raw, 174
materials requirement planning (MRP), 160
math skills, 165, 186
mathematics skills, 148
Mattel, 62, 79
mature phase in product life cycle, 175
maturity date, 544
maturity, emotional and social, 131
McDonnell Douglas, 245
mechanical aptitude, 165
mediator, 606
Medicare tax, 278-279
medium of exchange, money as, 312-313
mental health insurance, 587
merchandise trade balance, 384
Metrolaser, 578-579
Microsoft, 439
middle-level managers, 109
military assistance to developing nations, 410
minimum wage, 615-616
mining, career in, 268-269
mixed economies, 376
Miyares, Urban, 108-109
Model T, 89
modems, 388-389
moderate command economy, 372-373
monetary policy, 48, 332-340
money
    borrowing by business, 145
    characteristics of, 314-315
    creation of, 320-321
    functions of, 312-313
    kinds of, 315-316
    transfer of, 320
money and banking, 312-326
money management, 518-530
    balancing and adjusting budget, 525
    budget planning steps, 522-525
    computer for, 530
    defined, 518
    importance of budgeting, 520-522
    lifestyle costs, 518-520
    sample budget, 526-530
    See also banks and banking; saving(s)
money market accounts, 539, 566
money orders, 570
money supply, regulation of, 336-339
monopolies, 96, 262, 263, 439
monthly statement, 492-493
moral responsibility, to developing nations, 407
mortality table, 585
mortgage loan(s), 489, 548, 321-322
mortgage payments, 548
motivation
    consumer, 177-178
    of employees, 186, 132
motivations of business, 58-66
    competition, 60

on-line, 93
production decisions about, 29-31
providing of, 10-11
taxes on, 280-282
unions in, 606-607
See also production
shareholders, 545
Sherman Antitrust Act, 263
shipping goods, 174
shoppers, kinds of, 430
shopping
at sales, 431
comparison, 428-429, 444-445, 556, 585
electronic, 428
lists, 431
resisting pressure and gimmicks, 431-432
shortage, 77
sick days, 619
signature card, 560
sixteenth amendment, 277
skills
analysis, 28-29, 94-95, 216-217, 374-375, 478-479, 582-583
analytical, 148
communication, 113-114, 126-127, 165, 180-181, 186, 442-443, 460-461
computer, 148
employability, 10-11, 64-65, 112-113, 156-157, 232-233, 266-267, 506-507, 604-605, 642-643, 660-661
entrepreneurs and, 199
human relations, 186, 131
interpersonal, 114, 148
job, 652
listening, 113-114
math, 44-45, 76-77, 146-147, 148, 165, 186, 278-279, 300-301, 318-319, 338-339, 356-357, 390-391, 492-493, 526-527, 542-543, 562-563, 620-621
of finance employees, 148
of marketing employees, 185-186
of operations employees, 165-166
problem solving, 165, 186
science, 165
Slater, Samuel, 88
small business
defined, 196
employment in, 204
entrepreneurship and, 196-197
loans, 244-245
pattern of, 196-197
service industries and, 197
Small Business Administration (SBA), 247
loans by, 247
small claims courts, 462
Smoot-Hawley Tariff, 402
social needs, 176
social responsibility, 66
Social Security, 537
social security tax, 278-279
socialism, 372, 373

society, benefits of business to, 65-66
"soft assets," 148
sole proprietorship, advantages vs. disadvantages in, 226-228
sources of funding, 144, 145-146
Southwestern U.S., resources in, 30
specialization, 351, 352, 384, 407
specialty goods, 174
spending, government. *See* government spending
sponsors, 182
spreadsheets, electronic, 140-141
standard of living, 43, 376-377
standard of value, 313
standardization, 156
standards
quality, 163
work, 112
start-up capital, 237
start-up costs, 240
state banks, 323, 326, 335
state consumer protection, 456-457
state government spending, 298-299
state highways, 296
state individual income tax, 277-278
state insurance department, 579
statement of net worth, 250, 529-530
statistics
comparison of, 620-621
interpretation of, 582-583
statute, 260-261
statutory law, 260-261
stock, 146, 230, 231, 545-547
issuing, 231, 248
stock certificates, 546
stock exchange, 546
stock market quotations, 542-543
stockbroker, 546
stockholders, 230, 231, 248
stop payment order, 559
store of value, 313
stores, 423-428, 476
Strauss, Levi, 12
strike fund, 606
strikes, 606
strong command economy, 371-372
structure, organizational, 107-108
substitutes, changes in demand and, 79
Sudan, 27
Sun Coast Resources, 458-459
superstores, 426
suppliers, 248
supplies in business, 174
supply
changes in, 79-81
defined, 74
equilibrium price and, 78
law of, 75
surgical and medical insurance, 587
surplus, 76
trade, 384, 385
symbol, product, 179

T

take-home pay, 524
tariff(s), 282, 357-358, 360, 385-386, 402

taste, consumer, 79
tax
abatements, 269-270
base, 276
burden, 288
withholdings, 279-280
taxes and taxation, 276-288, 294
advantages for business, 269, 270
corporate, 231
criteria for, 286-287
cutting, 48
direct and indirect, 285, 287
economic activity and, 288
employee, 619
increasing, 48
investments and, 543
on goods and services, 280-282
on income, 276-280
on property, 282-284, 287
partnership, 229
progressive, 285, 286
proportional, 285, 286
real estate and, 548
regressive, 285, 286
sole proprietorship, 227
See also government spending
technical assistance to developing nations, 410
technical high schools, 644
technical workers, 601-602
technology
banking, 567
growth of, 625-626
rise of, 88-89
See also computer(s)
technology, focus on, 24-25, 80-81, 122-123, 140-141, 176-177, 200-201, 212-213, 282-283, 314-315, 334-335, 372-373, 388-389, 424-425, 474-475, 504-505, 520-521, 538-539, 558-559, 616-617, 638-639
telecommunications, in People's Republic of China, 31
telecommuting, 445
television commercials, 182
term insurance, 585-586
termination, 130
testing, 127
employment, 658
textile factory, 88
thank-you letter, job interview, 661-662
thrifts, 324
tight money policy, 332
time deposits, 319, 564
TLI, 354-355
top-level managers, 109
trade
balance of trade, 384-386
foreign policy, 353-355
government and, 353-361
restrictions of, 357-358
trade agreements, 360-361
General Agreement on Tariffs and Trade (GATT), 360

Credits

Photographs: **xviii** Holt Confer/Uniphoto Inc. **2** Jeff Greenberg/PhotoEdit **8** Tom McCarthy/PhotoEdit **13** Elena Rooraid/PhotoEdit **15** Dennis MacDonald/PhotoEdit **20** Bruce Hands/The Image Works **36** Mark Richards **41** Susan Lapides **54** Ron Coppock/Gamma-Liaison **56** Bob Daemmrich **59** Bob Daemmrich **61** Gary Matoso/Contact **70** Bob Daemmrich **86** J. Caputo/Gamma-Liaison **96** Amy Etra/PhotoEdit **102** David Hanover/Tony Stone Images **104** Chuck Keeler/Tony Stone Images **109** Courtesy Disabled Business Persons Association **118** T. Shambroom/Photo Researchers **123** NASA **129** Michael Newman/PhotoEdit **136** Robert Reichert/Gamma-Liaison **141** Courtesy Lotus, Inc. **152** Ken Whitmore/Tony Stone Images **162** David Young-Wolff/PhotoEdit **166** Chip Henderson/Tony Stone Images **170** Chuck Keeler/Tony Stone Images **177** Dan McCoy/Rainbow **185** Uniphoto, Inc. **192** Chuck Savage/The Stock Market **194** P.R. Production/Superstock **201** Michael Newman/PhotoEdit **208** Tony Freeman/PhotoEdit **211** Elizabeth Zuckerman/PhotoEdit **213** Jim Pickerell/The Image Works **214** McLaughlin/The Image Works **224** David Harry Stewart/Tony Stone Images **229** Courtesy Adcor Products, Inc. **231** William Strode/Woodfin Camp & Assoc. **238** Chris Jones/The Stock Market **241** Bill Bachmann/PhotoEdit **243** Courtesy Barden Companies, Inc. **245** T. Anderson/The Image Bank **256** Tim Bieber/The Image Bank **258** Dion Ogust/The Image Works **266** Tony Freeman/PhotoEdit **270** Lee Snider/The Image Works **274** Bob Daemmrich **283** Dan McCoy/Rainbow **292** Wernher Krutein/Gamma-Liaison **308** Peter Polides/Tony Stone Images **310** Tony Freeman/PhotoEdit **313** David Young-Wolff/PhotoEdit **325** Tony Freeman/PhotoEdit **330** Paul Conklin/PhotoEdit **346** Doug Armand/Tony Stone Images **348** Deborah Davis/PhotoEdit **355** Steve Leonard/Crain's Chicago Business **361** Adam Tannf/Comstock **366** Paul Conklin/PhotoEdit **370** Bob Daemmrich **373** Theodore Anderson/The Image Bank **382** Jeff Greenberg/PhotoEdit **387** Crandall/The Image Works **389** Dan McCoy/Rainbow **394** Bachmann/The Image Works **398** Tomas Spangler/The Image Works **418** Don Smetzer/Tony Stone Images **420** Richard Hutchings/PhotoEdit **425** Courtesy Symantec Corporation **432** Mary Kate Denny/PhotoEdit **436** Michael Newman/PhotoEdit **446** Bob Daemmrich/The Image Works **447** David Young-Wolff/PhotoEdit **452** Bob Daemmrich **457** Myrleen Ferguson/PhotoEdit **459** Mark Tucker **462** Rhoda Sidney/PhotoEdit **468** Paul Conklin/Uniphoto, Inc. **470** Mark Richards/PhotoEdit **475** Mitch Kezar/Tony Stone Images **484** David Young-Wolff/PhotoEdit **498** Charles Gupton/Tony Stone Images **505** Bonnie Kamin/PhotoEdit **514** Gary Gladstone/The Image Bank **516** Uniphoto, Inc. **521** Elena Rooraid/PhotoEdit **534** Bob Daemmrich/The Image Works **537** Richard Hutchings/PhotoEdit **539** Michael Newman/PhotoEdit **546** Myrleen Ferguson/PhotoEdit **550** Zigy Katuzny/Tony Stone Images **554** Comstock **559** David Young-Wolff/PhotoEdit **568** Ron Coppock/Gamma-Liaison **574** Myrleen Ferguson/PhotoEdit **579** Courtesy Metro Laser **587** Tom McCarthy/PhotoEdit **594** Comstock **596** David Burnett/Woodfin Camp & Assoc. **603** Greenlar/The Image Works **612** Michael Newman/PhotoEdit **617** Wernher Krutein/Gamma-Liaison **622** Michael L. Abramson/Woodfin Camp & Assoc. **626** Charles Gupton/Uniphoto, Inc. **632** Steven Peters/Tony Stone Images **634** Michael Newman/PhotoEdit **639** Roget Tully/Tony Stone Images **640** Dennis MacDonald/PhotoEdit **650** Allen McInnis/Gamma-Liaison **658** Bob Daemmrich/Uniphoto, Inc. **662** Michael Newman/PhotoEdit.